TV FACTS

by

Cobbett Steinberg

TV FACTS

by

Cobbett Steinberg

Facts On File Publications
New York, New York • Oxford, England

TV FACTS

Published by Facts on File, Inc.
460 Park Avenue South, New York, N.Y. 10016

Grateful acknowledgement is made to the following for permission to reprint the following material:

Ballantine Books: from the complete Directory to Prime Time Network TV Shows: 1946–Present by Tim Brooks and Earle Marsh, copyright 1979.

Cowles Broadcasting, Inc.: *Look* Annual Television Awards (1950–59).

Film Comment: "The Most Memorable Moments in TV History," dated Aug. 1979.

Praeger Publications: four charts from "The Mass Media."

Rand Corporation: charts from "TV and Human Behavior."

Time, The Weekly Newsmagazine: *Time* "TV's Ten Most" 1970–1979.

Variety Inc.: "Hit Movies on TV Since '61," dated 9/26/79; three charts from "A Prof's Survey of 20 Years of Network Primetime Series," dated 9/14/77.

Library of Congress Cataloging in Publication Data

Steinberg, Cobbett.
TV facts.

Includes index.
1. Television broadcasting—United States—Dictionaries.   2. Television industry—United States—Statistics.   I. Title.
PN1992.18.S75   384.55'0973
79-26912
ISBN 0-87196-312-4

9 8 7 6 5 4 3 2 1

Printed in the United States of America

For my sister Barbara
With profound thanks for her love and support.

TABLE OF CONTENTS

VI. THE NETWORKS AND STATIONS

ACKNOWLEDGEMENTS

I SHOULD LIKE to thank the following people and organizations for their generous help in providing material used in this book: the Academy of Television Arts and Sciences; Action for Children's Television; Broadcast Pioneers Library; Cable Television Information Center; Henry W. Grady School of Journalism, University of Georgia; Museum of Broadcasting; National Academy of Television Arts and Sciences; National Cable Television Association; A.C. Nielsen Company; Television Bureau of Advertising; Television Information Office; and Syd Silverman of Variety.

INTRODUCTION

TELEVISION RESEARCH SUFFERS from a double-headed problem: there's both too much material and too little. The TV industry produces programs at such a relentlessly prolific pace (more than 2,000 hours of new shows are aired each year during prime time alone) that any systematic research would seem difficult if not impossible. How can you wade through those hours and hours of programs with your sanity intact? There's almost too *much* TV for an archivist or scholar to handle.

And too little: the live programs from the early 1950s are, of course, lost forever; even recent shows are often routinely erased or destroyed; and credit listings are frequently hard to locate. During most of TV's thirty-five year history, the networks have not been interested in preserving their own past and the academic community has not deemed TV important enough to study.

Steps have been taken recently to correct this situation. The past few years have witnessed the publication of basic TV encyclopedias, dictionaries, and bibliographies. Courses in TV history are now offered in universities across the nation. And TV archives are rigorously preserving TV's past. *TV Facts* does, I hope, fill in a few more of the holes. Here are facts, figures, statistics, charts, and tables that cover the tube's history, from its earliest experimental days to the most recent TV season. Here are the programs, ratings, advertisers, networks, and viewers—the prizes, polls, and awards. In collecting these facts and figures, *TV Facts* will, I hope, prove useful and fun to those wanting to understand the medium that has been called everything from "democracy in its ugliest form" to "a saving radiance in the sky."

I. THE PROGRAMS

1/PRIME TIME SCHEDULES: 1950–1985

TELEVISION KEEPS BUSY, very busy. Networks broadcast throughout the day, evening, and night—seven days a week, 52 weeks a year. In 1979 the more than 700 commercial television stations in this country broadcast 4.7 million hours of programming, and that staggering, eye-opening figure does not even include the hours of public stations. Does any other medium consume so voraciously, produce so relentlessly? Does any other medium keep such strange hours?

Here are the "time cards" for TV's hours: a season-by-season record of its prime time programs. These schedules only record the fall line-up of shows. Any changes made during the season (and mid-season juggling has increased notoriously in recent years) are not included in these charts.

Even a cursory look at these schedules will tell you that something drastic has happened to TV programming; there's been a great move towards fewer and longer series. The schedules of the 1950s and early 1960s are dense and crowded. Half-hour shows are the general rule. By contrast, the late 1960s and 1970s schedules have fewer and fewer programs. One-hour and even two-hour shows have become popular.

In fact, according to a study by TV scholar Joel Persky, there were 123 prime time series on the air in 1956. By 1966 the number had decreased to 97, and by 1976 it had dwindled to 67. In 20 years the number of network shows had diminished by almost 50 percent!

Of course, this decrease is partially due to the 1975 change in the definition of prime time, which reduced the number of hours webs could broadcast each evening. Prior to the 1975/76 season, the networks had 3½ hours each evening to braodcast—basically from 7:30 pm to 11 pm. But during that season, the FCC reduced the networks' hours to three per evening, so that each web could no longer fit as many series into its schedules.

But the more important reason for the decrease in the number of series is the trend towards longer and longer shows. Consider, for example, the following table, also computed by Professor Persky:

Series	1956	1966	1976
Half-hour series	101	56	23
Hour series	20	36	37
Hour-and-a-half series	2	1	0
Two-hour series	0	4	6
Two-and-a-half hour series	0	0	1
TOTAL	123	97	67

Between 1956 and 1976, hour series almost doubled in number, while half-hour shows were slashed by more than 75 percent. And whereas two-hour series were unheard of in 1956, by 1976 there were 6 on the air each week.

A closer look at these season-by-season schedules reveals that not only the numbers but the kinds of TV series have changed during the past three decades. The tube could boast of more than 30 westerns during the 1959/60 season, for example, but by 1970 the number had nose-dived to 4. The years have similarly seen the rise and fall of variety series, dramatic anthologies, and prime time quiz shows. Only one night-time format has persisted throughout TV's history: the situation comedy. (In daytime TV, quiz shows and soap operas have demonstrated similar longevity.)

Consider, for example, the following statistics:

TYPE OF SHOW	NUMBER OF SHOWS			NUMBER OF HOURS		
	1956	1966	1976	1956	1966	1976
DRAMA						
Action/Adventure	10	15	4	6.5	12.5	4
Comedy	21	36	23	11	18.5	11.5
Crime/Detective	2	2	18	1	2	18
Domestic	29	5	6	17.5	4.5	7
Medical	1	3	2	.5	2	2
Motion Picture	3	4	6	3	8	12.5
Serial	0	3	0	0	1.5	0
Western	7	11	2	3.5	9.5	2
Miscellaneous	1	1	0	.5	.5	0
	74	80	61	43.5	59	57
TALKS						
Documentary	4	1	0	2	1	0
Game/Quiz Shows	16	3	1	8	1.5	1
Instructional	2	0	0	1	0	0
Panel Discussions	1	0	0	1	0	0
Religious Programs	2	0	0	1	0	0
Sports/Sports News	2	0	0	2	0	0
	27	4	1	14.5	2.5	1
VARIETY						
Comedy/Variety	6	3	2	4.5	3	2
Musical Variety	16	10	3	11	9	3
	22	13	5	11.5	12.0	5.0
TOTALS	123	97	67	73.5	73.5	63

There were 16 quiz shows on the air in 1956; 20 years later there was only one. Whereas crime and detective series only accounted for one hour of weekly prime time in 1956, they were on the air 18 hours each week by 1976.

What accounts for these and similar changes? Obviously some of the changes are due to shifts in national tastes: what is popular in 1956 will not necessarily be equally popular in 1966.

But economic pressures are responsible for many more of the shifts. When demographic analyses became fashionable in the late 1960s, for example, the very concept of a hit show changed: a smash series was no longer one that attracted a large audience but the right type of audience—an audience of young adults, with money, and preferably living in cities. Thus many series like *Mayberry, R.F.D.* and *Petticoat Junction* were cancelled despite good ratings because they were thought to attract the wrong kinds of audiences for advertisers.

Economics were also responsible for the demise of the crowning achievement of TV's Golden Age: the dramatic anthology. The anthology series were simply more expensive to produce than other kinds of shows. New characters, new scripts and new sets had to be mounted from scratch each week. Each week was a whole new ball game and what might work with an audience one week could fail the next. Unlike series with continuing situations and consistent characters, the dramatic anthologies did not have the self-promoting predictability necessary to attract a known, loyal audience.

This brings us to a third reason for some of these changes in series formats: the nature of TV itself. Because we watch TV in the comfort and supposed security of our own home, TV (it's often been said) needs to be safe and predictable. We don't want to invite into our homes especially dangerous or threatening characters, characters who would be tolerable if not downright attractive in the exotic darkness of a movie theater, but who simply are not appropriate for the domestic light of our living rooms. At home, we don't want many surprises or unhappy endings: we want to know what to expect.

TV's reputed penchant for predictability might explain why the series format has been more popular than, let's say, the anthology format and why certain types of series—like the sitcom with its lovable characters—are especially successful.

How do the networks decide what shows to air and when to schedule them? Each web has programming executives who choose which program more than 100 million Americans see each week, and as an 1980 New York *Times* article said, "in terms of exerting influence over the minds of a nation, history offers perhaps no parallels to the power wielded by the men and the few women who choose programs for the nation's television networks."

TV's most legendary programmer is Fred Silverman who has in fact been labelled "the most talked-about, joked-about, denounced and celebrated TV executive in network history." It was Silverman who maneuvered ABC's historic 1976 rise to the top-ranked web, and because of that coup Silverman moved from head of programming at ABC to the presidency of NBC.

Each network basically has three programming departments, one each for Sports, News, and Entertainment, and each of these is further subdivided so that the structure becomes nothing less than Byzantine. An entertainment programming department, for example, will typically have heads for prime time, daytime, children's specials, movies, late night and other such areas. That department will also have certain executives on the West Coast and their counterparts on the East Coast. Each exec will have his/her associate and assistant executive, and the entire programming department will be backed by a business affairs department to take care of the deals, contracts and budgets.

Although each of the various level executives can advocate that a certain new program be added to the web's schedule, most final decisions are made by a committee composed of the web's president, the chairman of the board, the programming vice-president, plus the vice-president of sales, research, affiliates, and so on and so on.

As you can guess, the chances of a show making it through all these trials-by-fire are slim indeed. "The odds for success," quips TV executive Bob Shanks, "are high enough to make Jimmy the Greek seek Social Security."

According to Martin Starger, a former ABC programmer, there are two major steps in producing a successful TV schedule: "first, developing good programs and second, the strategic placement of those programs within a weekly schedule." Starger's simple two-step strategy, though obviously sound, belies the complexity, the "gut-wrenching, pulse-pounding fun" of programming, as one TV executive has described it.

During an average week a TV programmer will receive as many as 30 written suggestions for new series and more than 100 phone calls about "original" program concepts—that's about 7,000 ideas a year! How does a programmer make his or her way through this miasma of scatter-brained notions and half-baked projects? What is he or she really looking for?

Not for something new, surprisingly enough. In *Cool Fire* (one of the most honest, amusing, and informative behind-the-scenes books about the TV industry) Bob Shanks confesses that there are no new ideas in TV: only new wine in old bottles. "No matter how extraordinary your idea may seem to be," Shanks advised TV writers, "the programmer has seen it. That's all right. No one is expecting or wanting anything else. . . As Samuel Goldwyn is alleged to have said, 'I'm sick of these old cliches. Get me some new ones.'"

Thus, Shanks points out that *All in the Family* is a "let-it-all-hang-out *Honeymooners* or *Life with Riley*. *M*A*S*H* is a cool and cynical *Bilko*. *Marcus Welby* is 50 different doctor shows. *The Streets of San Francisco* is *San Francisco Beat*. *The Rookies* is *Mod Squad* in a time that moved quickly from youth rebellion to law and order. *Sanford and Son* is a hip *Amos 'n' Andy*. *The Waltons* is *One Man's Family* and *The Grapes of Wrath*. *The Six Million Dollar Man* is *Superman* made with a Lockheed cost overrun. And Howard Cosell is sent in for Ed Sullivan."

Some programmers contend they pick shows that they themselves would want to watch. Programmers should stop guessing what "the public" wants, argues Martin Starger, "and start focusing on what truly excites them creatively, what they themselves really feel is excellent. The surest path to mediocrity in a network's television schedule is for the program director to sit in his office, stare out the window, and think, 'Now what do "they" want to see Wednesday at 8:30?' "

But other programmers disagree. "It's not what I personally like that matters," a former network vice-president confessed. "What you ask is, 'Will 30 million Americans watch this?' I'm not programming for my friends or your friends. I'm programming for people—people who are less educated than I am, who travel less, who read fewer books."

Once a web gives the go-ahead, plans are made to shoot a pilot for a proposed series. A cast and crew are assembled (more choices, more trials-by-fire) and the pilot is shown to a sample audience whose reactions to the show are carefully analyzed (more decisions, more predictions). If everything about the series bodes well, a slot for the show is found in the web's fall schedule (more questions: should the show follow the web's smash sitcom? should it precede the network's leading film series? is a weekend the best time for the new series?).

And then, when the show finally hits the air, the *real* problems begin. Until a few years ago, at least 13 episodes of a new show were shot and broadcast. A new series had breathing room—time to generate a loyal audience. But in the past few years, scheduling has grown more and more hysterical and a new show can now be cancelled after only two or three weeks. Today, new shows must win their audiences right away or not at all: there are no second chances.

In TV's early years there was basically one TV season per year, lasting from the fall through the following spring. A few years ago, a "second season" was added in January to replace shows canned during the autumn. But in today's competitive, kill-'em-in-the-ratings marketplace, there are really no seasons at all: every month is a juggling act in which programmers are constantly scheduling and rescheduling. Robert Daly, head of CBS entertainment programming, now likens his job to a football coach who "keeps shifting his lineup and reaching for the bench to add new strength and plug up holes in his defensive line."

And everyone thinks he knows the exact solution to the network's programming problems. "Wake the cleaning lady at 4:00 A.M.," Bob Shanks quips, "and she will tell you what to put in the schedule at 8:00 P.M. Saturday night or who to cast in the leads in a made-for-TV movie."

Programmers have to do so much hustling to get their shows on the air that after a while they begin to think the hustling *is* the programming. Or so argues Merrill Panitt in his essay "Television Today: The State of the Art." According to Panitt, network programmers appear to be "more concerned with audience manipulation than the showmanship that begins with outstanding entertainment, more involved with scheduling technique than creativity in programs. It is as if the programs themselves are only incidental to putting together the schedule that will attract most of the $6–$7 a thousand audience, most of the time."

So it should come as no surprise that despite the time and energy invested in a web's fall line-up, each year the new TV season is routinely—and resoundingly—booed. A TV season "without salt, without grit, without daring and most telling of all, without a trace of popular excitement. . . a quarter billion dollar's worth of unprecedented blandness," is how one angry critic described the 1966/67 season. "Pale, unimaginative imitations of other television series, which in turn, were pale imitations of other older television shows," ran an indictment of the 1970/71 season. "A menu of stale, unimaginative pap," attacked a critic of the 1979/80 season.

According to Michael J. Arlen (often considered the finest TV critic writing in America today), the bulk of television fare is deliberately banal. "It is not a question, then," writes Arlen, "of a critic dutifully seeking out the scarce wildflowers in a meadow; it is a matter of his wandering about in a garden which the gardener himself has painstakingly planted with weeds."

The networks of course counter such arguments: the public does get what it wants, web execs contend, otherwise would so many millions still be watching the tube? And in a world in which no medium—film, fiction, theater—has a perfect track record, why single out TV for such abuse? "With each of the three networks producing 22 hours a week of prime time programming," CBS' Robert Daly points out, "it is virtually impossible for every moment of television to be of high quality. Look at the movies, books—look how many bad books are written."

And so the debate goes on. Is TV fare so truly terrible? Do the networks foist whatever they can get away with onto an innocent public that has no real way of letting its desires be known? Or do Americans get what they really want—and deserve—on TV?

For the answers to these and other exciting questions, stay tuned. . .

PRIME TIME SCHEDULE: 1950/51

		AMERICAN ABC	COLUMBIA CBS	DUMONT	NATIONAL NBC
S U N D A Y	7:00 PM 7:30 PM	Paul Whiteman's Review	Gene Autry Show	Starlit Time	Leave It To The Girls
	7:30 PM 8:00 PM	Showtime, U.S.A.	This is Show Business	Starlit Time	Aldrich Family
	8:00 PM 8:30 PM	Hollywood Premiere Theatre	Toast of the Town	Rhythm Rodeo	Colgate Comedy Hour
	8:30 PM 9:00 PM	Sit or Miss	Toast of the Town		Colgate Comedy Hour
	9:00 PM 9:30 PM	Soap Box Theatre	Fred Waring Show	Arthur Murray Party	Philco TV Playhouse
	9:30 PM 10:00 PM	Marshall Plan in Action	Fred Waring Show	Arthur Murray Party	Philco TV Playhouse
	10:00 PM 10:30 PM	Old Fashioned Meeting	Celebrity Time	They Stand Accused	Garroway at Large
	10:30 PM 11:00 PM	Youth on the March	What's My Line	They Stand Accused	Take a Chance
M O N D A Y	7:00 PM 7:30 PM	Club Seven	Stork Club	Captain Video	Kukla, Fran & Ollie
	7:30 PM 8:00 PM	Hollywood Screen Test	/*Perry Como	*Susan Raye /*Manhattan Spotlight	*Mohawk Showroom
	8:00 PM 8:30 PM	Treasury Men in Action	Lux Video Theatre	Visit with the Armed Forces	Speidel Show
	8:30 PM 9:00 PM	Dick Tracy	Arthur Godfrey's Talent Scouts	Al Morgan	Voice of Firestone
	9:00 PM 9:30 PM	College Bowl	Horace Heidt Show	Wrestling from Columbia Park	Lights Out
	9:30 PM 10:00 PM	On Trial	The Goldbergs	Wrestling from Columbia Park	†Robert Montgomery Presents Lucky Strike Time †Musical Comedy Time
	10:00 PM 10:30 PM	Feature Film	Studio One	Wrestling from Columbia Park	†Robert Montgomery Presents Lucky Strike Time †Musical Comedy Time
	10:30 PM 11:00 PM	Feature Film	Studio One	Wrestling from Columbia Park	Who Said That?
T U E S D A Y	7:00 PM 7:30 PM	Club Seven	Stork Club	Captain Video	Kukla, Fran & Ollie
	7:30 PM 8:00 PM	Beulah	/*Faye Emerson	/*Joan Edwards /*Manhattan Spotlight	*Little Show
	8:00 PM 8:30 PM	Game of the Week	†Prudential Family Playhouse †Sure as Fate	Court of Current Issues	Texaco Star Theater
	8:30 PM 9:00 PM	Buck Rogers	†Prudential Family Playhouse †Sure as Fate	John Hopkins Science Review	Texaco Star Theater
	9:00 PM 9:30 PM	Billy Rose Show	Vaughn Monroe Musical Variety	Cavalcade of Bands	Fireside Theatre
	9:30 PM 10:00 PM	Can You Top This?	Suspense	Cavalcade of Bands	Circle Theatre
	10:00 PM 10:30 PM	Life Begins at Eighty	Danger	Star Time	Original Amateur Hour
	10:30 PM 11:00 PM	Roller Derby	We Take Your Word	Star Time	Original Amateur Hour
W E D N E S D A Y	7:00 PM 7:30 PM	Club Seven	Stork Club	Captain Video	Kukla, Fran & Ollie
	7:30 PM 8:00 PM	Chance of a Lifetime	/*Perry Como	*Most Important People /*Manhattan Spotlight	*Mohawk Showroom
	8:00 PM 8:30 PM	First Nighter	Arthur Godfrey and His Friends		Four Star Review
	8:30 PM 9:00 PM	First Nighter	Arthur Godfrey and His Friends		Four Star Review
	9:00 PM 9:30 PM	Don McNeil TV Club	Teller of Tales	Famous Jury Trials	Kraft Television Theatre
	9:30 PM 10:00 PM	Don McNeil TV Club	Teller of Tales	The Plainclothesman	Kraft Television Theatre
	10:00 PM 10:30 PM	Chicago Wrestling	Blue Ribbon Bouts	Broadway to Hollywood	Break the Bank
	10:30 PM 11:00 PM	Chicago Wrestling	Blue Ribbon Bouts		Stars Over Hollywood

* First quarter hour program   /* Second quarter hour program
† Program airs every other week
Note: Repeated names indicate the program extends into that half-hour time slot.

PRIME TIME SCHEDULE: 1950/51

		AMERICAN ABC	COLUMBIA CBS	DUMONT	NATIONAL NBC
T **H** **U** **R** **S** **D** **A** **Y**	7:00 PM 7:30 PM	Club Seven	Stork Club	Captain Video	Kukla, Fran & Ollie
	7:30 PM 8:00 PM	Lone Ranger	/*Faye Emerson	*Manhattan Spotlight /*Joan Edwards	*Little Show
	8:00 PM 8:30 PM	Stop the Music	Show Goes On		You Bet Your Life
	8:30 PM 9:00 PM	Stop the Music	Show Goes On		Hawkins Falls
	9:00 PM 9:30 PM	Holiday Hotel	The Alan Young Show	Adventures of Ellery Queen	Kay Kyser's Kollege of Musical Knowledge
	9:30 PM 10:00 PM	Blind Date	Big Town	Boxing from Dexter Arena	Kay Kyser's Kollege of Musical Knowledge
	10:00 PM 10:30 PM	I Cover Times Square	Truth or Consequences	Boxing from Dexter Arena	Martin Kane, Private Eye
	10:30 PM 11:00 PM	Roller Derby	Nash Airflyte Theater	Boxing from Dexter Arena	Wayne King
F **R** **I** **D** **A** **Y**	7:00 PM 7:30 PM	Club Seven	Stork Club	Captain Video	Kukla, Fran & Ollie
	7:30 PM 8:00 PM	Life with Linkletter	/*Perry Como	*Most Important People /*Manhattan Spotlight	*Mohawk Showroom
	8:00 PM 8:30 PM	Twenty Questions	Mama	Film Filler	Quiz Kids
	8:30 PM 9:00 PM	Pro Football Highlights	Man Against Crime	Hold That Camera	We, the People
	9:00 PM 9:30 PM	Pulitzer Prize Playhouse	†Ford Theatre †Magnavox Theater	Hands of Mystery	Bonny Maid Versatile Varieties
	9:30 PM 10:00 PM	Pulitzer Prize Playhouse	†Ford Theatre †Magnavox Theater	Inside Detective	†Big Story †The Clock
	10:00 PM 10:30 PM	Penthouse Party	Morton Downy Show	Cavalcade of Stars	Gillette Cavalcade of Sports
	10:30 PM 11:00 PM	Stud's Place	Beat the Clock	Cavalcade of Stars	*Gillette Cavalcade of Sports /*Greatest Fights
S **A** **T** **U** **R** **D** **A** **Y**	7:00 PM 7:30 PM	Sandy Dreams	Big Top	Captain Video	Hank McCune
	7:30 PM 8:00 PM	Stu Erwin Show	*Week in Review /*Faye Emerson		One Man's Family
	8:00 PM 8:30 PM	Paul Whiteman's Teen Club	Ken Murray Show	Country Style	Jack Carter Show
	8:30 PM 9:00 PM	Paul Whiteman's Teen Club	Ken Murray Show	Country Style	Jack Carter Show
	9:00 PM 9:30 PM	Roller Derby	Frank Sinatra Show	Madison Square Garden	Your Show of Shows
	9:30 PM 10:00 PM	Roller Derby	Frank Sinatra Show	Madison Square Garden	Your Show of Shows
	10:00 PM 10:30 PM	Roller Derby	Sing It Again	Madison Square Garden	Your Show of Shows
	10:30 PM 11:00 PM	Roller Derby	Sing It Again	Madison Square Garden	Your Hit Parade

* First quarter hour program   /* Second quarter hour program
† Program airs every other week
Note: Repeated names indicate the program extends into that half-hour time slot.

PRIME TIME SCHEDULE: 1951/52

	AMERICAN ABC	COLUMBIA CBS	DUMONT	NATIONAL NBC
SUNDAY				
7:00 PM 7:30 PM	Paul Whiteman's Goodyear Revue	Gene Autry Show		Chesterfield Sound Off Time
7:30 PM 8:00 PM	Music in Velvet	This is Show Business		Young Mr. Bobbin
8:00 PM 8:30 PM	Admission Free	Toast of the Town		Colgate Comedy Hour
8:30 PM 9:00 PM	Admission Free	Toast of the Town		Colgate Comedy Hour
9:00 PM 9:30 PM	Film Filler	Fred Waring Show	Rocky King, Detective	†Philco TV Playhouse †Goodyear TV Playhouse
9:30 PM 10:00 PM	Marshall Plan in Action	Fred Waring Show	The Plainclothesman	†Philco TV Playhouse †Goodyear TV Playhouse
10:00 PM 10:30 PM	Hour of Decision	Goodrich Celebrity Time	They Stand Accused	Red Skelton Show
10:30 PM 11:00 PM	Youth on the March	What's My Line	They Stand Accused	Leave It to the Girls
MONDAY				
7:00 PM 7:30 PM			Captain Video	Kukla, Fran & Ollie
7:30 PM 8:00 PM	Hollywood Screen Test	/*Perry Como		*Mohawk Showroom
8:00 PM 8:30 PM	†Mr. District Attorney †Amazing Mr. Malone	Lux Video Theatre	Stage Entrance	Speidel Show
8:30 PM 9:00 PM	Life Begins at Eighty	Arthur Godfrey's Talent Scouts	Johns Hopkins Science Review	Voice of Firestone
9:00 PM 9:30 PM	Curtain Up	I Love Lucy	Wrestling from Columbia Park	Lights Out
9:30 PM 10:00 PM	Curtain Up	It's News to Me	Wrestling from Columbia Park	†Robert Montgomery Presents †Somerset Maugham TV Theatre
10:00 PM 10:30 PM	Bill Gwinn Show	Studio One	Wrestling from Columbia Park	†Robert Montgomery Presents †Somerset Maugham TV Theatre
10:30 PM 11:00 PM	Stud's Place	Studio One	Wrestling from Columbia Park	
TUESDAY				
7:00 PM 7:30 PM			Captain Video	Kukla, Fran & Ollie
7:30 PM 8:00 PM	Beulah	/*Stork Club		*Little Show
8:00 PM 8:30 PM	Charlie Wild, Private Detective	Frank Sinatra Show	What's the Story?	Texaco Star Theater
8:30 PM 9:00 PM	How Did They Get That Way	Frank Sinatra Show	Keep Posted	Texaco Star Theater
9:00 PM 9:30 PM	United or Not	Crime Syndicated	Cosmopolitan Theatre	Fireside Theatre
9:30 PM 10:00 PM	On Trial	Suspense	Cosmopolitan Theatre	Armstrong Circle Theatre
10:00 PM 10:30 PM	Film Filler	Danger	Hands of Destiny	Original Amateur Hour
10:30 PM 11:00 PM	Chicago Symphony Chamber Orchestra			Original Amateur Hour
WEDNESDAY				
7:00 PM 7:30 PM			Captain Video	Kukla, Fran & Ollie
7:30 PM 8:00 PM	Chance of a Lifetime	/*Perry Como		*Mohawk Showroom
8:00 PM 8:30 PM	Paul Dixon Show	Arthur Godfrey and His Friends		Kate Smith Evening Hour
8:30 PM 9:00 PM	Paul Dixon Show	Arthur Godfrey and His Friends		Kate Smith Evening Hour
9:00 PM 9:30 PM	†Don McNeil TV Club †Arthur Murray Party	Strike It Rich	Gallery of Mme Liu-Tsong	Kraft Television Theatre
9:30 PM 10:00 PM	The Clock	The Web	Shadow of the Cloak	Kraft Television Theatre
10:00 PM 10:30 PM	†Celanese Theatre †King's Crossroads	Pabst Blue Ribbon Bouts		Break the Bank
10:30 PM 11:00 PM	†Celanese Theatre †King's Crosswords	*Pabst Blue Ribbon Bouts /*Sports Spot		Freddy Martin Show

* First quarter hour program   /* Second quarter hour program
† Program airs every other week
Note: Repeated names indicate the program extends into that half-hour time slot.

PRIME TIME SCHEDULE: 1951/52

		AMERICAN ABC	COLUMBIA CBS	DUMONT	NATIONAL NBC
T H U R S D A Y	7:00 PM 7:30 PM			Captain Video	Kukla, Fran & Ollie
	7:30 PM 8:00 PM	Lone Ranger	/*Stork Club		*Little Show
	8:00 PM 8:30 PM	Stop the Music	†George Burns & Gracie Allen †Garry Moore Show	Georgetown University Forum	You Bet Your Life
	8:30 PM 9:00 PM	Stop the Music	Amos 'n' Andy	Broadway to Hollywood	Treasury Men in Action
	9:00 PM 9:30 PM	Herb Shriner Show	The Alan Young Show	Adventures of Ellery Queen	Ford Festival
	9:30 PM 10:00 PM	Gruen Guild Theater	Big Town		Ford Festival
	10:00 PM 10:30 PM	Paul Dixon Show	Racket Squad	Bigelow Theatre	Martin Kane, Private Eye
	10:30 PM 11:00 PM	*Masland at Home Show /*Camel Myers Show	Crime Photographer	/*Football This Week	Wayne King
F R I D A Y	7:00 PM 7:30 PM			Captain Video	Kukla, Fran & Ollie
	7:30 PM 8:00 PM	†Say It With Acting †Life with Linkletter	/*Perry Como		*Mohawk Showroom
	8:00 PM 8:30 PM	Mystery Theatre	Mama	Twenty Questions	Quiz Kids
	8:30 PM 9:00 PM	Stu Erwin Show	Man Against Crime	You Asked for It	We, the People
	9:00 PM 9:30 PM	Crime with Father	Schlitz Playhouse of Stars	Down You Go	Big Story
	9:30 PM 10:00 PM	†Tales of Tomorrow †Versatile Varieties	Schlitz Playhouse of Stars	Front Page Detective	Aldrich Family
	10:00 PM 10:30 PM	Dell O'Dell Show	Live Like a Millionaire	Cavalcade of Stars	Gillette Cavalcade of Sports
	10:30 PM 11:00 PM	America in View	Hollywood Opening Night	Cavalcade of Stars	*Gillette Cavalcade of Sports /*Greatest Fights
S A T U R D A Y	7:00 PM 7:30 PM	Hollywood Theatre Time	Sammy Kaye Variety Show		American Youth Forum
	7:30 PM 8:00 PM	Jerry Colonna Show	Beat the Clock		One Man's Family
	8:00 PM 8:30 PM	Paul Whiteman's Teen Club	Ken Murray Show		All Star Revue
	8:30 PM 9:00 PM	Paul Whiteman's Teen Club	Ken Murray Show		All Star Revue
	9:00 PM 9:30 PM	Lesson in Safety	Fay Emerson's Wonderful Town		Your Show of Shows
	9:30 PM 10:00 PM	America's Health	Show Goes On	Wrestling from Chicago	Your Show of Shows
	10:00 PM 10:30 PM		Songs for Sale	Wrestling from Chicago	Your Show of Shows
	10:30 PM 11:00 PM		Songs for Sale	Wrestling from Chicago	Your Hit Parade

* First quarter hour program   /* Second quarter hour program
† Program airs every other week
Note: Repeated names indicate the program extends into that half-hour time slot.

PRIME TIME SCHEDULE: 1952/53

		AMERICAN ABC	COLUMBIA CBS	DUMONT	NATIONAL NBC
S U N D A Y	7:00 PM 7:30 PM	You Asked for It	Gene Autry Show	Georgetown University Forum	Red Skelton Show
	7:30 PM 8:00 PM	Hot Seat	This is Show Business		Doc Corkle
	8:00 PM 8:30 PM	All-Star News	Toast of the Town		Colgate Comedy Hour
	8:30 PM 9:00 PM	All-Star Shows	Toast of the Town		Colgate Comedy Hour
	9:00 PM 9:30 PM	Playhouse #7	Fred Waring Show	Rocky King, Detective	†Philco TV Playhouse †Goodyear TV Playhouse
	9:30 PM 10:00 PM	This is the Life	Break the Bank	The Plainclothesman	†Philco TV Playhouse †Goodyear TV Playhouse
	10:00 PM 10:30 PM	*Hour of Decision /*Film Filler	The Web	Arthur Murray Show	The Doctor
	10:30 PM 11:00 PM	Anywhere, U.S.A.	What's My Line	Youth on the March	
M O N D A Y	7:00 PM 7:30 PM			Captain Video	
	7:30 PM 8:00 PM	Hollywood Screen Test	/*Perry Como		*Those Two
	8:00 PM 8:30 PM	Inspector Mark Saber	Lux Video Theatre	Pentagon	What's My Name
	8:30 PM 9:00 PM	United or Not	Arthur Godfrey's Talent Scouts	Johns Hopkins Science Review	Voice of Firestone
	9:00 PM 9:30 PM	All Star News	I Love Lucy	Guide Right	Hollywood Opening Night
	9:30 PM 10:00 PM	All Star News	Life with Luigi	*Football Sidelines /*Famous Fights	Robert Montgomery Presents
	10:00 PM 10:30 PM		Studio One	Boxing from Eastern Parkway	Robert Montgomery Presents
	10:30 PM 11:00 PM		Studio One	Boxing from Eastern Parkway	Who Said That?
T U E S D A Y	7:00 PM 7:30 PM			Captain Video	/*Short Short Dramas
	7:30 PM 8:00 PM	Beulah	/*Heaven for Betsy		*Dinah Shore
	8:00 PM 8:30 PM		Leave it to Larry	Power of Women	Texaco Star Theater
	8:30 PM 9:00 PM		Red Buttons Show	Keep Posted	Texaco Star Theater
	9:00 PM 9:30 PM		†Crime Syndicated †City Hospital	Where Was I?	Fireside Theatre
	9:30 PM 10:00 PM		Suspense	Quick on the Draw	Armstrong Circle Theatre
	10:00 PM 10:30 PM		Danger		Two for the Money
	10:30 PM 11:00 PM				*Club Embassy /*On the Line with Considine
W E D N E S D A Y	7:00 PM 7:30 PM			Captain Video	
	7:30 PM 8:00 PM	Name's the Same	/*Perry Como	New York Giants Quarterback Huddle	*Those Two
	8:00 PM 8:30 PM	All-Star News	Arthur Godfrey and His Friends		I Married Joan
	8:30 PM 9:00 PM	All-Star News	Arthur Godfrey and His Friends	Trash or Treasure	†Scott Music Hall †Cavalcade of America
	9:00 PM 9:30 PM	Adventures of Ellery Queen	Strike It Rich	Stage a Number	Kraft Television Theatre
	9:30 PM 10:00 PM	Chicago Wrestling	Man Against Crime	Stage a Number	Kraft Television Theatre
	10:00 PM 10:30 PM	Chicago Wrestling	Pabst Blue Ribbon Bouts		This is Your Life
	10:30 PM 11:00 PM	Chicago Wrestling	*Pabst Blue Ribbon Bouts /*Sports Bouts		

* First quarter hour program   /* Second quarter hour program
† Program airs every other week
Note: Repeated names indicate the program extends into that half-hour time slot.

PRIME TIME SCHEDULE: 1952/53

		AMERICAN ABC	COLUMBIA CBS	DUMONT	NATIONAL NBC
THURSDAY	7:00 PM 7:30 PM			Captain Video	/*Short Short Dramas
	7:30 PM 8:00 PM	Lone Ranger	/*Heaven for Betsy		*Dinah Shore
	8:00 PM 8:30 PM	All-Star News	George Burns & Gracie Allen Show		You Bet Your Life
	8:30 PM 9:00 PM	Chance of a Lifetime	†Amos 'n' Andy †Four Star Playhouse	Broadway to Hollywood	Treasury Men in Action
	9:00 PM 9:30 PM	Politics on Trial	Pick the Winner	Pick the Winner	†Dragnet †Gangbusters
	9:30 PM 10:00 PM	On Guard	Big Town	What's the Story?	Ford Theatre
	10:00 PM 10:30 PM		Racket Squad	Author Meets the Critics	Martin Kane, Private Eye
	10:30 PM 11:00 PM		I've Got a Secret		
FRIDAY	7:00 PM 7:30 PM			Captain Video	*Herman Hickman Show
	7:30 PM 8:00 PM	Stu Erwin Show	/*Perry Como		*Those Two
	8:00 PM 8:30 PM	Adventures of Ozzie & Harriet	Mama	Steve Randall	RCA Victor Show
	8:30 PM 9:00 PM	All-Star News	My Friend Irma	Dark of Night	Gulf Playhouse
	9:00 PM 9:30 PM	All-Star News	Schlitz Playhouse of Stars	Life Begins at Eighty	Big Story
	9:30 PM 10:00 PM	Tales of Tomorrow	Our Miss Brooks		Aldrich Family
	10:00 PM 10:30 PM		Mr. & Mrs. North	Twenty Questions	Gillette Cavalcade of Sports
	10:30 PM 11:00 PM			Down You Go	*Gillette Cavalcade of Sports /*Greatest Fights
SATURDAY	7:00 PM 7:30 PM	Paul Whiteman's TV Teen Club	Stork Club		Mr. Wizard
	7:30 PM 8:00 PM	Live Like a Millionaire	Beat the Clock	Pet Shop	My Little Margie
	8:00 PM 8:30 PM	Feature Playhouse	Jackie Gleason Show		All Star Review
	8:30 PM 9:00 PM	Feature Playhouse	Jackie Gleason Show		All Star Revue
	9:00 PM 9:30 PM	Feature Playhouse	Jane Froman's U.S.A. Canteen		Your Show of Shows
	9:30 PM 10:00 PM	Feature Playhouse	Meet Millie	Wrestling from Chicago	Your Show of Shows
	10:00 PM 10:30 PM		†Balance Your Budget †Quiz Kids	Wrestling from Chicago	Your Show of Shows
	10:30 PM 11:00 PM		Battle of the Ages	Wrestling from Chicago	Your Hit Parade

* First quarter hour program   /* Second quarter hour program
† Program airs every other week
Note: Repeated names indicate the program extends into that half-hour time slot.

PRIME TIME SCHEDULE: 1953/54

		AMERICAN ABC	COLUMBIA CBS	DUMONT	NATIONAL NBC
S U N D A Y	7:00 PM 7:30 PM	You Asked for It	Quiz Kids	Georgetown University Forum	Paul Winchell Show
	7:30 PM 8:00 PM	*Frank Leahy Show /*Notre Dame Football	†Jack Benny Show †Private Secretary	Washington Exclusive	Mr. Peepers
	8:00 PM 8:30 PM	Notre Dame Football	Toast of the Town		Colgate Comedy Hour
	8:30 PM 9:00 PM	Notre Dame Football	Toast of the Town		Colgate Comedy Hour
	9:00 PM 9:30 PM	*Walter Winchell Show /*Orchid Award	†G.E. Theater †Fred Waring Show	Rocky King, Detective	†Philco TV Playhouse †Goodyear TV Playhouse
	9:30 PM 10:00 PM	Peter Potter Show	Man Behind the Badge	The Plainclothesman	†Philco TV Playhouse †Goodyear TV Playhouse
	10:00 PM 10:30 PM	Peter Potter Show	The Web	Dollar a Second	Letter to Loretta
	10:30 PM 11:00 PM	*Hour of Decision	What's My Line	Man Against Crime	Man Against Crime
M O N D A Y	7:00 PM 7:30 PM	*Walter Winchell		Captain Video	
	7:30 PM 8:00 PM	Jamie	/*Perry Como		*Arthur Murray Party
	8:00 PM 8:30 PM	Sky King	George Burns and Gracie Allen Show	Twenty Questions	Name That Tune
	8:30 PM 9:00 PM	Of Many Things	Arthur Godfrey's Talent Scouts	Big Issue	Voice of Firestone
	9:00 PM 9:30 PM	Junior Press Conference	I Love Lucy	Boxing from Eastern Parkway	RCA Victor Show Starring Dennis Day
	9:30 PM 10:00 PM	Big Picture	Red Buttons Show	Boxing from Eastern Parkway	Robert Montgomery Presents
	10:00 PM 10:30 PM	This is the Life	Studio One	Boxing from Eastern Parkway	Robert Montgomery Presents
	10:30 PM 11:00 PM		Studio One	Boxing from Eastern Parkway	Who Said That?
T U E S D A Y	7:00 PM 7:30 PM			*Captain Video	
	7:30 PM 8:00 PM	Cavalcade of America	/*Jane Froman		*Dinah Shore
	8:00 PM 8:30 PM		Gene Autry show	Life is Worth Living	Buick Berle Show
	8:30 PM 9:00 PM		Red Skelton Show	Pantomime Quiz	Buick Berle Show
	9:00 PM 9:30 PM	Make Room for Daddy	This is Show Business		Fireside Theatre
	9:30 PM 10:00 PM	†U.S. Steel Hour †Motorola TV Theatre	Suspense		Armstrong Circle Theatre
	10:00 PM 10:30 PM	†U.S. Steel Hour †Motorola TV Theatre	Danger		Judge for Yourself
	10:30 PM 11:00 PM	Name's the Same	See It Now		*On the Line with Considine /*It Happened in Sports
W E D N E S D A Y	7:00 PM 7:30 PM			Captain Video	
	7:30 PM 8:00 PM	Inspector Mark Saber	/*Perry Como		*Coke Time
	8:00 PM 8:30 PM	*At Issue/*Through the Curtain	Arthur Godfrey and His Friends	John Hopkins Science Review	I Married Joan
	8:30 PM 9:00 PM	America in View	Arthur Godfrey and His Friends	Joseph Schildkraut Presents	My Little Margie
	9:00 PM 9:30 PM	Wrestling from Rainbo	Strike It Rich	Colonel Humphrey Flack	Kraft Television Theatre
	9:30 PM 10:00 PM	Wrestling from Rainbo	I've Got a Secret	On Your Way	Kraft Television Theatre
	10:00 PM 10:30 PM	Wrestling from Rainbo	Pabst Blue Ribbon Bouts	Stars on Parade	This is Your Life
	10:30 PM 11:00 PM	Wrestling from Rainbo	*Pabst Blue Ribbon Bouts /*Sports Spot	Music Show	This is Your Life

* First quarter hour program   /* Second quarter hour program
† Program airs every other week
Note: Repeated names indicate the program extends into that half-hour time slot.

PRIME TIME SCHEDULE: 1953/54

		AMERICAN ABC	COLUMBIA CBS	DUMONT	NATIONAL NBC
T H U R S D A Y	7:00 PM 7:30 PM			Captain Video	
	7:30 PM 8:00 PM	Lone Ranger	/*Jane Froman		*Dinah Shore
	8:00 PM 8:30 PM	Quick as a Flash	Meet Mr. McNulty	New York Giants Quarterback Huddle	You Bet Your Life
	8:30 PM 9:00 PM	Where's Raymond	Four Star Playhouse	Broadway to Hollywood	Treasury Men in Action
	9:00 PM 9:30 PM	Back That Fact	Lux Video Theatre	What's the Story	Dragnet
	9:30 PM 10:00 PM	Kraft Television Theatre	Big Town		Ford Theatre
	10:00 PM 10:30 PM	Kraft Television Theatre	Philip Morris Playhouse		Martin Kane, Private Eye
	10:30 PM 11:00 PM		Place the Face		
F R I D A Y	7:00 PM 7:30 PM				
	7:30 PM 8:00 PM	Stu Erwin Show	/*Perry Como		*Coke Time
	8:00 PM 8:30 PM	Adventures of Ozzie & Harriet	Mama	Front Page Detective	Dave Garroway Show
	8:30 PM 9:00 PM	Pepsi-Cola Playhouse	Topper	Melody Street	Life of Riley
	9:00 PM 9:30 PM	Pride of the Family	Schlitz Playhouse of Stars	Life Begins at Eighty	Big Story
	9:30 PM 10:00 PM	Comeback Story	Our Miss Brooks	Nine Thirty Curtain	Campbell Soundstage
	10:00 PM 10:30 PM	Showcase Theater	My Friend Irma	Chance of a Lifetime	Gillette Cavalcade of Sports
	10:30 PM 11:00 PM		Person to Person	Down You Go	*Gillette Cavalcade of Sports /*Greatest Fights
S A T U R D A Y	7:00 PM 7:30 PM	Paul Whiteman's TV Teen Club	Meet Millie		Mr. Wizard
	7:30 PM 8:00 PM	Leave it to the Girls	Beat the Clock		Ethel & Albert
	8:00 PM 8:30 PM	Talent Patrol	Jackie Gleason Show	Pro Football	Bonino
	8:30 PM 9:00 PM	Music at the Meadowbrook	Jackie Gleason Show	Pro Football	Original Amateur Hour
	9:00 PM 9:30 PM	Saturday Night Fights	Two for the Money	Pro Football	Your Show of Shows
	9:30 PM 10:00 PM	/*Saturday Night Fights *Fight Talk	My Favorite Husband	Pro Football	Your Show of Shows
	10:00 PM 10:30 PM	Madison Square Garden Highlights	Medallion Theatre	Pro Football	Your Show of Shows
	10:30 PM 11:00 PM		Revlon Mirror Theatre	Pro Football	Your Hit Parade

* First quarter hour program   /* Second quarter hour program
† Program airs every other week
Note: Repeated names indicate the program extends into that half-hour time slot.

PRIME TIME SCHEDULE: 1954/55

		AMERICAN ABC	COLUMBIA CBS	DUMONT	NATIONAL NBC
S U N D A Y	7:00 PM 7:30 PM	You Asked for It	Lassie	Author Meets the Critic	People Are Funny
	7:30 PM 8:00 PM	Pepsi-Cola Playhouse	†Jack Benny Show †Private Secretary	Opera Cameos	Mr. Peepers
	8:00 PM 8:30 PM	Flight #7	Toast of the Town		Colgate Comedy Hour
	8:30 PM 9:00 PM	Big Picture	Toast of the Town		Colgate Comedy Hour
	9:00 PM 9:30 PM	*Walter Winchell Show /*Martha Wright Show	G.E. Theater	Rocky King, Detective	†Philco TV Playhouse †Goodyear TV Playhouse
	9:30 PM 10:00 PM	Dr. I.Q.	Honestly Celeste	Life Begins at Eighty	†Philco TV Playhouse †Goodyear TV Playhouse
	10:00 PM 10:30 PM	Break the Bank	Father Knows Best	Music Show	Loretta Young Show
	10:30 PM 11:00 PM		What's My Line		The Hunter
M O N D A Y	7:00 PM 7:30 PM	*Kukla, Fran & Ollie		*Captain Video	
	7:30 PM 8:00 PM	Name's the Same	/*Perry Como		*Tony Martin/
	8:00 PM 8:30 PM	Come Closer	George Burns and Gracie Allen Show	Ilona Massey Show	Caesar's Hour
	8:30 PM 9:00 PM	Voice of Firestone	Arthur Godfrey's Talent Scouts		Caesar's Hour
	9:00 PM 9:30 PM	Junior Press Conference	I Love Lucy	Boxing from St. Nicholas Arena	Medic
	9:30 PM 10:00 PM	Boxing from Eastern Parkway	December Bride	Boxing from St. Nicholas Arena	Robert Montgomery Presents
	10:00 PM 10:30 PM	Boxing from Eastern Parkway	Studio One	Boxing from St. Nicholas Arena	Robert Montgomery Presents
	10:30 PM 11:00 PM	Boxing from Eastern Parkway	Studio One	Boxing from St. Nicholas Arena	
T U E S D A Y	7:00 PM 7:30 PM	*Kukla, Fran & Ollie		*Captain Video	
	7:30 PM 8:00 PM	Cavalcade of America	/*Jo Stafford		*Dinah Shore
	8:00 PM 8:30 PM		Red Skelton Show	Life is Worth Living	Buick Berle Show
	8:30 PM 9:00 PM	Twenty Questions	Halls of Ivy	Studio 57	Buick Berle Show
	9:00 PM 9:30 PM	Make Room for Daddy	Meet Millie	One Minute Please	Fireside Theatre
	9:30 PM 10:00 PM	†U.S. Steel Hour †Elgin TV Hour	Danger		Armstrong Circle Theatre
	10:00 PM 10:30 PM	†U.S. Steel Hour †Elgin TV Hour	Life with Father		Truth or Consequences
	10:30 PM 11:00 PM	Stop the Music	See It Now		It's a Great Life
W E D N E S D A Y	7:00 PM 7:30 PM	*Kukla, Fran & Ollie		*Captain Video	
	7:30 PM 8:00 PM	Disneyland	/*Perry Como		*Coke Time/
	8:00 PM 8:30 PM	Disneyland	Arthur Godfrey and His Friends		I Married Joan
	8:30 PM 9:00 PM	Stu Erwin Show	Arthur Godfrey and His Friends		My Little Margie
	9:00 PM 9:30 PM	Masquerade Party	Strike It Rich	Chicago Symphony	Kraft Television Theatre
	9:30 PM 10:00 PM	Enterprise	I've Got a Secret	Chicago Symphony	Kraft Television Theatre
	10:00 PM 10:30 PM		Pabst Blue Ribbon Bouts	Down You Go	This is Your Life
	10:30 PM 11:00 PM		*Pabst Blue Ribbon Bouts /*Sports Spot		Big Town

* First quarter hour program   /* Second quarter hour program
† Program airs every other week
Note: Repeated names indicate the program extends into that half-hour time slot.

PRIME TIME SCHEDULE: 1954/55

		AMERICAN ABC	COLUMBIA CBS	DUMONT	NATIONAL NBC
T **H** **U** **R** **S** **D** **A** **Y**	7:00 PM 7:30 PM	*Kukla, Fran & Ollie		*Captain Video	
	7:30 PM 8:00 PM	Lone Ranger	/*Jane Froman		*Dinah Shore
	8:00 PM 8:30 PM	Mail Story	Ray Milland Show	They Stand Accused	You Bet Your Life
	8:30 PM 9:00 PM	Treasury Men in Action	Climax	They Stand Accused	Justice
	9:00 PM 9:30 PM	So You Want to Lead a Band	Climax	What's the Story?	Dragnet
	9:30 PM 10:00 PM	Kraft Television Theatre	Four Star Playhouse		Ford Theatre
	10:00 PM 10:30 PM	Kraft Television Theatre	Public Defender		Lux Video Theatre
	10:30 PM 11:00 PM		Name That Tune		Lux Video Theatre
F **R** **I** **D** **A** **Y**	7:00 PM 7:30 PM	*Kukla, Fran & Ollie		*Captain Video	
	7:30 PM 8:00 PM	Adventures of Rin Tin Tin	/*Perry Como		*Coke Time
	8:00 PM 8:30 PM	Adventures of Ozzie & Harriet	Mama		Red Buttons Show
	8:30 PM 9:00 PM	Ray Bolger Show	Topper		Life of Riley
	9:00 PM 9:30 PM	Dollar a Second	Schlitz Playhouse of Stars	The Stranger	Big Story
	9:30 PM 10:00 PM	The Vise	Our Miss Brooks		Dear Phoebe
	10:00 PM 10:30 PM		The Lineup	Chance of a Lifetime	Gillette Cavalcade of Sports
	10:30 PM 11:00 PM		Person to Person	Time Will Tell	*Gillette Cavalcade of Sports /*Great Moments in Sports
S **A** **T** **U** **R** **D** **A** **Y**	7:00 PM 7:30 PM		Gene Autry Show		Mr. Wizard
	7:30 PM 8:00 PM	Compass	Beat the Clock		Ethel & Albert
	8:00 PM 8:30 PM	Dolly Mack Show	Jackie Gleason Show	Pro Football	Mickey Rooney Show
	8:30 PM 9:00 PM	Dolly Mack Show	Jackie Gleason Show	Pro Football	Place the Face
	9:00 PM 9:30 PM	Saturday Night Fights	Two for the Money	Pro Football	Imogene Coca Show
	9:30 PM 10:00 PM	*Saturday Night Fights /*Fight Talk	My Favorite Husband	Pro Football	Texaco Star Theater
	10:00 PM 10:30 PM	Stork Club	That's My Boy	Pro Football	George Gobel Show
	10:30 PM 11:00 PM		Willy	Pro Football	Your Hit Parade

* First quarter hour program   /* Second quarter hour program
† Program airs every other week
Note: Repeated names indicate the program extends into that half-hour time slot.

PRIME TIME SCHEDULE: 1955/56

		AMERICAN ABC	COLUMBIA CBS	NATIONAL NBC
S U N D A Y	7:00 PM 7:30 PM	You Asked for It	Lassie	It's a Great Life
	7:30 PM 8:00 PM	Famous Film Festival	†Jack Benny Show †Private Secretary	Frontier
	8:00 PM 8:30 PM	Famous Film Festival	Ed Sullivan Show	Colgate Variety Hour
	8:30 PM 9:00 PM	Famous Film Festival	Ed Sullivan Show	Colgate Variety Hour
	9:00 PM 9:30 PM	Chance of a Lifetime	G.E. Theater	†Goodyear TV Playhouse †Alcoa Hour
	9:30 PM 10:00 PM	Original Amateur Hour	Alfred Hitchcock Presents	†Goodyear TV Playhouse †Alcoa Hour
	10:00 PM 10:30 PM	Life Begins at Eighty	$64,000 Challenge	Loretta Young Show
	10:30 PM 11:00 PM		What's My Line	Justice
M O N D A Y	7:00 PM 7:30 PM	*Kukla, Fran & Ollie		
	7:30 PM 8:00 PM	Topper	Adventures of Robin Hood	*Tony Martin Show
	8:00 PM 8:30 PM	TV Reader's Digest	George Burns and Gracie Allen Show	Caesar's Hour
	8:30 PM 9:00 PM	Voice of Firestone	Arthur Godfrey's Talent Scouts	Caesar's Hour
	9:00 PM 9:30 PM	Dolly Mack Show	I Love Lucy	Medic
	9:30 PM 10:00 PM	Medical Horizons	December Bride	Robert Montgomery Presents
	10:00 PM 10:30 PM	Big Picture	Studio One	Robert Montgomery Presents
	10:30 PM 11:00 PM			
T U E S D A Y	7:00 PM 7:30 PM	*Kukla, Fran & Ollie		
	7:30 PM 8:00 PM	Warner Brothers Presents	Name That Tune	*Dinah Shore Show
	8:00 PM 8:30 PM	Warner Brothers Presents	Navy Log	†Martha Raye Show †Milton Berle Show †Chevy Show
	8:30 PM 9:00 PM	Life and Legend of Wyatt Earp	You'll Never Get Rich	†Martha Raye Show †Milton Berle Show †Chevy Show
	9:00 PM 9:30 PM	Make Room for Daddy	Meet Millie	Fireside Theatre
	9:30 PM 10:00 PM	DuPont Cavalcade Theater	Red Skelton Show	†Armstrong Circle Theatre †Pontiac Presents Playwrights '56
	10:00 PM 10:30 PM	Talent Varieties	$64,000 Question	†Armstrong Circle Theatre †Pontiac Presents Playwrights '56
	10:30 PM 11:00 PM		My Favorite Husband	Big Town
W E D N E S D A Y	7:00 PM 7:30 PM	*Kukla, Fran & Ollie		
	7:30 PM 8:00 PM	Disneyland	Brave Eagle	*Coke Time
	8:00 PM 8:30 PM	Disneyland	Arthur Godfrey and His Friends	Screen Director's Playhouse
	8:30 PM 9:00 PM	MGM Parade	Arthur Godfrey and His Friends	Father Knows Best
	9:00 PM 9:30 PM	Masquerade Party	The Millionaire	Kraft Television Theatre
	9:30 PM 10:00 PM	Break the Bank	I've Got a Secret	Kraft Television Theatre
	10:00 PM 10:30 PM	Wednesday Night Fights	†20th Century-Fox Hour †U.S. Steel Hour	This is Your Life
	10:30 PM 11:00 PM	Wednesday Night Fights	†20th Century-Fox Hour †U.S. Steel Hour	Midwestern Hayride

* First quarter hour program   /* Second quarter hour program
† Program airs every other week
Note: Repeated names indicate the program extends into that half-hour time slot.

PRIME TIME SCHEDULE: 1955/56

		AMERICAN ABC	COLUMBIA CBS	NATIONAL NBC
T H U R S D A Y	7:00 PM 7:30 PM	*Kukla, Fran & Ollie		
	7:30 PM 8:00 PM	Lone Ranger	Sgt. Preston of the Yukon	*Dinah Shore Show
	8:00 PM 8:30 PM	Life Is Worth Living	Bob Cummings Show	You Bet Your Life
	8:30 PM 9:00 PM	Stop the Music	Climax	People's Choice
	9:00 PM 9:30 PM	Star Tonight	Climax	Dragnet
	9:30 PM 10:00 PM	Down You Go	Four Star Playhouse	Ford Theatre
	10:00 PM 10:30 PM	Outside U.S.A.	Johnny Carson Show	Lux Video Theatre
	10:30 PM 11:00 PM		Wanted	Lux Video Theatre
F R I D A Y	7:00 PM 7:30 PM	*Kukla, Fran & Ollie		
	7:30 PM 8:00 PM	Adventures of Rin Tin Tin	Adventures of Champion	*Coke Time
	8:00 PM 8:30 PM	Adventures of Ozzie & Harriet	Mama	Truth or Consequences
	8:30 PM 9:00 PM	Crossroads	Our Miss Brooks	Life of Riley
	9:00 PM 9:30 PM	Dollar a Second	The Crusader	Big Story
	9:30 PM 10:00 PM	The Vise	Schlitz Playhouse	Star Stage
	10:00 PM 10:30 PM	Ethel & Albert	The Lineup	Gillette Cavalcade of Sports
	10:30 PM 11:00 PM		Person to Person	*Gillette Cavalcade of Sports /*Red Barber's Corner
S A T U R D A Y	7:00 PM 7:30 PM		Gene Autry Show	
	7:30 PM 8:00 PM	Ozark Jubilee	Beat the Clock	Big Surprise
	8:00 PM 8:30 PM	Ozark Jubilee	Stage Show	Perry Como Show
	8:30 PM 9:00 PM	Ozark Jubilee	The Honeymooners	Perry Como Show
	9:00 PM 9:30 PM	Lawrence Welk Show	Two for the Money	People Are Funny
	9:30 PM 10:00 PM	Lawrence Welk Show	It's Always Jan	Texaco Star Theater Jimmy Durante
	10:00 PM 10:30 PM	Tomorrow's Careers	Gunsmoke	George Gobel Show
	10:30 PM 11:00 PM		Damon Runyon Theatre	Your Hit Parade

* First quarter hour program   /* Second quarter hour program
† Program airs every other week
Note: Repeated names indicate the program extends into that half-hour time slot.

PRIME TIME SCHEDULE: 1956/57

		AMERICAN ABC	COLUMBIA CBS	NATIONAL NBC
S U N D A Y	7:00 PM 7:30 PM	You Asked for It	Lassie	Tales of the 77th Bengal Lancers
	7:30 PM 8:00 PM	Original Amateur Hour	†Jack Benny Show †Private Secretary	Circus Boy
	8:00 PM 8:30 PM	Original Amateur Hour	Ed Sullivan Show	Steve Allen Show
	8:30 PM 9:00 PM	Press Conference	Ed Sullivan Show	Steve Allen Show
	9:00 PM 9:30 PM	Omnibus	G.E. Theater	†Goodyear TV Playhouse †Alcoa Hour
	9:30 PM 10:00 PM	Omnibus	Alfred Hitchcock Presents	†Goodyear TV Playhouse †Alcoa Hour
	10:00 PM 10:30 PM	Omnibus	$64,000 Challenge	Loretta Young Show
	10:30 PM 11:00 PM		What's My Line	National Bowling Champions
M O N D A Y	7:00 PM 7:30 PM	*Kukla, Fran & Ollie		
	7:30 PM 8:00 PM	Bold Journey	Adventures of Robin Hood	*Nat "King" Cole Show
	8:00 PM 8:30 PM	Danny Thomas Show	George Burns and Gracie Allen Show	Adventures of Sir Lancelot
	8:30 PM 9:00 PM	Voice of Firestone	Arthur Godfrey's Talent Scouts	Stanley
	9:00 PM 9:30 PM	Life is Worth Living	I Love Lucy	Medic
	9:30 PM 10:00 PM	Lawrence Welk Talent Show	December Bride	Robert Montgomery Presents
	10:00 PM 10:30 PM	Lawrence Welk Talent Show	Studio One	Robert Montgomery Presents
	10:30 PM 11:00 PM		Studio One	
T U E S D A Y	7:00 PM 7:30 PM	*Kukla, Fran & Ollie		
	7:30 PM 8:00 PM	†Conflict †Cheyenne	Name That Tune	*Jonathan Winters Show
	8:00 PM 8:30 PM	†Conflict †Cheyenne	Phil Silvers Show	Big Surprise
	8:30 PM 9:00 PM	Life and Legend of Wyatt Earp	The Brothers	Noah's Ark
	9:00 PM 9:30 PM	Broken Arrow	Herb Shriner Show	Jane Wyman Show
	9:30 PM 10:00 PM	DuPont Theater	Red Skelton Show	†Armstrong Circle Theatre †Kaiser Aluminum Hour
	10:00 PM 10:30 PM	It's Polka Time	$64,000 Question	†Armstrong Circle Theatre †Kaiser Aluminum Hour
	10:30 PM 11:00 PM		Do You Trust Your Wife?	Break the $250,000 Bank
W E D N E S D A Y	7:00 PM 7:30 PM	*Kukla, Fran & Ollie		
	7:30 PM 8:00 PM	Disneyland	Giant Step	*Eddie Fisher Show
	8:00 PM 8:30 PM	Disneyland	Arthur Godfrey Show	Adventures of Hiram Holliday
	8:30 PM 9:00 PM	Navy Log	Arthur Godfrey Show	Father Knows Best
	9:00 PM 9:30 PM	Adventures of Ozzie & Harriet	The Millionaire	Kraft Television Theatre
	9:30 PM 10:00 PM	Ford Theatre	I've Got a Secret	Kraft Television Theatre
	10:00 PM 10:30 PM	Wednesday Night Fights	†20th Century-Fox Hour †U.S. Steel Hour	This is Your Life
	10:30 PM 11:00 PM	Wednesday Night Fights	†20th Century-Fox Hour †U.S. Steel Hour	Twenty-One

* First quarter hour program /* Second quarter hour program
† Program airs every other week
Note: Repeated names indicate the program extends into that half-hour time slot.

PRIME TIME SCHEDULE: 1956/57

		AMERICAN ABC	COLUMBIA CBS	NATIONAL NBC
T H U R S D A Y	7:00 PM 7:30 PM	*Kukla, Fran & Ollie		
	7:30 PM 8:00 PM	Lone Ranger	Sgt. Preston of the Yukon	*Dinah Shore Show
	8:00 PM 8:30 PM	Circus Time	Bob Cummings Show	You Bet Your Life
	8:30 PM 9:00 PM	Circus Time	Climax	Dragnet
	9:00 PM 9:30 PM	Wire Service	Climax	People's Choice
	9:30 PM 10:00 PM	Wire Service	Playhouse 90	Ford Show Starring Tennessee Ernie Ford
	10:00 PM 10:30 PM	Ozark Jubilee	Playhouse 90	Lux Video Theatre
	10:30 PM 11:00 PM	Ozark Jubilee	Playhouse 90	Lux Video Theatre
F R I D A Y	7:00 PM 7:30 PM	*Kukla, Fran & Ollie		
	7:30 PM 8:00 PM	Adventures of Rin Tin Tin	My Friend Flicka	*Eddie Fisher Show
	8:00 PM 8:30 PM	Adventures of Jim Bowie	West Point Story	Life of Riley
	8:30 PM 9:00 PM	Crossroads	Dick Powell's Zane Grey Theater	Walter Winchell Show
	9:00 PM 9:30 PM	Treasure Hunt	The Crusader	On Trial
	9:30 PM 10:00 PM	The Vise	Schlitz Playhouse	Big Story
	10:00 PM 10:30 PM	Ray Anthony Show	The Lineup	Gillette Cavalcade of Sports
	10:30 PM 11:00 PM	Ray Anthony Show	Person to Person	*Gillette Cavalcade of Sports /*Red Barber's Corner
S A T U R D A Y	7:00 PM 7:30 PM		Beat the Clock	
	7:30 PM 8:00 PM	Famous Film Festival	The Buccaneers	People Are Funny
	8:00 PM 8:30 PM	Famous Film Festival	Jackie Gleason Show	Perry Como Show
	8:30 PM 9:00 PM	Famous Film Festival	Jackie Gleason Show	Perry Como Show
	9:00 PM 9:30 PM	Lawrence Welk Show	Gale Storm Show	Caesar's Hour
	9:30 PM 10:00 PM	Lawrence Welk Show	Hey Jeannie	Caesar's Hour
	10:00 PM 10:30 PM	Masquerade Party	Gunsmoke	George Gobel Show
	10:30 PM 11:00 PM		High Finance	Your Hit Parade

* First quarter hour program   /* Second quarter hour program
† Program airs every other week
Note: Repeated names indicate the program extends into that half-hour time slot.

PRIME TIME SCHEDULE: 1957/58

		AMERICAN ABC	COLUMBIA CBS	NATIONAL NBC
S U N D A Y	7:00 PM 7:30 PM	You Asked for It	Lassie	Original Amateur Hour
	7:30 PM 8:00 PM	Maverick	†Jack Benny Show †Bachelor Father	Sally
	8:00 PM 8:30 PM	Maverick	Ed Sullivan Show	Steve Allen Show
	8:30 PM 9:00 PM	Bowling Stars	Ed Sullivan Show	Steve Allen Show
	9:00 PM 9:30 PM	Open Hearing	G.E. Theater	Dinah Shore Chevy Show
	9:30 PM 10:00 PM	All-American Football Game of the Week	Alfred Hitchcock Presents	Dinah Shore Chevy Show
	10:00 PM 10:30 PM		$64,000 Challenge	Loretta Young Show
	10:30 PM 11:00 PM		What's My Line	
M O N D A Y	7:00 PM 7:30 PM			
	7:30 PM 8:00 PM	American Bandstand	Robin Hood	Price is Right
	8:00 PM 8:30 PM	Guy Mitchell Show	George Burns and Gracie Allen Show	Restless Gun
	8:30 PM 9:00 PM	Bold Journey	Arthur Godfrey's Talent Scouts	Tales of Wells Fargo
	9:00 PM 9:30 PM	Voice of Firestone	Danny Thomas Show	Twenty-One
	9:30 PM 10:00 PM	Lawrence Welk's Top Tunes and New Talent Show	December Bride	Turn of Fate
	10:00 PM 10:30 PM	Lawrence Welk's Top Tunes and New Talent Show	Studio One in Hollywood	Suspicion
	10:30 PM 11:00 PM		Studio One in Hollywood	Suspicion
T U E S D A Y	7:00 PM 7:30 PM			
	7:30 PM 8:00 PM	†Cheyenne †Sugarfoot	Name That Tune	Nat "King" Cole Show
	8:00 PM 8:30 PM	†Cheyenne †Sugarfoot	Phil Silvers Show	†Eddie Fisher Show †George Gobel Show
	8:30 PM 9:00 PM	Life and Legend of Wyatt Earp	Eve Arden Show	†Eddie Fisher Show †George Gobel Show
	9:00 PM 9:30 PM	Broken Arrow	To Tell the Truth	Meet McGraw
	9:30 PM 10:00 PM	Telephone Time	Red Skelton Show	Bob Cummings Show
	10:00 PM 10:30 PM	West Point Story	$64,000 Question	The Californians
	10:30 PM 11:00 PM		Assignment Foreign Legion	
W E D N E S D A Y	7:00 PM 7:30 PM			
	7:30 PM 8:00 PM	Disneyland	I Love Lucy	Wagon Train
	8:00 PM 8:30 PM	Disneyland	Big Record	Wagon Train
	8:30 PM 9:00 PM	Tombstone Territory	Big Record	Father Knows Best
	9:00 PM 9:30 PM	Adventures of Ozzie & Harriet	The Millionaire	Kraft Television Theatre
	9:30 PM 10:00 PM	Walter Winchell File	I've Got a Secret	Kraft Television Theatre
	10:00 PM 10:30 PM	Wednesday Night Fights	†Armstrong Circle Theatre †U.S. Steel Hour	This is Your Life
	10:30 PM 11:00 PM	*Wednesday Night Fights /*Famous Fights	†Armstrong Circle Theatre †U.S. Steel Hour	

* First quarter hour program   /* Second quarter hour program
† Program airs every other week
Note: Repeated names indicate the program extends into that half-hour time slot.

PRIME TIME SCHEDULE: 1957/58

		AMERICAN ABC	COLUMBIA CBS	NATIONAL NBC
T H U R S D A Y	7:00 PM 7:30 PM			
	7:30 PM 8:00 PM	Circus Boy	Sgt. Preston of the Yukon	Tic Tac Dough
	8:00 PM 8:30 PM	Zorro	Harbourmaster	You Bet Your Life
	8:30 PM 9:00 PM	Real McCoys	Climax	Dragnet
	9:00 PM 9:30 PM	Pat Boone-Chevy Showroom	Climax	People's Choice
	9:30 PM 10:00 PM	O.S.S.	Playhouse 90	Ford Show Starring Tennessee Ernie Ford
	10:00 PM 10:30 PM	Navy Log	Playhouse 90	Lux Show Starring Rosemary Clooney
	10:30 PM 11:00 PM		Playhouse 90	Jane Wyman Show
F R I D A Y	7:00 PM 7:30 PM			
	7:30 PM 8:00 PM	Adventures of Rin Tin Tin	Leave It to Beaver	Saber of London
	8:00 PM 8:30 PM	Adventures of Jim Bowie	Trackdown	Court of Last Resort
	8:30 PM 9:00 PM	Patrice Munsel Show	Dick Powell's Zane Grey Theater	Life of Riley
	9:00 PM 9:30 PM	Frank Sinatra Show	Mr. Adams & Eve	M Squad
	9:30 PM 10:00 PM	Dale with the Angels	Schlitz Playhouse	Thin Man
	10:00 PM 10:30 PM	Colt 45	The Lineup	Gillette Cavalcade of Sports
	10:30 PM 11:00 PM		Person to Person	*Gillette Cavalcade of Sports /*Red Barber's Corner
S A T U R D A Y	7:00 PM 7:30 PM			
	7:30 PM 8:00 PM	Keep It in the Family	Perry Mason	People Are Funny
	8:00 PM 8:30 PM	Country Music Jubilee	Perry Mason	Perry Como Show
	8:30 PM 9:00 PM	Country Music Jubilee	Dick & the Dutchess	Perry Como Show
	9:00 PM 9:30 PM	Lawrence Welk's Dancing Party	Gale Storm Show	†Polly Bergen Show †Club Oasis
	9:30 PM 10:00 PM	Lawrence Welk's Dancing Party	Have Gun, Will Travel	Gisele MacKenzie Show
	10:00 PM 10:30 PM	Mike Wallace Interviews	Gunsmoke	What's It For
	10:30 PM 11:00 PM			Your Hit Parade

* First quarter hour program   /* Second quarter hour program
† Program airs every other week
Note: Repeated names indicate the program extends into that half-hour time slot.

PRIME TIME SCHEDULE: 1958/59

		AMERICAN ABC	**COLUMBIA** CBS	**NATIONAL** NBC
S U N D A Y	7:00 PM 7:30 PM	You Asked for It	Lassie	Saber of London
	7:30 PM 8:00 PM	Maverick	†Jack Benny Show †Bachelor Father	Northwest Passage
	8:00 PM 8:30 PM	Maverick	Ed Sullivan Show	Steve Allen Show
	8:30 PM 9:00 PM	The Lawman	Ed Sullivan Show	Steve Allen Show
	9:00 PM 9:30 PM	Colt .45	G.E. Theater	Dinah Shore Chevy Show
	9:30 PM 10:00 PM	Encounter	Alfred Hitchcock Presents	Dinah Shore Chevy Show
	10:00 PM 10:30 PM	Encounter	$64,000 Question	Loretta Young Show
	10:30 PM 11:00 PM		What's My Line	
M O N D A Y	7:00 PM 7:30 PM			
	7:30 PM 8:00 PM	Jubilee U.S.A.	Name That Tune	Tic Tac Dough
	8:00 PM 8:30 PM	Jubilee U.S.A.	The Texan	Restless Gun
	8:30 PM 9:00 PM	Bold Journey	Father Knows Best	Tales of Wells Fargo
	9:00 PM 9:30 PM	Voice of Firestone	Danny Thomas Show	Peter Gunn
	9:30 PM 10:00 PM	Anybody Can Play	Ann Sothern Show	†Alcoa †Goodyear TV Playhouse
	10:00 PM 10:30 PM	This is Music	Desilu Playhouse	Arthur Murray Party
	10:30 PM 11:00 PM		Desilu Playhouse	
T U E S D A Y	7:00 PM 7:30 PM			
	7:30 PM 8:00 PM	†Cheyenne †Sugarfoot	Stars in Action	Dragnet
	8:00 PM 8:30 PM	†Cheyenne †Sugarfoot	Keep Talking	†George Gobel Show †Eddie Fisher Show
	8:30 PM 9:00 PM	Life and Legend of Wyatt Earp	To Tell the Truth	†George Gobel Show †Eddie Fisher Show
	9:00 PM 9:30 PM	The Rifleman	Arthur Godfrey Show	George Burns Show
	9:30 PM 10:00 PM	Naked City	Red Skelton Show	Bob Cummings Show
	10:00 PM 10:30 PM	Confession	Garry Moore Show	The Californians
	10:30 PM 11:00 PM		Garry Moore Show	
W E D N E S D A Y	7:00 PM 7:30 PM			
	7:30 PM 8:00 PM	Lawrence Welk's Plymouth Show	Twilight Theater	Wagon Train
	8:00 PM 8:30 PM	Lawrence Welk's Plymouth Show	Pursuit	Wagon Train
	8:30 PM 9:00 PM	Adventures of Ozzie & Harriet	Pursuit	Price is Right
	9:00 PM 9:30 PM	Donna Reed Show	The Millionaire	Milton Berle in the Kraft Music Hall
	9:30 PM 10:00 PM	Patti Page Olds Show	I've Got a Secret	Bat Masterson
	10:00 PM 10:30 PM	Wednesday Night Fights	†Armstrong Circle Theatre †U.S. Steel Hour	This is Your Life
	10:30 PM 11:00 PM	Wednesday Night Fights	†Armstrong Circle Theatre †U.S. Steel Hour	

* First quarter hour program   /* Second quarter hour program
† Program airs every other week
Note: Repeated names indicate the program extends into that half-hour time slot.

PRIME TIME SCHEDULE: 1958/59

		AMERICAN ABC	COLUMBIA CBS	NATIONAL NBC
T H U R S D A Y	7:00 PM 7:30 PM			
	7:30 PM 8:00 PM	Leave it to Beaver	I Love Lucy	Jefferson Drum
	8:00 PM 8:30 PM	Zorro	December Bride	Ed Wynne Show
	8:30 PM 9:00 PM	Real McCoys	Yancy Derringer	Twenty-One
	9:00 PM 9:30 PM	Pat Boone-Chevy Showroom	Dick Powell's Zane Grey Theatre	Behind Closed Doors
	9:30 PM 10:00 PM	Rough Riders	Playhouse 90	Ford Show Starring Tennessee Ernie Ford
	10:00 PM 10:30 PM	Traffic Court	Playhouse 90	You Bet Your Life
	10:30 PM 11:00 PM		Playhouse 90	Masquerade Party
F R I D A Y	7:00 PM 7:30 PM			
	7:30 PM 8:00 PM	Adventures of Rin Tin Tin	Your Hit Parade	Buckskin
	8:00 PM 8:30 PM	Walt Disney Presents	Trackdown	Adventures of Ellery Queen
	8:30 PM 9:00 PM	Walt Disney Presents	Jackie Gleason Show	Adventures of Ellery Queen
	9:00 PM 9:30 PM	Man with a Camera	Phil Silvers Show	M Squad
	9:30 PM 10:00 PM	77 Sunset Strip	†Lux Playhouse †Schlitz Playhouse	Thin Man
	10:00 PM 10:30 PM	77 Sunset Strip	The Lineup	Gillette Cavalcade of Sports
	10:30 PM 11:00 PM		Person to Person	*Gillette Cavalcade of Sports /*Fight Beat
S A T U R D A Y	7:00 PM 7:30 PM			
	7:30 PM 8:00 PM	Dick Clark Show	Perry Mason	People Are Funny
	8:00 PM 8:30 PM	Jubilee U.S.A.	Perry Mason	Perry Como Show
	8:30 PM 9:00 PM	Jubilee U.S.A.	Wanted: Dead or Alive	Perry Como Show
	9:00 PM 9:30 PM	Lawrence Welk's Dodge Dancing Party	Gale Storm Show	Steve Canyon
	9:30 PM 10:00 PM	Lawrence Welk's Dodge Dancing Party	Have Gun, Will Travel	Cimarron City
	10:00 PM 10:30 PM	Sammy Kaye's Music from Manhattan	Gunsmoke	Cimarron City
	10:30 PM 11:00 PM			Brains & Brawn

* First quarter hour program   /* Second quarter hour program
† Program airs every other week
Note: Repeated names indicate the program extends into that half-hour time slot.

PRIME TIME SCHEDULE: 1959/60

		AMERICAN ABC	COLUMBIA CBS	NATIONAL NBC
S U N D A Y	7:00 PM 7:30 PM	Colt .45	Lassie	Riverboat
	7:30 PM 8:00 PM	Maverick	Dennis the Menace	Riverboat
	8:00 PM 8:30 PM	Maverick	Ed Sullivan Show	Sunday Showcase
	8:30 PM 9:00 PM	The Lawman	Ed Sullivan Show	Sunday Showcase
	9:00 PM 9:30 PM	The Rebel	G.E. Theater	Dinah Shore Chevy Show
	9:30 PM 10:00 PM	The Alaskans	Alfred Hitchcock Presents	Dinah Shore Chevy Show
	10:00 PM 10:30 PM	The Alaskans	†Jack Benny Show †George Gobel Show	Loretta Young Show
	10:30 PM 11:00 PM	Dick Clark's World of Talent	What's My Line	
M O N D A Y	7:00 PM 7:30 PM			
	7:30 PM 8:00 PM	Cheyenne	Masquerade Party	Richard Diamond, Private Detective
	8:00 PM 8:30 PM	Cheyenne	The Texan	Love & Marriage
	8:30 PM 9:00 PM	Bourbon Street Beat	Father Knows Best	Tales of Wells Fargo
	9:00 PM 9:30 PM	Bourbon Street Beat	Danny Thomas Show	Peter Gunn
	9:30 PM 10:00 PM	Adventures in Paradise	Ann Sothern Show	†Alcoa †Goodyear TV Playhouse
	10:00 PM 10:30 PM	Adventures in Paradise	Hennesey	Steve Allen Plymouth Show
	10:30 PM 11:00 PM	Man with a Camera	DuPont Show with June Allyson	Steve Allen Plymouth Show
T U E S D A Y	7:00 PM 7:30 PM			
	7:30 PM 8:00 PM	†Sugarfoot †Bronco		Laramie
	8:00 PM 8:30 PM	†Sugarfoot †Bronco	Dennis O'Keefe Show	Laramie
	8:30 PM 9:00 PM	Life and Legend of Wyatt Earp	Many Loves of Dobie Gillis	Fibber McGee & Molly
	9:00 PM 9:30 PM	The Rifleman	Tightrope	Arthur Murray Party
	9:30 PM 10:00 PM	Philip Marlow	Red Skelton Show	Startime
	10:00 PM 10:30 PM	Alcoa Presents	Garry Moore Show	Startime
	10:30 PM 11:00 PM	Keep Talking	Garry Moore Show	
W E D N E S D A Y	7:00 PM 7:30 PM			
	7:30 PM 8:00 PM	Court of Last Resort	The Lineup	Wagon Train
	8:00 PM 8:30 PM	Hobby Lobby Show	The Lineup	Wagon Train
	8:30 PM 9:00 PM	Adventures of Ozzie & Harriet	Men into Space	Price is Right
	9:00 PM 9:30 PM	Hawaiian Eye	The Millionaire	Perry Como's Kraft Music Hall
	9:30 PM 10:00 PM	Hawaiian Eye	I've Got a Secret	Perry Como's Kraft Music Hall
	10:00 PM 10:30 PM	Wednesday Night Fights	†Armstrong Circle Theatre †U.S. Steel Hour	This is Your Life
	10:30 PM 11:00 PM	Wednesday Night Fights	†Armstrong Circle Theatre †U.S. Steel Hour	Wichita Town

* First quarter hour program   /* Second quarter hour program
† Program airs every other week
Note: Repeated names indicate the program extends into that half-hour time slot.

PRIME TIME SCHEDULE: 1959/60

		AMERICAN ABC	COLUMBIA CBS	NATIONAL NBC
T **H** **U** **R** **S** **D** **A** **Y**	7:00 PM 7:30 PM			
	7:30 PM 8:00 PM	Gale Storm Show	To Tell the Truth	Law of the Plainsman
	8:00 PM 8:30 PM	Donna Reed Show	Betty Hutton Show	Bat Masterson
	8:30 PM 9:00 PM	Real McCoys	Johnny Ringo	Staccato
	9:00 PM 9:30 PM	Pat Boone - Chevy Showroom	Dick Powell's Zane Grey Theatre	Bachelor Father
	9:30 PM 10:00 PM	The Untouchables	†Playhouse 90 †Big Party	Ford Show Starring Tennessee Ernie Ford
	10:00 PM 10:30 PM	The Untouchables	†Playhouse 90 †Big Party	You Bet Your Life
	10:30 PM 11:00 PM	Take a Good Look	†Playhouse 90 †Big Party	The Lawless Years

F **R** **I** **D** **A** **Y**	7:00 PM 7:30 PM			
	7:30 PM 8:00 PM	Walt Disney Presents	Rawhide	People Are Funny
	8:00 PM 8:30 PM	Walt Disney Presents	Rawhide	The Troubleshooters
	8:30 PM 9:00 PM	Man from Blackhawk	Hotel de Paree	Bell Telephone Hour
	9:00 PM 9:30 PM	77 Sunset Strip	Desilu Playhouse	Bell Telephone Hour
	9:30 PM 10:00 PM	77 Sunset Strip	Desilu Playhouse	M Squad
	10:00 PM 10:30 PM	Robert Taylor: The Detectives	Twilight Zone	Gillette Cavalcade of Sports
	10:30 PM 11:00 PM	Black Saddle	Person to Person	*Gillette Cavalcade of Sports /*Phillies Jackpot Bowling

S **A** **T** **U** **R** **D** **A** **Y**	7:00 PM 7:30 PM			
	7:30 PM 8:00 PM	Dick Clark Show	Perry Mason	Bonanza
	8:00 PM 8:30 PM	High Road	Perry Mason	Bonanza
	8:30 PM 9:00 PM	Leave It to Beaver	Wanted: Dead or Alive	Man & the Challenge
	9:00 PM 9:30 PM	Lawrence Welk Show	Mr. Lucky	The Deputy
	9:30 PM 10:00 PM	Lawrence Welk Show	Have Gun, Will Travel	Five Fingers
	10:00 PM 10:30 PM	Jubilee U.S.A.	Gunsmoke	Five Fingers
	10:30 PM 11:00 PM	Jubilee U.S.A.	Markham	It Could Be You

* First quarter hour program   /* Second quarter hour program
† Program airs every other week
Note: Repeated names indicate the program extends into that half-hour time slot.

PRIME TIME SCHEDULE: 1960/61

		AMERICAN ABC	COLUMBIA CBS	NATIONAL NBC
S U N D A Y	7:00 PM 7:30 PM	Walt Disney Presents	Lassie	Shirley Temple's Storybook
	7:30 PM 8:00 PM	Maverick	Dennis the Menace	Shirley Temple's Storybook
	8:00 PM 8:30 PM	Maverick	Ed Sullivan Show	National Velvet
	8:30 PM 9:00 PM	The Lawman	Ed Sullivan Show	Tab Hunter Show
	9:00 PM 9:30 PM	The Rebel	G.E. Theater	Dinah Shore Chevy Show
	9:30 PM 10:00 PM	The Islanders	Jack Benny Show	Dinah Shore Chevy Show
	10:00 PM 10:30 PM	The Islanders	Candid Camera	Loretta Young Show
	10:30 PM 11:00 PM	Walter Winchell Show	What's My Line	This is Your Life
M O N D A Y	7:00 PM 7:30 PM			
	7:30 PM 8:00 PM	Cheyenne	To Tell the Truth	Riverboat
	8:00 PM 8:30 PM	Cheyenne	Pete & Gladys	Riverboat
	8:30 PM 9:00 PM	Surfside Six	Bringing Up Buddy	Tales of Wells Fargo
	9:00 PM 9:30 PM	Surfside Six	Danny Thomas Show	Klondike
	9:30 PM 10:00 PM	Adventures in Paradise	Andy Griffith Show	Dante
	10:00 PM 10:30 PM	Adventures in Paradise	Hennesey	Barbara Stanwyck Show
	10:30 PM 11:00 PM	Peter Gunn	Presidential Countdown	Jackpot Bowling
T U E S D A Y	7:00 PM 7:30 PM	Expedition		
	7:30 PM 8:00 PM	Bugs Bunny Show		Laramie
	8:00 PM 8:30 PM	The Rifleman	Father Knows Best	Laramie
	8:30 PM 9:00 PM	Life and Legend of Wyatt Earp	Many Loves of Dobie Gillis	Alfred Hitchcock Presents
	9:00 PM 9:30 PM	Stagecoach West	Tom Ewell Show	Thriller
	9:30 PM 10:00 PM	Stagecoach West	Red Skelton Show	Thriller
	10:00 PM 10:30 PM	Alcoa Presents	Garry Moore Show	
	10:30 PM 11:00 PM		Garry Moore Show	
W E D N E S D A Y	7:00 PM 7:30 PM			
	7:30 PM 8:00 PM	Hong Kong	Aquanauts	Wagon Train
	8:00 PM 8:30 PM	Hong Kong	Aquanauts	Wagon Train
	8:30 PM 9:00 PM	Adventures of Ozzie & Harriet	Wanted: Dead or Alive	Price is Right
	9:00 PM 9:30 PM	Hawaiian Eye	My Sister Eileen	Perry Como's Kraft Music Hall
	9:30 PM 10:00 PM	Hawaiian Eye	I've Got a Secret	Perry Como's Kraft Music Hall
	10:00 PM 10:30 PM	Naked City	†Armstrong Circle Theatre †U.S. Steel Hour	Peter Loves Mary
	10:30 PM 11:00 PM	Naked City U.S. Steel Hour	†Armstrong Circle Theatre	

* First quarter hour program   /* Second quarter hour program
† Program airs every other week
Note: Repeated names indicate the program extends into that half-hour time slot.

PRIME TIME SCHEDULE: 1960/61

		AMERICAN ABC	COLUMBIA CBS	NATIONAL NBC
T **H** **U** **R** **S** **D** **A** **Y**	7:00 PM 7:30 PM			
	7:30 PM 8:00 PM	Guestward Hol	The Witness	The Outlaws
	8:00 PM 8:30 PM	Donna Reed Show	The Witness	The Outlaws
	8:30 PM 9:00 PM	Real McCoys	Dick Powell's Zane Grey Theatre	Bat Masterson
	9:00 PM 9:30 PM	My Three Sons	Angel	Bachelor Father
	9:30 PM 10:00 PM	The Untouchables	Peck's Bad Girl	Ford Show Starring Tennessee Ernie Ford
	10:00 PM 10:30 PM	The Untouchables	Person to Person	Groucho Show
	10:30 PM 11:00 PM	Take a Good Look	DuPont Show with June Allyson	
F **R** **I** **D** **A** **Y**	7:00 PM 7:30 PM			
	7:30 PM 8:00 PM	Matty's Funday Funnies	Rawhide	Dan Raven
	8:00 PM 8:30 PM	Harrigan & Son	Rawhide	Dan Raven
	8:30 PM 9:00 PM	The Flintstones	Route 66	The Westerner
	9:00 PM 9:30 PM	77 Sunset Strip	Route 66	Bell Telephone Hour
	9:30 PM 10:00 PM	77 Sunset Strip	Mr. Garlund	Bell Telephone Hour
	10:00 PM 10:30 PM	Robert Taylor: The Detectives	Twilight Zone	Michael Shayne
	10:30 PM 11:00 PM	Law & Mr. Jones	Eyewitness to History	Michael Shayne
S **A** **T** **U** **R** **D** **A** **Y**	7:00 PM 7:30 PM			
	7:30 PM 8:00 PM	Roaring Twenties	Perry Mason	Bonanza
	8:00 PM 8:30 PM	Roaring Twenties	Perry Mason	Bonanza
	8:30 PM 9:00 PM	Leave It to Beaver	Checkmate	Tall Man
	9:00 PM 9:30 PM	Lawrence Welk Show	Checkmate	The Deputy
	9:30 PM 10:00 PM	Lawrence Welk Show	Have Gun, Will Travel	Nation's Future
	10:00 PM 10:30 PM	Fight of the Week	Gunsmoke	Nation's Future
	10:30 PM 11:00 PM	*Fight of the Week /*Make That Spare		

* First quarter hour program   /* Second quarter hour program
† Program airs every other week
Note: Repeated names indicate the program extends into that half-hour time slot.

PRIME TIME SCHEDULE: 1961/62

		AMERICAN ABC	COLUMBIA CBS	NATIONAL NBC
S U N D A Y	7:00 PM 7:30 PM	Maverick	Lassie	Bullwinkle Show
	7:30 PM 8:00 PM	Follow the Sun	Dennis the Menace	Walt Disney's Wonderful World of Color
	8:00 PM 8:30 PM	Follow the Sun	Ed Sullivan Show	Walt Disney's Wonderful World of Color
	8:30 PM 9:00 PM	The Lawman	Ed Sullivan Show	Car 54, Where Are You?
	9:00 PM 9:30 PM	Bus Stop	G.E. Theater	Bonanza
	9:30 PM 10:00 PM	Bus Stop	Jack Benny Show	Bonanza
	10:00 PM 10:30 PM	Adventures in Paradise	Candid Camera	DuPont Show of the Week
	10:30 PM 11:00 PM	Adventures in Paradise	What's My Line	DuPont Show of the Week
M O N D A Y	7:00 PM 7:30 PM	Expedition		
	7:30 PM 8:00 PM	Cheyenne	To Tell the Truth	
	8:00 PM 8:30 PM	Cheyenne	Pete & Gladys	National Velvet
	8:30 PM 9:00 PM	The Rifleman	Window on Main Street	Price is Right
	9:00 PM 9:30 PM	Surfside Six	Danny Thomas Show	87th Precinct
	9:30 PM 10:00 PM	Surfside Six	Andy Griffith Show	87th Precinct
	10:00 PM 10:30 PM	Ben Casey	Hennesey	Thriller
	10:30 PM 11:00 PM	Ben Casey	I've Got a Secret	Thriller
T U E S D A Y	7:00 PM 7:30 PM			
	7:30 PM 8:00 PM	Bugs Bunny Show	Marshal Dillon	Laramie
	8:00 PM 8:30 PM	Bachelor Father	Dick Van Dyke Show	Laramie
	8:30 PM 9:00 PM	Calvin & the Colonel	Many Loves of Dobie Gillis	Alfred Hitchcock Presents
	9:00 PM 9:30 PM	New Breed	Red Skelton Show	Dick Powell Show
	9:30 PM 10:00 PM	New Breed	Ichabod & Me	Dick Powell Show
	10:00 PM 10:30 PM	Alcoa Premiere	Garry Moore Show	Cain's Hundred
	10:30 PM 11:00 PM	Alcoa Premiere	Garry Moore Show	Cain's Hundred
W E D N E S D A Y	7:00 PM 7:30 PM			
	7:30 PM 8:00 PM	Steve Allen Show	Alvin Show	Wagon Train
	8:00 PM 8:30 PM	Steve Allen Show	Father Knows Best	Wagon Train
	8:30 PM 9:00 PM	Top Cat	Checkmate	Joey Bishop Show
	9:00 PM 9:30 PM	Hawaiian Eye	Checkmate	Perry Como's Kraft Music Hall
	9:30 PM 10:00 PM	Hawaiian Eye	Mrs. G. Goes to College	Perry Como's Kraft Music Hall
	10:00 PM 10:30 PM	Naked City	†U.S. Steel Hour †Armstrong Circle Theatre	Bob Newhart Show
	10:30 PM 11:00 PM	Naked City	†U.S. Steel Hour †Armstrong Circle Theatre	David Brinkley's Journal

* First quarter hour program   /* Second quarter hour program
† Program airs every other week
Note: Repeated names indicate the program extends into that half-hour time slot.

PRIME TIME SCHEDULE: 1961/62

		AMERICAN ABC	COLUMBIA CBS	NATIONAL NBC
T H U R S D A Y	7:00 PM 7:30 PM			
	7:30 PM 8:00 PM	Adventures of Ozzie & Harriet	Frontier Circus	The Outlaws
	8:00 PM 8:30 PM	Donna Reed Show	Frontier Circus	The Outlaws
	8:30 PM 9:00 PM	Real McCoys	Bob Cummings Show	Dr. Kildare
	9:00 PM 9:30 PM	My Three Sons	The Investigators	Dr. Kildare
	9:30 PM 10:00 PM	Margie	The Investigators	Hazel
	10:00 PM 10:30 PM	The Untouchables	CBS Reports	Sing Along with Mitch
	10:30 PM 11:00 PM	The Untouchables	CBS Reports	Sing Along with Mitch
F R I D A Y	7:00 PM 7:30 PM			
	7:30 PM 8:00 PM	Straightway	Rawhide	International Showtime
	8:00 PM 8:30 PM	The Hathaways	Rawhide	International Showtime
	8:30 PM 9:00 PM	The Flintstones	Route 66	Robert Taylor's Detectives
	9:00 PM 9:30 PM	77 Sunset Strip	Route 66	Robert Taylor's Detectives
	9:30 PM 10:00 PM	77 Sunset Strip	Father of the Bride	†Bell Telephone Hour †Dinah Shore Show
	10:00 PM 10:30 PM	Target: The Corruptors	Twilight Zone	†Bell Telephone Hour †Dinah Shore Show
	10:30 PM 11:00 PM	Target: The Corruptors	Eyewitness	Here & Now
S A T U R D A Y	7:00 PM 7:30 PM	Matty's Funday Funnies		
	7:30 PM 8:00 PM	Roaring Twenties	Perry Mason	Tales of Wells Fargo
	8:00 PM 8:30 PM	Roaring Twenties	Perry Mason	Tales of Wells Fargo
	8:30 PM 9:00 PM	Leave It to Beaver	The Defenders	Tall Man
	9:00 PM 9:30 PM	Lawrence Welk Show	The Defenders	NBC Saturday Night Movie
	9:30 PM 10:00 PM	Lawrence Welk Show	Have Gun, Will Travel	NBC Saturday Night Movie
	10:00 PM 10:30 PM	Fight of the Week	Gunsmoke	NBC Saturday Night Movie
	10:30 PM 11:00 PM	*Fight of the Week /*Make That Spare	Gunsmoke	NBC Saturday Night Movie

* First quarter hour program   /* Second quarter hour program
† Program airs every other week
Note: Repeated names indicate the program extends into that half-hour time slot.

PRIME TIME SCHEDULE: 1962/63

		AMERICAN ABC	COLUMBIA CBS	NATIONAL NBC
S U N D A Y	7:00 PM 7:30 PM	Father Knows Best	Lassie	Ensign O'Toole
	7:30 PM 8:00 PM	Jetsons	Dennis the Menace	Walt Disney's Wonderful World of Color
	8:00 PM 8:30 PM	ABC Sunday Night Movie	Ed Sullivan	Walt Disney's Wonderful World of Color
	8:30 PM 9:00 PM	ABC Sunday Night Movie	Ed Sullivan	Car 54, Where Are You?
	9:00 PM 9:30 PM	ABC Sunday Night Movie	Real McCoys	Bonanza
	9:30 PM 10:00 PM	ABC Sunday Night Movie	G.E. True Theater	Bonanza
	10:00 PM 10:30 PM	Voice of Firestone	Candid Camera	DuPont Show of the Week
	10:30 PM 11:00 PM	Howard K. Smith	What's My Line	DuPont Show of the Week
M O N D A Y	7:00 PM 7:30 PM			
	7:30 PM 8:00 PM	Cheyenne	To Tell the Truth	It's a Man's World
	8:00 PM 8:30 PM	Cheyenne	I've Got a Secret	It's a Man's World
	8:30 PM 9:00 PM	Rifleman	Lucy Show	Saints & Sinners
	9:00 PM 9:30 PM	Stoney Burke	Danny Thomas Show	Saints & Sinners
	9:30 PM 10:00 PM	Stoney Burke	Andy Griffith Show	Price is Right
	10:00 PM 10:30 PM	Ben Casey	New Loretta Young Show	David Brinkley's Journal
	10:30 PM 11:00 PM	Ben Casey	Stump the Stars	
T U E S D A Y	7:00 PM 7:30 PM			
	7:30 PM 8:00 PM	Combat	Marshal Dillon	Laramie
	8:00 PM 8:30 PM	Combat	Lloyd Bridges Show	Laramie
	8:30 PM 9:00 PM	Hawaiian Eye	Red Skelton Hour	Empire
	9:00 PM 9:30 PM	Hawaiian Eye	Red Skelton Hour	Empire
	9:30 PM 10:00 PM	The Untouchables	Jack Benny Show	Dick Powell Show
	10:00 PM 10:30 PM	The Untouchables	Garry Moore Show	Dick Powell Show
	10:30 PM 11:00 PM	Bell & Howell Closeup	Garry Moore Show	Chet Huntley Reporting
W E D N E S D A Y	7:00 PM 7:30 PM			
	7:30 PM 8:00 PM	Wagon Train	CBS Reports	The Virginian
	8:00 PM 8:30 PM	Wagon Train	CBS Reports	The Virginian
	8:30 PM 9:00 PM	Going My Way	Many Loves of Dobie Gillis	The Virginian
	9:00 PM 9:30 PM	Going My Way	Beverly Hillbillies	Perry Como's Kraft Music Hall
	9:30 PM 10:00 PM	Our Man Higgins	Dick Van Dyke Show	Perry Como's Kraft Music Hall
	10:00 PM 10:30 PM	Naked City	†Armstrong Circle Theatre †U.S. Steel Hour	Eleventh Hour
	10:30 PM 11:00 PM	Naked City	†Armstrong Circle Theatre †U.S. Steel Hour	Eleventh Hour

* First quarter hour program   /* Second quarter hour program
† Program airs every other week
Note: Repeated names indicate the program extends into that half-hour time slot.

PRIME TIME SCHEDULE: 1962/63

		AMERICAN ABC	COLUMBIA CBS	NATIONAL NBC
T **H** **U** **R** **S** **D** **A** **Y**	7:00 PM 7:30 PM			
	7:30 PM 8:00 PM	Adventures of Ozzie & Harriet	Mr. Ed	Wide Country
	8:00 PM 8:30 PM	Donna Reed Show	Perry Mason	Wide Country
	8:30 PM 9:00 PM	Leave It to Beaver	Perry Mason	Dr. Kildare
	9:00 PM 9:30 PM	My Three Sons	The Nurses	Dr. Kildare
	9:30 PM 10:00 PM	McHale's Navy	The Nurses	Hazel
	10:00 PM 10:30 PM	Alcoa Premiere	Alfred Hitchcock Hour	Andy Williams Show
	10:30 PM 11:00 PM	Alcoa Premiere	Alfred Hitchcock Hour	Andy Williams Show
F **R** **I** **D** **A** **Y**	7:00 PM 7:30 PM			
	7:30 PM 8:00 PM	Gallant Men	Rawhide	International Showtime
	8:00 PM 8:30 PM	Gallant Men	Rawhide	International Showtime
	8:30 PM 9:00 PM	Flintstones	Route 66	Sing Along with Mitch
	9:00 PM 9:30 PM	I'm Dickens - He's Fenster	Route 66	Sing Along with Mitch
	9:30 PM 10:00 PM	77 Sunset Strip	Fair Exchange	Don't Call Me Charlie
	10:00 PM 10:30 PM	77 Sunset Strip	Fair Exchange	Jack Paar Show
	10:30 PM 11:00 PM		Eyewitness	Jack Paar Show
S **A** **T** **U** **R** **D** **A** **Y**	7:00 PM 7:30 PM	Beany & Cecil		
	7:30 PM 8:00 PM	Roy Rogers & Dale Evans Show	Jackie Gleason Show	Sam Benedict
	8:00 PM 8:30 PM	Roy Rogers & Dale Evans Show	Jackie Gleason Show	Sam Benedict
	8:30 PM 9:00 PM	Mr. Smith Goes to Washington	Defenders	Joey Bishop Show
	9:00 PM 9:30 PM	Lawrence Welk Show	Defenders	NBC Saturday Night Movie
	9:30 PM 10:00 PM	Lawrence Welk Show	Have Gun, Will Travel	NBC Saturday Night Movie
	10:00 PM 10:30 PM	Fight of the Week	Gunsmoke	NBC Saturday Night Movie
	10:30 PM 11:00 PM	*Fight of the Week /*Make That Spare	Gunsmoke	NBC Saturday Night Movie

* First quarter hour program   /* Second quarter hour program
† Program airs every other week
Note: Repeated names indicate the program extends into that half-hour time slot.

PRIME TIME SCHEDULE: 1963/64

		AMERICAN ABC	COLUMBIA CBS	NATIONAL NBC
S U N D A Y	7:00 PM 7:30 PM		Lassie	Bill Dana Show
	7:30 PM 8:00 PM	Travels of Jaimie McPheeters	My Favorite Martian	Walt Disney's Wonderful World of Color
	8:00 PM 8:30 PM	Travels of Jaimie McPheeters	Ed Sullivan Show	Walt Disney's Wonderful World of Color
	8:30 PM 9:00 PM	Arrest and Trial	Ed Sullivan Show	Grindl
	9:00 PM 9:30 PM	Arrest and Trial	Judy Garland Show	Bonanza
	9:30 PM 10:00 PM	Arrest and Trial	Judy Garland Show	Bonanza
	10:00 PM 10:30 PM	100 Grand	Candid Camera	DuPont Show of the Week
	10:30 PM 11:00 PM	ABC News Reports	What's My Line	DuPont Show of the Week
M O N D A Y	7:00 PM 7:30 PM			
	7:30 PM 8:00 PM	Outer Limits	To Tell the Truth	NBC Monday Night Movie
	8:00 PM 8:30 PM	Outer Limits	I've Got a Secret	NBC Monday Night Movie
	8:30 PM 9:00 PM	Wagon Train	Lucy Show	NBC Monday Night Movie
	9:00 PM 9:30 PM	Wagon Train	Danny Thomas Show	NBC Monday Night Movie
	9:30 PM 10:00 PM	Wagon Train	Andy Griffith Show	Hollywood & the Stars
	10:00 PM 10:30 PM	Breaking Point	East Side/West Side	Sing Along with Mitch
	10:30 PM 11:00 PM	Breaking Point	East Side/West Side	Sing Along with Mitch
T U E S D A Y	7:00 PM 7:30 PM			
	7:30 PM 8:00 PM	Combat	Marshal Dillon	Mr. Novak
	8:00 PM 8:30 PM	Combat	Red Skelton Hour	Mr. Novak
	8:30 PM 9:00 PM	McHale's Navy	Red Skelton Hour	Redigo
	9:00 PM 9:30 PM	Greatest Show on Earth	Petticoat Junction	Richard Boone Show
	9:30 PM 10:00 PM	Greatest Show on Earth	Jack Benny Show	Richard Boone Show
	10:00 PM 10:30 PM	The Fugitive	Garry Moore Show	Bell Telephone Hour
	10:30 PM 11:00 PM	The Fugitive	Garry Moore Show	Bell Telephone Hour
W E D N E S D A Y	7:00 PM 7:30 PM			
	7:30 PM 8:00 PM	Adventures of Ozzie & Harriet	†Chronicle †CBS Reports	The Virginian
	8:00 PM 8:30 PM	Patty Duke Show	†Chronicles †CBS Reports	The Virginian
	8:30 PM 9:00 PM	Price is Right	Glynis Johns Show	The Virginian
	9:00 PM 9:30 PM	Ben Casey	Beverly Hillbillies	Espionage
	9:30 PM 10:00 PM	Ben Casey	Dick Van Dyke Show	Espionage
	10:00 PM 10:30 PM	Channing	Danny Kaye Show	Eleventh Hour
	10:30 PM 11:00 PM	Channing	Danny Kaye Show	Eleventh Hour

* First quarter hour program   /* Second quarter hour program
† Program airs every other week
Note: Repeated names indicate the program extends into that half-hour time slot.

PRIME TIME SCHEDULE: 1963/64

		AMERICAN ABC	COLUMBIA CBS	NATIONAL NBC
T **H** **U** **R** **S** **D** **A** **Y**	7:00 PM 7:30 PM			
	7:30 PM 8:00 PM	The Flintstones	Password	Temple Houston
	8:00 PM 8:30 PM	Donna Reed Show	Rawhide	Temple Houston
	8:30 PM 9:00 PM	My Three Sons	Rawhide	Dr. Kildare
	9:00 PM 9:30 PM	Jimmy Dean Show	Perry Mason	Dr. Kildare
	9:30 PM 10:00 PM	Jimmy Dean Show	Perry Mason	Hazel
	10:00 PM 10:30 PM	†Edie Adams Show †Sid Caesar Show	The Nurses	Kraft Suspense Theater
	10:30 PM 11:00 PM		The Nurses	Kraft Suspense Theater
F **R** **I** **D** **A** **Y**	7:00 PM 7:30 PM			
	7:30 PM 8:00 PM	77 Sunset Strip	Great Adventure	International Showtime
	8:00 PM 8:30 PM	77 Sunset Strip	Great Adventure	International Showtime
	8:30 PM 9:00 PM	Burke's Law	Route 66	Bob Hope Presents the Chrysler Theatre
	9:00 PM 9:30 PM	Burke's Law	Route 66	Bob Hope Presents the Chrysler Theatre
	9:30 PM 10:00 PM	Farmer's Daughter	Twilight Zone	Harry's Girls
	10:00 PM 10:30 PM	Fight of the Week	Alfred Hitchcock Hour	Jack Paar Show
	10:30 PM 11:00 PM	*Fight of the Week /*Make That Spare	Alfred Hitchcock Hour	Jack Paar Show
S **A** **T** **U** **R** **D** **A** **Y**	7:00 PM 7:30 PM			
	7:30 PM 8:00 PM	Hootenanny	Jackie Gleason Show	The Lieutenant
	8:00 PM 8:30 PM	Hootenanny	Jackie Gleason Show	The Lieutenant
	8:30 PM 9:00 PM	Lawrence Welk Show	Phil Silvers	Joey Bishop Show
	9:00 PM 9:30 PM	Lawrence Welk Show	The Defenders	NBC Saturday Night Movie
	9:30 PM 10:00 PM	Jerry Lewis Show	The Defenders	NBC Saturday Night Movie
	10:00 PM 10:30 PM	Jerry Lewis Show	Gunsmoke	NBC Saturday Night Movie
	10:30 PM 11:00 PM	Jerry Lewis Show	Gunsmoke	NBC Saturday Night Movie

* First quarter hour program   /* Second quarter hour program
† Program airs every other week
Note: Repeated names indicate the program extends into that half-hour time slot.

PRIME TIME SCHEDULE: 1964/65

		AMERICAN ABC	COLUMBIA CBS	NATIONAL NBC
S U N D A Y	7:00 PM 7:30 PM		Lassie	Profiles in Courage
	7:30 PM 8:00 PM	Wagon Train	My Favorite Martian	Walt Disney's Wonderful World of Color
	8:00 PM 8:30 PM	Wagon Train	Ed Sullivan Show	Walt Disney's Wonderful World of Color
	8:30 PM 9:00 PM	Broadside	Ed Sullivan Show	Bill Dana Show
	9:00 PM 9:30 PM	ABC Sunday Night Movie	My Living Doll	Bonanza
	9:30 PM 10:00 PM	ABC Sunday Night Movie	Joey Bishop Show	Bonanza
	10:00 PM 10:30 PM	ABC Sunday Night Movie	Candid Camera	The Rogues
	10:30 PM 11:00 PM	ABC Sunday Night Movie	What's My Line	The Rogues
M O N D A Y	7:00 PM 7:30 PM			
	7:30 PM 8:00 PM	Voyage to the Bottom of the Sea	To Tell the Truth	90 Bristol Court
	8:00 PM 8:30 PM	Voyage to the Bottom of the Sea	I've Got a Secret	90 Bristol Court
	8:30 PM 9:00 PM	No Time for Sergeants	Andy Griffith Show	90 Bristol Court
	9:00 PM 9:30 PM	Wendy and Me	Lucy Show	Andy Williams Show
	9:30 PM 10:00 PM	Bing Crosby Show	Many Happy Returns	Andy Williams Show
	10:00 PM 10:30 PM	Ben Casey	Slattery's People	Alfred Hitchcock Hour
	10:30 PM 11:00 PM	Ben Casey	Slattery's People	Alfred Hitchcock Hour
T U E S D A Y	7:00 PM 7:30 PM			
	7:30 PM 8:00 PM	Combat	Marshal Dillon	Mr. Novak
	8:00 PM 8:30 PM	Combat	World War I	Mr. Novak
	8:30 PM 9:00 PM	McHale's Navy	Red Skelton Hour	Man from U.N.C.L.E.
	9:00 PM 9:30 PM	The Tycoon	Red Skelton Hour	Man From U.N.C.L.E.
	9:30 PM 10:00 PM	Peyton Place	Petticoat Junction	That Was the Week That Was
	10:00 PM 10:30 PM	The Fugitive	Doctors and the Nurses	Bell Telephone Hour
	10:30 PM 11:00 PM	The Fugitive	Doctors and the Nurses	Bell Telephone Hour
W E D N E S D A Y	7:00 PM 7:30 PM			
	7:30 PM 8:00 PM	Adventures of Ozzie & Harriet	CBS Reports	The Virginian
	8:00 PM 8:30 PM	Patty Duke Show	CBS Reports	The Virginian
	8:30 PM 9:00 PM	Shindig	Beverly Hillbillies	The Virginian
	9:00 PM 9:30 PM	Mickey	Dick Van Dyke Show	NBC Wednesday Night Movie
	9:30 PM 10:00 PM	Burke's Law	Cara Williams Show	NBC Wednesday Night Movie
	10:00 PM 10:30 PM	Burke's Law	Danny Kaye Show	NBC Wednesday Night Movie
	10:30 PM 11:00 PM	ABC Scope	Danny Kaye Show	NBC Wednesday Night Movie

* First quarter hour program   /* Second quarter hour program
† Program airs every other week
Note: Repeated names indicate the program extends into that half-hour time slot.

PRIME TIME SCHEDULE: 1964/65

		AMERICAN ABC	COLUMBIA CBS	NATIONAL NBC
T **H** **U** **R** **S** **D** **A** **Y**	7:00 PM 7:30 PM			
	7:30 PM 8:00 PM	The Flintstones	The Munsters	Daniel Boone
	8:00 PM 8:30 PM	Donna Reed Show	Perry Mason	Daniel Boone
	8:30 PM 9:00 PM	My Three Sons	Perry Mason	Dr. Kildare
	9:00 PM 9:30 PM	Bewitched	Password	Dr. Kildare
	9:30 PM 10:00 PM	Peyton Place	Baileys of Balboa	Hazel
	10:00 PM 10:30 PM	Jimmy Dean Show	The Defenders	Kraft Suspense Theater
	10:30 PM 11:00 PM	Jimmy Dean Show	The Defenders	Kraft Suspense Theater
F **R** **I** **D** **A** **Y**	7:00 PM 7:30 PM			
	7:30 PM 8:00 PM	Jonny Quest	Rawhide	International Showtime
	8:00 PM 8:30 PM	Farmer's Daughter	Rawhide	International Showtime
	8:30 PM 9:00 PM	Addams Family	The Entertainers	Bob Hope Presents the Chrysler Theatre
	9:00 PM 9:30 PM	Valentine's Day	The Entertainers	Bob Hope Presents the Chrysler Theatre
	9:30 PM 10:00 PM	Twelve O'Clock High	Gomer Pyle, U.S.M.C.	Jack Benny Program
	10:00 PM 10:30 PM	Twelve O'Clock High	The Reporter	Jack Paar Show
	10:30 PM 11:00 PM		The Reporter	Jack Paar Show
S **A** **T** **U** **R** **D** **A** **Y**	7:00 PM 7:30 PM			
	7:30 PM 8:00 PM	Outer Limits	Jackie Gleason Show	Flipper
	8:00 PM 8:30 PM	Outer Limits	Jackie Gleason Show	Famous Adventures of Mr. Magoo
	8:30 PM 9:00 PM	Lawrence Welk Show	Gilligan's Island	Kentucky Jones
	9:00 PM 9:30 PM	Lawrence Welk Show	Mr. Broadway	NBC Saturday Night Movie
	9:30 PM 10:00 PM	Hollywood Palace	Mr. Broadway	NBC Saturday Night Movie
	10:00 PM 10:30 PM	Hollywood Palace	Gunsmoke	NBC Saturday Night Movie
	10:30 PM 11:00 PM		Gunsmoke	NBC Saturday Night Movie

* First quarter hour program   /* Second quarter hour program
† Program airs every other week
Note: Repeated names indicate the program extends into that half-hour time slot.

PRIME TIME SCHEDULE: 1965/66

		AMERICAN ABC	COLUMBIA CBS	NATIONAL NBC
S U N D A Y	7:00 PM 7:30 PM	Voyage to the Bottom of the Sea	Lassie	†Bell Telephone Hour †Actuality Specials
	7:30 PM 8:00 PM	Voyage to the Bottom of the Sea	My Favorite Martian	Walt Disney's Wonderful World of Color
	8:00 PM 8:30 PM	The F.B.I.	Ed Sullivan Show	Walt Disney's Wonderful World of Color
	8:30 PM 9:00 PM	The F.B.I.	Ed Sullivan Show	Branded
	9:00 PM 9:30 PM	ABC Sunday Night Movie	Perry Mason	Bonanza
	9:30 PM 10:00 PM	ABC Sunday Night Movie	Perry Mason	Bonanza
	10:00 PM 10:30 PM	ABC Sunday Night Movie	Candid Camera	Wackiest Ship in the Army
	10:30 PM 11:00 PM	ABC Sunday Night Movie	What's My Line	Wackiest Ship in the Army
M O N D A Y	7:00 PM 7:30 PM			
	7:30 PM 8:00 PM	Twelve O'Clock High	To Tell the Truth	Hullabaloo
	8:00 PM 8:30 PM	Twelve O'Clock High	I've Got a Secret	John Forsythe Show
	8:30 PM 9:00 PM	Legend of Jesse James	Lucy Show	Dr. Kildare
	9:00 PM 9:30 PM	Man Called Shenandoah	Andy Griffith Show	Andy Williams Show
	9:30 PM 10:00 PM	Farmer's Daughter	Hazel	Andy Williams Show
	10:00 PM 10:30 PM	Ben Casey	Steve Lawrence Show	Run for Your Life
	10:30 PM 11:00 PM	Ben Casey	Steve Lawrence Show	Run for Your Life
T U E S D A Y	7:00 PM 7:30 PM			
	7:30 PM 8:00 PM	Combat	Rawhide	My Mother the Car
	8:00 PM 8:30 PM	Combat	Rawhide	Please Don't Eat the Daisies
	8:30 PM 9:00 PM	McHale's Navy	Red Skelton Hour	Dr. Kildare
	9:00 PM 9:30 PM	F Troop	Red Skelton Hour	NBC Tuesday Night Movie
	9:30 PM 10:00 PM	Peyton Place	Petticoat Junction	NBC Tuesday Night Movie
	10:00 PM 10:30 PM	The Fugitive	†CBS Reports †News Hour	NBC Tuesday Night Movie
	10:30 PM 11:00 PM	The Fugitive	†CBS Reports †News Hour	NBC Tuesday Night Movie
W E D N E S D A Y	7:00 PM 7:30 PM			
	7:30 PM 8:00 PM	Adventures of Ozzie & Harriet	Lost in Space	The Virginian
	8:00 PM 8:30 PM	Patty Duke Show	Lost in Space	The Virginian
	8:30 PM 9:00 PM	Gidget	Beverly Hillbillies	The Virginian
	9:00 PM 9:30 PM	Big Valley	Green Acres	Bob Hope Presents the Chrysler Theatre
	9:30 PM 10:00 PM	Big Valley	Dick Van Dyke Show	Bob Hope Presents the Chrysler Theatre
	10:00 PM 10:30 PM	Amos Burke - Secret Agent	Danny Kaye Show	I Spy
	10:30 PM 11:00 PM	Amos Burke - Secret Agent	Danny Kaye Show	I Spy

* First quarter hour program   /* Second quarter hour program
† Program airs every other week
Note: Repeated names indicate the program extends into that half-hour time slot.

PRIME TIME SCHEDULE: 1965/66

		AMERICAN ABC	COLUMBIA CBS	NATIONAL NBC
T	7:00 PM			
H	7:30 PM			
U	7:30 PM 8:00 PM	Shindig	The Munsters	Daniel Boone
R				
S	8:00 PM 8:30 PM	Donna Reed Show	Gilligan's Island	Daniel Boone
D				
A	8:30 PM 9:00 PM	O.K. Crackerby	My Three Sons	Laredo
Y				
	9:00 PM 9:30 PM	Bewitched	CBS Thursday Night Movie	Laredo
	9:30 PM 10:00 PM	Peyton Place	CBS Thursday Night Movie	Mona McCluskey
	10:00 PM 10:30 PM	Long, Hot Summer	CBS Thursday Night Movie	Dean Martin Show
	10:30 PM 11:00 PM	Long, Hot Summer	CBS Thursday Night Movie	Dean Martin Show
F	7:00 PM			
R	7:30 PM			
I	7:30 PM 8:00 PM	The Flintstones	Wild Wild West	Camp Runamuck
D				
A	8:00 PM 8:30 PM	Tammy	Wild Wild West	Hank
Y				
	8:30 PM 9:00 PM	Addams Family	Hogan's Heroes	Convoy
	9:00 PM 9:30 PM	Honey West	Gomer Pyle, U.S.M.C.	Convoy
	9:30 PM 10:00 PM	Peyton Place	Smothers Brothers Show	Mr. Roberts
	10:00 PM 10:30 PM	Jimmy Dean Show	Slattery's People	Man from U.N.C.L.E.
	10:30 PM 11:00 PM	Jimmy Dean Show	Slattery's People	Man from U.N.C.L.E.
S	7:00 PM			
A	7:30 PM			
T	7:30 PM 8:00 PM	Shindig	Jackie Gleason Show	Flipper
U				
R	8:00 PM 8:30 PM	King Family Show	Jackie Gleason Show	I Dream of Jeannie
D				
A	8:30 PM 9:00 PM	Lawrence Welk Show	Trials of O'Brien	Get Smart
Y				
	9:00 PM 9:30 PM	Lawrence Welk Show	Trials of O'Brien	Get Smart
	9:30 PM 10:00 PM	Hollywood Palace	The Loner	NBC Saturday Night Movie
	10:00 PM 10:30 PM	Hollywood Palace	Gunsmoke	NBC Saturday Night Movie
	10:30 PM 11:00 PM	ABC Scope	Gunsmoke	NBC Saturday Night Movie

* First quarter hour program   /* Second quarter hour program
† Program airs every other week
Note: Repeated names indicate the program extends into that half-hour time slot.

PRIME TIME SCHEDULE: 1966/67

		AMERICAN ABC	COLUMBIA CBS	NATIONAL NBC
S U N D A Y	7:00 PM 7:30 PM	Voyage to the Bottom of the Sea	Lassie	†Actuality Specials †Bell Telephone Hour
	7:30 PM 8:00 PM	Voyage to the Bottom of the Sea	It's About Time	Walt Disney's Wonderful World of Color
	8:00 PM 8:30 PM	The F.B.I.	Ed Sullivan Show	Walt Disney's Wonderful World of Color
	8:30 PM 9:00 PM	The F.B.I.	Ed Sullivan Show	Hey Landlord
	9:00 PM 9:30 PM	ABC Sunday Night Movie	Garry Moore Show	Bonanza
	9:30 PM 10:00 PM	ABC Sunday Night Movie	Garry Moore Show	Bonanza
	10:00 PM 10:30 PM	ABC Sunday Night Movie	Candid Camera	Andy Williams Show
	10:30 PM 11:00 PM	ABC Sunday Night Movie	What's My Line	Andy Williams Show
M O N D A Y	7:00 PM 7:30 PM			
	7:30 PM 8:00 PM	Iron Horse	Gilligan's Island	The Monkees
	8:00 PM 8:30 PM	Iron Horse	Run Buddy Run	I Dream of Jeannie
	8:30 PM 9:00 PM	Rat Patrol	Lucy Show	Roger Miller Show
	9:00 PM 9:30 PM	Felony Squad	Andy Griffith Show	Road West
	9:30 PM 10:00 PM	Peyton Place	Family Affair	Road West
	10:00 PM 10:30 PM	Big Valley	Jean Arthur Show	Run for Your Life
	10:30 PM 11:00 PM	Big Valley	I've Got a Secret	Run for Your Life
T U E S D A Y	7:00 PM 7:30 PM			
	7:30 PM 8:00 PM	Combat	Daktari	Man from U.N.C.L.E.
	8:00 PM 8:30 PM	Combat	Daktari	Man from U.N.C.L.E.
	8:30 PM 9:00 PM	The Rounders	Red Skelton Hour	Occasional Wife
	9:00 PM 9:30 PM	Pruitts of Southampton	Red Skelton Hour	NBC Tuesday Night Movie
	9:30 PM 10:00 PM	Love on a Rooftop	Petticoat Junction	NBC Tuesday Night Movie
	10:00 PM 10:30 PM	The Fugitive	CBS News Hour	NBC Tuesday Night Movie
	10:30 PM 11:00 PM	The Fugitive	CBS News Hour	NBC Tuesday Night Movie
W E D N E S D A Y	7:00 PM 7:30 PM			
	7:30 PM 8:00 PM	Batman	Lost in Space	The Virginian
	8:00 PM 8:30 PM	The Monroes	Lost in Space	The Virginian
	8:30 PM 9:00 PM	The Monroes	Beverly Hillbillies	The Virginian
	9:00 PM 9:30 PM	Man Who Never Was	Green Acres	Bob Hope Presents the Chrysler Theatre
	9:30 PM 10:00 PM	Peyton Place	Gomer Pyle, U.S.M.C.	Bob Hope Presents the Chrysler Theatre
	10:00 PM 10:30 PM	ABC Stage '67	Danny Kaye Show	I Spy
	10:30 PM 11:00 PM	ABC Stage '67	Danny Kaye Show	I Spy

* First quarter hour program   /* Second quarter hour program
† Program airs every other week
Note: Repeated names indicate the program extends into that half-hour time slot.

PRIME TIME SCHEDULE: 1966/67

		AMERICAN ABC	COLUMBIA CBS	NATIONAL NBC
T **H** **U** **R** **S** **D** **A** **Y**	7:00 PM 7:30 PM			
	7:30 PM 8:00 PM	Batman	Jericho	Daniel Boone
	8:00 PM 8:30 PM	F Troop	Jericho	Daniel Boone
	8:30 PM 9:00 PM	Tammy Grimes Show	My Three Sons	Star Trek
	9:00 PM 9:30 PM	Bewitched	CBS Thursday Night Movie	Star Trek
	9:30 PM 10:00 PM	That Girl	CBS Thursday Night Movie	The Hero
	10:00 PM 10:30 PM	Hawk	CBS Thursday Night Movie	Dean Martin Show
	10:30 PM 11:00 PM	Hawk	CBS Thursday Night Movie	Dean Martin Show
F **R** **I** **D** **A** **Y**	7:00 PM 7:30 PM			
	7:30 PM 8:00 PM	Green Hornet	Wild Wild West	Tarzan
	8:00 PM 8:30 PM	Time Tunnel	Wild Wild West	Tarzan
	8:30 PM 9:00 PM	Time Tunnel	Hogan's Heroes	Man from U.N.C.L.E.
	9:00 PM 9:30 PM	Milton Berle Show	CBS Friday Night Movie	Man from U.N.C.L.E.
	9:30 PM 10:00 PM	Milton Berle Show	CBS Friday Night Movie	T.H.E. Cat
	10:00 PM 10:30 PM	Twelve O'Clock High	CBS Friday Night Movie	Laredo
	10:30 PM 11:00 PM	Twelve O'Clock High	CBS Friday Night Movie	Laredo
S **A** **T** **U** **R** **D** **A** **Y**	7:00 PM 7:30 PM			
	7:30 PM 8:00 PM	Shane	Jackie Gleason Show	Flipper
	8:00 PM 8:30 PM	Shane	Jackie Gleason Show	Please Don't Eat the Daisies
	8:30 PM 9:00 PM	Lawrence Welk Show	Pistols'n' Petticoats	Get Smart
	9:00 PM 9:30 PM	Lawrence Welk Show	Mission: Impossible	NBC Saturday Night Movie
	9:30 PM 10:00 PM	Hollywood Palace	Mission: Impossible	NBC Saturday Night Movie
	10:00 PM 10:30 PM	Hollywood Palace	Gunsmoke	NBC Saturday Night Movie
	10:30 PM 11:00 PM	ABC Scope	Gunsmoke	NBC Saturday Night Movie

* First quarter hour program /* Second quarter hour program
† Program airs every other week
Note: Repeated names indicate the program extends into that half-hour time slot.

PRIME TIME SCHEDULE: 1967/68

		AMERICAN ABC	COLUMBIA CBS	NATIONAL NBC
S U N D A Y	7:00 PM 7:30 PM	Voyage to the Bottom of the Sea	Lassie	
	7:30 PM 8:00 PM	Voyage to the Bottom of the Sea	Gentle Ben	Walt Disney's Wonderful World of Color
	8:00 PM 8:30 PM	The F.B.I.	Ed Sullivan Show	Walt Disney's Wonderful World of Color
	8:30 PM 9:00 PM	The F.B.I.	Ed Sullivan Show	Mothers-in-Law
	9:00 PM 9:30 PM	ABC Sunday Night Movie	Smothers Brothers Comedy Hour	Bonanza
	9:30 PM 10:00 PM	ABC Sunday Night Movie	Smothers Brothers Comedy Hour	Bonanza
	10:00 PM 10:30 PM	ABC Sunday Night Movie	Mission: Impossible	High Chaparral
	10:30 PM 11:00 PM	ABC Sunday Night Movie	Mission: Impossible	High Chaparral
M O N D A Y	7:00 PM 7:30 PM			
	7:30 PM 8:00 PM	Cowboy in Africa	Gunsmoke	The Monkees
	8:00 PM 8:30 PM	Cowboy in Africa	Gunsmoke	Man from U.N.C.L.E.
	8:30 PM 9:00 PM	Rat Patrol	Lucy Show	Man from U.N.C.L.E.
	9:00 PM 9:30 PM	Felony Squad	Andy Griffith Show	Danny Thomas Hour
	9:30 PM 10:00 PM	Peyton Place	Family Affair	Danny Thomas Hour
	10:00 PM 10:30 PM	Big Valley	Carol Burnett Show	I Spy
	10:30 PM 11:00 PM	Big Valley	Carol Burnett Show	I Spy
T U E S D A Y	7:00 PM 7:30 PM			
	7:30 PM 8:00 PM	Garrison's Gorillas	Daktari	I Dream of Jeannie
	8:00 PM 8:30 PM	Garrison's Gorillas	Daktari	Jerry Lewis Show
	8:30 PM 9:00 PM	The Invaders	Red Skelton Hour	Jerry Lewis Show
	9:00 PM 9:30 PM	The Invaders	Red Skelton Hour	NBC Tuesday Night Movie
	9:30 PM 10:00 PM	N.Y.P.D.	Good Morning, World	NBC Tuesday Night Movie
	10:00 PM 10:30 PM	Hollywood Palace	CBS News Hour	NBC Tuesday Night Movie
	10:30 PM 11:00 PM	Hollywood Palace	CBS News Hour	NBC Tuesday Night Movie
W E D N E S D A Y	7:00 PM 7:30 PM			
	7:30 PM 8:00 PM	Legend of Custer	Lost in Space	The Virginian
	8:00 PM 8:30 PM	Legend of Custer	Lost in Space	The Virginian
	8:30 PM 9:00 PM	Second 100 Years	Beverly Hillbillies	The Virginian
	9:00 PM 9:30 PM	ABC Wednesday Night Movie	Green Acres	Kraft Music Hall
	9:30 PM 10:00 PM	ABC Wednesday Night Movie	He & She	Kraft Music Hall
	10:00 PM 10:30 PM	ABC Wednesday Night Movie	Dundee and the Culhane	Run For Your Life
	10:30 PM 11:00 PM	ABC Wednesday Night Movie	Dundee and the Culhane	Run For Your Life

* First quarter hour program   /* Second quarter hour program
† Program airs every other week
Note: Repeated names indicate the program extends into that half-hour time slot.

PRIME TIME SCHEDULE: 1967/68

		AMERICAN ABC	COLUMBIA CBS	NATIONAL NBC
T H U R S D A Y	7:00 PM 7:30 PM			
	7:30 PM 8:00 PM	Batman	Cimarron Strip	Daniel Boone
	8:00 PM 8:30 PM	Flying Nun	Cimarron Strip	Daniel Boone
	8:30 PM 9:00 PM	Bewitched	Cimarron Strip	Ironside
	9:00 PM 9:30 PM	That Girl	CBS Thursday Night Movie	Ironside
	9:30 PM 10:00 PM	Peyton Place	CBS Thursday Night Movie	Dragnet
	10:00 PM 10:30 PM	Good Company	CBS Thursday Night Movie	Dean Martin Show
	10:30 PM 11:00 PM		CBS Thursday Night Movie	Dean Martin Show
F R I D A Y	7:00 PM 7:30 PM			
	7:30 PM 8:00 PM	Off To See the Wizard	Wild Wild West	Tarzan
	8:00 PM 8:30 PM	Off To See the Wizard	Wild Wild West	Tarzan
	8:30 PM 9:00 PM	Hondo	Gomer Pyle, U.S.M.C.	Star Trek
	9:00 PM 9:30 PM	Hondo	CBS Friday Night Movie	Star Trek
	9:30 PM 10:00 PM	Guns of Will Sonnett	CBS Friday Night Movie	Accidental Family
	10:00 PM 10:30 PM	Judd, For the Defense	CBS Friday Night Movie	†Actuality Specials †Bell Telephone Hour
	10:30 PM 11:00 PM	Judd, For the Defense	CBS Friday Night Movie	†Actuality Specials †Bell Telephone Hour
S A T U R D A Y	7:00 PM 7:30 PM			
	7:30 PM 8:00 PM	Dating Game	Jackie Gleason Show	Maya
	8:00 PM 8:30 PM	Newlywed Game	Jackie Gleason Show	Maya
	8:30 PM 9:00 PM	Lawrence Welk Show	My Three Sons	Get Smart
	9:00 PM 9:30 PM	Lawrence Welk Show	Hogan's Heroes	NBC Saturday Night Movie
	9:30 PM 10:00 PM	Iron Horse	Petticoat Junction	NBC Saturday Night Movie
	10:00 PM 10:30 PM	Iron Horse	Mannix	NBC Saturday Night Movie
	10:30 PM 11:00 PM	ABC Scope	Mannix	NBC Saturday Night Movie

* First quarter hour program   /* Second quarter hour program
† Program airs every other week
Note: Repeated names indicate the program extends into that half-hour time slot.

PRIME TIME SCHEDULE: 1968/69

		AMERICAN ABC	COLUMBIA CBS	NATIONAL NBC
S U N D A Y	7:00 PM 7:30 PM	Land of the Giants	Lassie	New Adventures of Huck Finn
	7:30 PM 8:00 PM	Land of the Giants	Gentle Ben	Walt Disney's Wonderful World of Color
	8:00 PM 8:30 PM	The F.B.I.	Ed Sullivan Show	Walt Disney's Wonderful World of Color
	8:30 PM 9:00 PM	The F.B.I.	Ed Sullivan Show	Mothers-in-Law
	9:00 PM 9:30 PM	ABC Sunday Night Movie	Smothers Brothers Comedy Hour	Bonanza
	9:30 PM 10:00 PM	ABC Sunday Night Movie	Smothers Brothers Comedy Hour	Bonanza
	10:00 PM 10:30 PM	ABC Sunday Night Movie	Mission: Impossible	Beautiful Phyllis Diller Show
	10:30 PM 11:00 PM	ABC Sunday Night Movie	Mission: Impossible	Beautiful Phyllis Diller Show
M O N D A Y	7:00 PM 7:30 PM			
	7:30 PM 8:00 PM	The Avengers	Gunsmoke	I Dream of Jeannie
	8:00 PM 8:30 PM	The Avengers	Gunsmoke	Rowan & Martin's Laugh-In
	8:30 PM 9:00 PM	Peyton Place	Here's Lucy	Rowan & Martin's Laugh-In
	9:00 PM 9:30 PM	The Outcasts	Mayberry R.F.D.	NBC Monday Night Movie
	9:30 PM 10:00 PM	The Outcasts	Family Affair	NBC Monday Night Movie
	10:00 PM 10:30 PM	Big Valley	Carol Burnett Show	NBC Monday Night Movie
	10:30 PM 11:00 PM	Big Valley	Carol Burnett Show	NBC Monday Night Movie
T U E S D A Y	7:00 PM 7:30 PM			
	7:30 PM 8:00 PM	Mod Squad	Lancer	Jerry Lewis Show
	8:00 PM 8:30 PM	Mod Squad	Lancer	Jerry Lewis Show
	8:30 PM 9:00 PM	It Takes a Thief	Red Skelton Hour	Julia
	9:00 PM 9:30 PM	It Takes a Thief	Red Skelton Hour	NBC Tuesday Night Movie
	9:30 PM 10:00 PM	N.Y.P.D.	Doris Day Show	NBC Tuesday Night Movie
	10:00 PM 10:30 PM	That's Life	†CBS News Hour †60 Minutes	NBC Tuesday Night Movie
	10:30 PM 11:00 PM	That's Life	†CBS News Hour †60 Minutes	NBC Tuesday Night Movie
W E D N E S D A Y	7:00 PM 7:30 PM			
	7:30 PM 8:00 PM	Here Come the Brides	Daktari	The Virginian
	8:00 PM 8:30 PM	Here Come the Brides	Daktari	The Virginian
	8:30 PM 9:00 PM	Peyton Place	Good Guys	The Virginian
	9:00 PM 9:30 PM	ABC Wednesday Night Movie	Beverly Hillbillies	Kraft Music Hall
	9:30 PM 10:00 PM	ABC Wednesday Night Movie	Green Acres	Kraft Music Hall
	10:00 PM 10:30 PM	ABC Wednesday Night Movie	Jonathan Winters Show	The Outsider
	10:30 PM 11:00 PM	ABC Wednesday Night Movie	Jonathan Winters Show	The Outsider

* First quarter hour program   /* Second quarter hour program
† Program airs every other week
Note: Repeated names indicate the program extends into that half-hour time slot.

PRIME TIME SCHEDULE: 1968/69

		AMERICAN ABC	COLUMBIA CBS	NATIONAL NBC
T H U R S D A Y	7:00 PM 7:30 PM			
	7:30 PM 8:00 PM	Ugliest Girl in Town	Blondie	Daniel Boone
	8:00 PM 8:30 PM	Flying Nun	Hawaii Five-O	Daniel Boone
	8:30 PM 9:00 PM	Bewitched	Hawaii Five-O	Ironside
	9:00 PM 9:30 PM	That Girl	CBS Thursday Night Movie	Ironside
	9:30 PM 10:00 PM	Journey to the Unknown	CBS Thursday Night Movie	Dragnet
	10:00 PM 10:30 PM	Journey to the Unknown	CBS Thursday Night Movie	Dean Martin Show
	10:30 PM 11:00 PM		CBS Thursday Night Movie	Dean Martin Show
F R I D A Y	7:00 PM 7:30 PM			
	7:30 PM 8:00 PM	Operation: Entertainment	Wild Wild West	High Chaparral
	8:00 PM 8:30 PM	Operation: Entertainment	Wild Wild West	High Chaparral
	8:30 PM 9:00 PM	Felony Squad	Gomer Pyle, U.S.M.C.	Name of the Game
	9:00 PM 9:30 PM	Don Rickles Show	CBS Friday Night Movie	Name of the Game
	9:30 PM 10:00 PM	Guns of Will Sonnett	CBS Friday Night Movie	Name of the Game
	10:00 PM 10:30 PM	Judd, For the Defense	CBS Friday Night Movie	Star Trek
	10:30 PM 11:00 PM	Judd, For the Defense	CBS Friday Night Movie	Star Trek
S A T U R D A Y	7:00 PM 7:30 PM			
	7:30 PM 8:00 PM	Dating Game	Jackie Gleason Show	Adam 12
	8:00 PM 8:30 PM	Newlywed Game	Jackie Gleason Show	Get Smart
	8:30 PM 9:00 PM	Lawrence Welk Show	My Three Sons	Ghost & Mrs. Muir
	9:00 PM 9:30 PM	Lawrence Welk Show	Hogan's Heroes	NBC Saturday Night Movie
	9:30 PM 10:00 PM	Hollywood Palace	Petticoat Junction	NBC Saturday Night Movie
	10:00 PM 10:30 PM	Hollywood Palace	Mannix	NBC Saturday Night Movie
	10:30 PM 11:00 PM		Mannix	NBC Saturday Night Movie

* First quarter hour program /* Second quarter hour program
† Program airs every other week
Note: Repeated names indicate the program extends into that half-hour time slot.

PRIME TIME SCHEDULE: 1969/70

		AMERICAN ABC	COLUMBIA CBS	NATIONAL NBC
S U N D A Y	7:00 PM 7:30 PM	Land of the Giants	Lassie	Wild Kingdom
	7:30 PM 8:00 PM	Land of the Giants	To Rome with Love	Walt Disney's Wonderful World of Color
	8:00 PM 8:30 PM	The F.B.I.	Ed Sullivan Show	Bill Cosby Show
	8:30 PM 9:00 PM	The F.B.I.	Ed Sullivan Show	Bill Cosby Show
	9:00 PM 9:30 PM	ABC Sunday Night Movie	Leslie Uggams Show	Bonanza
	9:30 PM 10:00 PM	ABC Sunday Night Movie	Leslie Uggams Show	Bonanza
	10:00 PM 10:30 PM	ABC Sunday Night Movie	Mission: Impossible	Bold Ones
	10:30 PM 11:00 PM	ABC Sunday Night Movie	Mission: Impossible	Bold Ones
M O N D A Y	7:00 PM 7:30 PM			
	7:30 PM 8:00 PM	Music Scene	Gunsmoke	My World and Welcome to it
	8:00 PM 8:30 PM	Music Scene	Gunsmoke	Rowan & Martin's Laugh-In
	8:30 PM 9:00 PM	New People	Here's Lucy	Rowan & Martin's Laugh-In
	9:00 PM 9:30 PM	Harold Robbins' "The Survivors"	Mayberry R.F.D.	NBC Monday Night Movie
	9:30 PM 10:00 PM	Harold Robbins' "The Survivors"	Doris Day Show	NBC Monday Night Movie
	10:00 PM 10:30 PM	Love, American Style	Carol Burnett Show	NBC Monday Night Movie
	10:30 PM 11:00 PM	Love, American Style	Carol Burnett Show	NBC Monday Night Movie
T U E S D A Y	7:00 PM 7:30 PM			
	7:30 PM 8:00 PM	Mod Squad	Lancer	I Dream of Jeannie
	8:00 PM 8:30 PM	Mod Squad	Lancer	Debbie Reynolds Show
	8:30 PM 9:00 PM	Movie of the Week	Red Skelton Hour	Julia
	9:00 PM 9:30 PM	Movie of the Week	Red Skelton Hour	NBC Tuesday Night Movie
	9:30 PM 10:00 PM	Movie of the Week	Governor & J.J.	NBC Tuesday Night Movie
	10:00 PM 10:30 PM	Marcus Welby, M.D.	†CBS News Hour †60 Minutes	NBC Tuesday Night Movie
	10:30 PM 11:00 PM	Marcus Welby, M.D.	†CBS News Hour †60 Minutes	NBC Tuesday Night Movie
W E D N E S D A Y	7:00 PM 7:30 PM			
	7:30 PM 8:00 PM	Flying Nun	Glen Campbell Goodtime Hour	The Virginian
	8:00 PM 8:30 PM	Courtship of Eddie's Father	Glen Campbell Goodtime Hour	The Virginian
	8:30 PM 9:00 PM	Room 222	Beverly Hillbillies	The Virginian
	9:00 PM 9:30 PM	ABC Wednesday Night Movie	Medical Center	Kraft Music Hall
	9:30 PM 10:00 PM	ABC Wednesday Night Movie	Medical Center	Kraft Music Hall
	10:00 PM 10:30 PM	ABC Wednesday Night Movie	Hawaii Five-O	Then Came Bronson
	10:30 PM 11:00 PM	ABC Wednesday Night Movie	Hawaii Five-O	Then Came Bronson

* First quarter hour program   /* Second quarter hour program
† Program airs every other week
Note: Repeated names indicate the program extends into that half-hour time slot.

PRIME TIME SCHEDULE: 1969/70

		AMERICAN ABC	COLUMBIA CBS	NATIONAL NBC
T H U R S D A Y	7:00 PM 7:30 PM			
	7:30 PM 8:00 PM	Ghost & Mrs. Muir	Family Affair	Daniel Boone
	8:00 PM 8:30 PM	That Girl	Jim Nabors Hour	Daniel Boone
	8:30 PM 9:00 PM	Bewitched	Jim Nabors Hour	Ironside
	9:00 PM 9:30 PM	This is Tom Jones	CBS Thursday Night Movie	Ironside
	9:30 PM 10:00 PM	This is Tom Jones	CBS Thursday Night Movie	Dragnet
	10:00 PM 10:30 PM	It Takes a Thief	CBS Thursday Night Movie	Dean Martin Show
	10:30 PM 11:00 PM	It Takes a Thief	CBS Thursday Night Movie	Dean Martin Show
F R I D A Y	7:00 PM 7:30 PM			
	7:30 PM 8:00 PM	Let's Make a Deal	Get Smart	High Chaparral
	8:00 PM 8:30 PM	Brady Bunch	Good Guys	High Chaparral
	8:30 PM 9:00 PM	Mr. Deeds Goes to Town	Hogan's Heroes	Name of the Game
	9:00 PM 9:30 PM	Here Come the Brides	CBS Friday Night Movie	Name of the Game
	9:30 PM 10:00 PM	Here Come the Brides	CBS Friday Night Movie	Name of the Game
	10:00 PM 10:30 PM	Jimmy Durante Presents Lennon Sisters	CBS Friday Night Movie	Bracken's World
	10:30 PM 11:00 PM	Jimmy Durante Presents Lennon Sisters	CBS Friday Night Movie	Bracken's World
S A T U R D A Y	7:00 PM 7:30 PM			
	7:30 PM 8:00 PM	Dating Game	Jackie Gleason Show	Andy Williams Show
	8:00 PM 8:30 PM	Newlywed Game	Jackie Gleason Show	Andy Williams Show
	8:30 PM 9:00 PM	Lawrence Welk Show	My Three Sons	Adam 12
	9:00 PM 9:30 PM	Lawrence Welk Show	Green Acres	NBC Saturday Night Movie
	9:30 PM 10:00 PM	Hollywood Palace	Petticoat Junction	NBC Saturday Night Movie
	10:00 PM 10:30 PM	Hollywood Palace	Mannix	NBC Saturday Night Movie
	10:30 PM 11:00 PM		Mannix	NBC Saturday Night Movie

* First quarter hour program   /* Second quarter hour program
† Program airs every other week
Note: Repeated names indicate the program extends into that half-hour time slot.

PRIME TIME SCHEDULE: 1970/71

		AMERICAN ABC	COLUMBIA CBS	NATIONAL NBC
S U N D A Y	7:00 PM 7:30 PM	Young Rebels	Lassie	Wild Kingdom
	7:30 PM 8:00 PM	Young Rebels	Hogan's Heroes	Wonderful World of Disney
	8:00 PM 8:30 PM	The F.B.I.	Ed Sullivan Show	Wonderful World of Disney
	8:30 PM 9:00 PM	The F.B.I.	Ed Sullivan Show	Bill Cosby Show
	9:00 PM 9:30 PM	ABC Sunday Night Movie	Glen Campbell Goodtime Hour	Bonanza
	9:30 PM 10:00 PM	ABC Sunday Night Movie	Glen Campbell Goodtime Hour	Bonanza
	10:00 PM 10:30 PM	ABC Sunday Night Movie	Tim Conway Comedy Hour	Bold Ones
	10:30 PM 11:00 PM	ABC Sunday Night Movie	Tim Conway Comedy Hour	Bold Ones
M O N D A Y	7:00 PM 7:30 PM			
	7:30 PM 8:00 PM	Young Lawyers	Gunsmoke	Red Skelton Show
	8:00 PM 8:30 PM	Young Lawyers	Gunsmoke	Rowan & Martin's Laugh-In
	8:30 PM 9:00 PM	Silent Force	Here's Lucy	Rowan & Martin's Laugh-In
	9:00 PM 9:30 PM	ABC Monday Night Football	Mayberry R.F.D.	NBC Monday Night Movie
	9:30 PM 10:00 PM	ABC Monday Night Football	Doris Day Show	NBC Monday Night Movie
	10:00 PM 10:30 PM	ABC Monday Night Football	Carol Burnett Show	NBC Monday Night Movie
	10:30 PM 11:00 PM	ABC Monday Night Football	Carol Burnett Show	NBC Monday Night Movie
T U E S D A Y	7:00 PM 7:30 PM			
	7:30 PM 8:00 PM	Mod Squad	Beverly Hillbillies	Don Knotts Show
	8:00 PM 8:30 PM	Mod Squad	Green Acres	Don Knotts Show
	8:30 PM 9:00 PM	Movie of the Week	Hee Haw	Julia
	9:00 PM 9:30 PM	Movie of the Week	Hee Haw	NBC Tuesday Night Movie
	9:30 PM 10:00 PM	Movie of the Week	To Rome with Love	NBC Tuesday Night Movie
	10:00 PM 10:30 PM	Marcus Welby, M.D.	†CBS News Hour †60 Minutes	NBC Tuesday Night Movie
	10:30 PM 11:00 PM	Marcus Welby, M.D.	†CBS News Hour †60 Minutes	NBC Tuesday Night Movie
W E D N E S D A Y	7:00 PM 7:30 PM			
	7:30 PM 8:00 PM	Courtship of Eddie's Father	Storefront Lawyers	Men from Shiloh
	8:00 PM 8:30 PM	Make Room for Granddaddy	Storefront Lawyers	Men from Shiloh
	8:30 PM 9:00 PM	Room 222	Governor & J.J.	Men from Shiloh
	9:00 PM 9:30 PM	Johnny Cash Show	Medical Center	Kraft Music Hall
	9:30 PM 10:00 PM	Johnny Cash Show	Medical Center	Kraft Music Hall
	10:00 PM 10:30 PM	Dan August	Hawaii Five-O	Four in One
	10:30 PM 11:00 PM	Dan August	Hawaii Five-O	Four in One

* First quarter hour program   /* Second quarter hour program
† Program airs every other week
Note: Repeated names indicate the program extends into that half-hour time slot.

PRIME TIME SCHEDULE: 1970/71

		AMERICAN ABC	COLUMBIA CBS	NATIONAL NBC
T **H** **U** **R** **S** **D** **A** **Y**	7:00 PM 7:30 PM			
	7:30 PM 8:00 PM	Matt Lincoln	Family Affair	Flip Wilson Show
	8:00 PM 8:30 PM	Matt Lincoln	Jim Nabors Hour	Flip Wilson Show
	8:30 PM 9:00 PM	Bewitched	Jim Nabors Hour	Ironside
	9:00 PM 9:30 PM	Barefoot in the Park	CBS Thursday Night Movie	Ironside
	9:30 PM 10:00 PM	Odd Couple	CBS Thursday Night Movie	Nancy
	10:00 PM 10:30 PM	The Immortal	CBS Thursday Night Movie	Dean Martin Show
	10:30 PM 11:00 PM	The Immortal	CBS Thursday Night Movie	Dean Martin Show
F **R** **I** **D** **A** **Y**	7:00 PM 7:30 PM			
	7:30 PM 8:00 PM	Brady Bunch	The Interns	High Chaparral
	8:00 PM 8:30 PM	Nanny and the Professor	The Interns	High Chaparral
	8:30 PM 9:00 PM	Partridge Family	The Headmaster	Name of the Game
	9:00 PM 9:30 PM	That Girl	CBS Friday Night Movie	Name of the Game
	9:30 PM 10:00 PM	Love, American Style	CBS Friday Night Movie	Name of the Game
	10:00 PM 10:30 PM	This is Tom Jones	CBS Friday Night Movie	Bracken's World
	10:30 PM 11:00 PM	This is Tom Jones	CBS Friday Night Movie	Bracken's World
S **A** **T** **U** **R** **D** **A** **Y**	7:00 PM 7:30 PM			
	7:30 PM 8:00 PM	Let's Make a Deal	Mission: Impossible	Andy Williams Show
	8:00 PM 8:30 PM	Newlywed Game	Mission: Impossible	Andy Williams Show
	8:30 PM 9:00 PM	Lawrence Welk Show	My Three Sons	Adam 12
	9:00 PM 9:30 PM	Lawrence Welk Show	Arnie	NBC Saturday Night Movie
	9:30 PM 10:00 PM	Most Deadly Game	The Mary Tyler Moore Show	NBC Saturday Night Movie
	10:00 PM 10:30 PM	Most Deadly Game	Mannix	NBC Saturday Night Movie
	10:30 PM 11:00 PM		Mannix	NBC Saturday Night Movie

* First quarter hour program   /* Second quarter hour program
† Program airs every other week
Note: Repeated names indicate the program extends into that half-hour time slot.

PRIME TIME SCHEDULE: 1971/72

		AMERICAN ABC	COLUMBIA CBS	NATIONAL NBC
S U N D A Y	7:00 PM 7:30 PM			
	7:30 PM 8:00 PM		CBS Sunday Night Movie	Wonderful World of Disney
	8:00 PM 8:30 PM	The F.B.I.	CBS Sunday Night Movie	Wonderful World of Disney
	8:30 PM 9:00 PM	The F.B.I.	CBS Sunday Night Movie	Jimmy Stewart Show
	9:00 PM 9:30 PM	ABC Sunday Night Movie	CBS Sunday Night Movie	Bonanza
	9:30 PM 10:00 PM	ABC Sunday Night Movie	Cade's County	Bonanza
	10:00 PM 10:30 PM	ABC Sunday Night Movie	Cade's County	Bold Ones
	10:30 PM 11:00 PM	ABC Sunday Night Movie		Bold Ones
M O N D A Y	7:00 PM 7:30 PM			
	7:30 PM 8:00 PM			
	8:00 PM 8:30 PM	Nanny & Professor	Gunsmoke	Rowan & Martin's Laugh-In
	8:30 PM 9:00 PM		Gunsmoke	Rowan & Martin's Laugh-In
	9:00 PM 9:30 PM	ABC Monday Night Football	Here's Lucy	NBC Monday Night Movie
	9:30 PM 10:00 PM	ABC Monday Night Football	Doris Day Show	NBC Monday Night Movie
	10:00 PM 10:30 PM	ABC Monday Night Football	My Three Sons	NBC Monday Night Movie
	10:30 PM 11:00 PM	ABC Monday Night Football	Arnie	NBC Monday Night Movie
T U E S D A Y	7:00 PM 7:30 PM			
	7:30 PM 8:00 PM	Mod Squad	Glen Campbell Goodtime Hour	Ironside
	8:00 PM 8:30 PM	Mod Squad	Glen Campbell Goodtime Hour	Ironside
	8:30 PM 9:00 PM	Movie of the Week	Hawaii Five-O	Sarge
	9:00 PM 9:30 PM	Movie of the Week	Hawaii Five-O	Sarge
	9:30 PM 10:00 PM	Movie of the Week	Cannon	The Funny Side
	10:00 PM 10:30 PM	Marcus Welby, M.D.	Cannon	The Funny Side
	10:30 PM 11:00 PM	Marcus Welby, M.D.		
W E D N E S D A Y	7:00 PM 7:30 PM			
	7:30 PM 8:00 PM			
	8:00 PM 8:30 PM	Bewitched	Carol Burnett Show	Adam 12
	8:30 PM 9:00 PM	Courtship of Eddie's Father	Carol Burnett Show	NBC Mystery Movie
	9:00 PM 9:30 PM	Smith Family	Medical Center	NBC Mystery Movie
	9:30 PM 10:00 PM	Shirley's World	Medical Center	NBC Mystery Movie
	10:00 PM 10:30 PM	Man and the City	Mannix	Night Gallery
	10:30 PM 11:00 PM	Man and the City	Mannix	Night Gallery

* First quarter hour program   /* Second quarter hour program
† Program airs every other week
Note: Repeated names indicate the program extends into that half-hour time slot.

PRIME TIME SCHEDULE: 1971/72

		AMERICAN ABC	COLUMBIA CBS	NATIONAL NBC
T **H** **U** **R** **S** **D** **A** **Y**	7:00 PM 7:30 PM			
	7:30 PM 8:00 PM			
	8:00 PM 8:30 PM	Alias Smith & Jones	Bearcats	Flip Wilson Show
	8:30 PM 9:00 PM	Alias Smith & Jones	Bearcats	Flip Wilson Show
	9:00 PM 9:30 PM	Longstreet	CBS Thursday Night Movie	Nichols
	9:30 PM 10:00 PM	Longstreet	CBS Thursday Night Movie	Nichols
	10:00 PM 10:30 PM	Owen Marshall	CBS Thursday Night Movie	Dean Martin Show
	10:30 PM 11:00 PM	Owen Marshall	CBS Thursday Night Movie	Dean Martin Show
F **R** **I** **D** **A** **Y**	7:00 PM 7:30 PM			
	7:30 PM 8:00 PM			
	8:00 PM 8:30 PM	Brady Bunch	Chicago Teddy Bears	The D.A.
	8:30 PM 9:00 PM	Partridge Family	O'Hara, U.S. Treasury	NBC World Premiere Movie
	9:00 PM 9:30 PM	Room 222	O'Hara, U.S. Treasury	NBC World Premiere Movie
	9:30 PM 10:00 PM	Odd Couple	New CBS Friday Night Movies	NBC World Premiere Movie
	10:00 PM 10:30 PM	Love, American Style	New CBS Friday Night Movies	NBC World Premiere Movie
	10:30 PM 11:00 PM	Love, American Style	New CBS Friday Night Movies	
S **A** **T** **U** **R** **D** **A** **Y**	7:00 PM 7:30 PM			
	7:30 PM 8:00 PM			
	8:00 PM 8:30 PM	Getting Together	All in the Family	The Partners
	8:30 PM 9:00 PM	ABC Movie of the Weekend	Funny Face	The Good Life
	9:00 PM 9:30 PM	ABC Movie of the Weekend	New Dick Van Dyke Show	NBC Saturday Night Movie
	9:30 PM 10:00 PM	ABC Movie of the Weekend	The Mary Tyler Moore Show	NBC Saturday Night Movie
	10:00 PM 10:30 PM	The Persuaders	Mission: Impossible	NBC Saturday Night Movie
	10:30 PM 11:00 PM	The Persuaders	Mission: Impossible	NBC Saturday Night Movie

* First quarter hour program /* Second quarter hour program
† Program airs every other week
Note: Repeated names indicate the program extends into that half-hour time slot.

PRIME TIME SCHEDULE: 1972/73

		AMERICAN ABC	COLUMBIA CBS	NATIONAL NBC
S U N D A Y	7:00 PM 7:30 PM			
	7:30 PM 8:00 PM		Anna and the King	Wonderful World of Disney
	8:00 PM 8:30 PM	The F.B.I.	M*A*S*H	Wonderful World of Disney
	8:30 PM 9:00 PM	The F.B.I.	Sandy Duncan Show	NBC Sunday Mystery Movie
	9:00 PM 9:30 PM	ABC Sunday Night Movie	New Dick Van Dyke Show	NBC Sunday Mystery Movie
	9:30 PM 10:00 PM	ABC Sunday Night Movie	Mannix	NBC Sunday Mystery Movie
	10:00 PM 10:30 PM	ABC Sunday Night Movie	Mannix	Night Gallery
	10:30 PM 11:00 PM	ABC Sunday Night Movie		
M O N D A Y	7:00 PM 7:30 PM			
	7:30 PM 8:00 PM			
	8:00 PM 8:30 PM	The Rookies	Gunsmoke	Rowan & Martin's Laugh-In
	8:30 PM 9:00 PM	The Rookies	Gunsmoke	Rowan & Martin's Laugh-In
	9:00 PM 9:30 PM	ABC Monday Night Football	Here's Lucy	NBC Monday Night Movie
	9:30 PM 10:00 PM	ABC Monday Night Football	Doris Day Show	NBC Monday Night Movie
	10:00 PM 10:30 PM	ABC Monday Night Football	New Bill Cosby Show	NBC Monday Night Movie
	10:30 PM 11:00 PM	ABC Monday Night Football	New Bill Cosby Show	NBC Monday Night Movie
T U E S D A Y	7:00 PM 7:30 PM			
	7:30 PM 8:00 PM			
	8:00 PM 8:30 PM	Temperatures Rising	Maude	Bonanza
	8:30 PM 9:00 PM	Tuesday Movie of the Week	Hawaii Five-O	Bonanza
	9:00 PM 9:30 PM	Tuesday Movie of the Week	Hawaii Five-O	Bold Ones
	9:30 PM 10:00 PM	Tuesday Movie of the Week	New CBS Tuesday Night Movies	Bold Ones
	10:00 PM 10:30 PM	Marcus Welby, M.D.	New CBS Tuesday Night Movies	NBC Reports
	10:30 PM 11:00 PM	Marcus Welby, M.D.	New CBS Tuesday Night Movies	NBC Reports
W E D N E S D A Y	7:00 PM 7:30 PM			
	7:30 PM 8:00 PM			
	8:00 PM 8:30 PM	Paul Lynde Show	Carol Burnett Show	Adam 12
	8:30 PM 9:00 PM	Wednesday Movie of the Week	Carol Burnett Show	NBC Wednesday Mystery Movie
	9:00 PM 9:30 PM	Wednesday Movie of the Week	Medical Center	NBC Wednesday Mystery Movie
	9:30 PM 10:00 PM	Wednesday Movie of the Week	Medical Center	NBC Wednesday Mystery Movie
	10:00 PM 10:30 PM	Julie Andrews Hour	Cannon	Search
	10:30 PM 11:00 PM	Julie Andrews Hour	Cannon	Search

* First quarter hour program   /* Second quarter hour program
† Program airs every other week
Note: Repeated names indicate the program extends into that half-hour time slot.

PRIME TIME SCHEDULE: 1972/73

		AMERICAN ABC	COLUMBIA CBS	NATIONAL NBC
T **H** **U** **R** **S** **D** **A** **Y**	7:00 PM 7:30 PM			
	7:30 PM 8:00 PM			
	8:00 PM 8:30 PM	Mod Squad	The Waltons	Flip Wilson Show
	8:30 PM 9:00 PM	Mod Squad	The Waltons	Flip Wilson Show
	9:00 PM 9:30 PM	The Men	CBS Thursday Night Movie	Ironside
	9:30 PM 10:00 PM	The Men	CBS Thursday Night Movie	Ironside
	10:00 PM 10:30 PM	Owen Marshall	CBS Thursday Night Movie	Dean Martin Show
	10:30 PM 11:00 PM	Owen Marshall	CBS Thursday Night Movie	Dean Martin Show
F **R** **I** **D** **A** **Y**	7:00 PM 7:30 PM			
	7:30 PM 8:00 PM			
	8:00 PM 8:30 PM	Brady Bunch	Sonny & Cher Comedy Hour	Sanford & Son
	8:30 PM 9:00 PM	Partridge Family	Sonny & Cher Comedy Hour	Little People
	9:00 PM 9:30 PM	Room 222	CBS Friday Night Movie	Ghost Story
	9:30 PM 10:00 PM	Odd Couple	CBS Friday Night Movie	Ghost Story
	10:00 PM 10:30 PM	Love, American Style	CBS Friday Night Movie	Banyon
	10:30 PM 11:00 PM	Love, American Style	CBS Friday Night Movie	Banyon
S **A** **T** **U** **R** **D** **A** **Y**	7:00 PM 7:30 PM			
	7:30 PM 8:00 PM			
	8:00 PM 8:30 PM	Alias Smith & Jones	All in the Family	Emergency
	8:30 PM 9:00 PM	Alias Smith & Jones	Bridget Loves Bernie	Emergency
	9:00 PM 9:30 PM	Streets of San Francisco	The Mary Tyler Moore Show	NBC Saturday Night Movie
	9:30 PM 10:00 PM	Streets of San Francisco	The Bob Newhart Show	NBC Saturday Night Movie
	10:00 PM 10:30 PM	The Sixth Sense	Mission: Impossible	NBC Saturday Night Movie
	10:30 PM 11:00 PM	The Sixth Sense	Mission: Impossible	NBC Saturday Night Movie

* First quarter hour program   /* Second quarter hour program
† Program airs every other week
Note: Repeated names indicate the program extends into that half-hour time slot.

PRIME TIME SCHEDULE: 1973/74

		AMERICAN ABC	COLUMBIA CBS	NATIONAL NBC
S U N D A Y	7:00 PM 7:30 PM			
	7:30 PM 8:00 PM	The F.B.I.	New Adv. of Perry Mason	Wonderful World of Disney
	8:00 PM 8:30 PM	The F.B.I.	New Adv. of Perry Mason	Wonderful World of Disney
	8:30 PM 9:00 PM	ABC Sunday Night Movie	Mannix	NBC Sunday Mystery Movie
	9:00 PM 9:30 PM	ABC Sunday Night Movie	Mannix	NBC Sunday Mystery Movie
	9:30 PM 10:00 PM	ABC Sunday Night Movie	Barnaby Jones	NBC Sunday Mystery Movie
	10:00 PM 10:30 PM	ABC Sunday Night Movie	Barnaby Jones	NBC Sunday Mystery Movie
	10:30 PM 11:00 PM			
M O N D A Y	7:00 PM 7:30 PM			
	7:30 PM 8:00 PM			
	8:00 PM 8:30 PM	The Rookies	Gunsmoke	Lotsa Luck
	8:30 PM 9:00 PM	The Rookies	Gunsmoke	Diana
	9:00 PM 9:30 PM	ABC Monday Night Football	Here's Lucy	NBC Monday Night Movie
	9:30 PM 10:00 PM	ABC Monday Night Football	New Dick Van Dyke Show	NBC Monday Night Movie
	10:00 PM 10:30 PM	ABC Monday Night Football	Medical Center	NBC Monday Night Movie
	10:30 PM 11:00 PM	ABC Monday Night Football	Medical Center	NBC Monday Night Movie
T U E S D A Y	7:00 PM 7:30 PM			
	7:30 PM 8:00 PM			
	8:00 PM 8:30 PM	Temperatures Rising	Maude	Chase
	8:30 PM 9:00 PM	Tuesday Movie of the Week	Hawaii Five-O	Chase
	9:00 PM 9:30 PM	Tuesday Movie of the Week	Tuesday Night CBS Movie	The Magician
	9:30 PM 10:00 PM	Tuesday Movie of the Week	Tuesday Night CBS Movie	The Magician
	10:00 PM 10:30 PM	Marcus Welby, M.D.	Tuesday Night CBS Movie	Police Story
	10:30 PM 11:00 PM	Marcus Welby, M.D.	Tuesday Night CBS Movie	Police Story
W E D N E S D A Y	7:00 PM 7:30 PM			
	7:30 PM 8:00 PM			
	8:00 PM 8:30 PM	Bob & Carol & Ted & Alice	Sonny & Cher Comedy Hour	Adam 12
	8:30 PM 9:00 PM	Wednesday Movie of the Week	Sonny & Cher Comedy Hour	NBC Wednesday Mystery Movie
	9:00 PM 9:30 PM	Wednesday Movie of the Week	Cannon	NBC Wednesday Mystery Movie
	9:30 PM 10:00 PM	Wednesday Movie of the Week	Cannon	NBC Wednesday Mystery Movie
	10:00 PM 10:30 PM	Owen Marshall	Kojak	Love Story
	10:30 PM 11:00 PM	Owen Marshall	Kojak	Love Story

* First quarter hour program   /* Second quarter hour program
† Program airs every other week
Note: Repeated names indicate the program extends into that half-hour time slot.

PRIME TIME SCHEDULE: 1973/74

		AMERICAN ABC	COLUMBIA CBS	NATIONAL NBC
T **H** **U** **R** **S** **D** **A** **Y**	7:00 PM			
	7:30 PM			
	7:30 PM			
	8:00 PM			
	8:00 PM 8:30 PM	Toma	The Waltons	Flip Wilson Show
	8:30 PM 9:00 PM	Toma	The Waltons	Flip Wilson Show
	9:00 PM 9:30 PM	Kung Fu	CBS Thursday Night Movie	Ironside
	9:30 PM 10:00 PM	Kung Fu	CBS Thursday Night Movie	Ironside
	10:00 PM 10:30 PM	Streets of San Francisco	CBS Thursday Night Movie	NBC Follies
	10:30 PM 11:00 PM	Streets of San Francisco	CBS Thursday Night Movie	
F **R** **I** **D** **A** **Y**	7:00 PM			
	7:30 PM			
	7:30 PM			
	8:00 PM			
	8:00 PM 8:30 PM	Brady Bunch	Calucci's Dept.	Sanford & Son
	8:30 PM 9:00 PM	Odd Couple	Roll Out	The Girl with Something Extra
	9:00 PM 9:30 PM	Room 222	CBS Friday Night Movie	Needles & Pins
	9:30 PM 10:00 PM	Adam's Rib	CBS Friday Night Movie	Brian Keith Show
	10:00 PM 10:30 PM	Love, American Style	CBS Friday Night Movie	Dean Martin Show
	10:30 PM 11:00 PM	Love, American Style	CBS Friday Night Movie	Dean Martin Show
S **A** **T** **U** **R** **D** **A** **Y**	7:00 PM			
	7:30 PM			
	7:30 PM			
	8:00 PM			
	8:00 PM 8:30 PM	Partridge Family	All in the Family	Emergency
	8:30 PM 9:00 PM	ABC Suspense Movie	M*A*S*H	Emergency
	9:00 PM 9:30 PM	ABC Suspense Movie	The Mary Tyler Moore Show	NBC Saturday Night Movie
	9:30 PM 10:00 PM	ABC Suspense Movie	The Bob Newhart Show	NBC Saturday Night Movie
	10:00 PM 10:30 PM	Griff	Carol Burnett Show	NBC Saturday Night Movie
	10:30 PM 11:00 PM	Griff	Carol Burnett Show	NBC Saturday Night Movie

* First quarter hour program   /* Second quarter hour program
† Program airs every other week
Note: Repeated names indicate the program extends into that half-hour time slot.

PRIME TIME SCHEDULE: 1974/75

		AMERICAN ABC	COLUMBIA CBS	NATIONAL NBC
S **U** **N** **D** **A** **Y**	7:00 PM 7:30 PM			
	7:30 PM 8:00 PM		Apple's Way	Wonderful World of Disney
	8:00 PM 8:30 PM	Sonny Comedy Revue	Apple's Way	Wonderful World of Disney
	8:30 PM 9:00 PM	Sonny Comedy Revue	Kojak	NBC Sunday Mystery Movie
	9:00 PM 9:30 PM	ABC Sunday Night Movie	Kojak	NBC Sunday Mystery Movie
	9:30 PM 10:00 PM	ABC Sunday Night Movie	Mannix	NBC Sunday Mystery Movie
	10:00 PM 10:30 PM	ABC Sunday Night Movie	Mannix	NBC Sunday Mystery Movie
	10:30 PM 11:00 PM	ABC Sunday Night Movie		
M **O** **N** **D** **A** **Y**	7:00 PM 7:30 PM			
	7:30 PM 8:00 PM			
	8:00 PM 8:30 PM	Rookies	Gunsmoke	Born Free
	8:30 PM 9:00 PM	Rookies	Gunsmoke	Born Free
	9:00 PM 9:30 PM	ABC Monday Night Football	Maude	NBC Monday Night Movie
	9:30 PM 10:00 PM	ABC Monday Night Football	Rhoda	NBC Monday Night Movie
	10:00 PM 10:30 PM	ABC Monday Night Football	Medical Center	NBC Monday Night Movie
	10:30 PM 11:00 PM	ABC Monday Night Football	Medical Center	NBC Monday Night Movie
T **U** **E** **S** **D** **A** **Y**	7:00 PM 7:30 PM			
	7:30 PM 8:00 PM			
	8:00 PM 8:30 PM	Happy Days	Good Times	Adam 12
	8:30 PM 9:00 PM	Tuesday Movie of the Week	M*A*S*H	NBC World Premiere Movie
	9:00 PM 9:30 PM	Tuesday Movie of the Week	Hawaii Five-O	NBC World Premiere Movie
	9:30 PM 10:00 PM	Tuesday Movie of the Week	Hawaii Five-O	NBC World Premiere Movie
	10:00 PM 10:30 PM	Marcus Welby, M.D.	Barnaby Jones	Police Story
	10:30 PM 11:00 PM	Marcus Welby, M.D.	Barnaby Jones	Police Story
W **E** **D** **N** **E** **S** **D** **A** **Y**	7:00 PM 7:30 PM			
	7:30 PM 8:00 PM			
	8:00 PM 8:30 PM	That's My Mama	Sons & Daughters	Little House on the Prairie
	8:30 PM 9:00 PM	Wednesday Movie of the Week	Sons & Daughters	Little House on the Prairie
	9:00 PM 9:30 PM	Wednesday Movie of the Week	Cannon	Lucas Tanner
	9:30 PM 10:00 PM	Wednesday Movie of the Week	Cannon	Lucas Tanner
	10:00 PM 10:30 PM	Get Christie Love	Manhunter	Petrocelli
	10:30 PM 11:00 PM	Get Christie Love	Manhunter	Petrocelli

* First quarter hour program   /* Second quarter hour program
† Program airs every other week
Note: Repeated names indicate the program extends into that half-hour time slot.

PRIME TIME SCHEDULE: 1974/75

		AMERICAN ABC	COLUMBIA CBS	NATIONAL NBC
T H U R S D A Y	7:00 PM 7:30 PM			
	7:30 PM 8:00 PM			
	8:00 PM 8:30 PM	Odd Couple	The Waltons	Sierra
	8:30 PM 9:00 PM	Paper Moon	The Waltons	Sierra
	9:00 PM 9:30 PM	Streets of San Francisco	CBS Thursday Night Movie	Ironside
	9:30 PM 10:00 PM	Streets of San Francisco	CBS Thursday Night Movie	Ironside
	10:00 PM 10:30 PM	Harry-O	CBS Thursday Night Movie	Movin' On
	10:30 PM 11:00 PM	Harry-O	CBS Thursday Night Movie	Movin' On
F R I D A Y	7:00 PM 7:30 PM			
	7:30 PM 8:00 PM			
	8:00 PM 8:30 PM	Kodiak	Planet of the Apes	Sanford & Son
	8:30 PM 9:00 PM	Six Million Dollar Man	Planet of the Apes	Chico and the Man
	9:00 PM 9:30 PM	Six Million Dollar Man	CBS Friday Night Movie	Rockford Files
	9:30 PM 10:00 PM	Texas Wheelers	CBS Friday Night Movie	Rockford Files
	10:00 PM 10:30 PM	Kolchak: The Night Stalker	CBS Friday Night Movie	Police Woman
	10:30 PM 11:00 PM	Kolchak: The Night Stalker	CBS Friday Night Movie	Police Woman
S A T U R D A Y	7:00 PM 7:30 PM			
	7:30 PM 8:00 PM			
	8:00 PM 8:30 PM	The New Land	All in the Family	Emergency
	8:30 PM 9:00 PM	The New Land	Paul Sand in Friends and Lovers	Emergency
	9:00 PM 9:30 PM	Kung Fu	The Mary Tyler Moore Show	NBC Saturday Night Movie
	9:30 PM 10:00 PM	Kung Fu	The Bob Newhart Show	NBC Saturday Night Movie
	10:00 PM 10:30 PM	Nakia	Carol Burnett Show	NBC Saturday Night Movie
	10:30 PM 11:00 PM	Nakia	Carol Burnett Show	NBC Saturday Night Movie

* First quarter hour program   /* Second quarter hour program
† Program airs every other week
Note: Repeated names indicate the program extends into that half-hour time slot.

PRIME TIME SCHEDULE: 1975/76

		AMERICAN ABC	COLUMBIA CBS	NATIONAL NBC
S **U** **N** **D** **A** **Y**	7:00 PM 7:30 PM	Swiss Family Robinson	Three for the Road	Wonderful World of Disney
	7:30 PM 8:00 PM	Swiss Family Robinson	Three for the Road	Wonderful World of Disney
	8:00 PM 8:30 PM	Six Million Dollar Man	Cher	Family Holvak
	8:30 PM 9:00 PM	Six Million Dollar Man	Cher	Family Holvak
	9:00 PM 9:30 PM	ABC Sunday Night Movie	Kojak	NBC Sunday Mystery Movie
	9:30 PM 10:00 PM	ABC Sunday Night Movie	Kojak	NBC Sunday Mystery Movie
	10:00 PM 10:30 PM	ABC Sunday Night Movie	Bronk	NBC Sunday Mystery Movie
	10:30 PM 11:00 PM	ABC Sunday Night Movie	Bronk	NBC Sunday Mystery Movie
M **O** **N** **D** **A** **Y**	7:00 PM 7:30 PM			
	7:30 PM 8:00 PM			
	8:00 PM 8:30 PM	Barbary Coast	Rhoda	Invisible Man
	8:30 PM 9:00 PM	Barbary Coast	Phyllis	Invisible Man
	9:00 PM 9:30 PM	ABC Monday Night Football	All in the Family	NBC Monday Night Movie
	9:30 PM 10:00 PM	ABC Monday Night Football	Maude	NBC Monday Night Movie
	10:00 PM 10:30 PM	ABC Monday Night Football	Medical Center	NBC Monday Night Movie
	10:30 PM 11:00 PM	ABC Monday Night Football	Medical Center	NBC Monday Night Movie
T **U** **E** **S** **D** **A** **Y**	7:00 PM 7:30 PM			
	7:30 PM 8:00 PM			
	8:00 PM 8:30 PM	Happy Days	Good Times	Movin' On
	8:30 PM 9:00 PM	Welcome Back, Kotter	Joe and Sons	Movin' On
	9:00 PM 9:30 PM	The Rookies	Switch	Police Story
	9:30 PM 10:00 PM	The Rookies	Switch	Police Story
	10:00 PM 10:30 PM	Marcus Welby, M.D.	Beacon Hill	Joe Forrester
	10:30 PM 11:00 PM	Marcus Welby, M.D.	Beacon Hill	Joe Forrester
W **E** **D** **N** **E** **S** **D** **A** **Y**	7:00 PM 7:30 PM			
	7:30 PM 8:00 PM			
	8:00 PM 8:30 PM	When Things Were Rotten	Tony Orlando & Dawn	Little House on the Prairie
	8:30 PM 9:00 PM	That's My Mama	Tony Orlando & Dawn	Little House on the Prairie
	9:00 PM 9:30 PM	Baretta	Cannon	Doctors' Hospital
	9:30 PM 10:00 PM	Baretta	Cannon	Doctors' Hospital
	10:00 PM 10:30 PM	Starsky & Hutch	Kate McShane	Petrocelli
	10:30 PM 11:00 PM	Starsky & Hutch	Kate McShane	Petrocelli

* First quarter hour program   /* Second quarter hour program
† Program airs every other week
Note: Repeated names indicate the program extends into that half-hour time slot.

PRIME TIME SCHEDULE: 1975/76

		AMERICAN ABC	COLUMBIA CBS	NATIONAL NBC
T **H** **U** **R** **S** **D** **A** **Y**	7:00 PM 7:30 PM			
	7:30 PM 8:00 PM			
	8:00 PM 8:30 PM	Barney Miller	The Waltons	The Montefuscos
	8:30 PM 9:00 PM	On the Rocks	The Waltons	Fay
	9:00 PM 9:30 PM	Streets of San Francisco	CBS Thursday Night Movie	Ellery Queen
	9:30 PM 10:00 PM	Streets of San Francisco	CBS Thursday Night Movie	Ellery Queen
	10:00 PM 10:30 PM	Harry-O	CBS Thursday Night Movie	Medical Story
	10:30 PM 11:00 PM	Harry-O	CBS Thursday Night Movie	Medical Story
F **R** **I** **D** **A** **Y**	7:00 PM 7:30 PM			
	7:30 PM 8:00 PM			
	8:00 PM 8:30 PM	Mobile One	Big Eddie	Sanford & Son
	8:30 PM 9:00 PM	Mobile One	M*A*S*H	Chico and the Man
	9:00 PM 9:30 PM	ABC Friday Night Movie	Hawaii Five-O	Rockford Files
	9:30 PM 10:00 PM	ABC Friday Night Movie	Hawaii Five-O	Rockford Files
	10:00 PM 10:30 PM	ABC Friday Night Movie	Barnaby Jones	Police Woman
	10:30 PM 11:00 PM	ABC Friday Night Movie	Barnaby Jones	Police Woman
S **A** **T** **U** **R** **D** **A** **Y**	7:00 PM 7:30 PM			
	7:30 PM 8:00 PM			
	8:00 PM 8:30 PM	Saturday Night Live with Howard Cosell	The Jeffersons	Emergency
	8:30 PM 9:00 PM	Saturday Night Live with Howard Cosell	Doc	Emergency
	9:00 PM 9:30 PM	S.W.A.T.	The Mary Tyler Moore Show	NBC Saturday Night Movie
	9:30 PM 10:00 PM	S.W.A.T.	The Bob Newhart Show	NBC Saturday Night Movie
	10:00 PM 10:30 PM	Matt Helm	Carol Burnett Show	NBC Saturday Night Movie
	10:30 PM 11:00 PM	Matt Helm	Carol Burnett Show	NBC Saturday Night Movie

* First quarter hour program   /* Second quarter hour program
† Program airs every other week
Note: Repeated names indicate the program extends into that half-hour time slot.

PRIME TIME SCHEDULE: 1976/77

		AMERICAN ABC	COLUMBIA CBS	NATIONAL NBC
S U N D A Y	7:00 PM 7:30 PM	Cos	60 Minutes	Wonderful World of Disney
	7:30 PM 8:00 PM	Cos	60 Minutes	Wonderful World of Disney
	8:00 PM 8:30 PM	Six Million Dollar Man	Sonny & Cher Show	NBC Sunday Mystery Movie
	8:30 PM 9:00 PM	Six Million Dollar Man	Sonny & Cher Show	NBC Sunday Mystery Movie
	9:00 PM 9:30 PM	ABC Sunday Night Movie	Kojak	NBC Sunday Mystery Movie
	9:30 PM 10:00 PM	ABC Sunday Night Movie	Kojak	Big Event
	10:00 PM 10:30 PM	ABC Sunday Night Movie	Delvecchio	Big Event
	10:30 PM 11:00 PM	ABC Sunday Night Movie	Delvecchio	Big Event
M O N D A Y	7:00 PM 7:30 PM			
	7:30 PM 8:00 PM			
	8:00 PM 8:30 PM	Captain and Tennille	Rhoda	Little House on the Prairie
	8:30 PM 9:00 PM	Captain and Tennille	Phyllis	Little House on the Prairie
	9:00 PM 9:30 PM	ABC Monday Night Football	Maude	NBC Monday Night Movie
	9:30 PM 10:00 PM	ABC Monday Night Football	All's Fair	NBC Monday Night Movie
	10:00 PM 10:30 PM	ABC Monday Night Football	Executive Suite	NBC Monday Night Movie
	10:30 PM 11:00 PM	ABC Monday Night Football	Executive Suite	NBC Monday Night Movie
T U E S D A Y	7:00 PM 7:30 PM			
	7:30 PM 8:00 PM			
	8:00 PM 8:30 PM	Happy Days	Tony Orlando & Dawn Rainbow Hour	Baa Baa Black Sheep
	8:30 PM 9:00 PM	Laverne & Shirley	Tony Orlando & Dawn Rainbow Hour	Baa Baa Black Sheep
	9:00 PM 9:30 PM	Rich Man, Poor Man	M*A*S*H	Police Woman
	9:30 PM 10:00 PM	Rich Man, Poor Man	One Day at a Time	Police Woman
	10:00 PM 10:30 PM	Family	Switch	Police Story
	10:30 PM 11:00 PM	Family	Switch	Police Story
W E D N E S D A Y	7:00 PM 7:30 PM			
	7:30 PM 8:00 PM			
	8:00 PM 8:30 PM	Bionic Woman	Good Times	The Practice
	8:30 PM 9:00 PM	Bionic Woman	Ball Four	NBC Movie of the Week
	9:00 PM 9:30 PM	Baretta	All in the Family	NBC Movie of the Week
	9:30 PM 10:00 PM	Baretta	Alice	NBC Movie of the Week
	10:00 PM 10:30 PM	Charlie's Angels	Blue Knight	The Quest
	10:30 PM 11:00 PM	Charlie's Angels	Blue Knight	The Quest

* First quarter hour program   /* Second quarter hour program
† Program airs every other week
Note: Repeated names indicate the program extends into that half-hour time slot.

PRIME TIME SCHEDULE: 1976/77

		AMERICAN ABC	COLUMBIA CBS	NATIONAL NBC
T H U R S D A Y	7:00 PM 7:30 PM			
	7:30 PM 8:00 PM			
	8:00 PM 8:30 PM	Welcome Back, Kotter	The Waltons	Gemini Man
	8:30 PM 9:00 PM	Barney Miller	The Waltons	Gemini Man
	9:00 PM 9:30 PM	Tony Randall Show	Hawaii Five-O	NBC's Best Sellers
	9:30 PM 10:00 PM	Nancy Walker Show	Hawaii Five-O	NBC's Best Sellers
	10:00 PM 10:30 PM	Streets of San Francisco	Barnaby Jones	Van Dyke & Company
	10:30 PM 11:00 PM	Streets of San Francisco	Barnaby Jones	Van Dyke & Company
F R I D A Y	7:00 PM 7:30 PM			
	7:30 PM 8:00 PM		Campaign '76	
	8:00 PM 8:30 PM	Donny & Marie	Spencer's Pilots	Sanford & Son
	8:30 PM 9:00 PM	Donny & Marie	Spencer's Pilots	Chico and the Man
	9:00 PM 9:30 PM	ABC Friday Night Movie	CBS Friday Night Movie	Rockford Files
	9:30 PM 10:00 PM	ABC Friday Night Movie	CBS Friday Night Movie	Rockford Files
	10:00 PM 10:30 PM	ABC Friday Night Movie	CBS Friday Night Movie	Serpico
	10:30 PM 11:00 PM	ABC Friday Night Movie	CBS Friday Night Movie	Serpico
S A T U R D A Y	7:00 PM 7:30 PM			
	7:30 PM 8:00 PM			
	8:00 PM 8:30 PM	Holmes & Yo-Yo	The Jeffersons	Emergency
	8:30 PM 9:00 PM	Mr. T and Tina	Doc	Emergency
	9:00 PM 9:30 PM	Starsky & Hutch	The Mary Tyler Moore Show	NBC Saturday Night Movie
	9:30 PM 10:00 PM	Starsky & Hutch	The Bob Newhart Show	NBC Saturday Night Movie
	10:00 PM 10:30 PM	Most Wanted	Carol Burnett Show	NBC Saturday Night Movie
	10:30 PM 11:00 PM	Most Wanted	Carol Burnett Show	NBC Saturday Night Movie

* First quarter hour program   /* Second quarter hour program
† Program airs every other week
Note: Repeated names indicate the program extends into that half-hour time slot.

PRIME TIME SCHEDULE: 1977/78

		AMERICAN ABC	COLUMBIA CBS	NATIONAL NBC
S U N D A Y	7:00 PM 7:30 PM	†Hardy Boys Mysteries †Nancy Drew Mysteries	60 Minutes	Wonderful World of Disney
	7:30 PM 8:00 PM	†Hardy Boys Mysteries †Nancy Drew Mysteries	60 Minutes	Wonderful World of Disney
	8:00 PM 8:30 PM	Six Million Dollar Man	Rhoda	Wonderful World of Disney
	8:30 PM 9:00 PM	Six Million Dollar Man	On Our Own	Wonderful World of Disney
	9:00 PM 9:30 PM	ABC Sunday Night Movie	All in the Family	Big Event
	9:30 PM 10:00 PM	ABC Sunday Night Movie	Alice	Big Event
	10:00 PM 10:30 PM	ABC Sunday Night Movie	Kojak	Big Event
	10:30 PM 11:00 PM	ABC Sunday Night Movie	Kojak	Big Event
M O N D A Y	7:00 PM 7:30 PM			
	7:30 PM 8:00 PM			
	8:00 PM 8:30 PM	San Pedro Beach Bums	Young Dan'l Boone	Little House on the Prairie
	8:30 PM 9:00 PM	San Pedro Beach Bums	Young Dan'l Boone	Little House on the Prairie
	9:00 PM 9:30 PM	Monday Night Football	Betty White Show	NBC Monday Night Movie
	9:30 PM 10:00 PM	Monday Night Football	Maude	NBC Monday Night Movie
	10:00 PM 10:30 PM	Monday Night Football	Rafferty	NBC Monday Night Movie
	10:30 PM 11:00 PM	Monday Night Football	Rafferty	NBC Monday Night Movie
T U E S D A Y	7:00 PM 7:30 PM			
	7:30 PM 8:00 PM			
	8:00 PM 8:30 PM	Happy Days	The Fitzpatricks	Richard Pryor Show
	8:30 PM 9:00 PM	Laverne & Shirley	The Fitzpatricks	Richard Pryor Show
	9:00 PM 9:30 PM	Three's Company	M*A*S*H	Mulligan's Stew
	9:30 PM 10:00 PM	Soap	One Day at a Time	Mulligan's Stew
	10:00 PM 10:30 PM	Family	Lou Grant	Police Woman
	10:30 PM 11:00 PM	Family	Lou Grant	Police Woman
W E D N E S D A Y	7:00 PM 7:30 PM			
	7:30 PM 8:00 PM			
	8:00 PM 8:30 PM	Eight is Enough	Good Times	Life and Times of Grizzly Adams
	8:30 PM 9:00 PM	Eight is Enough	Busting Loose	Life and Times of Grizzly Adams
	9:00 PM 9:30 PM	Charlie's Angels	CBS Wednesday Movie	Oregon Trail
	9:30 PM 10:00 PM	Charlie's Angels	CBS Wednesday Movie	Oregon Trail
	10:00 PM 10:30 PM	Baretta	CBS Wednesday Movie	Big Hawaii
	10:30 PM 11:00 PM	Baretta	CBS Wednesday Movie	Big Hawaii

* First quarter hour program   /* Second quarter hour program
† Program airs every other week
Note: Repeated names indicate the program extends into that half-hour time slot.

PRIME TIME SCHEDULE: 1977/78

		AMERICAN ABC	COLUMBIA CBS	NATIONAL NBC
T H U R S D A Y	7:00 PM 7:30 PM			
	7:30 PM 8:00 PM			
	8:00 PM 8:30 PM	Welcome Back, Kotter	The Waltons	Chips
	8:30 PM 9:00 PM	What's Happening	The Waltons	Chips
	9:00 PM 9:30 PM	Barney Miller	Hawaii Five-O	Man from Atlantis
	9:30 PM 10:00 PM	Carter Country	Hawaii Five-O	Man from Atlantis
	10:00 PM 10:30 PM	Redd Foxx Show	Barnaby Jones	Rosetti and Ryan
	10:30 PM 11:00 PM	Redd Foxx Show	Barnaby Jones	Rosetti and Ryan
F R I D A Y	7:00 PM 7:30 PM			
	7:30 PM 8:00 PM			
	8:00 PM 8:30 PM	Donny & Marie	New Adventures of Wonder Woman	Sanford Arms
	8:30 PM 9:00 PM	Donny & Marie	New Adventures of Wonder Woman	Chico and the Man
	9:00 PM 9:30 PM	ABC Friday Night Movie	Logan's Run	Rockford Files
	9:30 PM 10:00 PM	ABC Friday Night Movie	Logan's Run	Rockford Files
	10:00 PM 10:30 PM	ABC Friday Night Movie	Switch	Quincy, M.E.
	10:30 PM 11:00 PM	ABC Friday Night Movie	Switch	Quincy, M.E.
S A T U R D A Y	7:00 PM 7:30 PM			
	7:30 PM 8:00 PM			
	8:00 PM 8:30 PM	Fish	The Bob Newhart Show	Bionic Woman
	8:30 PM 9:00 PM	Operation Petticoat	We've Got Each Other	Bionic Woman
	9:00 PM 9:30 PM	Starsky & Hutch	The Jeffersons	NBC Saturday Movie
	9:30 PM 10:00 PM	Starsky & Hutch	Tony Randall Show	NBC Saturday Movie
	10:00 PM 10:30 PM	Love Boat	Carol Burnett Show	NBC Saturday Movie
	10:30 PM 11:00 PM	Love Boat	Carol Burnett Show	NBC Saturday Movie

* First quarter hour program   /* Second quarter hour program
† Program airs every other week
Note: Repeated names indicate the program extends into that half-hour time slot.

PRIME TIME SCHEDULE: 1978/79

		AMERICAN ABC	COLUMBIA CBS	NATIONAL NBC
S U N D A Y	7:00 PM 7:30 PM	Hardy Boys Mysteries	60 Minutes	Wonderful World of Disney
	7:30 PM 8:00 PM	Hardy Boys Mysteries	60 Minutes	Wonderful World of Disney
	8:00 PM 8:30 PM	Battlestar Galactica	Mary	Big Event
	8:30 PM 9:00 PM	Battlestar Galactica	Mary	Big Event
	9:00 PM 9:30 PM	ABC Sunday Movie	All in the Family	Big Event
	9:30 PM 10:00 PM	ABC Sunday Movie	Alice	Big Event
	10:00 PM 10:30 PM	ABC Sunday Movie	Kaz	Lifeline
	10:30 PM 11:00 PM	ABC Sunday Movie	Kaz	Lifeline
M O N D A Y	7:00 PM 7:30 PM			
	7:30 PM 8:00 PM			
	8:00 PM 8:30 PM	Welcome Back, Kotter	WKRP in Cincinnati	Little House on the Prairie
	8:30 PM 9:00 PM	Operation Petticoat	People	Little House on the Prairie
	9:00 PM 9:30 PM	Monday Night Football	M*A*S*H	NBC Monday Movie
	9:30 PM 10:00 PM	Monday Night Football	One Day at a Time	NBC Monday Movie
	10:00 PM 10:30 PM	Monday Night Football	Lou Grant	NBC Monday Movie
	10:30 PM 11:00 PM	Monday Night Football	Lou Grant	NBC Monday Movie
T U E S D A Y	7:00 PM 7:30 PM			
	7:30 PM 8:00 PM			
	8:00 PM 8:30 PM	Happy Days	Paper Chase	Grandpa Goes to Washington
	8:30 PM 9:00 PM	Laverne & Shirley	Paper Chase	Grandpa Goes to Washington
	9:00 PM 9:30 PM	Three's Company	CBS Tuesday Movie	Big Event
	9:30 PM 10:00 PM	Taxi	CBS Tuesday Movie	Big Event
	10:00 PM 10:30 PM	Starsky and Hutch	CBS Tuesday Movie	Big Event
	10:30 PM 11:00 PM	Starsky and Hutch	CBS Tuesday Movie	Big Event
W E D N E S D A Y	7:00 PM 7:30 PM			
	7:30 PM 8:00 PM			
	8:00 PM 8:30 PM	Eight is Enough	The Jeffersons	Dick Clark's Live Wednesday
	8:30 PM 9:00 PM	Eight is Enough	In the Beginning	Dick Clark's Live Wednesday
	9:00 PM 9:30 PM	Charlie's Angels	CBS Wednesday Movie	NBC Wednesday Movie
	9:30 PM 10:00 PM	Charlie's Angels	CBS Wednesday Movie	NBC Wednesday Movie
	10:00 PM 10:30 PM	Vega$	CBS Wednesday Movie	NBC Wednesday Movie
	10:30 PM 11:00 PM	Vega$	CBS Wednesday Movie	NBC Wednesday Movie

* First quarter hour program   /* Second quarter hour program
† Program airs every other week
Note: Repeated names indicate the program extends into that half-hour time slot.

PRIME TIME SCHEDULE: 1978/79

		AMERICAN ABC	COLUMBIA CBS	NATIONAL NBC
T **H**	7:00 PM 7:30 PM			
U **R**	7:30 PM 8:00 PM			
S **D**	8:00 PM 8:30 PM	Mork & Mindy	The Waltons	Project U.F.O.
A **Y**	8:30 PM 9:00 PM	What's Happening	The Waltons	Project U.F.O.
	9:00 PM 9:30 PM	Barney Miller	Hawaii Five-O	Quincy, M.E.
	9:30 PM 10:00 PM	Soap	Hawaii Five-O	Quincy, M.E.
	10:00 PM 10:30 PM	Family	Barnaby Jones	W.E.B.
	10:30 PM 11:00 PM	Family	Barnaby Jones	W.E.B.
F **R**	7:00 PM 7:30 PM			
I **D**	7:30 PM 8:00 PM			
A **Y**	8:00 PM 8:30 PM	Donny and Marie	New Adventures of Wonder Woman	Waverly Wonders
	8:30 PM 9:00 PM	Donny and Marie	New Adventures of Wonder Woman	Who's Watching the Kids
	9:00 PM 9:30 PM	ABC Friday Movie	Incredible Hulk	Rockford Files
	9:30 PM 10:00 PM	ABC Friday Movie	Incredible Hulk	Rockford Files
	10:00 PM 10:30 PM	ABC Friday Movie	Flying High	Eddie Capra Mysteries
	10:30 PM 11:00 PM	ABC Friday Movie	Flying High	Eddie Capra Mysteries
S **A**	7:00 PM 7:30 PM			
T **U**	7:30 PM 8:00 PM			
R **D**	8:00 PM 8:30 PM	Carter Country	Rhoda	Chips
A **Y**	8:30 PM 9:00 PM	Apple Pie	Good Times	Chips
	9:00 PM 9:30 PM	Love Boat	American Girls	Specials
	9:30 PM 10:00 PM	Love Boat	American Girls	Specials
	10:00 PM 10:30 PM	Fantasy Island	Dallas	Sword of Justice
	10:30 PM 11:00 PM	Fantasy Island	Dallas	Sword of Justice

* First quarter hour program   /* Second quarter hour program
† Program airs every other week
Note: Repeated names indicate the program extends into that half-hour time slot.

PRIME TIME SCHEDULE: 1979/80

		AMERICAN ABC	COLUMBIA CBS	NATIONAL NBC
S **U** **N** **D** **A** **Y**	7:00 PM 7:30 PM	Out of the Blue	60 Minutes	Disney's Wonderful World
	7:30 PM 8:00 PM	New Kind of Family	60 Minutes	Disney's Wonderful World
	8:00 PM 8:30 PM	Mork & Mindy	Archie Bunker's Place	The Big Event
	8:30 PM 9:00 PM	The Associates	One Day at a Time	The Big Event
	9:00 PM 9:30 PM	Sunday Night Movie	Alice	The Big Event
	9:30 PM 10:00 PM	Sunday Night Movie	The Jeffersons	The Big Event
	10:00 PM 10:30 PM	Sunday Night Movie	Trapper John, M.D.	Prime Time Sunday
	10:30 PM 11:00 PM	Sunday Night Movie	Trapper John, M.D.	Prime Time Sunday
M **O** **N** **D** **A** **Y**	7:00 PM 7:30 PM			
	7:30 PM 8:00 PM			
	8:00 PM 8:30 PM	240-Robert	White Shadow	Little House on the Prairie
	8:30 PM 9:00 PM	240-Robert	White Shadow	Little House on the Prairie
	9:00 PM 9:30 PM	NFL Monday Night Football	M*A*S*H	Monday Night at the Movies
	9:30 PM 10:00 PM	NFL Monday Night Football	W.K.R.P. in Cincinnati	Monday Night at the Movies
	10:00 PM 10:30 PM	NFL Monday Night Football	Lou Grant	Monday Night at the Movies
	10:30 PM 11:00 PM	NFL Monday Night Football	Lou Grant	Monday Night at the Movies
T **U** **E** **S** **D** **A** **Y**	7:00 PM 7:30 PM			
	7:30 PM 8:00 PM			
	8:00 PM 8:30 PM	Happy Days	California Fever	Misadventures of Sherif Lobo
	8:30 PM 9:00 PM	Angie	California Fever	Misadventures of Sherif Lobo
	9:00 PM 9:30 PM	Three's Company	Tuesday Night Movie	Tuesday Night at the Movies
	9:30 PM 10:00 PM	Taxi	Tuesday Night Movie	Tuesday Night at the Movies
	10:00 PM 10:30 PM	Lazurus Syndrome	Tuesday Night Movie	Tuesday Night at the Movies
	10:30 PM 11:00 PM	Lazurus Syndrome	Tuesday Night Movie	Tuesday Night at the Movies
W **E** **D** **N** **E** **S** **D** **A** **Y**	7:00 PM 7:30 PM			
	7:30 PM 8:00 PM			
	8:00 PM 8:30 PM	Eight is Enough	Last Resort	Real People
	8:30 PM 9:00 PM	Eight is Enough	Struck by Lightning	Real People
	9:00 PM 9:30 PM	Charlie's Angels	Wednesday Night Movies	Diff'rent Strokes
	9:30 PM 10:00 PM	Charlie's Angels	Wednesday Night Movies	Hello, Larry
	10:00 PM 10:30 PM	Vega$	Wednesday Night Movies	From Here to Eternity
	10:30 PM 11:00 PM	Vega$	Wednesday Night Movies	From Here to Eternity

* First quarter hour program   /* Second quarter hour program
† Program airs every other week
Note: Repeated names indicate the program extends into that half-hour time slot.

PRIME TIME SCHEDULE: 1979/80

		AMERICAN ABC	COLUMBIA CBS	NATIONAL NBC
T **H** **U** **R** **S** **D** **A** **Y**	7:00 PM 7:30 PM			
	7:30 PM 8:00 PM			
	8:00 PM 8:30 PM	Laverne & Shirley	The Waltons	Buck Rogers in the 25th Century
	8:30 PM 9:00 PM	Benson	The Waltons	Buck Rogers in the 25th Century
	9:00 PM 9:30 PM	Barney Miller	Hawaii Five-O	Quincy, M.E.
	9:30 PM 10:00 PM	Soap	Hawaii Five-O	Quincy, M.E.
	10:00 PM 10:30 PM	20/20	Barnaby Jones	Kate Columbo
	10:30 PM 11:00 PM	20/20	Barnaby Jones	Kate Columbo
F **R** **I** **D** **A** **Y**	7:00 PM 7:30 PM			
	7:30 PM 8:00 PM			
	8:00 PM 8:30 PM	Fantasy Island	Incredible Hulk	Shirley
	8:30 PM 9:00 PM	Fantasy Island	Incredible Hulk	Shirley
	9:00 PM 9:30 PM	Friday Night Movie	Dukes of Hazzard	Rockford Files
	9:30 PM 10:00 PM	Friday Night Movie	Dukes of Hazzard	Rockford Files
	10:00 PM 10:30 PM	Friday Night Movie	Dallas	Eischied
	10:30 PM 11:00 PM	Friday Night Movie	Dallas	Eischied
S **A** **T** **U** **R** **D** **A** **Y**	7:00 PM 7:30 PM			
	7:30 PM 8:00 PM			
	8:00 PM 8:30 PM	The Ropers	Working Stiffs	Chips
	8:30 PM 9:00 PM	Detective School	Bad News Bears	Chips
	9:00 PM 9:30 PM	The Love Boat	Big Shamus, Little Shamus	B.J. & the Bear
	9:30 PM 10:00 PM	The Love Boat	Big Shamus, Little Shamus	B.J. & the Bear
	10:00 PM 10:30 PM	Hart to Hart	Paris	Man Called Sloane
	10:30 PM 11:00 PM	Hart to Hart	Paris	Man Called Sloane

* First quarter hour program   /* Second quarter hour program
† Program airs every other week
Note: Repeated names indicate the program extends into that half-hour time slot.

PRIME TIME SCHEDULE: 1980/81‡

		AMERICAN ABC	COLUMBIA CBS	NATIONAL NBC
S **U** **N** **D** **A** **Y**	7:00 PM 7:30 PM	Those Amazing Animals	60 Minutes	Disney's Wonderful World
	7:30 PM 8:00 PM	Those Amazing Animals	60 Minutes	Disney's Wonderful World
	8:00 PM 8:30 PM	Charlie's Angels	Archie Bunker's Place	Chips
	8:30 PM 9:00 PM	Charlie's Angels	One Day at a Time	Chips
	9:00 PM 9:30 PM	ABC Sunday Movie	Alice	The Big Event
	9:30 PM 10:00 PM	ABC Sunday Movie	The Jeffersons	The Big Event
	10:00 PM 10:30 PM	ABC Sunday Movie	Trapper John, M.D.	The Big Event
	10:30 PM 11:00 PM	ABC Sunday Movie	Trapper John, M.D.	The Big Event
M **O** **N** **D** **A** **Y**	7:00 PM 7:30 PM			
	7:30 PM 8:00 PM			
	8:00 PM 8:30 PM	That's Incredible	Flo	Little House on the Prairie
	8:30 PM 9:00 PM	That's Incredible	Ladies' Man	Little House on the Prairie
	9:00 PM 9:30 PM	Monday Night Football	M*A*S*H	NBC Monday Movie
	9:30 PM 10:00 PM	Monday Night Football	House Calls	NBC Monday Movie
	10:00 PM 10:30 PM	Monday Night Football	Lou Grant	NBC Monday Movie
	10:30 PM 11:00 PM	Monday Night Football	Lou Grant	NBC Monday Movie
T **U** **E** **S** **D** **A** **Y**	7:00 PM 7:30 PM			
	7:30 PM 8:00 PM			
	8:00 PM 8:30 PM	Happy Days	White Shadow	Misadventures of Sherif Lobo
	8:30 PM 9:00 PM	Laverne & Shirley	White Shadow	Misadventures of Sherif Lobo
	9:00 PM 9:30 PM	Three's Company	CBS Tuesday Movie	B.J. & the Bear
	9:30 PM 10:00 PM	Too Close for Comfort	CBS Tuesday Movie	B.J. & the Bear
	10:00 PM 10:30 PM	Hart to Hart	CBS Tuesday Movie	Steve Allen Comedy Hour
	10:30 PM 11:00 PM	Hart to Hart	CBS Tuesday Movie	Steve Allen Comedy Hour
W **E** **D** **N** **E** **S** **D** **A** **Y**	7:00 PM 7:30 PM			
	7:30 PM 8:00 PM			
	8:00 PM 8:30 PM	Eight is Enough	Enos	Real People
	8:30 PM 9:00 PM	Eight is Enough	Enos	Real People
	9:00 PM 9:30 PM	Taxi	CBS Wednesday Movie	Diff'rent Strokes
	9:30 PM 10:00 PM	Soap	CBS Wednesday Movie	Facts of Life
	10:00 PM 10:30 PM	Vega$	CBS Wednesday Movie	Quincy, M.E.
	10:30 PM 11:00 PM	Vega$	CBS Wednesday Movie	Quincy, M.E.

‡ Season delayed due to actors' strike.
* First quarter hour program   /* Second quarter hour program
† Program airs every other week
Note: Repeated names indicate the program extends into that half-hour time slot.

PRIME TIME SCHEDULE: 1980/81 ‡

		AMERICAN ABC	COLUMBIA CBS	NATIONAL NBC
T H U R S D A Y	7:00 PM 7:30 PM			
	7:30 PM 8:00 PM			
	8:00 PM 8:30 PM	Mork & Mindy	The Waltons	Games People Play
	8:30 PM 9:00 PM	Bosom Buddies	The Waltons	Games People Play
	9:00 PM 9:30 PM	Barney Miller	Magnum, P.I.	NBC Thursday Movie
	9:30 PM 10:00 PM	It's a Living	Magnum, P.I.	NBC Thursday Movie
	10:00 PM 10:30 PM	20/20	Knot's Landing	NBC Thursday Movie
	10:30 PM 11:00 PM	20/20	Knot's Landing	NBC Thursday Movie
F R I D A Y	7:00 PM 7:30 PM			
	7:30 PM 8:00 PM			
	8:00 PM 8:30 PM	Benson	Incredible Hulk	Marie
	8:30 PM 9:00 PM	I'm a Big Girl Now	Incredible Hulk	Marie
	9:00 PM 9:30 PM	ABC Friday Movie	Dukes of Hazzard	Speak Up America
	9:30 PM 10:00 PM	ABC Friday Movie	Dukes of Hazzard	Speak Up America
	10:00 PM 10:30 PM	ABC Friday Movie	Dallas	NBC Magazine with David Brinkley
	10:30 PM 11:00 PM	ABC Friday Movie	Dallas	NBC Magazine with David Brinkley
S A T U R D A Y	7:00 PM 7:30 PM			
	7:30 PM 8:00 PM			
	8:00 PM 8:30 PM	Breaking Away	WKRP in Cincinnati	Barbara Mandrell & the Mandrell Sisters
	8:30 PM 9:00 PM	Breaking Away	Tim Conway Show	Barbara Mandrell & the Mandrell Sisters
	9:00 PM 9:30 PM	The Love Boat	Freebie and the Bean	Walking Tall
	9:30 PM 10:00 PM	The Love Boat	Freebie and the Bean	Walking Tall
	10:00 PM 10:30 PM	Fantasy Island	Secrets of Midland Heights	Hill Street Blues
	10:30 PM 11:00 PM	Fantasy Island	Secrets of Midland Heights	Hill Street Blues

‡ Season delayed due to actors' strike.
* First quarter hour program   /* Second quarter hour program
† Program airs every other week
Note: Repeated names indicate the program extends into that half-hour time slot.

PRIME TIME SCHEDULE: 1981/82

		AMERICAN ABC	COLUMBIA CBS	NATIONAL NBC
S U N D A Y	7:00 PM 7:30 PM	Code Red	60 Minutes	Flintstones
	7:30 PM 8:00 PM	Code Red	60 Minutes	Here's Boomer!
	8:00 PM 8:30 PM	Today's FBI	Archie Bunker's Place	Chips
	8:30 PM 9:00 PM	Today's FBI	One Day at a Time	Chips
	9:00 PM 9:30 PM	ABC Sunday Movie	Alice	NBC Sunday Movie
	9:30 PM 10:00 PM	ABC Sunday Movie	The Jeffersons	NBC Sunday Movie
	10:00 PM 10:30 PM	ABC Sunday Movie	Trapper John, M.D.	NBC Sunday Movie
	10:30 PM 11:00 PM	ABC Sunday Movie	Trapper John, M.D.	NBC Sunday Movie
M O N D A Y	7:00 PM 7:30 PM			
	7:30 PM 8:00 PM			
	8:00 PM 8:30 PM	That's Incredible	Private Benjamin	Little House on the Prairie
	8:30 PM 9:00 PM	That's Incredible	Two of Us	Little House on the Prairie
	9:00 PM 9:30 PM	ABC Monday Football	M*A*S*H	NBC Monday Movie
	9:30 PM 10:00 PM	ABC Monday Football	House Calls	NBC Monday Movie
	10:00 PM 10:30 PM	ABC Monday Football	Lou Grant	NBC Monday Movie
	10:30 PM 11:00 PM	ABC Monday Football	Lou Grant	NBC Monday Movie
T U E S D A Y	7:00 PM 7:30 PM			
	7:30 PM 8:00 PM			
	8:00 PM 8:30 PM	Happy Days	Simon & Simon	Father Murphy
	8:30 PM 9:00 PM	Laverne & Shirley	Simon & Simon	Father Murphy
	9:00 PM 9:30 PM	Three's Company	CBS Tuesday Movie	Bret Maverick
	9:30 PM 10:00 PM	Too Close for Comfort	CBS Tuesday Movie	Bret Maverick
	10:00 PM 10:30 PM	Hart to Hart	CBS Tuesday Movie	Flamingo Road
	10:30 PM 11:00 PM	Hart to Hart	CBS Tuesday Movie	Flamingo Road
W E D N E S D A Y	7:00 PM 7:30 PM			
	7:30 PM 8:00 PM			
	8:00 PM 8:30 PM	Greatest American Hero	Mr. Merlin	Real People
	8:30 PM 9:00 PM	Greatest American Hero	WKRP in Cincinnati	Real People
	9:00 PM 9:30 PM	Fall Guy	Nurse	Facts of Life
	9:30 PM 10:00 PM	Fall Guy	Nurse	Love, Sidney
	10:00 PM 10:30 PM	Dynasty	Shannon	Quincy, M.E.
	10:30 PM 11:00 PM	Dynasty	Shannon	Quincy, M.E.

* First quarter hour program   /* Second quarter hour program
† Program airs every other week
Note: Repeated names indicate the program extends into that half-hour time slot.

PRIME TIME SCHEDULE: 1981/82

		AMERICAN ABC	COLUMBIA CBS	NATIONAL NBC
T **H** **U** **R** **S** **D** **A** **Y**	7:00 PM 7:30 PM			
	7:30 PM 8:00 PM			
	8:00 PM 8:30 PM	Mork & Mindy	Magnum, P.I.	Harper Valley
	8:30 PM 9:00 PM	Best of the West	Magnum, P.I.	Lewis & Clark
	9:00 PM 9:30 PM	Bosom Buddies	Knot's Landing	Diff'rent Strokes
	9:30 PM 10:00 PM	Taxi	Knot's Landing	Gimme a Break
	10:00 PM 10:30 PM	20/20	Jessica Novak	Hill Street Blues
	10:30 PM 11:00 PM	20/20	Jessica Novak	Hill Street Blues
F **R** **I** **D** **A** **Y**	7:00 PM 7:30 PM			
	7:30 PM 8:00 PM			
	8:00 PM 8:30 PM	Benson	Incredible Hulk	NBC Magazine
	8:30 PM 9:00 PM	Open All Night	Incredible Hulk	NBC Magazine
	9:00 PM 9:30 PM	Maggie	Dukes of Hazzard	McClain's Law
	9:30 PM 10:00 PM	Making a Living	Dukes of Hazzard	McClain's Law
	10:00 PM 10:30 PM	Strike Force	Dallas	Devlin Connection
	10:30 PM 11:00 PM	Strike Force	Dallas	Devlin Connection
S **A** **T** **U** **R** **D** **A** **Y**	7:00 PM 7:30 PM			
	7:30 PM 8:00 PM			
	8:00 PM 8:30 PM	King's Crossing	Walt Disney	Barbara Mandrell & the Mandrell Sisters
	8:30 PM 9:00 PM	King's Crossing	Walt Disney	Barbara Mandrell & the Mandrell Sisters
	9:00 PM 9:30 PM	The Love Boat	CBS Saturday Movie	Nashville Palace
	9:30 PM 10:00 PM	The Love Boat	CBS Saturday Movie	Nashville Palace
	10:00 PM 10:30 PM	Fantasy Island	CBS Saturday Movie	Fitz & Bones
	10:30 PM 11:00 PM	Fantasy Island	CBS Saturday Movie	Fitz & Bones

* First quarter hour program   /* Second quarter hour program
† Program airs every other week
Note: Repeated names indicate the program extends into that half-hour time slot.

PRIME TIME SCHEDULE: 1982/83

		AMERICAN ABC	COLUMBIA CBS	NATIONAL NBC
S U N D A Y	7:00 PM 7:30 PM	Ripley's Believe It or Not	60 Minutes	Voyagers
	7:30 PM 8:00 PM	Ripley's Believe It or Not	60 Minutes	Voyagers
	8:00 PM 8:30 PM	Matt Houston	Archie Bunker's Place	Chips
	8:30 PM 9:00 PM	Matt Houston	Gloria	Chips
	9:00 PM 9:30 PM	ABC Sunday Movie	The Jeffersons	NBC Sunday Movie
	9:30 PM 10:00 PM	ABC Sunday Movie	One Day at a Time	NBC Sunday Movie
	10:00 PM 10:30 PM	ABC Sunday Movie	Trapper John, M.D.	NBC Sunday Movie
	10:30 PM 11:00 PM	ABC Sunday Movie	Trapper John, M.D.	NBC Sunday Movie
M O N D A Y	7:00 PM 7:30 PM			
	7:30 PM 8:00 PM			
	8:00 PM 8:30 PM	That's Incredible	Square Pegs	Little House: A New Beginning
	8:30 PM 9:00 PM	That's Incredible	Private Benjamin	Little House: A New Beginning
	9:00 PM 9:30 PM	ABC Monday Football	M*A*S*H	NBC Monday Movie
	9:30 PM 10:00 PM	ABC Monday Football	Newhart	NBC Monday Movie
	10:00 PM 10:30 PM	ABC Monday Football	Cagney & Lacey	NBC Monday Movie
	10:30 PM 11:00 PM	ABC Monday Football	Cagney & Lacey	NBC Monday Movie
T U E S D A Y	7:00 PM 7:30 PM			
	7:30 PM 8:00 PM			
	8:00 PM 8:30 PM	Happy Days	Bring 'Em Back Alive	Father Murphy
	8:30 PM 9:00 PM	Laverne & Shirley	Bring 'Em Back Alive	Father Murphy
	9:00 PM 9:30 PM	Three's Company	CBS Tuesday Movie	Gavilan
	9:30 PM 10:00 PM	9 to 5	CBS Tuesday Movie	Gavilan
	10:00 PM 10:30 PM	Hart to Hart	CBS Tuesday Movie	St. Elsewhere
	10:30 PM 11:00 PM	Hart to Hart	CBS Tuesday Movie	St. Elsewhere
W E D N E S D A Y	7:00 PM 7:30 PM			
	7:30 PM 8:00 PM			
	8:00 PM 8:30 PM	Tales of the Gold Monkey	Seven Brides for Seven Brothers	Real People
	8:30 PM 9:00 PM	Tales of the Gold Monkey	Seven Brides for Seven Brothers	Real People
	9:00 PM 9:30 PM	Fall Guy	Alice	Facts of Life
	9:30 PM 10:00 PM	Fall Guy	Mama Malone	Family Ties
	10:00 PM 10:30 PM	Dynasty	Tucker's Witch	Quincy, M.E.
	10:30 PM 11:00 PM	Dynasty	Tucker's Witch	Quincy, M.E.

* First quarter hour program   /* Second quarter hour program
† Program airs every other week
Note: Repeated names indicate the program extends into that half-hour time slot.

PRIME TIME SCHEDULE: 1982/83

		AMERICAN ABC	COLUMBIA CBS	NATIONAL NBC
T **H** **U** **R** **S** **D** **A** **Y**	7:00 PM 7:30 PM			
	7:30 PM 8:00 PM			
	8:00 PM 8:30 PM	Joanie Loves Chachi	Magnum, P.I.	Fame
	8:30 PM 9:00 PM	Star of the Family	Magnum, P.I.	Fame
	9:00 PM 9:30 PM	Too Close for Comfort	Simon & Simon	Cheers
	9:30 PM 10:00 PM	IT Takes Two	Simon & Simon	Taxi
	10:00 PM 10:30 PM	20/20	Knot's Landing	Hill Street Blues
	10:30 PM 11:00 PM	20/20	Knot's Landing	Hill Street Blues
F **R** **I** **D** **A** **Y**	7:00 PM 7:30 PM			
	7:30 PM 8:00 PM			
	8:00 PM 8:30 PM	Benson	Dukes of Hazzard	Powers of Matthew Star
	8:30 PM 9:00 PM	New Odd Couple	Dukes of Hazzard	Powers of Matthew Star
	9:00 PM 9:30 PM	Greatest American Hero	Dallas	Knight Rider
	9:30 PM 10:00 PM	Greatest American Hero	Dallas	Knight Rider
	10:00 PM 10:30 PM	The Quest	Falcon Crest	Remington Steele
	10:30 PM 11:00 PM	The Quest	Falcon Crest	Remington Steele
S **A** **T** **U** **R** **D** **A** **Y**	7:00 PM 7:30 PM			
	7:30 PM 8:00 PM			
	8:00 PM 8:30 PM	T.J. Hooker	Walt Disney	Diff'rent Strokes
	8:30 PM 9:00 PM	T.J. Hooker	Walt Disney	Silver Spoons
	9:00 PM 9:30 PM	The Love Boat	CBS Saturday Movie	Gimme a Break
	9:30 PM 10:00 PM	The Love Boat	CBS Saturday Movie	Love, Sidney
	10:00 PM 10:30 PM	Fantasy Island	CBS Saturday Movie	Devlin Connection
	10:30 PM 11:00 PM	Fantasy Island	CBS Saturday Movie	Devlin Connection

* First quarter hour program /* Second quarter hour program
† Program airs every other week
Note: Repeated names indicate the program extends into that half-hour time slot.

PRIME TIME SCHEDULE: 1983/84

		AMERICAN ABC	COLUMBIA CBS	NATIONAL NBC
S	7:00 PM 7:30 PM	Ripley's Believe It or Not	60 Minutes	First Camera
U **N**	7:30 PM 8:00 PM	Ripley's Believe It or Not	60 Minutes	First Camera
D	8:00 PM 8:30 PM	Hardcastle & McCormick	Alice	Knight Rider
A **Y**	8:30 PM 9:00 PM	Hardcastle & McCormick	One Day at a Time	Knight Rider
	9:00 PM 9:30 PM	ABC Sunday Movie	The Jeffersons	NBC Sunday Movie
	9:30 PM 10:00 PM	ABC Sunday Movie	Goodnight, Beantown	NBC Sunday Movie
	10:00 PM 10:30 PM	ABC Sunday Movie	Trapper John, M.D.	NBC Sunday Movie
	10:30 PM 11:00 PM	ABC Sunday Movie	Trapper John, M.D.	NBC Sunday Movie
M	7:00 PM 7:30 PM			
O **N**	7:30 PM 8:00 PM			
D	8:00 PM 8:30 PM	That's Incredible	Scarecrow & Mrs. King	Boone
A **Y**	8:30 PM 9:00 PM	That's Incredible	Scarecrow & Mrs. King	Boone
	9:00 PM 9:30 PM	ABC Monday Football	After M*A*S*H	NBC Monday Movie
	9:30 PM 10:00 PM	ABC Monday Football	Newhart	NBC Monday Movie
	10:00 PM 10:30 PM	ABC Monday Football	Emerald Point, N.A.S.	NBC Monday Movie
	10:30 PM 11:00 PM	ABC Monday Football	Emerald Point, N.A.S.	NBC Monday Movie
T	7:00 PM 7:30 PM			
U **E** **S**	7:30 PM 8:00 PM			
D	8:00 PM 8:30 PM	Just Our Luck	Mississippi	The A-Team
A **Y**	8:30 PM 9:00 PM	Happy Days	Mississippi	The A-Team
	9:00 PM 9:30 PM	Three's Company	CBS Tuesday Movie	Remington Steele
	9:30 PM 10:00 PM	Oh Madeline	CBS Tuesday Movie	Remington Steele
	10:00 PM 10:30 PM	Hart to Hart	CBS Tuesday Movie	Bay City Blues
	10:30 PM 11:00 PM	Hart to Hart	CBS Tuesday Movie	Bay City Blues
W	7:00 PM 7:30 PM			
E **D** **N**	7:30 PM 8:00 PM			
E **S**	8:00 PM 8:30 PM	Fall Guy	Whiz Kids	Real People
D **A**	8:30 PM 9:00 PM	Fall Guy	Whiz Kids	Real People
Y	9:00 PM 9:30 PM	Dynasty	CBS Wednesday Movie	Facts of Life
	9:30 PM 10:00 PM	Dynasty	CBS Wednesday Movie	Family Ties
	10:00 PM 10:30 PM	Hotel	CBS Wednesday Movie	St. Elsewhere
	10:30 PM 11:00 PM	Hotel	CBS Wednesday Movie	St. Elsewhere

* First quarter hour program   /* Second quarter hour program
† Program airs every other week
Note: Repeated names indicate the program extends into that half-hour time slot.

PRIME TIME SCHEDULE: 1983/84

		AMERICAN ABC	COLUMBIA CBS	NATIONAL NBC
T H U R S D A Y	7:00 PM 7:30 PM			
	7:30 PM 8:00 PM			
	8:00 PM 8:30 PM	Trauma Center	Magnum, P.I.	Gimme a Break
	8:30 PM 9:00 PM	Trauma Center	Magnum, P.I.	Mama's Family
	9:00 PM 9:30 PM	9 to 5	Simon & Simon	We Got It Made
	9:30 PM 10:00 PM	It's Not Easy	Simon & Simon	Cheers
	10:00 PM 10:30 PM	20/20	Knot's Landing	Hill Street Blues
	10:30 PM 11:00 PM	20/20	Knot's Landing	Hill Street Blues
F R I D A Y	7:00 PM 7:30 PM			
	7:30 PM 8:00 PM			
	8:00 PM 8:30 PM	Benson	Dukes of Hazzard	Mr. Smith
	8:30 PM 9:00 PM	Webster	Dukes of Hazzard	Jennifer Slept Here
	9:00 PM 9:30 PM	Lottery	Dallas	Manimal
	9:30 PM 10:00 PM	Lottery	Dallas	Manimal
	10:00 PM 10:30 PM	Matt Houston	Falcon Crest	For Love and Honor
	10:30 PM 11:00 PM	Matt Houston	Falcon Crest	For Love and Honor
S A T U R D A Y	7:00 PM 7:30 PM			
	7:30 PM 8:00 PM			
	8:00 PM 8:30 PM	T.J. Hooker	Cutter to Houston	Diff'rent Strokes
	8:30 PM 9:00 PM	T.J. Hooker	Cutter to Houston	Silver Spoon
	9:00 PM 9:30 PM	The Love Boat	CBS Saturday Movie	Rousters
	9:30 PM 10:00 PM	The Love Boat	CBS Saturday Movie	Rousters
	10:00 PM 10:30 PM	Fantasy Island	CBS Saturday Movie	Yellow Rose
	10:30 PM 11:00 PM	Fantasy Island	CBS Saturday Movie	Yellow Rose

* First quarter hour program   /* Second quarter hour program
† Program airs every other week
Note: Repeated names indicate the program extends into that half-hour time slot.

PRIME TIME SCHEDULE: 1984/85

		AMERICAN ABC	COLUMBIA CBS	NATIONAL NBC
S **U**	7:00 PM 7:30 PM	Ripley's Believe It or Not	60 Minutes	Silver Spoons
N **D**	7:30 PM 8:00 PM	Ripley's Believe It or Not	60 Minutes	Punky Brewster
A **Y**	8:00 PM 8:30 PM	ABC Sunday Night Movie	Murder, She Wrote	Knight Rider
	8:30 PM 9:00 PM	ABC Sunday Night Movie	Murder, She Wrote	Knight Rider
	9:00 PM 9:30 PM	ABC Sunday Night Movie	Crazy Like A Fox	NBC Sunday Night at the Movies
	9:30 PM 10:00 PM	ABC Sunday Night Movie	Crazy Like A Fox	NBC Sunday Night at the Movies
	10:00 PM 10:30 PM	ABC Sunday Night Movie	Trapper John, M.D.	NBC Sunday Night at the Movies
	10:30 PM 11:00 PM	ABC Sunday Night Movie	Trapper John, M.D.	NBC Sunday Night at the Movies
M **O**	7:00 PM 7:30 PM			
N **D**	7:30 PM 8:00 PM			
A **Y**	8:00 PM 8:30 PM	Hardcastle & McCormick	Scarecrow & Mrs. King	TV's Bloopers & Practical Jokes
	8:30 PM 9:00 PM	Hardcastle & McCormick	Scarecrow & Mrs. King	TV's Bloopers & Practical Jokes
	9:00 PM 9:30 PM	ABC Monday Night Movie	Kate & Allie	NBC Monday Night at the Movies
	9:30 PM 10:00 PM	ABC Monday Night Movie	Newhart	NBC Monday Night at the Movies
	10:00 PM 10:30 PM	ABC Monday Night Movie	Cagney & Lacey	NBC Monday Night at the Movies
	10:30 PM 11:00 PM	ABC Monday Night Movie	Cagney & Lacey	NBC Monday Night at the Movies
T **U**	7:00 PM 7:30 PM			
E **S**	7:30 PM 8:00 PM			
D **A**	8:00 PM 8:30 PM	Three's A Crowd	Jeffersons	The A-Team
Y	8:30 PM 9:00 PM	Who's The Boss	Alice	The A-Team
	9:00 PM 9:30 PM	MacGruder & Loud	CBS Tuesday Night Movie	Riptide
	9:30 PM 10:00 PM	MacGruder & Loud	CBS Tuesday Night Movie	Riptide
	10:00 PM 10:30 PM	Call to Glory	CBS Tuesday Night Movie	Remington Steele
	10:30 PM 11:00 PM	Call to Glory	CBS Tuesday Night Movie	Remington Steele
W **E**	7:00 PM 7:30 PM			
D **N**	7:30 PM 8:00 PM			
E **S**	8:00 PM 8:30 PM	The Fall Guy	Charles In Charge	Highway to Heaven
D **A**	8:30 PM 9:00 PM	The Fall Guy	E/R	Highway to Heaven
Y	9:00 PM 9:30 PM	Dynasty	CBS Wednesday Night Movie	Facts of Life
	9:30 PM 10:00 PM	Dynasty	CBS Wednesday Night Movie	Sara
	10:00 PM 10:30 PM	Arthur Hailey's "Hotel"	CBS Wednesday Night Movie	St. Elsewhere
	10:30 PM 11:00 PM	Arthur Hailey's "Hotel"	CBS Wednesday Night Movie	St. Elsewhere

* First quarter hour program   /* Second quarter hour program
† Program airs every other week
Note: Repeated names indicate the program extends into that half-hour time slot.

PRIME TIME SCHEDULE: 1984/85

		AMERICAN ABC	COLUMBIA CBS	NATIONAL NBC
T H U R S D A Y	7:00 PM 7:30 PM			
	7:30 PM 8:00 PM			
	8:00 PM 8:30 PM	ABC Thursday Night Movie	Magnum, P.I.	The Bill Cosby Show
	8:30 PM 9:00 PM	ABC Thursday Night Movie	Magnum, P.I.	Family Ties
	9:00 PM 9:30 PM	ABC Thursday Night Movie	Simon & Simon	Cheers
	9:30 PM 10:00 PM	ABC Thursday Night Movie	Simon & Simon	Night Court
	10:00 PM 10:30 PM	20/20	Knot's Landing	Hill Street Blues
	10:30 PM 11:00 PM	20/20	Knot's Landing	Hill Street Blues
F R I D A Y	7:00 PM 7:30 PM			
	7:30 PM 8:00 PM			
	8:00 PM 8:30 PM	Benson	Dukes of Hazzard	Code Name: Foxfire
	8:30 PM 9:00 PM	Webster	Dukes of Hazzard	Code Name: Foxfire
	9:00 PM 9:30 PM	Street Hawk	Dallas	V
	9:30 PM 10:00 PM	Street Hawk	Dallas	V
	10:00 PM 10:30 PM	Matt Houston	Falcon Crest	Miami Vice
	10:30 PM 11:00 PM	Matt Houston	Falcon Crest	Miami Vice
S A T U R D A Y	7:00 PM 7:30 PM			
	7:30 PM 8:00 PM			
	8:00 PM 8:30 PM	T.J. Hooker	Otherworld	Diff'rent Strokes
	8:30 PM 9:00 PM	T.J. Hooker	Otherworld	Double Trouble
	9:00 PM 9:30 PM	The Love Boat	Airwolf	Gimme A Break
	9:30 PM 10:00 PM	The Love Boat	Airwolf	It's Your Move
	10:00 PM 10:30 PM	Finder of Lost Loves	Cover-Up	Berrenger's
	10:30 PM 11:00 PM	Finder of Lost Loves	Cover-Up	Berrenger's

* First quarter hour program   /* Second quarter hour program
† Program airs every other week
Note: Repeated names indicate the program extends into that half-hour time slot.

2/THE LONGEST RUNNING TV SERIES

HERE ARE TV's longest running series—those series that were aired for seven or more seasons. Again, a few explanatory notes are in order:

(1) Only prime time (6 p.m. to 11 p.m.) programs are included here. Had daytime shows also been considered, *Meet the Press* would head the list, but only its 18 nighttime seasons are shown here. And had late night programs been included, *The Tonight Show* would appear with 30 seasons.

(2) Similarly, a show's syndicated or local seasons are not counted here. Only national network programs are considered. For example, *The Lawrence Welk Show* was aired for 17 seasons between 1955 and 1971 and thereafter was syndicated for many years. But only the 17 prime time network seasons show up here.

(3) Newscasts are excluded from this list as well.

(4) A series is counted as having aired in a season even if it was broadcast during only one month of that season.

(5) A series' prime time reruns are shown here. For example, *Father Knows Best* ran for six years with original episodes. CBS then scheduled reruns in prime time for another two seasons, and then ABC reran them for still another prime time season after that. So *Father Knows Best* shows up with nine, not six, seasons.

(6) Changes in a show's format can also be tricky when counting a program's longevity. Should *Mayberry R.F.D.*, for example, be considered a continuation of *The Andy Griffith Show* or a whole new series? (A new series, by my thinking.) And is *Archie Bunker's Place* a new show or a part of *All in the Family*? (By my thinking, a part of *All in the Family*.) If you consider all of Lucille Ball's many TV shows as merely variations of a single series (as many TV fans do in fact consider them), then Lucy would chalk up some 23 prime time seasons. But I divide Lucy's shows into two groups: *I Love Lucy* (1951–67) and *The Lucy Show* (1962–74). In short, the "accuracy" of some of these statistics is debatable.

(7) The 1983/84 season is the last one counted here.

(8) Alternate titles and other qualifying information are included in parentheses.

Variety programs show up on this list more often than any other series format: 24 musical or comedy variety shows are included here. Situation comedies come in second place, with 22 entries, followed by dramatic anthologies (16), quiz and game shows (14), police and detective series (11), westerns (9), news and documentary programs (6), sports (5) and children's shows (4). The category of "variety" shows is really a mixed one, encompassing musical variety (*The Bell Telephone Hour*), comedy variety (*The Steve Allen Show*) and general variety (*The Ed Sullivan Show*). Hence, the most successful series format that can be more strictly defined is really the sitcom: of the 123 shows that have been aired for (7) or more seasons, 22 (or nearly 18 percent) have been situation comedies. Which sitcoms have enjoyed the longest runs? *I Love Lucy* (15 seasons), *The Adventures of Ozzie & Harriet* (14), *The Danny Thomas Show* (13), *All in the Family* (also 13), *The Lucy Show* (12) and *My Three Sons* (also 12).

It's been said that every television program has a single purpose: to put another off the air. Here, then, are TV's greatest "killers."

29 SEASONS

Disney's Wonderful World (*Disneyland, Walt Disney Presents, Walt Disney's Wonderful World of Color, The Wonderful World of Disney*)

24 SEASONS

The Ed Sullivan Show (*The Toast of the Town*)

21 SEASONS

*ABC Sunday Night Movie (*Hollywood Special*)

20 SEASONS

Gunsmoke
The Red Skelton Show (*The Red Skelton Hour*)

18 SEASONS

Meet the Press (Does not include daytime seasons)
What's My Line? (Does not include syndicated seasons)

17 SEASONS

I've Got a Secret (Does not include syndicated seasons)
Lassie
The Lawrence Welk Show (*Lawrence Welk's Dodge Dancing Party*, Does not include syndicated seasons)
Saturday Night at the Movies

*Still on the air, prime time.

16 SEASONS

The Jack Benny Show (Includes August 1977 prime time reruns)
**NBC Monday Night Movie*
**60 Minutes* (Includes seasons as an occasional series)

15 SEASONS

I Love Lucy (*Sunday Lucy Show, Lucy in Connecticut, Top 10 Lucy Shows, Lucy-Desi Comedy Hour*)
The Jackie Gleason Show (*The Honeymooners, The Jackie Gleason Show: The American Scene Magazine*)
The Perry Como Show (*The Chesterfield Supper Club*)

14 SEASONS

ABC Monday NFL Football
The Adventures of Ozzie & Harriet (*The Adventures of the Nelson Family*)
Armstrong Circle Theatre (*Circle Theatre*)
Bonanza
Gillette Cavalcade of Sports (*The Cavalcade of Sports*)

13 SEASONS

All in the Family (*Archie Bunker's Place*)
The Danny Thomas Show (*Make Room for Daddy, Make Room for Granddaddy*)
The Dinah Shore Show (*The Dinah Shore Chevy Show. Does not include daytime syndicated seasons*)
Monday Night Baseball (Summer series only)
Twentieth Century (*Twenty-first Century*)

12 SEASONS

Dragnet
Hawaii Five-O
Kraft Television Theatre (Does not include seasons as *Kraft Mystery Theatre* or *Kraft Suspense Theatre*)
The Lucy Show (*Here's Lucy*)
My Three Sons
The Original Amateur Hour
Pabst Blue Ribbon Bouts (*International Boxing Club*)

11 SEASONS

Arthur Godfrey's Talent Scouts
The Arthur Murray Party (*The Arthur Murray Show*)
Candid Camera (*Candid Microphone*)
The Carol Burnett Show
CBS Reports (*CBS News Hour, CBS News Special*)
Fireside Theatre (*Jane Wyman's Fireside Theatre, The Jane Wyman Show*)
General Electric Theater (*General Electric True*)
*Happy Days
M*A*S*H

The Milton Berle Show (*Texaco Star Theatre, The Buick-Berle Show, Milton Berle Starring in the Kraft Music Hall*)
Pantomime Quiz (*Stump the Stars*)
To Tell the Truth
The Voice of Firestone
You Bet Your Life (*The Groucho Show*)
Your Hit Parade (Includes August 1974 season)

10 SEASONS

Alfred Hitchcock Presents (*The Alfred Hitchcock Hour*)
Arthur Godfrey and His Friends (*The Arthur Godfrey Show*)
The F.B.I. (*The New F.B.I.*)
The Jeffersons
Perry Mason (*The New Adventures of Perry Mason*)
The Steve Allen Show (*The Steve Allen Plymouth Show, The Steve Allen Comedy Hour*)
Studio One
The U.S. Steel Hour

9 SEASONS†

The Andy Williams Show
Beat the Clock
The Beverly Hillbillies
Break the Bank
The Dean Martin Show
Father Knows Best (Includes prime time rerun seasons)
The Garry Moore Show
The George Burns & Gracie Allen Show (*The George Burns Show*)
Goodyear TV Playhouse (*Goodyear Theater*)
Masquerade Party
Little House on the Prairie (*Little House on the Prairie: A New Beginning*)
One Day at a Time
This is Your Life
The Virginian (*The Men from Shiloh*)
The Waltons
You Asked for It (*The Art Baker Show*)

8 SEASONS

Alice
The Alcoa Hour (*Alcoa Theatre, Alcoa Presents, Alcoa Premiere*)
The Andy Griffith Show (Does not include *Mayberry, R.F.D.*)
Barnaby Jones
Barney Miller
The Bell Telephone Hour
Bewitched (Does not includes sequel, *Tabitha*)

The Big Story
Cheyenne
The Donna Reed Show
Ironside
The Lone Ranger
The Loretta Young Show (Letter to Loretta)
Lux Video Theatre (Lux Playhouse)
Mama
Mannix
Mark Saber (Mystery Theater, Inspector Mark Saber—Homicide Squad, The Vise, Saber of London)
Midwestern Hayride
Person to Person
Rawhide
Robert Montgomery Presents
Schlitz Playhouse of Stars (Schlitz Playhouse)
*Three's Company
Wagon Train

7 SEASONS

Adam 12
Captain Video and His Video Rangers
*Dallas
The Eddie Fisher Show (Coke Time with Eddie Fisher)
*Fantasy Island
The Gene Autry Show
Hollywood Palace
Kukla, Fran & Ollie
Life Begins at Eighty
The Life of Riley
*The Love Boat
Marcus Welby, M.D.
The Mary Tyler Moore Show
McCloud
Medical Center
Mission: Impossible
Name That Tune
People Are Funny
Petticoat Junction
Philco TV Playhouse
The Price Is Right (Does not include daytime seasons)
The Quiz Kids
Red Barber's Corner (Red Barber's Clubhouse, The Peak of the Sport News)
Suspense
This Is Show Business
Who Said That?

*Still on the air, prime time.

3/THE COST OF TV PROGRAMS

TO CELEBRATE ITS 50th Anniversary in 1953, Ford presented a TV special. It was an elaborate production—"a panoramic capsule history of the past 50 years, recreating in song, dance, comedy and drama famous events between 1903 and 1953." Mary Martin and Ethel Merman sang, Edward R. Murrow narrated, Oscar Hammerstein II acted, Jerome Robbins choreographed, Irene Sharaff designed the costumes, and Greta Garbo, Rudolph Valentino and Charlie Chaplin were featured in film clips. Sports highlights included a Jack Dempsey fight, Babe Ruth's 60th homer and Lou Gehrig's 1939 Yankee Stadium farewell. Leaders in science, industry and government joined the cast which also included Eddie Fisher, Frank Sinatra and Rudy Vallee. According to a *TV Guide* "Close-UP," the show required three studios, eight cameras, 25 stagehands, 45 engineers, a cast of more than 50, and a 24-piece orchestra, quite a complicated production during TV's early keep-it-simple years.

The cost for this two-hour extravaganza? Half a million dollars—an unheard of sum of money in those days when budgets ran from $2,500 for every 30-minute *Arthur Godfrey's Talent Scouts* to $30,000 for each one-hour *Studio One*.

It should come as no surprise that in today's inflated market, money doesn't go as far. During the 1983/84 season, a single one-hour episode of a network series cost more than $650,000, and that's just an average price. ABC shells out $850,000 for each segment of *Dynasty*, as does CBS for each episode of *Dallas*. Situation comedies now go for approximately $350,000 per half-hour segment. But if the series features a star in command of a hefty salary, the show's price rises accordingly. During the 1978/79 season, for example, CBS paid $195,000 for each installment of *Alice*, but $290,000 for each episode of *All in the Family* with Carroll O'Connor.

The most expensive two-hour shows on the 1983/84 agenda are the various film series, with an average price of $2.1 million for each movie. ABC's *NFL Monday Night Football*, at $2 million per show, comes a close second. Of course, mini-series are in another price category entirely. ABC reportedly paid some $40 million for its 18-hour *The Winds of War* series, aired during the 1982/83 season. That's almost $2.25 million per hour—among the costliest per-hour productions in ABC's history.

The real bargain in night-time TV is the news and documentary programs. The hour-long *60 Minutes* and *20/20*

each cost the webs approximately $450,000 per episode during the 1983/84 season.

Of course, these figures apply only to prime time. Programs aired during the mornings and afternoons are more of a "bargain." During the late 1970s, an entire week of a soap opera—five segments—cost a network approximately $250,000, or the price of one prime time sitcom at the time. A week of daytime game shows went for even less—about $200,000 for five episodes. And the two-hour *Today* show during the late 1970s cost $350,000 per week, or only $35,000 per hour.

Where does this money go? According to industry guidelines, here's a typical budget for a $200,000+ half-hour program during the late 1970s.

ABOVE THE LINE	
Story	$15,000
Executive Producer	16,000
Producer	14,000
Director	6,000
Performers	54,000
Union Benefits	7,000
	$112,000

BELOW THE LINE	
Production Staff	$4,000
Camera	5,000
Set Design	3,000
Set Construction	4,000
Set Operation	4,000
Electrical	5,000
Special Effects	1,000
Set Dressing	3,000
Props	2,000
Wardrobe	2,000
Makeup	1,000
Production Sound	2,000
Transportation	2,000
Dailies	8,000
Editing	8,000
Music	3,000
Post Prod. Sound	4,000
Stock Film	1,000
Titles	1,000
Opticals	2,000
Lab Processing	6,000
Union Benefits	12,000
	$83,000

OTHER COSTS (PRO RATA)	
Testing	$2,000
Administrative	3,000

Promotion	4,000
Facilities	30,000
	$39,000
TOTAL (ABOVE, BELOW, & OTHER):	**$234,000**

The following charts list typical prices per episode for various series from the past decades. If you read across these charts, you can see how the price of a particular series has changed during the past decade. Read down these charts and you'll learn how the series compare in price to one another within a particular year.

HALF-HOUR SERIES: ESTIMATED COST PER EPISODE

	1970/ 71 (000)	1971/ 72 (000)	1972/ 73 (000)	1973/ 74 (000)	1974/ 75 (000)	1975/ 76 (000)	1976/ 77 (000)	1977/ 78 (000)	1978/ 79 (000)	1979/ 80 (000)	1980/ 81 (000)	1981/ 82 (000)	1982/ 83 (000)	1983/ 84 (000)
Adam 12	$ 90													
Alice							110	165	195	220	300	325		375
All in the Family		95	105	115	118	130	225	270	290	250	325	350		
Barney Miller							125	175	185	215	230	300	325	
Benson										210	275	300		375
Beverly Hillbillies	100													
Bewitched	115	115												
Bob Newhart Show			100	105	106	120	200	200						
Chico and the Man						90	105	180	170					
Diff'rent Strokes										220	275	325		375
Happy Days						105	130	180	200	265	265	300	325	375
Here's Lucy	130	130	125	125										
Hogan's Heroes	100													
The Jeffersons							110	170	180	200	220	300	300	375
Laverne & Shirley								160	190	250	250	280	325	
Let's Make a Deal	35													
The Mary Tyler Moore Show	110	110	100	110	110	130	225							
M*A*S*H			95	105	105	130	190	210	235	240	325	350		
Maude			95	105	105	120	190	190						
Mork & Mindy									190	250	300	325		
My Three Sons	120	125												
Newlywed Game	35													
The Odd Couple	90	95	103	110	106									
One Day At a Time								160	175	195	215	300	325	375
Rhoda						105	120	180	190	200				
Sanford & Son			90	100	105	130	220							
Soap								165	205	225	300			
Taxi											300	325		
Three's Company									160	215	300	325		375
Welcome Back, Kotter						95	150	165	250					

ONE-HOUR SERIES: ESTIMATED COST PER EPISODE

	1970/71 (000)	1971/72 (000)	1972/73 (000)	1973/74 (000)	1974/75 (000)	1975/76 (000)	1976/77 (000)	1977/78 (000)	1978/79 (000)	1979/80 (000)	1980/81 (000)	1981/82 (000)	1982/83 (000)	1983/84 (000)
Baretta						260	350	390						
Battlestar Galactica									750					
Beacon Hill						240								
Bonanza		220	225											
Buck Rogers in 25th Century										750				
Carol Burnett Show	210	210	230	230	245	260	280	310						
Charlie's Angels							310	390	440	450	650			
Dallas									380	420	650	800		850
Dean Martin Comedy Hour	225	230	230	230										
Disney's Wonderful World	225	225	200	215	245	275	385	800	440	450	600	600		
Donnie & Marie							230	300	330					
Dukes of Hazzard										420	620	700		700
Dynasty												600		850
Ed Sullivan Show	220													
Eight is Enough								350	420	430	620			
Fantasy Island									425	450	600	600		675
The F.B.I.	210	225	200											
Flip Wilson Show	180	205	205	210										
Gunsmoke	215	215	215	230	230									
Hart to Hart										420	600	600		725
Hawaii Five-O	210	210	210	215		270	385	390	430	450				
Hill Street Blues											550	600		925
Incredible Hulk									395	550	650	650		
Ironside	200	210	215	220	260									
Kojak				200	200	270	360	280						
Little House on the Prairie					225	260	320	270	425	435	625	650		
Lou Grant								370	415	425	600	625		
Love, American Style		190	200	200										
Love Boat								380	425	450	650	650		725
Magnum, P.I.											565	600		700
Mannix	200													
Medical Center	195	200	200	210	205	265								
Marcus Welby, M.D.	190	210	200	210	205	285								
Mission: Impossible	210	220	225											
Mod Squad	210	215	225											
Police Woman					210	250	360	380						
Rockford Files					235	265	365	380	420					
Rowan & Martin's Laugh In		210	200											
Six Million Dollar Man					225	280	370	410						
Sixty Minutes	130						200	270	175	190	300	350		450
Sonny & Cher Show			195	200		250	240							
Starsky & Hutch						245	340	395	430					
Streets of San Francisco			210	210	225	280	350							
Trapper John, M.D.										410	575	600		650
20/20										190	300	350		450
The Waltons			195	200	205	240	320	375	415	425	625			

II. THE VIEWERS

1/THE NUMBER OF TV HOUSEHOLDS IN AMERICA

IN DECEMBER 1945 George Gallup was asking Americans:

"Do you know what television is?"

"Have you ever seen a television set in operation?"

Today these questions sound preposterous, so popular—and powerful—has television become. TV is so firmly entrenched in American life that it is now the central medium of entertainment and information. By 1979, 98 percent of all American households were equipped with TV sets, and that's a higher percentage than own refrigerators or indoor toilets. In fact, by 1982 the United States had become the first nation in the world with enough TV sets to distribute two to each household: according to *Television Digest*, there were 170.8 million sets for 82.3 million households, or 2.075 TV sets per household, far more than any other nation. (The Soviet Union trailed a distant second with 70 to 80 million sets, followed by Japan with 29.8 million, England with 26 million, West Germany with 24.5 million and France with 15.6 million.) It has been estimated that the United States now has one-third of the world's total supply of TV sets.

Television now commands more of our time than any other activity except sleeping or working; the average household watches TV seven hours a day now. According to recent surveys, more Americans look to TV as their primary news source than to any other medium—newspapers, magazines or radio.* And in a country that's glued to the tube, is it any surprise than the largest magazine in circulation is *TV Guide*?

As social critic Louis Kronenberger has said, television is not just a great force in modern life—TV virtually is modern life. "Nothing approaches it, either in the abundance, variety and immediacy of its offerings, or the vastness, heterogeneity and attendance record of its audiences. . . TV is a truly stupendous addition to American life."

TV's conquest of America was unprecedently swift. In 1950 a mere nine percent of American homes owned TV sets. Just four years later the proportion had leaped to 54 percent. By 1960 there were more than 45 million TV households in this country. Radio took 32 years to reach that number of homes and the telephone 87 years.

Nothing could withstand TV's onslaught in those early years. Movies, theaters and nightclubs all fell under the giant advance of the tiny screen. TV historian Erik Barnouw recounts how in the early 1950s cities saw a drop in taxicab receipts. "Jukebox receipts were down. Public libraries, including the New York Public Library, reported a drop in book circulation, and many book stores reported sales down. Radio listening was off in television cities; the Bob Hope rating dropped from 23.8 in 1949 to 12.7 in 1951 and continued downward."

And of course movie theaters closed in waves: 70 closings in eastern Pennsylvania, 134 in southern California, 61 in Massachusetts, 64 in the Chicago area and 55 in New York City. According to Barnouw, in 1951 alone almost all television cities reported a 20 to 40 percent drop in movie attendance, whereas in non-TV cities movie attendance remained high or even grew.

Sales of TV sets boomed; there were almost twice as many sets sold in 1950 alone as had been purchased during the entire previous decade, as the following statistics show:

Year	Total	Cumulative Total
1941-49	—	3,602,872
1950	6,132,000	9,734,872
1951	5,905,000	15,639,872
1952	6,144,989	21,784,861
1953	6,370,571	28,155,432
1954	7,317,034	35,472,466
1955	7,421,084	42,893,550
1956	6,804,783	49,698,333
1957	6,560,220	56,258,553
1958	5,140,000	61,396,000
1959	5,749,000	67,145,000

And by the 1970s and early 1980s, when families were replacing older models and adding TV sets to almost every room in the house, sales reached astronomical heights:

Year	Total
1970	12,220,000
1971	14,921,000
1972	17,084,000
1973	17,368,000
1974	15,279,000
1975	10,637,000

*Since 1959, the Roper Organization has conducted national opinion polls to determine TV's influence. According to the 1980 survey, 64 percent of respondents selected TV as their principal news source, followed by newspapers (44 percent), radio (18 percent) and magazines (5 percent). It was in 1963 that TV surpassed newspapers for the first time. As *Variety* (April 15, 1981) noted, 1963 was also the year of the first half-hour evening network news.

1976	14,131,000
1977	15,431,000
1978	17,406,000
1979	16,619,000
1980	18,532,000
1981	18,479,000

TV, in short, has enjoyed unparalleled success in this country. "In only two decades of massive national existence," writes communications expert George Gerbner, "television has transformed the political life of the nation, has changed the daily habits of our people, has molded the style of the generation, made overnight global phenomena out of local happenings, and redirected the flow of information and values from traditional channels into centralized networks reaching into every home."

Here are the number of TV households in the United States from 1950 to 1985:

Number of TV Households in America

Year	Number of TV Households	% of American Homes with TV
1950	3,880,000	9.0
1951	10,320,000	23.5
1952	15,300,000	34.2
1953	20,400,000	44.7
1954	26,000,000	55.7
1955	30,700,000	64.5
1956	34,900,000	71.8
1957	38,900,000	78.6
1958	41,920,000	83.2
1959	43,950,000	85.9
1960	45,750,000	87.1
1961	47,200,000	88.8
1962	48,855,000	90.0
1963	50,300,000	91.3
1964	51,600,000	92.3
1965	52,700,000	92.6
1966	53,850,000	93.0
1967	55,130,000	93.6
1968	56,670,000	94.6
1969	58,250,000	95.0
1970	59,550,000	95.2
1971	60,900,000	95.5
1972	62,350,000	95.8
1973	65,600,000	96.0
1974	66,800,000	97.0
1975	68,500,000	97.0
1976	69,600,000	97.0
1977	71,200,000	97.0
1978	72,900,000	98.0
1979	74,500,000	98.0
1980	76,300,000	98.0
1981	77,800,000	98.0
1982	81,500,000	98.0
1983	83,300,000	98.0
1984	83,800,000	98.0
1985	84,900,000	98.0

Source: A.C. Nielsen Co.

2/Viewers with Color TV

Color TV was here before most of us even knew about black-and-white television. As early as 1929 Bell Telephone laboratories had demonstrated a rudimentary color TV broadcast. By the end of World War II, CBS had actually perfected a color system capable of transmitting brilliant, realistic colors. Unfortunately, the CBS system was incompatible with the black-and-white sets that had been sold before the war, and the Federal Communications Commission (FCC) was not happy about the incompatibility. RCA—which had also been experimenting with color since the 1930s—promised the FCC that the company would shortly develop a color system that could work with existing sets. And in the fall of 1946, RCA delivered its promise. There was only one problem—RCA's color was of very poor quality.

The FCC was thus faced with a dilemma: whether to approve CBS's superior but incompatible system or RCA's inferior but adaptable method. In 1947 the commission announced that it would postpone any final color decisions on color TV but that it would give the go-ahead to resume black-and-white production. (A halt on the manufacture of TV sets had been in effect since 1942.) TV historian Jeff Greenfield has pointed out that "had the FCC approved the CBS system in 1947—when fewer than 250,000 existing sets were in use—America might never have passed through the era of black-and-white television. As it delayed the decision, the more black-and-white sets that were sold, the more important it became to develop a system that could be received on those sets."

So during the late 1940s, when Americans were first experiencing the pleasures of black-and-white TV, many companies were trying to find a color system the FCC would approve. Like CBS and RCA, DuMont and Chromatic TV, Inc. were also experimenting with color. CBS clearly had the superior system, but its detractors did everything possible to point out its shortcomings. DuMont went so far as to contend that the CBS method, which used a spinning disk, would present a threat to families if the disk (which DuMont argued would be seven feet in diameter and achieve a speed of 360 miles per hour) should break loose from the TV set.

Nevertheless the FCC approved the CBS system in 1950, and the Supreme Court upheld that decision the following year. In June 1951 CBS broadcast an hour-long color program to New York, Boston, Philadelphia, Baltimore and Washington, D.C., and it appeared that CBS would be the winner in the race for approval of a color sys-

tem. But in 1953, when there were already more than 20 million households with black-and-white sets, the FCC reversed its decision and gave the nod to RCA, which by that time had spent $21 million pushing its color system. The cost of conversion under the CBS method would simply be too expensive, the FCC argued.

NBC's first color broadcast was aired in 1953; it starred Kukla, Fran and Ollie with the Boston Pops Orchestra. Although only one percent of American households owned color sets in 1954, both CBS and NBC began broadcasting in color. There were only 68 hours of color transmission during all of 1954; by 1960 there were 32 hours per week of color programming. NBC was the most active promoter of color shows, since its parent company, RCA, was one of the largest manufacturers of color sets. In September 1957 the NBC peacock—one of the most familiar sights to audiences in the late 1950s and early 1960s—was born. By the fall of 1965 both CBS and NBC had become virtually all-color networks. ABC followed the next year.

But it was not until the 1970s that color TV really took command of America. Even as late as 1970 only 39.3 percent of TV households had color sets. Two years later the figure finally passed the 50 percent mark, and by 1985, color television had conquered 91.5 percent of TV households, as the following chart shows:

COLOR TELEVISIONS

Year	Number of Color TV Households	% of TV Households with Color TV
1964	1,610,000	3.1
1966	5,220,000	9.6
1968	13,700,000	24.2
1970	23,400,000	39.3
1971	27,600,000	45.2
1972	32,800,000	52.6
1973	39,400,000	60.1
1974	44,950,000	67.3
1975	48,500,000	70.8
1976	51,200,000	74.0
1977	54,900,000	77.0
1978	56,900,000	78.0
1979	60,300,000	81.0
1980	63,400,000	83.0
1981	66,250,000	85.2
1982	71,390,000	87.6
1983	73,890,000	88.7

1984	75,810,000	90.5
1985	77,660,000	91.5

Source: A.C. Nielsen Co.

The 1970s also witnessed another first—in 1972 sales of color sets surpassed those of black and white:

TELEVISION SALES

Year	Color TV Sales	Black-and-White TV Sales	Total
1970	5,320,000	6,900,000	12,220,000
1971	7,274,000	7,647,000	14,921,000
1972	8,845,000	8,239,000	17,084,000
1973	10,071,000	7,297,000	17,368,000
1974	8,411,000	6,868,000	15,279,000
1975	6,219,000	4,418,000	10,637,000
1976	8,194,000	5,937,000	14,131,000
1977	9,341,000	6,090,000	15,431,000
1978	10,674,000	6,732,000	17,406,000
1979	10,043,000	6,576,000	16,619,000
1980	11,803,000	6,729,000	18,532,000
1981	12,423,000	6,056,000	18,479,000

Source: EIA, Domestic & Import

Not surprisingly, upper-income households bought color TV in larger numbers than lower-income households. In 1969 only 15 percent of lower-income TV households (under $5,000 per year) owned color TV sets; 31 percent of middle-income TV families ($5,000-$9,999 per year) had color sets and 57 percent of upper-income TV households (more than $10,000 per year) enjoyed color. By 1978, 63 percent of lower-income families (now defined as earning under $10,000 per year) had purchased color sets, 79 percent of middle-income TV households ($10,000-$14,999 per year) had color television and 91 percent of upper-income families (more than $15,000 per year) were color TV households.

Education also influenced color TV ownership. In 1969, 21 percent of those TV households with a grade school education owned color sets, whereas 41 percent of college-educated TV households had color TVs. By 1978 those figures had risen to 65 percent of grade school-educated TV households and 81 percent of college-educated TV families.

In film and TV, technology often affects aesthetics. Has color TV changed the nature of television? Jeff Greenfield argues that with the advance of color TV, the closeup human conflict dramas in which early TV excelled gave way to the graphic "big screen" movie values of color, movement and action, thus changing the face of TV drama in the late 1950s. "In effect," Greenfield concludes, "the advent of color gave television a chance to satisfy an audience less by what it said than by the way it said—and showed—it." And Erik Barnouw has pointed out that the shift to color film in 1965-66 affected some TV topics, including war. "Mud and blood were indistinguishable in black and white; in color, blood was blood."

3/VIEWERS WITH CABLE TV

TV'S POWERS HAVE been evident ever since the 1950s when millions and millions of Americans got "hooked" on the tube. But there was one thing television couldn't do in its early days: move mountains. I mean that literally. Many communities across the nation were not able to receive TV signals because of surrounding mountains or forests. To solve this and similar reception problems, several towns in the late 1940s and early 1950s began constructing large antennae that could pick up TV signals and feed them directly into home television sets via a series of cables, for which service viewers paid a small monthly charge. Thus was born cable television or Community Antenna Television (CATV), as it was then called.

Initially cable TV was perceived as a mere accessory to standard broadcasting—it was simply a means of extending the reach of commercial TV. A town with only one or two stations, for example, could receive several big city channels with a cable hook-up. Or an isolated community with little or no reception could immensely improve its reception through the use of cable. The networks did not object to cable TV at first because they were not threatened by it; cable TV only served to make their large audience even larger.

But in the 1960s the true potential of cable TV began to emerge, and network brass grew nervous over the possible competition. Cable TV had clear advantages over standard broadcasting. For one thing, cable greatly increased the number of stations available to TV viewers. Standard broadcasting, for example, could provide a city with a maximum of seven UHF stations. By contrast, cable could easily handle 60 channels. With such an abundance of stations, many groups that had been denied access to TV broadcasting would now have an opportunity to use the medium. Educational, artistic and community services could be revolutionized; TV would no longer be just a commercial enterprise.

Another advantage of cable was the potential it offered for two-way transmissions. Cable would finally let us "talk back" to our set—we could pay bills, cast votes, take classes or make purchases, all with the touch of a few buttons connected to our cable TVs. The possibilities of bidirectional transmission were mind-boggling.

Finally, cable companies in the 1960s realized that instead of merely retransmitting standard broadcasts, they could also offer specialized fare, programs the general public could not watch on commercial TV. Why just duplicate what already existed when you could offer more ex-

citing entertainment? Thus, cable companies started making plans to offer first-run films, special sports events and other highly attractive viewing.

When the Brooklyn Dodgers and the New York Giants moved to California in the early 1960s, for example, it was arranged that their games would not be carried by the commercial networks, but by a new pay-TV service called Subscription TV, Inc. In addition to carrying the ball games, this company would also provide its subscribers with first-run films and other unique programming. Needless to say, the networks were not happy about the arrangement and a campaign was waged to stop the advance of pay TV. In 1964 a statewide referendum in California actually outlawed pay TV. When the state supreme court ruled the referendum unconstitutional, Subscription TV, Inc. was too weak to survive.

The California case was merely one battle in a long and heated war over cable TV. Millions of dollars have been spent in the conflict and all levels of government—municipal, state and federal—have been involved. At first the FCC was not even sure whether it had jurisdiction over cable television. Because it only received and did not actually transmit electrical waves into the air, there was some question about whether cable TV even fit under the rubric of "broadcasting."

The commission had permitted experiments in over-the-air pay TV as early as 1950 and by the mid-1950s was seriously studying the possibilities of subscription TV; the views of more than 25,000 people were examined. After issuing three preliminary reports, in 1957, 1958 and 1959, the FCC began accepting applications for over-the-air pay TV, and on June 22, 1960 a Hartford, Conn. station asked permission to conduct a three-year trial run. Because of further legal complications—which have plagued pay TV thoughout its history—the station did not begin operations until June 1962.

Using data from the Hartford experiment, the FCC in December 1968 issued its decisions regarding over-the-air pay TV. There could be only one pay TV station in each market, and only those communities with at least four existing stations could be given the go-ahead for pay TV. At least 10% of the programming had to consist of shows other than movies and sports, and even the kinds of movies and sports programs were strictly regulated. In short, regulations were so stiff that commercial television was not threatened.

These regulations applied only to over-the-air pay TV. It took much longer to legislate policy for cable TV. In fact, it was not until 1966 that the FCC formally began studying the problems of cable television and then only at the urging of Congress and broadcasters across the nation who believed a national cable TV policy was necessary. While gathering its information, the commission put severe limitations on cable TV in the Top 100 markets, limitations that brought the growing cable industry to a virtual standstill.

On February 12, 1972 the FCC finally issued its report. (The report was revised slightly that July, and revisions have been made several times since.) According to the new regulations, a cable system had to carry the signals of all TV stations within 35 miles of its home base. The system, moreover, had to be able to carry at least 20 channels, and systems in top markets had to have the capacity for two-way transmissions, even if bidirectional transmissions were not currently in use. Several special channels had to be set aside, including at least one each for public access, educational and local government use. The program content of these special channels could not be censored by the cable company. And to protect commercial TV, special regulations dictated what kinds of programs and sports events could be carried on cable.

Several cable companies began offering "pay-cable" channels in 1972. That is, in addition to the retransmission of existing programs, the company would—for a second monthly service charge—provide a special entertainment channel offering unedited first-run films, special sports events and the like. Pay cable was successful; cities that had not taken to cable TV because it only duplicated commercial television now started subscribing to pay cable.

Because of this success, cable companies asked the FCC in 1975 to remove some of the strict regulations regarding cable TV. The networks, feeling their position threatened, waged an all-out war to stop cable's advance. According to the doomsayers, cable TV could ruin the pleasures of television. If cable continued to grow, we would have all to pay for what we now got free, and the poor and the elderly might be deprived of TV altogether.

The FCC did change its rulings in 1975 and neither the networks nor the cable industry liked the changes. Both appealed the decisions. In 1976 the House Communications Subcommittee issued a report which concluded that "constraints should not be imposed upon cable television simply to protect broadcasting from competition." And a year later the District of Columbia U.S. Circuit Court of Appeals declared the 1975 rules unconstitutional.

Cable TV has had to face enormous opposition, but today most TV experts agree that by the end of the decade, the majority of the nation's viewers will be hooked on cable. There are several national cable systems now, including Home Box Office, a subsidiary of Time-Life, Inc. And other signs of success are evident. According to a Nielsen study issued in September 1979, pay-cable homes use their "feevee" channels even when heavyweight network programming is on the air, suggesting that pay cable can compete with network shows. *TV Guide* now carries cable information; in January 1980 almost half of its 101 editions contained listings of cable TV shows. The National Cable Television Association has just established its own programming award: the ACE (Awards for Cablecasting Excellence).

As of 1978, California had the most cable subscribers (1,681,000), followed by Pennsylvania (1,210,040) and New York (987,756). Pennsylvania had the largest number of cable systems (328), with California (290) and Texas (255) in second and third places respectively. The average price for the regular cable service was $8 to $10 per month, with an additional $8 to $10 per month for the pay-cable channel. Cable and pay cable have spread to all 50 states. *New York Times* TV reviewer Les Brown estimated that it costs between $14 and $20 million to wire a city with cable TV, and the cost of wiring the entire nation would be $123 billion. Here's how cable has grown over the past 20 years:

CABLE TELEVISION

Year	Operating Systems	Total Subscribers	% of TV Households
1960	640	650,000	1.4
1965	1,325	1,275,000	2.4
1970	2,490	4,500,000	7.6
1971	2,570	5,300,000	8.7
1972	2,655	6,000,000	9.6
1973	2,991	7,300,000	11.1
1974	3,158	8,700,000	13.0
1975	3,450	9,800,000	14.3
1976	3,651	10,800,000	15.5
1977	3,801	11,900,000	16.7
1978	4,030	12,900,000	17.7
1979	3,997	14,100,000	19.1
1980	4,048	15,200,000	20.5
1981	4,300	17,000,000	22.0
1982	4,300	21,000,000	25.8
1983	5,600	25,000,000	30.0
1984	6,200	30,000,000	36.0

Source: *Television Digest*

4/Viewing Habits and Attitudes

On 14, June 1975 Abigail Van Buren—better known to most of us as "Dear Abby"—published a letter that even in the context of her characteristically quirky and amusing column seemed especially remarkable. "This may sound crazy," the letter began, "but I need your advice. I am divorced and the mother of a sweet, four-year-old boy named Ronnie."

It seems that mother and child were at home one day when confronted by an armed intruder. The man was "gentle," according to the mother; he wanted only money and promised to hurt no one. Both robber and mother explained to Ronnie that his mother would have to be tied up and gagged. Ronnie was told to turn the TV on and only when the program was over (in about 20 minutes), could he call for help. Thus, the mother was bound, gagged and moved to another room. The intruder took the money and ran. And Ronnie sat down to watch television.

"Abby," the mother wrote in despair, "my son spent the next three hours watching TV, while I was bound and utterly helpless." Finally, the woman managed to tell her son, through the gag, to go for help. "Could Ronnie possibly have some hostility toward me?" she wondered. "Should I see a psychologist? Please answer."

This "Dear Abby" incident is but one of the many signs of TV's strange seductive powers. Ever since television began conquering Americans by the millions in the early 1950s, it has been evident that TV is a "greedy" medium. It wants—and can win—our attention even under the most unusual circumstances. According to the latest statistics, almost 90 million Americans watch TV each night. Is it any wonder that the tube is so often likened to a drug? As ABC executive Bob Shanks said, Americans simply do not want to turn the TV off. "Television is a massage," Shanks says, "a 'there, there,' a need, an addiction, a psychic fortress—a friend."

Most TV experts agree, in fact, that viewers do not turn on the set to watch programs but to watch television. As George Comstock and his colleagues summarize in *Television and Human Behavior*, most viewers decide first whether to view TV and only second what to view. "In the ordinary situation any program largely draws its audience from those who are committed to viewing something at that time... to a large degree television viewing in America is a largely passive activity where acceptance rather than enthusiasm is the rule." Much of this section is adapted from Comstock's wonderfully useful book.

Quite simply, the more we watch TV, the more we want (need?) to watch TV. Our tolerance levels increase each year, as the following chart (based on annual industry estimates) demonstrates:

Year	Average Amount of Time Per Day Spent Watching TV
1958	5 hrs. 5 min.
1959	5 hrs. 2 min.
1960	5 hrs. 6 min.
1961	5 hrs. 7 min.
1962	5 hrs. 6 min.
1963	5 hrs. 13 min.
1964	5 hrs. 13 min.
1965	5 hrs. 29 min.
1966	5 hrs. 32 min.
1967	5 hrs. 42 min.
1968	5 hrs. 46 min.
1969	5 hrs. 48 min.
1970	n.a.
1971	5 hrs. 59 min.
1972	6 hrs. 2 min.
1973	6 hrs. 12 min.
1974	6 hrs. 12 min.
1975	6 hrs. 14 min.
1976	6 hrs. 7 min.
1977	6 hrs. 18 min.
1978	6 hrs. 10 min.
1979	6 hrs. 28 min.
1980	6 hrs. 36 min.
1981	6 hrs. 45 min.
1982	6 hrs. 48 min.
1983	7 hrs. 2 min.
1984	7 hrs. 8 min.

Source: A.C. Nielsen Co.

Although there have been slight fluctuations from year to year in the average number of hours viewed per day, the general trend has been upward. Americans now watch TV an hour more a day than they did 15 years ago. And remember, these figures are yearly averages; the winter statisics are considerably higher. In 1978, for example, the average TV household had the set on for seven hours six minutes during January and for five hours 13 minutes during July, making a yearly average of six hours 10 minutes. That's quite a lot of TV at any time of the year.

In fact, according to a mid-1960s survey of TV use, TV wins more of Americans' time than does any other leisure activity:

Activity	% of Total Free Time
Television viewing	31
Newspaper reading	8
All other mass media use	6
Study	4
Religion and organizations	5
Socializing and conversation (home and away)	27
Leisure travel	6
Outdoors, sports, cultural, entertainment	5
Resting	3
Other leisure activity	6

As you can see, TV occupied nearly one-third of all our leisure time and three-quarters of all time devoted to mass media. And TV's dominance would have been even stronger had the researchers included in their study children and the retired, for both the young and the elderly are among TV's most ardent fans. Moreover, all "secondary" TV viewing—that is, viewing accompanied by other activities such as eating or housekeeping—was excluded from these statistics. (As we shall see later, TV viewing is in fact often accompanied by other activities.) Thus, even these overwhelming statistics still understated television's true conquest of American life.

Sunday evening attracts the largest audiences in this country, Friday the smallest (although Friday does win most of the youngsters). TV viewing is minimal in the early morning, increases is minimal in the early morning, increases throughout the day, hits a peak between 8:00 and 10:00 p.m. and declines considerably after 11:00 p.m. Almost 90% of TV households have their sets in the living room or den. In multi-set families 90% of the second TVs are located in bedrooms.

Of course, all TV viewers are not alike in their viewing habits. Education, sex, age, race, income—each can influence what, when and why we watch TV. According to Nielsen Demographic Reports, for example, TV viewing changes with education.

Households whose head has less than one year of college education watch TV more than those families whose head has one or more years of college, and this difference in viewing habits has been consistent over the past 13 years. It's interesting to note that television use in the former category rose most sharply between 1963 and 1970, while the sharpest rise in TV use in the latter occurred between 1970 and 1976. The industry does not really know how to explain this difference.

Age and sex also influence viewing habits.

As the editors of *Television and Human Behavior* have noted, several patterns are evident:

—Children watch about the same amount of television per week as adults, although at different times. Children from two to five years watch somewhat more than those six to 11 years old.

—Teenagers watch the fewest hours of television. The 21.9 hours they averaged in the fall of 1976 was almost seven hours less than the norm for all age groups.

—Men from 18 to 49 watch less television than the other adult groups, although there was an increase of 5.1 hours per week between 1967 and 1976. This remarkable 26 percent increase is the most dramatic of any group.

—Men over 50 years old watch more TV than do men under 50. Their total viewing increased from 27.1 hours in 1967 to 31.9 hours a week in 1976, which is about seven hours more than younger men spent looking at TV that year.

—Women from 18 to 49 watch TV more hours than men the same age watch. In the fall of 1976 the viewing time of these younger adult women was almost seven hours per week more than that of younger adult men. Their total viewing increased by more than four hours in the last three years, and they remain above the overall average for individual viewing, with over 31 hours a week.

—Women over 50 watch far more television than any of the other groups. In short, viewing declines between elementary school and high school, rises in adulthood and rises again after age 50.

Sex and age influence not only how much television we watch but also when we watch it. Children, of course, lead very different lives than adults—kids have their own schedules, their own rhythms—and their TV habits reflect such differences.

Preschool children, for example, are very likly to watch television in the morning. At that time older brothers and sisters are in school; mothers, if not at work, are likely to be busy with household chores and morning TV caters to young children's tastes. According to 1976 Nielsen statistics, nearly 20 percent of all preschoolers watch TV between 8:00 and 10:00 a.m. In the late morning and early afternoon, when TV soap operas prevail, that level drops to 10 percent. Preschoolers' viewing picks up again in the late afternoon, hitting an afternoon peak between 5:00 and 5:30 p.m., when almost 45 percent of all preschool children are watching TV. That level drops a bit between 6:00 and 7:00 p.m., when most children are eating dinner and most television is devoted to evening news. But preschool viewing climbs again right after dinner, reaching its apex at 8:00 p.m., when approximately 47 percent of all children five years and under are glued to the tube. Thereafter their viewing declines; 26 percent of all preschoolers are watching TV at 9:00 p.m., 11 percent at 10:00 p.m.

Elementary shcool children have different TV habits, due of course to the fact that most of them are in shcool all day. There is some early morning viewing among six-to-11-year-olds; at 8:00 a.m. approximately 15 percent of elementary school kids watch television. But TV viewing is minimal between 8:00 a.m. and 2:30 p.m. for kids in this age group. The pattern changes, however, when the kids come home from school. Between 5:00 and 6:00 p.m., almost 40 percent of elementary school children are plopped down in front of the tube. After a short dinnertime dip in viewing, another peak is reached between 8:00 and 9:00 p.m., when 56 percent of six-to 11-year-olds are watching

TV. That considerable proportion drops to 36 percent between 9:00 and 10:00 p.m. and to 20 percent at 10:30 p.m. (Many adults are surprised to learn that 20 percent of children are still watching TV as late as 10:30 p.m.)

As already mentioned, teenagers watch TV less than any other age group. There is little teenage viewing from early morning through midafternoon. Even at 5:30 p.m. only 30 percent of all teenagers are watching the tube; this is 10 to 15 percent less than the percentage of their younger brothers and sisters. Teenage viewing hits its peak at 8:30 p.m., when almost 40 percent of adolescents are in front of television sets. By 11:00 p.m. their level has dropped to 16 percent, compared to 30 percent of adults.

Sex does not significantly affect the viewing habits of children and teenagers, but it does influence adult TV watching; women generally watch more TV than men do. Women between the ages of 18 and 49 begin to watch TV early in the morning and their numbers increase steadily through midafternoon. By 3:00 p.m., 25 percent of all women 18 to 49 years old are watching TV. Viewing drops from 4:00 to 5:00 p.m., but begins to rise thereafter, hitting a peak between 9:00 and 10:00, when almost 53 percent of all women in this age group are in front of their sets. TV use declines after 11:00 p.m., although at midnight 15 percent of women between the ages of 18 and 49 are still watching TV.

Because most men who are 18 to 49 years of age work during the day, TV viewing for this age group is minimal until 5:00 p.m., when their use of TV begins to climb rapidly. Thirty percent of all men 18 to 49 years old are watching television between 6:00 and 7:00 p.m. Viewing continues to rise, reaching its top level between 9:00 and 10:00 p.m. Even at that peak, however, fewer men than women are watching TV. After 11:00 p.m. patterns for men 18 to 49 years of age are quite similar to those of their female peers.

Viewing habits for people over 50 are generally similar to those of younger adults with a few exceptions. Women 50 years and older begin to watch TV earlier in the day, and TV viewing by all people over 50 peaks sooner: between 8:00 and 9:00 p.m. instead of the 9:00 to 10:00 p.m. peak for younger adults. Between 7:00 and 10:00 p.m. more than 50 percent of all people over 50 are watching TV.

The chart on page 95 draws a convenient profile of the television audience. Reading across the chart reveals audience composition for a particular time of day. Reading down the chart shows the viewing habits of a particular age group.

As you can see, at any given time during the Week, women 18 to 49 years old are the single largest group of viewers. Only on weekends do women in this age group finish in second place; on Saturday mornings, for example, 50% of the viewers are children 11 years or younger.

So far we've been discussing when and how much people watch TV. But why people watch TV and in what manner they watch it are also interesting matters. Do viewers really watch television or do they merely turn it on for background noise? Are most viewers drawn to the tube for specific programs, general entertainment, or information and education?

According to surveys conducted in 1960 (by G.A. Steiner) and in 1970 (by R.T. Bower), most viewers say they watch TV to see a specific program they enjoy very much. The 1970 poll repeated most of the questions asked in 1960 for comparison's sake; more than 2,000 people were polled in each survey and the results of both surveys were remarkably similar.

	% of Adults Saying They "Usually" Watch TV For a Given Reason	
Reasons for Watching TV	1960	1970
To see a specific program I enjoy very much.	80	81
Because it's a pleasant way to spend a night.	55	41
To see a specific program I've heard a lot about.	54	50
Because I feel like watching television.	50	46
Because I think I can learn something.	36	34

Motives changed very little during the decade. The only significant difference between the two surveys is in the use of TV as a pleasant way to spend an evening. Fifty-five percent of the adults polled in 1960 felt that they usually watched TV as a general diversion; by 1970 that level had dropped to 41 percent. Entertainment is the general motivation for most viewers as you can see, only one-third of those polled turned on the tube to be educated. (In another survey, only 12 percent claimed that they watched TV to be informed or to learn.) Few people in either the 1960 or 1970 survey said they viewed TV to be sociable, to escape or for background noise.

There is, however, evidence to the contrary. For years TV critics and social historians have suspected that many people may turn on TV without really watching it. And according to two studies—one performed in the early 1960s, the other in the early 1970s—people don't always pay much attention to television. In both studies, cameras were placed in sample house-holds to monitor TV use. The 1960s study found that 19 percent of the time the TV was on, nobody was even in the room, and that another 21 percent of the time, nobody was really paying attention to it even when someone was in the room. In short, 40 percent of the viewing time was really non-viewing time. And the level of inattentiveness climbed even higher during commercials; during 48 percent of the time commercials were on the air, either no one was in the room or, if they were in the room, they were not watching the set.

The early 1970s survey confirmed many of the previous study's findings. In addition, the second study ranked attentiveness according to type of program:

Type of Programming	% of Time Watched
Movies	76.0
Children's	71.4
Suspense	68.1
Religious	66.7
Family	66.4
Game Show	65.9
Talk Show	63.7
Melodrama	59.3
Sports events	58.7
News	55.2
Commercials	54.8

If people aren't always watching the set when it's on, what are they doing? Mostly talking and eating, according to the early 1970s study. But that's just the beginning of the "extracurricula" activities. The researchers expressed surprise at the astounding variety of activities that accompany TV viewing: looking out window, picking nose, scratching (someone else and self), doing homework, smoking, rocking, reading, dancing, lying (on floor, couch, table), untying knots, sorting wash, preparing meals, setting table, ironing, dressing, undressing, posing, doing exercises, singing, pacing, asking questions about the television program, reciting, wrestling, fighting, crying, throwing objects (toys, books, paper airplanes), scolding children, mimicking the television portrayal, conversing with the television set, sleeping, playing cards, playing board games (Monopoly, Scrabble), answering the phone, crawling, teasing, combing hair and, occasionally, making love.

Despite their inattentiveness, most viewers think favorably of television. Intellectuals, politicans and parents-teachers associations have been attacking TV for decades now, but most Americans remain true-blue to the tube. There may be differences in opinions—people with more education hold TV in less esteem then do those with less education—but TV remains in the public's favor.

Most Americans even think children are better off with TV than without. More than three-quarters of those polled in Bower's 1972 survey believed TV was generally beneficial for kids. Television is especially praised in comparison to other media. For example:

Public Opinion in Early 1970s on Value of Different Media, by % (bracketed figures are percentage change over decade)

"Which one of these would you say...	TV	Magazines	Newspapers	Radio	Don't Know
Is the most entertaining?	72[+4]	5[−4]	9[−4]	14[+5]	0[−1]
Presents things most intelligently?	38[+11]	18[−9]	28[−5]	9[+1]	8[+3]
Is the most educational?	46[+14]	20[−11]	26[−5]	4[+1]	5[+2]
Does the most for the public?	48[+14]	2[−1]	28[−16]	13[+2]	10[+2]
Is getting worse all the time?	41[+17]	18[+1]	14[+4]	5[−9]	22[−13]
Is the least important to you?	13[−2]	53[+4]	9[+2]	20[+5]	5[−2]
Creates most interest in new things?	61[+5]	16[−2]	14[−4]	5[+1]	5[+1]
Does the least for the public?	10[−3]	50[+3]	7[+2]	13[+1]	20[−3]
Is getting better all the time?	38[−11]	8[−3]	11[0]	15[+5]	28[+5]
You most want to keep?"	59[+17]	4[0]	19[−13]	17[−2]	1[−2]

As you can see, people think TV is the most interesting, the most educational, the most intelligent and the most beneficial medium. TV is the one medium they would want to keep if they had to give up all others. More than 40 percent of those polled did say, however, that TV was getting worse, but that didn't signficantly influence their other favorable attitudes toward the tube. Television has replaced the newspaper as the number one medium in this country.

All of these statistics point to TV's overwhelming presence in American life. As on TV critic has said, when the question "What do Americans do?" is asked, it's now possible to answer, "Watch television."

SEGMENTS OF AUDIENCE

Time of Day	Children		Teen-agers	Women		Men		Total Viewers (in millions)	Viewers in This Time Period as % of Total Potential Audience
	2-5	6-11	12-17	18-49	50+	18-49	50+		
Mon.-Fri. 7-10 a.m.	17.4%	12.6%	6.7%	23.3%	20.6%	8.5%	11.0%	14.6	7.3
Mon.-Fri. 10 a.m-1 p.m.	9.8	4.9	5.4	33.3	25.3	9.0	12.3	20.6	10.2
Mon.-Fri. 1-4:30 p.m.	8.0	7.5	7.6	34.6	25.0	8.0	9.4	28.8	14.3
Mon.-Fri. 4:30-7:30 p.m.	9.0	13.5	10.7	21.0	18.1	14.5	13.2	61.4	30.5
Mon-Sun. 8-11 p.m.	3.7	8.8	10.0	25.9	16.6	21.7	13.2	89.2	44.3
Mon.-Sun. 11:30 p.m.- 1 a.m.	1.0	2.9	7.4	31.5	15.5	28.0	13.6	28.4	14.1
Sat. 7 a.m. -1 p.m.	19.5	31.3	14.0	13.2	5.7	10.9	5.5	27.6	13.7
Total persons in TV Households									
in millions	**12.8**	**21.1**	**24.5**	**46.6**	**28.7**	**43.3**	**23.4**		
% of total	**6.4**	**10.5**	**12.2**	**23.2**	**14.3**	**22.0**	**11.6**		**100.0**

III. THE RATINGS

1/THE WHO'S AND HOW'S OF TV RATINGS

WHEN IT COMES to knowing its audience, television certainly has its problems. Book publishers keep reliable tabs on how many volumes a particular title has sold; Hollywood dependably calculates what various films gross; theater companies determine through box office receipts just how many tickets have been sold to a particular play; and newspapers and magazines must keep precise circulation figures. But TV producers often remain in the dark about the exact number of viewers. Because television is consumed free of charge in the privacy of our homes, knowing who is watching what and when can be quite a tricky business, at best an educated guess and at worst a sloppy and controversial mess.

The Nielsens—TV's most important and hotly-debated audience measurements—are computed by the A. C. Nielsen Company, a marketing research firm whose expertise in evaluating consumer use of various food and drug products led manufacturers in the 1930s to ask the company to find a way to measure radio audiences. After acquiring the rights to an electronic gadget invented by Robert F. Elder and Louis Woodruff called the "Audimeter" which could record what station a radio was tuned in to, Nielsen launched its radio audience measurement service in 1942. When TV showed signs of budding popularity, the company adapted its radio Audimeter to the new medium. TV Nielsens were first computed in September 1950 for nationally sponsored shows and in April 1954 for audiences in various local TV markets. The national statistics are known as the Nielsen Television Index (NTI), the locals as the Nielsen Stations Index (NSI).

How does Nielsen rate TV shows?

To compute the NTI, the company places an Audimeter—now better known as the "little black box"—in approximately 1,200 households across the nation. (Nielsen's Statistical Research Department uses the latest U.S. Census figures to produce an accurate sample.) Everytime a TV, even a battery-operated model, is turned on in one of the monitored households, the Audimeter records, minute by minute, the time of viewing, the length of viewing and the channel being viewed.

Originally, this minute-by-minute data was stored in the Audimeter and had to be mailed in to the company where it was then processed, but now each Audimeter is directly connected to a central computer which "calls" the Aumdimeter twice a day to retrieve (in five seconds!) its data. The Audimeter is kept out of sight—in a closet, or in the basement—and requires no care from any household member. Each box has its own power source in case of black-outs. A family is paid $25 when the Audimeter is first installed, $2 a month thereafter, and Nielsen agrees to pay 50% of the household's TV repair bills. Approximately 20% of the panel households are replaced each year, so that no household is monitored for more than five years.

To supplement data recorded by Audimeters, Nielsen asks 2,300 households (called the National Audience Composition, or NAC) to keep a log of its TV viewing. Each TV in a NAC household is equipped with a Recordimeter, which tallies the total number of hours a TV is used each day. The specifics of what was watched and by whom are written down by a household member in a diary called the Audilog. Whereas the Audimeter can only record when a TV is on and what channel is being viewed, the Audilog can reveal important demographic information—the sex, age, education and income of the individual viewers. Neilsen maintains the NAC survey 34 weeks per year, distributed throughout the four viewing seasons.

After processing data from these Audimeters and Audilogs, Nielsen publishes the national ratings in *The Nielsen National TV Rating Report*, popularly known in the industry as the "Pocketpiece," because it fits in the inside coat pocket of network salesmen. The Pocketpiece contains a wealth of information: audience composition breakdowns by age, sex, race, education and income; TV usage by time periods; overall TV usage comparisons versus one year ago; program type averages (are comedies doing better than action adventure series?); season-to-date averages for all network programs; and of course the ratings themselves for those weeks covered by that particular edition of the Pocketpiece.

Each network program has not one but three rating statisitics:

(1) The Total Audience Rating (TA) is the percentage of all TV households that watched a particular program for six minutes or more. If a show had a TA of 25.6, it means that 25.6% of all American TV homes viewed at least 6 minutes of the show.

(2) The Average Audience Rating (AA), the most widely-reported of the 3 statistics, is the percentage of all TV households that watched a particular program during an average minute of its telecast. If a show has an AA rating of 29.2, it means that 29.2% of all American TV households watched that program during an average minute of its broadcast. Of course, the TA will always be

slightly larger than the AA, but if there is little disparity between the two figures it implies that viewers liked the show, that they did not turn to another channel while the program was still on. On the other hand, a large difference between TA and AA ratings suggests the program did not satisfy its viewers, that the viewers were quick to switch to another channel. As of August 1983, each full rating point represented 838,000 homes, according to Nielsen estimates. That is, if a show earned a 20.0 rating, it was viewed in 16.76 million homes (838,000 × 20).

(3) The Share-of-Audience (or simply "share") indicates a program's ability to command an audience in relation to the programs opposite it; the share is a comparative and hence competitive figure. Whereas the AA ratings is the percentage of *all* American TV households, the share is based only on those households using TV at that *Particular* time.

Let's say, for example, that there are 100 sets in America, and 30 of these sets are watching *I Love Lucy*. This means that *I Love Lucy* has a 30.0 rating. But of those 100 sets only 60 are actually in use during *I Love Lucy's* time slot, which means that *I Love Lucy* has 30 out of 60 sets, or a 50 share. *I Love Lucy* would then have a 30.0 rating and a 50.0 share.

According to an industry rule-of-thumb, a show must have a share of at least 30 to survive, that is, the show must command at least one third of the network audience, there being three major networks. (ABC, CBS and NBC have a combined share of 90%; the other 10% goes to PBS, cable or independent stations.)

Because the Pocketpiece contains demographic data, it's possible to make important comparisons between various viewing groups. Do TV habits, for example, change with education and income? According to a 1968 *TV Guide* study: Yes. For a 6-week period ending Dec. 3, 1967, the Top 10 shows looked like this:

U.S. TOP 10	TOP 10 FOR INCOMES UNDER $5,000	TOP 10 FOR INCOMES $10,000 & OVER
Lucy Show	Lucy Show	Saturday Movies
Andy Griffith	Gunsmoke	Dean Martin
Bonanza	Andy Griffith	Friday Movies
Red Skelton	Red Skelton	Andy Griffith
Gunsmoke	Lawrence Welk	Thursday Movies
Family Affair	Bonanza	Smothers Bros.
Jackie Gleason	Gomer Pyle	Family Affair
Gomer Pyle	Family Affair	Jackie Gleason
Saturday Movies	Ed Sullivan	Tuesday Movies
Beverly Hillbillies	Virginian	FBI
Friday Movies		

The preferences of the lower income households were generally similar to those of the nation of a whole: there were seven shows in common. The main difference in tastes was for movies: no film series made the lower income's list.

Movies, on the other hand, were quite successful with the upper income households, whose Top 10 included

four(!) film series. Only five of the upper income's favorites coincided with the nation's as whole. The lower income households tended to watch Westerns and sit-coms, the uppers preferred movies and dramas. When it came to variety shows, the uppers liked Jackie Gleason, Dean Martin, and the Smothers Brothers, the lowers chose Red Skilton, Lawrence Welk, and Ed Sullivan.

According to the same *TV Guide* article, tastes changed again with education:

U.S. TOP 10	TOP 10: GRADE SCHOOL EDUCATION	TOP 10: 1 + YEARS OF COLLEGE
Lucy Show	Lucy Show	Saturday Movies
Andy Griffith	Andy Griffith	Mission: Impossible
Bonanza	Gunsmoke	Smothers Brothers
Red Skelton	Red Skelton	Dean Martin
Gunsmoke	Bonanza	Jackie Gleason
Family Affair	Gomer Pyle	Tuesday Movies
Jackie Gleason	Family Affair	Bewitched
Gomer Pyle	Lawrence Welk	NFL Football
Saturday Movies	Virginian	Thursday Movies
Beverly Hillbillies	Jackie Gleason	Get Smart
Friday Movies		

The grade school-educated households' tastes were quite similar to the nation's: eight shows were on both lists. The college-educated families, by contrast, had quite dissimilar preferences: only two of their favorite programs were also on the nation's Top 10.

The NTI provides many other services than the Pocketpiece, including overnight ratings, fast weekly household ratings, fast evening persons audience profiles and fast multi-networks area ratings. Moreover, NTI publishes one of the most comprehensive collections of statistics in the TV industry—the two-volume *NTI/NAC Audience Demographics* (NAD). Volume I provides an overview of American TV usage, including a 32-person categories breakdown. Volume II reports demographics by household size, income and education, and overall TV usage by 38 day parts.

Nielsen's local ratings (NSI) are computed in a slightly different fashion than its nationals (NTI). Whereas data for the NTI comes from both diaries and electronic meters, the NSI depends primarily upon diaries. Only in certain key cities—New York, Los Angeles, Chicago and San Francisco—are Audimeters used in computing the NSI.

Households in the NSI sample are contacted first by telephone (both listed and unlisted numbers are culled from a pool of more than 57 million residential telephone numbers) and then are sent NSI diaries (there are editions in Spanish as well as in English). The sample household is asked to keep a log of stations, channels and programs viewed for more than five minutes per quarter hour. Specifics about which member of the household watched what are also kept.

After the data has been processed, NSI published its *Viewers in Profile* (VIP), the NSI equivalent of the Pocketpiece. The VIPs are issued from three to eight times a year, depending upon the size of the local market: the larger the market, the more frequently the VIP is published. (NSI tabulates data for more than 200 local American markets.)

Like the Pocketpiece, the VIP collects a vast array of information; age and sex demographics (total adults in households, total working women, number of children, etc.); usage by time of day; audience data for individual programs; and each station's weekly cumulative audiences, to name but a few of the many VIP statistics. Ratings for syndicated programs are published in one of NSI's supplementary reports.

Is there a considerable difference between the TV habits of one part of the country and another? According to the forementioned *TV Guide* article, there is. Here are the Top 10 programs for the same 6 week period ending Dec. 3, 1967:

U.S. TOP 10	TOP 10 IN THE SOUTH	TOP 10 IN NORTHEAST
Lucy Show	Gunsmoke	Jackie Gleason
Andy Griffith	Bonanza	Smothers Brothers
Bonanza	Andy Griffith	Dean Martin
Red Skelton	Lucy Show	Ed Sullivan
Gunsmoke	Gomer Pyle	Friday Movies
Family Affair	Red Skelton	Saturday Movies
Jackie Gleason	Family Affair	Lucy Show
Gomer Pyle	Virginian	Thursday Movies
Saturday Movies	Daniel Boone	Tuesday Movies
Beverly Hillbillies	Beverly Hillbillies	My Three Sons
Friday Movies		

As you can see, the South's preferences were very similar to the nation's as a whole: eight shows made it on both lists. By contrast, the Northeast had only four programs in common with the U.S. list—missing were the Westerns and rural sit-coms like *Gomer Pyle* and *The Andy Griffith Show*. There were four film series among the Northeast's favorites, none among the South's.

If these Nielsen statistics sound precise and scientific, remember both their reliability and usefulness have been frequently challenged. As former Federal Communications Commission member Margita White has said, the rating system—"by encouraging imitation rather than innovation, by overemphasizing 'the numbers' at the expense of quality and encouraging bland programming to the lowest common denominator—may be the single major obstacle to better-quality programming."

Audimeters, it should be remembered, can only record whether a TV set in a monitored household is on or off, and not whether the household actually *enjoyed* the program. Audimeter data, in short, is quantitative not qualitative. (And even the Audimeter's quantitative data is limited: Audimeters tally the number of households and not the number of *viewers*.) Members of a monitored household could be chattering away, or someone could be asleep in front of the tube, or no one may be in the room at all, but as long as the set was on, that little box would never know the difference. As one TV reviewer has said,

the Nielsens are not so much inaccurate as irrelevant: they simply don't measure what's important—satisfaction.

In all fairness, it should be pointed out that Nielsen has ever claimed to measure quality. "As far as we're concerned, there is no such thing as a TV rating," the company says in a booklet *Everything You've Always Wanted to Know About TV Ratings but Were Maybe Too Skeptical To Ask.* "The word 'rating' is a misnomer because it implies a measurement of program quality—and this we never do. NEVER!"

Nielsen sampling procedures have also come under repeated attack. There are approximately 74.8 million American TV households, Nielsen monitors 1,200 of these, or only 1 of every 62,000. Nielsen of course contends the sample is large enough: "When a doctor takes a blood test," the company says, "even people who are hopelessly skeptical about samples agree there's no need to be pumped dry!" Many statisticians, however, have argued that the Nielsen panel simply isn't large enough to be a true reflection of American TV viewing. As TV producer Bob Shanks has complained, it is doubtful that "ever in history have so few had so much influence over so many."

If the Nielsens are plagued by these serious limitations, why then are they given so much importance, so much power? The answer is easy—money. Nielsen statistics may serve a variety of functions: a social historian could analyze Nielsen data to learn something about American values and attitudes, and of course network programmers use Nielsen ratings all the time to make scheduling decisions—to decide which shows should stay on the air, which should be cancelled, and which should be moved to a different time slot. But the primary use of Nielsens is financial: networks use ratings to determine how much to charge advertisers, and advertisers use ratings to decide which show is the best market for their commercials. Many of us assume that TV is in the business of selling programs to viewers, but it would be more accurate to say that TV sells viewers to advertisers: ratings set the going price.

Four times a year—in February, May, July and November—Nielsen conducts what the industry calls "the sweeps"—ratings for each individual station in the country which determine how much a station can charge an advertiser. In order to win the highest ratings and hence charge the highest prices, networks go crazy during the sweeps, scheduling the best and the brightest: blockbuster movies, guest superstars, extravagant specials. For example, on Feb. 11, 1979 (now a legendary night in sweeps history—the "Götterdammerung" of the "hellzapoppin' chess match of the Nielsen Sweeps," one TV critic tagged it), NBC ran the Oscar-winning *One Flew Over the Cuckoo's Nest*, CBS fought back with part I of *Gone With the Wind*, and ABC played its hand with a film bio of Elvis Presley.

"Television would be much better off and the public better served," CBS chairman William S. Paley has observed, "if the numbers race were not so important. But ratings are terribly important. Advertising revenues depend upon how many viewers the sponsor is reaching with his commercials. So the financial well-being of each network does depend on ratings."

It has been claimed, in fact, that a single rating point can be worth millions in prime time advertising revenue. By the end of the fall 1978 TV season, for example, ABC was the top-ranked web with a 20.2 average rating. CBS came in with an 18.2. Because of those two rating points, ABC generated $22 million more in prime time ad revenues that fall than CBS!

Does the Nielsen Company itself make much money from the ratings? Although the company is of course best-known for its TV measurements, only 10% of its annual revenues ($300 million in 1978) are derived from its TV audience research. Each of the three major networks pays Nielsen $1 million a year for its services, and Nielsen also sells its reports to advertisers, ad agencies and the like. When Nielsen surveyed cable TV in 1979, for example, the report went for $6,000.

Nielsen has no real competition when it comes to national ratings, but there is another important research firm that measures local TV audiences—the American Research Bureau (ARB). The bureau's rating service is known as Arbitron and it has been estimating audience size for TV programs since 1949 and for radio shows since 1965.

Initially, diaries were the main source of information for the Arbitrons, but the service now incorporates electronic metering of viewing. Arbitron divides the nation into 208 Areas of Dominant Influence (ADIs) and for each ADI calculates demographic breakdowns. Arbitron also estimates the number of households with cable TV, color TV, UHF TV, multiple sets, etc.

To supplement information obtained from the diary households, Arbitron also uses telephone surveys, personal interviews and—in New York, Chicago and Los Angeles—electronic meters. Arbitron ratings are also used during the "sweeps."

Like the Nielsens, Arbitrons are quantitative measurements. Are there any qualitative ratings for TV? Throughout the past 25 years there have been several attempts to measure quality, but none of them has truly succeeded in this country, although there are quality ratings in France and England. Since 1973 British law, for example, has required "Appreciation Indices" to be computed for commercial TV shows. Sample households are mailed questionnaires that allow viewers to rate recently-aired programs according to how *good* the shows were. And according to its charter, the BBC (the public TV network in England) must supplement its numbers ratings with "Reaction Indices."

Quality ratings have once again become a "hot" issue in this country. In 1977 the National Citizens Committee for Broadcasting—funded by a General Foods grant—researched the possibility of qualitative ratings. Approximately 200 households in the Washington, D.C. area were asked to keep TV diaries for one week, ranking each program according to its importance and its entertainment value. Although the sample simply was not large enough to be statistically reliable, there were consederable—and suggestive—discrepancies between the Nielsens and the quality ratings. *Happy Days*, for example, ranked third in the ratings that week, but 27th in the Quality Index. *I, Claudius*, on the other hand, came in 46th in the ratings, but first in the Quality Index.

In Seattle the R.D. Percy Co. has installed in 200 randomly-selected households electronic gadgets which can record much more information than the Nielsen's Audimeters: with the Percy "VoxBox" a viewer can push various buttons to indicate whether he/she finds a TV show informative, entertaining or dull. There's even a "Zap" button that blacks out the show for as long as the button is held! Data from the Vox Box is transmitted to a main computer, which records the reactions while the show is still on the air.

And in 1982, Television Audience Assessment Inc. issued its qualitative report "The Audience Rates Television," in which 3,000 viewers in two cable-access areas (Kansas City, Missouri, and New Britain, Connecticut) were asked to monitor their viewing habits, according to both attention paid to and enjoyment derived from each program. Based on viewers' diaries, each program was given two qualitative ratings—a Program Impact Index and a Program Appeal Index. The report, funded by a $1.5 million grant from the John and Mary R. Markle Foundation, was issued in the belief that counting the number of bodies that are supposedly watching their TV sets—even if the rating service can further identify these bodies by age, sex and income—"is no longer adequate when so many people have access to 30 or more channels. With so much television to choose from, viewers have become very restless. They're constantly sampling new channels, new programs." Hence, the need to measure not quantity, but "the overall entertainment value of a television program" and "the degree of intellectual and emotional stimulation a program gives its viewers." The company hoped to conduct a national survey in the near future to further test the possibilities of qualitative ratings.

Quality ratings could result in a greater diversity of TV fare. As Donald Thurston, chairman of the National Association of Broadcasters has pointed out, "If a show came in with good but not great ratings, but the Q-factor showed that it left viewers with wonderful feelings, it might have a chance to stay on the air."

Are networks then enthusiastic about qualitative ratings? Not exactly. The Coporation for Public Broadcasting has voiced interest in the enterprise. "The public broadcaster's mandate is to provide an 'alternative' source of programming, that is, to satisfy viewer needs left unfulfilled by commercial programming," says CPB president

Cortland Anderson. "A qualitative rating system woud provide us with a way to measure our success in meeting the goal."

The commercial networks, however, are not as enthusiastic. Would quality ratings result in increased revenues? Don't numbers ratings already provide enough information for advertisers to buy air time? Wouldn't Q-ratings make the complicated pricing procedures even more Byzantine? And network executives have pointed out that there are some kind of "quality ratings" in use right now: concept testing and pilot testing. Before a show even gets on the air, networks will ask a sample audience if it likes a pilot episode, if it thought the show was good and worth watching.

Meanwhile, the ratings debate continues. More than 20 years ago CBS president Frank Stanton observed that "ratings, properly taken, serve a useful purpose. They provide a yardstick for the measurement of audiences. But what ratings do, at best, is to reveal the choice that viewers have made among the programs available. . . . But beyond ratings, both quantitative and qualitative, we need to know something else—what people *want* to look at. It is not satisfactory to have indications of approval or disapproval of what we are doing. We need constantly to know what the audience thinks we *ought* to be doing."

Twenty years later, networks are still in the dark.

2/Top-Rated TV Series

Here are the annual top-rated series from 1950/51 through 1983/84. Because Nielsen changed its rating methodology in 1960, precise comparisons between pre-and-post 1960 figures are not really possible. Also remember that because the size of the American TV audience has been growing over the years, a show that captured 29.8% of the audience in 1979 would obviously have been seen by more people than a show that captured 29.8% of the audience in 1961. In short, with these figures we do not know the *number of people* who saw a particular program, only the percentage *of households.*

The ratings in this chapter are seasonal averages. Obviously, a particular *episode* of a series may have had a much higher of much lower rating than the series' seasonal average. What then are the top-rated *individual* episodes of all time? According to Nielsen statistics, the Top 20 since 1960 (when the new rating system was established) are as follows:

	Show	Net-work	Date	Rating
1.	M*A*S*H (Finale)	CBS	2/28/83	60.2
2.	Dallas ("Who Shot J.R.?")	CBS	11/21/80	53.3
3.	The Fugitive (the famous final episode of the series)	ABC	8/29/64	45.9
4.	Ed Sullivan Show	CBS	2/9/64	44.6
5.	Beverly Hillbillies	CBS	1/8/64	44.0
6.	Ed Sullivan Show	CBS	2/16/64	43.2
7.	Beverly Hillbillies	CBS	1/15/64	42.8
8.	Beverly Hillbillies	CBS	2/26/64	42.4
9.	Beverly Hillbillies	CBS	3/25/64	42.2
10.	Beverly Hillbillies	CBS	2/5/64	42.0
11.	Beverly Hillbillies	CBS	1/29/64	41.9
12.	Beverly Hillbillies	CBS	1/1/64	41.8
13.	Bonanza	NBC	3/8/64	41.6
14.	Beverly Hillbillies	CBS	1/22/64	41.5
15.	Bonanza	NBC	2/16/64	41.4
16.	Bonanza	NBC	2/9/64	41.0
17.	Gunsmoke	CBS	2/28/61	40.9
18.	Bonanza	NBC	3/28/65	40.8
19.	Bonanza	NBC	3/7/65	40.7
	All in the Family	CBS	1/8/72	40.7

The obvious champion here is *Beverly Hillbillies,* with 8 appearances on the list. *Bonanza* comes in second, with 5 episodes in the Top 20. Winter 1964 certainly was a good season for TV: 13 of the Top 20 episodes were broadcast then. By the way, the *I Love Lucy* episode in which Lucy gave birth to Little Ricky is said to have captured 71.7% of the audience.

Who are the record-breakers when it comes to the annual lists? The various Lucy shows appear 17 times on these lists; *Red Skelton* and *Gunsmoke* 16 times each; Ed Sullivan 13 times; and *Bonanza* and the various Disney series 12 times each.

What are the highest seasonal averages ever posted by a series?

Pre-1960 Seasonal

Show	Average	Year
1. I Love Lucy	67.3	1952/53
2. Texaco Star Theatre	61.6	1950/51
3. I Love Lucy	58.8	1953/54
4. Arthur Godfrey's Talent Scouts	53.8	1951/52
5. I Love Lucy	49.3	1954/55

Post-1960 Seasonal

Show	Average	Year
1. Beverly Hillbillies	39.1	1963/64
2. Gunsmoke	37.3	1960/61
3. Bonanza	36.3	1964/65
4. Beverly Hillbillies	36.0	1962/63
5. Dallas	34.5	1980/81

The following is a list of the top-rated TV series by year:

1950/51

1.	Texaco Star Theater	NBC	61.6
2.	Fireside Theatre	NBC	52.6
3.	Philco TV Playhouse	NBC	45.3
4.	Your Show of Shows	NBC	42.6
5.	The Colgate Comedy Hour	NBC	42.0
6.	Gillette Cavalcade of Sports	NBC	41.3
7.	The Lone Ranger	ABC	41.2
8.	Arthur Godfrey's Talent Scouts	CBS	40.6
9.	Hopalong Cassidy	NBC	39.9
10.	Mama	CBS	39.7
11.	Robert Montgomery Presents	NBC	38.8
12.	Martin Kane, Private Eye	NBC	37.8
13.	Man Against Crime	CBS	37.4
14.	Kraft Television Theatre	NBC	37.0
15.	The Toast of the Town	CBS	36.5

1951/52

1.	Arthur Godfrey's Talent Scouts	CBS	53.8
2.	Texaco Star Theater	NBC	52.0
3.	I Love Lucy	CBS	50.9
4.	The Red Skelton Show	NBC	50.2
5.	The Colgate Comedy Hour	NBC	45.3

6.	Arthur Godfrey and His Friends	CBS	43.3
7.	Fireside Theatre	NBC	43.1
8.	Your Show of Shows	NBC	43.0
9.	The Jack Benny Show	CBS	42.8
10.	You Bet Your Life	NBC	42.1
11.	Mama	CBS	41.3
12.	Philco TV Playhouse	NBC	40.4
13.	Amos 'n' Andy	CBS	38.9
14.	Gangbusters	NBC	38.7
15.	Big Town	CBS	38.5

1952/53

1.	I Love Lucy	CBS	67.3
2.	Arthur Godfrey's Talent Scouts	CBS	54.7
3.	Arthur Godfrey and His Friends	CBS	47.1
4.	Dragnet	NBC	46.8
5.	Texaco Star Theater	NBC	46.7
6.	The Buick Circus Hour	NBC	46.0
7.	The Colgate Comedy Hour	NBC	44.3
8.	Gangbusters	NBC	42.4
9.	You Bet Your Life	NBC	41.6
10.	Fireside Theatre	NBC	40.6
11.	The Red Buttons Show	CBS	40.2
12.	The Jack Benny Show	CBS	39.0
13.	Life with Luigi	CBS	38.5
14.	Pabst Blue Ribbon Bouts	CBS	37.9
15.	Goodyear TV Playhouse	NBC	37.8

1953/54

1.	I Love Lucy	CBS	58.8
2.	Dragnet	NBC	53.2
3.	Arthur Godfrey's Talent Scouts	CBS	43.6
	You Bet Your Life	NBC	43.6
5.	The Chevy Show (Bob Hope)	NBC	41.4
6.	The Milton Berle Show	NBC	40.2
7.	Arthur Godfrey and His Friends	CBS	38.9
8.	The Ford Show	NBC	38.8
9.	The Jackie Gleason Show	CBS	38.1
10.	Fireside Theatre	NBC	36.4
11.	The Colgate Comedy Hour	NBC	36.2
	This Is Your Life	NBC	36.2
13.	The Red Buttons Show	CBS	35.3
14.	The Life of Riley	NBC	35.0
15.	Our Miss Brooks	CBS	34.2

1954/55

1.	I Love Lucy	CBS	49.3
2.	The Jackie Gleason Show	CBS	42.4
3.	Dragnet	NBC	42.1
4.	You Bet Your Life	NBC	41.0
5.	The Toast of the Town	CBS	39.6
6.	Disneyland	ABC	39.1
7.	The Chevy Show (Bob Hope)	NBC	38.5
8.	The Jack Benny Show	CBS	38.3
9.	The Martha Raye Show	NBC	35.6
10.	The George Gobel Show	NBC	35.2
11.	Ford Theater	NBC	34.9
12.	December Bride	CBS	34.7
13.	Buick-Berle Show	NBC	34.6

14.	This Is Your Life	NBC	34.5
15.	I've Got a Secret	CBS	34.0

1955/56

1.	The $64,000 Question	CBS	47.5
2.	I Love Lucy	CBS	46.1
3.	The Ed Sullivan Show	CBS	39.5
4.	Disneyland	ABC	37.4
5.	The Jack Benny Show	CBS	37.2
6.	December Bride	CBS	37.0
7.	You Bet Your Life	NBC	35.4
8.	Dragnet	NBC	35.0
9.	The Millionaire	CBS	33.8
10.	I've Got a Secret	CBS	33.5
11.	General Electric Theater	CBS	32.9
12.	Private Secretary	CBS	32.4
	Ford Theater	NBC	32.4
14.	The Red Skelton Show	CBS	32.3
15.	The George Gobel Show	NBC	31.9

1956/57

1.	I Love Lucy	CBS	43.7
2.	The Ed Sullivan Show	CBS	38.4
3.	General Electric Theater	CBS	36.9
4.	The $64,000 Question	CBS	36.4
5.	December Bride	CBS	35.2
6.	Alfred Hitchcock Presents	CBS	33.9
7.	I've Got a Secret	CBS	32.7
	Gunsmoke	CBS	32.7
9.	The Perry Como Show	NBC	32.6
10.	The Jack Benny Show	CBS	32.3
11.	Dragnet	NBC	32.1
12.	Arthur Godfrey's Talent Scouts	CBS	31.9
13.	The Millionaire	CBS	31.8
	Disneyland	ABC	31.8
15.	The Red Skelton Show	CBS	31.4

1957/58

1.	Gunsmoke	CBS	43.1
2.	The Danny Thomas Show	CBS	35.3
3.	Tales of Wells Fargo	NBC	35.2
4.	Have Gun Will Travel	CBS	33.7
5.	I've Got a Secret	CBS	33.4
6.	The Life and Legend of Wyatt Earp	ABC	32.6
7.	General Electric Theater	CBS	31.5
8.	The Restless Gun	NBC	31.4
9.	December Bride	CBS	30.7
10.	You Bet Your Life	NBC	30.6
11.	The Perry Como Show	NBC	30.5
12.	Alfred Hitchcock Presents	CBS	30.3
	Cheyenne	ABC	30.3
14.	The Ford Show	NBC	29.7
15.	The Red Skelton Show	CBS	28.9
16.	The Gale Storm Show	CBS	28.8
17.	The Millionaire	CBS	28.5
18.	The Lineup	CBS	28.4
19.	This is Your life	NBC	28.1
	The $64,000 Question	CBS	28.1

1958/59

1.	Gunsmoke	CBS	39.6
2.	Wagon Train	NBC	36.1
3.	Have Gun Will Travel	CBS	34.3
4.	The Rifleman	ABC	33.1
5.	The Danny Thomas Show	CBS	32.8
6.	Maverick	ABC	30.4
7.	Tales of Wells Fargo	NBC	30.2
8.	The Real McCoys	ABC	30.1
9.	I've Got a Secret	CBS	29.8
10.	The Life and Legend of Wyatt Earp	ABC	29.1
11.	The Price Is Right	NBC	28.6
12.	The Red Skelton Show	CBS	28.5
13.	Zane Grey Theater	CBS	28.3
	Father Knows Best	CBS	28.3
15.	The Texan	CBS	28.2
16.	Wanted: Dead or Alive	CBS	28.0
	Peter Gunn	NBC	28.0
18.	Cheyenne	ABC	27.9
19.	Perry Mason	CBS	27.5
20.	The Ford Story	NBC	27.2

1959/60

1.	Gunsmoke	CBS	40.3
2.	Wagon Train	NBC	38.4
3.	Have Gun Will Travel	CBS	34.7
4.	The Danny Thomas Show	CBS	31.1
5.	The Red Skelton Show	CBS	30.8
6.	Father Knows Best	CBS	29.7
	77 Sunset Strip	ABC	29.7
8.	The Price Is Right	NBC	29.2
9.	Wanted: Dead or Alive	CBS	28.7
10.	Perry Mason	CBS	28.3
11.	The Real McCoys	ABC	28.2
12.	The Ed Sullivan Show	CBS	28.0
13.	The Bing Crosby Show	ABC	27.7
14.	The Rifleman	ABC	27.5
15.	The Ford Show	NBC	27.4
16.	The Lawman	ABC	26.2
17.	Dennis the Menace	CBS	26.0
18.	Cheyenne	ABC	25.9
19.	Rawhide	CBS	25.8
20.	Maverick	ABC	25.2

1960/61

1.	Gunsmoke	CBS	37.3
2.	Wagon Train	NBC	34.2
3.	Have Gun Will Travel	CBS	30.9
4.	The Andy Griffith Show	CBS	27.8
5.	The Real McCoy	ABC	27.7
6.	Rawhide	CBS	27.5
7.	Candid Camera	CBS	27.3
8.	The Untouchables	ABC	27.0
	The Price Is Right	NBC	27.0
10.	The Jack Benny Show	CBS	26.2
11.	Dennis the Menace	CBS	26.1
12.	The Danny Thomas Show	CBS	25.9
13.	My Three Sons	ABC	25.8
	77 Sunset Strip	ABC	25.8

15.	The Ed Sullivan Show	CBS	25.0
16.	Perry Mason	CBS	24.9
17.	Bonanza	NBC	24.8
18.	The Flintstones	ABC	24.3
19.	The Red Skelton Show	CBS	24.0
20.	Alfred Hitchcock Presents	CBS	23.8

1961/62

1.	Wagon Train	NBC	32.1
2.	Bonanza	NBC	30.0
3.	Gunsmoke	CBS	28.3
4.	Hazel	NBC	27.7
5.	Perry Mason	CBS	27.3
6.	The Red Skelton Show	CBS	27.1
7.	The Andy Griffith Show	CBS	27.0
8.	The Danny Thomas Show	CBS	26.1
9.	Dr. Kildare	NBC	25.6
10.	Candid Camera	CBS	25.5
11.	My Three Sons	ABC	24.7
12.	The Garry Moore Show	CBS	24.6
13.	Rawhide	CBS	24.5
14.	The Real McCoys	ABC	24.2
15.	Lassie	CBS	24.0
	Sing Along With Mitch	NBC	24.0
17.	Dennis the Menace	CBS	23.8
	Gunsmoke	CBS	23.8
19.	Ben Casey	ABC	23.7
20.	The Ed Sullivan Show	CBS	23.5

1962/63

1.	The Beverly Hillbillies	CBS	36.0
2.	Candid Camera	CBS	31.1
	The Red Skelton Show	CBS	31.1
4.	Bonanza	NBC	29.8
	The Lucy Show	CBS	29.8
6.	The Andy Griffith Show	CBS	29.7
7.	Ben Casey	ABC	28.7
	The Danny Thomas Show	CBS	28.7
9.	The Dick Van Dyke Show	CBS	27.1
10.	Gunsmoke	CBS	27.0
11.	Dr. Kildare	NBC	26.2
	The Jack Benny Show	CBS	26.2
13.	What's My Line	CBS	25.5
14.	The Ed Sullivan Show	CBS	25.3
15.	Hazel	NBC	25.1
16.	I've Got a Secret	CBS	24.9
17.	The Jackie Gleason Show	CBS	24.1
18.	The Defenders	CBS	23.9
19.	The Garry Moore Show	CBS	23.3
	To Tell the Truth	CBS	23.3

1963/64

1.	The Beverly Hillbillies	CBS	39.1
2.	Bonanza	NBC	36.9
3.	The Dick Van Dyke Show	CBS	33.3
4.	Petticoat Junction	CBS	30.3
5.	The Andy Griffith Show	CBS	29.4
6.	The Lucy Show	CBS	28.1
7.	Candid Camera	CBS	27.7
8.	The Ed Sullivan Show	CBS	27.5

9.	The Danny Thomas Show	CBS	26.7
10.	My Favorite Martian	CBS	26.3
11.	The Red Skelton Show	CBS	25.7
12.	I've Got a Secret	CBS	25.0
	Lassie	CBS	25.0
	The Jack Benny Show	CBS	25.0
15.	The Jackie Gleason Show	CBS	24.6
16.	The Donna Reed Show	ABC	24.5
17.	The Virginian	NBC	24.0
18.	The Patty Duke Show	ABC	23.9
19.	Dr. Kildare	NBC	23.6
20.	Gunsmoke	CBS	23.5

1964/65

1.	Bonanza	NBC	36.3
2.	Bewitched	ABC	31.0
3.	Gomer Pyle, U.S.M.C.	CBS	30.7
4.	The Andy Griffith Show	CBS	28.3
5.	The Fugitive	ABC	27.9
6.	The Red Skelton Hour	CBS	27.4
7.	The Dick Van Dyke Show	CBS	27.1
8.	The Lucy Show	CBS	26.6
9.	Peyton Place II	ABC	26.4
10.	Combat	ABC	26.1
11.	Walt Disney's Wonderful World of Color	NBC	25.7
12.	The Beverly Hillbillies	CBS	25.6
13.	My Three Sons	ABC	25.5
14.	Branded	NBC	25.3
15.	Petticoat Junction	CBS	25.2
	The Ed Sullivan Show	CBS	25.2
17.	Lassie	CBS	25.1
18.	The Munsters	CBS	24.7
	Gilligan's Island	CBS	24.7
20.	Peyton Place	ABC	24.6

1965/66

1.	Bonanza	NBC	31.8
2.	Gomer Pyle, U.S.M.C.	CBS	27.8
3.	The Lucy Show	CBS	27.7
4.	The Red Skelton Hour	CBS	27.6
5.	Batman	ABC	27.0
6.	The Andy Griffith Show	CBS	26.9
7.	Bewitched	ABC	25.9
	The Beverly Hillbillies	CBS	25.9
9.	Hogan's Heroes	CBS	24.9
10.	Batman	ABC	24.7
11.	Green Acres	CBS	24.6
12.	Get Smart	NBC	24.5
13.	The Man from U.N.C.L.E.	NBC	24.0
14.	Daktari	CBS	23.9
15.	My Three Sons	CBS	23.8
16.	The Dick Van Dyke Show	CBS	23.6
17.	Walt Disney's Wonderful World of Color	NBC	23.2
	The Ed Sullivan Show	CBS	23.2
19.	The Lawrence Welk Show	ABC	22.4
	I've Got a Secret	CBS	22.4

1966/67

1.	Bonanza	NBC	29.1
2.	The Red Skelton Hour	CBS	28.2
3.	The Andy Griffith Hour	CBS	27.4
4.	The Lucy Show	CBS	26.2
5.	The Jackie Gleason Show	CBS	25.3
6.	Green Acres	CBS	24.6
7.	Daktari	CBS	23.4
	Bewitched	ABC	23.4
	The Beverly Hillbillies	CBS	23.4
10.	Gomer Pyle, U.S.M.C.	CBS	22.8
	The Virginian	NBC	22.8
	The Lawrence Welk Show	ABC	22.8
	The Ed Sullivan Show	CBS	22.8
14.	The Dean Martin Show	NBC	22.6
	Family Affair	CBS	22.6
16.	The Smothers Brothers Comedy Hour	CBS	22.2
17.	Friday Night Movies	CBS	21.8
	Hogan's Heroes	CBS	21.8
19.	Walt Disney's Wonderful World of Color	NBC	21.5
20.	Saturday Night at the Movies	NBC	21.4

1967/68

1.	The Andy Griffith Show	CBS	27.6
2.	The Lucy Show	CBS	27.0
3.	Gomer Pyle, U.S.M.C.	CBS	25.6
4.	Gunsmoke	CBS	25.5
	Family Affair	CBS	25.5
	Bonanza	NBC	25.5
7.	The Red Skelton Show	CBS	25.3
8.	The Dean Martin Show	NBC	24.8
9.	The Jackie Gleason Show	CBS	23.9
10.	Saturday Night at the Movies	NBC	23.6
11.	Bewitched	ABC	23.5
12.	The Beverly Hillbillies	CBS	23.3
13.	The Ed Sullivan Show	CBS	23.2
14.	The Virginian	NBC	22.9
15.	Friday Night Movie	CBS	22.8
	Green Acres	CBS	22.8
17.	The Lawrence Welk Show	ABC	21.9
18.	The Smothers Brothers Comedy Hour	CBS	21.7
19.	Gentle Ben	CBS	21.5
20.	Tuesday Night at the Movies	NBC	21.4

1968/69

1.	Rowan & Martin's Laugh-In	NBC	31.8
2.	Gomer Pyle, U.S.M.C.	CBS	27.2
3.	Bonanza	NBC	26.6
4.	Mayberry R.F.D.	CBS	25.4
5.	Family Affair	CBS	25.2
6.	Gunsmoke	CBS	24.9
7.	Julia	NBC	24.6
8.	The Dean Martin Show	NBC	24.1
9.	Here's Lucy	CBS	23.8
10.	The Beverly Hillbillies	CBS	23.5
11.	Mission: Impossible	CBS	23.3
	Bewitched	ABC	23.3

The Red Skelton Hour	CBS	23.3
14. My Three Sons	CBS	22.8
15. The Glen Campbell Goodtime Hour	CBS	22.5
16. Ironside	NBC	22.3
17. The Virginian	NBC	21.8
18. The F.B.I.	ABC	21.7
19. Green Acres	CBS	21.6
20. Dragnet	NBC	21.4

1969/70

1. Rowan & Martin's Laugh-In	NBC	26.3
2. Gunsmoke	CBS	25.9
3. Bonanza	NBC	24.8
4. Mayberry R.F.D.	CBS	24.4
5. Family Affair	CBS	24.2
6. Here's Lucy	CBS	23.9
7. The Red Skelton Hour	CBS	23.8
8. Marcus Welby, M.D.	ABC	23.7
9. Walt Disney's Wonderful World of Color	NBC	23.6
10. The Doris Day Show	CBS	22.8
11. The Bill Cosby Show	NBC	22.7
12. The Jim Nabors Hours	CBS	22.4
13. The Carol Burnett Show	CBS	22.1
14. The Dean Martin Show	NBC	21.9
15. My Three Sons	CBS	21.8
Ironside	NBC	21.8
The Johnny Cash Show	ABC	21.8
18. The Beverly Hillbillies	CBS	21.7
19. Hawaii Five-O	CBS	21.1
20. The Glen Campbell Goodtime Hour	CBS	21.0
Hee Haw	CBS	21.0

1970/71

1. Marcus Welby, M.D.	ABC	29.6
2. The Flip Wilson Show	NBC	27.9
3. Here's Lucy	CBS	26.1
4. Ironside	NBC	25.7
5. Gunsmoke	CBS	25.5
6. ABC Movie of the Week	ABC	25.1
7. Hawaii Five-O	CBS	25.0
8. Medical Center	CBS	24.5
9. Bonanza	NBC	23.9
10. The F.B.I.	ABC	23.0
11. Mod Squad	ABC	22.7
12. Adam-12	NBC	22.6
13. Rowan & Martin's Laugh-In	NBC	22.4
The Wonderful World of Disney	NBC	22.4
15. Mayberry R.F.D.	CBS	22.3
16. Hee Haw	CBS	21.4
17. Mannix	CBS	21.3
18. The Men from Shiloh	NBC	21.2
19. My Three Sons	CBS	20.8
20. The Doris Day Show	CBS	20.7

1971/72

1. All in the Family	CBS	34.0
2. The Flip Wilson Show	NBC	28.2
3. Marcus Welby, M.D.	ABC	27.8
4. Gunsmoke	CBS	26.0

5. ABC Movie of the Week	ABC	25.6
6. Sanford & Son	NBC	25.2
7. Mannix	CBS	24.8
8. Funny Face	CBS	23.9
Adam 12	NBC	23.9
10. The Mary Tyler Moore Show	CBS	23.7
Here's Lucy	CBS	23.7
12. Hawaii Five-O	CBS	23.6
13. Medical Center	CBS	23.5
14. The NBC Mystery Movie	NBC	23.2
15. Ironside	NBC	23.0
16. The Partridge Family	ABC	22.6
17. The F.B.I.	ABC	22.4
18. The New Dick Van Dyke Show	CBS	22.2
19. The Wonderful World of Disney	NBC	22.0
20. Bonanza	NBC	21.9

1972/73

1. All in the Family	CBS	33.3
2. Sanford & Son	NBC	27.6
3. Hawaii Five-O	CBS	25.2
4. Maude	CBS	24.7
5. Bridget Loves Bernie	CBS	24.2
Sunday Mystery Movie	NBC	24.2
7. The Mary Tyler Moore Show	CBS	23.6
Gunsmoke	CBS	23.6
9. The Wonderful World of Disney	NBC	23.5
10. Ironside	NBC	23.4
11. Adam 12	NBC	23.3
12. The Flip Wilson Show	NBC	23.1
13. Marcus Welby, M.D.	ABC	22.9
14. Cannon	CBS	22.4
15. Here's Lucy	CBS	21.9
16. The Bob Newhart Show	CBS	21.8
17. Tuesday Movie of the Week	ABC	21.5
18. ABC NFL Football	ABC	21.0
19. The Partridge Family	ABC	20.6
The Waltons	CBS	20.6

1973/74

1. All in the Family	CBS	31.2
2. The Waltons	CBS	28.1
3. Sanford & Son	NBC	27.5
4. M*A*S*H	CBS	25.7
5. Hawaii Five-O	CBS	24.0
6. Maude	CBS	23.5
7. Kojak	CBS	23.3
The Sonny and Cher Hour	CBS	23.3
9. The Mary Tyler Moore Show	CBS	23.1
Cannon	CBS	23.1
11. The Six Million Dollar Man	ABC	22.7
12. The Bob Newhart Show	CBS	22.3
The Wonderful World of Disney	NBC	22.3
14. The NBC Sunday Mystery Movie	NBC	22.2
15. Gunsmoke	CBS	22.1
16. Happy Days	ABC	21.4
Barnaby Jones	CBS	21.4
19. ABC Monday Night Football	ABC	21.2
CBS Friday Night Movie	CBS	21.2

1974/75

1.	All in the Family	CBS	30.2
2.	Sanford & Son	NBC	29.6
3.	Chico and The Man	NBC	28.5
4.	The Jeffersons	CBS	27.6
5.	M*A*S*H	CBS	27.4
6.	Rhoda	CBS	26.3
	Good Times	CBS	26.3
8.	The Waltons	CBS	25.5
9.	Maude	CBS	24.9
10.	Hawaii Five-O	CBS	24.8
11.	The Mary Tyler Moore Show	CBS	24.0
12.	The Rockford Files	NBC	23.7
13.	Little House on the Prairie	NBC	23.5
14.	Kojak	CBS	23.3
15.	Police Woman	NBC	22.8
16.	S.W.A.T.	ABC	22.6
17.	The Bob Newhart Show	CBS	22.4
18.	The Wonderful World of Disney	NBC	22.0
	The Rookies	ABC	22.0
20.	Mannix	CBS	21.6
	Cannon	CBS	21.6

1975/76

1.	All in the Family	CBS	30.1
2.	Rich Man, Poor Man	ABC	28.0
3.	Laverne & Shirley	ABC	27.5
4.	Maude	CBS	25.0
5.	The Bionic Woman	ABC	24.9
6.	Phyllis	CBS	24.5
7.	Sanford & Son	NBC	24.4
	Rhoda	CBS	24.4
9.	The Six Million Dollar Man	ABC	24.3
10.	ABC Monday Night Movie	ABC	24.2
11.	Happy Days	ABC	23.9
12.	One Day at a Time	CBS	23.1
13.	ABC Sunday Night Movie	ABC	23.0
14.	The Waltons	CBS	22.9
	M*A*S*H	CBS	22.9
16.	Starsky and Hutch	ABC	22.5
	Good Heavens	ABC	22.5
18.	Welcome Back, Kotter	ABC	22.1
19.	The Mary Tyler Moore Show	CBS	21.9
20.	Kojak	CBS	21.8

1976/77

1.	Happy Days	ABC	31.5
2.	Laverne & Shirley	ABC	30.9
3.	ABC Monday Night Movie	ABC	26.0
4.	M*A*S*H	CBS	25.9
5.	Charlie's Angels	ABC	25.8
6.	The Big Event	NBC	24.4
7.	The Six Million Dollar Man	ABC	24.2
8.	ABC Sunday Night Movie	ABC	23.4
	Baretta	ABC	23.4
	One Day at a Time	CBS	23.4
11.	Three's Company	ABC	23.1
12.	All in the Family	CBS	22.9
13.	Welcome Back, Kotter	ABC	22.7
14.	The Bionic Woman	ABC	22.4

15.	The Waltons	CBS	22.3
	Little House on the Prairie	NBC	22.3
17.	Barney Miller	ABC	22.2
18.	60 Minutes	CBS	21.9
	Hawaii Five-O	CBS	21.9
20.	NBC Monday Night Movie	NBC	21.8

1977/78

1.	Laverne & Shirley	ABC	31.6
2.	Happy Days	ABC	31.4
3.	Three's Company	ABC	28.3
4.	60 Minutes	CBS	24.4
	Charlie's Angels	ABC	24.4
	All in the Family	CBS	24.4
7.	Little House on the Prairie	NBC	24.1
8.	Alice	CBS	23.3
	M*A*S*H	CBS	23.3
10.	One Day at a Time	CBS	23.0
11.	How the West Was Won	ABC	22.5
12.	Eight is Enough	ABC	22.2
13.	Soap	ABC	22.0
14.	The Love Boat	ABC	21.9
15.	NBC Monday Night Movie	NBC	21.7
16.	Monday Night Football	ABC	21.5
17.	Fantasy Island	ABC	21.4
	Barney Miller	ABC	21.4
19.	The Amazing Spider-Man	CBS	21.2
	Project U.F.O.	NBC	21.2

1978/79

1.	Laverne & Shirley	ABC	30.5
2.	Three's Company	ABC	30.3
3.	Mork & Mindy	ABC	28.6
	Happy Days	ABC	28.6
5.	Angie	ABC	26.7
6.	60 Minutes	CBS	25.5
7.	M*A*S*H	CBS	25.4
8.	The Ropers	ABC	25.2
9.	All in the Family	CBS	24.9
	Taxi	ABC	24.9
11.	Eight Is Enough	ABC	24.8
12.	Charlie's Angels	ABC	24.4
13.	Alice	CBS	23.2
14.	Little House on the Prairie	NBC	23.1
15.	ABC Sunday Night Movie	ABC	22.6
	Barney Miller	ABC	22.6
17.	The Love Boat	ABC	22.1
18.	One Day at a Time	CBS	21.6
19.	Soap	ABC	21.3
20.	The Dukes of Hazzard	CBS	21.0

1979/80

1.	60 Minutes	CBS	28.4
2.	Three's Company	ABC	26.3
3.	That's Incredible	ABC	25.8
4.	Alice	CBS	25.3
	M*A*S*H	CBS	25.3
	Dallas	CBS	25.3
7.	Flo	CBS	24.4
8.	The Jeffersons	CBS	24.3

9.	The Dukes of Hazzard	CBS	24.1
10.	One Day at a Time	CBS	23.0
11.	Archie Bunker's Place	CBS	22.9
12.	Eight Is Enough	ABC	22.8
13.	Taxi	ABC	22.4
14.	House Calls	CBS	22.1
15.	Real People	NBC	21.8
	Little House on the Prairie	NBC	21.8
17.	Happy Days	ABC	21.7
18.	Chips	NBC	21.5
19.	Trapper John, M.D.	CBS	21.2
20.	Charlie's Angels	ABC	20.9

1980/81

1.	Dallas	CBS	34.5
2.	The Dukes of Hazzard	CBS	27.3
3.	60 Minutes	CBS	27.0
4.	M*A*S*H	CBS	25.7
5.	The Love Boat	ABC	24.3
6.	The Jeffersons	CBS	23.5
7.	Alice	CBS	22.9
8.	House Calls	CBS	22.4
	Three's Company	ABC	22.4
10.	Little House on the Prairie	NBC	22.1
11.	One Day at a Time	CBS	22.0
12.	Real People	NBC	21.5
13.	Archie Bunker's Place	CBS	21.4
14.	Magnum, P.I.	CBS	21.0
15.	Happy Days	ABC	20.8
	Too Close for Comfort	ABC	20.8
17.	Fantasy Island	ABC	20.7
	Trapper John, M.D.	CBS	20.7
	Diff'rent Strokes	NBC	20.7
20.	Monday Night Football	ABC	20.6
	Laverne & Shirley	ABC	20.6

1981/82

1.	Dallas	CBS	28.4
2.	60 Minutes	CBS	27.7
3.	The Jeffersons	CBS	23.4
4.	Joanie Loves Chachi	ABC	23.3*
	Three's Company	ABC	23.3
6.	Alice	CBS	22.7
7.	The Dukes of Hazzard	CBS	22.6
	Too Close for Comfort	ABC	22.6
9.	ABC Monday Movie	ABC	22.5
10.	M*A*S*H	CBS	22.3
11.	One Day at a Time	CBS	22.0
12.	NFL Monday Football	ABC	21.8
13.	Archie Bunker's Place	CBS	21.6
14.	Falcon Crest	CBS	21.4
15.	The Love Boat	ABC	21.2
16.	Hart to Hart	ABC	21.1
	Trapper John, M.D.	CBS	21.1
18.	Magnum, P.I.	CBS	20.9
19.	Happy Days	ABC	20.6
20.	Dynasty	ABC	20.2

1982/83

1.	60 Minutes	CBS	25.5
2.	Dallas	CBS	24.6
3.	M*A*S*H	CBS	22.6
	Magnum, P.I.	CBS	22.6
5.	Dynasty	ABC	22.4
6.	Three's Company	ABC	21.2
7.	Simon & Simon	CBS	21.0
8.	Falcon Crest	CBS	20.7
9.	The Love Boat	ABC	20.3
10.	The A-Team	NBC	20.1
	NFL Monday Night Football	ABC	20.1
12.	The Jeffersons	CBS	20.0
	The Bob Newhart Show	CBS	20.0
14.	The Fall Guy	ABC	19.4
	The Mississippi	CBS	19.4
16.	Nine to Five	ABC	19.3
17.	One Day at a Time	ABC	19.1
18.	Hart to Hart	ABC	18.9
19.	Gloria	CBS	18.7
	Trapper John, M.D.	CBS	18.7
	Goodnight, Beantown	CBS	18.7

1983/84

1.	Dallas	CBS	25.7
2.	60 Minutes	CBS	24.2
3.	Dynasty	ABC	24.1
4.	The A Team	NBC	24.0
5.	Simon & Simon	CBS	23.8
6.	Magnum, P.I.	CBS	22.4
7.	Falcon Crest	CBS	22.0
8.	Kate & Allie	CBS	21.9
9.	Hotel	ABC	21.1
10.	Cagney & Lacey	CBS	20.9
11.	Knots Landing	CBS	20.8
12.	ABC Sunday Movie	ABC	20.4
	ABC Monday Movie	ABC	20.4
14.	TV's Bloopers & Practical Jokes	NBC	20.3
15.	Aftermash	CBS	20.1
16.	The Fall Guy	ABC	19.9
17.	The Love Boat	ABC	19.0
18.	Riptide	NBC	18.8
19.	The Jeffersons	CBS	18.6
20.	Scarecrow & Mrs. King	CBS	18.3

*Limited exposure: five airings or less.

3/TOP-RATED MOVIES ON TV

MOVIES AND TV are natural enemies, right? Well, not exactly. Yes, it has been repeatedly argued that the birth of television almost caused the death of movies, and yes, some movie moguls in the 1950s were so anxious about TV's growing success that they actually forbade their stars to appear on the tube. The very word *television* could be uttered on the silver screen not at all or only in derision. ("Rehearse for television? Television *is* a rehearsal!" quips George Sanders in *All About Eve*.) But for years now, the studios have depended upon the networks for whopping profits from selling films to the tube, and the webs have similarly been relying on movies for blockbuster ratings. Movies and TV—once bitter enemies—are now willing, and at times even friendly, collaborators.

When did the truce begin? On Sept. 23, 1961, when the first prime time weekly film series on television, NBC's *Saturday Night at the Movies*, made its debut with *How to Marry a Millionaire*, an ironic film presentation, perhaps, since that 1953 film—lavishly shot in Cinemascope with superstars Marilyn Monroe, Betty Grable and Lauren Bacall—was originally made to lure viewers *away* from their TV sets and back into the movie house.

Of course, there had been movies on television prior to 1961, but the films shown on TV during the late 1940s and throughout the 1950s were seldom recent releases or big hits. The major studios simply were not willing to sell their best products to the small screen, so that in its infancy TV had to depend upon independent producers and small studios like Monogram and Republic for its film fare.

In 1955 ABC had presented a package of 100 films from British filmmaker J. Arthur Rank, and in 1956 RKO sold more than 700 of its films to C & C Super Corp., which in turn, leased them to the networks. But none of these aired films had been theatrically released after 1948: Hollywood still held back its recent goods.

In 1960, however, NBC negotiated with 20th Century Fox and purchased broadcast rights to 30 feature films (vintage 1951 through 1955) for the 1961/62 season: thus, *Saturday Night at the Movies* was born.

The show proved so successful* that in 1962 ABC followed with its own movie series, and in 1963 NBC even added another film series, *Monday Night at the Movies*, to its prime time schedule. CBS, the third big network, began purchasing rights to movies in December 1964, so that by the end of the 1960s, as many as nine movies a week could be seen on national television.

Movies were so dominant during those years that a 1968 *Variety* headline nervously asked "Can TV Conquer the Movie Menace?" According to the article, the networks, in their reckless race for rating points, had turned themselves into "neighborhood theatres seven nights a week.... Are motion pictures destroying the television business? Fifteen years ago the question went the other way around."

Here's a chart that records the growing popularity of movies on TV during the 1960s boom:

	Saturday Night at the Movies (NBC)		Sunday Night at the Movies (ABC)	
	Rating	Share	Rating	Share
1962/63	19.3	32	16.2	24
1963/64	19.2	32	18.8	31
1964/65	21.0	37	19.0	32
1965/66	21.0	36	19.0	32
1966/67	21.6	37	20.7	35
1967/68	24.3	42	19.5	33

The success of movies on television gave birth to a new baby: the made-for-TV movie. *See How They Run*, starring John Forsythe and Senta Berger, was aired Oct. 7, 1964 and hailed as the first movie made especially for television. *The Killers*—with Lee Marvin, Angie Dickinson and Ronald Reagan in his last screen role—was supposed to be the first made-for-TV flick, but in the aftermath of the Kennedy assassination, it was deemed too violent for television and, hence, was released theatrically.

By 1969, made-for-TV movies were becoming so successful that ABC had an entire weekly series, *ABC Movie of the Week*, and the popularity, as well as the prestige, of made-for-TV movies have been increasing ever since. In recent years, actors of the caliber of Henry Fonda, Peter O'Toole, Marlon Brando and Joanne Woodward have appeared in TV movies. Critics, who once dismissed made-for-TV movies as "formula quickies" or "substandard grade C hackwork," have come to praise TV flicks for courageously tackling subjects that Hollywood films have found too controversial or too "uncommercial"—subjects like rape (*Born Innocent*), homosexuality (*That Certain Summer*), teen-age prostitution (*Little Ladies of the Night*), and nuclear holocaust (*The Day After*).*

Saturday Night at the Movies lasted until 1978, when it was the second longest-lived prime time series on TV. Only Walt Disney had lasted longer.

*Of course, other critics ridicule TV movies exactly because of this penchant for "controversial" issues. The television movie, according to *New York Times* critic John J. O'Connor, is "notorious for its preoccupation with inspirational fluff and disease of the week...."

"You can do things in television, strangely enough, that you can never do in movies," Lee Rich, president of Lorimar, told the *New York Times* in 1979. "We did *Sybil* as a TV movie. I couldn't sell that script as a motion picture. The movie community doesn't believe that kind of stuff will make any money." As Patrick McGilligan wrote in the March 1980 issue of *American Film*: "the television movie sphere is pulsating with experimentation and activity, with recent honors and growing prestige. It is no longer in the shadow of the film industry: it is a richly expending and parallel one."

The success of made-for-TV movies produced a new format in TV programming: the mini-series. The groundbreaking success was *Rich Man, Poor Man* (1975), followed by the blockbuster *Roots* (1977). All eight episodes of thats mash mini-series were among the Top 50 broadcasts of all time, and the show's final episode had the honor of being the highest-rated program in TV history: a 51.1 rating with a 71 share. (This record has since been broken.) These figures, as one *Variety* writer gushed, are "mind-boggling statistics, replete with 'firsts' 'bests,' and 'never befores,' beyond count. . . . In one fell swoop, the mini-series established a standard by which program productivity must be measured, set in motion changes in programming concepts and patterns that will profoundly alter traditional methods, and guaranteed that ABC will win its first primtetime season ever." In fact, *Roots* gave ABC what was then the highest weekly average in TV history: 35.5.

The growing success of made-for-TV movies (or "vidpics" as *Variety* likes to call them) is also reflected in their increasing predominance on the airwaves. A 1979 ABC study, for example, revealed that made-for-TV pictures had risen from 32% to 57% of the total films on TV between the 1975/76 and 1978/79 seasons. Feature films, by contrast, had decreased from 68% to 43%.

What accounts for the diminishing number of theatricals on TV? For one thing, Hollywood during the 1970s was making fewer and fewer films each year, so that the networks had fewer movies to fight over. Censorship concerns—most feature films are too violent and sexy by TV standards—further complicate the move from silver screen to TV tube. Then there are the demographics: studies indicate that the largest audience for movies consists of teenage males between 17 and 19. TV advertisers, on the other hand, want to capture the female 18 to 34 market, since they are the biggest consumers. And the growing popularity of pay TV—particularly services such as HBO, Showtime and Cinemax—has further decreased the value of theatricals on network TV: by the time a theatrical gets aired on prime time network, it has likely had repeated showings on cable. "A prime time showing of a major film has lost the excitement, glamor, and uniqueness it once

had because of paycable saturation," Tony Thomopoulous, president of ABC Entertainment, told *Variety* in 1980.

In reply, the studios have argued that paycable has diminished network share of *all* forms of programming, not just movies, and that one of the reasons why movies are not winning as high ratings as they have in the past is that the three networks tend to play one blockbuster against another during the fevered ratings "sweeps" of November and February. (The most notorious example of such network battles was the evening of Feb. 11, 1979, when CBS opened with the first installment of *Gone with the Wind*, NBC countered with the television premiere of the Oscar-winning *One Flew over the Cuckoo's Nest*, and ABC offered *Elvis*, a three-hour made-for-TV flick. Much to everyone's surprise, the TV movie won the night. As the *New York Times* reported, "if anyone in the entertainment business held lingering doubts about the rise of the television movie, those doubts were forever shattered the night *Elvis* beat Clark Gable and Jack Nicholson.")

Theatricals, in short, no longer automatically capture the high ratings they once did. When the blockbuster *Saturday Night Fever* was aired in 1979, it was expected to chalk up a mid-40s share, but it won only a 26.7 rating and a 38 share. By the fall of 1981, the percentage of theatricals to reach or top a 20 rating (26.9%) almost exactly equaled the percentage of vidpics reaching that mark (26.7%). As *Variety* summed it up, "vidpics have virtually equalled the ratings muscle of theatricals"—another reason why the number of theatricals on television has decreased in recent years.*

And then, of course, there's money: theatricals are much more expensive than made-for-TV films. Made-for-TV flicks are "so reasonably priced compared to theatricals," one top-level network executive has confessed, "you have to wonder why we're in theatricals at all."

How much *does* a studio charge a network to air a film? For its first historic season of *Saturday Night at the Movies*, NBC paid 20th Century Fox $5.5 million for 30 films, or approximately $180,000 per feature, and needless to say, prices have been skyrocketing ever since. In 1977 the average price per play of a feature film on TV was $500,000; in 1979, $1.2 million. The largest fee ever paid for a single film in the history of TV was the $35 million CBS forked over to MGM for 20 showings in 20 years of *Gone with the Wind*. On per-run basis, the richest deal ever made was the $25–$26 million CBS reportedly paid to 20th Century Fox for 3 runs of *Star Wars*, then the top-grossing film of all time. ABC reportedly paid $25 million for the air rights to *Jaws I* and *Jaws II*. NBC was willing to pay $21.5 million to air *The Sound of Music* 20 times in 22

---

*Theatricals, however, still win higher ratings in reruns. According to a 1980 survey conducted by Warner Brothers executive Ed Bleir, between 1975 and 1980, the networks played 567 theatricals for the first time and 516 repeats. The figures for vidpics, by comparison, were 607 first runs and only 262 reruns. The theatrical reruns averaged a 26 share, while TV movie repeats only earned an average 21 share (*Variety*, Dec. 24, 1980).

years. And CBS purchased 4 airings of *Rocky II* with an additional broadcast of *Rocky I* for $20 million.

Networks usually purchase films in packages: in 1980, for example, ABC obtained air rights from Columbia Pictures for 11 films (including *Kramer vs. Kramer, Chapter Two, California Suite* and *Midnight Express*) for a minimum of $60 million. A network will sometimes buy the TV rights to a film before it has even been made—a risky business, to be sure. CBS, for example, paid $6.5 million for three runs of *Butch Cassidy and the Sundance Kid: The Early Years* while that film was still in production. The movie was a box office flop when it was released, and CBS would not have had to pay such a hefty sum if it had waited.

On the other hand, CBS—in another preproduction deal—gave only $2 million for the TV rights to *Foul Play* because the movie had no superstars. The film, however, became one of the big hits of 1978, and many industry experts estimate that CBS would have had to pay at least three times the money if it had bought the film after its release. (Today, when studios presell a film to TV, an escalation clause is often written into the contract, providing extra money should the film be a substantial box office hit.)

Movies have obviously been quite good at winning big ratings for the networks, but are they very profitable given their high costs? Not particularly. The profit potential of an average two-hour movie aired during the 1978/79 season was $200,000 to $400,000, or $50,000 to $100,000 per half hour. By comparison, and episode of a successful series like *Three's Company* could generate a profit of $330,000 during the fall/winter and $430,000 during summer reruns.

The networks do make money from movies in another way: in recent years Hollywood has turned to TV as one of the best ways to advertise its current crop of films. Industry statistics show investments in TV time by film studios jumped more than 200% from 1975 to 1979. "Filmmakers are now utilizing their one-time archenemy, television, to sell their own product," says Arthur Trudeau Jr., an executive of the Television Bureau of Advertising.

In 1973, when Warner Brothers launched its successful reissue of *Billy Jack* with a TV campaign, television accounted for a mere 15% of the total media expenditure. By comparison, when Warner spent $55.7 million to promote its 14 Christmas releases in 1979, $20 million of that sum, or 36%, was spent on TV. In fact, statistics from *Broadcast Advertisers Reports* show a record $175 million was spent to type 452 films in 1979. And by 1980, motion pictures made it into the top 20 network ad categories for the first time, coming in 16th place overall.

What accounts for this dramatic rise in Hollywood's dependence on TV advertising? One undeniable factor is the change in distribution patterns. In previous decades a film would be distributed on a strictly timed multistep schedule—first in certain big cities, then in certain towns, and then across the nation. Today, a film is often released simultaneously in theaters throughout the entire country: hence, national TV advertising becomes attractive.

Local TV stations can choose from more thant 20,000 feature films to show on their film series. Which pictures are the most popular? In 1977 *TV Guide* asked program directors across the nation to name the 10 most popular, most often shown movies in their market. The results:

1. *Casablanca* (1943)
2. *King Kong* (1933)
3. *The Magnificant Seven* (1960)
4. *The Maltese Falcon* (1941)
5. *The Adventures of Robin Hood* (1938)
6. *The African Queen* (1951)
7. *The Birds* (1963)
8. *Citizen Kane* (1941)
9. *Miracle on 34th Street* (1941)
10. *Girls! Girls! Girls!* (1962)
11. *King Solomon's Mines* (1950)
12. *The Treasure of the Sierra Madre* (1948)
13. *The War of the Worlds* (1953)

The same survey revealed the most popular *series* of movies to be the Sherlock Holmes pictures starring Basil Rathbone and Nigel Bruce.

What are the highest-rated films on TV? The following chart lists the top-rated movies on television between September 1961 and September 1984. This list is selected from *Variety*'s much longer and more comprehensive compilation that ranks every movie that has earned a national Nielsen rating of 24.0 or better.

Variety's list is composed of 425 individual titles: 252 theatricals and 173 made-for-TVs. For the first seven years, the big movies on TV were all theatricals, but in recent years, as mentioned, several vidpics have enjoyed enormous success.

The Wizard of Oz is cited 15 times on *Variety*'s list, a record. *The Homecoming* (the source of *The Waltons* series), with five appearances on the list, holds the repeat record for made-for-TVs.

When reading this chart, please keep in mind that *Variety* does *not* consider mini-series to be made-for-TV films: hence, no mini-series is included below.

HIGHEST-RATED FILMS ON TV

Rank	Title	Web	Day	Date	Rtg.	Share
1.	*Gone with the Wind* —Part 1	NBC	Sun	11/7/76	47.7	65
2.	*Gone with the Wind* —Part 2	NBC	Mon	11/8/76	47.4	64
3. *	*The Day After*	ABC	Sun	11/20/83	46.0	62
4.	*Airport*	ABC	Sun	11/11/73	42.3	63
	Love Story	ABC	Sun	10/1/72	42.3	62
6.	*The Godfather* —Part 2	NBC	Mon	11/18/74	39.4	57
7.	*Jaws*	ABC	Sun	11/4/79	39.1	57
8.	*Poseidon Adventure*	ABC	Sun	10/27/74	39.0	62
9.	*True Grit*	ABC	Sun	11/12/72	38.9	63
	The Birds	NBC	Sat	1/6/68	38.9	59

11.	Patton	ABC	Sun	11/19/72	38.5	65
12.	Bridge on the River					
	Kwai	ABC	Sun	9/25/66	38.3	61
13. *	Helter Skelter					
	—Part 2	CBS	Fri	4/2/76	37.5	60
	Jeremiah Johnson	ABC	Sun	1/18/76	37.5	56
15.	Ben-Hur	CBS	Sun	2/14/71	37.1	56
	Rocky	CBS	Sun	2/4/79	37.1	53
17.	The Godfather					
	—Part 1	NBC	Sat	11/16/74	37.0	61
18. *	Little Ladies of the					
	Night	ABC	Sun	1/16/77	36.9	53
19.	Wizard of Oz (R)	CBS	Sun	12/13/59	36.5	58
20.	Wizard of Oz (R)	CBS	Sun	1/26/64	35.9	59
21.	Planet of the Apes	CBS	Fri	9/14/73	35.2	60
*	Helter Skelter					
	—Part 1	CBS	Thu	4/1/76	35.2	57
23.	Wizard of Oz (R)	CBS	Sun	1/17/65	34.7	49
24.	Born Free	CBS	Sun	2/22/70	34.2	53
25.	Wizard of Oz	CBS	Sat	11/3/56	33.9	53
26.	Sound of Music	ABC	Sun	2/29/76	33.6	49
27. *	The Waltons' Thanks-					
	giving Story	CBS	Thu	11/15/73	33.5	51
28.	Bonnie & Clyde	CBS	Thu	9/20/73	33.4	38
29.	Ten Commandments	ABC	Sun	2/18/73	33.2	54
*	Night Stalker	ABC	Tue	1/11/72	33.2	48
31.	The Longest Yard	ABC	Sun	9/25/77	33.1	53
*	A Case of Rape	NBC	Wed	2/20/74	33.1	49
33.	Wizard of Oz (R)	CBS	Sun	12/9/62	33.0	55
*	Dallas Cowboys					
	Cheerleaders	ABC	Sun	1/14/79	33.0	48
35. *	Brian's Song	ABC	Tue	11/30/71	32.9	48
36.	Wizard of Oz (R)	CBS	Sun	12/11/60	32.7	52
37.	Beneath the Planet of					
	the Apes	CBS	Fri	10/26/73	32.6	54
38.	Wizard of Oz (R)	CBS	Sun	12/10/61	32.5	53
39. *	Women in Chains	ABC	Tue	1/24/72	32.3	48
	Cat on a Hot Tin					
	Roof	CBS	Thu	9/28/67	32.3	50
42.	Sky Terror	ABC	Sun	9/19/76	32.0	51
	Apple Dumpling Gang	NBC	Sun	11/14/76	32.0	47
44.	Butch Cassidy & the					
	Sundance Kid	ABC	Sun	9/26/76	31.9	51
	The Sting	ABC	Sun	11/5/78	31.9	48
*	Something About					
	Amelia	ABC	Mon	1/9/84	31.9	46
47. *	Heidi	NBC	Sun	11/17/68	31.8	47
	Smokey & the Bandit	NBC	Sun	11/25/79	31.8	44
49.	Oh, God!	CBS	Sun	11/25/79	31.7	45
*	Guyana Tragedy: The					
	Story of Jim Jones					
	—Part 2	CBS	Wed	4/16/80	31.7	50
*	My Sweet Charlie	NBC	Tue	1/20/70	31.7	48
52.	Airport 1975	NBC	Mon	9/20/76	31.6	46
*	Feminist and the Fuzz	ABC	Tue	1/26/71	31.6	46
54. *	Something for Joey	CBS	Wed	4/6/77	31.5	51
*	Dawn: Portrait of a					
	Teenage Runaway	NBC	Mon	9/27/76	31.5	46
56.	Great Escape—Part 2	CBS	Fri	9/15/67	31.3	55
*	Kenny Rogers as the					
	Gambler	CBS	Tue	4/8/80	31.3	50
58.	McLintock!	CBS	Fri	11/3/67	31.2	54
59.	Ballad of Josie	NBC	Tue	9/16/69	31.1	56
	Great Escape—Part 1	CBS	Thu	9/14/67	31.1	51
	Wizard of Oz (R)	CBS	Sun	1/9/66	31.1	49

	Goldfinger	ABC	Sun	9/17/72	31.1	49
*	Coward of the County	CBS	Wed	10/7/81	31.1	48
64. *	Amazing Howard					
	Hughes—Part 2	CBS	Thu	4/14/77	31.0	53
	The Robe	ABC	Sun	3/26/67	31.0	53
*	Sarah T.—Portrait of					
	a Teenage Al-					
	coholic	NBC	Tue	2/11/75	31.0	44
67. *	Call Her Mom	ABC	Tue	2/15/72	30.9	46
68. *	A Death of Innocence	CBS	Fri	11/26/71	30.8	55
	Ten Commandments					
	—Part 2 (R)	ABC	Mon	2/18/74	30.8	48
*	Autobiography of Miss					
	Jane Pitman	CBS	Thu	1/31/74	30.8	47
71. *	Charlie's Angels	ABC	Sun	3/21/76	30.7	49
72.	Three Days of the					
	Condor	CBS	Sun	11/27/77	30.5	47
	The Graduate	CBS	Thu	11/8/73	30.5	48
74. *	Rescue from Gilli-					
	gan's Island					
	—Part 1	NBC	Sat	10/14/78	30.4	52
	The Dirty Dozen	CBS	Thu	9/24/70	30.4	53
*	Tribes	ABC	Tue	11/10/70	30.4	45
*	Yuma	ABC	Tue	3/2/71	30.4	44
*	Brian's Song (R)	ABC	Tue	11/21/72	30.4	43
79. *	Mr. & Mrs. Bo-Jo					
	Jones	ABC	Tue	11/16/71	30.2	45
	Superman—Part 2	ABC	Mon	2/8/82	30.2	42
81.	Earthquake —Part 2	NBC	Sun	10/3/76	30.1	46
82.	The War Wagon	NBC	Sat	10/31/70	30.0	53
	Lilies of the Field	CBS	Fri	3/24/67	30.0	50
	Airport (R)	ABC	Sun	2/9/75	30.0	42
85. *	Melvin Purvis, G-Man	ABC	Tue	4/9/74	29.8	49
86.	Your Cheatin' Heart	CBS	Fri	4/5/68	29.7	50
87.	Gidget Goes Hawai-					
	ian	CBS	Thu	3/31/66	29.6	49
	Superman—Part 1	ABC	Sun	2/7/82	29.6	42
*	The Gambler–The Ad-					
	venture Continues					
	—Part 2	CBS	Tue	11/29/83	29.6	45
90. *	The Gambler–The Ad-					
	venture Continues					
	—Part 1	CBS	Mon	11/28/83	29.5	42
*	Mrs. Sundance	ABC	Tue	4/9/74	29.5	43
92. *	The Waltons' Easter					
	Story	CBS	Thu	4/19/73	29.4	48
*	Charlie's Angels (R)	ABC	Tue	9/14/76	29.4	47
*	Maybe I'll Come					
	Home in the Spring	ABC	Tue	2/16/71	29.4	42
	Five Branded Women	CBS	Fri	1/6/67	29.4	42
96. *	Jesus of Nazareth					
	—Part 2	NBC	Sun	4/10/77	29.3	48
*	Alias Smith and					
	Jones	ABC	Tue	1/5/71	29.3	44
98.	Hooper	CBS	Sun	2/8/80	29.2	41
	Every Which Way but					
	Loose	CBS	Sun	11/1/81	29.2	42
100.	P.T. 109	CBS	Fri	1/13/67	29.1	50
	Escape from the					
	Planet of the Apes	CBS	Fri	11/6/73	29.1	50
	Roustabout	ABC	Wed	1/3/68	29.1	48
	Hombre	ABC	Sun	1/25/70	29.1	45
	Harper Valley PTA	NBC	Sun	2/24/80	29.1	42
105. *	Guyana Tragedy: The					
	Story of Jim Jones					
	—Part 1	CBS	Tue	4/15/80	28.9	46
	Green Berets	NBC	Sat	11/18/72	28.9	45

*Denotes made-for-TV movie.

West Side Story						
—Part 1	NBC	Tue	3/14/72	28.9	41	
108. Cat Ballou	ABC	Wed	10/2/68	28.8	48	
* Raid on Entebbe	NBC	Sun	1/9/77	28.8	41	
Gone with the Wind						
(R)—Part 2	CBS	Mon	2/12/79	28.8	40	
* Help Wanted: Male	CBS	Sat	1/16/82	28.8	47	
112. Valley of the Dolls	CBS	Fri	9/22/72	28.7	50	
* The Homecoming (R)	CBS	Fri	12/7/73	28.7	49	
* Sybil—Part 2	NBC	Mon	11/15/76	28.7	43	
115. Wizard of Oz (R)	CBS	Sun	2/12/67	28.6	50	
Splendor in the Grass	CBS	Thu	10/12/67	28.6	47	
Walking Tall (R)	ABC	Sun	11/9/75	28.6	46	
Survive!	ABC	Sun	2/27/77	28.6	44	
The Hospital	ABC	Sun	11/18/73	28.6	44	
* Incredible Journey of						
Dr. Meg Laurel	CBS	Tue	1/2/79	28.6	42	
In Harm's Way						
—Part 2	ABC	Mon	1/25/71	28.6	42	
9 to 5	CBS	Sun	2/27/83	28.6	42	
123. To Kill a Mockingbird	NBC	Sat	11/9/68	28.5	49	
Mario Puzo's The						
Godfather—Part 4	NBC	Tue	11/15/77	28.5	43	
* Gidget Gets Married	ABC	Tue	1/14/72	28.5	40	
126. * The Jericho Mile	ABC	Sun	3/18/79	28.4	46	
* The Runaways	CBS	Tue	4/1/75	28.4	44	
* Dr. Cook's Garden	ABC	Tue	1/19/71	28.4	41	
* Fallen Angel	CBS	Tue	2/24/81	28.4	42	
130. W.W. & the Dixie						
Dancekings	ABC	Sun	1/2/77	28.3	43	
131. * Flying High	CBS	Mon	8/28/78	28.2	46	
That Touch of Mink	NBC	Tue	1/9/68	28.2	43	
* The Women's Room	ABC	Sun	9/14/80	28.2	45	
134. Cactus Flower	NBC	Sat	9/30/72	28.1	46	
* The Last Child	ABC	Tue	10/15/71	28.1	44	
* Battlestar Galactica	ABC	Sun	9/17/78	28.1	43	
137. * SST—Death Flight	ABC	Fri	2/25/77	28.0	47	
Buster and Billie	ABC	Mon	3/22/76	28.0	44	
Mario Puzo's The						
Godfather—Part 3	NBC	Mon	11/14/77	28.0	42	
140. Madame X	NBC	Mon	9/16/68	27.9	47	
Oklahoma	CBS	Thu	11/26/70	27.9	47	
The Outlaw Josey						
Wales (R)	NBC	Sun	10/19/80	27.9	44	
143. North by Northwest	CBS	Fri	9/29/67	27.8	50	
Tora! Tora! Tora!	CBS	Fri	9/21/73	27.8	47	
Serpico	ABC	Sun	9/21/75	27.8	47	
* Girl Most Likely To	ABC	Tue	11/6/73	27.8	42	
The Cowboys	ABC	Tue	11/13/73	27.8	42	
Earthquake—Part 1	NBC	Sun	9/26/76	27.8	41	
The End	NBC	Tue	2/19/80	27.8	41	
150. Wizard of Oz (R)	NBC	Sun	3/15/70	27.7	50	
Second Time Around	NBC	Tue	10/3/67	27.7	48	
Sons of Katie Elder	ABC	Sun	11/17/68	27.7	46	
* In Search of America	ABC	Tue	3/23/71	27.7	42	
154. What a Way to Go!	NBC	Sat	9/16/67	27.6	50	
The Carpetbaggers	ABC	Sun	2/16/69	27.6	48	
* Cry Rape!	CBS	Tue	11/27/73	27.6	43	
* Wild Women	ABC	Tue	10/20/70	27.6	41	
158. * Doomsday Flight	NBC	Tue	12/13/66	27.5	48	
Billy Jack	NBC	Sat	11/20/76	27.5	46	
What's Up, Doc?	ABC	Fri	1/23/76	27.5	44	
* Longest Hundred						
Miles	NBC	Sat	1/21/67	27.5	43	
* Run, Simon, Run	ABC	Tue	12/1/70	27.5	43	
* The Red Pony	NBC	Sun	3/18/73	27.5	42	

164. Ten Commandments						
(R)	ABC	Sun	3/25/79	27.4	48	
Send Me No Flowers	NBC	Tue	9/19/67	27.4	47	
I Want to Live!	CBS	Thu	2/15/68	27.4	43	
* It Happened One						
Christmas	ABC	Sun	12/11/77	27.4	42	
* Elvis	ABC	Sun	2/11/79	27.4	40	
* Second Chance	ABC	Tue	2/8/72	27.4	40	
* Jacqueline Bouvier						
Kennedy	ABC	Wed	10/14/81	27.4	42	
171. * Man from Atlantis	NBC	Fri	3/4/77	27.3	46	
* Smash-Up on Inter-						
state 5	ABC	Fri	12/3/76	27.3	45	
Blue Hawaii	NBC	Tue	11/29/66	27.3	45	
* Jane Eyre	NBC	Wed	3/24/71	27.3	43	
That's Entertainment	CBS	Tue	11/18/75	27.3	41	
176. Spencers' Mountain	CBS	Fri	10/13/67	27.2	49	
Battle of the Bulge						
—Part 2	CBS	Fri	2/19/71	27.2	43	
* Victims	ABC	Mon	1/11/82	27.2	40	
Hawaii	CBS	Fri	1/11/74	27.2	42	
* A Taste of Evil	ABC	Tue	10/12/71	27.2	41	
* Hardcase	ABC	Tue	2/1/72	27.2	40	
* The Victim	ABC	Tue	11/14/72	27.2	40	
183. McLintock! (R)	NBC	Sat	2/27/71	27.1	44	
Stepford Wives	ABC	Sun	10/24/76	27.1	43	
* Loneliest Runner	NBC	Mon	12/20/76	27.1	42	
West Side Story						
—Part 2	NBC	Wed	3/15/72	27.1	42	
Diary of a Mad						
Housewife	NBC	Mon	1/24/73	27.1	42	
The Mating Game	NBC	Mon	10/21/63	27.1	41	
In Harm's Way						
—Part 1	ABC	Sun	1/24/71	27.1	41	
* V—Part 2	NBC	Mon	5/2/83	27.1	40	
191. Walking Tall	ABC	Sat	3/1/75	27.0	45	
* Girl Who Came Gift-						
Wrapped	ABC	Tue	1/29/74	27.0	40	
193. Hot Spell	NBC	Wed	3/17/65	26.9	44	
* She Waits	CBS	Fri	1/28/72	26.9	44	
African Queen	CBS	Thu	3/5/70	26.9	43	
Gator	CBS	Sun	2/12/78	26.9	41	
* Savage Bees	NBC	Mon	11/22/76	26.9	41	
* Sybil—Part 1	NBC	Sun	11/14/76	26.9	40	
* Crowhaven Farm	ABC	Tue	11/24/70	26.9	40	

*Denotes made-for-TV movie.

4/TOP-RATED PROGRAMS OF ALL TIME

HERE ARE THE top-rated broadcasts of all time, from July 1960 (when Nielsen established its current rating system) through September 1983. Please keep in mind that joint-network telecasts are excluded from this list. According to Nielsen counts, 96.1 percent of all American TV households watched at least part of the Kennedy assassination and its four-day aftermath. The Apollo moon mission attracted 93.9 percent of the nation's TV households during July 14 to 27, 1969—an estimated 53.5 million households.

Sunday certainly is a good day for television according to this list: 24 of the Top 50 programs were aired on that day. January wins the honor of being the most popular month: more than half (28) of these top shows were broadcast during the year's first month, when many Americans like to stay at home after the hectic and expensive Christmas holidays. February, when the networks fight their ratings "sweeps," comes in second place, with 9 of the Top 50.

There are 16 episodes of regularly scheduled series on this list, 13 Super Bowl events, 11 segments of mini-series, only 4 movies (counting *Gone with the Wind* twice because of its two-part telecast), 2 Academy Award ceremonies, 2 Bob Hope Christmas shows, 1 Miss America Pageant, 1 NFC Football Championship and 1 musical special—*Cinderella*. Of the 16 episodes of regularly scheduled series that made it to this list, 8 were *The Beverly Hillbillies*. And of the 11 segments of mini-series on this list, 7 belonged to the indomitable *Roots*.

How are these high raters distributed among the three networks? CBS aired 22; ABC 16; and NBC 13.

Postscript: Shortly after this list was compiled, *The Day After*, a made-for-TV movie, won a large 52.2 rating, making it the third highest-rated program of all time.

TOP-RATED PROGRAMS OF ALL TIME

Rank Title	Web	Day	Date	Rating
1. *M*A*S*H* (Final episode)	CBS	Mon.	2/28/83	60.2
2. *Dallas* ("Who Shot J.R.?")	CBS	Fri.	11/21/80	53.3
3. *Roots*—Part 8	ABC	Sun.	1/30/77	51.1
4. *Super Bowl XVI*	CBS	Sun.	1/24/82	51.0
5. *Super Bowl XVII*	NBC	Sun.	1/30/83	48.6
6. *Gone with the Wind* —Part 1	NBC	Sun.	11/7/76	47.7
7. *Gone with the Wind* —Part 2	NBC	Mon.	11/8/76	47.4
8. *Super Bowl XII*	CBS	Sun.	1/15/78	47.2
9. *Super Bowl XIII*	NBC	Sun.	1/21/79	47.1
10. *Bob Hope Christmas Show*	NBC	Thurs.	1/15/70	46.6
11. *Super Bowl XIV*	CBS	Sun.	1/20/80	46.3
12. *Roots*—Part 6	ABC	Fri.	1/28/77	45.9
The Fugitive (Final episode)	ABC	Tues.	8/29/67	45.9
14. *Roots*—Part 5	ABC	Thurs.	1/27/77	45.7
15. *Bob Hope Christmas Show*	NBC	Thurs.	1/14/71	45.0
16. *Roots*—Part 3	ABC	Tues.	1/25/77	44.8
17. *Ed Sullivan Show*	CBS	Sun.	2/9/64	44.6
18. *Super Bowl XI*	NBC	Sun.	1/9/77	44.4
Super Bowl XV	NBC	Sun.	1/25/81	44.4
20. *Super Bowl VI*	CBS	Sun.	1/16/72	44.2
21. *Roots*—Part 2	ABC	Mon.	1/24/77	44.1
22. *Beverly Hillbillies*	CBS	Wed.	1/8/64	44.0
23. *Roots*—Part 4	ABC	Wed.	1/26/77	43.8
24. *Academy Awards*	ABC	Tues.	4/7/70	43.4
25. *Ed Sullivan Show*	CBS	Sun.	2/16/64	43.2
Thorn Birds—Part 3	ABC	Tues.	3/29/83	43.2
27. *Thorn Birds*—Part 4	ABC	Wed.	3/30/83	43.1
28. *Beverly Hillbillies*	CBS	Wed.	1/15/64	42.8
29. *Super Bowl VII*	NBC	Sun.	1/14/73	42.7
30. *Thorn Birds*—Part 2	ABC	Mon.	3/28/83	42.5
31. *Super Bowl IX*	NBC	Sun.	1/12/75	42.4
Beverly Hillbillies	CBS	Wed.	2/26/64	42.4
33. *Super Bowl X*	CBS	Sun.	1/18/76	42.3
Airport (The movie)	ABC	Sun.	11/11/73	42.3
Love Story (The movie)	ABC	Sun.	10/1/72	42.3
Cinderella	CBS	Mon.	2/22/65	42.3
Roots—Part 7	ABC	Sat.	1/29/77	42.3
38. *Beverly Hillbillies*	CBS	Wed.	3/25/64	42.2
39. *Super Bowl XII*—Kickoff	CBS	Sun.	1/15/78	42.1
40. *Beverly Hillbillies*	CBS	Wed.	2/5/64	42.0
41. *Beverly Hillbillies*	CBS	Wed.	1/29/64	41.9
42. *Miss America Pageant*	CBS	Sat.	9/9/61	41.8
Beverly Hillbillies	CBS	Wed.	1/1/64	41.8
44. *Super Bowl VIII*	CBS	Sun.	1/13/74	41.6
Bonanza	NBC	Sun.	3/8/64	41.6
46. *Beverly Hillbillies*	CBS	Wed.	1/22/64	41.5
47. *Bonanza*	NBC	Sun.	2/16/64	41.4
48. *Academy Awards*	ABC	Mon.	4/10/67	41.2
49. *Bonanza*	NBC	Sun.	2/9/64	41.0
Winds of War—Part 7	ABC	Sun.	2/13/83	41.0
NFC Football Championship	CBS	Sun.	1/10/82	41.0

IV. THE ADVERTISERS

1/THE IN'S AND OUT'S OF TELEVISION ADVERTISING

DURING A 1966 conference on "The Meaning of Commercial Television" sponsored by Stanford University, the University of Texas and *TV Guide*, social historian David Potter posed an intriguing question: is television primarily a medium of public entertainment which happens to be supported financially by advertising, or is it primarily an apparatus for the marketing of consumer goods which happens to use public entertainment as part of the marketing process?

The question, of course, is practically impossible to answer. To the millions and millions of Americans who relax each night in front of the tube, TV is obviously a form of entertainment. And to the few networks who make millions and millions of dollars from selling those viewers to advertisers, TV is defenitely a business—big business.

"Television is another industry in America," says one of TV's most successful producers, Norman Lear. "It gets enormous attention because of its visibility. But it's run like all of those other industries." In short, for profit.

But this wasn't always the case: the first years of broadcasting were actually commercial free. Radio manufacturers, eager to increase sales, were often willing to subsidize programs in the hope that more people would want to buy radio sets if there were more shows on the air. But as the shows grew both in number and in cost, it became obvious that another means of supporting radio broadcasts had to be found.

Some suggested a tax be levied on each set sold. Others advocated an endowment plan by which wealthy donors support stations much as Andrew Carnegie had endowed libraries across the nation. And still others proposed that state and city governments support broadcasting as they were already financing schools, museums and hospitals.

There was almost no talk of selling advertising: radio was a public service, not a commercial venture. So when A.T.&T. announced in February 1922 that it was going to conduct an experiment in "toll broadcasting" whereby it would sell radio time to anyone who wanted to buy it, the proposal met universal condemnation. The first Washington Radio Conference soundly opposed the very notion of "ether advertising." The trade magazine *Radio Dealer* foresaw "a man-sized vocal rebellion." *Printer's Ink* predicted commercial radio would prove "positively offensive to great numbers of people." And Herbert Hoover, then Secretary of Commerce, warned the quickest way to kill broadcasting would be to use it for "direct advertising." It was inconceivable, Hoover later said, that we should allow

"so great a possibility for service" to be drowned in "advertising chatter."

Despite such vehement criticism, A.T.&T. continued its plans, and on Aug. 16, 1922 its first "toll" station, WEAF, opened for business. Two weeks later, the real estate firm of Queensboro Corporation paid $50 for a 10-minute late-afternoon time slot.

"Let me enjoin you," urged the voice of a Queensboro executive, "as you value your health and your hopes and your home happiness, get away from the solid masses of brick, where the meager opening admitting a slant of sunlight is mockingly called a light shaft, and where children grow up starved for a run over a patch of grass and the sight of a tree."

As a result of that ad, Queensboro sold suburban apartments. As David Potter has pointed out, WEAF had stumbled upon *the* axiomatic reality of broadcasting: broadcasters really have nothing to sell except access to a mass audience and the only parties who have reason to pay for such access are advertisers. This was, as Potter wryly notes, "the most far-reaching discovery since Columbus encountered the Americas as unsuspected obstacles in his path west-ward to the Indies." Thus, the age of commercials was born.

Nevertheless, business at WEAF was not exactly booming. During August and September total revenues for A.T.&T.'s toll broadcasting amounted to a mere $550. Only two other companies—American Express and Tidewater Oil—had joined Queensboro Corporation as radio sponsors. But gradually radio advertising became more attractive to businesses: in January 1923 the cosmetic Minerva sponsored a talk by actress Marion Davies on "How I Make Up for the Movies." During the talk a free autographed photo of Davies was offered to listeners who then wrote in by the hundreds. By February WEAF boasted 14 sponsors and other stations began following WEAF's suit: approximately 150 of the 561 stations on the air accepted sponsors by the end of 1924.

Radio's first commercials were definitely "soft sell" by today's standards: prices were not cited, store locations remained unmentioned, and products were left undescribed. Some sponsors bought time without even mentioning their products. The shows merely took the name of the products—the Goodrich Silverstone Orchestra, the A.&P. Gypsies, the Kodak Chorus, etc. "These clients neither describe their product nor name its price but simply depend on the good-will that results from their contribution of good programs," said NBC's first president Merlin H. Aylesworth in 1928 about the "institutional advertising" policies of early radio shows.

Although even this indirect advertising had its opponents—"outrageous rubbish," *Century* magazine tagged it in 1924—radio advertising was winning favor. "The commercially sponsored program spells, in a large measure, the future of radio," wrote Aylesworth in a 1928 *New York Times* article. "Dispensers of woe, who foretold the death of broadcasting when stations began selling time, have been met with ever improving programs, not in spite of time selling, but because of it."

And thus, not surprisingly, restrictions started going by the wayside. Although the first N.A.B. code in 1928 had prohibited commercials between 7:00 and 11:00 P.M., commercials started popping up at all hours. And products began "telling all": prices, store locations, detailed descriptions, etc. The air, as Sen. Burton K. Wheeler said, was turning into a "pawnshop."

In 1927 approximately 20% of radio network time was sponsored. By 1931 more than 36% was, and by the early 1940s, the majority of network time was being sold to advertisers. Advertising had become the prime support for station operation. The medium, as Jeff Greenfield has said, had become a marketplace.

Because the sponsors during those years often produced their own shows, they were able to call the shots. The sponsor, according to broadcasting historian Erik Barnouw, was "king." "He decided on programming. If he decided to change programs, network assent was considered *pro forma*. The sponsor was assumed to hold a 'franchise' on his time period or periods. Many programs were advertising agency creations, designed to fulfill specific sponsor objectives. The director was likely to be an advertising agency staff employee. During dress rehearsals an official of the sponsoring company was often on hand in the sponsor's booth, prepared to order last-minute changes. In 'Radio City'—completed in 1933—every studio had a sponsor's booth."

When television became a reality after World War II, it was assumed the new medium would merely adopt the advertising policies of radio. Yes, there was some talk in those early years of "free TV"—that is, TV without commercials—but for the most part, television just followed radio's example: time was sold to advertisers, the sponsors were in control, and TV became a mere extension of the advertising industry.

Many early television shows were, of course, named after their sponsors: *Texaco Star Theatre, Philco TV Playhouse, The Colgate Comedy Hour, Gillette Cavalcade of Sports, Kraft Television Theatre, The Buick Circus Hour, The Chevy Show*, etc. The sponsors in many cases actually produced the shows and were thus able to determine their content. The early history of TV abounds with examples of sponsor control. According to *New York Times* TV critic Les Brown, Chevrolet once removed "fording a

stream" from a show's dialogue because the phrase contained the name of its main competitor—Ford. And while sponsoring a drama about the Nuremberg Trials, the American Gas Company scratched all references to the fact that the Nazis had used gas to exterminate Jews—the company did not want TV viewers to think badly of its product.

One vice-president of a top advertising agency confessed that in shows sponsored by filter cigarettes, the villains would have to smoke non-filters, while on shows sponsored by non-filter cigarettes, the heavies were ordered to smoke filters. TV writers were given constant instructions: no one could cough on *Man Against Crime* sponsored by Camel cigarettes, and doctors could be shown only in "the most commendable light" lest they start to publish reports on the health effects of smoking.

And sponsor power was not limited to behind-the-scenes strategies. Many sponsors found clever ways to insinuate themselves on the programs. On *Beat the Clock*, the face of the clock read "Hazel Bishop." And on *What's My Line*, mystery guests signed in on a blackboard with "Stopette" deodorant emblazoned across the top.

But then a sponsor went too far: in late 1959 it was revealed that Charles Revson, the sponsor of the extremely popular *The $64,000 Question*, had actually dictated which contestants should win and which should lose. During the ensuing "TV Quiz Show Scandal," the networks decided to restructure their advertising policies: the networks themselves and not the sponsors would now produce the shows. "We will be masters of our own house," said CBS president Frank Stanton, as the "magazine concept of advertising"—by which advertisers merely buy inserts into programs and not the programs themselves—was launched. (The magazine approach had been advocated by NBC president Pat Weaver as early as 1953, when it had met stiff opposition from the ad agencies who predicted that sponsors would withdraw from TV if advertisers "could not be identified whith the particular program of their choice.")*

So today advertisers are merely sold spots on a show. Each year's fall line-up is announced the preceding spring, when the networks invite big advertisers for a meeting: schedules are discussed, pilot episodes are screened, series are outlined. These meeting, says TV producer Bob Shanks, are the "Rites of Television Spring, the Selling Season, the Mating Season, when advertising agency buyers are avidly sought by the network salesmen." By the end of June, 50-70% of the next year's total prime time has been sold.

How much is an advertiser charged to show his commercial on TV? The exact prices paid by advertisers are not generally released by the networks, and not every

---

*Although the magazine concept of advertising restricted sponsor control, it may have ironically harmed television's diversity. As TV historian Jeff Greenfield has noted, in the early days a sponsor might present a program not to reach large numbers but for the prestige of the show. Once the networks took total control, however, the game was to win the biggest audience: the networks could no longer risk minority programming.

buyer will pay the same price for a commercial on the same program: an advance buyer with a long-standing commitment to a particular show might pay 20% to 30% less than a "scatter" buyer in a crowded market. But those two qualifiers aside, it's safe to say that prices for TV commercials are primarily determined by a show's rating: the higher the rating, the higher the price.

During the 1980/81 season, for example, CBS charged approximately $150,000 for each 30-second commercial on its top-rated show *60 Minutes*, while ABC asked for about $100,000 for each half-minute ad on *Benson*, and NBC charged in the neighborhood of $60,000 for a 30-second spot on *Games People Play*. If these prices seem high, keep in mind that prices for ads on each year's highest-rated shows (like the Super Bowl, the World Series and the Oscars) command even higher fees: during the 1981/82 season, for example, CBS was charging a hefty $345,000 per 30-second spot during its broadcast of Super Bowl XVI.

It's easy to see that such prices for a mere 30 seconds can generate enormous revenues for the webs. During the October to mid-December peak of the 1980/81 season, for example, CBS's weekly prime time ad revenues were on the order of $29.7 million; ABC, $27.7 million; and NBC, slightly more than $26 million.

How much of these revenues is profit? Although profits and costs of network entertainment are generally closely guarded secrets, *Variety* reporter Jack Loftis has published statistics for various NBC shows aired during the first two months of 1980. These statistics provide a rare insight into how much money the networks make and spend on TV programming:

	Net Revenues (per episode)	Program Costs (per episode)	Profit (per episode)
PRIME TIME			
Little House on the Prairie	$775,000	$375,000	$400,000
Chips	574,000	276,000	298,000
Real People	443,000	291,000	152,000
Diff'rent Strokes	279,000	159,000	120,000
Walt Disney	694,000	677,000	17,000
Buck Rogers	365,000	381,000	- 16,000
LATE NIGHT			
Tonight	190,000	59,000	131,000
Saturday Night Live	455,000	295,000	160,000
Midnight Special	101,000	88,000	13,000
Tomorrow	14,000	12,000	2,000
Late Movie	12,000	79,000	- 67,000
DAYTIME			
Another World	230,000	71,000	159,000
Days of Our Lives	131,000	52,000	79,000
Hollywood Squares	34,000	18,000	16,000
Password	30,000	16,000	14,000

These above figures are, of course, for first-run episodes. Revenues and costs change dramatically during summer

reruns. During the 1978/79 season, for example, ABC sold each 30-second spot on *Three's Company* for $105,000, generating approximately $525,000 in revenues per half-hour episode. Since ABC paid approximately $205,000 per show to the producers, the network enjoyed a $330,000 profit for each first-run episode. During summer re-runs, the finances change: because of smaller summer audiences, the price per 30 seconds dropped and $470,000 worth of revenues were generated. But the cost of the show also drops: ABC basically had to pay only residuals, approximately $41,000 per show, which meant that each summer re-run episode earned $429,000 in profits—$100,000 more than when it was originally aired in the fall or winter.*

Because prime time shows are the highest-rated, the evening hours account for almost half of all advertising revenues, as the following chart from Broadcast Advertisers Reports demonstrates:

NETWORK BILLINGS BY DAYPART

Daypart	Days of Week	Revenues (in millions)	% of Total
Prime Time	Mon.-Sun.	$1,952.6	47.6%
Daytime	Mon.-Fri.	833.7	20.3%
Sports	Mon.-Fri.	618.5	15.1%
News	Mon.-Sun.	286.7	7.0%
Late Night	Mon.-Sun.	213.9	5.2%
Kids' Shows	Mon.-Fri.		
	(CBS)	142.1	3.5%
	Sat.-Sun. (All)		
Early Morning	Mon.-Fri.	53.3	1.3%
Other (political, etc)		4.3	0.1%

Given the high prices of TV commercials, why do advertisers use TV so frequently? Actually, television is *not* so expensive if, rather than considering the absolute costs, you consider the cost of reaching each would-be customer (or "cost-per-1,000," as industry executives say). During the 1980/81 season, for example, each episode of *M*A*S*H* was seen by approximately 30 million households. If each 30-second commercial on *M*A*S*H* cost approximately $150,000, that means reaching 1,000 homes only cost $5—which is, all things considered, quite inexpensive.

Television commercials have been both routinely condemned and widely celebrated. They've been attacked for undermining the morals of an entire nation and praised as the best thing on TV—"the greatest stories ever sold" as a *Village Voice* article called them.

Few disagree, however, that television commercials no longer do what they were originally intended to do: provide concrete information about a particular product or

---

*Actually, all of this $429,000 is not really profit. The network has to pay its affiliate stations a fee for carrying the show, and of course it has to pay its own overhead—employee salaries, facilities, etc. Even so, it's easy to see that TV is a very lucrative business.

service. As Erik Barnouw notes in his excellent book *The Sponsor*, there is scarcely time in a 30-second spot for "technical persuasions, documentation, 'reason-why' advertising. Everyone knows what the job is: instant drama, posing threat and promise." Thus, writes Barnouw, a network commercial is likely "to promote not only a product but a way of life, a view of the world, a philosophy."

What is the "philosophy" of most TV commercials? According to Barnouw, it basically comes down to this: "the work of Creation has been largely a disaster, functionally and aesthetically. Almost everything done in the making of man and his environment was a mistake; fortunately, man himself has invented products to correct the errors. . . For the unfortunate races on whom Nature has bestowed curly hair, man has developed straightening products; for those with the humiliating heritage of straight hair, curling products. . . Products are also available for 'moisturizing' dry skin and drying oily skin. . . Commercials have worked—with success—toward revision of many traditional tenets of our society. As we have seen, reverence for nature has been replaced by a determination to process it. Thrift has been replaced by the duty to buy. The work ethic has been replaced by the consumption ethic." TV commercials, in short, create new desires more than they satisfy old ones.

Commercials have been attacked for jarringly interrupting the continuity of programs: "you can be watching a story about children starving in Biafra," writes TV critic Marvin Kitman, "and suddenly there will be a commercial for dog food, or even special food for the poor fat dogs who have to slim down." And commercials have also been attacked for the exact opposite reason—for being a mere extension of TV program ideology. Many programs, says Erik Barnouw, are hard to distinguish from commercials. Quiz shows shower contestants with products; daytime serials immerse us in high-consumption living; situation comedies, like commercials, have neat, clean-cut solutions.

What do viewers themselves think about commercials? When Robert T. Bower surveyed adults across the nation for his book *Television and the Public* (1973), approximately three-quarters of those surveyed agreed that "there are just too many commercials." But roughly the same number admitted that "commercials are a fair price to pay for the entertainment you get."

Other findings?

—65% agreed that commercials were long.

—43% said commercials were annoying and in bad taste.

—54% agreed that some commercials were helpful and informative.

—54% believed that some commercials were more entertaining than the programs.

When asked to volunteer complaints, 15% agreed that commercials were stupid, unrealistic, or silly. Only 8% believed commercials were misleading or dis-

honest, only 2% said commercials were too hard sell, and only 1% found commercials boring or dull.

Since 1960, the F.C.C. has maintained a separate Complaints and Compliance Division in its Broadcast Bureau, and although the division handles inquiries about both radio and television, the majority of citizens' complaints are leveled against TV. In 1976, for example, 1,145 protests were received about the bad taste of TV commercials. Radio commercials received only 119 similar complaints. What gets people so angly about TV advertising? According to F.C.C. records for 1977, when 2,137 complaints about TV commercials were received, 772 people argued that the commercials were offensive, 333 complained about ads for alcoholic beverages, 276 about the sheer number of ads, 259 about the increased sound volume of commercials, and 227 about the false and misleading nature of ads. Surprisingly, only 36 viewers complained that commercials interrupted pogramming, and only 20 registered complaints concerning advertising for children.

How are commercials made? With great care and at great expense. Because advertisers have only 30 or 60 seconds to convey their messages, every second counts. Nothing is left to chance: scripts are scrutinzed word by word; casts are assembled from huge, exhaustive auditions; locations are thoroughly scouted; lighting is tested and retested. No detail is too small to neglect. Everything is analyzed, computed, calculated and planned, making TV commercials the "most rigidly managed form of cinema yet devised" according to critic Richard Goldstein.

Such control, of course, costs money. In 1960 a commercial might run between $10,000 and $20,000 to produce, but in today's inflated marketplace, it's not uncommon to spend $100,000 to make a 30-second spot. One commercial featuring tap dancer Ann Miller with a chorus of Busby Berkeley showgirls reportedly cost a staggering $250,000 to film! You can imagine what a feature-length movie would cost on that kind of scale.

Because of such high budgets, TV is not for firms with small pocketbooks: only Big Business can afford network advertising. Not surprisingly, the Top Ten Advertisers are among the most familiar corporations in the country, as the following list shows:

TV'S TOP TEN ADVERTISERS

	1956	1967	1979
1.	Procter & Gamble ($55,477,411)	Procter & Gamble ($192,052,300)	Procter Gamble ($289,600,000)
2.	General Motors ($48,981,798)	General Foods ($93,812,000)	General Foods ($203,200,000)
3.	Colgate-Palmolive ($29,566,513)	Bristol-Myers ($74,273,000)	American Home Products ($122,600,000)
4.	General Foods ($27,646,261)	Colgate-Palmolive ($71,087,800)	General Motors ($117,300,000)
5.	Chrysler Corp. ($26,923,885)	American Home Products ($57,230,300)	Bristol-Myers ($117,000,000)

6.	General Electric ($25,026,555)	Lever Bros. ($55,969,400)	Ford Motor Co. ($97,000,000)
7.	Ford Motor Co. ($21,793,953)	American Tobacco ($45,869,700)	Philip Morris ($86,400,000)
8.	American Home Products ($18,979,916)	Gillette ($43,068,600)	General Mills ($85,600,000)
9.	General Mills ($17,930,233)	General Mills ($42,555,200)	Johnson & Johnson ($83,700,000)
10.	Gillette ($17,930,233)		Pepsico ($72,300,000)

Each year these corporations may spend millions of dollars on air time, but are they getting their money's worth? Do commercials really work? Do viewers pay attention to them? ABC producer Bob Shanks has tagged TV "the most potent merchandising vehicle ever devised," and there's plenty of evidence to back up that claim:

—In 1950 Hazel Bishop earned $50,000 selling cosmetics. Then the company began advertising on TV. By 1952, sales had skyrocketed to $4,500,000.

—In the mid-1970s a new perfume hit the markets: Aviance. Its TV ads showed a housewife stripping to the song "I've been sweet, and I've been good." Within six months, Aviance was the #1 selling new fragrance in the country.

—When L'eggs panty hose began advertising on TV with a large production number in which women danced through a supermarket singing "Our L'eggs fit your legs, they'll hold you, they'll squeeze you, they'll never let you go," Hanes captured a considerable 30% share of the panty hose market. A few years earlier, the leader had only 4% of that market.

—A stork who sounds just like Groucho Marx and who delivers pickles instead of babies is the central character in Vlasic pickle commercials. In just a few years of TV exposure, that stork has won Vlasic 24% of the pickle market, more than double that of the century-old Heinz corporation.

What makes a commercial successful? According to advertising expert Harvey Wayne McMahan, approximately three-quarters of today's moneymaking commercials take one of two strategies: 42% use a jingle and 33% use a familiar personality—either a celebrity (22%) like O.J. Simpson or Laurence Olivier, or a continuing central character (11%) like the Vlasic stork, Madge the Manicurist, Mr. Whipple (who's been urging frustrated housewives "Please don't squeeze the Charmin" since 1964), and Morris the Cat (whose death last year was front page news around the nation).

Despite the success of these and other star-studded ads, there is evidence that many commercials are not especially effective. When media analyst Daniel Stack studied audience response to 1,800 TV commercials in the late 1960s, he found that only one of every six viewers could name the sponsor, and one of every 12 misnamed him. And in 1970, Edward H. Meyer, then president of the Association of National Advertisers, revealed that during the early 1960s sponsors lost 15% to 18% of the audience during commercials, but by the end of the decade the figure had risen to an alarming 50%!

In TV's early days most commercials lasted 60 seconds. But with rising costs, networks found it more lucrative to show two 30-second spots in that minute frame. Today more than 80% of all TV commercials are only 30-seconds long as the following chart demonstrates:

LENGTH OF COMMERCIALS

	Non-Network				Network			
	1965	1970	1975	1980	1965	1970	1975	1980
10 sec.	17%	12%	9%	8%	—	—	—	1%
20 sec.	13	6	1	—	—	—	—	—
30 sec.	2	45	77	85	—	20	79	96
60's piggybacked	4	8	1	—	23	48	15	11
60 sec.	64	29	12	7	77	32	6	2
	100%	100%	100%	100%	100%	100%	100%	100%

It has been said that commercials have changed the quality of American life, that they've strongly influenced where we eat, what we wear, even how we vote. The all-important relationship between politics and television began during the 1952 presidential election, when both Adlai Stevenson and Dwight D. Eisenhower were buying television time to help their respective campaigns. Stevenson's TV strategy was direct: he would simply sit before the cameras for a half-hour and address the issues. His speeches were often brilliant—eloquent, articulate and witty.

Eisenhowever, however, took a different tactic. Under the advice of top advertising agency Batten, Barton, Durstine and Osborn (who also handled U.S. Steel, DuPont and General Electric), Eisenhower would only speak for 20 of the 30 minutes of his programs. The first five minutes of the half-hour would show Eisenhower's arrival: cameras would be Strategically placed, crowds would cheer, Maime would smile. The closing five minutes would show a similarly carefully-planned exit. The half-hour program would not be so much a speech as a drama—a play with beginning, middle and end.

And for the final two weeks of the campaign, Eisenhower's advisers had a special TV trick up their sleeves: a barrage of 20-second "spot" announcements that first showed citizens from around the country asking Ike a question ("What about the cost of living, General?"), followed by Ike's I-can-handle-it answer ("My wife, Mamie, worries about the same thing, I tell here it's our job to change that on November fourth").

All of Eisenhower's 50 answers were filmed during one day in a New York TV commercial film studio. Stevenson, hearing of Eisenhower's $1.5 million "spot" barrage, refused to follow suit. He most definitely would not be merchandized "like a breakfast food." Stevenson, in short, was making speeches. Eisenhower was making commercials. Thus, argue many media experts, was the age of TV politics born.

Television has of course considerably changed—some might say "revolutionized"—American politics. Everything from the agenda of political conventions to the clothes of political conventions to the clothes of political candidates has been influenced by TV's relentless demands for "image."

The lesson of the 1952 campaign has not been lost on politicans: by 1956 even Adlai Stevenson—who argued the commercialization of politics would be "the ultimate indignity" to the democratic process— hired an advertising agency to oversee his campaign. Noramn, Craig & Kummel—who handled Chanel, Bon Ami and Maidenform bras—took the 1956 Democratic account. And Hollywood mogul Dory Schary even produced some footage for Stevenson.*

TV's role in politics grew even larger during the 1960 presidential campaign. "We wouldn't have had a prayer without that gadget," confessed John F. Kennedy while watching a videotape of one of his TV appearances. It is Kennedy—whose tanned, good looks are thought to have won many votes during the famous Nixon-Kennedy debates—who has been named the first "TV President."

By 1964 TV itself was the target of presidential debate. Republicans and Democratics alike began attacking each other's TV campaigns as crooked and dishonest. Even *Time* and network news programs ran stories about the candidates' TV strategies. Candidates became so enamored and afraid of TV newsmen that during the 1964 Republican convention, Goldwater supporters wore buttons urging viewers to "Stamp Out Huntley-Brinkley." It was during that convention that NBC news-caster John Chancellor was arrested on camera.

By 1968, Republicans and Democrats were spending more than $28 million on TV air time—almost double the expenditures of 1964, triple those of 1960 and quadruple those of 1956. Political advertising leveled during the 1972 presidential campaign, as the following chart demonstrates:

POLITICAL BROADCAST ACTIVITY

YEAR	POLITICAL BROADCASTING ADVERTISING		TV ADVERTISING BY POLITICAL PARTY			TV POLITICAL ADVERTISING BY LEVEL		
	Television	Radio	Democrat	Republican	Other	Network	Station	Cable
1956*	$ 6,685,709	$ 3,221,297	$ 2,769,053	$ 3,760,175	$ 156,481	$2,930,514	$ 3,755,195	
1960	10,052,322	4,142,956	4,414,862	5,431,293	206,167	2,927,235	7,125,087	
1964	17,496,405	7,207,584	7,715,094	9,431,110	350,201	3,807,011	13,689,394	
1968	28,087,027	13,316,471	10,423,940	15,122,872	1,480,215	1,362,240	19,724,787	
1972	24,566,710	13,501,005	11,433,097	11,618,558	1,515,055	4,911,383	19,655,327	$50,189

Note: 1956 figures are from 85th Congress, 1st session, "1956 General Election Campaign," exhibit 24. All other figures are from FCC Survey Political Broadcasting.
*Revised figures.

During television's early years, most candidates bought half-hour time slots to discuss the issues, but by the 1960s, most candidates were purchasing mere 20- and 60-second "spots." Just over 91% of the total 1968 charges went for spot commercials, only 9% for program time. And by 1970, 95% of the total charges went for spots. In 30 or 60 seconds, candidates can't discuss the issues. They can only be "packaged" and promoted like any other product sold via commercials— Campbell's Chunky soup, Charmin toilet paper or Ban underarm deodorant. The tactics used, say many TV critics, are all the same.

*American politics have been "going Hollywood" ever since. During the 1980 primaries, top film director Francis Coppola offered his filmmaking services to presidential aspirant, Jerry Brown.

2/TV Advertising Revenues, 1949–78

IT HAS BEEN argued often that television is about one thing and one thing only: the dollar sign. Unfortunately, the data collected here would do little to deflate that argument. Looking over these statistics, you might think it impossible for the industry to *lose* money. Is television, as N.A.B. president Vincent T. Wasilewski once boasted, "the most successful and universally acknowledged business enterprise in history"?

TV's moneymaking days certainly came quickly. Yes, in 1948 NBC was losing $13,000 a day on its television operations, and losses throughout the industry amounted to $25 million during 1949.

But revenues more than tripled in 1950 and then doubled in 1951—the first year the industry crossed over into the black. And it has remained in the black ever since: the industry has never lost money since 1950! In fact, only one year—1971—ever saw a decline in advertising revenues from the preceding year.

Many years have seen revenues jump by leaps and bounds that are just short of phenomenal. During 1976, for example, pretax profits jumped a whopping 60.3% and cleared the $1 billion hurdle for the first time in history. It was, as *Variety* said in its inimitable prose, the "$pirit of 76" as industry coffers bulged beyond belief.

Television in no other country enjoys such success. Advertisers in England spent $875 million on TV during 1977; in America, more than $6 billion!

Two sets of figures are collected here: the first provides an overview of industry finances from 1949 to the present; the second gives a year-by-year detailed analysis. All statistics are computed by the Federal Communications Commission.

TV INDUSTRY FINANCES 1949–80

Time Sales

	Network Time Sales (000)	National & Regional Time Sales (000)	Local Time Sales (000)	Total Revenues from Time Sales (000)	Total Broadcast Revenues (000)	Total Broadcast Expenses (000)	Total Broadcast Income (Before Federal Income Tax) (000)
1949	$ 10,796	7,275	9,460	27,530	34,330	59,600	−25,262
1950	35,210	25,034	30,384	90,630	105,915	115,129	−9,214
1951	97,558	59,733	51,304	208,595	235,684	194,086	41,598
1952	137,498	80,045	64,851	282,394	323,594	267,900	55,692
1953	171,900	124,318	88,474	383,692	431,777	360,514	71,263
1954	241,225	176,766	120,131	538,122	592,937	502,637	90,300
1955	308,900	222,400	149,800	681,100	744,700	594,500	150,200
1956	367,700	281,200	174,200	823,100	896,900	707,300	189,600
1957	394,200	300,500	174,000	868,700	943,200	783,200	160,000
1958	424,500	345,200	181,300	951,000	1,030,000	858,100	171,900
1959	445,800	424,200	200,600	1,070,600	1,163,900	941,600	222,300
1960	471,600	459,200	215,800	1,146,600	1,268,600	1,024,500	244,100
1961	480,300	468,500	211,200	1,160,000	1,318,300	1,081,300	237,000
1962	521,500	539,500	242,500	1,303,500	1,486,200	1,174,600	311,600
1963	537,900	600,700	256,100	1,394,700	1,597,200	1,254,200	343,200
1964	563,400	659,500	297,000	1,549,900	1,793,300	1,377,700	415,600
1965	585,100	764,500	324,100	1,673,700	1,964,800	1,516,900	447,900
1966	616,700	871,700	346,400	1,834,800	2,203,000	1,710,100	492,900
1967	609,600	871,700	365,300	1,846,600	2,275,400	1,860,800	414,600
1968	637,100	998,000	452,500	2,087,600	2,520,900	2,026,100	494,800
1969	1,569,600	1,119,100	546,800	3,235,500	2,796,200	2,242,600	553,600
1970	1,551,100	1,102,600	589,100	3,242,800	2,808,200	2,354,400	453,800
1971	1,490,400	1,022,800	665,600	3,178,800	2,750,300	2,361,300	389,200
1972	1,687,500	1,177,400	810,100	3,675,000	3,179,400	2,627,300	552,200
1973	1,839,700	1,230,200	932,200	4,002,100	3,464,800	2,811,700	653,100
1974	2,005,300	1,336,100	1,012,400	4,353,800	3,776,300	3,039,200	737,100
1975	2,156,700	1,449,200	1,116,200	4,722,100	4,094,100	3,313,800	780,300
1976	2,674,900	1,922,600	1,431,900	6,029,300	5,198,500	3,948,300	1,250,200
1977	3,241,200	1,967,300	1,630,900	6,839,300	5,889,000	4,488,000	1,401,000
1978	3,725,800	2,336,100	2,039,900	8,101,800	6,913,000	5,265,900	1,647,100
1979	4,310,500	2,573,600	2,297,800	9,181,900	7,875,100	6,184,900	1,690,200
1980	4,808,100	2,928,900	2,542,000	10,279,000	8,707,700	7,154,200	1,653,500

1949 Broadcasting Revenues

Item	4 networks and their 13 owned and operated stations	85 other stations[1]	Industry total
Revenues from network time sales	$ 8,862,399	$ 1,933,113	$ 10,795,512
Revenue from sale of time to national and regional advertisers and sponsors	2,965,594	4,309,419	7,275,013
Revenues from sale of time to local advertisers and sponsors	2,295,468	7,164,140	9,459,608
Total revenues from time sales	14,123,461	13,406,672	27,530,133
Commissions paid to representatives, etc	2,273,333	1,805,394	4,078,727
Incidental broadcast revenues:			
Revenues from sale of talent, etc	4,490,492	1,521,237	6,011,729
Furnishing material or service	2,005,437	1,396,458	3,401,895
Other incidental revenues	547,983	916,943	1,464,926
Total broadcast revenues	18,894,040	15,435,916	34,329,956
Total broadcast expenses	30,635,895	28,956,011	59,591,906
Total broadcast losses	(11,741,855)	(13,520,095)	(25,261,950)
Investment in tangible broadcast property:			
Original cost	19,084,764	36,790,819	55,875,583
Depreciation to date	4,350,273	6,583,841	10,934,114
Depreciated cost	14,734,491	30,206,978	44,941,469

[1] 1 station was an experimental station operating commercially.
( ) indicates loss

1950 Broadcasting Revenues

Item	4 networks and their 14 owned and operated stations	93 other stations	Industry total
Revenues from network time sales	$ 27,312,824	$ 7,897,652	$ 35,210,476
Revenue from sale of time to national and regional advertisers and sponsors	8,207,754	16,826,579	25,034,333
Revenues from sale of time to local advertisers and sponsors	6,857,926	23,526,985	30,384,911
Total revenues from time sales	42,378,504	48,251,216	90,629,720
Commissions paid to representatives, etc	7,415,806	6,892,987	14,308,793
Incidental broadcast revenues:			
Revenues from sale of talent, etc	10,860,695	4,300,804	15,161,499
Furnishing material or service	7,223,049	3,062,665	7,223,049
Other incidental revenues	2,429,603	1,717,225	7,209,493
Total broadcast revenues	55,476,045	50,438,923	105,914,968
Total broadcast expenses	65,506,575	49,622,386	115,128,961
Total broadcast income or loss	(10,030,530)	816,537	(9,213,993)
Investment in tangible broadcast property:			
Original cost	25,504,165	44,756,253	70,260,418
Depreciation to date	7,547,824	12,454,185	20,002,009
Depreciation cost	17,956,341	32,302,068	50,258,409

( ) indicates loss

1951 Broadcasting Revenues

Item	4 networks and their 15 owned and operated stations (000)	93 other stations (000)	Industry total (000)
Revenues from network time sales	$ 72,871	$ 24,687	$ 97,558
Revenue from sale of time to national and regional advertisers and sponsors	17,513	42,220	59,733
Revenues from sale of time to local advertisers and sponsors	11,638	39,666	51,304
Total revenues from time sales	102,022	106,573	208,595
Commissions paid to representatives, etc	18,881	14,457	33,338
Incidental broadcast revenues:			
Revenues from sale of talent, etc	27,453	5,473	33,016
Furnishing material or service	8,368	6,624	14,992
Other incidental revenues	9,330	3,089	12,419
Total broadcast revenues	128,382	107,302	235,684
Total broadcast expenses	117,401	76,685	194,086
Total broadcast income	10,981	30,617	41,598
Investment in tangible broadcast property:			
Original cost	37,902	55,080	92,982
Depreciation to date	11,094	18,738	29,832
Depreciation cost	26,808	36,342	63,150

1952 Broadcasting Revenues

Item	4 networks and their 15 owned and operated stations (000)	93 other stations[1] (000)	Industry total (000)
Revenues from network time sales	$101,484	$ 36,014	$137,498
Revenue from sale of time to national and regional advertisers and sponsors	21,781	58,264	80,045
Revenues from sale of time to local advertisers and sponsors	16,623	48,228	64,851
Total revenues from time sales	139,888	142,506	282,394
Commissions paid to representatives, etc	27,509	18,923	46,432
Incidental broadcast revenues:			
Revenues from sale of talent, etc	47,504	8,700	56,204
Furnishing material or service	10,352	7,580	17,932
Other incidental revenues	9,969	3,527	13,496
Total broadcast revenues	180,204	143,390	323,594
Total broadcast expenses	170,301	97,601	267,902
Total broadcast income (before federal income tax)	9,903	45,789	55,692
Investment in tangible broadcast property:			
Original cost	61,019	63,110	124,129
Depreciation to date	14,589	24,739	39,328
Depreciated cost	46,430	38,371	84,801

[1]Excludes 14 stations which commenced operations during 1952, having TV broadcast revenues, expenses, and loss of $629,247, $824,314 and ($195,067) respectively.

1953 Broadcasting Revenues

Item	4 networks and their 16 owned and oper- ated TV stations (000)	244 other TV stations[1] (000)	Total 4 networks and 260 TV stations (000)
Revenues from the sale of time:			
Network time sales:			
Nationwide networks	$126,541	$ 45,270	$171,811
Miscellaneous networks and stations	——	89	89
Revenue from network time sales	126,541	45,359	171,900
Non-network time sales to:			
National and regional advertisers and sponsors	36,870	87,448	124,318
Local advertisers and sponsors	19,576	68,898	88,474
Total revenues from non-network time sales	56,446	156,346	212,792
Total revenues from time sales	182,987	201,705	384,692
Deduct commissions to regularly established agencies, representatives, brokers and others	[2]34,999	27,462	62,461
Net revenues from time sales	147,988	174,243	322,231
Revenues from incidental broadcast activities:			
Talent	60,888	9,681	70,569
Sundry broadcast revenues	22,792	16,185	38,977
Total revenues from incidental broadcast activities	83,680	25,866	109,546
Total broadcast revenues	231,668	200,109	431,777
Total broadcast expenses of networks and stations	213,661	146,853	360,514
Broadcast income before Federal income tax	18,007	53,256	71,263

[1]Excludes data for 74 stations with less than $25,000 in time sales. Such stations report only total revenues and total expenses.
[2]Of this amount $26,211,189 is applicable to the total sale of network time.

1954 Broadcasting Revenues

Item	4 networks and their 16 owned and oper- ated TV stations (000)	380 other TV stations (000)	Total 4 networks and 396 TV stations[1] (000)
Revenues from the sale of time:			
Network time sales:			
Nationwide networks	$177,212	$ 64,013	$241,225
Miscellaneous networks and stations	——	——	——
Revenue from network time sales	177,212	64,013	241,225
Non-network time sales to:			
National and regional advertisers and sponsors	46,849	129,917	176,766
Local advertisers and sponsors	22,542	97,589	120,134
Total revenues from non-network time sales	69,391	227,506	296,897
Total revenues from time sales	246,603	291,519	538,122
Deduct—Commissions to regularly established agencies, representatives, brokers and others	[2]47,504	38,413	85,917
Net revenues from time sales	199,099	253,106	452,205
Revenues from incidental broadcast activities:			
Talent	75,850	9,137	84,987
Sundry broadcast revenues	31,731	24,014	55,745
Total revenues from incidental broadcast activities	107,581	33,151	140,732
Total broadcast revenues	306,680	286,257	592,937
Total broadcast expenses of networks and stations	270,159	232,478	502,637
Broadcast income before Federal income tax	36,521	53,779	90,300

[1]Excludes data for 14 stations with less than $25,000 in time sales. Such stations report only total revenues and total expenses.
[2]Of this amount $36,757,871 is applicable to the total sale of network time.

1955 Broadcasting Revenues

Item	4 networks and their 16 owned and oper-ated TV stations[1] (mil.)	421 other TV stations (millions) (mil.)	Total 4 networks and 437 TV stations[1] (mil.)
Revenues from the sale of time:			
Network time sales:			
Nationwide networks	$225.7	$ 83.0	$308.7
Miscellaneous networks and stations	—	.2	.2
Total network time sales	225.7	83.2	308.9
Non-network time sales to:			
National and regional advertisers	47.6	174.8	222.4
Local advertisers	24.8	125.0	149.8
Total non-network time sales	72.4	299.8	372.2
Total time sales	298.1	383.0	681.1
Deduct—Commissions to agencies, representatives, etc	[2]57.9	50.8	108.7
Net time sales	240.2	332.2	572.4
Revenues from incidental broadcast activities:			
Talent	102.1	10.4	112.5
Sundry broadcast revenues	31.8	28.0	59.8
Total incidental broadcast activities	133.9	38.4	172.3
Total broadcast revenues	374.1	370.6	744.7
Total broadcast expenses of networks and stations	306.0	288.5	594.5
Broadcast income before Federal income tax	68.1	82.1	150.2

[1] 3 networks after Sept. 15, 1955, when DuMont ceased network operations.
[2] Of this amount 47.0 million is applicable to the total sale of network time.

1956 Broadcasting Revenues

Item	3 networks and their 15 owned and operated TV stations (mil.)	459 other TV stations (millions) (mil.)	Total 3 networks and 474 TV stations (mil.)
Revenues from the sale of time:			
Network time sales:			
Nationwide networks	$269.1	$ 98.6	$367.7
Miscellaneous networks and stations	—	—	—
Total network time sales	269.1	98.6	367.7
Non-network time sales to:			
National and regional advertisers	55.7	225.5	281.2
Local advertisers	22.9	151.3	174.2
Total non-network time sales	78.6	376.8	455.4
Total time sales	347.7	475.4	823.1
Deduct—Commissions to agencies, representatives, etc	[1]70.9	63.1	134.0
Net time sales	276.8	412.3	689.1
Revenues from incidental broadcast activities:			
Talent	135.1	11.3	146.4
Sundry broadcast revenues	30.4	31.0	61.4
Total incidental broadcast activities	165.5	42.3	207.8
Total broadcast revenues	442.3	454.6	896.9
Total broadcast expenses of networks and stations	356.9	350.4	707.3
Broadcast income before Federal income tax	85.4	104.2	189.6

[1] Of this amount $55.7 million is applicable to the total sale of network time.

1957 Broadcasting Revenues

Item	3 networks and their 16 owned and operated TV stations (mil.)	485 other TV stations (mil.)	Total 3 networks and 501 TV stations (mil.)
Revenues from the sale of time:			
Network time sales:			
Nationwide networks	$287.7	$106.5	$394.2
Miscellaneous networks and stations	—	—	—
Total network time sales	287.7	106.5	394.2
Non-network time sales:			
National and regional advertisers	58.5	237.9	300.5
Local advertisers	23.4	154.7	174.0
Total non-network time sales	81.9	392.6	474.5
Total time sales	369.6	499.1	868.7
Deduct—Commissions to agencies, representatives, etc	175.9	66.5	142.4
Net time sales	293.7	432.6	726.3
Revenues from incidental broadcast activities:			
Talent	144.5	11.5	156.0
Sundry broadcast revenues	29.7	31.2	60.9
Total incidental broadcast activities	174.2	42.7	216.9
Total broadcast revenues	467.9	475.3	943.2
Total broadcast expenses of networks and stations	397.2	386.0	783.2
Broadcast income (before federal income tax)	70.7	89.3	160.0

[1]Of this amount $59.6 million is applicable to the total sale of network time.

1958 Broadcasting Revenues

Item	3 networks and their 19 owned and operated TV stations (mil.)	495 other TV stations (mil.)	Total 3 networks and 514 TV stations (mil.)
Revenues from the sale of time:			
Network time sales:			
Nation-wide networks	$306.7	$117.8	$424.5
Miscellaneous networks and stations	—	—	—
Total network time sales	306.7	117.8	424.5
Non-network time sales:			
National and regional advertisers	73.5	271.7	345.2
Local advertisers	24.6	156.7	181.3
Total non-network time sales	98.1	428.4	526.5
Total time sales	404.8	546.2	951.0
Deduct—Commissions to agencies, representatives, etc	183.4	75.9	159.3
Net time sales	321.4	470.3	791.7
Revenues from incidental broadcast activities:			
Talent	161.8	10.4	172.2
Sundry broadcast revenues	33.5	32.6	66.1
Total incidental broadcast activities	195.3	43.0	288.3
Total broadcast revenues	516.7	513.3	1030.0
Total broadcast expenses of networks and stations	439.7	418.4	858.1
Broadcast income (before federal income tax)	77.0	94.9	171.9

[1]Of this amount $64.5 million is applicable to the total sale of network time.

1959 Broadcasting Revenues

Item	3 networks (mil.)	17 networks owned and operated TV stations[1] (mil.)	502 other TV stations (mil.)	Total 3 networks and 519 TV stations (mil.)
Revenues from the sale of time:				
Network time sales:				
Sale of network time to advertisers	$443.3	——	——	——
Total network time sales	443.3	——	——	——
Deductions from networks' revenue from sale of time to advertisers	——	——	——	——
Paid to owned and operated stations	30.5	——	——	——
Paid to affiliated stations	125.0	——	——	——
Total participation by others (excluding commissions) in revenue from sale of network time	155.5	——	——	——
Total retentions from sale of network time	287.8	$ 30.5	[2]$127.5	$445.8
Non-network time sales:				
National and regional advertisers		92.6	331.6	424.2
Local advertisers	——	27.3	173.3	200.6
Total non-network time sales	——	119.9	504.9	624.8
Total time sales	287.8	150.4	632.4	1,070.6
Deduct—Commissions to agencies, representatives, etc	66.7	21.9	91.6	180.2
Net time sales	221.1	128.5	540.8	890.4
Revenues from incidental broadcast activities:				
Talent	181.7	4.4	10.9	197.0
Sundry broadcast revenues	35.7	4.7	36.1	76.5
Total incidental broadcast activities	217.4	9.1	47.0	273.5
Total broadcast revenues	438.5	137.6	587.8	1,163.9
Total broadcast expenses	406.5	81.7	453.4	941.6
Broadcast income (before federal income tax)	32.0	55.9	134.4	222.3

[1]Includes data for 2 network owned and operated UHF stations that were sold prior to Dec. 31, 1959.
[2]Total retentions from sale of network time of $127.5 million by 502 other TV stations includes revenues received from miscellaneous TV networks in addition to receipts from the 3 national TV networks.

1960 Broadcasting Revenues

Item	3 networks (mil.)	15 networks owned and operated TV stations[1] (mil.)	515 other TV stations (mil.)	Total 3 networks and 530 TV stations (mil.)
Revenues from the sale of time:				
Network time sales:				
Sale of network time to advertisers	$468.8	——	——	——
Total network time sales	468.8	——	——	——
Deductions from networks' revenue from sale of time to advertisers	——	——	——	——
Paid to owned and operated stations	29.9	——	——	——
Paid to affiliated stations	132.0	——	——	——
Total participation by others (excluding commissions) in revenue from sale of network time	161.9	——	——	——
Total retentions from sale of network time	306.9	$ 29.9	[1]$134.8	$471.6
Non-network time sales:				
National and regional advertisers	——	100.3	358.9	459.2
Local advertisers	——	30.8	185.0	215.8
Total non-network time sales	——	131.1	543.9	675.0
Total time sales	306.9	161.0	678.7	1,146.6
Deduct—Commissions to agencies, representatives, etc	70.4	24.6	99.7	194.7
Net time sales	236.5	136.4	579.0	951.9
Revenues from incidental broadcast activities:				
Talent	220.1	3.6	10.6	234.3
Sundry broadcast revenues	38.2	5.9	38.3	82.4
Total incidental broadcast activities	258.3	9.5	48.9	316.7
Total broadcast revenues	494.8	145.9	627.9	1,268.6
Total broadcast expenses	461.2	84.3	479.0	1,024.5
Broadcast income (before federal income tax)	33.6	61.6	148.9	244.1

[1]Total retentions from sale of network time of $134.8 million by 515 other TV stations includes revenues received from miscellaneous TV networks in addition to receipts from the 3 national TV networks.

1961 Broadcasting Revenues

Item	Networks (mil.)	15 networks owned and operated TV stations[1] (mil.)	525 other TV stations (mil.)	Total 3 networks and 540 TV stations (mil.)
Revenues from the sale of time:				
Network time sales:				
Sale of network time to advertisers	$476.8	——	——	——
Total network time sales	476.8	——	——	——
Deductions from networks' revenue from sale of time to advertisers				
Paid to owned and operated stations	32.8	——	——	——
Paid to affiliated stations	148.1	——	——	——
Total participation by others (excluding commissions) in revenue from sale of network time	180.9	——	——	——
Total retentions from sale of network time	295.9	$ 32.8	[1]$151.6	$480.3
Non-network time sales:				
National and regional advertisers	——	102.8	365.7	468.5
Local advertisers	——	30.6	180.6	211.2
Total non-network time sales	——	133.4	546.3	679.7
Total time sales	295.9	166.2	697.9	1,160.0
Deduct—Commissions to agencies, representatives, etc	71.5	25.4	101.1	198.0
Net time sales	224.4	140.8	596.8	962.0
Revenues from incidental broadcast activities:				
Talent	273.0	3.4	10.3	286.7
Sundry broadcast revenues	29.1	4.6	35.9	69.6
Total incidental broadcast activities	302.1	8.0	46.2	356.3
Total broadcast revenues	526.5	148.8	643.0	1,318.3
Total broadcast expenses	501.8	86.5	493.0	1,081.3
Broadcast income (before federal income tax)	24.7	62.3	150.0	237.0

[1]Total retentions from sale of network time of $151.6 million by 525 other TV stations includes revenues received from miscellaneous TV networks in addition to receipts from the 3 national TV networks.

1962 Broadcasting Revenues

Item	Networks (mil.)	15 networks owned and operated TV stations[1] (mil.)	539 other TV stations (mil.)	Total 3 networks and 554 TV stations (mil.)
Revenues from the sale of time:				
Network time sales:				
Sale of network time to advertisers	$520.2	——	——	——
Deductions from networks' revenue from sale of time to advertisers				
Paid to owned and operated stations	36.1	——	——	——
Paid to affiliated stations	164.5	——	——	——
Total participation by others (excluding commissions) in revenue from sale of network time	200.6	——	——	——
Total retentions from sale of network time	319.6	$ 36.1	[1]$165.8	$521.5
Non-network time sales:				
National and regional advertisers	——	114.8	424.7	539.5
Local advertisers	——	38.4	204.1	242.6
Total non-network time sales	——	153.2	628.8	782.0
Total time sales	319.6	189.3	794.6	1,303.5
Deduct—Commissions to agencies, representatives, etc	77.9	28.5	113.7	220.1
Net time sales	241.7	160.8	680.9	1,083.4
Revenues from incidental broadcast activities:				
Talent and programs	310.4	3.5	8.6	322.5
Sundry broadcast revenues	32.6	5.2	42.5	80.3
Total incidental broadcast revenues	343.0	8.7	51.1	402.8
Total broadcast revenues	584.7	169.5	732.0	1,486.2
Total broadcast expenses	548.0	94.8	531.8	1,174.6
Broadcast income (before federal income tax)	36.7	74.7	200.2	311.6

[1]Total retentions from sale of network time of $165.8 million by 539 other TV stations includes revenues received from miscellaneous TV networks in addition to receipts from the 3 national TV networks.

1963 Broadcasting Revenues

Item	Net-works (mil.)	15 own-ed and oper-ated TV stations (mil.)	550 other TV sta-tions (mil.)	Total 3 networks and 565 stations (mil.)	Percent change from previous year
Revenues from the sale of time:					
Network time sales:					
Sale of network time to advertisers	$537.0	—	—	—	—
Deductions from networks' revenue from sale of time to advertisers					
Paid to owned and operated stations	34.9	—	—	—	—
Paid to affiliated stations	166.9	—	—	—	—
Total participation by others (excluding commissions) in revenue from sale of network time	201.8	—	—	—	—
Total retentions from sale of network time	335.2	$ 34.9	[1]$167.8	$537.9	3.1
Non-network time sales:					
National and regional advertisers	—	131.8	468.9	600.7	11.3
Local advertisers	—	42.2	213.9	256.1	5.6
Total non-network time sales	—	174.0	682.8	856.8	9.6
Total time sales	335.2	208.9	850.6	1,394.7	7.0
Deduct—Commissions to agencies, representatives, etc	80.6	32.7	123.0	236.3	7.4
Net time sales	254.6	176.2	727.6	1,158.4	6.9
Revenues from incidental broadcast activities:					
Talent and programs	345.8	3.0	8.4	357.2	10.8
Sundry broadcast revenues	35.4	5.3	40.9	81.6	1.6
Total incidental broadcast revenues	381.2	8.3	49.3	438.8	8.9
Total broadcast revenues	635.8	184.5	776.9	1,597.2	7.5
Total broadcast expenses	579.4	104.7	569.9	1,254.0	6.8
Broadcast income (before federal income tax)	56.4	79.8	207.0	343.2	10.1

[1]Total retentions from sale of network time of $167.8 million by 550 other TV stations includes revenues received from miscellaneous TV networks in addition to receipts from the 3 national TV networks.

1964 Broadcasting Revenues

Item	Net- works (mil.)	15 own- ed and oper- ated TV stations (mil.)	560 other TV sta- tions (mil.)	Total 3 networks and 575 stations (mil.)	Percent change from previous year
Revenues from the sale of time:					
Network time sales:					
Sale of network time to advertisers	$562.8	—	—	—	—
Deductions from networks' revenue from sale of time to advertisers					
Paid to owned and operated stations	36.7	—	—	—	—
Paid to affiliated stations	177.2	—	—	—	—
Total participation by others (excluding commissions) in revenue from sale of network time	213.9	—	—	—	—
Total retentions from sale of network time	348.9	$ 36.7	[1]$177.8	$563.4	4.7
Non-network time sales:					
National and regional advertisers	—	162.8	526.7	689.5	14.8
Local advertisers	—	47.6	249.4	297.0	16.0
Total non-network time sales	—	210.4	776.1	986.5	15.1
Total time sales	348.9	247.1	953.9	1,549.9	11.1
Deduct—Commissions to agencies, representatives, etc	83.5	39.6	140.4	263.5	11.5
Net time sales	265.4	207.5	813.5	1,286.4	11.0
Revenues from incidental broadcast activities:					
Talent and programs	409.2	3.0	9.7	421.9	18.1
Sundry broadcast revenues	37.9	5.7	41.3	84.9	4.0
Total incidental broadcast activities	447.1	8.7	51.0	506.8	15.5
Total broadcast revenues	712.5	216.2	864.6	1,793.3	12.3
Total broadcast expenses	652.3	119.9	605.5	1,377.7	9.9
Broadcast income (before federal income tax)	60.2	96.3	259.1	415.6	21.1

[1]Total retentions from sale of network time of $177.8 million by 560 other TV stations includes revenues received from miscellaneous TV networks in addition to receipts from the 3 national TV networks.

1965 Broadcasting Revenues

Item	Net-works (mil.)	15 own-ed and oper-ated TV stations (mil.)	573 other TV sta-tions (mil.)	Total 3 networks and 588 stations (mil.)	Percent change from previous year
Revenues from the sale of time:					
Network time sales:					
Sale of network time to advertisers	$581.3	——	——	——	—
Deductions from networks' revenue from sale of time to advertisers					
Paid to owned and operated stations	38.4	——	——	——	—
Paid to affiliated stations	[1]188.0	——	——	——	—
Total participation by others (excluding commissions) in revenue from sale of network time	226.4	——	——	——	—
Total retentions from sale of network time	354.9	$ 38.4	[1]$191.8	$585.1	3.9
Non-network time sales:					
National and regional advertisers	——	179.5	585.0	764.5	10.9
Local advertisers	——	54.2	269.9	324.1	9.1
Total non-network time sales	——	233.7	854.9	1,088.6	10.3
Total time sales	354.9	272.1	1046.7	1,673.7	8.0
Deduct—Commissions to agencies, representatives, etc	79.3	44.4	156.3	280.0	6.3
Net time sales	275.6	227.7	890.4	1,393.7	8.3
Revenues from incidental broadcast activities:					
Talent and programs	473.1	1.6	9.7	484.8	14.8
Sundry broadcast revenues	39.9	5.9	40.9	86.7	2.1
Total incidental broadcast activities	513.0	7.5	50.6	571.1	12.7
Total broadcast revenues	788.6	235.2	941.0	1,964.8	9.6
Total broadcast expenses	729.2	133.0	654.7	1,516.9	10.1
Broadcast income (before federal income tax)	59.4	102.2	286.3	447.9	7.8

[1]Total retentions from sale of network time of $191.8 million by 573 other TV stations includes revenues received from miscellaneous TV networks in addition to receipts from the 3 national TV networks. Of the revenues received from miscellaneous networks ($3.8), approximately $3.1 million was reported by stations in Puerto Rico.

1966 Broadcasting Revenues

Item	networks (Mil.)	Percent of change from previous year (Mil.)	15 owned and operated TV stations (Mil.)	Percent of change from previous year	593 other TV stations (Mil.)	Percent of change from previous year	Total 3 networks and 608 stations (Mil.)	Percent of change from previous year
Revenues from the sale of time:								
Network time sales to advertisers .	$614.1	[1]4.0	——	——	——	——	——	——
Deductions from network revenue from sale of time to advertisers:								
Paid to owned and operated stations	40.6	5.7	——	——	——	——	——	——
Paid to affiliated stations	[3]201.0	6.9	——	——	——	——	——	——
Total participation by others (excluding commissions) in revenue from sale of network time	241.6	6.7	——	——	——	——	——	——
Total retentions from sale of network time	372.5	[1]2.4	40.6	5.7	[3]$203.6	6.2	$616.7	[1]3.8
Non-network time sales:								
National and regional advertisers	——	——	230.9	[2]15.0	640.8	9.5	871.7	[3]10.9
Local advertisers	——	——	34.7	[2]5.2	311.7	15.5	346.4	[2]14.4
Total non-network time sales	——	——	265.6	13.6	952.5	11.4	1,218.1	11.9
Total time sales	372.5	2.4	306.2	12.6	1,156.1	10.5	1,834.8	9.1
Deduct commissions to agencies, representatives, etc	91.7	[1]4.0	50.4	13.5	172.2	10.2	314.3	[1]8.7
Net time sales	280.8	1.9	255.8	12.4	983.9	10.5	1,520.5	9.1
Revenues from incidental broadcast activities:								
Talent and programs	582.8	23.2	1.1	(31.2)	9.3	(4.1)	593.2	22.5
Sundry broadcast revenues	40.3	1.0	5.5	(6.8)	43.5	6.4	89.3	3.0
Total from incidental broadcast activities	623.1	21.5	6.6	(12.0)	52.8	4.3	682.5	19.5
Total broadcast revenues	903.9	14.6	262.4	11.6	1,036.7	10.2	2,203.0	12.1
Total broadcast expenses	825.2	13.2	154.3	16.1	730.6	11.6	1,710.1	12.7
Broadcast income (before federal income tax)	78.7	32.5	108.1	5.8	306.6	6.9	492.9	10.0

[1]Information received after publication of the 1965 report indicated an understatement of $8.9 million in 1965 for each of these items: sales of network time to advertisers, total retentions from sales of network time, and commissions to agencies and representatives. The percentage changes from 1965 are based on the revised figures.

[2]Information received after publication of the 1965 report indicated that in 1965 nonnetwork time sales to local advertisers were overstated by $11.2 million and non-network time sales to national and regional advertisers understated by the same amount. The percentage changes from 1965 are based on the revised figures.

[3]Total retentions from sale of network time of $203.6 million by 593 other TV stations includes revenues received from miscellaneous TV networks in addition to receipts from the 3 national TV networks.

( ) Indicates decline.

1967 Broadcasting Revenues

Item	Networks (Mil.)	Percent of change from previous year (Mil.)	15 owned and operated TV stations (Mil.)	Percent of change from previous year	604 other TV stations (Mil.)	Percent of change from previous year	Total 3 networks and 619 stations (Mil.)	Percent of change from previous year
Revenues from the sale of time:								
Network time sales to advertisers .	$606.9	(1.2)	—	—	—	—	—	—
Deductions from network revenue from sale of time to advertisers:								
Paid to owned and operated stations	40.7	0.2	—	—	—	—	—	—
Paid to affiliated stations	1202.5	0.7	—	—	—	—	—	—
Total participation by others (excluding commissions) in revenue from sale of network time	243.2	0.7	—	—	—	—	—	—
Total retentions from sale of network time	363.7	(2.4)	$40.7	0.2	1$205.2	0.8	$609.6	(1.2)
Non-network time sales:								
National and regional advertisers	—	—	228.8	(0.9)	642.0	0.3	871.7	.0
Local advertisers	—	—	37.4	7.8	327.9	5.2	365.3	5.5
Total non-network time sales	—	—	266.2	0.2	970.8	1.9	1,237.0	1.6
Total time sales	363.7	(2.4)	306.9	0.2	1,176.0	1.7	1,846.6	0.6
Deduct—Commissions to agencies, representatives, etc	90.9	(0.9)	50.3	(0.2)	172.4	0.1	313.6	(0.2)
Net time sales	272.8	(2.8)	256.6	0.3	1,003.6	2.0	1,533.0	0.8
Revenues from incidental broadcast activities:								
Talent and programs	637.0	9.3	1.0	(9.1)	9.3	0.0	647.3	9.1
Sundry broadcast revenues	43.5	7.9	5.7	3.6	45.9	5.5	95.1	6.5
Total from incidental broadcast activities	680.5	9.2	6.7	1.5	55.2	4.5	742.4	8.8
Total broadcast revenues	953.3	5.5	263.3	0.3	1,058.8	2.1	2,275.4	3.3
Total broadcast expenses	897.5	8.8	159.0	3.0	804.3	10.1	1,860.8	8.8
Broadcast income (before federal income tax)	55.8	(29.1)	104.3	(3.5)	254.5	(16.9)	414.6	(15.9)

[1]Total retentions from sale of network times of $205.2 million by 604 other TV stations includes revenues received from miscellaneous TV networks in addition to receipts from the 3 national TV networks.

( ) Indicates decline.

1968 Broadcasting Revenues

Item	Networks (Mil.)	Percent of change from previous year (Mil.)	15 owned and operated TV stations (Mil.)	Percent of change from previous year	627 other TV stations (Mil.)	Percent of change from previous year	Total 3 networks and 642 stations (Mil.)	Percent of change from previous year
Revenues from the sale of time:								
Network time sales to advertisers .	$633.7	4.4	——	——	——	——	——	——
Deductions from network revenue from sale of time to advertisers:								
Paid to owned and operated stations	40.5	(.5)	——	——	——	——	——	——
Paid to affiliated stations	¹203.7	0.7	——	——	——	——	——	——
Total participation by others (excluding commissions) in revenue from sale of network time	244.2	0.5	——	——	——	——	——	——
Total retentions from sale of network time	389.5	7.0	$40.5	(0.5)	¹$207.1	0.9	$637.1	4.5
Non-network time sales:								
National and regional advertisers	——	——	257.1	12.4	741.0	15.3	998.0	14.5
Local advertisers	——	——	42.1	12.6	410.4	25.2	452.5	23.9
Total non-network time sales	——	——	299.1	12.4	1,151.4	18.6	1,450.6	17.3
Total time sales	389.5	7.0	339.6	10.7	1,358.5	15.5	2,087.6	13.1
Deduct—Commissions to agencies, representatives, etc	95.2	4.8	56.3	11.9	204.4	18.6	355.9	13.5
Net time sales	294.3	7.8	283.4	10.4	1,154.0	15.0	1,731.8	13.0
Revenues from incidental broadcast activities:								
Talent and programs	669.1	5.0	0.7	(33.5)	8.7	(6.5)	678.4	4.8
Sundry broadcast revenues	53.1	22.1	7.5	31.4	50.2	9.4	110.7	16.4
Total from incidental broadcast activities	722.1	6.1	8.2	21.3	58.8	6.5	789.1	6.3
Total broadcast revenues	1,016.4	6.6	291.5	10.7	1,212.9	14.6	2,520.9	10.8
Total broadcast expenses	960.0	7.0	169.2	6.4	897.0	11.5	2,026.1	8.9
Broadcast income (before federal income tax)	56.4	1.1	122.4	17.4	316.0	24.2	494.8	19.3

¹Total retentions from sale of network times of $207,1 million by 627 other TV stations includes revenues received from miscellaneous TV networks in addition to receipts from the 3 national TV networks.

Note: In some cases, last digits of figures do not add because of rounding.

( ) Indicates decline.

1969 Broadcasting Revenues

Item	Networks (Mil.)	Percent of change from previous year[2] (Mil.)	15 owned and operated TV stations (Mil.)	Percent of change from previous year[2]	658 other TV stations (Mil.)	Percent of change from previous year	Total 3 networks and 673 stations[1] (Mil.)	Percent of change from previous year[2]
Sales to advertisers for time, programs talent, facilities, and services								
Network sales	[1]$1,571.2	10.6	—	—	—	—	—	—
Deduct: Payments to owned and operated stations	42.4	4.8	—	—	—	—	—	—
Deduct: Payments to other affiliated stations	213.2	4.7	—	—	—	—	—	—
Retained from network sales	1,315.5	11.8	42.4	4.8	211.7	2.2	1,569.6	10.2
Non-network sales								
To national and regional advertisers	—	—	279.5	8.5	839.6	11.6	1,119.1	10.8
To local advertisers	—	—	55.5	30.1	[4]491.3	11.8	546.8	13.4
Total non-network sales	—	—	335.0	11.6	1,330.9	11.7	1,665,9	11.7
Total sales to advertisers	1,315.5	11.8	337.4	10.8	1,542.6	10.3	3,235.5	10.9
Sales to other than advertisers	64.3	21.2	8.2	15.5	17.1	(7.5)	89.7	13.9
Total sales	1,379.7	12.2	385.7	10.9	1,559.7	10.0	3,325.1	11.0
Deduct: Commissions to agencies, representatives, etc	[3]235.7	10.5	62.4	10.9	230.8	12.9	528.9	11.6
Total revenues	1,144.1	12.6	323.3	10.9	1,328.9	9.6	2,796.2	10.9
Total expenses	1,051.3	9.5	189.9	12.2	1,001.3	11.6	2,242.6	10.7
Total income (before federal income tax)	92.7	64.4	133.4	9.0	327.5	3.6	553.6	11.9

[1]Include 56 satellites 22 of which filed combined reports with their parent stations.

[2]See Broadcast Financial data of three national TV networks and 658 stations, 1968.

[3]Advertising agency commissions on network billings are paid directly by the advertiser to the agency. These commissions estimated at $235.7 million (15% of network advertising revenues) have been included in each of the footnoted entries above. Data previously published by the FCC did not include the entire amount of agency commissions.

[4]Includes $290 thousand from stations reporting less than $25,000 in time sales.

Note: Last digits may not add because of rounding.

( ) Indicates decline.

1970 Broadcasting Revenues

Item	Networks (Mil.)	Percent of change from previous year (Mil.)	15 owned and operated TV stations (Mil.)	Percent of change from previous year	671 other TV stations[1] (Mil.)	Percent of change from previous year	Total 3 networks and 686 stations[1] (Mil.)	Percent of change from previous year
Sales to advertisers for time, programs talent, facilities, and services								
Network sales	$1,546.5	(1.6)	——	——				
Deduct: Payments to owned and operated stations	39.4	(7.1)	——	——				
Deduct: Payments to other affiliated stations	196.2	(8.0)	——	——				
Retained from network sales . . .	1,311.0	(0.4)	$ 39.4	(7.1)	$ 200.7	(5.2)	$1,551.1	(1.2)
Non-network sales								
To national and regional advertisers	——	——	270.2	(3.3)	832.3	(0.9)	1,102.6	(1.5)
To local advertisers	——	——	58.1	4.7	531.0	8.1	589.1	7.7
Total non-network sales	——	——	328.3	(2.0)	1,363.4	2.4	1,691.7	1.5
Total sales to advertisers . . .	1,311.0	(0.4)	367.6	(2.6)	1,564.1	1.4	3,242.8	0.2
Sales to other than advertisers	66.5	3.4	6.2	(24.4)	21.1	23.4	93.8	4.6
Total sales	1,377.5	(0.2)	373.8	(3.1)	1,585.2	1.6	3,396.6	0.3
Deduct: Commissions to agencies, representatives, etc	[2]233.0	(1.7)	61.4	(1.6)	234.0	1.4	528.4	(0.1)
Total Revenues	1,144.6	(0.0)	312.5	(3.4)	1,351.1	1.7	2,808.2	0.4
Total Expenses	1,094.5	4.1	195.1	2.7	1,064.7	6.3	2,354.4	5.0
Total Income (before federal income tax)	50.1	(46.0)	11.73	(12.1)	286.4	(12.6)	453.6	(18.0)

[1]Include 63 satellites 27 of which filed combined reports with their parent stations.

[2]Advertising agency commissions on network billings are paid directly by the advertiser to the agency. These commissions estimated at $233.0 million have been included in each of the footnoted entries above.

Note: Last digits may not add because of rounding.

( ) Indicates decline.

1971 Broadcasting Revenues

Item	Networks (Mil.)	Percent of change from previous year (Mil.)	15 owned and operated TV stations (Mil.)	Percent of change from previous year	673 other TV stations[1] (Mil.)	Percent of change from previous year	Total 3 networks and 688 stations[1] (Mil.)	Percent of change from previous year
Sales to advertisers for time, programs talent, facilities, and services								
Network sales	$1,487.5	(3.8)	—	—				
Deduct: Payments to O & O stations	35.7	(9.4)	—	—				
Deduct: Payments to other affiliated stations	191.3	(2.5)	—	—				
Retained from network sales	1,260.3	(3.8)	[2]35.9	(8.9)	[2]194.0	(3.4)	1,490.4	(3.9)
Non-network sales								
To national & regional	—	—	236.4	(12.5)	786.4	(5.5)	1,022.8	(7.2)
To local	—	—	68.6	18.2	596.4	12.4	655.6	13.0
Total non-network sales	—	—	305.0	(7.1)	1,393.4	1.5	1,688.4	(0.2)
Total sales to advertisers	1,260.5	(3.8)	340.9	(7.3)	1,577.4	0.8	3,178.8	(2.0)
Sales to other than advertisers	57.5	(13.2)	5.6	(14.8)	21.7	3.2	84.7	(9.7)
Total sales	1,318.2	(4.3)	346.2	(7.4)	1,599.2	0.9	3,263.5	(2.2)
Deduct: Commissions to agencies, etc	224.1	(3.8)	[3]61.4	0.0	227.7	(2.7)	513.2	(2.9)
Total Revenues	1,094.1	(4.4)	[3]284.8	(8.9)	1,371.4	1.5	2,750.3	(2.1)
Total Expenses	1,040.5	(4.9)	[3]193.6	(0.8)	1,127.2	5.9	2,361.2	0.3
Total Income (before federal income tax)	53.7	7.2	91.2	(22.3)	244.3	(14.7)	389.2	(14.2)

[1]Include 66 satellites 28 of which filed combined reports with their parent stations.

[2]Includes payments from networks other than ABC, CBS, or NBC.

[3]In 1970 and in prior years, the commissions paid on non-network sales by one network's owned-and-operated stations to a sales representative firm owned by the same network were reported as selling expenses of the stations rather than as deductions from sales. Starting with 1971, the owned and operated station of all three national networks report station representative fees as a deduction from sales, if this network's stations had reported under its old procedure, the 1971 broadcast revenue and broadcast expense figures would be slightly higher and commissions would be lower. Income figures are not affected.

Note: Last digits may not add because of rounding.

( ) Indicates decline.

1972 Broadcasting Revenues

Item	Networks (Mil.)	Percent of change from previous year (Mil.)	15 owned and operated TV stations (Mil.)	Percent of change from previous year	675 other TV stations[1] (Mil.)	Percent of change from previous year	Total 3 networks and 690 stations (Mil.)	Percent of change from previous year
Sales to advertisers for time, programs talent, facilities, and services								
Network sales	$1,682.6	13.1						
Deduct: Payments to O&O Stations	34.2	(3.9)						
Deduct: Payments to other affiliated stations	185.4	(3.1)						
Retained from network sales	1,463.0	16.1	[2]34.2	4.2	[2]190.1	(2.0)	1,687.5	13.2
Non-network sales								
To national & regional	——	——	272.7	15.4	904.7	15.0	1,177.4	15.1
To local	——	——	84.2	22.7	725.9	21.6	810.1	21.7
Total non-network sales	——	——	356.9	17.0	1,630.6	17.9	1,987.5	17.7
Total sales to advertisers	1,463.0	16.1	391.3	14.0	1,820.7	15.4	3,675.0	15.5
Sales to other than advertisers	51.7	6.9	6.1	15.1	26.9	24.0	94.7	11.8
Total sales	1,524.7	15.7	397.4	14.8	1,847.6	15.5	3,789.7	15.5
Deduct: Commissions to agencies, etc	253.4	13.1	70.3	14.5	266.6	17.1	590.3	15.0
Total Revenues	1,271.3	16.2	327.1	14.9	1,581.1	15.3	3,179.4	15.6
Total Expenses	1,160.4	11.5	224.6	18.0	1,242.8	10.2	2,627.3	11.3
Total Income (before federal income tax)	110.9	106.5	102.5	12.4	338.8	33.7	552.2	41.9

[1]Include 59 satellites 27 of which filed combined reports with their parent stations.
[2]Includes payments from networks other than ABC, CBS, or NBC.
Note: Last digits may not add because of rounding.
( ) Indicates decline.

1973 Broadcasting Revenues

Item	Networks (Mil.)	Percent of change from previous year (Mil.)	15 owned and operated TV stations (Mil.)	Percent of change from previous year	677 other TV stations (Mil.)	Percent of change from previous year	Total 3 networks and 692 stations (Mil.)	Percent of change from previous year
Sales to advertisers for time, programs, talent, facilities, and service								
Network sales	$1,853.3	9.1						
Deduct: Payments to O&O Stations	36.2	29						
Deduct: Payments to other affiliated stations	193.3	4.3						
Retained from network sales	1,607.7	9.8	35.4	2.9	197.6	3.9	1,839.7	9.0
Non-network sales								
To national & regional	——	——	273.4	.2	956.7	5.7	1,230.2	4.5
To local	——	——	113.4	34.7	818.8	12.8	932.2	15.1
Total non-network sales	——	——	386.8	8.4	1,775.6	8.9	2,162.4	8.8
Total sales to advertisers . . .	1,606.7	9.8	422.3	7.9	1,973.1	8.4	4,002.1	8.9
Sales to other than advertisers	74.9	21.4	5.8	(4.9)	24.6	(8.6)	105.2	11.1
Total Sales	1,681.6	10.3	428.1	7.7	1,997.7	8.1	4,107.3	9.0
Deduct: Commissions to agencies, etc	276.7	9.2	74.9	6.5	240.9	9.1	642.5	8.8
Total Revenues	1,404.9	10.5	363.1	7.9	1,706.8	7.9	3,464.8	9.0
Total Expenses	1,220.0	5.1	250.3	11.4	1,341.4	8.0	2,811.7	7.3
Total Income (before federal income tax)	184.8	66.6	102.8	.3	365.4	7.8	653.1	18.0

[1]Include 59 satellites, 29 of which filed combined reports with their parent stations.

[2]Includes payments from networks other than ABC, CBS, or NBC.

[3]A part of the increase in local sales for both the network owned-and-operated and all other stations is due to a change in the way some stations classified national and local sales in 1973. These stations apparently reported as local sales some sales that would have been classified as national/regional in prior years. Although the full extent of this shift is unknown, comparisons of 1973 data for these categories with data for prior years should only be made with this in mind. These shifts would not affect total non-network sales, and year-to-year comparison would be valid.

Note: Last digits may not add because of rounding.

( ) Indicates decline.

1974 Broadcasting Revenues

Item	Networks (Mil.)	Percent of change from previous year (Mil.)	15 owned and operated TV stations (Mil.)	Percent of change from previous year	679 other TV stations[1] (Mil.)	Percent of change from previous year	Total 3 networks and 694 stations[1] (Mil.)	Percent of change from previous year
Sales to advertisers for time, programs, talent, facilities, and services								
Network sales	$2,000.7	9.0						
Deduct: Payments to O&O Stations	37.4	5.9						
Deduct: Payments to other affiliated stations	206.2	6.7						
Retained from network sales	1,757.1	9.4	[2]37.5	5.9	[2]210.7	6.6	[3]2,005.3	9.0
Non-network sales								
To national & regional[3]	——	——	286.4	4.8	1,049.7	9.7	1,336.1	8.6
To local[3]	——	——	125.2	10.4	887.2	8.4	1,012.4	8.6
Total non-network sales	——	——	411.6	6.4	1,036.9	9.1	2,348.5	8.6
Total sales to advertisers	1,747.1	9.4	449.1	6.3	2,147.6	8.8	4,353.8	8.8
Sales to other than advertisers	90.2	20.4	5.7	(1.8)	28.9	17.5	124.8	18.6
Total sales	1,847.3	9.8	454.9	6.3	2,076.5	9.0	4,478.7	9.0
Deduct: Commissions to agencies, etc	301.3	8.9	79.8	6.5	321.2	10.4	702.4	9.3
Total Revenues	1,545.9	10.0	375.2	6.2	1,855.2	8.7	3,776.3	9.0
Total Expenses	1,320.3	8.3	269.5	7.7	1,448.9	8.0	3,039.2	8.1
Total Income (before federal income tax)	225.1	21.8	105.7	2.8	406.3	11.2	737.1	12.9

[1]Include 60 satellites, 25 of which filed combined reports with their parent stations.
[2]Includes payments from networks other than ABC, CBS, or NBC.
[3]Includes sales of programs, materials, facilities, and service made in connection with sales of time. Exclude sales made by five commercial stations that obtained most of their revenues from contributions: National and Regional—$1,077,882 and Local—$2,393,218. Because stations are not consistent in the way they classify National/Regional versus local sales, year to year comparisons should be with caution.
Note: Last digits may not add because of rounding.
( ) Indicates decline.

1975 Broadcasting Revenues

Item	Networks (Mil.)	Percent of change from previous year (Mil.)	15 owned and operated TV stations (Mil.)	Percent of change from previous year	678 other TV stations (Mil.)[1]	Percent of change from previous year	Total 3 networks and 693 stations (Mil.)	Percent of change from previous year
Sales to advertisers for time, programs, talent, facilities, and services								
Network sales	$2,154.7	7.7	——	——	——	——	——	——
Deduct: Payments to owned-and-operated stations	38.9	4.0	——	——	——	——	——	——
Deduct: Payments to other affiliated stations	217.4	5.9	——	——	——	——	——	——
Retained from network sales	1,898.4	8.0	[2]39.0	4.0	[2]$219.3	3.9	[3]2,156.7	7.5
Non-network sales								
To national and regional advertisers	——	——	290.7	1.5	1,158.5	10.2	1,449.2	8.4
To local advertisers[3]	——	——	145.1	15.9	971.1	9.3	1,116.2	10.1
Total non-network sales	——	——	435.8	5.9	2,129.6	9.8	2,565.4	9.1
Total sales to advertisers ...	1,898.4	8.0	474.8	5.7	2,348.9	9.2	4,722.1	8.4
Sales to other than advertisers	99.7	10.5	6.2	6.9	32.1	1.6	138.0	8.2
Total sales	1,998.1	8.2	481.0	5.7	2,381.0	9.1	4,860.1	8.4
Deduct: Commissions to agencies, representatives, etc	324.4	7.7	85.4	7.0	356.3	10.8	766.1	9.0
Total broadcast revenues	1,673.8	8.3	395.6	5.4	2,024.8	8.9	4,094.1	8.3
Total broadcast expenses	1,465.3	10.9	290.0	7.6	1,558.6	7.3	3,313.8	8.9
Total income (before federal income tax)	208.5	(7.4)	105.7	0	466.1	14.4	780.3	5.7

[1]Include 58 satellites, 24 of which filed combined reports with their parent stations.

[2]Includes payments from networks other than ABC, CBS, or NBC.

[3]Includes sales of programs, materials, facilities, and service in connection with sales of time. Exclude sales made by five commercial stations that obtained most of their revenues from contributions: National and Regional—$1,077,882 and Local—$2,393,218. Because stations are not consistent in the way they classify National/Regional versus local sales, year-to-year comparisons should be with made caution.

( ) Indicates decline.

Note: Last digits may not add because of rounding.

1976 Broadcasting Revenues

Item	Networks (Mil.)	Percent of change from previous year (Mil.)	15 owned and operated TV stations (Mil.)	Percent of change from previous year	686 other TV stations (Mil.)[1]	Percent of change from previous year	Total 3 networks and 701 stations (Mil.)	Percent of change from previous year
Sales to advertisers for time, programs, talent, facilities, and services:								
Network sales	$2,669.7	23.9	—	—	—	—	—	—
Deduct: Payments to owned and operated stations	401.2	3.2	—	—	—	—	—	—
Deduct: Payments to other affiliated stations	224.6	3.3	—	—	—	—	—	—
Retained from network sales	2,405.0	26.7	$40.2	2.9	[2]$229.7	4.7	[3]2,674.9	24.0
Non-network sales								
To national and regional advertisers[3]	—	—	375.5	22.9	1,565.1	35.1	1,922.6	32.7
To local advertisers[3]	—	—	193.3	33.2	1,238.6	27.5	1,431.9	28.2
Total non-network sales	—	—	550.8	26.4	2,803.7	31.7	3,354.5	30.8
Total sales to advertisers . . .	2,405.0	26.7	591.0	24.5	3,033.4	29.1	6,029.3	27.7
Sales to other than advertisers	114.5	14.9	4.1	(38.3)	42.3	31.8	160.9	16.6
Total sales	2,519.5	26.1	595.1	23.7	3,075.7	29.2	6,190.2	27.4
Deduct: Commissions to agencies, representatives, etc	402.0	23.9	108.2	26.7	481.6	35.2	991.8	29.5
Total broadcast revenues	2,117.5	26.5	486.9	23.1	2,594.1	28.1	5,198.5	27.0
Total broadcast expenses	1,821.9	24.3	327.9	13.1	1,798.5	15.4	3,948.3	19.1
Total income	295.6	41.8	159.0	50.4	795.6	70.7	1,250.2	60.3

[1]Include 58 satellites, 21 of which filed combined reports with their parent stations.
[2]Includes payments from networks other than ABC, CBS, or NBC.
[3]Includes sales of programs, materials, facilities, and service in connection with sales of time. Exclude sales made by five commercial stations that obtained most of their revenues from contributions: National and Regional—$1,414,738 and Local—$1,047,834. Because stations are not consistent in the way they classify National/Regional versus local sales, year-to-year comparisons should be made with caution.
Note: Last digits may not add because of rounding.
( ) Indicates decline.

1977 Broadcasting Revenues

Item	Networks (Mil.)	15 Owned and Operated TV Stations (Mil.)	682 Other TV Stations[1] (Mil.)	Total 3 Networks and 697 Stations[1] (Mil.)
Sales to advertisers for time, programs talent, facilities, and services				
Network sales	$3,234.3			
Deduct: Payments to owned and operated stations	41.4			
Deduct: Payment to other affiliated stations	239.6			
Retained from network sales (line 2 minus lines 3 and 4) .	2,953.3	$ 41.6	$246.3	$3,241.2
Non-network sales				
To national and regional advertisers[3]	——	348.4	1,618.9	1,967.3
To local advertisers[3]	——	219.9	1,411.0	1,630.9
Total non-network sales (line 7 plus 8)	——	568.2	3,029.9	3,598.2
Total sales to advertisers (line 5 plus 9)	2,953.3	609.8	3,276.2	6,839.3
Sales to other than advertisers	114.6	3.5	41.3	159.3
Total sales (line 10 plus 11)	3,067.9	613.3	3,317.5	6,998.7
Deduct: Commission to agencies, representatives, etc. ...	486.5	109.7	513.4	1,109.6
Total broadcast revenues (line 12 minus 13)	2,581.4	503.5	2,804.1	5,889.0
Total broadcast expense	2,175.3	354.2	1,958.5	4,488.0
Total income (before federal income tax) (line 14 minus 15) ..	406.1	149.3	845.7	1,401.0

[1]Includes 61 satellites 27 of which filed combined reports with their parent stations.
[2]Includes payments from networks other than ABC, CBS or NBC.
[3]Includes sales of programs, materials, facilities and service made in connection with sales of time. Excludes sales made by 16 commercial stations that obtained most of their revenues from contributions: National and Regional—$4,092,537 and Local—$3,363,006. Because stations are not consistent in the way they classify National/Regional versus local sales, year to year comparisons should be made with caution.

1978 Broadcasting Revenues

Item	Networks (Mil.)	15 Owned and Operated TV Stations (Mil.)	708 Other TV Stations (Mil.)	Total 3 Networks and 708 Stations (Mil.)
Sales to advertisers for time, programs, talent, facilities and services	$3,410.8	$708.0	$3,939.7	$8,058.5
Network sales	3,714.2			
Deduct: Payments to owned and operated stations	42.9			
Deduct: Payments to other affiliated stations	260.5			
Retained from network sales (line 2 minus lines 3 and 4) .	3,410.8	43.4	314.0	3,724.8
Non-network sales		664.6	4,333.7	4,333.7
To national and regional advertisers	——	371.9	2,304.2	2,304.2
To local advertisers	——	292.7	2,029.5	2,029.5
Total non-network sales (line 7 plus 8)	——	664.6	4,333.7	4,333.7
Total sales to advertisers (line 5 plus 9)	3,410.8	708.0	4,647.7	8,058.5
Sales to other than advertisers	111.7	3.8	50.2	161.9
Total sales (line 10 plus 11)	3,522.5	711.8	4,697.9	8,220.4
Deduct: Commissions to agencies, representatives, etc. ..	557.9	127.2	749.4	1,307.3
Total broadcast revenues (line 12 minus 13)	2,964.6	584.5	3,984.4	6,913.0
Total broadcast expense	2,591.1	398.2	2,276.6	5,265.9
Total income (before federal income tax) (line 14 minus 15) ..	373.5	186.3	1,067.3	1,647.1

3/Top 10 Advertising Markets, 1966–1980

THE F.C.C. has been keeping tabs on television's advertising revenues from the very first days of the industry. But not until 1966 did the Commission publish statistics on individual TV markets—on which cities generated what kind of revenues.

The lists printed below are adapted from annual F.C.C. data. But whereas the F.C.C.'s top markets are listed alphabetically—everything from Albany to Youngstown—our charts are by revenues: these are the top 10 markets.

Between 1966 and 1976, there was no change in the top seven ranks: each year New York, Los Angeles, Chicago, Philadelphia, San Francisco-Oakland, Boston and Detroit won the first seven places. The 8th, 9th and 10th places, however, saw several changes as cities in the "sun belt"—Miami, Dallas-Fort Worth, Houston—grew considerably larger. By 1980, Dallas had passed Detroit in TV advertising revenues.

One thing becomes clear from these charts: the power of urban TV viewers. In 1966, the five largest TV markets (New York, Los Angeles, Chicago, Philadelphia, and San Francisco-Oakland) had only 5% of the total number of stations, but accounted for 29% of total station revenues, 37% of total national spot business, and a considerable 49% of total station profits! It's easy to understand why "urban/rural" demographics became important in the late 1960s and early 1970s: the big money has been in big cities.

Here, then, are the Top Ten advertising markets for each year from 1966 to 1980.

1966 Top 10 Advertising Markets

TIME SALES

Market & Rank	# of Stations in Operation	Network	National & Regional[1]	Local[1]	Total Stations Reporting	Total Revenues[2]	Total Expenses	Total Income[3]
1. New York	7	$15,321,344	$111,144,064	$12,778,957	7	$124,224,557	$80,162,591	$44,061,966
2. Los Angeles	10[4]	8,134,921	83,158,394	20,587,074	9	92,610,148	61,105,599	31,504,549
3. Chicago	6[4]	7,775,643	61,821,842	11,863,198	6	72,160,764	48,319,665	23,841,099
4. Philadelphia	6	6,785,089	35,318,293	9,647,692	6	43,483,095	26,832,297	16,650,798
5. San Francisco-Oakland	5[4]	4,444,475	33,393,469	10,276,438	4	41,501,957	19,853,162	21,648,795
6. Boston	4	4,943,724	29,086,815	8,756,162	4	35,513,590	16,576,891	18,936,699
7. Detroit	4	5,460,184	21,793,742	7,106,295	4	29,974,441	17,168,441	12,806,000
8. Cleveland	3	4,447,066	20,256,179	6,141,209	3	28,524,335	14,058,959	14,465,376
9. Pittsburgh	3	4,143,809	18,121,798	5,890,099	3	24,036,805	13,506,925	10,529,800
10. Washington, D.C.	6[4]	3,068,381	17,954,765	4,092,515	6	23,373,780	17,735,780	5,638,000

[1]Before commissions to agencies, representatives and others
[2]Total revenues consist of total time sales less commissions plus talent and program sales
[3]Before Federal Income Tax
[4]Not all stations in the market operated a full year during 1966.

1967 Top 10 Advertising Markets

TIME SALES

Market & Rank	# of Stations in Operation	Network	National & Regional[1]	Local[1]	Total Stations Reporting	Total Revenues[2]	Total Expenses	Total Income[3]
1. New York	7	$15,552,173	$115,708,148	$14,201,466	7	$129,484,267	$85,312,073	$44,172,194
2. Los Angeles*	11	8,175,377	82,824,136	20,459,788	11	92,635,836	65,992,606	26,643,230
3. Chicago	6	7,769,775	64,664,181	13,020,910	6	75,903,192	51,763,650	24,139,542
4. Philadelphia	6	6,491,095	36,388,601	10,413,616	6	45,041,578	30,415,101	14,626,477
5. San Francisco-Oakland	5	4,376,621	34,985,118	8,656,627	5	41,338,355	22,717,487	18,620,868
6. Boston	5	4,898,657	30,910,789	9,096,073	5	37,111,549	21,850,459	15,261,090
7. Detroit	4	5,253,757	23,370,927	7,193,849	4	31,175,422	18,425,541	12,749,881
8. Cleveland	3	4,636,070	20,855,790	7,516,471	3	30,749,454	14,899,536	15,849,918
9. Washington, D.C.	6	3,065,017	19,049,092	4,137,281	6	24,514,815	19,679,846	4,834,969
10. Pittsburgh	3	4,059,664	16,980,737	5,805,030	3	22,723,260	14,352,887	8,370,373

[1]Before commissions to agencies, representatives and others
[2]Total times sales less commissions, plus talent and program sales
[3]Before Federal Income Tax
* One station operated for only part of the year.

1968 Top 10 Advertising Markets

TIME SALES

Market & Rank	# of Stations in Operation	Network	National & Regional[1]	Local[1]	Total Stations Reporting	Total Revenues[2]	Total Expenses	Total Income[3]
1. New York	8[4]	$15,726,171	$133,048,019	$17,965,494	8	$147,315,530	$93,484,886	$53,830,644
2. Los Angeles	11	8,086,427	90,923,106	29,066,707	11	106,771,401	69,793,549	36,977,852
3. Chicago	6	7,545,853	73,149,039	13,013,494	6	83,362,204	56,916,628	26,445,576
4. Philadelphia	6	6,531,859	41,551,206	11,678,291	6	50,144,993	33,908,966	16,236,027
5. San Francisco-Oakland	8[4]	4,273,136	39,944,244	12,684,376	8	48,582,010	31,255,277	17,326,733
6. Boston	5	4,826,342	37,741,019	9,191,657	5	42,548,777	24,046,289	18,502,488
7. Detroit	5[4]	5,132,728	27,189,825	11,917,062	5	38,035,032	21,455,120	16,579,912
8. Cleveland	5[4]	4,658,559	23,341,808	9,782,862	5	34,784,942	19,732,009	15,016,933
9. Washington, D.C.	6	2,954,303	22,392,982	6,448,899	6	29,202,385	22,057,177	7,145,208
10. Dallas-Fort Worth	7[4]	2,772,330	15,822,045	8,865,802	6	24,695,832	17,202,757	7,493,075

[1]Before commissions to agencies, representatives and others
[2]Total times sales less commissions, plus talent and program sales
[3]Before Federal Income Tax
[4]One station operated for only part of the year.

1969 Top 10 Advertising Markets

TIME SALES

Market & Rank	# of Stations in Operation	Network	National & Regional[1]	Local[1]	Total Stations Reporting	Total Revenues[2]	Total Expenses	Total Income[3]
1. New York	8	$16,457,442	$145,976,431	$18,773,802	8	$159,117,500	$106,715,498	$52,402,002
2. Los Angeles	11	8,497,971	93,529,476	37,373,608	10	117,396,337	81,011,435	36,383,902
3. Chicago	7[4]	7,988,211	79,574,063	17,978,676	7	92,698,872	60,382,593	32,316,279
4. Philadelphia	6	6,921,449	45,864,367	13,750,647	6	55,919,249	38,942,516	16,976,733
5. San Francisco-Oakland	8	4,428,808	45,304,221	11,961,595	8	52,423,454	35,288,918	17,134,536
6. Boston	5	4,888,762	42,016,401	11,332,104	5	47,784,904	26,635,066	21,149,838
7. Detroit	5	5,322,253	32,939,854	12,320,866	5	42,918,522	23,771,940	19,146,582
8. Cleveland	5	4,837,176	26,621,576	10,958,327	5	37,588,587	24,002,231	13,586,356
9. Washington, D.C.	6	3,065,953	25,133,769	8,190,683	6	33,532,963	27,212,734	6,320,229
10. Dallas-Fort Worth	7	2,926,703	18,718,611	10,928,792	5	28,885,449	17,902,795	10,982,744

[1]Before commissions to agencies, representatives and brokers. Because clarifying instructions were issued in 1969 regarding the classification of time sales into national and local, caution should be used in comparing these figures with figures for prior years.
[2]Total times sales less commissions, plus sales of programs, materials, facilities and services, plus other broadcast revenues.
[3]Before Federal Income Tax.
[4]One or more stations did not report data for the full year.

1970 Top 10 Advertising Markets

TIME SALES

Market & Rank	# of Stations in Operation	Network	National & Regional[1]	Local[1]	Total Stations Reporting	Total Revenues[2]	Total Expenses	Total Income[3]
1. New York	8	$15,187,248	$137,309,499	$21,154,703	8	$152,555,355	$108,744,524	$43,810,831
2. Los Angeles	11[4]	7,859,849	93,839,921	39,199,637	11	118,087,665	86,208,554	31,879,111
3. Chicago	8[4]	7,484,627	72,481,522	21,018,333	7	89,145,279	63,301,074	25,844,205
4. Philadelphia	6	6,715,149	44,182,114	15,806,760	6	56,027,740	39,921,773	16,105,967
5. San Francisco-Oakland	8[4]	4,160,607	45,427,719	12,810,434	8	52,144,953	37,374,996	14,769,957
6. Boston	5	4,578,860	42,308,645	11,656,936	5	47,882,263	29,270,440	18,611,823
7. Detroit	5	4,958,561	33,835,723	13,079,854	5	43,859,827	25,280,650	18,579,177
8. Cleveland	5	4,579,655	24,565,934	11,524,054	5	36,575,704	24,895,426	11,680,278
9. Washington, D.C.	6	2,847,963	25,405,071	9,112,762	6	33,727,359	28,478,067	5,249,292
10. Dallas-Fort Worth	6[4]	2,713,416	19,131,930	12,217,188	5	30,564,459	19,418,889	11,145,570

[1]Before commissions to agencies, representatives, and brokers. Because clarifying instructions were issued in 1969.
[2]Total times sales less commissions to advertising agencies, representatives and brokers, plus sales of programs, materials, facilities and services, plus other broadcast revenues.
[3]Before Federal Income Tax.
[4]One or more stations did not report data for the full year.

1971 Top 10 Advertising Markets

TIME SALES

Market & Rank	# of Stations in Operation	Network	National & Regional[1]	Local[1]	Total Stations Reporting	Total Revenues[2]	Total Expenses	Total Income[3]
1. New York	8	$13,738,011	$119,440,240	$28,139,479	8	$140,159,479	$108,563,665	$31,595,814
2. Los Angeles	11	7,117,479	82,951,588	39,549,509	11	110,424,336	88,707,916	21,716,420
3. Chicago	8[4]	6,896,932	67,678,938	20,847,147	7	83,548,465	64,037,038	19,511,427
4. Philadelphia	6	6,403,409	38,807,789	22,397,798	6	57,352,765	45,174,530	12,178,235
5. San Francisco-Oakland	7[4]	3,900,700	41,147,334	13,604,071	6	48,568,216	35,457,017	13,111,199
6. Boston	5	4,402,232	38,920,292	13,863,285	5	47,266,049	31,945,756	15,320,293
7. Detroit	5	4,753,448	31,670,946	13,912,817	5	42,956,883	27,161,673	15,795,210
8. Cleveland	5	4,212,355	22,638,256	11,959,035	5	34,308,456	25,224,185	9,084,271
9. Washington, D.C.	6	2,551,498	23,288,383	10,928,617	6	31,751,494	28,503,960	3,247,534
10. Dallas-Fort Worth	6[4]	2,592,096	17,551,327	12,464,237	6	29,555,326	20,509,989	9,045,428

[1]Before commissions to agencies, representatives, and brokers. Because clarifying instructions were issued in 1969 regarding the classification of time sales into national and local, caution should be used in comparing these figures with figures for years prior to 1969.
[2]Total times sales less commissions to advertising agencies, representatives and brokers, plus sales of programs, materials, facilities and services, plus other broadcast revenues.
[3]Before Federal Income Tax.
[4]One or more stations did not report data for the full year.

1972 Top 10 Advertising Markets

TIME SALES

Market & Rank	# of Stations in Operation	Network	National & Regional[1]	Local[1]	Total Stations Reporting	Total Revenues[2]	Total Expenses	Total Income[3]
1. New York	8	$13,475,818	$138,978,060	$30,974,587	8	$159,428,748	$121,065,443	$38,363,305
2. Los Angeles	12	6,825,959	91,715,250	50,002,407	10	127,462,037	98,844,341	28,617,696
3. Chicago	7	6,532,784	76,810,149	27,660,254	7	97,089,400	72,625,504	24,463,986
4. Philadelphia	6	6,289,525	44,589,811	24,947,552	6	63,194,128	47,120,793	16,073,335
5. San Francisco-Oakland	8[4]	3,751,054	46,695,376	18,583,475	7	57,535,823	40,614,259	16,921,564
6. Boston	5	4,428,900	43,521,890	19,062,921	5	56,069,462	39,000,110	17,069,352
7. Detroit	5	4,499,297	32,614,515	18,718,728	5	47,365,698	30,533,533	16,832,165
8. Washington, D.C.	6[4]	2,480,430	27,031,541	14,202,700	6	37,574,581	31,855,311	5,719,270
9. Cleveland	5	4,186,480	24,989,124	12,619,478	3	36,773,706	27,094,867	9,678,839
10. Dallas-Fort Worth	6	2,498,762	21,026,693	14,062,127	5	34,087,916	23,051,685	11,036,231

[1]Before commissions to agencies, representatives, and brokers. Because clarifying instructions were issued in 1969 regarding the classification of time sales into national and local, caution should be used in comparing these figures with figures for years prior to 1969.
[2]Total times sales less commissions to advertising agencies, representatives and brokers, plus sales of programs, materials, facilities and services, plus other broadcast revenue.
[3]Before Federal Income Tax.
[4]One or more stations did not report data for the full year.

1973 Top 10 Advertising Markets

TIME SALES

Market & Rank	# of Stations in Operation	Network	National & Regional[1]	Local[1]	Total Stations Reporting	Total Revenues[2]	Total Expenses	Total Income[3]
1. New York	9[4]	$13,991,581	$138,864,961	$46,833,892	9	$173,358,789	$132,851,477	$40,507,312
2. Los Angeles	13	7,140,713	94,794,108	54,932,428	11	134,100,087	105,683,554	28,416,533
3. Chicago	7	6,844,817	76,302,345	34,668,868	7	102,482,936	75,691,902	26,791,034
4. Philadelphia	6	6,248,686	46,427,385	26,228,075	6	66,054,484	49,969,362	16,085,122
5. San Francisco-Oakland	8	3,870,970	39,825,065[5]	30,115,510[5]	6	62,336,820	45,409,396	16,927,424
6. Boston	5	4,262,116	44,053,189	20,755,103	5	58,167,118	42,608,473	15,558,645
7. Detroit	5	4,872,794	37,068,723	20,041,514	5	52,070,521	32,746,289	19,324,232
8. Washington, D.C.	6[4]	2,612,397	28,750,350	16,929,473	6	41,877,772	36,686,655	5,191,117
9. Cleveland	5	4,439,473	26,672,745	15,101,105	5	39,348,383	28,563,849	10,784,535
10. Dallas-Fort Worth	6[4]	2,581,490	21,523,713	14,767,030	5	35,274,419	23,668,644	11,605,775

[1]Before commissions to agencies, representatives, and brokers. Because clarifying instructions were issued in 1969 regarding the classification of time sales into national and local, caution should be used in comparing these figures with figures for years prior to 1969.
[2]Total times sales less commissions to advertising agencies, representatives and brokers, plus sales of programs, materials, facilities and services, plus other broadcast revenues.
[3]Before Federal Income Tax.
[4]One or more stations did not report data for the full year.
[5]A significant portion of the reported 1973 local time sales for this market came from a shift in the way one station allocated sales between national and local categories.

1974 Top 10 Advertising Markets

TIME SALES

Market & Rank	# of Stations in Operation	Network	National & Regional[1]	Local[1]	Total Stations Reporting	Total Revenues[2]	Total Expenses	Total Income[3]
1. New York	10[4]	$14,489,749	$143,007,221	$49,517,680	10	$176,779,491	$141,656,666	$35,122,825
2. Los Angeles	12	7,561,859	98,343,461	60,123,403	11	142,483,712	114,879,243	27,604,469
3. Chicago	7	7,111,914	85,184,789	36,828,945	7	110,972,039	80,501,049	30,470,990
4. Philadelphia	6	6,756,825	47,451,564	26,732,168	6	67,717,095	50,931,370	16,785,725
5. San Francisco-Oakland	7	3,903,332	44,066,640	32,426,013	6	67,454,723	49,078,523	18,738,200
6. Boston	5	4,461,043	47,387,938	21,598,086	5	62,227,822	45,950,562	16,277,260
7. Detroit	5	5,373,956	40,055,937	19,946,200	5	54,977,956	35,404,132	19,573,824
8. Washington, D.C.	6[4]	2,725,016	32,345,139	18,299,226	5	45,844,356	40,328,199	5,482,157
9. Cleveland	5	4,513,077	27,070,842	17,662,190	5	42,147,000	32,863,826	9,292,174
10. Miami	6	2,187,094	24,472,517	17,592,576	6	37,500,343	26,035,793	11,464,550
Dallas-Fort Worth	4	2,774,054	23,635,263	16,229,361	4	37,465,900	21,739,372	15,726,528

[1]Before commissions to agencies, representatives, and brokers. Because stations are not consistent in the way they classify national/regional versus local sales, year-to-year comparisons in these categories should be made with caution.
[2]Total times sales less commissions to advertising agencies, representatives and brokers, plus sales of programs, materials, facilities and services, plus other broadcast revenue.
[3]Before Federal Income Tax.
[4]One or more stations did not report data for the full year.

1975 Top 10 Advertising Markets

TIME SALES

Market & Rank	# of Stations in Operation	Network	National & Regional[1]	Local[1]	Total Stations Reporting	Total Revenues[2]	Total Expenses	Total Income[3]
1. New York	10	$14,985,805	$141,611,761	$64,817,822	9	$188,059,442	$144,580,480	$43,478,962
2. Los Angeles	13	8,060,130	104,396,731	64,522,244	11	153,856,923	127,360,526	26,496,397
3. Chicago	7	7,280,133	90,417,680	40,764,841	7	117,721,874	84,755,112	32,966,762
4. Philadelphia	6	70,078,803	56,946,000	28,455,430	6	76,657,029	55,668,817	20,988,212
5. San Francisco-Oakland	9[4]	4,000,042	50,126,321	31,480,535	7	71,355,306	52,691,179	18,664,127
6. Boston	5	4,874,937	48,901,812	21,012,693	5	63,049,681	47,339,676	15,710,005
7. Detroit	6[4]	5,411,241	40,103,334	21,189,500	5	55,850,860	38,758,750	17,092,110
8. Washington, D.C.	5	2,812,459	39,296,683	20,217,447	5	53,408,494	45,195,660	8,212,834
9. Cleveland	5[4]	4,671,173	32,453,427	18,904,547	5	47,871,794	33,300,590	14,571,204
10. Dallas-Fort Worth	5	2,783,253	27,296,963	18,982,428	4	43,188,280	26,633,315	16,554,965

[1]Before commissions to agencies, representatives, and brokers. Because stations are not consistent in the way they classify national/regional versus local sales, year-to-year comparisons in these categories should be made with caution.
[2]Total times sales less commissions to advertising agencies, representatives and brokers, plus sales of programs, materials, facilities and services, plus other broadcast revenue.
[3]Before Federal Income Tax.
[4]One or more stations did not report data for full year.

1976 Top 10 Advertising Markets

TIME SALES

Market & Rank	# of Stations in Operation	Network	National & Regional[1]	Local[1]	Total Stations Reporting	Total Revenues[2]	Total Expenses	Total Income[3]
1. New York	9	$15,379,902	$166,665,127	$94,776,373	9	$234,235,145	$170,254,550	$63,980,595
2. Los Angeles	13	8,591,340	140,776,834	92,189,700	11	213,349,461	149,860,317	63,489,144
3. Chicago	8	7,567,361	116,247,596	53,246,319	8	146,608,629	96,838,582	49,770,047
4. Philadelphia	7	7,170,064	79,024,984	35,059,836	7	99,577,567	62,615,490	36,962,077
5. San Francisco-Oakland	9	4,174,373	67,935,349	44,672,110	8	97,069,616	62,400,089	34,669,527
6. Boston	5	4,946,738	62,966,462	29,268,478	5	81,015,289	52,881,696	28,133,593
7. Detroit	6	5,653,619	52,726,687	29,786,390	6	73,885,035	46,129,777	27,755,258
8. Washington, D.C.	5	3,039,880	51,469,739	23,671,392	5	64,434,325	49,768,971	14,665,354
9. Dallas-Fort Worth	5	2,723,682	41,787,939	24,355,333	5	59,605,832	32,229,621	27,336,211
10. Cleveland	4	4,701,339	39,916,239	24,368,690	4	58,463,280	36,506,202	21,957,078

[1]Before commissions to agencies, representatives, and brokers. Because stations are not consistent in the way they classify national/regional versus local sales, year to year comparisons in these categories should be made with caution.
[2]Total times sales less commissions to advertising agencies, representatives and brokers, plus sales of programs, facilities and services, plus other broadcast revenue.
[3]Before Federal Income Tax.

1977 Top 10 Advertising Markets

TIME SALES

Market & Rank by Revenue	# of Stations in Operation	# of Stations Reporting	Total Revenues	Total Expenses	Total Income[1]
1. New York	9	9	$242,790,055	$184,956,310	$57,833,745
2. Los Angeles		12	224,526,041	159,740,101	64,785,940
3. Chicago	8	8	146,807,393	103,692,853	43,114,540
4. Philadelphia	7	7	103,393,441	64,917,151	38,476,290
5. San Francisco-Oakland	9	8	101,393,441	68,968,521	32,834,275
6. Boston	5	5	84,118,599	57,526,707	26,591,892
7. Detroit	6	5	77,089,168	51,410,129	25,679,039
8. Washington, D.C.		5	67,453,782	52,276,205	15,177,577
9. Dallas-Fort Worth	5	4	67,199,529	30,946,519	36,253,010
10. Houston-Galveston	5	5	64,845,883	28,464,877	36,381,006

[1]Before federal income tax.

1978 Top 10 Advertising Markets

TIME SALES

Market & Rank by Revenue	# of Stations in Operation	# of Stations Reporting	Total Revenues	Total Expenses	Total Income[1]
1. New York	10	9	$282,695,936	$208,796,524	$73,899,412
2. Los Angeles	14	12	265,809,168	186,355,848	79,453,320
3. Chicago	8	8	177,916,901	118,350,478	59,566,423
4. San Francisco-Oakland	9	9	123,238,237	81,182,911	42,055,326
5. Philadelphia	7	7	115,808,804	73,790,531	42,018,273
6. Boston					
7. Detroit	6	6	93,764,046	60,777,271	32,986,775
8. Dallas-Fort Worth	5	5	87,280,070	37,337,917	49,942,153
9. Houston-Galveston	5	5	81,470,447	34,776,882	46,693,565
10. Washington, D.C.	6	5	79,658,216	58,575,125	21,083,091

[1]Before federal income tax.

1979 Top 10 Advertising Markets

TIME SALES

Market & Rank by Revenue	# of Stations in Operation	# of Stations Reporting	Total Revenues	Total Expenses	Total Income[1]
1. New York	10	9	$311,557,455	$229,500,094	$82,057,361
2. Los Angeles	14	12	292,093,338	197,170,062	94,923,276
3. Chicago	8	8	186,142,279	130,774,540	55,367,739
4. San Francisco-Oakland	9	9	139,236,740	95,519,650	43,717,090
5. Philadelphia	7	7	126,453,759	87,128,323	39,325,436
6. Boston	6	6	115,272,937	79,687,760	35,585,177
7. Detroit	6	6	104,607,093	70,371,697	34,235,396
8. Dallas-Fort Worth	5	5	96,426,066	42,951,387	53,474,679
9. Houston-Galveston	5	5	92,291,752	41,197,902	51,093,850
10. Washington, D.C.	6	5	87,782,681	64,987,482	22,795,199

[1]Before federal income tax.

1980 Top 10 Advertising Markets

TIME SALES

Market & Rank by Revenue	# of Stations in Operation	# of Stations Reporting	Total Revenues	Total Expenses	Total Income[1]
1. New York	10	10	$362,032,920	$267,453,306	$94,579,614
2. Los Angeles	13	11	332,773,340	238,478,629	94,294,711
3. Chicago	8	8	206,694,445	152,218,865	54,475,580
4. San Francisco-Oakland	9	8	154,115,287	109,498,959	44,616,328
5. Philadelphia	7	7	140,888,506	100,798,541	40,089,965
6. Boston	6	6	132,822,322	96,171,227	36,651,095
7. Dallas-Fort Worth	5	6	117,835,499	55,818,336	62,017,163
8. Detroit	6	6	110,248,398	78,449,944	31,798,454
9. Houston-Galveston	5	5	108,386,612	49,516,574	58,870,038
10. Washington, D.C.	6	6	101,008,308	75,189,249	25,819,059

[1]Before federal income tax.

4/TV REVENUES VS. RADIO REVENUES

WHEN THE MANUFACTURING of TV sets was resumed after World War II, the most important broadcasting medium was, of course, radio: radio, not TV, was the big money-maker. But as the following chart (adapted from F.C.C. statistics) shows, it did not take long for television first to catch up with radio and then to take over the #1 spot.

In 1949, for example, radio revenues were almost 12 times as large as those of the fledgling TV industry. But just four years later in 1954, television revenues actually surpassed those of radio. It was, to say the least, a quick conquest, and TV has not given up the lead since.

By 1958, when TV revenues jumped the $1 billion mark for the first time, radio revenues were only half that sum: another decade would have to pass before the radio industry could boast of billion dollar revenues. By that time TV would have already cleared the $2 billion hurdle. TV's lead has been increasing ever since: today TV revenues are nearly three times as large as those of radio.

TV REVENUES VS. RADIO REVENUES

Year	Radio (Mil)	Television (Mil)
1949	$415,200	$34,300
1950	444,500	105,900
1951	450,400	235,700
1952	469,700	323,600
1953	475,300	431,800
1954	449,500	593,000
1955	453,400	744,700
1956	480,600	896,900
1957	518,300	943,200
1958	523,100	1,030,000
1959	560,000	1,163,900
1960	597,700	1,268,600
1961	590,700	1,318,300
1962	636,100	1,486,200
1963	681,100	1,597,200
1964	732,000	1,793,300
1965	792,500	1,964,800
1966	872,100	2,203,000
1967	907,300	2,275,000
1968	1,022,900	2,520,000
1969	1,085,900	2,796,000
1970	1,136,900	2,808,000
1971	1,260,000	2,750,000
1972	1,400,000	3,180,000
1973	1,510,000	3,460,000
1974	1,603,100	3,776,000
1975	1,725,000	4,100,000
1976	2,019,400	5,198,000
1977	2,274,500	5,889,000
1978	2,635,300	6,913,000
1979	2,873,600	7,875,100
1980	3,206,000	8,807,700

5/TV's Share of the American Advertising Dollar

TELEVISION IS A big moneymaker, but is it the country's #1 advertising medium? Only when it comes to nationwide ads, where TV has captured an impressive 49.1% of the market. On a local level, however, newspapers (with 68.8% of the market) wins first place, followed by TV (with 15.6%).

TV'S SHARE OF THE AMERICAN ADVERTISING DOLLAR: 1981*

	Advertising Revenue (billion)	% of Total
1. TOTAL ADVERTISING VOLUME		
1. Newspapers	$17.420	28.4
2. Television	12,650	20.6
3. Radio	4,212	6.9
4. Magazines	3,533	5.8
5. Business Papers	1,841	3.0
6. Outdoor	650	1.1
7. All Others	21,014	34.2
2. NATIONAL ADVERTISING INVESTMENTS IN MAJOR MEDIA		
1. Television	$9,305	49.1
a. Network	5,575	29.4
b. Spot	3,730	19.7
2. Magazines	3,533	18.7
3. Newspapers	2,729	14.4
4. Business Papers	1,841	9.7
5. Radio	1,116	5.9
6. Outdoor	419	2.2
3. LOCAL ADVERTISING INVESTMENTS IN MAJOR MEDIA		
1. Newspapers	$14,691	68.8
2. Television	3,345	15.6
3. Radio	3,096	14.5
4. Outdoor	231	1.1

*Source: McCann-Erickson

V. THE AWARDS

1/THE EMMYS (ACADEMY OF TELEVISION ARTS AND SCIENCES)

THE NATIONAL ACADEMY of Television Arts and Sciences (NATAS) was formed in 1946. Its aim (to quote its own credo) has been to "advance the arts and sciences of television, and to foster creative leadership in the television industry for artistic, cultural, educational and technological purposes," a credo that is suspiciously reminiscent of that of another arts organization—the Academy of Motion Picture Arts and Sciences.

Like the Motion Picture Academy, the Television Academy established its annual awards soon after its creation. The first annual Emmys presentation was rather a simple affair: 600 people gathered at the Hollywood Athletic Club on Jan. 25, 1949 to watch the presentation of a mere six awards. Not much hoopla, little fanfare, no TV cameras. In fact, by 1951 a Los Angeles critic was already complaining that the Emmys affairs looked like a Union City fish fry—"raggedly timed and boringly slow moving." Throughout the 1950s and 1960s award categories were added, revised, redefined and broadened. There were only six awards for the first presentation in 1949, but by the 1955 awards the number of categories had jumped to 41, and the proliferation of awards continued until a record peak was hit for the 1977/78 prizes: 349 nominations in 75 categories, with 50 programs and 298 individuals up for prizes!

As if the marked increase in prime time awards was not enough to make the Emmys practically unmanageable, regional awards were added for Los Angeles achievements in 1952, followed by similar awards for New York (1956), Chicago and Washington, D.C. (1958), Arizona (1959), Seattle (1962), Columbus and San Francisco (1963), Cleveland (1969), San Diego and Atlanta (1974). (These local awards are not listed below.) Then came the daytime awards in 1973/74.

It is little wonder that the Emmys have been so routinely criticized and attacked: the methods of determining the winners have been constantly revised, and the categories of awards can seem arbitrary at best. On May 12, 1964 Fred W. Friendly (then vice-president of CBS News) was so dismayed by the whole Emmy procedure that he withdrew his division from the Emmys ceremony. ABC News soon followed suit. NBC then provided $25,000 to finance a study to improve the award procedure, and a multiple award system was established for the 1964/65 prizes. Multiple awards, however, were not very popular (competition is more newsworthy), and the single-award

system (with further modifications) returned the following year.

The Academy's most serious attack occurred 10 years later, in 1976. At that time NATAS consisted of 13 chapters with a total membership of around 11,000. Some 4,800 of those members belonged to the Hollywood chapter alone, which believed that the Emmys should be decided not by the Academy at large, but only by those members directly involved in producing national prime time TV shows—namely, the Hollywood branch.

The National Academy first rejected the Hollywood chapter's demands and then revoked that chapter's charter. The Hollywood branch, incensed, boycotted the 1977 ceremony. Big names like Norman Lear, Mary Tyler Moore, Carroll O'Connor, James Garner and Jean Stapleton refused to take part in the presentations. The Awards were cancelled.

After a series of lawsuits and heated debates, a compromise was reached. A new organization—the Academy of Television Arts & Sciences (ATAS)—was formed from the old Hollywood branch. This new organization got the prime time Emmys; the old organization (NATAS) got the daytime Emmys, as well as the news and documentary Emmys. NATAS also won the right to continue publishing *Television Quarterly*. ATAS soon began publishing its own journal, simply titled *Emmy*.

Ballots for prime time Emmys are now mailed to all active members of ATAS and to those members of NATAS (located in New York) who are involved in producing national prime time shows. The votes are tabulated by a computer, and those entries receiving the most votes are placed into nomination. A blue-ribbon panel of TV professionals (some ATAS members, some not) then decides the winners.

The Emmy statuette—of a winged woman holding aloft a sphere—was designed by Louis McManus, who himself received a special 1948 Emmy for that design. The statuette has been variously described as "Oscar's kid sister" and as a "golden portrait of a woman trying to put a hatbox on a top shelf."

How did the statuette get the name "Emmy"? Although many people initially assumed that it had been named after a particular woman, it was soon revealed that Harry R. Lubcke (then president of the Academy) had given the statuette its name from the word "immy," which was TV jargon for an image orthicon camera tube.

The Emmys were first televised on March 7, 1955. NBC carried the event through the 1965/66 awards, when a rotating system among all three major webs was established.

1948

(Presented January 25, 1949)

OUTSTANDING TELEVISION PERSONALITY
☐ Shirley Dinsdale (and her puppet Judy Splinters) (KTLA)
Rita LeRoy (KTLA)
Patricia Morrison
Mike Stokey (KTLA)
Bill Welsh (KTLA)

MOST POPULAR TELEVISION PROGRAM
☐ *Pantomime Quiz Time* (KTLA)
Armchair Detective (KTLA)
Don Lee Music Hall (KTSL)
Felix De Cola Show (KTLA)
Judy Splinters (KTLA)
Mabel's Fables (KTLA)
Masked Spooner (KTSL)
Treasure of Literature (KFI-TV)
Tuesday Varieties (KTLA)
What's the Name of That Song? (KTSL)

BEST FILM MADE FOR TELEVISION
☐ "The Necklace," *Your Show Time*
Christopher Columbus
Hollywood Brevities
It Could Happen to You
Telltale Heart
Time Signal

STATION AWARD
☐ *KTLA,* for outstanding overall achievements in 1948

TECHNICAL AWARD
☐ *Charles Mesak,* Don Lee Television, for the phase finder, in recognition of an outstanding advancement in the video field

SPECIAL AWARD
☐ *Louis McManus,* for his original design of the Emmy

1949

(Presented January 27, 1950)

BEST LIVE SHOW
☐ *Ed Wynn Show* (KTTV)
Pantomime Quiz (KTTV)
Your Witness (KECA-TV)

BEST KINESCOPE SHOW
☐ *Texaco Star Theater* (NBC)
Fred Waring (CBS)
The Goldbergs (CBS)
Studio One (CBS)

BEST CHILDREN'S SHOW
☐ *Time for Beany* (KTLA)

☐ Indicates winner

Cyclone Malone (KNBH)
Kukla, Fran and Ollie (KNBH)

OUTSTANDING LIVE PERSONALITY
☐ Ed Wynn (KTTV)
Tom Harmon (KTTV, KFI, KECA)
Mike Stokey (KTTV, KTLA)
Bill Welsh (KFI, KTLA)

OUTSTANDING KINESCOPE PERSONALITY
☐ Milton Berle (NBC)
Fran Allison (NBC)
Arthur Godfrey (CBS)

BEST FILM MADE FOR TELEVISION
☐ *Life of Riley* (KNBH)
Guiding Star (KTTV)
Lone Ranger (KECA)
Time Bomb (KNBH)
Vain Glory (KNBH)
Your Showtime

BEST PUBLIC SERVICE, CULTURAL OR EDUCATIONAL PROGRAM
☐ *Crusade in Europe* (KECA, KTTV)
Ford News and Weather (KNBH)
Kathy Fiscus Rescue (KTLA)
Man's Best Friend (KTLA)
Nuremberg Trials (KTSL)
Teleforum (KTLA)

BEST SPORTS COVERAGE
☐ Wresting (KTLA)
Amateur Boxing (KTLA)
Baseball (KLAC)
College Basketball (KTTV)
Ice Hockey (KTLA)
USC-UCLA Football (KECA)

STATION ACHIEVEMENT
☐ *KTLA,* for outstanding overall achievements in 1949
☐ *KECA TV,* honorable mention

BEST COMMERCIAL MADE FOR TELEVISION
☐ *Lucky Strike,* N.W. Ayer & Son, Inc. for the American Tobacco Company

TECHNICAL AWARD
☐ *Harold W. Jury,* KTSL, Los Angeles, for the synchronizing coordinator which allows superimposition from more than one location

1950

(Presented January 23, 1951)

BEST VARIETY SHOW
☐ *The Alan Young Show* (CBS)
Four Star Revue (NBC)
Ken Murray (CBS)
Show of Shows (NBC)
Texaco Star Theatre (NBC)

BEST DRAMATIC SHOW
☐ *Pulitzer Prize Playhouse* (KECA-TV)
Fireside Theater (KTLA)

I Remember Mama (CBS)
Philco TV Playhouse (NBC)
Studio One (CBS)

BEST CULTURAL SHOW
☐ *Campus Chorus and Orchestra* (KTSL)
Designed for Women (KNBH)
Sunset Service (KNBH)
Vienna Philharmonic (KTTV)
The Woman's Voice (KTTV)

BEST SPORTS PROGRAM
☐ *Rams Football* (KNBH)
College Basketball Games (CBS)
College Football Games (CBS)
Hollywood Baseball (KLAC)
Los Angeles Baseball (KFI-TV)

BEST EDUCATIONAL SHOW
☐ *KFI-TV University* (KFI-TV)
Kieran's Kaleidoscope (KECA-TV)
Know Your Schools (KFI-TV)
Magazine of the Week (KTLA)
Zoo Parade (KNBH)

BEST CHILDREN'S SHOW
☐ *Time for Beauty* (KTLA)
Cisco Kid (KNBH)
Jump Jump (KTTV)
Kukla, Fran and Ollie (NBC)
Lone Ranger (KTLA)

BEST NEWS PROGRAM
☐ *KTLA Newsreel* (KTLA)
Clete Roberts (KLAC)
Fleetwood Lawton (KTSL)
Ford News and Weather (KNBH)

BEST GAME AND AUDIENCE PARTICIPATION SHOW
☐ *Truth or Consequences* (CBS)
Kay Kyser College of Musical Knowledge (NBC)
Life with Linkletter (KECA-TV)
Pantomine Quiz (CBS)
You Bet Your Life (NBC)

BEST PUBLIC SERVICE
☐ *City at Night* (KTLA)
Classified Column (KTTV)
Community Chest Kickoff in Our Time (KTTV)
Marshall Plan (KECA-TV)
Teleforum (KTLA)

SPECIAL EVENTS
☐ *Departure of Marines for Korea* (KFMB-TV, KTLA)
Arrival of Cruiser from Korea (KTLA)
Commissioning of Hospital Ship Haven
Election Coverage (KECA-TV)
Tournament of Roses (KECA-TV)

BEST ACTOR
☐ Alan Young (CBS)
Sid Caesar (NBC)
Jose Ferrer
Stan Freberg as Cecil the Sea Serpent (KTLA)
Charles Ruggles (KECA-TV)

BEST ACTRESS
☐ Gertrude Berg (CBS)
  Judith Anderson
  Imogene Coca (NBC)
  Helen Hayes (KECA-TV)
  Betty White (KLAC)

MOST OUTSTANDING PERSONALITY
☐ Groucho Marx (NBC)
  Sid Caesar (NBC)
  Faye Emerson (KTTV, KECA-TV)
  Dick Lane (KTLA)
  Alan Young (CBS)

STATION ACHIEVEMENT
☐ *KTLA*

TECHNICAL ACHIEVEMENT
☐ Orthogram TV Amplifier by KNBH, NBC

1951

(Presented February 18, 1952)

BEST DRAMATIC SHOW
☐ *Studio One* (CBS)
  Celanese Theatre (ABC)
  Philco-Goodyear TV Playhouse (NBC)
  Pulitzer Prize Playhouse (ABC)
  Robert Montgomery Presents (NBC)

BEST COMEDY SHOW
☐ *Red Skelton Show* (NBC)
  Burns & Allen (CBS)
  Groucho Marx (NBC)
  Herb Shriner Show (ABC)
  I Love Lucy (CBS)

BEST VARIETY SHOW
☐ *Your Show of Shows* (NBC)
  All Star Revue (NBC)
  Comedy Hour (NBC)
  Fred Waring (CBS)
  Toast of the Town (CBS)

BEST ACTOR
☐ Sid Caesar
  Walter Hampden
  Charlton Heston
  Robert Montgomery
  Thomas Mitchell
  Vaughn Taylor

BEST ACTRESS
☐ Imogene Coca
  Helen Hayes
  Maria Riva
  Mary Sinclair
  Margaret Sullavan

BEST COMEDIAN OR COMEDIENNE
☐ Red Skelton (NBC)
  Lucille Ball (CBS)
  Sid Caesar (NBC)
  Imogene Coca (NBC)
  Jimmy Durante (NBC)
☐ Indicates winner

Dean Martin, Jerry Lewis (NBC)
Herb Shriner (ABC)

SPECIAL ACHIEVEMENT AWARDS
☐ Sen. Estes Kefauver for outstanding public service on television
  American Telephone and Telegraph Co. for the transcontinental Micro-Wave Relay System
  Jack Burrell of Station KNBH of Los Angeles, for the development of an independent TV transmission Mobile Unit

1952

(Presented February 5, 1953)

BEST DRAMATIC PROGRAM
☐ *Robert Montgomery Presents* (NBC)
  Celanese Theatre (ABC)
  Kraft TV Theatre (NBC)
  Philco-Goodyear TV Playhouse (NBC)
  Studio One (CBS)

BEST VARIETY PROGRAM
☐ *Your Show of Shows* (NBC)
  Arthur Godfrey and His Friends (CBS)
  Colgate Comedy Hour (NBC)
  Jackie Gleason Show (CBS)
  Toast of the Town (CBS)

BEST PUBLIC AFFAIRS PROGRAM
☐ *See It Now* (CBS)
  Bishop Fulton J. Sheen (Syndicated)
  Camel News Caravan (NBC)
  Meet the Press (NBC)
  Victory at Sea (NBC)

BEST MYSTERY, ACTION OR ADVENTURE PROGRAM
☐ *Dragnet* (NBC)
  Big Story (NBC)
  Foreign Intrigue (Syndicated)
  Martin Kane (NBC)
  Racket Squad (CBS)

BEST SITUATION COMEDY
☐ *I Love Lucy* (CBS)
  Amos 'n' Andy (CBS)
  Burns & Allen (CBS)
  Mr. Peepers (NBC)
  Our Miss Brooks (CBS)
  Ozzie and Harriet (ABC)

BEST AUDIENCE PARTICIPATION, QUIZ, OR PANEL PROGRAM
☐ *What's My Line?* (CBS)
  Down You Go
  This Is Your Life (NBC)
  Two For the Money (CBS)
  You Bet Your Life (NBC)

BEST CHILDREN'S PROGRAM
☐ *Time for Beany* (KTLA)
  Big Top (CBS)
  Gabby Hayes
  Howdy Doody (NBC)
  Kukla, Fran and Ollie (NBC)

Super Circus (NBC)
Zoo Parade (NBC)

BEST ACTOR
☐ Thomas Mitchell
  John Forsythe
  Charlton Heston
  John Newland
  Vaughn Taylor
  Jack Webb

BEST ACTRESS
☐ Helen Hayes
  Sarah Churchill
  June Lockhart
  Maria Riva
  Peggy Wood

BEST COMEDIAN
☐ Jimmy Durante (NBC)
  Sid Caesar (NBC)
  Wally Cox (NBC)
  Jackie Gleason (CBS)
  Herb Shriner (ABC)

BEST COMEDIENNE
☐ Lucille Ball (CBS)
  Eve Arden (CBS)
  Imogene Coca (NBC)
  Joan Davis (NBC)
  Martha Raye (NBC)

MOST OUTSTANDING PERSONALITY
☐ Bishop Fulton J. Sheen (Dumont)
  Lucille Ball (CBS)
  Arthur Godfrey (CBS)
  Jimmy Durante (NBC)
  Edward R. Murrow (CBS)
  Donald O'Connor (NBC)
  Adlai Stevenson (NBC)

1953

(Presented February 11, 1954)

BEST DRAMATIC PROGRAM
☐ *U.S. Steel Hour* (ABC)
  Kraft Television Theatre (NBC)
  Philco-Goodyear TV Playhouse (NBC)
  Robert Montgomery Presents (NBC)
  Studio One (CBS)

BEST SITUATION COMEDY
☐ *I Love Lucy* (CBS)
  Burns & Allen (CBS)
  Mr. Peepers (NBC)
  Our Miss Brooks (CBS)
  Topper (CBS)

BEST VARIETY PROGRAM
☐ *Omnibus* (CBS)
  Colgate Comedy Hour (NBC)
  Jackie Gleason Show (CBS)
  Your Show of Shows (NBC)
  Toast of the Town (CBS)

BEST PROGRAM OF NEWS OR SPORTS
☐ *See It Now* (CBS)
Camel News Caravan (NBC)
Gillette Cavalcade of Sports (NBC)
NCAA Football (NBC)
Pabst Fight (CBS)
Professional Football (Dumont)

BEST PUBLIC AFFAIRS PROGRAM
☐ *Victory at Sea* (NBC)
Adventure (CBS)
Bishop Fulton J. Sheen (Syndicated)
Meet the Press (NBC)
Person to Person (CBS)

BEST CHILDREN'S PROGRAM
☐ *Kukla, Fran and Ollie* (NBC)
Big Top (CBS)
Ding Dong School (NBC)
Super Circus (NBC)
Zoo Parade (NBC)

BEST NEW PROGRAMS
☐ *Make Room for Daddy* (ABC)
☐ *U.S. Steel Hour* (ABC)
Adventure (CBS)
Ding Dong School (NBC)
Letter to Loretta (NBC)
Person to Person (CBS)

BEST MYSTERY, ACTION OR ADVENTURE PROGRAM
☐ *Dragnet* (NBC)
Foreign Intrigue (NBC)
I Led Three Lives
Suspense (CBS)
The Web (CBS)

BEST AUDIENCE PARTICIPATION, QUIZ OR PANEL PROGRAM
☐ *This Is Your Life* (NBC)
☐ *What's My Line?* (CBS)
I've Got a Secret (CBS)
Two For the Money (CBS)
You Bet Your Life (NBC)

BEST MALE STAR OF REGULAR SERIES
☐ Donald O'Connor, *Colgate Comedy Hour* (NBC)
Sid Caesar, *Your Show of Shows* (NBC)
Wally Cox, *Mr. Peepers* (NBC)
Jackie Gleason, *Jackie Gleason Show* (CBS)
Jack Webb, *Dragnet* (NBC)

BEST FEMALE STAR OF REGULAR SERIES
☐ Eve Arden, *Our Miss Brooks* (CBS)
Lucille Ball, *I Love Lucy* (CBS)
Imogene Coca, *Your Show of Shows* (NBC)
Dinah Shore, *Dinah Shore Show* (NBC)
Loretta Young, *Letter to Loretta* (NBC)

☐ Indicates winner

BEST SERIES SUPPORTING ACTOR
☐ Art Carney, *Jackie Gleason Show* (CBS)
Ben Alexander, *Dragnet* (NBC)
William Frawley, *I Love Lucy* (CBS)
Tony Randall, *Mr. Peepers* (NBC)
Carl Reiner, *Your Show of Shows* (NBC)

BEST SERIES SUPPORTING ACTRESS
☐ Vivian Vance, *I Love Lucy* (CBS)
Bea Benedaret, *Burns & Allen* (CBS)
Ruth Gilbert, *Milton Berle Show* (NBC)
Marion Lorne, *Mr. Peepers* (NBC)
Audrey Meadows, *Jackie Gleason Show* (CBS)

MOST OUTSTANDING PERSONALITY
☐ Edward R. Murrow (CBS)
Arthur Godfrey (CBS)
Martha Raye (NBC)
Bishop Fulton J. Sheen (Syndicated)
Jack Webb (NBC)

1954

(Presented March 7, 1955)

Program Awards

BEST MYSTERY OR INTRIGUE SERIES
☐ *Dragnet* (NBC)
Foreign Intrigue (NBC)
I Led Three Lives (Syndicated)
Racket Squad (Syndicated)
Waterfront (Syndicated)

BEST VARIETY SERIES INCLUDING MUSICAL VARIETIES
☐ *Disneyland* (ABC)
George Gobel Show (NBC)
Jack Benny Show (CBS)
Jackie Gleason Show (CBS)
Toast of the Town (CBS)
Your Hit Parade (NBC)

BEST SITUATION COMEDY SERIES
☐ *Make Room for Daddy* (ABC)
Burns & Allen (CBS)
I Love Lucy (CBS)
Mr. Peepers (NBC)
Our Miss Brooks (CBS)
Private Secretary (CBS)

BEST DRAMATIC SERIES
☐ *U.S. Steel Hour* (ABC)
Four Star Playhouse (CBS)
Medic (NBC)
Philco Television Playhouse (NBC)
Studio One (CBS)

BEST CULTURAL, RELIGIOUS OR EDUCATIONAL PROGRAM
☐ *Omnibus* (CBS)
Life is Worth Living (Dumont)

Meet the Press (NBC)
Person to Person (CBS)
See it Now (CBS)

BEST SPORTS PROGRAM
☐ *Gillette Cavalcade of Sports* (NBC)
Blue Ribbon Bouts (CBS)
Forest Hills Tennis Matches (NBC)
Greatest Moments in Sports (NBC)
NCAA Football (ABC)
Professional Football (Dumont)

BEST WESTERN OR ADVENTURE SERIES
☐ *Stories of the Century* (Syndicated)
Annie Oakley (Syndicated)
Death Valley Days (CBS)
Roy Rogers Show (NBC)
Wild Bill Hickok (Syndicated)

BEST CHILDREN'S PROGRAM
☐ *Lassie* (CBS)
Art Linkletter and the Kids (Syndicated)
Ding Dong School (NBC)
Kukla, Fran and Ollie (ABC)
Time for Beany (Syndicated)
Zoo Parade (NBC)

BEST DAYTIME PROGRAM
☐ *Art Linkletter's House Party* (CBS)
Betty White Show (NBC)
Bob Crosby Show (CBS)
Garry Moore Show (CBS)
Robert Q. Lewis (CBS)

BEST INDIVIDUAL PROGRAM OF THE YEAR
☐ "Operation Undersea," *Disneyland* (ABC)
Diamond Jubilee of Light (4 networks)
"White is the Color," *Medic* (NBC)
"A Christmas Carol," *Shower of Stars* (CBS)
"Twelve Angry Men," *Studio One* (CBS)

BEST AUDIENCE, GUEST PARTICIPATION OR PANEL PROGRAM
☐ *This Is Your Life* (NBC)
Masquerade Party (ABC)
People Are Funny (NBC)
What's My Line? (CBS)
You Bet Your Life (NBC)

Performance Awards

BEST ACTOR IN A SINGLE PERFORMANCE
☐ Robert Cummings, "Twelve Angry Men," *Studio One* (CBS)
Frank Lovejoy, "Double Indemnity," *Lux Video Theatre* (CBS)
Fredric March, "A Christmas Carol," *Shower of Stars* (CBS)
Thomas Mitchell, "Good of His Soul," *Ford Theatre* (NBC)
David Niven, "The Answer," *Four Star Playhouse* (CBS)

BEST ACTRESS IN A SINGLE PERFORMANCE

☐ Judith Anderson, "Macbeth," *Hallmark Hall of Fame* (NBC)
Ethel Barrymore, "The 13th Chair," *Climax* (CBS)
Beverly Garland, "White Is the Color," *Medic* (NBC)
Ruth Hussey, "Craig's Wife," *Lux Video Theatre* (NBC)
Dorothy McGuire, "The Giaconda Smile," *Climax* (CBS)

BEST ACTOR STARRING IN A REGULAR SERIES

☐ Danny Thomas, *Make Room for Daddy* (ABC)
Richard Boone, *Medic* (NBC)
Robert Cummings, *My Hero* (Syndicated)
Jackie Gleason, *Jackie Gleason Show* (CBS)
Jack Webb, *Dragnet* (NBC)

BEST ACTRESS STARRING IN A REGULAR SERIES

☐ Loretta Young, *Loretta Young Show* (NBC)
Eve Arden, *Our Miss Brooks* (CBS)
Gracie Allen, *Burns & Allen Show* (CBS)
Lucille Ball, *I Love Lucy* (CBS)
Ann Sothern, *Private Secretary* (CBS)

BEST SUPPORTING ACTOR IN A REGULAR SERIES

☐ Art Carney, *Jackie Gleason Show* (CBS)
Ben Alexander, *Dragnet* (NBC)
Don DeFore, *The Adventures of Ozzie and Harriet* (ABC)
William Frawley, *I Love Lucy* (CBS)
Gale Gordon, *Our Miss Brooks* (CBS)

BEST SUPPORTING ACTRESS IN A REGULAR SERIES

☐ Audrey Meadows, *Jackie Gleason Show* (CBS)
Bea Benedaret, *Burns & Allen Show* (CBS)
Jean Hagen, *Make Room for Daddy* (ABC)
Marion Lorne, *Mr. Peepers* (NBC)
Vivian Vance, *I Love Lucy* (CBS)

BEST MALE SINGER

☐ Perry Como (NBC)
Eddie Fisher (NBC)
Frankie Laine (Syndicated)
Tony Martin (NBC)
Gordon MacRae (NBC)

BEST FEMALE SINGER

☐ Dinah Shore (NBC)
Jane Froman (CBS)
Peggy King (NBC)
Gisele Mackenzie (NBC)
Jo Stafford (CBS)

☐ Indicates winner

BEST NEWS REPORTER OR COMMENTATOR

☐ John Daly (ABC)
Douglas Edwards (CBS)
Clete Roberts (Syndicated)
Eric Sevareid (CBS)
John Cameron Swayze (NBC)

MOST OUTSTANDING NEW PERSONALITY

☐ George Gobel (NBC)
Richard Boone (NBC)
Walt Disney (ABC)
Tennessee Ernie Ford (CBS)
Preston Foster (Syndicated)
Michael O'Shea (NBC)
Fess Parker (ABC)

Craft and Technical Awards

BEST DIRECTION

☐ Franklin Schaffner, "Twelve Angry Men," *Studio One* (CBS)
Robert Florey, "The Clara Schumann Story," *Loretta Young Show* (NBC)
Clark Jones, *Your Hit Parade* (NBC)
Roy Kellino, "The Answer," *Four Star Playhouse* (CBS)
Ted Post, "Christmas on the Waterfront," *Waterfront* (CBS)
Alex Segal, *U.S. Steel Hour* (ABC)

BEST WRITTEN DRAMATIC MATERIAL

☐ Reginald Rose, "Twelve Angry Men," *Studio One* (CBS)
Paddy Chayefsky, *Philco Television Playhouse* (NBC)
David Dortort, "An Error in Chemistry," *Climax* (CBS)
Leonard Freeman, "The Answer," *Four Star Playhouse* (CBS)
James Moser, "White Is the Color," *Medic* (NBC)

BEST WRITTEN COMEDY MATERIAL

☐ James Allardice, Jack Douglass, Hal Kanter, Harry Winkler, *George Gobel Show* (NBC)
George Balzer, Milt Josefsberg, Sam Perrin, Jack Tackaberry, *Jack Benny Show* (CBS)
James Fritzell, Everett Greenbaum, *Mr. Peepers* (NBC)
Jackie Gleason (and staff writers), *Jackie Gleason Show* (CBS)
Jess Oppenheimer, Robert G. Carroll, Madelyn Pugh, *I Love Lucy* (CBS)
Danny Thomas (and staff writers), *Make room for Daddy* (ABC)

BEST ART DIRECTION OF A LIVE SHOW

☐ Bob Markell, "Mallory's Tragedy on Mt. Everest," *You Are There* (CBS)
Robert Tyler Lee, *Shower of Stars* (CBS)
Carl Macauley, *Space Patrol* (ABC)

William T. Martin, *Dinah Shore Show* (NBC)
James Vance, *Climax* (CBS)

BEST ART DIRECTION OF A FILMED SHOW

☐ Ralph Berger, Albert Pyke, "A Christmas Carol," *Shower of Stars* (CBS)
Duncan Cramer, *Four Star Playhouse* (CBS)
Frank Durlauf, *Ozzie and Harriet Show* (ABC)
Caludio Guzman, *Ray Bolger Show* (ABC)
Serge Krizman, "The Roman and the Renegade," *Schlitz Playhouse of Stars* (CBS)

BEST DIRECTION OF PHOTOGRAPHY

☐ Lester Shorr, "I Climb the Stairs," *Medic* (NBC)
Norbert Brodine, "The Clara Schumann Story," *Loretta Young Show* (NBC)
George T. Clemens, "The Roman and the Renegade," *Schlitz Playhouse of Stars* (CBS)
Edward Colman, "The Big Bible," *Dragnet* (NBC)
Harold E. Stine, "Night Call," *Cavalcade of America* (Syndicated)

BEST TECHNICAL ACHIEVEMENT

☐ John West; Color TV Policy; Burbank Color (NBC)

BEST ENGINEERING EFFECTS

☐ Robert Shelby, (Four Quadrant Screen) 1954 National Election Coverage (NBC)
Electronic Editing, *Background* (NBC)—John Goetz; Walter O'Meara; Daniel Zampino
Jackie Gleason Show (CBS)—Jackie Gleason Enterprises
Space Patrol (ABC)—Cameron Pierce

BEST TELEVISION SOUND EDITING

☐ George Nicholson, *Dragnet* (NBC)
Cathey Burrow, *Waterfront* (CBS)
Johnny Bushelman, *Ramar of the Jungle* (Syndicated)
Stanley Callahan, *Rin Tin Tin* (ABC)
Josef von Stroheim, "Red Christmas," *Medic* (NBC)

BEST TELEVISION FILM EDITING

☐ Grant Smith; Lynn Harrison, "Operation Undersea," *Disneyland* (ABC)
George Amy, "The Roman and the Renegade," *Schlitz Playhouse of Stars* (CBS)
Samuel E. Beetley, "The Answer," *Four Star Playhouse* (CBS)
Jodie Copelan, "White Is the Color," *Medic* (NBC)

Chester W. Schaeffer, "Davy Crockett Indian Fighter," *Disneyland* (ABC)

BEST ORIGINAL MUSIC COMPOSED FOR TV

☐ Walter Schumann, *Dragnet* (NBC)
Bernard Hermann, "A Christmas Carol," *Shower of Stars* (CBS)
Gian Carlo Menotti, "Amahl and the Night Visitors," *Hallmark Hall of Fame* (NBC)
Victor Young, *Diamond Jubilee of Light* (4 networks)
Victor Young, *Medic* (NBC)

BEST SCORING OF A DRAMATIC OR VARIETY PROGRAM

☐ *Diamond Jubilee of Light* (4 networks)
Buddy Bregman, "Anything Goes," *Colgate Comedy Hour* (NBC)
Gordon Jenkins, *Shower of Stars* (first show) (CBS)
Nelson Riddle, *Satins and Spurs*
Walter Scharf, "Here Comes Donald," *Texaco Star Theater* (NBC)

BEST CHOREOGRAPHER

☐ June Taylor, *Jackie Gleason Show* (CBS)
Rod Alexander, *Max Liebman Spectaculars* (NBC)
Tony Charmoli; Bod Herget, *Your Hit Parade* (NBC)
Louis Da Pron, "Here Comes Donald," *Texaco Star Theater* (NBC)

1955

(Presented March 17, 1956)

Program Awards

BEST ACTION OR ADVENTURE SERIES

☐ *Disneyland* (ABC)
Alfred Hitchcock Presents (CBS)
Dragnet (NBC)
Gunsmoke (CBS)
Line-Up (CBS)

BEST COMEDY SERIES

☐ *Phil Silvers' You'll Never Get Rich* (CBS)
Jack Benny Show (CBS)
Bob Cummings Show (CBS)
Caesar's Hour (NBC)
George Gobel Show (NBC)
Make Room for Daddy (ABC)

BEST VARIETY SERIES

☐ *Ed Sullivan Show* (CBS)
Dinah Shore Show (NBC)
Ford Star Jubilee (CBS)
Perry Como Show (NBC)
Shower of Stars (CBS)

BEST MUSIC SERIES

☐ *Your Hit Parade* (NBC)

☐ Indicates winner

Coke Time—Eddie Fisher (NBC)
Dinah Shore Show (NBC)
Perry Como Show (NBC)
Voice of Firestone (CBS)

BEST DRAMATIC SERIES

☐ *Producers' Showcase* (NBC)
Alcoa-Goodyear TV Playhouse (NBC)
Climax (CBS)
Studio One (CBS)
U.S. Steel Hour (CBS)

BEST SINGLE PROGRAM OF THE YEAR

☐ "Peter Pan," *Producers' Showcase* (NBC)
"The American West," *Wide Wide World* (NBC)
"Caine Mutiny Court-Martial," *Ford Star Jubilee* (CBS)
"Davy Crockett and River Pirates," *Disneyland* (ABC)
"No Time for Sergeants," *U.S. Steel Hour* (ABC)
"Peter Pan Meets Rusty Williams," *Make Room for Daddy* (ABC)
"The Sleeping Beauty," *Producers' Showcase* (NBC)

BEST CHILDREN'S SERIES

☐ *Lassie* (CBS)
Ding Dong School (NBC)
Howdy Doody (NBC)
Kukla, Fran and Ollie (ABC)
Mickey Mouse Club (ABC)
The Pinky Lee Show (NBC)

BEST CONTRIBUTION TO DAYTIME PROGRAMMING

☐ *Matinee Theatre* (NBC)
The Bob Crosby Show (CBS)
The Garry Moore Show (CBS)
Home Arlene Francis (NBC)
Today Dave Garroway (NBC)

BEST SPECIAL EVENTS OR NEWS PROGRAM

☐ *A-Bomb Test Coverage* (CBS)
Academy of Motion Picture Arts and Science Awards (NBC)
Academy of Television Arts and Sciences Awards (NBC)
Football—Rose Bowl (NBC)
Baseball—World Series (NBC)

BEST DOCUMENTARY PROGRAM (RELIGIOUS, INFORMATIONAL, EDUCATIONAL OR INTERVIEW)

☐ *Omnibus* (CBS)
Meet the Press (NBC)
Person to Person (CBS)
See It Now (CBS)
Wide Wide World (NBC)

BEST AUDIENCE PARTICIPATION SERIES (QUIZ, PANEL ETC.)

☐ *$64,000 Question* (CBS)
I've Got a Secret (CBS)
People Are Funny (NBC)
What's My Line? (CBS)
You Bet Your Life (NBC)

Performance Awards

BEST ACTOR (SINGLE PERFORMANCE)

☐ Lloyd Nolan, "The Caine Mutiny Court-Martial," *Ford Star Jubilee* (CBS)
Ralph Bellamy, "Fearful Decision," *U.S. Steel Hour* (CBS)
Jose Ferrer, "Cyrano de Bergerac," *Producers' Showcase* (NBC)
Everett Sloane, "Patterns," *Kraft Theatre* (NBC)
Barry Sullivan, "Caine Mutiny Court-Martial," *Ford Star Jubilee* (CBS)

BEST ACTRESS (SINGLE PERFORMANCE)

☐ Mary Martin, "Peter Pan," *Producers' Showcase* (NBC)
Julie Harris, "Wind From the South," *U.S. Steel Hour* (CBS)
Eva Marie Saint, "Our Town," *Producers' Showcase* (NBC)
Jessica Tandy, "The Fourposter," *Producers' Showcase* (NBC)
Loretta Young, "Christmas Stopover," *Loretta Young Show* (NBC)

BEST ACTOR (CONTINUING PERFORMANCE)

☐ Phil Silvers, *You'll Never Get Rich* (CBS)
Bob Cummings, *Bob Cummings Show* (CBS)
Jackie Gleason, *The Honeymooners* (CBS)
Danny Thomas, *Make Room for Daddy* (ABC)
Robert Young, *Father Knows Best* (CBS)

BEST ACTRESS (CONTINUING PERFORMANCE)

☐ Lucille Ball, *I Love Lucy* (CBS)
Gracie Allen, *Burns & Allen* (CBS)
Eve Arden, *Our Miss Brooks* (CBS)
Jean Hagen, *Make Room for Daddy* (ABC)
Ann Sothern, *Private Secretary* (CBS)

BEST ACTOR IN A SUPPORTING ROLE

☐ Art Carney, *The Honeymooners* (CBS)
Ed Begley, "Patterns," *Kraft Theatre* (NBC)
William Frawley, *I Love Lucy* (CBS)
Carl Reiner, *Caesar's Hour* (NBC)
Cyril Ritchard, "Peter Pan," *Producers' Showcase* (NBC)

BEST ACTRESS IN A SUPPORTING ROLE

☐ Nanette Fabray, *Caesar's Hour* (NBC)
Ann B. Davis, *Bob Cummings Show* (CBS)
Jean Hagan, *Make Room for Daddy* (ABC)
Audrey Meadows, *The Honeymooners* (CBS)

Thelma Ritter, "A Catered Affair," *Alcoa-Goodyear Playhouse* (NBC)

BEST COMEDIAN
☐ Phil Silvers (CBS)
Jack Benny (CBS)
Sid Caesar (NBC)
Art Carney (CBS)
George Gobel (NBC)

BEST COMEDIENNE
☐ Nanette Fabray (NBC)
Gracie Allen (CBS)
Eve Arden (CBS)
Lucille Ball (CBS)
Ann Sothern (CBS)

BEST MALE SINGER
☐ Perry Como (NBC)
Harry Belafonte
Eddie Fisher (NBC)
Gordon MacRae (NBC)
Frank Sinatra (NBC)

BEST FEMALE SINGER
☐ Dinah Shore (NBC)
Rosemary Clooney (Syndicated)
Judy Garland (CBS)
Peggy Lee
Gisele Mackenzie (NBC)

BEST MC OR PROGRAM HOST (MALE OR FEMALE)
☐ Perry Como (NBC)
Alistair Cooke (CBS)
John Daly (CBS)
Dave Garroway (NBC)
Alfred Hitchcock (CBS)

BEST NEWS COMMENTATOR OR REPORTER
☐ Edward R. Murrow (CBS)
John Daly (ABC)
Douglas Edwards (CBS)
Clete Roberts (CBS)
John Cameron Swayze (NBC)

BEST SPECIALTY ACT (SINGLE OR GROUP)
☐ Marcel Marceau (NBC)
Harry Belafonte (NBC)
Victor Borge
Sammy Davis, Jr.
Donald O'Connor (NBC)

Craft and Technical Awards

BEST ORIGINAL TELEPLAY WRITING
☐ Rod Serling, "Patterns," *Kraft TV Theatre* (NBC)
David Davidson, "Thunder Over Washington," *Alcoa-Goodyear Playhouse* (NBC)
Robert Alan Authur, "A Man Is Ten Feet Tall," *Philco Playhouse* (NBC)
Paddy Chayefsky, "A Catered Affair," *Alcoa-Goodyear Playhouse* (NBC)

☐ Indicates winner

Cyril Hume, Richard Maibaum, "Fearful Decision," *U.S. Steel Hour* (CBS)

BEST COMEDY WRITING
☐ Nat Hiken, Barry Blitser, Arnold Auerbach, Harvey Orkin, Vincent Bogert, Arnold Rosen, Coleman Jacoby, Tony Webster, Terry Ryan, *You'll Never Get Rich* (CBS)
Hal Kanter, Howard Leeds, Everett Greenbaum, Harry Winkler, *George Gobel Show* (NBC)
Jess Oppenheimer, Madelyn Pugh, Bob Carroll, Jr., Bob Schiller, Bob Weiskopf, *I Love Lucy* (CBS)
Sam Perrin, George Balzer, Hal Goldman, Al Gordon, *Jack Benny Show* (CBS)
Mel Tolkin, Selma Diamond, Larry Gelbart, Mel Brooks, Sheldon Keller, *Caesar's Hour* (NBC)

BEST TELEVISION ADAPTATION
☐ Paul Gregory, Franklin Schaffner, "The Caine Mutiny Court-Martial," *Ford Star Jubilee* (CBS)
David Dortort, "The Ox-Bow Incident," *20th Century-Fox Hour* (CBS)
John Monks, Jr., "Miracle on 34th Street," *20th Century-Fox Hour* (CBS)
Rod Serling, "The Champion," *Climax* (CBS)
David Shaw, "Our Town," *Producers' Showcase* (NBC)

BEST MUSICAL CONTRIBUTION
☐ Sammy Cahn, James Van Heusen, "Love and Marriage," from "Our Town" *Producers' Showcase* (NBC)
The arranging of "Camarata" for "Together with Music," *Four Star Jubilee* ; Mary Martin; Noel Coward (CBS)
The score of "Our Town" by Sammy Cahn and James Van Heusen, *Producers' Showcase* (NBC)
The arranging of Nelson Riddle for "Our Town" *Producers' Showcase* (NBC)
The series scoring by David Broekman for *Wide Wide World* (NBC)

BEST PRODUCER (LIVE SERIES)
☐ Fred Coe, *Producers' Showcase* (NBC)
Herbert Brodkin, *Alcoa-Goodyear Playhouse* (NBC)
Hal Kanter, *George Gobel Show* (NBC)
Martin Manulis, *Climax* (CBS)
The Theatre Guild, *U.S. Steel Hour* (CBS)
Barry Wood, *Wide Wide World* (NBC)

BEST PRODUCER (FILM SERIES)
☐ Walt Disney, *Disneyland* (ABC)
James D. Fonda, *You Are There* (CBS)
Paul Henning, *Bob Cummings Show* (CBS)

Nat Hiken, *Phil Silvers Show, You'll Never Get Rich* (CBS)
Frank La Tourette, *Medic* (NBC)

BEST DIRECTOR (LIVE SERIES)
☐ Franklin Schaffner, "The Caine Mutiny Court-Martial," *Ford Star Jubilee* (CBS)
John Frankenheimer, "Portrait in Celluloid," *Climax* (CBS)
Clark Jones, "Peter Pan," *Producers' Showcase* (NBC)
Delbert Mann, "Our Town," *Producers' Showcase* (NBC)
Alex Segal, "No Time for Sergeants," *U.S. Steel Hour* (CBS)

BEST DIRECTOR (FILM SERIES)
☐ Nat Hiken, *You'll Never Get Rich* (CBS)
Rod Amateau, "Return of the Wolf," *Bob Cummings Show* (CBS)
Bernard Girard, "Grant and Lee at Appomatox," *You Are There* (CBS)
Alfred Hitchcock, "The Case of Mr. Pelham," *Alfred Hitchcock Presents* (CBS)
Sheldon Leonard, *Make Room for Daddy* (ABC)
Jack Webb, "Christmas Story," *Dragnet* (NBC)

BEST ART DIRECTION (LIVE SERIES)
☐ Otis Riggs, *Playwrights '56* and *Producers' Showcase* (NBC)
Carl Kent, *U.S. Steel Hour* (CBS)
Jan Scott, *Hallmark Hall of Fame* (NBC)
Don Shirley, *Perry Como Show* (NBC)
William Craig Smith, *Lux Video Theatre* (NBC)
James D. Vance, *Climax* (CBS)

BEST ART DIRECTION (FILM SERIES)
☐ William Ferrari, *You Are There* (CBS)
Duncan Cramer, *Four Star Playhouse* (CBS)
Ernst Fegte, *Medic* (NBC)
Serge Krizman, *Schlitz Playhouse*
Peter Proud, *Robin Hood*

BEST CINEMATOGRAPHY FOR TELEVISION
☐ William Scikner, "Black Friday," *Medic* (NBC)
Norbert Brodine, "I Remember the Rani," *Loretta Young Show* (NBC)
Edward Colman, *Dragnet* (NBC)
George Diskant, "The Collar," *Four Star Playhouse* (CBS)
Robert Pittack, *Private Secretary* (CBS)

BEST CAMERA WORK (LIVE SHOW)
☐ T. Miller, *Studio One* (CBS)
A. J. Cunningham, *Climax* (CBS)
Joe Strauss, *Lux Video Theatre* (NBC)
Les Vaught, *Art Linkletter's House Party* (CBS)

BEST EDITING OF A TELEVISION FILM
☐ Edward W. Williams, "Breakdown" *Alfred Hitchcock Presents* (CBS)
Samuel E. Beetley, "The Collar," *Four Star Playhouse* (CBS)
Jason H. Bernie, "Operation 3 in 1," *Navy Log* (CBS)
Stanley Frazen; Guy Scarpitta, "Miss Coffee Break," *Bob Cummings Show* (CBS)
Daniel Nathan, "Little Guy," *Fireside Theatre* (NBC)

BEST CHOREOGRAPHER
☐ Tony Charmoli, "Show Biz," *Your Hit Parade* (NBC)
Rod Alexander, *Max Liebman Spectaculars* (NBC)
Jerome Robbins, "Peter Pan," *Producers' Showcase* (NBC)
James Starbuck, *Max Liebman Presents* and *Shower of Stars with Ethel Merman* (NBC, CBS)
June Taylor, *Jackie Gleason Show* (CBS)

BEST ENGINEERING TECHNICAL ACHIEVEMENT
☐ RCA Tricolor Picture Tube, which made the commercial color receiver practical
Automatic Iris Control for NBC pick-up of complete atom blast at Yucca Flats
Color wipe Amplifier developed by CBS Engineering
Dumont Electronicam
Electronic Editing Machine developed at the Disney Studios
Ultra-Violet Kinescope Recording of RCA which improved the quality of television recording

BEST COMMERCIAL CAMPAIGN
☐ Ford Motor Co.
Bank of America
Chrysler Corp.
Hamm's Beer Co.
Piel's Beer Co.

Special Awards

GOVERNOR'S AWARD (THE FIRST PRESIDENTIAL-SIZE EMMY)
☐ President Dwight D. Eisenhower, for his use and encouragement of television

☐ Indicates winner

1956

(Presented March 16, 1957)

Program Awards

BEST SINGLE PROGRAM OF THE YEAR
☐ "Requiem for a Heavyweight," *Playhouse 90* (CBS)
"A Night to Remember," *Kraft Television Theatre* (NBC)
"Leonard Bernstein," *Omnibus* (CBS)
"Secret Life of Danny Kaye," *See It Now* (CBS)
Victor Borge Show

BEST NEW PROGRAM SERIES
☐ *Playhouse 90* (CBS)
Air Power (CBS)
The Chevy Show—Dinah Shore (NBC)
Ernie Kovacs Show (NBC)
Steve Allen Sunday Show (NBC)

BEST SERIES (HALF HOUR OR LESS)
☐ *Phil Silvers Show* (CBS)
Alfred Hitchcock Presents (CBS)
Father Knows Best (NBC)
Jack Benny Show (CBS)
Person to Person (CBS)

BEST SERIES (ONE HOUR OR MORE)
☐ *Caesar's Hour* (NBC)
Climax (CBS)
Ed Sullivan Show (CBS)
Omnibus (CBS)
Perry Como Show (NBC)

BEST PUBLIC SERVICE SERIES
☐ *See It Now* (CBS)
Meet the Press (NBC)
NBC Opera (NBC)
Wide Wide World (NBC)
You Are There (CBS)

BEST COVERAGE OF A NEWSWORTHY EVENT
☐ *Years of Crisis*, year-end report with Edward R. Murrow and other correspondents (CBS)
Andrea Doria Sinking (CBS)
Andrea Doria Survivors Arrive in New York (NBC)
National Political Conventions (ABC)
National Political Conventions (NBC)

Performance Awards

BEST CONTINUING PERFORMANCE BY AN ACTOR IN A DRAMATIC SERIES
☐ Robert Young, *Father Knows Best* (NBC)
James Arness, *Gunsmoke* (CBS)
Charles Boyer, *Four Star Playhouse* (CBS)
Hugh O'Brien, *Wyatt Earp* (ABC)

David Niven, *Four Star Playhouse* (CBS)

BEST CONTINUING PERFORMANCE BY AN ACTRESS IN A DRAMATIC SERIES
☐ Loretta Young, *Loretta Young Show* (NBC)
Jan Clayton, *Lassie* (CBS)
Ida Lupino, *Four Star Playhouse* (CBS)
Peggy Wood, *Mama* (CBS)
Jane Wyman, *Jane Wyman Theatre* (NBC)

BEST CONTINUING PERFORMANCE BY A COMEDIAN IN A SERIES
☐ Sid Caesar, *Caesar's Hour* (NBC)
Jack Benny, *Jack Benny Show* (CBS)
Bob Cummings, *Bob Cummings Show* (CBS)
Ernie Kovacs, *Ernie Kovacs Show* (NBC)
Phil Silvers, *Phil Silvers Show* (CBS)

BEST CONTINUING PERFORMANCE BY A COMEDIENNE IN A SERIES
☐ Nanette Fabray, *Caesar's Hour* (NBC)
Edie Adams, *Ernie Kovacs Show* (NBC)
Gracie Allen, *Burns & Allen* (CBS)
Lucille Ball, *I Love Lucy* (CBS)
Ann Sothern, *Private Secretary* (CBS)

BEST SINGLE PERFORMANCE BY AN ACTOR
☐ Jack Palance, "Requiem for a Heavyweight," *Playhouse 90* (CBS)
Lloyd Bridges, "Tragedy in a Temporary Town," *Alcoa-Goodyear Playhouse* (NBC)
Frederic March, "Dodsworth," *Producers' Showcase* (NBC)
Sal Mineo, "Dino," *Studio One* (CBS)
Red Skelton, "The Big Slide," *Playhouse 90* (CBS)

BEST SINGLE PERFORMANCE BY AN ACTRESS
☐ Claire Trevor, "Dodsworth," *Producers' Showcase* (NBC)
Edna Best, "This Happy Breed," *Ford Star Jubilee* (CBS)
Gracie Fields, "Old Lady Shows Her Medals," *U.S. Steel Hour* (CBS)
Nancy Kelly, "The Pilot," *Studio One* (CBS)
Evelyn Rudie, "Eloise," *Playhouse 90* (CBS)

BEST SUPPORTING PERFORMANCE BY AN ACTOR
☐ Carl Reiner, *Caesar's Hour* (NBC)
Art Carney, *Jackie Gleason Show* (CBS)
Paul Ford, *Phil Silvers Show* (CBS)
William Frawley, *I Love Lucy* (CBS)
Ed Wynn, "Requiem for a Heavyweight," *Playhouse 90* (CBS)

BEST SUPPORTING PERFORMANCE BY AN ACTRESS
☐ Pat Carroll, *Caesar's Hour* (CBS)
Ann B. Davis, *Bob Cummings Show* (CBS)
Audrey Meadows, *Jackie Gleason Show* (CBS)
Mildred Natwick, "Blithe Spirit," *Ford Star Jubilee* (CBS)
Vivian Vance, *I Love Lucy* (CBS)

BEST MALE PERSONALITY (CONTINUING PERFORMANCE)
☐ Perry Como (NBC)
Steve Allen (NBC)
Leonard Bernstein (CBS)
Tennessee Ernie Ford (NBC)
Alfred Hitchcock (CBS)
Bishop Fulton J. Sheen (Dumont)

BEST FEMALE PERSONALITY (CONTINUING PERFORMANCE)
☐ Diah Shore (NBC)
Rosemary Clooney (Syndicated)
Faye Emerson (CBS)
Arlene Francis (NBC)
Gisele Mackenzie (NBC)

BEST NEWS COMMENTATOR
☐ Edward R. Murrow (CBS)
Walter Cronkite (CBS)
John Daly (ABC)
Douglas Edwards (CBS)
Chet Huntley (NBC)

Craft and Technical Awards

BEST TELEPLAY WRITING (HALF HOUR OR LESS)
☐ James P. Cavanagh, "Fog Closes In," *Alfred Hitchcock Presents* (CBS)
Morton Fine, David Friedkin, "Patrol," *Frontier* (NBC)
Richard Morris, "The Pearl," *Loretta Young Show* (NBC)
John Nesbitt, "Man with the Bear," *Telephone Time* (ABC)
Dan Ullman, "The Buntline," *Wyatt Earp* (ABC)

BEST TELEPLAY WRITING (ONE HOUR OR MORE)
☐ Rod Serling, "Requiem for a Heavyweight," *Playhouse 90* (CBS)
Louis Peterson, "Joey," *Alcoa Hour-Goodyear Playhouse* (NBC)
George Roy Hill, John Whedon, "A Night to Remember," *Kraft Television Theatre* (NBC)
Elick Moll, "Seldman and Son," *Playhouse 90* (CBS)
Reginald Rose, "Tragedy in a Temporary Town," *Alcoa Hour-Goodyear Playhouse* (NBC)

☐ Indicates winner

BEST COMEDY WRITING (VARIETY OR SITUATION COMEDY)
☐ Nat Hiken, Billy Friedberg, Tony Webster, Leonard Stern, Arnold Rosen, Coleman Jacoby, *Phil Silvers Show* (CBS)
Goodman Ace, Jay Burton, Mort Green, Geroge Foster, *Perry Como Show* (NBC)
Ernie Kovacs, Louis M. Heyward, Rex Lardner, Mike Marmer, *Ernie Kovacs Show* (NBC)
Sam Perrin, George Balzer, Hal Goldman, Al Gordon, *Jack Benny Show* (CBS)
Mel Tolkin, Gary Belkin, Mel Brooks, Sheldon Keller, Neil Simon, Larry Gelbart, Mike Stewart, *Caesar's Hour* (NBC)

BEST DIRECTION (HALF HOUR OR LESS)
☐ Sheldon Leonard, "Danny's Comeback," *Danny Thomas Show* (ABC)
George Archainbaud, "The Traitor," *77th Bengal Lancers* (NBC)
Herschel Gaugherty, "The Road That Led Afar," *G.E. Theatre* (CBS)
William Russell, "First Moscow Purge Trial," *You Are There* (CBS)
Clay Yurdin, "As I Lay Dying," *Camera Three* (CBS)

BEST DIRECTION (ONE HOUR OR MORE)
☐ Ralph Nelson, "Requiem for a Heavyweight," *Playhouse 90* (CBS)
Lewis Allen, "Child of the Regiment," *20th Century-Fox Hour* (CBS)
Bob Banner, "October 5 with Sinatra," *Chevy Show—Dinah Shore* (NBC)
Kirk Browning, "La Boheme," *NBC Opera Theatre* (NBC)
John Frankenheimer, "Forbidden Area," *Playhouse 90* (CBS)
George Roy Hill, "A Night to Remember," *Kraft Television Theatre* (NBC)

BEST ART DIRECTION (HALF HOUR OR LESS)
☐ Paul Barnes, *Your Hit Parade* (NBC)
Warren Clymer, *Frontiers of Faith* (NBC)
Grover Cole, *Adventure* (CBS)
Martin Obzina, John Robert Lloyd, John J. Lloyd, John Meehan, George Patrick, *G.E. Theatre* (CBS)
Franklin Swig, *Dinah Shore Show* (NBC)

BEST ART DIRECTION (ONE HOUR OR MORE)
☐ Albert Heschong, "Requiem for a Heavyweight," *Playhouse 90* (CBS)
Henry May, *Omnibus* (CBS)
Duane McKinney, *Kraft Television Theatre* (NBC)

Jan Scott, *Kraiser Aluminum Hour* (NBC)
Don Shirley, *Perry Como Show* (NBC)

BEST CINEMATOGRAPHY FOR TELEVISION
☐ Norbert Brodine, "The Pearl," *Loretta Young Show* (NBC)
Lloyd Ahem, "Stranger in the Night," *20th Century-Fox Hour* (CBS)
George E. Diskant, "Tunnel of Fear," *Four Star Playhouse* (CBS)
Robert W. Pittack, "The Glorious Gift of Molly Malloy," *G.E. Theatre* (CBS)
John L. Russell, "The Night Goes On," *G.E. Theatre* (CBS)

BEST EDITING OF A FILM FOR TELEVISION
☐ Frank Keller, "Our Mr. Sun," *A.T. & T. Science Series* (CBS)
Samuel E. Beetley, "Tunnel of Fear," *Four Star Playhouse* (CBS)
Richard Fantl, "Betty's Birthday," *Father Knows Best* (NBC)
Daniel A. Nathan, "Between Jobs," *Jane Wyman Theatre* (NBC)
Robert Watts, "Bounty Killers," *Cheyenne* (ABC)

BEST MUSICAL CONTRIBUTION FOR TELEVISION
☐ Leonard Bernstein, "Composing, Conducting," *Omnibus* (CBS)
Sidney Fine for orchestration of Victor Young's music on *Medic* (NBC)
Nelson Riddle for arrangement of musical score on *Rosemary Clooney Show* (Syndicated)
Walter Schumann for vocal arrangements on *Tennessee Ernie Ford Show* (NBC)
Oliver Wallace for composing score on *Disneyland TV Show* (ABC)

BEST LIVE CAMERA WORK
☐ "A Night to Remember," *Kraft Television Theatre* (NBC)
"An American Sunday," *Wide Wide World* (NBC)
"Jack and the Beanstalk," *Producers' Showcase* (NBC)
Republican Convention, (ABC-CBS-NBC Pool)
"Requiem for a Heavyweight," *Playhouse 90* (CBS)

BEST ENGINEERING OR TECHNICAL ACHIEVEMENT
☐ Development of video tape by Ampex and further development and practical applications by SBS. Dual entry.
Application of Lenticular Film to recording process for colored delayed release (NBC)
Development of the truly portable "Creepie Peepie" for television pick-up by RCA

Telescopic lens with 100-inch focal length ("Big Jake") developed and used by ABC

Wide Wide World live pick-up from Havana, Cuba **(NBC)**

1957

(Presented April 15, 1958)

Program Awards

BEST SINGLE PROGRAM OF THE YEAR

☐ "The Comedian," *Playhouse 90* (CBS)
Edsel Show (CBS)
"Green Pastures," *Hallmark Hall of Fame* (NBC)
"Helen Morgan Story," *Playhouse 90* (CBS)

BEST NEW PROGRAM SERIES OF THE YEAR

☐ *Seven Lively Arts* (CBS)
Leave It to Beaver (CBS)
Maverick (ABC)
Tonight (NBC)
Wagon Train (NBC)

BEST DRAMATIC ANTHOLOGY SERIES

☐ *Playhouse 90* (CBS)
Alfred Hitchcock Presents (CBS)
Climax (CBS)
Hallmark Hall of Fame (NBC)
Studio One (CBS)

BEST DRAMATIC SERIES WITH CONTINUING CHARACTERS

☐ *Gunsmoke* (CBS)
Lassie (CBS)
Maverick (ABC)
Perry Mason (CBS)
Wagon Train (NBC)

BEST COMEDY SERIES

☐ *Phil Silvers Show* (CBS)
Bob Cummings Show (CBS, NBC)
Caesar's Hour (NBC)
Father Knows Best (NBC)
Jack Benny Show (CBS)

BEST MUSICAL, VARIETY, AUDIENCE PARTICIPATION OR QUIZ SERIES

☐ *Dinah Shore—Chevy Show* (NBC)
Ed Sullivan Show (CBS)
Perry Como Show (NBC)
Steve Allen Show (NBC)
Tonight (NBC)

BEST PUBLIC SERVICE PROGRAM OR SERIES

☐ *Omnibus* (ABC, NBC)
Bell Telephone Science Series (NBC)
Person to Person (CBS)
See It Now (CBS)
Wide Wide World (NBC)

☐ Indicates winner

BEST COVERAGE OF AN UNSCHEDULED NEWSWORTHY EVENT

☐ Coverage of the Rikers Island, New York, plane crash, *World News Round-up* (CBS)
Four newsmen interview **Governor Orval Faubus** of Arkansas in Little Rock (ABC)
New coverage of the integration story in Little Rock and other southern cities (NBC)
Coverage of the Little Rock School Riot, as presented on *Little Rock, 1957* (CBS)
News coverage of first Russian sputnik, the U.S. satellite launching efforts and Vanguard failure (NBC)

Performance Awards

BEST CONTINUING PERFORMANCE BY AN ACTOR IN A LEADING ROLE IN A DRAMATIC OR COMEDY SERIES

☐ Robert Young, *Father Knows Best* (NBC)
James Arness, *Gunsmoke* (CBS)
Bob Cummings, *Bob Cummings Show* (CBS, NBC)
Phil Silvers, *Phil Silvers Show* (CBS)
Danny Thomas, *Danny Thomas Show* (ABC, CBS)

BEST CONTINUING PERFORMANCE BY AN ACTRESS IN A LEADING ROLE IN A DRAMATIC OR COMEDY SERIES

☐ Jane Wyatt, *Father Knows Best* (NBC)
Eve Arden, *Eve Arden Show* (CBS)
Spring Byington, *December Bride* (CBS)
Jan Clayton, *Lassie* (CBS)
Ida Lupino, *Mr. Adam and Eve* (CBS)

BEST CONTINUING PERFORMANCE (MALE) IN A SERIES BY A COMEDIAN, SINGER, HOST, DANCER, MC, ANNOUNCER, NARRATOR, PANELIST OR ANY PERSON WHO ESSENTIALLY PLAYS HIMSELF

☐ Jack Benny, *Jack Benny Show* (CBS)
Steve Allen, *Steve Allen Show* (NBC)
Sid Caesar, *Caesar's Hour* (NBC)
Perry Como, *Perry Como Show* (NBC)
Jack Paar, *Tonight* (NBC)

BEST CONTINUING PERFORMANCE (FEMALE) IN A SERIES BY A COMEDIENNE, SINGER, HOSTESS, DANCER, MC, ANNOUNCER, NARRATOR, PANELIST OR ANY PERSON WHO ESSENTIALLY PLAYS HERSELF

☐ Dinah Shore, *Dinah Shore Chevy Show* (CBS)
Gracie Allen, *Burns & Allen Show* (CBS)

Lucille Ball, *I Love Lucy* (CBS)
Dody Goodman, *Tonight* (NBC)
Loretta Young, *Loretta Young Show* (NBC)

ACTOR—BEST SINGLE PERFORMANCE (LEAD OR SUPPORT)

☐ Peter Ustinov, "The Life of Samuel Johnson," *Omnibus* (NBC)
Lee J. Cobb, "No Deadly Medicine," *Studio One* (CBS)
Mickey Rooney, "The Comedian," *Playhouse 90* (CBS)
David Wayne, "Heartbeat," *Suspicion* (NBC)
Ed Wynn, "On Borrowed Time," *Hallmark Hall of Fame* (NBC)

ACTRESS—BEST SINGLE PERFORMANCE (LEAD OR SUPPORT)

☐ Polly Bergen, "Helen Morgan Story," *Playhouse 90* (CBS)
Julie Andrews, *Cinderella* (CBS)
Helen Hayes, "Mrs. Gilling and the Skyscraper," *Alcoa Hour* (NBC)
Piper Laurie, "The Deaf Heart," *Studio One* (CBS)
Teresa Wright, "The Miracle Worker," *Playhouse 90* (CBS)

BEST CONTINUING SUPPORTING PERFORMANCE BY AN ACTOR IN A DRAMATIC OR COMEDY SERIES

☐ Carl Reiner, *Caesar's Hour* (NBC)
Paul Ford, *Phil Silvers Show* (CBS)
William Frawley, *I Love Lucy* (CBS)
Louis Nye, *Steve Allen Show* (NBC)
Dennis Weaver, *Gunsmoke* (CBS)

BEST CONTINUING SUPPORTING PERFORMANCE BY AN ACTRESS IN A DRAMATIC OR COMEDY SERIES

☐ Ann B. Davis, *Bob Cummings Show* (CBS, NBC)
Pat Carroll, *Caesar's Hour* (NBC)
Verna Felton, *December Bride* (CBS)
Marion Lorne, *Sally* (NBC)
Vivian Vance, *I Love Lucy* (CBS)

BEST NEWS COMMENTARY

☐ Edward R. Murrow, *See It Now* (CBS)
John Daly, *News* (ABC)
Douglas Edwards, *News* (CBS)
Chet Huntley, David Brinkley, *News* (NBC)
Eric Sevareid. *World News Round-up* (CBS)

Craft and Technical Awards

BEST TELEPLAY WRITING (HALF HOUR OR LESS)

☐ Paul Monash, "The Lonely Wizard," *Schlitz Playhouse of Stars* (CBS)
Joe Connelly, Bob Mosher, "Beaver Gets Spelled," *Leave It to Beaver* (CBS)

John Meston, "Born to Hang," *Gunsmoke* (CBS)

Roswell Rogers, "Margaret Hires a Gardener," *Father Knows Best* (NBC)

Morton Wishengrad, "A Chassidic Tale," *Frontiers of Faith* (NBC)

BEST TELEPLAY WRITING (ONE HOUR OR MORE)

☐ Rod Serling, "The Comedian," *Playhouse 90* (CBS)

Marc Connelly, "Green Pastures," *Hallmark Hall of Fame* (NBC)

William Gibson, "Miracle Worker," *Playhouse 90* (CBS)

Arthur Hailey, "No Deadly Medicine," *Studio One* (CBS)

James Lee, "Life of Samuel Johnson," *Omnibus* (NBC)

BEST COMEDY WRITING

☐ Nat Hiken, Billy Friedberg, Phil Sharp, Terry Ryan, Coleman Jacoby, Arnold Rosen, Sidney Zelinka, A.J. Russell, Tony Webster, *Phil Silvers Show* (CBS)

Ernie Kovacs, *Ernie Kovacs Show* (No Dialogue Show) (NBC)

Sam Perrin, George Balzer, Al Gordon, Hal Goldman, *Jack Benny Show* (CBS)

Mel Tolkin, Larry Gelbart, Mel Brooks, Neil Simon, Sheldon Keller, Mike Stewart, Gary Belkin, *Caesar's Hour* (NBC)

Roswell Rogers, Paul West, *Father Knows Best* (NBC)

BEST DIRECTION (HALF HOUR OR LESS)

☐ Robert Stevens, "The Glass Eye," *Alfred Hitchcock Presents* (CBS)

Bill Hobin, *Your Hit Parade* (NBC)

Clark Jones, *Patrice Munsel Show* (ABC)

Sheldon Leonard, *Danny Thomas Show* (ABC, CBS)

Peter Tewksbury, *Father Knows Best* (NBC)

BEST DIRECTION (ONE HOUR OR MORE)

☐ Bob Banner, *Dinah Shore Chevy Show* (NBC)

John Frankenheimer, "The Comedian," *Playhouse 90* (CBS)

George Roy Hill, "Helen Morgan Story," *Playhouse 90* (CBS)

Arthur Penn, "Miracle Worker," *Playhouse 90* (CBS)

George Schaefer, "Green Pastures," *Hallmark Hall of Fame* (NBC)

BEST ART DIRECTION

☐ Rouben Ter-Arutunian, "Twelfth Night," *Hallmark Hall of Fame* (NBC)

Beulah Frankel, "Don't Ever Come Back," *Climax* (CBS)

☐ Indicates winner

Howard E. Johnson, *Wagon Train* (NBC)

Robert Kelly, *George Gobel Show* (NBC)

Don Shirley, *Perry Como Show* (NBC)

BEST CINEMATOGRAPHY FOR TELEVISION

☐ Harold E. Wellman, "Hemo the Magnificent," *Bell Telephone Science Series* (CBS)

Norbert Brodine, "Miss Ashley's Demon," *Loretta Young Show* (NBC)

Robert De Grasse, *Danny Thomas Show* (ABC, CBS)

George E. Diskant, "Voice in the Fog," *Goodyear Theatre* (NBC)

William Margulies, "Outlaw," *Have Gun, Will Travel* (CBS)

BEST LIVE CAMERA WORK

☐ *Playhouse 90* (CBS)

Annie Get Your Gun (NBC)

Cinderella (CBS)

General Motors 50th Anniversary Show (NBC)

Wide Wide World (NBC)

BEST EDITING OF A FILM FOR TELEVISION

☐ Mike Pozen, "How to Kill a Woman," *Gunsmoke* (CBS)

Samuel E. Beetley, "The Tinhorn," *Schlitz Playhouse of Stars* (CBS)

Danny Landres, "Lonely Wizard," *Schlitz Playhouse of Stars* (CBS)

Michael R. McAdam, "Trail to Christmas," *G.E. Theatre* (CBS)

Robert Sparr, "The Quick and the Dead," *Maverick* (ABC)

BEST MUSICAL CONTRIBUTION FOR TELEVISION

☐ Leonard Bernstein, "Conducting and Analyzing Music of Johann Sebastian Bach," *Omnibus* (ABC)

Mitchell Ayres for musical direction, *Perry Como Show* (NBC)

Robert Russell Bennett for arranging and conducting "The Innocent Years," *Project* (NBC)

Nelson Riddle for arranging and conducting, *Frank Sinatra Show* (ABC)

Richard Rodgers for music score, *Cinderella* (CBS)

BEST ENGINEERING OR TECHNICAL ACHIEVEMENT

☐ Engineering and camera techniques on *Wide Wide World* (NBC)

Chroma Key System as developed by Frank Gaskins, Milt Altman, and Associate at NBC

Color mating amplifier (CBS)

Dage Fidicon Camera adapted as a portable TV Camera—Thompson Products Co

Live pick-up from Havana over the Horizon (NBC)

Special Awards

TRUSTEES' AWARD

☐ **Jack Benny,** for his significant contributions to the television industry as a showman; for the high standard, for all to emulate, set by his personal skill and excellence as a performer; for the consistency, quality, and good taste of his programs through many years and many media.

1958/59

(Presented May 6, 1959 for programs telecast between January 1, 1958 and February 28, 1959)

Program Awards

MOST OUTSTANDING SINGLE PROGRAM OF THE YEAR

☐ *An Evening with Fred Astaire* (NBC)

"Child of Our Time," *Playhouse 90* (CBS)

"Little Moon of Alban," *Hallmark Hall of Fame* (NBC)

"The Old Man," *Playhouse 90* (CBS)

BEST DRAMATIC SERIES (ONE HOUR OR LONGER)

☐ *Playhouse 90* (CBS)

U.S. Steel Hour (CBS)

BEST DRAMATIC SERIES (LESS THAN ONE HOUR)

☐ *Alcoa-Goodyear Theatre* (NBC)

Alfred Hitchcock Presents (CBS)

G.E. Electric Theatre (CBS)

Loretta Young Show (NBC)

The Naked City (ABC)

Peter Gunn (NBC)

BEST COMEDY SERIES

☐ *Jack Benny Show* (CBS)

Bob Cummings Show (NBC)

Danny Thomas Show (CBS)

Father Knows Best (CBS, NBC)

Phil Silvers Show (CBS)

Red Skelton Show (CBS)

BEST MUSICAL OR VARIETY SERIES

☐ *Dinah Shore Chevy Show* (NBC)

Perry Como Show (NBC)

Steve Allen Show (NBC)

BEST WESTERN SERIES

☐ *Maverick* (ABC)

Gunsmoke (CBS)

Have Gun, Will Travel (CBS)

The Rifleman (ABC)

Wagon Train (NBC)

BEST PUBLIC SERVICE PROGRAM OR SERIES

☐ *Omnibus* (NBC)

Bold Journey (ABC)

Meet the Press (NBC)

Small World (CBS)
The Twentieth Century (CBS)
Young People's Concert—N.Y. Philharmonic (CBS)

BEST PANEL, QUIZ OR AUDIENCE PARTICIPATION SERIES
☐ *What's My Line?* (CBS)
I've Got a Secret (CBS)
Keep Talking (CBS)
The Price Is Right (NBC)
This Is Your Life (NBC)
You Bet Your Life (NBC)

BEST NEWS REPORTING SERIES
☐ *Huntley-Brinkley Report* (NBC)
Douglas Edwards with the News (CBS)
John Daly and the News (ABC)

BEST SPECIAL DRAMATIC PROGRAM (ONE HOUR OR LONGER)
☐ "Little Moon of Alban," *Hallmark Hall of Fame* (NBC)
"The Bridge of San Luis Rey," *Du Pont Show of the Month* (CBS)
"Hamlet," *Du Pont Show of the Month* (CBS)
"The Hasty Heart," *Du Pont Show of the Month* (CBS)
"Johnny Belinda," *Hallmark Hall of Fame* (NBC)

BEST SPECIAL MUSICAL OR VARIETY PROGRAM (ONE HOUR OR LONGER)
☐ *An Evening with Fred Astaire* (NBC)
Art Carney Meets "Peter and the Wolf" (ABC)

BEST SPECIAL NEWS PROGRAM
☐ *Face of Red China* (CBS)
"American GI's in Lebanon," *Outlook* (NBC)
Election Night Returns (CBS)
Projection '59 (NBC)
"The Story of Atlas 10B," *Chet Huntley Reporting* (NBC)
Where We Stand II (CBS)
Years of Crisis (CBS)

Performance Awards

BEST ACTOR IN A LEADING ROLE (CONTINUING CHARACTER) IN A DRAMATIC SERIES
☐ Raymond Burr, *Perry Mason* (CBS)
James Arness, *Gunsmoke* (CBS)
Richard Boone, *Have Gun, Will Travel* (CBS)
James Garner, *Maverick* (ABC)
Craig Stevens, *Peter Gunn* (NBC)
Efrem Zimbalist, Jr., *'77 Sunset Strip* (ABC)

BEST ACRESSS IN A LEADING ROLE (CONTINUING CHARACTER) IN A DRAMATIC SERIES
☐ Loretta Young, *Loretta Young Show* (NBC)

☐ Indicates winner

Phyllis Kirk, *The Thin Man* (NBC)
June Lockhart, *Lassie* (CBS)
Jane Wyman, *Jane Wyman Show* (NBC)

BEST ACTOR IN A LEADING ROLE (CONTINUING CHARACTER) IN A COMEDY SERIES
☐ Jack Benny, *Jack Benny Show* (CBS)
Walter Brennan, *The Real McCoys* (ABC)
Bob Cummings, *Bob Cummings Show* (NBC)
Phil Silvers, *Phil Silvers Show* (CBS)
Danny Thomas, *Danny Thomas Show* (CBS)
Robert Young, *Father Knows Best* (CBS, NBC)

BEST ACTRESS IN A LEADING ROLE (CONTINUING CHARACTER) IN A COMEDY SERIES
☐ Jane Wyatt, *Father Knows Best* (CBS, NBC)
Gracie Allen, *Burns & Allen* (CBS)
Spring Byington, *December Bride* (CBS)
Ida Lupino, *Mr. Adams and Eve* (CBS)
Donna Reed, *Donna Reed Show* (ABC)
Ann Sothern, *Ann Sothern Show* (CBS)

BEST SUPPORTING ACTOR (CONTINUING CHARACTER) IN A DRAMATIC SERIES
☐ Dennis Weaver, *Gunsmoke* (CBS)
Herschel Bernardi, *Peter Gunn* (NBC)
Johnny Crawford, *The Rifleman* (ABC)
William Hopper, *Perry Mason* (CBS)

BEST SUPPORTING ACTRESS (CONTRIBUTING CHARACTER) IN A DRAMATIC SERIES
☐ Barbara Hale, *Perry Mason* (CBS)
Lola Albright, *Peter Gunn* (NBC)
Amanda Blake, *Gunsmoke* (CBS)
Hope Emerson, *Peter Gunn* (NBC)

BEST SUPPORTING ACTOR (CONTINUING CHARACTER) IN A COMEDY SERIES
☐ Tom Poston, *Steve Allen Show* (NBC)
Richard Crenna, *The Real McCoys* (ABC)
Paul Ford, *Phil Silvers Show* (CBS)
Maurice Gosfield, *Phil Silvers Show* (CBS)
Billy Gray, *Father Knows Best* (CBS, NBC)
Harry Morgan, *December Bride* (CBS)

BEST SUPPORTING ACTRESS (CONTINUING CHARACTER) IN A COMEDY SERIES
☐ Ann B. Davis, *Bob Cummings Show* (NBC)
Rosemary De Camp, *Bob Cummings Show* (NBC)

Elinor Donahue, *Father Knows Best* (CBS, NBC)
Verna Felton, *December Bride* (CBS)
Kathy Nolan, *The Real McCoys* (ABC)
Zasu Pitts, *Oh Susanna* (CBS)

BEST PERFORMANCE BY AN ACTOR (CONTINUING CHARACTER) IN A MUSICAL OR VARIETY SERIES
☐ Perry Como, *Perry Como Show* (NBC)
Steve Allen, *Steve Allen Show* (NBC)
Jack Paar, *Jack Paar Show* (NBC)

BEST PERFORMANCE BY AN ACTRESS (CONTINUING CHARACTER) IN A MUSICAL OR VARIETY SERIES
☐ Dinah Shore, *Dinah Shore Chevy Show* (NBC)
Patti Page, *Patti Page Show* (ABC)

BEST SINGLE PERFORMANCE BY AN ACTOR
☐ Fred Astaire, *An Evening with Fred Astaire* (NBC)
Robert Crawford, "Child of Our Time," *Playhouse 90* (CBS)
Paul Muni, "Last Clear Chance," *Playhouse 90* (CBS)
Christopher Plummer, "Little Moon of Alban," *Hallmark Hall of Fame* (NBC)
Mickey Rooney, "Eddie," *Alcoa-Goodyear Theatre* (NBC)
Rod Steiger, "A Town Has Turned to Dust," *Playhouse 90* (CBS)

BEST SINGLE PERFORMANCE BY AN ACTRESS
☐ Julie Harris, "Little Moon of Alban," *Hallmark Hall of Fame* (NBC)
Judith Anderson, "Bridge of San Luis Rey," *Du Pont Show of the Month* (CBS)
Helen Hayes, "One Red Rose for Christmas," *U.S. Steel Hour* (CBS)
Piper Laurie, "Days of Wine and Roses," *Playhouse 90* (CBS)
Geraldine Page, "The Old Man," *Playhouse 90* (CBS)
Maureen Stapleton, "All the King's Men," *Kraft Theatre* (NBC)

BEST NEWS COMMENTATOR OR ANALYST
☐ Edward R. Murrow (CBS)
John Daly (ABC)
Chet Huntley (NBC)

Craft and Technical Awards

BEST DIRECTION OF A SINGLE PROGRAM OF A DRAMATIC SERIES (LESS THAN ONE HOUR)
☐ Jack Smight, "Eddie," *Alcoa-Goodyear Theatre* (NBC)
Herschel Daugherty, "One is a Wanderer," *General Electric Theatre* (CBS)

Blake Edwards, "The Kill," *Peter Gunn* (NBC)

Alfred Hitchcock, "Lamb to the Slaughter," *Alfred Hitchcock Presents* (CBS)

James Neilson, "Kid at the Stick," *General Electric Theatre* (CBS)

BEST DIRECTION OF A SINGLE DRAMATIC PROGRAM (ONE HOUR OR LONGER)

☐ George Schaefer, "Little Moon of Alban," *Hallmark Hall of Fame* (NBC)

George Roy Hill, "Child of Our Time," *Playhouse 90* (CBS)

John Frankenheimer, "A Town Has Turned to Dust," *Playhouse 90* (CBS)

BEST DIRECTION OF A SINGLE PROGRAM OF A COMEDY SERIES

☐ Peter Tewksbury, "Medal for Margaret," *Father Knows Best* (CBS)

Hy Averback, "Kate's Career," *The Real McCoys* (ABC)

Seymour Berns, "Jack Benny Show with Gary Cooper," *Jack Benny Show* (CBS)

Richard Kinon, "The Interview," *Mr. Adams and Eve* (CBS)

Sheldon Leonard, "Pardon My Accent," *Danny Thomas Show* (CBS)

BEST DIRECTION OF A SINGLE MUSICAL OR VARIETY PROGRAM

☐ Bud Yorkin, *An Evening with Fred Astaire* (NBC)

Clark Jones, "Perry Como Show with Maureen O'Hara, Robert Preston," *Perry Como Show* (NBC)

Gower Champion and Joe Cates, "Accent on Love," *Pontiac Star Parade* (NBC)

BEST WRITING OF A SINGLE PROGRAM OF A DRAMATIC SERIES (LESS THAN ONE HOUR)

☐ Alfred Brenner; Ken Hughes, "Eddie," *Alcoa-Goodyear Theatre* (NBC)

Roald Dahl, "Lamb to the Slaughter," *Alfred Hitchcock Presents* (CBS)

Blake Edwards, "The Kill," *Peter Gunn* (NBC)

Christopher Knopf, "The Loudmouth," *Alcoa-Goodyear Theatre* (NBC)

Samuel Taylor, "One Is a Wanderer," *General Electric Theatre* (CBS)

BEST WRITING OF A SINGLE DRAMATIC PROGRAM (ONE HOUR OR LONGER)

☐ James Costigan, "Little Moon of Alban," *Hallmark Hall of Fame* (NBC)

Horton Foote, "The Old Man," *Playhouse 90* (CBS)

☐ Indicates winner

J.P. Miller, "Days of Wine and Roses," *Playhouse 90* (CBS)

Irving Gaynor Neiman, "Child of Our Time," *Playhouse 90* (CBS)

Rod Serling, "A Town Has Turned to Dust," *Playhouse 90* (CBS)

BEST WRITING OF A SINGLE PROGRAM OF A COMEDY SERIES

☐ Sam Perrin, George Balzer, Hal Goldman, Al Gordon, "Jack Benny Show with Ernie Kovacs," *Jack Benny Show* (CBS)

Billy Freidberg, Arnie Rosen, Coleman Jacoby, "Bilko's Vampire," *Phil Silvers Show* (CBS)

Paul Henning, Dick Wesson, "Grandpa Clobbers the Air Force," *Bob Cummings Show* (NBC)

Roswell Rogers, "Medal for Margaret," *Father Knows Best* (CBS)

Bill Manhoff, "Once There Was a Traveling Salesman," *The Real McCoys* (ABC)

BEST WRITING OF A SINGLE MUSICAL OR VARIETY PROGRAM

☐ Bud Yorkin, Herbert Baker, *An Evening with Fred Astaire* (NBC)

Goodman Ace, Mort Green, George Foster, Jay Burton, *Perry Como Show* (with Pier Angeli, Andy Griffith, Helen O'Connell) (NBC)

Larry Gelbart, Woody Allen, *Sid Caesar's Chevy Show* (with Shirley MacLaine, Art Carney, Jo Stafford) (NBC)

A. J. Russell, *Art Carney meets Peter and the Wolf* (ABC)

Leonard Stern, Stan Burns, Herb Sargent, Bill Dana, Don Hinkley, Hal Goldman, Larry Klein, *Steve Allen Show* (with Peter Ustinov, Louis Armstrong, Van Cliburn) (NBC)

BEST CINEMATOGRAPHY FOR TELEVISION

☐ Ellis W. Carter, "Alphabet Conspiracy," *Bell Telephone Special* (NBC)

Fred Jackman, Jr., "Corporal Hardy," *Alcoa-Goodyear Theatre* (NBC)

William Margulies, "Ella West," *Have Gun, Will Travel* (CBS)

Mack Stengler, "Day of Glory," *Jane Wyman Show* (NBC)

Harold Stine, "Shady Deal at Sunny Acres," *Maverick* (ABC)

Ralph Woolsey, "Diamond in the Rough," *Maverick* (ABC)

BEST LIVE CAMERA WORK

☐ *An Evening with Fred Astaire* (NBC)

"The Bridge of San Luis Rey," *Du Pont Show of the Month* (CBS)

"Child of Our Time," *Playhouse 90* (CBS)

"A Town Has Turned to Dust," *Playhouse 90* (CBS)

"The Old Man," *Playhouse 90* (CBS)

BEST ART DIRECTION IN A TELEVISION FILM

☐ Claudio Guzman, "Bernadette," *Westinghouse Desilu Playhouse* (CBS)

Ralph Berger, Charles F. Pyke, "The Duchess of Denver," *The Texan* (CBS)

John McCormack, "Corporal Hardy," *Alcoa-Goodyear Theatre* (NBC)

Albert M. Pyke, "Man From Paris," *The Californians* (NBC)

Frank Sylos, "Most Honorable Day," *Loretta Young Show* (NBC)

BEST ART DIRECTION IN A LIVE TELEVISION PROGRAM

☐ Edward Stephenson, *An Evening with Fred Astaire* (NBC)

Warren Clymer, "Little Moon of Alban," *Hallmark Hall of Fame* (NBC)

Walter Cott Herndon, "The Old Man," *Playhouse 90* (CBS)

Bob Markell, "Hamlet," *Du Pont Show of the Month* (CBS)

Jan Scott, "Hans Brinker of the Silver Skates," *Hallmark Hall of Fame* (NBC)

Robert Wade, "Count of Monte Cristo," *Du Pont Show of the Month* (CBS)

BEST EDITING OF A FILM FOR TELEVISION

☐ Silvio D'Alisera, "Meet Mr. Lincoln," *Project XX* (NBC)

Robert Crawford, "Grandpa Clobbers the Air Force," *Bob Cummings Show* (NBC)

Richard Fantl, "Eddie," *Alcoa-Goodyear Theatre* (NBC)

Danny B. Landres, "Long Distance," *Schlitz Playhouse* (CBS)

Robert T. Sparr, "Rope of Cards," *Maverick* (ABC)

Richard Van Enger, "Two Graves for Swan Valley," *Bat Masterson* (NBC)

Robert Watts, "Saga of Waco Williams," *Maverick* (ABC)

BEST MUSICAL CONTRIBUTION TO A TELEVISION PROGRAM

☐ *David Rose*, for the musical direction of *An Evening with Fred Astaire* (NBC)

Frank De Vol for musical direction of *Lux Show* starring Rosemary Clooney (NBC)

Bernard Green for musical direction of "Johnny Belinda," *Hallmark Hall of Fame* (NBC)

Henry Mancini for composing *Peter Gunn* theme (NBC)

Eddy Manson for composing and conducting music for "Harvey," *Du Pont Show of the Month* (CBS)

Paul Weston for composing and conducting music for *Art Carney Meets "Peter and the Wolf"* (ABC)

BEST CHOREOGRAPHY FOR TELEVISION
☐ Hermes Pan, *An Evening with Fred Astaire* (NBC)
Gene Kelly, "Dancing is a Man's Game," *Omnibus* (NBC)

BEST ENGINEERING OR TECHNICAL ACHIEVEMENT
☐ Industry-wide improvement of editing video tape as exemplified by ABC, CBS, and NBC
☐ Practical application of automation to TV program switching (NBC), Washington, D.C.
☐ RCA development of color video tape

BEST ON-THE-SPOT COVERAGE OF A NEWS EVENT
☐ Cuban Revolution: Jack Fern (film director); Stuart Novins, Richard Bate (reporters); Frank Donghi (coordinator); Paul Rubenstein, Ralph Santos, Larry Smith (cameramen) (CBS)
Lebanon Civil War Street Battle: Frank Kearns (correspondent); Paul Bruck (cameraman) (CBS)
First Air Force attempt to probe the moon: Frank McGee, Roy Neal (reporters); Chet Hagan (producer); Jim Kitchell (director) (NBC)
Election of Pope John XXIII: John Secondari; Marshall Diskin (director) (ABC)
Chicago Fire at Our Lady of Angels parochial school: George Faber (producer); Joe Sauris, Hugh Hill, Frank Reynolds (reporters); Maury Bleckman, John Richardson, Irv Heberg, Welsey Marks (cameramen) (CBS)
Crash of American Airlines Electra off LaGuardia into Flushing Bay: Paul Levitan (producer); Don Hewitt (director); Tom Costigan (correspondent); Phil Scheffler, Charles Kuralt, Sam Jaffe, Bob Schakne (reporters); Arthur Kinghan, George Snyder, Larry Racies, Lou Hutt, Mike Evdokimoff, Irving Heitzner (cameramen) (CBS)

Special Awards

TRUSTEES' AWARD
☐ Bod Hope Presented with appreciation and admiration for bringing the great gift of laughter to all peoples of all nations; for selflessly entertaining American troops throughout the world over many years; and for making television finer by these deeds and by the consistently high quality of his television programs through the years.

☐ Indicates winner

1959/60

(Presented June 20, 1960 for programs telecast between March 1, 1959 and March 31, 1960)

Program Awards

OUTSTANDING PROGRAM ACHIEVEMENT IN THE FIELD OF HUMOR
☐ *Art Carney Special* (NBC)
Danny Thomas Show (CBS)
Father Knows Best (CBS)
Jack Benny Show (CBS)
Red Skelton Show (CBS)

OUTSTANDING PROGRAM ACHIEVEMENT IN THE FIELD OF DRAMA
☐ *Playhouse 90* (CBS)
"Ethan Frome," *Du Pont Show of the Month* (CBS)
The Moon and Sixpence (NBC)
"The Turn of the Screw," *Ford Startime* (NBC)
The Untouchables (ABC)

OUTSTANDING PROGRAM ACHIEVEMENT IN THE FIELD OF VARIETY
☐ *Fabulous Fifties* (CBS)
Another Evening with Fred Astaire (NBC)
Dinah Shore Chevy Show (NBC)
Garry Moore Show (CBS)
"Tonight with Belafonte," *Revlon Revue* (CBS)

OUTSTANDING PROGRAM ACHIEVEMENT IN THE FIELD OF NEWS
☐ *Huntley-Brinkley Report* (NBC)
Chet Huntley Reporting (NBC)
Douglas Edwards with the News (CBS)
Journey to Understanding (NBC)
"Khrushchev's Arrival, Appearance at National Press Club, Speech to the Nation," *Journey to Understanding* (NBC)

OUTSTANDING PROGRAM ACHIEVEMENT IN THE FIELD OF PUBLIC AFFAIRS AND EDUCATION
☐ *Twentieth Century* (CBS)
Meet the Press (NBC)
"The Population Explosion," *CBS Reports* (CBS)
Small World (CBS)
Winter Olympics (CBS)

OUTSTANDING ACHIEVEMENT IN THE FIELD OF CHILDREN'S PROGRAMMING
☐ *Huckleberry Hound* (Syndicated)
Captain Kangaroo (CBS)
Lassie (CBS)
Quick Draw McGraw (Syndicated)
Watch Mr. Wizard (NBC)

OUTSTANDING ACHIEVEMENT IN THE FIELD OF MUSIC
☐ *Leonard Bernstein and the New York Philharmonic* (CBS)
Bell Telephone Hour (NBC)
"Green Pastures," *Hallmark Hall of Fame* (NBC)
"Music of Gershwin," *Bell Telephone Hour* (NBC)
"Young People's Concerts," with Leonard Bernstein (CBS)

Performance Awards

OUTSTANDING SINGLE PERFORMANCE BY AN ACTOR (LEAD OR SUPPORT)
☐ Laurence Olivier, *The Moon and Sixpence* (NBC)
Lee J. Cobb, "Project Immortality," *Playhouse 90* (CBS)
Alec Guinness, "The Wicked Scheme of Jebal Deeks," *Ford Startime* (NBC)

OUTSTANDING SINGLE PERFORMANCE BY AN ACTRESS (LEAD OR SUPPORT)
☐ Ingrid Bergman, "The Turn of the Screw," *Ford Startime* (NBC)
Julie Harris, "Ethan Frome," *Du Pont Show of the Month* (CBS)
Teresa Wright, "Margaret Bourke-White Story," *Breck Sunday Showcase* (NBC)

OUTSTANDING PERFORMANCE BY AN ACTOR IN A SERIES (LEAD OR SUPPORT)
☐ Robert Stack, *The Untouchables* (ABC)
Richard Boone, *Have Gun, Will Travel* (CBS)
Raymond Burr, *Perry Mason* (CBS)

OUTSTANDING PERFORMANCE BY AN ACTRESS IN A SERIES (LEAD OR SUPPORT)
☐ Jane Wyatt, *Father Knows Best* (CBS)
Donna Reed, *Donna Reed Show* (ABC)
Loretta Young, *Loretta Young Show* (NBC)

OUTSTANDING PERFORMANCE IN A VARIETY OR MUSICAL PROGRAM OR SERIES
☐ Harry Belafonte, "Tonight with Belafonte," *Revlon Revue* (CBS)
Fred Astaire, *Another Evening with Fred Astaire* (NBC)
Dinah Shore, *Dinah Shore Chevy Show* (NBC)

OUTSTANDING WRITING ACHIEVEMENT IN DRAMA
☐ Rod Serling, *Twilight Zone* (CBS)
James Costigan, "The Turn of the Screw," *Ford Startime* (NBC)

Loring Mandel, "Project Immortality," *Playhouse 90* (CBS)

Craft and Technical Awards

OUTSTANDING WRITING ACHIEVEMENT IN COMEDY
☐ Ralph Levy, Bud Yorkin, *Jack Benny Hour Specials* (CBS)
Dorothy Cooper, Roswell Rogers, *Father Knows Best* (CBS)
Nat Hiken, *Ballad of Louis the Louse* (CBS)

OUTSTANDING DIRECTIONAL ACHIEVEMENT IN DRAMA
☐ Robert Mulligan, *The Moon and Sixpence* (NBC)
John Frankenheimer, "The Turn of the Screw," *Ford Startime* (NBC)
Phil Karlson, "The Untouchables," *Westinghouse-Desilu Playhouse* (CBS)

OUTSTANDING WRITING ACHIEVEMENT IN THE DOCUMENTARY FIELD
☐ Howard K. Smith, Av Westin, *The Population Explosion* (CBS)
James Benjamin, "From Kaiser to Fuehrer," *Twentieth Century* (CBS)
Richard F. Hanser, "Life in the Thirties," *Project XX* (NBC)

OUTSTANDING DIRECTIONAL ACHIEVEMENT IN COMEDY
☐ Ralph Levy, Bud Yorkin, *Jack Benny Hour Specials* (CBS)
Seymour Berns, *Red Skelton Show* (CBS)
Sheldon Leonard, *Danny Thomas Show* (CBS)

OUTSTANDING ACHIEVEMENT IN ART DIRECTION AND SCENIC DESIGN
☐ Ralph Berger, Frank Smith, "The Untouchables," *Westinghouse-Desilu Playhouse* (CBS)
Charles Lisanby, *Garry Moore Show* (CBS)
John J. Lloyd, *Alfred Hitchcock Presents* (CBS)

OUTSTANDING ACHIEVEMENT IN CINEMATOGRAPHY FOR TELEVISION
☐ Charles Straumer, "The Untouchables," *Westinghouse-Desilu Playhouse* (CBS)
William Margulies, "The Morrison Story," *The Lawless Years* (NBC)
Ralph Woolsey, "Secret Island," *77 Sunset Strip* (ABC)

OUTSTANDING ACHIEVEMENT IN ELECTRONIC CAMERA WORK
☐ *Winter Olympics* (CBS)
Playhouse 90 (CBS)

☐ Indicates winner

"The Turn of the Screw," *Ford Startime* (NBC)

OUTSTANDING ACHIEVEMENT IN FILM EDITING FOR TELEVISION
☐ Ben H. Ray, Robert L. Swanson, *The Untouchables* (ABC)
Dan Landres, "The Patsy," *General Electric Theatre* (CBS)
Edward Williams, "Man from the South," *Alfred Hitchcock Presents* (CBS)

BEST ENGINEERING OR TECHNICAL ACHIEVEMENT
☐ The new General Electric supersensitive camera tube permitting colorcasting in no more light than is needed for black and white
The British Broadcasting Corp. and the National Broadcasting Co. for the development of the cable film process speeding the transmission of overseas events

Special Awards

TRUSTEES' AWARD
☐ Dr. Frank Stanton, president, the Columbia Broadcasting System, Inc. by forthright and courageous action, ahs advanced immeasurably the freedom of television as an arm of the free press and in so doing has strengthened the total freedom of television. In honoring Dr. Stanton, the Trustees seek to express their deep concern for television's freedom to carry out its vital responsibilities as a medium of information and discussion.

TRUSTEES' CITATION
☐ *The Ampex Corp.*, Radio Corporation of America, Michael P. Gargiulo, Richard Gillaspy In recognition of the corporate effort of all phases of television production. For capturing on video tape the Nixon-Khrushchev debate of July 25, 1959 in Moscow at the American Color Television Exhibit; and for making the extraordinary public event available to the American people through its television network.

1960/61

(Presented May 16, 1961 for programs telecast between April 1, 1960 and April 15, 1961)

Program Awards

THE PROGRAM OF THE YEAR
☐ "Macbeth," *Hallmark Hall of Fame* (NBC)

Astaire Time (NBC)
Convention Coverage (NBC)
An Hour with Danny Kaye (CBS)
Sacco-Vanzetti (NBC)

OUTSTANDING PROGRAM ACHIEVEMENT IN THE FIELD OF HUMOR
☐ *Jack Benny Show* (CBS)
Andy Griffith Show (CBS)
Bob Hope Buick Show (NBC)
Candid Camera (CBS)
Flintstones (ABC)

OUTSTANDING PROGRAM ACHIEVEMENT IN THE FIELD OF VARIETY
☐ *Astaire Time* (NBC)
Belafonte (CBS)
Garry Moore Show (CBS)
An Hour with Danny Kaye (CBS)
Jack Paar Show (NBC)

OUTSTANDING PROGRAM ACHIEVEMENT IN THE FIELD OF DRAMA
☐ "Macbeth," *Hallmark Hall of Fame* (NBC)
Naked City (ABC)
Sacco-Vanzetti (NBC)
Twilight Zone (CBS)
The Untouchables (ABC)

OUTSTANDING PROGRAM ACHIEVEMENT IN THE FIELD OF NEWS
☐ *Huntley-Brinkley Report* (NBC)
Convention Coverage (NBC)
Douglas Edwards with the News (CBS)
Eyewitness to History (CBS)
President Kennedy's Live News Conferences (ABC, CBS, NBC)

OUTSTANDING PROGRAM ACHIEVEMENT IN THE FIELD OF PUBLIC AFFAIRS AND EDUCATION
☐ *Twentieth Century* (CBS)
CBS Reports (CBS)
Project XX (NBC)
"The U-2 Affair," *NBC White Paper* (NBC)
Winston Churchill: The Valiant Years (ABC)

OUTSTANDING ACHIEVEMENT IN THE FIELD OF CHILDREN'S PROGRAMMING
☐ "Aaron Copland's Birthday Party," *Young People's Concert* (CBS)
Captain Kangaroo (CBS)
Huckleberry Hound (Syndicated)
Shari Lewis Show (NBC)
Shirley Temple Show (NBC)

Performance Awards

OUTSTANDING SINGLE PERFORMANCE BY AN ACTOR IN A LEADING ROLE
☐ Maurice Evans, "Macbeth," *Hallmark Hall of Fame* (NBC)

Cliff Robertson, "The Two Worlds of Charlie Gordon," *U.S. Steel Hour* (CBS)

Ed Wynn, "The Man in the Funny Suit," *Westinghouse-Desilu Playhouse* (CBS)

OUTSTANDING SINGLE PERFORMANCE BY AN ACTRESS IN A LEADING ROLE

☐ Judith Anderson, "Macbeth," *Hallmark Hall of Fame* (NBC)

Ingrid Bergman, *24 Hours in a Woman's Life* (CBS)

Elizabeth Montgomery, "The Rusty Heller Story," *The Untouchables* (ABC)

OUTSTANDING PERFORMANCE BY AN ACTOR IN A SERIES (LEAD)

☐ Raymond Burr, *Perry Mason* (CBS)

Jackie Cooper, *Hennesey* (CBS)

Robert Stack, *The Untouchables* (ABC)

OUTSTANDING PERFORMANCE BY AN ACTRESS IN A SERIES (LEAD)

☐ Barbara Stanwyck, *Barbara Stanwyck Show* (NBC)

Donna Reed, *Donna Reed Show* (ABC)

Loretta Young, *Loretta Young Show* (NBC)

OUTSTANDING PERFORMANCE IN A SUPPORTING ROLE BY AN ACTOR OR ACTRESS IN A SINGLE PROGRAM

☐ Roddy McDowall, "Not Without Honor," *Equitable's American Heritage* (NBC)

Charles Bronson, "Memory in White," *G.E. Theatre* (CBS)

Peter Falk, "Cold Turkey," *The Law and Mr. Jones* (ABC)

OUTSTANDING PERFORMANCE IN A SUPPORTING ROLE BY AN ACTOR OR ACTRESS IN A SERIES

☐ Don Knotts, *Andy Griffith Show* (CBS)

Abby Dalton, *Hennesey* (CBS)

Barbara Hale, *Perry Mason* (CBS)

OUTSTANDING PERFORMANCE IN A VARIETY OR MUSICAL PROGRAM OR SERIES

☐ Fred Astaire, *Astaire Time* (NBC)

Harry Belafonte, *Belafonte N.Y.* (CBS)

Dinah Shore, *Dinah Shore Chevy Show* (NBC)

Craft and Technical Awards

OUTSTANDING ACHIEVEMENT IN THE FIELD OF MUSIC FOR TELEVISION

☐ Leonard Bernstein, *Leonard Bernstein and the New York Philharmonic* (NBC)

☐ Indicates winner

Andre Previn, *The Donald O'Connor Show* (NBC)

Pete Rugolo, Jerry Goldsmith, *The Thriller* (NBC)

OUTSTANDING WRITING ACHIEVEMENT IN DRAMA

☐ Rod Serling, *The Twilight Zone* (CBS)

Reginald Rose, *Sacco-Vanzetti* (NBC)

Dale Wasserman, "The Lincoln Murder Case," *Du Pont Show of the Month* (CBS)

OUTSTANDING WRITING ACHIEVEMENT IN COMEDY

☐ Sherwood Schwartz, Dave O'Brien, Al Schwartz, Martin Ragaway, Red Skelton, *Red Skelton Show* (CBS)

Richard Baer, *Hennesey* (CBS)

Charles Stewart, Jack Elinson, *The Danny Thomas Show* (CBS)

OUTSTANDING WRITING ACHIEVEMENT IN THE DOCUMENTARY FIELD

☐ Victor Wolfson, *Winston Churchill: The Valiant Years* (ABC)

Arthur Barron, Al Wasserman, "The U-2 Affair," *NBC White Paper* (NBC)

Fred Friendly, David Lowe, Edward R. Murrow, "Harvest of Shame," *CBS Reports* (CBS)

OUTSTANDING DIRECTORIAL ACHIEVEMENT IN DRAMA

☐ George Schaefer, "Macbeth," *Hallmark Hall of Fame* (NBC)

Sidney Lumet, *Sacco-Vanzetti* (NBC)

Ralph Nelson, "The Man in the Funny Suit," *Westinghouse-Desilu Playhouse* (CBS)

OUTSTANDING DIRECTORIAL ACHIEVEMENT IN COMEDY

☐ Sheldon Leonard, *Danny Thomas Show* (CBS)

Jack Shea, Richard McDonough, *Bob Hope Buick Show* (NBC)

Peter Tewksbury, *My Three Sons* (ABC)

OUTSTANDING ACHIEVEMENT IN ART DIRECTION AND SCENIC DESIGN

☐ John L. Lloyd, *Checkmate* (CBS)

Gary Smith, *Perry Como's Kraft Music Hall* (NBC)

Jac Venza, *24 Hours in a Woman's Life* (CBS)

OUTSTANDING ACHIEVEMENT IN CINEMATOGRAPHY FOR TELEVISION

☐ George Clemens, *The Twilight Zone* (CBS)

William Margulies, "Outrage at Pawnee Bend," *Outlaws* (NBC)

Walter Strenge, "Sam Elder Story," *Wagon Train* (NBC)

OUTSTANDING ACHIEVEMENT IN FILM EDITING FOR TELEVISION

☐ Harry Coswick, Aaron Nibley, Milton Shifman, *The Naked City* (ABC)

Richard H. Cahoon, John Faure, *Perry Mason* (CBS)

Edward W. Williams, "Incident in a Small Jail," *Alfred Hitchcock Presents* (NBC)

OUTSTANDING ACHIEVEMENT IN ELECTRONIC CAMERA WORK

☐ "Sounds of America," *Bell Telephone Hour* (RED-EO-TAPE Mobile Unit for NBC)

Dinah Shore Chevy Show (NBC)

"Journey to the Day," *Playhouse 90* (CBS)

Wrangler (KTLA-Hollywood Camera Crew for NBC)

OUTSTANDING ENGINEERING OR TECHNICAL ACHIEVEMENT

☐ Radio Corporation of America and Marconi's Wireless Telegraph Company, Ltd.—English Electric Valve Company Ltd., for the independent development of the 4 1/2 inch image orthicon tube and cameras.

Special Awards

TRUSTEES' AWARDS

☐ *National Educational Television* and Radio Center and its affiliated stations, for its foresight and perseverance in promoting the development of educational television in the United States; and for its stimulation and transmission of the imaginative educational programs produced by the individual educational television stations.

☐ *Joyce C. Hall*, President of Hallmark Cards, Inc., for his personal interest in uplifting the standards of television through complete sponsorship over a 10-year period of *Hallmark Hall of Fame*, which has brought many enriching hours of entertainment to the viewing public; and for furthering the interests of young playwrights by establishing the Hallmark Teleplay-Writing Competition.

1961/62

(Presented May 22, 1962 for programs telecast between April 16, 1961 and April 14, 1962)

Program Awards

PROGRAM OF THE YEAR

☐ "Victoria Regina," *Hallmark Hall of Fame* (NBC)

"Biography of a Bookie Joint," *CBS Reports* (CBS)
Judy Garland Show (CBS)
Vincent Van Gogh: A Self Portrait (NBC)
"Walk in My Shoes," *Bell and Howell Close Up* (ABC)

OUTSTANDING PROGRAM ACHIEVEMENT IN THE FIELD OF HUMOR
☐ *Bob Newhart Show* (NBC)
Andy Griffith Show (CBS)
Car 54, Where Are You? (NBC)
Hazel (NBC)
Red Skelton Show (CBS)

OUTSTANDING PROGRAM ACHIEVEMENT IN THE FIELD OF DRAMA
☐ *The Defenders* (CBS)
Ben Casey (ABC)
Dick Powell Show (NBC)
Naked City (ABC)
"People Need People," *Alcoa Premiere* (ABC)
"Victoria Regina," *Hallmark Hall of Fame* (NBC)

OUTSTANDING PROGRAM ACHIEVEMENT IN THE FIELDS OF VARIETY OR MUSIC
☐ *Garry Moore Show* (CBS) for Variety
☐ *Leonard Bernstein and the New York Philharmonic in Japan* (CBS) for Music
Here's Edie (ABC)
Judy Garland Show (CBS)
Perry Como's Kraft Music Hall (NBC)
Walt Disney's Wonderful World of Color (NBC)
Bell Telephone Hour (NBC)
NBC Opera (NBC)
The Thief and the Hangman (ABC)

OUTSTANDING PROGRAM ACHIEVEMENT IN THE FIELD OF NEWS
☐ *Huntley-Brinkley Report* (NBC)
Capital Cities Broadcasting for the Eichman Trial (Syndicated)
Douglas Edwards with the News (CBS)
Eyewitness with Walter Cronkite (CBS)
NBC-TV Gulf Instant News Specials (NBC)

OUTSTANDING PROGRAM ACHIEVEMENT IN THE FIELD OF EDUCATIONAL AND PUBLIC AFFAIRS
☐ *David Brinkley's Journal* (NBC)
ABC's Wide World of Sports (ABC)
Bell and Howell Close Up (ABC)
CBS Reports (CBS)
Howard K. Smith—News and Comment (ABC)
NBC White Paper (NBC)
☐ Indicates winner

OUTSTANDING PROGRAM ACHIEVEMENT IN THE FIELD OF CHILDREN'S PROGRAMMING
☐ *New York Philharmonic Young People's Concerts with Leonard Bernstein* (CBS)
Captain Kangaroo (CBS)
1, 2, 3 Go! (NBC)
Shari Lewis Show (NBC)
Update (NBC)
Walt Disney's Wonderful World of Color (NBC)

OUTSTANDING DAYTIME PROGRAM
☐ *Purex Specials for Women* (NBC)
Art Linkletter's House Party (CBS)
Calendar (CBS)
Today (NBC)
Verdict Is Yours (CBS)

Performance Awards

OUTSTANDING SINGLE PERFORMANCE BY AN ACTOR IN A LEADING ROLE
☐ Peter Falk, "The Price of Tomatoes," *Dick Powell Show* (NBC)
Milton Berle, "Against the House," *Dick Powell Show* (NBC)
James Donal, "Victoria Regina," *Hallmark Hall of Fame* (NBC)
Lee Marvin, "People Need People," *Alcoa Premiere* (ABC)
Mickey Rooney, "Somebody's Waiting," *Dick Powell Show* (NBC)

OUTSTANDING SINGLE PERFORMANCE BY AN ACTRESS IN A LEADING ROLE
☐ Julie Harris, "Victoria Regina," *Hallmark Hall of Fame* (NBC)
Geraldine Brooks, "Call Back Yesterday," *Bus Stop* (ABC)
Suzanne Pleshette, "Shining Image," *Dr. Kildare* (NBC)
Inger Stevens, "The Price of Tomatoes," *Dick Powell Show* (NBC)
Ethel Waters, "Goodnight Sweet Blues," *Route 66* (CBS)

OUTSTANDING CONTINUED PERFORMANCE BY AN ACTOR IN A SERIES (LEAD)
☐ E.G. Marshall, *The Defenders* (CBS)
Paul Burke, *Naked City* (ABC)
Jackie Cooper, *Hennesey* (CBS)
Vincent Edwards, *Ben Casey* (ABC)
George Maharis, *Route 66* (CBS)

OUTSTANDING CONTINUED PERFORMANCE BY AN ACTRESS IN A SERIES (LEAD)
☐ Shirley Booth, *Hazel* (NBC)
Gertrude Berg, *Gertrude Berg Show* (CBS)
Donna Reed, *Donna Reed Show* (ABC)
Mary Stuart, *Search For Tomorrow* (CBS)

Cara Williams, *Pete and Gladys* (CBS)

OUTSTANDING PERFORMANCE IN A SUPPORTING ROLE BY AN ACTOR
☐ Don Knotts, *Andy Griffith Show* (CBS)
Sam Jaffe, *Ben Casey* (ABC)
Barry Jones, "Victoria Regina," *Hallmark Hall of Fame* (NBC)
Horace McMahon, *Naked City* (ABC)
George C. Scott, "I Remember a Lemon Tree," *Ben Casey* (ABC)

OUTSTANDING PERFORMANCE IN A SUPPORTING ROLE BY AN ACTRESS
☐ Pamela Brown, "Victoria Regina," *Hallmark Hall of Fame* (NBC)
Jeanne Cooper, "But Linda Only Smiled," *Ben Casey* (ABC)
Colleen Dewhurst, *Focus* (NBC)
Joan Hackett, "A Certain Time, A Certain Darkness," *Ben Casey* (ABC)
Mary Wickes, *Gertrude Berg Show* (CBS)

OUTSTANDING PERFORMANCE IN A VARIETY OR MUSICAL PROGRAM OR SERIES
☐ Carol Burnett, *Garry Moore Show* (CBS)
Edie Adams, *Here's Edie* (ABC)
Perry Como, *Perry Como's Kraft Music Hall* (NBC)
Judy Garland, *Judy Garland Show* (CBS)
Yves Montand, *Yves Montand on Broadway* (ABC)

Craft and Technical Awards

OUTSTANDING ACHIEVEMENT IN ORIGINAL MUSIC COMPOSED FOR TELEVISION
☐ Richard Rodgers, *Winston Churchill: The Valiant Years* (ABC)
Jacques Belasco, *Vincent Van Gogh: A Self Portrait* (NBC)
Robert Russell Bennett, *Project XX* (NBC)
Leith Stevens, "The Price of Tomatoes," *Dick Powell Show* (NBC)
John Williams, *Alcoa Premiere* (ABC)

OUTSTANDING WRITING ACHIEVEMENT IN DRAMA
☐ Reginald Rose, *The Defenders* (CBS)
Henry F. Greenberg, "People Need People," *Alcoa Premiere* (ABC)
Jack Lair, "I Remember a Lemon Tree," *Ben Casey* (ABC)
Rod Serling, *Twilight Zone* (CBS)
Richard Alan Simmons, "The Price of Tomatoes," *Dick Powell Show* (NBC)

OUTSTANDING WRITING ACHIEVEMENT IN COMEDY

☐ Carl Reiner, *Dick Van Dyke Show* (CBS)

Stan Freberg, *Chunking Chow Mein Hour* (ABC)

Nat Hiken, Tony Webster, Terry Ryan, *Car 54, Where Are You?* (NBC)

Roland Kibbee, Bob Newhart, Don Hinkley, Milt Rosen, Ernie Chambers, Dean Hargrove, Robert Kaufman, Norm Liebman, Charles Sherman, Howard Snyder, Larry Siegel, *Bob Newhart Show* (NBC)

Ed Simmons, David O'Brien, Marty Ragaway, Arthur Phillips, Al Schwartz, Sherwood Schwartz, Red Skelton, *Red Skelton Show* (CBS)

OUTSTANDING WRITING ACHIEVEMENT IN THE DOCUMENTARY FIELD

☐ Lou Hazam, *Vincent Van Gogh: A Self Portrait* (NBC)

Arthur Holch, "Walk in My Shoes," *Bell and Howell Close Up* (ABC)

George Lefferts, *Purex Specials for Women* (NBC)

Jay McMullen, "Biography of a Bookie Joint," *CBS Reports* (CBS)

Al Wasserman, Arthur Zegart, "Battle of Newburgh," *NBC White Paper* (NBC)

OUTSTANDING DIRECTORIAL ACHIEVEMENT IN DRAMA

☐ Franklin Schaffner, *The Defenders* (CBS)

Arthur Hiller, *Naked City* (ABC)

Buzz Kulik, "Shining Image," *Dr. Kildaire* (NBC)

George Schaefer, "Victoria Regina," *Hallmark Hall of Fame* (NBC)

Alex Segal, "People Need People," *Alcoa Premiere* (ABC)

Jack Smight, "Come Again to Carthage," *Westinghouse Presents* (CBS)

OUTSTANDING DIRECTORIAL ACHIEVEMENT IN COMEDY

☐ Nat Hiken, *Car 54, Where Are You?* (NBC)

Seymour Berns, *Red Skelton Show* (CBS)

Dave Giesel, *Garry Moore Show* (CBS)

John Rich, *Dick Van Dyke Show* (CBS)

Bud Yorkin, *Henry Fonda and the Family* (CBS)

OUTSTANDING ACHIEVEMENT IN ART DIRECTION AND SCENIC DESIGN

☐ Gary Smith, *Perry Como's Kraft Music Hall* (NBC)

Philip Barber, *Twilight Zone* (CBS)

Charles Lisanby, *Garry Moore Show* (CBS)

☐ Indicates winner

Jan Scott, *Theatre '62* (NBC)

Burr Smidt, *The Power and the Glory* (CBS)

OUTSTANDING ACHIEVEMENT IN CINEMATOGRAPHY FOR TELEVISION

☐ John S. Priestley, *The Naked City* (ABC)

Guy Blanchard, *Vincent Van Gogh: A Self Portrait* (NBC)

Walter Castle, Haskell Boggs, *Bonanza* (NBC)

George Clemens, *Twilight Zone* (CBS)

Walter Stenge, *Wagon Train* (NBC)

Ted Voightlander, *Ben Casey* (ABC)

OUTSTANDING ACHIEVEMENT IN ELECTRONIC CAMERA WORK

☐ Ernie Kovacs, *Ernie Kovacs Show* (ABC)

Lou Onofrio, *Judy Garland Show* (CBS)

Heino Rippe, *Perry Como's Kraft Music Hall* (NBC)

O. Tamburri, "Victoria Regina," *Hallmark Hall of Fame* (NBC)

OUTSTANDING ACHIEVEMENT IN FILM EDITING FOR TELEVISION

☐ Hugh Chaloupka, Aaron Nibley, Charles L. Freeman, *The Naked City* (ABC)

Aram Boyajian, Robert Collinson, Bernard Friend, Lora Hays, Walter Katz, Lawrence Silk, Harold Silver, Leo zochling, *Twentieth Century* (CBS)

Marston Fay, Gene Palmer, *Wagon Train* (NBC)

Constantine Gochis, *U.S. 1: American Profile* (NBC)

Richard L. Van Enger, *Bus Stop* (ABC)

OUTSTANDING ENGINEERING OR TECHNICAL ACHIEVEMENT

☐ ABC Video Tape Expander, or VTX— slow motion tape developed by ABC—**Albert Malang**, chief engineer, Video Facilities **(ABC)**

Amtec, a device to correct timing faults on tape playbacks

Interleaved Sound, an NBC development which provides an emergency circuit available whenever there is a failure of the regular network television sound

Slow Motion Kinescope, as developed by CBS

Special Awards

TRUSTEES' AWARD

☐ *CBS News*, for the special program *A Tour of the White House.* The Columbia Broadcasting System created and produced the biggest housewarming of the year. The CBS News team brought its cameras into the home of the Chief Executive,

gave the nation a bright, fresh look at their historic White House. For one of the major highlights of an exciting television year.

☐ *Jacqueline Kennedy.* The television tour of the White House brought to the TV screen a memorable hour, alive with a singular experience. The Academy Trustees wish to honor, on behalf of the membership, the concept and star of that program. For her gracious invitation, extended to millions of Americans, to see the White House, and through this tour to learn of the historical and cultural background of this national monument; for making history a living thing and for making the entire country feel at home.

☐ *David Sarnoff.* The Trustees of the Television Academy have voted this year to honor an illustrious statesman of our industry. He has been both pioneer and prophet. He has inspired and supported many of television's finest cultural achievements. He has laid many of our cornerstones, blueprinted much of our future and has been the leading architect in the development of color television. For his many years of vision and accomplishment.

☐ The heads of the News Departments of ABC, CBS and NBC. The Trustees of the Television Academy have voted to honor an exciting television adventure which dramatically demonstrated to the world our country's policy of open reporting. By sending John Glenn and Friendship VII into space in front of the nation's TV cameras, more than a hundred million of us saw. . . as it happened. . . a thrilling advance of science. Our three National networks offered a coverage at once complete and dynamic demonstrating the full range of TV's creative resource. In salute to all those who opened this window of history: the reporters, technicians, directors, cameramen— a veritable army of skilled associates.

1962/63

(Presented May 26, 1963 for programs telecast April 15, 1962 and April 14, 1963)

Program Awards

PROGRAM OF THE YEAR

☐ *The Tunnel* (NBC)

*The Danny Kaye Show with Lucille
Ball* (NBC)
"The Madman," *The Defenders* (CBS)
"The Voice of Charlie Pont," Premiere,
Presented by Fred Astaire (ABC)

OUTSTANDING PROGRAM ACHIEVEMENT IN THE FIELD OF HUMOR
☐ *The Dick Van Dyke Show* (CBS)
The Beverly Hillbillies (CBS)
*The Danny Kaye Show with Lucille
Ball* (NBC)
McHale's Navy (ABC)

OUTSTANDING PROGRAM ACHIEVEMENT IN THE FIELD OF DRAMA
☐ *The Defenders* (CBS)
*Alcoa Premiere/Premiere, Presented
by Fred Astaire* (ABC)
The Dick Powell Theatre (NBC)
The Eleventh Hour (NBC)
Naked City (ABC)

OUTSTANDING PROGRAM ACHIEVEMENT IN THE FIELD OF MUSIC
☐ *Julie and Carol at Carnegie Hall* (CBS)
Bell Telephone Hour (NBC)
*Judy Garland and Her Guests Phil
Silvers and Robert Goulet* (CBS)
The Lively Ones (NBC)
NBC Opera (NBC)

OUTSTANDING PROGRAM ACHIEVEMENT IN THE FIELD OF VARIETY
☐ *Andy Williams Show* (NBC)
Carol and Company (CBS)
Garry Moore Show (CBS)
Here's Edie (ABC)
Red Skelton Show (CBS)

OUTSTANDING PROGRAM ACHIEVEMENT IN THE FIELD OF PANEL, QUIZ OR AUDIENCE PARTICIPATION
☐ *G.E. College Bowl* (CBS)
Password (CBS)
To Tell the Truth (CBS)

OUTSTANDING PROGRAM ACHIEVEMENT IN THE FIELD OF DOCUMENTARY PROGRAMS
☐ *The Tunnel* (NBC)
"Emergency Ward," *Du Pont Show of
the Week* (NBC)
"He is Risen," *Project XX* (NBC)
The River Nile (NBC)

OUTSTANDING PROGRAM ACHIEVEMENT IN THE FIELD OF CHILDREN'S PROGRAMMING
☐ *Walt Disney's Wonderful World of
Color* (NBC)
Captain Kangaroo (CBS)
Discovery '62-'63 (ABC)
Shari Lewis Show (NBC)
Update with Robert Abernathy (NBC)
☐ Indicates winner

Watch Mr. Wizard (NBC)

OUTSTANDING ACHIEVEMENT IN THE FIELD OF NEWS
☐ *Huntley-Brinkley Report* (NBC)
*CBS News Evening Report with Walter
Cronkite* (CBS)
Eyewitness (CBS)
*NBC Special News Reports, Gulf Oil
Corporation* (NBC)

OUTSTANDING PROGRAM ACHIEVEMENT IN THE FIELD OF NEWS COMMENTARY OR PUBLIC AFFAIRS
☐ *David Brinkley's Journal* (NBC)
Bell & Howell Close Up! (ABC)
CBS Reports (CBS)
Howard K. Smith, News and Comment
(ABC)
Twentieth Century (CBS)

OUTSTANDING ACHIEVEMENT IN INTERNATIONAL REPORTING OR COMMENTARY
☐ Piers Anderton, *The Tunnel* (NBC)
John Rich, *Germany: Fathers and
Sons* (NBC)
Marvin Kalb, Moscow Correspondent,
for general reporting (CBS)
James Robinson, Southeast Asia, for
general reporting (NBC)
John Secondari, "The Vatican," *Bell &
Howell Close Up* (ABC)

Performance Awards

OUTSTANDING SINGLE PERFORMANCE BY AN ACTOR IN A LEADING ROLE
☐ Trevor Howard, "The Invincible Mr.
Disraeli," *Hallmark Hall of Fame*
(NBC)
Bradford Dillman, "The Voice of
Charlie Pont," *Premiere, Presented
by Fred Astaire* (ABC)
Don Gordon, "The Madman," *The
Defenders* (CBS)
Walter Matthau, "Big Deal in Laredo,"
Du Pont Show of the Week (NBC)
Joseph Schildkraut, "Hear the Mellow
Wedding Bells," *Sam Benedict*
(NBC)

OUTSTANDING SINGLE PERFORMANCE BY AN ACTRESS IN A LEADING ROLE
☐ Kim Stanley, "Cardinal Act of Mercy,"
Ben Casey (ABC)
Diahann Carroll, "A Horse Has a Big
Head, Let Him Worry," *Naked City*
(ABC)
Diana Hyland, "The Voice of Charlie
Pont," *Premiere, Presented by Fred
Astaire* (ABC)
Eleanor Parker, "Why Am I Grown So
Cold?," *The Eleventh Hour* (NBC)
Sylvia Sidney, "The Madman," *The
Defenders* (CBS)

OUTSTANDING CONTINUED PERFORMANCE BY AN ACTOR IN A SERIES (LEAD)
☐ E.G. Marshall, *The Defenders* (CBS)
Ernest Borgnine, *McHale's Navy* (ABC)
Paul Burke, *Naked City* (ABC)
Vic Morrow, *Combat* (ABC)
Dick Van Dyke, *The Dick Van Dyke
Show* (CBS)

OUTSTANDING CONTINUED PERFORMANCE BY AN ACTRESS IN A SERIES (LEAD)
☐ Shirley Booth, *Hazel* (NBC)
Lucille Ball, *The Lucille Ball Show*
(CBS)
Shirl Conway, *The Nurses* (CBS)
Mary Tyler Moore, *The Dick Van Dyke
Show* (CBS)
Irene Ryan, *The Beverly Hillbillies*
(CBS)

OUTSTANDING PERFORMANCE IN A SUPPORTING ROLE BY AN ACTOR
☐ Don Knotts, *Andy Griffith Show* (CBS)
Tim Conway, *McHale's Navy* (ABC)
Paul Ford, "Teahouse of the August
Moon," *Hallmark Hall of Fame*
(NBC)
Hurd Hatfield, "The Invincible Mr.
Disraeli," *Hallmark Hall of Fame*
(NBC)
Robert Redford, "The Voice of Charlie
Pont," *Premiere, Presented by Fred
Astaire* (ABC)

OUTSTANDING PERFORMANCE IN A SUPPORTING ROLE BY AN ACTRESS
☐ Glenda Farrell, "A Cardinal Act of
Mercy," *Ben Casey* (ABC)
Davey Davison, "Of Roses and
Nightingales and Other Lovely
Things," *The Eleventh Hour* (NBC)
Nancy Malone, *Naked City* (ABC)
Rose Marie, *The Dick Van Dyke Show*
(CBS)
Kate Reid, "The Invincible Mr.
Disraeli," *Hallmark Hall of Fame*
(NBC)

OUTSTANDING PERFORMANCE IN A VARIETY OR MUSICAL PROGRAM OR SERIES
☐ Carol Burnett, *Julie and Carol at
Carnegie Hall* (CBS); *Carol and
Company* (CBS)
Edie Adams, *Here's Edie* (ABC)
Merv Griffin, *The Merv Griffin Show*
(NBC)
Danny Kaye, *Danny Kaye Show with
Lucille Ball* (NBC)
Andy Williams, *Andy Williams Show*
(NBC)

Craft and Technical Awards

OUTSTANDING ACHIEVEMENT IN COMPOSING ORIGINAL MUSIC FOR TELEVISION

☐ Robert Russell Bennett, "He is Risen," *Project XX* (NBC)
Eddy Manson, *The River Nile* (NBC)
Gian Carlo Menotti, "Labyrinth," *NBC Opera* (NBC)
Joseph Mullendore, *The Dick Powell Theatre* (NBC)
Johnny Williams, *Premiere, Presented by Fred Astaire* (ABC)

OUTSTANDING ACHIEVEMENT IN ART DIRECTION AND SCENIC DESIGN

☐ Carroll Clark, Marvin Aubrey Davis, *Walt Disney's Wonderful World of Color* (NBC)
Warren Clymer, *Hallmark Hall of Fame* (NBC)
Willard Levitas, *The Defenders* (CBS)
Hal Pereira, Earl Hedrick, *Bonanza* (NBC)
George W. Davis, Merrill Pye, *The Eleventh Hour* (NBC)
Jan Scott, *Du Pont Show of the Week* (NBC)

OUTSTANDING WRITING ACHIEVEMENT IN DRAMA

☐ Robert Thom, Reginald Rose, "The Madman," *The Defenders* (CBS)
Sidney Carroll, "Big Deal in Laredo," *Du Pont Show of the Week* (NBC)
Norman Katkov, "A Cardinal Act of Mercy," *Ben Casey* (ABC)
James Lee, "The Invincible Mr. Disraeli," *Hallmark Hall of Fame* (NBC)
Halsted Welles, "The Voice of Charlie Pont," *Premiere, Presented by Fred Astaire* (ABC)

OUTSTANDING WRITING ACHIEVEMENT IN COMEDY

☐ Carl Reiner, *Dick Van Dyke Show* (CBS)
Sam Perrin, George Balzer, Hal Goldman, Al Gordon, *The Jack Benny Program* (CBS)
Paul Henning, *The Beverly Hillbillies* (CBS)
Nat Hiken, *Car 54, Where Are You?* (NBC)
Ed Simmons, Dave O'Brien, Martin A. Ragaway, Arthur Phillips, Larry Rhine, Mort Greene, Hugh Wedlock, Red Skelton, Bruce Howard, Rich Mittleman, *The Red Skelton Hour* (CBS)

☐ Indicates winner

OUTSTANDING DIRECTORIAL ACHIEVEMENT IN DRAMA

☐ Stuart Rosenberg, "The Madman," *The Defenders* (CBS)
Fielder Cook, "Big Deal in Laredo," *Du Pont Show of the Week* (NBC)
Robert Ellis Miller, "The Voice of Charlie Pont," *Premiere, Presented by Fred Astaire* (ABC)
Sydney Pollack, "A Cardinal Act of Mercy," *Ben Casey* (ABC)
George Schaefer, "The Invincible Mr. Disraeli," *Hallmark Hall of Fame* (NBC)

OUTSTANDING DIRECTORIAL ACHIEVEMENT IN COMEDY

☐ John Rich, *Dick Van Dyke Show* (CBS)
Seymour Berns, *The Red Skelton Hour* (CBS)
Frederick De Cordova, *The Jack Benny Program* (CBS)
David Geisel, *The Garry Moore Show* (CBS)
Richard Whorf, *The Beverly Hillbillies* (CBS)

OUTSTANDING ACHIEVEMENT IN CINEMATOGRAPHY FOR TELEVISION

☐ John S. Priestley, *The Naked City* (ABC)
Guy Blanchard, *Shakespeare: Soul of an Age* (NBC); *The River Nile* (NBC)
George T. Clemens, Robert W. Pittack, *Twilight Zone* (CBS)
Robert Hauser, *Combat* (ABC)
Joe Vadala, "Comedian Backstage," *Du Pont Show of the Week* (NBC)
William Hartigan, Edmondo Ricci, "The Vatican," *Bell & Howell Close Up!* (ABC)

OUTSTANDING ACHIEVEMENT IN ELECTRONIC CAMERA WORK

☐ "The Invincible Mr. Disraeli," *Hallmark Hall of Fame* (NBC)
Here's Edie (ABC)
The Lively Ones (NBC)
ABC's Wide World of Sports (ABC)

OUTSTANDING ACHIEVEMENT IN FILM EDITING FOR TELEVISION

☐ Sid Katz, *The Defenders* (CBS)
James Ballas, George Boemler, Al Clark, Mike Pozen, Aaron Stell, *Ben Casey* (ABC)
David E. Roland, "Comedian Backstage," *Du Pont Show of the Week* (NBC)
Hugh Chaloupka, Aaron Nibley, Charles Freeman, Harry Coswick, Jack Gleason, *Naked City* (ABC)
Howard Epstein, Richard Belding, Tony Martinelli, *Premiere, Presented by Fred Astaire* (ABC)

Special Awards

INTERNATIONAL AWARD

☐ *War and Peace* (Granada TV Network, Ltd. of England) "The Bird," *Steptoe and Son* (British Broadcasting Corp.)
"Caesarian Section," *Your Life in Their Hands* (British Broadcasting Corp.)
The Offshore Island (Canadian Broadcasting Corp.)
Takajoh, English Title: *Young Hawk, Old Hawk* (Nippon Television Network Corp.)

THE STATION AWARD

☐ *Superfluous People* (WCBS-TV, New York)
The Dark Corner (WBAL-TV, Baltimore)
Suspect (KING-TV, Seattle)
Time's Man (WKY-TV, Oklahoma City)
The Wasted Years (WBBM-TV, Chicago)
Operation SOS (KMTV, Omaha)
Burden of Shame (KNXT, Los Angeles)
Conformity (WCAU-TV, Philadelphia)

TRUSTEES' AWARD

☐ *American Telephone and Telegraph Co.* For conceiving and developing Telstar 1 and Telstar 2. The launching of these satellites into the skies has spanned the oceans with a measureless gift—the promise of instant television communication between the peoples of the world.
☐ *Dick Powell.* In grateful memory of his conspicuous contributions to and relfections of credit upon the industry as an actor, director, producer, and executive; and for his consistent and unselfish cooperation with and support of the Academy.

TRUSTEES' CITATION

☐ This citation is presented to the President of the United States. Because you have initiated and have continued to make your news conferences available to television. Because this willingness to expose to the public the thoughts and feelings of your Office was further reflected in a specially scheduled news conference as a part of the first Telstar broadcast; and because by participating in the program. *Conversation with the President*, a new dimension was reached in communication between the White House and the people. For these reasons and in honor of your continued recognition of television's importance to the dialogues of a free society, this citation is extended by the Board of Trustees of the National Academy of Television Arts and Sciences to the President of the

United States, John Fitzgerald Kennedy.

1963/64

(Presented May 25, 1964 for programs telecast between April 15, 1963 and April 12, 1964)

Program Awards

THE PROGRAM OF THE YEAR
☐ *The Making of the President 1960* (ABC)
American Revolution of '63 (NBC)
"Balcklist," *The Defenders* (CBS)
The Kremlin (NBC)
Town Meeting of the World (CBS)

OUTSTANDING PROGRAM ACHIEVEMENT IN THE FIELD OF COMEDY
☐ *Dick Van Dyke Show* (CBS)
The Bill Dana Show (NBC)
The Farmer's Daughter (ABC)
McHale's Navy (ABC)
That Was the Week That Was (NBC)

OUTSTANDING PROGRAM ACHIEVEMENT IN THE FIELD OF DRAMA
☐ *The Defenders* (CBS)
Bob Hope Presents the Chrysler Theatre (NBC)
East Side, West Side (CBS)
Mr. Novak (NBC)
Richard Boone Show (NBC)

OUTSTANDING PROGRAM ACHIEVEMENT IN THE FIELD OF MUSIC
☐ *Bell Telephone Hour* (NBC)
The Lively Ones (NBC)
New York Philharmonic Young People's Concerts with Leonard Bernstein (CBS)

OUTSTANDING PROGRAM ACHIEVEMENT IN THE FIELD OF VARIETY
☐ *Danny Kaye Show* (CBS)
Andy Williams Show (NBC)
Garry Moore Show (CBS)
Judy Garland Show (CBS)
Tonight Show Starring Johnny Carson (NBC)

OUTSTANDING PROGRAM ACHIEVEMENT IN THE FIELD OF CHILDREN'S PROGRAMMING
☐ *Discovery '63-'64* (ABC)
Exploring (NBC)
NBC Children's Theatre (NBC)
Science All Stars (ABC)
Wild Kingdom (NBC)

☐ Indicates winner

OUTSTANDING PROGRAM ACHIEVEMENT IN THE FIELD OF DOCUMENTARY PROGRAMS
☐ *The Making of the President 1960* (ABC)
Greece: The Golden Age (NBC)
The Kremlin (NBC)
"Manhattan Battleground," *Du Pont Show of the Week* (NBC)
Saga of Western Man (ABC)
The Twentieth Century (CBS)

OUTSTANDING PROGRAM ACHIEVEMENT IN THE FIELD OF NEWS REPORTS
☐ *Huntley-Brinkley Report* (NBC)
CBS Evening News with Walter Cronkite (CBS)
NBC Special News Reports (NBC)
Ron Cochran with the News (ABC)

OUTSTANDING PROGRAM ACHIEVEMENT IN THE FIELD OF NEWS COMMENTARY OR PUBLIC AFFAIRS
☐ "Cuba: Part I and II—The Bay of Pigs and The Missile Crisis," *NBC White Paper* (NBC)
American Revolution of '63 (NBC)
CBS Reports (CBS)
Chronicle (CBS)
Town Meeting of the World (CBS)

Performance Awards

OUTSTANDING SINGLE PERFORMANCE BY AN ACTOR IN A LEADING ROLE
☐ Jack Klugman, "Blacklist," *The Defenders* (CBS)
James Earl Jones, "Who Do You Kill?," *East Side, West Side* (CBS)
Roddy McDowall, "Journey Into Darkness," *Arrest and Trial* (ABC)
Jason Robards, Jr., "Abe Lincoln in Illinois," *Hallmark Hall of Fame* (NBC)
Rod Steiger, "A Slow Fade to Black," *Bob Hope Presents the Chrysler Theatre* (NBC)
Harold J. Stone, "Nurse Is a Feminine Noun," *The Nurses* (CBS)

OUTSTANDING SINGLE PERFORMANCE BY AN ACTRESS IN A LEADING ROLE
☐ Shelley Winters, "Two Is the Number," *Bob Hope Presents the Chrysler Theatre* (NBC)
Ruby Dee, "Express Stop From Lenox Avenue," *The Nurses* (CBS)
Bethel Leslie, "Statement of Fact," *Richard Boone Show* (NBC)
Jeanette Nolan, "Vote No on 11l," *Richard Boone Show* (NBC)
Diana Sands, "Who Do You Kill?" *East Side, West Side* (CBS)

OUTSTANDING CONTINUED PERFORMANCE BY AN ACTOR IN A SERIES (LEAD)
☐ Dick Van Dyke, *Dick Van Dyke Show* (CBS)
Richard Boone, *Richard Boone Show* (NBC)
Dean Jagger, *Mr. Novak* (NBC)
David Janssen, *The Fugitive* (ABC)
George C. Scott, *East Side, West Side* (CBS)

OUTSTANDING CONTINUED PERFORMANCE BY AN ACTRESS IN A SERIES (LEAD)
☐ Mary Tyler Moore, *Dick Van Dyke Show* (CBS)
Shirley Booth, *Hazel* (NBC)
Patty Duke, *Patty Duke Show* (ABC)
Irene Ryan, *The Beverly Hillbillies* (CBS)
Inger Stevens, *The Farmer's Daughter* (ABC)

OUTSTANDING PERFORMANCE IN A SUPPORTING ROLE BY AN ACTOR
☐ Albert Paulsen, "One Day in the Life of Ivan Denisovich," *Bob Hope Presents the Chrysler Theatre* (NBC)
Sorrell Booke, "What's God to Julius?" *Dr. Kildare* (NBC)
Conlan Carter, "The Hostages," *Combat* (ABC)
Carl Lee, "Express Stop From Lenox Avenue," *The Nurses* (CBS)

OUTSTANDING PERFORMANCE IN A SUPPORTING ROLE BY AN ACTRESS
☐ Ruth White, "Little Moon of Alban," *Hallmark Hall of Fame* (NBC)
Martine Bartlett, "Journey Into Darkness," *Arrest and Trial* (ABC)
Anjanette Comer, "Journey Into Darkness," *Arrest and Trial* (ABC)
Rose Marie, *Dick Van Dyke Show* (CBS)
Claudia McNeil, "Express Stop From Lenox Avenue," *The Nurses* (CBS)

OUTSTANDING PERFORMANCE IN A VARIETY OR MUSICAL PROGRAM OR SERIES
☐ Danny Kaye, *Danny Kaye Show* (CBS)
Judy Garland, *Judy Garland Show* (CBS)
Barbra Streisand, *Judy Garland Show* (CBS)
Burr Tillstrom, *That Was the Week That Was* (NBC)
Andy Williams, *Andy Williams Show* (NBC)

Craft and Technical Award

OUTSTANDING ACHIEVEMENT IN COMPOSING ORIGINAL MUSIC FOR TELEVISION

☐ Elmer Bernstein, *The Making of the President 1960* (ABC)

George Auric, *The Kremlin* (NBC)

John Barry, *Elizabeth Taylor in London* (CBS)

Kenyon Hopkins, *East Side, West Side* (CBS)

George Kleinsinger, *Greece: The Golden Age* (NBC)

Ulpio Minucci, Joe Moon, Rayburn Wright, *Saga of Western Man* (ABC)

OUTSTANDING ACHIEVEMENT IN ART DIRECTION AND SCENIC DESIGN

☐ Warren Clymer, *Hallmark Hall of Fame* (NBC)

Robert Kelly, Gary Smith, *Judy Garland Show* (CBS)

Jack Poplin, *The Outer Limits* (ABC)

Edward Stephenson, *Danny Kaye Show* (CBS)

OUTSTANDING WRITING ACHIEVEMENT IN DRAMA (ORIGINAL)

☐ Ernest Kinoy, "Blacklist," *The Defenders* (CBS)

Arnold Perl, "Who Do You Kill?", *East Side, West Side* (CBS)

David Rayfiel, "Something About Lee Wiley," *Bob Hope Presents the Chrysler Theatre* (NBC)

Allan Sloane, "And James Was a Very Small Snail," *Breaking Point* (ABC)

Adrian Spies, "What's God to Julius?" *Dr. Kildare* (NBC)

OUTSTANDING WRITING ACHIEVEMENT IN DRAMA (ADAPTATION)

☐ Rod Serling, "It's Mental Work," *Bob Hope Presents the Chrysler Theatre* (NBC)

James Bridges, "The Jar," *Alfred Hitchcock Hour* (CBS)

Robert Hartung, "The Patriots," *Hallmark Hall of Fame* (NBC)

Walter Brown Newman, "The Hooligan," *Richard Boone Show* (NBC)

OUTSTANDING WRITING ACHIEVEMENT IN COMEDY OR VARIETY

☐ Carl Reiner, Sam Denoff, Bill Persky, *Dick Van Dyke Show* (CBS)

Herbert Baker, Mel Tolkin, Ernest Chambers, Saul Ilson, Sheldon Keller, Paul Mazursky, Larry Tucker, Gary Belkin, Larry Gelbart, *Danny Kaye Show* (CBS)

Robert Emmett, Gerald Gardner, Saul Turtletaub, David Panich, Tony

☐ Indicates winner

Webster, Thomas Meehan, Ed Sherman, *That Was the Week That Was* (NBC)

Steven Gethers, Jerry Davis, Lee Loeb, John McGreevey, *The Farmer's Daughter* (ABC)

OUTSTANDING DIRECTORIAL ACHIEVEMENT IN DRAMA

☐ Tom Gries, "Who Do You Kill?" *East Side, West Side* (CBS)

Paul Bogart, "Moment of Truth," *The Defenders* (CBS)

Sydney Pollack, "Something About Lee Wiley," *Bob Hope Presents the Chrysler Theatre* (NBC)

Stuart Rosenberg, "Blacklist," *The Defenders* (CBS)

George Schaefer, "The Patriots," *Hallmark Hall of Fame* (NBC)

OUTSTANDING DIRECTORIAL ACHIEVEMENT IN COMEDY

☐ Jerry Paris, *Dick Van Dyke Show* (CBS)

Sidney Lanfield, *McHale's Navy* (ABC)

Paul Nickell, William Russell, Don Taylor, *The Farmer's Daughter* (ABC)

Richard Whork, *The Beverly Hillbillies* (CBS)

OUTSTANDING DIRECTORIAL ACHIEVEMENT IN VARIETY OR MUSIC

☐ Robert Scheerer, *Danny Kaye Show* (CBS)

Roger Englander, "A Tribute to Teachers," *New York Philharmonic Young People's Concerts with Leonard Bernstein* (CBS)

Bob Henry, *Andy Williams Show* (NBC)

Marshall Jamison, *That Was the Week That Was* (NBC)

Clark Jones, Sid Smith, *Bell Telephone Hour* (NBC)

OUTSTANDING ACHIEVEMENT IN CINEMATOGRAPHY FOR TELEVISION

☐ J. Baxter Peters, *The Kremlin* (NBC)

John S. Priestley, *East Side, West Side* (NBC)

Bradford Kress, *Greece: The Golden Age* (NBC)

Ellis F. Thackery, "Once Upon a Savage Night," *Kraft Suspense Theatre* (NBC)

OUTSTANDING ACHIEVEMENT IN ELECTRONIC PHOTOGRAPHY

☐ *Danny Kaye Show* (CBS)

Bell Telephone Hour (NBC)

The Lively Ones (NBC)

"Ride with Terror," *Du Pont Show of the Week* (NBC)

OUTSTANDING ACHIEVEMENT IN FILM EDITING FOR TELEVISION

☐ William T. Cartwright, *The Making of the President 1960* (ABC)

James Algie, Samuel Cohen, Hans Dudelheim, Walter Essenfeld, Alexander Hamilton, Edward Lempa, Walter Moran, Nils Rasmussen, John Roberts, Robert Sanbo, Edward Shea, *Saga of Western Man* (ABC)

Abram Boyajian, *The Kremlin* (NBC)

Constantine S. Gochis, *Greece: The Golden Age* (NBC)

Danny Landres, Milton Shifman, Richard Wray, *Arrest and Trial* (ABC)

THE INTERNATIONAL AWARD

☐ *Les Raisins Verts* (Radiodiffusion Television Française)

Bunraku Dolls (NHK, Japan Broadcasting Corp.)

Pale Horse, Pale Rider (Canadian Broadcasting Corp.)

THE STATION AWARD

☐ *Operation Challenge—A Study in Hope* (KSD-TV, St. Louis)

The Case of the Limited Child (KPIX, San Francisco)

Child Beating (WMAL-TV, Washington, D.C.)

Date Line: Chicago Composite (WNBQ, Chicago)

The Last Prom (WLW-TV, Cincinnati)

The Next Revolution (WCBS-TV, New York)

Poison in the Air (KNXT, Los Angeles)

Wednesday's Child (KGW-TV, Portland)

Without Violence (WBRZ-TV, Baton Rouge)

1964/65

(Presented September 12, 1965 for programs telecast between April 13, 1964 and April 30, 1965)

Program Awards

OUTSTANDING PROGRAM ACHIEVEMENTS IN ENTERTAINMENT

☐ *Dick Van Dyke Show* (CBS)

☐ "The Magnificent Yankee," *Hallmark Hall of Fame* (NBC)

☐ *My Name is Barbra* (CBS)

☐ "What is Sonata Form?", *New York Philharmonic Young People's Concerts with Leonard Bernstein* (CBS)

The Andy Williams Show (NBC)

Bob Hope Presents the Chrysler Theatre (NBC)

The Defenders (CBS)

Hallmark Hall of Fame (NBC)
The Man from U.N.C.L.E. (NBC)
Mr. Novak (NBC)
Profiles in Courage (NBC)
Walt Disney's Wonderful World of Color (NBC)
The Wonderful World of Burlesque (NBC)
Xerox Specials: "Carol for Another Christmas," (ABC); "Who Has Seen the Wind?" (ABC)

OUTSTANDING PROGRAM ACHIEVEMENTS IN NEWS, DOCUMENTARIES, INFORMATION AND SPORTS

☐ "I, Leonardo da Vinci," *Saga of Western Man* (ABC)
☐ *The Louvre* (NBC)
NBC Convention Coverage (NBC)
"The Decision to Drop the Bomb," *NBC White Paper* (NBC)

Individual Achievement Awards in Entertainment

ACTORS AND PERFORMERS

☐ Leonard Bernstein, *New York Philharmonic Young People's Concerts with Leonard Bernstein* (CBS)
Lynn Fontanne, "The Magnificent Yankee," *Hallmark Hall of Fame* (NBC)
Alfred Lunt, "The Magnificent Yankee," *Hallmark Hall of Fame* (NBC)
Barbra Streisand, *My Name is Barbra* (CBS)
Dick Van Dyke, *Dan Van Dyke Show* (CBS)
Julie Andrews, *Andy Williams Show* (NBC)
Johnny Carson, *The Tonight Show Starring Johnny Carson* (NBC)
Gladys Cooper, *The Rogues* (NBC)
Robert Coote, *The Rogues* (NBC)
Richard Crenna, *Slattery's People,* (CBS)
Julie Harris, "The Holy Terror," *Hallmark Hall of Fame* (NBC)
Bob Hope, *Chrysler Presents a Bob Hope Comedy Special* (NBC)
Dean Jagger, *Mr. Novak* (NBC)
Danny Kaye, *The Danny Kaye Show* (CBS)
David McCallum, *The Man from U.N.C.L.E.* (NBC)
Red Skelton, *Red Skelton Hour* (CBS)

WRITERS

☐ David Karp, "The 700-Year-Old-Gang," *The Defenders* (CBS)
William Boardman, Dee Caruso, Robert Emmett, David Frost, Gerald Gardner, Buck Henry, Joseph Hurley, Tom Meehan, Herb Sargent, Larry Siegel, Gloria Steinem, Jim

☐ Indicates winner

Stevenson, Calvin Trillin, Saul Turteltaub, *That Was the Week That Was* (NBC)
Robert Hartung, "The Magnificent Yankee," *Hallmark Hall of Fame* (NBC)
Coleman Jacoby, Arnie Rosen, *The Wonderful World of Burlesque* (NBC)
Carl Reiner, "Never Bathe On Saturday," *Dick Van Dyke Show* (CBS)

DIRECTORS

☐ Paul Bogart, "The 700-Year-Old Gang," *The Defenders* (CBS)
Dwight Hemion, *My Name is Barbra* (CBS)
George Schaefer, "The Magnificent Yankee," *Hallmark Hall of Fame* (NBC)

CONCEPTION CHOREOGRAPHY, AND STAGING

☐ Joe Layton, *My Name is Barbra* (CBS)

ART DIRECTORS AND SET DECORATORS

☐ Warren Clymer, "The Holy Terror," *Hallmark Hall of Fame* (NBC)
☐ Tom John (art director), Bill Harp (set decorator), *My Name Is Barbra* (CBS)
Gene Callahan (art director), Jack Wright, Jr (set decorator), "Carol For Another Christmas," *Xerox Special* (ABC)
Warren Clymer, "The Magnificent Yankee," *Hallmark Hall of Fame* (NBC)
Noel Taylor (costume designer), "The Magnificent Yankee," *Hallmark Hall of Fame* (NBC)

MAKE-UP ARTIST

☐ Robert O'Bradovich, "The Magnificent Yankee," *Hallmark Hall of Fame* (NBC)

MUSICIANS

☐ Peter Matz, *My Name Is Barbra* (CBS)
☐ Herbert Grossman, "The Fantasticks," *Hallmark Hall of Fame* (NBC)

CINEMATOGRAPHERS

☐ William Spencer, *Twelve O'Clock High* (ABC)
Haskell Boggs, William Whitley, *Bonanza* (NBC)
Fred Koenekamp, *The Man from U.N.C.L.E.* (NBC)

LIGHTING DIRECTOR

☐ Phil Hymes, "The Magnificent Yankee," *Hallmark Hall of Fame* (NBC)

SPECIAL PHOTOGRAPHIC EFFECTS

☐ L. B. Abbott, *Voyage to the Bottom of the Sea* (ABC)
Production team effort, *The Man from U.N.C.L.E.* (NBC)

COLOR CONSULTANT

☐ Edward Ancona, *Bonanza* (NBC)

TECHNICAL DIRECTOR

☐ Clair McCoy, *The Wonderful World of Burlesque* (NBC)

FILM EDITORS

Henry Berman, Joseph Dervin, Will Gulick, *The Man from U.N.C.L.E.* (NBC)

Individual Achievement Awards in News, Documentaries, Information and Sports

DIRECTORS

☐ John L. Sughrue, *The Louvre* (NBC)
Frank De Felitta, *Battle of the Bulge* (NBC)
Marshall Flaum, *Let My People Go* (Syndicated)
Tom Priestley, *John F. Kennedy Remembered* (NBC)
Helen Jean Rogers, "I, Leonardo da Vinci," *Saga of Western Man* (ABC)

WRITERS

☐ Sidney Carroll, *The Louvre* (NBC)
John H. Secondari, "I, Leonardo de Vinci," *Saga of Western Man* (ABC)

FILM EDITORS

☐ Aram Boyajian, *The Louvre* (NBC)
Walter Essenfeld, Nils Rasmussen, "I, Leonardo da Vinci," *Saga of Western Man* (ABC)
Angelo Farina, Ben Schiller, *Battle of the Bulge* (NBC)

CINEMATOGRAPHERS

☐ Tom Priestley, *The Louvre* (NBC)
Dexter Alley, Richar Norling, *The Journals of Lewis & Clark* (NBC)
William B. Hartigan, "I, Leonardo da Vinci," *Saga of Western Man* (ABC)

MUSICIANS

☐ Norman Dello Joio, *The Louvre* (NBC)
Ulpio Minucci (Composer), Rayburn Wright (Conductor), "I, Leonardo da Vinci," *Saga of Western Man* (ABC)

NARRATORS

☐ Richard Basehart, *Let My People Go* (Syndicated)
Charles Boyer, *The Louvre* (NBC)

Special Awards

THE INTERNATIONAL AWARD

☐ *Le Barbier de Seville* (Canadian Broadcasting Corp.)
Antonio e Cleopatra (RAI-Radiotelevisione Italiana)
Bilder Aus Der Sowjet-Union: Sibirien—Traum Und Wirklichkeit (Norddeutscher Rundfunk)
Island Yearbook (Sveriges Radio, Sweden)

Seven Up (Granada Television Limited, England)
Show Becaud (Office de Radiodiffusion—Television Française)

THE STATION AWARD
□ *Ku Klux Klan* (WDSU-TV, New Orleans)
Conversation with James Emory Bond (WBAL-TV, Baltimore)
Korean Legacy (KTLA, Los Angeles)
My Childhood (WNEW-TV, New York)
No Room at the Bottom (KSD-TV, St. Louis)
The Outsiders (WOW-TV, Omaha)
Roses Have Thorns (WOOD-TV, Grand Rapids)
Strangers in the Shadows (WBNS-TV, Columbus)

1965/66

(Presented May 22, 1966 for programs telecast between May 1, 1965 and April 10, 1966)

Program Awards

OUTSTANDING COMEDY SERIES
□ *Dick Van Dyke Show* (CBS)
Batman (ABC)
Bewitched (ABC)
Get Smart! (NBC)
Hogan's Heroes (CBS)

OUTSTANDING VARIETY SERIES
□ *Andy Williams Show* (NBC)
Danny Kaye Show (CBS)
Hollywood Palace (ABC)
Red Skelton Hour (CBS)
Tonight Show Starring Johnny Carson (NBC)

OUTSTANDING VARIETY SPECIAL
□ *Chrysler Presents the Bob Hope Christmas Special* (NBC)
An Evening with Carol Channing (CBS)
Jimmy Durante Meets the Lively Arts (ABC)
Julie Andrews Show (NBC)
The Swinging World of Sammy Davis Jr. (Syndicated)

OUTSTANDING DRAMATIC SERIES
□ *The Fugitive* (ABC)
Bonanza (NBC)
I Spy (NBC)
The Man from U.N.C.L.E. (CBS)
Slattery's People (CBS)

OUTSTANDING DRAMATIC PROGRAM
□ *Ages of Man* (CBS)
"Eagle in a Cage," *Hallmark Hall of Fame* (NBC)

□ Indicates winner

"Inherit the Wind," *Hallmark Hall of Fame* (NBC)
"Rally Round Your Own Flag, Mister," *Slattery's People* (CBS)

OUTSTANDING MUSICAL PROGRAM
□ *Frank Sinatra: A Man and His Music* (NBC)
Bell Telephone Hour (NBC)
The Bolshoi Ballet (Syndicated)
Color Me Barbra (CBS)
New York Philharmonic Young People's Concerts with Leonard Bernstein (CBS)

OUTSTANDING CHILDREN'S PROGRAM
□ *A Charlie Brown Christmas* (CBS)
Captain Kangaroo (CBS)
Discovery (ABC)
"Further Adventures of Gallagher," *Walt Disney's Wonderful World of Color* (NBC)
"The World of Stuart Little," *NBC Children's Theatre* (NBC)

Performance Awards

OUTSTANDING PERFORMANCE BY AN ACTOR IN A LEADING ROLE IN A DRAMA
□ Cliff Robertson, "The Game," *Bob Hope Presents the Chrysler Theatre* (NBC)
Ed Begley, "Inherit the Wind," *Hallmark Hall of Fame* (NBC)
Melvyn Douglas, "Inherit the Wind," *Hallmark Hall of Fame* (NBC)
Trevor Howard, "Eagle in a Cage," *Hallmark Hall of Fame* (NBC)
Christopher Plummer, *Hamlet* (Syndicated)

OUTSTANDING SINGLE PERFORMANCE BY AN ACTRESS IN A LEADING ROLE IN A DRAMA
□ Simone Signoret, "A Small Rebellion," *Bob Hope Presents the Chrysler Theatre* (NBC)
Eartha Kitt, "Angle for the Loser," *I Spy* (NBC)
Margaret Leighton, "Behold the Great Man," "A Life for a Life," "Web of Hate," "Horizontal Hero," *Dr. Kildare* (NBC)
Shelley Winters, "Back to Back," *Bob Hope Presents the Chrysler Hour* (CBS)

OUTSTANDING CONTINUED PERFORMANCE BY AN ACTOR IN A LEADING ROLE IN A DRAMATIC SERIES
□ Bill Cosby, *I Spy* (NBC)
Richard Crenna, *Slattery's People* (CBS)
Robert Culp, *I Spy* (NBC)
David Janssen, *The Fugitive* (ABC)
David McCallum, *The Man from U.N.C.L.E.* (NBC)

OUTSTANDING CONTINUED PERFORMANCE BY AN ACTRESS IN A LEADING ROLE IN A DRAMATIC SERIES
□ Barbara Stanwyck, *The Big Valley* (ABC)
Anne Francis, *Honey West* (ABC)
Barbara Parkins, *Peyton Place* (ABC)

OUTSTANDING CONTINUED PERFORMANCE BY AN ACTOR IN A LEADING ROLE IN A COMEDY SERIES
□ Dick Van Dyke, *Dick Van Dyke Show* (CBS)
Don Adams, *Get Smart!* (NBC)
Bob Crane, *Hogan's Heroes* (CBS)

OUTSTANDING CONTINUED PERFORMANCE BY AN ACTRESS IN A LEADING ROLE IN A COMEDY SERIES
□ Mary Tyler Moore, *Dick Van Dyke Show* (CBS)
Lucille Ball, *The Lucy Show* (CBS)
Elizabeth Montgomery, *Bewitched* (ABC)

OUTSTANDING PERFORMANCE BY AN ACTOR IN A SUPPORTING ROLE IN A DRAMA
□ James Daly, "Eagle in a Cage," *Hallmark Hall of Fame* (NBC)
David Burns, *Trials of O'Brien* (CBS)
Leo G. Carroll, *The Man from U.N.C.L.E.* (NBC)

OUTSTANDING PERFORMANCE BY AN ACTRESS IN A SUPPORTING ROLE IN A DRAMA
□ Lee Grant, *Peyton Place* (ABC)
Diane Baker, "Inherit The Wind," *Hallmark Hall of Fame* (NBC)
Pamela Franklin, "Eagle in a Cage," *Hallmark Hall of Fame* (NBC)
Jeanette Nolan, "The Conquest of Maude Murdock," *I Spy* (NBC)

OUTSTANDING PERFORMANCE BY AN ACTOR IN A SUPPORTING ROLE IN A COMEDY
□ Don Knotts, "The Return of Barney Fife," *Andy Griffith Show* (CBS)
Morey Amsterdam, *Dick Van Dyke Show* (CBS)
Frank Gorshin, "Hi Di-dle Riddle," *Batman* (ABC)
Werner Klemperer, *Hogan's Heroes* (CBS)

OUTSTANDING PERFORMANCE BY AN ACTRESS IN A SUPPORTING ROLE IN A COMEDY
□ Alice Pearce, *Bewitched* (ABC)
Agnes Moorehead, *Bewitched* (ABC)
Rose Marie, *Dick Van Dyke Show* (CBS)

Writing and Directing Awards

OUTSTANDING WRITING ACHIEVEMENT IN DRAMA

☐ Millard Lampell, "Eagle in a Cage," *Hallmark Hall of Fame* (NBC)

Morton Fine, David Friedkin, "A Cup of Kindness," *I Spy* (NBC)

S. Lee Pogostin, "The Game," *Bob Hope Presents the Chrysler Theatre* (NBC)

OUTSTANDING WRITING ACHIEVEMENT IN COMEDY

☐ Bill Persky, Sam Denoff, "Coast to Coast Big Mouth," *Dick Van Dyke Show* (CBS)

Mel Brooks, Buck Henry, "Mr. Big," *Get Smart* (NBC)

Bill Persky, Sam Denoff, "The Ugliest Dog in the World," *Dick Van Dyke Show* (CBS)

OUTSTANDING WRITING ACHIEVEMENT IN VARIETY

☐ Al Gordon, Hal Goldman, Sheldon Keller, *An Evening with Carol Channing* (CBS)

Ernest Chambers, Pat McCormick, Ron Friedman, Larry Tucker, Paul Mazursky, Billie Barnes, Bernard Rothman, Norman Barasch, Carrol Moore, *The Danny Kaye Show* (CBS)

Bill Persky, Sam Denoff, *The Julie Andrews Show* (NBC)

OUTSTANDING DIRECTORIAL ACHIEVEMENT IN DRAMA

☐ Sidney Pollack, "The Game," *Bob Hope Presents the Chrysler Theatre* (NBC)

Sheldon Leonard, "So Long, Patrick Henry," "A Cup of Kindness," "Carry Me Back to Old Tsing-Tao," *I Spy* (NBC)

George Schaefer, "Eagle in a Cage," *Hallmark Hall of Fame* (NBC)

George Schaefer, "Inherit the Wind," *Hallmark Hall of Fame* (NBC)

OUTSTANDING DIRECTORIAL ACHIEVEMENT IN COMEDY

☐ William Asher, *Bewitched* (ABC)

Paul Bogart, "Diplomat's Daughter," *Get Smart!* (NBC)

Jerry Paris, *Dick Van Dyke Show* (CBS)

OUTSTANDING DIRECTORIAL ACHIEVEMENT IN VARIETY OR MUSIC

☐ Alan Handley, *Julie Andrews Show* (NBC)

Greg Garrison, *Dean Martin Show* (NBC)

Dwight Hemion, *Frank Sinatra: A Man and His Music* (NBC)

☐ Indicates winner

Dwight Himion, *Color Me Barbra* (CBS)

Bob Henry, *Andy Williams Show* (NBC)

Craft and Programming Awards*

ACHIEVEMENTS IN NEWS AND DOCUMENTARIES:

Programs:

☐ *American White Paper: United States Foreign Policy* (NBC)

"KKK—The Invisible Empire," *CBS Reports* (CBS)

☐ *Senate hearings on Vietnam* (NBC)

CBS Reports (CBS)

Coverage of Papal Visit (NBC)

KTLA Coverage of Watts Riots (ABC, CBS, NBC), KTLA News Department

Huntley-Brinkley Report (NBC)

The Making of the President 1964 (CBS)

Michelangelo: The Last Giant (NBC)

National Drivers Test (CBS)

Twentieth Century (CBS)

Individuals:

William Boardman, Lisa Commager, Diana Fetter, Robert Rickner (researchers) "Beethoven: Ordeal and Triumph," *Saga of Western Man* (ABC)

Walter Cronkite (commentator), *CBS Evenings News with Walter Cronkite* (CBS)

Lou Hazam (writer), *Michelangelo: The Last Giant* (NBC)

Chet Huntley and David Brinkley (commentators), *Huntley-Brinkley Report* (NBC)

David Lowe (writer), "KKK—The Invisible Empire," *CBS Reports* (CBS)

Frank McGee (commentator), *The Frank McGee Report* (NBC)

Frank McGee (commentator), *The Papal Visit* (NBC)

Tom Priestley (director), *Michelangelo: The Last Giant* (NBC)

Harry Reasoner (narrator), *The Great Love Affair* (CBS)

Richard Schneider (director), *Papal Mass* (ABC, CBS, NBC)

Eric Sevareid (commentator), *CBS Evening News with Walter Cronkite* (CBS)

Howard K. Smith (commentator), "United States Policy on Vietnam," *Issues and Answers* (ABC)

Mel Stuart (director), *The Making of the President 1964* (CBS)

Peter Ustinov (voice of Michelangelo), *Michelangelo: The Last Giant* (NBC)

Theodore H. White (writer), *The Making of the President 1964* (CBS)

* possibility of multiple awards

ACHIEVEMENT IN DAYTIME PROGRAMMING

Programs:

☐ *Camera Three* (CBS)

☐ *Mutual of Omaha's Wild Kingdom* (NBC)

"A Tribute to Stevenson," *Today* (NBC)

ACHIEVEMENTS IN SPORTS

Programs:

☐ *ABC Wide World of Sports* (ABC)

☐ *CBS Golf Classic* (CBS)

☐ *Shell's Wonderful World of Golf* (NBC)

NFL Game of the Week (CBS)

U.S.-Russian Track Meet (ABC)

Individuals:

Vin Scully (sports announcer), *The World Series* (NBC)

ACHIEVEMENTS IN EDUCATIONAL TELEVISION

Programs:

America's Crisis: Trouble in the Family (NET)

An Hour with Joan Sutherland (NET)

"A Roomful of Music," *Festival of Arts* (NET)

Baldwin vs. Buckley (NET)

History of the Negro People (NET)

"Poland," *Changing World* (NET)

"The Dance Theatre of Jose Limon," *Festival of Arts* (NET)

Individuals:

☐ Julia Child (instructor and hostess), *The French Chef* (NET)

Karl Genus (writer and director), *Sibelius, A Symphony of Finland* (NET)

Lane Slate (director), *The Creative Person* (NET)

Tom Wicker, Max Frankel, Lester Markel (commentators), *News in Perspective* (NET)

ACHIEVEMENTS IN MUSIC

Composition:

☐ Laurence Rosenthal, *Michelangelo: The Last Giant* (NBC)

Jerry Goldsmith, *The Man from U.N.C.L.E.* (NBC)

Earle Hagen, *I Spy* (NBC)

David Rose, *Bonanza* (NBC)

Pete Rugolo, *Run for Your Life* (NBC)

Lalo Schifrin, *The Making of the President 1964* (CBS)

Morton Stevens, "Seven Hours to Dawn," *Gunsmoke* (CBS)

Conducting:

Mitchell Ayres, *The Hollywood Palace* (ABC)

Irwin Kostal, *Julie Andrews Show* (NBC)

Gordon Jenkins, Nelson Riddle, *Frank Sinatra: A Man and His Music* (NBC)

Erich Leinsdorf, "Beethoven: Ordeal and Triumph," *Saga of Western Man* (ABC)

Laurence Rosenthal, *Michelangelo: The Last Giant* (NBC)

Donald Voorhees, *Bell Telephone Hour* (NBC)

Arranging:

Joe Lipman, *The Hollywood Palace* (ABC)

Marty Paich, *Alice in Wonderland or What's a Nice Kid Like You Doing in a Place Like This?* (ABC)

Special:

Ray Charles (special vocal material), *Julie Andrews Show* (NBC)

Claude Frank (pianist), "Beethoven: Ordeal and Triumph," *Saga of Western Man* (ABC)

INDIVIDUAL ACHIEVEMENTS IN ART DIRECTION AND ALLIED ARTS

Art direction:

☐ James Trittipo, *Hollywood Palace* (ABC)

Carroll Clark, William Tuntke, "Further Adventures of Gallegher," *Walt Disney's Wonderful World of Color* (NBC)

William J. Creber, *Voyage to the Bottom of the Sea* (ABC)

George Davis, Merrill Pye, James Sullivan, *The Man from U.N.C.L.E.* (NBC)

Tom John, *Color Me Barbra* (CBS)

Edward Stephenson, *Andy Williams Show* (NBC)

Set decoration:

Henry Grace, Francisco Lombardo, Jack Mills, Charles Thompson, *The Man from U.N.C.L.E.* (NBC)

Bill Harp, *Color Me Barbra* (CBS)

Norman Rockett, *Voyage to the Bottom of the Sea* (ABC)

Costume Design:

Ray Aghayan, Bob Mackie, "Wonderful World of Burlesque II," *Danny Thomas Special* (NBC)

Wardrobe

Ed Smith, *Hollywood Palace* (ABC)

Make-up:

Bod O'Bradovich, "Inherit the Wind," *Hallmark Hall of Fame* (NBC)

Special:

Arnold Goode, Bill Graham, Bob Murdock (creation of unusual props) *The Man from U.N.C.L.E.* (NBC)

Robert Tait (mechanical effects) *Voyage to the Bottom of the Sea* (ABC)

INDIVIDUAL ACHIEVEMENTS IN CINEMATOGRAPHY

☐ Winton C. Hoch, *Voyage to the Bottom of the Sea* (ABC)

☐ Indicates winner

Haskell Boggs, William F. Whitley, *Bonanza* (NBC)

Fred Koenekamp, *The Man from U.N.C.L.E.* (NBC)

Lionel Lindon, "The Cold, Cold War of Paul Bryan," *Run for Your Life* (NBC)

Meredith M. Nicholson, *The Fugitive* (ABC)

Tom Priestley, *Michelangelo: The Last Giant* (NBC)

Ted Voightlander, *The Wild, Wild West* (CBS)

INDIVIDUAL ACHIEVEMENTS IN CINEMATOGRAPHY: SPECIAL

☐ L.E. Abbott, Howard Lydecker (photographie effects), *Voyage to the Bottom of the Sea* (ABC)

L.B. Abbott, Howard Lydecker (photographic effects), *Lost in Space* (CBS)

Edward Ancon (color coordinator), *Bonanza* (NBC)

INDIVIDUAL ACHIEVEMENTS IN FILM EDITING

☐ David Blewitt, William T. Cartwright, *The Making of the President 1964* (CBS)

Marvin Coil, Everett Douglas, Ellsworth Hoagland, *Bonanza* (NBC)

James Baiotto, Robert Belcher, Richard Wormell, *Voyage to the Bottom of the Sea* (ABC)

Henry Berman, Joseph Dervin, William Gulick, *The Man from U.N.C.L.E.* (NBC)

Loftus McDonough, *Michelangelo: The Last Giant* (NBC)

INDIVIDUAL ACHIEVEMENTS IN SOUND EDITING

☐ James Bourgeois, *Mutual of Omaha's Wild Kingdom* (NBC)

Robert Cornett, Don Hall, Jr., Donald Higgins, Elwell Jackson, *Voyage to the Bottom of the Sea* (ABC)

Richard Legrand, Ross Taylor, Harold Wooley, Ralph Hickey, *Batman* (ABC)

John J. Lipow, William Rival, *The Man from U.N.C.L.E.* (NBC)

INDIVIDUAL ACHIEVEMENTS IN ELECTRONIC PRODUCTION

Audio engineering:

☐ Laurence Schneider, "Seventh Annual Young Performers Program," *New York Philharmonic Young People's Concerts with Leonard Bernstein* (CBS)

William Cole, *Andy Williams Show* (NBC)

Herman Lewis, *Perry Mason* (CBS)

Video tape editing:

☐ Craig Curtis, Art Schneider, *Julie Andrews Show* (NBC)

Stan Chlebek, Craig Curtis, Art Schneider, *Lorne Greene's American West* (NBC)

Video control:

Arnold Dick, *Bell Telephone Hour* (NBC)

Lighting:

☐ Lon Stucky, *Frank Sinatra: A Man and His Music* (NBC)

Robert Barry, *Color Me Barbra* (CBS)

John Freschi, *Andy Williams Show* (NBC)

Phil Hymes, *Bell Telephone Hour* (NBC)

Technical directors:

☐ O. Tamburri, "Inherit the Wind," *Hallmark Hall of Fame* (NBC)

Karl Messerschmidt, *Dean Martin Show* (NBC)

Electronic Cameramen:

Mike English, Emil Husni, Al Loreto, John Lincoln, *The Strollin' '20s* (CBS)

Special electronic effects:

Milt Altman, *Julie Andrews Show* (NBC)

INDIVIDUAL ACHIEVEMENTS IN ENGINEERING DEVELOPMENT

☐ Stop Action Playback (MVR Corp., CBS)

☐ Early Bird Satellite (Hughes Aircraft Co. and Communication Satellite Corp.)

SPECIAL CLASSIFICATIONS OF INDIVIDUAL ACHIEVEMENTS

☐ Burr Tillstrom (hand ballet), "Berlin Wall," *That Was the Week That Was* (NBC)

Art Carney (performer), "The Adoption," *Jackie Gleason Show* (CBS)

Nick Castle (choreographer), *Andy Williams Show* (NBC)

Tony Charmoli (choreographer), *Danny Kaye Show* (CBS)

Tony Charmoli (choreographer), *Julie Andrews Show* (NBC)

Robert Hartung (adaptation), "Inherit the Wind," *Hallmark Hall of Fame* (NBC)

Gene Kelly (performer), *Julie Andrews Show* (NBC)

Carl Reiner (voices), *Linus the Lionhearted* (CBS)

Charles Schultz (writer), *A Charlie Brown Christmas* (CBS)

THE INTERNATIONAL AWARD: NON-FICTION

☐ "Wyvern at War—No. 2," *Breakout* (Westward Television Limited, England)

The House on the Beach (Rediffusion Television Limited, England)

Mozart in Prague (Osterreichischer Rundfunk, Austria)

THE INTERNATIONAL AWARD: FICTION

Stasera Rita (RAI-Radiotelevisione Italiana, Italy)

The Successor (ANGLIA Television, Limited, England)

The Tale of Genji (Mainichi Broadcasting System, Japan)

THE STATION AWARD

☐ *I See Chicago* (WBBM-TV, Chicago)

As They Like It (KGW-TV, Portland)

The Corner (KTVI, St. Louis)

Government by Gaslight (KJXT-TV, Jacksonville)

Guns Are for Killing (KPRC-TV, Houston)

Make a Joyful Sound (WCBS-TV, New York)

The Miner's Story (WCAU-TV, Philadelphia)

No Deposit, No Return (KRON-TV, San Francisco)

Viet Nam '65: A Distant Christmas (WWL-TV, New Orleans)

TRUSTEES' AWARD

☐ *Edward R. Murrow.* For 40 years, broadcasting—first radio and then television—has bred men whose wit, intelligence, insight and personal magnetism have literally filled the air and made us all look with a clearer eye and listen with a more attentive ear. The annals of journalism are filled with tales of men of courage whose integrity, whose commitment to the search for truth and whose devotion to its revelation have made this land of ours truly a democracy. It was given to one man, however, to bring together these highest qualities of broadcasting and journalism so that he became a symbol to colleagues and the public alike of the complete broadcast journalist. He was born, it seems, with a deep-rooted fundamental belief in the rights of man—individually and collectively. And as a reporter—whether of the issues and events of the Second World War from Great Britain; the problems and inequities experienced by the migrant worker, the fettered scientist or the underpaid and underrated educator here at home; or the corrosive tyranny of the McCarthy era which he exposed and so helped bring to an end—he exemplified the courage, the sensitivity and the devotion to truth and duty to which all free men aspire. For all of these reasons, the Trustees of the National Academy of Television Arts and Sciences—with the keenest regret that he is no longer here to shed his light and to

accept this honor—present this Trustees' Award to Edward R. Murrow.

☐ *Xerox Corporation.* Rarely, in the history of television, have there been sponsors who have subordinated their interest in television as an advertising medium to their interest in its capacity to inform, to enlighten and to entertain on the highest level. One sponsor has come to the forefront of our attention in the past several years because of its presentation of some of the finest art, news and historical documentaries and because of its zealous support of democratic institutions—both in the United States and internationally. Because this company has contributed significantly to upgrading the quality of television while presenting its commercial message modestly and tastefully so that the American viewing public has been the beneficiary of its use of television, the Board of Trustees of the National Academy of Television Arts and Sciences presents its Trustees' Award to the Xerox Corp.

1966/67

(Presented June 4, 1967 for programs telecast between March 25, 1966 and April 16, 1967)

Program Awards

OUTSTANDING COMEDY SERIES

☐ *The Monkees* (NBC)

Bewitched (ABC)

Get Smart! (NBC)

Andy Griffith Show (CBS)

Hogan's Heroes (CBS)

OUTSTANDING VARIETY SERIES

☐ *Andy Williams Show* (NBC)

Dean Martin Show (NBC)

Jackie Gleason Show (CBS)

Hollywood Palace (ABC)

Smothers Brothers Comedy Hour Starring Tom and Dick Smothers (ABC)

Tonight Show Starring Johnny Carson (NBC)

OUTSTANDING VARIETY SPECIAL

☐ *The Sid Caesar, Imogene Coca, Carl Reiner, Howard Morris Special* (CBS)

Chrysler Presents the Bob Hope Christmas Special (NBC)

"A Time for Laughter: A Look at Negro Humor in America," *ABC Stage '67* (ABC)

Dick Van Dyke (CBS)

OUTSTANDING DRAMATIC SERIES

☐ *Mission: Impossible* (CBS)

The Avengers (ABC)

I Spy (NBC)

Run for Your Life (ABC)

Star Trek (NBC)

OUTSTANDING DRAMATIC PROGRAM

☐ *Death of a Salesman* (CBS)

"A Christmas Memory," *ABC Stage '67* (ABC)

"The Final War of Olly Winter," *CBS Playhouse* (CBS)

"The Glass Menagerie," *CBS Playhouse* (CBS)

"The Love Song of Barney Kempinski," *ABC Stage '67* (ABC)

Mark Twain Tonight! (CBS)

OUTSTANDING MUSICAL PROGRAM

☐ *Brigadoon* (ABC)

Frank Sinatra: A Man and His Music Part 2 (CBS)

"Toscanini: The Maestro Revisited," *Bell Telephone Hour* (NBC)

OUTSTANDING CHILDREN'S PROGRAM

☐ *Jack and the Beanstalk* (NBC)

Charlie Brown's All Stars (CBS)

Discovery '66-'67 (ABC)

It's the Great Pumpkin, Charlie Brown (CBS)

Performance Awards

OUTSTANDING SINGLE PERFORMANCE BY AN ACTOR IN A LEADING ROLE IN A DRAMA

☐ Peter Ustinov, "Barefoot in Athens," *Hallmark Hall of Fame* (NBC)

Alan Arkin, "The Love Song of Barney Kempinski," *ABC Stage '67* (ABC)

Lee J. Cobb, *Death of a Salesman* (CBS)

Ivan Dixon, "The Final War of Olly Winter," *CBS Playhouse* (CBS)

Hal Holbrook, *Mark Twain Tonight!* (CBS)

OUTSTANDING SINGLE PERFORMANCE BY AN ACTRESS IN A LEADING ROLE IN A DRAMA

☐ Geraldine Page, "A Christmas Memory," *ABC Stage 67* (ABC)

Shirley Booth, "The Glass Menagerie," *CBS Playhouse* (CBS)

Mildred Dunnock, *Death of a Salesman* (CBS)

Lynn Fontanne, "Anastasia," *Hallmark Hall of Fame* (NBC)

Julie Harris, "Anastasia," *Hallmark Hall of Fame* (NBC)

OUTSTANDING CONTINUED PERFORMANCE BY AN ACTOR IN A LEADING ROLE IN A DRAMATIC SERIES

☐ Bill Cosby, *I Spy* (NBC)

Robert Culp, *I Spy* (NBC)
Ben Gazzara, *Run for Your Life* (NBC)
David Janssen, *The Fugitive* (ABC)
Martin Landau, *Mission: Impossible* (CBS)

OUTSTANDING CONTINUED PERFORMANCE BY AN ACTRESS IN A LEADING ROLE IN A DRAMATIC SERIES

☐ Barbara Bain, *Mission: Impossible* (CBS)
Diana Rigg, *The Avengers* (ABC)
Barbara Stanwyck, *The Big Valley* (ABC)

OUTSTANDING CONTINUED PERFORMANCE BY AN ACTOR IN A LEADING ROLE IN A COMEDY SERIES

☐ Don Adams, *Get Smart!* (NBC)
Bob Crane, *Hogan's Heroes* (CBS)
Brian Keith, *Family Affair* (CBS)
Larry Storch, *F Troop* (ABC)

OUTSTANDING CONTINUED PERFORMANCE BY AN ACTRESS IN A LEADING ROLE IN A COMEDY SERIES

☐ Lucille Ball, *The Lucy Show* (CBS)
Elizabeth Montgomery, *Bewitched* (ABC)
Agnes Moorehead, *Bewitched* (ABC)
Mario Thomas, *That Girl* (ABC)

OUTSTANDING PERFORMANCE BY AN ACTOR IN A SUPPORTING ROLE IN A DRAMA

☐ Eli Wallach, "The Poppy is also a Flower," *Xerox Special* (ABC)
Leo G. Carroll, *The Man From U.N.C.L.E.* (NBC)
Leonard Nimoy, *Star Trek* (NBC)

OUTSTANDING PERFORMANCE BY AN ACTRESS IN A SUPPORTING ROLE IN A DRAMA

☐ Agnes Moorehead, "Night of the Vicious Valentine," *Wild, Wild West* (CBS)
Tina Chen, "The Final War of Olly Winter," *CBS Playhouse* (CBS)
Ruth Warrick, *Peyton Place* (ABC)

OUTSTANDING PERFORMANCE BY AN ACTOR IN A SUPPORTING ROLE IN A COMEDY

☐ Don Knotts, "Barney Comes to Mayberry," *Andy Griffith Show* (CBS)
Gale Gordon, *The Lucy Show* (CBS)
Werner Klemperer, *Hogan's Heroes* (CBS)

OUTSTANDING PERFORMANCE BY AN ACTRESS IN A SUPPORTING ROLE IN A COMEDY

☐ Francis Bavier, *Andy Griffith Show* (CBS)
Nancy Kulp, *The Beverly Hillbillies* (CBS)

☐ Indicates winner

Marion Lorne, *Bewitched* (ABC)

Writing and Directing Awards

OUTSTANDING WRITING ACHIEVEMENT IN DRAMA

☐ Bruce Geller, *Mission: Impossible* (CBS)
Robert Culp, "The Warlord," *I Spy* (NBC)
Ronald Ribman, "The Final War of Olly Winter," *CBS Playhouse* (CBS)

OUTSTANDING WRITING ACHIEVEMENT IN COMEDY

☐ Buck Henry, Leonard Stern, *Get Smart!* (NBC)
Edmund Hartmann, "Buffy," *Family Affair* (CBS)
Sidney Sheldon, *I Dream of Jeannie* (NBC)

OUTSTANDING WRITING ACHIEVEMENT IN VARIETY

☐ Mel Brooks, Sam Denoff, Bill Persky, Carl Reiner, Mel Tolkin, *The Sid Caesar, Imogene Coca, Carl Reiner, Howard Morris Speical* (CBS)
Harry Crane, Rich Eustis, Lee Hale, Paul Keyes, Al Rogers, *Dean Martin Show* (NBC)
Marvin Marx, Walter Stone, Rod Parker, *Jackie Gleason Show* (CBS)

OUTSTANDING DIRECTORIAL ACHIEVEMENT IN DRAMA

☐ Alex Segal, *Death of a Salesman* (CBS)
Paul Bogart, "The Final War of Olly Winter," *CBS Playhouse* (CBS)
Paul Bogart, *Mark Twain Tonight!* (CBS)
George Schaefer, "Anastasia," *Hallmark Hall of Fame* (NBC)

OUTSTANDING DIRECTORIAL ACHIEVEMENT IN COMEDY

☐ James Frawley, "Royal Flush," *The Monkees* (NBC)
William Asher, *Bewitched* (ABC)
Earl Bellamy, "One of Our Bombs Is Missing," *I Spy* (NBC)
William Russell, *Family Affair* (CBS)
Maury Thompson, *The Lucy Show* (CBS)

OUTSTANDING DIRECTORIAL ACHIEVEMENT IN VARIETY OR MUSIC

☐ Fielder Cook, *Brigadoon* (ABC)
Greg Garrison, *Dean Martin Show* (NBC)
Dwight Hemion, *Frank Sinatra: A Man and His Music Part 2* (CBS)
Bob Henry, *Andy Williams Show* (NBC)
Bill Hobin, *The Sid Caesar, Imogene Coca, Carl Reiner, Howard Morris Special* (CBS)

The Craft and Programming Area*

PROGRAM ACHIEVEMENTS IN NEWS AND DOCUMENTARIES

☐ *China: The Roots of Madness* (Syndicated)
☐ *Hall of Kings* (ABC)
☐ *The Italians* (CBS)
CBS Reports (CBS)
"The Homosexuals," *CBS Reports* (CBS)
If It's Tuesday, This Must Be Belgium (CBS)
"Organized Crime in America," *American White Paper* (NBC)

INDIVIDUAL ACHIEVEMENTS IN NEWS AND DOCUMENTARIES

☐ Theodore H. White (writer), *China: The Roots of Madness* (Syndicated)
Luigi Barzini (narrator), *The Italians* (CBS)
Luigi Barzini, Perry Wolff (writers), *The Italians* (CBS)
Walter Cronkite (commentator), *CBS Evening News with Walter Cronkite* (CBS)
Chet Huntley and David Brinkley (commentators), *Huntley-Brinkley Report* (NBC)
James Mason (narrator), *Hall of Kings* (ABC)
Frank McGee (commentator), *The Frank McGee Report* (NBC)
Budd Schulberg (writer), *The Angry Voices of Watts* (NBC)
Eric Sevareid (commentator), *CBS Evening News with Walter Cronkite* (CBS)
Howard K. Smith (commentator), *Elections '66* (ABC)

PROGRAM ACHIEVEMENTS IN DAYTIME PROGRAMMING

☐ *Mutual of Omaha's Wild Kingdom* (NBC)
G.E. College Bowl (NBC)
Mike Douglas Show (Syndicated)

INDIVIDUAL ACHIEVEMENTS IN DAYTIME PROGRAMMING

☐ Mike Douglas (m.c.) *Mike Douglas Show* (Syndicated)
Tom Kennedy (m.c.), *You Don't Say* (NBC)
Gene Rayburn (m.c.), *Match Game* (NBC)

PROGRAM ACHIEVEMENTS IN SPORTS

☐ *ABC Wide World of Sports* (ABC)
Portrait of Willie Mays (ABC)
Shell's Wonderful World of Golf (NBC)

* possibility of one award, more than one award or no award

INDIVIDUAL ACHIEVEMENTS IN SPORTS

Jim McKay (commentator), *Fifth Anniversary Program ABC Wide World of Sports* (ABC)

Chris Schenkel (commentator), *Portrait of a Team* (ABC)

Chris Schenkel (commentator), *NBA Basketball* (ABC)

INDIVIDUAL ACHIEVEMENTS IN MUSIC

Composition:

Aaron Copland, *CBS Playhouse* (CBS)

Earle Hagen, *I Spy* (NBC)

Pete Rugolo, *Run for Your Life* (NBC)

Lalo Schifrin, *Mission: Impossible* (CBS)

Conductors:

Gordon Jenkins, Nelson Riddle, *Frank Sinatra: A Man and His Music Part 2* (CBS)

Arranging:

Ray Ellis, Lennie Hayton, *Lena* (Syndicated)

Gordon Jenkins, Nelson Riddle, *Frank Sinatra: A Man and His Music Part 2* (CBS)

Routines and Choral Direction:

Ticker Freeman, George Wyle, *Andy Williams Show* (NBC)

INDIVIDUAL ACHIEVEMENTS IN ART DIRECTION AND ALLIED CRAFTS:

Art Direction:

Earl G. Carlson (set decorator), *Death of a Salesman* (CBS)

Tom John (art director), *Death of a Salesman* (CBS)

Costume Design:

☐ Ray Aghayan, Bob Mackie, *Alice Through the Looking Glass* (NBC)

Make-up:

☐ Dick Smith, *Mark Twain Tonight!* (CBS)

Claude Thompson, *Alice Through the Looking Glass* (NBC)

Mechanical Special Effects:

Jim Rugg, *Star Trek* (NBC)

Robert Tait, *Voyage to the Bottom of the Sea* (ABC)

INDIVIDUAL ACHIEVEMENTS IN CINEMATOGRAPHY

Cinematography

Haskell Boggs, William F. Whitely, *Bonanza* (NBC)

Photographic Special Effects:

☐ L. B. Abbott, *Time Tunnel* (ABC)

L. B. Abbot, *Voyage to the Bottom of the Sea* (ABC)

Darrell Anderson, Linwood G. Dunn, Joseph Westheimer, *Star Trek* (NBC)

INDIVIDUAL ACHIEVEMENTS IN FILM AND SOUND EDITING

☐ Paul Krasny and Robert Watts (film editors), *Mission: Impossible* (CBS)

☐ Don Hall, Dick Legrand, Daniel Mandell and John Mills (sound editors), *Voyage to the Bottom of the Sea* (ABC)

Douglas H. Grindstaff (sound editor), *Star Trek* (NBC)

INDIVIDUAL ACHIEVEMENTS IN ELECTRONIC PRODUCTION

Technical Directors:

☐ A. C. Cunningham, *Brigadoon* (ABC)

A.C. Cunningham, *Death of a Salesman* (CBS)

Karl Messerschmidt, *Dean Martin Show* (NBC)

Joseph Strauss, *Frank Sinatra: A Man and His Music Part 2* (CBS)

O. Tamburri, *Damn Yankees* (NBC)

Lighting Directors:

☐ Leard Davis, *Brigadoon* (ABC)

Leard Davis, *Death of a Salesman* (CBS)

John Freschi, *Andy Williams Show* (NBC)

Lon Stucky, *Frank Sinatra: A Man and His Music* (CBS)

Video Tape Editing:

James E. Brady, *Death of a Salesman* (CBS)

James E. Brady, *Brigadoon* (ABC)

Lewis W. Smith, *Red Skelton Hour* (CBS)

Audio Engineering:

☐ Bill Cole, *Frank Sinatra: A Man and His Music Part 2* (CBS)

Ray Kemper, *Brigadoon* (ABC)

Sound Recording:

Fred Bosch, "The Cleveland Orchestra: One Man's Triumph," *Bell Telephone Hour* (NBC)

Electronic Cameramen:

☐ Robert Dunn, Gorm Erickson, Ben Wolf, Nick Demos, *Brigadoon* (ABC)

Robert Dunn, Gorm Erickson, Fred Gough, Jack Jennings, Dick Nelson, *Death of a Salesman* (CBS)

INDIVIDUAL ACHIEVEMENTS IN ENGINEERING DEVELOPMENT

☐ Plumbicon Tube, N. V. Philips Gloeilampenfabrieken

☐ High-Band Video Tape Recorder, Ampex Co.

SPECIAL CLASSIFICATIONS OF INDIVIDUAL ACHIEVEMENTS

☐ Art Carney, *Jackie Gleason Show* (CBS)

☐ Truman Capote, Eleanor Perry (adaptation), "A Christmas Memory," *ABC Stage '67* (ABC)

☐ Arthur Miller (adaptation), *Death of a Salesman* (CBS)

Peter Gennaro (choreographer), *Brigadoon* (ABC)

Sheldon Keller and Glenn Wheaton (writers), *Frank Sinatra: A Man and His Music Part 2* (CBS)

Bill Lelendez (director), *It's the Great Pumpkin, Charlie Brown* (CBS)

Charles Schulz (writer), *It's the Great Pumpkin, Charlie Brown* (CBS)

Charles Schulz (writer), *Charlie Brown's All Stars* (CBS)

Burr Tillstrom (puppeteer), *Perry Como's Kraft Music Hall* (NBC)

Special Awards

INTERNATIONAL AWARD

Documentary:

☐ *Big Deal at Gothenburg* (Tyne Tees Television Limited, England)

Darwin—The Galapagos (Canadian Broadcasting Corp., Ottawa)

Family of Man (Film Polski, Poland)

Entertainment:

☐ *The Caretaker* (Rediffusion Television Limited, England)

D.H. Lawrence—The Blind Man (Granada Television Network Limited, England)

Phedre (Office de Radiodiffusion-Television Française, France)

Bernard Shaw (Societe Suisse de Radiodiffusion et Television, Switzerland)

STATION AWARD

☐ The Road to Nowhere (KLZ-TV, Denver)

Assignment: 1747 Randolph Street (WFIL-TV, Philadelphia)

A Baby is a Wonderful Thing (WBAL-TV, Baltimore)

The Face of a Genius (WBZ-TV, Boston)

Five Civilized Tribes: An Unfinished Journey (KTUL-TV, Tulsa)

The Golden Calf (KGW-TV, Portland)

I See Chicago: The Illinois Voter's Test (WBBM-TV, Chicago)

The Lengthening Shadow (KSD-TV, St. Louis)

Medal of Valor (KTTV, Hollywood)

TRUSTEES' AWARD

☐ *Sylvester "Pat" Weaver, Jr.*. For his constant conviction that the American public deserves better than it gets on the television screen; for introducing the special to television, thus breathing new life into the weekly schedule; for having the foresight to predict that there could be an audience for an early morning information show and a late night entertainment show, thus providing us with *Today* and *Tonight*, two programs which have demonstrated their validity by having remained on the air with great success for more than a decade; but finally and most importantly, for the imagination, leadership, courage and integrity which he has brought to our medium during the 18 years he has been a part of it.

1967/68

(Presented May 19, 1968)

Entertainment Program Awards

OUTSTANDING COMEDY SERIES
□ *Get Smart* (NBC)
  Bewitched (ABC)
  Family Affair (CBS)
  Hogan's Heroes (CBS)
  Lucy Show (CBS)

OUTSTANDING DRAMATIC SERIES
□ *Mission: Impossible* (CBS)
  The Avengers (ABC)
  I Spy (NBC)
  NET Playhouse (NET)
  Run for Your Life (NBC)
  Star Trek (NBC)

OUTSTANDING DRAMATIC PROGRAM
□ "Elizabeth the Queen," *Hallmark Hall of Fame* (NBC)
  "Do Not Go Gentle into That Good Night," *CBS Playhouse* (CBS)
  "Dear Friends," *CBS Playhouse* (CBS)
  The Strange Case of Dr. Jekyll and Mr. Hyde (ABC)
  "Uncle Vanya," *NET Playhouse* (NET)
  "Luther," *Xerox Special Events* (ABC)

OUTSTANDING MUSICAL OR VARIETY SERIES
□ *Rowan and Martin's Laugh-In* (NBC)
  Bell Telephone Hour (NBC)
  Carol Burnett Show (CBS)
  Dean Martin Show (NBC)
  Smothers Brothers Comedy Hour (CBS)

OUTSTANDING MUSICAL OR VARIETY PROGRAM
□ *Rowan and Martin's Laugh-In Special* (NBC)
  A Man and His Music + Ella + Jobim (NBC)
  "Chrysler Presents the Bob Hope Christmas Special," *Chrysler Presents the Bob Hope Show* (NBC)
  "Five Ballets of the Five Senses," *Lincoln Center/Stage* (NET)

□ Indicates winner

Entertainment Performance Awards

OUTSTANDING SINGLE PERFORMANCE BY AN ACTOR IN A LEADING ROLE IN A DRAMA
□ Melvyn Douglas, "Do Not Go Gentle into That Good Night" *CBS Playhouse* (CBS)
  Raymond Burr, *Ironside World Premiere* (NBC)
  Van Heflin, *A Case of Libel* (ABC)
  George C. Scott, *The Crucible* (CBS)
  Eli Wallach, "Dear Friends," *CBS Playhouse* (CBS)

OUTSTANDING SINGLE PERFORMANCE BY AN ACTRESS IN A LEADING ROLE IN A DRAMA
□ Maureen Stapleton, "Among the Paths to Eden," *Xerox Special Event* (ABC)
  Dame Judith Anderson, "Elizabeth the Queen," *Hallmark Hall of Fame* (NBC)
  Genevieve Bujold, "Saint Joan," *Hallmark Hall of Fame* (NBC)
  Colleen Dewhurst, *The Crucible* (CBS)
  Anne Jackson, "Dear Friends," *CBS Playhouse* (CBS)

OUTSTANDING CONTINUED PERFORMANCE BY AN ACTOR IN A LEADING ROLE IN A DRAMATIC SERIES
□ Bill Cosby, *I Spy* (NBC)
  Raymond Burr, *Ironside* (NBC)
  Robert Culp, *I Spy* (NBC)
  Ben Gazzara, *Run for Your Life* (NBC)
  Martin Landau, *Mission: Impossible* (CBS)

OUTSTANDING CONTINUED PERFORMANCE BY AN ACTRESS IN A LEADING ROLE IN A DRAMATIC SERIES
□ Barbara Bain, *Mission: Impossible* (CBS)
  Diana Rigg, *The Avengers* (ABC)
  Barbara Stanwyck, *The Big Valley* (ABC)

OUTSTANDING CONTINUED PERFORMANCE BY AN ACTOR IN A LEADING ROLE IN A COMEDY SERIES
□ Don Adams, *Get Smart* (NBC)
  Richard Benjamin, *He and She* (CBS)
  Sebastian Cabot, *Family Affair* (CBS)
  Brian Keith, *Family Affair* (CBS)
  Dick York, *Bewitched* (ABC)

OUTSTANDING CONTINUED PERFORMANCE BY AN ACTRESS IN A LEADING ROLE IN A COMEDY SERIES
□ Lucille Ball, *The Lucy Show* (CBS)
  Barbara Feldon, *Get Smart* (NBC)
  Elizabeth Montgomery, *Bewitched* (ABC)

Paula Prentiss, *He and She* (CBS)
Mario Thomas, *That Girl* (ABC)

OUTSTANDING PERFORMANCE BY AN ACTOR IN A SUPPORTING ROLE IN A DRAMA
□ Milburn Stone, *Gunsmoke* (CBS)
  Joseph Campanella, *Mannix* (CBS)
  Lawrence Dobkin, "Do Not Go Gentle into That Good Night," *CBS Playhouse* (CBS)
  Leonard Nimoy, *Star Trek* (NBC)

OUTSTANDING PERFORMANCE BY AN ACTRESS IN A SUPPORTING ROLE IN A DRAMA
□ Barbara Anderson, *Ironside* (NBC)
  Linda Cristal, *The High Chaparral* (NBC)
  Tessie O'Shea, *The Strange Case of Dr. Jekyll and Mr. Hyde* (ABC)

OUTSTANDING PERFORMANCE BY AN ACTOR IN A SUPPORTING ROLE IN A COMEDY
□ Werner Klemperer, *Hogan's Heroes* (CBS)
  Jack Cassidy, *He and She* (CBS)
  William Demarest, *My Three Sons* (CBS)
  Gale Gordon, *The Lucy Show* (CBS)

OUTSTANDING PERFORMANCE BY AN ACTRESS IN A SUPPORTING ROLE IN A COMEDY
□ Marion Lorne, *Bewitched* (ABC)
  Agnes Moorehead, *Bewitched* (ABC)
  Marge Redmond, *The Flying Nun* (ABC)
  Nita Talbot, "The Hostage," *Hogan's Heroes* (CBS)

Entertainment Craft and Technical Awards

OUTSTANDING WRITING ACHIEVEMENT IN DRAMA
□ Loring Mandel, "Do Not Go Gentle into that Good Night," *CBS Playhouse* (CBS)
  Allan Balter, William Read Woodfield, "The Seal," *Mission: Impossible* (CBS)
  Don M. Mankiewicz, *Ironside World Premiere* (NBC)
  Reginald Rose, "Dear Friends," *CBS Playhouse* (CBS)

OUTSTANDING WRITING ACHIEVEMENT IN COMEDY
□ Alan Burns, Chris Hayward, "The Coming-Out Party," *He and She* (CBS)
  Danny Arnold, Ruth Brooks Flippen, "The Mailman Cometh," *That Girl* (ABC)
  Ray Singer, Milt Josefsberg, "Lucy Gets Jack Benny's Account," *The Lucy Show* (CBS)

Leonard Stern, Arne Sultan, "The Old Man and the She," *He and She* (CBS)

OUTSTANDING WRITING ACHIEVEMENT IN MUSIC OR VARIETY

☐ Paul Keyes, Hugh Wedlock, Allan Manings, Chris Beard, David Panich, Phil Hahn, Jack Hanrahan, Coslough Johnson, Marc London, Digby Wolfe, *Rowan and Martin's Laugh-In* (NBC)

Bill Angelos, Stan Burns, Don Hinkley, Buz Kohan, Mike Marmer, Gail Parent, Arnie Rosen, Kenny Solms, Saul Turtletaub, *The Carol Burnett Show* (CBS)

Chris Beard, Phil Hahn, Jack Hanrahan, Coslough Johnson, Paul Keyes, Marc London, Allan Manings, David Panich, Hugh Wedlock, Digby Wolfe, *Rowan and Martin's Laugh-In* (NBC)

Ted Bergman, Allan Blye, Sam Bobrick, Ernest Chambers, Ron Clark, Gene Farmer, Hal Goldman, Al Gordon, Saul Ilson, Jerry Music, Mason Williams, *The Smothers Brothers Comedy Hour* (CBS)

OUTSTANDING DIRECTORIAL ACHIEVEMENT IN DRAMA

☐ Paul Bogart, "Dear Friends," *CBS Playhouse* (CBS)

Lee H. Katzin, "The Killing," *Mission: Impossible (CBS)*

George Schaefer, "Do Not Go Gentle into That Good Night," *CBS Playhouse* (CBS)

Alex Segal, *The Crucible* (CBS)

OUTSTANDING DIRECTORIAL ACHIEVEMENT IN COMEDY

☐ Bruce Bilson, "Maxwell Smart, Private Eye," *Get Smart* (NBC)

Danny Arnold, "The Apartment," *That Girl* (ABC)

James Frawley, "The Devil and Peter Tork," *The Monkees* (NBC)

OUTSTANDING DIRECTORIAL ACHIEVEMENT IN MUSIC OR VARIETY

☐ Jack Haley, Jr. *Movin' with Nancy* (NBC)

Bill R. Foster, *Rowan and Martin's Laugh-In Special* (NBC)

Greg Garrison, *Dean Martin Show* (NBC)

Dwight Hemion, *Herb Alpert and the Tijuana Brass Special* (NBC)

Gordon W. Wiles, *Rowan and Martin's Laugh-In* (NBC)

OUTSTANDING ACHIEVEMENT IN MUSICAL COMPOSITION

☐ Earle Hagen, "Laya," *I Spy* (NBC)

Bernard Green, "My Father and My Mother," *CBS Playhouse* (CBS)

☐ Indicates winner

Pete Rugolo, "Cry Hard, Cry Fast," *Run for Your Life* (NBC)

Lalo Schifrin, "The Seal," *Mission: Impossible* (CBS)

Morton Stevens, "Major Glory," *Gunsmoke* (CBS)

Harry Sukman, "The Champion of the Western World," *The High Chaparral* (NBC)

OUTSTANDING ACHIEVEMENT IN ART DIRECTION AND SCENIC DESIGN

☐ James W. Trittipo, *The Fred Astaire Show* (NBC)

Warren Clymer, "Elizabeth the Queen," *Hallmark Hall of Fame* (NBC)

Jan Scott (art director), George Gaines (set director), "Kismet," *Armstrong Circle Theatre* (ABC)

Romain Johnston, (art director), Charles Kreiner (set director), *Smothers Brothers Comedy Hour* (CBS)

William P. Ross, "Echo of Yesterday," *Mission: Impossible* (CBS)

OUTSTANDING ACHIEVEMENT IN CINEMATOGRAPHY

☐ Ralph Woolsey, "A Thief is a Thief is a Thief," *It Takes a Thief* (ABC)

Gordon Avil, "How to Escape from a Prison Camp Without Really Leaving," *Hogan's Heroes* (CBS)

Winton C. Hoch, "Raiders from Outerspace," *Time Tunnel* (ABC)

Michel Hugo, "The Killing," *Mission: Impossible* (CBS)

Vilis Lapenieks, *Movin' with Nancy* (NBC)

Ted Voigtlander, "Search for Survival," *Cowboy in Africa* (ABC)

OUTSTANDING ACHIEVEMENT IN ELECTRONIC CAMERA WORK

☐ A.J. Cunningham (technical director), Edward Chaney, Robert Fonorow, Harry Tatarian, Ben Wolf (cameramen), "Do Not Go Gentle into That Good Night," *CBS Playhouse* (CBS)

Heino Rippe (technical director), *Herb Alpert and the Tijuana Brass Special* (CBS)

Joe Strauss (technical director), Richard Durham, Ray Figelski, Roy Holm, Robert Keys, Carl Pitsch, Ron Sheldon, Tony Yarlett (cameramen), *Fred Astaire Show* (NBC)

Chuck Howard (director of program production), *10th World Olympic Games* (ABC)

OUTSTANDING ACHIEVEMENT IN FILM EDITING

☐ Peter Johnson, "The Sounds and Sights of Chicago," *Bell Telephone Hour* (NBC)

Richard Brockway, Donn Cambern, John C. Fuller, *Chrysler Presents the Bob Hope Christmas Special* (NBC)

Peter V. Punzi, "Four Days to Omaha," *NBC Experiment in Television* (NBC)

Donald R. Rode, "The Doomsday Machine," *Star Trek* (NBC)

Donald D. Wages, "The Photographer," *Mission: Impossible* (CBS)

Robert Watts, "The Traitor," *Mission: Impossible* (CBS)

The Areas*

OUTSTANDING ACHIEVEMENT IN CHILDREN'S PROGRAMMING

Programs:

He's Your Dog, Charlie Brown (CBS)
Mister Rogers' Neighborhood (NET)
You're In Love, Charlie Brown (CBS)

Individuals:

Fred Rogers (host), *Mister Rogers' Neighborhood* (NET)

OUTSTANDING ACHIEVEMENT IN DAYTIME

Program:

☐ *Today* (NBC)
Camera Three (CBS)
The Mike Douglas Show (Syndicated)

Individuals:

MacDonald Carey, *Days of Our Lives* (NBC)

Joan Bennett, *Dark Shadows* (ABC)

Celeste Holm, *Fat Hands and a Diamond Ring* (Syndicated)

OUTSTANDING ACHIEVEMENT IN SPORTS PROGRAMMING

Programs:

☐ *ABC's Wide World of Sports* (ABC)
The American Sportsman (ABC)
The Flying Fisherman (Syndicated)
10th Winter Olympic Games (ABC)

Individuals:

☐ Jim McKay (sports commentator), *ABC's Wide World of Sports* (ABC)

Dick Button (sports commentator), *10th Winter Olympic Games* (ABC)

Chris Schenkel (sports commentator), *NCAA Football* (ABC)

SPECIAL CLASSIFICATION OF INDIVIDUAL ACHIEVEMENTS

☐ Art Carney (performer), *The Jackie Gleason Show* (CBS)

☐ Pat Paulsen (performer), *The Smothers Brothers Comedy Hour* (CBS)

The Westheimer Co. (special photographic effects), "Metamorphosis," *Star Trek* (NBC)

* possibility of one award, more than one award or no award

Joseph G. Sorokin (sound editor), "The Survivors," *Mission: Impossible* (CBS)

Charles M. Schulz (writer), *You're in Love, Charlie Brown* (CBS)

Bill Melendez (director), *You're In Love, Charlie Brown* (CBS)

David Winters (choreographer), *Movin' with Nancy* (NBC)

OUTSTANDING INDIVIDUAL ACHIEVEMENT IN MUSIC (OTHER THAN COMPOSER)

Mitchell Ayres (conductor), *The Hollywood Palace* (ABC)

Arthur Fiedler (conductor), "A Boston Pops Concert for Youngsters," *Children's Theatre* (NBC)

Neal Hefti (conductor), *The Fred Astaire Show* (NBC)

Sammy Cahn (lyricist), *The Legend of Robin Hood* (NBC)

Lee Hale (special musical material), *The Dean Martin Christmas Show* (NBC)

Arthur Malvin (special musical material), *A Man and His Music + Ella + Jobim* (NBC)

OUTSTANDING INDIVIDUAL ACHIEVEMENT IN THE VISUAL ARTS

Bert Gordon (graphic design), *The Strange Case of Dr. Jekyll and Mr. Hyde* (ABC)

Dick Smith (make up), *The Strange Case of Dr. Jekyll and Mr. Hyde* (ABC)

Dan Striepeke (make-up), "The Space Destructors," *Lost In Space* (CBS)

OUTSTANDING INDIVIDUAL ACHIEVEMENT IN ELECTRONIC PRODUCTION

☐ Arthur Schneider (tape editor), *Rowan and Martin's Laugh-In Special* (NBC)

William M. Klages (lighting director), *Herb Alpert and the Tijuana Brass* (CBS)

Lon Stucky (lighting director), "Carousel," *Armstrong Circle Theatre* (ABC)

Bill Cole (audio engineer), *The Fred Astaire Show* (NBC)

Robert H. Guhl (audio engineer), "Home to Judgement," *I Spy* (NBC)

Nick V. Giordano (tape editor), *The Hollywood Palace* (ABC)

Jerry Smith (video control), "Carousel," *Armstrong Circle Theatre* (ABC)

Herb Weiss (video control), *The Hollywood Palace* (ABC)

THE INTERNATIONAL AWARD:

Entertainment:

☐ *Call Me Daddy* (ABC Television Limited, England)

☐ Indicates winner

Swan Lake (Canadian Broadcasting Corp., Canada)

The Good and Faithful Servant (Rediffusion Television Limited, England)

Riedaiglia (Sveriges Radio, Sweden)

Die Ofarims (Westdeutscher Rundfunk, Germany)

THE INTERNATIONAL AWARD

Documentary:

☐ *La Section Anderson* (Office de Radiodiffusion Television Française, France)

The Enchanted Isles (Anglia Television Limited, England)

High Street—Mayfair (ATV Network Limited, England)

The Price of a Record (Four Companies Productions, England)

Contract 736 (Scottish Television Limited, Scotland)

The Servants (Tyne Tees Television Limited, England)

THE STATION AWARD

☐ *Now Is the Time* (WCAU-TV, Philadelphia)

Operation Thanks (KFMB-TV, San Diego)

Albania: Ghetto of the Mind (KGW-TV, Portland)

Our Kind of World (KRMA-TV, Denver)

What's a Man Worth? (KSD-TV, St. Louis)

The Dropout Drugs (KUTV, Salt Lake City)

A Matter of Life (WNBC-TV, New York)

The Giants and the Common Men (WMAQ-TV, Chicago)

The Other Washington (WRC-TV, Washington, D.C.)

SPECIAL CITATION FOR THE PROGRAM OR SERIES DEALING WITH DISADVANTAGED YOUNG PEOPLE, YOUTH OPPORTUNITY, OR WHICH ATTEMPTS TO DETER CIVIL UNREST

☐ *The Other Side of the Shadow* (WWL-TV, New Orleans)

The Other Washington (WRC-TV, Washington, D.C.)

Tony McBride (KDKA-TV, Pittsburgh)

Poverty's Children Are Not Alike (KLZ-TV, Denver)

The Invisible Minority (KNBC-TV, Los Angeles)

What's a Man Worth? (KSD-TV, St. Louis)

Six Days in July (WWJ-TV, Detroit)

TRUSTEES' AWARD

☐ *Donald H. McGannon*, president and chairman of the Board of Directors of Group W (Westinghouse Broadcasting Company). For his creative and executive leadership of one of the most dynamic groups of radio and television stations in the United States; for innovating and encouraging the development by a Station Group of public service and entertainment programs of unparalleled scope and quality; for the sponsorship of six Public Service Programming Conferences, enabling all broadcasters better to serve the public on vital issues; for his leadership qualities which have been expressed through his service as adviser or trustee to six universities, through his work in a number of government posts, and through his commitment as officer or director of many broadcast organizations; and finally, for his early recognition of broadcasting's need to train and employ individuals from minority groups and his chairmanship of the Broadcast Skills Bank.

OUTSTANDING ACHIEVEMENT IN ENGINEERING DEVELOPMENT

☐ *British Broadcasting Corporation.* For the Electronic Field—Store Color Television Standards Converter. By converting television pictures instantaneously from the 525 line/60-field NTSC system used in America and other countries to the 626-line/50-field PAL or SECAM systems used in Europe and in other parts of the world, the Color Television Standards Converter facilitates immediate and world-wide color television broadcast of events and entertainment of major importance via setellite.

News and Documentary Awards*

OUTSTANDING ACHIEVEMENT WITHIN REGULARLY SCHEDULED NEWS PROGRAMS

Programs:

☐ "Crisis in the Cities," *Public Broadcast Laboratory* (NET)

"Coverage of the Milwaukee Open Housing Crisis, Father Groppi, Demonstrations and Riots," *The Huntley-Brinkley Report* (NBC)

"Immediate and On-The-Spot Coverage of the Tet Attacks," *The Huntley-Brinkley Report* (NBC)

"The Police Chief Executing VC During Tet Attack," *The Huntley-Brinkley Report* (NBC)

"Sgt. Simpson: Vietnam," *Peter Jennings with the News* (ABC)

---

* possibility of one award, more than one award or no award

Individuals:

☐ John Laurence (CBS News correspondent), Keith Kay (CBS News cameraman), "1st Cavalry," "Con Thien" and other segments, *CBS Evening News with Walter Cronkite* (CBS)

Dean Brelis (reporter), (coverage of attack on Hills 882 and 875) *The Huntley-Brinkley Report* (NBC)

Kirk Browning (director), "Crisis in the Cities," *Public Broadcast Laboratory* (NET)

Winston Burdett (CBS News correspondent), (Middle East coverage), *CBS Evening News with Walter Cronkite* and CBS News Special Reports (CBS)

Walter Cronkite (CBS News correspondent), (Vietnam coverage), *CBS Evening News with Walter Cronkite* and *Report From Vietnam by Walter Cronkite*

David Douglas Duncan (photographer), still photo essays on the Marines under bombardment at Con Thien and Khe Sanh, *ABC Evening News with Bob Young* (ABC)

Don Farmer (correspondent), reports on the black and white communities preparing for another apparently long hot summer, *ABC Evening News with Bob Young* (ABC)

Peter Jennings (reporter), dramatic report on Fred Esherick, a 15 year old boy facing death for killing his father, *ABC Evening News with Bob Young* (ABC)

Charles Kuralt (CBS News correspondent), James Wilson (CBS News cameraman), "On the Road," *CBS Evening News with Walter Cronkite* (CBS)

Walter Lippman, "Walter Lippmann on Vietnam and Politics" *Public Broadcast Laboratory* (NET)

Edward P. Mogan (program commentator), *Public Broadcast Laboratory* particularly "A Conversation with Dean Acheson" (NET)

Eric Sevareid (CBS News national correspondent), *CBS Evening News with Walter Cronkite* (CBS)

Howard K. Smith, John Scali, William H. Lawrence, and Joseph C. Harsch (commentators), commentaries on Vietnam, politics and various domestic issues, *Evening News* (ABC)

Howard Tuckner (reporter), reporting while wounded in Vietnam, *The Huntley Brinkley-Report* (NBC)

Av Westin (executive producer), *Public Broadcast Laboratory*, particularly "George Wallace's America" (NET)

☐ Indicates winner

OUTSTANDING ACHIEVEMENT IN COVERAGE OF SPECIAL EVENTS

Programs:

☐ "News Analysis," *State of the Union/68* (NET)

"CBS News Continuous Coverage of War in Middle East," *CBS News Special Reports and Special Broadcasts* (CBS)

CBS News Special Report: Vietnam Perspective: The Ordeal of Con Thien (CBS)

Complete Live Coverage of the United Nations During The Middle East Crisis (NBC)

"Coverage of the Middle East War and Other Specials from the U.N.," *War in the Middle East* (ABC)

Satellite Coverage of Adenauer's Funeral (NBC)

Satellite Coverage of Pope's Visit to Fatima (NBC)

Individuals:

☐ Frank McGee (commentator), *Satellite Coverage of Adenauer's Funeral* (NBC)

Walter Cronkite (CBS News correspondent), *CBS news Special Report: The Flight of Apollo 4* (CBS)

OUTSTANDING ACHIEVEMENT IN NEWS DOCUMENTARIES

Programs:

☐ *Africa* (ABC)

☐ *Summer '67: What We Learned* (NBC)

ABC Scope: The Vietnam War (ABC)

"CBS News Inquiry: The Warren Report," *CBS News Hour* (CBS)

CBS News Special: Destination: North Pole (CBS)

"CBS News Special: Viet Cong," *CBS News Hour* (CBS)

"CBS News Special Report: Morley Safer's Red China Diary," *CBS News Hour* (CBS)

"CBS Report: What About Ronald Reagan?" *CBS News Hour* (CBS)

Israel: Victory or Else (NBC)

Khrushchev in Exile (NBC)

"On Face Value," *Your Dollar's Worth* (NET)

"The Poor Pay More," *NET Journal* (NET)

Same Mud, Same Blood (NBC)

Southern Accents, Northern Ghettos (ABC)

Soviets in Space (NBC)

War in the Skies (ABC)

"The Way It Is," *NET Journal* (NET)

"What Harvest for the Reaper?" *NET Journal* (NET)

"Where Is Prejudice?", *NET Journal* (NET)

Who in '68? (ABC)

Individuals:

☐ Harry Reasoner (writer), *CBS Reports: What About Ronald Reagan?* (CBS)

☐ Vo Huynh (cameraman), *Same Mud, Same Blood* (NBC)

Ethel Huber (music supervision), *CBS News Special: Road Signs on a Merry-Go-Round* (CBS)

John Laurence (correspondent), *CBS News Special Report: Vietnam Perspective: The Ordeal of Con Thien* (CBS)

Peter McIntyre (soundman), *Same Mud, Same Blood* (NBC)

Masaki Shiihara (soundman), *Same Mud, Same Blood* (NBC)

Jeri Sopanen (cameraman), "The Way It Is," *NET Journal* (NET)

OUTSTANDING ACHIEVEMENT IN CULTURAL DOCUMENTARIES

Programs:

☐ "CBS News Special: Eric Hoffer: The Passionate State of Mind," *CBS News Hour* (CBS)

☐ "CBS News Special: Gauguin in Tahiti: The Search For Paradise," *CBS News Hour* (CBS)

☐ *John Steinbeck's "America and Americans"* (NBC)

☐ "Dylan Thomas: The World I Breathe," *NET Festival* (NET)

"American Profile: Music from the Land," *American Profile* (NBC)

"American Profile: The National Gallery of Art," *American Profile* (NBC)

An Evening at Tanglewood (NBC)

Can You Hear Me? (ABC)

CBS News Special: Galileo Galilei (CBS)

CBS News Special: Road Signs on a Merry-Go-Round (CBS)

Dialogue: Martin Buber and Israel (NET)

Duke Ellington: Love You Madly (NET)

Everett Dirksen's Washington (ABC)

Life and Times of John Huston, Esquire (NET)

Mr. Dickens of London (ABC)

Robert Scott and the Race for the South Pole (ABC)

"The Law and the Prophets," *Project 20* (NBC)

The Pursuit of Excellence—The Vienna Choir Boys (ABC)

The Rise and Fall of the Third Reich (ABC)

"The Wyeth Phenomenon," "Who, What, When, Where, Why with Harry Reasoner," *CBS News Hour* (CBS)

Individuals:

☐ Nathaniel Dorsky (art photography), "CBS News Special: Gauguin in Tahiti: The Search for Paradise," *CBS News Hour* (CBS)

☐ Harry Morgan (writer), "The Wyeth Phenomenon," "Who, What, When, Where, Why with Harry Reasoner," *CBS News Hour* (CBS)

Thomas A. Priestley (director of photography), Robert Loweree (film editor), *John Steinbeck's "American and Americans"* (NBC)

Martin Carr (writer), "CBS News Special: Gauguin in Tahiti: The Search for Paradise," *CBS News Hour* (CBS)

Gerald Fried (composer), "CBS News Special: Gauguin in Tahiti: The Search for Paradise," *CBS News Hour* (CBS)

William B. Hartigan (director of photography), *Robert Scott and the Race for the South Pole* (ABC)

Louis J. Hazam (writer), "American Profile: The National Gallery of Art," *American Profile* (NBC)

Peter Moseley (film editor), *Life and Times of John Huston, Esquire* (NET)

Eric Sevareid (interviewer), "CBS News Special: Eric Hoffer: The Passionate State of Mind," *CBS News Hour* (CBS)

John Wilcox (cinematographer), "CBS News Special: Gauguin in Tahiti: The Search for Paradise," *CBS News Hour* (CBS)

Robert Young (cinematographer), *Dialogue: Martin Buber and Israel* (NET)

OTHER NEWS AND DOCUMENTARY ACHIEVEMENTS

Programs:

☐ *The 21st Century* (CBS)
☐ "Science and Religion: Who Will Play God?" *CBS News* (CBS)
Animal Secrets (NBC) "A Conversation with Svetllana Alliluyeva," *NET Journal* (NET)
Boston Pops Concert for Youngsters (NBC)
Directions (ABC)
Discovery '68 (ABC)
The Learning Process (NBC) "New Morality: Challenge of the Student Generation," *CBS News Special* (CBS)
Our World (NET)
The Shephardes Playe (ABC)

Individuals:

☐ Georges Delerue (composer), *Our World* (NET)

1968/69

(Presented June 8, 1969 for programs telecast between March 7, 1968 and March 16, 1969)

OUTSTANDING COMEDY SERIES

☐ *Get Smart* (CBS)

☐ Indicates winner

Bewitched (ABC)
Family Affair (CBS)
The Ghost and Mrs. Muir (NBC)
Julia (NBC)

OUTSTANDING DRAMATIC SERIES

☐ *NET Playhouse* (NET)
The FBI (ABC)
Ironside (NBC)
Judd for the Defense (ABC)
The Name of the Game (NBC)
Mission: Impossible (CBS)

OUTSTANDING DRAMATIC PROGRAM

☐ "Teacher, Teacher" *Hallmark Hall of Fame* (NBC)
"The Execution," *Mission: Impossible* (CBS)
Heidi (NBC)
A Midsummer Night's Dream (CBS)
"The People Next Door," *CBS Playhouse* (CBS)
"Talking to a Stranger," *NET Playhouse* (NET)

OUTSTANDING MUSICAL OR VARIETY SERIES

☐ *Rowan and Martin's Laugh-In* (NBC)
Carol Burnett Show (CBS)
Dean Martin Show (NBC)
Smothers Brothers Comedy Hour (CBS)
That's Life (ABC)

OUTSTANDING MUSICAL OR VARIETY PROGRAM

☐ The Bill Cosby Special (NBC)
Barbra Streisand: A Happening in Central Park (CBS)
"Duke Ellington Concert of Sacred Music," *NET Playhouse* (NET)
Francis Albert Sinatra Does His Thing (CBS)
Rowan and Martin's Laugh-In (with Marcel Marceau) (NBC)
"The Rite of Spring," *NET Festival* (NBC)
Vladimir Horowitz: A Television Concert at Carnegie Hall (CBS)

Entertainment Program Awards

OUTSTANDING SINGLE PERFORMANCE BY AN ACTOR IN A LEADING ROLE

☐ Paul Scofield, "Male of the Species," *Prudential's on Stage* (NBC)
☐ Ossie Davis, "Teacher, Teacher," *Hallmark Hall of Fame* (NBC)
☐ David McCallum, "Teacher, Teacher," *Hallmark Hall of Fame* (NBC)
☐ Bill Travers, "The Admirable Crichton," *Hallmark Hall of Fame* (NBC)

OUTSTANDING SINGLE PERFORMANCE BY AN ACTRESS IN A LEADING ROLE

☐ Geraldine Page, *The Thanksgiving Visitor* (ABC)
Anne Baxter, "The Bobbie Currier Story," *The Name of the Game* (NBC)
Lee Grant, "The Gates of Cerberus," *Judd for the Defense* (ABC)

OUTSTANDING CONTINUED PERFORMANCE BY AN ACTOR IN A LEADING ROLE IN A DRAMATIC SERIES

☐ Carl Betz, *Judd for the Defense* (ABC)
Raymond Burr, *Ironside* (NBC)
Peter Graves, *Mission: Impossible* (CBS)
Martin Landau, *Mission: Impossible* (CBS)
Ross Martin, *The Wild, Wild West* (CBS)

OUTSTANDING CONTINUED PERFORMANCE BY AN ACTRESS IN A LEADING ROLE IN A DRAMATIC SERIES

☐ Barbara Bain, *Mission: Impossible* (CBS)
Joan Blondell, *Here Comes the Brides* (ABC)
Peggy Lipton, *The Mod Squad* (ABC)

OUTSTANDING CONTINUED PERFORMANCE BY AN ACTOR IN A LEADING ROLE IN A COMEDY SERIES

☐ Don Adams, *Get Smart* (NBC)
Brian Keith, *Family Affair* (CBS)
Edward Mulhare, *The Ghost and Mrs. Muir* (NBC)
Lloyd Nolan, *Julia* (NBC)

OUTSTANDING CONTINUED PERFORMANCE BY AN ACTRESS IN A LEADING ROLE IN A COMEDY SERIES

☐ Hope Lange, *The Ghost and Mrs. Muir* (NBC)
Diahann Carroll, *Julia* (NBC)
Barbara Feldon, *Get Smart* (NBC)
Elizabeth Montgomery, *Bewitched* (ABC)

OUTSTANDING SINGLE PERFORMANCE BY AN ACTRESS IN A SUPPORTING ROLE

☐ Anna Calder-Marshall, "Male of the Species," *Prudential's on Stage* (NBC)
Pamela Brown, "The Admirable Crichton," *Hallmark Hall of Fame* (NBC)
Irene Harvey, "The O'Casey Scandal," *My Three Sons* (CBS)
Nancy Kovak, "The Girl Who Came in with the Tide," *Mannix* (CBS)

OUTSTANDING SINGLE PERFORMANCE BY AN ACTOR IN A SUPPORTING ROLE

☐ Ned Glass, "A Little Chicken Soup Never Hurt Anybody," *Julia* (NBC)
Hal Holbrook, *The Whole World is Watching* (NBC)
Billy Schulman, "Teacher, Teacher," *Hallmark Hall of Fame* (NBC)

OUTSTANDING CONTINUED PERFORMANCE BY AN ACTOR IN A SUPPORTING ROLE IN A SERIES

☐ Werner Klemperer, *Hogan's Heroes* (CBS)
Greg Morris, *Mission: Impossible* (CBS)
Leonard Nimoy, *Star Trek* (NBC)

OUTSTANDING CONTINUED PERFORMANCE BY AN ACTRESS IN A SUPPORTING ROLE IN A SERIES

☐ Susan Saint James, *The Name of the Game* (NBC)
Barbara Anderson, *Ironside* (NBC)
Agnes Moorehead, *Bewitched* (ABC)

Entertainment Craft and Technical Awards

OUTSTANDING WRITING ACHIEVEMENT IN DRAMA

☐ J.P. Miller, "The People Next Door," *CBS Playhouse* (CBS)
Alan E. Sloane, "Teacher, Teacher," *Hallmark Hall of Fame* (NBC)
Ellen M. Violett, "The Experiment," *CBS Playhouse* (CBS)

OUTSTANDING WRITING ACHIEVEMENT IN COMEDY, VARIETY OR MUSIC

☐ Alan Blye, Bob Einstein, Murray Roman, Carl Gottlieb, Jerry Music, Steve Martin, Cecil Tuck, Paul Wayne, Cy Howard, Mason Williams, *Smothers Brothers Comedy Hour* (CBS)
Paul W. Keyes, Hugh Wedlock Jr., Allan S. Manings, Chris Beard, David Panich, Coslough H. Johnson, Marc London, Dave Cox, Jim Carlson, Jack Mendelsohn, James Mulligan, Lorne E. Michaels, Hart Pomerantz, *Rowan and Martin's Laugh-In* (NBC)
Arnie Rosen, Stan Burns, Mike Marmer, Hal Goldman, Al Gordon, Don Hinkley, Kenny Solms, Gail Parent, Bill Angelos, Alan Kohan, *The Carol Burnett Show* (CBS)

OUTSTANDING DIRECTORIAL ACHIEVEMENT IN DRAMA

☐ David Greene, "The People Next Door," *CBS Playhouse* (CBS)
Paul Bogart, "Secrets," *CBS Playhouse* (CBS)
Fielder Cook, "Teacher, Teacher," *Hallmark Hall of Fame* (NBC)

☐ Indicates winner

OUTSTANDING DIRECTORIAL ACHIEVEMENT IN COMEDY, VARIETY OR MUSIC

☐ Greg Garrison, *The Dean Martin Show* (NBC)
Bill Hobin, *Bill Cosby Special* (NBC)
Gordon Wiles, *Rowan and Martin's Laugh-In* (NBC)

OUTSTANDING ACHIEVEMENT IN MUSICAL COMPOSITION

☐ John T. Williams, *Heidi* (NBC)
Jacques Belasco, *Hemingway's Spain—A Love Affair* (ABC)
Hugo Montenegro, "Take Your Lover in the Ring," *The Outcasts* (ABC)
Lalo Schifrin, "The Heir Apparent," *Mission: Impossible* (CBS)
Morton Stevens, "Hawaii Five O," *CBS Friday Night at the Movies* (CBS)

OUTSTANDING ACHIEVEMENT IN ART DIRECTION AND SCENIC DESIGN

☐ William P. Ross (art director), Lou Hafley (set decorator), "The Bunker," *Mission: Impossible* (CBS)
Walter M. Jefferies Jr. (art director), John Dwyer (set decorator), "All Our Yesterdays," *Star Trek* (NBC)
Ken Johnson, *Rowan and Martin's Laugh-In* (NBC)

OUTSTANDING ACHIEVEMENT IN CINEMATOGRAPHY

☐ George Folsey, *Here's Peggy Fleming* (NBC)
Frank Phillips, "Up-Tight," *Hawaii Five-O* (CBS)
Robert Riger, *19th Summer Olympic Games* (ABC)
Howard Schwartz, "The Crash," *Land of the Giants* (ABC)

OUTSTANDING ACHIEVEMENT IN ELECTRONIC CAMERAWORK

☐ A.J. Cunningham (technical director), Nick DeMos, Bob Fonarow, Fred Gough, Jack Jennings, Dick Nelson, Rick Tanzi, Ben Wolf (cameramen), "The People Next Door," *CBS Playhouse* (CBS)
Frank Biondo (cameraman), "Our First Fight," *That's Life* (ABC)
Karl Messerschmidt (technical director), Roy Holm, Bob Keyes, Wayne Nostaja, Tony Yarlett (cameramen), *Petula* (NBC)

OUTSTANDING ACHIEVEMENT IN FILM EDITING

☐ Bill Mosher, "An Elephant in a Cigar Box," *Judd for the Defense* (ABC)
John C. Fuller, Patrick Kennedy, Igo Kantor, Frank McKelvey, *Chrysler Presents The Bob Hope Christmas Special* (NBC)
Sidney Katz, "Teacher, Teacher," *Hallmark Hall of Fame* (NBC)

Donald R. Rode, "Assignment: Earth," *Star Trek* (NBC)

The Areas*

OUTSTANDING ACHIEVEMENT IN CHILDREN'S PROGRAMMING

Programs:
Mister Rogers' Neighborhood (NET)
Walt Disney's Wonderful World of Color (NBC)

Individuals:
Bob Keeshan (performer), *Captain Kangaroo* (CBS)
Burr Tillstrom (performer), "The Reluctant Dragon," *NBC Children's Theatre* (NBC)

OUTSTANDING ACHIEVEMENT IN DAYTIME PROGRAMMING

Programs:
☐ *The Dick Cavett Show* (ABC)
The Hollywood Squares (NBC)

Individuals:
Hugh Downs (host), *Concentration* (NBC)

OUTSTANDING ACHIEVEMENT IN SPORTS PROGRAMMING

Programs:
☐ *19th Summer Olympics Games* (ABC)
ABC's Wide World of Sports (ABC)

Individuals:
☐ Bill Bennington, Mike Freedman, Mac Memion, Robert Riger, Marv Schlenker, Andy Sidaris, Lou Volpicelli and Doug Wilson (directors); *19th Summer Olympic Games* (ABC)
Chris Schenkel (commentator), *19th Summer Olympic Games* (ABC)

SPECIAL CLASSIFICATION ACHIEVEMENTS

Programs:
☐ *Firing Line with William F. Buckley, Jr.* (Syndicated)
☐ *Mutual of Omaha's Wild Kingdom* (NBC)
Broadway '68—The Tony Awards (NBC)
1969 Tournament of Roses Parade (CBS)

Individuals (Variety Performances):
☐ Arte Johnson, *Rowan and Martin's Laugh-In* (NBC)
☐ Harvey Korman *The Carol Burnett Show* (CBS)
Ruth Buzzi, *Rowan and Martin's Laugh-In* (NBC)
Goldie Hawn, *Rowan and Martin's Laugh-In* (NBC)

* possibility of one award, more than one award or no award

Individuals (Special Photographic Effects):
Van Der Veer Photo Effects, Howard A. Anderson Co., The Westheimer Co., Cinema Research, "The Tholian Web," *Star Trek* (NBC)

OUTSTANDING INDIVIDUAL ACHIEVEMENT IN MUSIC

☐ Mort Lindsey (musical director), *Barbra Streisand: A Happening in Central Park* (CBS)
Tom Adair, John Scott Trotter (words and music), *Barbar the Elephant* (NBC)
Herb Alpert (arranger and conductor), *The Beat of the Brass* (CBS)
Billy Barnes (special material), *Rowan and Martin's Laugh-In* (NBC)

OUTSTANDING INDIVIDUAL ACHIEVEMENT IN THE VISUAL ARTS

Ray Aghayan (costume designer), *Carol Channing and Pearl Bailey on Broadway* (ABC)
Angel G. Esparza (graphic designer), "U.S.S. Pueblo Court of Inquiry," *The Huntley-Brinkley Report* (NBC)
Bod Mackie (costume designer), *The Carol Burnett Show* (CBS)
Claude Thompson (make-up artist), *And Debbie Makes Six* (CBS)

OUTSTANDING INDIVIDUAL ACHIEVEMENT IN ELECTRONIC PRODUCTION

Bill Cole (audio engineer), *TCB* (NBC)
John Freschi (lighting director), *H. Andrew Williams Kaleidoscope Co.* (NBC)
Robert Guhl, Jim Stewart, Larry Jones (audio engineers), "A Hint of Darkness, A Hint of Light," *The Mod Squad* (ABC)
Arthur Schneider (video tape editor), *Rowan and Martin's Laugh-In* (NBC)
Bruce Verran and John Teele (video tape editors), *Rowan and Martin's Laugh-In* (NBC)

Special Awards

STATION AWARD
☐ *Pretty Soon Runs Out* (WHA-TV, Madison)
Appalachian Heritage (WLWT, Cincinnati)
Beggar at the Gates (WBZ-TV, Boston)
Color Me Somebody (KING-TV, Seattle)
Heal the Hurt Child (KSD-TV, St. Louis)
Job Man Caravan (SCE-TV, Columbia)
Mister Rogers' Special Program for Parents (WQED, Pittsburgh)
Operation Thanks, Parts I and II (KFMB-TV, San Diego)
☐ Indicates winner

Something for Nothing (WFIL-TV, Philadelphia)
We Are All Policemen (WNBC-TV, New York)

INTERNATIONAL AWARD
☐ (Entertainment) "A Scent of Flowers," *CBC-TV Festival* (Canadian Broadcasting Corporation, Canada)
Blesseth Is One (Hiroshima Telecasting Company, Ltd., Japan)
Pavoncello (Film Polski, Poland)
Star Quality (Thames Television Limited, England)
The Caesars—Claudius (Granada Television Limited, England)
☐ (Documentary) *The Last Campaign of Robert Kennedy* (Swiss Broadcasting and Television, Switzerland)
An Expedition into the Stone Age (Nippon Television Network, Japan)
Archaeology (Film Polski, Poland)
Christmas Eve in Biafra (Independent Television News, England)

THE SPECIAL CITATION
☐ *Assignment: The Young Greats* (WFIL-TV, Philadelphia)
Job Man Caravan (SCE-TV, Columbia)
Opportunity Line (KNXT-TV, Los Angeles)
Project Summer (WMAL-TV, Washington, D.C.)
Tell It Like It Is (KPRC-TV, Houston)
The New Generation and the Establishment (WHA-TV, Madison)
The School That Would Not Die (WDSU-TV, New Orleans)
The Urban Battleground (WIIC-TV, Pittsburgh)
To Be Somebody (WTIC-TV, Hartford)
Ya Es Tiempo (WNJU-TV, Newark)

TRUSTEES' AWARD
☐ William D. McAndrew, 1914-1968, "who shaped television news to be his permanent memorial by imposing on it early the American news tradition—honesty, bravery and public enlightenment. Television journalism took giant strides in its frist two decades under the dedicated leadership of a newsman motivated by his experience and his personality to lift its standards even higher while magnifying its public usefulness. As reporter, editor and finally president of NBC News, Bill McAndrew was always a newsman, was always an innovator and always a gentleman."
☐ Apollo VII, VIII, IX and X Space Missions; Apollo VII Astronauts **Walter Schirra, Donn Eisele, Walter Cunningham;** Apollo VIII Astronauts **Frank Borman, James A. Lovell, Jr., William A. Anders;** Apollo IX Astronauts **James A. McDivitt, David**

R. Scott, Russell L. Schweickart; Apollo X Astronauts **Thomas B. Stafford, Eugene A. Cernan, John W. Young** For sharing with the American public and the rest of the world the incredible experience of the unfolding of the mysteries of outer space and the surface of the moon via live television.

CITATION
☐ Billy Schulman. For recognition of an extraordinary achievement in the television drama, "Teacher, Teacher," presented by Hallmark Hall of Fame. Billy, who is retarded, has demonstrated that a mentally retarded person, given love and understanding, can achieve far more than anyone might have expected, and that he can indeed compete and accomplish as much or more than any youngsters his age.
☐ CBS. For the development of the digital Control Technique used in the Minicam miniaturized television color camera, which provides a new degree of mobility by permitting control via a substantially smaller and mobile connecting cable or, alternatively, a single wireless channel.

OUTSTANDING ACHIEVEMENT IN ENGINEERING DEVELOPMENT
☐ Eastman Kodak Co. for the ME-4 Process, making it possible to develop color film with greater speed and sharper images than ever before, materially facilitating the presentation of news and other programs.

News and Documentary Awards*

OUTSTANDING ACHIEVEMENT WITHIN REGULARLY SCHEDULED NEWS PROGRAMS

Programs:
☐ "Coverage of Hunger in the United States," *The Huntley-Brinkley Report* (NBC)
"Debate between Senator Robert F. Kennedy and Senator Eugene McCarthy," *Issues and Answers* (ABC)
"Recap of Senator Robert F. Kennedy Funeral," *The ABC Weekend News* (ABC)

Individuals:
☐ Charles Kuralt (correspondent), James Wilson (cameraman), Robert Funk (soundman), "On the Road," *CBS*

* possibility of one award, more than one award or no award

Evening News with Walter Cronkite (CBS)

☐ John Laurence (correspondent), "Police After Chicago," *CBS Evening News with Walter Cronkite* (CBS)

Frank Bourgholtzer (reporter), "Coverage of Russian Naval Emergence in Mediterranean," *The Frank McGee Report* (NBC)

Fred Briggs (reporter), "Coverage of the Campaign to Obtain Black Lung Compensation," *The Huntley-Brindley Report* (NBC)

Heywood Hale Broun (special correspondent), "Special Sports Reporting," *CBS Evening News with Roger Mudd—Saturday* (CBS)

John Chancellor (reporter), "Coverage of 1968 Political Campaign," *The Huntley-Brinkley Report* (NBC)

Peter Jennings (reporter), "Report on Slaughter of Baby Seals," *ABC News with Frank Reynolds* (ABC)

Frank Reynolds, "Commentaries," *ABC Evening News with Frank Reynolds* (ABC)

Morley Safer (correspondent), "Nigerian-Biafran War," *CBS Evening News with Walter Cronkite* (CBS)

Eric Sevaried (correspondent), "Analysis," *CBS Evening News with Walter Cronkite* (CBS)

Howard K. Smith, "Commentaries," *ABC Evening News with Frank Reynolds* (ABC)

Liz Trotta (reporter), "Vietnam War," *The Huntley-Brinkley Report* (NBC)

OUTSTANDING ACHIEVEMENT IN COVERAGE OF SPECIAL EVENTS

Programs:

☐ "Coverage of Martin Luther King Assassination and Aftermath," *CBS News Special Reports and Special Broadcasts* (CBS)

"Apollo: A Journey to the Moon (Flight Nos., VII, VIII and IX," *NBC News Special* (NBC)

Assassination and Funeral of Senator Robert F. Kennedy (ABC)

"Jules Bergman and Ralph Lapp Discussions on Manned Space Programs— Apollo VIII," *Space '68* (ABC)

"Chicago Democratic Convention Coverage," *NBC News Special* (NBC)

"Coverage of the Democratic Convention and Surrounding Events," *CBS News Special Reports and Special Broadcasts* (CBS)

"Coverage of Robert F. Kennedy Assassination and Aftermath," *CBS News Special Reports and Special Broadcasts* (CBS)

☐ Indicates winner

"News Analysis," *The President's Farewell* (NET)

"News Analysis," *The Nixon Administration* (NET)

"The Invasion of Czechoslovakia—August 20, 1968," *NBC News Special* (NBC)

"Unconventional Convention Coverage," *The Race to the White House* (ABC)

Individuals:

Jules Bergman (science editor), *Space '68* (ABC)

William Boyle, Dennis Dalton, Gene Farinet and Arthur Lord (writers), "Apollo: A Journey to the Moon," *NBC News Special* (NBC)

Vern Diamond (director), "Coverage of the Democratic Convention and Surrounding Events," *CBS News Special Reports and Special Broadcasts* (CBS)

Delos Hall (cameraman), "Coverage of the Democratic Convention and Surrounding Events," *CBS News Special Reports and Special Broadcasts* (CBS)

Chet Huntley, David Brinkley, Sandy Vanocur, John Chancellor, Frank McGee and Edwin Newman (news reporters), "Chicago Democratic Convention," *NBC News Special* (NBC)

William H. Lawrence (national affairs editor), *Assassination and Funeral of Senator Robert F. Kennedy* (ABC)

Frank McGee (reporter), "Apollo: A Journey to the Moon," *NBC News Special* (NBC)

Anthony Messuri (director), "Apollo: A Journey to the Moon," *NBC News Special* (NBC)

Dan Rather (reporter), "Coverage of the Democratic Convention and Surrounding Events," *CBS News Special Reports and Special Broadcasts* (CBS)

Frank Reynolds (commentator), *Assassination and Funeral of Robert F. Kennedy* (ABC)

Howard K. Smith (commentator), *The Race to the White House* (ABC)

Mike Wallace (reporter), "Coverage of the Democratic Convention and Surrounding Events," *CBS News Special Reports and Special Broadcasts* (CBS)

OUTSTANDING NEWS DOCUMENTARY PROGRAM ACHIEVEMENT

Programs:

☐ "CBS Reports: Hunger in America," *CBS News Hour* (CBS)

☐ "Law and Order," *Public Broadcast Laboratory* (NET)

"Appalachia: Rich Land, Poor People," *Net Journal* (NET)

"Bias and the Mass Media, Part I," *Time for Americans* (ABC)

"CBS Reports: Campaign American Style," *CBS News Hour* (CBS)

"Cities Have No Limits," *White Paper: The Ordeal of the American City* (NBC)

Elegy and Memory (ABC)

"Free at last (Martin Luther King)," *Public Broadcast Laboratory* (NET)

"Hanoi: A Report by Charles Collingwood," *CBS News Hour* (CBS)

Heart Attack! (ABC)

"Home Country, USA," *American Profile* (NBC)

Robert Kennedy Remembered (ABC, CBS, NBC)

"Of Black America," *CBS News Hour* (CBS)

"Russia in the Mediterranean," *NBC News Special* (NBC)

"Still a Brother," *NET Journal* (NET)

"The Cities: A City Is to Live in, Dilemma in Black and White, To Build the Future," *CBS News Hour* (CBS)

View from Space (ABC)

"The Whole World is Watching," *Public Broadcasting Laboratory* (NET)

Individuals:

☐ Perry Wolff and Andy Rooney (writers) "Black History: Lost Stolen or Strayed—Of Black America," *CBS News Hour* (CBS)

Charles Austin (cinematographer), "Cities Have No Limits," *White Paper: The Ordeal of the American City* (NBC)

Mili Bonsignori (film editor), "CBS Reports. Hunger in America," *CBS News Hour* (CBS)

Mili Bonsignori and Morton Rosenfeld (film editors), *View from Space* (ABC)

Rene Bras (animation) *View from Space* (ABC)

Bill Brayne (cameraman), "Law and Order," *Public Broadcast laboratory* (NET)

Charles Collingwood (reporter), "Hanoi: A Report by Charles Collingwood," *CBS News Hour* (CBS)

David Culhane (reporter), "CBS Reports: Hunger in America," *CBS News Hour* (CBS)

Joseph Louw (reporter), "Free at Last (Martin Luther King)," *Public Broadcast Laboratory* (NET)

Desmond McElroy and Darold Murray (film editors), *Home Country, USA— American Profile* (NBC)

Darold Murray (supervising film editor), "Cities Have No Limits," *White Paper: The Ordeal of the American City* (NBC)

Richard Norling (cameraman), Home Country USA—*American Profile* (NBC)

Richard Roy (cameraman), *Heart Attack!* (ABC)

Frederick Wiseman (director), "Law and Order," *Public Broadcast Laboratory* (NET)

Frederick Wiseman (writer), "Law and Order," *Public Broadcast Laboratory* (NET)

OUTSTANDING CULTURAL DOCUMENTARY AND "MAGAZINE-TYPE" PROGRAMS OR SERIES ACHIEVEMENT

Programs:

☐ "Don't Count the Candles," *CBS News Hour* (CBS)

☐ "Justice Black and The Bill of Rights," *CBS News Hour* (CBS)

☐ "Man Who Dances: Edward Villella," *Bell Telephone Hour* (NBC)

☐ "The Great American Novel," *CBS News Hour* (CBS)

"Birth and Death," *Public Broadcast Laboratory* (NET)

"Black Journal No. 1," *NET Journal* (NET)

Children's Letters to God (NBC)

"Cosmopolis: Big City, 2000 A.D.," *Man and His Universe* (ABC)

"Down to the Sea in Ships," *Project XX* (NBC)

"Ecce Homo," *The Southern Baptist Hour* (NBC)

First Tuesday (NBC)

Hemingway's Spain—A Love Affair (ABC)

How Life Begins (ABC)

"Ingmar Bergman Interview," *Public Broadcast Laboratory* (NET)

"Jazz: The Intimate Art," *Bell Telephone Hour* (NBC)

Jesse Owens Returns to Berlin (Syndicated)

John Steinbeck's Travels with Charley (NBC)

"Love in a Sexy Society," *One Reach One* (Syndicated)

"Margaret Mead's New Guinea Journal," *NET Festival* (NET)

"Once Upon a Wall—The Great Age of Fresco," *CBS News Hour* (CBS)

One Nation Indivisible (Syndicated)

One Reach One (Syndicated)

"Rembrandt and the Bible," *Directions* (ABC)

"Reptiles and Amphibians" *National Geographic Special* (CBS)

60 Minutes (CBS)

"Sunken Treasure," *The Undersea World of Jacques Cousteau* (ABC)

☐ Indicates winner

The Actor (ABC)

"The American Alcoholic," *NBC News Special* (NBC)

"The Big Little World of Roman Vishniac," *NBC News Special* (NBC)

The Confrontation (ABC)

"The Endless Thread," *One Reach One* (Syndicated)

"The New Voices of Watts," *NBC Experiment in Television* (NBC)

"The Road to Gettysburg," *The Saga of Western Man* (ABC)

"The Savage Heart: A Conversation with Eric Hoffer," *CBS News Hour* (CBS)

The Secret of Michelangelo: Every Man's Dream (ABC)

The Sense of Wonder (ABC)

"The Unexpected Voyage of Pepito and Cristobal," *The Undersea World of Jacques Cousteau* (ABC)

"Whales," *The Undersea World of Jacques Cousteau* (ABC)

"What Color is the Wind," *NBC Experiment in Television* (NBC)

What Manner of Man (Syndicated)

Individuals:

☐ Walter Dombrow and Jerry Sims (cinematographers), "The Great American Novel," *CBS News Hour* (CBS)

☐ Tom Petit (producer), "CBW: The Secrets of Secrecy," *First Tuesday* (NBC)

☐ Lord Snowdon (cinematographer), "Don't Count the Candles," *CBS News Hour* (CBS)

☐ Ralph Bellamy (host), *One Reach One* (Syndicated)

Warren V. Bush (writer), "Sunken Treasure," *The Undersea World of Jacques Cousteau* (ABC)

Patrick Carey, Ron Headford, James Godfrey and Lewis McLeod (cameramen) *Hemingway's Spain— A Love Affair* (ABC)

Walt DeFaria and Sheldon Fay, Jr. (directors), *John Steinbeck's Travels with Charley* (NBC)

Walter Essenfeld, Nils Rasmussen and Samuel Cohen (film editors), "The Road to Gettysburg," *The Saga of Western Man* (ABC)

Joseph Fackovec, Reg Browne and Pierre Vacho (film editors), *What Manner of Man* (Syndicated)

Sheldon Fay, Jr. (cameraman), *John Steinbeck's Travels with Charley* (NBC)

Arthur Fillmore and Laszlo Pal (cameramen), *What Manner of Man* (Syndicated)

Milton A. Fruchtman (director), *The Secret of Michelangelo: Every Man's Dream* (ABC)

Craig Gilbert (director), "Margaret Mead's New Guinea Journal," *NET Festival* (NET)

Craig Gilbert (writer), "Margaret Mead's New Guinea Journal," *NET Festival* (NET)

Leon Gluckman (director), *The Actor* (ABC)

Allan Grant (cameraman), "What Color Is the Wind?" *NBC Experiment in Television* (NBC)

Marshall Flaum (writer) "What Color Is the Wind?" *NBC Experiment in Television* (NBC)

Bud Greenspan (director), *Jesse Owens Returns to Berlin* (Syndicated)

Bud Greenspan (writer), *Jesse Owens Returns to Berlin* (Syndicated)

William B. Hartigan (cameraman), "The Road to Gettysburg," *The Saga of Western Man* (ABC)

Dick Hubert, Sr. (writer), *One Nation Indivisible* (Syndicated)

Mike Jackson (director), "Man Who Dances: Edward Villella," *Bell Telephone Hour* (NBC)

Norton Juster and Stuart Hample (writers), *Children's Letters to God* (NBC)

Alan Landsburg and Walon Green (writers), "Reptiles and Amphibians," *National Geographic Special* (CBS)

Jules Laventhol (film editor), "Don't Count the Candles," *CBS News Hour* (CBS)

Richard Leiterman (director of photography), "Margaret Mead's New Guinea Journal," *NET Festival* (NET)

Abbot Mills (cameraman), "Man Who Dances: Edward Villella," *Bell Telephone Hour* (NBC)

John Oettinger, Frank Host, Paul Galan (film editors), *One Nation Indivisible* (Syndicated)

Laurence D. Savadove (writer), "Whales," *The Undersea World of Jacques Cousteau* (ABC)

John H. Secondari (writer), "Cosmopolis: Big City, 2000 A.D.," *Man and His Universe* (ABC)

John H. Secondari (writer), "The Road to Gettysburg," *The Saga of Western Man* (ABC)

John Soh (film editor), "Whales" and "Sunken Treasure," *The Undersea World of Jacques Cousteau* (ABC)

John Steinbeck (writer), *John Steinbeck's Travels with Charley* (NBC)

Shelby Storck (narrator), *What Manner of Man* (Syndicated)

Shelby Storck (writer), *What Manner of Man* (Syndicated)

Walker Stuart (director), *Hemingway's Spain—A Love Affair* (ABC)

John Teeple (film editor), "Ecce Homo," *The Southern Baptist Hour* (NBC)

Thomas Tomizawa (producer), "College for the New Generation," *First Tuesday* (NBC)

Kenneth Tynan (writer), "The Actor," (ABC)

Joseph Vadala (photographer), "Ecce Homo" *The Southern Baptist Hour* (NBC)

Mike Wallace and Harry Reasoner (reporters), "60 Minutes," *CBS News Hour* (CBS)

1969/70

(Presented June 7, 1970 for programs aired between March 17, 1969 and March 15, 1970)

Entertainment Program Awards

OUTSTANDING COMEDY SERIES
☐ *My World and Welcome To It* (NBC)
The Bill Cosby Show (NBC)
The Courtship of Eddie's Father (ABC)
Love, American Style (ABC)
Room 222 (ABC)

OUTSTANDING DRAMATIC SERIES
☐ *Marcus Welby, M.D.* (ABC)
The Forsyte Saga (NET)
Ironside (NBC)
The Mod Squad (ABC)
The Name of the Game (NBC)
NET Playhouse (NET)

OUTSTANDING DRAMATIC PROGRAM
☐ "A Storm in Summer," *Hallmark Hall of Fame* (NBC)
David Copperfield (NBC)
"Hello, Goodbye, Hello," *Marcus Welby, M.D.* (ABC)
My Sweet Charlie (NBC)

OUTSTANDING VARIETY OR MUSICAL SERIES
☐ *The David Frost Show* (Syndicated)
The Carol Burnett Show (CBS)
The Dean Martin Show (NBC)
The Dick Cavett Show (ABC)
Rowan and Martin's Laugh-In (NBC)

OUTSTANDING VARIETY OR MUSICAL PROGRAM
Variety and popular music:
☐ *Annie, The Women in the Life of a Man* (CBS)
The Friars Club "Roasts" Jack Benny (NBC)
The Second Bill Cosby Special (NBC)
Sinatra (CBS)
The Sound of Burt Bacharach (NBC)
☐ Indicates winner

Classical music:
☐ *Cinderella.* National Ballet of Canada (NET)
S. Hurok Presents—Part III (CBS)
Sounds of Summer (NET)
The Switched-On Symphony (NBC)

OUTSTANDING NEW SERIES
☐ *Room 222* (ABC)
The Bill Cosby Show (NBC)
The Forsyte Saga (NET)
Marcus Welby, M.D. (ABC)
Sesame Street (NET)

Entertainment Performance Awards

OUTSTANDING SINGLE PERFORMANCE BY AN ACTOR IN A LEADING ROLE
☐ Peter Ustinov, "A Storm in Summer," *Hallmark Hall of Fame* (NBC)
Al Freeman Jr. *My Sweet Charlie* (NBC)
Laurence Olivier, *David Copperfield* (NBC)

OUTSTANDING SINGLE PERFORMANCE BY AN ACTRESS IN A LEADING ROLE
☐ Patty Duke, *My Sweet Charlie* (NBC)
Dame Edith Evans, *David Copperfield* (NBC)
Shirley Jones, *Silent Night, Lonely Night* (NBC)

OUTSTANDING CONTINUED PERFORMANCE BY AN ACTOR IN A LEADING ROLE IN A DRAMATIC SERIES
☐ Robert Young, *Marcus Welby, M.D.* (ABC)
Raymond Burr, *Ironside* (NBC)
Mike Connors, *Mannix* (CBS)
Robert Wagner, *It Takes a Thief* (ABC)

OUTSTANDING CONTINUED PERFORMANCE BY AN ACTRESS IN A LEADING ROLE IN A DRAMATIC SERIES
☐ Susan Hampshire, *The Forsyte Saga* (NET)
Joan Blondell, *Here Come the Brides* (ABC)
Peggy Lipton, *The Mod Squad* (ABC)

OUTSTANDING CONTINUED PERFORMANCE BY AN ACTOR IN A LEADING ROLE IN A COMEDY SERIES
☐ William Windom, *My World and Welcome To It* (NBC)
Bill Cosby, *The Bill Cosby Show* (NBC)
Lloyd Haynes, *Room 222* (ABC)

OUTSTANDING CONTINUED PERFORMANCE BY AN ACTRESS IN A LEADING ROLE IN A COMEDY SERIES
☐ Hope Lange, *The Ghost and Mrs. Muir* (ABC)

Elizabeth Montgomery, *Bewitched* (ABC)
Marlo Thomas, *That Girl* (ABC)

OUTSTANDING PERFORMANCE BY AN ACTOR IN A SUPPORTING ROLE IN DRAMA
☐ James Brolin, *Marcus Welby, M.D.* (ABC)
Tige Andrews, *The Mod Squad* (ABC)
Greg Morris, *Mission: Impossible* (CBS)

OUTSTANDING PERFORMANCE BY AN ACTRESS IN A SUPPORTING ROLE IN DRAMA
☐ Gail Fisher, *Mannix* (CBS)
Barbara Anderson, *Ironside* (NBC)
Susan Saint James, *The Name of the Game* (NBC)

OUTSTANDING PERFORMANCE BY AN ACTOR IN A SUPPORTING ROLE IN COMEDY
☐ Michael Constantine, *Room 222* (ABC)
Werner Klemperer, *Hogan's Heroes* (CBS)
Charles Nelson Reilly, *The Ghost and Mrs. Muir* (ABC)

OUTSTANDING PERFORMANCE BY AN ACTRESS IN A SUPPORTING ROLE IN COMEDY
☐ Karen Valentine, *Room 222* (ABC)
Agnes Moorehead, *Bewitched* (ABC)
Lurene Tuttle, *Julia* (NBC)

Entertainment Craft and Technical Awards

OUTSTANDING WRITING ACHIEVEMENT IN DRAMA
☐ Richard Levinson, William Link, *My Sweet Charlie* (NBC)
George Bellak, "Sadbird," *CBS Playhouse* (CBS)
Don M. Mankiewicz, "Marcus Welby, M.D.," *The ABC Wednesday Night Movie* (ABC)

OUTSTANDING WRITTING ACHIEVEMENT IN COMEDY, VARIETY OR MUSIC
☐ Gary Belkin, Peter Bellwood, Herb Sargent, Thomas Meehan, Judith Viorst, *Annie, The Women in the Life of a Man* (CBS)
Paul W. Keyes, David Panich, Marc London, Coslough Johnson, Jim Carlson, Jim Mulligan, John Carsey, Gene Farmer, Jeremy Lloyd, John Rappaport, Stephen Spears, Jack Douglas, Allan Manings, *Rowan and Martin's Laugh-In* (with Buddy Hackett) (NBC)
Allan Manings, David Panich, Coslough Johnson, John Carsey, Stephen Spears, John Rappaport, Jim Carlson, Marc London, Chet Dowling, Jim Abell, Barry Took, Jack

Douglas, Jim Mulligan, Gene Farmer, Jeremy Lloyd, *Rowan and Martin's Laugh-In* (with Nancy Sinatra) (NBC)

OUTSTANDING DIRECTORIAL ACHIEVEMENT IN DRAMA

☐ Paul Bogart, "Shadow Game," *CBS Playhouse* (CBS)

Buzz Kulik, "A Storm in Summer," *Hallmark Hall of Fame* (NBC)

Lamont Johnson, *My Sweet Charlie* (NBC)

OUTSTANDING DIRECTORIAL ACHIEVEMENT IN COMEDY, VARIETY OR MUSIC

☐ Dwight A. Hemion, "The Sound of Burt Bacharach," *Kraft Music Hall* (NBC)

Seymour Berns, *The Second Bill Cosby Special* (NBC)

Roger Englander, "Berlioz Takes A Trip," *N.Y. Philharmonic Young People's Concerts* (CBS)

OUTSTANDING ACHIEVEMENT IN CHOREOGRAPHY

☐ Morman Maen, *This Is Tom Jones* (ABC)

Tom Hansen, *The Red Skelton Show* (with Walter Brennan) (CBS)

David Winters, *Ann Margret—From Hollywood with Love* (CBS)

OUTSTANDING ACHIEVEMENT IN MUSIC COMPOSITION

For a series or a single program of a series (in its first year only):

☐ Morton Stevens, "A Thousand Pardons, You're Dead," *Hawaii Five-O* (CBS)

Quincy Jones, *The Bill Cosby Show* (NBC)

Franklyn Marks, "Charlie, The Lonesome Cougar," *The Wonderful World of Disney* (NBC)

For a special program:

☐ Pete Rugolo, "The Challengers," *CBS Friday Night Movie* (CBS)

Van Alexander, *Gene Kelly's Wonderful World of Girls With 50 Girls, Count 'Em, 50* (NBC)

Jacques Belasco, "The Threshold," *Apollo: Journey To the Moon* (NBC)

OUTSTANDING ACHIEVEMENT IN MUSIC DIRECTION OF A VARIETY, MUSICAL OR DRAMATIC PROGRAM

☐ Peter Matz, "The Sound of Burt Bacharach," *Kraft Music Hall* (NBC)

Mort Lindsey, *The Merv Griffin Show* (with Chuck Connors, Joey Heatherton, Buddy Greco, Jack E. Leonard, Jerry Van Dyke) (CBS)

Johnnie Spence, *This Is Tom Jones* (ABC)

☐ Indicates winner

OUTSTANDING ACHIEVEMENT IN MUSIC, LYRICS AND SPECIAL MATERIAL

For a single program of a series or a special program written for television:

☐ Arnold Margolin, Charles Fox, *Love, American Style* (ABC)

Charles Aidman, Naomi C. Hirshhorn, *Spoon River* (CBS)

Billy Barnes, *Rowan and Martin's Laugh-In* (with Carol Channing) (NBC)

OUTSTANDING ACHIEVEMENT IN ART DIRECTION OR SCENIC DESIGN

For a dramatic program or feature length film made for television for a series, a single program of a series or a special program:

☐ Jan Scott (art director), Earl Carlson (set decorator), "Shadow Game," *CBS Playhouse* (CBS)

Gibson Holley (art director), Lucien M. Hafley (set decorator), "The Falcon" (3 parts), *Mission: Impossible* (CBS)

Hugh Gray Raisky (art director), Wesley Laws (set decorator), *Man on the Moon: The Epic Journey of Apollo XI* (CBS)

James Trittipo (art director), "The File on Devlin," *Hallmark Hall* (NBC)

OUTSTANDING ACHIEVEMENT IN ART DIRECTION OR SCENIC DESIGN

For a musical or variety single program of a series or a special program:

☐ E. Jay Krause (art director) *Mitzi's 2nd Special* (NBC)

Paul Barnes and Robert Sansom (art directors), Bill Harp (set decorator), *The Carol Burnett Show* (CBS)

Rene Lagler (art director), Robert Checchi (set decorator), *The Glen Campbell Goodtime Hour* (with Tom Jones, Totie Fields, Jackie DeShannon) (CBS)

OUTSTANDING ACHIEVEMENT IN LIGHTING DIRECTION

☐ Leard Davis, Ed Hill "Appalachian Autumn," *CBS Playhouse* (CBS)

John Freschi, *The Switched-On Symphony* (NBC)

Jim Kilgore, *The Johnny Cash Show* (with Rod McKuen, the Everly Brothers, Dusty Springfield) (ABC)

William Klages, *Kraft Music Hall* (with Petula Clark, Anthony Newley, Lou Rawls) (NBC)

OUTSTANDING ACHIEVEMENT IN COSTUME DESIGN

☐ Bod Mackie, *Diana Ross and the Supremes and the Temptations on Broadway* (NBC)

Michael Travis, *Rowan and Martin's Laugh-In* (with Danny Kaye) (NBC)

George R. Whittaker, *The Don Adams Special: Hooray for Hollywood* (CBS)

OUTSTANDING ACHIEVEMENT IN MAKE-UP

☐ Ray Sebastien, Louis A. Phillippi, *The Don Adams Special: Hooray for Hollywood* (CBS)

Shirley Muslin, Marie Roche, *This is Tom Jones* (with Mary Hopkins, Jose Feliciano, Shelley Berman) (ABC)

OUTSTANDING ACHIEVEMENT IN CINEMATOGRAPHY FOR ENTERTAINMENT PROGRAMMING

☐ Walter Strenge, "Hello, Goodbye, Hello," *Marcus Welby, M.D.* (ABC)

Harvey Genkins, *N.Y.P.D.* (ABC)

Al Francis, "The Amnesiac," *Mission Impossible* (CBS)

OUTSTANDING ACHIEVEMENT IN CINEMATOGRAPHY FOR ENTERTAINMENT PROGRAMMING

For a special or feature length program made for television:

☐ Lionel Lindon, "Ritual of Evil," *NBC Monday Night at the Movies* (NBC)

Gene Polito, "My Sweet Charlie," *World Premiere* (NBC)

Howard R. Schwartz, "The Immortal," *ABC Movie of the Week* (ABC)

OUTSTANDING ACHIEVEMENT IN CINEMATOGRAPHY FOR NEWS AND DOCUMENTARY PROGRAMMING

For a regularly scheduled news programs and coverage of special events:

☐ Edward Winkle, "Model Hippie," *The Huntley-Brinkley Report* (NBC)

Charles W. Boyle, "Middle Town U.S.A.," *The Huntley-Brinkley Report* (NBC)

James P. Watt Jr., "High School Profile," *The Huntley-Brinkley Report* (NBC)

For a documentary, magazine-type or mini-documentary programs:

☐ Thomas A. Priestley, *Sahara: La Caravane du Sel* (NBC)

Chuck Austin, ASC, "The Ordeal of the American City—Confrontation," *NBC White Paper* (NBC)

Ronald W. Van Nostrand, "Hide and Go Seek," *First Tuesday* (NBC)

OUTSTANDING ACHIEVEMENT IN FILM EDITING FOR ENTERTAINMENT PROGRAMMING

For a series or a single program of a series:

☐ Bill Mosher, "Sweet Smell of Failure," *Bracken's World* (NBC)

Arthur David Hilton, "The Falcon" (3 parts), *Mission: Impossible* (CBS)

Axel R. Hubert, "The Great Power Failure," *The Ghost and Mrs. Muir* (ABC)

For a special or feature length program made for television:

☐ Edward M. Abroms, "My Sweet Charlie," *World Premiere* (NBC)

Igo Kantor, James Henrikson, Stan Siegel, Tony Carras, Frank McKelvey, *Bob Hope Christmas Special* (NBC)

Gene Palmer, "Marcus Welby, M.D.," *ABC Wednesday Night Movie* (ABC)

For a regularly scheduled news programs and coverage of special events:

☐ Michael C. Shugrue, "The High School Profile," *The Huntley-Brinkley Report* (NBC)

Raymond L. Elberfeld and Richard A. Hessel, "Eisenhower Funeral," *The Huntley-Brinkley Report* (NBC)

Fred Flamenhalt, Martin Sheppard, Tom Dunphy, Pat Minerva, Ken Shea, George Johnson, *The Huntley-Brinkley Report* (NBC)

For documentary, magazine-type or mini-documentary programs:

☐ John Soh, "The Desert Whales," *The Undersea World of Jacques Cousteau* (ABC)

Peter C. Johnson, *The Mystery of Animal Behavior* (CBS)

Robert B. Loweree and Hank Grennon, *Arthur Rubinstein* (NBC)

OUTSTANDING ACHIEVEMENT IN FILM SOUND EDITING

☐ Douglas H. Grindstaff, Alex Bamattre, Michael Colgan, Bill Lee, Joe Kavigan, Josef E. Von Stroheim, "The Immortal," *Movie of the Week* (ABC)

☐ Richard E. Raderman, Norman Karlin, "Charlie Noon," *Gunsmoke* (CBS)

Don Hall, Jr., Larry Meek, William Howard, John Kline, Robert Cornett, Frank R. White, "A Small War," *Land of the Giants* (ABC)

OUTSTANDING ACHIEVEMENT IN FILM SOUND MIXING

☐ Gordon L. Day, Dominick Gaffey, "The Submarine," *Mission: Impossible* (CBS)

Melvin M. Metcalfe, Sr., John A. Stransky, Jr., Clarence Self, Roger Heman, "My Sweet Charlie," *World Premiere* (NBC)

Roger Gary Andrews, "Some Footnotes to 25 Nuclear Years," *First Tuesday* (NBC)

☐ Indicates winner

OUTSTANDING ACHIEVEMENT IN LIVE OR TAPE SOUND MIXING

☐ Bill Cole, Dave Williams, *The Switched-On Symphony* (NBC)

Mahlon H. Fox, "The Sound of Burt Bacharach," *Kraft Music Hall* (NBC)

Neal Weinstein, *The Jim Nabors Hour* (with Vickki Carr) (CBS)

OUTSTANDING ACHIEVEMENT IN VIDEO TAPE EDITING

☐ John Shultis, "The Sound of Burt Bacharach," *Kraft Music Hall* (NBC)

Nick Giordano, "Finale," *The Hollywood Palace* (ABC)

Armond Poitras, *An Evening with Julie Andrews and Harry Belafonte* (NBC)

OUTSTANDING ACHIEVEMENT IN TECHNICAL DIRECTION AND ELECTRONIC CAMERAWORK

☐ Heino Ripp (technical director), Al Camonin, Gene Martin, Donald Mulvaney and Cal Shadwell (cameramen), "The Sound of Burt Bacharach," *Kraft Music Hall* (NBC)

Charles Franklin and Ken Lamkin (technical directors), Robert Fonarow, Nick DeMos and Ben Wolf (cameramen), "A Storm in Summer," *Hallmark Hall of Fame* (NBC)

O. Tamburri (technical director), Gene Schwartz, Robert Keyes, Kurt Tonnessen, Ronald Sheldon, Roy Holm and Wayne Osterhout (cameramen), *An Evening with Julie Andrews and Harry Belafonte* (NBC)

The Areas*

OUTSTANDING ACHIEVEMENT IN CHILDREN'S PROGRAMMING

Programs:

☐ *Sesame Street* (NET)

The Wonderful World of Disney (NBC)

Individuals:

☐ Joe Raposo and Jeffrey Moss (music and lyrics), "This Way to Sesame Street," *Sesame Street* (NET)

☐ Jon Stone, Jeffrey Moss, Ray Sipherd, Jerry Juhl, Dan Wilcox, Dave Connell, Bruce Hart, Carole Hart and Virginia Schone (writers), "Sally Sees Sesame Street," *Sesame Street* (NET)

Michael Loewenstein (scenic design), *Kukla, Fran and Ollie* (NET)

OUTSTANDING ACHIEVEMENT IN DAYTIME PROGRAMMING

Programs:

☐ *Today* (NBC)

The Galloping Gourmet (Syndicated)

Individuals:

Hugh Downs, *Today* (NBC)

* possibility of one award, more than one award or no award

Joe Garagiola, *Today* (NBC)

OUTSTANDING ACHIEVEMENT IN SPORTS PROGRAMMING

Programs:

☐ *The NFL Games* (CBS)

☐ *ABC'S Wide World of Sports* (ABC)

1969 World Series (NBC)

Individuals:

☐ Robert R. Forte (film editing), "Pre-game Program," *Pro-Bowl Games* (CBS)

Robert Riger (director), "International Ski Championships Val D'Isere, France," *ABC's Wide World of Sports* (ABC)

SPECIAL CLASSIFICATION OF OUTSTANDING PROGRAM AND INDIVIDUAL ACHIEVEMENT

Programs:

☐ *Mutual of Omaha's Wild Kingdom* (NBC)

☐ "Fellini—A Director's Notebook," *NBC Experiment in Television* (NBC)

Individuals:

Goldie Hawn, *Rowan and Martin's Laugh-In* (NBC)

Arte Johnson, *Rowan and Martin's Laugh-In* (NBC)

OUTSTANDING ACHIEVEMENT IN ANY AREA OF CREATIVE TECHNICAL CRAFTS

Jonnie Burke (special visual effects), "Time Bomb," *Mission: Impossible* (CBS)

Howard A. Anderson, Jr., Wilfrid Cline and Bill Hansard (special photographic effects), "Rally 'Round the Flag Boys," *My World and Welcome To It* (NBC)

Edie J. Panda (hair styling), *The Don Adams Special—Hooray for Hollywood* (CBS)

Special Awards

OUTSTANDING ACHIEVEMENT IN ENGINEERING DEVELOPMENT

Apollo color television from space. For the conceptual aspects, an Emmy Award was presented to the Video Communication Division of NASA, and for development of the camera, an Emmy Award was presented to the Westinghouse Electric Corporation.

Citation:

Ampex Corporation for the development of the HS-200 color television production system.

THE STATION AWARD

☐ *The Slow Guillotine* (KNBC-TV, Los Angeles)

City in Crisis (WDSU-TV, New Orleans)

Job Man Caravan (SCE-TV, Columbia)

Journey to a Pine Box (WRC-TV, Washington, D.C.)
New Voices in the Wilderness (WNBC-TV, New York)
The Savage Root (WBZ-TV, Boston)
Urban Mythology (WGTV, Athens)
A Visit to Allenville (KOOL-TV, Phoenix)
Young, Black and Explosive (KOMO-TV, Seattle)

Special Citation:
□ *The Other Americans* (WJZ-TV Baltimore)
Honorable Mention—Young, Black and Explosive (KOMO-TV, Seattle)
The Children Are Waiting (WBBM-TV, Chicago)
The First Step (WETK-TV, Winooski, Vermont)
Sickle Cell Anemia (WABC-TV, New York)
What's So Special About Warrendale (WIIC-TV, Pittsburgh)
Whose Museum (KPIX-TV, San Francisco)

THE TRUSTEES AWARD
The Presidents of television's network News Division, the personnel of NASA and the 3M Company were each honored with special awards by the Trustees of the National Academy of Television Arts and Sciences at the annual Emmy Awards ceremonies:
The Trustees Award presented to the Presidents of the News Divisions cited them for "safeguarding the public's right to full information, at a time when the constitutional right of freedom of the press is under its strongest attack."
The first two Trustee Citations went to the hundreds of men comprising the staff of NASA who were saluted for television coverage of the Apollo II moon landing which "made it possible for hundreds of millions of people throughout the world to witness history being made 238,000 miles away."
The Trustees of the Academy also cited the 3M Company for "having presented some of the finest art, cultural, scientific and entertainment programs in the public interest. This company has contributed significantly to upgrading the quality of television while presenting its sales message with modesty and taste."

□ Indicates winner

News and Documentary Program and Individual Achievement*

OUTSTANDING ACHIEVEMENT WITHIN REGULARLY SCHEDULED NEWS PROGRAMS

Programs:
□ "An Investigation of Teenage Drug Addiction—Odyseey House," *The Huntley-Brinkley Report* (NBC)
□ "Can the World Be Saved?" *CBS Evening News with Walter Cronkite* (CBS)
"Chicago Conspiracy Trial," *CBS Evening News with Walter Cronkite* (CBS)
"Coverage of Hurricane Camille," *ABC Evening News with Frank Reynolds and Howard K. Smith* (ABC)
"Coverage of the Nigerian/Biafran Conflict," *ABC Evening News with Frank Reynolds and Howard K. Smith* (ABC)
The Huntley-Brinkley Report (NBC)
"J. Edgar Hoover and the FBI," *CBS Morning News with Joseph Benti* (CBS)
"Man and His Environment," *ABC Evening News with Frank Reynolds and Howard K. Smith* (ABC)
"Moratorium and the Silent Majority," *ABC Evening News with Frank Reynolds and Howard K. Smith* (ABC)

Individuals:
Heywood Hale Broun (special correspondent), "Special Sports Reporting," *CBS Evening News with Roger Mudd* (CBS)
John Chancellor (correspondent), "Coverage of the Poison Grain Incident," *The Huntley-Brinkley Report* (NBC)
Robert Goralski (correspondent), "Investigation of the Green Beret Case," *The Huntley-Brinkley Report* (NBC)
Chet Huntley (correspondent), "Coverage of the West German Elections," *The Huntley-Brinkley Report* (NBC)
Frank Reynolds, Howard K. Smith, "News Commentaries," *ABC Evening News with Frank Reynolds and Howard K. Smith* (ABC)
Mike Wallace (correspondent), "Interviews with Meadlo and Medina," *Evening News with Walter Cronkite* (CBS)

* possibility of one award, more than one award or no award

OUTSTANDING ACHIEVEMENT IN COVERAGE OF SPECIAL EVENTS

Programs:
□ *Apollo: A Journey to the Moon* (NBC)
□ *Solar Eclipse: A Darkness at Noon* (NBC)
Coverage of the ABM Hearings (NBC)
Dwight David Eisenhower: 1890-1969 (CBS)
Footsteps on the Moon: The Flight of Apollo XI (ABC)
Man on the Moon: The Epic Journey of Apollo XI (CBS)
Mr. Nixon in Asia (ABC)
Solar Eclipse: Darkness at Midday (ABC)

Individuals:
□ Walter Cronkite (reporter), *Man on the Moon: The Epic Journey of Apollo XI* (CBS)
Joel Banow (director), *Man on the Moon: The Epic Journey of Apollo XI* (CBS)
Jules Bergman (co anchorman), *Footsteps on the Moon: The Flight of Apollo XI* (ABC)
Frank McGee, Chet Huntley and David Brinkley (reporters), *Apollo: A Journey to the Moon* (NBC)
John Chancellor, Frank McGee and Jack Perkins (reporters), *Solar Eclipse: A Darkness at Noon* (NBC)
Gene Farinet, Dennis Dalton, Arthur Lord and Ken Donoghue (writers), *Apollo: A Journey to the Moon* (NBC)
Robert J. Le Donne (news editor), *Footsteps on the Moon: The Flight of Apollo XI* (ABC)
Larry Pickard (news editor), *Footsteps on the Moon: The Flight of Apollo XI* (ABC)
Frank Reynolds (co-anchorman), *Footsteps on the Moon: The Flight of Apollo XI* (ABC)
Fred Rheinstein (director), *Solar Eclipse: A Darkness at Noon* (NBC)
Walter M. Schirra, Jr. (commentator), *Man on the Moon: The Epic Journey of Apollo XI* (CBS)

OUTSTANDING ACHIEVEMENT IN NEWS DOCUMENTARY PROGRAMMING

Programs:
□ "Hospital," *Net Journal* (NET)
□ *The Making of the President, 1968* (CBS)
"Abortion," *Summer Focus* (ABC)
Adventures at the Jade Sea (CBS)
"The Battle of East St. Louis," *CBS News Hours* (CBS)
"Black Fiddler: Prejudice and the Negro": *Summer Focus* (ABC)
"CBS Reports: A Timetable for Vietnam," *CBS News Hour* (CBS)

"Do You Think a Job Is the Answer,"
Public Broadcast Laboratory (NET)

"Fasten Your Seatbelts," *NET Journal*
(NET)

From Here to the Seventies (NBC)

*The Great Dollar Robbery: Can We
Arrest Inflation?* (ABC)

"LBJ: Why I Chose Not to Run," *CBS
News Hour* (CBS)

*The Natural History of Our World: The
Time of Man* (CBS)

"The Ordeal of the American City—
Confrontation," *NBC White Paper*
(NBC)

"The Walting Game," *Lifewatch Six*
(Syndicated)

"Who Invited Us?" *NET Journal* (NET)

Who Killed Lake Erie? (NBC)

"Who Speaks for Man?" *NET Journal*
(NET)

"Wild River," *National Geographic
Special* (CBS)

Individuals:

□ Frederick Wiseman (director),
"Hospital," *NET Journal* (NET)

Richard Basehart (narrator), *The
Natural History of Our World: The
Time of Man* (CBS)

Charles Collingwood (reporter), "CBS
Reports: A Timetable for Vietnam,"
CBS News Hour (CBS)

Walter Cronkite (reporter), "LBJ: Why I
Chose Not to Run," *CBS News
Hour* (CBS)

Peter Davis (writer), "The Battle of
East St. Louis," *CBS News Hour*
(CBS)

Marshall Flaum (writer), *The Natural
History of Our World: The Time of
Man* (CBS)

Gary Gilson (reporter-writer), "Do You
Think a Job Is the Answer?" *Public
Broadcast Laboratory* (NET)

Douglas Leiterman (writer-director),
Fasten Your Seatbelts (NET)

Frank McGee (reporter), "The Ordeal
of the American City—
Confrontation," *NBC White Paper*
(NBC)

Frank McGee (reporter), *Who Killed
Lake Erie?* (NBC)

NBC News Team (commentators),
From Here to the Seventies (NBC)

Robert Northshield (writer), *From Here
to the Seventies* (NBC)

Hughes Rudd (reporter), "The Battle
of East St. Louis," *CBS News Hour*
(CBS)

Louis Rukeyser (correspondent-writer),
*The Great Dollar Robbery: Can We
Arrest Inflation* (ABC)

David Seltzer (writer), *Adventures at
the Jade Sea* (CBS)

Arthur Zegart (writer-director), "Who
Speaks for Man?" *NET Journal*
(NET)

□ Indicates winner

OUTSTANDING ACHIEVEMENT IN MAGAZINE-TYPE PROGRAMMING

Programs:

□ *Black Journal* (NET)

60 Minutes (CBS)

"Some Footnotes to 25 Nuclear
Years," *First Tuesday* (NBC)

"Voices on the Inside," *First Tuesday*
(NBC)

Individuals:

□ Tom Pettit (reporter-writer), "Some
Footnotes to 25 Nuclear Years,"
First Tuesday (NBC)

Len Giovannitti and Rafael Abramovitz
(directors), "Voices on the Inside"
First Tuesday (NBC)

Harry Reasoner (reporter), *60 Minutes*
(CBS)

Mike Wallace (reporter), *60 Minutes*
(CBS)

OUTSTANDING ACHIEVEMENT IN CULTURAL DOCUMENTARY PROGRAMMING

Programs:

□ *Arthur Rubinstein* (NBC)

□ "Fathers and Sons," *CBS News Hour*
(CBS)

□ "The Japanese," *CBS News Hour*
(CBS)

The Ballad of the Iron Horse (ABC)

Charlie Brown and Charles Schulz
(CBS)

"The Desert Whales," *The Undersea
World of Jacques Cousteau* (ABC)

"Ferment and the Catholic Church,"
Summer Focus (ABC)

Hollywood: The Selznick Years (NBC)

"In Search of Rembrandt," *NET
Festival* (NET)

The Journey of Robert F. Kennedy
(ABC)

The Man Hunters (NBC)

"Modern Man: The Loser," *Directions*
(ABC)

"The Mystery of Animal Behavior,"
National Geographic Special (CBS)

Sahara: La Caravane Du Sel (NBC)

"Siberia: The Endless Horizon,"
National Geographic Special (CBS)

Survival on the Prairie (NBC)

*Three Young Americans in Search of
Survival* (ABC)

"Volcano: Birth of an Island," *CBS
News Hour* (CBS)

The Warren Years (NET)

Individuals:

□ Edwin O. Reischauer (commentator),
"The Japanese," *CBS News Hour*
(CBS)

□ Arthur Rubinstein (commentator),
Arthur Rubinstein (NBC)

James Benjamin (writer), "Ferment
and the Catholic Church," *Summer
Focus* (ABC)

Warren Bush (writer), "The Desert
Whales," *The Undersea World of
Jacques Cousteau* (ABC)

Hugh Downs (reporter), *Survival on the
Prairie* (NBC)

Marshall Flaum (writer), *Hollywood:
The Selznick Years* (NBC)

Stephen Fleischman (writer), *Three
Young Americans in Search of
Survival* (ABC)

Lou Hazam (writer) *Sahara: La
Caravane du Sel* (NBC)

John Huston (narrator), *The Journey of
Robert F. Kennedy* (ABC)

Charles Kuralt (reporter), "Volcano:
Birth of an Island," *CBS News Hour*
(CBS)

James Mason (host and narrator), "In
Search of Rembrandt," *NET Festival*
(NET)

Harry Morgan (writer), "Fathers and
Sons," *CBS News Hour* (CBS)

Nicolas Noxon (writer), *The Man
Hunters* (NBC)

Nicolas Noxon (director), *The Man
Hunters* (NBC)

Thomas A. Priestly (director), *Sahara:
La Cavarane du Sel* (NBC)

Helen Jean Rogers (director), *The
Ballad of the Iron Horse* (ABC)

Arthur Schlesinger, Jr. (writer), *The
Journey of Robert F. Kennedy* (ABC)

John H. Secondari (writer), *The Ballad
of the Iron Horse* (ABC)

Richard F. Siemanowski (writer), "In
Search of Rembrandt," *NET Festival*
(NET)

Mel Stuart (director), *The Journey of
Robert F. Kennedy* (ABC)

Bud Wiser (writer), "Siberia: The
Endless Horizon," *National
Geographic Special* (CBS)

Perry Wolff (writer), "The Japanese,"
CBS News Hour (CBS)

1970/71

*(Presented May 9, 1971 for programs
aired between March 16, 1970 and
March 16, 1971)*

Entertainment Program Awards

OUTSTANDING SERIES—COMEDY

□ *All in the Family* (CBS)

Arnie (CBS)

Love, American Style (ABC)

The Mary Tyler Moore Show (CBS)

The Odd Couple (ABC)

OUTSTANDING SERIES—DRAMA

□ *The Senator—The Bold Ones* (NBC)

"The First Churchills," *Masterpiece
Theatre* (PBS)

Ironside (NBC)

NET Playhouse (NET)
Marcus Welby, M.D. (ABC)

OUTSTANDING SINGLE PROGRAM—DRAMA OR COMEDY

☐ "The Andersonville Trial," *Hollywood Television Theatre* (PBS)
"Hamlet," *Hallmark Hall of Fame* (NBC)
"The Price," *Hallmark Hall of Fame* (NBC)
"They're Tearing Down Tim Riley's Bar," *Rod Serling's Night Gallery* (NBC)
"Vanished—Parts I and II," *World Premiere* (NBC)

OUTSTANDING VARIETY SERIES— MUSICAL

☐ *The Flip Wilson Show* (NBC)
The Carol Burnett Show (CBS)
Rowan and Martin's Laugh-In (NBC)

OUTSTANDING VARIETY SERIES— TALK

☐ *The David Frost Show* (Syndicated)
The Dick Cavett Show (ABC)
The Tonight Show Starring Johnny Carson (NBC)

OUTSTANDING SINGLE PROGRAM—VARIETY OR MUSICAL

Variety and popular music:
☐ *Singer Presents Burt Bacharach* (CBS)
Another Evening with Burt Bacharach (NBC)
Harry and Lena (ABC)

Classical Music:
☐ "Leopold Stokowski," *NET Festival* (PBS)
"Queen of Spades," *Fanfare—NET Opera Theatre* (PBS)
"Swan Lake," *Fanfare* (PBS)

OUTSTANDING NEW SERIES

☐ *All in the Family* (CBS)
The Mary Tyler Moore Show (CBS)
The Odd Couple (ABC)
The Senator—The Bold Ones (NBC)
The Flip Wilson Show (NBC)

Entertainment Performance Awards

OUTSTANDING SINGLE PERFORMANCE BY AN ACTOR IN A LEADING ROLE

☐ George C. Scott, "The Price," *Hallmark Hall of Fame* (NBC)
Jack Cassidy, "The Andersonville Trial," *Hollywood Television Theatre* (PBS)
Hal Holbrook, "A Clear and Present Danger," *World Premiere* (NBC)
Richard Widmark, "Vanished, Parts I and II," *World Premiere* (NBC)
Gig Young, "The Neon Ceiling," *World Premiere* (NBC)

☐ Indicates winner

OUTSTANDING SINGLE PERFORMANCE BY AN ACTRESS IN A LEADING ROLE

☐ Lee Grant, "The Neon Ceiling," *World Premiere* (NBC)
Colleen Dewhurst, "The Price," *Hallmark Hall of Fame* (NBC)
Lee Grant, "Ransom For A Dead Man," *World Premiere* (NBC)

OUTSTANDING CONTINUED PERFORMANCE BY AN ACTOR IN A LEADING ROLE IN A DRAMATIC SERIES

☐ Hal Holbrook, *The Senator—The Bold Ones* (NBC)
Raymond Burr, *Ironside* (NBC)
Mike Connors, *Mannix* (CBS)
Robert Young, *Marcus Welby, M.D.* (ABC)

OUTSTANDING CONTINUED PERFORMANCE BY AN ACTRESS IN A LEADING ROLE IN A DRAMATIC SERIES

☐ Susan Hampshire, "The First Churchils," *Masterpiece Theatre* (PBS)
Linda Cristal, *The High Chaparral* (NBC)
Peggy Lipton, *The Mod Squad* (ABC)

OUTSTANDING CONTINUED PERFORMANCE BY AN ACTOR IN A LEADING ROLE IN A COMEDY SERIES

☐ Jack Klugman, *The Odd Couple* (ABC)
Ted Bessell, *That Girl* (ABC)
Bill Bixby, *The Courtship of Eddie's Father* (ABC)
Carroll O'Connor, *All in the Family* (CBS)
Tony Randall, *The Odd Couple* (ABC)

OUTSTANDING CONTINUED PERFORMANCE BY AN ACTRESS IN A LEADING ROLE IN A COMEDY SERIES

☐ Jean Stapleton, *All in the Family* (CBS)
Mary Tyler Moore, *The Mary Tyler Moore Show* (CBS)
Marlo Thomas, *That Girl* (ABC)

OUTSTANDING PERFORMANCE BY AN ACTOR IN A SUPPORTING ROLE IN DRAMA

☐ David Burns, "The Price," *Hallmark Hall of Fame* (NBC)
James Brolin, *Marcus Welby, M.D.* (ABC)
Robert Young, "Vanished, Parts I and II," *World Premiere* (NBC)

OUTSTANDING PERFORMANCE BY AN ACTRESS IN A SUPPORTING ROLE IN DRAMA

☐ Margaret Leighton, "Hamlet," *Hallmark Hall of Fame* (NBC)
Gail Fisher, *Mannix* (CBS)

Susan Saint James, *The Name of the Game* (NBC)
Elena Verdugo, *Marcus Welby, M.D.* (ABC)

OUTSTANDING PERFORMANCE BY AN ACTOR IN A SUPPORTING ROLE IN COMEDY

☐ Ed Asner, *The Mary Tyler Moore Show* (CBS)
Michael Constantine, *Room 222* (ABC)
Gale Gordon, *Here's Lucy* (CBS)

OUTSTANDING PERFORMANCE BY AN ACTRESS IN A SUPPORTING ROLE IN A COMEDY

☐ Valerie Harper, *The Mary Tyler Moore Show* (CBS)
Agnes Moorehead, *Bewitched* (ABC)
Karen Valentine, *Room 222* (ABC)

ENTERTAINMENT CRAFT AND TECHNICAL AWARDS

Outstanding directorial achievement in drama a single program:
☐ Fielder Cook, "The Price," *Hallmark Hall of Fame* (NBC)
Peter Wood, "Hamlet," *Hallmark Hall of Fame* (NBC)
Joseph Sargent, "Tribes," *Movie of the Week on ABC* (ABC)
James Goldstone, "A Clear and Present Danger," *World Premiere* (NBC)

OUTSTANDING DIRECTORIAL ACHIEVEMENT IN DRAMA

A single program of a series:
☐ Daryl Duke, "The Day the Lion Died," *The Bold Ones—The Senators* (NBC)
Bob Sweeney, "Over 50? Steal," *Hawaii Five-O* (CBS)
John M. Badham, "A Single Blow of a Sword," *The Bold Ones—The Senators* (NBC)

OUTSTANDING DIRECTORIAL ACHIEVEMENT IN COMEDY

A single program of a series with continuing characters and or theme:
☐ Jay Sandrich, "Toulouse Lautrec Is One of My Favorite Artists," *The Mary Tyler Moore Show* (CBS)
Alan Rafkin, "Support Your Local Mother," *The Mary Tyler Moore Show* (CBS)
John Rich, "Gloria's Pregnancy," *All in the Family* (CBS)

OUTSTANDING DIRECTORIAL ACHIEVEMENT IN VARIETY OR MUSIC

A single program of a series:
☐ Mark Warren, *Rowan and Martin's Laugh-In* (with Orson Welles) (NBC)
Art Fisher, "Andy Williams Christmas Show," *The Andy Williams Show* (NBC)

Tim Kiley, *The Flip Wilson Show* (with David Frost, James Brown, The Muppets) (NBC)

A special program:

☐ Sterling Johnson, *Timex Presents Peggy Fleming at Sun Valley* (NBC)

Walter C. Miller, Martin Charnin, "George M!" *Bell System Family Theatre* (NBC)

Roger Englander, "The Anatomy of a Symphony Orchestra," *New York Philharmonic Young People's Concert* (CBS)

OUTSTANDING ACHIEVEMENT IN CHOREOGRAPHY

☐ Ernest O. Flatt, *The Carol Burnett Show* (with Nanette Fabray, Ken Berry) (CBS)

Claude Chagrin, "Hamlet," *Hallmark Hall of Fame* (NBC)

Alan Johnson, "George M!" *Bell System Family Theatre* (NBC)

OUTSTANDING WRITING ACHIEVEMENT

In drama for a single program of a series with continuing characters and/or theme:

☐ Joel Oliansky, "To Taste of Death but Once," *The Bold Ones—The Senator Segment* (NBC)

David W. Rintels, "A Continual Roar of Musketry, Parts I & II," *The Bold Ones—The Senator Segment* (NBC)

Jerrold Freedman, "In Death's Other Kingdom," *The Psychiatrist, Four-In-One* (NBC)

OUTSTANDING WRITING ACHIEVEMENT

In drama, original teleplay for a single program:

☐ Tracy Keenan Wynn, Marvin Schwartz, "Tribes," *Movie of the Week on ABC* (ABC)

William Read Woodfield, Allan Balter, "San Francisco International Airport," *World Premiere NBC Tuesday Night at the Movies* (NBC)

David Karp, "The Brotherhood of the Bell," *CBS Thursday Night Movies* (CBS)

OUTSTANDING WRITING ACHIEVEMENT

In drama adaptation for a single program:

☐ Saul Levitt, "The Andersonville Trial," *Hollywood Television Theatre* (PBS)

John Barton, "Hamlet," *Hallmark Hall of Fame* (NBC)

Dean Riesner, "Vanished," *World Premiere NBC Monday & Tuesday Night at the Movies* (NBC)

☐ Indicates winner

OUTSTANDING WRITING ACHIEVEMENT IN COMEDY

For a single program of a series with continuing characters and/or theme:

☐ James L. Brooks, Allan Burns, "Support Your Local Mother," *The Mary Tyler Moore Show* (CBS)

Norman Lear, "Meet the Bunkers," *All in the Family* (CBS)

Stanley Ralph Ross, "Oh, My Aching Back," *All in the Family* (CBS)

Bob Carroll, Jr., Madelyn Davis, "Lucy Meets the Burtons," *Here's Lucy* (CBS)

OUTSTANDING WRITING ACHIEVEMENT IN VARIETY OR MUSIC FOR A SINGLE PROGRAM OF A SERIES

☐ Herbert Baker, Hal Goodman, Larry Klein, Bob Weiskopf, Bob Schiller, Norman Steinberg, Flip Wilson, *The Flip Wilson Show* (with Lena Horne, Tony Randall) (NBC)

☐ Arthur Julian, Don Hinkley, Jack Mendelsohn, Stan Hart, Larry Siegel, Woody Kling, Rodger Beatty, Arnie Rosen, Kenny Solms, Gail Parent, *The Carol Burnett Show* (with Rita Hayworth) (CBS)

Danny Simon, Marty Farrell, Norman Barasch, Carroll Moore, Tony Webster, Coleman Jacoby, Bob Ellison, "The Kopykats Kopy TV," *Kraft Music Hall* (NBC)

OUTSTANDING WRITING ACHIEVEMENT IN COMEDY, VARIETY OR MUSIC FOR A SPECIAL PROGRAM:

☐ Bob Ellison, Marty Farrell, *Singer Presents Burt Bacharach* (CBS)

Hal Goldman, Al Gordon, Hilliard Markes, Hugh Wedlock, Jr., *Timex Presents Jack Benny's 20th TV Anniversary Special* (NBC)

Saul Ilson, Ernest Chambers, Gary Belkin, Alex Barris, *The Doris Mary Anne Kappelhoff Special* (CBS)

OUTSTANDING ACHIEVEMENT IN MUSIC COMPOSITION FOR A SERIES OR A SINGLE PROGRAM OF A SERIES (IN THE FIRST YEAR OF MUSIC'S USE ONLY)

☐ David Rose, "The Love Child," *Bonanza* (NBC)

Robert Prince, Billy Goldenberg, "LA 2017," *The Name of the Game* (Gene Barry segment) (NBC)

Frank Comstock, "Elegy for a Pig," *Adam 12* (NBC)

Charles Fox, *Love American Style* (ABC)

OUTSTANDING ACHIEVEMENT IN MUSIC COMPOSITION

For a special program:

☐ Walter Scharf, "The Tragedy of the Red Salmon," *The Undersea World of Jacques Cousteau* (ABC)

John Addison, "Hamlet," *Hallmark Hall of Fame* (NBC)

Pete Rugolo, "Do You Take This Stranger," *World Premiere NBC Monday Night at the Movies* (NBC)

OUTSTANDING ACHIEVEMENT IN MUSIC DIRECTION OF A VARIETY, MUSICAL OR DRAMATIC PROGRAM

☐ Dominic Frontiere, *Swing Out, Sweet Land* (NBC)

John Addison, "Hamlet," *Hallmark Hall of Fame* (NBC)

Mort Lindsey, "Big Band Salute, Parts I & II," *The Merv Griffin Show* (CBS)

OUTSTANDING ACHIEVEMENT IN MUSIC, LYRICS AND SPECIAL MATERIAL FOR A SERIES OR A SINGLE PROGRAM OF A SERIES OR A SPECIAL PROGRAM WRITTEN

☐ Ray Charles, *The First Nine Months Are the Hardest* (NBC)

Billy Barnes, *Clairol Command Performance Presents... Pure Goldie* (NBC)

Lee Hale, *The Dean Martin Show* (NBC)

William Goldenberg, David Wilson, "All the Old Familiar Faces," *The Name of the Game* (Gene Barry segment) (NBC)

OUTSTANDING ACHIEVEMENT IN CINEMATOGRAPHY FOR ENTERTAINMENT PROGRAMMING

For a series or a single program of a series:

☐ Jack Marta, "Cynthia Is Alive and Living in Avalon," *The Name of the Game* (Gene Barry segment) (NBC)

Ted Voigtlander, ASC, "The Love Child," *Bonanza* (NBC)

Walter Strenge, ASC, "A Spanish Saying I Made Up," *Marcus Welby, M.D.* (ABC)

For a special or feature length program made for television

☐ Lionel Lindon, ASC, "Vanished, Parts I & II," *World Premiere NBC Monday & Tuesday Night at the Movies* (NBC)

☐ Bob Collins, *Timex Presents Peggy Fleming at Sun Valley* (NBC)

Russell L. Metty, ASC, "Tribes," *Movie of the Week on ABC* (ABC)

Edward Rosson, "The Neon Ceiling," *World Premiere NBC Monday Night at the Movies* (NBC)

OUTSTANDING ACHIEVEMENT IN CINEMATOGRAPHY FOR NEWS AND DOCUMENTARY PROGRAMMING

For a series, a single program of a series, a special program, program segment or elements within: Regularly scheduled news program and coverage of special events:

☐ Larry Travis, "Los Angeles-Earthquake," (Sylmar V.A. Hospital) *CBS Evening News with Walter Cronkite* (CBS)

James Watt, "Cattle Drive Parts I & II," *The Huntley-Brinkley Report* (NBC)

Houston Hall, "They Paved Paradise," *The Huntley-Brinkley Report* (NBC)

Documentary, magazine-type or mini-documentary programs:

☐ Jacques Renoir, "The Tragedy of the Red Salmon," *The Undersea World of Jacques Cousteau* (ABC)

Philippe Cousteau, "Lagoon of Lost Ships," *The Undersea World of Jacques Cousteau* (ABC)

Michel De Loire, Jacques Renoir, "The Dragons of Galapagos," *The Undersea World of Jacques Cousteau* (ABC)

James S. Wilson, Guy Adenis, George Apostolides, Joe Bardo-Yesko, Tony Coggans, Michael Dugan, J. Barry Herron, Robert E. Thomas, Larry Travis, "Wildfire," *GE Monogram Series* (NBC)

OUTSTANDING ACHIEVEMENT IN ART DIRECTION OR SCENIC DESIGN

For a dramatic program or feature length film, a single program of a series or a special program:

☐ Peter Roden, "Hamlet," *Hallmark Hall of Fame* (NBC)

John J. Lloyd (art director), Rudy R. Levitt (set decorator), "Vanished, Parts I & II," *World Premiere NBC Monday and Tuesday Night at the Movies* (NBC)

Jan Scott, "Montserrat," *Hollywood Television Theatre* (PBS)

John Clements, "The Price," *Hallmark Hall of Fame* (NBC)

J. M. Van Tamelen (art director), Fred Price (set decorator), "The Mouse That Died" *Mannix* (CBS)

For a musical or variety single program of a series, or a special program:

☐ James W. Trittiop (art director), George Gaines (set decorator), "Robert Young and the Family" (CBS)

Rene Lagler (art director), Robert Checci (set decorator), *The Glen*

☐ Indicates winner

Campbell Goodtime Hour (with Neil Diamond, Linda Ronstadt) (CBS)

Romain Johnston, *The Flip Wilson Show* (with Robert Goulet, Lola Falana) (NBC)

Fred Luff, "Love Is," *Oral Roberts Valentine Special—Contact* (Syndicated)

OUTSTANDING ACHIEVEMENT IN COSTUME DESIGN

☐ Martin Baugh, David Walker, "Hamlet," *Hallmark Hall of Fame* (NBC)

Robert Carlton, *Bing Crosby—Cooling It* (NBC)

Ret Turner, "Andy Williams Christmas Show," *The Andy Williams Show* (NBC)

Patricia Segnan, *They've Killed President Lincoln* (NBC)

OUTSTANDING ACHIEVEMENT IN MAKE-UP

☐ Robert Dawn, "Catafalque," *Mission: Impossible* (CBS)

Marie Roche, "Hamlet," *Hallmark Hall of Fame* (NBC)

Rolf J. Miller, "Samantha's Old Man," *Bewitched* (ABC)

Perc Westmore, Harry C. Blake, *The Third Bill Cosby Show* (NBC)

OUTSTANDING ACHIEVEMENT IN FILM EDITING FOR ENTERTAINMENT PROGRAMMING

For a series or a single program of a series:

☐ Michael Economou, "A Continual Roar of Musketry, Parts I & II," *The Bold Ones—The Senator Segment* (NBC)

Arthur David Hilton, "Over 50? Steal," *Hawaii Five-O* (CBS)

Douglas Stewart, "To Taste of Death But Once," *The Bold Ones—The Senator Segment* (NBC)

For a special or feature length program made for television:

☐ George J. Nicholson "Longstreet," *Movie Of The Week On ABC* (ABC)

Robert F. Shugrue, "The Neon Ceiling," *World Premiere NBC Monday Night at the Movies* (NBC)

Robert Watts, "Vanished, Parts I & II," *World Premiere NBC Monday and Tuesday Night at the Movies* (NBC)

OUTSTANDING ACHIEVEMENT IN FILM EDITING FOR NEWS AND DOCUMENTARY PROGRAMMING

Regularly scheduled news programs and coverage of special events:

☐ George L. Johnson, "Prisons, Parts I thru IV," *NBC Nightly News* (NBC)

Michael C. Shugrue, "The Welfare Worker," *NBC Nightly News* (NBC)

Louis Buchignani, "L.A. Earthquake," *ABC Evening News with Howard K. Smith and Harry Reasoner* (ABC)

Documentary, Magazine-type or Mini-documentary programs:

☐ Robert B. Loweree, Henry J. Grennon, *Cry Help! An NBC White Paper on Mentally Disturbed Youth* (NBC)

David E. Blewitt, "The Tragedy of the Red Salmon," *The Undersea World of Jacques Cousteau* (ABC)

Dena Levitt, *CBS Reports: The Selling of the Pentagon* (CBS)

John F. Teeple, "The Prado," *The Southern Baptist Hour* (NBC)

OUTSTANDING ACHIEVEMENT IN FILM SOUND EDITING

☐ Don Hall, Jr., Jack Jackson, Bob Weatherford, Dick Jensen, "Tribes," *Movie of the Week on ABC* (ABC)

Douglas H. Grindstaff, Frank R. White, Joe Kavigan, Don Crosby, Chuck Perry, "The Blast," *Mission: Impossible* (CBS)

Douglas H. Grindstaff, Edward L. Sandlin, Josef E. Von Stroheim, Seth D. Larsen, Bill Rivol, Billie Owens, "Sunburst," *Mannix* (CBS)

OUTSTANDING ACHIEVEMENT IN FILM SOUND MIXING

☐ Theodore Soderberg, "Tribes," *Movie of the Week on ABC* (ABC)

Joel F. Moss, Don Rush, "Sunburst," *Mannix* (CBS)

Ronald K. Pierce, James Z. Flaster, "Vanished, Parts I & II," *World Premiere NBC Monday and Tuesday Night at the Movies* (NBC)

Roger Parish, Robert L. Hoyt, "San Francisco International Airport," *World Premiere NBC Tuesday Night at the Movies* (NBC)

OUTSTANDING ACHIEVEMENT IN LIGHTING DIRECTION FOR

A single program of a series or a special program produced for electronic television only:

☐ John Rook, "Hamlet," *Hallmark Hall of Fame* (NBC)

Kenneth Dettling, "The Andersonville Trial," *Hollywood Television Theatre* (PBS)

John Freschi, "Andy Williams Christmas Show," *The Andy Williams Show* (NBC)

Carl Gibson, "Love Is," *Oral Roberts Valentine Special—Contact* (Syndicated)

OUTSTANDING ACHIEVEMENT IN LIVE OR TAPE SOUND MIXING

☐ Henry Bird, "Hamlet," *Hallmark Hall of Fame* (NBC)

Dave Williams, *The Flip Wilson Show* (with Lena Horne, Tony Randall) (NBC)

Marshall King, *Swing Out, Sweet Land* (NBC)

OUTSTANDING ACHIEVEMENT IN VIDEO TAPE EDITING
☐ Marco Zappia, *Hee-Haw* (with Roger Miller, Peggy Little) (CBS)
Ray Knipe, "Hamlet," *Hallmark Hall of Fame* (NBC)
Steven Orland, Martin J. Peters, *Clairol Command Performance Presents... Pure Goldie* (NBC)

OUTSTANDING ACHIEVEMENT IN TECHNICAL DIRECTION AND ELECTRONIC CAMERAWORK FOR A
Single program of a series of a special program:
☐ Gordon Baird (technical director), Tom Ancell, Rick Bennewitz, Larry Bentley and Jack Reader (cameramen), "The Andersonville Trail," *Hollywood Television Theatre* (PBS)
Louis Fusari (technical director), Tony Yarlett, Ray Figelski, Marvin Ault and Jon Olson (cameramen), *Rowan and Martin's Laugh-In* (NBC)
Bill Schertle (technical director), Barney Neeley, Tom McConnell and Alan Latter (cameramen), *Apollo 14 Recovery Aboard the USS New Orleans* (Pool Coverage)

The Areas*

OUTSTANDING ACHIEVEMENT IN CHILDREN'S PROGRAMMING
Programs:
☐ *Sesame Street* (PBS)
Kukla, Fran and Ollie (PBS)
Individuals:
☐ Burr Tillstrom (performer), *Kukla, Fran and Ollie* (PBS)
George W. Riesenberger (lighting director), *Sesame Street* (PBS)

OUTSTANDING ACHIEVEMENT IN DAYTIME PROGRAMMING
Programs:
☐ *Today* (NBC)
The Galloping Gourmet (Syndicated)
Individuals:
James Angerame (technical director), *Love Is a Many Splendored Thing* (CBS)
Victor L. Paganuzzi (art director), John A. Wendell (set decorator), *Love Is a Many Splendored Thing* (CBS)

OUTSTANDING ACHIEVEMENT IN SPORTS PROGRAMMING
Programs:
☐ *ABC'S Wide World of Sports* (ABC)
34th Masters Tournament (CBS)
NFL Monday Night Football (ABC)

* possibility of one award, more than one award or no award
☐ Indicates winner

Individuals:
☐ Jim McKay (commentator), *ABC'S Wide World of Sports* (ABC)
Don Meredith (commentator), *NFL Monday Night Football* (ABC)
Walt Kubilus (technical director), Dick Kerr, John Morrealle, Mike Rebich, Stuart Goodman, Mort Levin, Sal Folino, Don Langford, and Ed Payne (cameramen), *NCAA Football* (ABC)

SPECIAL CLASSIFICATION OF OUTSTANDING PROGRAM AND INDIVIDUAL ACHIEVEMENT

Programs:
The Wonderful World of Disney (NBC)
Mutual of Omaha's Wild Kingdom (NBC)

Individuals:
☐ Harvey Korman (performer), *The Carol Burnett Show* (CBS)
Lilly Tomlin (performer), *Rowan and Martin's Laugh-In* (NBC)
Artie Johnson (performer), *Rowan and Martin's Laugh-In* (NBC)

OUTSTANDING ACHIEVEMENT IN ANY AREA OF CREATIVE TECHNICAL CRAFTS
☐ Lenwood B. Abbott and John C. Caldwell (special photographic effects), "City Beneath the Sea," *World Premiere NBC Monday Night at the Movies* (NBC)
☐ Gene Widhoff (graphic art—courtroom sketches), "Manson Trial," *The Huntley-Brinkley Report—NBC Nightly News* (NBC)
Albert J. Whitlock (special photographic effects), "Vanished, Parts I & II," *World Premiere NBC Monday and Tuesday Night at the Movies* (NBC)

Special Awards

TRUSTEES AWARD
Ed Sullivan. For serving as a founder of The National Academy and its first National President; for pioneering in the variety format which has become a backbone of television programming; for having the foresight and courage to provide network exposure for minority performers; for bringing to millions of Americans cultural performances from ballet to opera to legitimate drama; for introducing performers from throughout the world to audiences who would otherwise never have known them, and, finally, for his showmanship, taste and personal commitment in entertaining a nation for 23 years.

OUTSTANDING ACHIEVEMENT IN ENGINEERING DEVELOPMENT
The Columbia Broadcasting System. For the development of the Color Corrector which can provide color uniformity between television picture segments and scenes shot and recorded under different conditions at different times and locations.
The American Broadcasting Co. For the development of an "Open-Loop" Synchronizing System which enables the simultaneous synchronization of any number of color programs from remote locations.

CITATIONS
General Electric for the development of the Portable Earth Station Transmitter which has provided the only means of getting color television pictures of Apollo splashdowns and recoveries via satellite to the mainland for worldwide distribution to the viewing public.
Stefan Kudelski, for his design of the NAGRA IV Recorder which has achieved wide acceptance for sound recording of motion pictures filmed for television.

THE STATION AWARD
☐ *If You Turn On* (KNXT, Los Angeles)
Are We Killing the Gulf? (KPRC-TV, Houston)
Father Mountain's Christmas (KOOL-TV, Phoenix)
Hey Doc (WCAU-TV, Philadelphia)
Homes Like These (WLBT, Jackson)
The Lost—The Lonely (WJW-TV, Cleveland)
Nine Heroes (WGBH, Educational Station, Allston, Massachusetts)
No Place To Hide (WBBM-TV, Chicago)
Out City's History—Boston: June 1970 (WNAC-TV, Boston)
Timetable for Disaster (WMC-TV, Memphis)

News and Documentary Program and Individual Achievement*

OUTSTANDING ACHIEVEMENT WITHIN REGULARLY SCHEDULED NEWS PROGRAMS
Programs:
☐ "Five Part Investigation of Welfare," *NBC Nightly News* (NBC)
"Coverage of the Indo China War," *ABC Evening News* (ABC)
"Coverage of the Pakistani Tidal Wave Disaster," *NBC Nightly News* (NBC)

* possibility of one award, more than one award or no award

"Coverage of the Middle East Plane Hijackings," *NBC Nightly News* (NBC)

Individuals:

☐ Bruce Morton (correspondent), "Reports from the Lt. Calley Trial," *CBS Evening News with Walter Cronkite* (CBS)

Phil Brade (correspondent), "Investigation of GI Drug Addiction In Vietnam," *NBC Nightly News* (NBC)

OUTSTANDING ACHIEVEMENT IN COVERAGE OF SPECIAL EVENTS

Programs:

☐ CBS News Space Coverage for 1970-71: "Aquarius on the Moon: The Flight of Apollo 13" and "Ten Years Later: The Flight of Apollo 14" (CBS)

Earth Day: A Question of Survival (CBS)

NBC news Coverage of the Southern California Earthquake (NBC)

Individuals:

☐ Walter Cronkite (correspondent), "CBS News Space Coverage for 1970-71: Aquarius On The Moon: The Flight of Apollo 13" and "Ten Years Later: The Flight of Apollo 14" (CBS)

Douglas Kiker (correspondent), *The War in Jordan* (NBC)

OUTSTANDING ACHIEVEMENT IN NEWS DOCUMENTARY PROGRAMMING

Programs:

☐ *The Selling of the Pentagon* (CBS)
☐ *The World of Charlie Company* (CBS)
☐ *NBC White Paper: Pollution Is a Matter of Choice* (NBC)

Individuals:

☐ John Laurence (correspondent), *The World of Charlie Company* (CBS)
☐ Fred Freed (writer) *NBC White Paper: Pollution Is a Matter of Choice* (NBC)

Denis Sanders and Robert Fresco (directors), "Trial: The City and County of Denver vs. Lauren R. Watson" *NET Journal* (PBS)

OUTSTANDING ACHIEVEMENT IN MAGAZINE-TYPE PROGRAMMING

Programs:

☐ "Gulf of Tonkin Segment," *60 Minutes* (CBS)
☐ *The Great American Dream Machine* (PBS)

Black Journal (PBS)

Individuals:

☐ Mike Wallace (correspondent), *60 Minutes* (CBS)

Morley Safer (correspondent), "Gulf of Tonkin Segment," *60 Minutes* (CBS)

☐ Indicates winner

Elinor Bunin (director of animated film), *The Great American Dream Machine* (PBS)

OUTSTANDING ACHIEVEMENT IN CULTURAL DOCUMENTARY PROGRAMMING

Programs:

☐ *The Everglades* (NBC)
☐ *The Making of "Butch Cassidy & The Sundance Kid"* (NBC)
☐ *Arthur Penn 1922: Themes and Variants* (PBS)

"Gertrude Stein: When This You See, Remember Me," *Fanfare* (PBS)

Which Way America? (NBC)

Individuals:

☐ Nana Mahomo (narrator), *A Balck View of South Africa* (CBS)
☐ Robert Guenette and Theodore H. Strauss (writers), *They've Killed President Lincoln* (NBC)
☐ Robert Young (director), *The Eskimo: Fight for Life* (CBS)

Craig Gilbert (director-writer), *The Triumph of Christy Brown* (PBS)

Gerge C. Scott (narrator), *A Man Named Lombardi* (NBC)

Jerry Izenberg (writer), *A Man Named Lombardi* (NBC)

Perry Miller Adato (director), "Gertrude Stein: When This You See, Remember Me" (PBS)

Nathan Kroll (director), "Helen Hayes—Portrait of an American Actress," *NET Playhouse* (PBS)

1971/72

(Presented May 6, 1972 and May 14, 1972 for programs aired between March 17, 1971 and March 12, 1972)

Entertainment Program Awards

OUTSTANDING SERIES—COMEDY

☐ *All in the Family* (CBS)

The Mary Tyler Moore Show (CBS)

The Odd Couple (ABC)

Sanford and Son (NBC)

OUTSTANDING SERIES—DRAMA

☐ "Elizabeth R," *Masterpiece Theater* (PBS)

Columbo (NBC)

Mannix (CBS)

Marcus Welby, M.D. (ABC)

The Six Wives of Henry VIII (CBS)

OUTSTANDING SINGLE PROGRAM—DRAMA OR COMEDY

☐ "Brian's Song," *Movie of the Week* (ABC)

"Jane Seymour," *The Six Wives of Henry VIII* (CBS)

"The Lion's Cub," *Elizabeth R, Masterpiece Theatre* (PBS)

"Sammy's Visit," *All in the Family* (CBS)

"The Snow Goose," *Hallmark Hall of Fame* (NBC)

OUTSTANDING VARIETY SERIES—MUSICAL

☐ *The Carol Burnett Show* (CBS)

The Dean Martin Show (NBC)

The Flip Wilson Show (NBC)

The Sonny & Cher Comedy Hour (CBS)

OUTSTANDING VARIETY SERIES—TALK

☐ *The Dick Cavett Show* (ABC)

The David Frost Show (Syndicated)

The Tonight Show Starring Johnny Carson (NBC)

OUTSTANDING SINGLE PROGRAM—VARIETY OR MUSICAL

Variety and popular music:

☐ "Jack Lemon in 'S Wonderful, 'S Marvelous, 'S Gershwin," *Bell System Family Theater* (NBC)

The Flip Wilson Show (with Sammy Davis, Jr., Lily Tomlin, Ed McMahon) (NBC)

Julie and Carol at Lincoln Center (CBS)

The Sonny and Cher Comedy Hour (with Tony Randall) (CBS)

Classical music:

☐ *Beethoven's Birthday: A Celebration in Vienna with Leonard Bernstein* (CBS)

"Heifetz," *Bell System Family Theatre* (NBC)

The Peking Ballet: First Spectacular From China (NBC)

"The Trial of Mary Lincoln," *NET Opera Theatre* (PBS)

OUTSTANDING NEW SERIES

"Elizabeth R," *Masterpiece Theatre* (PBS)

Columbo (NBC)

Sanford and Son (NBC)

The Six Wives of Henry VIII (CBS)

The Sonny & Cher Comedy Hour (CBS)

Entertainment Performance Awards

OUTSTANDING SINGLE PERFORMANCE BY AN ACTOR IN A LEADING ROLE

☐ Keith Mitchell, "Catherine Howard," *The Six Wives of Henry VIII* (CBS)

James Caan, "Brian's Song," *Movie of the Week* (ABC)

Richard Harris, "The Snow Goose," *Hallmark Hall of Fame* (NBC)

George C. Scott, "Jane Eyre," *Bell System Family Theatre* (NBC)

Billy Dee Williams, "Brian's Song," *Movie of the Week* (ABC)

OUTSTANDING SINGLE PERFORMANCE BY AN ACTRESS IN A LEADING ROLE

☐ Glenda Jackson, "Shadow In the Sun," *Elizabeth R, Masterpiece Theatre* (PBS)

Glenda Jackson, "The Lion's Cub," *Elizabeth R, Masterpiece Theatre* (PBS)

Helen Hayes, "Do Not Fold, Spindle or Mutilate," *Movie of the Week* (ABC)

Patricia Neal, *The Homecoming—A Christmas Story* (CBS)

Susannah York, "Jane Eyre," *Bell System Family Theatre* (NBC)

OUTSTANDING CONTINUED PERFORMANCE BY AN ACTOR IN A LEADING ROLE IN A DRAMATIC SERIES

☐ Peter Falk, *Columbo* (NBC)

Raymond Burr, *Ironside* (NBC)

Mike Connors, *Mannix* (CBS)

Keith Mitchell, *The Six Wives of Henry VIII* (CBS)

Robert Young, *Marcus Welby, M.D.* (ABC)

OUTSTANDING CONTINUED PERFORMANCE BY AN ACTRESS IN A LEADING ROLE IN A DRAMATIC SERIES

☐ Glenda Jackson, "Elizabeth R," *Masterpiece Theatre* (PBS)

Peggy Lipton, *The Mod Squad* (ABC)

Susan Saint James, *McMillan & Wife* (NBC)

OUTSTANDING CONTINUED PERFORMANCE BY AN ACTOR IN A LEADING ROLE IN A COMEDY SERIES

☐ Caroll O'Connor, *All in the Family* (CBS)

Redd Foxx, *Sanford and Son* (NBC)

Jack Klugman, *The Odd Couple* (ABC)

Tony Randall, *The Odd Couple* (ABC)

OUTSTANDING CONTINUED PERFORMANCE BY AN ACTRESS IN A LEADING ROLE IN A COMEDY SERIES

☐ Jean Stapleton, *All in the Family* (CBS)

Sandy Duncan, *Funny Face* (CBS)

Mary Tyler Moore, *The Mary Tyler Moore Show* (CBS)

OUTSTANDING PERFORMANCE BY AN ACTOR IN A SUPPORTING ROLE IN DRAMA

☐ Jack Warden, "Brian's Song," *Movie of the Week* (ABC)

James Brolin, *Marcus Welby, M.D.* (ABC)

Greg Morris, *Mission: Impossible* (CBS)

☐ Indicates winner

OUTSTANDING PERFORMANCE BY AN ACTRESS IN A SUPPORTING ROLE IN DRAMA

☐ Jenny Agutter, "The Snow Goose," *Hallmark Hall of Fame* (NBC)

Gail Fisher, *Mannix* (CBS)

Elena Verdugo, *Marcus Welby, M.D.* (ABC)

OUTSTANDING PERFORMANCE BY AN ACTOR IN A SUPPORTING ROLE IN COMEDY

☐ Edward Asner, *The Mary Tyler Moore Show* (CBS)

Ted Knight, *The Mary Tyler Moore Show* (CBS)

Rob Reiner, *All in the Family* (CBS)

OUTSTANDING PERFORMANCE BY AN ACTRESS IN A SUPPORTING ROLE IN COMEDY

☐ Valerie Harper, *The Mary Tyler Moore Show* (CBS)

☐ Sally Struthers, *All in the Family* (CBS)

Cloris Leachman, *The Mary Tyler Moore Show* (CBS)

OUTSTANDING ACHIEVEMENT BY A PERFORMER IN MUSIC OR VARIETY

☐ Harvey Korman, *The Carol Burnett Show* (CBS)

Ruth Buzzi, *Rowan and Martin's Laugh-In* (NBC)

Lily Tomlin, *Rowan and Martin's Laugh-In* (NBC)

Craft and Technical Awards

OUTSTANDING DIRECTORIAL ACHIEVEMENT IN DRAMA

For a single program of a series with continuing characters and/or theme:

☐ Alexander Singer "The Invasion of Kevin Ireland," *The Bold Ones—The Lawyers* (NBC)

Edward M. Abroms, "Short Fuse," *Columbo* (NBC)

Daniel Petrie, "Hands of Love," *The Man and the City* (ABC)

A single program:

☐ Tom Gries, "The Glass House," *The New CBS Friday Night Movies* (CBS)

Paul Bogart, "Look Homeward, Angel," *CBS Playhouse 90* (CBS)

Fielder Cook, *The Homecoming—A Christmas Story* (CBS)

Patrick Garland, "The Snow Goose," *Hallmark Hall of Fame* (NBC)

Buzz Kulik, "Brian's Song," *Movie of The Week* (ABC)

OUTSTANDING DIRECTORIAL ACHIEVEMENT IN COMEDY

For a single program of a series with continuing characters and/or theme:

☐ John Rich, "Sammy's Visit," *All in the Family* (CBS)

Peter Baldwin, "Where There's Smoke, There's Rhoda," *The Mary Tyler Moore Show* (CBS)

Jay Sandrich, "Thoroughly Unmilitant Mary," *The Mary Tyler Moore Show* (CBS)

OUTSTANDING DIRECTORIAL ACHIEVEMENT IN COMEDY, VARIETY OR MUSIC FOR

A single program of a series:

☐ Art Fisher, *The Sonny & Cher Comedy Hour* (with Tony Randall) (CBS)

Tim Kiley, *The Flip Wilson Show* (with Petula Clark, Redd Foxx) (NBC)

David Powers, *The Carol Burnett Show* (with Carol Channing, Steve Lawrence) (CBS)

A special program:

☐ Walter C. Miller, Martin Charnin, "Jack Lemmon in 'S Wonderful, 'S Marvelous, 'S Gershwin," *Bell System Family Theatre* (NBC)

Roger Englander, "Liszt and the Devil," *New York Philharmonic Young People's Concert* (CBS)

Davis P. Powers, *Julie and Carol at Lincoln Center* (CBS)

OUTSTANDING ACHIEVEMENT IN CHOREOGRAPHY

☐ Alan Johnson, "Jack Lemmon in 'S Wonderful, 'S Marvelous, 'S Gershwin," *Bell System Family Theatre* (NBC)

Ernest O. Flatt, *The Carol Burnett Show* (with Mel Torme, Nanette Fabray) (CBS)

Tom Hansen, *The Fabulous Fordies* (NBC)

OUTSTANDING WRITING ACHIEVEMENT IN DRAMA FOR A SINGLE PROGRAM OF A SERIES WITH CONTINUING CHARACTERS AND/OR THEME

☐ Richard L. Levinson, William Ling, "Death Lends A Hand," *Columbo* (NBC)

Steven Bochco, "Murder by the Book," *Columbo* (NBC)

Jackson Gillis, "Suitable for Framing," *Columbo* (NBC)

OUTSTANDING WRITING ACHIEVEMENT IN DRAMA, ORIGINAL TELEPLAY FOR A SINGLE PROGRAM

☐ Allan Sloane, *To All My Friends on Shore* (CBS)

John D.F. Black, "Thief," *Movie of the Weekend* (ABC)

Jack Sher, "Goodbye, Raggedy Ann," *The New CBS Friday Night Movies* (CBS)

OUTSTANDING WRITING ACHIEVEMENT IN DRAMA, ADAPTATION FOR A SINGLE PROGRAM

☐ William Blinn, "Brian's Song," *Movie of the Week* (ABC)

Paul W. Gallico, "The Snow Goose," *Hallmark Hall of Fame* (NBC)

Earl Hamner, Jr., *The Homecoming—A Christmas Story* (CBS)

Tracy Keenan Wynn, "The Glass House," *The New CBS Friday Night Movies* (CBS)

OUTSTANDING WRITING ACHIEVEMENT IN COMEDY FOR A SINGLE PROGRAM OF A SERIES WITH CONTINUING CHARACTERS AND/OR THEME

☐ Burt Styler, "Edith's Problem," *All in the Family* (CBS)

Burt Styler, Norman Lear, "The Saga of Cousin Oscar," *All in the Family* (CBS)

Philip Mishkin, Alan J. Levitt, "Mike's Problem," *All in the Family* (CBS)

OUTSTANDING WRITING ACHIEVEMENT IN VARIETY OR MUSIC FOR A SINGLE PROGRAM OF A SERIES

☐ Don Hinkley, Stan Hart, Larry Siegel, Woody Kling, Roger Beatty, Art Baer, Ben Joelson, Stan Burns, Mike Marmer, Arnie Rosen, *The Carol Burnett Show* (with Tim Conway, Ray Charles) (CBS)

Herbert Baker, Hal Goodman, Larry Klein, Bob Schiller, Bob Weiskopf, Sid Green, Dick Hills, Flip Wilson, *The Flip Wilson Show* (with Sammy Davis, Jr., Lily Tomlin, Ed McMahon) (NBC)

Phil Hahn, Paul Wayne, George Burditt, Coslough Johnson, Bob Einstein, Allan Blye, Chris Bearde, *The Sonny & Cher Comedy Hour* (with Carroll O'Connor) (CBS)

A special program:

☐ Anne Howard Bailey, "The Trial of Mary Lincoln," *NET Opera Theatre* (PBS)

Martin Charnin, "Jack Lemmon in 'S Wonderful, 'S Marvelous, 'S Gershwin," *Bell System Family Theatre* (NBC)

Bob Ellison, Marty Farrell, Ken and Mitzie Welch, *Julie and Carol at Lincoln Center* (CBS)

☐ Indicates winner

OUTSTANDING ACHIEVEMENT IN MUSIC COMPOSITION

For a series or a single program of a series:

☐ Pete Fugolo, "In Defense of Ellen McKay," *The Bold Ones—The Lawyers* (NBC)

Charles Fox, *Love American Style* (ABC)

William Goldenberg, "Lady in Waiting," *Columbo* (NBC)

For a special program:

☐ John T. Williams, "Jane Eyre," *Bell System Family Theatre* (NBC)

Carl Davis, "The Snow Goose," *Hallmark Hall of Fame* (NBC)

Michel Legrand, "Brian's Song," *Movie of The Week* (ABC)

OUTSTANDING ACHIEVEMENT IN MUSIC DIRECTION OF A VARIETY, MUSICAL OR DRAMATIC PROGRAM

☐ Elliot Lawrence, "Jack Lemmon in 'S Wonderful, 'S Marvelous, 'S Gershwin," *Bell System Family Theatre* (NBC)

Van Alexander, *The Golddiggers Chevrolet Show* (with Fess Parker) (Syndicated)

James E. Dale, *The Sonny & Cher Comedy Hour* (with Jean Stapleton, Mike Connors) (CBS)

OUTSTANDING ACHIEVEMENT IN MUSIC, LYRICS AND SPECIAL MATERIAL FOR A SERIES OR A SINGLE PROGRAM OF A SERIES OR A SPECIAL PROGRAM WRITTEN FOR TELEVISION

☐ Ray Charles, "The Funny Side of Marriage," *The Funny Side* (NBC)

Billy Barnes, *Rowan and Martin's Laugh-In* (with Liza Minnelli) (NBC)

Earl Brown, *The Sonny and Cher Comedy Hour* (CBS)

OUTSTANDING ACHIEVEMENT IN ART DIRECTION OR SCENIC DESIGN

For a dramatic program or feature length film made for television, a single program of a series or a special program:

☐ Jan Scott, "The Scarecrow," *Hollywood Television Theatre* (PBS)

Ben Edwards, "Look Homeward, Angel," *CBS Playhouse 90* (CBS)

Gibson Holley (art director), Lucien Hafley (set decorator), "Encore," *Mission: Impossible* (CBS)

Stanley Morris, "The Snow Goose," *Hallmark Hall of Fame* (NBC)

For a Musical or Variety single program of a series or a special program:

☐ E. Jay Krause, *Dianal* (ABC) Paul Barnes and Bob Sansom (art directors), Bill Harp (set decorator),

The Carol Burnett Show, (with Vincent Price, Eydie Gorme) (CBS)

Romain Johnston, *The Flip Wilson Show* (with Petula Clark, Redd Foxx) (NBC)

Rene Lagener (art director), Robert Checchi (set decorator), *The Glen Campbell Show* (with John Wayne) (CBS)

OUTSTANDING ACHIEVEMENT IN COSTUME DESIGN

☐ Elizabeth Waller, "The Lion's Cub," *Elizabeth R, Masterpiece Theatre* (PBS)

Bob Mackie, Ret Turner, *The Sonny & Cher Comedy Hour* (with Art Carney) (CBS)

Ret Turner, *The Fabulous Forties* (NBC)

OUTSTANDING ACHIEVEMENT IN MAKE-UP

☐ Frank Westmore, "Kung Fu," *Movie of the Week* (ABC)

Harry C. Blake, "Gideon," *Hallmark Hall of Fame* (NBC)

Nick Marcellino, Leonard Engelman, John F. Chambers, "Pickman's Model," *Rod Serling's Night Gallery* (NBC)

OUTSTANDING ACHIEVEMENT IN CINEMATOGRAPHY FOR ENTERTAINMENT PROGRAMMING

For a series or a single program of a series:

☐ Lloyd Ahern, ASC, "Blue Print for Murder," *Columbo* (NBC)

Charles G. Clarke, "The Only Way to Go," *Arnie* (CBS)

Robert L. Morrison, *Hawaii Five-O* (CBS)

For a special or feature length program made for television:

☐ Joseph Biroc, "Brian's Song," *Movie of the Week* (ABC)

Ray Henman, "The Snow Goose," *Hallmark Hall of Fame* (NBC)

Jack A. Marta, "Duel," *Movie of the Weekend* (ABC)

OUTSTANDING ACHIEVEMENT IN CINEMATOGRAPHY FOR NEWS AND DOCUMENTARY PROGRAMMING

Regularly scheduled News programs and coverage of Special Events:

☐ Peter McIntyre, Lim Youn Choul, "Dacca," *NBC Nightly News* (NBC)

William Bryan, "Pontiac Bussing," *NBC Nightly News* (NBC)

Vo Huynh, "Beautiful Vietnam," *NBC Nightly News* (NBC)

Kyung Mo Lee, "Seoul Hotel Fire," *NBC Nightly News* (NBC)

Hoang Trong Nghia, Vo Suu, "Viet Casualties," *NBC Nightly News* (NBC)

Charles A. Ray, "West Virginia Flood," *NBC Nightly News* (NBC)

Larry Travis, "Nitrogen Kills Columbia River Fish," *CBS Evening News with Walter Cronkite* (CBS)

Documentary, Magazine-type or Mini-documentary programs:
☐ Thomas Priestley, *Venice Be Damned!* (NBC)

Philippe Cousteau, "Forgotten Mermaids," *The Undersea World of Jacques Cousteau* (ABC)

Philippe Cousteau, Michel Deloire, "The Unsinkable Sea Otter," *The Undersea World of Jacques Cousteau* (ABC)

Michel Deloire, "Octopus, Octopus," *The Undersea World of Jacques Cousteau* (ABC)

Jacques Renoir, "A Sound of Dolphins," *The Undersea World of Jacques Cousteau* (ABC)

OUTSTANDING ACHIEVEMENT IN FILM EDITING FOR ENTERTAINMENT PROGRAMMING

For a series or a single program of a series:
☐ Edward M. Abroms, "Death Lends a Hand," *Columbo* (NBC)

Richard Bracken, Gloryette Clark, Terry Williams, *The Bold Ones—The Lawyers* (NBC)

Joseph T. Dervin, Sr., "Spell Legacy Like Death," *Longstreet* (ABC)

For a special or feature length program made for television:
☐ Bud S. Isaacs, "Brian's Song," *Movie of the Week* (ABC)

Gene Folwer, "The Glass House," *The New CBS Friday Night Movies* (CBS)

Ken Pearce, "The Snow Goose," *Hallmark Hall of Fame* (NBC)

OUTSTANDING ACHIEVEMENT IN FILM EDITING FOR NEWS AND DOCUMENTARY PROGRAMMING

Regularly scheduled News programs and coverage of Special Events:
☐ Darold Murray, "War Song," *NBC Nightly News* (NBC)

Gerald C. Breese, "Native Hawaiians," *NBC Nightly News* (NBC)

George L. Johnson, "Slaughter in East Pakistan Village of Subhadya," *NBC Nightly News* (NBC)

Documentary, Magazine-type or Mini-documentary programs:
☐ Spencer David Saxon, "Monkeys, Apes and Man," *National Geographic Society* (CBS)

☐ Indicates winner

Samuel Cohen, James Flanagan, "Earthquake!" *The Monday Night Special* (ABC)

John Soh, "The Forgotten Mermaids," *The Undersea World of Jacques Cousteau* (ABC)

OUTSTANDING ACHIEVEMENT IN FILM SOUND EDITING
☐ Jerry Christian, James Troutman, Ronald LaVine, Sidney Lubow, Richard Raderman, Dale Johnston, Sam Caylor, John Stacy, Jack Kirschner, "Duel," *Movie of the Weekend* (ABC)

Colin C. Mouat, Charles L. Campbell, Roger A. Sword, "The Forgotten Mermaids," *The Undersea World of Jacques Cousteau* (ABC)

Harold E. Wooley, Paul Laune, Marvin Kosberg, George Emick, Ralph Hickey, Wayne Fury, Monty Pearce, "Brian's Song," *Movie of the Week* (ABC)

OUTSTANDING ACHIEVEMENT IN FILM SOUND MIXING
☐ Theodore Soderberg, Richard Overton, "Fireball Forward," *The ABC Sunday Night Movie* (ABC)

William J. Montague, Alfred E. Overton, "Brian's Song," *Movie of the Week* (ABC)

George Porter, Roy Granville, Ed Nelson, "The Forgotten Mermaids," *The Undersea World of Jacques Cousteau* (ABC)

OUTSTANDING ACHIEVEMENT IN TECHNICAL DIRECTION AND ELECTRONIC CAMERAWORK
☐ Heino Ripp (technical director), Albert Camoin, Frank Gaeta, Gene Martin and Donald Mulvaney (cameramen), "Jack Lemmon in 'S Wonderful, 'S Marvelous, 'S Gershwin," *Bell System Family Theatre* (NBC)

Louis Fusari (technical director), Ray Figelski, Rick Lombardo, Wayne Osterhoudt and Jon Olson (cameramen), *The Flip Wilson Show* (with Petula Clark, Redd Foxx) (NBC)

O. Tamburri (technical director), Don Mulvaney, Jon Olson and Bob Keys (cameramen), "Gideon," *Hallmark Hall of Fame* (NBC)

OUTSTANDING ACHIEVEMENT IN LIGHTING DIRECTION FOR A SINGLE PROGRAM OF A SERIES OR A SPECIAL PROGRAM, PRODUCED FOR ELECTRONIC TELEVISION ONLY
☐ John Freschi, "Gideon," *Hallmark Hall of Fame* (NBC)

William Klages, *Good Vibrations from Central Park* (ABC)

John R. Nance, *The Flip Wilson Show* (with Petula Clark, Redd Foxx) (NBC)

OUTSTANDING ACHIEVEMENT IN VIDEO TAPE EDITING
☐ Pat McKenna "Hogan's Goat," *Special of the Week* (PBS)

Frank Herold, "Paradise Lost—Part II," *NET Playhouse on the 30's* (PBS)

Mike Wenig, "The Twentieth Century Follies," *The ABC Comedy Hour* (ABC)

OUTSTANDING ACHIEVEMENT IN LIVE OR TAPE SOUND MIXING
☐ Norman H. Dewes, "The Elevator Story," *All in the Family* (CBS)

Bill Cole, *Bing Crosby and His Friends* (NBC)

Dave Williams, *The Flip Wilson Show* (with Petula Clark, Redd Foxx) (NBC)

The Areas*

SPECIAL CLASSIFICATION OF OUTSTANDING PROGRAM AND INDIVIDUAL ACHIEVEMENT

General Programming:
☐ "The Pentagon Papers," *PBS Special* (PBS)

The Advocates (PBS)

The French Chef (PBS)

Mutual of Omaha's Wild Kingdom (Syndicated)

The Wonderful World of Disney (NBC)

Docu-Drama:
☐ *The Search for the Nile—Parts I-VI* (NBC)

"The Plot to Murder Hitler," *Appointment with Destiny* (CBS)

Individuals:
☐ Michael Hastings and Derek Marlow (writers), *The Search for the Nile—Parts I-VI* (NBC)

Jess Paley (cinematographer), "The Plot to Murder Hitler," *Appointment with Destiny* (CBS)

Brian Tufano and John Baker (cinematographers), *The Search for the Nile—Parts I-VI* (NBC)

George Porter, David Ronne, Roy Granville and Edward Nelson (film sound mixers), "Showdown at O.K. Corral," *Appointment with Destiny* (CBS)

William Morris (technical director), Robert Bernstein, Philip Fontana, Richard Kerr, Jessel Kohn, Morton Levin, John Morreale and Michael Rebich (cameramen), *25th Annual Antoinette Perry (Tony) Awards* (ABC)

* possibility of one award, more than one award or no award

OUTSTANDING ACHIEVEMENT IN SPORTS PROGRAMMING

Programs:
☐ *ABC'S Wide World of Sports* (ABC)
NFL Monday Night Football (ABC)
Rose Bowl Game (NBC)
World Series (baseball) (NBC)
Jack Perkins (correspondent), "The Perkins Piece," *XI Olympic Winter Games* (NBC)

Individuals:
☐ William P. Kelley (technical director), Jim Culley, Jack Bennett, Buddy Joseph, Mario Ciarlo, Frank Manfredi, Corey Leible, Gene Martin, Cal Shadwell, Billy Barnes and Ron Charbonneau (cameramen), *AFC Championship Game* (NBC)

OUTSTANDING ACHIEVEMENT IN CHILDREN'S PROGRAMMING

Programs:
☐ *Sesame Street* (PBS)
The Electric Company (PBS)

Individuals:
George W. Riesenberger (lighting director), *Sesame Street* (PBS)
John Scott Trotter (music director), *Play It Again, Charlie Brown* (CBS)

OUTSTANDING ACHIEVEMENT IN DAYTIME DRAMA

Programs:
☐ *The Doctors* (NBC)
General Hospital (ABC)

Individuals:
John L. Coffey (technical director), and Selwyn Reed, Louis Gerard and Gene Martin (cameramen), *Another World* (NBC)
Mel Handelsman (lighting director), *All My Children* (ABC)

OUTSTANDING ACHIEVEMENT IN DAYTIME PROGRAMMING

(No awards presented)

Programs:
Dinah's Place (NBC)
The Hollywood Squares (NBC)

Individuals:
Paul Lynde, *The Hollywood Squares* (NBC)
Peter Marshall, *The Hollywood Squares* (NBC)

OUTSTANDING ACHIEVEMENT IN RELIGIOUS PROGRAMMING

Programs:
Insight (Syndicated)
This Is The Life (Syndicated)

Individuals:
☐ Alfredo Antonini (music director), *And David Wept* (CBS)
☐ Lon Stucky (lighting director), "A City of the King," *Contact* (Syndicated)

☐ Indicates winner

OUTSTANDING ACHIEVEMENT IN ANY AREA OF CREATIVE TECHNICAL CRAFTS

☐ Pierre Goupil, Michel Deloire and Yves Omer (underwater cameramen), "Secrets of the Sunken Caves," *The Undersea World of Jacques Cousteau* (ABC)
Robert Guenette, David Wolper, Warren Bush, Nicholas Webster and Robert Larson (re-creation of vintage films), "The Plot to Murder Hitler," "The Last Days of John Dillinger," "Showdown at O.K. Corral," *Appointment with Destiny* (CBS)
Edie Panda (hairstylist), "U.S.A.," *Hollywood Television Theatre* (PBS)

Special Awards

TRUSTEES AWARDS

Bill Lawrence, National Affairs Editor, ABC News (deceased). For dedicating more than four decades of his life to reporting the news of the nation, the last one of which was devoted to television; ranging from internal politics to international affairs and global combat; with that degree of objectivity, that devotion to truth, that professional preeminence which can only serve as a model for all television newsmen.
Dr. Frank Stanton, President CBS. For his selfless leadership and unwavering principle in defense of our industry under attack, his outspoken stance and courageous posture in protecting the right of the people to know, frequently in the face of potential dangers, both personal and professional, from those many forces which have attempted to abridge or even to abolish that right.

OUTSTANDING ACHIEVEMENT IN ENGINEERING DEVELOPMENT

Lee Harrison, III. For the development of Scanimate, a unique electronic means of generating picture animation.

CITATIONS

Richard E. Hill and Electronic Engineering Company of California. For the development of a time code and equipment to facilitate the editing of magnetic video tape.
National Broadcasting System. For the development of the Hum Bucker, which provides a practical means to correct a picture transmission defect commonly encountered on remote pickups.

THE STATION AWARD

☐ *Sickle Cell Disease: Paradox of Neglect* (WZZM-TV, Grand Rapids)
All About Welfare (WITF-TV, Hershey)
The Awkward Age (WCKT-TV, Miami)
Drug Crises in East Harlem (WABC-TV, New York)
Inside Parish Prison (WWL-TV, New Orleans)
Louisville: Open City (WHAS, Louisville)
Make No Mistake About It: The President Came to Iowa (KDIN-TV, Educational Station, Des Moines)
A Place for Music (WHDH-TV, Boston)
Probe. . . And Throw Away the Key (WRC-TV, Washington, D.C.)
. . . Still Got Life To Go (WKY-TV, Oklahoma City)

News and Documentary Program and Individual Achievements*

OUTSTANDING ACHIEVEMENT WITHIN REGULARLY SCHEDULED NEWS PROGRAMS

Programs:
"Defeat of Dacca," *NBC Nightly News* (NBC)
"Coverage of President Nixon's Visit to China," *NBC Nightly News* (NBC)
"Howard Hughes Phone Interview," *NBC Nightly News* (NBC)

Individuals:
☐ Phil Brady (reporter), "Defeat of Dacca," *NBC Nightly News* (NBC)
☐ Bod Schieffer, Phil Jones, Don Webster and Bill Plante (correspondents), "The Air War," *CBS Evening News with Walter Cronkite* (CBS)
David Brinkley (correspondent), "David Brinkley's Journal," *NBC Nightly News* (NBC)
John Chancellor (correspondent), "President Nixon's Visit to China," *NBC Nightly News* (NBC)

OUTSTANDING ACHIEVEMENT FOR REGULARLY SCHEDULED MAGAZINE-TYPE PROGRAMS

Programs:
☐ *Chronolog* (NBC)
☐ *The Great American Dream Machine* (PBS)
60 Minutes (CBS)

Individuals:
☐ Mike Wallace (correspondent), *60 Minutes* (CBS)
Tom Pettit (reporter), "The Business of Blood," *Chronolog* (NBC)

* possibility of one award, more than one award or no award

Andrew A. Rooney (writer), "An Essay on War," *The Great American Dream Machine* (PBS)

Morley Safer (correspondent), *60 Minutes* (CBS)

OUTSTANDING ACHIEVEMENT IN COVERAGE OF SPECIAL EVENTS

Programs:
☐ *The China Trip* (ABC)
☐ *June 30, 1971, A Day for History: The Supreme Court and the Pentagon Papers* (NBC)
☐ *A Ride on the Moon: The Flight of Apollo 15* (CBS)
Louis Armstrong 1900-1971 (CBS)
The President in China (CBS)

Individuals:
Joel Banow (director), *Louis Armstrong 1900-1971* (CBS)
Anthony C. Messuri (director), *The Flight of Apollo 15: A Journey To Hadley Rille* (NBC)

OUTSTANDING DOCUMENTARY PROGRAM ACHIEVEMENT

Programs—Current Significance:
☐ "A Night in Jail, A Day in Court," *CBS Reports* (CBS)
☐ *This Child Is Rated X: An NBC News White Paper on Juvenile Justice* (NBC)
"Justice in America—Parts II and III" *CBS Reports* (CBS)
"Some Are More Equal Than Others," *Justice in America—CBS Reports* (CBS)
"Under Surveillance" *CBS Reports* (CBS)

Programs—Cultural:
☐ "Hollywood: The Dream Factory," *The Monday Night Special* (ABC)
☐ "A Sound of Dolphins," *The Undersea World of Jacques Cousteau* (ABC)
☐ "The Unsinkable Sea Otter," *The Undersea World of Jacques Cousteau* (ABC)
The American West of John Ford (CBS)
"The Forgotten Mermaids," *The Undersea World of Jacques Cousteau* (ABC)
"Picasso Is 90," *CBS Reports* (CBS)

Individuals:
☐ Louis J. Hazam (writer), *Venice Be Damned!* (NBC)
☐ Robert Northshield (writer), *Suffer the Little Children—An NBC News White Paper on Northern Ireland* (NBC)
Martin Carr (writer), *This Child Is Rated X: An NBC White Paper on Juvenile Justice* (NBC)
Fred Flamenhaft (director), *Suffer the Little Children—An NBC News White Paper on Northern Ireland* (NBC)

☐ Indicates winner

Andy White (writer), "Octopus, Octopus," *The Undersea World of Jacques Cousteau* (ABC)

1972/73

(For programs aired between March 13, 1972 and March 18, 1973. Entertainment awards presented May 20, 1973. News and Documentary Awards presented May 22, 1973)

Entertainment Program Awards

OUTSTANDING COMEDY SERIES
☐ *All in the Family* (CBS)
The Mary Tyler Moore Show (CBS)
*M*A*S*H* (CBS)
Maude (CBS)
Sanford and Son (NBC)

OUTSTANDING DRAMA SERIES—CONTINUING
☐ *The Waltons* (CBS)
Cannon (CBS)
Columbo (NBC)
Hawaii Five-O (CBS)
Kung Fu (ABC)
Mannix (CBS)

OUTSTANDING DRAMA/COMEDY—LIMITED EPISODES
☐ "Tom Brown's Schooldays," *Masterpiece Theatre* (PBS)
"The Last of the Mohicans," *Masterpiece Theatre* (PBS)
The Life of Leonardo da Vinci (CBS)

OUTSTANDING VARIETY MUSICAL SERIES
☐ *The Julie Andrews Hour* (ABC)
The Carol Burnett Show (CBS)
The Dick Cavett Show (ABC)
The Flip Wilson Show (NBC)
The Sonny & Cher Comedy Hour (CBS)

OUTSTANDING SINGLE PROGRAM—DRAMA OR COMEDY
☐ "A War of Children," *The New CBS Tuesday Night Movies* (CBS)
Long Day's Journey Into Night (ABC)
"The Marcus Nelson Murders," *The CBS Thursday Night Movies* (CBS)
"The Red Pony," *Bell System Family Theatre* (NBC)
"That Certain Summer," *Wednesday Movie of the Week* (ABC)

OUTSTANDING SINGLE PROGRAM—VARIETY AND POPULAR MUSIC
☐ *Singer Presents Liza with a "Z"* (NBC)
Applause (CBS)
Once Upon a Mattress (CBS)

OUTSTANDING SINGLE PROGRAM—CLASSICAL MUSIC
☐ *The Sleeping Beauty* (PBS)
"Bernstein in London," *Special of the Week* (PBS)
The Metropolitan Opera Salute to Sir Rudolf Bing (CBS)

OUTSTANDING NEW SERIES
☐ *America* (NBC)
The Julie Andrews Hour (ABC)
Kung Fu (ABC)
*M*A*S*H* (CBS)
Maude (CBS)
The Waltons (CBS)

OUTSTANDING PROGRAM ACHIEVEMENT IN DAYTIME DRAMA
☐ *The Edge of Night* (CBS)
Days of Our Lives (NBC)
The Doctors (NBC)
One Life to Live (ABC)

OUTSTANDING PROGRAM ACHIEVEMENT IN DAYTIME
☐ *Dinah's Place* (NBC)
The Hollywood Squares (NBC)
Jeopardy (NBC)
The Mike Douglas Show (Syndicated)
Password (ABC)

Entertainment Performance Awards

OUTSTANDING SINGLE PERFORMANCE BY AN ACTOR IN A LEADING ROLE
☐ Laurence Olivier, *Long Day's Journey Into Night* (ABC)
Henry Fonda, "The Red Pony," *Bell System Family Theatre* (NBC)
Hal Holbrook, "That Certain Summer," *Wednesday Movie of the Week* (ABC)
Telly Savalas, "The Marcus Nelson Murders," *The CBS Thursday Night Movies* (CBS)

OUTSTANDING SINGLE PERFORMANCE BY AN ACTRESS IN A LEADING ROLE
☐ Cloris Leachman, "A Brand New Life," *Tuesday Movie of the Week* (ABC)
Lauren Bacall, *Applause* (CBS)
Hope Lange, "That Certain Summer," *Wednesday Movie of the Week* (ABC)

OUTSTANDING CONTINUED PERFORMANCE BY AN ACTOR IN A LEADING ROLE

Drama series—continuing:
☐ Richard Thomas, *The Waltons* (CBS)
David Carradine, *Kung Fu* (ABC)
Mike Connors, *Mannix* (CBS)
William Conrad, *Cannon* (CBS)
Peter Falk, *Columbo* (NBC)

Drama/comedy—limited episodes:

☐ Anthony Murphy, "Tom Browns's Schooldays," *Masterpiece Theatre* (PBS)

John Abineri, "The Last of the Mohicans," *Masterpiece Theatre* (PBS)

Philippe LeRoy, *The Life of Leonardo daVinci* (CBS)

OUTSTANDING CONTINUED PERFORMANCE BY AN ACTRESS IN A LEADING ROLE

Drama series—continuing:

☐ Michael Learned, *The Waltons* (CBS)

Linda Day George, *Mission: Impossible* (CBS)

Susan Saint James, *McMillan & Wife* (NBC)

Drama/comedy—limited episodes:

☐ Susan Hampshire, "Vanity Fair," *Masterpiece Theatre* (PBS)

Vivien Heilbron, "The Moonstone," *Masterpiece Theatre* (PBS)

Margaret Tyzack, "Cousin Bette," *Masterpiece Theatre* (PBS)

OUTSTANDING CONTINUED PERFORMANCE BY AN ACTOR IN A LEADING ROLE IN A COMEDY SERIES

☐ Jack Klugman, *The Odd Couple* (ABC)

Alan Alda, *M*A*S*H* (CBS)

Redd Foxx, Sanford and Son (NBC)

Carroll O'Connor, *All in the Family* (CBS)

Tony Randall, *The Odd Couple* (ABC)

OUTSTANDING CONTINUED PERFORMANCE BY AN ACTRESS IN A LEADING ROLE IN A COMEDY SERIES

☐ Mary Tyler Moore, *The Mary Tyler Moore Show* (CBS)

Beatrice Arthur, *Maude* (CBS)

Jean Stapleton, *All in the Family* (CBS)

OUTSTANDING PERFORMANCE BY AN ACTOR IN A SUPPORTING ROLE IN DRAMA

☐ Scott Jacoby, "That Certain Summer," *Wednesday Movie of the Week* (ABC)

Will Geer, *The Waltons* (CBS)

James Brolin, *Marcus Welby, M.D.* (ABC)

OUTSTANDING PERFORMANCE BY AN ACTRESS IN A SUPPORTING ROLE IN DRAMA

☐ Ellen Corby, *The Waltons* (CBS)

Gail Fisher, *Mannix* (CBS)

Nancy Walker, *McMillan & Wife* (NBC)

OUTSTANDING PERFORMANCE BY AN ACTOR IN A SUPPORTING ROLE IN COMEDY

☐ Ted Knight, *The Mary Tyler Moore Show* (CBS)

☐ Indicates winner

Edward Asner, *The Mary Tyler Moore Show* (CBS)

Gary Burghoff, *M*A*S*H* (CBS)

Rob Reiner, *All in the Family* (CBS)

McLean Stevenson, *M*A*S*H* (CBS)

OUTSTANDING PERFORMANCE BY AN ACTRESS IN A SUPPORTING ROLE IN COMEDY

☐ Valerie Harper, *The Mary Tyler Moore Show* (CBS)

Cloris Leachman, *The Mary Tyler Moore Show* (CBS)

Sally Struthers, *All in the Family* (CBS)

OUTSTANDING ACHIEVEMENT BY A SUPPORTING PERFORMER IN MUSIC OR VARIETY

☐ Tim Conway, *The Carol Burnett Show* (CBS)

Harvey Korman, *The Carol Burnett Show* (CBS)

Liza Minnelli, *A Royal Gala Variety Performance in the Presence of Her Majesty the Queen* (ABC)

Lily Tomlin, *Rowan and Martin's Laugh-In* (NBC)

Entertainment, Craft and Technical Awards

OUTSTANDING DIRECTORIAL ACHIEVEMENT IN DRAMA (A SINGLE PROGRAM OF A SERIES)

☐ Jerry Thorpe, "An Eye for an Eye," *Kung Fu* (ABC)

Edward M. Abroms, "The Most Dangerous Match," *Columbo* (NBC)

Lee Philips, "The Love Story," *The Waltons* (CBS)

OUTSTANDING DIRECTORIAL ACHIEVEMENT IN DRAMA (A SINGLE PROGRAM)

☐ Joseph Sargent, "The Marcus-Nelson Murders," *The CBS Thursday Night Movies* (CBS)

Lamont Johnson, "That Certain Summer," *Wednesday Movie of the Week* (ABC)

George Schaefer, "A War of Children," *The New CBS Tuesday Night Movies* (CBS)

OUTSTANDING DIRECTORIAL ACHIEVEMENT IN COMEDY A SINGLE PROGRAM OF A SERIES WITH CONTINUING CHARACTERS AND/OR THEME

☐ Jay Sandrich, "It's Whether You Win or Lose," *The Mary Tyler Moore Show* (CBS)

Gene Reynolds, "P-I-L-O-T," *M*A*S*H* (CBS)

John Rich, Bob LaHendro, "The Bunkers and the Swingers," *All in the Family* (CBS)

OUTSTANDING DIRECTORIAL ACHIEVEMENT IN VARIETY OR MUSIC A SINGLE PROGRAM OF A SERIES

☐ Bill Davis, *The Julie Andrews Hour* (with "Liza Doolittle," "Mary Poppins") (ABC)

Art Fisher, *The Sonny & Cher Comedy Hour* (with Mike Connors) (CBS)

Tim Kiley, *The Flip Wilson Show* (with Roberta Flack, Burt Reynolds) (NBC)

OUTSTANDING DIRECTORIAL ACHIEVEMENT IN COMEDY, VARIETY OR MUSIC FOR A SPECIAL PROGRAM

☐ Bob Fosse, *Singer Presents Liza with a "Z"* (NBC)

Martin Charnin, Dave Wilson, *Jack Lemmon—Get Happy* (NBC)

Stan Harris, *Duke Ellington. . . We Love You Madly* (CBS)

Walter C. Miller, "You're a Good Man Charlie Brown," *Hallmark Hall of Fame* (NBC)

Dave Powers, Ron Field, *Once Upon a Mattress* (CBS)

OUTSTANDING WRITING ACHIEVEMENT IN DRAMA FOR A SINGLE PROGRAM OF A SERIES WITH CONTINUING CHARACTERS AND/OR THEME

☐ John McGreevey, "The Scholar," *The Waltons* (CBS)

Steven Bochco, "Etude in Black," *Columbo* (NBC)

Earl Hamner, Jr., "The Love Story," *The Waltons* (CBS)

OUTSTANDING WRITING ACHIEVEMENT IN DRAMA, ORIGINAL TELEPLAY FOR A SINGLE PROGRAM

☐ Abby Mann, "The Marcus-Nelson Murders," *The CBS Thursday Night Movies* (CBS)

David Karp, "Hawkins on Murder," *The New CBS Tuesday Night Movies* (CBS)

Richard Levinson, William Ling, "That Certain Summer," *Wednesday Movie of the Week* (ABC)

OUTSTANDING WRITING ACHIEVEMENT IN DRAMA, ADAPTATION FOR A SINGLE PROGRAM OF A SERIES WITH CONTINUING CHARACTERS AND/OR THEME

☐ Eleanor Perry, *The House Without a Christmas Tree* (CBS)

Robert Totten, Ron Bishop, "The Red Pony," *Bell System Family Theatre* (NBC)

Ellen M. Violett, "Go Ask Alice," *Wednesday Movie of the Week* (ABC)

OUTSTANDING WRITING ACHIEVEMENT IN COMEDY FOR A SINGLE PROGRAM OF A SERIES WITH CONTINUING CHARACTERS AND/OR THEME

☐ Michael Ross, Bernie West and Lee Kalcheim, "The Bunkers and the Swingers," *All in the Family* (CBS)

Allan Burns, James L. Brooks, "The Good-Time News," *The Mary Tyler Moore Show* (CBS)

Larry Gelbart, "P-I-L-O-T," *M*A*S*H* (CBS)

OUTSTANDING WRITING ACHIEVEMENT IN VARIETY OR MUSIC FOR A SINGLE PROGRAM OF A SERIES

☐ Stan Hart, Larry Siegel, Gail Parent, Woody Kling, Roger Beatty, Tom Patchett, Jay Tarses, Robert Hilliard, Arnie Kogen, Bill Angelos, Buz Kohan, *The Carol Burnett Show* (with Steve Lawrence, Lily Tomlin) (CBS)

Herbert Baker, Mike Marmer, Stan Burns, Don Hinkley, Dick Hills, Sid Green, Paul McCauley, Peter Gallay, Flip Wilson, *The Flip Wilson Show* (with Sammy Davis, Jr., Ed Sullivan, Marilyn Michaels) (NBC)

Bob Ellison, Hal Goodman, Larry Kelin, Jay Burton, George Bloom, Lila Garrett, John Aylesworth, Frank Peppiatt, *The Julia Andrews Hour* (with "Eliza Doolittle," "Mary Poppins") (ABC)

OUTSTANDING WRITING ACHIEVEMENT IN COMEDY, VARIETY OR MUSIC FOR A SPECIAL PROGRAM

☐ Renee Taylor, Joseph Bologna, *Acts of Love—And Other Comedies* (ABC)

Fred Ebb, *Singer Presents Liza with a "Z"* (NBC)

Allan Manings, Ann Elder, Karyl Geld, Richard Pryor, John Rappaport, Jim Rusk, Lily Tomlin, Jane Wagner, Rod Warren, George Yanok, *The Lily Tomlin Show* (CBS)

OUTSTANDING ACHIEVEMENT IN CHOREOGRAPHY

☐ Bob Fosse, *Singer Presents Liza with a "Z"* (NBC)

Tony Charmoli, *The Julie Andrews Hour* (with Robert Goulet, Joel Grey) (ABC)

Ernest O. Flatt, "Family Show," *The Carol Burnett Show* (CBS)

☐ Indicates winner

OUTSTANDING ACHIEVEMENT IN MUSIC COMPOSITION FOR A SERIES OR A SINGLE PROGRAM OF A SERIES (IN THE FIRST YEAR OF MUSIC'S USE ONLY)

☐ Charles Fox, *Love, American Style* (ABC)

Alexander Courage, "Cycle of Peril," *Medical Center* (CBS)

Marty Paich, *Ironside* (NBC)

For a special program:

☐ Jerry Goldsmith, "The Red Pony," *Bell System Family Theatre* (NBC)

Fred Ebb, John Kander, *Singer Presents Liza with a "Z"* (NBC)

Billy Goldenberg, "A Brand New Life," *Tuesday Movie of the Week* (ABC)

OUTSTANDING ACHIEVEMENT IN MUSIC DIRECTION OF A VARIETY, MUSICAL OR DRAMATIC PROGRAM

☐ Peter Matz, *The Carol Burnett Show* (with Anthony Newley, Bernadette Peters) (CBS)

Van Alexander, *The Wacky World of Jonathan Winters* (with Debbie Reynolds) (Syndicated)

Irwin Kostal, *Dr. Jekyll and Mr. Hyde* (NBC)

OUTSTANDING ACHIEVEMENT IN MUSIC, LYRICS AND SPECIAL MATERIAL FOR A SERIES OR A SINGLE PROGRAM OF A SERIES OR A SPECIAL PROGRAM WRITTEN FOR TELEVISION

☐ Fred Ebb, John Kander, *Singer Presents Liza with a "Z"* (NBC)

Earl Brown, "The Gloria Majestic Story," *The Sonny and Cher Comedy Hour* (with Jean Stapleton) (CBS)

Billy Goldenberg, Bobby Russell, "The Marcus-Nelson Murders," *The CBS Thursday Night Movies* (CBS)

OUTSTANDING ACHIEVEMENT IN ART DIRECTION OR SCENIC DESIGN

For a dramatic program or feature length film made for television; for a series, a single program of a series or a special program:

☐ Tom John, *Much Ado About Nothing* (CBS)

Robert Boyle and James Hulsey (art directors), John Kurl (set decorator), "The Red Pony," *Tuesday Movie of the Week* (ABC)

William Campbell, "Night of Terror," *Tuesday Movie of the Week* (ABC)

Gibson Holly (art director), Lucien M. Hafley (set decorator), "Western," *Mission: Impossible* (CBS)

Jan Scott, "Another Part of the Forest," *Hollywood Television Theatre Special of the Week* (PBS)

Jan M. Van Tamelen (art director), Fred R. Price (set decorator), *Mannix* (CBS)

For a Musical or Variety single program of a series or a special program:

☐ Brian Bartholomew, Keaton S. Walker, *The Julie Andrews Hour* (with "Eliza Doolittle," "Mary Poppins") (ABC)

Paul Barnes and Bob Sansom (art directors), Bill Harp (set decorator), "The Doily Sisters," *The Carol Burnett Show* (CBS)

Romain Johnston, *The Flip Wilson Show* (with Burt Reynolds, Tim Conway, Roberta Flack) (NBC)

OUTSTANDING ACHIEVEMENT IN LIGHTING DIRECTION FOR A SINGLE PROGRAM OF A SERIES OR A SPECIAL PROGRAM, PRODUCED FOR ELECTRONIC TELEVISION ONLY

☐ John Freschi, John Casagrande, *44th Annual Oscar Awards* (NBC)

Truck Krone, "Christmas Show," *The Julie Andrews Hour* (ABC)

John R. Beam, *The Sonny and Cher Comedy Hour* (with William Conrad) (CBS)

OUTSTANDING ACHIEVEMENT IN COSTUME DESIGN

☐ Jack Bear, *The Julie Andrews Hour* (with Ken Berry, Jack Cassidy) (ABC)

Theoni V. Aldredge, *Much Ado About Nothing* (CBS)

Grady Hunt, "Dagger of the Mind," *Columbo* (NBC)

Emma Porteous, *Dr. Jekyll and Mr. Hyde* (NBC)

Christina Von Humboldt, "Cortez and Montezuma," *Appointment with Destiny* (CBS)

OUTSTANDING ACHIEVEMENT IN MAKE-UP

☐ Del Armstrong, Ellis Burman, Stan Winston, "Gargoyles," *The New CBS Tuesday Night Movies* (CBS)

Robert A. Sidell, "The Actress," *The Waltons* (CBS)

Neville Smallwood, *Dr. Jekyll and Mr. Hyde* (NBC)

Allan Snyder, Richard Cobos, "The Red Pony," *Bell System Family Theatre* (NBC)

Frank C. Westmore, "Chains," *Kung Fu* (ABC)

Michael Westmore, Marvin Westmore, *Frankenstein—Parts I and II* (ABC)

OUTSTANDING ACHIEVEMENT IN CINEMATOGRAPHY FOR ENTERTAINMENT PROGRAMMING

For a series or a single program of a series:

☐ Jack Woolf, "Eye for an Eye," *Kung Fu* (ABC)

Sam Leavitt, "Banacek," *NBC Wednesday Mystery Movie* (NBC)

Russell L. Metty, *The Waltons* (CBS)

For a special or feature length program made for television:

☐ Howard Schwartz, ASC, "Night of Terror," *Tuesday Movie of the Week* (ABC)

Andrew Jackson, "The Red Pony," *Bell System Family Theatre* (NBC)

Owen Roizman, *Singer Presents Liza with a "Z"* (NBC)

OUTSTANDING ACHIEVEMENT IN FILM EDITING FOR ENTERTAINMENT PROGRAMMING

For a series or a single program of a series:

☐ Gene Fowler, Jr., Marjorie Fowler, Anthony Wollner, "The Literary Man," *The Waltons* (CBS)

Douglas Hines, *The Mary Tyler Moore Show* (CBS)

Stanford Tischler, Fred W. Berger, *M*A*S*H* (CBS)

For a special or feature length program made for television:

☐ Peter C. Johnson, Ed Spiegel, "Surrender at Appomattox," *Apppointment with Destiny* (CBS)

Henry Berman, ACE, "Go Ask Alice," *Wednesday Movie of the Week* (ABC)

Alan Heim, *Singer Presents Liza with a "Z"* (NBC)

OUTSTANDING ACHIEVEMENT IN FILM SOUND EDITING

☐ Ross Taylor, Fred Brown, David Marshall, "The Red Pony," *Bell System Family Theatre* (NBC)

Peter Berkos, John Singleton, Brian Courcier, Gordon Ecker, John Stacy, James Nownes, George Luckenbacher, Walter Jenevein, Sidney Lubow, "Short Walk to Daylight," *Tuesday Movie of the Week* (ABC)

Charles L. Campbell, Roger A. Sword, Robert H. Cornett, Jerry R. Stanford, "The Smile of the Walrus," *The Undersea World of Jacques Cousteau* (ABC)

OUTSTANDING ACHIEVEMENT IN FILM SOUND MIXING

☐ Richard J. Wagner, George E. Porter, Eddie J. Nelson, Fred Leroy Granville, "Surrender at Appomattox, *Appointment with Destiny* (CBS)

☐ Indicates winner

Melvin M. Metcalf, Sr., Thom Piper, "That Certain Summer," *Wednesday Movie of the Week* (ABC)

George Porter, Eddie Nelson, Hoppy Mehterian, "The Singing Whale," *The Undersea World of Jacques Cousteau* (ABC)

OUTSTANDING ACHIEVEMENT IN LIVE OR TAPE SOUND MIXING

☐ Al Gramaglia, Mahlon Fox, *Much Ado About Nothing* (CBS)

William J. Levitsky, *44th Annual Oscar Awards* (NBC)

Philip Ramone, *Duke Ellington. . . We Love You Madly* (CBS)

OUTSTANDING ACHIEVEMENT IN VIDEO TAPE EDITING

☐ Nick Giordano, Arthur Schneider, *The Julie Andrews Hour* (with "Eliza Doolittle," "Mary Poppins") (ABC)

William H. Breshears, Andrew McIntyre, *Ed Sullivan Presents the TV Comedy Years* (CBS)

James H. Rose, *Burt Bacharach in Shangri-La* (ABC)

Charles Shadel, Walter Balderson, "Democratic Convention Highlights," *NBC Nightly News* (NBC)

Mike Wenig, *Love Is. . . Barbara Eden* (ABC)

OUTSTANDING ACHIEVEMENT IN TECHNICAL DIRECTION AND ELECTRONIC CAMERAWORK

☐ Ernie Buttelman (technical director), and Robert A. Kemp, James Angel, James Balden and Dave Hilmer (cameramen), *The Julie Andrews Hour* (with "Mary Poppins," "Eliza Doolittle") (ABC)

Charles Franklin (technical director), and Gorme Erickson, Jack Jennings, Tom McConnell, Richard Nelson and Barney Neeley (cameramen), *The Sonny & Cher Comedy Hour* (with Mike Connors) (CBS)

E. G. Johnson (technical director), Sam Drummy (cameraman), *Apollo 17 Splashdown* (Pool Coverage)

OUTSTANDING ACHIEVEMENT BY INDIVIDUALS IN DAYTIME DRAMA

☐ Mary Fickett (performer), *All My Children* (ABC)

Macdonald Carey (performer), *Days of Our Lives* (NBC)

Norman Hall (director) *The Doctors* (NBC)

H. Wesley Kenney (director), *Days of Our Lives* (NBC)

Peter Levin (director), *Love Is a Many Splendored Thing* (CBS)

David Pressman (director), *One Life To Live* (ABC)

Victor Paganuzzi (scenic designer), John A. Wendell (set decorator),

Love Is a Many Splendored Thing (CBS)

The Areas*

OUTSTANDING ACHIEVEMENT BY INDIVIDUALS IN DAYTIME PROGRAMMING

An award for individual achievements which do not qualify in Daytime Drama:

Bill Cullen (host), *Three on a Match* (NBC)

Paul Lynde (performer), *The Hollywood Squares* (NBC)

Peter Marshall (host), *The Hollywood Squares* (NBC)

OUTSTANDING ACHIEVEMENT IN CHILDREN'S PROGRAMMING

Entertainment/Fictional:

☐ *Sesame Street* (PBS)

☐ *Zoom* (PBS)

☐ Tom Whedon, John Boni, Sara Compton, Tom Dunsmuir, Thad Mumford, Jeremy Stevens and Jim Thurman (writers), *The Electric Company* (PBS)

Henry Bahar (director), *The Electric Company* (PBS)

Robert G. Myhrum (director), *Sesame Street* (PBS)

Charles M. Schulz (writer), *You're Elected, Charlie Brown* (CBS)

Joe Raposo (music director), *Sesame Street* (PBS)

Informational/Factual:

☐ "Last of the Curlews," *The ABC Afterschool Special* (ABC)

☐ Shari Lewis (performer), "A Picture of Us," *NBC Children's Theatre* (NBC)

In the News (CBS)

Make a Wish (ABC)

Jameson Brewer (writer), "Last of the Curlews," *The ABC Afterschool Special* (ABC)

OUTSTANDING ACHIEVEMENT IN SPORTS PROGRAMMING

☐ *ABC'S Wide World of Sports* (ABC)

☐ *1972 Summer Olympic Games* (ABC)

☐ John Croak, Charles Gardner, Jakob Hierl, Conrad Kraus, Edward McCarthy, Nick Mazur, Alex Moskovic, James Parker, Louis Rende, Ross Skipper, Robert Steinback, John DeLisa, George Boettcher, Merrit Roesser, Leo Scharf, Randy Cohen, Vito Gerardi, Harold Byers, Winfield Gross, Paul Scoskie, Peter Fritz, Leo Stephan, Gerber McBeath, Louis Torino, Michael Wenig, Tom Wight and James Kelley (video tape editors),

*possibility of one award, more than one award or no award

1972 Summer Olympic Games (ABC)
NCAA College Football (ABC)
NFL Monday Night Football (ABC)
Super Bowl VII (NBC)
Keith Jackson (commentator), *1972 Summer Olympic Games* (ABC)
Jim McKay (commentator), *1972 Summer Olympic Games* (ABC)

Special Awards

OUTSTANDING ACHIEVEMENT IN ENGINEERING DEVELOPMENT

Sony. For the development of the Trinitron, a picture tube providing good picture quality in color television receivers.

CMX Systems, a CBS/Memorex company. For the development of a video tape editing system, utilizing a computer to aid the decision-making process, store the editing decisions and implement them in the final assembly of takes.

THE NATIONAL AWARD FOR COMMUNITY SERVICE

☐ *Take Des Moines. . . Please* (KDIN-TV, educational station, Des Moines)
Bars to Progress (WMAR-TV, Baltimore)
Carrascolendas (KLRN-TV, educational station, Austin)
Egypt Valley—An Epitaph/A Call to Conscience (montage) (WKYC-TV, Cleveland)
The Green Grass of Home (KFDA-TV, Amarillo)
In a Class. . . All by Himself (KNBC-TV, Los Angeles)
Newsign 4 (KRON-TV, San Francisco)
One and One Is. . . Dos (WZZM-TV, Grand Rapids)
A Seed of Hope (WTVJ-TV, Miami)
Willowbrook: The Last Great Disgrace (WABC-TV, New York)

News and Documentary Program and Individual Achievements*

OUTSTANDING ACHIEVEMENT WITHIN REGULARLY SCHEDULED NEWS PROGRAMS

An award for program segments, i.e. the presentation of individual stories (in single or multi-part) or elements within the program:

☐ "The US/Soviet Wheat Deal: Is There a Scandal?" *CBS Evening News with Walter Cronkite* (CBS)
"Coverage of the Return of the POW'S," *NBC Nightly News* (NBC)

*possibility of one award, moe than one award or no award
☐ Indicates winner

"Coverage of the Shooting of Governor Wallace," *CBS Evening News with Walter Cronkite* (CBS)
"The Tasaday Tribe of the Philippines," *NBC Nightly News* (NBC)
"The Watergate Affair," *CBS Evening News with Walter Cronkite* (CBS)

An award for individuals contributing to the program segments:

☐ Walter Cronkite, Dan Rather, Daniel Schorr and Joel Blocker (correspondents), "The Watergate Affair," *CBS Evening News with Walter Cronkite* (CBS)
☐ David Dick, Dan Rather, Roger Mudd and Walter Cronkite (correspondents), "Coverage of the Shooting of Governor Wallace," *CBS Evening News with Walter Cronkite* (CBS)
☐ Eric Sevareid (correspondent), "LBJ—The Man and the President," *CBS Evening News with Walter Cronkite* (CBS)
John Chancellor (correspondent), "Coverage of President Nixon's Visit to Russia," *NBC Nightly News* (NBC)
Jack Reynolds (reporter), "The Tasaday Tribe of the Philippines," *NBC Nightly News; April 7-11, 1972* (NBC)
Eric Sevareid (correspondent), "The Paradox of Special Privilege: Executive Immunity and Shield Laws," *CBS Evening News with Walter Cronkite* (CBS)

OUTSTANDING ACHIEVEMENT FOR REGULARLY SCHEDULED MAGAZINE-TYPE PROGRAMS

An award for programs, program segments or series:

☐ "The Poppy Fields of Turdey—The Heroin Labs Of Marseilles—The N.Y. Connection," *60 Minutes* (CBS)
☐ "The Selling of Colonel Herbert," *60 Minutes* (CBS)
☐ *60 Minutes* (CBS)
First Tuesday (NBC)
Today (NBC)

An award for individuals contributing to the program, program segments or series achievements:

☐ Mike Wallace (correspondent), "The Selling of Colonel Hebert," *60 Minutes* (CBS)
☐ Mike Wallace (correspondent), *60 Minutes* (CBS)
Morley Safer (correspondent), *60 Minutes* (CBS)
Mike Wallace (correspondent), "Dita Beard Interview," *60 Minutes* (CBS)

Edwin Newman (writer), "No Contest," *Today* (NBC)

OUTSTANDING ACHIEVEMENT IN COVERAGE OF SPECIAL EVENTS

An award for program achievements:

☐ "Coverage of the Munich Olympic Tragedy," *ABC Special* (ABC)
"The 1972 Democratic National Convention," *NBC News Special* (NBC)
"Election Night '72," *NBC News Special* (NBC)
"Jackie Robinson," *CBS News Special* (CBS)
"The Return of the POW'S," *NBC News Special* (NBC)

An award for individuals contributing to the program achievement:

☐ Jim McKay (commentator), "Coverage of the Munich Olympic Tragedy," *ABC Special* (ABC)
John Chancellor, David Brinkley, Edwin Newman, Catherine Mackin, Douglas Kiker and Garrick Utley (correspondents), "Election Night '72," *NBC News Special* (NBC)
Harry Reasoner and Howard K. Smith (anchormen), "Elections '72," *ABC News Special* (ABC)
David Fox (director), *Apollo 17: Astronauts Splashdown in Pacific* (Pool Coverage)
Edwin Newman (writer), "Decision '72: It Starts Tomorrow," *NBC News Special* (NBC)

OUTSTANDING DOCUMENTARY PROGRAM ACHIEVEMENT

An award for documentary programs dealing with events or matters of current significance:

☐ "The Blue Collar Trap," *NBC News White Paper* (NBC)
☐ "The Mexican Connection," *CBS Reports* (CBS)
☐ "One Billion Dollar Weapon and Now the War Is Over—The American Military in the 70's," *NBC Reports* (NBC)
"If You Want Us To Stand Down, Tell Us and Now the War Is Over—The American Military in the 70's," *NBC Reports* (NBC)
"Pensions: The Broken Promise," *NBC Reports* (NBC)

An award for documentary programs dealing with artistic, historical or cultural subjects:

☐ *America* (NBC)
☐ *Jane Goodall and the World of Animal Behavior*, "The Wild Dogs of Africa," (ABC)
☐ "The Cave People of the Philippines," *NBC Reports* (NBC)

The Incredible Flight of the Snow Geese (NBC)
In Search of Ancient Astronauts (NBC)

An award for individuals contributing to documentary programs:
☐ Alistair Cook (narrator), *America* (NBC)
☐ Alistair Cooke (writer), "A Firebell in the Night," *America* (NBC)
☐ Hugo Van Lawick (director), *Jane Goodall and the World of Animal Behavior*, "The Wild Dogs of Africa" (ABC)
Marshall Flaum and Bill Travers (writers), *Jane Goodall and the World of Animal Behavior*, "The Wild Dogs of Africa" (ABC)
Tom Priestley (director), "The Forbidden City," *NBC Reports* (NBC)

SPECIAL CLASSIFICATION OF OUTSTANDING PROGRAM AND INDIVIDUAL ACHIEVEMENT
☐ *The Advocates* (PBS)
☐ "VD Blues," *Special of the Week* (PBS)
LBJ: The Last Interview (CBS)
Dick Cavett (host), "VD Blues," *Special of the Week* (PBS)
Walter Cronkite (correspondent), *LBJ: The Last Interview* (CBS)

OUTSTANDING ACHIEVEMENT IN RELIGIOUS PROGRAMMING
☐ *Duty Bound* (NBC)
Insight (Syndicated)
Martin Hoade (director), *Duty Bound* (NBC)
John B. Boxer (costume designer), *Duty Bound* (NBC)

OUTSTANDING ACHIEVEMENT IN ANY AREA OF CREATIVE TECHNICAL CRAFTS
☐ Donald Feldstein, Robert Fontana and Joe Zuckerman, (animation layout of da Vinci's art), *Leonardo: To Know How To See* (NBC)
Philippe Cousteau (underwater cameraman), "The Singing Whale," *The Undersea World of Jacques Cousteau* (ABC)
Biddy Chrystal (hairdresser), *Dr. Jekyll and Mr. Hyde* (NBC)

One Award Only in Each of the Following Categories

OUTSTANDING ACHIEVEMENT IN CINEMATOGRAPHY FOR NEWS AND DOCUMENTARY PROGRAMMING

Regularly scheduled News programs and coverage of Special Events:
☐ Laurens Pierce, "Coverage of the Schooting of Governor Wallace,"

☐ Indicates winner

CBS Evening News with Walter Cronkite (CBS)
Isadore Bleckman, "Roadside Garden: On the Road," *CBS Evening News with Walter Cronkite* (CBS)
Dang Van Minh, "Vietnamese Orphans," *ABC Evening News with Howard K. Smith and Harry Reasoner* (ABC)

Documentary, Magazine-type or Mini-documentary programs:
☐ Des and Jen Bartlett, *The Incredible Flight of the Snow Geese* (NBC)
Philippe Cousteau, Jacques Renoir, "The Smile of the Walrus," *The Undersea World of Jacques Cousteau* (ABC)
Philippe Cousteau, François Charlet, Walter Bal, "The Singing Whale," *The Undersea World of Jacques Cousteau* (ABC)

OUTSTANDING ACHIEVEMENT IN FILM EDITING FOR NEWS AND DOCUMENTARY PROGRAMMING

Regularly scheduled news programs and coverage of Special Events:
☐ Patrick Minerva, Martin Sheppard, George Johnson, William J. Freeda, Miguel E. Portillo, Albert J. Helias, Irwin Graf, Jean Venable, Rick Hessel, Loren Berry, Nick Wilkins, Gerry Breese, Michael Shugrue, K. Su, Edwin Einarsen, Thomas Dunphy, Russel Moore, Robert Mole, *NBC Nightly News* (NBC)
Michael C. Shugrue, "I Am Woman," *NBC Nightly News* (NBC)
Patrick Minerva, Thomas Dunphy, Jean Venable, Edwin Einarsen, Gerald Breese, "Coverage of President Nixon's Trip to Russia," *NBC Nightly News* (NBC)

Documentary, magazine-type or mini-documentary programs:
☐ Les Parry, *The Incredible Flight of the Snow Geese* (NBC)
Carl Kress, "The Singing Whale," *The Undersea World of Jacques Cousteau* (ABC)
John Soh, "The Smile of the Walrus," *The Undersea World of Jacques Cousteau* (ABC)

1973/74

(For programs aired between March 19, 1973 and March 17, 1974. Entertainment awards presented May 28, 1974; Daytime awards presented May 28, 1974; News and documentary

awards presented March 19, 1974 for programs aired between March 19, 1973 and June 30, 1974.)

Prime Time Entertainment Program Awards

OUTSTANDING COMEDY SERIES
☐ *M*A*S*H* (CBS)
The Mary Tyler Moore Show (CBS)
All in the Family (CBS)
The Odd Couple (ABC)

OUTSTANDING DRAMA SERIES
☐ "Upstairs, Downstairs," *Masterpiece Theatre* (PBS)
Kojak (CBS)
The Streets of San Francisco (ABC)
Policy Story (NBC)
The Waltons (CBS)

OUTSTANDING MUSIC—VARIETY SERIES
☐ *The Carol Burnett Show* (CBS)
The Sonny & Cher Comedy Hour (CBS)
The Tonight Show Starring Johnny Carson (NBC)

OUTSTANDING LIMITED SERIES
☐ *Columbo* (NBC)
McCloud (NBC)
The Blue Knight (NBC)

OUTSTANDING SPECIAL—COMEDY OR DRAMA
☐ *The Autobiography of Miss Jane Pittman* (CBS)
"The Migrants," *CBS Playhouse 90* (CBS)
"The Execution of Private Slovic," *NBC Wednesday Night at the Movies* (NBC)
"Steambath," *Hollywood Television Theatre* (PBS)
6 RMS RIV VU (CBS)

OUTSTANDING COMEDY-VARIETY, VARIETY OR MUSIC SPECIAL
☐ *Lily* (CBS)
Barbra Streisand. . . and Other Musical Instruments (CBS)
Magnavox Presents Frank Sinatra (NBC)
The John Denver Show (ABC)

OUTSTANDING CHILDREN'S SPECIAL (FOR PROGRAMS BROADCAST DURING THE EVENING)
☐ *Marlo Thomas and Friends in Fee To Be. . . You and Me* (ABC)

"The Borrowers," *Hallmark Hall of Fame* (NBC)
A Charlie Brown Thanksgiving (CBS)

Prime Time Entertainment Performance Awards

BEST LEAD ACTOR IN A COMEDY SERIES
☐ Alan Alda, *M*A*S*H* (CBS)
Redd Foxx, *Sanford and Son* (NBC)
Jack Klugman, *The Odd Couple* (ABC)
Carroll O'Connor, *All in the Family* (CBS)
Tony Randall, *The Odd Couple* (ABC)

BEST LEAD ACTOR IN A DRAMA SERIES
☐ Telly Savalas, *Kojak* (CBS)
William Conrad, *Cannon* (CBS)
Karl Malden, *The Streets of San Francisco* (ABC)
Richard Thomas, *The Waltons* (CBS)

BEST LEAD ACTOR IN A LIMITED SERIES
☐ William Holden, *The Blue Knight* (NBC)
Peter Falk, *Columbo* (NBC)
Dennis Weaver, *McCloud* (NBC)

BEST LEAD ACTOR IN A DRAMA (FOR A SPECIAL PROGRAM—COMEDY OR DRAMA—OR A SINGLE APPEARANCE IN A DRAMA OR COMEDY SERIES)
☐ Hal Holbrook, "Pueblo," *ABC Theatre* (ABC)
Dick Van Dyke, "The Morning After," *Wednesday Movie of the Week* (ABC)
Laurence Olivier, "The Merchant of Venice," *ABC Theatre* (ABC)
Martin Sheen, "The Execution of Private Slovik," *NBC Wednesday Night At the Movies* (NBC)
Alan Alda, *6 RMS RIV VU* (CBS)

ACTOR OF THE YEAR—SERIES
☐ Alan Alda, *M*A*S*H* (CBS)

ACTOR OF THE YEAR—SPECIAL
☐ Hal Holbrook, "Pueblo," *ABC Theatre* (ABC)

BEST LEAD ACTRESS IN A COMEDY SERIES
☐ Mary Tyler Moore, *The Mary Tyler Moore Show* (CBS)
Bea Arthur, *Maude* (CBS)
Jean Stapleton, *All in the Family* (CBS)

BEST LEAD ACTRESS IN A DRAMA SERIES
☐ Michael Learned, *The Waltons* (CBS)
Jeanette Nolan, *Dirty Sally* (CBS)
Jean Marsh, "Upstairs, Downstairs," *Masterpiece Theatre* (PBS)

☐ Indicates winner

BEST LEAD ACTRESS IN A LIMITED SERIES
☐ Mildred Natwick, "The Snoop Sisters," *NBC Tuesday Mystery Movie* (NBC)
Lee Remick, *The Blue Knight* (NBC)
Helen Hayes, "The Snoop Sisters," *NBC Tuesday Mystery Movie* (NBC)

BEST LEAD ACTRESS IN A DRAMA (FOR A SPECIAL PROGRAM—COMEDY OR DRAMA—OR A SINGLE APPEARANCE IN A DRAMA OR COMEDY SERIES)
☐ Cicely Tyson, *The Autobiography of Miss Jane Pittman* (CBS)
Elizabeth Montgomery, "A Case of Rape," *NBC Wednesday Night at the Movies* (NBC)
Katharine Hepburn, *The Glass Menagerie* (ABC)
Cloris Leachman, "The Migrants," *CBS Playhouse 90* (CBS)
Carol Burnett, *6 RMS RIV VU* (CBS)

ACTRESS OF THE YEAR—SERIES
☐ Mary Tyler Moore, *The Mary Tyler Moore Show* (CBS)

ACTRESS OF THE YEAR—SPECIAL
☐ Cicely Tyson, *The Autobiography of Miss Jane Pittman* (CBS)

BEST SUPPORTING ACTOR IN COMEDY
☐ Rob Reiner, *All in the Family* (CBS)
Ted Knight, *The Mary Tyler Moore Show* (CBS)
Ed Asner, *The Mary Tyler Moore Show* (CBS)
Gary Burghoff, *M*A*S*H* (CBS)
McLean Stevenson, *M*A*S*H* (CBS)

BEST SUPPORTING ACTOR IN DRAMA
☐ Michael Moriarty, *The Glass Menagerie* (ABC)
Michael Douglas, *The Streets of San Francisco* (ABC)
Will Geer, *The Waltons* (CBS)
Sam Waterson, *The Glass Menagerie* (ABC)

BEST SUPPORTING ACTOR IN COMEDY-VARIETY, VARIETY OR MUSIC
☐ Harvey Korman, *The Carol Burnett Show* (CBS)
Tim Conway, *The Carol Burnett Show* (with Tim Conway, Petula Clark) (CBS)
Foster Brooks, *The Dean Martin Comedy Hour* (NBC)

SUPPORTING ACTOR OF THE YEAR
☐ Michael Moriarty, *The Glass Menagerie* (ABC)

BEST SUPPORTING ACTRESS IN DRAMA
☐ Joanna Miles, *The Glass Menagerie* (ABC)

Ellen Corby, *The Waltons* (CBS)
Nancy Walker, *McMillan and Wife* (NBC)

BEST SUPPORTING ACTRESS IN COMEDY
☐ Cloris Leachman, "The Lars Affair," *The Mary Tyler Moore Show* (CBS)
Valerie Harper, *The Mary Tyler Moore Show* (CBS)
Loretta Swit, *M*A*S*H* (CBS)
Sally Struthers, *All in the Family* (CBS)

BEST SUPPORTING ACTRESS IN COMEDY-VARIETY, VARIETY OR MUSIC
☐ Brenda Vaccaro, *The Shape of Things* (CBS)
Vicki Lawrence, *The Carol Burnett Show* (CBS)
Lee Grant, *The Shape of Things* (CBS)
Ruth Buzzi, *The Dean Martin Comedy Hour* (NBC)

SUPPORTING ACTRESS OF THE YEAR
☐ Joanna Miles, *The Glass Menagerie* (ABC)

Prime Time Entertainment Craft and Technical Awards

BEST DIRECTING IN DRAMA (A SINGLE PROGRAM OF A SERIES)
☐ Robert Butler, *The Blue Knight, Part III* (NBC)
Harry Harris, "The Journey," *The Waltons* (CBS)
Philip Leacock, "The Thanksgiving Story," *The Waltons* (CBS)

BEST DIRECTING IN DRAMA (A SINGLE PROGRAM—COMEDY OR DRAMA)
☐ John Korty, *The Autobiography of Miss Jane Pittman* (CBS)
Tom Gries, "The Migrants," *CBS Playhouse 90* (CBS)
Boris Sagal, "A Case of Rape," *NBC Wednesday Night at the Movies* (NBC)
Anthony Page, "Pueblo," *ABC Theatre* (ABC)
Lamont Johnson, "The Execution of Private Slovik," *NBC Wednesday Night at the Movies* (NBC)

BEST DIRECTING IN COMEDY FOR A SINGLE PROGRAM OF A SERIES WITH CONTINUING CHARACTERS AND/OR THEME
☐ Jackie Cooper, "Cary On Hawkeye," *M*A*S*H* (CBS)
Jay Sandrich, "Lou's First Date," *The Mary Tyler Moore Show* (CBS)
Gene Reynolds, "Deal Me Out," *M*A*S*H* (CBS)

BEST DIRECTING IN VARIETY OR MUSIC FOR A SINGLE PROGRAM OF A SERIES

☐ Dave Powers, "The Australia Show," *The Carol Burnett Show* (CBS)

Art Fisher, *The Sonny and Cher Comedy Hour* (with Ken Berry and George Foreman) (CBS)

Joshua White, "In Concert (with Cat Stevens)," *ABC Wide World of Entertainment* (ABC)

BEST DIRECTING IN COMEDY-VARIETY, VARIETY OR MUSIC FOR A SPECIAL PROGRAM

☐ Dwight Hemion, *Barbra Streisand. . . and Other Musical Instruments* (CBS)

Marty Pasetta, *Magnavox Presents Frank Sinatra* (NBC)

Tony Charmoli, *Mitzi. . . A Tribute to the American Housewife* (CBS)

Sterling Johnson, "Peggy Fleming Visits the Soviet Union," *Bell System Family Theatre* (NBC)

DIRECTOR OF THE YEAR—SERIES

☐ Robert Butler, *The Blue Knight, Part III* (NBC)

DIRECTOR OF THE YEAR—SPECIAL

☐ Dwight Hemion, *Barbra Streisand. . . and Other Musical Instruments* (CBS)

BEST WRITING IN DRAMA A SINGLE PROGRAM OF A SERIES WITH CONTINUING CHARACTERS AND/OR THEME

☐ Joanna Lee, "The Thanksgiving Story," *The Waltons* (CBS)

Gene R. Kearney, "Death Is Not a Passing Grade," *Kojak* (CBS)

John McGreevey, "The Easter Story," *The Waltons* (CBS)

BEST WRITING IN DRAMA (ORIGINAL TELEPLAY) FOR A SINGLE PROGRAM-COMEDY OR DRAMA

☐ Fay Kanin, "Tell Me Where It Hurts," *GE Theater* (CBS)

Will Lorin, "Cry Rape!" *The New CBS Tuesday Night Movie* (CBS)

Lanford Wilson, "The Migrants," *CBS Playhouse 90* (CBS)

BEST WRITING IN DRAMA (ADAPTION) FOR A SINGLE PROGRAM-COMEDY OR DRAMA

☐ Tracy Keenan Wynn, *The Autobiography of Miss Jane Pittman* (CBS)

Bruce Jay Friedman, "Steambath," *Hollywood Television Theatre* (PBS)

Richard Levinson, William Link, "The Execution of Private Slovik," *NBC Wednesday Night at the Movies* (NBC)

☐ Indicates winner

BEST WRITING IN COMEDY FOR A SINGLE PROGRAM OF A SERIES WITH CONTINUING CHARACTERS AND/OR THEME

☐ Treva Silverman, "The Lou and Edie Story," *The Mary Tyler Moore Show* (CBS)

Linda Bloodworth, Mary Kay Place, "Hot Lips and Empty Arms," *M*A*S*H* (CBS)

McLean Stevenson, "The Trial of Henry Blake," *M*A*S*H* (CBS)

BEST WRITING IN VARIETY OR MUSIC FOR A SINGLE PROGRAM OF A SERIES

☐ Ed Simmons, Gary Belkin, Roger Beatty, Arnie Kogen, Bill Richmond, Gene Perret, Rudy De Luca, Barry Levinson, Dick Clair, Jenna McMahon, Barry Harman, *The Carol Burnett Show* (with Tim Conway, Bernadette Peters) (CBS)

Chris Bearde, Allan Blye, Bob Arnott, George Burditt, Bob Einstein, Phil Hahn, Coslough Johnson, Jim Mulligan, Paul Wayne, *The Sonny and Cher Comedy Hour* (with Chuck Connors, Howard Cosell) (CBS)

Stan Hart, Larry Siegel, Gail Parent, Woody Kling, Roger Beatty, Tom Patchett, Jay Tarses, Robert Hilliard, Arnie Kogen, Buz Kohan, Bill Angelos, "The Family Show," *The Carol Burnett Show* (CBS)

BEST WRITING IN COMEDY-VARIETY, VARIETY OR MUSIC FOR A SPECIAL PROGRAM

☐ Herb Sargent, Rosalyn Drexler, Lorne Michaels, Richard Pryor, Jim Rusk, James R. Stein, Robert Illes, Lily Tomlin, George Yanok, Jane Wagner, Rod Warren, Ann Elder, Karyl Geld, *Lily* (CBS)

Larry Gelbart, Mitzie Welch, Ken Welch, *Barbra Streisand. . . and Other Musical Instruments* (CBS)

Renee Taylor, Joseph Bologna, *Paradise* (CBS)

WRITER OF THE YEAR—SERIES

☐ Treva Silverman, "The Lou and Edie Story," *The Mary Tyler Moore Show* (CBS)

WRITER OF THE YEAR—SPECIAL

☐ Fay Kanin, "Tell Me Where It Hurts," *GE Theater* (CBS)

OUTSTANDING ACHIEVEMENT IN CHOREOGRAPHY

☐ Tony Charmoli, *Mitzi. . . A Tribute to the American Housewife* (CBS)

Ernest O. Flatt, "The Australia Show," *The Carol Burnett Show* (CBS)

Carl Jablonski, *Sammy Davis Starring in NBC Follies* (with Milton Berle, Johnny Brown, Michael Landon, Carol Lawrence) (NBC)

BEST MUSIC COMPOSITION FOR A SERIES OR A SINGLE PROGRAM OF A SERIES (IN THE FIRST YEAR OF MUSIC'S USE ONLY)

☐ Morton Stevens, "Hookman," *Hawaii Five-O* (CBS)

Don B. Ray, "Nightmare in Blue," *Hawaii Five-O* (CBS)

Bruce Broughton, "The $100,000 Nickel," *Hawaii Five-O* (CBS)

For a special program:

☐ Fred Karlin, *The Autobiography of Miss Jane Pittman* (CBS)

Billy Goldenberg, "The Migrants," *CBS Playhouse 90* (CBS)

Laurence Rosenthal, *Portrait: A Man Whose Name Was John* (ABC)

BEST SONG OR THEME FOR A SERIES OR A SINGLE PROGRAM OF A SERIES OR A SPECIAL PROGRAM WRITTEN FOR TELEVISION

☐ Mary and David Paich, "Light The Way," "Once More for Joey," *Ironside* (NBC)

Fred Karlin, "The Love That Lights Our Way," *The Autobiography of Miss Jane Pittman* (CBS)

Billy Goldenberg, *Kojak* (CBS)

BEST MUSIC DIRECTION OF A VARIETY, MUSICAL OR DRAMATIC PROGRAM

☐ Jack Parnell, Ken Welch, Mitzie Welch, *Barbra Streisand. . . and Other Musical Instruments* (CBS)

Peter Matz, "The Australia Show," *The Carol Burnett Show* (CBS)

Marty Paich, "The Sonny and Cher Years," *The Sonny and Cher Comedy Hour* (CBS)

MUSICIAN OF THE YEAR

☐ Jack Parnell, Ken Welch, Mitzie Welch, *Barbra Streisand. . . and Other Musical Instruments* (CBS)

BEST ART DIRECTION OR SCENIC DESIGN

For a dramatic program or feature length film made for television; for a series, a single program of a series, or a special program:

☐ Jan Scott (art director), Charles Kreiner (set decorator), "The Lie," *CBS Playhouse 90* (CBS)

Michael Haller, *The Autobiography of Miss Jane Pittman* (CBS)

Walter H. Tyler (art director), Richard Friedman (set director), "The Execution of Private Slovik," *NBC Wednesday Night at the Movies* (NBC)

For a Musical or Variety single program of a series or a special

program:

☐ Brian C. Bartholomew, *Barbra Streisand. . . and Other Musical Instruments* (CBS)

Paul Barnes and Bob Sansom (art directors), Bill Harp (set decorator), *The Carol Burnett Show* (with Bernadette Peters, Tim Conway) (CBS)

Rene Lagler and Lynn Griffin (art directors), *The Andy Williams Christmas Show* (NBC)

ART DIRECTOR AND SET DECORATOR OF THE YEAR

☐ Jan Scott (art director), Charles Kreiner (set director), "The Lie," *CBS Playhouse 90* (CBS)

OUTSTANDING ACHIEVEMENT IN COSTUME DESIGN

☐ Bruce Walkup, Sandy Stewart, *The Autobiography of Miss Jane Pittman* (CBS)

Grady Hunt, "The Devil Made Me Do It," *The Snoop Sisters* (NBC)

Barbara Murphy, *The New Treasure Hunt* (Syndicated)

Ret Turner, Bob Mackie, "The Sonny and Cher Years," *The Sonny and Cher Comedy Hour* (CBS)

Charles Knode, concluding episode, *War And Peace* (PBS)

OUTSTANDING ACHIEVEMENT IN MAKE-UP

☐ Stan Winston, Rick Baker, *The Autobiography of Miss Jane Pittman* (CBS)

Nick Marcellino, James Lee McCoy, *Portrait: A Man Whose Name Was John* (ABC)

Ben Nye II, "Judgment—The Trial of Julius and Ethel Rosenberg," *ABC Theatre* (ABC)

William Tuttle, "The Phantom of Hollywood," *The New CBS Tuesday Night Movies* (CBS)

BEST CINEMATOGRAPHY FOR ENTERTAINMENT PROGRAMMING

For a series or a single program of a series:

☐ Harry Wolf, ASC, "Any Old Port in a Storm," *Columbo* (NBC)

Gerald Perry Finnerman, ASC, *Kojak* (CBS)

Robert Morrison, Jack Whitman, Bill Huffman, *Hawaii Five-O* (CBS)

For a special or feature length program made for television:

☐ Ted Voigtlander, ASC, "It's Good To Be Alive," *GE Theater* (CBS)

Richard C. Kratina, "The Migrants," *CBS Playhouse 90* (CBS)

Walter Strenge, ASC, *Portrait: A Man Whose Name Was John* (ABC)

☐ Indicates winner

Andrew Laszlo, *The Man Without a Country* (ABC)

Fred Mandl, "Trapped," *Wednesday Movie of the Week* (ABC)

CINEMATOGRAPHER OF THE YEAR

☐ Ted Voigtlander, ASC, "It's Good To Be Alive," *GE Theater* (CBS)

BEST FILM EDITING FOR ENTERTAINMENT PROGRAMMING

For a series or a single program of a series:

☐ Gene Fowler, Jr., Marjorie Fowler and Samuel E. Beetley, *The Blue Knight* (NBC)

Douglas Hines, Bud Isaacs, *The Mary Tyler Moore Show* (CBS)

Stanford Tischler, Fred W. Berger, *M*A*S*H* (CBS)

For a special or feature length program made for television:

☐ Frank Morriss, "The Execution of Private Slovik," *NBC Wednesday Night at the Movies* (NBC)

Richard Bracken, "A Case of Rape," *NBC Wednesday Night at the Movies* (NBC)

Sidney Levin, *The Autobiography of Miss Jane Pittman* (CBS)

FILM EDITOR OF THE YEAR

☐ Frank Morriss, "The Execution of Private Slovik," *NBC Wednesday Night at the Movies* (NBC)

OUTSTANDING ACHIEVEMENT IN FILM SOUND EDITING

☐ Bud Nolan, "Pueblo," *ABC Theatre* (ABC)

Sid Lubow, Sam Caylor, Jack Kirschner, Richard Raderman, Stanley Frazen, John Singleton, "Marker for a Dead Bookie," *Kojak* (CBS)

Jerry Rosenthal, Ron Ashcroft, Al Kajita, Richard Burrow, Jack Milner, Tony Garber, William M. Andrews, Edward L. Sandlin, Milton C. Burrow, "Collision Course," *Police Story* (NBC)

OUTSTANDING ACHIEVEMENT IN FILM OR TAPE SOUND MIXING

☐ Albert A. Gramaglia, Michael Shindler, "Pueblo," *ABC Theatre* (ABC)

John K. Kean, Thom K. Piper, "The Execution of Private Slovik," *NBC Wednesday Night at the Movies* (NBC)

Charles T. Knight, Don Minkler, *The Autobiography of Miss Jane Pittman* (CBS)

OUTSTANDING ACHIEVEMENT IN VIDEO TAPE EDITING

☐ Alfred Muller, "Pueblo," *ABC Theatre* (ABC)

Lewis W. Smith, "The Lie," *CBS Playhouse 90* (CBS)

Nick V. Giordano, George Gurunian, *The John Denver Show* (ABC)

OUTSTANDING ACHIEVEMENT IN TECHNICAL DIRECTION AND ELECTRONIC CAMERAWORK

☐ Gerry Bucci (technical director), and Kenneth Tamburri, Dave Hilmer, Dave Smith, Jim Balden and Ron Brooks (cameramen) "In Concert (with Cat Stevens)," *ABC Wide World of Entertainment* (ABC)

Parker Roe (technical director) and Lew Adams, Ken Lamkin, John Poliak, and Gary Stantor (cameramen), "Judgment—The Trial of Julius and Ethel Rosenberg," *ABC Theatre* (ABC)

Lou Marchand (technical director) and Richard Kerr, Morris Mann, John Morreale, Michael W. Rebich and Robert Wolff (cameramen), "Pueblo," *ABC Theatre* (ABC)

OUTSTANDING ACHIEVEMENT IN LIGHTING DIRECTION A SINGLE PROGRAM OR A SERIES OR A SPECIAL PROGRAM, PRODUCED FOR ELECTRONIC TELEVISION ONLY

☐ William M. Klages, "The Lie," *CBS Playhouse 90* (CBS)

John Freschi, *Mitzi. . . A Tribute to the American Housewife* (CBS)

Lon Stucky, John Nance, *Dean Martin Presents Music Country* (with Johnny Cash, Loretta Lynn) (NBC)

The Areas*

OUTSTANDING INDIVIDUAL ACHIEVEMENT IN CHILDREN'S PROGRAMMING

☐ Charles M. Schulz (writer), *A Charlie Brown Thanksgiving* (CBS)

☐ William Zaharuk (art director), Peter Razmofski (set decorator), "The Borrowers," *Hallmark Hall of Fame* (NBC)

Dame Judith Anderson (performer), "The Borrowers," *Hallmark Hall of Fame* (NBC)

Walter C. Miller (director), "The Borrowers," *Hallmark Hall of Fame* (NBC)

Bill Davis (director), *Marlo Thomas and Friends in Free To Be. . . You and Me* (ABC)

Juul Haalmeyer (costume designer), "The Borrowers," *Hallmark Hall of Fame* (NBC)

SPECIAL CLASSIFICATION OF OUTSTANDING PROGRAM AND INDIVIDUAL ACHIEVEMENT

☐ *The Dick Cavett Show* (ABC)

---

* possibility of one award, more than one award or no award

☐ Tom Snyder (host), *Tomorrow* (NBC)
"Warner Bros. Movies—A 50 Year Salute," *ABC Wide World of Entertainment* (ABC)
CBS All-American Thanksgiving Day Parade (CBS)
Paul Lynde (performer), *The Hollywood Squares* (NBC)
Bette Davis (hostess), "Warner Bros. Movies—A 50 Year Salute," *ABC Wide World of Entertainment* (ABC)

OUTSTANDING ACHIEVEMENT IN SPORTS PROGRAMMING
☐ *ABC'S Wide World of Sports* (ABC)
☐ Jim McKay (host), *ABC'S Wide World of Sports* (ABC)
Bobby Riggs vs. Billie Jean King, Tennis Battle of Sexes (ABC)
1973 World Series (NBC)
Monday Night Football (ABC)
Howard Cosell (announcer), *Monday Night Football* (ABC)
Frank Gifford (announcer), *Monday Night Football* (ABC)
Tony Verna (director), *The Triple Crown of Racing: The Kentucky Derby, The Preakness and The Belmont Stakes* (CBS)
Harry Coyle (director), *1973 World Series* (NBC)

OUTSTANDING ACHIEVEMENTS IN ANY AREA OF CREATIVE TECHNICAL CRAFTS
☐ Lynda Gurasich (hair stylist), *The Autobiography of Miss Jane Pittman* (CBS)
Jordon Whitelaw (orchestral treatment director), *Evening at Pops* (with Ella Fitzgerald) (PBS)
Rena Leuschner (hairdresser), *The Sonny and Cher Comedy Hour* (with Paul Anka, Neil Sedaka) (CBS)

Special Awards

OUTSTANDING ACHIEVEMENT IN ENGINEERING DEVELOPMENT
☐ *Consolidated Video Systems, Inc.* For the application of digital video technique to the Time Base Corrector, permitting use of smaller lighter weight, more portable video tape equipment on news and other outside events in television broadcasting.
☐ *RCA.* For its leading role in the development of the quadruplex video tape cartridge equipment, providing improved production reliability and efficiency in broadcasting video taped program segments, promos and commercials.

☐ Indicates winner

THE INTERNATIONAL AWARDS
Non-Fiction:
☐ *Horizon: The Making of a Natural History Film* (British Broadcasting Corporation, London)
Omnibus: Fidelio Fincke, Where Are You Now? (British Broadcasting Corporation, London)
Grey Owl (Canadian Broadcasting Corporation, Toronto)
Bunny (Thames Television Limited, London)
Too Long A Winter (Yorkshire Television Ltd., London)
Fiction:
☐ *La Cabina* (Television Espanola, Madrid)
High Summer (Armchair Theatre; Thames Television Limited, London)
Country Matters: The Little Farm (Granada Television Ltd., Manchester, England)
The Duchess of Malfi (British Broadcasting Corporaton, London)
Sarah (Yorkshire Television, Yorkshire, England)

THE INTERNATIONAL DIRECTORATE EMMY AWARD
☐ Charles Curran, President, European Broadcasting Union, Director-General, British Broadcasting Corporation

THE NATIONAL AWARD FOR COMMUNITY SERVICE
☐ *Through the Looking Glass Darkly* (WKY-TV, Oklahoma City)
From Protest to Politics (WXYZ-TV, Southfield)
The Rape of Paulette (WBBM-TV, Chicago)
Probe: Uncle Sam Is a Slumlord (WRC-TV, Washington, D.C.)
Living with Death (WCCO-TV, Minneapolis)
Focus 30 (KYTV, Springfield)
Medicine: Where Does It Hurt? (WNBC-TV, New York)
The Frightening Feeling You're Going To Die (WCVB-TV, Needham)
A Matter of Life and Debt (KOOL-TV, Phoenix)
What Happens to Me? (KPEC-TV, Tacoma)
The Nine-Year-Old in Norfolk Prison (WTIC-TV, Hartford)
The Elders (KDIN, Des Moines)

Daytime Program and Individual Achievements*

OUTSTANDING DRAMA SERIES, DAYTIME PROGRAMMING
☐ *The Doctors* (NBC)
General Hospital (ABC)

* Only one award in each of the following categories

Days Of Our Lives (NBC)

OUTSTANDING DRAMA SPECIAL, DAYTIME PROGRAMMING
☐ "The Other Woman," *ABC Matinee Today* (ABC)
"A Special Act of Love," *ABC Afternoon Playbreak* (ABC)
"Tiger on a Chain," *CBS Daytime 90* (CBS)

OUTSTANDING GAME SHOW DAYTIME PROGRAMMING
☐ *Password* (ABC)
The Hollywood Squares (NBC)
Jeopardy (NBC)

OUTSTANDING TALK, SERVICE OR VARIETY SERIES, DAYTIME PROGRAMMING
☐ *The Merv Griffin Show* (Syndicated)
Dinah's Place (NBC)
The Mike Douglas Show (Syndicated)

OUTSTANDING ENTERTAINMENT CHILDREN'S SERIES FOR PROGRAMS WHICH WERE BROADCAST DURING THE DAYTIME
☐ *Zoom* (PBS)
Captain Kangaroo (CBS)
Fat Albert and the Cosby Kids (CBS)
Star Trek (NBC)

OUTSTANDING ENTERTAINMENT CHILDREN'S SPECIAL FOR PROGRAMS WHICH WERE BROADCAST DURING THE DAYTIME
☐ "Rookie of the Year," *The ABC Afterschool Special* (ABC)
"My Dad Lives in a Downtown Hotel," *The ABC Afterschool Special* (ABC)
"The Swiss Family Robinson," *Famous Classic Tales* (CBS)

BEST ACTOR IN DAYTIME DRAMA
For a series:
☐ Macdonald Carey, *Days of Our Lives* (NBC)
John Beradino, *General Hospital* (ABC)
Peter Hansen, *General Hospital* (ABC)
For a special program:
☐ Pat O'Brien, "The Other Woman," *ABC Matinee Today* (ABC)
Peter Coffield, "Legacy of Fear," *CBS Daytime 90* (CBS)
Don Porter, "Mother of the Bride," *ABC Afternoon Playbreak* (ABC)

DAYTIME ACTOR OF THE YEAR
☐ Pat O'Brien, "The Other Woman," *ABC Matinee Today* (ABC)

BEST ACTRESS IN DAYTIME DRAMA
For a series:
☐ Elizabeth Hubbard, *The Doctors* (NBC)
Mary Stuart, *Search for Tomorrow* (CBS)
Rachel Ames, *General Hospital* (ABC)

Mary Fickett, *All My Children* (ABC)

For a special program:
☐ Cathleen Nesbit, "The Mask of Love," *ABC Matinee Today* (ABC)
Eve Arden, "Mother of the Bride," *ABC Afternoon Playbreak* (ABC)
Constance Towers, "Once in Her Life," *CBS Daytime 90* (CBS)

DAYTIME ACTRESS OF THE YEAR
☐ Cathleen Nesbit, "The Mask of Love," *ABC Matinee Today* (ABC)

BEST HOST OR HOSTESS IN A GAME SHOW, DAYTIME PROGRAMMING
☐ Peter Marshall, *The Hollywood Squares* (NBC)
Allen Ludden, *Password* (ABC)
Art Fleming, *Jeopardy!* (NBC)

BEST HOST OR HOSTESS IN A TALK, SERVICE OR VARIETY SERIES, DAYTIME PROGRAMMING
☐ Dinah Shore, *Dinah's Place* (NBC)
Mike Douglas, *The Mike Douglas Show* (Syndicated)
Merv Griffin, *The Merv Griffin Show* (Syndicated)
Barbara Walters, Not for Women Only (Syndicated)

DAYTIME HOST OF THE YEAR
☐ Peter Marshall, *The Hollywood Squares* (NBC)

BEST INDIVIDUAL DIRECTOR FOR A DRAMA SERIES, DAYTIME PROGRAMMING
☐ H. Wesley Kenney, *Days of Our Lives* (NBC)
Hugh McPhillips, *The Doctors* (NBC)
Norman Hall, *The Doctors* (NBC)

BEST INDIVIDUAL DIRECTOR FOR A SPECIAL PROGRAM, DAYTIME PROGRAMMING
☐ H. Wesley Kenney, "Miss Kline, We Love You," *ABC Afternoon Playbreak* (ABC)
Peter Levin, "The Other Woman," *ABC Matinee Today* (ABC)
Lela Swift, "The Gift of Terror," *ABC Afternoon Playbreak* (ABC)
Burt Brinkerhoff, "The Mask of Love," *ABC Matinee Today* (ABC)

BEST INDIVIDUAL DIRECTOR FOR A GAME SHOW, DAYTIME PROGRAMMING
☐ Mike Gargiulo, *Jackpot!* (NBC)
Jerome Shaw, *The Hollywood Squares* (NBC)
Stuart Phelps, *Password* (with Carol Burnett, Elizabeth Montgomery) (ABC)

☐ Indicates winner

BEST INDIVIDUAL DIRECTOR FOR A TALK, SERVICE OR VARIETY PROGRAM, DAYTIME PROGRAMMING
☐ Dick Carson, *The Merv Griffin Show* (with Rosemary Clooney, Helen O'Connell, Fran Warren, Kay Starr) (Syndicated)
Ron A. Appling *The Merv Griffin Show* (with Clint Eastwood, Forrest Tucker, Stanley Myron Handleman) (Syndicated)
Glen Swanson, *Dinah's Place* (with Jose Feliciano) (NBC)

DAYTIME DIRECTOR OF THE YEAR
☐ H. Wesley Kenney, "Miss Kline, We Love You," *ABC Afternoon Playbreak* (ABC)

BEST WRITING FOR A DRAMA SERIES, DAYTIME PROGRAMMING
☐ Henry Slesar, *The Edge of Night* (CBS)
Eileen and Robert Mason Pollock, James Lipton, *The Doctors* (NBC)
Frank and Doris Hursley, Bridget Dobson, Deborah Hardy, *General Hospital* (ABC)

BEST WRITING FOR A SPECIAL PROGRAM, DAYTIME PROGRAMMING
☐ Lila Garrett, Sandy Krinski, "Mother of the Bride," *ABC Afternoon Playbreak* (ABC)
Robert Shaw, "Once in Her Life," *CBS Daytime 90* (CBS)
Art Wallace, "Alone With Terror," *ABC Matinee Today* (ABC)

BEST WRITING FOR A GAME SHOW, DAYTIME PROGRAMMING
☐ Jay Redack, Harry Friedman, Harold Schneider, Gary Johnson, Steve Levitch, Rich Kellard, Rowby Goren, *The Hollywood Squares* (NBC)
Robert Sherman, Patrick Neary, Joe Neustein, Dick DeBartolo, *Match Game '74* (CBS)
Lynette Williams, Elizabeth M. Camp, Leslie Cooper, Mark Eisman, G. Ross Parker, James J. Thesing, *Jeopardy!* (NBC)

BEST WRITING FOR A TALK, SERVICE OR VARIETY PROGRAM, DAYTIME PROGRAMMING
☐ Tony Garafalo, Bob Murphy, Merv Griffin, *The Merv Griffin Show* (with Billie Jean King, Mark Spitz, Hank Aaron, Johnny Unitas) (Syndicated)
Bill Walker, Bob Howard, Fred Tatashore, "The Child Abuse Show," *Dinah's Place* (NBC)
Don Cornelius, *Soul Train* (with Johnny Mathis) (Syndicated)

DAYTIME WRITER OF THE YEAR
☐ Lila Garrett, Sandy Krinski, "Mother of the Bride," *ABC Afternoon Playbreak* (ABC)

OUTSTANDING MUSICAL DIRECTION, DAYTIME PROGRAMMING
☐ Richard Clements, "A Special Act of Love," *ABC Afternoon Playbreak* (ABC)
John Geller, *The Doctors* (NBC)
Paul Taubman, *Edge of Night* (CBS)

OUTSTANDING ART DIRECTION OR SCENIC DESIGN, DAYTIME PROGRAMMING
☐ Tom Trimble (art director), Brock Broughton (set decorator), *The Young and the Restless* (CBS)
☐ Otis Riggs, Jr., *Another World* (NBC)
Victor L. Paganuzzi (scenic designer), John Wendell (set decorator), "Once in Her Life," *CBS Daytime 90* (CBS)
Lloyd R. Evans, (scenic designer), Tom Cunningham and John Wendell (set decorators), *Love of Life* (CBS)

OUTSTANDING COSTUME DESIGN, DAYTIME PROGRAMMING
☐ Bill Jobe, "The Mask of Love," *ABC Matinee Today* (ABC)
Lewis Broan, *Another World* (ABC)
Julia Sze, *Somerset* (NBC)
Hazel Roy, *All My Children* (ABC)

OUTSTANDING MAKE-UP, DAYTIME PROGRAMMING
☐ Douglas D. Kelly, "The Mask of Love," *ABC Matinee Today* (ABC)
Andrew Eger, *The Edge of Night* (CBS)
Lee Baygan, *The Doctors* (NBC)
Sylvia Lawrence, *All My Children* (ABC)

OUTSTANDING TECHNICAL DIRECTION AND ELECTRONIC CAMERAWORK DAYTIME PROGRAMMING
☐ Lou Marchand (technical director) and Gerald M. Dowd, Frank Melchiorre and John Morris (cameramen) *One Life To Live* (ABC)
Harold Schutzman (technical director) and Hal Weldon, William Unkel and Robert Toerper (cameramen) *The Edge of Night* (CBS)
A. J. Cunningham (technical director) and Rick Tanzi, Joe Arvizu, Jack Jennings and Wayne Orr (cameramen) *The Price Is Right* (CBS)
Gordon C. James (technical director) and George Simpson, George Meyer and John Kullman (cameramen) *Days of Our Lives* (NBC)
Clive Bassett (technical director) and Paul Johnson, Rick Tanzi, Dick Ouderkirk, Marvin Dresser and

Gordon Sweeney (cameramen), *The Young and the Restless* (CBS)

J. J. Lupatkin and Bill Degenhardt (technical directors) and John Wodd, Frank Zuccaro, James Woodle, Joe Solomito, Al Gianetta, Len Gelardi (cameramen) *All My Children* (ABC)

OUTSTANDING LIGHTING DIRECTION, DAYTIME PROGRAMMING

☐ Richard Holbrook, *The Young and the Restless* (CBS)

Alan E. Scarlett, *Days of Our Lives* (NBC)

Ron Holden, *General Hospital* (ABC)

Mel Handelsman, *All My Children* (ABC)

OUTSTANDING SOUND MIXING DAYTIME PROGRAMMING

☐ Ernest Dellutri, *Days of Our Lives* (NBC)

Dick Ellis, *General Hospital* (ABC)

Albin S. Lemanski, *All My Children* (ABC)

OUTSTANDING EDITING, DAYTIME PROGRAMMING

☐ Gary Anderson, "Miss Kline, We Love You," *ABC Afternoon Playbreak* (ABC)

Jerry Greene, "The Mask of Love," *ABC Matinee Today* (ABC)

Jerry Laing, "Once In Her Life," *CBS Daytime 90* (CBS)

News and Documentary Program and Individual Achievements*

OUTSTANDING ACHIEVEMENT WITHIN REGULARLY SCHEDULED NEWS PROGRAMS

For program segments, i.e. the presentation of individual stories (in single or multi-part) or elements within the programs

☐ "Coverage of the October War from Israel's Northern Front," *CBS Evening New with Walter Cronkite* (CBS)

☐ "The Agnew Resignation," *CBS Evening News with Walter Cronkite* (CBS)

☐ "The Key Biscayne Bank Charter Struggle," *CBS Evening News with Walter Cronkite* (CBS)

☐ "Reports on World Hunger," *NBC Nightly News* (NBC)

"Inside China," *ABC Evening News* (ABC)

"The Arab World," *ABC Evening News* (ABC)

"Deprogramming: The Clash Between Religion and Civil Rights," *CBS Evening News with Walter Cronkite* (CBS)

OUTSTANDING ACHIEVEMENT FOR REGULARLY SCHEDULED MAGAZINE-TYPE PROGRAMS

For program segments, i.e. the presentation of individual stories, individual segments or a single program of a series

☐ "America's Nerve Gas Arsenal," *First Tuesday* (NBC)

☐ "The Adversaries," *Behind the Lines* (PBS)

☐ "A Question of Impeachment," *Bill Moyers' Journal* (PBS)

"It's Enough to Make You Sick," *The Reasoner Report* (ABC)

"The End of a Salesman," *60 Minutes* (CBS)

"Local News and the Rating War," *60 Minutes* (CBS)

OUTSTANDING ACHIEVEMENT IN COVERAGE OF SPECIAL EVENTS

For program achievements

☐ *Watergate: The White House Transcripts* (CBS)

☐ *Watergate Coverage* (PBS)
ABC News At Ease (ABC)
Watergate This Week (NBC)

OUTSTANDING DOCUMENTARY PROGRAM ACHIEVEMENTS

For documentary programs dealing with events or matters of current significance.

☐ "Fire," *ABC News Close Up* (ABC)

☐ *CBS News Special Report: The Senate and the Watergate Affair* (CBS)

☐ *Action Biography: Henry Kissinger* (ABC)

"Juvenile Court," *Special of the Week* (PBS)

"The Unquiet Death of Julius and Ethel Rosenberg," *Special of the Week* (PBS)

"Oil. The Policy Crisis," *ABC News Close-up* (ABC)

OUTSTANDING DOCUMENTARY PROGRAM ACHIEVEMENTS

For documentary programs dealing with artistic, historical or cultural subjects.

☐ "Journey to the Outer Limits," *National Geographic Society* (ABC)

☐ *The World at War* (Syndicated)

☐ *CBS Reports: The Rockefellers* (CBS)

☐ *The Baboons of Gombe* (ABC)

"Culture Thieves," *ABC News Close Up* (ABC)

"Raoul Walsh," *The Men Who Made the Movies* (PBS)

"Power and the Presidency," *The American Parade* (CBS)

OUTSTANDING INTERVIEW PROGRAM

For a single program or one entire program of a series produced by a network news division or dealing with public affairs exclusively

☐ "Solzhenitsyn," *CBS News Special* (CBS)

☐ "Henry Steele Commager," *Bill Moyers' Journal* (PBS)

"Watergate: An Interview with John Dean," *CBS News Special Report* (CBS)

"Crisis of the Presidency," *ABC News Special* (ABC)

OUTSTANDING TELEVISION NEWS BROADCASTER

☐ Harry Reasoner, *ABC News* (ABC)

☐ Bill Moyers, "Essay On Watergate," *Bill Moyers' Journal* (PBS)

Mike Wallace, *60 Minutes* (CBS)

Walter Cronkite, *CBS Evening News with Walter Cronkite* and various specials (CBS)

Carl Stern, "Coverage of Watergate and Justice Department," *NBC Nightly News* (NBC)

John Chancellor, *NBC Nightly News* (NBC)

OUTSTANDING INDIVIDUAL ACHIEVEMENT IN CHILDREN'S PROGRAMMING

☐ Ronald Baldwin (art director), Nat Mongioi (set decorator), *The Electric Company* (PBS)

☐ The Muppets (Jim Henson, Frank Oz, Carroll Spinney, Jerry Nelson, Richard Hunt and Fran Brill, performers) *Sesame Street* (PBS)

Jon Stone, Joseph A. Bailey, Jerry Juhl, Emily Perl Kingsley, Jeffrey Moss, Ray Sipherd and Norman Stiles (writers), *Sesame Street* (PBS)

Henry Behar (director), *The Electric Company* (PBS)

Thomas A. Whedon, John Boni, Sara Compton, Tom Dunsmuir, Thad Mumford, Jeremy Stevens and Jim Thurman (writers), *The Electric Company* (PBS)

OUTSTANDING ACHIEVEMENT IN RELIGIOUS PROGRAMMING

☐ Ken Lamkin (technical director) and Sam Drummy, Gary Stanton and Robert Hatfield (cameramen) "Gift of Tears," *This Is the Life* (Syndicated)

John Ward (scenic designer), Myron Bleam (set decorator) "St. Francis of Assisi," "The Tower of Babel," "David and Goliath," *Marshall Efron's Illustrated, Simplified and Painless Sunday School* (CBS)

Holy Land (NBC)

Directions (ABC)

Christmas in Wales (ABC)

* possibility of one award, more than one award or no award.
☐ Indicates winner

OUTSTANDING ACHIEVEMNT IN NEWS AND DOCUMENTARY DIRECTING

☐ Pamela Hill, "Fire," *ABC News Close-up* (ABC)

Victoria Hochberg, "The Right To Die," *ABC News Close-up* (ABC)

William E. Linden, "Watergate: The White House Transcripts," *CBS News Special Report* (CBS)

OUTSTANDING ACHIEVEMENT IN NEWS AND DOCUMENTARY WRITING

☐ Robert Northshield, "The Sins of the Fathers," *NBC Reports* (NBC)

Marlene Sanders, "The Right to Die," *ABC News Close-up* (ABC)

Howard Stringer, Burton Benjamin, *The Rockfellers; CBS Reports* (CBS)

Alvin H. Goldstein, "The Unquiet Death of Julius and Ethel Rosenberg," *Special of the Week* (PBS)

OUTSTANDING ACHIEVEMENT IN ANY AREA OF CREATIVE TECHNICAL CRAFTS

☐ Philippe Cousteau (under-ice photography), "Beneath the Frozen World," *The Undersea World of Jacques Cousteau* (ABC)

☐ John Chambers and Tom Burman (make-up), "Struggle for Survival," *Primal Man* (ABC)

☐ Aggie Whelan (courtroom drawings), "The Mitchell-Stans Trial," *CBS Evening News with Walter Cronkite* (CBS)

François Charlet (aerial photography), "Beneath the Frozen World," *The Undersea World of Jacques Cousteau* (ABC)

Robert R. Dunn (cameraman), C. Fred Gayton (videotape recorder operator), "The Hearst Kidnapping," *CBS Evening News* (CBS)

OUTSTANDING INFORMATIONAL CHILDREN'S SERIES

☐ *Make A Wish* (ABC)
The Electric Company (PBS)
In the News (CBS)

One Award in Each of the Four Categories

OUTSTANDING INFORMATIONAL CHILDREN'S SPECIAL

☐ *The Runaways* (ABC)
What's Impeachment All About? (CBS)
What's the Energy Crisis All About? (CBS)

OUTSTANDING INSTRUCTIONAL CHILDREN'S PROGRAMMING

☐ *Inside Out* (Syndicated)
Mister Rogers' Neighborhood (PBS)
Multiplication Rock (ABC)

☐ Indicates winner

Sesame Street (PBS)

BEST CINEMATOGRAPHY FOR NEWS AND DOCUMENTARY PROGRAMMING

Regularly scheduled news programs and coverage of special events:

☐ Delos Hall, "Clanking Savannah Blacksmith; On the Road with Charles Kuralt," *CBS Evening news with Walter Cronkite* (CBS)

Robert O. Brown, Elia Ravasz, "SLA Shootout Los Angeles," *CBS Evening News with Dan Rather* (CBS)

Isadore Bleckman, "Bird Lady," "On the Road with Charles Kuralt," *CBS Evening News with Walter Cronkite* (CBS)

Documentary, magazine-type or mini-documentary programs:

☐ Walter Dombrow, "Ballerina," *60 Minutes* (CBS)

Philippe Cousteau, "Beneath the Frozen World," *The Undersea World of Jacques Cousteau* (ABC)

John J. Landi, Ralph Mayher, "Fire," *ABC News Close-up* (ABC)

Dick Mingalone, "Inside Attica," *The Reasoner Report* (ABC)

BEST MUSIC COMPOSITION

☐ Walter Scharf, "Beneath the Frozen World," *The Undersea World of Jacques Cousteau* (ABC)

Lyn Murray, "Struggle For Survival," *Primal Man* (ABC)

Billy Goldenberg, "Journey to the Outer Limits," *National Geographic Society* (ABC)

BEST ART DIRECTION OR SCENIC DESIGN

☐ William Sunshine, *60 Minutes* (CBS)

Frank Skinner, "Soviet Prison Camps," *NBC Presents: Special Edition* (NBC)

Merrill Sindler, "The Cost of Living: Up, Up and Away," *Today* (NBC)

BEST FILM EDITING FOR NEWS AND DOCUMENTARY PROGRAMMING

Regularly scheduled news programs and coverage of special events:

☐ William J. Freeda, "Profile of Poverty in Appalachia," *NBC Nightly News* (NBC)

Patrick Minerva, Thomas E. Dunphy, William J. Freeda, Irwin Graf, Albert J. Helias, George Johnson, Miguel Portillo, Martin Sheppard, Jean Venable, Edwin Einarsen, Constantine S. Gochis, Loftus McDonough, Desmond McElroy, Robert Mole, Russell Moore, Loren Berry, Tina Gruettner, Nick Wilkins, Gerry Bresse, K. Tu-Huei Su,

Michael Shugrue, Nina Jackson *NBC Nightly News* (NBC)

Gilbert LeVeque, "SLA Shootout," *CBS Evening News with Dan Rather* (CBS)

Documentary, magazine-type or mini-documentary programs:

☐ Ann Chegwidden, "The Baboons of Gombe," *Jane Goodall and the World of Animal Behavior (ABC)*

David H. Newhouse, "Journey to the Outer Limits," *National Geographic Society* (ABC)

John Soh, "Beneath the Frozen World," *The Undersea World of Jacques Cousteau* (ABC)

BEST FILM OR TAPE SOUND MIXING FOR A SERIES, A SINGLE PROGRAM OF A SERIES OR A SPECIAL PROGRAM

☐ Peter Pilafian, George E. Porter, Eddie J. Nelson, Robert L. Harman, "Journey to the Outer Limits," *National Geographic Society* (ABC)

Robert L. Harman, George E. Porter, Eddie J. Nelson, Guy Jouas, "The Flight of the Penguins," *The Undersea World of Jacques Cousteau* (ABC)

George E. Porter, Eddie J. Nelson, Roy Granville, "South to Fire and Ice," *The Undersea World of Jacques Cousteau* (ABC)

Robert L. Harman, George E. Porter, Eddie J. Nelson, "The Baboons of Gombe," *Jane Goodall and the World of Animal Behavior* (ABC)

BEST FILM SOUND EDITING FOR A SERIES, A SINGLE PROGRAM OF A SERIES OR A SPECIAL PROGRAM

☐ Charles L. Campbell, Robert Cornett, Larry Carow, Larry Kaufman, Colin Mouat, Don Warne, Frank R. White, "The Baboons of Gombe," *Jane Goodall and the World of Animal Behavior* (ABC)

Stephen E. Price, "Bigger is Better," *60 Minutes* (CBS)

Charles L. Campbell, Colin Mouat, Jerry R. Stanford, Larry Carow, "The Flight of the Penguins," *The Undersea World of Jacques Cousteau* (ABC)

BEST VIDEO TAPE EDITING

☐ Gary Anderson, "Paramount Presents...," *ABC Wide World of Entertainment* (ABC)

George Kiyak, Robert Baiy, Lloyd Campbell, Joseph D. Colvin, Don Dunn, Buddy Fleck, Vincent Gabriele, Richard Leible, Ralph Martucci, Arthur Schweiger, Morton Smith, Jerry Valdivia, Richard Wedeking, "Watergate. This Week," *NBC News Special* (NBC)

Jack Stanley, Ernest Allen Tobin, "Watergate Hearings," *CBS Evening News with Walter Cronkite* (CBS)

BEST TECHNICAL DIRECTION AND ELECTRONIC CAMERAWORK
□ Carl Schutzman (technical director), Joseph Schwartz, William Bell (cameramen), *60 Minutes* (CBS)
David Fee (technical director), and Stuart Goodman, Richard Kerr, Eugene Wood and Phil Fontana (cameraman), "Goodnight America," *ABC Wide World of Entertainment* (ABC)
Martin Solomon (technical director), and Harry Haigood, David Dorsett, and Cass Gaylord (cameramen), *CBS Evening News with Walter Cronkite* (CBS)

1974/75

(For programs aired between March 18, 1974 and March 10, 1975. Prime time awards presented May 19, 1975. Daytime awards presented May 15, 1975.)

Prime Time Program Awards

OUTSTANDING COMEDY SERIES
□ *The Mary Tyler Moore Show* (CBS)
*M*A*S*H* (CBS)
All in the Family (CBS)
Rhoda (CBS)

OUTSTANDING DRAMA SERIES
□ "Upstairs, Downstairs," *Masterpiece Theatre* (PBS)
The Streets of San Francisco (ABC)
Policy Story (NBC)
The Waltons (CBS)
Kojak (CBS)

OUTSTANDING COMEDY-VARIETY OR MUSIC SERIES
□ *The Carol Burnett Show* (CBS)
Cher (CBS)

OUTSTANDING LIMITED SERIES
□ *Benjamin Franklin* (CBS)
McCloud (NBC)
Columbo (NBC)

OUTSTANDING SPECIAL—DRAMA OR COMEDY
□ "The Law," *NBC World Premiere Movie* (NBC)
"The Missiles of October," *ABC Theatre* (ABC)
Queen of the Stardust Ballroom (CBS)
"Love among the Ruins," *ABC Theatre* (ABC)
"QB VII, Parts 1 and 2," *ABC Movie Special* (ABC)

□ Indicates winner

OUTSTANDING SPECIAL—COMEDY-VARIETY OR MUSIC
□ *An Evening with John Denver* (ABC)
Lily (ABC)
Shirley MacLaine: If They Could See Me Now (CBS)

OUTSTANDING CLASSICAL MUSIC PROGRAM
□ "Profile in Music: Beverly Sills," *Festival '75* (PBS)
"Rubinstein," *Great Performances* (PBS)
"Bernstein at Tanglewood," *Great Performances* (PBS)
Evening at Pops (PBS)

OUTSTANDING CHILDREN'S SPECIAL (BROADCAST DURING THE EVENING)
□ *Yes, Virginia, There Is a Santa Claus* (ABC)
Be My Valentine, Charlie Brown (CBS)
Dr. Seuss' The Hoober-Bloob Highway (CBS)
It's the Easter Beagle, Charlie Brown (CBS)

OUTSTANDING SPORTS EVENT (FOR A NON-EDITED PROGRAM)
□ *Jimmy Connors vs. Rod Laver Tennis Challenge* (CBS)
NFL Monday Night Football (ABC)
NCAA Football (ABC)
ABC Championship Golf (ABC)
NBA Championship Game (CBS)
National Football League Game— Washington vs. Dallas (CBS)
Jackie Gleason Inverrary Classic (HTN)
Andy Williams San Diego Open (HTN)
Madison Square Garden events (HTN)
1974 World Series (NBC)
NBC Monday Night Baseball (NBC)
AFC Football Playoffs (NBC)
Spalding International Mixed Doubles Tennis Championship (PBS)
National Bicycle Track Championships (PBS)
ATP Summer Tennis Tour (PBS)
World Football League Championship (TVS)
UCLA-Notre Dame Basketball (TVS)
NCAA Basketball (TVS)

OUTSTANDING SPORTS PROGRAM (FOR AN EDITED PROGRAM)
□ *Wide World of Sports* (ABC)
The Superstars (ABC)
The American Sportsman (ABC)
CBS Sports Spectacular (CBS)
NFL on CBS (CBS)
NBA on CBS (CBS)
The Baseball World of Joe Garagiola (NBC)
Super Bowl IX Pre-Game Show (NBC)
The Way It Was (PBS)
Victor Awards (TVS)
USA-China Basketball Highlights (TVS)

Prime Time Performance Awards

OUTSTANDING SPORTS BROADCASTER
□ Jim McKay, *Wide World of Sports* (ABC)
Howard Cosell, *Monday Night Football* (ABC)
Keith Jackson, *NCAA Football* (ABC)
Frank Gifford, *Monday Night Football* (ABC)
Chris Schenkel, *ABC Championship Golf* (ABC)
Vin Scully, *Jimmy Connors vs. Rod Laver Tennis Challenge* (CBS)
Pat Summerall, *NFL Football* (CBS)
Brent Musburger, *NBA Basketball* (CBS)
Jack Whitaker, *NBA All Star Game* (CBS)
Ken Squier, *CBS Sports Spectacular* (CBS)
Curt Gowdy, *AFC Football Playoffs* (NBC)
Don Meredith, *Super Bowl IX* (NBC)
Joe Garagiola, *The Baseball World of Joe Garagiola* (NBC)
Jim Simpson, *Wimbledon Tennis* (NBC)
Tim Ryan, *1974 Stanley Cup Playoffs* (NBC)
Budd Collins, *Spalding International Mixed Doubles Tennis Championship* (PBS)
Judy Dixon, *Spalding International Mixed Doubles Tennis Championship* (PBS)
Curt Gowdy, *The Way It Was* (PBS)

OUTSTANDING LEAD ACTOR IN A COMEDY SERIES
□ Tony Randall, *The Odd Couple* (ABC)
Alan Alda, *M*A*S*H* (CBS)
Jack Albertson, *Chico and the Man* (NBC)
Jack Klugman, *The Odd Couple* (ABC)
Carroll O'Connor, *All in the Family* (CBS)

OUTSTANDING LEAD ACTOR IN A DRAMA SERIES
□ Karl Blake, *Baretta* (ABC)
Karl Malden, *The Streets of San Francisco* (ABC)
Barry Newman, *Petrocelli* (NBC)
Telly Savalas, *Kojak* (CBS)

OUTSTANDING LEAD ACTOR IN A LIMITED SERIES
□ Peter Falk, *Columbo* (NBC)
Dennis Weaver, *McCloud* (NBC)

OUTSTANDING CONTINUING PERFORMANCE BY A SUPPORTING ACTOR IN A DRAMA SERIES (FOR A REGULAR OR LIMITED SERIES)
□ Will Geer, *The Waltons* (CBS)

Michael Douglas, *The Streets of San Francisco* (ABC)

J.D. Cannon, "McCloud," *NBC Sunday Mystery Movie* (NBC)

OUTSTANDING CONTINUING OR SINGLE PERFORMANCE BY A SUPPORTING ACTOR IN VARIETY OR MUSIC (FOR A CONTINUING ROLE IN A REGULAR OR LIMITED SERIES, OR A ONE-TIME APPEARANCE IN A SERIES, OR A SPECIAL)

☐ Jack Albertson, *Cher* (CBS)

Tim Conway, *The Carol Burnett Show* (CBS)

John Denver, *Doris Day Today* (CBS)

OUTSTANDING SINGLE PERFORMANCE BY A SUPPORTING ACTOR IN A COMEDY OR DRAMA SPECIAL

☐ Anthony Quale, "QB VII, Parts 1 & 2," *ABC Movie Special* (ABC)

Ralph Bellamy, "The Missiles of October," *ABC Theatre* (ABC)

Trevor Howard, "The Count of Monte Cristo," *Bell System Family Theatre* (NBC)

Jack Hawkins, "QB VII, Parts 1 & 2," *ABC Movie Special* (ABC)

OUTSTANDING SINGLE PERFORMANCE BY A SUPPORTING ACTOR IN A COMEDY OR DRAMA SERIES (FOR A ONE-TIME APPEARANCE IN A REGULAR OR LIMITED SERIES)

☐ Patrick McGoohan, "By Dawn's Early Light," *Columbo* (NBC)

Lew Ayres, "The Vanishing Image," *Kung Fu* (ABC)

Harold Gould, "Fathers and Sons," *Police Story* (NBC)

Harry Morgan, "The General Flipped at Dawn," *M*A*S*H* (CBS)

OUTSTANDING CONTINUING PERFORMANCE BY A SUPPORTING ACTRESS IN A COMEDY SERIES (FOR A REGULAR OR LIMITED SERIES)

☐ Betty White, *The Mary Tyler Moore Show* (CBS)

Julie Kavner, *Rhoda* (CBS)

Nancy Walker, *Rhoda* (CBS)

Loretta Swit, *M*A*S*H* (CBS)

OUTSTANDING CONTINUING PERFORMANCE BY A SUPPORTING ACTRESS IN A DRAMA SERIES (FOR A REGULAR OR LIMITED SERIES)

☐ Ellen Corby, *The Waltons* (CBS)

Nancy Walker, "McMillan & Wife," *NBC Sunday Mystery Movie* (NBC)

Angela Baddeley, "Upstairs, Downstairs," *Masterpiece Theatre* (PBS)

☐ Indicates winner

OUTSTANDING LEAD ACTOR IN A SPECIAL PROGRAM—DRAMA OR COMEDY (FOR A SPECIAL PROGRAM, OR FOR A SINGLE APPEARANCE IN A DRAMA OR COMEDY SERIES)

☐ Laurence Olivier, "Love Among the Ruins," *ABC Theatre* (ABC)

Richard Chamberlain, "The Count of Monte Cristo," *Bell System Family Theatre* (NBC)

William Devane, "The Missiles of October," *ABC Theatre* (ABC)

Charles Durning, "Queen of the Stardust Ballroom" (CBS)

Henry Fonda, "IBM Presents Clarence Darrow," (NBC)

OUTSTANDING LEAD ACTRESS IN A COMEDY SERIES

☐ Valerie Harper, *Rhoda* (CBS)

Mary Tyler Moore, *The Mary Tyler Moore Show* (CBS)

Jean Stapleton, *All in the Family* (CBS)

OUTSTANDING LEAD ACTRESS IN A DRAMA SERIES

☐ Jean Marsh, "Upstairs, Downstairs," *Masterpiece Theatre* (PBS)

Angie Dickinson, *Police Woman* (NBC)

Michael Learned, *The Waltons* (CBS)

OUTSTANDING LEAD ACTRESS IN A LIMITED SERIES

☐ Jessica Walter, "Amy Prentiss," *NBC Sunday Mystery Movie* (NBC)

Susan Saint James, "McMillan & Wife," *NBC Sunday Mystery Movie* (NBC)

OUTSTANDING LEAD ACTRESS IN A SPECIAL PROGRAM—DRAMA OR COMEDY (FOR A SPECIAL PROGRAM, OR A SINGLE APPEARANCE IN A DRAMA OR COMEDY SERIES)

☐ Katharine Hepburn, "Love Among the Ruins," *ABC Theatre* (ABC)

Jill Clayburgh, "Hustling," *Special World Premiere ABC Saturday Night Movie* (ABC)

Elizabeth Montgomery, "The Legend of Lizzie Borden," *Special World Premiere ABC Monday Night Movie* (ABC)

Diana Rigg, "In This House of Brede," *GE Theater* (CBS)

Maureen Stapleton, *Queen of the Stardust Ballroom* (CBS)

OUTSTANDING CONTINUING PERFORMANCE BY A SUPPORTING ACTOR IN A COMEDY SERIES (FOR A REGULAR OR LIMITED SERIES)

☐ Ed Asner, *The Mary Tyler Moore Show* (CBS)

Rob Reiner, *All in the Family* (CBS)

Ted Knight, *The Mary Tyler Moore Show* (CBS)

Gary Burghoff, *M*A*S*H* (CBS)

McLean Stevenson, *M*A*S*H* (CBS)

OUTSTANDING CONTINUING OR SINGLE PERFORMANCE BY A SUPPORTING ACTRESS IN VARIETY OR MUSIC (FOR A CONTINUING ROLE IN A REGULAR OR LIMITED SERIES OR A ONE-TIME APPEARANCE IN A SERIES OR A SPECIAL)

☐ Cloris Leachman, *Cher* (CBS)

Rita Moreno, *Out to Lunch* (ABC)

Vicki Lawrence, *The Carol Burnett Show* (CBS)

OUTSTANDING SINGLE PERFORMANCE BY A SUPPORTING ACTRESS IN A COMEDY OR DRAMA SPECIAL

☐ Juliet Mills, "QB VII—Parts 1 & 2," *ABC Movie Special* (ABC)

Charlotte Rae, *Queen of the Stardust Ballroom* (CBS)

Lee Remick, "QB VII—Parts 1 & 2," *ABC Movie Special* (ABC)

Eileen Heckart, "Wedding Band," *ABC Theatre* (ABC)

OUTSTANDING SINGLE PERFORMANCE BY A SUPPORTING ACTRESS IN A COMEDY OR DRAMA SERIES (FOR A ONE-TIME APPEARANCE IN A REGULAR OR LIMITED SERIES)

☐ Cloris Leachman, "Phyllis Whips Inflation," *The Mary Tyler Moore Show* (CBS)

☐ Zohra Lampert, "Queen of the Gypsies," *Kojak* (CBS)

Shelley Winters, "The Barefoot Girls of Bleecker Street," *McCloud* (NBC)

Prime Time Craft and Technical Awards

OUTSTANDING DIRECTING IN A DRAMA SERIES (FOR A SINGLE EPISODE OF A REGULAR OR LIMITED SERIES WITH CONTINUING CHARACTERS AND/OR THEME)

☐ Bill Bain, "A Sudden Storm," *Upstairs, Downstairs* (PBS)

Harry Falk, "The Mask of Death," *The Streets of San Francisco* (ABC)

David Friedkin, "Cross Your Heart and Hope to Die," *Kojak* (CBS)

Telly Savalas, "I Want to Report a Dream. . .," *Kojak* (CBS)

Glenn Jordan, "The Ambassador," *Benjamin Franklin* (CBS)

OUTSTANDING DIRECTING IN A COMEDY SERIES (FOR A SINGLE EPISODE OF A REGULAR OR LIMITED SERIES WITH CONTINUING CHARACTERS AND/OR THEME)

☐ Gene Reynolds, "O.R.," *M*A*S*H* (CBS)

Hy Averback, "Alcoholics Unanimous," *M*A*S*H* (CBS)

Alan Alda, "Bulletin Board," *M*A*S*H* (CBS)

OUTSTANDING DIRECTING IN A COMEDY-VARIETY OR MUSIC SERIES (FOR A SINGLE EPISODE OF A REGULAR OR LIMITED SERIES)

☐ Dave Powers, *The Carol Burnett Show* (with Alan Alda), (CBS)

Art Fisher, *Cher* (with Bette Midler, Flip Wilson, Elton John), (CBS)

OUTSTANDING DIRECTING IN A COMEDY-VARIETY OR MUSIC SPECIAL

☐ Bill Davis, *An Evening with John Denver* (ABC)

Robert Scheerer, *Shirley MacLaine: If They Could See Me Now* (CBS)

Dwight Hemion, *Ann-Margret Olsson* (NBC)

OUTSTANDING DIRECTING IN A SPECIAL PROGRAM—DRAMA OR COMEDY

☐ George Cukor, "Love Among the Ruins," *ABC Theatre* (ABC)

John Badham, "The Law," *NBC World Premiere Movie* (NBC)

Sam O'Steen, *Queen of the Stardust Ballroom* (CBS)

Tom Gries, "QB VII—Parts 1 & 2," *ABC Movie Special* (ABC)

Anthony Page, "The Missiles of October," *ABC Theatre* (ABC)

OUTSTANDING WRITING IN A DRAMA SERIES (FOR A SINGLE EPISODE OF A REGULAR OR LIMITED SERIES WITH CONTINUING CHARACTERS AND/OR THEME)

☐ Howard Fast, "The Ambassador," *Benjamin Franklin* (CBS)

Robert Collins, "Robbery: 48 Hours," *Police Story* (NBC)

Alfred Shaughnessy, "Miss Forrest," *Upstairs, Downstairs* (PBS)

Loring Mandel, "The Whirlwind," *Benjamin Franklin* (CBS)

John Hawkesworth, "The Bolter," *Upstairs, Downstairs* (PBS)

OUTSTANDING WRITING IN A COMEDY SERIES (FOR A SINGLE EPISODE OR A REGULAR OR LIMITED SERIES WITH CONTINUING CHARACTERS AND/OR THEME)

☐ Ed Weinberger, Stan Daniels, "Mary Richards Goes to Jail," *The Mary Tyler Moore Show* (CBS)

David Lloyd, "Lou and That Woman," *The Mary Tyler Moore Show* (CBS)

Norman Barasch, Carroll Moore, David Lloyd, Lorenzo Music, Allan Burns, James L. Brooks, David Davis, "Rhoda's Wedding," *Rhoda* (CBS)

☐ Indicates winner

OUTSTANDING WRITING IN A COMEDY-VARIETY OR MUSIC SERIES (FOR A SINGLE EPISODE OF A REGULAR OR LIMITED SERIES)

☐ Ed Simmons, Gary Belkin, Roger Beatty, Arnie Kogen, Bill Richmond, Gene Perret, Rudy DeLuca, Barry Levinson, Dick Clair, Jenna McMahon, *The Carol Burnett Show* (with Alan Alda) (CBS)

Digby Wolfe, Don Reo, Alan Katz, Iris Rainer, David Panich, Ron Pearlman, Nick Arnold, John Boni, Ray Taylor, George Schlatter, *Cher* (with Raquel Welch, Tatum O'Neal, Wayne Rogers) (CBS)

OUTSTANDING WRITING A COMEDY-VARIETY OR MUSIC SPECIAL

☐ Bob Wells, John Bradford, Cy Coleman, *Shirley MacLaine: If They Could See Me Now* (CBS)

Sybil Adelman, Barbara Gallagher, Gloria Banta, Pat Nardo, Stuart Birnbaum, Matt Newman, Lorne Michales, Marilyn Miller, Earl Pomerantz, Rosie Ruthchild, Lily Tomlin, Jane Wagner, *Lily* (ABC)

OUTSTANDING WRITING IN A SPECIAL PROGRAM—DRAMA OR COMEDY—ORIGINAL TELEPLAY

☐ James Costigan, "Love Among the Ruins," *ABC Theatre* (ABC)

Jerome Kass, *Queen of the Stardust Ballroom* (CBS)

Stanley R. Greenberg, "The Missiles of October," *ABC Theatre* (ABC)

Fay Kanin, "Hustling," *Special World Premiere ABC Saturday Night Movie* (ABC)

Joel Oliansky, story by William Sackheim and Joel Oliansky, "The Law," *NBC World Premiere Movie* (NBC)

OUTSTANDING WRITING IN A SPECIAL PROGRAM—DRAMA OR COMEDY—ADAPTATION

☐ David W. Rintels, *IBM Presents Clarence Darrow* (NBC)

Edward Anhalt, "QB VII—Parts 1 & 2," *ABC Movie Special* (ABC)

OUTSTANDING ACHIEVEMENT IN CHOREOGRAPHY FOR A SINGLE EPISODE OF A SERIES OR A SPECIAL PROGRAM

☐ Marge Champion, *Queen of the Stardust Ballroom* (CBS)

Alan Johnson, *Shirley MacLaine: If They Could See Me Now* (CBS)

Dee Dee Wood, *Cher* (with Freddie Prinze, The Pointer Sisters) (CBS)

OUTSTANDING ACHIEVEMENT IN MUSIC COMPOSITION FOR A SERIES FOR DRAMATIC UNDERSCORE FOR A SINGLE EPISODE OF A REGULAR OR LIMITED SERIES

☐ Billy Goldenberg, "The Rebel," *Benjamin Franklin* (CBS)

Pat Williams, "One Last Shot," *The Streets of San Francisco* (ABC)

OUTSTANDING ACHIEVEMENT IN MUSIC COMPOSITION FOR A SPECIAL FOR DRAMATIC UNDERSCORE

☐ Jerry Goldsmith, "QB VII—Parts 1 & 2," *ABC Movie Special* (ABC)

Billy Goldenberg, Alan and Marilyn Bergman, *Queen of the Stardust Ballroom* (CBS)

OUTSTANDING ACHIEVEMENT IN ART DIRECTION OR SCENIC DESIGN FOR A SINGLE EPISODE OF A COMEDY, DRAMA OR LIMITED SERIES

☐ Charles Lisanby (art director), Robert Checchi (set director), "The Ambassador," *Benjamin Franklin* (CBS)

Michael Baugh (art director), Jerry Adam (set decorator), "Playback," *Columbo* (NBC)

OUTSTANDING ACHIEVEMENT IN ART DIRECTION OR SCENIC DESIGN FOR A SINGLE EPISODE OF A COMEDY-VARIETY OF MUSIC SERIES OR A COMEDY-VARIETY OR MUSIC SPECIAL

☐ Robert Kelly (art director), Robert Checchi (set decorator), *Cher* (with Bette Midler, Flip Wilson, Elton John) (CBS)

OUTSTANDING ACHIEVEMENT IN ART DIRECTION OR SCENIC DESIGN FOR A DRAMATIC SPECIAL OR A FEATURE LENGTH FILM MADE FOR TELEVISION

☐ Carmen Dillon (art director), Tessa Davies (set decorator), "Love Among the Ruins," *ABC Theatre* (ABC)

Jack De Shields (art director), Harry Gordon (set decorator), "The Legend of Lizzie Borden," *Special World Premiere ABC Monday Night Movie* (ABC)

Ross Bellah and Maurice Fowler (art directors), Audrey Blesdel-Goddard and Terry Parr (set decorators), "QB VII—Parts 1 & 2," *ABC Movie Special* (ABC)

OUTSTANDING ACHIEVEMENT IN GRAPHIC DESIGN AND TITLE SEQUENCES FOR A SINGLE EPISODE OF A SERIES OR FOR A SPECIAL PROGRAM. THIS INCLUDES ANIMATION ONLY WHEN CREATED FOR USE IN TITLING

☐ Phil Norman, "QB VII—Parts 1 & 2," *ABC Movie Special* (ABC)

Rick Andreoli, *The Tonight Show Starring Johnny Carson* (NBC)

Susan Cuscuna, *The Tonight Show Starring Johnny Carson* (NBC)

OUTSTANDING ACHIEVEMENT IN CINEMATOGRAPHY FOR ENTERTAINMENT PROGRAMMING FOR A SERIES FOR A SINGLE EPISODE OF A REGULAR OR LIMITED SERIES

☐ Richard C. Glouner, "Playback," *Columbo* (NBC)

William Jurgensen, "Bombed," *M*A*S*H* (CBS)

Vilis Lapenieks, Sol Negrin, "Wall Street Gunslinger," *Kojak* (CBS)

OUTSTANDING ACHIEVEMENT IN CINEMATOGRAPHY FOR ENTERTAINMENT PROGRAMMING FOR A SPECIAL OR FEATURE LENGTH PROGRAM MADE FOR TELEVISION

☐ David M. Walsh, *Queen of the Stardust Ballroom* (CBS)

Howard Schwartz, "Sad Figure, Laughing," *Sandburg's Lincoln* (NBC)

Paul Beeson, Robert L. Morrison, *QB VII—Parts 1 & 2* (ABC)

Michael Chapman, "Death Be Not Proud," *Tuesday Movie of the Week* (ABC)

OUTSTANDING FILM EDITING FOR ENTERTAINMENT PROGRAMMING FOR A SERIES FOR A SINGLE EPISODE OF A COMEDY SERIES

☐ Douglas Hines, "An Affair to Forget," *The Mary Tyler Moore Show* (CBS)

Stanford Tischler, Fred W. Berger, "The General Flipped at Dawn," *M*A*S*H* (CBS)

OUTSTANDING FILM EDITING FOR ENTERTAINMENT PROGRAMMING FOR A SPECIAL OR FILM MADE FOR TELEVISION

☐ John A. Martinelli, *The Legend of Lizzie Borden* (ABC)

Byron "Buzz" Brandt, Irving C. Rosenblum, *QB VII—Parts 1 & 2* (ABC)

Jerry Young, *Attack on Terror: The FBI Versus the Ku Klux Klan*—Parts 1 & 2 (CBS)

☐ Indicates winner

OUTSTANDING ACHIEVEMENT IN FILM SOUND EDITING (FOR A SINGLE EPISODE OF A REGULAR OR LIMITED SERIES OR FOR A SPECIAL PROGRAM)

☐ Marvin, I. Kosberg, Richard Burrow, Milton C. Burrow, Jack Milner, Ronald Ashcroft, James Ballas, Josef Von Stroheim, Jerry Rosenthal, William Andrews, Edward Sandlin, David Horton, Alvin Kajita, Tony Garber, Jeremy Hoenack, *QB VII—Parts 1 & 2* (ABC)

David Isaacs, Don Higgins, Larry Kaufman, Jack Kirschner, Dick LeGrand, Gary Vaughan, Gene Wahrman, Frank White, Harold Wooley, *The Legend of Lizzie Borden* (ABC)

OUTSTANDING ACHIEVEMENT IN FILM OR TAPE SOUND MIXING (FOR A SINGLE EPISODE OF A REGULAR OR LIMITED SERIES, OR FOR A SPEICAL PROGRAM)

☐ Marshall King, *The American Film Institute Salute to James Cagney* (CBS)

Doug Nelson, *The Missiles of October* (ABC)

Doug Nelson, Norm Schwartz, "California Jam," *Wide World in Concert* (ABC)

OUTSTANDING ACHIEVEMENT IN VIDEO TAPE EDITING (FOR A SINGLE EPISODE OF A REGULAR OR LIMITED SERIES, OR FOR A SPECIAL PROGRAM)

☐ Gary Anderson, Jim McElroy, "Judgment: The Court-Martial of Lt. William Calley," *ABC Theatre* (ABC)

Nick V. Giordan, George Gurunian, "California Jam," *Wide World in Concert* (ABC)

Jerry Greene, *The Missiles of October* (ABC)

OUTSTANDING ACHIEVEMENT IN TECHNICAL DIRECTION AND ELECTRONIC CAMERA WORK (FOR A SINGLE EPISODE OR A REGULAR OR LIMITED SERIES: OR FOR A SPECIAL PROGRAM)

☐ Ernie Buttelman (technical director), and Jim Angel, Jim Balden, Ron Brooks and Art LaCombe (cameramen), *The Missiles of October* (ABC)

Heino Ripp (technical director), and Jon Olson, Bob Keys, John James and Kurt Tonnessen (cameramen), *IBM Presents Clarence Darrow* (NBC)

Heino Ripp and Lou Fusari (technical directors), and Roy Holm, Tony Yarlett, Rick Lombardo, Bob Keys and Ray Figelski (cameramen), *The Perry Como Christmas Show* (CBS)

OUTSTANDING ACHIEVEMENT IN LIGHTING DIRECTION (FOR A SINGLE EPISODE OF A REGULAR OR LIMITED SERIES OR FOR A SPECIAL PROGRAM)

☐ John Freschi, *The Perry Como Christmas Show* (CBS) Lon Stucky, *IBM Presents Clarence Darrow* (NBC)

The Areas*

SPECIAL CLASSIFICATION OF OUTSTANDING PROGRAM AND INDIVIDUAL ACHIEVEMENT

☐ *The American Film Institute Salute to James Cagney* (CBS)

The American Film Institute Salute to Orson Welles (CBS)

☐ Alistair Cooke (host), *Masterpiece Theatre* (PBS)

The Dick Cavett Show (ABC)

"That's Entertainment: 50 Years of MGM," *ABC Wide World of Entertainment* (ABC)

86th Annual Pasadena Tournament of Roses Parade (NBC)

Tom Snyder (host) *Tomorrow* (NBC)

Jack Stewart (art director), John Hueners (set decorator), *Bicentennial Minutes* (CBS)

OUTSTANDING ACHIEVEMENT IN SPECIAL MUSICAL MATERIAL

Alan and Marilyn Bergman, Billy Goldenberg, *Queen of the Stardust Ballroom* (CBS)

Cy Coleman, Bob Well, *Shirley MacLaine: If They Could See Me Now* (CBS)

Morton Stevens, *Police Woman* (theme) (NBC)

Earl Brown, Billy Barnes, *Cher* (with Bette Midler, Flip Wilson, Elton John) (CBS)

Jose and Janna Merlyn Feliciano, *Chico and The Man* (theme) (NBC)

OUTSTANDING ACHIEVEMENT IN COSTUME DESIGN

☐ Guy Verhille, "The Legend Of Lizzie Borden," *Special World Premiere ABC Monday Night Movie* (ABC)

☐ Margaret Furse, "Love Among the Ruins," *ABC Theatre* (ABC)

Bruce Walkup, *Queen of the Stardust Ballroom* (CBS)

Bob Mackie, *Cher* (with Bette Midler, Flip Wilson, Elton John) (CBS)

Ret Turner, *The Sonny Comedy Revue* (with McLean Stevenson, Joey Heatherton) (ABC)

* possibility of one award, more than one award or no award

OUTSTANDING ACHIEVEMENT IN MAKE-UP

Harry Blake, Stan Winston, Jim Kail, Ralph Gulko, Bob Ostermann, Tom Cole, Larry Abbott, *Masquerade Party* (Syndicated)

Mark R. Bussan, *The Ambassador: Benjamin Franklin* (CBS)

Dan Striepeke, John Chambers, *Twigs* (CBS)

OUTSTANDING ACHIEVEMENT IN ANY AREA OF CREATIVE TECHNICAL CRAFTS

□ Edie Panda (hairstylist), *The Ambassador: Benjamin Franklin* (CBS)

□ Doug Nelson and Norm Schwartz (double system sound editing and synchronization for stereophonic broadcasting of television programs), *Wide World in Concert* (ABC)

Larry Germain (hairstylist), "If I Should Wake Before I Die," *Little House on the Prairie* (NBC)

OUTSTANDING INDIVIDUAL ACHIEVEMENT IN SPORTS PROGRAMMING

□ Gene Schwartz (technical director), *1974 World Series* (NBC)

□ Herb Altman (film editor), *The Baseball World of Joe Garagiola* (NBC)

□ Corey Leible, Len Basile, Jack Bennett, Lou Gerad and Ray Figelski (electronic cameramen), *1974 Stanley Cup Playoffs* (NBC)

□ John Pumo, Charles D'Onofrio, Frank Florio (technical directors) George Klimcsak, Robert Kania, Harold Hoffmann, Herman Lang, George Drago, Walt Deniear, Stan Gould, Al Diamond, Charles Armstrong, Al Brantley, Sig Meyers, Frank McSpedon, George F. Naeder, James Murphy, James McCarthy, Vern Surphlis, Al Loreto, Gordon Sweeney, Jo Sidlo, William Hathaway, Gene Pescalek and Curly Fonorow (cameramen), *Masters Tournament* (CBS)

Lary Kamm, Lou Volpicelli, Brice Weisman, Ned Steckel, Andy Sidaris and Chet Forte (directors), *Wide World of Sports* (ABC)

Werner Gunther, John Broderick and John Irvine (technical directors), Andy Armentani, Drew DeRosa, Jim Heneghan, John Morreale, Joe Nesi, Mike Rebich, Jack Himelfarb, Steve Ciliberto, Jesse Kohn, Joe Stefanoni, Stu Goodman, Joe Schiavo, Bob Hammond, Art Peffer, Dick Spanos, Art Ferrare, Gene Wood, Roy Hutchings, Bill Karvelas, Ronnie Sterckx, Joe Sapienza, Bob Wolfe, John Cronin, Carl Brown, Robert

□ Indicates winner

Copper, Dick Kerr, Mort Levin, Bob Bernstein, Jerry Doud, Jack Dorfman (cameramen), *U.S. Open* (ABC)

William Morris and Werner Gunther (technical directors), and Andy Armentani, Drew DeRosa, Jim Heneghan, John Morreale, Joe Nesi, Mike Rebich, Jack Himmelfarb, Steve Ciliberto, Jesse Kohn, Joe Stefanoni, Stu Goodman, Joe Schiavo, Bill Sullivan, Steve Nikifor, Jack Dorfman, Bob Lopes (cameramen), *Indianapolis 500* (ABC)

John Peterson and Tony Zaccaro (film editors), *Wide World Of Sports* (ABC)

John Croak, John DeLisa, Chester Pawlak, Marv Gench, Alex Moskovic, Jack Hierl, Tony Greco, Erskine Roberts, Art Volk and Harvey Beal (video tape editors), *Wide World of Sports* (ABC)

John Croak, John DeLisa, Art Volk, Ron Ackerman, Marv Gench, Alex Moskovic, Nick Mazur (video tape editors), *The Superstars* (ABC)

Pat Smith (writer), *The American Sportsman* (ABC)

Jack Simon (director), *New York Mets Baseball* (HTN)

Joe O'Rourke (director), *Professional Championship Golf* (HTN)

Harry Coyle (director), *1974 World Series* (NBC)

Ted Nathanson (director), *AFC Football Playoffs* (NBC)

Howard Neef and Barry Winnik (cinematographers), *The Baseball World of Joe Garagiola; Gates Brown—Parts 1 & 2* (NBC)

Murray Vecchio, Bill Tobey, Bill Rose and John O'Connor (videotape [slow motion] editors), *Orange Bowl* (NBC)

Sandy Bell, Frank Vilot, Chuck Franklin, Jim Angerami and John Burkhart (technical directors), and Dick Douglas, George Klimcsak, Al Diamond, Frank McSpedon, John Lincoln, Phil Walsh, Stan Gould, Mike English, Robert Heller, David Graham, Walt Deniear, Robert Chandler, Harold Hoffman, Gene Savitt, Dave Levenson, George Erickson, Curly Fonarow, Tom McConnell, Fred Dansereau, Bob Faeth, George Drago, Jim Murphy, George F. Naeder, Jo Sokota, Pat McBride, Al Loreto, Dave Leavel, Jerry Weaver, Bob Chaney, Fred Schultz, Tony Butts, Danny Ireland (cameramen), *NBA Basketball* (CBS)

Angelo J. Gulino, Bob Brown, Ed Dahlberg, Dick Ohldacker, Sam Lane, Tom Duffy, Frank Hicks (sound mixers), *NBA Basketball* (CBS)

Pete Reed (sound mixer), *Jimmy Connors vs. Rod Laver Tennis Challenge* (CBS)

Sandy Grossman (director), *NBA Basketball* (CBS)

Bob Dailey (director), *Jimmy Connors vs. Rod Laver Tennis Challenge* (CBS)

Special Awards

OUTSTANDING ACHIEVEMENT IN ENGINEERING DEVELOPMENT

□ *CBS.* For spearheading the development and realization of the Electronic News Gathering System.

□ *Nippon Electric Co.* For development of digital television Frame Synchronizers.

Citation to The Society of Motion Picture and Television Engineers. For the technical development of the Universal Tape Time Code.

TRUSTEES' AWARDS

□ *Elmer Lower*, Vice President, Corporate Affairs, ABC, Inc.

□ *Dr. Peter Goldmark*, President, Goldmark Laboratories.

THE NATIONAL AWARD FOR COMMUNITY SERVICE

□ *The Willowbrook Case: The People vs. the State of New York* (WABC-TV, New York)

Breast Surgery: Rebirth or Betrayal (WXYZ-TV, Detroit)

Focus 30 (KYTV, Springfield)

Grandpeople (WPBT, Miami)

The Occupant in the Single Room (WNET, New York)

Senility, a State of Mind (KSL, Salt Leke City)

Smoke and Steel (WKY-TV, Oaklahoma City)

Trouble in the Ghetto (WAGA-TV, Atlanta)

Why Me? (KNXT, Los Angeles)

Without Fear (WKYC-TV, Cleveland)

THE INTERNATIONAL AWARDS

Fiction:

□ *Comets Among the Stars* (ATV Network Limited, Hertfordshire, England)

Mad in Austria (ORF, Vienna)

Jennie: His Borrowed Plumes (Thames Television Ltd., London)

Mr. Sing My Hearts Delight (Radio Telefis Eireann, Dublin)

□ *The Evacuees* (BBC, London)

De Verrassing (Nederlandse Omroop Stichting, the Netherlands)

Non-Fiction:

□ *Inside Story: Marek* (BBC, London)

Travels Through Life with Leacock (Canadian Broadcasting Corp., Ontario)

After 3 Years in the Jungle: Homecoming of a Japanese Soldier (Fuji Telecasting Company, Ltd., Tokyo)

Pilger: Mr. Nixon's Secret Legacy (ATV Network Ltd., Hertfordshire, England)

The Search for the Shinohara (Survival Anglia Ltd., London)

INTERNATIONAL DIRECTORATE AWARD
☐ Mr. Junzo Imamichi, Chariman of the Board, Tokyo Broadcasting System, Inc.

Daytime Awards

OUTSTANDING DAYTIME DRAMA SERIES
☐ *The Young and the Restless* (CBS)
Days of Our Lives (NBC)
Another World (NBC)

OUTSTANDING DAYTIME DRAMA SPECIAL
The Girl Who Couldn't Lose (ABC)
The Last Bride of Salem (ABC)

OUTSTANDING GAME OR AUDIENCE PARTICIPATION SHOW
☐ *Hollywood Squares* (NBC)
The $10,000 Pyramid (ABC)
Jeopardy! (NBC)
Let's Make a Deal (ABC)

OUTSTANDING TALK, SERVICE OR VARIETY SERIES
☐ *Dinah!* (Syndicated)
The Mike Douglas Show (Syndicated)
Today (NBC)

OUTSTANDING ENTERTAINMENT CHILDREN'S SPECIAL
☐ *Harlequin* (CBS)
Ailey Celebrates Ellington (CBS)
What Makes a Gershwin Tune a Gershwin Tune? (CBS)

OUTSTANDING ENTERTAINMENT CHILDREN'S SERIES
☐ *Star Trek* (NBC)
Captain Kangaroo (CBS)
The Pink Panther (NBC)

OUTSTANDING ACTOR IN A DAYTIME DRAMA SERIES
☐ Macdonald Carey, *Days of Our Lives* (NBC)
John Beradino, *General Hospital* (ABC)
Bill Hayes, *Days of Our Lives* (NBC)

OUTSTANDING ACTOR IN A DAYTIME DRAMA SPECIAL
☐ Bradford Dillman, *The Last Bride of Salem* (ABC)
Jack Carter, *The Girl Who Couldn't Lose* (ABC)
Bert Convey, *Oh! Baby, Baby, Baby...* (ABC)

☐ Indicates winner

OUTSTANDING ACTRESS IN A DAYTIME DRAMA SERIES
☐ Susan Flannery, *Days of Our Lives* (NBC)
Rachel Ames, *General Hospital* (ABC)
Susan Seaforth, *Days of Our Lives* (NBC)
Ruth Warrick, *All My Children* (ABC)

OUTSTANDING ACTRESS IN A DAYTIME DRAMA SPECIAL
☐ Kay Lenz, *Heart in Hiding* (ABC)
Diane Baker, *Can I Save My Children?* (ABC)
Julie Kavner, *The Girl Who Couldn't Lose* (ABC)
Lois Nettleton, *The Last Bride of Salem* (ABC)

OUTSTANDING HOST IN A GAME OR AUDIENCE PARTICIPATION SHOW
☐ Peter Marshall, *Hollywood Squares* (NBC)
Monty Hall, *Let's Make a Deal* (ABC)
Gene Rayburn, *Match Game '75* (CBS)

OUTSTANDING HOST OR HOSTESS IN A TALK, SERVICE OR VARIETY SERIES
☐ Barbara Walters, *Today* (NBC)
Mike Douglas, *The Mike Douglas Show* (Syndicated)
Dinah Shore, *Dinah!* (Syndicated)
Jim Hartz, *Today* (NBC)

OUTSTANDING INDIVIDUAL DIRECTOR FOR A DAYTIME DRAMA SERIES (FOR A SINGLE EPISODE)
☐ Richard Dunlap, *The Young and the Restless* (CBS)
Ira Cirker, *Another World* (NBC)
Joseph Behar, *Days of Our Lives* (NBC)

OUTSTANDING INDIVIDUAL DIRECTOR FOR A DAYTIME SPECIAL PROGRAM
☐ Mort Lachman, *The Girl Who Couldn't Lose* (ABC)
Walter C. Miller, *Can I Save My Children?* (ABC)

OUTSTANDING INDIVIDUAL DIRECTOR FOR A GAME OR AUDIENCE PARTICIPATION SHOW (FOR A SINGLE EPISODE)
☐ Jerome Shaw, *Hollywood Squares* (NBC)
Joseph Behar, *Let's Make a Deal* (ABC)

OUTSTANDING INDIVIDUAL DIRECTOR FOR A DAYTIME

VARIETY PROGRAM (FOR A SINGLE EPISODE)
☐ Glen Swanson, *Dinah!* (with Ethel Merman, Bobby Morse, Michelle Lee, Phil Silvers, Jack Cassidy) (Syndicated)
Dick Carson, *The Merv Griffin Show* (with Robert Goulet, Louis Prima, Shecky Greene) (Syndicated)

OUTSTANDING WRITING FOR A DAYTIME DRAMA SERIES (FOR A SINGLE EPISODE OF A SERIES OF FOR THE ENTIRE SERIES)
☐ Harding Lemay, Tom King, Charles Kozloff, Jan Merlin and Douglas Marland, *Another World* (NBC)
William J. Bell, *The Young and the Restless* (CBS)
William J. Bell, Pat Falken Smith and Bill Rega, *Days of Our Lives* (NBC)

OUTSTANDING WRITING FOR A DAYTIME SPECIAL PROGRAM
☐ Audrey Davis Levin, *Heart in Hiding* (ABC)
Ruth Brooks Flippen, *Oh! Baby, Baby, Baby...* (ABC)
Lila Garrett and Sanford Krinski, *The Girl Who Couldn't Lose* (ABC)

OUTSTANDING INDIVIDUAL ACHIEVEMENT IN DAYTIME PROGRAMMING (FOR A SINGLE EPISODE OF A SERIES OR FOR A SPECIAL PROGRAM)
Paul Lynde (performer), *Hollywood Squares* (NBC)
Jay Redack, Harry Friedman, Gary Johnson, Harold Schneider, Rick Kelford and Steve Levitch (writers), *Hollywood Squares* (NBC)
Stas Pyka (graphic design and title sequence), *How To Survive a Marriage* (NBC)

OUTSTANDING INDIVIDUAL ACHIEVEMENT IN CHILDREN'S PROGRAMMING (FOR A SINGLE EPISODE OF A SERIES, OR FOR A SPECIAL PROGRAM)
☐ Elinor Bunin (graphic design and title sequences), *Funshine Saturday & Sunday* (ABC)
Bob Keeshan (performer), *Captain Kangaroo* (CBS)
Bill Cosby, (performer), *Highlights of Ringling Bros. Barnum & Bailey Circus* (NBC)
Charles M. Schultz (writer), *Be My Valentine, Charlie Brown* (CBS)

1975/76

(For programs aired between March 11, 1975 and March 15, 1976. Entertainment program and individual achievements presented May 17, 1976. Creative Arts in Entertainment awards presented May 15, 1976. Daytime awards presented May 11, 1976.)

Prime Time Program Awards

OUTSTANDING COMEDY SERIES
□ *The Mary Tyler Moore Show* (CBS)
All in the Family (CBS)
*M*A*S*H* (CBS)
Welcome Back, Kotter (ABC)
Barney Miller (ABC)

OUTSTANDING DRAMA SERIES
□ *Police Story* (NBC)
Baretta (ABC)
Columbo (NBC)
The Streets of San Francisco (ABC)

OUTSTANDING COMEDY-VARIETY OR MUSIC SERIES
□ *NBC'S Saturday Night* (NBC)
The Carol Burnett Show (CBS)

OUTSTANDING LIMITED SERIES
□ *Upstairs, Downstairs* (PBS)
Jennie: Lady Randolph Churchill (PBS)
Rich Man, Poor Man (ABC)
The Adams Chronicles (PBS)
The Law (NBC)

OUTSTANDING SPECIAL—DRAMA OR COMEDY
□ *Eleanor and Franklin* (ABC)
Babe (CBS)
A Moon for the Misbegotten (ABC)
Fear on Trial (CBS)
The Lindbergh Kidnapping Case (NBC)

OUTSTANDING SPECIAL—COMEDY-VARIETY OR MUSIC
□ *Gypsy in My Soul* (CBS)
The Monty Python Show (PBS)
John Denver Rocky Mountain Christmas (ABC)
Steve and Eydie: Our Love Is Here to Stay (CBS)
Lily Tomlin (ABC)

OUTSTANDING CLASSICAL MUSIC PROGRAM, FOR A SPECIAL PROGRAM OR FOR A SERIES
□ *Bernstein and the New York Philharmonic* (PBS)
Three by Balanchine with the New York City Ballet (PBS)
Arthur Rubinstein—Chopin (PBS)
Dance in America: City Center Joffrey Ballet (PBS)
Live From Lincoln Center (PBS)

□ Indicates winner

OUTSTANDING CHILDREN'S SPECIAL, FOR SPECIALS WHICH WERE BROADCAST DURING THE EVENING
□ *You're a Good Sport, Charlie Brown* (CBS)
□ *Huckleberry Finn* (ABC)

OUTSTANDING LIVE SPORTS SPECIAL
□ *1975 World Series* (NBC)
NCAA Basketball Championship (NBC)
Rose Bowl (NBC)
The Super Bowl Today and Super Bowl X (CBS)
1975 Masters Golf Tournament

OUTSTANDING LIVE SPORTS SERIES
□ *NFL Monday Night Football* (ABC)
NCAA College Football (ABC)
ABC's Golf (ABC)
NFL Football on CBS (CBS)

OUTSTANDING EDITED SPORT SPECIAL
□ *XII Winter Olympic Games* (ABC)
□ *Triumph and Tragedy. . . The Olympic Experience* (ABC)

OUTSTANDING EDITED SPORTS SERIES
□ *ABC's Wide World of Sports* (ABC)
The Superstars (ABC)
Baseball World of Joe Garagiola (NBC)
The Way It Was (PBS)

THE NATIONAL AWARD FOR COMMUNITY SERVICE
□ *Forgotten Children* (WBBM-TV, Chicago)
A Day Without Sunshine (WPBT, North Miami)
The Gift of Life (KWTV, Oklahoma City)
Blood Bank (WCIX-TV, Miami)
Centre Four (WJXT-TV, Jacksonville)
Closing the Gap (WITF-TV, Hershey)
Buddy, Can You Spare a Dime? (WBAL-TV, Baltimore)
The Edlein Conviction (WGBH, Boston)

Prime Time Performance Awards

OUTSTANDING SPORTS PERSONALITY
□ Jim McKay, *ABC's Wide World of Sports; ABC's XII Winter Olympics* (ABC)
Joe Garagiola, *1975 World Series—Game 6* (NBC)
Frank Gifford, *NFL Monday Night Football; ABC's XII Winter Olympics* (ABC)
Vin Scully, *Masters Golf* (CBS)
Heywood Hale Broun, *CBS Sports Programs* (CBS)

OUTSTANDING LEAD ACTOR IN A COMEDY
□ Jack Albertson, *Chico and the Man* (NBC)
Hal Linden, *Barney Miller* (ABC)
Alan Alda, *M*A*S*H* (CBS)
Henry Winkler, *Happy Days* (ABC)

OUTSTANDING LEAD ACTOR IN A DRAMA SERIES
□ Peter Falk, *Columbo* (NBC)
Karl Malden, *The Streets of San Francisco* (ABC)
James Garner, *The Rockford Files* (NBC)

OUTSTANDING LEAD ACTOR IN A LIMITED SERIES
□ Hal Holbrook, *Sandburg's Lincoln* (NBC)
Nick Nolte, *Rich Man, Poor Man* (ABC)
Peter Strauss, *Rich Man, Poor Man* (ABC)
George Grizzard, *The Adams Chronicles* (PBS)

OUTSTANDING LEAD ACTOR IN A DRAMA OR COMEDY SPECIAL
□ Anthony Hopkins, *The Lindbergh Kidnapping Case* (NBC)
William Devane, *Fear on Trial* (CBS)
Jack Lemmon, *The Entertainer* (NBC)
Edward Herrmann, *Eleanor and Franklin* (ABC)
Jason Robards, *A Moon for the Misbegotten* (ABC)

OUTSTANDING LEAD ACTOR FOR A SINGLE APPEARANCE IN A DRAMA OR COMEDY SERIES
□ Edward Asner, *Rich Man, Poor Man* (ABC)
Robert Reed, "The Fourth Sex," *Medical Center* (CBS)
Tony Musante, "The Quality of Mercy," *Medical Story* (NBC)
Bill Bixby, "Police Buff," *The Streets of San Francisco* (ABC)

OUTSTANDING LEAD ACTRESS IN A COMEDY SERIES
□ Mary Tyler Moore, *The Mary Tyler Moore Show* (CBS)
Beatrice Arthur, *Maude* (CBS)
Valerie Harper, *Rhoda* (CBS)
Lee Grant, *Fay* (NBC)
Cloris Leachman, *Phyllis* (CBS)

OUTSTANDING LEAD ACTRESS IN A DRAMA SERIES
□ Michael Learned, *The Waltons* (CBS)
Anne Meara, *Kate McShane* (CBS)
Angie Dickinson, *Police Woman* (NBC)
Brenda Vaccaro, *Sara* (CBS)

OUTSTANDING LEAD ACTRESS IN A LIMITED SERIES
□ Rosemary Harris, "Notorious Woman," *Masterpiece Theatre* (PBS)
Lee Remick, *Jennie: Lady Randolph Churchill* (PBS)

Susan Blakely, *Rich Man, Poor Man* (ABC)

Jean Marsh, "Upstairs, Downstairs," *Masterpiece Theatre* (PBS)

OUTSTANDING LEAD ACTRESS IN A DRAMA OR COMEDY SPECIAL
□ Susan Clark, *Babe* (CBS)

Colleen Dewhurst, *A Moon for the Misbegottn* (ABC)

Jane Alexander, *Eleanor and Franklin* (ABC)

Sada Thompson, *The Entertainer* (NBC)

OUTSTANDING LEAD ACTRESS FOR A SINGLE APPEARANCE IN A DRAMA OR COMEDY SERIES
□ Kathryn Walker, "John Adams, Lawyer," *The Adams Chronicles* (PBS)

Helen Hayes, "Retire in Sunny Hawaii. . . Forever," *Hawaii Five-O* (CBS)

Sheree North, "How Do You Know What Hurts Me?", *Marcus Welby, M.D.* (ABC)

Pamela Payton-Wright, "John Quincy Adams, Diplomat," *The Adams Chronicles* (PBS)

Martha Raye, "Greed," *McMillan & Wife* (NBC)

OUTSTANDING CONTINUING PERFORMANCE BY A SUPPORTING ACTOR IN A COMEDY SERIES, FOR A REGULAR OR LIMITED SERIES
□ Ted Knight, *The Mary Tyler Moore Show* (CBS)

Gary R. Burghoff, *M*A*S*H* (CBS)

Abe Vigoda, *Barney Miller* (ABC)

Edward Asner, *The Mary Tyler Moore Show* (CBS)

Harry Morgan, *M*A*S*H* (CBS)

OUTSTANDING CONTINUING PERFORMANCE BY A SUPPORTING ACTOR IN A DRAMA SERIES, FOR A REGULAR OR LIMITED SERIES
□ Anthony Zerbe, *Harry O* (ABC)

Will Geer, *The Waltons* (CBS)

Ray Milland, *Rich Man, Poor Man* (ABC)

Robert Reed, *Rich Man, Poor Man* (ABC)

Michael Douglas, *The Streets of San Francisco* (ABC)

OUTSTANDING CONTINUING OR SINGLE PERFORMANCE BY A SUPPORTING ACTOR IN VARIETY OR MUSIC, FOR A CONTINUING ROLE IN REGULAR OR LIMITED SERIES, OR A ONE-TIME APPEARANCE IN A SERIES, OR A SPECIAL
□ Chevy Chase, *NBC'S Saturday Night* (NBC)

□ Indicates winner

Harvey Korman, *The Carol Burnett Show* (CBS)

Tim Conway, *The Carol Burnett Show* (CBS)

OUTSTANDING SINGLE PERFORMANCE BY A SUPPORTING ACTOR IN A COMEDY OR DRAMA SPECIAL
□ Ed Flanders, *A Moon for the Misbegotten* (ABC)

Art Carney, *Katherine* (ABC)

Ray Bolger, *The Entertainer* (NBC)

OUTSTANDING SINGLE PERFORMANCE BY A SUPPORTING ACTOR IN A COMEDY OR DRAMA SERIES, FOR A ONE-TIME APPEARANCE IN A REGULAR OR LIMITED SERIES
□ Gordon Jackson, "The Beastly Hun," *Upstairs, Downstairs* (PBS)

Roscoe Lee Browne, "The Escape Artist," *Barney Miller* (ABC)

Bill Bixby, *Rich Man, Poor Man* (ABC)

Norman Fell, *Rich Man, Poor Man* (ABC)

Van Johnson, *Rich Man, Poor Man* (ABC)

OUTSTANDING CONTINUING PERFORMANCE BY A SUPPORTING ACTRESS IN A COMEDY SERIES, FOR A REGULAR OR LIMITED SERIES
□ Betty White, *The Mary Tyler Moore Show* (CBS)

Georgia Engel, *The Mary Tyler Moore Show* (CBS)

Nancy Walker, *Rhoda* (CBS)

Julie Kavner, *Rhoda* (CBS)

Loretta Swit, *M*A*S*H* (CBS)

OUTSTANDING CONTINUING PERFORMANCE BY A SUPPORTING ACTRESS IN A DRAMA SERIES, FOR A REGULAR OR LIMITED SERIES
□ Ellen Corby, *The Waltons* (CBS)

Susan Howard, *Petrocelli* (NBC)

Angela Baddeley, *Upstairs, Downstairs* (PBS)

Dorothy McGuire, *Rich Man, Poor Man* (ABC)

Sada Thompson, *Sandburg's Lincoln* (NBC)

OUTSTANDING CONTINUING OR SINGLE PERFORMANCE BY A SUPPORTING ACTRESS IN VARIETY OR MUSIC, FOR A CONTINUING ROLE IN A REGULAR OR LIMITED SERIES, OR ONE-TIME APPEARANCE IN A SERIES, OR A SPECIAL
□ Vicki Lawrence, *The Carol Burnett Show* (CBS)

Cloris Leachman, *Telly. . . Who Loves Ya, Baby?* (CBS)

OUTSTANDING SINGLE PERFORMANCE BY A SUPPORTING ACTRESS IN A COMEDY OR DRAMA SPECIAL
□ Rosemary Murphy, *Eleanor and Franklin* (ABC)

Irene Tedrow, *Eleanor and Franklin* (ABC)

Lilia Skala, *Eleanor and Franklin* (ABC)

Lois Nettleton, *Fear on Trial* (CBS)

OUTSTANDING SINGLE PERFORMANCE BY A SUPPORTING ACTRESS IN A COMEDY OR DRAMA SERIES, FOR A ONE-TIME APPEARANCE IN A REGULAR OR LIMITED SERIES
□ Fionnuala Flanagan, *Rich Man, Poor Man* (ABC)

Eileen Heckart, "Mary's Aunt," *The Mary Tyler Moore Show* (CBS)

Ruth Gordon, "Kiss Your Epaulets Goodbye," *Rhoda* (CBS)

Kim Darby, *Rich Man, Poor Man* (ABC)

Kay Lenz, *Rich Man, Poor Man* (ABC)

Prime Time Time Writing and Directing Awards

OUTSTANDING DIRECTING IN A DRAMA SERIES, FOR A SINGLE EPISODE OF A REGULAR OR LIMITED SERIES WITH CONTINUING CHARACTERS AND/OR THEME
□ David Greene, *Rich Man, Poor Man,* Episode 8 (ABC)

James Cellan Jones, *Jennie: Lady Randolph Churchill,* Part IV (PBS)

Boris Sagal, *Rich Man, Poor Man,* Episode 5 (ABC)

George Schaefer, "Crossing Fox River," *Sandburg's Lincoln* (NBC)

Fielder Cook, *Beacon Hill* (CBS)

Christopher Hodson, "Women Shall Not Weep," *Upstairs, Downstairs* (PBS)

OUTSTANDING DIRECTING IN A COMEDY SERIES, FOR A SINGLE EPISODE OF A REGULAR OR LIMITED SERIES WITH CONTINUING CHARACTERS AND/OR THEME
□ Gene Reynolds, "Welcome to Korea," *M*A*S*H* (CBS)

Hal Cooper, "The Analyst," *Maude* (CBS)

Joan Darling, "Chuckles Bites the Dust," *The Mary Tyler Moore Show* (CBS)

Alan Alda, "The Kids," *M*A*S*H* (CBS)

OUTSTANDING DIRECTING IN A COMEDY-VARIETY OR MUSIC SERIES, FOR A SINGLE EPISODE OF A REGULAR OR LIMITED SERIES
□ Dave Wilson, *NBC'S Saturday Night* with host Paul Simon (NBC)

Dave Powers, *The Carol Burnett Show* with Maggie Smith (CBS)

Tim Kiley, *The Sonny and Cher Show* (CBS)

OUTSTANDING DIRECTING IN A COMEDY-VARIETY OR MUSIC SPECIAL

☐ Dwight Hemion, *Steve and Eydie: Our Love is Here to Stay* (CBS)

Bill Davis, *John Denver Rocky Mountain Christmas* (ABC)

Tony Charmoli, *Mitzi. . . Roarin' in the 20's* (CBS)

OUTSTANDING DIRECTING IN A SPECIAL PROGRAM—DRAMA OR COMEDY

☐ Daniel Petrie, *Eleanor and Franklin* (ABC)

Lamont Johnson, *Fear on Trial* (CBS)

Buzz Kulik, *Babe* (CBS)

Jose Quintero, and Gordon Rigsby, *A Moon for the Misbegotten* (ABC)

OUTSTANDING WRITING IN A DRAMA SERIES, FOR A SINGLE EPISODE OF A REGULAR OR LIMITED SERIES WITH CONTINUING CHARACTERS AND/OR THEME

☐ Sherman Yellen, "John Adams, Lawyer," *The Adams Chronicles* (PBS)

Dean Riesner, *Rich Man, Poor Man* (ABC)

Julian Mitchell, *Jennie: Lady Randolph Churchill* (PBS)

Joel Oliansky, "Complaint Amended," *The Law* (NBC)

Alfred Shaughnessy, "Another Year," *Upstairs, Downstairs* (PBS)

OUTSTANDING WRITING IN A COMEDY SERIES, FOR A SINGLE EPISODE OR A REGULAR OR LIMITED SERIES WITH CONTINUING CHARACTERS AND/OR THEME

☐ David Lloyd, "Chuckles Bites the Dust," *The Mary Tyler Moore Show* (CBS)

Danny Arnold and Chris Hayward, "The Hero," *Barney Miller* (ABC)

Jay Folb, "The Analyst," *Maude* (CBS)

Larry Gelbart and Gene Reynolds, "The More I See You," *M*A*S*H* (CBS)

Larry Gelbart and Simon Muntner, "Hawkeye," *M*A*S*H* (CBS)

OUTSTANDING WRITING IN A COMEDY-VARIETY OR MUSIC SERIES, FOR A SINGLE EPISODE OR A REGULAR OR LIMITED SERIES

☐ Anne Beatts, Chevy Chase, Al Franken, Tom Davis, Lorne Michaels, Marilyn Suzanne Miller, Michael O'Donoghue, Herb Sargent, Tom Schiller, Rosie Shuster, and

Alan Zweibel, *NBC'S Saturday Night*, (with host Elliott Gould) (NBC)

Ed Simmons, Gary Belkin, Roger Beatty, Bill Richmond, Gene Perret, Arnie Kogen, Ray Jessel, Rudy DeLuca, Barry Levinson, Dick Clair and Jenna McMahon, *The Carol Burnett Show*, (with Jim Nabors) (CBS)

Phil Hahn, Bob Arnott, Jeanine Burnier, Coslough Johnson, Iris Rainier, Stuart Gillard, Frank Peppiatt, John Aylesworth, Ted Zeigler, *The Sonny and Cher Show*.

OUTSTANDING WRITING IN A COMEDY-VARIETY OR MUSIC SPECIAL

☐ Jane Wagner, Lorne Michaels, Ann Elder, Christopher Guest, Earl Pomerantz, Jim Rusk, Lily Tomlin, Rod Warren and George Yanok, *Lily Tomlin* (ABC)

Fred Ebb, *Gypsy in My Soul* (NBC)

Dick Van Dyke, Allan Blye, Bob Einstein, James Stein, George Burditt, Robert Illes, Steve Martin, Jack Mendelsohn, Rich Mittleman, *Van Dyke and Company* (NBC)

Jerry Mayer, *Mitzi. . . Roarin' in the 20's* (CBS)

OUTSTANDING WRITING IN A SPECIAL PROGRAM—DRAMA OR COMEDY—ORIGINAL TELEPLAY

☐ James Costigan, *Eleanor and Franklin* (ABC)

Joanna Lee, *Babe* (CBS)

J.P. Miller, *The Lindbergh Kidnapping Case* (NBC)

Nicholas Meyer, Anthony Wilson, *The Night That Panicked America* (ABC)

Jeb Rosebrook, *Theodore Strauss, I Will Fight No More Forever* (ABC)

OUTSTANDING WRITING IN A SPECIAL PROGRAM—DRAMA OR COMEDY—ADAPTATION

☐ David W. Rintels, *Fear on Trial* (CBS)

Jeanne Wakatsuki, James D. Houston, John Korty, *Farewell to Manzanar* (NBC)

Elliott Baker, *The Entertainer* (NBC)

The Areas*

SPECIAL CLASSIFICATION OF OUTSTANDING PROGRAM AND INDIVIDUAL ACHIEVEMENT

☐ *Bicentennial Minutes* (CBS)

☐ *The Tonight Show Starring Johnny Carson* (NBC)

☐ Ann Marcus, Jerry Adelman, Daniel Gregory Browne. Writers, *Mary Hartman, Mary Hartman* (Syndicated)

The American Film Institute Salute to William Wyler (CBS)

Tomorrow (NBC)

Mary Hartman, Mary Hartman (Syndicated)

Tom Snyder, (host), *Tomorrow* (NBC)

Louise Lasser, (performer) *Mary Hartman, Mary Hartman* (Syndicated)

Artie Malvin, Ken Welch, Mitzie Welch, Mini Musical—Irving Berlin Finale, *The Carol Burnett Show* (CBS)

OUTSTANDING INDIVIDUAL ACHIEVEMENT IN SPORTS PROGRAMMING

☐ Andy Sidaris, Don Ohlmeyer, Roger Goodman, Larry Kamm, Ronnie Hawkins, and Ralph Mellanby (directors), *XII Winter Olympic Games* (ABC)

The Creative Arts Awards*

OUTSTANDING ACHIEVEMENT IN CHOREOGRAPHY, (FOR A SINGLE EPISODE OF A SERIES OR A SPECIAL PROGRAM)

Jaime Rogers, *Mary's Incredible Dream* (CBS)

Ernest O. Flatt, *The Carol Burnett Show* (with Roddy McDowall and Bernadette Peters) (CBS)

☐ Tony Charmoli, *Gypsy in My Soul* (CBS)

Rob Iscove, *Ann-Margaret Smith* (NBC)

Lester Wilson, *Lola!* (ABC)

OUTSTANDING ACHIEVEMENT IN MUSIC COMPOSITION—DRAMATIC UNDERSCORE—FOR A SINGLE EPISODE OF A REGULAR OR LIMITED SERIES

John Cacavas, "A Question Of Answers," *Kojak* (CBS)

Jack Urbont, "Next of Kin," *Bronk* (CBS)

☐ Alex North, *Rich Man, Poor Man* (ABC)

David Rose, "Remember Me (Parts 1 & 2)," *Little House on the Prairie* (NBC)

OUTSTANDING ACHIEVEMENT IN MUSIC COMPOSITION FOR A SPECIAL DRAMATIC UNDERSCORE

Cy Coleman, *Gypsy in My Soul* (CBS)

Billy Goldenberg, *Dark Victory* (NBC)

☐ Jerry Goldsmith, *Babe* (CBS)

Jack Urbont, *Supercops* (CBS)

☐ Indicates winner

* possibility of one award, more than one award or no award

* One award only in each category

OUTSTANDING ACHIEVEMENT IN MUSIC DIRECTION, FOR A SINGLE EPISODE OF A SERIES OR A SPECIAL PROGRAM WHETHER IT BE VARIETY OR MUSIC

Donn Trenner (conductor) Cy Coleman (arranger), *Gypsy in My Soul* (ABC)

Seiji Ozawa, *Central Park in the Dark/ A Hero's Life* (PBS)

OUTSTANDING ACHIEVEMENT IN ART DIRECTION OR SCENIC DESIGN, FOR A SINGLE EPISODE OF A COMEDY, DRAMA OR LIMITED SERIES

Ed Wittstein (art director), *The Adams Chronicles* (PBS)

William Hiney, (art director) Joseph J. Stone (set decorator), *Rich Man, Poor Man* (ABC)

□ Tom John (art director), John Wendell and Wes Laws (set decorators), *Beacon Hill* (CBS)

Michael Hall and Fred Pusey (scenic designers), *Jennie: Lady Randolph Churchill* (PBS)

OUTSTANDING ACHIEVEMENT IN ART DIRECTION OR SCENIC DESIGN, FOR A SINGLE EPISODE OF A COMEDY-VARIETY OR MUSIC SERIES, OR FOR A COMEDY-VARIETY OR MUSIC SPECIAL

□ Raymond Klausen (art director) Robert Checchi (set decorator), *Cher* (with Anthony Newley, Ike and Tina Turner) (CBS)

Eugene T. McAvoy (art director), *Mary's Incredible Dream* (CBS)

Ken Johnson (art director), *John Denver Rocky Mountain Christmas* (ABC)

Paul Barnes, Bob Sansom (art directors), Bill Harp (set decorator), *The Carol Burnett Show* (with The Pointer Sisters) (CBS)

OUTSTANDING ACHIEVEMENT IN ART DIRECTION OR SCENIC DESIGN, FOR A DRAMATIC SPECIAL OR A FEATURE LENGTH FILM MADE FOR TELEVISION

Jack F. De Shields (art director) and Red Allen (set decorator), *Barbary Coast* (ABC)

□ Jan Scott (art director) and Anthony Mondello (set decorator), *Eleanor and Franklin* (ABC)

Roy Christopher (art director) and Frank Lombardo (set decorator), *The Legendary Curse of the Hope Diamond* (CBS)

□ Indicates winner

OUTSTANDING ACHIEVEMENT IN GRAPHIC DESIGN AND TITLE SEQUENCES, FOR A SINGLE EPISODE OF A SERIES, OR FOR A SPECIAL PROGRAM

Phill Norman, *The New, Original Wonder Woman* (ABC)

Anthony Goldschmidt, *Eleanor and Franklin* (ABC)

□ Norman Sunshine, *Addie and the King of Hearts* (CBS)

Girish Bhargava and Bill Mandel, *The Adams Chronicles* (PBS)

Edie Baskin, *NBC's Saturday Night* (with host Buck Henry) (NBC)

OUTSTANDING ACHIEVEMENT IN COSTUME DESIGN FOR A DRAMA SPECIAL

□ Joe I. Tompkins, *Eleanor and Franklin* (ABC)

Bob Christenson and Denita Cavett, *The Lindbergh Kidnapping Case* (NBC)

OUTSTANDING ACHIEVEMENT IN COSTUME DESIGN FOR A MUSIC-VARIETY, FOR A SINGLE EPISODE OF A SERIES, OR FOR A SPECIAL PROGRAM

Bob Mackie and Ret Turner, *Cher* (with Wayne Rogers and Nancy Walker) (CBS)

□ Bob Mackie, *Mitzi. . . Roarin' in the 20's* (CBS)

OUTSTANDING ACHIEVEMENT IN COSTUME DESIGN FOR A DRAMA OR COMEDY SERIES, FOR A SINGLE EPISODE OF A DRAMA, COMEDY OR LIMITED SERIES

Charles Waldo, *Rich Man, Poor Man* (ABC)

□ Jane Robinson, "Recovery" *Jennie: Lady Randolph Churchill* (PBS)

Alvin Colt, "John Adams, Diplomat," *The Adams Chronicles* (PBS)

OUTSTANDING ACHIEVEMENT IN MAKE-UP, FOR A SINGLE EPISODE OF A SERIES OR FOR A SPECIAL PROGRAM

Allan Whitey Snyder, *The 1975 Fashion Awards* (ABC)

□ Del Armstrong and Mike Westmore, *Eleanor and Franklin* (ABC)

William Tuttle, *Babe* (CBS)

OUTSTANDING ACHIEVEMENT IN CINEMATOGRAPHY FOR ENTERTAINMENT PROGRAMMING FOR A SERIES, FOR A SINGLE EPISODE OF A REGULAR OR LIMITED SERIES

□ Harry L. Wolf, ASC, "Keep Your Eye on the Sparrow," *Baretta* (ABC)

Ted Voigtlander, "Remember Me (Parts 1 & 2)," *Little House on the Prairie* (NBC)

Howard Schwartz, *Rich Man, Poor Man* (ABC)

Sol Negrin, "A Question of Answers," *Kojak* (CBS)

William Jurgensen, "Hawkeye," *M*A*S*H* (CBS)

OUTSTANDING ACHIEVEMENT IN CINEMATOGRAPHY FOR ENTERTAINMENT PROGRAMMING FOR A SPECIAL, FOR A SPECIAL OR FEATURE LENGTH PROGRAM MADE FOR TELEVISION

Charles F. Wheeler, *Babe* (CBS)

Hiro Narita, *Farewell to Manzanar* (NBC)

□ Paul Lohmann and Edward R. Brown, Sr., *Eleanor and Franklin* (ABC)

Richard C. Glouner, *Griffin and Phoenix, A Love Story* (ABC)

James Crabe, *The Entertainer* (NBC)

OUTSTANDING FILM EDITING FOR ENTERTAINMENT PROGRAMMING FOR A SERIES, FOR A SINGLE EPISODE OF A COMEDY SERIES

Douglas Hines, "Chuckles Bites the Dust," *The Mary Tyler Moore Show* (CBS)

□ Stanford Tischler and Fred W. Berger, "Welcome to Korea," *M*A*S*H* (CBS)

OUTSTANDING FILM EDITING FOR ENTERTAINMENT PROGRAMMING FOR A SERIES, FOR A SINGLE EPISODE OF A DRAMA OR LIMITED SERIES

Douglas Stewart, *Rich Man, Poor Man* (ABC)

Dick Van Enger, Jr., "The Right to Die," *Medical Story* (NBC)

Richard Bracken, *Rich Man, Poor Man* (ABC)

□ Samuel E. Beetley and Ken Zemkie, "The Quality of Mercy," *Medical Story* (NBC)

OUTSTANDING FILM EDITING FOR ENTERTAINMENT PROGRAMMING FOR A SPECIAL OR FILM MADE FOR TELEVISION

Henry Berman, *Babe* (CBS)

Bud S. Isaacs, Tony Radecki and George Nicholson, *The Night That Panicked America* (ABC)

□ Michael Kahn, *Eleanor and Franklin* (ABC)

Robert K. Lambert, *I Will Fight No More Forever* (ABC)

Rita Roland, *The Lindbergh Kidnapping Case* (NBC)

OUTSTANDING ACHIEVEMENT IN FILM SOUND EDITING, FOR A SINGLE EPISODE OF A REGULAR OR LIMITED SERIES

Jerry Christian, Ken Sweet, Thomas M. Patchlett, Jack Jackson, David A. Schonleber, John W. Singleton, Dale

Johnston, George E. Luckenbacher, Walter Jenevein and Dennis Diltz, "The Secret of Bigfoot (Parts 1 & 2)," *The Six Million Dollar Man* (ABC)

☐ Douglas H. Grindstaff, Al Kajita, Marvin Kosberg, Hans Newman, Leon Selditz, Dick Friedman, Stan Gilbert, Hank Salerno, Larry Singer and William Andrews, "The Quality of Mercy," *Medical Story* (NBC)

Marvin I. Kosberg, Bob Human, Hans Newman, Leon Selditz, Jeremy Hoenack, Jack Milner, Al Kajita, Luke Wolfram, Dick Friedman, Hank Salerno, Larry Singer, Stan Gilbert and William Andrews, "Task Force (Parts 1 & 2)," *Police Woman* (NBC)

OUTSTANDING ACHIEVEMENT IN FILM SOUND EDITING, FOR A SPECIAL PROGRAM

Don Hall, William Hartman, Mike Corrigan, Ed Rossi, Dick Sperber, Ron Smith, John Jolliffe, Bob Pearson, John Kline, Al La Mastra and Jay Engel, *Eleanor and Franklin* (ABC)

Marvin I. Kosberg, Larry Kaufman, Jack Milner and William Andrews, *The Lindbergh Kidnapping Case* (NBC)

☐ Charles L. Campbell, Larry Neiman, Colin Mouat, Larry Carow, Don Warner, John Singleton, Tom McMullen, Joseph DiVitale, Carl Kress, John Kline and John Hanley, *The Night That Panicked America* (ABC)

OUTSTANDING ACHIEVEMENT IN FILM SOUND MIXING, FOR A SINGLE EPISODE OF A REGULAR OR LIMITED SERIES, OR FOR A SPECIAL PROGRAM

☐ Don Bassmann and Don Johnson, *Eleanor and Franklin* (Parts 1 & 2) (ABC)

Charles Lewis, Robert L. Harman, George Porter and Eddie Nelson, "Prairie Lawyer," *Sandburg's Lincoln* (NBC)

OUTSTANDING ACHIEVEMENT IN TAPE SOUND MIXING, FOR A SINGLE EPISODE OF A REGULAR OR LIMITED SERIES, OR FOR A SPECIAL PROGRAM

☐ Dave Williams, "Anniversary Show," *The Tonight Show Starring Johnny Carson* (NBC)

Vernon Coleman, *New Year's Eve at Pops* (PBS)

John F. Pfeiffer, *Live From Lincoln Center* (PBS)

☐ Indicates winner

OUTSTANDING ACHIEVEMENT IN VIDEO TAPE EDITING FOR A SERIES, FOR A SINGLE EPISODE OF A REGULAR OR LIMITED SERIES

Ken Denisoff and Robert Veatch, "Earthquake II," *Sanford and Son* (NBC)

Susan Jenkins and Manuel Matinez, "The Telethon," *Welcome Back Kotter* (ABC)

Holmes Powell, Fred Golan and Paul Schatzkin, "Happy New Year," *Barney Miller* (ABC)

☐ Girish Bhargava and Manford Schorn, *The Adams Chronicles* (PBS)

OUTSTANDING ACHIEVEMENT IN VIDEO TAPE EDITING FOR A SPECIAL

Roy Stewart, *The Hemingway Play* (PBS)

☐ Nick V. Gordani, *Alice Cooper—The Nightmare* (ABC)

Hal Collins and Danny White, *Texaco Presents a Quarter Century of Bob Hope on Television* (NBC)

Rex Bagwell and Frank Phillips, *Mitzi... Roarin' in the 20's* (CBS)

OUTSTANDING ACHIEVEMENT IN TECHNICAL DIRECTION AND ELECTRONIC CAMERAWORK, FOR A SINGLE EPISODE OF A REGULAR OR LIMITED SERIES, OR FOR A SPECIAL PROGRAM

Ken Lamkin (Technical Director), Lew Adams, John Poliak, S. E. Dowlen (Cameramen), *Mary's Incredible Dream* (CBS)

Louis Fusari (Technical Director), Jon Olson, Roy Holm, Rick Lombardo and Ian Taylor (Cameramen), *Mitzi and a Hundred Guys* (CBS)

☐ Leonard Chumbley (Technical Director), Walter Edel, John Feher, Steve Zink (Cameramen), *The Adams Chronicles* (PBS)

Jerry Weiss (Technical Director), Fred Donelson, Bruce Gray, George Meyer and Roy Holm (Cameramen), *Mitzi... Roarin' in the 20's* (CBS)

OUTSTANDING ACHIEVEMENT IN LIGHTING DIRECTION, FOR A SINGLE EPISODE OR A REGULAR OR LIMITED SERIES, OR FOR A SPECIAL PROGRAM

Billy Knight and Dick Weiss, "John Quincy Adams-Diplomat," *The Adams Chronicles* (PBS)

☐ William Klages and Lon Stucky, *Mitzi and a Hundred Guys* (CBS)

☐ John Freschi, *Mitzi... Roarin' in the 20's* (CBS)

The Creative Arts Areas

OUTSTANDING ACHIEVEMENT IN SPECIAL MUSICAL MATERIAL

☐ Ken Welch, Mitzie Welch, Artie Malvin, "Cinderella Gets It On," *The Carol Burnett Show* (with The Pointer Sisters.) (CBS)

Cy Coleman and Fred Ebb, *Gypsy In My Soul.* (With Shirley MacLaine) (CBS)

OUTSTANDING ACHIEVEMENT IN ANY AREA OF CREATIVE TECHNICAL CRAFTS

☐ Jean Burt Reilly, Billie Laughridge (hairstylists), "Eleanor and Franklin," *ABC Theatre* (ABC)

☐ Donald Sahlin, Kermit Love, Caroly Wilcox, John Lovelady and Rollie Krewson (costumes and props for The Muppets) *Sesame Street* (PBS)

John Leay and Mark Schubin, Live stereo simulcast nationwide, first stereo simulcast via satellite, *Live From Lincoln Center* with Andre Previn and Van Cliburn (PBS)

Werner G. Sherer. Hairdresser, *First Ladies' Diaries: Martha Washington* (NBC)

Louis Schmitt, Sophie Quinn, Trudy Philion, (animated character designers) "The Tiny Tree," *Bell System Family Theatre* (NBC)

OUTSTANDING INDIVIDUAL ACHIEVEMENT IN DAYTIME PROGRAMMING

☐ Rene Lagler (art director), Richard Harvey (set decorator), *Dinah!* (Syndicated)

Stas Pyka (graphic design and title sequence), *First Ladies' Diaries: Edith Wilson* (NBC)

Lee Baygan (make-up), *First Ladies' Diaries: Martha Washington* (NBC)

Richard W. Wilson (tape sound mixer), *The Merv Griffin Show* (with Tony Bennett, Peggy Lee, Fred Astaire) (Syndicated)

OUTSTANDING INDIVIDUAL ACHIEVEMENT IN SPORTS PROGRAMMING

☐ John Cohan, Joe Aceti, John Delisa, Lou Frederick, Jack Gallivan, Jim Jennett, Carol Lehti, Howard Shapiro, Katsumi Aseada, John Fernandez, Peter Fritz, Eddie C. Joseph, Ken Klingbeil, Leo Stephan, Ted Summers, Michael Wenig, Ron Ackerman, Michael Bonifazio, Barbara Bowman, Charlie Burnham, John Croak, Charles Gardner, Marvin Gench, Victor Gonzales, Jakob Hierl, Nick Mazur, Ed McCarthy, Alex Moskovic, Arthur Nace, Lour Rende, Erskin Roberts, Merritt Roesser, Arthur Volk, Roger

Haenelt, Curt Brand, Phil Mollica, George Boettcher, Herb Ohlandt (video tape editors), *XII Winter Olympic Games* (ABC)
☐ Dick Roes, Jack Kelly, Bill Sandreuter, Frank Bailey, Jack Kestenbaum (tape sound mixers), *XII Winter Olympic Games* (ABC)
Larry Cansler, (music composition), *CBS Sports Spectacular* (CBS)
Mike Delaney, Harvey Harrison, Harry Hart, D'arcy March, Bruce Buckley, Don Shapiro, Eric Van Haren Noman (cameramen), *XII Olympic Winter Games* (ABC)
John Petersen, Tony Zaccaro, Don Shoemaker, Peter Silver, Alan Spencer, Irwin Krechaf, Margaret Murphy (film editors), *XII Olympic Winter Games* (ABC)

OUTSTANDING ACHIEVEMENT IN RELIGIOUS PROGRAMMING
☐ Joseph J. H. Vadala (cinematographer), *A Determining Force* (NBC)
Sharon Kaufman (film sound editor), *The Will To Be Free* (ABC)
Harvey Holocker (make-up), "Good News," *The Rex Humbard World Outreach Ministry* (Syndicated)

OUTSTANDING INDIVIDUAL ACHIEVEMENT IN CHILDREN'S PROGRAMMING
☐ Bud Nolan, Jim Cookman (film sound editors), *Bound for Freedom* (NBC)
Robert L. Harman, Ted Gomillion, Bill Edmundson (film sound mixers), "Pape and Me," *Special Treat* (NBC)
Gerri Brioso (graphic design), *Sesame Street* (PBS)
Michael Westmore, Louis Phillippi (make-up), "Blackout," *Land of The Lost* (NBC)

Special Awards

OUTSTANDING ACHIEVEMENT IN ENGINEERING DEVELOPMENT
☐ Sony Corp for the U-matic video cassette concept.
☐ Eastman Kodak for the development of Eastman Ektachrome Video News Film.
☐ Citation to Tektronix for leadership in development of equipment for verifying television transmission performance in the vertical interval.

Daytime Awards

OUTSTANDING DAYTIME DRAMA SERIES
☐ *Another World* (NBC)
Days of Our Lives (NBC)
The Young and the Restless (CBS)
All My Children (ABC)
☐ Indicates winner

OUTSTANDING DAYTIME DRAMA SPECIAL
☐ *First Ladies' Diaries: Edith Wilson* (NBC)
First Ladies' Diaries: Rachel Jackson (NBC)
First Ladies' Diaries: Martha Washington (NBC)

OUTSTANDING DAYTIME GAME OR AUDIENCE PARTICIPATION SHOW
The Price is Right (CBS)
Match Game '75 (CBS)
☐ *The $20,000 Pyramid* (ABC)
Hollywood Squares (NBC)
Let's Make a Deal (ABC)

OUTSTANDING DAYTIME TALK, SERVICE OR VARIETY SERIES
Good Morning America (ABC)
☐ *Dinah!* (Syndicated)
The Mike Douglas Show (Syndicated)

OUTSTANDING ACTOR IN A DAYTIME DRAMA SERIES
John Beradino, *General Hospital* (ABC)
Bill Hayes, *Days of Our Lives* (NBC)
MacDonald Carey, *Days of Our Lives* (NBC)
Shepperd Strudwick, *One Life to Live* (ABC)
☐ Larry Haines, *Search for Tomorrow* (CBS)
Michael Nouri, *Search for Tomorrow* (CBS)

OUTSTANDING ACTOR IN A DAYTIME DRAMA SPECIAL
☐ Gerald Gordon, *First Ladies' Diaries: Rachel Jackson* (NBC)
☐ James Luisi, *First Ladies' Diaries: Martha Washington* (NBC)

OUTSTANDING ACTRESS IN A DAYTIME DRAMA SERIES
Susan Seaforth Hayes, *Days of Our Lives* (NBC)
☐ Helen Gallagher, *Ryan's Hope* (ABC)
Mary Stuart, *Search for Tomorrow* (CBS)
Denise Alexander, *General Hospital* (ABC)
Frances Heflin, *All My Children* (ABC)

OUTSTANDING ACTRESS IN A DAYTIME DRAMA SPECIAL
Susan Browning, *First Ladies' Diaries: Martha Washington* (NBC)
☐ Elizabeth Hubbard, *First Ladies' Diaries: Edith Wilson* (NBC)

OUTSTANDING HOST OR HOSTESS IN A GAME OR AUDIENCE PARTICIPATION SHOW
Peter Marshall, *Hollywood Squares* (NBC)
☐ Allen Ludden, *Password* (ABC)
Geoff Edwards, *Jackpot* (NBC)

OUTSTANDING HOST OR HOSTESS IN A TALK, SERVICE OR VARIETY SERIES
David Hartman, *Good Morning America* (ABC)
☐ Dinah Shore, *Dinah!* (Syndicated)
Mike Douglas, *The Mike Douglas Show* (Syndicated)
Merv Griffin, *The Merv Griffin Show* (Syndicated)

OUTSTANDING INDIVIDUAL DIRECTOR FOR A DRAMA SERIES—A SINGLE EPISODE
Hugh McPhillips, *The Doctors* (NBC)
☐ David Pressman, *One Life to Live* (ABC)
Richard Dunlap, *The Young and the Restless* (CBS)

OUTSTANDING INDIVIDUAL DIRECTOR FOR A SPECIAL PROGRAM
John J. Desmond, *First Ladies' Diaries: Martha Washington* (NBC)
☐ Nicholas Havings, *First Ladies' Diaries: Edith Wilson* (NBC)
Ira Cirker, *First Ladies' Diaries: Rachel Jackson* (NBC)

OUTSTANDING INDIVIDUAL DIRECTOR FOR A GAME OR AUDIENCE PARTICIPATION SHOW—A SINGLE EPISODE
☐ Mike Gargiulo, *The $20,000 Pyramid* (ABC)
Jerome Shaw, *Hollywood Squares* (NBC)

OUTSTANDING INDIVIDUAL DIRECTOR FOR A VARIETY PROGRAM—A SINGLE EPISODE
☐ Glen Swanson, "Dinah Salutes Tony Orlando and Dawn on Their 5th Anniversary," *Dinah!* (Syndicated)
Donald R. King, *The Mike Douglas Show* (with Fred Astaire and Gene Kelly) (Syndicated)

OUTSTANDING WRITING FOR A DRAMA SERIES, FOR A SINGLE EPISODE OF A SERIES, OR FOR THE ENTIRE SERIES
Henry Slesar, *The Edge of Night* (ABC)
Jerome Dobson, Birdget Dobson and Jean Rouverol, *The Guiding Light* (CBS)
☐ William J. Bell, Kay Lenard, Pat Falken Smith, Bill Rega, Margaret Stewart, Sheri Anderson and Wanda Coleman, *Days of Our Lives* (NBC)
William J. Bell and Kay Alden, *The Young and the Restless* (ABC)
Agnes Nixon, *All My Children* (ABC)

OUTSTANDING WRITING FOR A SPECIAL PROGRAM
☐ Audrey Davis Levin, *First Ladies' Diaries: Edith Wilson* (NBC)

Ethel Frank, *First Ladies' Diaries: Martha Washington* (NBC)

OUTSTANDING ENTERTAINMENT CHILDREN'S SERIES
☐ Big Blue Marble (Syndicated)
Captain Kangaroo (CBS)
Zoom (PBS)
Fat Albert and the Cosby Kids (CBS)

OUTSTANDING ENTERTAINMENT CHILDREN'S SPECIAL
☐ *Danny Kaye's Look-In at the Metropolitan Opera* (CBS)
Me and Dad's New Wife (ABC)
It Must Be Love (Cause I Feel So Dumb!) (ABC)
"What Is Noise? What is Music?," *New York Philharmonic Young People's Concert* (CBS)
Papa and Me (NBC)

OUTSTANDING INFORMATIONAL CHILDREN'S SERIES, FOR THE PERIOD 7/1/74—3/15/76
The Electric Company (PBS)
☐ *Go* (NBC)
Make a Wish (ABC)

OUTSTANDING INFORMATIONAL CHILDREN'S SERIES, FOR THE PERIOD 7/1/74—3/15/76
What are the Loch Ness and Other Monsters All About? (CBS)
☐ *Happy Anniversary, Charlie Brown* (CBS)
Winning and Losing: Diary of a Campaign (ABC)

OUTSTANDING INSTRUCTIONAL CHILDREN'S PROGRAMMING— SERIES AND SPECIALS
Mister Rogers' Neighborhood (PBS)
Sesame Street (PBS)
☐ *Grammar Rock* (ABC)

The Daytime Areas*

OUTSTANDING INDIVIDUAL ACHIEVEMENT IN DAYTIME PROGRAMMING
Paul Lynde (performer), *The Hollywood Squares* (NBC)

OUTSTANDING INDIVIDUAL ACHIEVEMENT IN CHILDREN'S PROGRAMMING
☐ *The Muppets* (Jim Henson, Frank Oz, Jerry Nelson, Carroll Spinney, and Richard Hunt) (performers) *Sesame Street* (PBS)

---

* possibility of one award, more than one award or no award
☐ Indicates winner

1976/77

(For programs aired between March 16, 1976 and March 13, 1977. Entertainment program and individual achievement awards presented September 11, 1977. Creative Arts in Television Awards presented September 10, 1977. Daytime awards presented May 12, 1977. Sports programming awards presented November 6, 1977.)

Prime Time Program Awards

OUTSTANDING COMEDY SERIES
☐ *The Mary Tyler Moore Show* (CBS)
All in the Family (CBS)
Barney Miller (ABC)
The Bob Newhart Show (CBS)
*M*A*S*H* (CBS)

OUTSTANDING DRAMA SERIES
☐ "Upstairs, Downstaires," *Masterpiece Theatre* (PBS)
Baretta (ABC)
Columbo (NBC)
Family (ABC)
Police Story (NBC)

OUTSTANDING COMEDY-VARIETY OR MUSIC SERIES
☐ *Van Dyke and Company* (NBC)
The Carol Burnett Show (CBS)
Evening at Pops (PBS)
The Muppet Show (Syndicated)
NBC's Saturday Night (NBC)

OUTSTANDING LIMITED SERIES
☐ *Roots* (ABC)
The Adams Chronicles (PBS)
Captains and the Kings (NBC)
"Madame Bovary," *Masterpiece Theatre* (PBS)
The Moneychangers (NBC)

OUTSTANDING SPECIAL—DRAMA OR COMEDY
☐ *Eleanor and Franklin: The White House Years* (ABC)
☐ *Sybil*
Harry S Truman: Plain Speaking (PBS)
Raid On Entebbe (NBC)
21 Hours at Munich (ABC)

OUTSTANDING SPECIAL—COMEDY-VARIETY OR MUSIC
☐ *The Barry Manilow Special* (ABC)
Doug Henning's World of Magic (NBC)
The Neil Diamond Special (NBC)
The Shirley MacLaine Special: Where Do We Go From Here? (CBS)
Sills and Burnett at the Met (CBS)

OUTSTANDING CLASSICAL PROGRAM IN THE PERFORMING ARTS
☐ "American Ballet Theatre: Swan Lake," *Live From Lincoln Center, Great Performances* (PBS)
"American Ballet Theatre," *Dance in America, Great Performances* (PBS)
"Arthur Rubinstein at 90," *Great Performances* (PBS)
The Bolshoi Ballet: Romeo and Juliet (CBS)
"Martha Graham Dance Company," *Dance in America, Great Performances* (PBS)

OUTSTANDING CHILDREN'S SPECIAL (FOR SPECIALS WHICH WERE BROADCAST DURING THE EVENING)
☐ "Ballet Shoes, Parts 1 & 2," *Piccadilly Circus* (PBS)
It's Arbor Day, Charlie Brown (CBS)
"Peter Pan," *Hallmark Hall of Fame* (NBC)
Pinocchio (CBS)
The Little Drummer Boy—Book II (NBC)

OUTSTANDING ACHIEVEMENT IN COVERAGE OF SPECIAL EVENTS— PROGRAMS
The Good Old Days of Radio (PBS)
Grammy Awards Show (CBS)
The 28th Annual Emmy Awards (ABC)
30th Annual Tony Awards (ABC)
48th Annual Oscar Awards (ABC)

SPECIAL CLASSIFICATION OF OUTSTANDING PROGRAM ACHIEVEMENT
☐ *The Tonight Show Starring Johnny Carson* (NBC)
Bicentennial Minutes (CBS)
The First Fifty Years, The Big Event (NBC)
Life Goes to the Movies (NBC)
The Wonderful World of Disney (NBC)

Prime Time Performance Awards

OUTSTANDING LEAD ACTOR IN A COMEDY SERIES
☐ Carroll O'Connor, *All in the Family* (CBS)
Jack Albertson, *Chico and the Man* (NBC)
Alan Alda, *M*A*S*H* (CBS)
Hal Linden, *Barney Miller* (ABC)
Henry Winkler, *Happy Days* (ABC)

OUTSTANDING LEAD ACTOR IN A DRAMA SERIES
☐ James Garner, *The Rockford Files* (NBC)
Robert Blake, *Baretta* (ABC)
Peter Falk, *Columbo* (NBC)
Jack Klugman, *Quincy, M.E.* (NBC)

Karl Malden, *The Streets of San Francisco* (ABC)

OUTSTANDING LEAD ACTOR IN A LIMITED SERIES

☐ Christopher Plummer, *The Moneychangers* (NBC)
  Stanley Baker, "How Green Was My Valley," *Masterpiece Theatre* (PBS)
  Richard Jordan, *Captains and the Kings* (NBC)
  Steven Keats, *Seventh Avenue* (NBC)

OUTSTANDING LEAD ACTOR IN A DRAMA OR COMEDY SPECIAL

☐ Ed Flanders, *Harry S Truman: Plain Speaking* (PBS)
  Peter Boyle, *Tail Gunner Joe* (NBC)
  Peter Finch, *Raid on Entebbe* (NBC)
  Edward Herrmann, *Eleanor and Franklin: The White House Years* (ABC)
  George C. Scott, "Beauty and the Beast," *Hallmark Hall of Fame* (NBC)

OUTSTANDING LEAD ACTOR FOR A SINGLE PERFORMANCE IN A DRAMA OR COMEDY SERIES

☐ Louis Gossett, Jr., *Roots*—Part 2 (ABC)
  John Amos, *Roots*—Part 5 (ABC)
  Levar Burton, *Roots*—Part 1 (ABC)
  Ben Vereen, *Roots*—Part 6 (ABC)

OUTSTANDING LEAD ACTRESS IN A COMEDY SERIES

☐ Beatrice Arthur, *Maude* (CBS)
  Valerie Harper, *Rhoda* (CBS)
  Mary Tyler Moore, *The Mary Tyler Moore Show* (CBS)
  Suzanne Pleshette, *The Bob Newhart Show* (CBS)
  Jean Stapleton, *All in the Family* (CBS)

OUTSTANDING LEAD ACTRESS IN A DRAMA SERIES

☐ Lindsay Wagner, *The Bionic Woman* (ABC)
  Angie Dickinson, *Police Woman* (NBC)
  Kate Jackson, *Charlie's Angels* (ABC)
  Michael Learned, *The Waltons* (CBS)
  Sada Thompson, *Family* (ABC)

OUTSTANDING LEAD ACTRESS IN A LIMITED SERIES

☐ Patty Duke Astin, *Captains and the Kings* (NBC)
  Susan Flannery, *The Moneychangers* (NBC)
  Dori Brenner, *Seventh Avenue* (NBC)
  Eva Marie Saint, *How the West Was Won* (ABC)
  Jane Seymour, *Captains and the Kings* (NBC)

OUTSTANDING LEAD ACTRESS IN A DRAMA OR COMEDY SPECIAL

☐ Sally Field, *Sybil* (NBC)
☐ Indicates winner

Jane Alexander, *Eleanor and Franklin: The White House Years* (ABC)
Susan Clark, *Amelia Earhart* (NBC)
Julie Harris, *The Last of Mrs. Lincoln* (PBS)
Joanne Woodward, *Sybil* (NBC)

OUTSTANDING LEAD ACTRESS FOR A SINGLE PERFORMANCE IN A DRAMA OR COMEDY SERIES

☐ Beulah Bondi, "The Pony Cart," *The Waltons* (CBS)
  Susan Blakely, *Rich Man, Poor Man Book II, Ch. 1* (ABC)
  Made Sinclair, *Roots*—Part 4 (ABC)
  Leslie Uggams, *Roots*—Part 6 (ABC)
  Jessica Walter, "Til Death Do Us Part," *The Streets of San Francisco* (ABC)

OUTSTANDING CONTINUING PERFORMANCE BY A SUPPORTING ACTOR IN A COMEDY SERIES

☐ Gary Burghoff, *M*A*S*H* (CBS)
  Ed Asner, *The Mary Tyler Moore Show* (CBS)
  Ted Knight, *The Mary Tyler Moore Show* (CBS)
  Harry Morgan, *M*A*S*H* (CBS)
  Abe Vigoda, *Barney Miller* (ABC)

OUTSTANDING CONTINUING PERFORMANCE BY A SUPPORTING ACTOR IN A DRAMA SERIES

☐ Gary Frank, *Family* (ABC)
  Noah Beery, *The Rockford Files* (NBC)
  David Doyle, *Charlie's Angels* (ABC)
  Tom Ewell, *Baretta* (ABC)
  Will Geer, *The Waltons* (CBS)

OUTSTANDING CONTINUING OR SINGLE PERFORMANCE BY A SUPPORTING ACTOR IN VARIETY OR MUSIC

☐ Tim Conway, *The Carol Burnett Show* (CBS)
  John Belushi, *NBC's Saturday Night Live* (with Candace Bergen) (NBC)
  Chevy Chase, *NBC's Saturday Night Live* (with Elliott Gould) (NBC)
  Harvey Korman, *The Carol Burnett Show* (CBS)
  Ben Vereen, *The Bell Telephone Jubilee* (NBC)

OUTSTANDING PERFORMANCE BY A SUPPORTING ACTOR IN A COMEDY OR DRAMA SPECIAL

☐ Burgess Meredith, *Tail Gunner Joe* (NBC)
  Martin Balsam, *Raid on Entebbe* (NBC)
  Mark Harmon, *Eleanor and Franklin: The White House Years* (ABC)
  Yaphet Kotto, *Raid on Entebbe* (NBC)
  Walter McGinn, *Eleanor and Franklin: The White House Years* (ABC)

OUTSTANDING SINGLE PERFORMANCE BY A SUPPORTING ACTOR IN A COMEDY OR DRAMA SERIES

☐ Ed Asner, *Roots*—Part 1 (ABC)
  Charles Durning, *Captains and the Kings*—Chapter 2 (NBC)
  Moses Gunn, *Roots*—Part 1 (ABC)
  Robert Reed, *Roots*—Part 5 (ABC)
  Ralph Waite, *Roots*—Part 1 (ABC)

OUTSTANDING CONTINUING PERFORMANCE BY A SUPPORTING ACTRESS IN A COMEDY SERIES

☐ Mary Kay Place, *Mary Hartman, Mary Hartman* (Syndicated)
  Georgia Engel, *The Mary Tyler Moore Show* (CBS)
  Julie Kavner, *Rhoda* (CBS)
  Loretta Swit, *M*A*S*H* (CBS)
  Betty White, *The Mary Tyler Moore Show* (CBS)

OUTSTANDING CONTINUING PERFORMANCE BY A SUPPORTING ACTRESS IN A DRAMA SERIES

☐ Kristy McNichol, *Family* (ABC)
  Meredith Baxter Birney, *Family* (ABC)
  Ellen Corby, *The Waltons* (CBS)
  Lee Meriwether, *Barnaby Jones* (CBS)
  Jacqueline Tong, "Upstairs, Downstairs," *Masterpiece Theatre* (PBS)

OUTSTANDING CONTINUING OR SINGLE PERFORMANCE BY A SUPPORTING ACTRESS IN VARIETY OR MUSIC

☐ Rita Moreno, *The Muppet Show* (Syndicated)
  Vicki Lawrence, *The Carol Burnett Show* (CBS)
  Gilda Radner, *NBC's Saturday Night Live* (with Steve Martin) (NBC)

OUTSTANDING PERFORMANCE BY A SUPPORTING ACTRESS IN A COMEDY OR DRAMA SPECIAL

☐ Diana Hyland, *The Boy in the Plastic Bubble* (ABC)
  Ruth Gordon, *The Great Houdinis* (ABC)
  Rosemary Marphy, *Eleanor and Franklin: The White House Years* (ABC)
  Patricia Neal, *Tail Gunner Joe* (NBC)
  Susan Oliver, *Amelia Earhart* (NBC)

OUTSTANDING SINGLE PERFORMANCE BY A SUPPORTING ACTRESS IN A COMEDY OR DRAMA SERIES

☐ Olivia Cole, *Roots*—Part 8 (ABC)
  Sandy Duncan, *Roots*—Part 5 (ABC)
  Eileen Heckart, "Lou Proposes," *The Mary Tyler Moore Show* (CBS)
  Cicely Tyson, *Roots*—Part 1 (ABC)
  Nancy Walker, "The Separation," *Rhoda* (CBS)

Prime Time Directing and Writing Awards

OUTSTANDING WRITING IN A COMEDY SERIES

☐ Allan Burns, James L. Brooks, Ed Weinberger, Stan Daniels, David Lloyd, Bob Ellison, "The Last Show," *The Mary Tyler Moore Show* (CBS)

Alan Alda, "Dear Sigmund," *M*A*S*H* (CBS)

Danny Arnold, Tony Sheehan, "Quarantine—Part 2," *Barney Miller* (ABC)

David Lloyd, "Mary Midwife," *The Mary Tyler Moore Show* (CBS)

Earl Pomerantz, "Ted's Change of Heart," *The Mary Tyler Moore Show* (CBS)

OUTSTANDING WRITING IN A DRAMA SERIES

☐ Ernest Kinoy, William Blinn, *Roots*—Part 2 (ABC)

James Lee, *Roots*—Part 4 (ABC)

Roger O. Hirson, "Charles Francis Adams: Minister to Great Britain," *The Adams Chronicles* (PBS)

M. Charles Cohen, *Roots*—Part 8 (ABC)

Tad Mosel, "John Quincy Adams: President," *The Adams Chronicles* (PBS)

OUTSTANDING WRITING IN A COMEDY-VARIETY OR MUSIC SERIES

☐ Annie Beatts, Dan Aykroyd, Al Franken, Tom Davis, James Downey, Lorne Michaels, Marilyn Suzanne Miller, Michael O'Donoghue, Herb Sargent, Tom Schiller, Rosie Shuster, Alan Zweibel, John Belushi, Bill Murray, *NBC's Saturday Night Live* (with Sissy Spacek) (NBC)

Jim Henson, Jack Burns, Marc London, Jerry Juhl, *The Muppet Show* (with Paul Williams) (Syndicated)

Anne Beatts, Chevy Chase, Al Franken, Tom Davis, Lorne Michaels, Marilyn Suzanne Miller, Michael O'Donoghue, Herb Sargent, Tom Schiller, Rosie Schuster, Alan Zweibel, *NBC's Saturday Night Live* (with Elliot Gould) (NBC)

Ed Simmons, Roger Beatty, Elias Davis, David Pollock, Rich Hawkins, Liz Sage, Adele Styler, Burt Styler, Tim Conway, Bill Richmond, Gene Perret, Dick Clair, Jenna McMahon, *The Carol Burnett Show* (with Eydie Gorme) (CBS)

Bob Einstein, Allan Blye, George Burditt, Garry Ferrier, Ken Kinkelman, Mitch Markowitz, Tommy McLoughlin, Don Novello, Pat Proft, Leonard Ripps, Mickey Rose, Aubrey Tadman, Dick Van Dyke, Paul Wayne, *Van Dyke & Company* (with John Denver) (NBC)

OUTSTANDING WRITING IN A COMEDY-VARIETY OR MUSIC SPECIAL

☐ Alan Buz Kohan, Ted Strauss, *America Salutes Richard Rodgers: The Sound of His Music* (CBS)

Alan Thicke, Don Clark, Susan Clark, Ronny Pearlman, Steve Binder, Barry Manilow, Bruce Vilanch, *the Barry Manilow Special* (ABC)

Bill Dyer, Notzake Shange, *An Evening with Diana Ross* (NBC)

Ken Welch, Mitzie Welch, Kenny Solms, Gail Parent, *Sills and Burnett at the Met* (CBS)

Digby Wolfe, George Schlatter, *John Denver and Friend* (ABC)

OUTSTANDING WRITING IN A SPECIAL PROGRAM—DRAMA OR COMEDY—ORIGINAL TELEPLAY

☐ Lane Slate, *Tail Gunner Joe* (NBC)

Barry Beckerman, *Raid on Entebbe* (NBC)

James Costigan, *Eleanor and Franklin: The White House Years* (ABC)

Ernest Kinoy, *Victory at Entebbe* (ABC)

Douglas Day Stewart (teleplay), Joe Morgenstern, Douglas Day Stewart (story) *The Boy in the Plastic Bubble* (ABC)

OUTSTANDING WRITING IN A SPECIAL PROGRAM—DRAMA OR COMEDY—ADAPTATION

☐ Stewart Stern, *Sybil* (NBC)

William Bast, "The Man in the Iron Mask," *The Bell System Presents* (NBC)

John McGreevey, *Judge Horton and the Scottsboro Boys* (NBC)

Carol Sobieski, *Harry S Truman: Plain Speaking* (PBS)

Steven Gethers, *A Circle of Children* (CBS)

OUTSTANDING DIRECTING IN A COMEDY SERIES

☐ Alan Alda, "Dear Sigmund," *M*A*S*H* (CBS)

Paul Bogart, "The Draft Dodger," *All in the Family* (CBS)

Joan Darling, "The Nurses," *M*A*S*H* (CBS)

Alan Rakfin, "Radar O'Reilley," *M*A*S*H* (CBS)

Jay Sandrich, "The Last Show," *The Mary Tyler Moore Show* (CBS)

OUTSTANDING DIRECTING IN A DRAMA SERIES

☐ David Greene, *Roots*—Part 1 (ABC)

Marvin Chomsky, *Roots*—Part 3 (ABC)

Fred Coe, "John Quincy Adams: President," *The Adams Chronicles* (PBS)

John Erman, *Roots*—Part 2 (ABC)

Gilbert Moses, *Roots*—Part 6 (ABC)

OUTSTANDING DIRECTING IN A SPECIAL PROGRAM—DRAMA OR COMEDY

☐ Daniel Petrie, *Eleanor and Franklin: The White House Years* (ABC)

Fielder Cook, *Judge Horton and the Scottsboro Boys* (NBC)

Tom Gries, *Helter Skelter* (CBS)

Irvin Kershner, *Raid on Entebbe* (NBC)

Jud Taylor, *Tail Gunner Joe* (NBC)

OUTSTANDING DIRECTING IN A COMEDY-VARIETY OR MUSIC SERIES

☐ Dave Powers, *The Carol Burnett Show* (with Eydie Gorme) (CBS)

John C. Moffitt, *Van Dyke & Company* (with John Denver) (NBC)

Dave Wilson, *NBC's Saturday Night Live* (with Paul Simon) (NBC)

OUTSTANDING DIRECTING IN A COMEDY-VARIETY OR MUSIC SPECIAL

☐ Dwight Hemion, *America Salutes Richard Rodgers: The Sound of His Music* (CBS)

Steve Binder, *The Barry Manilow Special* (ABC)

Tony Charmoli, *The Shirley MacLaine Special: Where Do We Go From Here?* (CBS)

Walter C. Miller, *Doug Henning's World of Magic* (NBC)

David Powers, *Sills and Burnett at the Met* (CBS)

OUTSTANDING ACHIEVEMENT IN COVERAGE OF SPECIAL EVENTS—INDIVIDUALS

☐ John C. Moffit (Director), *The 28th Annual Emmy Awards* (ABC)

Helen O'Connell (Hostess), *Miss Universe Beauty Pagent* (CBS)

Marty Pasetta (Director), *48th Annual Oscar Awards* (ABC)

Creative Arts and Television Awards

OUTSTANDING ART DIRECTION OR SCENIC DESIGN FOR A COMEDY SERIES

☐ Thomas E. Azzari (art director), "The Really Longest Day," *Fish* (ABC)

Seymour Klate (art director), Mary Ann Biddle (set decorator), "The Happy Hooker," *Sirota's Court* (NBC)

C. Murawski (art director), "Walter's Crisis," *Maude* (CBS)

Don Roberts (art director), "The Unemployment Story—Part 2," *All in the Family* (CBS)

☐ Indicates winner

Roy Christopher (art director), Mary Ann Biddle (set decorator), "The Americanization of Michi," *Mr. T & Tina* (ABC)

OUTSTANDING ART DIRECTION OR SCENIC DESIGN FOR A DRAMA SERIES

☐ Tim Harvey (scenic designer), *The Pallisers*—Episode 1 (PBS)

John Corso (art director), Jerry Adams (set decorator), *Captains and the Kings*—Chapter 2 (NBC)

Joseph R. Jennings (art director), Solomon Brewer (set decorator), *Roots*—Part 6 (ABC)

Jan Scott (art director), Charles Bennett (set decorator), *Roots*—Part 2 (ABC)

Ed Wittstein (production designer), "John Quincy Adams: Congressman," *The Adams Chronicles* (PBS)

OUTSTANDING ART DIRECTION OR SCENIC DESIGN FOR A COMEDY-VARIETY OR MUSIC SERIES

☐ Romain Johnston (art director), *The Mac Davis Show* (with Susan Saint James, The Pointer Sisters, Shields & Yarnell) (NBC)

Paul Barnes and Bob Sansom (art directors), Bill Harp (set decorator), *The Carol Burnett Show* (with Glen Campbell) (CBS)

Bill Bohnert (art director), John Told (set decorator), *Donny and Marie* (with Chad Everett and Florenece Henderson) (ABC)

Eugene Lee, Leo Yoshimura, Franne Lee, *NBC's Saturday Night Live* (with Sissy Spacek) (NBC)

OUTSTANDING ART DIRECTION OR SCENIC DESIGN FOR A DRAMATIC SPECIAL

☐ Jan Scott (art director), Anne D. McCulley (set decorator), *Eleanor and Franklin, The White House Years* (ABC)

William H. Tuntke (art director), Richard Friedman (set decorator), *Amelia Earhart* (NBC)

Roy Christopher (art director), Beulah Frankel (set decorator), *The Last of Mrs. Lincoln* (PBS)

Trevor Williams (art director), Robert Checchi (set decorator), "Eccentricities of a Nightingale," *Theater In America, Great Performances* (PBS)

OUTSTANDING ART DIRECTION OR SCENIC DESIGN FOR A COMEDY-VARIETY OR MUSIC SPECIAL

☐ Robert Kelly (art director), *America Salutes Richard Rodgers: The Sound of His Music* (CBS)

☐ Indicates winner

Jac Venza (scenic designer), "Billy the Kid, American Ballet Theatre," *Dance in America, Great Performances* (PBS)

Roy Christopher (art director) John Hueners (set decorator) *The George Burns Comedy Special* (CBS)

William Mickley (art director), "Les Patineurs, American Ballet Theatre," *Dance in America, Great Performances* (PBS)

OUTSTANDING ACHIEVEMENT IN CHOREOGRAPHY

☐ Ron Field, *America Salutes Richard Rodgers: The Sound of His Music* (CBS)

David Blair, "Swan Lake," *Live from Lincoln Center, Great Performances* (PBS)

Ernest O. Flatt, *The Carol Burnett Show* (with the Pointer Sisters) (CBS)

Alan Johnson, *The Shirley MacLaine Special: Where Do We Go From Here?* (CBS)

Donald McKayle, *Minstrel Man* (CBS)

OUTSTANDING CINEMATOGRAPHY IN ENTERTAINMENT PROGRAMMING FOR A SERIES

☐ Ric Waite, *Captains and the Kings*—Chapter 1 (NBC)

Joseph Biroc, *The Moneychangers*—Part 1 (NBC)

John J. Jones, *Once An Eagle*—Part 1 (NBC)

William Burgensen, "Dear Sigmund," *M*A*S*H* (CBS)

Sherman Kunkel, "Soldier in the Jungle," *Baretta* (ABC)

Steven Larner, *Roots*—Part 2 (ABC)

Sol Negrin, "A Shield for Murder—Part 2," *Kojak* (CBS)

Joseph M. Wilcots, *Roots*—Part 7 (ABC)

OUTSTANDING CINEMATOGRAPHY IN ENTERTAINMENT PROGRAMMING FOR A SPECIAL

☐ Wilmer C. Butler, *Raid on Entebbe* (NBC)

James Crabe, *Eleanor and Franklin: The White House Years* (ABC)

Mario Tosi, *Sybil* (NBC)

Ted Voigtlander, *The Loneliest Runner* (NBC)

Ric Waite, *Tail Gunner Joe* (NBC)

OUTSTANDING ACHIEVEMENT IN COSTUME DESIGN FOR A DRAMA OR COMEDY SERIES

☐ Raymond Hughes, *The Pallisers*—Episode 1 (PBS)

Alvin Colt, "Henry Adams: Historian," *The Adams Chronicles* (PBS)

Jack F. Martell, *Roots*—Part 1 (ABC)

Joan Ellacott, "Madame Bovary—Part 3," *Masterpiece Theatre* (PBS)

Grady Hunt, "Prairie Woman," *The Quest* (NBC)

OUTSTANDING ACHIEVEMENT IN COSTUME DESIGN FOR MUSIC-VARIETY

☐ Jan Skalicky, "The Barber of Seville," *Live From Lincoln Center, Great Performances* (PBS)

Bill Hargate, *Neil Sedaka Steppin' Out* (NBC)

Frank Thompson, *America Salutes Richard Rodgers: The Sound of His Music* (CBS)

Ret Turner, Bob Mackie, *The Sonny & Cher Show* (with Barbara Eden and the Smothers Brothers) (CBS)

Bob Mackie, *An Evening with Diana Ross* (NBC)

OUTSTANDING ACHIEVEMENT IN COSTUME DESIGN FOR A DRAMA SPECIAL

☐ Joe I. Tompkins, *Eleanor and Franklin: The White House Years* (ABC)

Olga Lehmann, "The Man in the Iron Mask," *A Bell System Special* (NBC)

Albert Wolsky, "Beauty and the Beast," *Hallmark Hall of Fame* (NBC)

OUTSTANDING FILM EDITING IN A COMEDY SERIES

☐ Douglas Hines, "Murray Can't Lose," *The Mary Tyler Moore Show* (CBS)

Samuel E. Beetley, Stanford Tischler, "Dear Sigmund," *M*A*S*H* (CBS)

OUTSTANDING FILM EDITING IN A DRAMA SERIES

☐ Neil Travis, *Roots*—Part 1 (ABC)

James T. Heckert, *Roots*—Part 8 (ABC)

Peter Kirby, *Roots*—Part 3 (ABC)

Jerrold Ludwig, *Rich Man, Poor Man*—Book II, Ch. 3 (ABC)

Neil Travis, James Heckert, *Roots*—Part 2 (ABC)

OUTSTANDING FILM EDITING FOR A SPECIAL

☐ Rita Roland, Michael S. McLean, *Eleanor and Franklin: The White House Years* (ABC)

Byron "Buzz" Brandt, Bud Isaacs, *Helter Skelter* (CBS)

Ronald J. Fagan, *21 Hours at Munich* (ABC)

Bud S. Isaacs, Art Seid, Nick Archer, *Raid on Entebbe* (NBC)

John L. Loeffler, *The Loneliest Runner* (NBC)

OUTSTANDING ACHIEVEMENT IN FILM SOUND EDITING FOR A SERIES

☐ Larry Carow, Larry Neiman, Don Warner, Colin Mouat, George Fredrick, Dave Pettijohn, Paul Bruce Richardon, *Roots*—Part 2 (ABC)

Dale Johnston, James A. Bean, Carl J. Brandon, Joe Divitale, Don Tomlinson, Don Weinman, Gene Craig, "The Return of Bigfoot—Part 1," *The Six Million Dollar Man* (ABC)

Douglas H. Grindstaff, Richard Raderman, Sid Lubow, Hans Newman, Al Kajita, Luke Wolfram, Don V. Isaacs, Hank Salerno, Larry Singer, Stanley M. Gilbert, "Atlantium" *Fantastic Journey* (NBC)

Jerry Rosenthal, William L. Stevenson, Michael Corrigan, "The Mexican Connection," *Charlie's Angels* (ABC)

OUTSTANDING ACHIEVEMENT IN FILM SOUND EDITING FOR A SPECIAL

☐ Bernard F. Pincus, Milton C. Burrow, Gene Eliot, Don Ernst, Tony Garber, Don V. Issacs, Larry Kaufman, William L. Manger, A. David Marshall, Richard Oswald, Edward L. Sandlin, Russ Tinsley, *Raid on Entebbe* (NBC)

Douglas H. Grindstaff, Don V. Isaacs, Larry Kaufman, Bob Human, Buzz Cooper, Jack A. Finley, Marvin I. Kosberg, Harold Lee Chaney, Dick Friedman, Bill Andrews, Richard Raderman, Larry Singer, Stanley M. Gilbert, Hank Salerno, Al Kajita, Jack Milner, *The Quest* (NBC)

Richard Harrison, *Eleanor and Franklin: The White House Years* (ABC)

Jerry Rosenthal, William Phillips, John Strauss, William Jackson, James Yant, Jerry Pirozzi, Bruce Bell, *The Boy in the Plastic Bubble* (ABC)

OUTSTANDING ACHIEVEMENT IN FILM SOUND MIXING

☐ Alan Bernard, George E. Porter, Eddie J. Nelson, Robert L. Harman, *The Savage Bees* (NBC)

Willie D. Burton, George E. Porter, Eddie J. Nelson, Robert L. Hartman, *Roots*—Part 4 (ABC)

Hoppy Mehterian, George E. Porter, Eddie J. Nelson, Arnold Braun, *Roots*—Part 7 (ABC)

George E. Porter, Eddie J. Nelson, Robert L. Hartman, Arnold Braun, *Roots*—Part 8 (ABC)

Richard Portman, David Roone, Daonal W. MacDougall, Edward "Curly" Thirlwell, *Eleanor and Franklin: The White House Years* (ABC)

Bill Varney, Leonard Peterson, Robert Litt, Willie D. Burton, *Roots*—Part 1 (ABC)

☐ Indicates winner

OUTSTANDING ACHIEVEMENT IN GRAPHIC DESIGN AND TITLE SEQUENCES

☐ Eytan Keller, Stu Bernstein, *Bell Telephone Jubilee* (NBC)

Phill Norman, *The Moneychangers*—Part 1 (NBC)

Gene Piotrowsky, "The Gardener's Son," *Visions* (PBS)

Martine Sheon, David Summers, "Mozart as Keyboard Prodigy," *Previn and The Pittsburgh* (PBS)

OUTSTANDING ACHIEVEMENT IN LIGHTING DIRECTION

☐ William M. Klages, Peter Edwards *The Dorothy Hamill Special* (ABC)

Imero Fiorentino, Scott Johnson, *The Neil Diamond Special* (NBC)

George Risenberger, William Knight, "John Quincy Adams: President," *The Adams Chronicles* (PBS)

Dick Weiss, William Knight, "Henry Adams: Historian," *The Adams Chronicles* (PBS)

Ken Dettling, Leard Davis, "Gold Watch," *Visions* (PBS)

OUTSTANDING ACHIEVEMENT IN MAKE-UP

☐ Ken Chase (make-up design), Joe Dibella (make-up artist), *Eleanor and Franklin: The White House Years* (ABC)

Del Acevedo, John Chambers, Dan Striepeke, "Beauty and the Beast," *Hallmark Hall of Fame* (NBC)

Dick Smith, *Harry S Truman: Plain Speaking* (PBS)

Michael G. Westmore, Ed Butterworth, Charlie Schram, *The Million Dollar Rip-Off* (NBC)

Stan Winston, *An Evening with Diana Ross* (NBC)

OUTSTANDING ACHIEVEMENT IN MUSIC COMPOSITION FOR A SERIES (DRAMATIC UNDERSCORE)

Quincy Jones, Gerald Fried, *Roots*—Part 1 (ABC)

Elmer Bernstein, *Captain and the Kings*—Chapter 8 (NBC)

Gerald Fried, *Roots*—Part 8 (ABC)

Dick De Benedictis, "Monster Manor," *Police Story* (NBC)

Jack Urbont, "The Vigilant," *Bronk* (CBS)

OUTSTANDING ACHIEVEMENT IN MUSIC COMPOSITION FOR A SPECIAL (DRAMATIC UNDERSCORE)

☐ Leonard Rosenman, Alan Bergman, Marilyn Bergman, *Sybil* (NBC)

John Barry, *Eleanor and Franklin: The White House Years* (ABC)

Fred Karlin, *Minstrel Man* (CBS)

David Shire, *Raid on Entebbe* (NBC)

Billy Goldenberg, *Helter Skelter* (CBS)

OUTSTANDING ACHIEVEMENT IN MUSIC DIRECTION

☐ Ian Fraser, *America Salutes Richard Rodgers: The Sound of His Music* (CBS)

Andre Previn, "Mozart As Keyboard Prodigy," *Previn and The Pittsburgh* (PBS)

Jack Urbont, "The Vigilante," *Bronk* (CBS)

Peter Matz, *Sills and Burnett at the Met* (CBS)

Ralph Kubelik, "New York Philharmonic: Rafael Kubelik," *Live From Lincoln Center, Great Performances* (PBS)

OUTSTANDING ACHIEVEMENT IN SPECIAL MUSICAL MATERIAL

Bill Dyer, Billy Goldenberg, *An Evening with Diana Ross* (NBC)

Jerrold Immel, (Series Theme) *How the West Was Won* (ABC)

Fred Karlin (music), Meg Karlin (lyrics), "Early in the Morning," *Minstrel Man* (CBS)

Morton Stevens (music), Hermine Hilton (lyrics), "Leave Me Tomorrow," "Killer Cowboys," *Police Woman* (NBC)

Larry Grossman, *America Salutes Richard Rodgers: The Sound of His Music* (CBS)

OUTSTANDING ACHIEVEMENT IN TAPE SOUND MIXING

☐ Doug Nelson, *John Denver and Friend* (ABC)

Michael T. Gannon, Jerry Clemans, Tom Huth, Phil Seretti, "Ice Time," *Police Story* (NBC)

Doug Nelson, Norman H. Schwartz, John Black, *The American Music Awards* (ABC)

Emil Neroda, "John Quincy Adams. President," *The Adams Chronicles* (PBS)

OUTSTANDING ACHIEVEMENT IN TECHNICAL DIRECTION AND ELECTRONIC CAMERAWORK

☐ Karl Messerschmidt (technical director), Jon Olson, Bruce Gray, John Gutierrez, Jim Dodge, Wayne McDonald (cameramen), *Doug Henning's World of Magic* (NBC)

Ernie Buttelman (technical director), David Hilmer, James Balden, Jack Denton, Mayo Partee (cameramen), *A Special Olivia Newton-John* (ABC)

Gene Crowe (technical director), Samuel E. Dowlen, Tom Doakes, Larry Heider, Bob Keys, Wayne Orr, Bill Philbin, Ron Sheldon (cameramen), *The Neil Diamond Special* (NBC)

Ken Lamkin (technical director) Lew Adams, Mike Keeler, Gary Stanton,

Samuel E. Dowlen (cameramen), *Victory at Entebbe* (ABC)

Ken Anderson (technical director), Arthur G. Vogel, Jr. (cameraman), *Harry S Truman: Plain Speaking* (PBS)

OUTSTANDING ACHIEVEMENT IN VIDEO TAPE EDITING FOR A SERIES

□ Roy Stewart, "The War Widow," *Visions* (PBS)

Terry Pickford, *Meetings of Minds*—Episode 3 (PBS)

Ken Denisoff, Stowell Werden, "Sharkey Boogies on Down," *C.P.O. Sharkey* (NBC)

Jimmy B. Frazier, "Ice Time," *Police Story* (NBC)

OUTSTANDING ACHIEVEMENT IN VIDEO TAPE EDITING FOR A SPECIAL

□ Gary H. Anderson, *American Bandstand's 25th Anniversary* (ABC)

Thomas Klein, Bill Breshears, *The Barry Manilow Special* (ABC)

Susan Jenkins, Manuel Martinez, *The Captain and Tennille Special* (ABC)

Jimmy B. Frazier, Danny White, *The Dorothy Hamill Special* (ABC)

James McElroy, Mike Gavaldon, David Saxon, *Victory at Entebbe* (ABC)

William Breshears, Barbara Babcock, *The Neil Diamond Special* (NBC)

OUTSTANDING INDIVIDUAL ACHIEVEMENT IN ANY AREA OF CREATIVE TECHNICAL CRAFTS*

□ Emma di Vittorio (hairstylist), Vivienne Walker (hairstylist), *Eleanor and Franklin: The White House Years* (ABC)

Larry Germain (hairstylist), "To Live with Fear," *Little House on the Prairie* (NBC)

Naomi Cavin (hairstylist), *The Great Houndinis* (ABC)

Dick Wilson (live sound mixing), Doug Nelon (live sound mixing), *The 28th Annual Emmy Awards* (ABC)

Robert Biggart (tape sound editing), Patrick Somerset (tape sound editing), *Victory at Entebbe* (ABC)

SPECIAL CLASSIFICATION OF OUTSTANDING INDIVIDUAL ACHIEVEMENT*

□ Allen Brewster, Bob Roethle, William Lorenz, Manuel Martinez, Ron Fleury, Mike Welch, Jerry Burling, Walter Balderson, Chuck Droege (video tape editing), *The First Fifty Years* (NBC)

---

* possibility of one award, more than one award or no award
* possibility of one award, more than one award or no award
□ Indicates winner

□ George Pitts, Clay Cassell (film editing), *The First Fifty Years* (NBC)

Enzo Martinelli (cinematography), "Mystery of the Haunted House," *Nancy Drew/Hardy Boys Mysteries* (ABC)

Robert K. Lambert, Peter C. Johnson (film editing), *Life Goes to the Movies* (NBC)

OUTSTANDING INDIVIDUAL ACHIEVEMENT IN CHILDREN'S PROGRAMMING*

□ Jean De Joux (videoanimation), Elizabeth Savel (videoanimation), "Peter Pan," *Hallmark Hall of Fame* (NBC)

□ Bill Hargate (costume designer), *Pinocchio* (CBS)

□ Jerry Greene (video tape editor), *Pinocchio* (CBS)

Michael Tilson Thomas (music director), "Making Pictures with Music," *CBS Festival of Lively Arts for Young People, New York Philharmonic Young People's Concert*

Stan Winston (make-up designer), Larry Abbott (make-up artist), Ed Butterworth (make-up artist), *Pinocchio* (CBS)

OUTSTANDING ACHIEVEMENT IN COVERAGE OF SPECIAL EVENTS— INDIVIDUALS*

□ Brian C. Bartholomew, Keaton S. Walker (art directors), *The 28th Annual Emmy Awards* (ABC)

OUTSTANDING ACHIEVEMENT IN BROADCAST JOURNALISM

□ *MacNeil-Lehrer Report*
□ Eric Sevareid
□ League of Women Voters
□ *60 minutes*

OUTSTANDING ACHIEVEMENT IN ENGINEERING DEVELOPMENT

□ ABC, for leadership in establishing Circularly Polarized Transmission to improve television reception.

Citation to Varian Associates for improving the efficiency of UHF Klystrons.

Daytime Awards

OUTSTANDING DAYTIME TALK, SERVICE OR VARIETY SERIES

Emmy(s) to executive producer(s) and producer(s):

Dinah! Henry Jaffe and Carolyn Raskin (executive producers), Fred Tatashore (producer) (Syndicated)

The Gong Show Chuck Barris (executive producer), Gene Banks (producer) (NBC)

□ *The Merv Griffin Show* Bob Murphy (producer) (Syndicated)

The Mike Douglas Show David Salzman (executive producer), Jack Reilly (producer) (Syndicated)

OUTSTANDING HOST OR HOSTESS IN A TALK, SERVICE OR VARIETY SERIES

□ Phil Donahue, *Donahue* (Syndicated)

Mike Douglas, *The Mike Douglas Show* (Syndicated)

Merv Griffin, *The Merv Griffin Show* (Syndicated)

Dinah Shore, *Dinah!* (Syndicated)

OUTSTANDING INDIVIDUAL DIRECTOR FOR A DAYTIME VARIETY PROGRAM

For a single episode:

Dick Carson, *The Merv Griffin Show*, "Merv Griffin in Israel" (Syndicated)

John Dorsey, *The Gong Show*, November 23, 1976 (NBC)

□ Donald R. King, *The Mike Douglas Show*, "Mike in Hollywood" (with Ray Charles and Michel Le Grand) (Syndicated)

Glen Swanson, *Dinah!* "Dinah from Australia" (Syndicated)

OUTSTANDING GAME OR AUDIENCE PARTICIPATION SHOW

For daytime programs, Emmy(s) to executive producer(s) and producer(s):

The $20,000 Pyramid, Bob Stewart (executive Producer), Anne Marie Schmitt (producer) (ABC)

□ *Family Feud*, Howard Felsher (producer) (ABC)

Hollywood Squares, Robert Quigley and Merrill Heatter (executive producers), Jay Redack (producer) (NBC)

Match Game '76, Ira Skutch (producer) (CBS)

Tattletales, Ira Skutch (executive producer), Paul Alter (producer) (CBS)

OUTSTANDING HOST OR HOSTESS IN A GAME OR AUDIENCE PARTICIPATION SHOW

For daytime programs:

Dick Clark, *The $20,000 Pyramid* (ABC)

□ Bert Convy, *Tattletales* (CBS)

Gene Rayburn, *Match Game '76* (CBS)

OUTSTANDING INDIVIDUAL DIRECTOR FOR A GAME OR AUDIENCE PARTICIPATION SHOW

For a single episode of a daytime series:

Joseph Behar, *Let's Make a Deal*, May 5, 1976 (ABC)

□ Mike Gargiulo, *The $20,000 Pyramid* (with Tony Randall and Jo Anne Worley), August 10, 1976 (ABC)

OUTSTANDING ENTERTAINMENT, CHILDREN'S SERIES

Emmy(s) to executive producer(s) and producer(s):

Captain kangaroo, Jim Hirschleld (producer) (CBS)

David Copperfield, *Once Upon a Classic*, Jay Rayvid (executive producer), John McRae and Don Coney (producers) (PBS)

"Heidi," *Once upon a Classic*, Jay Rayvid (executive producer), John McRae and Don Coney (producers) (PBS)

"The Prince and the Pauper," *Once upon a Classic*, Ray Rayvid (executive producer), Barry Letts and Don Coney (producers) (PBS)

☐ *Zoom*, Cheryl Susheel Bibbs (executive producer), Monia Joblin and Mary Benjamin (producers) (PBS)

OUTSTANDING ENTERTAINMENT, CHILDREN'S SPECIAL

Emmy(s) to executive producer(s) and producer(s):

☐ "Big Henry and the Polka Dot Kid," *Special Treat*, Linda Gottlieb (procuder), November 9, 1976 (NBC)

"Blind Sunday," *ABC Afterschool Specials*, Daniel Wilson (producer), April 21, 1976 (ABC)

"Francesca Baby," *ABC Afterschool Specials*, Martin Tahse (producer), October 6, 1976 (ABC)

"Luke Was There," *Special Treat*, Linda Gottlieb (executive producer), Richard Marquand (producer), October 5, 1976 (NBC)

"The Original Rompin' Stompin' Hot and Heavy, Cool and Groovy All Star Jazz Show," *The CBS Festival of Lively Arts for Young People*, Ron Kass and Edgar Bronfman, Jr. (executive producers), Gary Keys (producer), April 13, 1976 (CBS)

"P.J. And The President's Son," *ABC Afterschool Specials*, Danny Wilson (executive producer), Fran Sears (producer), November 10, 1976 (ABC)

OUTSTANDING INFORMATIONAL CHILDREN'S SERIES

Emmy(s) to executive producer(s) and producer(s):

ABC Minute Magazine, Thomas H. Wolf (producer) (ABC)

America Rock, Tom Yohe (executive producer), Radford Stone (producer) (ABC)

Animals Animals Animals, Lester Cooper (executive producer), Peter Weinberg, (producer) (ABC)

☐ Indicates winner

☐ *The Electric Company*, Samuel Y. Gibbon Jr. (executive producer) (PBS)

OUTSTANDING INFORMATIONAL CHILDREN'S SPECIAL

Emmy(s) to executive producer(s) and producer(s):

How to Follow the Election, Sid Darion (producer), October 31, 1976 (ABC)

☐ "My Mom's Having a Baby," *ABC Afterschool Specials*, David H. DePatie and Friz Freleng (executive producers), Bob Chenault (producer), February 16, 1977 (ABC)

OUTSTANDING INSTRUCTIONAL CHILDREN'S PROGRAMMING—SERIES AND SPECIALS

Emmy(s) to executive producer(s) and producer(s):

☐ *Sesame Street*, Jon Stone (executive producer), Duley Singer (producer), Series (PBS)

Villa Alegre, Claudio Guzman (executive producer), Larry Gottlieb (producer), Series (PBS)

OUTSTANDING ACTRESS IN A DAYTIME DRAMA SERIES

Nancy Addision, *Ryan's Hope* (ABC)

☐ Helen Gallagher, *Ryan's Hope* (ABC)

Beverlee McKinsey, *Another World* (NBC)

Mary Stuart, *Search for Tomorrow* (CBS)

Ruth Warrick, *All My Children* (ABC)

OUTSTANDING ACHIEVEMENT IN DAYTIME DRAMA SPECIALS

☐ Gaby Monet (producer), *The American Woman: Portraits of Courage*, May 20, 1976 (ABC)

OUTSTANDING WRITING FOR A DAYTIME DRAMA SERIES

For a single episode of a series or for the entire series:

William J. Bell, Pat Falken Smith, William Rega, Kay Lenard, Margaret Stewart, *Days of Our Lives*, Series (NBC)

☐ Claire Labine, Paul Avila Mayer, Mary Munisteri, *Ryan's Hope* Series (ABC)

Harding Lemay, Tom King, Peter Swet, Barry Berg, Jan Merlin, Arthur Giron, Kathy Callaway, *Another World*, Series (NBC)

Agnes Nixon, Wisner Washam, Kathryn McCabe, Mary K. Wells, Jack Wood, *All My Children*, Series (ABC)

Robert Soderberg, Edith Sommer, Ralph Ellis, Eugenie Hunt, Theodore Apstein, Gillian Spencer, *As the World Turns*, October 27, 1976 (CBS)

OUTSTANDING ACTOR IN A DAYTIME DRAMA SERIES

☐ Val Dufour, *Search for Tomorrow* (CBS)

Farley Granger, *One Life to Live* (ABC)

Larry Haines, *Search for Tomorrow* (CBS)

Lawrence Keith, *All My Children* (ABC)

James Pritchett, *The Doctors* (NBC)

OUTSTANDING INDIVIDUAL DIRECTOR FOR A DAYTIME DRAMA SERIES

For a single episode:

Joseph Behar, *Days of Our Lives*, March 8, 1977 (NBC)

Ira Cirker, *Another World*, November 10, 1976 (NBC)

Paul E. Davis, Leonard Valenta, *As the World Turns*, January 14, 1977 (CBS)

Al Rabin, *Days of Our Lives*, "Julie and Doug's Wedding," October 1, 1976 (NBC)

John Sedwick, *The Edge of Night*, August 6, 1976 (ABC)

☐ Lela Swift, *Ryan's Hope*, February 8, 1977 (ABC)

OUTSTANDING DAYTIME DRAMA SERIES

Emmy(s) to executive producer(s) and producer(s):

All My Children, Bud Kloss and Agnes Nixon (producers) (ABC)

Another World, Paul Rauch (Executive producer), Mary S. Bonner and Joseph H. Rothenberger (producers) (NBC)

Days of Our Lives, Mrs. Ted Corday (executive producer), H. Wesley Kenney and Jack Herzberg (producers) (NBC)

The Edge of Night, Erwin Nicholson (producer) (ABC)

☐ *Ryan's Hope*, Paul Avila Mayer and Claire Labine (executive producers), Robert Costello (producer) (ABC)

Sports Programming Awards

OUTSTANDING LIVE SPORTS SPECIAL

Emmy(s) to executive producer(s) and producer(s):

Super Bowl XI, Scotty Connal (executive producer), George Finkel and Ted Nathanson (producers), January 9, 1977 (NBC)

1976 Masters Golf Tournament, Frank Chirkinian (producer), April 9-10, 1976 (CBS)

1976 World Series, Scotty Connal (executive producer), Roy Hammerman (producer), October 16–21, 1976 (NBC)

1977 Rose Bowl, Scotty Connal (executive producer), Dick Auerbach (producer), January 1, 1977 (NBC)

☐ *1976 Olympic Games*, (Montreal, Canada), Roone Arledge (executive producer), Chuck Howard, Don Ohlmeyer, Chet Forte, Dennis Lewin, Bob Goodrich, Geoffrey Mason, Terry Jastrow, Eleanor Riger, Ned Steckel, Brice Weisman, John Wilcox and Doug Wilson (producers), July 17–August 1, 1976 (ABC)

OUTSTANDING LIVE SPORT SERIES

Emmy(s) to executive producer(s) and producer(s):

ABC'S NCAA Football, Roone Arledge (executive producer), Chuck Howard and Terry Jastrow (producers) (ABC)

ABC'S NFL Monday Night Football, Roone Arledge (executive producer), Don Ohlmeyer and Dennis Lewin (producers) (ABC)

College Basketball 1977, Scotty Connal (executive producer), George Finkel and Roy Hammerman (producers) (NBC)

NFL Football, Scotty Connal (executive producer), Dick Auerback, George Finkel, Roy Hammerman, Ted Nathanson, Larry Circillo and Jim Marooney (producers) (NBC)

☐ *The NFL Today/NFL Football on CBS*, Michael Pearl, Hal Classon and Sid Kaufman (producers) (CBS)

OUTSTANDING EDITED SPORTS SPECIAL

Emmy(s) to executive producer(s) and producer(s):

Baseball World of Joe Garagiola ("World Series pregame"), Joe Garagiola (executive producer), Ginny Seipt (producer), October 16–21, 1976 (NBC)

The Glory of Their Times, Cappy Petrash Greenspan (executive producer), Bud Greenspan (producer), January 31, 1977 (PBS)

To the Top of the World: An Assault on Everest, Ed Goren and Mike Hoover (producers), January 7, 1977 (CBS)

Wide World of Sports 15th Anniversary Special, Roone Arledge (executive producer), Dennis Lewin, (producer), April 24, 1976 (ABC)

☐ *A Special Preview Of The 1976 Olympic Games From Montreal, Canada*, Roone Arledge (executive producer), Chuck Howard, Don Ohlmeyer, Chet Forte, Dennis Lewin, Bob Goodrich, Geoffrey Mason, Terry Jastrow, Eleanor Riger, Nid Steckel, Brice Weisman, John

☐ Indicates winner

Wilcox and Doug Wilson (producers), July 17, 1976 (ABC)

OUTSTANDING EDITED SPORTS SERIES

Emmy(s) to executive producer(s) and producer(s):

ABC'S Wide World of Sports, Roone Arledge (executive producer), Dennis Lewin, Red Steckel, Doug Wilson, Chet Forte and Chuck Howard (producers) (ABC)

Grandstand, Don Ellis (executive producer), Bill Fitts (producer) (NBC)

☐ *The Olympiad*, Cappy Petrash Greenspan (executive producer), Bud Greenspan (producer) (PBS)

The Way it Was, Gerry Gross (executive producer), Gary Brown and Dick Enberg (producers) (PBS)

OUTSTANDING SPORTS PERSONALITY

Jim McKay (ABC)
☐ Frank Gifford (ABC)
Keith Jackson (ABC)
Don Meredith (NBC)
Joe Garagiola (NBC)

OUTSTANDING DIRECTING IN SPORTS PROGRAMMING

Harry Coyle, *World Series of Baseball* (Yankees vs. Cincinnati), October 16, 1976 (NBC)

☐ Chet Forte, *ABC NFL Monday Night Football*, September 19–December 17, 1976 (ABC)

Ronald Hawkins, Joe Aceti, Chet Forte, Roger Goodman, Larry Kamm, Don Ohlmeyer, Andy Sidaris, Lou Volpicelli, Robert Riger, Ralph Mellaney, *1976 Olympic Games: Montreal, Canada*, July 17–August 1, 1976 (ABC)

Robert Riger, *ABC's Wide World of Sports*, "Men's World Cup Downhill Skiing Championships" (Laax, Switzerland), February 27, 1977 (ABC)

Doug Wilson, *ABC's Wide World of Sports*, "Grand Prix of Monaco," June 5, 1976 (ABC)

OUTSTANDING INDIVIDUAL ACHIEVEMENT IN SPORTS PROGRAMMING

For a single episode of a series or for a special program. The following are "Areas," where there is a possibility of one award, more than one award or no award:

Cinematography

☐ Peter Henning, Harvey Harrison, Harry Hart, D'Arcy March, Don Shapiro, Don Shoemaker and Joe Valentine, *1976 Olympic Games*, July 17–August 1, 1976 (ABC)

Tape Sound Mixing

Dick Ross, Rich Sloan, Jack Black, Gary Larkins, Bill Sandrueter, John McCullough, Willie Earl, Art Morganstern, Jack Brandes, Charles Buckage, Wayne Caluger, Max Goldstein, Jack Hughes, Les Scheyer and Ray Tomaszeski, *1976 Olympic Games*, July 17–August 1, 1976 (ABC)

Graphic Design

Michael Webster and Jim Duffy, *Challenge of the Sexes—Show #1*, January 16, 1977 (CBS)

Film Editing

☐ John Petersen, Angelo Bernaducci, Irwin Krechaf, Margaret Murphy, Vincent Reda and Anthony Zaccaro, *1976 Olympic Games*, July 17–August 1, 1976 (ABC)

Engineering Supervision/Technical Direction/Electronic Camerawork

Julius Barnathan, Phil Levens, Joe Debonis, Joe Maltz, Ben Greenberg, William H. Johnson, Abdelnour Tadros, Jack Neitlich, Herb Kraft, Jacques Lesgards, Bob Czinke, Frank Genereux, Dick Horan, Mel Morehouse, Mort Romanoff and Jack Wilkey (engineering supervisors), Ernie Buttleman, Bill Morris, Dave Smith, Gene Affrunti, Bob Myers, Vic Bary, John Allen, John Broderick, Charlie Giles, Tom Sumner, Werner Gunther, Bob Bernthal and Joe Nesi (technical directors), Keith Brock, Evan Baker, John Lee, Bill Sullivan, Simon Melpose, Jim Angel, Andy Armentani, John Cronin, Drew Derosa, Jack Dorfman, Sal Folino, James Hennegahan, William Karvelas, Mort Levin, John Morreale, Steve Nikifor, Roger Pierce, Mike Rebich, Joe Sapienza, Joe Scarpa. Joe Stefanoni. Larry Stenman, Joe Talosi, and Dale Walsh (electronic cameramen), *1976 Olympic Games*, July 17–August 1, 1976 (ABC)

Videotape Editing (includes associate direction)

Carol Lehti, Dick Buffinton, Jeff Cohan, Vince DeDario, John DeLisa, Lou Frederick, Jack Gallivan, Jim Jennett, Bob Lanning, Jean MacLean, Dave Malenofski, Norm Samet, Howard Shapiro and Stan Spiro (associate directors), Emil Rich, John Stevens, Mike Raffaele, Ron Ackerman, Harry Allen, Harvey Beal, Ronald Blachut, Barbara Bowman, Bud Crowe, Peter Fritz, Charles Gardner, Vito Gerardi, Nick Giordano, James Hepper, Jacob Hierl, Hector Kicelian, Conrad Kraus, Fred Labib, Hal Lea, Pat Malik, Ed

McCarthy Peter Mecca, Alex Moskovic, Harvey Otto, Nicholas Pantelakis, Chester Pawlak, Carl Pollack, Douglas Ridsel, Erskin Roberts, Danny Rosenson, Winston Saddo, Gene Smejkal, Leo Stephen, Ted Summers, Martin Thibeau, Arthur Volk, Mike Wenig, Mike Biondi, Rocco Cotugno, Jim Florence, Marvin Gench, Victor Gonzalez, Frank Guigliano, Galon Halloway, Emerson Lawson, Nick Mazur, Merrit Roesser, Nathan Rogers, Mario Schencman, Truett Smith, Charles Stephenson, George Stevens, Tom Wight, Hector Kierl and Ken Klingbeil (videotape editors), *1976 Olympic Games*, July 17–August 1, 1976 (ABC)

1977/78

(For program aired between March 14, 1977 and June 30, 1978. Primetime program and individual achievements awards presented September 17, 1978. Creative Arts awards presented September 9, 1978. Daytime awards presented June 7, 1978. Sports programming awards presented February 13, 1979. National Award for Community Service presented November 21, 1977. Science of Television Engineering Award presented September 2, 1978.)

Prime Time Program Awards

OUTSTANDING COMEDY SERIES
☐ *All in the Family* (CBS)
Barney Miller (ABC)
*M*A*S*H* (CBS)
Soap (ABC)
Three's Company (ABC)

OUTSTANDING DRAMA SERIES
☐ *The Rockford Files* (NBC)
Columbo (NBC)
Family (ABC)
Lou Grant (CBS)
Quincy (CBS)

OUTSTANDING COMEDY-VARIETY OR MUSIC SERIES
☐ *The Muppet Show* (Syndicated)
America 2 Night (Syndicated)
The Carol Burnett Show (CBS)
Evening At Pops (PBS)
NBC's Saturday Night Live (NBC)

OUTSTANDING LIMITED SERIES
☐ *Holocaust* (NBC)
King (NBC)
Washington: Behind Closed Doors (ABC)

☐ Indicates winner

"Anna Karenina," *Masterpiece Theatre* (PBS)
"I, Claudius," *Masterpiece Theatre* (PBS)

OUTSTANDING SPECIAL—DRAMA OR COMEDY
☐ *The Gathering* (ABC)
A Death in Cannan (CBS)
Jesus of Nazareth (NBC)
"Our Town," *Bell System Special* (NBC)
Young Joe, The Forgotten Kennedy (ABC)

OUTSTANDING SPECIAL—COMEDY-VARIETY OR MUSIC
☐ *Bette Midler—Ol' Red Hair Is Back* (NBC)
Doug Henning's World of Magic (NBC)
The George Burns One-Man Show (CBS)
Neil Diamond: I'm Glad You're Here With Me Tonight (NBC)
The Second Barry Manilow Special (ABC)

OUTSTANDING CLASSICAL PROGRAM IN THE PERFORMING ARTS
☐ "American Ballet Theatre's 'Giselle,'" *Live From Lincoln Center* (PBS)
"American Ballet Theatre," *Live From Lincoln Center* (PBS)
Dance in America: Choreography by Balanchine (PBS)
"La Boheme," *Live From the Met* (PBS)
The Nutcracker (Baryshnikov) (CBS)

OUTSTANDING CHILDREN'S SPECIAL (FOR SPECIALS WHICH WERE BORADCAST IN THE EVENING)
☐ *Halloween Is Grinch Night* (ABC)
A Connecticut Yankee in King Arthur's Court (PBS)
The Fat Albert Christmas Special (CBS)
Once Upon a Brothers Grimm (CBS)
Peter Lundy and the Medicine Hat Stallion (NBC)

OUTSTANDING INFORMATIONAL SERIES
☐ *The Body Human* (CBS)
Between the Wars (Syndicated)
Cousteau Oasis in Space (PBS)
Mutual of Omaha's Wild Kingdom (Syndicated)
Nova (PBS)

OUTSTANDING INFORMATIONAL SPECIAL
☐ *The Great Whales, National Geographic* (PBS)
Bing Crosby: His Life and Legend (ABC)
"Calypso's Search for Atlantis," *Cousteau Odyssey* (PBS)

The Treasures of Tutankhamun (PBS)
Tut: The Boy King (NBC)

OUTSTANDING ACHIEVEMENT IN COVERAGE OF SPECIAL EVENTS—PROGRAMS*
50th Annual Awards of the Academy of Motion Picture Arts and Sciences (ABC)

SPECIAL CLASSIFICATION OF OUTSTANDING PROGRAM ACHIEVEMENT*
☐ *The Tonight Show Starring Johnny Carson* (NBC)
The American Film Institute Salute to Bette Davis (CBS)
The American Film Institute Salute to Henry Fonda (CBS)
The Dick Cavett Show (PBS)
NBC: The First Fifty Years—A Closer Look (NBC)

Prime Time Performance Awards*

OUTSTANDING LEAD ACTOR IN A COMEDY SERIES
☐ Caroll O'Connor, *All in the Family* (CBS)
Alan Alda, *M*A*S*H* (CBS)
Hal Linden, *Barney Miller* (ABC)
John Ritter, *Three's Company* (ABC)
Henry Winkler, *Happy Days* (ABC)

OUTSTANDING LEAD ACTOR IN A DRAMA SERIES
☐ Ed Asner, *Lou Grant* (CBS)
James Broderick, *Family* (ABC)
Peter Falk, *Columbo* (NBC)
James Garner, *Rockford Files* (NBC)
Jack Klugman, *Quincy* (NBC)
Ralph White, *The Waltons* (CBS)

OUTSTANDING LEAD ACTOR IN A LIMITED SERIES
☐ Michael Moriarty, *Holocaust* (NBC)
Hal Holbrook, *The Awakening Land* (NBC)
Jason Robards, Jr., *Washington: Behind Closed Doors* (ABC)
Fritz Weaver, *Holocaust* (NBC)
Paul Winfield, *King* (NBC)

OUTSTANDING LEAD ACTOR IN A DRAMA OR COMEDY SPECIAL
☐ Fred Astaire, *A Family Upside Down* (NBC)
Alan Alda, *Kill Me If You Can* (NBC)
Hal Holbrook, "Our Town," *Bell System* (NBC)
Martin Sheen, "Taxi," *Hallmark Hall of Fame* (NBC)
James Stacy, *Just a Little Incovenience* (NBC)

* possibility of one award, more than one award or no award

OUTSTANDING LEAD ACTOR FOR A SINGLE APPEARANCE IN A DRAMA OR COMEDY SERIES

☐ Barnard Hughes, "Judge," *Lou Grant* (CBS)
David Cassidy, "A Chance to Live," *Police Story* (NBC)
Will Geer, "The Old Man and the Runaway," *The Love Boat* (ABC)
Judd Hirsch, "Rhoda Likes Mike," *Rhoda* (CBS)
John Rubinstein, "And Baby Makes Three," *Family* (ABC)
Keenan Wynn, "Good Old Uncle Ben," *Police Woman* (NBC)

OUTSTANDING LEAD ACTRESS IN A COMEDY SERIES

☐ Jean Stapleton, *All in the Family* (CBS)
Beatrice Arthur, *Maude* (CBS)
Cathryn Damon, *Soap* (ABC)
Valerie Harper, *Rhoda* (CBS)
Katherine Helmond, *Soap* (ABC)
Suzanne Pleshette, *The Bob Newhart Show* (CBS)

OUTSTANDING LEAD ACTRESS IN A DRAMA SERIES

☐ Sada Thompson, *Family* (ABC)
Melissa Sue Anderson, *Little House on the Prairie* (NBC)
Fionnula Flanagan, *How the West Was Won* (ABC)
Kate Jackson, *Charlie's Angels* (ABC)
Michael Learned, *The Waltons* (CBS)
Susan Sullivan, *Julie Farr, M.D.* (ABC)

OUTSTANDING LEAD ACTRESS IN A LIMITED SERIES

☐ Meryl Streep, *Holocaust* (NBC)
Rosemary Harris, *Holocaust* (NBC)
Elizabeth Montgomery, *The Awakening Land* (NBC)
Lee Remick, *Wheels* (NBC)
Cicely Tyson, *King* (NBC)

OUTSTANDING LEAD ACTRESS IN A DRAMA OR COMEDY SPECIAL

☐ Joanne Woodward, *See How She Runs* (CBS)
Helen Hayes, *A Family Upside Down* (NBC)
Eva Marie Saint, "Taxi," *Hallmark Hall of Fame* (NBC)
Maureen Stapleton, *The Gathering* (ABC)
Sada Thompson, "Our Town," *Bell System* (NBC)

OUTSTANDING LEAD ACTRESS FOR A SINGLE APPEARANCE IN A DRAMA OR COMEDY SERIES

☐ Rita Moreno, "The Paper Palace," *The Rockford Files* (NBC)
Patty Duke Astin, *Having Babies* (ABC)
Kate Jackson, "James at 15," *James at 15/16* (NBC)

☐ Indicates winner

Jayne Meadows, "Luther, Volatire, Plato, Nightingale," *Meeting of Minds* (PBS)
Irene Tedrow, "Ducks," *James at 15/16* (NBC)

OUTSTANDING CONTINUING PERFORMANCE BY A SUPPORTING ACTOR IN A COMEDY SERIES

☐ Rob Reiner, *All in the Family* (CBS)
Tom Bosley, *Happy Days* (ABC)
Gary Burghoff, *M*A*S*H* (CBS)
Harry Morgan, *M*A*S*H* (CBS)
Vic Tayback, *Alice* (CBS)

OUTSTANDING CONTINUING PERFORMANCE BY A SUPPORTING ACTOR IN A DRAMA SERIES

☐ Robert Vaughn, *Washington: Behind Closed Doors* (ABC)
Ossie Davis, *King* (NBC)
Will Geer, *The Waltons* (CBS)
Sam Wanamaker, *Holocaust* (NBC)
David Warner, *Holocaust* (NBC)

OUTSTANDING CONTINUING OR SINGLE PERFORMANCE BY A SUPPORTING ACTOR IN VARIETY OR MUSIC

☐ Tim Conway, *The Carol Burnett Show* (CBS)
Dan Aykroyd, *NBC's Saturday Night Live* (NBC)
John Belushi, *NBC's Saturday Night Live* (NBC)
Louis Gossett, Jr., *The Sentry Collection Presents Ben Vereen— His Roots* (ABC)
Peter Sellers, *The Muppet Show* (Syndicated)

OUTSTANDING PERFORMANCE BY A SUPPORTING ACTOR IN A COMEDY OR DRAMA SPECIAL

☐ Howard Da Silva, "Verna: USO Girl," *Great Performances* (PBS)
James Farentino, *Jesus of Nazareth* (NBC)
Burgess Meredith, "The Last Hurrah," *Hallmark Hall of Fame* (NBC)
Donald Pleasance, *The Defection of Simas Kudirka* (CBS)
Efrem Zimbalist, Jr., *A Family Upside Down* (NBC)

OUTSTANDING SINGLE PERFORMANCE BY A SUPPORTING ACTOR IN A COMEDY OR DRAMA SERIES

☐ Ricardo Montalban, *How the West Was Won—Part II* (ABC)
Will Geer, "Yes, Nicholas There Is a Santa Claus," *Eight Is Enough* (ABC)
Larry Gelman, "Goodbye Mr. Fish—Part II," *Barney Miller* (ABC)
Harold Gould, "Happy Anniversary," *Rhoda* (CBS)
Abe Vigoda, "Goodbye Mr. Fish—Part II," *Barney Miller* (ABC)

OUTSTANDING CONTINUING PERFORMANCE BY A SUPPORTING ACTRESS IN A COMEDY SERIES

☐ Julie Kavner, *Rhoda* (CBS)
Polly Holliday, *Alice* (CBS)
Sally Struthers, *All in the Family* (CBS)
Loretta Swit, *M*A*S*H* (CBS)
Nancy Walker, *Rhoda* (CBS)

OUTSTANDING CONTINUING PERFORMANCE BY A SUPPORTING ACTRESS IN A DRAMA SERIES

☐ Nancy Marchand, *Lou Grant* (CBS)
Meredith Baxter Birney, *Family* (ABC)
Tovah Feldshuh, *Holocaust* (NBC)
Linda Kelsey, *Lou Grant* (CBS)
Kristy McNichol, *Family* (ABC)

OUTSTANDING CONTINUING OR SINGLE PERFORMANCE BY A SUPPORTING ACTRESS IN VARIETY OR MUSIC

☐ Gilda Radner, *NBC's Saturday Night Live* (NBC)
Beatrice Arthur, *Laugh-In* (NBC)
Jane Curtin, *NBC's Saturday Night Live* (NBC)
Dolly Parton, *Cher. . . Special* (ABC)
Bernadette Peters, *The Muppet Show* (Syndicated)

OUTSTANDING PERFORMANCE BY A SUPPORTING ACTRESS IN A DRAMA OR COMEDY SPECIAL

☐ Eva Le Gallienne, *The Royal Family* (PBS)
Patty Duke Astin, *A Family Upside Down* (NBC)
Tyne Daly, *Intimate Strangers* (ABC)
Mariette Hartley, "The Last Hurrah," *Hallmark Hall of Fame* (NBC)
Cloris Leachman, *It Happened One Christmas* (ABC)
Viveca Lindfors, *A Question of Guilt* (CBS)

OUTSTANDING SINGLE PERFORMANCE BY A SUPPORTING ACTRESS IN A COMEDY OR DRAMA SERIES

☐ Blanche Baker, *Holocaust—Part I* (NBC)
Ellen Corby, "Grandma Comes Home," *The Waltons* (CBS)
Jeanette Nolan, *The Awakening Land—Part I* (NBC)
Beulah Quo, "Tz'u-Hsi, Becaria, De Sade," *Meeting of Minds* (PBS)
Beatrice Straight, *The Dain Curse—Part I* (CBS)

Prime Time Writing and Directing Awards

OUTSTANDING WRITING IN A COMEDY SERIES

☐ Bob Weiskopt, Bob Schiller (teleplay), Barry Harman, Harve Brosten (story), "Cousin Liz," *All in the Family* (CBS)

Alan Alda, "Fallen Idol," *M*A*S*H* (CBS)

Mel Tolkin, Larry Rhine (teleplay), Erik Tarloff (story), "Edith's Crisis Of Faith—Part II," *All in the Family* (CBS)

Bob Weiskopf, Bob Schiller, "Edith's 50th Birthday," *All in the Family* (CBS)

OUTSTANDING WRITING IN A DRAMA SERIES
☐ Gerald Green, *Holocaust* (NBC)
Steve Allen, *Meeting of Minds* (PBS)
Alan Ayckbourn, *The Norman Conquest* (PBS)
Robert W. Lenski, *The Dain Curse* (CBS)
Abby Mann, *King* (NBC)

OUTSTANDING WRITING IN A COMEDY-VARIETY OR MUSIC SERIES
☐ Ed Simmons, Roger Beatty, Rick Hawkins, Liz Sage, Robert Illes, James Stein, Franelle Silver, Larry Siegel, Tim Conway, Bill Richmond, Gene Perret, Dick Clair, Jenna McMahon, *The Carol Burnett Show* (with Steve Martin, Betty White) (CBS)
Jerry Juhl, Don Hinkley, Joseph Bailey, Jim Henson, *The Muppet Show* (with Dom De Luise) (Syndicated)
Alan Thicke, John Boni, Norman Stiles, Jeremy Stevens, Tom Moore, Robert Illes, James Downey, Brian Doyle-Murray, Al Franken, Lorne Michaels, Marilyn Suzanne Miller, Don Novello ,Michael O'Donoghue, Herb Sargent, Tom Schiller, Rosie Shuster, Alan Zweibel, *NBC's Saturday Night Live* (with Steve Martin) (NBC)

OUTSTANDING WRITING IN A COMEDY-VARIETY OR MUSIC SPECIAL
☐ Lorne Michaels, Paul Simon, Chevy Chase, Tom Davis, Al Franken, Charles Grodin, Lily Tomlin, Alan Zweibel, *The Paul Simon Special* (NBC)
Alan Buz Kohan, Rod Warren, Pat McCormick, Tom Eyen, Jerry Blatt, Bette Midler, Bruce Vilanch, *Bette Midler—Ol' Red Hair Is Back* (NBC)
Elon Packard, Fred Fox, Seaman Jacobs, *The George Burns One-Man Show* (CBS)
Ernest Chambers, Barry Manilow, *The Second Manilow Special* (ABC)
Michael H. Kagan, *The Sentry Collection Presents Ben Vereen— His Roots* (ABC)

☐ Indicates winner

OUTSTANDING WRITING IN A SPECIAL PROGRAM—DRAMA OR COMEDY—ORIGINAL TELEPLAY
☐ George Rubino, *The Last Tenant* (ABC)
Bruce Feldman, *The Defection of Simas Kudirka* (CBS)
Richard Levinson, William Link, *The Storyteller* (NBC)
Loring Mandel, *Breaking Up* (ABC)
Jerry McNeely, *Something for Joey* (CBS)
James Poe, *The Gathering* (ABC)

OUTSTANDING WRITING IN A SPECIAL PROGRAM—DRAMA OR COMEDY—ADAPTATION
☐ Caryl Ledner, *Mary White* (ABC)
Blanche Hanalis, *A Love Affair: The Eleanor and Lou Gehrig Story* (NBC)
Albert Innaurato, "Verna: USO Girl," *Great Performances* (PBS)
Jerome Lawrence, Robert E. Lee, *Actor* (PBS)
Barbara Turner, *The War Between The Tates* (NBC)

OUTSTANDING DIRECTING IN A COMEDY SERIES
☐ Paul Bogart, "Edith's 50th Birthday," *All in the Family* (CBS)
Hal Cooper, "Vivian's Decision," *Maude* (CBS)
Burt Metcalfe, Alan Alda, "Comrades In Arms—Part I *M*A*S*H* (CBS)
Jerry Paris, "Richie Almost Dies," *Happy Days* (ABC)
Jay Sandrich, *Soap*—#24 (ABC)

OUTSTANDING DIRECTING IN A DRAMA SERIES
☐ Marvin J. Chomsky, *Holocaust* (NBC)
Abby Mann, *King* (NBC)
Gary Nelson, *Washington: Behind Closed Doors* (ABC)
E. W. Swackhamer, *The Dain Curse* (CBS)
Herbert Wise, "I, Claudius," *Masterpiece Theatre* (PBS)

OUTSTANDING DIRECTING IN A SPECIAL PROGRAM—DRAMA OR COMEDY
☐ David Lowell Rich, *The Defection of Simas Kudirka* (CBS)
Lou Antonio, *Something For Joey* (CBS)
Randal Kleiser, *The Gathering* (ABC)
Delbert Mann, *Breaking Up* (ABC)
Ronald Maxwell, "Verna: USO Girl," *Great Performances* (PBS)
George Schaefer, "Our Town," *Bell System* (NBC)

OUTSTANDING DIRECTING IN A COMEDY-VARIETY OR MUSIC SERIES
☐ Dave Powers, *The Carol Burnett Show* (with Steve Martin, Betty White) (CBS)

Steve Binder, *Shields and Yarnell with John Aylesworth* (CBS)
Peter Harris, *The Muppet Show* (with Elton John) (Syndicated)
John C. Moffitt, *The Richard Pryer Show* (with Paul Kelly) (NBC)
Dave Wilson, *NBC's Saturday Night Live* (with Steve Martin) (NBC)

OUTSTANDING DIRECTING IN A COMEDY-VARIETY OR MUSIC SPECIAL
☐ Dwight Hemion, *The Sentry Collection Presents Ben Vereen—His Roots* (ABC)
Tony Charmoli, *Mitzi. . . Zings Into Spring* (CBS)
Walter C. Miller, *Doug Henning's World of Magic* (NBC)
George Schaefer, *The Second Barry Manilow Special* (ABC)
Dave Wilson, *The Paul Simon Special* (NBC)

Creative Arts Awards

OUTSTANDING ART DIRECTION FOR A COMEDY SERIES
☐ Edward Stephenson (production designer), Robert Checchi (set decorator), *Soap*—#1 (ABC)
Thomas E. Azzari, "In the Balck," *Hudson Street* (ABC)
Roy Christopher (art director), James Shanahan (art director), "Barbarino in Love—Part I," *Welcome Back, Kotter* (ABC)
Paul Sylos, Eugene H. Harris (art directors), Robert Signorellia, John McCarthy (set decorators), *The Love Boat* (ABC)
C. Murawski, "The Wake," *Maude* (CBS)

OUTSTANDING ART DIRECTION FOR A DRAMA SERIES
☐ Tim Harvey, "I, Claudius—Part 1," *Masterpiece Theatre* (PBS)
Jack De Shields (production designer), James F. Claytor (art director), Barbara Kreiger (set decorator), *Washington: Behing Closed Doors*—Episode #3 (ABC)
Derek Dodd, "Anna Karenina," *Masterpiece Theatre*—Episode #1 (PBS)
Wilfred J. Shingleton (production designer), Theo Harisch, Jurgen Kiebach (art directors), Maxi Hareiter (set decorator), *Holocaust* (NBC)

OUTSTANDING ART DIRECTION FOR A COMEDY-VARIETY OR MUSIC SERIES
☐ Roy Christopher, *The Richard Pryor Show* (NBC)
Paul Barnes, Bob Sansom (art directors), Bill Harp (set decorator),

The Carol Burnett Show (the final show) (CBS)

Bill Bohnert (art director), Arlene Alen (set decorator), *Donny and Marie* (opening show) (ABC)

Romain Johnston, *Captain and Tenille* (ABC)

Eugene Lee, Leo Yoshimura (art directors), Franne Lee, Lee Mayman (set decorator), *NBC's Saturday Night Live* (with Steve Martin) (NBC)

OUTSTANDING ART DIRECTION FOR A DRAMATIC SPECIAL

☐ John De Cuir (production designer), Richard C. Goddard (set decorator), *Ziegfeld: The Man and His Women* (NBC)

Roy Christopher (production designer), James Shanahan (set decorator), "Our Town," *Bell System* (NBC)

John J. Lloyd (art director), Hal Guasman (set decorator), *It Happened One Christmas* (ABC)

Loyd S. Papez (art director), Richard Friedman (set decorator), *The Bastard* (Syndicated)

Jan Scott (art director), Anne D. McCulley (set decorator), *The Gathering* (ABC)

OUTSTANDING ART DIRECTION FOR A COMEDY-VARIETY OR MUSIC SPECIAL

☐ Romain Johnston (art director), Kerry Joyce (set decorator), *The Sentry Collection Presents Ben Vereen— His Roots* (ABC)

Brian C. Bartholomew, *Cher. . . Special* (ABC)

Roy Christopher (art director), Don Remacle (set decorator), *How To survive the 70s and Maybe Even Bump Into Happiness* (CBS)

Romain Johnston, John Dapper (art directors), Robert Checci (set decorator), *They Said It With Music: Yankee Doodle to Ragtime* (CBS)

Robert Kelly, *Mitzi. . . Zings Into Spring* (CBS)

OUTSTANDING ACHIEVEMENT IN CHOREOGRAPHY

☐ Ron Field, *The Sentry Collection Presents Ben Vereen—His Roots* (ABC)

George Balanchine, Alexandra Danilova, "New York City Ballet: Coppelia," *Live From Lincoln Center* (PBS)

Tom Charmoli, *Mitzi. . . Zings Into Spring* (CBS)

Ernest O. Flatt, *The Carol Burnett Show* (the final show) (CBS)

Miriam Nelson, *Ziegfeld: The Man and His Woman* (NBC)

☐ Indicates winner

OUTSTANDING CINEMATOGRAPHY IN ENTERTAINMENT PROGRAMMING FOR A SERIES

☐ Ted Voigtlander, "The Fighter," *Little House on the Prairie* (NBC)

Lloyd Ahern, "The Inspector," "A Very Special Girl," "Until the Last Goodbye," *The Love Boat* (ABC)

Joseph Biroc, *Washington: Behind Closed Doors*—Part I (ABC)

Robert Hauser, *Roll of Thunder, Hear My Cry* (ABC)

Michel Hugo, *The Awakening Land* (NBC)

OUTSTANDING CINEMATOGRAPHY IN ENTERTAINMENT PROGRAMMING FOR A SPECIAL

☐ Gerald Perry Finnerman, *Ziegfeld: The Man and His Women* (NBC)

Joseph Biroc, *A Family Upside Down* (NBC)

Sol Negrin, *The Last Tenant* (ABC)

Howard Schwartz, *The Ghost of Flight 401* (NBC)

Richard Waite, *The Life and Assassination of The Kingfish* (NBC)

OUTSTANDING ACHIEVEMENT IN COSTUME DESIGN FOR A DRAMA OR COMEDY SERIES

☐ Peggy Farrell, Edith Almoslino, *Holocaust* (NBC)

Don Feld, "Anschluss '77," *The New Adventures of Wonder Woman* (CBS)

Grady Hunt, "The Emperor's Quasi Norms—Part II," *Quark* (NBC)

Bill Jobe, *Testimony of Two Men*—Part III (Syndicated)

Yvonne Wood, *79 Park Avenue* (NBC)

OUTSTANDING ACHIEVEMENT IN COSTUME DESIGN FOR MUSIC-VARIETY

☐ Bob Mackie, Ret Turner, *Mitzi. . . Zings Into Spring* (CBS)

David Doucette, *Dorothy Hamill Presents Winners* (ABC)

Bill Hargate, *Doug Henning's World of Magic* (NBC)

Warden Neil, *The John Davidson Christmas Special* (ABC)

Sandra Stewart, *Cindy* (ABC)

OUTSTANDING ACHIEVEMENT IN COSTUME DESIGN FOR A DRAMA SPECIAL

☐ Noel Taylor, *Actor* (PBS)

Jean-Pierre Dorleac, *The Bastard* (Syndicated)

Grady Hunt, *Ziegfeld: The Man and His Women* (NBC)

Bill Jobe, *The Dark Secret of Harvest Home* (NBC)

Olga Lehmann, "The Four Feathers," *Bell System* (NBC)

OUTSTANDING FILM EDITING IN A COMEDY SERIES

☐ Ed Cotter, "Richie Almost Dies," *Happy Days* (ABC)

M. Pam Blumenthal, "A Jackie Story," *The Bob Newhart Show* (CBS)

Stanford Tischler, Larry L. Mills, "Fade Out, Fade In," *M*A*S*H* (CBS)

Norman Wallerstein, Robert Moore, "Masquerade," "The Caper," "Eyes of Love," "Hollywood Royalty," *The Love Boat* (ABC)

OUTSTANDING FILM EDITING IN A DRAMA SERIES

☐ Stephen A. Rotter, Robert M. Reitano, Craig McKay, Alan Heim, Brian Smedley-Aston, *Holocaust* (NBC)

David G. Blangsted, Howard Terrill, "Yes, Nicholas, There Is a Santa Claus," *Eight Is Enough* (ABC)

Byron "Buzz" Brandt, Richard Meyer, David Berlatsky, *King* (NBC)

Jim Faris, "Acts of Love—Part 1," *Family* (ABC)

Bill Mosher, "Grandma Comes Home," *The Waltons* (CBS)

Robert Watts, "How To Dial a Murder," *Columbo* (NBC)

OUTSTANDING FILM EDITING FOR A SPECIAL

☐ John A. Martinelli, *The Defection of Simas Kudirka* (CBS)

Ronald J. Fagan, *Young Joe, The Forgotten Kennedy* (ABC)

Leslie L. Green, *Ziegfeld: The Man and His Women* (NBC)

Harry Kaye, Donald Rode, *To Kill a Cop* (NBC)

Kenneth R. Koch, *Mary Jame Harper Cried Last Night* (CBS)

Bernald J. Small, *Just a Little Inconvenience* (NBC)

Ken Zemke, *A Killing Affair* (CBS)

OUTSTANDING ACHIEVEMENT IN FILM EDITNG FOR A SERIES

☐ Douglas H. Grindstaff, Hank Salerno, Larry Singer, Christopher Chulack, Richard Raderman, Don Crosby, H. Lee Chaney, Mark Dennis, Don V. Isaacs, Steve Olson, Al Kajita, "River of Promises," *Police Story* (NBC)

Larry Carow, David Pettijohn, Don Warner, Colin Mouat, Chuck Moran, Pieter Hubbard, "The Hawk Field on Sunday," *Baa Baa Black Sheep/ Black Sheep Squadron* (NBC)

Tony Garber, Dale Johnston, Ron Clark, "Nazi," *Lou Grant* (CBS)

Douglas H. Grindstaff, Larry Singer, Hank Salerno, Christopher Chulack, Luke Wolfram, Al Kajita, Dwayne Avery, Richard Friedman, Don V. Isaacs, "Racer and Lady of the Evening," *Fantasy Island* (ABC)

William Stevenson, Richard Raderman, *Roll of Thunder, Hear My Cry* (ABC)

OUTSTANDING ACHIEVEMENT IN FILM SOUND EDITING FOR A SPECIAL

☐ Jerry Rosenthal, Michael Corrigan, Jerry Pirozzi, William Jackson, James Yant, Richard LeGrand, Donald Higgins, John Strauss, John Kline, *The Amazing Howard Hughes* (CBS)

Douglas H. Grindstaff, H. Lee Chaney, Don V. Isaacs, Larry Kaufman, Steve Olson, Don Crosby, Al Kajita, Bob Human, Hank Salerno, Larry Singer, "The Last Hurrah," *Hallmark Hall of Fame* (NBC)

Douglas H. Grindstaff, Hank Salerno, Larry Singer, Christopher Chulack, Mark Dennis, Don Crosby, H. Lee Chaney, Don V. Isaacs, *To Kill a Cop*—Part I (NBC)

Don Hall, Dwayne Avery, Tom Burke, Chick Camera, *Standing Tall* (NBC)

Bernard F. Pincus, Patrick R. Somerset, Jeffrey Bushelman, A. Jeremy Hoenarc, John Bushelman, Edward L. Sandlin, Robert A. Biggart, Jerry Rosenthal, *The Dark Secret of Harvest Home* (NBC)

Don Warner, Larry Carow, Colin Mouat, David Pettijohn, Gary Vaughan, Chuck Moran, Pieter Hubbard, Fred Stafford, *Tarantulas: The Deadly Cargo* (CBS)

OUTSTANDING ACHIEVEMENT IN FILM SOUND MIXING

☐ William Teague, George E. Porter, Eddie J. Nelson, Robert L. Harman, *Young Joe, The Forgotten Kennedy* (ABC)

Alan Bernard, George E. Porter, Eddie J. Nelson, Hoppy Mehterian, *Having Babies II* (ABC)

Eddie Knowles, George E. Porter, Eddie J. Nelson, J. Robert Pettis, *Tarantulas: The Deadly Cargo* (CBS)

Hoppy Mehterian, George E. Porter, Eddie J. Nelson, Dean Hodges, *A Sensitive, Passionate Man* (NBC)

J. Robert Pettis, George E. Porter, Eddie J. Nelson, Cabell Smith, *See How She Runs* (CBS)

Tommy Thompson, George E. Porter, Eddie J. Nelson, Hoppy Mehterian, *In the Matter Of Karen Ann Quinlan* (NBC)

OUTSTANDING ACHIEVEMENT IN GRAPHIC DESIGN AND TITLE SEQUENCES

☐ Bill Davis, *NBC: The First Fifty Years—A Closer Look* (NBC)

Eytan Keller, Stewart Bernstein, *50th Annual Awards of the Academy of Motion Pictures Arts and Sciences* (ABC)

Maury Nemoy, Robert Branham, John De Cuir, *Ziegfeld: The Man and His Women* (NBC)

Phill Norman, *Washington: Behind Close Doors* (ABC)

OUTSTANDING ACHIEVEMENT IN LIGHTING DIRECTION

☐ Greg Brunton, *Cher. . . Special* (ABC)

Leard Davis, (lighting designer), Ken Dettling (lighting director), "You Can Run, But You Can't Hide," *Visions* (PBS)

Imero Fiorentino, *The Neil Diamond Special: I'm Glad You're Here With Me Tonight* (NBC)

Fred McKinnon, Carl J. Vitelli, Jr., *Happy Brithday, Las Vegas* (ABC)

Alan K. Walker, Bill Klages, *Olivia* (ABC)

George Riesenberger, "The Great Trolley Strike of 1895," *Best of Families* (PBS)

OUTSTANDING ACHIEVEMENT IN MAKE-UP

☐ Richard Cobos, Walter Schenck, *How the West Was Won*—Part I (ABC)

Hank Edds, Allan "Whitey" Snyder, "The Fighter," *Little House on the Prairie* (NBC)

Christina Smith, *King* (NBC)

Frank C. Westmore, Michael G. Westmore, *A Love Affair: The Eleanor and Lou Gehrig Story* (NBC)

Michael G. Westmore, Hank Edds, Lynn Reynolds, *The Amazing Howard Hughes* (CBS)

OUTSTANDING ACHIEVEMENT IN MUSIC COMPOSITION FOR A SERIES (DRAMATIC UNDERSCORE)

☐ Billy Goldenberg, *King* (NBC)

Morton Gould, *Holocaust* (NBC)

Fred Karlin, *The Awakening Land* (NBC)

Morton Stevens, *Wheels* (NBC)

Patrick Williams, "Try and Catch Me," *Columbo* (NBC)

OUTSTANDING ACHIEVEMENT IN MUSIC COMPOSITION FOR A SPECIAL (DRAMATIC UNDERSCORE)

☐ Jimmie Haskell, *See How She Runs* (CBS)

Dick De Benedictis, *Ziegfeld: The Man and His Women* (NBC)

Bill Goldenberg, *Actor* (PBS)

David Shire, *The Defection of Simas Kudirka* (CBS)

OUTSTANDING ACHIEVEMENT IN MUSIC DIRECTION

☐ Ian Fraser, *The Sentry Collection Presents Ben Vereen—His Roots* (ABC)

Jimmie Haskell, *The Second Barry Manilow Special* (ABC)

Zubin Mehta, *The New York Philharmonic/Mehta, Live From Lincoln Center* (PBS)

Andred Previn, "The Music That Made The Movies," *Previn and The Pittsburgh* (PBS)

OUTSTANDING ACHIEVEMENT IN SPECIAL MUSICAL MATERIAL

☐ Stan Freeman, Arthur Malvin (music and lyrics) for the Mini Musical "Hi-Hat," *The Carol Burnett Show* (CBS)

☐ Mitzie Welch, Ken Welch (music and lyrics) for the song "See You Tomorrow In Class," *The Sentry Collection Presents Ben Vereen—His Roots* (ABC)

Earl Brown for the Song "Leading Lady," *The Donny and Marie Show* (ABC)

Bill Dyer, (lyrics), Dick De Benedictis (music) for the song "Until the Music Ends," *Ziegfeld: The Man and His Women* (NBC)

Kenyon Emrys-Roberts, for the Poldark Theme, "Poldark," *Masterpiece Theatre* (PBS)

OUTSTANDING ACHIEVEMENT IN TAPE SOUND MIXING

☐ Thomas J. Huth, Edward J. Green, Ron Bryan, *Bette Midler—Ol' Red Hair Is Back* (NBC)

Ron Estes, "Our Town," *Bell System* (NBC)

Philip J. Seretti, Bob Gaudio, Val Garay, Rick Ruggieri, John Walker, *The Neil Diamond Special: I'm Glad You're Here with Me Tonight* (NBC)

Larry Stephens, Thomas J. Huth, Ron Bryan, Eric Levinson, Grover Helsley, *Perry Como's Easter By the Sea* (ABC)

Dick Wilson, *The Lawrence Welk Show* (with Roger Williams) (Syndicated)

OUTSTANDING ACHIEVEMENT IN TECHNICAL DIRECTION AND ELECTRONIC CAMERAWORK

☐ Gene Crowe, (technical director), Wayne Orr, Larry Heider, Dave Hilmer, Bob Keys (cameramen), *The Sentry Collection Presents Ben Vereen—His Roots* (ABC)

Charles Franklin, Steve Cunningham, Harry Tatarian, Mark Miller (technical directors), Gorman Erickson, John Aguirre, Stanley Zitnick, David Finch, Richard Nelson, Hector Ramirez, Louis Shore, Ben Wolf, Thomas Brown, Grodon Sweeney, Robert Welsh, Brian Cunneen (cameramen), *CBS: On the Air* (CBS)

Louis Fusari (technical director), Rodger Harbaugh, Roy Holm, Rick Lombardoo, Peggy Mahoney

☐ Indicates winner

(cameramen), *Mitzi. . . What's Hot, What's Not* (CBS)

Karl Messerschmidt (technical director), Jon Olson, Mike Stramisky, George Loomis, George Falardeau, Mike Higuera, Jim Dodge (cameramen), *Doug Hennings' World of Magic* (NBC)

O. Tamburri (technical director), Jon Olson, Roy Holm, Reed Howard (cameramen), "Our Town," *Bell System* (NBC)

OUTSTANDING ACHIEVEMENT IN VIDEO TAPE EDITING FOR A SERIES

☐ Tucker Wiard, *The Carol Burnett Show* (the final show) (CBS)

Gary H. Anderson, *Soap*, Episode #2 (ABC)

Ed J. Brennan, *Laugh-In*, Show #6 (NBC)

Chip Brooks, *The Berry White Show* (pilot) (CBS)

Jerry Davis, "Chrissy, Come Home," *Three's Company* (ABC)

Marco Zappia, "The One Where Everybody Is Looking For a Little Action," *Husbands, Wives & Lovers* (CBS)

OUTSTANDING ACHIEVEMENT IN VIDEO TAPE EDITING FOR A SPECIAL

☐ Pam Marshall, Andy Zall, *The Sentry Collection Presents Ben Vereen— His Roots* (ABC)

Ed J. Brennan, *The Goldie Hawn Special* (CBS)

Chip Brooks, Hal Collins, *Texaco Presents Bob Hope in a Very Special Special—On the Road with Bing* (NBC)

Jimmy B. Frazier, *The Carpenters— Space Encounters* (ABC)

Marco Zappia, Terry Greene, Harvey Berger, Jimmy F. Fizier, *Superstunt* (NBC)

OUTSTANDING INDIVIDUAL ACHIEVEMENT IN ANY AREA OF CREATIVE TECHNICAL CRAFTS*

☐ William F. Bronwell, John H. Kantrowe Jr. (sound effects), "Our Town," *Bell System* (NBC)

Sugar Blymer (haristylist), *The Awakening Land—Part III* (NBC)

Larry Germain, Gladys Witten (hairstylists), "Here Comes the Brides," *Little House on the Prairie* (NBC)

Mark Schubin (technical director), *Live From Lincoln Center* (PBS)

Frank Van Der Veer (optical effects), L.B. Abbott (special photographic

---

effects), *The Return on Captain Nemo* (CBS)

SPECIAL CLASSIFICATION OF OUTSTANDING INDIVIDUAL ACHIEVEMENT*

☐ William Pitkin (costume design), *Romeo and Juliet* (PBS)

Mikhail Baryshnikov (dancer), *The Nutcracker* (CBS)

William T. Cartwright (film editor), Jeffrey Weston (film editor), *Oscar Presents the War Movies and John Wayne* (ABC)

Jan Scott (production designer), Earl Carlson (set decorator), *CBS: On the Air* (CBS)

OUTSTANDING INDIVIDUAL ACHIEVEMENT IN CHILDREN'S PROGRAMMING*

☐ Ken Johnson (art director), Robert Checchi (set decorator), *Once Upon a Brothers Grimm* (CBS)

☐ Bill Hargate (costume designer), *Once Upon a Brothers Grimm* (CBS)

Jerry Greene (video tape editor), *Once Upon a Brothers Grimm* (CBS)

Nicholas Spies, Robert Millslagle (video tape editors), *A Connecticut Yankee In King Arthur's Court* (PBS)

Tommy Cole, Larry Abbott, Michael G. Westmore (make-up), *Once Upon a Brothers Grimm* (CBS)

OUTSTANDING ACHIEVEMENT IN COVERAGE OF SPECIAL EVENTS— INDIVIDUALS*

Rodger Harbaugh (aerial photography), *The 29th Annual Emmy Awards Show* (NBC)

William W. Landers (technical direction and electronic camerawork), *The 29th Annual Emmy Awards Show* (NBC)

Alan Buz Kohan (music), *50th Annual Awards of the Academy of Motion Picture Arts and Sciences*, for the opening production number, "Look How Far We've Come" (ABC)

Clark Jones (director), *Footlights: The 1978 Tony Awards* (CBS)

OUTSTANDING ACHIEVEMENT IN BROADCAST JOURNALISM

☐ Charles Kuralt, "On the Road," *CBS News*

☐ Bill Moyer, *CBS Reports*

☐ *The Fire Next Door*, *CBS Reports*

☐ *Exploding Gas Tanks*, *20/20*

OUTSTANDING ACHIEVEMENT IN ENGINEERING DEVELOPMENT

☐ Petro Vlahos of Vlahos-Gottschalk Research Corporation for the invention and development of the ULTIMATTE video-matting device.

Citation to Society of Motion Picture and Television Engineers for expeditiously achieveing the difficult

---

task of obtaining industry agreement on the ONe-Inch Type C Continuous Field Helical Recording Standards.

GOVERNORS AWARDS

☐ *Larry Stewart*, President of ATAS, 1975–1977

☐ *William S. Paley*, Chairman of the Board, (CBS)

☐ *Frederick Wolcott*, for his 30 years of service on the ATAS Engineering Awards Panel.

Daytime Awards

OUTSTANDING DAYTIME DRAMA SERIES

Emmy(s) to executive producer(s) and producer(s):
All My Children (producers), Bud Klossand Anges Nixon (ABC)

☐ *Days of Our Lives*, Betty Corday and H. Wesley Kenny (executive producers), Jack Herzberg (producer) (NBC)

Ryan's Hope, Claire Labine and Paul Avila Mayer (executive producers), Robert Costello (producer) (ABC)

The Young and the Restless, John Conboy (executive producer), Patricia Wenig (producer) (CBS)

OUTSTANDING GAME OR AUDIENCE PARTICIPATION SHOW

Emmy(s) to executive producer(s) and producer(s):
Family Feud, Howard Felsher (producer) (ABC)

☐ *Hollywood Squares*, Merrill Heatter and Bob Quigley (executive producers), Jay Redack (producer) (NBC)

The $20,000 Pyramid, Bob Stewart (executive producer), Ann Marie Schmitt (producer) (ABC)

OUTSTANDING TALK, SERVICE OR VARIETY SERIES

Emmy(s) to executive producer(s) and producer(s):
Dinah!, Henry Jaffe (executive producer), Fred Tatashore (producer) (Syndicated)

Merv Griffin Show, Bob Murphy (producer) (Syndicated)

The Mike Douglas Show, Frank Miller (executive producer), Brad Lachman (producer) (Syndicated)

☐ *Donahue*, Richard Mincer (executive producer), Patricia McMillen (producer) (Syndicated)

OUTSTANDING ACTOR IN A DAYTIME DRAMA SERIES

Matthew Cowles, *All My Children* (ABC)

Larry Keith, *All My Children* (ABC)

Michael Levin, *Ryan's Hope* (ABC)

☐ James Pritchett, *The Doctors* (NBC)

Andrew Robinson, *Ryan's Hope* (ABC)

---

* possibility of one award, more than one award or no award

☐ Indicates winner

Michael Storm, *One Life to Live* (ABC)

OUTSTANDING ACTRESS IN A DAYTIME SERIES

Mary Fickett, *All My Children* (ABC)
Susan Seaforth Hayes, *Days of Our Lives* (NBC)
Jennifer Harmon, *One Life to Live* (ABC)
☐ Laurie Heineman, *Another World* (NBC)
Susan Lucci, *All My Children* (ABC)
Beverlee McKinsey, *Another World* (NBC)
Victoria Wyndham, *Another World* (NBC)

OUTSTANDING HOST OR HOSTESS IN A GAME OR AUDIENCE PARTICIPATION SHOW

Dick Clark, *The $20,000 Pyramid* (ABC)
☐ Richard Dawson, *Family Feud* (ABC)
Gene Rayburn, *Match Game* (CBS)
Chuck Woolery, Host; Susan Stafford, Hostess, *Wheel of Fortune* (NBC)

OUTSTANDING HOST OR HOSTESS IN A TALK, SERVICE OR VARIETY SERIES

James Crockett, *Crockett's Victory Garden* (PBS)
☐ Phil Donahue, *Donahue* (Syndicated)
Jim Nabors, *The Jim Nabors Show* (Syndicated)
Dinah Shore, *Dinah!* (Syndicated)

OUTSTANDING INDIVIDUAL DIRECTOR FOR A DAYTIME DRAMA SERIES

For a single episode:
Ira Cirker, *Another World*, December 20, 1977 (NBC)
☐ Richard Dunlap, *The Young and the Restless*, March 3, 1978 (CBS)
Richard T. McCue, *As the World Turns*, March 15, 1977 (CBS)
Robert Myhrum, *Love of Live*, August 31, 1977 (CBS)
Al Rabin, *Days of Our Lives* ("Julie's Rape"), February 21, 1978 (NBC)
Lela Swift, *Ryan's Hope*, November 3, 1977 (ABC)

OUTSTANDING INDIVIDUAL DIRECTOR FOR A DAYTIME GAME OR AUDIENCE PARTICIPATION SHOW

For a single episode:
Paul Alter, *Family Feud* ("Valentine's Day Celebration Special"), February 14, 1978 (ABC)
☐ Mike Gargiulo, *The $20,000 Pyramid*, June 20, 1977 (ABC)

☐ Indicates winner

OUTSTANDING INDIVIDUAL DIRECTOR FOR A VARIETY PROGRAM

For a single episode:
Donald R. King, *The Mike Douglas Show*, "Mike in Hollywood," February 9, 1978 (Syndicated)
☐ Martin Haig Mackey, *Over Easy*, March 20, 1978 (PBS)
Glen Swanson, *Dinah!*, "(Dinah Salutes Philadelphia"), February 28, 1978 (Syndicated)

OUTSTANDING WRITING FOR A DAYTIME DRAMA SERIES

For a single episode of a series or for the entire series:
William J. Bell, Kay Lenard, Bill Rega, Pat Falken Smith, Margaret Stewart, *Days of Our Lives*, April 18, 1977 (NBC)
Jerome and Bridget Dobson, Nancy Ford, Jean Ruverol, Robert and Phyllis White, *The Guiding Light* (CBS)
☐ Claire Labine, Paul Avila Mayer, Mary Munisteri, Allan Leicht, Judith Pinsker, *Ryan's Hope* (ABC)
Agnes Nixon, Cathy Chicos, Doris Frankel, Ken Harvey, Kathryn McCabe, Wisner Washam, Mary K. Wells, Jack Wood, *All My Children* (ABC)
Ann Marcus, Ray Goldstone, Joyce Perry, Michael Robert David, Laura Olsher, Rocci Chatfield, Elizabeth Harrower, *Days of Our Lives* (NBC)

OUTSTANDING CHILDREN'S ENTERTAINMENT SPECIAL

Emmy(s) to executive producer(s) and producer(s):
"A Piece of Cake", *Special Treat*, Marilyn Olin and Lee Polk (producers) (NBC)
☐ "Hewitt's Just Different," *ABC Afterschool Special*, Daniel Wilson (executive producer, Fran Sears (producer) (ABC)
"How the Beatles Changed the World," *Special Treat*, Charles E. Andrews and Ken Greengrass (executive producers) (NBC)
"I Can," *The Winners*, Robert Guenette (executive producer), Paul Asselin and Diane Asselin (producers) (CBS)
"Journey Together," *The Winners*, Robert Guenette (executive producer), Paul Asselin and Diane Asselin (producers) (CBS)
"Man From Nowhere," *Once upon a Classic*, George Gallicco (executive producer), Jay Rayvid (producer) (PBS)
"The Pinballs," *ABC Afterschool Special*, Martin Tahse (producer) (ABC)

OUTSTANDING CHILDREN'S ENTERTAINMENT SERIES

Emmy(s) to executive producer(s) and producer(s):
☐ *Captain Kangaroo*, Jim Hirschfeld (producer) (CBS)
"Robin Hood," *Once upon a Classic*, George Gallicco (executive producer), Jay Rayvid (producer) (PBS)
Zoom, Terri Payne Francis (producer), Bob Glover, Janet Weaver (producers) (PBS)

OUTSTANDING CHILDREN'S INFORMATIONAL SERIES

Emmy(s) to executive producer(s) and producer(s):
ABC Minute Magazine, Tom Wolf (executive producer) (ABC)
☐ *Animals Animals Animals*, Lester Cooper (executive producer), Peter Weinberg (producer) (ABC)
Villa Alegre, Claudio Guzman (executive producer), Larry Gotlieb (producer) (PBS)

OUTSTANDING CHILDREN'S INFORMATIONAL SPECIAL

Emmy(s) to executive producer(s) and producer(s):
"Henry Winkler Meets William Shakespeare," *Festival of Lively Arts for Young People*, Daniel Wilson (producer) (CBS)
☐ "Very Good Friends," *ABC Afterschool Special*, Martin Tahse (producer) (ABC)

OUTSTANDING CHILDREN'S INSTRUCTIONAL SERIES

Emmy(s) to executive producer(s) and producer(s):
☐ *Schoolhouse Rock*, Tom Yohe (executive producer), Radford Stone, George Newall (producers) (ABC)
Sesame Street, Al Hyslop (producer) (PBS)

OUTSTANDING ACHIEVEMENT IN RELIGIOUS PROGRAMMING

An award for program—series and specials. (possibility of one award, more than one award or no award):
Directions Series, Sid Darion (executive producer) (ABC)
Francis of Assisi: A Search for the Man and His Meaning, Doris Ann (executive producer), Martin Hoade (producer), December 11, 1977 (NBC)
Woman of Valor, Doris Ann (executive producer), Martin Hoade (producer) March 20, 1977 (NBC)

SPECIAL CLASSIFICATION OF OUTSTANDING PROGRAM ACHIEVEMENT

An award for unique program achievements that do not fall into a specific category or are not otherwise recognized.

(Possibility of one award, more than one award or no award):

Camera Three, John Musilli (executive producer), John Musilli, Roger Englander (producers) (CBS)

Good Morning America Series, Woody Fraser (executive producer), George Merlis, Merrill Mazuer, Bob Blum (producers) (ABC)

☐ *Live from Lincoln Center: Recital of Tenor Luciano Pavarotti from the Met*, John Goberman (executive producer) (PBS)

Mutual of Omaha's Wild Kingdom, Don Meier (executive producer) (Syndicated)

OUTSTANDING ACHIEVEMENT IN COVERAGE OF SPECIAL EVENTS

An award for program and individual achievements. A special event is a single program presented as live coverage; i.e., parades, pageants, awards presentations, salutes and coverage of other live events that were not covered by the news division.

(Possibility of one award, more than one award or no award):

All-American Thanksgiving Day Parade, Mike Gargiulo (executive producer), Vern Diamond, Clarence Schimmel, Jim Hirschfeld, Wilfred Fielding and Malachy Wienges (producers), November 24, 1977 (CBS)

Tournament of Roses Parade and Pageant, Mike Gargiulo (executive producer), Vern Diamond (producer), January 2, 1978 (CBS)

Fourth Annual Daytime Emmy Awards, Walter Miller (producer), May 12, 1977 (NBC)

Macy's 51st Annual Thanksgiving Day Parade, Dick Schneider (producer), November 24, 1977 (NBC)

☐ *The Great English Garden Party—Peter Ustinov Looks at 100 Years of Wimbledon*, Ken Ashton, Allison Hawkes and Pamela Moncur (producers), June 18, 1977 (NBC)

OUTSTANDING INDIVIDUAL ACHIEVEMENT IN CHILDREN'S PROGRAMMING

For a single episode of a series or for a special program.

☐ Indicates winner

(Possibility of one award, more than one award or no award):

☐ Tom Aldredge (Role: William Shakespeare), "Henry Winkler Meets William Shakespeare," *CBS Festival of Lively Arts for Young People*, March 20, 1977 (CBS)

Frank Cady (Role: Mr. Minney), "The Winged Colt," *ABC Weekend Specials*, September 10, 1977 (ABC)

Jack Elam (Role: Sam), "The Ransom of Red Chief," *ABC Weekend Specials*, October 22, 1977 (ABC)

Al Freeman Jr. (Role: Jerry Hudson), "A Piece of Cake," *Special Treat*, October 11, 1977 (NBC)

"The Muppets" (Performers: Jim Henson, Richard Hunt, Jenny Nelson, Frank Oz, Carroll Spinney), *Sesame Street*, January 16, 1978 (PBS)

Strother Martin (Role: Billy), "The Ransom of Red Chief," *ABC Weekend Special*, October 22, 1977 (ABC)

Slim Pickens (Role: Uncle Coot), "The Winged Colt," *ABC Weekend Specials*, September 10, 1977 (ABC)

Robert Behrens (director), *Kidsworld*, November 19, 1977 (Syndicated)

Nicholas J. De Noia (director), "The Magic Hat," *Unicorn Tales*, December 5, 1977 (Syndicated)

Arthur Nadel (director), "Life Begins at 300," *Space Academy*, November 12, 1977 (CBS)

Richard Slote (director), "The Cruise of the Courageous," *The Winners*, February 9, 1978 (CBS)

James G. Stewart (director), "Maro and the Magic Movie Machine," December 25, 1977 (Syndicated)

Alistair Bell (writer), "Robin Hood," Episode 1, *Once upon a Classic*, October 6, 1977 (PBS)

Mark Fink (writer), "Soup and Me," *ABC Weekend Specials*, February 4, 1978 (ABC)

☐ Jan Hartman (writer), "Hewitt's Just Different," *ABC Weekend Specials*, October 12, 1977 (ABC)

Jim Inman (writer), "The Winged Colt," *ABC Weekend Specials*," September 10, 1977 (ABC)

☐ David Wolf (writer), "The Magic Hat," *Unicorn Tales*, December 5, 1977 (Syndicated)

Ronald Baldwin (art director), "Marlo and the Magic Movie Machine," April 3, 1977 (Syndicated)

Michael Baugh (art director), "Parenting for All," *Villa Alegre*, November 12, 1977 (PBS)

Ray Markham (art director), "The Winged Colt," *ABC Weekend Specials*, September 10, 1977 (ABC)

Robert F. Brunner (music composition and direction), Bruce Belland (Lyricist), *The New Mickey Mouse Club*, May 11, 1977 (Syndicated)

Hod David (music composition), "Very Good Friends," *ABC Afterschool Specials*, April 6, 1977 (ABC)

Jack Feldman, Bruce H. Sussman (music composition), "The Magic Hat," *Unicorn Tales*, December 5, 1977 (Syndicated)

Carole M. Carter (costume design), "The Pinballs," *ABC Afterschool Specials*, May 18, 1977 (ABC)

Jeffrey Ullman, Helen Butler (costume design), "Big Apple Birthday," *Unicorn Tales*, February 7, 1978 (NBC)

Bob Mills (makeup), "The Winged Colt," *ABC Weekend Specials*, September 10, 1977 (ABC)

Monty Westmore (makeup), "The Ransom of Red Chief," *ABC Weekend Specials*, October 22, 1977 (ABC)

Nils Johnson (technical director), Howard Smith, Tore Askeland, Tom Lang (cameramen), "Marlo and the Magic Movie Machine," December 25, 1977 (Syndicated)

☐ Tony Di Girolamo (lighting director), "Henry Winkler Meets William Shakespeare," *CBS Festival of Lively Arts for Young People*, March 20, 1978 (CBS)

George Reisenberger (lighting director), "Hawaii Remote," *Sesame Street*, January 18, 1978 (Syndicated)

Mike Elliot (film editor), "It Isn't Easy Being a Teenage Millionaire," *ABC Afterschool Special*, March 8, 1978 (ABC)

Vince Humphrey (film editor), "Very Good Friends," *ABC Afterschool Special*, April 6, 1977 (ABC)

☐ Bonnie Karrin (film editor), "Big Apple Birthday," *Unicorn Tales*, February 7, 1978 (Syndicated)

Phillip Kellison (film editor), "The Winged Colt," *ABC Weekend Special*, September 10, 1977 (ABC)

Peter Parasheles (film editor), "The Winged Colt," *ABC Weekend Specials*, September 10, 1977 (ABC)

Clay Rawson, Tom Schachte, Dave Sherwin, Joy I. Stephens, Chris Stock, Robert Behrens, (film editors), *Kidsworld*, November 19, 1977 (Syndicated)

Bruce Bisenz (film sound editor), "The Pinballs," *ABC Afterschool Special*, May 18, 1977 (ABC)

John Christophel (film Sound Editor), "Marlo and the Magic Movie Machine," December 25, 1977 (Syndicated)

Bob Behrens (videotape editor), *Kidsworld*, November 19, 1977 (Syndicated)

Girish Bhargava, Al Mueller (videotape editors), *The National Kids' Quiz*, January 28, 1978 (NBC)

Marty Krofft, Sid Krofft, Ben Boyle (graphic design and title sequence), *Krofft Supershow*, September 10, 1977 (ABC)

Rick Reinert (graphic design and title sequence), "The Winged Colt," *ABC Weekend Specials*, September 10, 1977 (ABC)

Bob Collins (cinematographer), "The Pinballs," *ABC Afterschool Specials*, May 18, 1977 (ABC)

Elmer Cossey (cinematographer), "Robin Hood," Episode 3, *Once upon a Classic*, October 20, 1977 (PBS)

John R Hill (cinematographer) "Zoom", February 13, 1978 (PBS)

Henry Johnson (cinematographer), *Zoom*, February 12, 1977 (PBS)

Ken Lamkin (cinematographer), "Mobile Maidens," *The Winners*, November 10, 1977 (CBS)

William Markle (cinematographer), "The Stowaway," *Unicorn Tales*," November 22, 1977 (Syndicated)

□ Brianne Murphy (cinematographer), "Five Finger Discount," *Special Treat*, November 1, 1977 (NBC)

Otto Nemenz (cinematographer), "The Winged Colt," *ABC Weekend Specials*, September 10, 1977 (ABC)

Al Niggemeyer (cinematographer), "It Isn't Easy Being a Teenage Millionaire," *ABC Afterschool Specials*, March 8, 1978 (ABC)

Don Herbert (cinematographer), *Mr. Wizard Close-Ups* (NBC)

OUTSTANDING INDIVIDUAL ACHIEVEMENT IN DAYTIME PROGRAMMING

For a single episode of a series: or for a special program.

(Possibility of one award, more than one award or no award):

Charles Brandon (scenic designer), Robert Hoppe (assistant scenic designer), *One Life to Live*, March 22, 1978 (ABC)

Sy Tomashoff (scenic designer), *Ryan's Hope*, March 15, 1978 (ABC)

Elmon Webb (art director), *The Doctors* ("Fire at Andres' "), February 21, 1978 (NBC)

Milton Delugg (music composition/direction), *Gong Show*, March 9, 1978 (NBC)

John Geller (music director), *The Doctors*, February 14, 1978 (NBC)

□ Indicates winner

James Reichert (music composition/direction), *All My Children*, January 31, 1978 (ABC)

Jack Urbont (music composition), *One Life to Live*, November 17, 1977 (ABC)

Sybil Weinberger (music director), *Ryan's Hope*, December 16, 1977 (ABC)

Doreen Ackerman (costume design), *The Edge of Night*, January 20, 1978 (ABC)

Joseph Markham (costume design), *Days of Our Lives*, March 3, 1978 (NBC)

□ Connie Wexler (costume design), *Search for Tomorrow*, February 14, 1978 (CBS)

Mark R. Bussan (makeup), *The Young and the Restless*, May 2, 1977 (CBS)

Andrew Eger, Irene B. Hamalain (makeup), *The Edge of Night*, March 6, 1978 (ABC)

Lee Halls, Sheila King (makeup), *Love of Life*, December 30, 1977 (CBS)

Frank Bianco (hair design), *Search for Tomorrow*, February 11, 1978 (CBS)

Nick Troiano (hair design), *Love of Life*, December 30, 1977 (CBS)

Clive Basset (technical director), Keith Lawrence, Ed Chaney, Toby Brown, Glen Swanson (cameramen), *Dinah!* ("Dinah Salutes Philadelphia"), February 28, 1978 (Syndicated)

□ Steve Cunningham (technical director), Hector Ramirez, Sheldon Mooney, Martin Wagner, Dave Finch (cameramen), *After Hours: Singin', Swingin' & All That Jazz*, December 6, 1977 (CBS)

□ Steve Cunningham (technical director), Fred Gough, Mike Stitch, Joe Vicens (cameramen), *The Young and the Restless*, March 3, 1978 (CBS)

Wally Stanard (technical director), Charles Barrett, Barry Kirstein, Luis Rojas, Bill McCloud, Dale Walsh, Joe Tolasi (cameramen), *Family Feud*, ("Valentine's Day Special"), February 14, 1978 (ABC)

Jay Adams (lighting director), *Family Feud*, ("Valentine's Day Special"), February 14, 1978 (ABC)

□ David M. Clark (lighting director), *The Mike Douglas Show* (The New York Remotes), November 8, 1977 (Syndicated)

Ronald R. Holden, Thomas Markel, John Zak (lighting director), *General Hospital*, March 10, 1978 (ABC)

Jonathan M. Lory, Frances Gertler (tape sound mixing), *Ryan's Hope*, December 1, 1977 (ABC)

Terry Ross (tape sound mixing), *Ryan's Hope*, December 15, 1977 (ABC)

Jean L. Dadario, Roger Haenelt, Nathan Rogers (videotape editing), *All My Children*, March 17, 1978 (ABC)

□ Joyce Tamara Grossman (videotape editing), *Family Feud*, ("Valentine's Day Special"), February 14, 1978 (ABC)

Brian McCullough (videotape editing), *The Doctors*, March 21, 1978 (NBC)

Lou Dorfsman, Vahe Kirishjian, Frank Guido (graphic design and title sequences), *Love of Life*, August 19, 1977 (CBS)

Donald Spagnolia, Jim House (design and title sequences), *The Mike Douglas Show*, January 30, 1978 (Syndicated)

OUTSTANDING INDIVIDUAL ACHIEVEMENT IN RELIGIOUS PROGRAMMING

For a single episode of a series or for a special program.

(Possibility of one award, more than one award, or no award):

□ Carolee Campbell (performer), *This Is My Son*, June 19, 1977 (NBC)

Edward Power (performer), "Lost, One Modern Prophet," *This Is the Life*, September 18, 1977 (Syndicated)

Carol Tzitel (performer), *Woman of Valor*, March 20, 1977 (NBC)

□ Douglass Watson (performer), *Continuing Creation*, February 19, 1978 (NBC)

Martin Hoade (director), *Woman of Valor*, March 20, 1977 (NBC)

Lynwood King (director), *This Is My Son*, June 19, 1977 (NBC)

Ken Lamkin (director), "All the Days of My life," *This Is the Life*, September 25, 1977 (Syndicated)

Marc Siegel (writer), "The Panama Canal—A Test of Conscience," *Directions Series*, April 3, 1977 (ABC)

Richard Wendley (writer), "All the Days of My Life," *This Is the Life*, October 25, 1977 (Syndicated)

Fred Luff (art direction), *Oral Roberts and You*, February 5, 1978 (Syndicated)

George Maly (film sound editor), "All the Days of My Life," *This Is the Life*, September 25, 1977 (Syndicated)

Janet Riley (film sound editor), "Lost, One Modern Prophet," *This Is the Life*, September 18, 1977 (Syndicated)

□ Joseph Vadala (cinematographer), *Continuing Creation*, February 19, 1978 (NBC)

Ken Lamkin (cinematographer), "Lost, One Modern Prophet," *This Is the*

Life, September 18, 1977
(Syndicated)

SPECIAL CLASSIFICATION OF OUTSTANDING INDIVIDUAL ACHIEVEMENT

An award for unique individual achievement that does not fall into a specific category or is not otherwise recognized.

(Possibility of one award, more than one award or no award):

Dick Clark (host), *American Bandstand*, October 8, 1977 (ABC)

Paul Lynde (panelist), *Hollywood Squares*, December 16, 1977 (NBC)

Victoria Mallory (singer), *After Hours*, "Singin', Swingin', and All That Jazz," December 6, 1977 (CBS)

Dick Chapin, Jim Fuller Jr., Mark Maxwell-Smith, R. Patrick Neary (writers), *Knockout*, March 10, 1978 (NBC)

Harry Friedman, Gary Johnson, Philip Kellard, Jay Redack, Brian Pollack, Justin Antonow, Steve Kreinberg (writers), *Hollywood Squares*, November 10, 1977 (NBC)

Phil Black (choreographer), "The Stowaway," *Unicorn Tales*, November 22, 1977 (NBC)

John Musilli (director), "BeauBourg," *Camera Three*, November 13, 1977 (CBS)

OUTSTANDING ACHIEVEMENT IN ANY AREA OF CREATIVE TECHNICAL CRAFTS

An award for individual technical craft achievement that does not fall into a specific category and is not otherwise recognized.

(Possibility of one award, more than one award or no award):

Caroly Wilcox, Kermit Love, John Lovelady, Donald Sahlin costumes and props for "The Muppets," *Sesame Street* (PBS)

Sports Programming Awards

OUTSTANDING LIVE SPORTS SPECIALS

Emmy(s) to executive producer(s) and producer(s):

1977 League Championship Series—American and National Leagues, Scotty Connal (executive producer), Roy Hammerman, George Finkel and Mike Weisman (producers), October 4–9, 1977 (NBC)

Masters Golf Tournament, Frank Chirkinian (producer), April 8–9, 1977 (CBS)

NCAA Basketball Championship Game, Don Ohlmeyer (executive

☐ Indicates winner

producer), George Finkel (producer), March 27, 1978 (NBC)

Superbowl XII, Robert Stenner (producer), January 15, 1978 (CBS)

U.S. Open Tennis Championships, Frank Chirkinian (executive producer), Bernie Hoffman (producer), September 3, 4, 5, 10, 11, 1977 (CBS)

☐ *World Championship Boxing* (Ali/Spinks), Frank Chirkinian (producer), February 15, 1978 (CBS)

OUTSTANDING LIVE SPORTS SERIES

Emmy(s) to executive producer(s) and producer(s):

Major League Baseball: Game of the Week, Scotty Connal (executive producer), Jim Marooney, David Stern, Larry Cirillo, Mike Weisman, Roy Hammerman and George Finkel (producers) (NBC)

NCAA Basketball, Don Ohlmeyer (executive producer), David Stern, Dick Auerback, Jim Marooney, George Finkel, Roy Hammerman and Mike Weisman (producers) (NBC)

NFL Football, Scotty Connal (executive producer), Jim Marooney, David Stern, Ken Edmondson, Sam Kirschman, Larry Cirillo, Mike Weisman, Roy Hammerman, George Finkel and Dick Auerback (producers) (NBC)

☐ *The NFL Today/NFL Football on CBS*, Michael Pearl (producer) (CBS)

OUTSTANDING EDITED SPORTS SPECIAL

Emmy(s) to executive producer(s) and producer(s):

The Baseball World of Joe Garagiola, Joe Garagiola (executive producer), Ginny Seipt (producer), July 19, 1977 (NBC)

☐ *The Impossible Dream: Ballooning Across the Atlantic*, Ed Goren (producer), February 5, 1978 (CBS)

Target: New Orleans, ("NFL Preview '77"), Michael Pearl (producer), August 28, 1977 (CBS)

OUTSTANDING EDITED SPORTS SERIES

Emmy(s) to executive producer(s) and producer(s):

CBS Sports Spectacular, Ed Goren (producer) (CBS)

Soccer Made in Germany, Joerg Klebe (executive producer), Christian Viertel (producer) (PBS)

Sportsworld, Don Ohlmeyer (executive producer), Don Ellis (coordinating producer), Larry Cirillo, Peter Diamond, Les Dennis, Ken Edmundson, Chris Glidden, Linda

Jonsson, Rex Lardner Jr., Jim Marooney, Don McGuire, Ginny Seipt, David Stern, Mike Weisman, Dick Auerback, Geoff Mason, Ted Nathanson, John Kerwin, George Finkel, Ed Connel, Bill Sheehan, Peter Bonventre and Bud Greenspan (producers) (NBC)

☐ *The Way It Was*, Gerry Gross (executive producer), Gary Brown and Dick Enberg (producers) (Syndicated)

OUTSTANDING SPORTS PERSONALITY

Dick Enberg (NBC)

Al McGuire (NBC)

Brent Musburger (CBS)

Vince Scully (CBS)

Pat Summerall (CBS)

☐ Jack Whitaker (CBS)

OUTSTANDING DIRECTING IN SPORTS PROGRAMMING

Frank Chirkinian, *World Championship Boxing*, (Ali/Spinks), February 15, 1978 (CBS)

Harry Coyle, *NCAA College Basketball Championships*, March 27, 1978 (NBC)

☐ Ted Nathanson, *AFC Championship Football*, December 24, 1977 (NBC)

Tony Verna, *Superbowl XII*, January 15, 1978 (CBS)

OUTSTANDING INDIVIDUAL ACHIEVEMENT IN SPORTS PROGRAMMING

The following are "Areas," where there is a possibility of one award, more than one award or no award:

Writing

☐ Steve Sabol, "Joe and the Magic Bean: The Story of Superbowl III" (segment of *NFL Today*), December 1977 (CBS)

Cinematrography

Joe Jay Jalbert and Kim Takal, "Aerial Acrobatic Sking Championship" (segment of *Sportsworld*), March 26, 1978 (NBC)

☐ Steve Sabol, "Skateboard Fever," *Sportsworld*), Febrrary 1978 (NBC)

Barry Winik, *Downhill Skiing*, February 12, 1978 (NBC)

Film editing

Joe Jay Jalbert and Kim Takal, "Aerial Acrobatic Skiing Championship" (segment of *Sportsworld*, March 26, 1978 (NBC)

Yale Nelson, *Downhill Skiing*, February 12, 1978 (NBC)

☐ Steve Sabol, "Skateboard Fever," (*Sportsworld*), February 1978 (NBC)

Norm Smith, *The Impossible Dream: Ballooning Across the Atlantic*, February 5, 1978 (CBS)

Engineering supervision/Technical direction/Electronic camerawork
James Martens (engineering supervisor), Robert Brown (technical director), *The NFL Today* Series (CBS)
☐ Arthur Tinn (engineering supervisor), *The Superbowl Today/Superbowl XII*, January 15, 1978 (CBS)
William Tobey (technical director), Phil Cantrell, Roger Habaugh, Buddy Joseph, Bill Landers, George Loomis, Donald J. Mulvaney, Roy V. Ratliff and Mike Stramisky (electronic cameramen), *American League Championship, 5th Game—Yankees at Kansas City*, October 8, 1977 (NBC)

Videotape editing (includes associate directors)
☐ Bob Levy (associate director), Jerome Haggart, Richard Leible, Charles Liotta and John Olszewski (videotape editors), *Sportsworld* Series (NBC)
Joe Bill Worthington (videotape editor), *Colgate Triple Crown LPGA Match Play Championships*, January 29, 1978 (PBS)

Art direction/Scenic design and graphic design/Title sequences
Neil DeLuca (scenic designer), *NFL Today*, Series (CBS)
☐ Matthew F. McCarthy and Peter Caesar (graphic designers), *Sportsworld*, Series (NBC)

SPECIAL AWARDS

National Award for Community Service:
Volunteer-a-Thon, (WRAL-TV, Raleigh, North Carolina)
Hot Spot: A Report On Rocky Flats, (KMGH-TV, Denver, Colorado)
Bubble Gum Digest, (WMAQ-TV, Chicago, Illinois)
One Man's Strugle, (WBAL-TV, Baltimore, Maryland)
Misery, Money and Whitewash, (KBTV, Denver, Colorado)
CO-OP Conspiracy: Pyramid of Shame, (KTVI-TV, St. Louis, Missouri)
Dying to Grow Up, (WCVB-TV, Needham, Massachusetts)
☐ *Water*, (KOOL-TV, Phoenix, Arizona)

Outstanding Achievement in the Science of Television Engineering:
CBS, Inc.
PBS Engineering
Thomson–CSF Laboratories
☐ Indicates winner

1978/79

(For programs aired between July 1, 1978 to June 30, 1979. Entertainment program and individual achievement awards presented September 9, 1979. Creative Arts awards presented September 8, 1979. Daytime awards presented May 17, 1979 for programs aired between March 22, 1978 and March 5, 1979. Science of Television Engineering Award presented September 17, 1979. Sports awards presented March 4, 1980.)

Prime Time Program Awards

OUTSTANDING COMEDY SERIES
☐ *Taxi* (ABC)
Mork & Mindy (ABC)
*M*A*S*H* (CBS)
Barney Miller (CBS)
All in the Family (CBS)

OUTSTANDING COMEDY-VARIETY OR MUSIC PROGRAM
☐ *Steve & Eydie Celebrate Irving Berlin* (NBC)
Shirley MacLaine at the Lido (CBS)
NBC's Saturday Night Live (NBC)
The Muppet Show (Syndicated)
Arthur Fiedler: Just Call Me Maestro (PBS)

OUTSTANDING DRAMA SERIES
☐ *Lou Grant* (CBS)
The Rockford Files (NBC)
The Paper Chase (CBS)

OUTSTANDING LIMITED SERIES
☐ *Roots: The Next Generations* (ABC)
Blind Ambition (CBS)
Backstairs at the White House (NBC)

OUTSTANDING DRAMA OR COMEDY SPECIAL
☐ *Friendly Fire* (ABC)
Summer of My German Soldier (NBC)
The Jericho Mile (ABC)
First You Cry (CBS)
Dummy (CBS)

OUTSTANDING INFORMATIONAL PROGRAM
Scared Straight! (Syndicated)
Who are the DeBolts—And Where Did They Get 19 Kids? (ABC)
The Body Human: The Sexes (CBS)

OUTSTANDING CLASSICAL PROGRAM IN THE PERFORMING ARTS
☐ "Balanchine IV," *Dance in America, Great Performances* (PBS)
Live From Lincoln Center (with Luciano Pavarotti and Joan Sutherland) (PBS)
Live From Lincoln Center: The American Ballet Theatre: The Sleeping Beauty (PBS)
Giulini's Beethoven's 9th Live—A Gift From Los Angeles (PBS)
"Balanchine III," *Dance in America, Great Performances* (PBS)

OUTSTANDING ANIMATED PROGRAM*
☐ *The Lion, The Witch and the Wardrobe* (CBS)
You're the Greatest, Charlie Brown (CBS)
Happy Birthday, Charlie Brown (CBS)

OUTSTANDING CHILDREN'S PROGRAM*
☐ *Christmas Eve on Sesame Street* (PBS)
Once Upon a Classic (PBS)
Benji's Very Own Christmas Story (ABC)
A Special Sesame Street Christmas (CBS)

OUTSTANDING PROGRAM ACHIEVEMENT—SPECIAL EVENTS*
☐ *51st Annual Awards Presentation of the Academy of Motion Picture Arts and Sciences* (ABC)
Good Luck Tonight—The 1979 Tony Awards (CBS)
Baryshnikov At the White House (PBS)

OUTSTANDING PROGRAM ACHIEVEMENT—SPECIAL CLASS*
☐ *The Tonight Show Starring Johnny Carson* (NBC)
☐ *Lifeline* (NBC)
Steve Allen's Meeting of Minds (PBS)
The Dick Cavett Show (PBS)

Prime Time Performing Awards

OUTSTANDING SUPPORTING ACTRESS IN A COMEDY OR COMEDY-VARIETY OR MUSIC SERIES
☐ Sally Struthers, "California Here We Are," *All in the Family* (CBS)
Polly Holliday, *Alice* (CBS)
Marion Ross, *Happy Days* (ABC)
Loretta Swit, *M*A*S*H* (CBS)

OUTSTANDING SUPPORTING ACTOR IN A COMEDY OR COMEDY-VARIETY OR MUSIC SERIES
☐ Robert Guillaume, *Soap* (ABC)
Gary Burghoff, *M*A*S*H* (CBS)
Danny De Vito, *Taxi* (ABC)
Max Gail, *Barney Miller* (ABC)
Harry Morgan, *M*A*S*H* (CBS)

OUTSTANDING SUPPORTING ACTRESS IN A DRAMA SERIES
☐ Kristy McNichol, *Family* (ABC)

* possibility of one award, more than one award or no award

Linda Kelsey, *Lou Grant* (CBS)
Nancy Marchand, *Lou Grant* (CBS)

OUTSTANDING SUPPORTING ACTOR IN A DRAMA SERIES

☐ Stuart Margolin, *The Rockford Files* (NBC)
Mason Adams, *Lou Grant* (CBS)
Noah Berry, *The Rockford Files* (NBC)
Joe Santos, *The Rockford Files* (NBC)
Robert Walden, *Lou Grant* (CBS)

OUTSTANDING SUPPORTING ACTRESS IN A LIMITED SERIES OR A SPECIAL

☐ Esther Rolle, *Summer of My German Solider* (NBC)
Ruby Dee, *Roots: The Next Generations* (ABC)
Colleen Dewhurst, *Silent Victory: The Kitty O'Neil Story* (CBS)
Eileen Heckart, *Backstairs at the White House* (NBC)
Celeste Holm, *Backstairs at the White House* (NBC)

OUTSTANDING SUPPORTING ACTOR IN A LIMITED SERIES OR A SPECIAL

☐ Marlon Brando, *Roots: The Next Generations*—Episode 7 (ABC)
Ed Flanders, *Backstairs at the White House*—Book Two (NBC)
Al Freeman Jr., *Roots: The Next Generations*—Episode 7 (ABC)
Robert Vaughn, *Backstairs at the White House*—Book One (NBC)
Paul Winfield, *Roots: The Next Generations*—Episode 5 (ABC)

OUTSTANDING LEAD ACTRESS IN A COMEDY SERIES

☐ Ruth Gordon, "Sugar Mama," *Taxi* (ABC)
Katherine Helmond, *Soap* (ABC)
Linda Lavin, *Alice* (CBS)
Isabel Sanford, *The Jeffersons* (CBS)
Jean Stapleton, *All in the Family* (CBS)

OUTSTANDING LEAD ACTOR IN A COMEDY SERIES

☐ Carroll O'Connor, *All in the Family* (CBS)
Alan Alda, *M*A*S*H* (CBS)
Judd Hirsch, *Taxi* (ABC)
Hal Linden, *Barney Miller* (ABC)
Robin Williams, *Mork & Mindy* (ABC)

OUTSTANDING LEAD ACTRESS IN A DRAMA SERIES

☐ Mariette Hartley, "Married," *The Incredible Hulk* (CBS)
Barbara Bel Geddes, *Dallas* (CBS)
Rita Moreno, "Rosendahl and Gilda Stern Are Dead," *The Rockford Files* (NBC)
Sada Thompson, *Family* (ABC)

☐ Indicates winner

OUTSTANDING LEAD ACTOR IN A DRAMA SERIES

☐ Ron Leibman, *Kaz* (CBS)
Ed Asner, *Lou Grant* (CBS)
James Garner, *The Rockford Files* (NBC)
Jack Klugman, *Quincy, M.E.* (NBC)

OUTSTANDING LEAD ACTRESS IN A LIMITED SERIES OR A SPECIAL

☐ Bette Davis, *Strangers: The Story of a Mother and Daughter* (CBS)
Carol Burnett, *Friendly Fire* (ABC)
Olivia Cole, *Backstairs at the White House* (NBC)
Katharine Hepburn, *The Corn Is Green* (CBS)
Mary Tyler Moore, *First You Cry* (CBS)

OUTSTANDING LEAD ACTOR IN A LIMITED SERIES OR A SPECIAL

☐ Peter Strauss, *The Jericho Mile* (NBC)
Ned Beatty, *Friendly Fire* (ABC)
Louis Gosset Jr., *Backstairs at the White House* (NBC)
Kurt Russell, *Elvis* (ABC)

Prime Time Writing and Directing Awards

OUTSTANDING DIRECTING IN A COMEDY OR COMEDY-VARIETY OR MUSIC SERIES

☐ Noam Pitlik, "The Harris Incident," *Barney Miller* (ABC)
Alan Alda, "Dear Sis," *M*A*S*H* (CBS)
Paul Bogart, "California Here We Are—Part II," *All in the Family* (CBS)
Charles Dubin, "Point of View," *M*A*S*H* (CBS)
Jay Sandrich, *Soap*—Episode 27 (ABC)

OUTSTANDING DIRECTING IN A DRAMA SERIES

☐ Jackie Cooper, *The White Shadow* (pilot) (CBS)
Burt Brinckerhoff, "Schools," *Lou Grant* (CBS)
Mel Damski, "Murder," *Lou Grant* (CBS)
Gene Reynolds, "Prisoner," *Lou Grant* (CBS)

OUTSTANDING DIRECTING IN A LIMITED SERIES OR A SPECIAL

☐ David Greene, *Friendly Fire* (ABC)
Lou Antonio, *Silent Victory: The Kitty O'Neil Story* (CBS)
Glenn Jordan, *Les Miserables* (CBS)

OUTSTANDING WRITING IN A COMEDY OR COMEDY-VARIETY OR MUSIC SERIES

☐ Alan Alda, "Inga," *M*A*S*H* (CBS)
Dan Aykroyd, Anne Beatts, Tom Davis, James Downey, Brain Doyle-Murry, Al Franken, Brian McConnachie,

Lorne Michaels, Don Novello, Herb Sargent, Tom Schiller, Rosie Shuster, Walter Williams, Alan Zweibel, *NBC's Saturday Night Live* (with Richard Benjamin) (NBC)
Milt Josefsberg, Phil Sharp, Bob Schiller, Bob Weiskopt, "California Here We Are—Part Two," *All in the Family* (CBS)
Michael Leeson, "Blind Date," *Taxi* (ABC)
Ken Livine and David Isaacs, "Point of View," *M*A*S*H* (CBS)

OUTSTANDING WRITING IN A DRAMA SERIES

☐ Michele Gallery, "Dying," *Lou Grant* (CBS)
Jim Bridges, "The Late Mr. Hart," *The Paper Chase* (CBS)
Gene Reynolds, "Marathon," *Lou Grant* (CBS)
Leon Tokatyan, "Vet," *Lou Grant* (CBS)

OUTSTANDING WRITING IN A LIMITED SERIES OR A SPECIAL

☐ Patrick Nolan, Michael Mann, *The Jericho Mile* (ABC)
Gwen Bagni, Paul Dubov, *Backstairs at the White House*—Book One (NBC)
Jane Howard Hammerstein, *Summer of My German Solider* (NBC)
Fay Kanin, *Friendly Fire* (ABC)
Ernest Kinoy, *Roots: The Next Generations*—Episode 1 (ABC)

Special Individual Achievement Awards

OUTSTANDING INDIVIDUAL ACHIEVEMENT—ANIMATION PROGRAM*

Bill Melendez, David Connell (writers), *The Lion, the Witch and the Wardrobe* (CBS)

OUTSTANDING INDIVIDUAL ACHIEVEMENT—INFORMATIONAL PROGRAM* * possibility of one award, more than one award or no award

☐ John Korty (director), *Who Are the DeBolts—And Where Did They Get 19 Kids?* (ABC)
Arnold Shapiro (writer), *Scared Straight!* (Syndicated)

OUTSTANDING INDIVIDUAL ACHIEVEMENT—SPECIAL EVENTS* * possibility of one award, more than one award or no award

☐ Mikhail Baryshnikov, *Baryshnikov At the White House* (PBS)

A SPECIAL PRESENTATION

☐ Milton Berle, "Mr. Television"

* possibility of one award, more than one award or no award

SECOND ANNUAL ATAS GOVERNORS AWARD
Walter Cronkite

ACADEMY TRIBUTE TO
Don Harris, Robert Brown, Bill Stewart, news broadcasters who lost their lives in Guyana and Nicaragua

Creative Arts Awards

OUTSTANDING ACHIEVEMENT IN ENGINEERING DEVELOPMENT
☐ *Ampex Corp.* for the development of their Automatic Scan Tracking system for helical video tape equipment.

OUTSTANDING ART DIRECTION FOR A SERIES
☐ Howard E. Johnson (art director), Richard B. Goddard (set decorator), *Little Women*—Part I (NBC)
John E. Chilberg II (art director), "Saga of a Star World," *Battlestar Galactica* (ABC)
Rene Lagler (art director), Earl Carlson (set decorator), *The Mary Tyler Moore Hour* (with Gene Kelly) (CBS)

OUTSTANDING ART DIRECTION FOR A LIMITED SERIES OR A SPECIAL
☐ Jan Scott (art director and production designer), Bill Harp (set decorator), *Studs Lonigan*—Part III (NBC)
Michael Baugh (art director), Robert Checchi (set decorator), Arthur Jeph Parker (set decorator), *Blind Ambition*—Part 3 (CBS)
Richard Y. Haman (art director), Anne D. McCulley (set decorator), *Backstairs At the White House*—Book One (NBC)
Jan Scott (art director and production designer), Edward J. McDonald (set decorator), *Studs Lonigan*—Part I (NBC)
Jack Senter (production designer), John W. Corso (art director), Sherman Lourdermilk (art director), Joseph J. Stone (set decorator), John M. Dwyer (set decorator), Robert G. Freer (set decorator), "The Shepherds," *Centennial* (NBC)

OUTSTANDING ACHIEVEMENT IN CHOREOGRAPHY
☐ Kevin Carlisle, *The 3rd Barry Manilow Special* (ABC)
Martha Graham, "The Martha Graham Dance Company: Clytemnestra," *Dance In America, Great Performances* (PBS)
Anita Mann, *The Muppets Go Hollywood* (CBS)

☐ Indicates winner

OUTSTANDING CINEMATOGRAPHY FOR A SERIES
☐ Ted Voigtlander, "The Craftsman," *Little House on the Prairie* (NBC)
Joseph Biroc, *Little Women*—Part II (NBC)
William W. Spencer, "Memory of a Nightmare," *Barnaby Jones* (CBS)

OUTSTANDING CINEMATOGRAPHY FOR A LIMITED SERIES OR A SPECIAL
☐ Howard Schwartz, *Rainbow* (NBC)
Arch R. Dalzell, Freddie Young, *Ike*—Part II (ABC)
Dennis Dalzell, *The Winds of Kitty Hawk* (NBC)
Donald M. Morgan, *Elvis* (ABC)

OUTSTANDING COSTUME DESIGN FOR A SERIES
☐ Jean-Pierre Dorleac, "Furlon," *Battlestar Galactica* (ABC)
Alfred E. Lehamn, "The Third Annual Shotz Talent Show," *Laverne & Shirley* (ABC)

OUTSTANDING COSTUME DESIGN FOR A LIMITED SERIES OR A SPECIAL
☐ Ann Hollowood, Sue Le Cash, Christine Wilson, "King At Last," *Edward the King* (Syndicated)
Bob Mackie, Ret Turner, *Cher. . . And Other Fantasies* (NBC)
Warden Neil, *The John Davidson Christmas Show* (ABC)
David Walker, *The Corn Is Green* (CBS)

OUTSTANDING FILM EDITING FOR A SERIES
☐ M. Pam Blumenthal, "Paper Marriage," *Taxi* (ABC)
Fred W. Berger, "Reunion—Part II," *Dallas* (CBS)
James Galloway, "Hooker," *Lou Grant* (CBS)
Larry L. Mills, Stanford Tischler, "The Billfold Syndrome," *M*A*S*H* (CBS)

OUTSTANDING FILM EDITING FOR A LIMITED SERIES OR A SPECIAL
☐ Arthur Schmidt, *The Jericho Mile* (NBC)
James Galloway, *First You Cry* (CBS)
John A. Martinelli, *The Winds of Kitty Hawk* (NBC)
Robert Watts, "Only the Rocks Live Forever," *Centennial* (CBS)
John M. Woodcock, Bill Lenny, Paul Dixon, *Ike*—Part III (ABC)

OUTSTANDING ACHIEVEMENTS IN FILM SOUND EDITING
☐ William H. Wistrom, *Friendly Fire* (ABC)
Douglas H. Grindstaff, Don Isaacs, Mark Dennis, Bob Human, Larry

Kaufman, Larry Singer, Hank Salerno, *A Fire in the Sky* (NBC)
Lawrence E. Neiman, Charles L. Campbell, Colin Nouat, Don Warner, David Pettijohn, Pieter S. Hubbard, Gary Vaughan, Charles E. Moran, Bob Canton, Martin Varno, *The Triangle Factory Fire Scandal* (NBC)
Michael Redbourn, Peter Harrison, Russ Tinsley, Linda Dove, Leonard Corso, *Ike*—Part II (ABC)

OUTSTANDING ACHIEVEMENT IN FILM SOUND MIXING
☐ Bill Teague, George E. Porter, Eddie J. Nelson, Ray West, *The Winds of Kitty Hawk* (NBC)
Stanley P. Gordon, George E. Porter, Eddie J. Nelson, Hoppy Mehterian, *A Christmas to Remember* (CBS)
George E. Porter, Eddie J. Nelson, Ray West, Maury Harris, *The Triangle Factory Fire Scandal* (NBC)
Bill Teague, George E. Porter, Eddie J. Nelson, Hoppy Mehterian, *Ike*—Part II (ABC)

OUTSTANDING ACHIEVEMENT IN GRAPHIC DESIGN AND TITLE SEQUENCES
☐ Stu Bernstein, Eytan Keller, *Cinderella at the Palace* (CBS)
Phill Norman, "Centerfold," *Vega$* (ABC)

OUTSTANDING ACHIEVEMENT IN LIGHTING DIRECTION (ELECTRONIC)
☐ George Riesenberger (lighting consultant & designer), Roy A. Barnett (director of photography), *You Can't Take It With You* (CBS)
William M. Klages, George Riesenberger, *A Salute to American Imagination* (CBS)
William Knight, "The Homecoming," *Mourning Becomes Electra, Great Performances* (PBS)
Fred McKinnon, *Cinderella at the Palace* (CBS)

OUTSTANDING ACHIEVEMENT IN MAKEUP
☐ Tommy Cole, Mark Bussan, Ron Walters, *Backstairs at the White House*—Book Four (NBC)
Ken Chase (makeup artist), Joe DiBella (makeup artist), Zoltan Elek (makeup artist), Tom Miller (makeup artist), David Dittmar (makeup artist), *Roots: The Next Generations*—Episode 3 (ABC)
Leo L. Lotito, Jr., Nick Pagliaro, *Lady of the House* (NBC)
Marvin G. Westmore, *Elvis* (ABC)

OUTSTANDING ACHIEVEMENT IN HAIRSTYLING
☐ Janice D. Brandow, *The Triangle Factory Fire Scandal* (NBC)

Susan Germaine, Lola Kemp, Vivian McAteer, *Backstairs at the White House*—Book Four (NBC)

Jean Burt Reilly, *Ike*—Part III (ABC)

OUTSTANDING MUSIC COMPOSITION FOR A SERIES

☐ David Rose, "The Craftsman," *Little House on the Prairie* (NBC)

Dick DeBenedictis, Dean DeBenedicitis, *Dear Detective* (CBS)

Charles Fox, Norman Gimbel (lyrics), "A Day in the Life," *The Paper Chase* (CBS)

Patrick Williams, "Prisoner," *Lou Grant* (CBS)

OUTSTANDING MUSIC COMPOSITION FOR A LIMITED SERIES OR A SPECIAL

☐ Leonard Rosenman, *Friendly Fire* (ABC)

Peter Matz, *First You Cry* (CBS)

Alex North, *The Word* (CBS)

Ken Welch, Mitzie Welch, *The Hal Linden Special* (ABC)

OUTSTANDING ACHIEVEMENT IN TAPE SOUND MIXING

☐ Ed Greene, Phillip J. Seretti, Dennis S. Sands, Garry Ylmer, *Steve & Edyie Celebrate Irving Berlin* (NBC)

Ed Greene, *The Muppets Go Hollywood* (CBS)

Gordon Klimuck, Tom Huth, *Perry Como's Early American Christmas* (ABC)

Doug Nelson, *The 3rd Barry Manilow Special* (ABC)

Georja Skinner, Phillip J. Seretti, "Return Engagement," *Hallmark Hall of Fame* (NBC)

OUTSTANDING ACHIEVEMENT IN TECHNICAL DIRECTION AND ELECTRONIC CAMERAWORK

☐ Jerry Weiss (technical director), Don Barker, Peggy Mahoney, Reed Howard, Jurt Tonnessen, William Landers, Louis Cywinski, George Loomis, Brian Sherriffe (camerapersons), *Dick Clark's Live Wednesday*—Show # 1 (NBC)

Robert G. Holmes (technical director), Bruce Bottone, Jim Herring, Royden Holm, Bill Landers, Peggy Mahoney (camerapersons), *The Midnight Special* (with Dolly Parton) (NBC)

Robert C. Jones (technical director), Barry A. Brown, Larry Heider, Wayne Orr, Hank Geving, Dianne Biederbeck, Richard Price, Tom Karnowski, Dave Levisohn (camerapersons), *You Can't Take It With You* (CBS)

Heino Ripp (technical director), Al Camoin, Peter Basil, Tom De Zendorf, John Pinto, Vine Di Pietro

☐ Indicates winner

(camerapersons), *NBC's Saturday Night Live* (with Richard Benjamin) (NBC)

OUTSTANDING VIDEO TAPE EDITING FOR A SERIES

☐ Andy Zall, *Stockard Channing In Just Friends* (pilot) (CBS)

Hal Collins, Harvey Berger, *The 200th Episode Celebration of All in the Family* (CBS)

OUTSTANDING VIDEO TAPE EDITING FOR A LIMITED SERIES OR A SPECIAL

☐ Ken Denisoff, Tucker Wiard, Janet McFadden, *The Scarlett Letter*—Part Two (PBS)

Darryl Sutton, *The Muppets Go Hollywood* (CBS)

Andy Zall, *Cheryl Ladd Special* (ABC)

Marco Zappia, *Liberace—A Valentine Special* (CBS)

OUTSTANDING INDIVIDUAL ACHIEVEMENT—ANIMATION PROGRAM*

Johnny Bradford (lyrics), Doug Goodwin (music), *A Pink Christmas*, main title song (ABC)

Doug Goodwin (music & lyrics), *A Pink Christmas* (songs) (ABC)

Peter Yarrow and David Campell (music and lyrics), *Puff the Magic Dragon* (CBS)

OUTSTANDING INDIVIDUAL ACHIEVEMENT—CHILDREN'S PROGRAM

☐ Gerri Brioso (graphic artist), *Christmas Eve on Sesame Street* (PBS)

Tony Di Girolamo (lighting director), Dave Clark (lighting director), *Christmas Eve on Sesame Street* (PBS)

OUTSTANDING INDIVIDUAL ACHIEVEMENT—CREATIVE TECHNICAL CRAFTS

☐ John Dykstra (special effects coordinator), Richard Edlund (director of miniature photography), Joseph Goss (mechanical special effects), "Saga Of a Star World," *Battlestar Galactica* (ABC)

☐ Tom Ancell (live stereo sound mixing), *Giulini's Beethoven's 9th Live—A Gift From Los Angeles* (PBS)

Joe Unsinn (special effects, explosion and destruction, pyrotechnical work) *A Fire in the Sky* (NBC)

Dick Wilson (sound effects), "Barbarino's Baby," *Welcome Back Kotter* (ABC)

* possibility of one award, more than one award or no award

OUTSTANDING INDIVIDUAL ACHIEVEMENT—INFORMATION PROGRAM

☐ Robert Niemack (film editor), *Scared Straight!* (Syndicated)

OUTSTANDING INDIVIDUAL ACHIEVEMENT—SPECIAL CLASS

Harry Blake, Bob Ostermann, David A. Dittmar (makeup artists), *General Electric's All-Star Anniversary* (ABC)

William M. Klages (lighting director), *Rockette: A Tribute to Radio City Music Hall* (NBC)

Carl Vitelli (lighting director), *A Gift of Song—The Music for UNICEF Special* (NBC)

Dave Clark (lighting designer), Michael Rosatti, Harry Bottorf (lighting directors), *Baryshnikov at the White House* (PBS)

David W. Foster, Eddie C. Joseph (videotape editors), *The Television Annual: 1978/79* (ABC)

OUTSTANDING INDIVIDUAL ACHIEVEMENT—SPECIAL EVENTS

Michael L. Wenig, Terry Pickford (videotape editors), *51st Annual Awards Presentation of the Academy of Motion Picture Arts and Sciences* (ABC)

Roy Christopher (art director), *51st Annual Awards Presentation of the Academy of Motion Picture Arts and Sciences* (ABC)

Daytime Awards

OUTSTANDING DAYTIME DRAMA SERIES

Emmy(s) to executive producer(s) and producer(s):

All My Children, Agnes Nixon (executive producer), Bud Kloss (producer) (ABC)

Days of Our Lives, Betty Corday and H. Wesley Kenney (executive producers), Jack Herzberg (producer) (NBC)

☐ *Ryan's Hope*, Claire Labine and Paul Avila Mayer (executive producers), Ellen Barrett and Robert Costello (producers) (ABC)

The Young and the Restless, John Conboy (executive producer), Ed Scott (producer) (CBS)

OUTSTANDING GAME OR AUDIENCE PARTICIPATION SHOW

Emmy(s) to executive producer(s) and producer(s):

Family Feud, Mark Goodson and Bill Todman (executive producers), Howard Felsher (producer) (ABC)

☐ *Hollywood Squares*, Merrill Heatter and Bob Quigley (executive producers), Jay Redack (producer) (NBC)

The $20,000 Pyramid, Bob Stewart (executive producer), Anne Marie Schmitt (producer) (ABC)

OUTSTANDING TALK, SERVICE OR VARIETY SERIES

Emmy(s) to executive producer(s) and producer(s):

Dinah!, Henry Jaffe (executive producer), Fred Tatashore (producer) (Syndicated)

☐ *Donahue*, Richard Mincer (executive producer), Patricia McMillen (producer) (Syndicated)

Good Morning America, George Merlis (senior producer), Jack Reilly, Sonya Selby-Wright and John Kippycash (producers) (ABC)

Mike Douglas Show, Frank R. Miller (executive producer), Vince Calandra and E. V. DiMassa Jr. (producers) (Syndicated)

OUTSTANDING CHILDREN'S ENTERTAINMENT SERIES

Emmy(s) to executive producer(s) and producer(s):

Captain Kangaroo, Joel Kosofsky and Frank Alesia (producers) (CBS)

John Halifax: Gentleman, "Once upon a Classic," Jay Rayvid (executive producer), John McRae and James A. DeVinney (producer) (ABC)

☐ *Kids Are People Too*, Lawrence Einhorn (producer) (ABC)

Lorna Doone, "Once upon a Classic," Jay Rayvid (executive producer), Barry Letts and Shep Greene (producers) (PBS)

The Secret Garden, "Once upon a Classic," Jay Rayvid (executive producer), Dorothea Brooking and James A. DeVinney (producers) (PBS)

OUTSTANDING CHILDREN'S ENTERTAINMENT SPECIAL

Emmy(s) to executive producer(s) and producer(s):

Joey and Redhawk (December 4–8, 1978), Daniel Wilson (executive producer), Fran Sears (producer) (CBS)

"Make Believe Marriage," *ABC Afterschool Special*, February 14, 1979, Linda Gottlieb (executive producer), Evelyn Barron (producer) (ABC)

"Mom and Dad Can't Hear Me," *ABC Afterschool Special*, April 4, 1978, Daniel Wilson (executive producer), Fran Sears (producer) (ABC)

"New York City Too Far From Tamps Blues," *Special Treat*, February 20, 1979, Daniel Wilson (executive producer), Linda Marmelstein and Phyllis Minoff (producers) (NBC)

☐ Indicates winner

"Rodeo Red and the Runaway," *Special Treat*, November 28, 1978, Linda Gottlieb (executive producer), Doro Bachrach (producer) (NBC)

☐ "The Tap Dance Kid," *Special Treat*, October 24, 1978, Linda Gottlieb (executive producer), Evelyn Barron (producer) (NBC)

OUTSTANDING CHILDREN'S INFORMATIONAL SERIES

Emmy(s) to executive producer(s) and producer(s):

30 Minutes, Joel Heller (executive producer), Madeline Amgott, Elliot Bernstein, JoAnn Caplin, Christine Huneke, Robert Rubin, Patti Obrow White (producers) (CBS)

ABC Minute Magazine, Thomas H. Wolf (producer) (ABC)

Animals, Animals, Animals, Lester Cooper (executive producer), Peter Weinberg (producer) (ABC)

☐ *Big Blue Marble*, Robert Wiemer (executive producer), Richard Berman (producer) (Syndicated)

In the News, Joel Heller (executive producer), Susan Mills (producer) (CBS)

When You Turn Off the Set, Turn On a Book, Mary Alice Dwyer (executive producer), George Newall and Tom Yohe (producers) (NBC)

OUTSTANDING CHILDREN'S INFORMATIONAL SPECIAL

Emmy(s) to executive producer(s) and producer(s):

☐ *Razzmatazz*, February 1, 1979, Joel Heller (executive producer), Vern Diamond (producer) (CBS)

"The Secret of Charles Dickens," *CBS Festival of Live, Arts for Young People*—April 16, 1978, Daniel Wilson (executive producer), Linda Marmelstein (producer) (CBS)

OUTSTANDING CHILDREN'S INSTRUCTIONAL SERIES

Emmy(s) to executive producer(s) and producer(s):

"Dear Alex and Annie," *Kids Are People Too*, Ken Greengrass and Phil Lawrence (executive producers), Lynn Ahrens (producer) (ABC)

Metric Marvels, George Newall and Tom Yohe (producers) (NBC)

Sesame Street, David D. Connell (vice president for production), Al Hyslop (producer) (PBS)

☐ "Science Rock," *Schoolhouse Rock*, Tom Yohe (executive producer), George Newall and Radford Stone (producers) (ABC)

OUTSTANDING ACTOR IN A DAYTIME DRAMA SERIES

Jed Allan, *Days of Our Lives* (NBC)

Nicholas Benedict, *All My Children* (ABC)

John Clarke, *Days of Our Lives* (NBC)

Joel Crothers, *The Edge of Night* (ABC)

☐ Al Freeman Jr., *One Life to Live* (ABC)

Michael Levin, *Ryan's Hope* (ABC)

OUTSTANDING ACTRESS IN A DAYTIME DRAMA SERIES

Nancy Addison, *Ryan's Hope* (ABC)

☐ Irene Dailey, *Another World* (NBC)

Helen Gallagher, *Ryan's Hope* (ABC)

Beverlee McKinsey, *Another World* (NBC)

Susan Seaforth Hayes, *Days of Our Lives* (NBC)

Victoria Wyndham, *Another World* (NBC)

OUTSTANDING SUPPORTING ACTOR IN A DAYTIME DRAMA SERIES

Lewis Arlt, *Search for Tomorrow* (CBS)

Bernard Barrow, *Ryan's Hope* (ABC)

Joe Gallison, *Days of Our Lives* (NBC)

Ron Hale, *Ryan's Hope* (ABC)

☐ Peter Hansen, *General Hospital* (ABC)

Mandel Kramer, *The Edge of Night* (ABC)

OUTSTANDING SUPPORTING ACTRESS IN A DAYTIME DRAMA SERIES

Rachel Ames, *General Hospital* (ABC)

Susan Brown, *General Hospital* (ABC)

Lois Kibbee, *The Edge of Night* (ABC)

Francis Reed, *Days of Our Lives* (NBC)

☐ Suzanne Rogers, *Days of Our Lives* (NBC)

OUTSTANDING HOST OR HOSTESS IN A GAME OR AUDIENCE PARTICIPATION SHOW

Bob Barker, *The Price Is Right* (CBS)

☐ Dick Clark, *The $20,000 Pyramid* (ABC)

Peter Marshall, *The Hollywood Squares* (NBC)

OUTSTANDING HOST OR HOSTESS IN A TALK, SERVICE OR VARIETY SHOW

John Bennett-Perry, *Everyday* (Syndicated)

☐ Phil Donahue, *Donahue* (Syndicated)

Stephanie Edwards, *Everyday* (Syndicated)

OUTSTANDING DIRECTION FOR A DAYTIME DRAMA SERIES

For the entire series:

Ira Cirker, Melvin Bernhardt, Paul Lammers, Robert Calhoun, *Another World* (NBC)

Jack Coffee, Del Hughes, Henry Kaplan, *All My Children* (ABC)

Richard Dunlap, Bill Glenn, *The Young and the Restless* (CBS)

☐ Jerry Evans, Lela Swift, *Ryan's Hope* (ABC)

Al Rabin, Joe Behar, Frank Pacelli, *Days of Our Lives* (NBC)

John Sedwick, Richard Pepperman, *The Edge of Night* (ABC)

OUTSTANDING INDIVIDUAL DIRECTION FOR A GAME OR AUDIENCE PARTICIPATION SHOW
For a single episode:
Mike Gargiulo, *The $20,000 Pyramid*, September 4, 1978 (ABC)

Richard Schneider, *Jeopardy*, January 8, 1979 (NBC)

☐ Jerome Shaw, *Hollywood Squares*, June 20, 1978 (NBC)

OUTSTANDING INDIVIDUAL DIRECTION FOR A VARIETY PROGRAM
For a single episode:
Donald R. King, *America Alive*, November 7, 1978 (NBC)

☐ Ron Wiener, *Donahue*, "The Nazis and the Klan," July 7, 1978 (Syndicated)

Glen Swanson, *Dinah!*, "The Fifth Anniversary Show," November 13, 1978 (Syndicated)

OUTSTANDING WRITING FOR A DAYTIME DRAMA SERIES
For the entire series:
William J. Bell, Kay Alden, Elizabeth Harrower, *The Young and the Restless* (CBS)

☐ Claire Labine, Paul Avila Mayer, Mary Munisteri, Judith Pinsker, Jeffrey Lane, *Ryan's Hope* (ABC)

Ann Marcus, Michael Robert David, Raymond E. Goldstone, Joyce Perry, Elizabeth Harrower, Rocci Chatfield, Laura Olsher, *Days of Our Lives* (NBC)

Agnes Nixon, Wisner Washam, Jack Wood, Mary K. Wells, Kenneth Harvey, Cathy Chicos, Caroline Franz, Doris Frankel, William Delligan, *All My Children* (ABC)

OUTSTANDING ACHIEVEMENT IN TECHNICAL EXCELLENCE FOR A DAYTIME DRAMA SERIES
Emmys to program representative and respective individuals:
All My Children, J.J. Lupatkin and Joseph Solomito (technical directors), Sherrell Hoffman and Jean Dadario (associated directors), Len Walas and John Monteleone (video), Nat Rogers and Roger Haenelt (videotape editors), Al Lamanski and Sy Chaiken (audio), Barry Klemons, Barry Considine, Joe Cotugno and Larry Hammond (camerapersons), James Reichert (music composer/music director), Ed Blainey (sound effects) (NBC)

Another World, Frank DeRienzo, Frank Gaeta and Bill Hildreth (technical directors), John C. LiBretto, Kevin Kelly and David Handler (associate directors), Arnold Dick and Harold Mofsen (video), Lloyd G. Campbell and John J. O'Conner (videotape editors), Mel Hench and Phil Berge (audio), Olonzo Roberts and Barry Frischer (camerapersons), music by Score productions, Art Cooper (sound effects) (NBC)

☐ *The Edge of Night*, William Edwards (technical director), Joanne Goodhart (associate director), Paul York (video), Edward R. Atchison (audio), William Hughes, Arie Hefter and Jay Millard (camerapersons), music by Elliot Lawrence Productions, Barbara Miller (music coordinator), Robert Saxon (sound effects technician), Roman Spinner (teleprompter) (ABC)

One Life to Live, Lou Marchand and Martin Gavrin (technical Directors), J. W. Sullivan (associate director), Herbert Segall (video), Anthony Greco and Albert Forman (videotape editors), Frank W. Bailey (audio), Robert L. Knudsen, Al Gianetta, Thomas L. Franch, Richard Westline and John Morris (camerapersons), Jack Urbont (music composer), Irving Robbins and John D. Anthony (music directors), Robert J. Prescott Jr. (sound effects) (ABC)

Ryan's Hope, George Whitaker (technical director), Suelle Goldstein (associate director), Rucy Piccirillo and Dick Williams (video), Pau Malik and Dan Rosenson (videotape editors), Dick Kerr, Mary Flood and Frank J. Merklein (camerapersons), Kenneth B. Weaver (audio), Carey Gold (music composer), Sybil Weinberger (music supervisor) (ABC)

The Young and the Restless, Steve Cunningham (technical director), Howard Quinn (associate director), David Fisher and Al Latter (video), Dan Brumett (videotape editor), Bud Lindquist, Luis E. Godinez, Jim Williams, Ralph Cummings, Frank Carter and Tom Hanley (audio), Michael Stich, Fred Gough, Joe Vicens, Pat Kenny and Barney Neeley (camerapersons), Patti Bereyso and Sally Anlauf (music coordinators), Gus Bayz (sound effects) (CBS)

OUTSTANDING ACHIEVEMENT IN DESIGN EXCELLENCE FOR A DAYTIME DRAMA SERIES
Emmy to program representative and respective individuals:
Days of Our Lives, Barry Williams and Arnold Shyler (art directors and

scenic designers), Herbert Margolis and Dick Pickens (lighting directors), Joseph R. Markham (costume designer), Bess Keiser and Joan Lawrence (makeup designers), Alfie Rodriguez (hairstylist) (NBC)

☐ *Love of Live*, Lloyd R. Evans (scenic designer), Wesley Laws (set decorator), Dean Nelson (lighting director), Bob Anton (costume designer), Lee Halls (makeup designer), Phyllis Sagnelli (hairdresser), Lou Dorfsman (graphic design/title sequence) (CBS)

One Life to Live, Charles Brandon (scenic designer), Howard Sharrott and Donald R. Gavitt (lighting directors), George Drew (costume designer), Dennis Eger and Harry Buchman (makeup designers), Willis Hanchett and Roberto Donzi (hairdressers) (ABC)

Ryan's Hope, Sy Tomashoff (scenic designer), Herb Gruber (scenic artists), John Connolly (lighting director), Honore Walsh (costume designer), David Lawrence and Jim Cola (makeup artists), John K. Quinn (hairstylist) (ABC)

Daytime Awards*

OUTSTANDING INDIVIDUAL ACHIEVEMENT IN CHILDREN'S PROGRAMMING
For a single episode of a series or for a special program:
☐ Geraldine Fitzgerald (performer), "Rodeo Red and the Runaway," *Special Treat*, November 28, 1978 (NBC)

☐ Jack Gilford (performer) "Hello in There," *Big Blue Marble*, September 16, 1978 (Syndicated)

☐ Jim Henson, Frank Oz, Carroll Spinney, Jerry Nelson, Richard Hunt (performers), "The Muppets of Sesame Street," *Sesame Street*, November 27, 1978 (PBS)

Lester Cooper (writer), "Doves and Pigeons," *Animals, Animals, Animals*, September 10, 1978 (ABC)

Art Wallace (writer), "Joey and Redhawk," *CBS Afternoon Playhouse*, December 4-8, 1978 (CBS)

☐ Larry Elikann (director), "Mom and Dad Can't Hear Me," *ABC Afterschool Special*, April 4, 1978 (ABC)

Frank Marrero (director), "Art for Whose Sake," *Mundo Real*, September 1, 1978 (Syndicated)

* possibility of one award, more than one award or no award

◻ Charles Gross (composer), "Rodeo Red and the Runaway," *Special Treat*, November 28, 1978 (NBC)

◻ John Morris (composer), "The Tap Dance Kid," *Special Treat*, October 24, 1978 (NBC)

Jack Kestenbaum (tape sound mixing), *Kids Are People Too*, February 4, 1979 (ABC)

◻ Dick Maitland and Roy Carch (sound effects), *Sesame Street*, April 20, 1978 (PBS)

◻ Gene Piotrowsky (tape sound mixing), "A Special Day in the Year of the Child," *CBS Festival of Lively Arts for Young People* (CBS)

◻ Michael Baugh (art director), "Todos los ninos del mundo," *Villa Alegre*, November 9, 1978, (PBS)

Neil DeLuca (scenic designer), *Razzmatazz*, February 1, 1979 (CBS)

Bil Mikulewicz (art director/scenic designer), "Mr. Pennywhistle/ Cafeteria," *Captain Kangaroo*, October 4, 1978 (CBS)

Peter D. Altobelli (makeup designer), "A Home Run for Love," *ABC Afterschool Special*, October 11, 1978 (ABC)

◻ Dorothy Weaver (costume designer), "Rodeo Red and the Runaway," *Special Treat*, November 28, 1978 (NBC)

Tony DiGirolamo (lighting director), "Hooper Goes to the Hospital," *Sesame Street*, December 12, 1978 (PBS)

◻ Rene Verzier (cinematographer), *Big Blue Marble*, November 18, 1978 (Syndicated)

◻ Dick Young (cinematographer), "Day of the Jouster," *Big Blue Marble*, September 16, 1978 (Syndicated)

◻ Norman Gay (film editor), *The Tap Dance Kid*, October 24, 1978 (NBC)

◻ Vince Humphrey (film editor), *Gaucho*, October 25, 1978 (ABC)

◻ Ian Maitland (cinematographer), "Rodeo Red and the Runaway," *Special Treat*, November 28, 1978 (NBC)

◻ Michael Baugh (graphic designer/ titles), "Todos los ninos del mundo," *Villa Alegre*, November 9, 1978 (PBS)

◻ Jack Regas, Harvey Berger and Ron Hays (graphic designers/titles), *Krofft Superstar Hour*, (starring The Bay City Rollers), September 9, 1978 (NBC)

◻ Harvey Berger (videotape editor), *Krofft Superstar Hour*, (starring The Bay City Rollers), September 9, 1978 (NBC)

◻ Ken Gutstein (videotape editor), "The Secret of Charles Dickens *Festival of Lively Arts for Young People* (CBS)

◻ Roy Stewart (videotape editor), "Flat," *Freestyle!*, October 27, 1978 (PBS)

OUTSTANDING INDIVIDUAL ACHIEVEMENT IN RELIGIOUS PROGRAMMING

For a single episode of a series or for a special program:

Lee Bryant (performer), "The Scoop," *This Is the Life*, October 8, 1978 (Syndicated)

David Hooks (performer), "The Sexton," *This Is the Life*, October 1, 1978 (Syndicated)

◻ Rolanda Mendels (performer), *Interrogation in Budapest*, December 17, 1978 (NBC)

Marc Siegel (writer), *Interrogation in Budapest*, December 17, 1978 (NBC)

◻ Martin Hoad (director), *Interrogation in Budapest*, December 17, 1978 (NBC)

◻ Joseph J.H. Vadala (cinematographer), *This Other Eden*, February 4, 1979 (NBC)

Sports Awards

OUTSTANDING LIVE SPORTS SPECIAL

Emmy(s) to executive producer(s) and producer(s):

The Masters Golf Tournament, Frank Chirkinian (executive producer), April 14–15, 1979 (CBS)

NCAA Basketball Championship, Don Ohlmeyer (executive producer), George Finkel (producer), March 26, 1979 (NBC)

◻ *Super Bowl XIII*, Don Ohlmeyer (executive producer), George Finkel and Michael Weisman (producers), January 21, 1979 (NBC)

U.S. Open Tennis Championships, Frank Chirkinian (executive producer), August 30–September 10, 1979 (CBS)

Wimbledon '79, Don Ohlmeyer (executive producer), Geoff Mason and Ted Nathanson (producers), June 30, July 1–7, 1979 (NBC)

1978 World Series, Don Ohlmeyer (executive producer), George Finkel and Michael Weisman (producers), October 10, 11, 13, 14, 15, 17, 1979 (NBC)

OUTSTANDING LIVE SPORTS SERIES

Emmy(s) to executive producer(s) and producer(s):

◻ ABC's NFL Monday Night Football, Roone Arledge (executive producer),

Dennis Lewin (producer), Series (ABC)

AFC/NFL Football, Don Ohlmeyer (executive producer), Michael Wiesman, David Stern, Jim Marooney, George Finkel, Larry Cirillo, Roy Hammerman and Kenneth Edmundson (producers) Series (NBC)

Major League Baseball, Don Ohlmeyer (executive producer), Michael Weisman, George Finkel, David Stern and Jim Marooney (producers), Series (NBC)

NCAA Basketball, Don Ohlmeyer (executive producer), Roy Hammerman, George Finkel, Michael Wiesman, David Stern and Kenneth Edmundson (producers), Series (NBC)

The NFL Today/NFL Football on CBS, Michael Pearl (producer), *NFL Today*, Bill Barnes, David Fox, Bob Rowe, Perry Smith, Bob Stenner, Chuck Will, Tom O'Neil, Howard Reifsnyder and Chuck Milton (producers), *NFL Football on CBS*, Series (CBS)

OUTSTANDING EDITED SPORTS SPECIAL

Emmy(s) to executive producer(s) and producer(s):

Indianapolis 500, Roone Arledge (executive producer), Chuck Howard and Bob Goodrich (producers), May 27, 1979 (ABC)

Olympic Diary, Don Ohlmeyer (executive producer), Bernie Hoffman and Peter Diamond (producers), January 28, 1979 (NBC)

Pan American Games, Eddie Einhorn (executive producer), Ed Goren (producer), July 1–15, 1979 (CBS)

◻ *Spirit of '78—The Flight of Double Eagle II*, Roone Arledge (executive producer), John Wilcox (producer), August 27, 1978 (ABC)

Super Bowl XIII—Pre-Game, Don Ohlmeyer (executive producer), Don McGuire (producer), January 21, 1979 (NBC)

OUTSTANDING EDITED SPORTS SERIES

Emmy(s) to executive producer(s) and producer(s):

ABC's Wide World of Sports, Roone Arledge (executive producer), Chet Forte, Chuck Howard, Doug Wilson, Ned Steckel, Bob Goodrich, Dennis Lewin, Eleanor Riger, Carol Lehti, Joe Aceti and Terry O'Neil (producers), Series (ABC)

◻ *The American Sportsman*, Roone Arledge (executive producer), John Wilcox, Series produce (ABC), Bob

Duncan, Curt Gowdy and Bob Nixon (Producers) Series (ABC)

Sportsworld, Don Ohlmeyer, (executive producer), Linda Jonsson, Virginia Seipt, Hilary Cosell, Ted Nathanson, Michael Wiesman, Jim Marooney, Bernie Hoffman, Matthew McCarthy, David Stern, George Finkel, Larry Cirillo and Don McGuire (producers), Series (NBC)

OUTSTANDING DIRECTING SPORTS PROGRAMMING

Frank Chirkinian, Robert Dailey, *The Masters Golf Tournament*, April 14–15, 1979 (CBS)

☐ Harry Coyle, 1978 World Series, October 10, 11, 13, 14, 15, 17, 1978 (NBC)

Chet Forte, *ABC's NFL Monday Night Football*, Series (ABC)

Ted Nathanson, *Super Bowl XIII*, January 21, 1979 (NBC)

Andy Sidaris, *NCAA Football*, Fall 1978 (ABC)

OUTSTANDING INDIVIDUAL ACHIEVEMENT IN SPORTS PROGRAMMING*

Writting

Steve Sabol, Dave Morcom, "Pigskin Poetry," part of *NFL '78 for Pre-Game Show*, November 1978 (NBC)

Cinematography

☐ Bob Angelo, Ernie Ernst, Jay Gerber, Stan Leshner, Hank McElwee, Howard Neef, Jack Newman, Steve Sabol, Bob Smith, Art Spieller and Phil Tuckett (cinematographers for NFL Films), *NFL Game of the Week*, Series (Syndicated)

Technical direction/Engineering supervision/Electronic camerawork

☐ Sandy Bell, Bob Brown (technical directors), Ralph Savignano, Art Tinn (engineering supervisors), Barry Drago, Jim McCarthy, Joe Sokota, George Rothweiler, George Naeder, John Lincoln, Tom McCarthy, Hans Singer, Keeth Lawrence, Jim Murphy, Neil McCaffrey, Herman Lang, Sig Meyers and Frank McSpedon (electronic camerapersons), Anthony Hlavaty, Wayne Wright, Johnny Morris, Ed Ambrosini, Frank Florio and Tom Spalding (electronic camerapersons for Minicam and Microwave Systems; Operation of NR and minicam equipment for coverage of pit areas, camera in driver's car and microwave systems), *Daytona 500*, February 18, 1979 (CBS)

Sandy Bell, Charles D'Onofrio (technical directors), Art Tinn, Lou Scannapieco (engineering supervisors), George Klimcsak, Fred Holst, Gavin Blane, David Graham, Harry Haigood, George Rothweiler, Herman Lang, Hans Singer, Frank McSpedon, Barry Drago, James Murphy, Alan Diamond, Neil McCaffrey, George Naeder, James McCarthy, Alfred Loreto, John Linclon, Dennis McBride, Stanley Gould, Robert Welsh, David Finch, Gordon Sweeney, Joseph Vincens, Bob Skorup and Ken Woehlck (electronic camerapersons), *The Masters Golf Tournament*, April 14–15, 1979 (CBS)

☐ Horace Ruiz (technical director), Joe Commare, Bob McKearnin and Jack Bennett (engineering supervisors), George Loomis, Rodger Harbaugh, William W. Landers, Michael C. Stramisky, Roy V. Ratliff, Leonard Basile, Mario J. Ciarlo, Tom C. Dezondorf, Steve Cimino, William M. Goetz, Louis Gerard, Len Stucker, Steven H. Gonzales, Jim Johnson, Cory Lieble, Don Mulvaney, Al Rice Jr., and Russ K. Ross (electronic camerapersons), *Super Bowl XIII*, January 21, 1979 (NBC)

☐ Horace Ruiz, Dick Roecker, Ray Figelski (technical directors), Robert McKearnin, Jack Bennett, Ernest Thiel, Jerry Ireland and Bob Brown (engineering supervisors), Leonard G. Basile, Mario J. Ciarlo, Roy Ratliff, George Loomis, Bernard Joseph, Louis Gerard, Steve Cimino, Mike Stramisky, Rodger Harbaugh, Al Rice Jr., William M. Goetz, Jim Johnson, Brian Cherriffe, Phil Cantrell, Steven H. Gonzales, Russ K. Ross, Art Parker, Bill Landers, Jim Bragg, James Culley, Cory Liebele and Len Stucker (electronic camerapersons), *1978 World Series*, October 10, 11, 13, 14, 15, 17, 1979 (NBC)

Bob Vernum, Charles D'Onofrio (technical directors), Joseph Tier (Engineering supervisor), James McCarthy, Rick Blane, George Klimcsak, Al Diamond, Hans Singer, Frank McSpedon, David Graham, Dick Douglas, Barry Drago, Al Loreto, Steve Gorsuch, Herman Lang, Fred Holst and Arthur Jackson (electronic camerapersons), *U.S. Open Tennis Championship*, August 30–September 10, 1978 (CBS)

Associate direction/Videotape editing

Ted Shaker, Richard Drake and Rick Sharp (associate directors), Jeff Ringel, Jeff Laing, Bob Hickson,

Chris Balomatis (videotape editors), *Daytona 500*, February 18, 1979 (CBS)

Bob Levy and Matthew McCarthy (associate directors), Richard Lieble, Mark Beltran and Mark Jankeloff (videotape editors), *Sports World*, Series (NBC)

Ralph J. Mole (associate director), Oden Kitzmiller, Cyrus McRoe, Ed Eblik, Len Jordan, Hal Sommer and Frank O'Connel (videotape editors), *Pan American Games*, July 1–15, 1979 (CBS)

Music composition/Direction

Roger Nichols, *Olympathon '79*, ("Olympic Theme"), April 21, 1979 (NBC)

Graphic design/Title sequence

Robert Angelo and Jay Gerber (graphic designers), *The NFL Today*, Series (CBS)

☐ James M. Grau (graphic designer), "Closing Logo," *CBS Sports Programs* (CBS)

SPECIAL CLASSIFICATIONS OF OUTSTANDING PROGRAM AND INDIVIDUAL ACHIEVEMENT*

Emmy(s) to producing organization(s) or individual(s), whichever applicable:

Program

Sportsjournal, "The Cocaine Connection: Ken Stabler and the Set-Up?," Don Ohlmeyer (executive producer), Hilary Cosell (producer), February 11, 1979 (NBC)

Individual

Tom Spalding (inventor/developer of the In-Car Racing System), *Daytona 500*, February 18, 1979 (CBS)

OUTSTANDING SPORTS PERSONALITY

Dick Enberg (NBC)
Frank Gifford (ABC)
Keith Jackson (ABC)
☐ Jim McKay (ABC)
Merlin Olsen (NBC)
Pat Summerall (CBS)
Jack Whitaker (CBS)

NATIONAL AWARD FOR COMMUNITY SERVICE

The Welfare Blues: New York City Blues (WABC-TV, New York City)

A Case of Neglect (KPNX, Phoenix, Arizona)

Angel Death (KTTV-TV, Los Angeles, California)

Wednesday's Child (KOCO-TV, Oklahoma City, Oklahoma)

Politics of Poison (KRON-TV, San Francisco, California)

---

* possibility of one award, more than one award or no award
☐ Indicates winner

---

* possibility of one award, more than one award or no award

□ *Agent Orange: The Human Harvest*
(WBBM-TV, Chicago, Illinois)
Slow Motion Tragedy (WSM-TV,
Nashville, Tennessee)
Seven On Your Side (WJLA-TV,
Washington, D.C.)
The Last Hurrah: Chicago Style (WLS-
TV, Chicago, Illinois)
"Piney"—The Rural Face of Jersey
(WNEW-TV, New York City)
Emergency Medical Services—Probe
(WDVM-TV, Washington, D.C.)

OUTSTANDING ACHIEVEMENT IN THE SCIENCE OF TELEVISION ENGINEERING

□ *Ampex Corporation*
□ *Sony Video Products Company*
□ *Society of Motion Picture and Television Engineers*

TRUSTEES AWARD

□ **William S. Paley,** for continued
distinguished service to television
and the audience it serves

1979/80

*(For programs aired between July 1,
1979 and June 30, 1980.
Entertainment program and individual
achievement awards presented
September 7, 1980. Creative Arts
awards presented September 6, 1980.
Daytime awards presented June 2 and
June 4, 1980. News and Documentary
awards presented April 13, 1981 for
programs aired between June 1, 1979
and November 14, 1980. Sports
awards presented December 10, 1980
for programs aired between July 19,
1979 and July 15, 1980. Science of
Engineering in Television award
presented September 15, 1980.)*

Prime Time Program Awards

OUTSTANDING COMEDY SERIES

**Emmy(s) to executive producer(s)
and or producer(s):**

□ *Taxi*, James L. Brooks, Stan Daniels,
Ed Weinberger (executive
producers), Glen Charles, Les
Charles (producers) (ABC)
Barney Miller, Danny Arnold (executive
producer), Tony Sheehan, Noam
Pitlik (producers), Gary Shaw (co-
producer) (ABC)
*M*A*S*H*, Burt Metcalfe (executive
producer), Jim Mulligan, John
Rappaport (producers) (CBS)
Soap, Paul Junger Witt, Tony Thomas
(executive producers), Susan Harris
(producer) (ABC)

□ Indicates winner

WKRP in Cincinnati, Hugh Wilson
(executive producer), Rod Daniel
(producer) (CBS)

OUTSTANDING DRAMA SERIES

**Emmy(s) to executive producer(s)
and producer(s):**

□ *Lou Grant*, Gene Reynolds (executive
producer), Seth Freeman (producer)
(CBS)
Dallas, Philip Capice, Lee Rich
(executive producers), Leonard
Katzman (producer) (CBS)
Family, Aaron Spelling, Leonard
Goldberg (executive producers),
Edward Zwick (producer) (ABC)
The Rockford Files, Meta Rosenberg
(executive producer), Stephen J.
Cannell (supervising producer),
David Chase, Chas Floyd Johnson,
Juanita Bartlett (producers) (NBC)
The White Shadow, Bruce Paltrow
(executive producer), Mark Tinker
(producer) (CBS)

OUTSTANDING LIMITED SERIES

**Emmy(s) to executive producer(s)
and producer(s):**

□ *Edward & Mrs. Simpson*, Andrew
Brown (producer) (Syndicated)
"Disraeli: Portrait of a Romantic,"
Masterpiece Theatre, Joan Wilson
(series producer), Cecil Clarke
(producer) (PBS)
"The Duchess of Duke Street II,"
Masterpiece Theatre, Joan Wilson
(series producer), John
Hawkesworth (producer) (PBS)
Moviola, David L. Wolper (executive
producer), Stan Margulies (producer)
(NBC)

OUTSTANDING VARIETY OR MUSIC PROGRAM

**For a special or a series. Emmy(s)
to executive producer(s),
producer(s) and star(s), if
applicable:**

□ *IBM Presents Baryshnikov on
Broadway*, Herman Krawitz
(executive producer), Gary Smith,
Dwight Hemion (producers), Mikhail
Baryshnikov (star), April 24, 1980
(ABC)
The Benny Hill Show, Philip Jones
(executive producer), Keith Beckett,
David Bell, Ronald Fouracre, Peter
Frazer Jones, Dennis Kirkland, John
Robbins, Mark Stuart (producers),
Benny Hill (star), Series (Syndicated)
Goldie and Liza Together, George
Schlatter (executive producer), Don
Mischer, Fred Ebb (producers),
Goldie Hawn, Liza Minnelli (stars),
February 19, 1980 (CBS)
The Muppet Show, David Lazer
(executive producer), Jim Henson
(producer), Dave Goelz, Louise

Gold, Jim Henson, Richard Hunt,
Kathryn Mullen, Jerry Nelson, Frank
Oz, Steve Whitmire (stars)
(Syndicated)
*Shirley MacLaine. . . "Every Little
Movement,"* Gary Smith, Dwight
Hemion (producers), Shirley
Maclaine (star), May 22, 1980 (CBS)

OUTSTANDING DRAMA OR COMEDY SPECIAL

**Emmy(s) to executive producer(s)
and producer(s):**

□ *The Miracle Worker*, Raymond Katz,
Sandy Gallin (executive producers),
Fred Coe (producer), October 14,
1979 (NBC)
"All Quiet on the Western Front,"
Hallmark Hall of Fame, Martin
Starger (executive producer),
Norman Rosemont (producer),
November 14, 1979 (CBS)
Amber Waves, Philip Mandelker
(executive producer), Stanley Kallis
(producer), March 9, 1980 (ABC)
"Gideon's Trumpet," *Hallmark Hall of
Fame*, John Houseman (executive
producer), David W. Rintels
(producer), April 30, 1980 (CBS)
*Guyana Tragedy: The Story of Jim
Jones*, Frank Konigsberg (executive
producer), Ernest Tidyman, Sam
Manners (producers), April 15 and
16, 1980 (CBS)

OUTSTANDING CLASSICAL PROGRAM IN THE PERFORMING ARTS

**For a special or a series. Emmy(s)
to executive producer(s),
producer(s) and star(s), if
applicable:**

□ *Live from Studio 8H: A Tribute to
Toscanini*, Alvin Cooperman, Judith
De Paul (producers), January 9,
1980 (NBC)
*Agnes deMille and the Joffrey Ballet in
Conversations About the Dance*,
Loring d'Usseau (producer), Agnes
deMille (star), January 28, 1980
(PBS)
Beverly Sills in Concert, Thomas L.
Merklinger (executive producer),
Beverly Sills (star), June 28, 1980
(PBS)
*Luciano Pavarotti and the New York
Philharmonic Live from Lincoln
Center*, John Goberman (producer),
Luciano Pavarotti (star), January 14,
1980 (PBS)

OUTSTANDING INFORMATIONAL PROGRAM

**For a special or a series. Emmy(s)
to executive producer(s),**

producer(s) and star(s), if applicable:

☐ *The Body Human: The Magic Sense*, Thomas W. Moore (executive producer), Alfred R. Kelman, Robert E. Fuisz, M.D. (producers), Charles A. Bangert, Vivian R. Moss (co-producers), September 6, 1979 (CBS)

Bill Moyers' Journal, Joan Konner (executive producer), Bill Moyers (star), Series (PBS)

The Body Human: The Body Beautiful, Thomas W. Moore (executive producer), Alfred R. Kelman, Robert E. Fuisz, M.D. (producers), Charles A. Bangert, Geof Bartz, Vivian R. Moss (co-producers), April 16, 1980 (CBS)

"The Nile," *The Cousteau Odyssey*, Jacques-Yves Cousteau, Philippe Cousteau (executive producers), December 9 and 10, 1979 (PBS)

Picasso—A Painter's Diary, George Page (executive producer), Perry Miller Adato (producer), June 2, 1980 (PBS)

OUTSTANDING PROGRAM ACHIEVEMENT—SPECIAL EVENTS

An award for special event programming. Emmy(s) to executive producer(s) and producer(s).

(Possibility of one award, more than one award or no award):

☐ *The 34th Annual Tony Awards*, Alexander H. Cohen (executive producer), Hildy Parks (producer), Roy A. Somlyo (co-producer), June 8, 1980 (CBS)

The American Film Institute Salute to Jimmy Stewart, George Stevens Jr. (producer), March 16, 1980 (CBS)

52nd Annual Awards Presentation of the Academy of Motion Picture Arts and Sciences, Howard W. Koch (producer), April 14, 1980 (ABC)

The Kennedy Center Honors: A Celebration of the Performing Arts, George Stevens Jr., Nick Vanoff (producers), December 29, 1979 (CBS)

OUTSTANDING PROGRAM ACHIEVEMENT—SPECIAL CLASS

An award for unique program achievement that does not fall into a specific category and is not otherwise recognized. Emmy(s) to executive producer(s), producer(s) and star(s), if applicable.

(Possibility of one award, more than one award or no award):

☐ *Fred Astaire: Change Partners and Dance*, George Page, Jac Venza (executive producers), David Heeley (producer), March 14, 1980 (PBS)

☐ Indicates winner

Fred Astaire: Puttin' on His Top Hat, George Page, Jac Venza (executive producers), David Heeley (producer), March 10, 1980 (PBS)

Real People, George Schlatter (executive producer), John Barbour, Bob Wynn (producers), Series (NBC)

The Tonight Show Starring Johnny Carson, Fred de Cordova (executive producer), Peter Lassally (producer), Johnny Carson (star), Series (NBC)

Winter Olympics '80—The World Comes to America, Roone Arledge (executive producer), Doug Wilson (producer), January 12, 1980 (ABC)

OUTSTANDING CHILDREN'S PROGRAM

For a special or a series. Emmy(s) to executive producer(s) and producer(s).

(Possibility of one award, more than one award or no award):

Benji at Work, Joe Camp (executive producer), Fielder Baker (producer), May 2, 1980 (ABC)

The Halloween that Almost Wasn't, Richard Barclay (executive producer), Gaby Monet (producer), October 28, 1979 (ABC)

Sesame Street in Puerto Rico, al Hyslop (executive producer), Michael Cozell (producer), November 24, 1979 (PBS)

OUTSTANDING ANIMATED PROGRAM

For a special or a series. Emmy(s) to executive producer(s) and producer(s).

(Possibility of one award, more than one award or no award):

☐ *Carlton Your Doorman*, Lorenzo Music, Barton Dean (producers), May 21, 1980 (CBS)

Dr. Seuss' Pontoffel Pock, Where Are You?, David H. De Patie, Friz Freleng (executive producers), Ted Geisel (producer), May 2, 1980 (ABC)

Pink Panther in Olym-Pinks, David H. De Paite, Friz Freleng (producers), February 22, 1980 (ABC)

She's a Good Skate, Charlie Brown, Lee Mendelson (executive producer), Bill Melendez (producer), February 25, 1980 (CBS)

Prime Time Performing Awards

OUTSTANDING LEAD ACTOR IN A COMEDY SERIES

For a continuing or single performance in a regular series:

☐ Richard Mulligan, *Soap* (ABC)

Alan Alda, *M*A*S*H* (CBS)

Robert Guillaume, *Benson* (ABC)

Judd Hirsch, *Taxi* (ABC)

Hal Linden, *Barney Miller* (ABC)

OUTSTANDING LEAD ACTOR IN A DRAMA SERIES

For a continuing or single performance in a regular series:

☐ Ed Asner, *Lou Grant* (CBS)

James Garner, *The Rockford Files* (NBC)

Larry Hagman, *Dallas* (CBS)

Jack Klugman, *Quincy, M.E.* (NBC)

OUTSTANDING LEAD ACTOR IN A LIMITED SERIES OR A SPECIAL

For a continuing role in a limited series or for a single appearance in a limited series or a special:

☐ Powers Boothe, *Guyana Tragedy: The Story of Jim Jones*, April 15 and 16, 1980 (CBS)

Tony Curtis, *Moviola: The Scarlett O'Hara War*, May 19, 1980 (NBC)

Henry Fonda, "Gideon's Trumpet," *Hallmark Hall of Fame*, April 30, 1980 (CBS)

Jason Robards, *F.D.R.: The Last Year*, May 15, 1980 (NBC)

OUTSTANDING LEAD ACTRESS IN A COMEDY SERIES

For a continuing or single performance in a regular series:

☐ Cathryn Damon, *Soap* (ABC)

Katherine Helmond, *Soap* (ABC)

Polly Holliday, *Flo* (CBS)

Sheree North, *Archie Bunker's Place* (CBS)

Isabel Sanford, *The Jeffersons* (CBS)

OUTSTANDING LEAD ACTRESS IN A DRAMA SERIES

For a continuing or single performance in a regular series:

☐ Barbara Bel Geddes, *Dallas* (CBS)

Lauren Bacall, *The Rockford Files*, "Lions, Tigers, Monkeys and Dogs," October 12, 1979 (NBC)

Mariette Hartley, *The Rockford Files*, "Paradise Cove," September 28, 1979 (NBC)

Kristy McNichol, *Family* (ABC)

Sada Thompson, *Family* (ABC)

OUTSTANDING LEAD ACTRESS IN A LIMITED SERIES OR A SPECIAL

For a continuing role in a limited series or for a single appearance in a limited series or a special:

☐ Patty Duke Astin, *The Miracle Worker*, October 14, 1979 (NBC)

Bette Davis, *White Mama*, March 5, 1980 (CBS)

Melissa Gilbert, *The Miracle Worker*, October 14, 1979 (NBC)

Lee Remick, *Haywire*, May 14, 1980 (CBS)

OUTSTANDING SUPPORTING ACTOR IN A COMEDY OR VARIETY OR MUSIC SERIES

For a continuing or single performance in a regular series:
☐ Harry Morgan, *M*A*S*H* (CBS)
Mike Farrell, *M*A*S*H* (CBS)
Max Gail, *Barney Miller* (ABC)
Howard Hesseman, *WKRP in Cincinnati* (CBS)
Steve Landesberg, *Barney Miller* (ABC)

OUTSTANDING SUPPORTING ACTOR IN A DRAMA SERIES

For a continuing or single performance in a regular series:
☐ Stuart Margolin, *The Rockford Files* (NBC)
Mason Adams, *Lou Grant* (CBS)
Noah Beery, *The Rockford Files* (NBC)
Robert Walden, *Lou Grant* (CBS)

OUTSTANDING SUPPORTING ACTOR IN A LIMITED SERIES OR A SPECIAL

For a continuing role in a limited series or for a single appearance in a limited series or a special:
☐ George Grizzard, *The Oldest Living Graduate*, April 7, 1980 (NBC)
Ernest Borgnine, "All Quiet on the Western Front," *Hallmark Hall of Fame*, November 14, 1979 (CBS)
John Cassavetes, *Flesh and Blood*, October 14 and 16, 1979 (CBS)
Charles Durning, *Attica*, March 2, 1980 (ABC)
Harold Gould, *Moviola* (NBC)

OUTSTANDING SUPPORTING ACTRESS IN A COMEDY OR VARIETY OR MUSIC SERIES

For a continuing or single performance in a regular series:
☐ Loretta Swit, *M*A*S*H* (CBS)
Loni Anderson, *WKRP in Cincinnati* (CBS)
Polly Holliday, *Alice* (CBS)
Inga Swenson, *Benson* (ABC)

OUTSTANDING SUPPORTING ACTRESS IN A DRAMA SERIES

For a continuing or single performance in a regular series:
☐ Nancy Marchand, *Lou Grant* (CBS)
Nina Foch, *Lou Grant*, "Hollywood," December 17, 1979 (CBS)
Linda Kelsey, *Lou Grant* (CBS)
Jessica Walter, *Trapper John, M.D.* (CBS)

☐ Indicates winner

OUTSTANDING SUPPORTING ACTRESS IN A LIMITED SERIES OR A SPECIAL

For a continuing role in a limited series or for a single appearance in a limited series or a special:
☐ Mare Winningham, *Amber Waves*, March 9, 1980 (ABC)
Eileen Heckart, *F.D.R.: The Last Year*, May 15, 1980 (NBC)
Patricia Neal, "All Quiet on the Western Front," *Hallmark Hall of Fame*, November 14, 1979 (CBS)
Carrie Nye, *Moviola: The Scarlett O'Hara War*, May 19, 1980 (NBC)

Prime Time Writing and Directing Awards

OUTSTANDING DIRECTING IN A COMEDY SERIES

For a single episode of a regular series:
☐ James Burrows, *Taxi*, "Louie and the Nice Girl," September 11, 1979 (ABC)
Alan Alda, *M*A*S*H*, "Dreams," February 18, 1980 (CBS)
Charles Dubin, *M*A*S*H*, "Period of Adjustment," October 22, 1979 (CBS)
Burt Metcalfe, *M*A*S*H*, "Bottle Fatigue," January 7, 1980 (CBS)
Harry Morgan, *M*A*S*H*, "Stars and Stripe," December 17, 1979 (CBS)

OUTSTANDING DIRECTING IN A DRAMA SERIES

For a single episode of a regular series:
☐ Roger Young, *Lou Grant*, "Cop," September 17, 1979 (CBS)
Burt Brinckerhoff, *Lou Grant*, "Hollywood," December 17, 1979 (CBS)
Peter Levin, *Lou Grant*, "Andrew, Part II Trial," December 10, 1979 (CBS)
Frank Perry, *Skag*, "Premiere," January 6, 1980 (NBC)
Gene Reynolds, *Lou Grant*, "Influence," March 10, 1980 (CBS)

OUTSTANDING DIRECTING IN A VARIETY OR MUSIC PROGRAM

For a single episode of a regular or limited series or for a special:
☐ Dwight Hemion, *IBM Presents Baryshnikov on Broadway*, April 24, 1980 (ABC)
Steve Binder, *The Big Show*, (with Mariette Hartley, Dean Martin), March 18, 1980 (NBC)
Tony Charmoli, *John Denver and the Muppets: A Christmas Together*, December 5, 1979 (ABC)
Peter Harris, *The Muppet Show*, (with Liza Minnelli), (Syndicated)

OUTSTANDING DIRECTING IN A LIMITED SERIES OR A SPECIAL

For a single episode of a limited series or for a special:
☐ Marvin J. Chomsky, *Attica*, March 2, 1980 (ABC)
John Erman, *Moviola: The Scarlett O'Hara War*, May 19, 1980 (NBC)
William A. Graham, *Guyana Tragedy: The Story of Jim Jones*, April 15 and 16, 1980 (CBS)
Delbert Mann, "All Quiet on the Western Front," *Hallmark Hall of Fame*, November 14, 1979 (CBS)
Joseph Sargent, *Amber Waves*, March 9, 1980 (ABC)

OUTSTANDING ACHIEVEMENT IN CHOREOGRAPHY

For a single episode of a regular of limited series, or for a special:
☐ Alan Johnson, *Shirley MacLaine... "Every Little Movement,"* May 22, 1980 (CBS)
Ron Field, *IBM Presents Baryshnikov on Broadway*, April 24, 1980 (ABC)
Lester Wilson, *Uptown—A Musical Comedy History of Harlem's Apollo Theatre*, May 30, 1980 (NBC)

OUTSTANDING WRITING IN A COMEDY SERIES

For a single episode of a regular series:
☐ Bob Colleary, *Barney Miller*, "Photographer," September 20, 1979 (ABC)
Glen Charles and Les Charles, *Taxi*, "Honor Thy Father," September 18, 1979 (ABC)
Stan Daniels and Ed Weinberger, *The Associates*, "The Censors," April 10, 1980 (ABC)
David Isaacs and Ken Levine, *M*A*S*H*, "Goodbye, Radar,"—Part II, October 15, 1979 (CBS)
Michael Leeson (Teleplay), Charlie Hauck (story), *The Associates*, "The First Day," September 23, 1979 (ABC)

OUTSTANDING WRITING IN A DRAMA SERIES

For a single episode of a regular series:
☐ Seth Freeman, *Lou Grant*, "Cop," September 17, 1979 (CBS)
Allan Burns and Gene Reynolds, *Lou Grant*, "Brushfire," January 7, 1980 (CBS)
Stephen J. Cannell, *Tenspeed and Brown Shoe*, "Pilot," January 27, 1980 (ABC)
Michele Gallery, *Lou Grant*, "Lou," February 11, 1980 (CBS)
Abby Mann, *Skag*, "Premiere," January 6, 1980 (NBC)

OUTSTANDING WRITING IN A VARIETY OR MUSIC PROGRAM

For a single episode of a regular or limited series or for a special:

☐ Buz Kohan, *Shirley MacLaine. . . "Every Little Movement,"* May 22, 1980 (CBS)

Peter Aykroyd, Anne Beatts, Tom Davis, James Downey, Brian Doyle-Murray, Al Franken, Tom Gammill, Lorne Michaels, Matt Neuman, Don Novello, Sarah Paley, Max Pross, Herb Sargent, Tom Schiller, Harry Shearer, Rosie Shuster, Alan Zweibel, *Saturday Night Live*, Teri Garr (host), January 26, 1980 (NBC)

Fred Ebb, *Goldie and Liza Together*, February 19, 1980 (CBS)

Jim Henson, Don Hinkley, Jerry Juhl, David Odell, *The Muppet Show*, (with Alan Arkin), (Syndicated)

Bob Arnott, Roger Beatty, Dick Clair, Tim Conway, Ann Elder, Arnie Kogen, Buz Kohan, Jenna McMahon, Kenny Solms, *Carol Burnett & Company*, (with Sally Field), September 8, 1979 (ABC)

OUTSTANDING WRITING IN A LIMITED SERIES OR A SPECIAL

For a single episode of a limited series or for a special, whether the writing is an original teleplay or an adaptation:

☐ David Chase, *Off the Minnesota Strip*, May 5, 1980 (ABC)

James S. Henerson, *Attica*, March 2, 1980 (ABC)

James Lee, *Moviola: This Year's Blonde*, May 18, 1980 (NBC)

David W. Rintels, "Gideon's Trumpet," *Hallmark Hall of Fame*, April 30, 1980 (CBS)

Ken Trevey, *Amber Waves*, March 9, 1980 (ABC)

Creative Arts Awards

OUTSTANDING CINEMATOGRAPHY FOR A SERIES

For a single episode of a regular series:

☐ Enzo A. Martinelli, A.S.C., *The Contender*, "Break-through," April 10, 1980 (CBS)

Emmett Bergholz, *Fantasy Island*, "The Wedding," November 3, 1979 (ABC)

Alric Edens, A.S.C., *Quincy, M.E.*, "Riot," January 31, 1980 (NBC)

Gerald Perry Finnerman, A.S.C., *From Here to Eternity*, "Pearl Harbor," March 10, 1980 (NBC)

John McPherson, A.S.C., *The Incredible Hulk*, "Broken Image," January 4, 1980 (CBS)

☐ Indicates winner

Ted Voightländer, A.S.C., *Little House on the Prairie*, "May We Make Them Proud," February 4, 1980 (NBC)

OUTSTANDING CINEMATOGRAPHY FOR A LIMITED SERIES OR A SPECIAL

For a single episode of a limited series or for a special:

☐ Gayne Rescher, A.S.C., *Moviola: The Silent Lovers*, May 20, 1980 (NBC)

Joe Biroc, A.S.C., *Kenny Rogers as the Gambler*, April 8, 1980 (CBS)

Ted Voigtländer, A.S.C., *The Miracle Worker*, October 14, 1979 (NBC)

Harry L. Wolf, A.S.C., *Brave New World*, March 7, 1980 (NBC)

OUTSTANDING ART DIRECTION FOR A SERIES

For a single episode of a regular series:

☐ James D. Bissell (art director), William Webb (set decorator), *Palmerstown, U.S.A.*, "The Old Sister," May 1, 1980 (CBS)

James J. Agazzi (art director), Paul Sylos (art director, Bob Signorelli (set director), *Hart to Hart*, "Man with Jade Eyes," December 11, 1979 (ABC)

Michael Baugh (production designer), Edward McDonald (set decorator), *Beyond Westworld*, "Pilot," March 5, 1980 (CBS)

Hub Braden (art director), Fred Luff (art director), Frank Lombardo (set decorator), *Buck Rogers in the 25th Century*, "Ardala Returns," January 24, 1980 (NBC)

David Marshall (art director), William Craig Smith (art director), Leonard Mazzola (set decorator), *Skag*, "Premiere," January 6, 1980 (NBC)

OUTSTANDING ART DIRECTION FOR A LIMITED SERIES OR A SPECIAL

For a single episode of a limited series or for a special:

☐ Wilfrid Shingleton (production designer), Julian Sacks (art director), Jean Taillandier (art director), Cheryal Kearney (set decorator), Robert Christides (set decorator), *Gauguin the Savage*, April 29, 1980 (CBS)

Michael Baugh (production designer), Jerry Adams (set decorator), *Moviola: The Silent Lovers*, May 20, 1980 (NBC)

Jack F. DeShields (art director), Ira Bates (set decorator), *The Ordeal of Dr. Mudd*, March 25, 1980 (CBS)

Tom H. John (art director), Mary Ann Biddle (set decorator), *Brave New World*, March 7, 1980 (NBC)

Jan Scott (art director and production designer), Bill Harp (set decorator), *Orphan Train*, December 22, 1979 (CBS)

John Stoll (production designer), Karel Vacek (art director), "All Quiet on the Western Front," *Hallmark Hall of Fame*, November 14, 1979 (CBS)

OUTSTANDING ART DIRECTION FOR A VARIETY OR MUSIC PROGRAM

For a single episode of a regular or limited series or for a special:

☐ Charles Lisanby (art director), Dwight Jackson (set decorator), *IBM Presents Baryshnikov on Broadway*, April 24, 1980 (ABC)

Brian C. Bartholomew, Bob Keene (production designers), Tom Bugenhagen (set decorator), *The Big Show*, (with Sarah Purcell and Flip Wilson), June 3, 1980 (NBC)

Romain Johnston (art director), Debe Hendricks (set decorator), *Shirley McLaine. . . "Every Little Movement,"* May 22, 1980 (CBS)

Malcolm Stone (art director), *The Muppet Show*, (with Beverly Sills) (Syndicated)

OUTSTANDING MUSIC COMPOSITION FOR A SERIES (DRAMATIC UNDERSCORE)

For a single episode of a regular series:

☐ Patrick Williams, *Lou Grant*, "Hollywood," December 17, 1979 (CBS)

Bruce Broughton, *Dallas*, "The Lost Child," November 2, 1979 (CBS)

John Cacavas, *Eischied*, "Only the Pretty Girls Die,"—Part II, September 28, 1979 (NBC)

Billy Goldenberg, *Skag*, "Premiere," January 6, 1980 (NBC)

Fred Karlin, *Paris*, "Decisions," December 18, 1979 (CBS)

OUTSTANDING ACHIEVEMENT IN MUSIC COMPOSITION FOR A LIMITED SERIES OR A SPECIAL (DRAMATIC UNDERSCORE)

For a single episode of a limited series or for a special:

☐ Jerry Fielding, *High Midnight*, November 27, 1979 (CBS)

Gerald Fried, *Moviola: The Silent Lovers*, May 20, 1980 (NBC)

Pete Rugolo, *The Last Convertible*, Episode 1, September 24, 1979 (NBC)

Harry Sukman, *Salem's Lot*, November 17 and 24, 1979 (CBS)

OUTSTANDING ACHIEVEMENT IN MUSIC DIRECTION

For a single episode of a regular or limited series or for a special, whether it be variety or music:
☐ Ian Fraser (music director), Ralph Burns and Billy Byers (principal arrangers), *IBM Presents Baryshnikov on Broadway*, April 24, 1980 (ABC)
Artie Butler, *Barry Manilow—One Voice*, May 19, 1980 (ABC)
Nick Perito (music director), Joe Lipman, Angela Morley and Peter Myers (principal arrangers), *The Big Show*, (with Steve Lawrence and Don Rickles), April 8, 1980 (NBC)

OUTSTANDING COSTUME DESIGN FOR A SERIES

For a single episode of a regular series:
☐ Pete Menefee, *The Big Show*, (with Tony Randall and Herve Villechaize, March 25, 1980 (NBC)
Jean-Pierre Dorleac, *Galactica 1980*, "Starbuck's Last Journey," May 4, 1980 (ABC)
Calista Hendrickson, *The Muppet Show*, (with Beverly Sills) (Syndicated)
Grady Hunt, *Fantasy Island*, "Tatoo: The Love God/Magnolia Blossom," September 21, 1979 (ABC)
Alfred E. Lehman, *Buck Rogers in the 25th Century*, "Flight of the War Witch," Part II, April 3, 1980 (NBC)

OUTSTANDING COSTUME DESIGN FOR A LIMITED SERIES OR A SPECIAL

For a single episode of a limited series or for a special:
☐ Travilla, *Moviola: The Scarlett O'Hara War*, May 19, 1980 (NBC)
Bill Belew, *The Carpenters—Music, Music, Music*, May 16, 1980 (ABC)
Grady Hunt, *The Dream Merchants* (Syndicated)
Bob Mackie, *Ann-Margret—Hollywood Movie Girls*, May 3, 1980 (ABC)
Ret Turner, *The Beatrice Arthur Special*, January 19, 1980 (CBS)

OUTSTANDING ACHIEVEMENT IN MAKEUP

For a single episode of a regular or limited series or for a special:
☐ Richard Blair, *Moviola: The Scarlett O'Hara War*, May 19, 1980 (NBC)
John Chambers and Robert A. Sidell, *Beyond Westworld*, "Pilot," March 5, 1980 (CBS)
Lorraine Dawkins, Anita Harris, Sheila Mann, Mary Southgate, Brenda Yewdell, "Disraeli: Portrait of a

☐ Indicates winner

Romantic," *Masterpiece Theatre*, "Dizzy," June 1, 1980 (PBS)
Jack Freeman, *Haywire*, May 14, 1980 (CBS)
Ben Lane and Jack Young, *S.M.A., Salem's Lot*, November 17 and 24, 1979 (CBS)

OUTSTANDING ACHIEVEMENT IN HAIRSTYLING

For a single episode of a regular or limited series or for a special:
☐ Larry Germain and Donna Gilbert, *The Miracle Worker*, October 14, 1979 (NBC)
Naoma Cavin and Mary Hadley, *Murder Can Hurt You!*, May 21, 1980 (ABC)
Leonard Drake, *Moviola: The Silent Lovers*, May 20, 1980 (NBC)
Carolyn Elias and Bette Iverson, *Haywire*, May 14, 1980 (CBS)
Joan Phillips, *Fantasy Island*, "Dr. Jekyll and Ms. Hyde/Aphrodite," February 2, 1980 (ABC)

OUTSTANDING ACHIEVEMENT IN GRAPHIC DESIGN AND TITLE SEQUENCES

For a single episode of a regular or limited series or for a special. This includes animation only when created for use in titling:
☐ Phill Norman, *The French Atlantic Affair*, Part I, November 15, 1979 (ABC)
Gene Kraft, *Salem's Lot*, November 17 and 24, 1979 (CBS)

OUTSTANDING ACHIEVEMENT IN FILM EDITING FOR A SERIES

For a single episode of a regular series:
☐ M. Pam Blumenthal, *Taxi*, "Louie and the Nice Girl," September 11, 1979 (ABC)
Sidney M. Katz, A.C.E., *Skag*, "Premiere," January 6, 1980 (NBC)
Larry Mills, and Stanford Tischler, *M*A*S*H*, "The Yalu Brick Road," November 19, 1979 (CBS)
Larry Armstrong, A.C.E., *Skag*, "The Working Girl," Part I, January 24, 1980 (NBC)

OUTSTANDING FILM EDITING FOR A LIMITED SERIES OR A SPECIAL

For a single episode of a limited series or for a special:
☐ Bill Blunden and Alan Pattillo, "All Quiet on the Western Front," *Hallmark Hall of Fame*, November 14, 1979 (CBS)
Paul La Mastra, *Attica*, March 2, 1980 (ABC)
Jerrold L. Ludwig, A.C.E., *Kenny Rogers as the Gambler*, April 8, 1980 (CBS)

John A. Martinelli, A.C.E. and Rusty Coppleman, *S.O.S. Titanic*, September 23, 1979 (ABC)
David Newhouse, A.C.E., *Moviola: The Silent Lovers*, May 20, 1980 (NBC)
John Woodcock, A.C.E., *When Hell Was in Session*, October 8, 1979 (NBC)

OUTSTANDING ACHIEVEMENT IN FILM SOUND EDITING

For a single episode of a regular or limited series or for a special:
☐ Don Crosby, Mark Dennis, Tony Garber, Doug Grindstaff, Don V. Isaacs, Hank Salerno, Larry Singer, *Power*, Part I, January 14, 1980 (NBC)
Tom Cornwell, Dave Elliott, Don Ernst, Dimitry Gortinsky, Peter Harrison, Andrew Herbert, Michael L. Hilkene, Fred Judkins, Jill Taggart, Russ Tinsley, Christopher T. Welch, *The Plutonium Incident*, March 11, 1980 (CBS)
Tom Cornwell, Peter Harrison, Andrew Herbert, Michael L. Hilkene, Fred Judkins, Jill Taggart, Russ Tinsley, *Amber Waves*, March 9, 1980 (ABC)
Tom Cornwell, Linda Dove, Don Ernst, Peter Harrison, Andrew Herbert, Fred Judkins, Michael Redbourn, Russ Tinsley, *Attica*, March 2, 1980 (ABC)

OUTSTANDING ACHIEVEMENT IN FILM SOUND MIXING

For a single episode of a regular or limited series or for a special:
☐ Ray Barons, David Campbell, Bob Pettis, John Reitz, *The Ordeal of Dr. Mudd*, March 25, 1980 (CBS)
David Campbell, Jacque Nosco, Bob Pettis, John Reitz, *Guyana Tragedy: The Story of Jim Jones*, Part II, April 16, 1980 (CBS)
Christopher Large, Eddie Nelson, George E. Porter, Terry Porter, *Amber Waves*, March 9, 1980 (ABC)
David E. Dockendorf, Robert L. Harman, William L. McCaughey, Jack Solomon, *Skag*, "Premiere," January 6, 1980 (NBC)
Robert Glass Jr., Patrick Mitchell, Robert Thirwell, John Wilkenson, *The Golden Moment: An Olympic Love Story*, May 25 and 26, 1980 (NBC)

OUTSTANDING ACHIEVEMENT IN TAPE SOUND MIXING

For a single episode of a regular or limited series or for a special:
☐ Bruce Burns and Jerry Clemans, *Sinatra: The First 40 Years*, January 3, 1980 (NBC)
Jerry Clemans, Gordon F. Klimuck, Doug Nelson, *Olivia Newton-John—*

Hollywood Nights, April 14, 1980 (ABC)

Jerry Clemans, Juergen Koppers, Doug Nelson, *The Donna Summer Special*, January 27, 1980 (ABC)

Jerry Clemans and Billy Sherrill, *Kenny Rogers and the American Cowboy*, November 28, 1979 (CBS)

Terry Farris, Tom Huth, Blake Norton, *The Crystal Gayle Special*, December 12, 1979 (CBS)

Donald Worsham, *The Oldest Living Graduate*, April 7, 1980 (NBC)

OUTSTANDING VIDEOTAPE EDITING FOR A SERIES

For a single episode of a regular series:

☐ John Hawkins, *The Muppet Show*, (with Liza Minnelli) (Syndicated)

Ken Denisoff, Kevin Muldoon, Andy Zall, *The Big Show*, (with Tony Randall and Herve Villechaize), March 25, 1980 (NBC)

Terry Pickford, *Fridays*, (with Boz Scaggs), May 16, 1980 (ABC)

Marco Zappia, *A New Kind of Family*, "I Do," September 16, 1979 (ABC)

OUTSTANDING VIDEOTAPE EDITING FOR A LIMITED SERIES OR A SPECIAL

For a single episode of a limited series or for a special:

☐ Danny White, *Olivia Newton-John—Hollywood Nights*, April 14, 1980 (ABC)

Terry Climer, *The Donna Summer Special*, January 27, 1980 (ABC)

Andy Zall, *IBM Presents Baryshnikov on Broadway*, April 24, 1980 (ABC)

Marco Zappia, *Perry Como's Christmas in New Mexico*, December 14, 1979 (ABC)

OUTSTANDING ACHIEVEMENT IN TECHNICAL DIRECTION AND ELECTRONIC CAMERAWORK

For a single episode of a regular or limited series or for a special program:

☐ Wayne Parsons (technical director), Tom Geren, Dean Hall, Bob Highton, William Landers, Ron Sheldon (camerapersons), *The Oldest Living Graduate*, April 7, 1980 (NBC)

Robert G. Holmes (technical director), Bruce Bottone, George Falardeau, William Landers, Peggy Mahoney, Mike Stramisky (camerapersons), *The Midnight Special*, Host: The Cars, September 28, 1979 (NBC)

Robert A. Kemp (technical director), Ralph Alcocer, Jim Angel, Dave Banks, Ron Brooks, Warren Cress, Jack Denton, Bud Holland, Art La Combe, Dan Langford, Wayne Orr,

☐ Indicates winner

Ken Tamburri (camerapersons), *Goldie and Liza Together*, February 19, 1980 (CBS)

Jerry Weiss (technical director), Leslie B. Atkinson, Roy Holm, Peggy Mahoney, Mike Stramisky (camerapersons), *The Magic of David Copperfield*, October 24, 1979 (CBS)

Jerry Weiss (technical director), Larry Heider, Roy Holm, William Landers, Peggy Mahoney, Wayne Orr, Mike Stramisky (camerapersons), *A Christmas Special. . . With Love, Mac Davis*, December 24, 1979 (NBC)

OUTSTANDING ACHIEVEMENT IN LIGHTING DIRECTION (ELECTRONIC)

For a single episode of a regular or limited series or for a special program:

☐ Peter G. Edwards, William Knight, Peter S. Passas, *F.D.R.: "The Last Year,"* May 15, 1980 (NBC)

Tony Di Girolamo, *Tender Land*, August 28, 1979 (PBS)

Daniel Flannery (Lighting Director), William M. Klages (lighting consultant), *Goldie and Liza Together*, February 19, 1980 (CBS)

William M. Klages, *The Big Show*, (with Sarah Purcell and Flip Wilson, June 2, 1980 (NBC)

Fred McKinnon and Mark Palius, *The Cheryl Ladd Special: Souvenirs*, May 19, 1980 (ABC)

George W. Riesenberger and John Freschi, *The Unbroken Circle: A Tribute to Mother Maybelle Carter*, November 28, 1979 (CBS)

OUTSTANDING INDIVIDUAL ACHIEVEMENT—SPECIAL EVENTS

(Possibility of one award, more than one award or no award):

Larry Grossman (music), Buz Kohan (lyrics), *52nd Annual Awards Presentation of the Academy of Motion Picture Arts and Sciences, "Dancin' on the Silver Screen,"* April 14, 1980 (ABC)

Ray Klausen (art director), *52nd Annual Awards Presentation of the Academy of Motion Picture Arts and Sciences*, April 14, 1980 (ABC)

Donald O'Connor (performer), *52nd Annual Awards Presentation of the Academy of Motion Picture Arts and Sciences, "Dancin' on the Silver Screen,"* April 14, 1980 (ABC)

Walter Painter (choreographer), *52nd Annual Awards Presentation of the Academy of Motion Picture Arts and Sciences, "Dancin' on the Silver Screen,"* April 14, 1980 (ABC)

Carl Vitelli (lighting director), *The 34th Annual Tony Awards*, June 8, 1980 (CBS)

OUTSTANDING INDIVIDUAL ACHIEVEMENT—INFORMATIONAL PROGRAM

(Possibility of one award, more than one award or no award):

☐ Bryan Anderson, Bob Elfstrom, Al Giddings (cinematographers), *Mysteries of the Sea*, May 18, 1980 (ABC)

☐ David Clark, Joel Fein, Robert L. Harman, George E. Porter (film sound mixers), "Dive to the Edge of Creation," *National Geographic Special,"* January 7, 1980 (PBS)

☐ Robert Eisenhardt, Hank O'Karma, Jane Kurson (film editors), *The Body Human: The Body Beautiful*, April 16, 1980 (CBS)

Henri Colpi and John Soh (film editors), "The Nile," *The Cousteau Odyssey*, December 9 and 10, 1979 (PBS)

Robert E. Fuisz M.D., Louis H. Gorfain (writers), *The Body Human: The Body Beautiful*, April 16, 1980 (CBS)

OUTSTANDING INDIVIDUAL ACHIEVEMENT—SPECIAL CLASS

(Possibility of one award, more than one award or no award):

☐ Geof Bartz (film editor), *Operation: Lifeline, Dr James "Red" Duke, Trauma Surgeon*, August 13, 1979 (NBC)

Harry Bottorf, John Gisondi, William Knight, Dick Weiss (lighting), *A Christmas Carol at Ford's Theatre*, December 15, 1979 (PBS)

Clifford L. Chally and Pat Zinn (costumes), *The Dream Merchants* (Syndicated)

Darryl Sutton (videotape editor), *Bob Hope's Overseas Christmas Tours: Around the World with the Troops (1941–1972)*, February 3 and 10, 1980 (NBC)

O. Tamburri (technical director), Reed Howard, William Landers, Victoria Walker (camerapersons), *Skinflint: A Country Christmas Carol*, December 18, 1979 (NBC)

OUTSTANDING INDIVIDUAL ACHIEVEMENT—CHILDREN'S PROGRAM

(Possibility of one award, more than one award or no award):

☐ Bob O'Bradovich (makeup), *The Halloween that Almost Wasn't*, October 28, 1979 (ABC)

Ozzie Alfonso (director), *Sesame Street in Puerto Rico*, November 24, 1979 (PBS)

Arthur Ginsburg (film editor), *The Halloween that Almost Wasn't*, October 28, 1979 (ABC)

Mariette Hartley (performer), *The Halloween that Almost Wasn't*, October 28, 1979 (ABC)

Nat Mongioi (art director), *Sesame Street in Puerto Rico*, November 24, 1979 (PBS)

OUTSTANDING INDIVIDUAL ACHIEVEMENT—ANIMATION PROGRAMS

(Possibility of one award, more than one award or no award):

Friz Freleng (director), *Pink Panther in Olym-Pinks*, February 22, 1980 (ABC)

Chuck Jones (director), *Bugs Bunny's Bustin' Out All Over*, May 21, 1980 (CBS)

OUTSTANDING ACHIEVEMENT IN ENGINEERING DEVELOPMENT

An award to an individual, a company or an organization for developments in engineering that are either so extensive an improvement on existing methods or so innovative in nature that they materially affect the transmission, recording or reception of television:

□ National Bureau of Standards, Public Broadcasting Service and American Broadcasting Company for their development of the Closed Captioninig for the Deaf system

Citation to **David Bargen** for the development of the "409" and "Trace" computer programs used in off-line videotape editing

Citation to **Vital Industries** for its pioneering development of digital video manipulation technology

Citation to **Convergence Corporation** for the videotape editing systems utilizing a "joystick" control, as incorporated in its ECS-100 Video Tape Editing Systems

OUTSTANDING INDIVIDUAL ACHIEVEMENT—CREATIVE TECHNICAL CRAFTS

(Possibility of one award, more than one award or no awards):

□ Scott Schachter (live audio mixing), *Live from Studio 8H: A Tribute to Toscanini*, January 9, 1980 (NBC)

□ Mark Schubin, "Live Stereo Simulcast," *Luciano Pavarotti and the New York Philharmonic, Live from Lincoln Center*, January 14, 1980 (PBS)

Leslie Asch, Ed Christie, Barbara Davis, Faz Fazakas, Nomi Fredrick, Michael Frith, Amy Van Gilder, Dave Goelz, Marianne Harms, Larry

□ Indicates winner

Jameson, Mari Kaestle, Rollin Krewson, Tim Miller, Robert Payne, Jan Rosenthal, Don Sahlin, Caroly Wilcox (Muppet design), *The Muppet Show*, (with Alan Arkin) (Syndicated)

Ed Christie, Barbara Davis, Faz Fazakas, Nomi Fredrick, Michael Frith, Amy Van Gilder, Dave Goelz, Larry Jameson, Mari Kaestle, Rollin Krewson, Tim Miller, Robert Payne, Jan Rosenthal, Don Sahlin, Caroly Wilcox (Muppet design), *The Muppet Show*, (with Kenny Rogers) (Syndicated)

Roy Whybrow (special effects—cinematography), "All Quiet on the Western Front," *Hallmark Hall of Fame*, November 14, 1979 (CBS)

THIRD ANNUAL ATAS GOVERNORS AWARD
□ To Johnny Carson

Daytime Awards

OUTSTANDING DAYTIME DRAMA SERIES

Emmy(s) to executive producer(s) and producer(s):

All My Children, Agnes Nixon (executive producer), Jorn Winther (producer) (ABC)

Another World, Paul Rauch (executive producer), Mary S. Bonner and Robert Costello (producers) (NBC)

□ *Guiding Light*, Allen M. Potter (executive producer), Leslie Kwartin and Joe Willmore (producers) (CBS)

OUTSTANDING GAME OR AUDIENCE PARTICIPATION SHOW

Emmy(s) to executive producer(s) and producer(s):

Family Feud, Mark Goodson (executive producer), Howard Felsher (producer) (ABC)

□ *Hollywood Squares*, Merrill Heatter and Robert Quigley (executive producers), Jay Redack (producer) (NBC)

□ *The $20,000 Pyramid*, Bob Stewart (executive producer), Anne Marie Schmitt and Jane Rothchild (producers) (ABC)

OUTSTANDING TALK, SERVICE OR VARIETY SERIES

Emmy(s) to executive producer(s) and producer(s):

□ *Donahue*, Richard Mincer (executive producer), Patricia McMillen (senior producer), Darlene Hayes and Sheri Singer (producers) (Syndicated)

Good Morning America, George Merlis (executive producer), John Kippycash, Jack Reilly, Jan Rifkinson, Sonya Selby-Wright and Susan Winston (producers) (ABC)

The Mike Douglas Show, Frank Miller (executive producer), Vince Calandra and E.V. DiMassa Jr. (producers) (Syndicated)

OUTSTANDING CHILDREN'S ENTERTAINMENT SPECIAL

Emmy(s) to executive producer(s) and producer(s):

"The Boy with Two Heads," *Once upon a Classic*, Jay Rayvid (executive producer), Frank Good and James A. DeVinney (producers), December 14, 1979 (PBS)

"The House at 12 Rose Street," *NBC Special Treat*, Daniel Wilson (executive producer), Fran Sears (producer), March 4, 1980 (NBC)

"I Don't Know Who I Am," *NBC Special Treat*, Daniel Wilson (executive producer), Joanne A. Curley (producer), November 20, 1979 (NBC)

□ "The Late Great Me: Story of a Teenage Alcoholic," *ABC Afterschool Special*, Daniel Wilson (executive producer), Linda Marmelstein (producer), November 14, 1979 (ABC)

"The Rocking Chair Rebellion," *NBC Special Treat*, Daniel Wilson (executive producer), Phyllis Minoff (producer), October 23, 1979 (NBC)

OUTSTANDING CHILDREN'S ENTERTAINMENT SERIES

Emmy(s) to executive producer(s) and producer(s):

Captain Kangaroo, Robert Keeshan (executive producer), Joel Kosofsky (producer) (CBS)

□ *Hot Hero Sandwich*, Bruce Hart and Carole Hart (executive producers), Howard G. Malley (producer) (NBC)

Kids Are People Too, Lawrence Einhorn (executive producer), Laura Schrock (producer), Noreen Conlin (co-producer) (ABC)

OUTSTANDING CHILDREN'S ANTHOLOGY/DRAMATIC PROGRAMMING

Emmy(s) to executive producer(s) and producer(s).

(Possibility of one award, more than one award or no award):

□ "Animal Talk," *CBS Library*, Diane Asselin (executive producer), Paul Asselin (producer), March 4, 1980 (CBS)

□ "The Gold Bug," *ABC Weekend Special*, Linda Gottlieb (executive producer), Doro Bachrach (producer), February 2 and 9, 1980 (ABC)

□ "Leatherstocking Tales," *Once upon a Classic*, Jay Rayvid (executive producer), Bob Walsh (producer),

January 21 and 28, February 4 and 11, 1980 (PBS)

☐ "Once Upon a Midnight Dreary," *CBS Library*, Diane Asselin and Paul Asselin (producers), October 21, 1979 (CBS)

"The Revenge of Red Chief," *ABC Weekend Special*, Robert Chenault (executive producer), December 15, 1979 (ABC)

OUTSTANDING CHILDREN'S INFORMATIONAL INSTRUCTIONAL SERIES/SPECIALS

Emmy(s) to executive producer(s) and producer(s).

(Possibility of one award, more than one award or no award):

Mister Rogers' Neighborhood, Fred Rogers (executive producer), Hugh Martin (producer) (PBS)

☐ *Sesame Street*, Al Hyslop (executive producer), Dave Freyss (producer) (PBS)

☐ *Thirty Minutes*, Joel Heller (executive producer), Allan Ducovny, Madeline Amgott, Diego Echevarria, Horace Jenkens, Elizabeth Lawrence, Patti Obrow White, Robert Rubin, Susan Mills, Catherine Olian and Virginia Gray (producers) (CBS)

"Make 'Em Laugh: A Young People's Comedy Concert," *CBS Festival of Lively Arts for Young People*, Jack Wohl and Bernard Rothman (executive producers), Robert Arnott and Sid Smith (producers), November 25, 1979 (CBS)

☐ "Why a Conductor?" *CBS Festival of Lively Arts for Young People*, Kirk Browning (executive producer), November 18, 1979 (CBS)

OUTSTANDING CHILDREN'S INFORMATIONAL/INSTRUCTIONAL PROGRAMMING—SHORT FORMAT

Emmy(s) to executive producer(s) and producer(s).

(Possibility of one award, more than one award or no award):

☐ *ABC Schoolhouse Rook*, Thomas Yohe (executive producer), George Newall and Radford Stone (producers) (ABC)

☐ *ASK NBC News*, Lester Crystal (senior executive producer), Beryl Pfizer (producer) (NBC)

☐ *H.E.L.P.!!! (Dr. Henry's Emergency Lessons for People)*, Ken Greengrass and Phil Lawrence (executive producers), Lynn Ahrens (producer) (ABC)

☐ *In the News*, Joel Heller (executive producer), Walter Lister (producer) (CBS)

When You Turn off the Set, Turn on a Book, Mary Alice Dwyer (executive

☐ Indicates winner

producer), George Newall and Tom Yohe (producers) (NBC)

OUTSTANDING ACHIEVEMENT IN RELIGIOUS PROGRAMMING— SERIES/SPECIALS

Emmy(s) to executive producer(s) and producer(s).

(Possibility of one award, more than one award or no award):

☐ *Directions*, Sid Darion (executive producer) (ABC)

☐ *For Our Times*, Pamela Ilott (executive producer), Joseph Clement, Chalmers Dale, Marlene DiDonato and Ted Holmes (producers) (CBS)

As We with Candles Do, Doris Ann (executive producer), February 24, 1980 (NBC)

A Conversation on Passover: Renewing Ancient Traditions, Doris Ann (executive producer), Martin Hoade (producer), April 8, 1979 (NBC)

A Talent for Life: Jews of the Italian Renaissance, Helen Marmor (executive producer), Martin Hoade (producer), December 2, 1979 (NBC)

OUTSTANDING ACHIEVEMENT IN COVERAGE OF SPECIAL EVENTS

Emmy(s) to executive producer(s) and producer(s).

(Possibility of one award, more than one award or no award):

☐ *La Gioconda*, Jeanne Mulcahy (executive producer), John Goberman (producer; for KCET Los Angeles), September 16, 1979 (PBS)

☐ *Macy's 53rd Annual Thanksgiving Day Parade*, Dick Schneider (producer), November 22, 1979 (NBC)

91st Tournament of Roses Parade, Dick Schneider (producer), January 1, 1980 (NBC)

SPECIAL CLASSIFICATION OF OUTSTANDING PROGRAM ACHIEVEMENT

For programs that are so unique and different that they do not fall into any other category or area. Emmy(s) to executive producer(s) and producer(s).

(Possibility of one award, more than one award or no award):

American Bandstand, Dick Clark (executive producer), Larry Klein (producer), Barry Glazer (co-producer) (ABC)

☐ *FYI*, Yanna Kroyt Brandt, (producer) (ABC)

Giselle, E. Grigorian (producer; for Gosteleradio—USSR), April 8, 1979 (NBC)

A Memorial Tribute to Jim Crockett, Russell Marash (producer; for WGBH-Boston), July 16, 1979 (PBS)

OUTSTANDING ACTOR IN A DAYTIME DRAMA SERIES

John Gabriel, *Ryan's Hope* (ABC)
Michael Levin, *Ryan's Hope* (ABC)
Franc Luz, *The Doctors* (NBC)
James Mitchell, *All My Children* (ABC)
William Mooney, *All My Children* (ABC)
☐ Douglass Watson, *Another World* (NBC)

OUTSTANDING ACTRESS IN A DAYTIME DRAMA SERIES

Julia Barr, *All My Children* (ABC)
Leslie Charleson, *General Hospital* (ABC)
Kim Hunter, *The Edge or Night* (ABC)
☐ Judith Light, *One Life to Live* (ABC)
Beverlee McKinsey, *Another World* (NBC)
Kathleen Noone, *All My Children* (ABC)

OUTSTANDING PERFORMANCE BY AN ACTOR IN A SUPPORTING ROLE FOR A DAYTIME DRAMA SERIES

Vasili Bogazianos, *The Edge of Night* (ABC)
☐ Warren Burton, *All My Children* (ABC)
Larry Haines, *Search for Tomorrow* (CBS)
Ron Hale, *Ryan's Hope* (ABC)
Julius LaRosa, *Another World* (NBC)
Shepperd Strudwick, *Love of Life* (CBS)

OUTSTANDING PERFORMANCE BY AN ACTRESS IN A SUPPORTING ROLE FOR A DAYTIME DRAMA SERIES

Deidre Hall, *Days of Our Lives* (NBC)
☐ Francesca James, *All My Children* (ABC)
Lois Kibbee, *The Edge of Night* (ABC)
Elaine Lee, *The Doctors* (NBC)
Valerie Mahaffey, *The Doctors* (NBC)
Louise Shaffer, *Ryan's Hope* (ABC)

OUTSTANDING GUEST/CAMEO APPEARANCE IN A DAYTIME DRAMA SERIES

(For five fewer appearances):

Sammy David Jr., *One Life to Live*, August 9, 10, 14, 15 and 20, 1979 (ABC)
Joan Fontaine, *Ryan's Hope*, January 28 and 30, February 4, 6, and 7, 1980 (ABC)
Kathryn Harrow, *The Doctors*, December 17 and 18, 1979, January 4, 7 and 8, 1980 (NBC)
☐ Hugh McPhillips, *Days of Our Lives*, December 27, 1979, January 2, 1980 (NBC)
Eli Mintz, *All My Children*, October 11, 1979 (ABC)

OUTSTANDING HOST OR HOSTESS IN A GAME OR AUDIENCE PARTICIPATION SHOW

Richard Dawson, *Family Feud* (ABC)
☐ Peter Marshall, *Hollywood Squares* (NBC)

OUTSTANDING HOST OR HOSTESS IN A TALK, SERVICE OR VARIETY SERIES

☐ Phil Donahue, *Donahue* (Syndicated)
Dinah Shore, *Dinah! and Friends* (Syndicated)

OUTSTANDING WRITING FOR A DAYTIME DRAMA SERIES

Agnes Nixon, Wisner Washam, Jack Wood, Caroline Franz, Mary K. Wells, Cathy Chicos, Clarice Balckburn, Anita Jaffe and Ken Harvey, *All My Children* (ABC)
Henry Slesar and Steve Lehrman, *The Edge of Night* (ABC)
Gordon Russell, Sam Hall, Peggy O'Shea, Don Wallace, Lanie Bertram, Cynthia Benjamin and Marisa Gioffre, *One Life to Live* (ABC)
☐ Claire Labine, Paul Avila Mayer, Mary Munisteri, Judith Pinsker and Jeffrey Lane, *Ryan's Hope* (ABC)

OUTSTANDING DIRECTION FOR A DAYTIME DRAMA SERIES

Henry Kaplan, Jack Coffey, Sherrell Hoffman and Jorn Winther, *All My Children* (ABC)
Ira Cirker, Melvin Bernhardt, Robert Calhoun, Barnet Kellman, Jack Hofsiss and Andrew Weyman, *Another World* (NBC)
John Sedwick and Richard Pepperman, *The Edge of Night* (ABC)
Marlena Laird, Alan Pultz and Phil Sogard, *General Hospital* (ABC)
Larry Auerbach and Robert Scinto, *Love of Life* (CBS)
☐ Lela Swift and Jerry Evans, *Ryan's Hope* (ABC)

OUTSTANDING ACHIEVEMENT IN TECHNICAL EXCELLENCE FOR A DAYTIME DRAMA SERIES

Emmys to individual team members:
☐ Joseph Solomito, Howard Zweig (technical directors), Lawrence Hammond, Robert Ambrico, Dianne Cates-Cantrell, Christopher N. Mauro, Larry Strack, Vincent Senatore (electronic camerapersons), Albin S. Lemanski (audio engineer), Len Walas (video engineer), Diana Wenman, Jean Dadario (associate directors), Roger Haenelt, John L. Grella (Videotape editors), Irving Robbin, Jim Reichert (music composers), Teri Smith

(music director), *All My Children* (ABC)
Frank Gaeta, Steve Cimino, Frank DeRienzo (technical directors), Carl Eckett, David Weinberg, Olonzo Roberts, Wayne Norman (electronic camerapersons), Philip Berge, Mel Hench (audio engineers), Arnold Dick, Harold Mofsen (video engineers), Kevin Kelley, John Libretto (associate directors), Lloyd Campbell, John O'Connor (videotape editors), Score Productions (music composer/director), *Another World* (NBC)
Raymond Barrett (technical director), Jack Dolan, Steve Jambeck, Jan Kasoff (electronic camerapersons), George Corrado (audio engineer), Frank Vierling (video engineer), David Handler (associate director), Lee Goldman (videotape editor), Bob Israel (music coordinator), John Geller (music director), *The Doctors* (NBC)
William Edwards (technical director), William Hughes, Thomas Stallone, Arie Hefter (electronic camerapersons), Edward Atchison (audio engineer), Robert Saxon (sound effects), John Valentino (video engineer), Joanne Goodhart (associate director), Stephen Scott, Lenny Davidowitz (videotape editors), Elliott Lawrence (music composer), Barbara Miller (music coordinator), *The Edge of Night* (ABC)
David Smith, John Cochran (technical directors), Dave Banks, Luis Rojas, Carol Wetovich, James Angel, Jack Denton (electronic camerapersons), Ken Quayle, Zoli Osaze (audio engineers), Nick Kleissas (sound effects), Sam Potter (video engineer), Hal Alexander, George Thompson (associate directors), Dan Blevens, Jack Moody (videotape editors), Charles Paul (music composer/director), *General Hospital* (ABC)
George Whitaker (technical director), Dick Kerr, Mary Flood, Frank J. Merklein (electronic camerapersons), William deBlock, Lee M. Goldman (audio engineers), Rudy Picarillo, Dick Williams, Linda Wallach (video engineers), Suellen Goldstein (associate director), Pat Malik, Walter Urbanski (videotape editors), Carey Gold (music composer), Sybil Weinberger (music supervisor), *Ryan's Hope* (ABC)

OUTSTANDING ACHIEVEMENT IN DESIGN EXCELLENCE FOR A DAYTIME DRAMA SERIES

Emmys to individual team members:
☐ William Mickley (scenic designer), William Itkin, Donna Larson, Mel Handelsman (lighting directors), Carol Luiken (costume designer), Sylvia Lawrence (makeup designer), Michael Huddle (hair designer), Hy Bley (graphic designer), *All My Children* (ABC)
Robert Franklin (art director), Russell Christian, Richard Hankins (scenic designers), Leo Farrenkopf, Maury Verschoore (lighting directors), Lewis Brown (costume designer), Frank Rubertone (hair designer), Edward Jackson (makeup designer), *Another World* (NBC)
Jim Ellingwood (art director), Mercer Barrows (set decorator), Grant Velie, John Zak, Tom Markle (lighting directors), George Whittaker (costume designer), Pam K. Cole (makeup designer), Kathy Kotarakos (hair designer), *General Hospital* (ABC)
Sy Tomashoff (scenic designer), Herb Gruber (scenic artist), John Connolly (lighting director), Bill Kellard (costume designer), James Cola (makeup designer), John K. Quinn (hair designer), *Ryan's Hope* (ABC)

OUTSTANDING INDIVIDUAL DIRECTION FOR A GAME OR AUDIENCE PARTICIPATION SHOW

For a single episode:
Paul Alter, *Family Feud*, April 10, 1979 (ABC)
☐ Jerome Shaw, *Hollywood Squares*, June 14, 1979 (NBC)

OUTSTANDING INDIVIDUAL DIRECTION FOR A TALK, SERVICE OR VARIETY SERIES

For a single episode:
☐ Duke Struck, "Henry Fonda Tribute," *Good Morning America*, February 2–8, 1980 (ABC)
Glen Swanson, *Dinah! and Friends in Singapore*, November 1, 1979 (Syndicated)
Ron Weiner, "Pimps," *Donahue*, February 28, 1980 (Syndicated)

OUTSTANDING INDIVIDUAL ACHIEVEMENT IN CHILDREN'S PROGRAMMING

For a single episode or for a special program.
(Possibility of one award, more than one award or no award):
☐ Melissa Sue Anderson (performer), "Which Mother is Mine?," *ABC Afterschool Special*, September 26, 1979 (ABC)

☐ Indicates winner

Rene Auberjonois (performer), "Once upon a Midnight Dreary," *CBS Library*, October 21, 1979 (CBS)

☐ Maia Danziger (performer), "The Late Great Me: Story of a Teenage Alcoholic," *ABC Afterschool Special*, November 14, 1979 (ABC)

Bob Keeshan (performer), *Captain Kangaroo*, October 9, 1979 (CBS)

☐ Butterfly McQueen (performer), "The Seven Wishes of a Rich Kid," *ABC Afterschool Special*, May 9, 1979 (ABC)

☐ Fred Rogers (performer), "Mister Rogers Goes to School," *Mister Rogers' Neighborhood*, August 29, 1979 (PBS)

Mary Batten (writer), "Forces/Friday," *3-2-1 Contact*, January 25, 1980 (PBS)

☐ David Axlerod, Joseçh A. Bailey, Andy Breckman, Richard Camp, Sherry Coben, Bruce Hart, Carole Hart and Marianne Mayer (writers), *Hot Hero Sandwich*, December 8, 1979 (NBC)

☐ Jan Hartman (writer), "The Late Great Me: Story of a Teenage Alcoholic," *ABC Afterschool Special*, November 14, 1979 (ABC)

John O'Toole (writer), "The Leatherstocking Tales," (4 parts), *Once upon a Classic*, January 21 and 18, February 4 and 11, 1980 (PBS)

Fred Rogers (writer), "Mister Rogers Goes to School," *Mister Rogers' Neighborhood*, August 29, 1979 (PBS)

Joseph Consentino (director), "Divorce," *Big Blue Marble*, December 29, 1979 (Syndicated)

☐ Anthony Lover (director), "The Late Great Me: Story of a Teenage Alcoholic," *ABC Afterschool Special*, November 14, 1979 (ABC)

J. Philip Miller (director), "The Bloodhound Gang," *3-2-1 Contact*, January 10, 1980 (PBS)

☐ Arthur Allen Seidelman (director), "Which Mother Is Mine?" *ABC Afterschool Special*, September 26, 1979 (ABC)

Thomas Trbovich (director), *Hot Hero Sandwich*, December 1, 1979 (NBC)

William P. Kelley (technical director), Gene Martin, John Pinto, Vincent DiPietro, Thomas C. Dezendorf, Edward Corsi and Donald Mulvaney (electronic camerapersons), *Hot Hero Sandwich*, December 1, 1979 (NBC)

☐ Steven Zink (director of photography [tape] single camera; film style), *Sesame Street*—Show #1320 (Puerto Rico), November 26, 1979 (PBS)

☐ George Alch (audio engineer), "A Special Gift," *ABC Afterschool Special*, October 24, 1979 (ABC)

☐ Lee Dichter (film sound mixer), *Big Blue Marble*, September 8, 1979 (Syndicated)

Peter Page (film sound mixer), "Shark," *Animals Animals Animals*, September 9, 1979 (ABC)

Scott Schachter and Joel G. Spector (tape sound mixers), *Hot Hero Sandwich*, December 1, 1979 (NBC)

Jerome Haggart, Harvey Berger and Bill Breshears (videotape editors), *Hot Hero Sandwich*, November 10, 1979 (NBC)

☐ John Gonzalez (associate director), Charles Liotta, John A. Servidio and George A. Magda (videotape editors), *Time Out* (short form), Shows #1, 7, 10, 12, 13 and 26 (NBC)

Don Sullivan (associate director), Jan Morgan (videotape editor), "Fast/Show," *3-2-1 Contact*, February 4, 1980 (PBS)

☐ John Beymer and Mike Fash (cinematographers), "A Movie Star's Daughter," *ABC Afterschool Special*, October 10, 1979 (ABC)

☐ Robert Collins (cinematographer), "Heartbreak Winner," *ABC Afterschool Special*, February 13, 1980 (ABC)

Tom McDonough (cinematographer), "Mountain Climbing (Hot/Cold)," *3-2-1 Contact*, February 25, 1980 (PBS)

☐ David Sanderson (cinematographer), "Once upon a Midnight Dreary," *CBS Library*, October 21, 1979 (CBS)

☐ Alex Thompson (cinematographer), "The Gold Bug," (2 parts), *ABC Weekend Special*, February 2 and 9, 1980 (ABC)

Norman Gay (film editor), "Communication—Mets," *3-2-1 Contact*, February 11, 1980 (PBS)

☐ Jack Sholder (film editor), "Noisy/Quiet—Hearing," *3-2-1 Contact*, January 15, 1980 (PBS)

☐ Vincent Sklena (film editor), "The Late Great Me: Story of a Teenage Alcoholic," *ABC Afterschool Special*, November 14, 1979 (ABC)

☐ Merle Worth (film editor), "Fast/Slow—Speed Up/Slow Down," *3-2-1 Contact*, February 4, 1980 (PBS)

Tom Anthony (music composer/director—theme), "Noisy/Quiet," *3-2-1 Contact*, January 14, 1980 (PBS)

Danny Epstein (music director), "Forces," *3-2-1 Contact*, January 22, 1980 (PBS)

Walt Levinsky (music Composer), "Forces," *3-2-1 Contact*, January 22, 1980 (PBS)

Glenn Paxton (music composer), "Which Mother Is Mine?" *ABC Afterschool Special*, September 26, 1979 (ABC)

Hod David Schudson (music composer), "Heartbreak Winner," *ABC Afterschool Special*, February 13, 1980 (ABC)

☐ Ronald Baldwin (art director), "Growth/Decay," *3-2-1 Contact*, January 31, 1980 (PBS)

Shawn Callahan and Henry Hubbert (set decorators), *Captain Kangaroo*, October 30, 1979 (CBS)

Bil Mikulewicz (art director/Scenic designer), "Space Chicken and the disappearing Stars," *Captain Kangaroo*, December 6, 1979 (CBS)

☐ Nat Mongioi (set decorator), "Hot/Cold," *3-2-1 Contact*, February 27, 1980 (PBS)

Tony DiGirolamo (lighting director), *Sesame Street*, April 13, 1979 (PBS)

☐ Steven Atha (makeup and hair designer), "The Gold Bug," (2 parts), *ABC Weekend Special*, February 2 and 9, 1980 (ABC)

Bill Griffin (costume designer), *Captain Kangaroo*, October 30, 1979 (CBS)

Constance Wexler (costume designer), "Growth/Decay," *3-2-1 Contact*, January 31, 1980 (PBS)

☐ Michael Baugh (graphic designer), "I Can Sing a Rainbow," *Villa alegre*, October 17, 1979 (PBS)

R. Greenberg (Greenberg Associates; graphic designer), "Noisy/Quiet," *3-2-1 Contact*, January 14, 1980 (PBS)

Robert Pook (designer of internal graphics), *Hot Hero Sandwich*, January 12, 1980 (NBC)

OUTSTANDING INDIVIDUAL ACHIEVEMENT IN RELIGIOUS PROGRAMMING

For a single episode of a series or for a special program.

(Possibility of one award, more than one award or no award):

Norman Rose (performer), *A Talent for Life: Jews of the Italian Renaissance*, December 2, 1979 (NBC)

William Schallert (performer), "The Stableboy's Christmas," *This Is the Life*, December 1, 1979 (Syndicated)

☐ Dean Jagger (performer), "Independence and 76," *This Is the Life*, September 16, 1979 (Syndicated)

☐ Richard F. Morean, "If No Birds Sang," *This Is the Life*, September 30, 1979 (Syndicated)

☐ Indicates winner

Allan E. Sloane (writer), *As We with Candles Do*, February 24, 1980 (NBC)

Arthur Zegart (writer), "Aging in Venice," *Directions*, December 2, 1979 (ABC)

Lynwood King (director), *As We with Candles Do*, February 24, 1980 (NBC)

Heino Ripp (technical director), Al Camoin, Gene Martin and Don Mulvaney (electronic camerapersons), *As We with Candles Do*, February 24, 1980 (NBC)

☐ Justus Taylor (sound recordist), "Seeds of Revolution," *Directions*, November 18, 1979 (ABC)

Edward R. Williams (film editor), *A Talent for Life: Jews of the Italian Renaissance*, December 2, 1979 (NBC)

☐ John Duffy (music composer/director), *A Talent for Life: Jews of the Italian Renaissance*, December 2, 1979 (NBC)

☐ Thomas E. Azzari (art director), "Stable Boy's Christmas," *This Is the Life*, December 1, 1979 (Syndicated)

SPECIAL CLASSIFICATION OF OUTSTANDING INDIVIDUAL ACHIEVEMENT

(Possibility of one award, more than one award or no award):
Jay Redack, Harry Friedman, Brian Pollack, Gary Johnson, Steve Kreinberg, Justin Antonow, Phil Kellard (writers), *Hollywood Squares* (NBC)

Michael R. Gargiulo (director), *FYI* (with Hal Linden) (ABC)

Joseph Carow (choreographer), Nightmare Ballet Sequence, "Witch's Sister," (Chapter 2), *Big Blue Marble*, December 1, 1979 (Syndicated)

☐ Danny Seagren, "Puppet Design and Construction, Miss Peach of the Kelly School," *The Annual Thanksgiving Turkey Day Raffle*, November 10, 1979 (Syndicated)

OUTSTANDING INDIVIDUAL ACHIEVEMENT IN COVERAGE OF SPECIAL EVENTS

(Possibility of one award, more than one award or no award):
☐ Luciano Pavarotti (performer), *La Gioconda*, September 16, 1979 (PBS)

☐ Renata Scotto (performer), *La Gioconda*, September 16, 1979 (PBS)

☐ Kirk Browning (director), *La Gioconda*, September 16, 1979 (PBS)

☐ Indicates winner

☐ Ron Graft (technical director), Kenneth Patterson, Gary Emrick, Luis A. Fuerte, Daniel J. Webb, Jack Reader, Thomas Tucker and William Kelsey (electronic camerapersons), *La Gioconda*, September 16, 1979 (PBS)

☐ Greg Harms (video engineer), *La Gioconda*, September 16, 1979 (PBS)

☐ Tom Ancell (audio mixer), *La Gioconda*, September 16, 1979 (PBS)

Val Riolo (associate director), Roy Stewart (videotape editor), *La Gioconda*, September 16, 1979 (PBS)

☐ Zack Brown (scenic designer/set decorator), *La Gioconda*, September 16, 1979 (PBS)

☐ Ken Dettling (lighting director), *La Gioconda*, September 16, 1979 (PBS)

☐ Zack Brown (costume designer), *La Gioconda*, September 16, 1979 (PBS)

OUTSTANDING INDIVIDUAL ACHIEVEMENT IN ANY AREA OF CREATIVE TECHNICAL CRAFTS

(Possibility of one award, more than one award or no award):
Mike Maloof (technical director), Dick Watson, Galen Westfall and John Gillis (electronic camerapersons), *Dinah! and Friends* (Syndicated)

Becky Greenlaw (associate director), Gary Nestra (videotape editor), *The Mike Douglas Show*, September 10, 1979 (Syndicated)

Joe Massimino (music composer/director), *The Mike Douglas Show* (Syndicated)

News and Documentary Awards

(Possibility of one award, more than one award or no award)

PROGRAMS AND PROGRAM SEGMENTS
"Aborted Raid Broadcast," *CBS Evening News with Walter Cronkite*, Sanford Socolow (executive producer), Mark Harrington, Sam Roberts, Lane Venardos and Linda Mason (producers), Walter Cronkite, Doug Tunnell, Ike Pappas, Lesley Stahl, Phil Jones and Marvin Kalb (correspondents), April 25, 1980 (CBS)

The Pope in America: Journey for Understanding, Jeff Gralnick (producer), Frank Reynolds (correspondent), October 2–5, 1979 (ABC)

☐ *Pope John Paul II in Poland*, Helen Marmor (producer), Philip Scharper (correspondent), June 10, 1979 (NBC)

☐ "Post Election Special Edition," *ABC News: Nightline*, Jeff Gralnick and William Lord (producers), Ted Koppel, Frank Reynolds, Barbara Walters, Max Robinson and Lynn Sherr (correspondents), November 5, 1980 (ABC)

"After the Deluge," segment: *CBS News: Sunday Morning*, James Houtrides (producer), Ed Rabel (correspondent), August 17, 1980 (CBS)

☐ "Fishing Boat Sinks," segment: *NBC Nightly News*, Nancy Fernandez and Jeff Weinstock (producers), Lee McCarthy (correspondent), July 1, 1980 (NBC)

"The Fixer," segment: *ABC News: 20/20'*, Lowell Bergman (producer), Geraldo Rivera (correspondent), February 28, 1980 (ABC)

"Hostages—300 Days," segment: *CBS Evening News with Walter Cronkite*, Rita Braver (producer), Diane Sawyer (correspondent), August 29, 1980 (CBS)

"Iran-Iraq War," 5-part segment: *CBS Evening News with Walter Cronkite*, William Willson (producer), Larry Pintak (correspondent), September 22–26, 1980 (CBS)

☐ "Murder of a Correspondent," segment: *ABC World News Tonight*, Ken Luckoff (producer), Al Dale (correspondent), June 21, 1979 (ABC)

"Campaign Report #3: The New Right, The Evangelicals," *Bill Moyers' Journal*, Martin Koughan (producer), Bill Moyers (correspondent), September 26, 1980 (PBS)

"Campaign Report #8: Essential Carter/Essential Reagan," *Bill Moyers' Journal*, Randy Bean and Howard Weinberg (producers), Bill Moyers (correspondent), October 31 1980 (PBS)

☐ *CBS Reports: Miami: The Trial that Sparked the Riots*, Eric F. Saltzman (producer), Ed Bradley (correspondent), August 27, 1980 (CBS)

☐ "Lights, Cameras... Politics," *ABC News: Closeup*, Ann G. Black and Tom Priestley (producers), Richard Reeves (correspondent), July 11, 1980 (ABC)

NBC White Paper: We're Moving Up: the Hispanic Migration, Anthony Potter (producer), Bill McLaughlin (correspondent), March 28, 1980 (NBC)

"B-52's: Too Old to Fly?" segment, *ABC News: 20/20*, Richard Clark (producer), Jules Bergman (correspondent), August 14, 1980 (ABC)

"Child Snatching," segment: *ABC News: 20/20*, David Meyer (producer), Bob Brown (correspondent), October 16, 1980 (ABC)

"Energy Alternatives: Beating Opec Now," 3-part special assignment segment: *ABC World News Tonight*, Sharon Young (producer), Roger Peterson (correspondent), October 9–11, 1979 (ABC)

"The Iran File," segment: *CBS News: 60 Minutes*, Barry Lando (producer), Mike Wallace (correspondent), March 2, 1980 (CBS)

"Money Talks," segment: *ABC News: 20/20*, Martin Clancy (producer), Barry Serafin (correspondent), July 14, 1980 (ABC)

☐ "Nicaragua," segment: *ABC News: 20/20*, Lowell Bergman and Neil Cunningham (producers), Dave Marash (correspondent), June 26, 1980 (ABC)

☐ Onward Christian Voters, segment: *CBS News: 60 Minutes*, Joel Bernstein (producer), Dan Rather (correspondent), September 21, 1980 (CBS)

☐ "Too Little, Too Late?" segment: *CBS News: Magazine*, Janet Roach (producer), Ed Bradley (correspondent), December 6, 1979 (CBS)

"Hot Shells: U.S. Arms for South Africa," *World*, William Cran (producer), January 29, 1980 (PBS)

NBC Reports: The Migrants, 1980, Morton Silverstein (producer), Chris Wallace (correspondent), August 15, 1980 (NBC)

"A Plague on Our Children," *Nova*, Robert Richter (producer/ correspondent), October 2, 1979 (PBS)

Song of the Canary, Josh Hanig and David Davis (producers), November 5, 1980 (PBS)

☐ "Who Killed Georgi Markov?" *World*, Phil Harding (producer), Michael Cockerrell (correspondent), October 9, 1979 (PBS)

☐ "Arson for Profit"—Part I and II, segment: *ABC News: 20/20*, Peter Lance (producer), Geraldo Rivera (correspondent), February 5, 1980 (ABC)

"Carnival Capers," segment: *ABC News: 20/20*, Barbara Newman (producer), Geraldo Rivera

(correspondent), August 7, 1980 (ABC)

"Equal Justice?" segment: *CBS News: 60 Minutes*, Leslie Edwards (producer), Dan Rather (correspondent), December 2, 1979 (CBS)

"Injustice for All," segment: *ABC News: 20/20*, Charles C. Thompson (producer), Geraldo Rivera (correspondent), April 17, 1980 (ABC)

"Prison Benefits," segment: *NBC News: Prime Time Saturday*, Beth Polson (producer), Jack Perkins (correspondent), May 17, 1980 (NBC)

"Scientology: The Clearwater Conspiracy," segment: *CBS News: 60 Minutes*, Allan Maraynes (producer), Mike Wallace (correspondent), April 13, 1980 (CBS)

☐ "Urethane," segment: *NBC News: Prime Time Saturday*, Peter Jeffries (producer), John Dancy (correspondent), February 9, 1980 (NBC)

☐ "VW Beetle: The Hidden Danger," segment: *ABC News: 20/20*, Jeff Diamond (producer), Sylvia Chase (correspondent), November 8, 1979 (ABC)

☐ *CBS Reports: Teddy*, Andrew Lack (producer), Roger Mudd (interviewer), November 4, 1979 (CBS)

"A Conversation with Zbigniew Brzezinski," *Bill Moyers' Journal*, Betsy McCarthy (producer), Bill Moyers (interviewer), November 14, 1980 (PBS)

"Judge,"—Parts I and II, *Bill Moyers' Journal*, Randy Bean (producer), Bill Moyers (interviewer), July 24, 31, 1980 (PBS)

"Lorin Hollander," *Old Friends. . . New Friends*, Jayne Adair (producer), Fred Rogers (interviewer), September 19, 1980 (PBS)

☐ "Bette Davis," segment: *CBS News: 60 Minutes*, Nancy Lea (producer), Mike Wallace (interviewer), January 20, 1980 (CBS)

☐ "Here's Johnny!" segment: *CBS News: 60 Minutes*, David Lowe Jr. (producer), Mike Wallace (interviewer), September 23, 1979 (CBS)

"The Ump (Ron Luciano)," segment: *ABC News: 20/20*, Bernard I. Cohen (producer/interviewer), September 20, 1979 (ABC)

"American Dream, American Nightmare," *CBS News Special Report*, Perry Wolff (executive producer), Shareen Blair Brysac

(producer), Harry Reasoner (correspondent), December 28, 29, 1979 (CBS)

☐ *CBS Reports: on the Road*, Bernard Birnbaum and Charles Kuralt (producers), Charles Kuralt (correspondent), June 8, 1979 (CBS)

CBS Reports: What Shall We Do About Mother?, Judy Reemtsma (producer), Marlene Sanders (correspondent), August 2, 1980 (CBS)

Choosing Suicide, Richard Ellison (producer/correspondent), June 16, 1980 (PBS)

"Dive to the Edge of Creation," *National Geographic Special*, James Lipscomb (producer), January 8, 1980 (PBS)

☐ "The Invisible World," *National Geographic Special*, Alex Pomasanoff (producer), March 3, 1980 (PBS)

☐ "Mysteries of the Mind," *National Geographic Special*, Irwin Rosten (producer), February 4, 1980 (PBS)

NBC Reports: To Be a Doctor, Tom Spain (producer), Tom Brokaw (correspondent), May 29, 1980 (NBC)

"To Die for Ireland," *ABC News: Closeup*, Alan Raymond and Susan Raymond (producers), June 12, 1980 (ABC)

"Anne Lindbergh," segment: *CBS News: 60 Minutes*, Joseph Wershba (producer), Morley Safer (correspondent), April 20, 1980 (CBS)

"Annie," segment: *NBC News: Prime Time Saturday*, Fred Flamenhaft (producer), Jessica Savitch (correspondent), February 2, 1980 (NBC)

"Back in the World: Vietnam Vets," segment: *CBS News: Sunday Morning*, William Moran (producer), Jerry Landay (correspondent), March 2, 1980 (CBS)

"Billy Joel," segment: *ABC News: 20/20*, Donovan Moore (producer), Tom Hoving (correspondent), May 1, 1980 (ABC)

"Billy Martin # 1," segment: *ABC News: 20/20*, Peggy Brim (producer), Sylvia Chase (correspondent), September 18, 1980 (ABC)

"The Endless War," segment *ABC News: 20/20*, Phyllis McGrady (producer), Sylvia Chase (correspondent), November 13, 1980 (ABC)

☐ "George Burns: An Update," segment: *ABC News: 20/20*, Betsy Osha (producer), Bob Brown

☐ Indicates winner

(correspondent), August 7, 1980 (ABC)

☐ "Heart Transplant," segment: *NBC News: Prime Time Sunday*, Robert Eaton, George Lewis and Arthur Lord (producers), Jack Perkins (correspondent), August 19, 1979 (NBC)

"Plenty for Everyone," segment: *CBS News: Magazine*, Jean Abounader (producer), Sharron Lovejoy (correspondent), December 6, 1979 (CBS)

"A Tale of Two Cities," segment: *CBS News: Sunday Morning*, Robert Northshield (executive producer), Elliot Bernstein (producer), Tom Fenton and Don Kladstrup (correspondents), September 9, 1979 (CBS)

"To Save a Life," segment: *ABC News: 20/20*, Peter W. Kunhardt (producer), Tom Jarriel (correspondent), April 24, 1980 (ABC)

"Walking Small in Pitkin County," segment: *CBS News: 60 Minutes*, Greg Cooke (producer), Morley Safer (correspondent), April 27, 1980 (CBS)

OUTSTANDING INDIVIDUAL ACHIEVEMENT IN NEWS AND DOCUMENTARY PROGRAMMING

Writing

Malcolm Clarke and Ray Bradbury, *Infinite Horizons: Space Beyond Apollo*, July 19, 1979 (ABC)

Lloyd Dobyns and Reuven Frank, *NBC White Paper: If Japan Can, Why Can't We?*, June 24, 1980 (NBC)

☐ Bill Moyers, "Our Times," *Bill Moyers' Journal*, January 31, 1980 (PBS)

Roger Mudd, *CBS Reports: Teddy*, November 4, 1979 (CBS)

☐ Irwin Rosten, "Mysteries of the Mind," *National Geographic Special*, February 4, 1980 (PBS)

☐ Marlene Sanders and Judy Towers Reemtsma, *CBS Reports: What Shall We Do About Mother?*, August 2, 1980 (CBS)

☐ Morton Silverstein and Chris Wallace, *NBC Reports: The Migrants, 1980*, August 15, 1980 (NBC)

☐ Perry Wolff, "American Dream, American Nightmare," *CBS News Special Report*, December 28, 29, 1979 (CBS)

Direction

☐ Patrick M. Cook, "Death in a Southwest Prison," *ABC News: Closeup*, September 23, 1980 (ABC)

Andrew Lack, "Inside Afghanistan," segment: *CBS News: 60 Minutes*, April 6, 1980 (CBS)

☐ Indicates winner

☐ Ray Lockhart, *NBC White Paper: If Japan Can, Why Can't We?*, June 24, 1980 (NBC)

☐ Roger Phenix, *NBC Reports: To Be a Doctor*, May 29, 1980 (NBC)

Dick Schneider, "Who's Choosing Our President?" *Bill Moyers' Journal*, June 12, 1980 (PBS)

☐ Morton Silverstein, *NBC Reports: The Migrants, 1980*, August 15, 1980 (NBC)

Technical direction/Electronic camera

☐ Jon Alpert (camera), *Third Avenue: Only the Strong Survive*, April 11, 1980 (PBS)

Don Basil (camera), "The Ump (Ron Luciano)," segment: *ABC News: 20/20*, September 20, 1980 (ABC)

☐ Jack Clark (camera), "Shooting of Bill Stuart—Nicaragua," segment: *ABC World News Tonight*, June 20, 1979 (ABC)

J. Randall Fairbairn (camera), "Haitians Expelled from Cayo Lobos," 3-part segment: *NBC Nightly News*, November 12–14, 1980 (NBC)

Martin Murphy, Bob McKenny and John Waszak (engineering supervisors), Gilbert A. Miller, Bob Vernum and Joseph Duenas (technical directors), "Democratic National Convention," *CBS News: Campaign '80*, August 11, 1980 (CBS)

Cinematography

Gregory Andracke, *Infinite Horizons: Space Beyond Apollo*, July 19, 1979 (ABC)

☐ Mike Edwards, "Inside Afghanistan," segment: *CBS News: 60 Minutes*, April 6, 1980 (CBS)

David Grubin, "The World of David Rockefeller," *Bill Moyers' Journal*, February 7, 1980 (PBS)

☐ Alan Raymond, "To Die for Ireland," *ABC News: Closeup*, June 12, 1980 (ABC)

Tom Spain and David Grubin, *NBC Reports: To Be a Doctor*, May 29, 1980 (NBC)

Ivan Strasburg and Richard Roy, "Escape from Justice: Nazi War Criminals in America," *ABC News: Closeup*, January 13, 1980 (ABC)

Associate direction and/or videotape editing

Jerry Chernak (associate director), Thomas R. Gubar (videotape editor), "The Ump (Ron Luciano)," segment: *ABC News: 20/20*, September 20, 1980 (ABC)

☐ John Godfrey, Jon Alpert and Keiko Tsuno (videotape editors), *Third Avenue: Only the Strong Survive*, April 11, 1980 (PBS)

☐ Ruth Neuwald (videotape editor), *CBS Reports: Miami: The Trial that Sparked the Riots*, August 27, 1980 (CBS)

Dennis S. Osik (associate director), Edward Buda, Consuelo Gonzalez and Peter Murphy (videotape editors), "The Elvis Coverup," segment: *ABC News: 20/20*, September 13, 1979 (ABC)

Mitchell Rudick (videotape editor), "The Iran File," segment: *CBS News: 60 Minutes*, March 2, 1980 (CBS)

Tressa Anne Verna (videotape editor), "Terry Bradshaw—Cashing In," segment: *NBC News: Prime Time Saturday*, May 17, 1980 (NBC)

Film editing

Kenneth J. Dalglish, "Leonard Bernstein," segment: *CBS News: 60 Minutes*, February 10, 1980 (CBS)

Richard Manichello, "Pavarotti," segment: *CBS News: 60 Minutes*, November 4, 1979 (CBS)

☐ Maurice Murad, *CBS Reports: The Saudis*, October 21, 1980 (CBS)

☐ Steve Sheppard, "Inside Afghanistan," segment: *CBS News: 60 Minutes*, April 6, 1980 (CBS)

☐ Kenneth E. Werner and Nils Rassmussen, "Death in a Southwest Prison," *ABC News: Closeup*, September 23, 1980 (ABC)

Merle Worth, *NBC Reports: To Be a Doctor*, May 29, 1980 (NBC)

Audio

☐ Jim Cefalo (sound recordist), "Shooting of Bill Stuart—Nicaragua," segment: *ABC World News Tonight*, June 20, 1979 (ABC)

Anthony Gambino (sound recordist), "The Ump (Ron Luciano)," segment: *ABC News: 20/20*, September 20, 1980 (ABC)

John Hampton (sound recordist— court), Ron Yoshida (sound recordist—location), "The Shooting of Big Man: Anatomy of a Criminal Case," *ABC News: Closeup*, June 8, 1979 (ABC)

☐ Robert Rogow (location sound recordist), Joel Dulberg (re-recording mixer), "Pavarotti," segment: *CBS News: 60 Minutes*, November 4, 1979 (CBS)

Scenic/Set design

David M. Carlk, Imero Fiorentino and George Honchar (scenic designers), *Democratic National Convention*, August 11, 1980 (Pool)

Victor Paganuzzi and Neil J. Deluca (set designers), "Sports," segment: *CBS News: Morning with Charles Kuralt*, November 10, 1980 (CBS)

Lighting direction
Carl Vitelli Jr. and Everett Melosh *Democratic National Convention*, August 11, 1980 (Pool)

Graphic design
William Sunshine and Ellen Denton, "Pavarotti," segment: *CBS News: 60 Minutes*, November 4, 1979 (CBS)

Music direction
☐ Lionel Hampton, *No Maps on My Taps*, April 25, 1980 (PBS)

Sports Awards

OUTSTANDING LIVE SPORTS SPECIAL

Emmy(s) to executive producer(s) and producer(s):
NCAA Championship Basketball, (Louisville vs. UCLA), Don Ohlmeyer (executive producer), George Finkel (producer), March 24, 1980 (NBC)
Super Bowl XIV, Robert Stenner (executive producer), January 20, 1980 (CBS)
Wimbledon '80, Don Ohlmeyer (executive producer), Geoffrey Mason (producer), Ted Nathanson (co-producer), June 27–July 5, 1980 (NBC)
☐ *1980 Winter Olympic Games*, (Lake Placid N.Y.), Roone Arledge (executive producer), Chuck Howard, Chet Forte and Dennis Lewin (senior producers), Bob Goodrich, Curt Gowdy Jr., Terry Jastrow, Terry O'Neil, Eleanor Riger, Ned Steckel and Doug Wilson (producers), Jeff Ruhe (coordinating producer), Brice Weisman (producer) for "Up Close and Personals," Robert Riger and Bud Greenspan (special projects producers), February 12–24, 1980 (ABC)
1979 World Series (Baltimore Orioles vs. Pittsburgh Pirates), Roone Arledge (executive producer), Chuck Howard (producer), October 7–17, 1980 (ABC)

OUTSTANDING LIVE SPORTS SERIES

Emmy(s) to executive producer(s) and producer(s):
ABC's Monday Night Football, Roone Arledge (executive producer), Dennis Lewin (producer), Series (ABC)
NCAA Basketball, Don Ohlmeyer (executive producer), George Finkel (coordinating producer), Ken Edmundson (producer), Series (NBC)
☐ *NCAA College Football*, Roone Arledge (executive producer), Chuck Howard (senior producer), Bob Goodrich (producer), Eleanor Riger, Curt Gowdy Jr., Dick Buffinton, Chirs

Carmody, Ned Steckel, Doug Wilson, Terry O'Neil (producers), Series (ABC)
NFL Football on CBS, Bill Barnes, David Fox, Robert Stenner, Robert Rowe, Perry Smith, Chuck Will, Tom O'Neil and Howard Reifsnyder, Series (CBS)
PGA on CBS, Frank Chirkinian (executive producer and producer), Series (CBS)

OUTSTANDING EDITED SPORTS SPECIAL

Emmy(s) to executive producer(s) and producer(s):
☐ *Gossamer Albatross—Flight of Imagination*, Eddie Einhorn (executive producer), Joseph A. Thompson (producer), June 15, 1980 (CBS)
1980 Indianapolis 500, Roone Arledge (executive producer), Chuck Howard and Bob Goodrich (producers), May 25, 1980 (ABC)
Olympic Trials, Don Ohlmeyer (executive producer), Don McGuire (coordinating producer), Peter Diamond, Bernie Hoffman and Linda Jonsson (producers), May 24–June 29, 1980 (NBC)
Upsets & Underdogs, Hot Dogs & Heroes: The Story of the 1979 NFL Season, Steve Sabol and Ed Sabol (producers), January 20, 1980 (NBC)
1980 Winter Olympic Preview Special; Adirondack Gold Rush, Roone Arledge (executive producer), Terry O'Neil (producer), February 11, 1980 (ABC)

OUTSTANDING EDITED SPORTS SERIES

Emmy(s) to executive producer(s) and producer(s):
ABC's Wide World of Sports, Roone Arledge (executive producer), Dennis Lewin (coordinating producer), Chuck Howard, Chet Forte, Joe Aceti, Carol Lehti, Terry O'Neil, Ned Steckel, Doug Wilson and Bob Goodrich (producers), Series (ABC)
American Sportsman, Roone Arledge (executive producer), John Wilcox (series producer), Robert Duncan, Curt Gowdy and Robert Nixon, Series (ABC)
CBS Sports Spectacular, Eddie Einhorn (executive producer), Ed Goren (coordinating producer), David Fox, Ted Shaker, Perry Smith, Brad Schrieber, Charles Milton, Jim Silman, Michael Pearl, Dave Berman, Ken Squier, Sherman Eagan, Tom O'Neil, Tony Verna, Robert Stenner, Howard Reifsnyder and Peter Bleckner (producers), Series (CBS)

☐ *NFL Game of the Week*, Ed Sabol (executive producer), Steve Sabol (producer), Series (Syndicated)
This Week in Baseball, Larry Parker (executive producer), Jody Shapiro and Geoff Belinfante (supervising producers), Tim Parker and Bill Brown (producers), Series (Syndicated)

OUTSTANDING DIRECTING IN SPORTS PROGRAMMING

Joe Aceti and Roger Goodman (coordinating directors), Chet Forte, John DeLisa, Jack Gallivan, Mac Hemion, Craig Janoff, Jim Jennett, Larry Kamm, Bob Lanning, Raimo Piltz, Andy Sidaris, Ken Wolfe, Lou Volpicelli, Larry Cavolina and Ron Harrison (directors), *1980 Winter Olympic Games*, (Lake Placid, N.Y.), February 12–24, 1980 (ABC)
Frank Chirkinian and Robert Daily, *The Masters*, April 12–13, 1980 (CBS)
Chet Forte, *1979 World Series*, October 7–17, 1980
☐ Sandy Grossman, *Super Bowl XIV*, January 20, 1980 (CBS)
Ted Nathanson, *Wimbledon '80* (Men's Finals—Borg vs. McEnroe), July 5, 1980 (NBC)
Duke Struck, Robert Dailey, Sandy Grossman, Marvin Mews, Jim Silman, Robert Dunphy, Chris Erskine, Tony Verna and John McDonough, *NFL Football on CBS*, Series (CBS)
Doug Wilson, "World Figure Skating Championships," *ABC'S Wide World of Sports*, March 16, 1980 (ABC)

OUTSTANDING INDIVIDUAL ACHIEVEMENT IN SPORTS PROGRAMMING

This is an "Area," where there is a possibility of one award, more than one award or no award:

Cinematography
☐ Bob Angelo, Ernie Ernst, Jay Gerber, Stan Leshner, Don Marx, Hank McElwee, Howard Neef, Jack Newman, Steve Sabol, Bob Smith, Art Spieller and Phil Tuckett (cinematographers), *NFL Game of the Week*, Decmeber 15, 1979 (Syndicated)
☐ Harvey Harrison, Harry Hart and Don Shapiro (cinematographers), "Up Close and Personals," *1980 Winter Olympic Games*, (Lake Placid, N.Y.), February 12–24, 1980 (ABC)

Associate direction/Videotape editing
☐ Barbara Bowman, Paul Fanelli, Charles Gardner, Marvin Gench, Roger Haenelt, Conrad Kraus, Alex Moscovic, Lou Rende, Nathan Rogers, Erskin Roberts, Mario

☐ Indicates winner

Schencman, Ann Stone, Arthur Volk, Francis Giugliano, Ronald Ackerman, Michael Altieri, Tom Capace, John Croak, Jack Hierl, Tony Jutchenko, Hector Kicelian, Ken Klingbeil, Pete Murphy, Hiorshi Nakamoto, Carl Pollack, Merrit Roesser, Winston Sadoo, Fausto Sanchez, Rene Sanchez, Leo Stephen, Richard Velasco and Ed Zlotnick (videotape editors), *1980 Winter Olympic Games*, (Lake Placid, N.Y.), February 12–24, 1980 (ABC)

Ron Ackerman, Tom Capace, Phil Mollica and Lou Rende (videotape editors), *ABC's NFL Monday Night Football*, December 17, 1979 (ABC)

Film editing
□ Angelo Bernarducci, Jon Day, Sam Fine, John Petersen, Vincent Reda, Anthony Scandiffio, Wayne Weiss and Ted Winterburn (film editors), "Up Close & Personals," *1980 Winter Olympic Games* (Lake Placid, N.Y.), February 12–24, 1980 (ABC)

Audio
□ Trevor Carless, George Hause, Jim Lynch, Dennis Fierman and Jan Schulte (location sound mixers), "Up Close & Personals," *1980 Winter Olympic Games*, (Lake Placid, N.Y.), February 12–24, 1980 (ABC)

Dick Roes, Jim Davis, Tom Glazner, Jack Hugues, George Meyer, Joe Vernum, Jonathan M. Lory (from West Coast), Gary Larson, D. Nelson, J. Eaton, R. Emerson and A. Morgenstern (live/tape sound mixers), *1980 Winter Olympic Games*, (Lake Placid, N.Y.), February 12–24, 1980 (ABC)

Lighting direction
Mel Handelsman (lighting director), *1980 Winter Olympic Games*, (Lake Placid, N.Y.), February 12–24, 1980 (ABC)

Music composition/Direction
□ Chuck Mangione (music composer/director), *1980 Winter Olympic Games*, (Lake Placid, N.Y.; including original theme, "Give It All You Got"), February 12–24, 1980 (ABC)

Engineering supervision/Technical direction/Electronic camerawork
□ Julius Barnathan, Joseph DeBonis, Bill Stone, Joseph A. Maltz, David E. Eschelbacher, Charles Baldour, David Linick, Eric Rosenthal, Abdelnour Tadros and Tony Uyttendaele (engineering supervisors), Dick Horan, Robert Armbruster, Bill Blumel, Loren Coltran, Geoffrey Felger, Mike Jochim, Jacques Lesgards, Bill

□ Indicates winner

Maier, Gary Larkins, Joseph Polito, Elliott R. Reed, Martin Sandberg, Tony Versley, Mike Fisher, Joseph Kresnicka (Chicago) and Bud Untiedt (West Coast) (technical managers), Les Weiss, Werner Gunther, Chester Mazurek, William Morris, Joseph Schiavo, Joe Nesi (from West Coast), Ernie Buttleman, J. Allen, Gerry Bucci, H. Falk and David Smith (technical directors), Dianne Cates-Cantrell, Gary Donatelli, Danny LaMothe, Charles Mitchell, Steve Nikifor, William Sullivan, Don Farnham (Chicago), Rick Knipe, Morton Lipow and Joseph Montesano (minicam) (electronic camerapersons), *1980 Winter Olympic Games*, (Lake Placid, N.Y.), February 12–24, 1980 (ABC)

Lou Scannapieco and Arthur Tinn (engineering supervisors), Charles D'Onofrio and Sandy Bell (technical directors), George Klimscak, George Rothweiler, David Graham, Herman Lang, Hans Singer, Harry Haigood, Rick Blane, Frank McSpedon, Barry Drago, Jim Murphy, Mike Zwick, George Naeder, Jim McCarthy, Al Loreto, Al Diamond, Mike English, John Lincoln, Pat McBride, Stan Gould, Joe Sokota, Neil McCaffrey, Bob Welsh, David Finch, Gordon Sweeney and Gorm Erickson (electronic camerapersons), *The Masters*, April 12–13, 1980 (CBS)

Loren Coltran (technical manager), Bill Morris (technical director), Andrew J. Armentani, Jack Dorfman, Steve Nikifor, Joe Cotugno, Gary Donatelli, Jim Heneghan, Roy Hutchings, Tom O'Connell, Jack Savoy and Jessel Kohn (electronic camerapersons), *ABC's NFL Monday Night Football*, December 17, 1979 (ABC)

Associate direction
Carol Lehti, Rob Beiner, Jeff Cohan, Vince DeDario, Bob Dekas, Lou Frederick, Bob Hersh, Ronald Hawkins, Jean MacLean, Norm Samet, Howard Shapiro, Toni Slotkin, Stan Spiro, Doug Towey and Pat Tuite (associate directors live/tape), *1980 Winter Olympic Games*, (Lake Placid, N.Y.), February 12–24, 1980 (ABC)

Graphic design
Roger Goodman (creative director in charge), Hy Bley (director of graphic arts), Maxwell Berry (director of electronic graphics), *1980 Winter Olympic Games*, (Lake Placid, N.Y.), February 12–24, 1980 (ABC)

SPECIAL CLASSIFICATION OF OUTSTANDING PROGRAM AND INDIVIDUAL ACHIEVEMENT
Emmy to producer for program; emmys to individuals for individual achievement:

Program:
A Tribute to Thurman Munson, (pre-empted regular Major League Baseball Pre-Game programming), Terry Ewert (producer), August 4, 1979 (NBC)

Individual
□ Jerry P. Caruso and Harry Smith (creators/developers of Radio Frequency Golf Cup Mic), *Bob Hope Golf Classic*, January 12–13, 1980 (NBC)

OUTSTANDING SPORTS PERSONALITY
Howard Cosell (ABC)
Frank Gifford (ABC)
Keith Jackson (ABC)
Al McGuire (NBC)
□ Jim McKay (ABC)
Don Meredith (ABC)
Vin Scully (CBS)
Jack Whitaker (CBS)

OUTSTANDING ACHIEVEMENT IN THE SCIENCE OF TELEVISION ENGINEERING
□ *Nippon Electric Company*
□ *Panasonic Company*
□ *Quantel Limited*
□ *Vital Industries*

TRUSTEES AWARD
□ Leonard H. Goldenson, for his role in forming the American Broadcasting Corporation and guiding its growth to become one of the leading forces in American communications

1980/81

(For programs aired between July 1, 1980 and June 30, 1981. Entertainment program and individual achievement awards presented September 13, 1981. Creative Arts awards presented September 12, 1981. Daytime awards presented May 19 and May 21, 1981 for programs aired between March 6, 1980 and March 5, 1981. Sports awards presented December 15, 1981 for programs aired between July 16, 1980 and July 15, 1981. Science of Television Engineering Award presented September 21, 1981. News and Documentary awards presented April 12, 1982.)

Prime Time Program Awards

OUTSTANDING COMEDY SERIES

Emmy(s) to executive producer(s) and producer(s):

☐ *Taxi*, James L. Brooks, Stan Daniels, Ed Weinberger (executive producers), Glen Charles, Les Charles (producers) (ABC)

Barney Miller, Danny Arnold (executive producer), Tony Sheehan, Noam Pitlik (producers), Gary Shaw (co-producer) (ABC)

*M*A*S*H*, Burt Metcalfe (executive producer), John Rappaport (producer) (CBS)

Soap, Paul Junger Witt, Tony Thomas, Susan Harris (executive producers), Stu Silver, Dick Clair, Jenna McMahon (producers) (ABC)

WKRP in Cincinnati, Hugh Wilson (executive producer), Rod Daniel (supervising producer), Blake Hunter, Steven Kampmann, Peter Torokvei (producers) (CBS)

OUTSTANDING DRAMA SERIES

Emmy(s) to executive producer(s) and producer(s):

☐ *Hill Street Blues*, Steven Bochco, Michael Kozoll (executive producers), Gregory Hoblit (producer) (NBC)

Dallas, Philip Capice (executive producer), Leonard Katzman (producer) (CBS)

Lou Grant, Gene Reynolds (executive producer), Seth Freeman (producer) (CBS)

Quincy, David Moessinger (executive producer), William O. Cairncorss, Lester William Berke (supervising producers), Sam Egan (producer) (NBC)

☐ Indicates winner

The White Shadow, Bruce Paltrow (executive producer), Mark Tinker (producer), John Masius (coordinating producer) (CBS)

OUTSTANDING LIMITED SERIES

Emmy(s) to executive producer(s) and producer(s):

☐ *Shogun*, James Clavell (executive producer), Eric Bercovici, (producer) (NBC)

John Steinbeck's East of Eden, Mace Neufeld (executive producer), Barney Rosenzweig (producer), Ken Wales (co-producer) (ABC)

Masada, George Eckstein (producer) (ABC)

"Rumpole of the Bailey," *Mystery!* Joan Wilson (series producer), Jacqueline Davis (producer) (PBS)

"Tinker, Tailor, Soldier, Spy," *Great Performances*, Jac Venza (executive producer), Jonathan Powell (producer), Samuel J. Paul III (series producer) (PBS)

OUTSTANDING VARIETY, MUSIC OR COMEDY PROGRAM

For a variety or music special or series or for a comedy special. Emmy(s) to executive producer(s), producer(s) and star(s), if applicable:

☐ *Lily: Sold Out*, Lily Tomlin, Jane Wagner (executive producers), Rocco Urbisci (producer), Lily Tomlin (star), February 2, 1981 (CBS)

The American Film Institute Salute to Fred Astaire, George Stevens Jr. (producer), April 18, 1981 (CBS)

The Benny Hill Show, John Robins, Dennis Kirkland, Mark Stuart, Keith Beckett (producers), Benny Hill (star), Series (Syndicated)

The Muppet Show, David Lazer (executive producer), Jim Henson (producer), Frank Oz, Jerry Nelson, Richard Hunt, Dave Goelz, Louise Gold, Steve Whitmire, Kathryn Mullen, Brian Muehl, Karen Prell, Jim Henson (stars), Series (Syndicated)

The Tonight Show Starring Johnny Carson, Fred de Cordova (producer), Peter Lassally (co-producer), Johnny Carson (star), Series (NBC)

OUTSTANDING DRAMA SPECIAL

Emmy(s) to executive producer(s) and producer(s):

☐ *Playing for Time*, Linda Yellen (executive producer and producer), John E. Quill (co-producer), September 30, 1980 (CBS)

Evita Peron, Harry Evans Sloan, Lawrence L. Kuppin, Selma Jaffe (executive producers), Fred Baum (supervising producer), Marvin

Chomsky (producer), David R. Ames (co-producer), February 23 and 24, 1981 (NBC)

Fallen Angel, Jim Green, Allen Epstein (executive producers), Lew Hunter, Audrey Blasdel-Goddard (producers), February 24, 1981 (CBS)

The Shadow Box, Jill Marti, Susan Kendall Newman (producers), December 28, 1980 (ABC)

The Women's Room, Philip Mandelker (executive producer), Glenn Jordan (supervising producer), Kip Gowans, Anna Cottle (producers), September 14, 1980 (ABC)

OUTSTANDING CLASSICAL PROGRAM IN THE PERFORMING ARTS

For a special or a series. Emmy(s) to executive producer(s), producer(s) and star(s), if applicable:

☐ *Live from Studio 8H: an Evening of Jerome Robbins' Ballets with Members of the New York City Ballet*, Alvin Cooperman, Judith DePaul (producers), July 2, 1980 (NBC)

Joan Sutherland, Marilyn Horne and Luciano Pavarotti, *Live from Lincoln Center*, John Goberman (producer), Joan Sutherland, Marilyn Horne, Luciano Pavarotti (stars), March 23, 1981 (PBS)

A Lincoln Center Special: Beverly! Her Farewell Performance, Great Performances, John Goberman (producer), Beverly Sills (star), January 5, 1981 (PBS)

"Nureyev and the Joffrey Ballet/In Tribute to Nijinsky," *Dance in America*, Jac Venza (executive producer), Emile Ardolino, Judy Kinberg (producers), Rudolf Nureyev (star), March 9, 1981 (PBS)

"Zubin Mehta, Itzhak Perlman and Pinchas Zukerman Celebrate Isaac Stern's 60th Birthday," *Live from Lincoln Center*, John Goberman (producer), Zubin Mehta, Itzhak Perlman, Pinchas Zukerman, Isaac Stern (stars), September 24, 1980 (PBS)

OUTSTANDING INFORMATIONAL SPECIAL

Emmy(s) to executive producer(s) and producer(s):

☐ *The Body Human: the Bionic Breakthrough*, Thomas W. Moore (executive producer), Alfred R. Kelman, Robert E. Fuisz, M.D. (producers), Charles A. Bangert, Nancy Smith (co-producers), May 12, 1981 (CBS)

The Body Human: the Sexes II, Thomas W. Moore (executive

producer), Alfred R. Kelman, Robert
E. Fuisz, M.D. (producers), Charles
A. Bangert, Vivian R. Moss (co-
producers), November 2, 1980
(CBS)
Gorilla, National Geographic Special,
Dennis B. Kane, Thomas Skinner
(executive producers), Barbara
Jampel (producer), April 8, 1981
(PBS)
Making M*A*S*H, Michael Hirsh
(producer), January 21, 1981 (PBS)
Starring Katharine Hepburn, George
Page (executive producer), David
Heely (producer), March 16, 1981
(PBS)

OUTSTANDING INFORMATIONAL SERIES

Emmy(s) to executive producer(s) and producer(s):
☐ *Steve Allen's Meeting of Minds*, Loring
d'Usseau (producer) (PBS)
The Barbara Walters Specials, Don
Mischer (executive producer), Jo
Ann Goldberg (producer) (ABC)
Cosmos, Adrian Malone (executive
producer), Geoffrey Haines-Stiles,
David Kennard (senior producers),
Gregory Andorfer (producer) (PBS)
Profile: Lillian Hellman, David Dowe
(producer) (PBS)
Real People, George Schlatter
(executive producer), John Barbour,
Bob Wynn (producers) (NBC)

OUTSTANDING CHILDREN'S PROGRAM

For a series or a special. Emmy(s) to executive producer(s) and producer(s):
☐ "Donahue and Kids," *Project Peacock*,
Walter Bartlett (executive producer),
Don Mischer (producer), Jan Cornell
(co-producer), March 16, 1981
(NBC)
"The Art of Disney Animation,"
Disney's Wonderful World, William
Robert Yates (executive producer),
Bob King, Phil May, William Reid
(producers), April 26, 1981 (NBC)
Emmet Otter's Jug-Band Christmas,
David Lazer (executive producer),
Jim Henson (producer), December
15, 1980 (ABC)
The Legend of Sleepy Hollow, Charles
E. Sellier Jr. (executive producer),
James L. Conway (producer),
October 31, 1980 (NBC)
Paddington Bear, Pepper Weiss
(executive producer), Renate Cole,
Graham Clutterbuck (producers),
Series (PBS)

☐ Indicates winner

OUTSTANDING ANIMATED PROGRAM

For a series or a special. Emmy(s) to executive producer(s) and producer(s):
☐ *Life is a Circus, Charlie Brown*, Lee
Mendelson (executive producer), Bill
Melendez (producer), October 24,
1980 (CBS)
Bugs Bunny: All American Hero, Hal
Geer (executive producer), Friz
Freleng (producer), May 4, 1981
(CBS)
Faeries, Thomas W. Moore, Jean
Moore Edwards, Anne E. Upson
(executive producers), Lee Mishkin,
Fred Hellmich, Norton Virgien
(producers), February 25, 1981
(CBS)
Gnomes, Thomas W. Moore, Anne E.
Upson (executive producers), Jack
Zander (producer), November 11,
1980 (CBS)
It's Magic, Charlie Brown, Lee
Mendelson (executive producer), Bill
Melendez (producer), April 28, 1981
(CBS)

Prime Time Performing Awards

OUTSTANDING LEAD ACTOR IN A COMEDY SERIES

For a continuing or single performance in a regular series:
☐ Judd Hirsch, *Taxi* (ABC)
Alan Alda, *M*A*S*H* (CBS)
Hal Linden, *Barney Miller* (ABC)
Richard Mulligan, *Soap* (ABC)
John Ritter, *Three's Company* (ABC)

OUTSTANDING LEAD ACTOR IN A DRAMA SERIES

For a continuing or single performance in a regular series:
☐ Daniel J. Travanti, *Hill Street Blues*
(NBC)
Edward Asner, *Lou Grant* (CBS)
Jim Davis, *Dallas* (CBS)
Louis Gossett Jr., *Palmerstown*,
"Future City," April 7, 1981 (CBS)
Larry Hagman, *Dallas* (CBS)
Pernell Roberts, *Trapper John, M.D.*
(CBS)

OUTSTANDING LEAD ACTOR IN A LIMITED SERIES OR A SPECIAL

For a continuing role in a limited series or for a single appearance in a limited series or a special:
☐ Anthony Hopkins, *The Bunker*, January
27, 1981 (CBS)
Richard Chamberlain, *Shogun* (NBC)
Toshiro Mifune, *Shogun* (NBC)
Peter O'Toole, *Masada* (ABC)
Peter Strauss, *Masada* (ABC)

OUTSTANDING LEAD ACTRESS IN A COMEDY SERIES

For a continuing or single performance in a regular series:
☐ Isabel Sanford, *The Jeffersons* (CBS)
Eileen Brennan, *Taxi*, "Thy Boss's
Wife," February 12, 1981 (ABC)
Cathryn Damon, *Soap* (ABC)
Katherine Helmond, *Soap* (ABC)
Lynn Redgrave, *House Calls* (CBS)

OUTSTANDING LEAD ACTRESS IN A DRAMA SERIES

For a continuing or single performance in a regular series:
☐ Barbara Babcock, *Hill Street Blues*,
"Fecund Hand Rose," March 25,
1981 (NBC)
Barbara Bel Geddes, *Dallas* (CBS)
Linda Gray, *Dallas* (CBS)
Veronica Hamel, *Hill Street Blues*
(NBC)
Michael Learned, *Nurse* (CBS)
Stefanie Powers, *Hart to Hart* (ABC)

OUTSTANDING LEAD ACTRESS IN A LIMITED SERIES OR A SPECIAL

For a continuing role in a limited series or for a single appearance in a limited series or a special:
☐ Vanessa Redgrave, *Playing for Time*,
September 30, 1980 (CBS)
Ellen Burstyn, *People vs. Jean Harris*,
May 7 and 8, 1981 (NBC)
Catherine Hicks, *Marilyn: The Untold
Story*, September 28, 1980 (ABC)
Yoko Shimada, *Shogun*, Series (NBC)
Joanne Woodward, *Crisis at Central
High*, February 4, 1981 (CBS)

OUTSTANDING SUPPORTING ACTOR IN A COMEDY OR VARIETY OR MUSIC SERIES

For a continuing or single performance in a regular series:
☐ Danny De Vito, *Taxi* (ABC)
Howard Hesseman, *WKRP in
Cincinnati* (CBS)
Steve Landesberg, *Barney Miller*
(ABC)
Harry Morgan, *M*A*S*H* (CBS)
David Ogden Stiers, *M*A*S*H* (CBS)

OUTSTANDING SUPPORTING ACTOR IN A DRAMA SERIES

For a continuing or single performance in a regular series:
☐ Michael Conrad, *Hill Street Blues*
(NBC)
Mason Adams, *Lou Grant* (CBS)
Charles Haid, *Hill Street Blues* (NBC)
Robert Walden, *Lou Grant* (CBS)
Bruce Weitz, *Hill Street Blues* (NBC)

OUTSTANDING SUPPORTING ACTOR IN A LIMITED SERIES OR A SPECIAL

For a continuing role in a limited series or for a single appearance in a limited series or a special:

☐ David Warner, *Masada* (ABC)

Andy Griffith, *Murder in Texas*, May 3 and 4, 1981 (NBC)

Yuki Meguro, *Shogun* (NBC)

Anthony Quayle, *Masada* (ABC)

John Rhys-Davies, *Shogun* (NBC)

OUTSTANDING SUPPORTING ACTRESS IN A COMEDY OR VARIETY OR MUSIC SERIES

For a continuing or single performance in a regular series:

☐ Eileen Brennan, *Private Benjamin* (CBS)

Loni Anderson, *WKRP in Cincinnati* (CBS)

Marla Gibbs, *The Jeffersons* (CBS)

Anne Meara, *Archie Bunker's Place* (CBS)

Loretta Swit, *M*A*S*H* (CBS)

OUTSTANDING SUPPORTING ACTRESS IN A DRAMA SERIES

For a continuing or single performance in a regular series:

☐ Nancy Marchand, *Lou Grant* (CBS)

Barbara Barrie, *Breaking Away* (ABC)

Barbara Bosson, *Hill Street Blues* (NBC)

Linda Kelsey, *Lou Grant* (CBS)

Betty Thomas, *Hill Street Blues* (NBC)

OUTSTANDING SUPPORTING ACTRESS IN A LIMITED SERIES OR A SPECIAL

For a continuing role in a limited series or for a single appearance in a limited series or a special:

☐ Jane Alexander, *Playing for Time*, September 30, 1980 (CBS)

Patty Duke Astin, *The Women's Room*, September 14, 1980 (ABC)

Colleen Dewhurst, *The Women's Room*, September 14, 1980 (ABC)

Shirley Knight, *Playing for Time*, September 30, 1980 (CBS)

Piper Laurie, *The Bunker*, January 27, 1981 (CBS)

Prime Time Writing and Directing Awards

OUTSTANDING DIRECTING IN A COMEDY SERIES

For a single episode of a regular series:

☐ James Burrows, *Taxi*, "Elaine's Strange Triangle," December 10, 1980 (ABC)

Alan Alda, *M*A*S*H*, "The Life You Save," May 4, 1981 (CBS)

☐ Indicates winner

Rod Daniel, *WKRP in Cincinnati*, "Venus Flytrap Explains the Atom," January 31, 1981 (CBS)

Linda Day, *Archie Bunker's Place*, "Tough Love," March 15, 1981 (CBS)

Burt Metcalfe, *M*A*S*H*, "No Laughing Matter," February 16, 1981 (CBS)

Jerry Paris, *Happy Days*, "Hello Mrs. Arcola," February 24, 1981 (ABC)

Noam Pitlik, *Barney Miller*, "Liquidation," May 21, 1981 (ABC)

OUTSTANDING DIRECTING IN A DRAMA SERIES

For a single episode of a regular series:

☐ Robert Butler, *Hill Street Blues*, "Hill Street Station," January 15, 1981 (NBC)

Corey Allen, *Hill Street Blues*, "Jungle Madness," May 26, 1981 (NBC)

Burt Brinckerhoff, *Lou Grant*, "Pack," October 27, 1980 (CBS)

Georg Stanford Brown, *Hill Street Blues*, "Up in Arms," February 21, 1981 (NBC)

Mel Damski, *American Dream*, "Pilot," April 26, 1981 (ABC)

Gene Reynolds, *Lou Grant*, "Strike," February 16, 1981 (CBS)

OUTSTANDING DIRECTING IN A VARIETY, MUSIC OR COMEDY PROGRAM

For a variety or music special or series or for a comedy special:

☐ Don Mischer, *The Kennedy Center Honors: A National Celebration of the performing Arts*, December 27, 1980 (CBS)

Emile Ardolino, "Nureyev and the Joffrey Ballet/In Tribute to Nijinsky," *Dance in America*, March 9, 1981 (PBS)

Tony Charmoli, *Sylvia Fine Kaye's Musical Comedy Tonight II*, February 11, 1981 (PBS)

Dwight Hemion, *Linda in Wonderland*, November 27, 1980 (CBS)

Bob Henry, *Barbara Mandrell and the Mandrell Sisters*, (with Dolly Parton and John Schneider), November 18, 1980 (NBC)

Marty Pasetta, *53rd Annual Academy Awards*, March 31, 1981 (ABC)

OUTSTANDING DIRECTING IN A LIMITED SERIES OR A SPECIAL

For a single episode of a limited series or for a special:

☐ James Goldstone, *Kent State*, February 8, 1981 (NBC)

Jerry London, *Shogun*—Episode 5, September 19, 1980 (NBC)

Paul Newman, *The Shadow Box*, December 28, 1980 (ABC)

Boris Sagal, *Masada*—Episode 4, April 8, 1981 (ABC)

Roger Young, *Bitter Harvest*, May 18, 1981 (NBC)

OUTSTANDING ACHIEVEMENT IN CHOREOGRAPHY

For a single episode of a regular or limited series or for a special:

☐ Walter Painter, *Lynda Carter's Celebration*, May 11, 1981 (CBS)

Tony Charmoli, *Lily: Sold Out*, February 2, 1981 (CBS)

Don Crichton, *The Tim Conway Show*—Episode 219, January 31, 1981 (CBS)

Michael Smuin, "The Tempest Live with the San Francisco Ballet," *Dance in America*, March 30, 1981 (PBS)

Lester Wilson, *Sixty Years of Seduction*, May 4, 1981 (ABC)

OUTSTANDING WRITING IN A COMEDY SERIES

For a single episode of a regular series:

☐ Michael Leeson, *Taxi*, "Tony's Sister and Jim," November 26, 1980 (ABC)

Stephen J. Cannell, *The Greatest American Hero*, "Pilot," March 18, 1981 (ABC)

Glen Charles, Les Charles, *Taxi*, "Going Home," December 17, 1980 (ABC)

Mike Farrell, John Rappaport, Dennis Koenig (teleplay), Thad Mumford, Dan Wilcox, Burt Metcalfe (story), *M*A*S*H*, "Death Takes the Holiday," December 15, 1980 (CBS)

David Lloyd, *Taxi*, "Elaine's Strange Triangle," December 10, 1980 (ABC)

OUTSTANDING WRITING IN A DRAMA SERIES

For a single episode of a regular series:

☐ Michael Kozoll, Steven Bochco, *Hill Street Blues*, "Hill Street Station," January 15, 1981 (NBC)

Michael Kozoll, Steven Bochco, Anthony Yerkovich, *Hill Street Blues*, "Jungle Madness," May 26, 1981 (NBC)

Ronald M. Cohen, Barbara Corday, Ken Hecht, *American Dream*, "Pilot," April 26, 1981 (ABC)

Seth Freeman, *Lou Grant*, "Rape," January 12, 1981 (CBS)

April Smith, *Lou Grant*, "Strike," February 16, 1981 (CBS)

OUTSTANDING WRITING IN A VARIETY, MUSIC OR COMEDY PROGRAM

For a variety or music special or series or for a comedy special:
☐ Jerry Juhl, David Odell, Chris Langham, *The Muppet Show*, (with Carol Burnett) (Syndicated)

Nancy Audley, Ann Elder, Irene Mecchi, Elaine Pope, Ziggy Steinberg, Rocco Urbisci, Jane Wagner, Rod Warren, *Lily: Sold Out*, February 2, 1981 (CBS)

Sylvia Fine Kaye, *Sylvia Fine Kaye's Musical Comedy Tonight II*, February 11, 1981 (PBS)

Raymond Siller, Hal Goodman, Larry Klein, Michael Barrie, Jim Mulholland, Kevin Mulholland, Robert Smith, Gary Murphy, Greg Fields, Pat McCormick, *The Tonight Show Starring Johnny Carson*, "18th Anniversary Show," September 29, 1980 (NBC)

George Stevens Jr., Joseph Mc Bride, *The American Film Institute Salute to Fred Astaire*, April 18, 1981 (CBS)

OUTSTANDING WRITING IN A LIMITED SERIES OR A SPECIAL

For a single episode of a limited series or for a special:
☐ Arthur Miller, *Playing for Time*, September 30, 1980 (CBS)

Eric Bercovici, *Shogun*—Episode 5, September 19, 1980 (NBC)

Michael Cristofer, *The Shadow Box*, December 28, 1980 (ABC)

Richard Friedenberg, *Bitter Harvest*, May 18, 1981 (NBC)

Joel Oliansky, *Masada*—Episode 4, April 8, 1981 (ABC)

Creative Arts Awards

OUTSTANDING CINEMATOGRAPHY FOR A SERIES

For a single episode of a regular series:
☐ William H. Cronjager, *Hill Street Blues*, "Hill Street Station," January 15, 1981 (NBC)

Ben Colman, A.S.C., *Buck Rogers*, "Hawk," January 9, 1981 (NBC)

Gerald Perry Finnerman, A.S.C., *The Gangster Chronicles*—Chapter 1, February 12, 1981 (NBC)

Brianne Murphy, A.S.C., *Breaking Away*, "La Strada," January 10, 1981 (ABC)

Charles W. Short, *Nero Wolfe*, "Death and the Dolls, April 10, 1981 (NBC)

Ted Voigtlander, A.S.C., *Little House on the Prairie*, "Sylvia," February 9 and 16, 1981 (NBC)

☐ Indicates winner

OUTSTANDING CINEMATOGRAPHY FOR A LIMITED SERIES OR A SPECIAL

For a single episode of a limited series or for a special:
☐ Arthur F. Ibbetson, B.S.C., *Littel Lord Fauntleroy*, November 25, 1980 (CBS)

Andrew Laszlo, *Shogun*—Episode 4, September 18, 1980 (NBC)

Terry K. Meade, *Marilyn: The Untold Story*, September 28, 1980 (ABC)

Gayne Rescher, A.S.C., *Bitter Harvest*, May 18, 1981 (NBC)

Frank W. Stanley, A.S.C., *John Steinbeck's East of Eden*—Episode 2, February 9, 1981 (ABC)

Ted Voigtländer, A.S.C., *The Diary of Anne Frank*, November 17, 1980 (NBC)

OUTSTANDING ART DIRECTION FOR A SERIES

For a single episode of a regular series:
☐ Howard E. Johnson (production designer), John M. Dwyer, Robert George Freer (Set decorators), *The Gangster Chronicles*—Chapter 11, May 1, 1981 (NBC)

James J. Agazzi, Paul Sylos (art directors), Robert Signorelli (set decorator), *Hart to Hart*, "Blue Chip Murders," May 26, 1981 (ABC)

Thomas E. Azzari (production designer), James I. Colburn (set decorator), *Goodtime Harry, Wally Smith*, July 26, 1980 (NBC)

John E. Chilberg II, Paul Sylos, Frank Swig (art directors), Brock Broughton (set decorator), *Dynasty*—Episode 1, January 12, 1981 (ABC)

Jeffrey L. Goldstein (art director), Joseph A. Armetta (set decorator), *Hill Street Blues*, "Hill Street Station," January 15, 1981 (NBC)

OUTSTANDING ART DIRECTION FOR A LIMITED SERIES OR A SPECIAL

For a single episode of a limited series or for a special:
☐ Ray Storey (art director), Dennis Peeples, David Love (set decorators), *John Steinbeck's East of Eden*—Episode 3, February 11, 1981 (ABC)

Robert Gundlach (art director), Gary Jones (set decorator), *Playing for Time*, September 30, 1980 (CBS)

Joseph R. Jennings (production designer), Yoshinobu Nishioka (art director), Thomas R. Pedigo, Shoichi Yasuda (set decorators), *Shogun*—Episode 5, September 19, 1980 (NBC)

Jan Scott, Sydney Z. Litwack (art directors), Bill Harp (set decorator), *Marilyn: The Untold Story*, September 28, 1980 (ABC)

John H. Senter (production designer), George Renne, Kuli Sanders (art directors), Joseph J. Stone, Edward M. Parker (set decorators), *Masada*—Episode 4, April 8, 1981 (ABC)

OUTSTANDING ART DIRECTION FOR A VARIETY OR A MUSIC PROGRAM

For a single episode of a regular or limited series or for a special:
☐ Roy Christopher (art director), *53rd Annual Academy Awards*, March 31, 1981 (ABC)

Romain Johnston (art director), Jim Wagner (set decorator), *Barbara Mandrell and the Mandrell Sisters*, (with Charlie Pride), December 6, 1980 (NBC)

Ray Klausen (art director), Walter L. Goodwin (set decorator), *Lynda Carter's Celebration*, May 11, 1981 (CBS)

Charles Lisanby (art director), Dwight Jackson (set decorator), *Diana*, March 2, 1981 (CBS)

John Shrum (art director), *The Tonight Show Starring Johnny Carson*, (with Charles Nelson Reilly), December 31, 1980 (NBC)

Malcolm Stone (art director), *The Muppet Show*, (with Brooke Shields) (Syndicated)

OUTSTANDING ACHIEVEMENT IN MUSIC COMPOSITION FOR A SERIES (DRAMATIC UNDERSCORE)

For a single episode of a regular series. Emmy(s) to composer(s):
☐ Bruce Broughton, *Buck Rogers*, "The Satyr," March 12, 1981 (NBC)

Billy Goldenberg, *The Gangster Chronicles*—Chapter 1, February 12, 1981 (NBC)

Mike Post, *Hill Street Blues*, "Hill Street Station," January 15, 1981 (NBC)

David Rose, *Little House on the Prairie*, "The Lost Ones," May 11, 1981 (NBC)

Patrick Williams, *Lou Grant*, "Stroke," May 4, 1981 (CBS)

OUTSTANDING ACHIEVEMENT IN MUSIC COMPOSITION FOR A LIMITED SERIES OR A SPECIAL (DRAMATIC UNDERSCORE)

For a single episode of a limited series or for a special. Emmy(s) to composer(s):
☐ Jerry Goldsmith, *Masada*—Episode 2, April 6, 1981 (ABC)

Paul Chihara, "The Tempest Live with the San Francisco Ballet," *Dance in America*, March 30, 1981 (PBS)

Fred Karlin, *Homeward Bound*, November 19, 1980 (CBS)

Pater Matz, *Father Damien: The Leper Priest*, October 27, 1980 (NBC)

Morton Stevens, *Masada*—Episode 4, April 8, 1981 (ABC)

OUTSTANDING ACHIEVEMENT IN MUSIC AND LYRICS

For a song (which *must* have both music and lyrics), whether it be for a single episode of a regular or limited series or for a special. Emmy(s) to composer(s) and lyricist(s):

☐ Ken Welch (composer), Mitzie Welch (lyricist), *Linda in Wonderland*, song: "This Is My Night," November 27, 1980 (CBS)

W. Earl Brown (composer and lyricist), *All Commercials*, song: "Truman Capote Jeans," September 30, 1980 (NBC)

Ray Charles (composer and lyricist), *Perry Como's Christmas In the Holy Land*, song: "The City of Tradition," December 13, 1980 (ABC)

Larry Grossman (composer), Sheldon Harnick (lyricist), *The Way They Were*, song: "In the Beginning" (Syndicated)

Fred Karlin (composer), David Pomranz (lyricist), *Homeward Bound*, song: "Home," November 19, 1980 (CBS)

OUTSTANDING ACHIEVEMENT IN MUSIC DIRECTION

For a single episode of a regular or limited series of for a special, whether it be variety or music. Emmy(s) to music director and principal arranger(s):

☐ Ian Fraser (music director), Billy Byers, Chris Boardman, Bob Florence (arrangers), *Linda in Wonderland*, November 27, 1980 (CBS)

Jack Elliott (music director), Alf Clausen, William Goldstein (arrangers), *Omnibus*, December 28, 1980 (ABC)

Earle Hagen (music director), Carl Brandt, Deane Hagen (arrangers), *Stand by Your Man*, May 13, 1981 (CBS)

Nick Perito (music director and arranger), *Perry Como's Christmas in the Holy Land*, December 13, 1980 (ABC)

George Wyle (music director), Sid Feller, Norman Mamey (arrangers), *The Magic of David Copperfield*, September 25, 1980 (CBS)

☐ Indicates winner

OUTSTANDING COSTUME DESIGN FOR A SERIES

For a single episode of a regular or limited series:

☐ Shin Nishida, *Shogun*—Episode 5, September 19, 1980 (NBC)

Grady Hunt, *Beulah Land*—Episode 3, October 9, 1980 (NBC)

Alfred E. Lehman, *Buck Rogers*, "The Dorian Secret," April 16, 1981 (NBC)

Nino Novarese, *Masada*—Episode 4, April 8, 1981 (ABC)

OUTSTANDING COSTUME DESIGN FOR A SPECIAL

For a comedy, drama, variety or music special:

☐ Willa Kim, "The Tempest Live with the San Francisco Ballet," *Dance in America*, March 30, 1981 (PBS)

Olga Lehmann, "A Tale of Two Cities," *Hallmark Hall of Fame*, December 2, 1980 (CBS)

Warden Neil, *The Jayne Mansfield Story*, October 29, 1980 (CBS)

Nino Novarese, *Peter and Paul*, April 12 and 14, 1981 (CBS)

Travilla, *Evita Peron*, February 23 and 24, 1981 (NBC)

OUTSTANDING ACHIEVEMENT IN MAKEUP

For a single episode of a regular or limited series or for a special:

☐ Albert Paul Jeyte, James Kail, *Peter and Paul*, April 12 and 14, 1981 (CBS)

Del Acevedo, Albert Paul Jeyte, *Masada*—Episode 4, April 8, 1981 (ABC)

Scott H. Eddo, Stan Smith, *The Diary of Anne Frank*, November 17, 1980 (NBC)

Alan Friedman, Lona Mardock Jeffers, *The Jayne Mansfield Story*, October 29, 1980 (CBS)

John Inzerella, *Father Damien: The Leper Priest*, October 27, 1980 (NBC)

Allan "Whitey" Snyder, *Marilyn: The Untold Story*, September 28, 1980 (ABC)

OUTSTANDING ACHIEVEMENT IN HAIRSTYLING

For a single episode of a regular or limited series or for a special:

☐ Shriley Padgett, *Madame X*, March 16, 1981 (NBC)

Sylvia Abascal, Janis Clark, *The Jayne Mansfield Story*, October 29, 1980 (CBS)

Jean Austin, *Lou Grant*, "Stroke," May 4, 1981 (CBS)

Janice D. Brandow, *Father Damien: The Leper Priest*, October 27, 1980 (NBC)

Larry Germain, *Little House on the Prairie*, "To See the Light," December 1 and 8, 1980 (NBC)

OUTSTANDING GRAPHIC DESIGN AND TITLE SEQUENCES

For a single episode of a regular or limited series or for a special:

☐ Phill Norman, *Shogun*—Episode 1, September 15, 1980 (NBC)

Gene Kraft, *Freebie and the Bean*, "Health Nuts," December 13, 1980 (CBS)

OUTSTANDING ACHIEVEMENT IN FILM EDITING FOR A SERIES

For a single episode of a regular series:

☐ M. Pam Blumenthal, Jack Michon, *Taxi*, "Elaine's Strange Triangle," December 10, 1980 (ABC)

Bernard Balmuth, A.C.E., *Palmerstown*, "Crossroads," June 9, 1981 (CBS)

Clay Bartels, *Hill Street Blues*, "Jungle Madness," May 26, 1981 (NBC)

Fred W. Berger, *Dallas*, "Ewing-Gate," May 1, 1981 (CBS)

Ray Daniels, A. David Marshall, *Hill Street Blues*, "Hill Street Station," January 15, 1981 (NBC)

Richard W. Darling Jr., *Dynasty*—Episode 3, January 26, 1981 (ABC)

Tony De Zarraga, *The White Shadow*, "A Day in the Life," March 16, 1981 (CBS)

James Galloway, A.C.E., *Lou Grant*, "Strike," February 16, 1981 (CBS)

Christopher Nelson, *The Greatest American Hero*, "Pilot," March 18, 1981 (ABC)

Thomas H. Stevens Jr., *Hill Street Blues*, "Rites of Spring," May 19, 1981 (NBC)

Stanford Tischler, A.C.E., Larry L. Mills, A.C.E., *M*A*S*H*, "Death Takes the Holiday," December 15, 1980 (CBS)

OUTSTANDING FILM EDITING FOR A LIMITED SERIES OR A SPECIAL

For a single episode of a limited series or for a special:

☐ John A. Martinelli, A.C.E., *Murder in Texas*, May 3 and 4, 1981 (NBC)

John Bloom (editorial consultant), "Edwin F. England, Peter Kirby," *Masada*—Episode 4, April 8, 1981 (ABC)

Barbara Dies, Michael S. McLean, A.C.E., *The Best Little Girl in the World*, May 11, 1981 (ABC)

Michael Eliot, Robert Florio, *A Whale for the Killing*, February 1, 1981 (ABC)

Thomas Fries, *Bitter Harvest*, May 18, 1981 (NBC)

Donald R. Rode, Benjamin A. Weissman, Jerry Young, Bill Luciano, *Shogun*—Episode 5, September 19, 1980 (NBC)

OUTSTANDING ACHIEVEMENT IN FILM SOUND EDITING

For a single episode of a regular or limited series or for a special:

☐ Samuel Horta (supervising editor), Robert Cornett, Denise Horta, Eileen Horta (editors), *Hill Street Blues*, "Hill Street Station," January 15, 1981 (ABC)

Michael Hilkene, Russ Tinsley (supervising editors), Albert Cavigga, Tom Cornwell, Linda Dove, Dave Elliott, Don Ernst, Dimitry Gortinsky, Peter Harrison, Jerry M. Jacobson, Fred Judkins, John Kline, Corinne Sessarego, Rusty Tinsley, Christopher T. Welch, (editors), *The Women's Room*, September 14, 1980 (ABC)

John Kline, Russ Tinsley (supervising editors), Tom Cornwell, Jere Golding, Dimitry Gortinsky, Michael Hilkene, Bill Manger, Bob Pearson, Christopher T. Welch, (editors), *A Whale for the Killing*, February 1, 1981 (ABC)

Stanley M. Paul (supervising editor), Bill Andrews, Leonard Corso, Dennis Dutton, Jack Finley, Bob Gutknecht, Sean Hanley, Pierre Jalbert, Jack Keath, Alan Nineberg, Lee Osborne, Talley Paulos (editors), *Shogun*—Episode 3, September 17, 1980 (NBC)

Russ Tinsley, Bill Wistrom (supervising editors), Tom Cornwell, Peter Harrison, Bill Manger, R. William Thiederman, Christopher T. Welch, (editors), *Evita Peron*—Part 1, February 23, 1981 (NBC)

OUTSTANDING VIDEOTAPE EDITING FOR A SERIES

For a single episode of a regular series:

☐ Andy Ackerman, *WKRP in Cincinnati*, "Bah, Humbug," December 20, 1980 (CBS)

Ken Dennisoff, Tom Faigh, *Barbara Mandrell and the Mandrell Sisters*, (with Ray Stevens), December 13, 1980 (NBC)

John Hawkins, *The Muppet Show*, (with Brooke Shields) (Syndicated)

Andy Zall, *Barbara Mandrell and the Mandrell Sisters*, (with Dolly Parton and John Schneider), November 18, 1980 (NBC)

☐ Indicates winner

OUTSTANDING VIDEOTAPE EDITING FOR A LIMITED SERIES OR A SPECIAL

For a single episode of a limited series or for a special:

☐ Marco Zappia (videotape editor), Branda S. Miller (film editor), *Perry Como's Christmas in the Holy Land*, December 13, 1980 (ABC)

Harvey W. Berger, Andy Schubert, *The American Film Institute Salute to Fred Astaire*, April 18, 1981 (CBS)

Raymond M. Bush, *Tom and Dick Smothers Brothers Special I*, November 1, 1980 (NBC)

Terry W. Greene, Ron Menzies, *Diana*, March 2, 1981 (CBS)

Pam Marshall, *John Schneider—Back Home*, September 24, 1980 (CBS)

OUTSTANDING FILM SOUND MIXING

For a single episode of a regular or limited series or for a special:

☐ William R. Teague (production mixer), Robert L. Harman, William L. McCaughey, Howard Wollman (rerecording mixers), *Evita Peron*—Part 1, February 23, 1981 (NBC)

Alan Bernard (production mixer), Robert L. Harman, William L. McCaughey, Howard Wollman (rerecording mixers), *Baby Comes Home*, October 16, 1980 (CBS)

Nick Gaffey (production mixer), Gary Bourgeois, Lee Minkler, Terry Porter (rerecording mixers), *Nero Wolfe*, "Gambit," April 3, 1981 (NBC)

Stanley P. Gordon (production mixer), Robert L. Harman, William L. McCaughey, Lee Minkler (rerecording mixers), *Dial "M" for Murder*, April 9, 1981 (NBC)

Rene Magnol (production mixer), Robert L. Harman, William L. McCaughey, Howard Wollman (rerecording mixers), *The Bunker*, January 27, 1981 (CBS)

John MacLeod (production mixer), Robert L. Harman, William L. McCaughey, Terry Porter (rerecording mixers), *Word of Honor*, January 6, 1981 (CBS)

Richard Raguse (production mixer), Robert L. Harman, William L. McCaughey, Howard Wollman (rerecording mixers), *The Killing of Randy Webster*, March 11, 1981 (CBS)

William R. Teague (production mixer), Joel Fein, George E. Porter, Howard Wollman (rerecording mixers), *A Time for Miracles*, December 21, 1980 (ABC)

Manuel Topete Blake (production mixer), Harry Alphin, Robert L.

Harman, William L. McCaughey (rerecording mixers), *A Rumor of War*, September 24 and 25, 1980 (CBS)

Blake Wilcox (production mixer), Robert L. Harman, William L. McCaughey, Howard Wollman (rerecording mixers), *Hart to Hart*, "Tis the Season to Be Murdered, December 16, 1980 (ABC)

OUTSTANDING ACHIEVEMENT IN TAPE SOUND MIXING

For a single episode of a regular or limited series or for a special:

☐ Jerry Clemans, Doug Nelson, Donald Worsham, *John Denver with His Special Guest George Burns: Two of a Kind*, March 30, 1981 (ABC)

Tom L. Ancell, *San Francisco Inaugural Gala*, September 16, 1980 (PBS)

Jerry Clemans, Ed Greene, Phillip J. Seretti, *Perry Como's Spring in San Francisco*, May 14, 1981 (ABC)

Jerry Clemans, Matthew Hyde, Donald Worsham, *Barbara Mandrell and the Mandrell Sisters*, (with the Gatlin Brothers), February 14, 1981 (NBC)

Don Johnson, Phillip J. Seretti, *Kent State*, February 8, 1981 (NBC)

OUTSTANDING ACHIEVEMENT IN TECHNICAL DIRECTION AND ELECTRONIC CAMERA WORK

For a single episode of a regular or limited series or for a special:

☐ Heino Ripp (technical director), Peter Basil, Al Camoin, Tom Dezendorf, Vince Di Pietro, Gene Martin (camerapersons), *Live from Studio 8H: An Evening of Jerome Robbins' Ballets with Members of the New York City Ballet*, July 2, 1980 (NBC)

John B. Field (technical director), Rick Caswell, Rocky Danielson, Bob Eberline, Hank Geving, Dean Hall, Larry Heider, Bob Heighton, Dave Hilmer, Dave Levisohn, Dan Preston, Larry Travis, Wayne Womack (camerapersons), *Kenny Rogers' America*, November 20, 1980 (CBS)

Crew A—Tom Sabol (technical director), George Ciliberto, Barry Frisher, Jodi Greenberg, Pamela Schneider (camerapersons), Crew B—O. Tamburri (technical director), George Loomis, Mike Stramisky (camerapersons), *Tomorrow Coast to Coast*, "Charles Manson Interview," June 12, 1981 (NBC)

O. Tamburri (technical director), George Falardeau, Royden Holm, Reed Howard (camerapersons), *People vs. Jean Harris*, May 7 and 8, 1981 (NBC)

Jerry Weiss (technical director), Don Barker, Bruce Bottone, Jim Hering,

Royden Holm (camerapersons), *The Magic of David Copperfield*, September 25, 1980 (CBS)

OUTSTANDING ACHIEVEMENT IN LIGHTING DIRECTION

For a single episode of a regular or limited series or for a special:
☐ Ralph Holmes, "Nureyev and the Joffrey Ballet/In Tribute to Nijinsky," *Dance in America*, March 9, 1981 (PBS)

Gregory Brunton, *Sixty Years of Seduction*, May 4, 1981 (ABC)

Gregory Brunton (lighting director), Allen Branton (lighting designer), *Diana*, March 2, 1981 (CBS)

Leard Davis, *The Osmond Family Christmas Show*, December 15, 1980 (NBC)

Fred McKinnon, *Command Performance: The Stars Salute to the President*, March 26, 1981 (NBC)

George W. Riesenberger, *A Bayou Legend*, June 15, 1981 (PBS)

Carl J. Vitelli Jr., *The 35th Annual Tony Awards*, June 7, 1981 (CBS)

OUTSTANDING INDIVIDUAL ACHIEVEMENT—ANIMATED PROGRAMMING

(Possibility of one award, more than one award or no award):
Hoyt S. Curtin (composer), *The Flinstones*, "Flintstones New Neighbors," September 26, 1980 (NBC)

Peter Aries (film editor), *Faeries*, February 25, 1981 (CBS)

Peter Aries (film sound editor), *Faeries*, Febuary 25, 1981 (CBS)

Alan Aldridge, Lee Mishkin (teleplay), Christopher Gore (story), *Faeries*, February 25, 1981 (CBS)

OUTSTANDING INDIVIDUAL ACHIEVEMENT—SPECIAL CLASS

(Possibility of one award, more than one or no award):
☐ Sarah Vaughn (performer), *Rhapsody and Song—A Tribute to George Gershwin*, May 9, 1981 (PBS)

Nick Perito (music director), Zubin Mehta, Michael Tilson Thomas, Alan Barker (guest conductors), *The Kennedy Center Honors: A National Celebration of the Performing Arts*, December 27, 1980 (CBS)

Rita Bennett (women's costumer), Bill Blackburn (men's costumer), *The Diary of Anne Frank*, November 17, 1980 (NBC)

Robert Magahay (men's costumer), Judy Truchan (women's costumer), *John Steinbeck's East of*

Eden—Episode 1, February 8, 1981 (ABC)

Adrianne Levesque (women's costumer), Harry Curtis (men's costumer), *Crazy Times*, April 10, 1981 (ABC)

OUTSTANDING INDIVIDUAL ACHIEVEMENT—CREATIVE TECHNICAL CRAFTS

(Possibility of one award, more than one award or no award):
☐ John Allison, Adolf Schaller, Don Davis, Rick Sternbach, Jon Lomberg Brown, Anne Norcia, Ernie Norcia (astronomical artists), *Cosmos*, "The Shores of the Cosmic Ocean," September 29, 1980 (PBS)

☐ Carey Melcher (technical designer), Bob Buckner, Steve Burum, Jim Dow, John Gale, Larry Heider, Mike Johnson, Robert C. King, Cleve Landsberg, Joseph Matza, George C. Reilly, Joe Wolcott (magicam Crew), *Cosmos*, "The Shores of the Cosmic Ocean," September 28, 1980 (PBS)

John L. Marlow, M.D., "Live Fetal Photography," *The Body Human: The Bionic Breakthrough*, May 12, 1981 (CBS)

Mark Schubin (technical designer), "Stereo Simulcast," *Joan Sutherland, Marilyn Horne and Luciano Pavarotti, Live from Lincoln Center*, March 23, 1981 (PBS)

Dick Wilson (sound effects), *Fridays*—Episode 8, November 14, 1980 (ABC)

OUTSTANDING INDIVIDUAL ACHIEVEMENT—CHILDREN'S PROGRAMMING

(Possibility of one award, more than one or no award):
Tom Wright (lighting), *Emmet Otter's Jug-Band Christmas*, December 15, 1980 (ABC)

Paul Williams (composer and lyricist), *Emmet Otter's Jug-Band Christmas*, song: "When the River Meets the Sea," December 15, 1980 (ABC)

Patty Duke Astin (performer), *Family Specials*, "Girl on the Edge of Town" (Syndicated)

Don Mischer (director), "Donahue and Kids," *Project Peacock*, March 16, 1981 (NBC)

Calista Hendrickson, Sherry Ammott (costume designers), *Emmet Otter's Jug-Band Christmas*, December 15, 1980 (ABC)

OUTSTANDING INDIVIDUAL ACHIEVEMENT—INFORMATIONAL PROGRAMMING

(Possibility of one award, more than one or no award):
☐ Kent Gibson, Gerald Zelinger (tape sound mixers), *Cosmos*, "Blues for a Red Planet," October 26, 1980 (PBS)

☐ Dick Rector (production mixer), Gary Bourgeois, Dave Dockendorf, John Mack (rerecording mixers), "Gorilla," *National Geographic Special*, April 8, 1981 (PBS)

Roy Stewart (videotape editor), *Cosmos*, "The Shores of the Cosmic Ocean," September 29, 1980 (PBS)

Kenneth Love (production mixer), Gary Bourgeois, Hoppy Mehterian, Howard Wollman (rerecording mixers), "Living Treasures of Japan," *National Geographic Special*, February 11, 1981 (PBS)

David Hughes (production mixer), Dave Dockendorf, Hoppy Mehterian, George E. Porter (rerecording mixers), "Etosha: Place of Dry Water," *National Geographic Special*, January 7, 1981 (PBS)

Chuck White (production mixer), Gary Bourgeois, George E. Porter, Terry Porter (rerecording mixers), "National Parks: Playground or Paradise," *National Geographic Special*, March 11, 1981 (PBS)

FOURTH ANNUAL ATAS GOVERNORS AWARD
☐ Elton H. Rule

OUTSTANDING ACHIEVEMENT IN ENGINEERING DEVELOPMENT

An award to an individual, a company or an organization for developments in engineering that are either so extensive an improvement on existing methods or so innovative in nature that they materially affect the transmission, recording or reception of television:
☐ Rank Precision Industries Ltd for the design and development of the Rank Cintel Mark III Flying Spot Telecine, which converts film to video

Daytime Awards

OUTSTANDING DAYTIME DRAMA SERIES

Emmy(s) to executive producer(s) and producer(s):
All My Children, Agnes Nixon (executive producer), Jorn Winther (producer) (ABC)

☐ *General Hospital*, Gloria Monty (producer) (ABC)

Ryan's Hope, Paul Avila Mayer and Claire Labine (executive producers), Ellen Barrett (producer) (ABC)

OUTSTANDING GAME OR AUDIENCE PARTICIPATION SHOW

Emmy(s) to executive producer(s) and producer(s):
Family Feud, Mark Goodson (executive producer), Howard Felsher (producer) (ABC)
Hollywood Squares, Merrill Heatter and Bob Quigley (executive producers), Jay Redack (producer) (NBC)
☐ *The $20,000 Pyramid*, Bob Stewart (executive producer), Anne Marie Schmitt and Jane Rothehild (producers) (ABC)

OUTSTANDING TALK/SERVICE SERIES

Emmy(s) to executive producer(s) and producer(s):
Over Easy, Richard R. Rector (executive producer), Jules Power (senior producer), Ben Bayol and Janice Tunder (studio producers) (PBS)
☐ *Donahue*, Richard Mincer (executive producer), Patricia McMillen (senior producer), Darlene Hayes and Sheri Singer (producers) (Syndicated)
The Richard Simmons Show, Woody Fraser (executive producer), Nora Fraser (producer) (Syndicated)

OUTSTANDING VARIETY SERIES

Emmy(s) to executive producer(s) and producer(s):
The David Letterman Show, Jack Rollins (executive producer), Barry Sand (producer) (NBC)
☐ *The Merv Griffin Show*, Peter Barsocchini (producer) (Syndicated)

OUTSTANDING CHILDREN'S ENTERTAINMENT SERIES (Tie!)

Emmy(s) to executive producer(s) and producer(s):
ABC Weekend Specials, Robert Chenault (executive producer) (ABC)
☐ *Captain Kangaroo*, Robert Keeshan (executive producer), Joel Kosofsky (producer) (CBS)
"The Legend of King Arthur," *Once upon a Classic*, Jay Rayvid (executive producer), James A. DeVinney and Ken Riddington (producers) (PBS)
☐ "A Tale of Two Cities," Once Upon a Classic, Jay Rayvid (executive producer), James A. DeVinney and Barry Letts (producers), Christine Ochtun (coproducer) (PBS)

☐ Indicates winner

OUTSTANDING CHILDREN'S ENTERTAINMENT SPECIAL

Emmy(s) to executive producer(s) and producer(s):
"Family of Strangers," *ABC Afterschool Special*, Linda Gottlieb (executive producer), Doro Bachrach and Franklin Getchell (producers), September 24, 1970 (ABC)
"I Think I'm Having a Baby," *CBS Afternoon Playhouse*, Joe Stern (executive producer), Eda Godel Hallinan and Keetje Van Benschoten (producers), March 3, 1981 (CBS)
☐ "A Matter of Time," *ABC Afterschool Special*, Martin Tashe (executive producer/producer), February 11, 1981 (ABC)
"Sunshine's on the Way," *NBC Special Treat*, Linda Gottlieb (executive producer), Doro Bachrach (producer), November 11, 1980 (NBC)

OUTSTANDING CHILDREN'S INFORMATIONAL/INSTRUCTIONAL SERIES

Emmy(s) to executive producer(s) and producer(s):
Animals Animals Animals, Lester Cooper (executive producer), Jake Haselkorn (producer) (ABC)
Kids are People Too, Laura Schrock (producer), Lyn Butler (coordinating producer), Burt Dubrow (studio producer) (ABC)
Sesame Street, Dulcy Singer (executive producer), Lisa Simon (producer) (PBS)
☐ *30 Minutes*, Joel Heller (executive producer), Madeline Amgott, Vern Diamond, Allen Ducovny, Diego Echeverria, Virginia Gray, Susan Mills, Patti Obrow White, Catherine Olian, Robert Rubin and Martin Smith (producers) (CBS)

OUTSTANDING CHILDREN'S INFORMATIONAL/INSTRUCTIONAL SPECIAL

Emmy(s) to executive producer(s) and producer(s):
☐ "Julie Andrews' Invitation to the Dance with Rudold Nureyev," *The CBS Festival of Lively Arts for Young People*, Jack Wohl and Bernard Rothman (producers), November 30, 1980 (CBS)
"Side by Side—Prejudice," *On the Level*, Lawrence Walcoff (executive producer), November 14, 1980 (PBS)

OUTSTANDING CHILDREN'S INFORMATIONAL/INSTRUCTIONAL PROGRAMMING—SHORT FORM

Emmy(s) to executive producer(s) and producer(s):
ABC Nutrition Spots, George Newall and Tom Yohe (executive producers) (ABC)
ASK NBC News, Beryl Pfizer (producer) (NBC)
The Doughnuts, Ken Greengrass and Phil Lawrence (executive producers), Lynn Ahrens (producer) (ABC)
☐ *In the News*, Joel Heller (executive producer), Walter Lister (producer) (CBS)

OUTSTANDING ACTOR IN A DAYTIME DRAMA SERIES
James Mitchell, *All My Children* (ABC)
☐ Douglass Watson, *Another World* (NBC)
Larry Bryggman, *As the World Turns* (CBS)
Henderson Forsythe, *As the World Turns* (CBS)
Anthony Geary, *General Hospital* (ABC)

OUTSTANDING ACTRESS IN A DAYTIME DRAMA SERIES
Julia Barr, *All My Children* (ABC)
Susan Lucci, *All My Children* (ABC)
☐ Judith Light, *One Life to Live* (ABC)
Robin Strasser, *One Life to Live* (ABC)
Helen Gallagher, *Ryan's Hope* (ABC)

OUTSTANDING ACTOR IN A SUPPORTING ROLE FOR A DAYTIME DRAMA SERIES
Matthew Cowles, *All My Children* (ABC)
William Mooney, *All My Children* (ABC)
Justin Deas, *As the World Turns* (CBS)
Richard Backus, *Ryan's Hope* (ABC)
☐ Larry Haines, *Search for Tomorrow* (CBS)

OUTSTANDING ACTRESS IN A SUPPORTING ROLE FOR A DAYTIME DRAMA SERIES
Elizabeth Lawrence, *All My Children* (ABC)
Lois Kibbee, *The Edge of Night* (ABC)
☐ Jane Elliot, *General Hospital* (ABC)
Jacklyn Zeman, *General Hospital* (ABC)
Randall Edwards, *The Edge of Night* (ABC)

OUTSTANDING HOST/HOSTESS IN A GAME OR AUDIENCE PARTICIPATION SHOW
Dick Clark, *The $20,000 Pyramid* (ABC)
Richard Dawson, *Family Feud* (ABC)
☐ Peter Marshall, *Hollywood Squares* (NBC)

OUTSTANDING HOST/HOSTESS IN A TALK/SERVICE SERIES
Phil Donahue, *Donahue* (Syndicated)
☐ Hugh Downs, *Over Easy* (PBS)

OUTSTANDING HOST/HOSTESS IN A VARIETY SERIES
Merv Griffin, *The Merv Griffin Show* (Syndicated)
☐ David Letterman, *The David Letterman Show* (NBC)
Dinah Shore, *Dinah and Friends* (Syndicated)

OUTSTANDING DIRECTION FOR A DAYTIME DRAMA SERIES
For the entire series:
Larry Auerbach, Jack Coffey, Sherrell Hoffman and Jorn Winther, *All My Children* (ABC)
☐ Marlena Laird, Alan Pultz and Phillip Sogard, *General Hospital* (ABC)
David Pressman, Peter Miner and Norman Hall, *One Life to Live* (ABC)

OUTSTANDING INDIVIDUAL DIRECTION FOR A GAME OR AUDIENCE PARTICIPATION SHOW
For a single episode:
Paul Alter, *Family Feud*, December 16, 1980 (ABC)
☐ Mike Gargiulo, *The $20,000 Pyramid*, May 15, 1980 (ABC)

OUTSTANDING INDIVIDUAL DIRECTION FOR A TALK/SERVICE SERIES
For a single episode:
Vincent Casalaina, *Over Easy*, October 14, 1980 (PBS)
☐ Jerry Kupcinet, *The Richard Simmons Show*, March 13, 1980 (Syndicated)
Ron Weiner, *Donahue—Wives Who Kill Husbands*, September 23, 1980 (Syndicated)

OUTSTANDING INDIVIDUAL DIRECTION FOR A VARIETY SERIES
For a single episode:
Dick Carson, *The Merv Griffin Show— Salute to New York Dance*, October 30, 1980 (Syndicated)
☐ Sterling Johnson, *Dinah and Friends in Israel*, September 10, 1980 (Syndicated)

OUTSTANDING WRITING FOR A DAYTIME DRAMA SERIES
For the entire series:
Agnes Nixon, Wisner Washam, Jack Wood, Mary K. Wells, Clarice Blackburn, Caroline Franz, Cathy Chicos and Cynthia Benjamin, *All My Children* (ABC)
Pat Falken Smith, Margaret DePriest, Sheri Anderson, Frank Salisbury and

Margaret Stewart, *General Hospital* (ABC)
☐ Douglas Marland, Robert Dwyer, Nancy Franklin and Harding Lemay, *The Guiding Light* (CBS)
Sam Hall, Peggy O'Shea, Don Wallace, Lanie Bertram, Gordon Russell and Fred Corke, *One Life to Live* (ABC)

OUTSTANDING ACHIEVEMENT IN TECHNICAL EXCELLENCE FOR A DAYTIME DRAMA SERIES

For the entire series—Emmys to individuals:
☐ *All My Children*, Joseph Solomito and Howard Zweig (technical directors), Lawrence Hammond, Dianne Cates-Cantrell, Robert Ambrico, Christopher Mauro, Larry Strack, Salvatore Augugliaro, Vincent Senatore and Thomas McGrath (electronic camera), Len Walas (senior video engineer), Albin S. Lemanski, Peter Bohm and Charles Eisen (senior audio engineers), Barbara Wood (sound effects engineer), Diana Wenman and Jean Dadario (associate directors), Roger Haenelt (videotape editor) (ABC)
General Hospital, John Cochran, David Smith and Jim Ralston (technical directors), Jack Denton, James Angel, David Banks, D.J. Diomedes, Bud Holland, Rich Kenney, Barry Kirstein, William Pope, John Rago, Luis Rojas, William Scott, Joseph Talosi, Dale Walsh, Carol Wetovich and Sal Folino (electronic camera), Victor Bagdadi, Sam Potter, Eric Clay and Richard Engstrom (senior video engineers), Robert Miller and Zoli Osaze (senior audio engineers), Hal Alexander and George Thompson (associate directors), Bob Lanham, Jose Galvez and Jack Moody (videotape editors) (ABC)
One Life to Live, Martin Gavrin and Louis Marchand (technical directors), John Morris, Thomas French, Eugene Kelly, Richard Westlein, John Wood, Earl Moore, Genevieve Twohig, Bill Phypers, Keith Morris and Nancy Kriegel (electronic camera), Herbert Segall (senior video engineer), Frank Bailey and Jeffrey Schloss (senior audio engineers), Jack Sullivan and Stuart Silver (associate directors), Tony Greco, Robert Steinbeck and Al Forman (videotape editors) (ABC)

OUTSTANDING ACHIEVEMENT IN DESIGN EXCELLENCE FOR A DAYTIME DRAMA SERIES
For the entire series—Emmys to individuals:
All My Children, William Mickley (scenic designer), William Itkin, Donna Larson and Donald Gavitt (lighting directors), Carol Luiken (costume designer), Sylvia Lawrence (makeup designer), Michael Huddle and Marie Ange Ripka (hair designers), Teri Smith (music director), Sid Ramin and Irving Robbins (music composers), Hy Bley (graphic designer) (ABC)
General Hospital, James Ellingwood (art director), Mercer Barrows (set decorator), Grant Velie, John Zak and Tom Markle (lighting directors), Jim O'Daniel and George Whittaker (costume designers), Pam K. Cole (makeup designer), Kathy Kotarakos (hair designer), Dominic Messinger and Jill Phelps (music directors), Charles Paul (music composer) (ABC)
One Life to Live, Charles Brandon (scenic designer), Howard Sharrot and Jo Mayer (lighting directors), Joseph Miller (costume designer), Josephine Foerderer and Tracey Kelley (makeup designers), Karen Crehan and Willis Hanchett (hair designers), Irving Robbins and John Anthony (music directors), Jack Urbont (music composer) (ABC)
☐ *Ryan's Hope*, Sy Tomashoff (scenic designer), John Connolly (lighting director), David Murin and Michele Reish (costume designers), James Cola (makeup designer), John K. Quinn (hair designer), Sybil Weinberger (music supervisor) (ABC)

Daytime Areas Awards*

OUTSTANDING INDIVIDUAL ACHIEVEMENT IN CHILDREN'S PROGRAMMING
For a single episode of a series or for a special program:
Performers
Julie Andrews, "Julie Andrews' Invitation to the Dance with Rudolf Nureyev," *The CBS Festival of Lively Arts for Young People*, November 30, 1980 (CBS)
Bill Bixby, "A Tale of Two Cities"—Part I, *Once upon a Classic*, October 4, 1980 (PBS)
☐ Bill Cosby, "The Secret," *The New Fat Albert Show*, September 13, 1980 (CBS)

---

* possibility of one award, more than one award or no award

☐ Indicates winner

Ken Howard, *The Body Human: Facts for Boys*, November 6, 1980 (CBS)

Marlo Thomas, *The Body Human: Facts for Girls*, October 7, 1980 (CBS)

Danny Aiello, "Family of Strangers," *ABC Afterschool Special*, September 24, 1980 (ABC)

Scott Baio, "Stoned," *ABC Afterschool Special*, November 12, 1980 (ABC)

Hal Linden, "Llama," *Animals Animals Animals*, September 28, 1980 (ABC)

Directors

John Herzfeld, "Stoned," *ABC Afterschool Special*, November 12, 1980 (ABC)

Don Roy King, *Kids Are People Too*, September 21, 1980 (ABC)

Writers

Bob Brush, *Captain Kangaroo*, December 26, 1980 (CBS)

Paul W. Cooper, "A Matter of Time," *ABC Afterschool Special*, February 11, 1981 (ABC)

Blossom Elfman, "I Think I'm Having a Baby," *The CBS Afternoon Playhouse*, March 3, 1981 (CBS)

Robert E. Fuisz M.D., *The Body Human: Facts for Girls*, October 7, 1980 (CBS)

John Herzfeld, "Stoned," *ABC Afterschool Special*, November 12, 1980 (ABC)

Mary Munisteri, "Mandy's Grandmother," *Young People's Special*, April 1, 1980 (Syndicated)

Norman Stiles, Sara Compton, Judy Freudberg, Tony Geiss, John Glines, Emily Kingsley, Louis Santeiro, Ray Sipherd and Peter Swet, *Sesame Street*, January 29, 1981 (PBS)

Electronic camera

Chuck Clifton, *Reflectons: From the Ghetto*, January 14, 1981 (PBS)

Cinematographers

Chuck Clifton, "Mandy's Grandmother," *Young People's Special*, April 1, 1981 (Syndicated)

Joe Consentino, "Globetrotter," *Big Blue Marble*, September 6, 1980 (Syndicated)

Robert Elfstrom, *The Body Human: Facts for Boys*, November 6, 1980 (CBS)

Larry Pizer, "Stoned," *ABC Afterschool Special*, November 12, 1980 (ABC)

Eric Van Heren Noman, "Egyptian Weavers," *Big Blue Marble*, September 13, 1980 (Syndicated)

Film editors

Geof Bartz, *The Body Human: Facts for Girls*, October 7, 1980 (CBS)

Peter Hammer, "Do Me a Favor. . .Don't Vote for My Mom"—Part 3, *Big Blue Marble*, November 22, 1980 (Syndicated)

Allen Kirkpatrick, "Bike Racing," *Big Blue Marble*, October 11, 1980 (Syndicated)

Lighting directors

Dave Clark and William Knight, *Sesame Street*, May 9, 1980 (PBS)

Audio

Dick Maitland (sound effects engineer), "Tuning the Engine," *Sesame Street*, April 14, 1980 (PBS)

Music composers and/or directors

Bob Cobert (composer/conductor), "I Think I'm Having a Baby," *The CBS Afternoon Playhouse*, March 3, 1981 (CBS)

Dick Hyman (composer), "Sunshine's on the Way," *NBC Special Treat*, November 11, 1980 (NBC)

Costume designers

Dianne Finn-Chapman, "Stoned," *ABC Afterschool Special*, November 12, 1980 (ABC)

Bill Kellard, *The Great Space Coaster*, January 6, 1981 (Syndicated)

Barbara Warwich, "A Matter of Time," *ABC Afterschool Special*, February 11, 1981 (ABC)

Dorothy Weaver, "Family of Strangers," *ABC Afterschool Special*, September 24, 1980 (ABC)

Makeup and hair designers

Christy Ann Newquist (makeup designer), "A Matter of Time," *ABC Afterschool Special*, February 11, 1981 (ABC)

Steve Atha (makeup and hair designer), "Sunshine's on the Way," *NBC Special Treat*, November 11, 1980 (NBC)

Graphics and animation designers

Gerri Brioso (graphic designer), *Sesame Street* (PBS)

Fred Crippen, Roy Morita, Rosemary O'Connor and Robert Zamboni (animation Layout designers), "The Incredible Book Escape," *The CBS Library*, June 3, 1980 (CBS)

Lewis Gifford, Paul Kim and Tom Yohe (animation layout designers), *Drawing Power*, October 11, 1980 (NBC)

OUTSTANDING ACHIEVEMENT IN RELIGIOUS PROGRAMMING

Emmy(s) to executive producer(s) and producer(s):

Directions, Sid Darion (producer) (ABC)

Insight, Ellwood E. Kieser, C.S.P., (executive producer), Mike Rhodes (producer) (Syndicated)

OUTSTANDING INDIVIDUAL ACHIEVEMENT IN RELIGIOUS PROGRAMMING

For a single episode of a series or for a special program:

Martin Sheen (performer), "Long Road Home," *Insight*, November 30, 1980 (Syndicated)

Joseph J.H. Vadala (cinematographer), *Work and Worship: The Legacy of St. Benedict*, April 27, 1980 (NBC)

C. Murawski and Dahl Delu (art directors), Scott Heineman (set decorator), "Long Road Home," *Insight*, November 30, 1980 (Syndicated)

SPECIAL CLASSIFICATION OF OUTSTANDING PROGRAM ACHIEVEMENT

For programs that are so unique and different that they do not fall into any other category or area. Emmy(s) to executive producer(s) and producer(s):

F.Y.I., Yanna Kroyt Brandt (producer), Mary Ann Donahue (coordinating producer) (ABC)

Good Morning America, George Merlis (executive producer), Jack Reilly, Susan Winston and Sonya Selby-Wright (producers), David Horwitz (senior producer of news) (ABC)

SPECIAL CLASSIFICATION OF OUTSTANDING INDIVIDUAL ACHIEVEMENT

Dick Clark (host), *American Bandstand*, February 28, 1981 (ABC)

Justin Antonow, Harry Friedman, Gary Johnson, Phil Kellard, Steve Kreinberg, Brian Pollack and Jay Redack (writers), *Hollywood Squares* (NBC)

Hal Linden (host), *F.Y.I.* (ABC)

Michael R. Gargiulo (director), *F.Y.I.* (ABC)

Barry Glazer (director), *American Bandstand*, February 28, 1981 (ABC)

Justin Antonow, Harry Friedman, Gary Johnson, Phil Kellard, Steve Kreinberg, Brian Pollack and Jay Redack (writers), *Hollywood Squares* (NBC)

Betty S. Cornfeld, Mary Ann Donahue and Ed Tivnan (writers), *F.Y.I.* (ABC)

Merrill Markoe, Rich Hall, David Letterman, Gerard Mulligan, Paul Raley and Ron Richards (writers), *The David Letterman Show* (NBC)

Caroly Wilcox, Cheryl Bi Alock and Edward G. Christie (puppet design, construction and costuming), *Sesame Street* (PBS)

□ Indicates winner

OUTSTANDING ACHIEVEMENT IN THE COVERAGE OF SPECIAL EVENTS

Emmy(s) to executive producer(s) and producer(s):

CBS Tournament of Roses Parade, Mike Gargiulo (executive producer), Vern Diamond (producer), January 1, 1981 (CBS)

Macy's Thanksgiving Day Parade, Dick Schneider (producer), November 27, 1980 (NBC)

The Seventh Annual Emmy Award for Daytime Programming, William Carruthers (executive producer), Joel Stein (producer), June 4, 1980 (NBC)

92nd Tournament of Roses Parade, Dick Schneider (producer), January 1, 1981 (NBC)

OUTSTANDING INDIVIDUAL ACHIEVEMENT IN THE COVERAGE OF SPECIAL EVENTS

Dick Schneider (director), *Macy's Thanksgiving Day Parade*, November 27, 1980 (NBC)

Barry E. Downes (writer), *Macy's Thanksgiving Day Parade*, November 27, 1980 (NBC)

Terry Rohnke (technical director), *Macy's Thanksgiving Day Parade*, November 27, 1980 (NBC)

Terry Rohnke (technical director), Peter Basil, Al Camoin, Tom Dezendorf, Barry Frischer, John Pinto, Bryan Russo and John Hillyer (electronic camera), *The Seventh Annual Emmy Awards for Daytime Programming*, June 4, 1980 (NBC)

Robert Warren Davis (lighting director), *The Seventh Annual Emmy Awards for Daytime Programming*, June 4, 1980 (NBC)

Milton Delugg (music director), *Macy's Thanksgiving Day Parade*, November 27, 1980 (NBC)

OUTSTANDING INDIVIDUAL ACHIEVEMENT IN ANY AREA OF CREATIVE TECHNICAL CRAFTS

For individual craft achievement not falling into a specific category and not otherwise recognized:

☐ Robert Hoffman (technical director), Anthony Gambino and Lawrence Hammond (electronic camera), Remote: Savannah, *All My Children*, February 23–24, 1981 (ABC)

Kathleen Ankers (art director), *The David Letterman Show*, October 24, 1980 (NBC)

Tony DiGirolamo (lighting director [location], Remote), "Anita Bryant Interview," *Donahue*, March 24, 1980 (Syndicated)

☐ Indicates winner

☐ Dayton Anderson (costume designer), *The Mike Douglas Show*, February 9, 1981 (Syndicated)

Elinor Bunin (graphic designer)—Title Sequence, *F.Y.I.*, "Premiere," March 2, 1981 (ABC)

☐ Michael Gass (graphic designer), *Good Morning America* (ABC)

Bob Pook and Bill Shortridge Jr. (graphic designers), *The David Letterman Show* (NBC)

☐ Donald Spagnolia (graphic designer)— Opening Logo, Thomas Burton and Claudio Zeitlin Burton (animation designers)—Opening, *The John Davidson Show*, June 30, 1980 (Syndicated)

Sports Awards

OUTSTANDING LIVE SPORTS SPECIAL

Emmy(s) to executive producer(s), producer(s) and director(s):

American & National League Championship Series, Roone Arledge (executive producer), Dennis Lewin (producer: National League), Joe Aceti (director: National League), Chuck Howard (producer: American League), Chet Forte (director: American League), October 8–12, 1980 (American League) and October 7, 8, 10–12, 1980 (National League) (ABC)

☐ *Kentucky Derby*, Roone Arledge (executive producer), Chuck Howard (producer), Chet Forte (director), May 2, 1981 (ABC)

Sugar Bowl, Roone Arledge (executive producer), Chuck Howard (producer), Andy Sidaris (director), January 1, 1981 (ABC)

Super Bowl XV, Don Ohlmeyer (executive producer), Ted Nathanson (coordinating producer), Larry Cirillo and George Finkel (producers), Ted Nathanson (director), Ken Fouts (replay director), January 25, 1981 (NBC)

1980 World Series, Don Ohlmeyer (executive producer), Michael Weisman (coordinating producer), George Finkel and Michael Weisman (producers), Harry Coyle and Ken Fouts (directors), October 14–21, 1980 (NBC)

OUTSTANDING LIVE SPORTS SERIES

Emmy(s) to executive producer(s), producer(s) and director(s):

1980–1981 College Basketball, Don Ohlmeyer (executive producer), George Finkel (coordinating producer), Kenneth Edmundson, George Finkel, David Stern and Michael Weisman (producers), Harry

Coyle, Ken Fouts, John Gonzalez and Andy Rosenberg (directors), Series (NBC)

1980–1981 NFL Football, Don Ohlmeyer (executive producer), Larry Cirillo, Kenneth Edmundson, Terry Ewert, George Finkel, J. Michael Hadley, Roy Hammerman, Don McGuire, Peter M. Rolfe, David Stern and Michael Weisman (producers), Richard Cline, Harry Coyle, Jim Cross, Ken Fouts, John Gonzalez, Jim Marcione, Ted Nathanson, Lou Rainone, Andy Rosenberg and Barry Stoddard (directors), Series (NBC)

NFL Monday Night Football, Roone Arledge (executive producer), Bob Goodrich (producer), Chet Forte (director), Series (ABC)

☐ *PGA Tour on CBS*, Frank Chirkinian (executive producer), Bob Dailey and Frank Chirkinian (directors), Series (CBS)

PRO Bowlers Tour, Roone Arledge (executive producer), Curt Gowdy Jr. and Peter Englehart (producers), Larry Cavolina, John DeLisa and Ralph Abraham (directors), Series (ABC)

OUTSTANDING EDITED SPORTS SPECIAL

Emmy(s) to executive producer(s), producer(s) and director(s):

☐ *ABC's Wide World of Sports 20th Anniversary Show*, Roone Arledge (executive producer), Dennis Lewin and Doug Wilson (producers), Larry Kamm (director), May 25, 1981 (ABC)

1981 Indianapolis 500, Roone Arledge (executive producer), Dennis Lewin (coordinating producer), Chuck Howard and Bob Goodrich (producers), Chet Forte and Roger Goodman (directors), May 24, 1981 (ABC)

NFL 80: Super Sunday Countdown, Don Ohlmeyer (executive producer), David Stern (producer), Les Dennis and David Neal (feature producers), Bob Levy (director), January 25, 1981 (NBC)

Sugar Ray Leonard vs. Roberto Duran II, Roone Arledge (executive producer), Bob Goodrich (producer), Chet Forte (director), December 19, 1980 (ABC)

Wimbledon 81, Don Ohlmeyer (executive producer), Geoff Mason and Ted Nathanson (producers), Terry Ewert (producer; tape), Ted Nathanson (director), Bob Levy (director; tape), June 27–July 4, 1981 (NBC)

OUTSTANDING EDITED SPORTS SERIES

Emmy(s) to executive producer(s), producer(s) and director(s):

ABC's Wide World of Sports, Roone Arledge (executive producer), Dennis Lewin (coordinating producer), Bob Goodrich, Eleanor Riger, Doug Wilson, Mike Pearl, Brice Weisman, Ralph Abraham, Ken Wolfe, Jeff Ruhe, Chuck Howard and Carol Lehti (producers), Larry Kamm, Chet Forte, Roger Goodman, Craig Janoff, Andy Sidaris, Jim Jennett, Joe Aceti and Lou Volpicelli (directors), Series (ABC)

☐ *American Sportsman*, Roone Arledge (executive producer), John Wilcox (series producer), Chris Carmody (coordinating producer), Robert Nixon and Curt Gowdy (producers), John Wilcox and Bob Nixon (directors), Series (ABC)

CBS Sports Saturday/Sunday, Terry O'Neil (executive producer), Jean Harper (coordinating producer), John Faratzis, David Dinkins, Ed Goren, David Winner, Dan Forer, Dan Lauck, George Veras, Sherman Eagan, Perry Smith, Chuck Milton, Ted Shaker and Mike Burks (producers), Richard Drake, Larry Cavolina, John McDonough, Andy Kindle, Bob Dunphy, Peter M. Bleckner and Bob Fishman (directors), Series (CBS)

NBC Sportsworld, Don Ohlmeyer (executive producer), Linda Jonsson (coordinating producer), Matthew McCarthy, Hilary Cosell, Terry Ewert, Michael Weisman, Ginny Seipt and Peter M. Rolfe (producers), Bob Levy (coordinating director), John Gonzalez, Ken Fouts, Richard Cline, Harry Coyle and Ted Nathanson (directors), Series (NBC)

NFL '80, Don Ohlmeyer (executive producer), David Stern (producer), Les Dennis, David Neal and David Israel (feature producers), Bob Levy (director), Series (NBC)

OUTSTANDING INDIVIDUAL ACHIEVEMENT IN SPORTS PROGRAMMING

(These are "Areas," where there is a possibility of one award, more than one award or no award):

Cinamatography

Edgar Boyles, David Conley, John Hammond, Peter Henning, Mike Hoover, D'Arcy Marsh, Dan Merkel, Stanton Waterman, Steve Petropoulos and Roger Brown (cinematographers), *American Sportsman*, April 5, 1981 (ABC)

☐ Indicates winner

Steve Sabol, Ernie Ernst, Howard Neef, Phil Tuckett, Bob Smith, Bob Angelo, Donnie Marx, Jay Gerber, Art Spieller, Jack Newman and Hank McElwee (cinamatographers), *The Super Seventies*, August 26, 1981 (NBC)

Associate direction/Videotape editing

☐ Rob Beiner, Dick Buffinton, Jeff Cohan, Kathy Cook, Vince Dedario, John Delisa, Joel Feld, Ben Harvey, Bob Hersh, Jack Graham, Bob Lanning, Peter Lasser, Carol Lehti, Brian McCullough, Dennis Mazzocco, Bob Rosburg, Norm Samet, Ned Simon, Toni Slotkin, Larry Carolina and Bob Dekas (associate directors), *ABC's Wide World of Sports*, July 19, 1980 (ABC)

☐ Tony Tocci, Ken Browne and Gary Bradley (videotape editors), *The Baseball Bunch*, May 1, 1981 (Syndicated)

☐ Matthew McCarthy (associate director), Mark Jankeloff, Richard Leible, Jim McQueen and Jeff U'Ren (videotape editors), *NBC Sportsworld*, July 20, 1980 (NBC)

Lou Rende, Ron Ackerman, Charles Gardner, Ron Feszchur, Martin Bell and Winston Sadoo (videotape editors), *NFL Football—Sunday Night*, October 26, 1980 (ABC)

☐ Cathy Barreto (associate director), Joel Aronowitz, Jack Black, Bob Coffey, Joe D'Ornellas, Stanley Faer, Bob Halper, Beth Hermelin, Howard N. Miller, Gady Reinhold, Roni Scherman, Steve Dellapietra and Barry Hicks (associate directors—Highlights and coords), George Palmisano and John Wells (senior video operator), Jim Alkins, Curtis Campbell, Bob Clark, Ted Demers, Joe Drake, Tom Durkin, Bob Foster, Harve Gilman, Al Golly, Sigismund Gordon, Elliott Greenblatt, Bob Hickson, Frank Hodnett, George Joanitis, Andy Klein, Gary Kozak, Ed Knudholt, Pete Lacorte, Marvin Lee, George Magee, Mario Marino, Walter Matwichuk, John Mayer, Henry Menusan, Jesse Michnick, Jeff Ringel, Charlotte Robinson, Allan Segal, Bill Vandenort, Irv Villafana, Hank Wolf and Bill Zizza (videotape editors), *NFL Today*, September 7, 1980 (CBS)

Tom Wight, Dick Velasco, Hector Kicelian, Bruce A. Gearraffa and Merrit Roesser (videotape editors), *Sugar Bowl*, January 1, 1981 (ABC)

Mike Kostel, Mario Bucich, Ken McIlwaine and Tony Tocci, *This*

Week in Baseball, October 11, 1980 (Syndicated)

Film editing

☐ Angelo Bernarducci, Vincent Reda, Richard Rossi, Anthony Scandiffio, Norman Smith, Chris Riger, Ted Winterburn and Anthony Zaccaro (film editors), *The American Sportsman*, April 5, 1981 (ABC)

☐ Mike Adams, Bob Ryan and Phil Tuckett (film editors), *NFL Symfunny*, January 17, 1981 (Syndicated)

Audio

Jack Newman, Dave Paul, Don Paravati and Bill Gray (location sound recordists), *Saviors, Saints and Sinners*, January 25, 1981 (NBC)

Engineering supervision (technical managers)

☐ Ray Savignano and Jesse Rineer (engineering supervisors), *1981 Daytona 500*, February 15, 1981 (CBS)

☐ Louis Scannapieco and Arthur Tinn (engineering supervisors), *The Masters*, April 11, 1981 (CBS)

☐ Walter Pile (engineering supervisor), *NFC Championship Game*, January 11, 1981 (CBS)

Martin Sandberg and Loren Coltran (engineering supervisors), *NFL Football—Sunday Night*, October 26, 1980 (ABC)

James Tonn (engineering supervisor), *NFL Today*, September 7, 1980 (CBS)

Bob Armbruster (engineering supervisor), *Sugar Bowl*, January 1, 1981 (ABC)

Technical direction/Senior video operators/Electronic camerawork

☐ Sandy Bell and Robert Brown (technical directors), Edward Ambrosini, Robert Squittieri and Ronald Resch (senior video operators), James Murphy, Neil McCaffrey, Herman Lang, Frank McSpedon, Thomas McCarthy, Barry Drago, Joseph Sokota, Stephen Gorsuch, George Rothweiler, George Naeder, David Graham, Jeffrey Pollack, James McCarthy, Hans Singer and Sigmund Meyers (electronic camerapersons), *1981 Daytona 500*, February 15, 1981 (CBS)

Ray Figelski and Keith Kniep (technical directors), Carroll Bolstad (senior video operator), Jim Bragg, Phillip E. Cantrell, Jim Herring, George Loomis, Hugh Morelli, Jay O'Neil, Michael C. Stramisky and Dan Sutton (electronic camerapersons), "John Denver Pro/Celebrity Ski

Tournament," *NBC Sportsworld*, March 22, 1981 (NBC)

☐ Charles D'Onofrio and Sandy Bell (technical directors), Robert Hanford, Edward Ambrosini, Robert Pieringer and Frank Florio (senior video operator, rich blane), George Klimcsak, George Naeder, James McCarthy, George Rothweiler, Al Loreto, Herman Lang, Hans Singer, Nicholas Lauria, James Murphy, Harry Haigood, Michael English, John Lincoln, Frank McSpedon, Stan Gould, Dennis McBride, Joseph Sokota, Barry Drago, Neil McCaffrey, David Graham, Walter Soucy, Robert Welch, David Finch, Richard E. Kearney, Joseph Sidlo and W. Haigood (electronic camerapersons), *The Masters*, April 11, 1981 (CBS)

William Toby (technical director), Lenny Stucker (facilities technical director), Bryan Russo, Mario Ciarlo, James J. Culley, Lenny Basile, Barry Jon Frischer, David A. Hagen, Lou Gerard, Jim Johnson, Steve Gonzalez, Don Mulvaney and Buddy Joseph (electronic camerapersons), *1981 NCAA College Basketball Championship*, March 30, 1981 (NBC)

John Allen (technical director), Ken Amow (senior video operator), Frank Melchiorre, John Morreale, Joe Puleo, Evan Baker, Ed Payne, Sal Folino, Mike Freedman, Warren Cress and John Dukewich (electronic camerapersons), *NCAA Football*, November 14, 1980 (ABC)

☐ Robert Brown and Edward Kushner (technical directors), Robert Hanford and Frank Florio (senior video operators), Rick Blane, Stan Gould, Stephen Gorsuch, John Lincoln, George Klimcsak, Robert Jamieson, David Graham, James Murphy, Frank McSpedon, Jeffrey Pollack, Joseph Vincens and David Finch (electronic camerapersons), *NFC Championship Game*, January 11, 1981 (CBS)

☐ Joe Schiavo (technical director), Joseph Lee (senior video operator), Drew Derosa, Jim Heneghan, Andrew Armentani, Gary Donatelli, Jack Dorfman, Jessel Kohn, Jack Savoy, Tom O'Connell, Steve Nikifor, Joe Cotugno and Roy Hutchings (electronic camerapersons), *NFL Football— Sunday Night*, October 26, 1980 (ABC)

☐ Gilbert A. Miller (technical director), Ronald Resch and Emanuel Kaufman (senior video operators), John Curtin, Thomas McCarthy,

James McCarthy, Neil McCaffrey, Stephen Gorsuch and Michael English (electronic camerapersons), *NFL Today*, September 7, 1980 (CBS)

John Allen (technical director), Ken Amow (senior video operator), John Morreale, John Dukewich, Evan Baker, Mike Freedman, Sal Folino, Frank Melchiorre and Warren Cress (electronic camerapersons), *Sugar Bowl*, January 1, 1981 (ABC)

Horace Ruiz (technical director), William Tobey (facilities technical director), Jim Marshall (senior vedeo operator), Lenny Basile, Mario Ciarlo, George Loomis, Victoria Walker, Lou Gerard, Phillip E. Cantrell, Bryan Russo, Brian D. Sherriffe, David A. Hagen, Jim Johnson, Cory Leible, Rodger G. Harbaugh, Jim Bragg, Steve Gonzalez, R.V. Ratliff, Michael C. Stramisky, Ken Harvey, Buddy Joseph, Albert Rice and George Ciliberto (electronic camerapersons), *Super Bowl XV*, January 25, 1981 (NBC)

Horace Ruiz (technical director), Bruce Berquist and William Tobey (facilities technical directors), Lenny Basile, Jim Bragg, Al Camoin, Phillip E. Cantrell, Mario Ciarlo, George Ciliberto, Louis Cywinski, Lou Gerard, Bill Goetz, David A. Hagen, Rodger G. Harbaugh, Ken Harvey, Jim Johnson, Buddy Joseph, Cory Leible, George Loomis, Don Mulvaney, Art Parker, R.V. Ratliff, Albert Rice, Bryan Russo, Brian D. Sherriffe, Michael C. Stramisky and Dan Sutton (electronic camerapersons), *1980–1981 World Series*, October 14–21, 1980 (NBC)

Primary graphic designers

☐ James W. Grau (graphic designer), *NBC on CBS* (show opening), November 27, 1980 (CBS)

Matthew McCarthy (graphic designer), *NBC Sports Presents: The Summer Season*, July 25, 1980 (NBC)

Roger Goodman (graphic designer), *Prudential College Scoreboard Show*, September 6, 1980 (ABC)

☐ James W. Grau (graphic designer), *U.S. Open* (show opening), August 26, 1980 (CBS)

Writing

Mark Durand, Mike Tollin and Gary Cohen (writers), *The Baseball Bunch*, May 1, 1981 (Syndicated)

Mark Durand, Warner Fusselle and Hal Fischer (writers), *This Week in Baseball*, August 1, 1980 (Syndicated)

SPECIAL CLASSIFICATION OF OUTSTANDING PROGRAM AND INDIVIDUAL ACHIEVEMENT

Emmy(s) to producer(s) for program; emmy(s) to individual(s) for individual achievement:

Program

☐ *The Baseball Bunch*, Larry Parker (executive producer), Jody Shapiro (producer), May 1, 1981 (Syndicated)

☐ "The Arlberg Kandahar Downhill from St. Anton," *NBC Sportsworld*, Don Ohlmeyer (executive producer), Linda Jonsson (coordinating producer), Terry Ewert and Geoff Mason (producers), Bob Levy (coordinating director/director), February 1, 1981 (NBC)

Individual

Amy Sacks (producer), *ABC Sports on-Air Promotions* (ABC)

☐ Don Ohlmeyer and Ted Nathanson (producers Louma Camera Crane), *Friday Night Fights* (NBC)

Dennis Lewin (producer Gondola Camera [over second base]), *1980 National League Championship Series* (ABC)

Bob Levy (coordinating director), *NBC Sportsworld* (NBC)

☐ Steve Gonzalez (electronic camera), *Super Bowl XV* (NBC)

Chuck Howard (producer; electronic camera Logistics), *U.S. Open Golf Championship* (ABC)

OUTSTANDING SPORTS PERSONALITY—HOST

(Play by play):

☐ Dick Enberg (NBC)

Keith Jackson (ABC)

Jim McCay (ABC)

Al Michaels (ABC)

Vin Scully (CBS)

OUTSTANDING SPORTS PERSONALITY—ANALYST

(Commentary):

☐ Dick Button (ABC)

Al McGuire (NBC)

Don Meredith (ABC)

Merlin Olsen (NBC)

Jack Whitaker (CBS)

OUTSTANDING ACHIEVEMENT IN THE SCIENCE OF TELEVISION ENGINEERING

☐ Ampex Corporation

☐ CBS Inc.

☐ Ikegami Electronics

☐ Marconi Electronics

☐ RCA CCSD Video Systems

TRUSTEES AWARD

☐ Agnes E. Nixon, for her distinguished creative contributions to daytime television

News and Documentary Awards

PROGRAMS AND PROGRAM SEGMENTS

"January 20, 1981," *NBC Nightly News*, Paul Greenberg (executive producer), Bill Wheatley (senior producer), Lloyd Siegel–domestic, Harry Griggs–Foreign, Bob McFarland–Washington, Joan Carrigan–Germany (producers), Jim Bitterman, John Hart, Judy Woodruff, Tom Pettit, John Palmer, Bob Jamieson, Linda Ellerbee (correspondents), January 20, 1981 (NBC)

"January 27, 1981," *NBC Nightly News*, Paul Greenberg (executive producer), Bill Wheatley (senior producer), Lloyd Siegel–domestic, Harry Griggs–foreign, Bob McFarland–Washington (producers), John Chancellor and Roger Mudd (anchors), Tom Pettit, John Palmer, John Dancy, Bob Jamieson, Robert Hager, John Cochran (correspondents), January 27, 1981 (NBC)

"El Salvador Firefight," *Today Show*, Dave Riggs (producer), Jim Cummins (correspondent), April 30, 1981 (NBC)

☐ "Inside Awacs," *'Magazine with David Brinkley'*, Sid Feders (producer), Garrick Utley (correspondent), September 18, 1981 (NBC)

"Italian Earthquake," *ABC World News Tonight*, Dean Johnson (producer), Gregg Dobbs and Bill Blakemore (correspondents), November 26—30, 1980 (ABC)

"Moment of Crisis—Hyatt Disaster," *20/20*, Stanhope Gould and Peter W. Kunhardt (producers), Tom Jarriel (correspondent), July 23, 1981 (ABC)

"The Other Egypt," *Magazine*, Sid Feders, Bill Theodore, Ron Bonn (producers), Garrick Utley (correspondent), October 9, 1981 (NBC)

"Reluctant Hero," *Magazine with David Brinkley*, Sid Feders (producer), Doug Kiker (correspondent), January 30, 1981 (NBC)

"Sadat," *CBS Evening News with Dan Rather*, Sanford Socolow, Mark Harrington, David Buksbaum, Linda Mason, Lane Venardos (producers), Dan Rather (correspondent), October 6, 1981 (CBS)

☐ *CBS Reports: Murder Teenage Style*, Irina Posner (producer), Ed Bradley

(correspondent), September 3, 1981 (CBS)

"The Shattered Badge," *Closeup*, Paul Altmeyer (producer/correspondent), December 27, 1980 (ABC)

☐ "Soldiers of the Twilight," *Closeup*, Malcolm Clarke (producer), Marshall Frady (correspondent), March 19, 1981 (ABC)

"Anatomy of a Manhunt," *Sunday Morning*, James Houtrides (producer), Ed Rabel (correspondent), September 27, 1981 (CBS)

"Art/Science," *Water Cronkite's Universe*, Michele Dumont (producer), Charles Osgood (correspondent), June 21, 1981 (CBS)

"Boston Irish-Ira," *Nightline*, Robert Jordan (producer), Mike Barnicle (correspondent), May 5, 1981 (ABC)

"The Cheapest Way To Go," *20/20*, Richard R. Clark (producer), John Stossel (correspondent), September 24, 1981 (ABC)

"Crime/Elderly," *Nightline*, Herb Holmes (producer), Bob Greene (correspondent), February 26, 1981 (ABC)

☐ "Death in the Fast Lane," *20/20*, Danny Schechter (producer), Catherine Mackin (correspondent), September 16, 1981 (ABC)

☐ "Ghost Town," *20/20*, Pete Simmons and Ellen Rossen (producers), John Laurence (correspondent), July 16, 1981 (ABC)

☐ "'Grain' a Few Minutes with Andy Rooney," *60 Minutes*, Andrew A. Rooney (producer/reporter), May 10, 1981 (CBS)

"Hunger in Africa," *CBS Evening News with Dan Rather*, Harry Radliffe (producer), Tom Fenton (correspondent), March 19, 1981 (CBS)

"Insanity and Murder," *NBC Nightly News*, Chuck Collins (producer), James Polk (correspondent), November 9–11, 1981 (NBC)

☐ "Libya," *ABC World News Tonight*, Liz Colton and Denise Schreiner (producers), Lou Cioffi (correspondent), June 16 and 17, 1981 (ABC)

"Magic Bullets," *Walter Cronkite's Universe*, Elena Mannes (producer), Jacqueline Adams (correspondent), July 14, 1981 (CBS)

"Northern Ireland's History," *CBS Evening News with Morton Dean*, Joan Richman (executive producer), Bill Higley (producer), John Blackstone (correspondent), July 5, 1981 (CBS)

"Rescuing the Hostages: The Untried Mission," *NBC Nightly News Special Segment*, Ellen McKeefe (producer), George Lewis, Mike Snyder–KXAS (correspondents), February 19 and 20, 1981 (NBC)

"The Rites of Passage," *20/20*, Jeff Diamond (producer), Bob Brown (correspondent), September 24, 1981 (ABC)

"Tough Guys/Tough Times," *CBS Evening News with Dan Rather*, Bob McNamara (producer/ correspondent), May 8, 1981 (CBS)

"Unemployment in Britain," *NBC Nightly News*, Dina Modianot (producer), John Hart (correspondent), July 16, 1981 (NBC)

☐ "The War on Opium," *Nightline*, Tom Yellin (producer), Mark Litke (correspondent), May 15, 1981 (ABC)

☐ *CBS Reports: The Defense of the United States: Nuclear Battlefield*, Judy Crichton (producer), Harry Reasoner (correspondent), June 15, 1981 (CBS)

☐ *CBS Reports: The Defense of the United States: The War Machine*, Craig Leake (producer), Richard Threlkeld (correspondent), June 17, 1981 (CBS)

"The Gene Merchants," *Closeup*, Stephen Fleischman (producer), Marshall Frady and William Sherman (correspondents), September 11, 1981 (ABC)

☐ *The Hunter and the Hunted*, Thomas F. Madigan (executive producer), John Oakley and Lisa Cantini-Sequin, Bill Bemister (producers), Bill Bemister (correspondent), October 21, 1981 (PBS)

☐ "Near Armageddon: The Spread of Nuclear Weapons in the Middle East," *Closeup*, Christopher Isham (producer), Marshall Frady and William Sherman (correspondents), April 27, 1981 (ABC)

☐ "Why America Burns," *Nova*, Brian Kaufman (producer), October 4, 1981 (PBS)

☐ "Formula for Disaster," *'20/20'*, John Fager (producer), Geraldo Rivera (correspondent), January 15, 1981 (ABC)

☐ "Killer Wheels," *60 Minutes*, Allan Maraynes (producer), Mike Wallace (correspondent), March 8, 1981 (CBS)

☐ "Rockets for Sale," *Magazine with David Brinkley*, Tony Van Witsen (producer), Garrick Utley (correspondent), March 20, 1981 (NBC)

☐ Indicates winner

☐ "Teen Models," *Magazine with David Brinkley*, Beth Polson (producer), Jack Perkins (correspondent), April 23, 1981 (NBC)

☐ "Unnecessary Surgery," *20/20*, Peter Lance and Janice Tomlin (producers), Peter Lance (correspondent), January 18, 1981 (ABC)

☐ "Clark Clifford on Presidents and Power"—Part 1, *Bill Moyers' Journal*, Douglas Lutz (producer), Bill Moyers (interviewer), March 6, 1981 (PBS)

☐ "George Steiner on Literature, Language & Culture," *Bill Moyers' Journal*, Douglas Lutz (producer), Bill Moyers (interviewer), May 22, 1981 (PBS)

☐ "The Last Mafioso (Jimmy Fratianno)," *60 Minutes*, Marion F. Goldin (producer), Mike Wallace (interviewer), January 4, 1981 (CBS)

"Sirhan-Shirhan," *Nightline*, David Bohrman, Bob Jordan, Susan Mercandetti (producers), Ted Koppel (interviewer), August 27 and 28, 1981 (ABC)

☐ "Wanted (Terpil/Korkala Interview)," *60 Minutes*, Barry Lando (producer), Mike Wallace (interviewer), November 8, 1981 (CBS)

☐ *Close Harmony*, Nigel Noble (producer), November 9, 1981 (PBS)

☐ "The Colonel Comes to Japan," *Enterprise*, John Nathan (producer), October 9, 1981 (PBS)

Eisenstaedt: Germany, Gordon Bowman (producer), November 2, 1981 (PBS)

"Chinese Island," *CBS Evening News with Dan Rather*, Barry Peterson (producer/correspondent), October 12, 1981 (CBS)

"The Holocaust," *'Nightline'*, Pamela L. Kahn (producer), June 19, 1981 (ABC)

☐ "Louis is 13," *Sunday Morning*, Lee Reichenthal (producer), Morton Dean (correspondent), October 25, 1981 (CBS)

☐ "Moment of Crisis: Berlin Wall," *20/20*, Richard O'Regan and Rolfe Tessem (producers), Tom Jarriel (correspondent), August 13, 1981 (ABC)

"Moment of Crisis: Vietnam Withdrawal," *20/20*, Peter W. Kunhardt (producer), Tom Jarriel (correspondent), April 30, 1981 (ABC)

"A Place To Go," *60 Minutes*, Joel Bernstein (producer), Dan Rather (correspondent), January 18, 1981 (CBS)

☐ "Ray Charles," *20/20*, Betsy Osha (producer), Bob Brown

☐ Indicates winner

(correspondent), November 12, 1981 (ABC)

"Romare Bearden," *Sunday Morning*, Kathy Sulkes (producer), David Culhane (correspondent), December 21, 1980 (CBS)

☐ "St. Paul's Bells," *ABC World News Tonight*, Phil Bergman (producer), Hughes Rudd (correspondent), July 7, 1981 (ABC)

"Sunshine Foundations," *Today Show*, Bert Medley (producer), Bob Dotson (correspondent), December 4, 1980 (NBC)

"A Time of Magic," *Sunday Morning*, Philip Garvin (producer), David Culhane (correspondent), September 20, 1981 (CBS)

OUTSTANDING INDIVIDUAL ACHIEVEMENT IN NEWS AND DOCUMENTARY PROGRAMMING

Writers

Pierre Salinger (narrative), George Orick (studio & background material), "America Held Hostage: The Secret Negotiations," *ABC News Special*, January 28, 1981 (ABC)

Lloyd Dobyns, Darold Murray and Pat Trese, "An American Adventure: The Rocket Pilots," *NBC News Special Program*, September 23, 1981 (NBC)

☐ Philip Buton Jr. and Larry L. King, *CBS Reports: The Best Little Statehouse in Texas*, August 26, 1981 (CBS)

Maurice Murad, *CBS Reports: The Defense of the United States: A Call to Arms*, June 16, 1981 (CBS)

☐ Walter Pincus, Andrew Lack, Howard Stringer and Bob Schieffer, *CBS Reports: The Defense of the United States: Ground Zero*, June 14, 1981 (CBS)

☐ Judy Crichton, Howard Stringer and Leslie Cockburn, *CBS Reports: The Defense of the United States: Nuclear Battlefield*, June 15, 1981 (CBS)

Andrew Lack, *CBS Reports: The Defense of the United States: The Russians*, June 18, 1981 (CBS)

Graig Leake and Richard Threlkeld, *CBS Reports: The Defense of the United States: The War Machine*, June 17, 1981 (CBS)

Irina Posner and Ed Bradley, *CBS Reports: Murder Teenage Style*, September 3, 1981 (CBS)

☐ Judy Towers Reemtsma and Marlene Sanders, *CBS Reports: Nurse, Where Are You?*, May 28, 1981 (CBS)

☐ Perry Wolff, "Inside Hollywood: The Movie Business," *A CBS News Special*, March 28, 1981 (CBS)

Helen Whitney, "The Monastery," *Closeup*, August 20, 1981 (ABC)

Lindsay Miller, "News in Review," *Sunday Morning*, July 19, 1981 (CBS)

Directors

☐ Craig Leake, *CBS Reports: The Defense of the United States: The War Machine*, June 17, 1981 (CBS)

Charles Heinz, "Four Presidents," *ABC World News Tonight*, October 8, 1981 (ABC)

Helen Whitney, "The Monastery," *Closeup*, August 20, 1981 (ABC)

Technical direction/Electronic camera

Don Basil, Richard Kuhne, John Cordone, John Landi, Elliot Butler, Jack Clark, Sidney Dobish, Ken Sanborn, Bob Freeman, Rupen Vosgimorukian, Tony Hirashiki, Ron Headford and Fabrice Moussus (electronic camera), "America Held Hostage: The Secret Negotiation," *ABC News Special*, January 28, 1981 (ABC)

☐ Richard Jeffreys (electronic camera), "The Assassination of Anwar Sadat," *CBS Evening News with Dan Rather*, October 6, 1981 (CBS)

Rolfe Tessem (electronic camera), "Carter's Final Hours," *Nightline*, January 28, 1981 (ABC)

John J. Landi (location & game), Les Solin, Gordon Hoover and Scott Levine–game (electronic camera), "If You Were the President," *'20/20'*, August 6, 1981 (ABC)

☐ Tom Woods (electronic camera), "Inside Afghanistan," *Magazine with David Brinkley*, January 30, 1981 (NBC)

☐ Rupen Vosgimorukian and Barry Fox (electronic camera), "Italian Earthquake—5 Part segment," *ABC World News Tonight*, November 26–30, 1980 (ABC)

☐ Stephen N. Stanford (electronic camera), "Monarch Butterflies," *20/20*, June 18, 1981 (ABC)

Henry Brown (electronic camera), "President Reagan Assassination Attempt," *ABC World News Tonight*, March 30, 1981 (ABC)

Sheldon Fielman (electronic camera), "President Reagan Shooting," *NBC News Special Report*, March 30, 1981 (NBC)

Fabrice Moussus (electronic camera), "Sadat Assassination," *ABC News Special Events*, October 6, 1981 (ABC)

Cinematography

☐ Billy Wagner, Jan Morgan, John Boulter and John Peters (cinematographers), *CBS Reports: The Defense of the United States:*

Nuclear Battlefield, June 15, 1981 (CBS)

Film editing

☐ John J. Martin (film editor), "An American Adventure: The Rocket Pilots," *An NBC News Special Program*, September 23, 1981 (NBC)

☐ Mili Bonsignori (film editor), *CBS Reports: The Defense of the United States: Call to Arms*, June 16, 1981 (CBS)

Peter Eliscu (film editor), *CBS Reports: The Defense of the United States: Nuclear Battlefield*, June 15, 1981 (CBS)

☐ Ara Chekmayan and Christopher Dalrymple (film editors), *CBS Reports: The Defense of the United States: The War Machine*, June 17, 1981 (CBS)

Alan Raymond and Nils Rasmussen (film editors), "Horay for Hollywood," *Closeup*, October 11, 1981 (ABC)

☐ David R. Ward (film editor), "Jackie Gleason: How Sweet It Is," *20/20*, February 22, 1981 (ABC)

Audio

Rudy Boyer, Anthony Pagano, Alfonso Burney, Mark French, Jay Lamonaco, Jack Gray, Neal Harvey, Jim Fitzgerald, Leonard Jensen, Alan Lewis, Ali Ashmawy (live/location tape sound recordists), George Myer (re-recording mixer/editor), "America Held Hostage: The Secret Negotiations," *ABC News Special*, January 28, 1981 (ABC)

☐ Ed Jennings (tape sound editor), "Carter's Final Hours," *Nightline*, January 28, 1981 (ABC)

James A. Cefalo (location sound recordist), "Monarch Butterflies," *20/20*, June 18, 1981 (ABC)

Harry Weldon (location sound recordist), "President Regan Assassination Attempt," *ABC World News Tonight*, March 30, 1981 (ABC)

Aly El Ashnawy (location sound recordist), "Sadat Assassination," *ABC News Special Events*, October 6, 1981 (ABC)

Associate direction and/or videotape editing

☐ Neil Philpson (senior associate director–post production), Jerry Chernak (associate director–post production), Ed Buda and Thomas R. Gubar (senior videotape editors), Sam Hadley, Robert Brandt, Alan Campbell, Henriette Huehne, David Harten, Robert Kerr, Vicki Papazian, Dave Rummel, Donna Rowlinson (videotape editors), Harvey Beal, Eileen Clancy, John Croak, Dean Irwin, Catherine Isabella, Conrad

☐ Indicates winner

Kraus, Mike Mazella, Tom Miller, Peter Murphy, Erskin Roberts, Mario Schencman, Mike Siegel, Barry Spitzer and Chris Von Benge (videotape editors–post production), "America Held Hostage: The Secret Negotiations," *ABC News Special*, January 28, 1981 (ABC)

☐ David G. Rummel Jr. (videotape editor), "Monarch Butterflies," *'20/20'*, June 18, 1981 (ABC)

John J. Gillen (videotape editor), "Robots: The Coming Revolution," *ABC World News Tonight*, June 12, 1981 (ABC)

Lighting Direction

Jerome Slattery (location lighting director), "America Held Hostage: The Secret Negotiations," *ABC News Special*, January 28, 1981 (ABC)

Graphic design

Barbara M. Incognito (electronic graphic designer), *20/20*, November 5, 1981 (ABC)

☐ Freida Reiter (graphic artist/illustrator), "America Held Hostage: The Secret Negotiations," *ABC News Special*, January 28, 1981 (ABC)

☐ Gerry Andrea (graphic designer/illustrator), "Shooting of Pope John Paul II," *ABC World News Tonight*, May 14–19, 1981 (ABC)

1981/82

(For programs aired between July 1, 1981 and June 30, 1982. Entertainment and individual achievement awards presented September 19, 1982. Creative Arts awards presented September 12, 1982. Daytime awards presented June 8 and June 11, 1982. News and Documentary awards presented October 17, 1983 for programs aired between November 15, 1981 and December 31, 1982. Sports awards presented March 1, 1983 for programs aired between July 16, 1981 and July 15, 1982. Science of Engineering in Television award presented September 29, 1982.)

Prime Time Program Awards

OUTSTANDING COMEDY SERIES

Emmy(s) to executive producer(s) and producer(s):

☐ *Barney Miller*, Danny Arnold, Roland Kibbee (executive producers), Frank Dungan, Jeff Stein (producers), Gary Shaw (co-producer) (ABC)

Love, Sidney, George Eckstein (executive producer), Ernest Chambers, Bob Brunner, Ken Hecht (supervising producers), April Kelly, Mel Tolkin, Jim Parker (producers) (NBC)

M*A*S*H, Burt Metcalfe (executive producer), John Rappaport (supervising producer), Thad Mumford, Dan Wilcox, Dennis Koenig (producers) (CBS)

Taxi, James L. Brooks, Stan Daniels, Ed Weinberger (executive producers), Glen Charles, Les Charles (supervising producers), Ken Estin, Howard Gewirtz, Ian Praiser (producers), Richard Sakai (co-producer) (ABC)

WKRP in Cincinnati, Hugh Wilson (executive producer), Blake Hunter, Peter Torokvei, Dan Guntzelman, Steve Marshall (producers) (CBS)

OUTSTANDING DRAMA SERIES

Emmy(s) to executive producer(s) and producer(s):

☐ *Hill Street Blues*, Steven Bochco (executive producer), Gregory Hoblit (supervising producer), David Anspaugh, Anthony Yerkovich (producers) (NBC)

Dynasty, Aaron Spelling, Douglas S. Cramer (executive producers), E. Duke Vincent (supervising producer), Ed Ledding, Elaine Rich (producers) (ABC)

Lou Grant, Gene Reynolds (executive producer), Seth Freeman (producer) (CBS)

Magnum, P.I., Donald P. Bellisario (executive producer), Douglas Green, Andrew Schneider, Rick Weaver (producers) (CBS)

Fame, William Blinn, Gerald I. Isenberg (executive producers), Stan Rogow, Mel Swope (producers) (NBC)

OUTSTANDING LIMITED SERIES

Emmy(s) to executive producer(s) and producer(s):

☐ *Marco Polo*, Vincenzo LaBella (producer) (NBC)

"Brideshead Revisited," *Great Performances*, Jac Venza, Robert Kotlowitz (executive producers), Sam Paul (series producer), Derek Granger (producer) (PBS)

"Flickers," *Masterpiece Theatre*, Joan Wilson (executive producer), Joan Brown (producer) (PBS)

"Oppenheimer," *American Playhouse*, Peter Goodchild (producer), Lindsay Law (coordinating producer), (PBS)

"A Town Like Alice," *Masterpiece Theatre*, Joan Wilson (executive producer), Henry Crawford (producer) (PBS)

OUTSTANDING VARIETY, MUSIC OR COMEDY PROGRAM

For a special or a series. Emmy(s) to executive producer(s), producer(s) and star(s), if applicable:

☐ *Night of 100 Stars*, Alexander H. Cohen (executive producer), Hildy Parks (producer), Roy A. Somlyo (co-producer), March 8, 1982 (ABC)

Ain't Misbehavin', Alvin Cooperman (executive producer), Alvin Cooperman, Buddy Bregman (producers), June 21, 1982 (NBC)

American Film Institute Salute to Frank Capra, George Stevens Jr. (producer), April 4, 1982 (CBS)

Baryshnikov in Hollywood, Herman E. Krawitz (executive producer), Don Mischer (producer), Mikhail Baryshnikov (star), April 21, 1982 (CBS)

SCTV Network, Andrew Alexander, Doug Holtby, Len Stuart, Jack Rhodes (executive producers), Patrick Whitley (supervising producer), Barry Sand, Don Novello (producers), Nicolas Wry (co-producer), Series (NBC)

OUTSTANDING CLASSICAL PROGRAM IN THE PERFORMING ARTS

For a special or a series. Emmy(s) to executive producer(s), producer(s) and star(s), if applicable:

☐ *La Bohème: Live from the Met*, Michael Bronson (executive producer), Clemente D'Alessio (producer), January 20, 1982 (PBS)

Bernstein/Beethoven, Horant H. Hohlfeld, Harry Kraut (executive producers), David Griffiths (producer), Leonard Bernstein (star), Series (PBS)

Horowitz in London: A Royal Concert, Peter Gelb, John Vernon (producers), Vladimir Horowitz (star), May 22, 1982 (PBS)

Live from Lincoln Center: An Evening with Danny Kaye and the New York Philharmonic, Herbert Bonis (executive producer), John Goberman (producer), Danny Kaye (star), September 23, 1981 (PBS)

Live from Lincoln Center: An Evening with Itzhak Perlman and the New York Philharmonic, John Goberman (producer), Itzhak Perlman (star), February 10, 1982 (PBS)

☐ Indicates winner

OUTSTANDING DRAMA SPECIAL

Emmy(s) to executive producer(s) and producer(s):

☐ *A Woman Called Golda*, Harve Bennett (executive producer), Gene Corman (producer) (Syndicated)

Bill, Alan Landsburg (executive producer), Mel Stuart (producer), December 22, 1981 (CBS)

The Elephant Man, Martin Starger (executive producer), Richmond Crinkley (producer), January 4, 1982 (ABC)

Inside the Third Reich, E. Jack Neuman (producer), May 9 and 10, 1982 (ABC)

Skokie, Herbert Brodkin (executive producer), Robert Berger (producer), November 17, 1981 (CBS)

OUTSTANDING INFORMATIONAL SPECIAL

Emmy(s) to executive producer(s) and producer(s):

☐ *Making of "Raiders of the Lost Ark,"* Sidney Ganis (executive producer), Howard Kazanjian (producer), November 28, 1981 (PBS)

Great Movie Stunts: "Raiders of the Lost Ark," Sidney Ganis (executive producer), Robert Guenette (producer), October 5, 1981 (CBS)

High Hopes: The Capra Years, Carl Pingitore, Frank Capra Jr. (producers), December 24, 1981 (NBC)

Hollywood: The Gift of Laughter, David L. Wolper (executive producer), Jack Haley Jr. (producer), May 16, 1982 (ABC)

Marva Collins: Excellence in Education, Kathleen Maloney (producer), February 16, 1982 (PBS)

OUTSTANDING CHILDREN'S PROGRAM

For a special or a series. Emmy(s) to executive producer(s) and producer(s):

☐ *The Wave*, Virginia L. Carter (executive producer), Fern Field (producer), October 4, 1981 (ABC)

"Alice at the Palace," Project Peacock, Joseph Papp (producer), January 16, 1982 (NBC)

"The Electric Grandmother," Project Peacock, Linda Gottlieb (executive producer), Doro Bachrach (producer), January 17, 1982 (NBC)

Please Don't Hit Me, Mom, Virginia L. Carter (executive producer), Fern Field (producer), September 20, 1981 (ABC)

Through the Magic Pyramid, Ron Howard (executive producer), Rance Howard, Herbert J. Wright (producers), December 6 and 13, 1981 (NBC)

OUTSTANDING INFORMATIONAL SERIES

Emmy(s) to executive producer(s) and producer(s):

☐ *Creativity with Bill Moyers*, Merton Koplin, Charles Grinker, Bill Moyers (executive producers), Betsy McCarthy (coordinating producer) (PBS)

The Barbara Walters Specials, Don Mischer (executive producer), Jo Ann Goldberg (producer) (ABC)

The Dick Cavett Show, Robin Breed (producer) (PBS)

Entertainment Tonight, Jim Bellows (executive producer), Andy Friendly, John Goldhammer, Vin DiBona (producers) (Syndicated)

Middletown, Peter Davis (producer) (PBS)

OUTSTANDING ANIMATED PROGRAM

For a special or a series. Emmy(s) to executive producers(s) and producer(s):

☐ *The Grinch Grinches the Cat in the Hat*, David H. DePatie (executive producer), Ted Geisel, Friz Freleng (producers), May 20, 1982 (ABC)

A Charlie Brown Celebration, Lee Mendelson, Bill Melendez (producers), May 24, 1982 (CBS)

The Smurf Springtime Special, Joseph Barbera, William Hanna (executive producers), Gerard Baldwin (producer), April 8, 1982 (NBC)

Smurfs, William Hanna, Joseph Barbera (executive producers), Gerard Baldwin, Kay Wright (producers), November 29, 1981 (NBC)

Someday You'll Find Her, Charlie Brown, Lee Mendelson (executive producer), Bill Melendez (producer), October 30, 1981 (CBS)

Prime Time Performing Awards

OUTSTANDING LEAD ACTOR IN A COMEDY SERIES

For a continuing or single performance in a regular series:

☐ Alan Alda, *M*A*S*H* (CBS)

Robert Guillaume, *Benson* (ABC)

Judd Hirsch, *Taxi* (ABC)

Hal Linden, *Barney Miller* (ABC)

Leslie Nielsen, *Police Squad!* (ABC)

OUTSTANDING LEAD ACTOR IN A LIMITED SERIES OR A SPECIAL

For a continuing role in a limited series or for a single appearance in a limited series or a special:

☐ Mickey Rooney, *Bill*, December 22, 1981 (CBS)

Anthomny Andrews, *Brideshead Revisited* (PBS)
Philip Anglim, *The Elephant Man*, January 4, 1982 (ABC)
Anthony Hopkins, "The Hunchback of Notre Dame," *Hallmark Hall of Fame*, February 4, 1982 (CBS)
Jeremy Irons, *Brideshead Revisited* (PBS)

OUTSTANDING LEAD ACTOR IN A DRAMA SERIES

For a continuing or single performance in a regular series:
□ Daniel J. Travanti, *Hill Street Blues* (NBC)
Edward Asner, *Lou Grant* (CBS)
John Forsythe, *Dynasty* (ABC)
James Garner, *Bret Maverick* (NBC)
Tom Selleck, *Magnum, P.I.* (CBS)

OUTSTANDING LEAD ACTRESS IN A COMEDY SERIES

For a continuing or single performance in a regular series:
□ Carol Kane, *Taxi*, "Simka Returns," February 4, 1982 (ABC)
Nell Carter, *Gimme a Break* (NBC)
Bonnie Franklin, *One Day at a Time* (CBS)
Swoosie Kurptz, *Love, Sidney* (NBC)
Charlotte Rae, *The Facts of Life* (NBC)
Isabel Sanford, *The Jeffersons* (CBS)

OUTSTANDING LEAD ACTRESS IN A DRAMA SERIES

For a continuing or single performance in a regular series:
□ Michael Learned, *Nurse* (CBS)
Debbie Allen, *Fame* (NBC)
Veronica Hamel, *Hill Street Blues* (NBC)
Michele Lee, *Knots Landing* (CBS)
Stefanie Powers, *Hart to Hart* (ABC)

OUTSTANDING LEAD ACTRESS IN A LIMITED SERIES OR A SPECIAL

For a continuing role in a limited series or for a single appearance in a limited series or a special:
□ Ingrid Bergman, *A Woman Called Golda* (Syndicated)
Glenda Jackson, *The Patricia Neal Story*, December 8, 1981 (CBS)
Ann Jillian, *Mae West*, May 2, 1982 (ABC)
Jean Stapleton, *Eleanor, First Lady of the World*, May 12, 1982 (CBS)
Cicely Tyson, "The Marva Collins Story," *Hallmark Hall of Fame*, December 1, 1981 (CBS)

□ Indicates winner

OUTSTANDING SUPPORTING ACTOR IN A COMEDY OR VARIETY OR MUSIC SERIES

For a continuing or single performance in a regular series:
□ Christopher Lloyd, *Taxi* (ABC)
Danny De Vito, *Taxi* (ABC)
Ron Glass, *Barney Miller* (ABC)
Steve Landesberg, *Barney Miller* (ABC)
Harry Morgan, *M*A*S*H* (CBS)
David Ogden Stiers, *M*A*S*H* (CBS)

OUTSTANDING SUPPORTING ACTOR IN A DRAMA SERIES

For a continuing or single performance in a regular series:
□ Michael Conrad, *Hill Street Blues* (NBC)
Taurean Blacque, *Hill Street Blues* (NBC)
Charles Haid, *Hill Street Blues* (NBC)
Michael Warren, *Hill Street Blues* (NBC)
Bruce Weitz, *Hill Street Blues* (NBC)

OUTSTANDING SUPPORTING ACTOR IN A LIMITED SERIES OR A SPECIAL

For a continuing role in a limited series or for a single appearance in a limited series or a special:
□ Laurence Olivier, *Brideshead Revisited*, "Brideshead Revisited," March 29, 1982 (PBS)
Jack Albertson, *My Body, My Child*, April 12, 1982 (ABC)
John Gielgud, *Brideshead Revisited*, "Et In Arcadia Ego," January 18, 1982 (PBS)
Derek Jacobi, *Inside the Third Reich*, May 9 and 10, 1982 (ABC)
Leonard Nimoy, *A Woman Called Golda* (Syndicated)

OUTSTANDING SUPPORTING ACTRESS IN A COMEDY OR VARIETY OR MUSIC SERIES

For a continuing or single performance in a regular series:
□ Loretta Swit, *M*A*S*H* (CBS)
Eileen Brennan, *Private Benjamin* (CBS)
Marla Gibbs, *The Jeffersons* (CBS)
Andrea Martin, *SCTV Network* (NBC)
Anne Meara, *Archie Bunker's Place*, "Relapse," March 14, 1982 (CBS)
Inga Swenson, *Benson* (ABC)

OUTSTANDING SUPPORTING ACTRESS IN A DRAMA SERIES

For a continuing or single performance in a regular series:
□ Nancy Marchand, *Lou Grant* (CBS)
Barbara Bosson, *Hill Street Blues* (NBC)
Julie Harris, *Knots Landing* (CBS)
Linda Kelsey, *Lou Grant* (CBS)

Betty Thomas, *Hill Street Blues* (NBC)

OUTSTANDING SUPPORTING ACTRESS IN A LIMITED SERIES OR A SPECIAL

For a continuing role in a limited series or for a single appearance in a limited series or a special:
□ Penny Fuller, *The Elephant Man*, January 4, 1982 (ABC)
Claire Bloom, *Brideshead Revisited*, "Sebastian Against the World," February 8, 1982 (PBS)
Judy Davis, *A Woman Called Golda* (CBS)
Vicki Lawrence, *Eunice*, March 15, 1982 (CBS)
Rita Moreno, *Portrait of a Showgirl*, May 4, 1982 (Syndicated)

Prime Time Writing and Directing Awards

OUTSTANDING DIRECTING IN A COMEDY SERIES

For a single episode of a regular series:
□ Alan Rafkin, *One Day at a Time*, "Barbara's Crisis," February 21, 1982 (CBS)
Alan Alda, *M*A*S*H*, "Where There's a Will, There's a War," February 22, 1982 (CBS)
Hy Averback, *M*A*S*H*, "Sons and Bowlers," March 22, 1982 (CBS)
James Burrows, *Taxi*, "Jim the Psychic," October 8, 1981 (ABC)
Charles S. Dubin, *M*A*S*H*, "Pressure Points," February 15, 1982 (CBS)
Burt Metcalfe, *M*A*S*H*, "Picture This," April 5, 1982 (CBS)

OUTSTANDING DIRECTING IN A DRAMA SERIES

For a single episode of a regular series:
□ Harry Harris, *Fame*, "To Soar and Never Falter, February 4, 1982 (NBC)
Jeff Bleckner, *Hill Street Blues*, "The World According to Freedom," January 7, 1982 (NBC)
Robert Butler, *Hill Street Blues*, "The Second Oldest Profession," November 19, 1981 (NBC)
Gene Reynolds, *Lou Grant*, "Hometown," November 23, 1981 (CBS)
Robert Scheerer, *Fame*, "Musical Bridge," April 1, 1982 (NBC)

OUTSTANDING DIRECTING IN A VARIETY OR MUSIC PROGRAM

For a single episode of a regular or limited series or for a special:
□ Dwight Hemion, *Goldie and Kids. . . Listen to Us*, May 8, 1982 (ABC)

Clark Jones, *Night of 100 Stars*, March 8, 1982 (ABC)

Don Mischer, *Baryshnikov in Hollywood*, April 21, 1982 (CBS)

Marty Pasetta, *The 54th Annual Academy Awards*, March 29, 1982 (ABC)

Robert Scheerer, *Live From Lincoln Center: An Evening with Danny Kaye and the New York Philharmonic*, September 23, 1981 (PBS)

OUTSTANDING DIRECTING IN A LIMITED SERIES OR A SPECIAL

For a single episode of a limited series or for a special:

☐ Marvin J. Chomsky, *Inside the Third Reich*, May 9 and 10, 1982 (ABC)

Lee Philips, *Mae West*, May 2, 1982 (ABC)

Charles Sturridge, Michael Lindsay-Hogg, *Brideshead Revisited*, "Et in Arcadia Ego," January 18, 1982 (PBS)

Herbert Wise, *Skokie*, November 17, 1981 (CBS)

OUTSTANDING WRITING IN A COMEDY SERIES

For a single episode of a regular series:

☐ Ken Estin, *Taxi*, "Elegant Iggy," March 18, 1982 (ABC)

Alan Alda, *M*A*S*H*, "Follies of the Living—Concerns of the Dead," January 4, 1982 (CBS)

Frank Dungan, Jeff Stein, Tony Sheehan, *Barney Miller*, "Landmark"—Part 3, May 20, 1982 (ABC)

Barry Kemp, (teleplay), Holly Holmberg Brooks (story), *Taxi*, "Jim the Psychic," October 8, 1982 (ABC)

David Zucker, Jim Abrahams, Jerry Zucker, *Police Squad!*, "A Substantial Gift," March 4, 1982 (ABC)

OUTSTANDING WRITING IN A VARIETY OR MUSIC PROGRAM

For a single episode of a regular or limited series or for a special:

☐ John Candy, Joe Flaherty, Eugene Levy, Andrea Martin, Rick Moranis, Catherine O'Hara, Dave Thomas, Dick Blasucci, Paul Flaherty, Bob Dolman, John McAndrew, Doug Steckler, Mert Rich, Jeffrey Barron, Michael Short, Chris Cluess, Stuart Kreisman, Brian McConnachie, *SCTV Network*, "Moral Majority Show," July 10, 1981 (NBC)

Richard Alfieri, Rita Mae Brown, Rick Mitz, Arthur Alan Seidelman, Norman Lear, *I Love Liberty*, March 21, 1982 (ABC)

☐ Indicates winner

John Candy, Joe Flaherty, Eugene Levy, Andrea Martin, Rick Moranis, Catherine O'Hara, Dave Thomas, Dick Blasucci, Paul Flaherty, Bob Dolman, John McAndrew, Doug Steckler, Jeffrey Barron, *SCTV Network*, "Cycle Two, Show Two," October 23, 1981 (NBC)

John Candy, Joe Flaherty, Eugene Levy, Andrea Martin, Rick Moranis, Catherine O'Hara, Dave Thomas, Dick Blasucci, Paul Flaherty, Bob Dolman, John McAndrew, Doug Steckler, Michael Short, Tom Couch, Eddie Gorodetsky, Don Novello, *SCTV Network*, (with Tony Bennett), April 16, 1982 (NBC)

John Candy, Joe Flaherty, Eugene Levy, Andrea Martin, Rick Moranis, Catherine O'Hara, Dave Thomas, Dick Blasucci, Paul Flaherty, Bob Dolman, John McAndrew, Doug Steckler, Mert Rich, Jeffrey Barron, *SCTV Network*, "Christmas Show," December 18, 1981 (NBC)

OUTSTANDING WRITING IN A DRAMA SERIES

For a single episode of a regular series:

☐ Steven Bochco, Anthony Yerkovich, Jeffrey Lewis, Michael Wagner (teleplay), Michael Kozoll, Steven Bochco (story), *Hill Street Blues*, "Freedom's Last Stand," January 28, 1982 (NBC)

Steven Bochco, Anthony Yerkovich, Robert Crais (teleplay), Michael Kozoll, Steven Bochco, Anthony Yerkovich (story), *Hill Street Blues*, "The Second Oldest Profession," November 19, 1981 (NBC)

Steven Bochco, Anthony Yerkovich, Jeffrey Lewis, Michael Wagner, *Hill Street Blues*, "Personal Foul," March 25, 1982 (NBC)

Seth Freeman, *Lou Grant*, "Blacklist," April 5, 1982 (CBS)

Michael Wagner, *Hill Street Blues*, "The World According to Freedom," January 7, 1982 (NBC)

OUTSTANDING WRITING IN A LIMITED SERIES OR A SPECIAL

For a single episode of a limited series or for a special:

☐ Corey Blechman (teleplay), Barry Morrow (story), "Bill," December 22, 1981 (CBS)

Oliver Hailey, *Sidney Shorr*, October 5, 1981 (NBC)

Ernest Kinoy, *Skokie*, November 17, 1981 (CBS)

John Mortimer, *Brideshead Revisited*, "Et in Arcadia Ego," January 18, 1982 (PBS)

Peter Prince, "Oppenheimer," *American Playhouse*—Part 5, June 8, 1982 (PBS)

Creative Arts Awards

OUTSTANDING CINEMATOGRAPHY FOR A SERIES

For a single episode of a regular series:

☐ William W. Spencer, A.S.C., *Fame*, "Alone in a Crowd," January 28, 1982 (NBC)

Robert F. Liu, *Lou Grant*, "Ghosts," January 11, 1982 (CBS)

Sol Negrin, A.S.C., *Baker's Dozen*, "A Class by Himself," March 24, 1982 (CBS)

Woody Omens, *Magnum, P.I.*, "Memories Are Forever," November 5, 1981 (CBS)

Ted Voigtlander, A.S.C., *Little House on the Prairie*, "He Was Only Twelve"—Part 2, May 10, 1982 (NBC)

OUTSTANDING CINEMATOGRAPHY FOR A LIMITED SERIES OR A SPECIAL

For a single episode of a limited series or for a special:

☐ James Crabe, A.S.C., *The Letter*, May 3, 1982 (ABC)

Pasqualino De Santis, *Marco Polo*—Part 4, May 19, 1982 (NBC)

Gayne Rescher, A.S.C., *The Princess and the Cabbie*, November 3, 1981 (CBS)

OUTSTANDING ART DIRECTION FOR A SERIES

For a single episode of a regular series:

James J. Agazzi, Paul Sylos (art directors), Robert Signorelli (set decorator), *Hart to Hart*, "The Hart of the Matter," February 16, 1982 (ABC)

☐ Ira Diamond (art director), Joseph Stone (set decorator), *Fame*, "Tomorrow's Farewell," January 21, 1982 (NBC)

Jeffrey L. Goldstein (art director), James G. Cane (set decorator), *Hill Street Blues*, "Personal Foul," March 25, 1982 (NBC)

Scott T. Ritenour (art director), Robert L. Zilliox (set decorator), *Bret Maverick*, "The Yellow Rose," December 22, 1981 (NBC)

OUTSTANDING ART DIRECTION FOR A LIMITED SERIES OR A SPECIAL

For a single episode of a limited series or for a special:

☐ James Hulsey (art director, Jerry Adams (set decorator), *The Letter*, May 3, 1982 (ABC)

Peter Phillips (production designer), *Brideshead Revisited*, "Et in Arcadia Ego," January 18, 1982 (PBS)

Luciano Ricceri (production designer), Bruno Cesari (set decorator), *Marco Polo*—Part 2, May 17, 1982 (NBC)

Rolf Zehetbauer (production designer), Kuli Sander, Herbert Strabel (art directors), "Inside the Third Reich," May 9 and 10, 1982 (ABC)

OUTSTANDING ART DIRECTION FOR A VARIETY OR MUSIC PROGRAM

For a single episode of a regular or limited series or for a special:

☐ Ray Klausen (art director), *The 54th Annual Academy Awards*, March 29, 1982 (ABC)

Roy Christopher (art director), *Baryshnikov in Hollywood*, April 21, 1982 (CBS)

Romain Johnston (art director), Jim Wagner (set decorator), *Barbara Mandrell and the Mandrell Sisters*, (with Tom Jones and R.C. Bannon), February 20, 1982 (NBC)

Kim Colefax (production designer), *Olivia Newton-John: Let's Get Physical*, February 8, 1982 (ABC)

Charles Lisanby (art director), Dwight Jackson (set decorator), "Working," *American Playhouse*, April 13, 1982 (PBS)

OUTSTANDING ACHIEVEMENT IN MUSIC COMPOSITION FOR A SERIES (DRAMATIC UNDERSCORE)

For a single episode of a regular series. Emmy(s) to composer(s):

☐ David Rose, *Little House on the Prairie*, "He Was Only Twelve"—Part 2, May 10, 1982 (NBC)

Bruce Broughton, *Dallas*, "The Search," January 8, 1982 (CBS)

Joe Harnell, *The Incredible Hulk*, "Triangle," November 13, 1981 (CBS)

Patrick Williams, *Lou Grant*, "Hometwon," November 23, 1981 (CBS)

OUTSTANDING ACHIEVEMENT IN MUSIC COMPOSITION FOR A LIMITED SERIES OR SPECIAL (DRAMATIC UNDERSCORE)

For a single episode of a limited series or for a special. Emmy(s) to composer(s):

☐ Patrick Williams, *The Princess and the Cabbie*, November 3, 1981 (CBS)

Bruce Broughton, *Killjoy*, October 22, 1981 (CBS)

Allyn Ferguson, *Ivanhoe*, February 23, 1982 (CBS)

☐ Indicates winner

Billy Goldenberg, *Jacqueline Bouvier Kennedy*, October 14, 1981 (ABC)

Michel Legrand, *A Woman Called Golda* (Syndicated)

Laurence Rosenthal, *The Letter*, May 3, 1982 (ABC)

OUTSTANDING ACHIEVEMENT IN MUSIC DIRECTION

For a single episode of a regular or limited series or for a special, whether it be variety or music. Emmy(s) to music director and principal arranger(s):

☐ Elliot Lawrence (music director), Bill Elton, Tommy Newsom, Torrie Zito, Lanny Meyers, Jonathan Tunick (principal arrangers), *Night of 100 Stars*, March 8, 1982 (ABC)

Allyn Ferguson (music director and principal arranger), *The American Movie Awards*, March 15, 1982 (NBC)

Ian Fraser (music director), Billy Byers, Chris Boardman (principal arrangers), *Walt Disney... One Man's Dream*, December 12, 1981 (CBS)

Luther Henderson (music director and principal arranger), *Ain't Misbehavin'*, June 21, 1982 (NBC)

Peter Matz (music director and principal arranger), *Shirley MacLaine... Illusions*, June 24, 1982 (CBS)

OUTSTANDING ACHIEVEMENT IN MUSIC AND LYRICS

For a song (which must have both music and lyrics), whether it be for a single episode of a regular or limited series or for a special. Emmy(s) to composer(s) and lyricist(s):

☐ Larry Grossman (composer), Alan Buz Kohan (lyricist), *Shirley MacLaine... Illusions*, song: "On the Outside Looking In," June 24, 1982 (CBS)

James Di Pasquale (composer), Carol Connors (lyricist), *Advice to the Lovelorn*, song: "If This Is Love," November 30, 1981 (NBC)

Stephen Geyer (composer and lyricist), *The Greatest American Hero*, "Dreams," song: "Dreams," March 17, 1982 (ABC)

Billy Goldenberg (composer), Harry Shannon (lyricist), *The Gift of Life*, song: "Just a Little More Love," March 16, 1982 (CBS)

Alan Buz Kohan (composer and lyricist), *Night of 100 Stars*, song: "What's Your Line?," March 8, 1982 (ABC)

Mitzie Welch, Ken Welch (composers and lyricists), *Walt Disney... One Man's Dream*, song: "Marceline," December 12, 1981 (CBS)

OUTSTANDING ACHIEVEMENT IN CHOREOGRAPHY

For a single episode of a regular or limited series or for a special:

☐ Debbie Allen, *Fame*, "Come One, Come All," March 11, 1982 (NBC)

Peter Anastos, Michael Kidd, *Baryshnikov in Hollywood*, April 21, 1982 (CBS)

Arthur Faria, *Ain't Misbehavin'*, June 21, 1982 (NBC)

Alan Johnson, *Shirley MacLaine... Illusions*, June 24, 1982 (CBS)

Walter Painter, *The 54th Annual Academy Awards*, March 29, 1982 (ABC)

OUTSTANDING COSTUME DESIGN FOR A REGULAR OR LIMITED SERIES

For a single episode of a regular or limited series:

☐ Enrico Sabbatini, *Marco Polo*—Part 4, May 18, 1982 (NBC)

Rickie A. Hansen, *Solid Gold*, (with Andy Gibb and Marilyn McCoo) (Syndicated)

Bill Hargate, *Barbara Mandrell and the Mandrell Sisters*, (with Brenda Lee and Paul Williams), November 28, 1981 (NBC)

Grady Hunt, *Fantasy Island*, "La Liberatora/Mr. Nobody," April 17, 1982 (ABC)

Jane Robinson, *Brideshead Revisited*, "Home and Abroad, January 25, 1982 (PBS)

OUTSTANDING COSTUME DESIGN FOR A SPECIAL

For a comedy, drama, variety or music special:

☐ Donald Brooks, *The Letter*, May 3, 1982 (ABC)

Jean-Pierre Dorleac, *Mae West*, May 2, 1982 (ABC)

Noel Taylor, *Eleanor, First Lady of the World*, May 12, 1982 (CBS)

Travilla, *Jacqueline Bouvier Kennedy*, October 14, 1981 (ABC)

Julie Weiss, *The Elephant Man*, January 4, 1982 (ABC)

OUTSTANDING ACHIEVEMENT IN MAKEUP

For a single episode of a regular or limited series or for a special:

☐ Paul Stanhope, *World War III*, January 31 and February 1, 1982 (NBC)

Del Acevedo (personal makeup artist to Mr. Scott), Pauline Heys, *Oliver Twist*, March 23, 1982 (CBS)

Richard Blair, *Mae West*, May 2, 1982 (ABC)

Jack Freeman, Jack Barron, *The Letter*, May 3, 1982 (ABC)

Leo L. Lotito Jr., Nora de la Torre, *Fantasy Island*, "Case Againt Mr. Roarke/Save Sherlock Holmes," February 6, 1982 (ABC)

OUTSTANDING ACHIEVEMENT IN HAIRSTYLING

For a single episode of a regular or limited series or for a special:

☐ Hazel Catmull, *Eleanor, First Lady of the World*, May 12, 1982 (CBS)

Emma Di Vittorio, Dione Taylor, *Jacqueline Bouvier Kennedy*, October 14, 1981 (ABC)

Renata Magnanti, Elda Magnanti, *Marco Polo—Part 4*, May 19, 1982 (NBC)

Gloria Montemayor, *Fame*, "The Strike," February 18, 1982 (NBC)

Steve Robinette, *Cagney & Lacey*, "Street Scene," June 21, 1982 (CBS)

OUTSTANDING FILM EDITING FOR A SERIES

For a single episode of a regular series:

☐ Andrew Chulack, *Hill Street Blues*, "Of Mouse and Man," February 11, 1982 (NBC)

Jeanene Ambler, *Quincy*, "For Love of Joshua," February 3, 1982 (NBC)

Fred W. Berger, A.C.E., *Dallas*, "The Split," November 27, 1981 (CBS)

Ray Daniels, *Hill Street Blues*, "The Second Oldest Profession," November 19, 1981 (NBC)

Michael A. Hoey, *Fame*, "Passing Grade," January 14, 1982 (NBC)

Mark Melnick, *Fame*, "Musical Bridge," April 1, 1982 (NBC)

OUTSTANDING FILM EDITING FOR A LIMITED SERIES OR A SPECIAL

For a single episode of a limited series or for a special:

☐ Robert F. Shugrue, *A Woman Called Golda* (Syndicated)

James T. Heckert, Richard Belding, Les Green, *Inside the Third Reich*, May 9 and 10, 1982 (ABC)

John A. Martinelli, A.C.E., *Marco Polo—Part 4*, May 19, 1982 (NBC)

Rita Roland, A.C.E., *A Piano for Mrs. Cimino*, February 3, 1982 (CBS)

OUTSTANDING ACHIEVEMENT IN FILM SOUND EDITING

For a single episode of a regular or limited series or for a special:

☐ William H. Wistrom, Russ Tinsley (supervising film sound editors), Peter Bond, Tom Cornwell, David Elliott, Tony Garber, Peter Harrison, Charles W. McCann, Joseph Mayer, Joseph Melody, R. William A.

☐ Indicates winner

Thiederman, Rusty Tinsley (editors), *Inside the Third Reich*, May 9 and 10, 1982 (ABC)

Jeff Bushelman, Steve Bushelman, Ian MacGregor-Scott (supervising editors), Barney Cabral, William De Nicholas, Jerelyn Golding, Frank Howard, Bobbe Kurtz, Lettie Odney, Bernard Pincus, Sam Shaw, Patrick Somerset, Frank Spencer, Dave Stone, Ascher Yates (editors), *Marco Polo—Part 4*, May 19, 1982 (NBC)

Joseph Melody, Russ Tinsley (supervising editors), Tom Cornwell, David Elliott, Don Ernst, Michael L. Hilkene, Fred Judkins, John Kline, R. William A. Thiederman, Rusty Tinsley (editors), *Marian Rose White*, January 19, 1982 (CBS)

Russ Tinsley, Michael L. Hilkene (supervising editors), Tom Cornwell, David Elliott, Peter Harrison, Fred Judkins, John Kline, Joseph Melody, R. William A. Thiederman, William H. Wistrom (editors), *The Capture of Grizzly Adams*, February 21, 1982 (NBC)

OUTSTANDING ACHIEVEMENT IN FILM SOUND MIXING

For a single episode of a regular or limited series or for a special:

☐ William Marky, C.A.S., (production mixer), Robert W. Glass Jr., William M. Nicholson, C.A.S., Howard Wilmarth (rerecording mixers), *Hill Street Blues*, "Personal Foul," March 25, 1982 (NBC)

Thomas Causey (production mixer), David J. Hudson, C.A.S., Mel Metcalfe, George R. West (rerecording mixers), *Fire on the Mountain*, November 23, 1981 (NBC)

William Marky, C.A.S., (production mixer), Donald Cahn, C.A.S., James R. Cook, C.A.S., Robert L. Harman, C.A.S., (rerecording mixers), *Hill Street Blues*, "The Second Oldest Profession," November 19, 1981 (NBC)

Jacques Nosco (production mixer), Donald Cahn, C.A.S., James R. Cook, C.A.S., Robert L. Harman, C.A.S., (rerecording mixers), *World War III*, January 31 and February 1, 1982 (NBC)

Eli Yarkoni, (production mixer), Donald Cahn, C.A.S., James R. Cook, C.A.S., Robert L. Harman, C.A.S., (rerecording mixers), *A Woman Called Golda* (Syndicated)

OUTSTANDING ACHIEVEMENT IN TAPE SOUND MIXING

For a single episode of a regular or limited series or for a special:

☐ Christopher L. Haire, Richard J. Masci, Doug Nelson, *Perry Como's Easter in Guadalajara*, April 3, 1982 (ABC)

Jerry Clemans, Matt Hyde, Don Worsham, *Barbara Mandrell and the Mandrell Sisters*, (with Ray Charles and Sylvia), January 23, 1982 (NBC)

Jerry Clemans, Joe Ralston, *Sinatra: The Man and His Music*, November 22, 1981 (NBC)

Bill Cole, Joe Ralston, Allen Patapoff, *Ain't Misbehavin'*, June 21, 1982 (NBC)

Christopher L. Haire, Don Worsham, Russell Terrana, *Debby Boone. . . One Step Closer*, April 26, 1982 (NBC)

OUTSTANDING VIDEOTAPE EDITING FOR A SERIES

For a single episode of a regular series:

☐ Ken Denisoff, *Barbara Mandrell and the Mandrell Sisters* (with Brenda Lee and Paul Williams), November 28, 1981 (NBC)

Andy Ackerman, *WKRP in Cincinnati*, "Fire," February 24, 1982 (CBS)

Raymond Bush, *Report to Murphy*, "High Noon," April 26, 1982 (CBS)

John Carrol, Mario DiMambro, Dave Goldson, Art Schneider, A.C.E., Roderic G. Stephens, A.C.E., *The Greatest American Hero*, "Lost Diablo Mine," December 16, 1981 (ABC)

OUTSTANDING VIDEOTAPE EDITING FOR A LIMITED SERIES OR A SPECIAL

For a single episode of a limited series or for a special:

☐ William H. Breshears Sr., Pam Marshall, Tucker Wiard, *American Bandstand's 30th Anniversary Special*, October 30, 1981 (ABC)

Ed J. Brennan, *Ain't Misbehavin'*, June 21, 1982 (NBC)

Jimmy B. Frazier, Ken Laski, *Lily for President?*, May 20, 1982 (CBS)

Pam Marshall, *Perry Como's French-Canadian Christmas*, December 12, 1981 (ABC)

Roy Stewart, "Working," *American Playhouse*, April 13, 1982 (PBS)

OUTSTANDING TECHNICAL DIRECTION AND ELECTRONIC CAMERAWORK

For a single episode of a regular or limited series or for a special:

☐ Jerry Weiss (technical director), Bruce Bottone, Ken Dahlquist, Dean Hall, James Herring, Royden Holm, Tom

Munshower, Wayne Nostaja, David Nowell (camerapersons), *The Magic of David Copperfield*, October 26, 1981 (CBS)

Gerry Bucci (technical director), Ron Brooks, Warren Cress, D.J. Diomedes, Don Langford, Jay Lowry, Bill Scott (camerapersons), *Lynda Carter: Street Life*, March 5, 1981 (CBS)

Terry Donohue (technical director), Rocky Danielson, Joe Epperson, John Gillis, Dean Hall, Don Jones, Mike Keeler, Bruce Oldham, Kenneth A. Patterson, John Repczynski, Ken Tamburri (camerapersons), *Rod Stewart—Tonight He's Yours* (Syndicated)

Karl Messerschmidt (technical director), Les Atkinson, George Falardeau, James Herring, Mike Higuera, Royden Holm, Mike Stramisky (camerapersons), *All the Way Home*, December 21, 1981 (NBC)

O. Tamburri (technical director), Donald Barker, George Falardeau, Mike Higuera, Royden Holm, Reed Howard (camerapersons), *Ain't Misbehavin'*, June 21, 1982 (NBC)

OUTSTANDING LIGHTING DIRECTION (ELECTRONIC)

For a single episode of a regular or limited series or for a special:
□ George W. Riesenberger (lighting designer), Ken Dettling (lighting director), "Working," *American Playhouse*, April 13, 1982 (PBS)

Gregory Brunton (lighting director), *Debby Boone. . .One Step Closer*, April 26, 1982 (NBC)

Leard Davis (lighting designer), *Nashville Palace* (with Tammy Wynette, George Jones and Minnie Pearl), November 14, 1981 (NBC)

Bob Dickinson (lighting consultant), Harold Guy (lighting director), *Solid Gold*, (with Marilyn McCoo and The Charlie Daniels Band) (Syndicated)

William Klages (lighting designer), *Night of 100 Stars*, March 8, 1982 (ABC)

Fred McKinnon, (lighting consultant), March Palius (lighting director), *I Love Liberty*, March 21, 1982 (ABC)

OUTSTANDING INDIVIDUAL ACHIEVEMENT—ANIMATED PROGRAMMING

(Possibility of one award, more than one award or no award):
Bill Perez (director), *The Grinch Grinches the Cat in the Hat*, May 20, 1982 (ABC)

□ Indicates winner

Phil Roman (director), *Someday You'll Find Her, Charlie Brown*, October 30, 1981 (CBS)

OUTSTANDING INDIVIDUAL ACHIEVEMENT—SPECIAL CLASS

(Possibility of one award, more than one award or no award):
□ Nell Carter (performer), *Ain't Misbehavin'*, June 21, 1982 (NBC)
□ Andre De Sheilds (performer), *Ain't Misbehavin'*, June 21, 1982 (NBC)
□ Marilyn Matthews (costume supervisor), *Fame*, "The Strike," February 18, 1982 (NBC)
Elsa Fennell (costume supervisor), Gloria Barnes (costume mistress), Colin Wilson (costume master), *Agatha Christie's "Murder Is Easy,"* January 2, 1982 (CBS)
Gregory Hines (performer), *I Love Liberty*, March 21, 1982 (ABC)

OUTSTANDING INDIVIDUAL ACHIEVEMENT—CREATIVE SPECIAL ACHIEVEMENT

(Possibility of one award, more than one award or no award):
□ Andy Zall (videotape editor), *Shirley MacLaine. . .Illusions*, June 24, 1982 (CBS)
Jeff Bushelman, Steve Bushelman, Ian MacGregor-Scott (supervising film sound editors), Barney Cabral, William De Nicholas, Jerelyn Golding, Bobbe Kurtz, Lette Odney, Patrick Somerset, Ascher Yates (film sound editors), *Marco Polo*—Part 4, May 19, 1982 (NBC)
William Mesa, Tim Donahue (graphic artists, *Inside the Third Reich*, May 9 and 10, 1982 (ABC)
Alex Tkach, Michael Gross, Wayne Schneider (graphic artists), *SCTV Network*, "Cycle Two, Show One," November 16, 1981 (NBC)

OUTSTANDING INDIVIDUAL ACHIEVEMENT—GRAPHIC DESIGN AND TITLE SEQUENCES

(Possibility of one award, more than one award or no award):
Michael Levine, Michael Hoey, *Fame*, "Metamorphosis," January 7, 1982 (NBC)
Robert Pook, William Shortridge Jr., Arlen Schumer, *Late Night with David Letterman* (with Ruth Norman and Vic Gold), April 29, 1982 (NBC)
Valerie Pye, *Brideshead Revisited*, "Brideshead Revisited," March 29, 1982 (PBS)

OUTSTANDING INDIVIDUAL ACHIEVEMENT—INFORMATIONAL PROGRAMMING

(Possibility of one award, more than one award or no award):
James Castle, Bruce Bryant (graphic artists), *Hollywood: The Gift of Laughter*, May 16, 1982 (ABC)
Ron Hays, Richard Froman (graphic artists), *Omni: The New Frontier*, "Terminal Man/Ciani" (Syndicated)
Phillip Schuman, Gil Hubbs (cinematographers), Great Movie Stunts: "Raiders of the Lost Ark," October 5, 1981 (CBS)
Peter Ustinov (host), *Omni: The New Frontier* (Syndicated)
David Wisnievitz (production mixer), Gary Bourgeois, Hoppy Mehterian, Howard Wollman (rerecording mixers), *Great Movie Stunts: "Raiders of the Lost Ark,"* October 5, 1981 (CBS)

OUTSTANDING INDIVIDUAL ACHIEVEMENT—CHILDREN'S PROGRAMMING

(Possibility of one award, more than one award or no award):
□ Ralph Holmes (lighting designer), "Alice at the Palace," *Project Peacock*, January 16, 1982 (NBC)
Theoni V. Aldredge (costume designer), "Alice at the Palace," *Project Peacock*, January 16, 1982 (NBC)
Byron "Buzz" Brandt, A.C.E., (film editor), *Rascals and Robbers—The Secret Adventures of Tom Sawyer and Huck Finn*, February 27, 1982 (CBS)
Albert Heschong (art director), Warren E. Welch (set decorator), *Rascals and Robbers—The Secret Adventures of Tom Sawyer and Huck Finn*, February 27, 1982 (CBS)
Keith A. Wester C.A.S., (production mixer), Robert W. Glass Jr., William A. Nicholson, C.A.S., Howard Wilmarth (rerecording mixers), Rascals and Robbers—The Secret Adventures of Tom Sawyer and Huck Finn, February 27, 1982 (CBS)

FIFTH ANNUAL ATAS GOVERNORS AWARD
□ Hallmark Cards Inc. for the *Hallmark Hall of Fame*. Dedicated to the standards of quality throughout the 31 years on television, the *Hallmark Hall of Fame* has brought millions of Americans an opportunity to see the classic dramas of the past and outstanding works of contemporary playwrights.

OUTSTANDING ACHIEVEMENT IN ENGINEERING DEVELOPMENT

An award to an individual, a company or an organization for developments in engineering that are either so extensive an improvement on existing metods or so innovative in nature that they materially affect the transmission, recording or reception of television:
- ☐ Hal Collins for his contributions to the art and development of videotape editing (posthumous)
- ☐ Dubner Computer Systems Inc. and the American Broadcasting Company for the Dubner CBG-2 electronic character and background generator

Citation to Chapman Studio Equipment for the development of crane systems

Daytime Awards

OUTSTANDING DAYTIME DRAMA SERIES

Emmy to executive producer(s) and producer(s)

All My Children, Jorn Winther (producer) (ABC)

General Hospital, Gloria Monty (producer) (ABC)
- ☐ *The Guiding Light*, Allen Potter (executive producer), Joe Willmore and Leslie Kwartin (producers) (CBS)

Ryan's Hope, Ellen Barrett (producer) (ABC)

OUTSTANDING ACTOR IN A DAYTIME DRAMA SERIES

James Mitchell, *All My Children* (Role: Palmer Cortlandt) (ABC)

Richard Shoberg, *All My Children* (Role: Tom Cudahy) (ABC)

Larry Bryggman, *As the World Turns* (Role: John Dixon) (CBS)

Stuart Damon, *General Hospital* (Role: Dr. Alan Quartemaine) (ABC)
- ☐ Anthony Geary, *General Hospital* (Role: Luke Spencer) (ABC)

OUTSTANDING ACTRESS IN A DAYTIME DRAMA SERIES

Susan Lucci, *All My Children* (Role: Erica Kane) (ABC)

Ann Flood, *The Edge of Night* (Role: Nancy Karr) (ABC)

Sharon Gabet, *The Edge of Night* (Role: Raven Whitney) (ABC)

Leslie Charleson, *General Hospital* (Role: Dr. Monica Quartermaine) (ABC)
- ☐ Robin Strasser, *One Life to Live* (Role: Dorian Lord Callison) (ABC)

☐ Indicates winner

OUTSTANDING ACTOR IN A SUPPORTING ROLE IN A DAYTIME DRAMA SERIES

Darnell Williams, *All My Children* (Role: Jesse Hubbard) (ABC)
- ☐ David Lewis, *General Hospital* (Role: Edward Quartermaine) (ABC)

Doug Sheehan, *General Hospital* (Role: Joe Kelly) (ABC)

Gerald Anthony, *One Life to Live* (Role: Marco Dane) (ABC)

OUTSTANDING ACTRESS IN A SUPPORTING ROLE IN A DAYTIME DRAMA SERIES

Elizabeth Lawrence, *All My Children* (Role: Myra Murdock) (ABC)
- ☐ Dorothy Lyman, *All My Children* (Role: Opal Gardner) (ABC)

Meg Mundy, *The Doctors* (Role: Mona Croft) (NBC)

Louise Shaffer, *Ryan's Hope* (Role: Rae Woodard) (ABC)

OUTSTANDING GAME OR AUDIENCE PARTICIPATION SHOW

Emmy to executive producer(s) and producer(s)

Family Feud, Mark Goodson (executive producer), Howard Felsher (producer) (ABC)
- ☐ *Password Plus*, Robert Sherman (producer) (NBC)

The Price Is Right, Frank Wayne (executive producer), Barbara Hunter, Phillip Wayne (co-producers) (CBS)

Wheel of Fortune, Nancy Jones (producer) (NBC)

OUTSTANDING VARIETY SERIES

Emmy to executive producer(s) and producer(s)

The John Davidson Show, Frank Brill (executive producer), Vince Calandra (producer) (Syndicated)

The Merv Show, Peter Barsocchini (producer) (Syndicated)
- ☐ *The Regis Philbin Show*, E.V. DiMassa Jr. and Fred Tatashore (producers) (NBC)

OUTSTANDING HOST OR HOSTESS IN A GAME OR AUDIENCE PARTICIPATION SHOW
- ☐ Bob Barker, *The Price Is Right* (CBS)

Bill Cullen, *Blockbusters* (NBC)

Richard Dawson, *Family Feud* (ABC)

OUTSTANDING HOST OR HOSTESS IN A VARIETY SERIES
- ☐ Merv Griffin, *The Merv Show* (Syndicated)

Mike Douglas, *The Mike Douglas Show* (Syndicated)

OUTSTANDING TALK OR SERVICE SERIES

Emmy to executive producer(s) and producer(s)

Louis Rukeyser's Business Journal, Paul Galan, Dick Hubert (executive producers), Graig Fisher (producer) (Syndicated)

Donahue, Richard Mincer (executive producer), Patricia McMillen (senior producer), Darlene Hayes and Sheri Singer (producers) (Syndicated)
- ☐ *The Richard Simmons Show*, Woody Fraser (executive producer), Nora Fraser (producer) (Syndicated)

Hour Magazine, Martin M. Berman (executive producer), Steve Clements (producer) (Syndicated)

OUTSTANDING HOST OR HOSTESS IN A TALK OR SERVICE SERIES
- ☐ Phil Donahue, *Donahue* (Syndicated)

Gary Collins, *Hour Magazine* (Syndicated)

OUTSTANDING WRITING FOR A DAYTIME DRAMA SERIES

Agnes Nixon, Wisner Washam, Jack Wood, Mary K. Wells, Clarice Blackburn, Lorraine Broderick, Cynthia Benjamin, John Saffron and Elizabeth Wallace, *All My Children* (ABC)

Henry Slesar and Lois Kibbee, *The Edge of Night* (ABC)
- ☐ Douglas Marland, Nancy Franklin, Patricia Mulcahey, Gene Palumbo and Frank Salisbury, *The Guiding Light* (CBS)

Sam Hall, Peggy O'Shea, Don Wallace, Lanie Bertram, Fred Corke and S. Michael Schnessel, *One Life to Live* (ABC)

OUTSTANDING DIRECTION FOR A DAYTIME DRAMA SERIES

Larry Auerbach, Jack Coffey, Sherrel Hoffman and Jorn Winther, *All My Children* (ABC)

Richard Pepperman and John Sedwick, *The Edge of Night* (ABC)
- ☐ Marlena Laird, Alan Pultz and Phillip Sogard, *General Hospital* (ABC)

Norman Hall, Peter Miner and David Pressman, *One Life to Live* (ABC)

OUTSTANDING CHILDREN'S ENTERTAINMENT SERIES

Emmy to executive producer(s) and producer(s)

ABC Weekend Specials, Robert Chenault (executive producer), Joe Ruby and Ken Spears (producers) (ABC)
- ☐ *Captain Kangaroo*, Robert Keeshan (executive producer), Joel Kosofsky (producer) (CBS)

OUTSTANDING PERFORMER IN CHILDREN'S PROGRAMMING

Mike Farrell, *The Body Human: Becoming a Man* (Role: Host) (CBS)
☐ Bob Keeshan, *Captain Kangaroo Show* (Role: Host) (CBS)
Rita Moreno, *Orphans, Waifs and Wards, CBS Library* (Role: Mirelli, the Gypsy) (CBS)
Cicely Tyson, *The Body Human: Becoming a Woman* (Role: Hostess) (CBS)

OUTSTANDING CHILDREN'S ENTERTAINMENT SPECIALS

Emmy to executive producer(s) and producer(s)

"Me and Mr. Stenner," *CBS Afternoon Playhouse*, Paul Freeman (producer), June 2, 1981 (CBS)
☐ "Starstruck," *ABC Afterschool Special*, Diana Kerew (executive producer), Patrick McCormick (producer), October 14, 1981 (ABC)

OUTSTANDING INDIVIDUAL DIRECTION IN CHILDREN'S PROGRAMMING

For a single episode of a series or for a special program

Jeff Bleckner, "Daddy, I'm Their Mama Now," *ABC Afterschool Special*, March 3, 1982 (ABC)
Jim Hirschfeld, *Captain Kangaroo Show*, February 8, 1982 (CBS)
☐ Arthur Allan Seidelman, "She Drinks a Little," *ABC Afterschool Special*, September 23, 1981 (ABC)

OUTSTANDING WRITING FOR CHILDREN'S PROGRAMMING

☐ Paul W. Cooper, "She Drinks a Little," *ABC Afterschool Special*, September 23, 1981 (ABC)
Robert E. Fuisz M.D., *The Body Human: Becoming a Woman*, October 27, 1981 (CBS)
Norman Stiles, Sara Compton, Tom Dunsmuir, Judy Freugberg, Tony Geiss, John Glines, Emily Kingsley, David Korr, Luis Santeiro, Ray Sipherd and Joe Bailey, *Sesame Street*, November 23, 1981 (PBS)

OUTSTANDING CHILDREN'S INFORMATIONAL/INSTRUCTIONAL SERIES

Emmy to executive producer(s) and producer(s)

Kids are People Too, Marilyn Olin (executive producer), Laura Schrock (producer) (ABC)
☐ *30 Minutes*, Joel Heller (executive producer), Madeline Amgott, John Block, Jo Ann Caplin, Vern Diamond, Nancy Duffy, Carolyn Kreskey, Irene Molnar, Susan Mills,

Robert Rubin, Martin Smith, Patti Obrow White (producers) (CBS)
Sesame Street, Dulcy Singer (executive producer), Lisa Simon (producer) (PBS)

OUTSTANDING INFORMATIONAL/ INSTRUCTIONAL PROGRAMMING— SHORT FORMAT

Emmy to executive producer(s) and producer(s)

ASK NBC News, Lester Crystal (executive producer), Beryl Pfizer (producer) (NBC)
Betcha Don't Know, Jim Benjamin, Chiz Schultz (executive producers), Bob Glover (producer) (NBC)
☐ *In the News*, Joel Heller (executive producer), Walter Lister (producer) (CBS)

OUTSTANDING CHILDREN'S INFORMATIONAL/INSTRUCTIONAL SPECIAL

The Body Human: Becoming a Man, Thomas W. Moore (executive producer), Alfred R. Kelman and Robert E. Fuisz M.D. (producer), Nancy Smith (co-producer) (CBS)
The Body Human: Becoming a Woman, Thomas W. Moore (executive producer), Alfred R. Kelman and Robert E. Fuisz, M.D. (producer), Nancy Smith (co-producer) (CBS)
☐ *Kathy*, Kier Cline and Barry Teicher (producers) (PBS)

OUTSTANDING MUSIC COMPOSITION/DIRECTION IN CHILDREN'S PROGRAMMING

For a single episode or a series or for a special program

Christopher Cerf, David Conner, Norman Stiles (composers), *Sesame Street*, December 18, 1981 (PBS)
☐ Eliot Lawrence (composer/director), "The Unforgiveable Secret," *ABC Afterschool Special*, February 10, 1982 (ABC)

OUTSTANDING CINEMATOGRAPHY IN CHILDREN'S PROGRAMMING

For a single episode of a series or for a special program

Hanania Baer, "Daddy, I'm Their Mama Now," *ABC Afterschool Special*, March 3, 1982 (ABC)
☐ Tom Hurwitz, "Horsemen of Inner Mongolia," *Big Blue Marble*, November 14, 1981 (Syndicated)
Don Lenzer, *The Body Human: Becoming a Woman*, October 27, 1981 (CBS)

OUTSTANDING FILM EDITING IN CHILDREN'S PROGRAMMING

Robert Eisenhardt, *The Body Human: Becoming a Woman*, October 27, 1981 (CBS)
☐ Peter Hammer, Allen Kirkpatrick, "Horsemen of Inner Mongolia," *Big Blue Marble*, November 14, 1981 (Syndicated)
Gloria Whittemore, "My Mother Was Never a Kid," *ABC Afterschool Special*, March 18, 1981 (ABC)

OUTSTANDING INDIVIDUAL DIRECTION FOR A TALK OR SERVICE SERIES

For a single episode

☐ Ron Weiner, *Donahue*, January 21, 1982 (Syndicated)
Glen Swanson, *Hour Magazine*, January 11, 1982 (Syndicated)

OUTSTANDING INDIVIDUAL DIRECTION FOR A GAME OR AUDIENCE PARTICIPATION SHOW

For a single episode

☐ Paul Alter, *Family Feud*, May 29, 1981 (ABC)
Dick Carson, *Wheel of Fortune*, March 3, 1982 (NBC)

OUTSTANDING ACHIEVEMENT IN TECHNICAL EXCELLENCE FOR A DAYTIME DRAMA SERIES

For the entire series. Emmys to individual team members

☐ Joseph Solomito, Howard Zweig (technical directors), Diana Wenman, Jean Dadario, Barbara Martin Simmons (associate directors), Lawrence Hammond, Robert Ambrico, Larry Strack, Vincent Senatore, Jay Kenn, Trevor Thompson (electronic cameramen), Len Walas (senior video engineer), Al Lemanski, Charles Eisen (audio engineers), Roger Haenelt (video tape editor), Barbara Wood (sound effects engineer), *All My Children* (ABC)
John Cochran, David Smith (technical directors), Ritch Kenney, John Rago, James Angel, Barry Kirstein, Jack Denton, David Banks, Jan Lowry, Blair White, Dale Walsh, Carol Wetovich, William Scott, D.J. Diomedes, Sal Folino, Bud Holland (electronic cameramen), Sam Potter, Victor Bagdadi (senior video engineers), Robert Miller, Zoli Osaze (senior audio engineers), Hal Alexander, George Thompson (associate directors), Bob Lanham, Jose Galvez, Jack Moody (videotape editors), Ralph Waldo Emerson III (special effects engineer), *General Hospital* (ABC)

☐ Indicates winner

OUTSTANDING ACHIEVEMENT IN DESIGN EXCELLENCE FOR A DAYTIME DRAMA SERIES

For the entire series. Emmy to individual team members

John Pitts (scenic designer), William Itkin, Donna Larson, Donald Gavitt (lighting directors), Carol Luiken (costume designer), Sylvia Lawrence, Scott Hersch (makeup designers), Marie Angeripka, Richard Green (hair designers), Teri Smith (music director), Sid Ramin, Irving Robbin (music composers), Hy Bley (graphic designer), *All My Children* (ABC)

☐ James Ellingwood (art director), Mercer Barrows (set decorator), Grant Velie, Thomas Markle, John Zak (lighting directors), Jim O'Daniel (costume designer), P.K. Cole, Vikki McCarter, Diane Lewis (makeup designers), Katherine Kotarakos, Debbie Holmes (hair designers), Dominic Missinger, Jill Farren Phelps (music directors), Charles Paul (music composer), *General Hospital* (ABC)

Sy Tomashoff (scenic designer), John Connolly, Dennis Size (lighting directors), Alex Tolken (costume designer), James Cola, Tracy Kelly McNevin (makeup designers), John Keith Quinn, John Delaat (hair designers), Sybil Weinberger (music director), *Ryan's Hope* (ABC)

OUTSTANDING INDIVIDUAL DIRECTION FOR A VARIETY SERIES, FOR A SINGLE EPISODE

Dick Carson, "The Merv Griffin Show in Paris," *The Merv Show*, November 10, 1981 (Syndicated)

☐ Barry Glazer, *American Bandstand*, April 18, 1981 (ABC)

PLEASE NOTE: ALL THE FOLLOWING ARE EMMY AWARD "AREAS," WHICH MEANS THAT THERE WAS A POSSIBILITY OF ONE AWARD, MORE THAN ONE AWARD, OR NO AWARD

OUTSTANDING INDIVIDUAL ACHIEVEMENT IN THE COVERAGE OF SPECIAL EVENTS—DIRECTING

Dick Schneider, *Macy's Thanksgiving Day Parade*, November 26, 1981 (NBC)

OUTSTANDING INDIVIDUAL ACHIEVEMENT IN THE COVERAGE OF SPECIAL EVENTS—TECHNICAL DIRECTION/ELECTRONIC CAMERA

Terry Rohnke (technical director), Tom Dezendorf, Vincent Dipietro, Carol Eckett, Eric Eisenstein, Barry Frischer, Bill Goetz, Steve Gonzalez,

Dave Hagen, John Hillyer, Jim Johnson, Gene Martin, Don Mulvaney, Al Roberts (electronic camera), *Macy's Thandsgiving Day Parade*, November 26, 1981 (NBC)

OUTSTANDING INDIVIDUAL ACHIEVEMENT IN THE COVERAGE OF SPECIAL EVENTS—MUSIC COMPOSITION/DIRECTION

Milton Delugg (composer/director), *Macy's Thanksgiving Day Parade*, November 26, 1981 (NBC)

Walter Levinsky (composer/director), *The Eighth Annual Emmy Awards for Daytime Programming*, May 21, 1981 (ABC)

OUTSTANDING PROGRAM ACHIEVEMENT IN THE COVERAGE OF SPECIAL EVENTS

For programs presented as live coverage, not covered by the news division. Emmy to executive producer(s) and producer(s)

Macy's Thanksgiving Day Parade, Dick Schneider (producer), November 26, 1981 (NBC)

The Eighth Annual Emmy Awards for Daytime Programming, William Carruthers (executive producer), Joel Stein (producer), May 21, 1981 (ABC)

SPECIAL CLASSIFICATION OF OUTSTANDING PROGRAM ACHIEVEMENT

For programs which are so unique and different that they do not fall into any other category or area. Emmy to executive producer(s) and producer(s)

☐ *FYI*, Yanna Kroyt Brandt (producer), Mary Ann Donahue (co-producer) (ABC)

The Body Human: The Loving Process—Men, Thomas W. Moore (executive producer), Alfred R. Kelman and Robert E. Fuisz, M.D. (producers) (CBS)

The Body Human: The Loving Process—Women, Thomas W. Moore (executive producer), Alfred R. Kelman and Robert E. Fuisz, M.D. (producers) (CBS)

SPECIAL CLASSIFICATION OF OUTSTANDING INDIVIDUAL ACHIEVEMENT—PERFORMERS

Hal Linden, *FYI* (Role: Host) (ABC)

SPECIAL CLASSIFICATION OF OUTSTANDING INDIVIDUAL ACHIEVEMENT—WRITING

☐ Elaine Meryl Brown, Betty Cornfeld, Mary Ann Donahue, Joe Gustaitis, Robin Westen, *FYI* (ABC)

Bernard N. Eismann, *The Body Human: The Loving Process— Women* (CBS)

SPECIAL CLASSIFICATION OF OUTSTANDING INDIVIDUAL ACHIEVEMENT—DIRECTING

Charles A. Bangert and Alfred R. Kelman, *The Body Human: The Loving Process—Men* (CBS)

Michael Gargiulo, *FYI* (ABC)

☐ Alfred R. Kelman, *The Body Human: The Loving Process—Women* (CBS)

OUTSTANDING ACHIEVEMENT IN RELIGIOUS PROGRAMMING SPECIALS

Emmy to executive producer(s) and producer(s)

Harry Chapin's Cotton Patch, Helen Marmor (executive producer), Stanley Losak (producer), February 28, 1982 (NBC)

What Shall We Do About the Children, Helen Marmor (executive producer), Stanley Losak (producer), September 27, 1982 (NBC)

OUTSTANDING ACHIEVEMENT IN RELIGIOUS PROGRAMMING— SERIES

Emmy to executive producer(s) and producer(s)

Directions, Sid Darion (executive producer), Della E. Lowe (producer) (ABC)

☐ *Insight*, Ellwood Kieser (executive producer), Mike Rhodes and Terry Sweeny (producers) (Syndicated)

OUTSTANDING INDIVIDUAL ACHIEVEMENT IN RELIGIOUS PROGRAMMING—PERFORMERS

Steve Allen, *Wait Till We're 65* (Role: Host), December 13, 1981 (NBC)

Edwin Newman, *Ambassadors of Hope* (Role: Moderator), May 3, 1981 (NBC)

OUTSTANDING INDIVIDUAL ACHIEVEMENT IN ANY AREA OF CREATIVE TECHNICAL CRAFTS— TECHNICAL DIRECTION/ ELECTRONIC CAMERAWORK

☐ Sanford Bell, Hal Classon (technical directors) Remote: Kent Falls State Park, Danbury, Connecticut, *The Guiding Light*, August 20–25, 1981 (CBS)

Frank Florio, Malachy G. Wienges (technical directors), Remote: Canary Island, Spain, *The Guiding Light*, November 4–December 17, 1981 (CBS)

Lawrence Hammond, Nicholas Hutak and Thomas Woods (electronic camera) Remote: Switzerland, *All My Children*, February 11, 19, 22, 1982 (ABC)

William H. Pope, (electronic camera) Remote: Luke and Laura's Wedding, *General Hospital*, November 15–16, 1981 (ABC)

OUTSTANDING ACHIEVEMENT IN ANY AREA OF CREATIVE TECHNICAL CRAFTS—ASSOCIATE DIRECTION/VIDEOTAPE EDITING
Nick Giordano, Lou Torino (videotape editors), Shelly Curtis (associate director) Remote: Luke and Laura's Wedding, *General Hospital*, November 15–16, 1981 (ABC)

OUTSTANDING ACHIEVEMENT IN ANY AREA OF CREATIVE TECHNICAL CRAFTS— CINEMATOGRAPHY
Chuck Levey, *The Body Human: The Loving Process – Men*. November 10 and 11, 1981. (CBS)

OUTSTANDING ACHIEVEMENT IN ANY AREA OF CREATIVE TECHNICAL CRAFTS—FILM EDITING
C. Bartz, *The Body Human: The Loving Process – Women*, November 3 & 4, 1981 (CBS)
Charlotte Grossman, *The Body Human: The Loving Process—Men*, November 10 and 11, 1981 (CBS)

OUTSTANDING ACHIEVEMENT IN ANY AREA OF CREATIVE TECHNICAL CRAFTS—ART DIRECTION/SCENIC DESIGN/SET DECORATION
☐ Bob Keene, Griff Lambert (art directors), *The Richard Simmons Show*, November 26, 1981 (Syndicated)
Jack McAdam, Kate Murphy (art directors), *The John Davidson Show*, December 14, 1981 (Syndicated)

OUTSTANDING ACHIEVEMENT IN ANY AREA OF CREATIVE TECHNICAL CRAFTS—LIGHTING DIRECTION
☐ Everett Melosh Remote: Gallery Basement, *One Life to Live*, December 30, 1981 (ABC)
James Tetlaw Remote: Switzerland, *All My Children*, February 11–15, 1982 (ABC)

OUTSTANDING ACHIEVEMENT IN ANY AREA OF CREATIVE TECHNICAL CRAFTS—COSTUME DESIGN
☐ Nancy Simmons, *The Richard Simmons Show* (Syndicated)

☐ Indicates winner

OUTSTANDING ACHIEVEMENT IN ANY AREA OF CREATIVE TECHNICAL CRAFTS—GRAPHIC DESIGN
Stas Pyka, *Louis Rukeyser's Business Journal*, February 13, 1982 (Syndicated)

OUTSTANDING INDIVIDUAL ACHIEVEMENT IN CHILDREN'S PROGRAMMING—TECHNICAL DIRECTION/ELECTRONIC CAMERAWORK
James Angerame (technical director), "An Orchestra Is a Team, Too!," *CBS Festival of the Lively Arts for Young People*, October 4, 1981 (CBS)
Frank Florio (technical director), "Orphans, Waifs and Wards," *CBS Library*, November 26, 1981 (CBS)

OUTSTANDING INDIVIDUAL ACHIEVEMENT IN CHILDREN'S PROGRAMMING—ART DIRECTION/ SCENIC DESIGN/SET DECORATION
☐ Claude Bonniere (art director), "My Mother was Never a Kid," *ABC Afterschool Special*, March 18, 1981 (ABC)
Cary White (art director), "Daddy, I'm Their Mama Now," *ABC Afterschool Special*, March 3, 1982 (ABC)

OUTSTANDING INDIVIDUAL ACHIEVEMENT IN CHILDREN'S AUDIO
☐ Steven J. Palecek (tape sound recordist), "An Orchestra Is a Team, Too!," *CBS Festival of the Lively Arts for Young People*, October 4, 1981 (CBS)

OUTSTANDING ACHIEVEMENT IN CHILDREN'S PROGRAMMING— LIGHTING DIRECTION
Randy Nordstrom, *Sesame Street* #1623, January 27, 1982 (PBS)

OUTSTANDING ACHIEVEMENT IN CHILDREN'S PROGRAMMING— COSTUME DESIGN
Jean Blackburn, "She Drinks a Little," *ABC Afterschool Special*, September 23, 1981 (ABC)
Alfred E. Lehman, "Billy Bixby and the Adventures of a Young Magician," *CBS Festival of the Lively Arts for Young People*, May 5, 1981 (CBS)
Delphine White, "My Mother Was Never a Kid," *ABC Afterschool Special*, March 18, 1981 (ABC)

OUTSTANDING INDIVIDUAL ACHIEVEMENT IN CHILDREN'S PROGRAMMING—MAKE-UP AND HAIR DESIGN
Nancy Ferguson (makeup designer), "She Drinks a Little," *ABC*

Afterschool Special, September 23, 1981 (ABC)
Shonagh Jabour (makeup designer), "My Mother Was Never a Kid," *ABC Afterschool Special*, March 18, 1981 (ABC)
☐ Judi Cooper Sealy (hair designer), "My Mother Was Never a Kid," *ABC Afterschool Special*, March 18, 1981 (ABC)

OUTSTANDING INDIVIDUAL ACHIEVEMENT IN CHILDREN'S PROGRAMMING—GRAPHIC DESIGN
☐ Ray Favata, Michael J. Smollin (graphic designers) Opening Animation, *The Great Space Coaster*—93, October 9, 1981 (Syndicated)
Lou Palisano, *An Orchestra is a Team, Too! CBS Festival of the Lively Arts for Young People*, October 4, 1981 (CBS)

News and Documentary Awards

FOR PROGRAMS OUTSTANDING COVERAGE OF A SINGLE BREAKING NEWS STORY
"Washington Monument Siege," *Nightline*, William Lord (executive producer), Stuart Schwartz, Tom Yellin (senior producers), Ted Koppel (anchorman), December 8, 1982 (ABC)
☐ "Disaster on the Potomac," *Nightline*, William Lord (executive producer), Stuart Schwartz (senior producer), Ted Koppel (anchorman), January 13, 1982 (ABC)
"Brezhnev Death," *Nightline*, William Lord (executive producer), Stuart Schwartz, Tom Yellin, Bill Moore (senior producers), John Martin, Barry Serafin, Carl Bernstein (reporters/correspondents), November 11, 1982 (ABC)

FOR SEGMENTS OUTSTANDING COVERAGE OF A SINGLE BREAKING NEWS STORY
"Amerasians Come Home," *CBS Evening News with DAn Rather*, Rita Braver (producer), Bruce Morton (reporter/correspondent), September 30, 1982 (CBS)
☐ "New Mexico's Yates Oil Company," *CBS Evening News with Dan Rather*, Steve Kroft (producer), Steve Kroft (reporter/correspondent), November 8, 1982 (CBS)
☐ "Personal Note/Beirut," *ABC World News Tonight*, John Boylan (producer), Peter Jennings (reporter/correspondent), August 2, 1982 (ABC)

"Heart Treatment," *World News Tonight*, Sally Holm (producer), George Strait (reporter/correspondent), January 11, 1982 (ABC)

☐ "Linda Down's Marathon," *World News This Morning*, Fred Wymore (producer), Fred Wymore (reporter/correspondent), October 25, 1982 (ABC)

FOR PROGRAMS OUTSTANDING COVERAGE OF A CONTINUING NEWS STORY

Small Business Failures, Kenneth Witty (producer), Robert MacNeil, Jim Lehrer, Charlayne Hunter-Gault, Joe Quinlan (reporters/correspondents), June 4, 1982 (PBS)

☐ *The Paterson Project*, Howard Husock (producer), Scott Simon (reporter/correspondent), October 27, 1982 (PBS)

"The War in Lebanon," *Nightline*, Stuart Schwartz (senior producer), Ted Koppel (anchorman), September 20, 1982 (ABC)

FOR SEGMENTS OUTSTANDING COVERAGE OF A CONTINUING NEWS STORY

El Salvador Reports, Jon Alpert (producer), Jon Alpert (reporter/correspondent), December 2, 18, 21, 1981; March 24; April 2, 1982 (NBC)

"You're Under Arrest," *60 Minutes*, James W. Jackson (producer), Harry Reasoner (reporter/correspondent), January 3, 1982 (CBS)

"To Serve and To Share," *Sunday Morning*, Larry Doyle (producer), David Culhane (reporter/correspondent), October 10, 1982 (CBS)

"Honor Thy Children," *60 Minutes*, Barry Lando (producer), Mike Wallace (reporter/correspondent), September 19, 1982 (CBS)

"Sad New Faces," *Sunday Morning*, Skip Brown (producer), Barry Petersen (reporter/correspondent), July 22, 1982 (CBS)

"Watergate: An Untold Story," *20/20*, Gordon Greedman (producer), Tom Jarriel (reporter/correspondent), June 17, 1982 (ABC)

☐ "Coverage of American Unemployment," *CBS Evening News with Dan Rather*, Rita Braver, David Browning, Quentin Neufeld, Terry Martin, David Gelber (producers), Bruce Morton, Jerry Bowen, Terry Drinkwater, Ed Rabel, Ray Brady (correspondents), October 13, March 4, April 6, August 19, December 3, 1982 (CBS)

☐ Indicates winner

FOR PROGRAMS OUTSTANDING BACKGROUND/ANALYSIS OF A SINGLE CURRENT STORY

Roses in December, Ana Carrigan, Bernard Stone (producers), David Meyer (co-producer), Ana Carrigan (reporter/correspondent), July 23, 1982 (PBS)

What Price Clean Air?, Robert Richter (producer), Robert Richter (reporter/correspondent), August, 13, 1982 (PBS)

Books Under Fire, Arnold Bennett, Grady Watts Jr. (producers), September 10, 1982 (PBS)

☐ *Chrysler: Once Upon a Time... and Now*, Shelby Newhouse (producer), Andrew Kokas (reporter/correspondent), July 2, 1982 (PBS)

☐ *From the Ashes... Nicaragua Today*, Helena Solberg Ladd, Glen Silber (producers), April 7, 1982 (PBS)

The Falklands/Oh What a Sorry War, Bill Brown (producer), Lloyd Dobyns (reporter/correspondent), June 26, 1982 (NBC)

☐ "Guatemala," *CBS Reports*, Martin Smith (producer), Ed Rabel (reporter/correspondent), September 1, 1982 (CBS)

Our Friends the Germans, Catherine Olian (producer), Bill Moyers (reporter/correspondent), June 9, 1982 (CBS)

"People Like Us," *CBS Reports*, Judy Towers Reemtsma (producer), Bill Moyers (reporter/correspondent), April 21, 1982 (CBS)

The American-Israeli Connection, Philip Burton Jr. (producer), Andrew Lack (reporter/correspondent), June 17, 1982 (CBS)

Fortress Israel, Judy Crichton (producer), Marshall Frady (reporter/correspondent), April 21, 1982 (ABC)

The Money Masters, Pamela Hill (executive producer), Richard Richter (senior producer), Richard Gerdau (producer & director), Dan Cordtz, Michael Connor (correspondents), December 12, 1982 (ABC)

"Drug Smuggling," *Nightline*, Herbert Holmes (producer), David Garcia (reporter/correspondent), August 30, 1982 (ABC)

FOR SEGMENTS OUTSTANDING BACKGROUND/ANALYSIS OF A SINGLE CURRENT STORY

"Saving the Smallest Humans," *NBC Nightly News*, Mary Laurence Flynn (producer), Robert Bazell (reporter/correspondent), January 11–12, 1982 (NBC)

☐ "College Sports, The Money Game," *NBC Nightly News*, ML Flynn, Paul Hazzard, Barry Hohlfelder (producers), Bob Jamieson (co-producer), Bob Jamieson (reporter/correspondent), March, 23, 24, 25, 1982 (NBC)

"Title V," *CBS Evening News*, Elena Mannes (producer), Bill Moyers (reporter/correspondent), September 7, 1982 (CBS)

"Homeless," *60 Minutes*, Joel Bernstein (producer), Ed Bradley (reporter/correspondent), January 10, 1982 (CBS)

"The Alaska Gas Pipeline Rip-Off," *CBS Evening News*, Martin Koughan (producer), Bill Moyers (reporter/correspondent), December 8, 1981 (CBS)

"... To Tax, Value, Judge," *Sunday Morning*, James Houtrides, Robert Northshield (producers), David Culhane (reporter/correspondent), May 23, 1982 (CBS)

"Inside Iran," *CBS Evening News with Dan Rather*, Harry Radcliffe (producer), Tom Fenton (reporter/correspondent), November 22, 1982 (CBS)

"Crime and Punishment," *20/20*, Peter W. Kunhardt (producer), Tom Jarriel (reporter/correspondent), May 20, 1982 (ABC)

"Under the Israeli Thumb," *20/20*, Stanhope Gould (producer), Tom Jarriel (reporter/correspondent), February 4, 1982 (ABC)

☐ " 'Tanks'—A Few Minutes with Andy Rooney," *60 Minutes*, Jane Bradford (producer), Andrew A. Rooney (reporter/correspondent), March 7, 1982 (CBS)

"Candle in the Dark," *60 Minutes*, Al Wasserman (producer), Harry Reasoner (reporter/correspondent), February 7, 1982 (CBS)

☐ "Welcome to Palermo," *60 Minutes*, William McClure (producer), Harry Reasoner (reporter/correspondent), December 31, 1981 (CBS)

"Martina," *60 Minutes*, Grace Deikhaus (producer), Mike Wallace (reporter/correspondent), December 26, 1982 (CBS)

"Life After Doomsday?" *20/20*, Danny Schechter, Bill Lichtenstein (producers), Tom Jarriel (reporter/correspondent), April 15, 1982 (ABC)

"Out Atomic Legacy: A Special Report on Nuclear Testing and Its Effects," *Good Morning America*, Thomas A. Ryder, Steve Fox (producers), Steve Fox (reporter/correspondent) (ABC)

"Lest We Forget," *60 Minutes*, Tom Bettag (producer), Morley Safer (reporter/correspondent), October 10, 1982 (CBS)

FOR PROGRAMS OUTSTANDING INTERVIEW/INTERVIEWER(S)

☐ "The Palestinian Viewpoint," *Nightline*, Bob Jordan (producer), Ted Koppel (interviewer), March 16, 1982 (ABC)

☐ *The Barbara Walters Special*, Beth Polson (producer), Barbara Walters (interviewer), December 24, 1982 (ABC)

The Lawmakers, Gregg Ramshaw (producer), Paul Duke, Linda Wertheimer (interviewers), September 9, 1982 (PBS)

News in the Network, Joe Russin (producer), Hodding Carter (interviewer), April 23, 1982 (PBS)

Absence of Malice: Fact or Fiction, Lois Cuniff (producer), Joe Russin (co-producer), Hodding Carter (interviewer), January 22, 1982 (PBS)

FOR SEGMENTS OUTSTANDING INTERVIEW/INTERVIEWER(S)

"Jacobo Timerman," *60 Minutes*, Barry Lando (producer), Mike Wallace (interviewer), December 5, 1982 (CBS)

"Richard Nixon," *CBS Morning News*, Shirley Wershba (producer), Diane Sawyer (interviewer), June 1, 2, 3, 4, 1982 (CBS)

"Best in the West," *60 Minutes*, Steve Glauber (producer), Ed Bradley (interviewer), January 24, 1982 (CBS)

☐ "In the Belly of the Beast," *60 Minutes*, Monika Jensen (producer), Ed Bradley (interviewer), April 18, 1982 (CBS)

FOR PROGRAMS SPECIAL CLASSIFICATION FOR OUTSTANDING PROGRAM ACHIEVEMENT

Fire on the Water, Robert Hillmann (producer), September 17, 1982 (PBS)

"Central America in Revolt," *CBS Reports*, Martin Smith, Craig Leake, Barry Lando (producers), March 20, 1982 (CBS)

Eye on the Media: Business and the Press, Mary Drayne (producer), December 25, 1982 (CBS)

☐ *Vietnam Requiem*, Jonas McCord, William Couturie (producers), July 15, 1982 (ABC)

FOR SEGMENTS SPECIAL CLASSIFICATION FOR OUTSTANDING PROGRAM ACHIEVEMENT

DPT Vaccine, Lea Thompson, Stewart Dan (producers), April 20, 1982 (NBC)

"Hot Property," *NBC Magazine*, Robert Lissit (producer), Douglas Kiker (reporter), November 20, 1981 (NBC)

"Getting Straight," *NBC Magazine*, Beth Polson (producer), Jack Perkins (reporter), April 24, 1982 (NBC)

Survival in America, Steve Friedman (producer), Jon Alpert (correspondent), June 2, March 1, December 28, August 5, December 11, 1982 (NBC)

☐ "It Didn't Have to Happen," *60 Minutes*, Norman Gorin (producer), Morley Safer (correspondent), February 28, 1982 (CBS)

FOR PROGRAMS OUTSTANDING INFORMATIONAL, CULTURAL OR HISTORICAL PROGRAMMING

☐ *Here's Looking at You, Kid*, Andrew McGuire (producer), November 9, 1982 (PBS)

Japan: Myths Behind the Miracle, Malcolm Clarke (producer), Jim Laurie (reporter/correspondent), December 31, 1981 (ABC)

☐ *The Taj Mahal*, James M. Messenger, Stuart Sillery (producers), September 27, 1982 (PBS)

"Egypt: Quest For Eternity," *National Geographic Special*, Miriam Birch (producer), Richard Basehart (reporter/correspondent), February 3, 1982 (PBS)

Don't Touch that Dial, Julian Krainin (producer), Morley Safer (reporter/correspondent), December 23, 1982 (CBS)

Middletown: The Campaign, Peter Davis (producer), March 24, 1982 (PBS)

"Jean Seberg," *The Mike Wallace Profiles*, Harry Moses (producer), Mike Wallace (reporter/correspondent), November 17, 1981 (CBS)

A Portrait of Maya Angelou, David Grubin (producer), Bill Moyers (reporter/correspondent), January 8, 1982 (PBS)

FOR SEGMENTS OUTSTANDING INFORMATIONAL, CULTURAL OR HISTORICAL PROGRAMMING

"Nathan Milstein," *Sunday Morning*, Alan Harper (producer), Eugenia Zukerman (reporter/correspondent), November 28, 1982 (CBS)

"Salta Province," *NBC Nightly News*, Charles McLean (producer), Dan Molina (reporter/correspondent), May 28, 1982 (NBC)

"Cuban Missile Crisis 1962," *Nightline*, William Lord (executive producer), Robert J. LeDonne, Jay LaMonica (producers), Jay LaMonica (reporter), October 22, 1982 (ABC)

"A Regal Way with Words," *Sunday Morning*, Kathy Sulkes (producer), Charles Kuralt (reporter/correspondent), January 17, 1982 (CBS)

☐ "Eclectic: A Profile of Quincy Jones," *Sunday Morning*, Brett Alexander (producer), Billy Taylor (reporter/correspondent), August 1, 1982 (CBS)

"Some of Our Airmen Are Home," *Sunday Morning*, James Houtrides (producer), John Blackstone (reporter/correspondent), October 31, 1982 (CBS)

"Musician Plays the Glasses," *CBS Evening News with Dan Rather*, Charles Kuralt (producer), Charles Kuralt (reporter/correspondent), July 8, 1982 (CBS)

"Keith Haring, Subway Artist," *CBS Evening News with Dan Rather*, Peter Schweitzer (producer), Charles Osgood (reporter/correspondent), October 20, 1982 (CBS)

"Monkey See," *Walter Cronkite's Universe*, Ruth Streeter (producer), Walter Cronkite (reporter/correspondent), June 8, 1982 (CBS)

☐ "Sid Caesar," *20/20*, Betsy Osha (producer), Dick Schaap (reporter/correspondent), December 23, 1982 (ABC)

Orbis (Distant Visions), Richard R. Clark (producer), Geraldo Rivera (reporter/correspondent), June 17, 1982 (ABC)

"Dreams Do Come True," *20/20*, Rolfe Tessem (producer), Steve Fox (reporter/correspondent), June 24, 1982 (ABC)

"The Best Movie Ever Made (Casablanca)," *60 Minutes*, Drew Phillips (producer), Harry Reasoner (reporter/correspondent), November 15, 1981 (CBS)

"Name Brands, No Brands," *20/20*, Bob Lange (producer), John Stossel (reporter/correspondent), November 11, 1982 (ABC)

"Tina Turner," *20/20*, Chip Kurzenhauser, Danny Schechter (producers), Steve Fox (reporter/correspondent), February 4, 1982 (ABC)

"Sex & Scents," *20/20*, Bob Lange (producer), John Stossel (reporter/correspondent), December 17, 1981 (ABC)

"Great Arctic Adventure," *20/20*, Richard R. Clark (producer), Garaldo Rivera (reporter/correspondent), May 6, 1982 (ABC)

☐ "Lena," *60 Minutes*, Jeanne Solomon (producer), Ed Bradley (reporter/correspondent), December 27, 1981 (CBS)

☐ Indicates winner

"Moment of Crisis: The Munich Massacre," *20/20*, Judith Moses (producer), Tom Jarriel (reporter/correspondent), September 2, 1982 (ABC)

FOR PROGRAMS OUTSTANDING INVESTIGATIVE JOURNALISM

☐ *Frank Terpil: Confessions of a Dangerous Man*, David Fanning (producer), Antony Thomas (reporter/correspondent), January 11, 1982 (PBS)

The Man who Shot the Pope: A Study in Terrorism, Anthony Potter, (executive producer), Marvin Kalb, Bill McLaughlin (reporters/correspondents), September 21, 1982 (NBC)

J. Edgar Hoover, Tom Bywaters (producer), Marshall Frady (correspondent), Pat Lynch (reporter), June 3, 1982 (ABC)

Rain of Terror, Steve Singer (producer), Bill Redeker (reporter/correspondent), December 21, 1981 (ABC)

FOR SEGMENTS OUTSTANDING INVESTIGATIVE JOURNALISM

"Land Hustles," *NBC Nightly News*, Robert Windrem, Charles Collins (co-producers), Mark Nykanen (reporter/correspondent), October 11, December 7, 1982 (NBC)

"Small Town," *60 Minutes*, William H. Wilson (producer), Mike Wallace (reporter/correspondent), October 2, 1982 (CBS)

☐ "The Nazi Connection," *60 Minutes*, Ira Rosen (producer), Mike Wallace (reporter/correspondent), May 16, 1982 (CBS)

"The Trouble with Temik," *CBS Evening News with Dan Rather*, Elizabeth Karnes, Martin Koughan (producers), Bill Moyers (reporter/correspondent), August 5–6, 1982 (CBS)

"Mariel Cubans Spread Crime," *CBS Evening News with Dan Rather*, Andrew Heyward (producer), Bernard Goldberg (reporter/correspondent), February 2, 1982 (CBS)

"Formaldehyde: The Danger Within," *20/20*, Peter Lance, Bill Lichtenstein (co-producers), Peter Lance (reporter/correspondent), February 4, 1982 (CBS)

☐ "Air Force Surgeon," *60 Minutes*, Tom Bettag (producer), Morley Safer (reporter/correspondent), January 24, 1982 (CBS)

"Apache: The Tank Chopper," *20/20*, Jeff Diamond, Jay LaMonica (producers), Tom Jarriel (reporter/

☐ Indicates winner

correspondent), August 12, 1982 (ABC)

Throwaway Kids, Bill Lichtenstein, Karen Burnes (co-producers), Sylvia Chase (reporter/correspondent), December 16, 1982 (ABC)

"Deadly Chemicals: Deadly Oil," *20/20*, Janice Tomlin (producer), Peter Lance (reporter/correspondent), December 17, 1981 (ABC)

"Willowbrook—Ten Years After," *20/20*, Kerry Smith (producer), Geraldo Rivera (reporter/correspondent), January 7, 1982 (ABC)

FOR OUTSTANDING INDIVIDUAL ACHIEVEMENT IN NEWS AND DOCUMENTARY PROGRAMMING

Writers

Joseph Angier, Jim Laurie, Malcolm Clarke, "Japan: Myths Behind the Miracle," *ABC News Closeup*, December 31, 1981 (ABC)

David Brinkley, Richard Threlkeld, Ann Black, Richard Gerdau, Tom Priestly, Kathy Slobogin, Steve Zousmer, Peter Jennings, Richard O'Regan, *FDR*, January 29, 1982 (ABC)

Perry Wolff, *Pablo Picasso: A Retrospective, Once in a Lifetime*, March 27, 1982 (CBS)

Catherine Olian, Perry Wolff, *Our Friends the Germans*, June 2, 1982 (CBS)

☐ Sharon Blair Brysac, Perry Wolff, *Juilliard and Beyond: A Life in Music*, July 24, 1982 (CBS)

☐ Charles Kuralt, "Cicada Invasion," *CBS Evening News with Dan Rather*, June 18, 1982 (CBS)

Morley Safer, "Don't Touch That Dial," *CBS Reports*, December 23, 1982 (CBS)

Marvin Kalb, Bill McLaughlin, Anthony Potter, *The Man Who Shot the Pope: A Study in Terrorism*, September 21, 1982 (NBC)

Miriam Birch, "Egypt: Quest For Eternity," *National Geographic Special*, February 3, 1982 (PBS)

Theodore Strauss, *Hillary's Challenge: Race to the Sky*, May 12, 1982 (PBS)

Shelby Newhouse, Dan McCosh, Andrew Kokas, Ed Baumeister, *Chrysler: Once Upon a Time. . . and Now*, July 2, 1982 (PBS)

James Lipscomb, "Polar Bear Alert," *National Geographic Special*, March 10, 1982 (PBS)

Nicolas Noxon, "The Sharks," *National Geographic Special*, January 13, 1982 (PBS)

Directors

Paul R. Fine, *The Saving of the President*, April 1, 1982 (ABC)

Anthony Potter, *The Man Who Shot the Pope: A Study in Terrorism*, September 21, 1982 (NBC)

☐ Jonas McCord, William Couturie, *Vietnam Requiem*, July 15, 1982 (ABC)

☐ Bill Jersey, *Children of Violence*, August 20, 1982 (PBS)

Malcolm Clarke, *Japan: Myths Behind the Miracle*, December 31, 1982 (ABC)

Catherine Olian, *Our Friends the Germans*, June 9, 1982 (CBS)

Antony Thomas, *Frank Terpil: Confessions of a Dangerous Man*, January 11, 1982 (PBS)

Tom Cohen, *Family Business*, April 14, 1982 (PBS)

Cinematographers

Ted Haimes, *Vietnam Requiem*, July 15, 1982 (ABC)

Jeri Sopanen, Robert Leacock, Victor Losick, *Juilliard and Beyond: A Life in Music*, July 24, 1982 (CBS)

☐ Norris Brock, "Egypt: Quest for Eternity," *National Geographic Special*, February 3, 1982 (PBS)

John Else, *Palace of Delights*, March 7, 1982 (PBS)

☐ Arnie Serlin, *The Taj Mahal*, September 27, 1982 (PBS)

☐ James Deckard, James Lipscomb, "Polar Bear Alert," *National Geographic Special*, March 10, 1982 (PBS)

Bill Bacon, Bill Sweney, Garry Russell, Lisle Hebert, Joel Bennett, Ron Eagle, Peter Pilafian, George Lukens Jr., Larry Golden, Bo Boudart, Wolfgang Bayer, *Alaska: Story of a Dream*, April 24, 1982 (Syndicated)

Electronic camerapersons: Videographers

Chester Panzer (videographer), "Plane Disaster," *World News Tonight & Nighline*, January 13–14, 1982 (ABC)

Alan Debos (cameraperson), "Ceasefire," *CBS Evening News with Dan Rather*, June 11, 1982 (CBS)

Jon Alpert (electronic camera), *El Salvador Reports*, December 2, 18, 21, 1982, March 23, April 2, 1982 (NBC)

Erik P. Prentnieks (videographer), "Palace of Gold," *CBS Morning News* (CBS)

☐ David Green (cameraperson), "Guerillas in Usulatan," *CBS Evening News with Dan Rather*, March 29, 1982 (CBS)

John Landi, Fabrice Moussust (electronic camera), *Assassination of*

Anwar Sadat, October 21, 1982 (ABC)

Izzy Bleckman (cameraperson), "Woman Flyer," *CBS Evening News with Dan Rather*, November 3, 1982 (CBS)

☐ George Fridrick (electronic camera), *Along Route 30*, August 4–25, 1982 (NBC)

Steve Byerly (electronic camera), *Epidemic: Why Your Kid is on Drugs*, February 12, 1982 (Syndicated)

Associate directors

Larry M. Weisman, "Throwaway Kids," *20/20*, December 16, 1982 (ABC)

☐ Consuelo Gonzalez, Neill Phillipson, *FDR*, January 29, 1982 (ABC)

Stanley Spiro, "Barbara Mandrell," *20/20*, October 21, 1982 (ABC)

Sound

Gary Bourgeois (re-recording artist), Leo Chaloukian (sound director), Kenneth Love (production mixer), Elliot Tyson (re-recording mixer), Troy S. Porter (sound recordist), "Egypt: Quest for Eternity," *National Geographic Special*, February 3, 1982 (PBS)

Vincent R. Perry (audio engineer), Paul H. Glazer (audio engineer), "Nuclear Arms: What to Do About Them," *Nightline*, April 22, 1982 (ABC)

Alan Berliner (sound editor), *Battleships*, December 23, 1982 (ABC)

Larry Loewinger, Francis Daniel, Michael Lonsdale, Peter Miller, David Moshlak (sound recordists), *Juilliard and Beyond: A Life in Music*, July 24, 1982 (CBS)

☐ Tom Cohen (sound recordist), *The Campaign*, March 24, 1982 (PBS)

Peter Miller (sound recordist), Lee Dichter (film sound mixer & re-recording mixer), *The Family Business*, November 14, 1982 (PBS)

Emily Paine (audio sweetening–sound editor), *Community of Praise*, April 7, 1982 (PBS)

☐ Simon Jones, Mike Lonsdale, David Moshlak, Kim Ornitz (film recordists), Rudy Boyer, Ken Blaylock, Jack Gray, Bill Barry, Jeffrey Cree (video recordists), Jonathan M. Lory, Tom Glazner, Kathleen Jalbert, Morley Lang, Don V. Scholtes, Hesh Q. Yarmark (audio post production), Roy Carch, Al James (post production–sound effects), Alan Berliner, Seymour Hymowitz, Frank Martinez, Robert Sandbo (sound editors), Tom Fleischman (re-recording mixer), *FDR*, January 29, 1982 (ABC)

☐ Indicates winner

Videotape editors, videotape post production editors

☐ Edward Buda, Ruth Iwano (videotape editors), Chris Von Benge, Kathy Black, Dean Irwin, Catherine Isabella, Michael Siegel, Carla Morgenstern (videotape post production editors), *FDR*, January 29, 1982 (ABC)

Dean Irwin (videotape post production editor), "Throwaway Kids," *20/20*, December 16, 1982 (ABC)

Tim Gibney (videotape editor), "Saving the Smallest Humans," *NBC Nightly News*, January 11, 1982 (NBC)

John Matejko (videotape editor), *Viewpoint*, August 12, 1982 (ABC)

Mitch Udoff (videotape editor), "Vacation Dream, Vacation Nightmare/Time Sharing Condos," *20/20*, April 8, 1982 (ABC)

Robert Shattuck, Susan Ottalini (videotape editors), "Central America in Revolt," *El Salvador Segment*, March 20, 1982 (CBS)

☐ Thomas Micklas (videotape editor), "Ice Sculptor," *CBS Evening News with Dan Rather*, July 2, 1982 (CBS)

Bernard Altman (videotape editor), "Monkey See," *Walter Cronkite's Universe*, June 8, 1982 (CBS)

☐ Anthony Ciccimarro, Kathy Hardigan, Don Orrico, Matty Powers (videotape editors), *The Man Who Shot the Pope: A Study in Terrorism*, September 21, 1982 (NBC)

John J. Godfrey, Jon Alpert (videotape editors), *El Salvador Reports*, December 2, 18, 21, 1981, March 23, April 2, 1982 (NBC)

Arden Rynew, Caren Myers, Bruce Ochmanek (videotape editors), *Artists in the Lab*, November 5, 1982 (PBS)

Thomas C. Goodwin, Bill Coyle, Gerardine Wurzburg (videotape editors), *We Dig Coal, A Portrait of Three Women*, June 25, 1982 (PBS)

Film editors and film post production editors

Rob Wallace (film editor), "Merle Haggard, A Profile," *20/20*, February 11, 1982 (ABC)

Lisa Shreve (film editor), "Recipes for Life," *20/20*, November 25, 1982 (ABC)

☐ James Flanagan, Nils Rasmussen, William Longo, Walter Essenfeld (film editors), *FRD*, January 29, 1982 (ABC)

Nancy Kanter (film editor), *Japan: Myths Behind the Miracle*, December 31, 1981 (ABC)

☐ Nobuko Oganesoff (film editor), *Juilliard and Beyond: A Life in Music*, July 24, 1982 (CBS)

☐ Bob Brady (film editor), *The Campaign*, March 24, 1982 (PBS)

Tom Haneke (film editor), *Second Time Around*, April 21, 1982 (PBS)

Barry Nye (film editor), *National Geographic Special*, January 13, 1982 (PBS)

Michael Chandler (film editor), *Fire on the Water*, September 17, 1982 (PBS)

Stephen Stept (film editor), *Vietnam Requiem*, July 15, 1982 (ABC)

John J. Martin, Elizabeth Ackerman, Otto Pfeffer (film editors), *Bataan: The Forgotten Hell*, December 5, 1982 (NBC)

Graphic designers, electronic graphics, graphic illustrators, electronic & film animation

Bruce Soloway (graphic designer), *World News Tonight* (ABC)

☐ Rebecca Allen (graphic designer), *Walter Cronkite's Universe*, June 8, 1982 (CBS)

Gerry Andrea (graphic illustrator), "The Falklands," *World News Tonight*, May 3, 5, 12, 26, 1982 (ABC)

☐ David Millman (graphic artist illustrator), "The Cuban Missile Crisis," *Nightline*, October 22, 1982 (ABC)

Tony Cacioppo (art director), Gary Petrini, Joanne Dominick (graphic designers), *CBS Evening News with Dan Rather*, February 22, 1982 (CBS)

Barbara M. Incognito, Madeline DeVito (electronic animators), *20/20*, November 25, 1982 (ABC)

Music composers

Ken Melville, Dawn Atkinson (music composers), *Vietnam Requiem*, July 15, 1982 (ABC)

☐ James G. Pirie (music composer, conductor), *Alaska: Story of a Dream*, April 24, 1982 (Syndicated)

Chris Adelman (composer), *Battleship*, December 23, 1982 (ABC)

Sports Awards

OUTSTANDING LIVE SPORTS SERIES

Emmy(s) to executive producer(s) and producer(s) and director(s):

ABC's NFL Monday Night Football, Roone Arledge (executive producer), Bob Goodrich (producer), Chet Forte (director), September 7–December 21, 1981 (ABC)

NCAA Football, Roone Arledge (executive producer), Chuck Howard (senior producer), Curt Gowdy Jr., Ken Wolfe and Eleanor Sanger Riger (producers), Andy Sidaris, Jim Jennett, Larry Kamm and Ken Fouts (directors), September 5–December 19, 1981 (ABC)

☐ *NFL Football*, Terry O'Neil (executive producer), Charles H. Milton III (senior producer), Michael Burks, David Dinkins Jr., Sherman Eagan, John Faratis, Ed Goren, Bob Rowe, Perry Smith, Jim Silman, Robert D. Stenner and David Winner (producers), Peter Bleckner, Larry Cavolina, Joe Carolie, Bob Dailey, Bob Dunphy, Robert Fishman, Sandy Grossman, Andy Kindle, John McDonough, Jim Silman and Tony Verna (directors), September 6, 1981–January 10, 1982 (CBS)

The NBA on CBS, James F. Harrington (executive producer), Michael Burks and Robert Stenner (producers), Sandy Grossman and Tony Verna (directors), October 30, 1981–June 8, 1982 (CBS)

NCAA Basketball, Kevin O'Malley (executive producer), Rick Sharp, David Dinkins Jr., George Veras, David Michaels, Dave Blatt, Bob Mansbach, Jean Harper and Ted Shaker (directors), November 28, 1982–March 7, 1982 (CBS)

OUTSTANDING EDITED SPORTS SERIES/ANTHOLOGIES

Emmy(s) to executive producer(s) and producer(s) and director(s):
ABC Sportsbeat, August 30, 1981–July 11, 1982 (ABC)
CBS Sports Saturday, Terry O'Neil (executive producer), David Winner and Jean Harper (coordinating producers), Michael Arnold, Michael Burks, David Blatt, Bill Brown, David Dinkins Jr., Bob Dekas, Sherman Eagan, John Faratzis, Robert Fishman, Daniel H. Forer, Ed Goren, Dan Lauck, Robert Matina, David Michaels, Charles H. Milton III, Bob Mansbach, Pat O'Brien, David Segal, Craig Silver, Perry Smith, Robert D. Stenner, George Veras, John Tesh and Mark Wolff (producers), Peter Bleckner, Cathy Barreto, Larry Cavolina, Bob Dailey, Richard Drake, Bob Dekas, Bob Dunphy, Robert Fishman, Sandy Grossman, Andy Kindle, John McDonough, Arthur Struck, Patti Tuite (directors) (CBS)
The NFL Today, Ted Shaker (producer), Daniel H. Forer (coordinating producer), Sherman Eagan, Jean Harper, Andy Kindle, Bob Mansbach and David Winner (feature producers), Richard Drake (director) (CBS)
☐ *The American Sportsman*, Roone Arledge (executive producer), John Wilcox (series producer), Chris Carmody (coordinating producer),

Bob Nixon and Curt Gowdy (producers), April 4–July 11, 1982 (ABC)
ABC's Wide World of Sports, Roone Arledge (executive producer), Dennis Lewin (coordinating producer), Chuck Howard, Mike Pearl, Jeff Ruhe, Brice Weisman, Doug Wilson, Eleanor Sanger Riger, Ken Wolfe, Bob Goodrich, Curt Gowdy Jr. and Carol Lehti (producers), Craig Janoff, Larry Kamm, Ralph Abraham, Jim Jennett, Joe Aceti, Rogert Goodman, Ken Fouts, Chet Forte and Andy Sidaris (directors), July 16, 1981–July 11, 1982 (ABC)

OUTSTANDING INDIVIDUAL ACHIEVEMENT IN SPORTS PROGRAMMING

This is an "Area" where there is a possibility of one award, more than one award or no award. Nominations in this "Area" include:

Associate directors:
John C. McDonough Jr., *The Super Bowl XVI Close*—"The Winner Takes It All," January 24, 1982 (CBS)
☐ Jeff Cohan, Bob Lanning and Ned Simon, *1982 Indianapolis "500"*, May 30, 1982 (ABC)
Cathy Barreto, Steve Deliapiatra and Danny Lew, *Superbowl Today*, January 24, 1982 (CBS)
Dick Buffinton, Kathy Cook, Vince Dedario, John Delisa, Jack Graham, Ben Harvey, Bob Hersh, Paul Hutchinson, Peter Lasser, Dennis Mazzocco, Brian McCullough, Norman Samet, Toni Slotkin and Meg Streeter, *ABC's Wide World of Sports*, July 18, 1981–July 11, 1982 (ABC)
Bob Dekas and Patti Tuite, *NCAA Basketball Championship Final—Feature Endpiece*, March 29, 1982 (CBS)
Joel Aronowitz, Cathy Barreto, Bob Coffey, Steve Deliapiatra, Stan Faer, Bob Halper, Beth Hermelin, Barry Hicks, Dave Kaplan, Danny Lew, Muffy McDonough, Howard Miller, Gady Reinhold, Roni Scherman Stein and Tommy Simpson, *NFL Today* (CBS)

OUTSTANDING INDIVIDUAL ACHIEVEMENT IN SPORTS PROGRAMMING

This is an "Area" where there is a possibility of one award, more than one award or no award. Nomination in this "Area" include:

Cinematographers:
Joseph H. Klimovitz, *A Celebration of Sports*, July 2, 1982 (NBC)

James W. Grau and James W. Barry Grau, *Super Bowl XVI Time Capsule, Program Titles*, January 24, 1982 (CBS)
☐ Ernie Ernst, Hand McElwee, Howard Neef, Steve Sabol and Phil Tuckett, *Sports Illustrated: A Series for Television*, May 26, 1982 (Syndicated)
Paul Bellinger, Edgar Boyles, Jon Hammond, Peter Henning, Mike Hoover, D'Arcy Marsh, Stanton Waterman and Jonathan Wright, *The American Sportsman*, April 4–July 11, 1982 (ABC)

Videotape/Film editors
☐ Steve Purcell, *Reggie Jackson*, May 23, 1982 (CBS)
Rasha Drachkovitch, *Legend of Larry Mahan*, "Greatest Sports Legends," April 1, 1982 (Syndicated)
Joe Drake, Bob Hickson and George Joanitis, *NCAA Basketball Championship Final*, "Feature Endpiece," March 29, 1982 (CBS)
Phil Tuckett, *NFL Weekly Magazine*, "Week 14," December 7, 1981 (Syndicated)
Scott L. Rader, *The Spirit of Competition*—"A Celebration of Sports Segment: 'Secretariat' ", July 3, 1982 (NBC)
Mario Bucich, Ken McIlwaine, Bob Klug, Andy Praskai, Bruce Schechter, Tony Tocci and Mike Kostel, *This Week in Baseball*, "Episode #615," July 10, 1982 (Syndicated)
Jimmy Alkins, Steve Babb, Art Buckner, Curtis Campbell, Summer Demar, David Diaz, Joe Drake, Tom Durkin, Bob Enrione, Al Golly, Sig Gordon, Frank Hodnett, Bernie Jacobs, Mike Kayatta, Andy Klein, Gary Kozak, Jeff Laing, Mark Lioczko, George Magee, Walter Matwichuk, John Mayer, Gary Mazzacca, Henry Menusan, Jesse Michnick, George Palmisano, Fred Pinciaro, Jeff Ringel, Charlotte Robinson, Brian Rosner, Joe Scholnick, Allan Segal, Tom Ferrante, Larry Shellenberger, Bill Vandennoort, Jim Warden, John Wells and Bill Zizza, *NFL Today* (CBS)
Andrew Squicciarini, *The Heisman Trophy Award '81*, December 5, 1981 (Syndicated)
Rich Domich, Ken McIlwaine, Bruce Schechter and Tony Tocci, *The Baseball Bunch*, " #4," March 22, 1982 (Syndicated)
Angelo Bernarducci, Richard Rossi, Anthony Scandiffio, Ted Winterburn and Anthony Zaccaro, *The American*

☐ Indicates winner

Sportsman, April 4–July 11, 1982 (ABC)

☐ Martin Bell, Joe Clark, Finbar Collins, Ron Feszchur, Chuck Gardner, Bruce Giaraffe, Clare Gilmour, Hector Kicilian, M. Schencman, Mike Seigel, Mike Wenig and Tom White, *Indianapolis "500"*, May 29, 1982 (ABC)

Finbar Collins, Clare Gilmour, Phil Jackson, Dale Sills, Art Volk, Paul Weber, Mike Wenig and Tom White, *U.S. Open*, June 20, 1982 (ABC)

Martin Bell, Ron Feschur, Chuck Gardner, Lou Rende, Winston Sadoo and Ed Zlotnik, *NFL Football*, December 17, 1981 (ABC)

Nat Chomsky, Bruce Giarraffa, Hector Kicelian, Merritt Roesser, Mike Wenig and Tom White, *Sugar Bowl*, January 1, 1982 (ABC)

OUTSTANDING EDITED SPORTS SPECIAL

Emmy(s) to executive producer(s) and producer(s) and director(s):

☐ *1982 Indianapolis "500"*, Roone Arledge (executive producer), Mike Pearl and Bob Goodrich (producers), Chuck Howard (coordinating producer), Larry Kamm and Roger Goodman (directors), May 30, 1982 (ABC)

1981 National Sports Festival, Roone Arledge (executive producer), Chuck Howard (senior producer), Mike Pearl, Doug Wilson, Jeff Ruhe, Peter Lasser and Ned Simon (producers), Joe Aceti, Andy Sidaris, Larry Kamm, John DeLisa and Ken Fouts (directors), July 26–August 2, 1981 (ABC)

WBC World Heavyweight Championship, "Larry Holmes vs. Gerry Cooney," Roone Arledge (executive producer), Chet Forte (producer), Joe Aceti (director), June 25, 1982 (ABC)

OUTSTANDING EDITED SPORTS SPECIAL

Emmy(s) to executive producer(s) and producer(s) and director(s)

The Super Bowl Today, Ted Shaker (producer), Daniel H. Forer (co-ord feature producer), Andy Kindle, Dan Lauck and David Winner (segment producers), David Michaels and George Veras (remote producers), Richard Drake (director), Jim Silman and Patti Tuite (remote directors), January 24, 1982 (CBS)

The Heisman Trophy Award '81, Michael Lepiner (executive producer), Cappy Petrash Greenspan (senior producer), Nancy Beffa (producer), Bud Greenspan

☐ Indicates winner

(director), December 5, 1981 (Syndicated)

OUTSTANDING INDIVIDUAL ACHIEVEMENT IN SPORTS PROGRAMMING

This is an "Area" where there is a possibility of one award, more than one award or no award.
Nominations in this 'Area' include:

Technical/Engineering supervisors:

Bill Freiberger, Geoff Felger, Verne Kerrick, Rick Okulski, Frank Quitoni and Harold Robbins, *New York Marathon*, October 25, 1981 (ABC)

Jesse Rineer and Joseph Tier, *U.S. Open Tennis* (CBS)

Louis Scannapieco and Arthur Tinn, *1982 Masters* (CBS)

Robert Armbruster, *U.S. Open*, June 20, 1982 (ABC)

Verne Kerrick, *Indianapolis "500"*, May 29, 1982 (ABC)

Loren Coltran, *NFL Football*, December 17, 1981 (ABC)

Robert Armbruster, *Sugar Bowl*, January 1, 1982 (ABC)

☐ James Patterson, Jesse Rineer, Louis Scanna, Arthur Tinn and Philip Wilson, *Super Bowl XVI*, January 24, 1982 (CBS)

Walter Pile and Arthur Tinn, *1982 Daytona 500* (CBS)

Doug Fleetham, *NCAA Basketball Championship Final*, March 29, 1982 (CBS)

Lighting directors:

Nat Albin, *Indianapolis "500"*, May 29, 1982 (ABC)

Tony Azzolino, *Sugar Bowl*, January 1, 1982 (ABC)

Technical directors, electronic camerapersons, senior video operators:

Charles D'Onofrio and Robert Vernum (technical directors), Edward Ambrosini, William Berridge, Louis Leger and Robert Pieringer (senior video operators), James McCarthy, George Rothweiler, Patti McBride, Frank McSpedon, Hans Singer, Roy Jackson, Rick Blane, George Klimcsak, Barry Drago, Alfred Loreto, Neil McCaffrey, Robert Jamieson, William Murphy and Herman Lang (electronic camerapersons), *U.S. Open Tennis* (CBS)

Sanford Bell and Charles D'Onofrio (technical directors), William Berridge, Thomas DeLilla, D. Ohrlich, Frank Fosso and Louis Leger (senior video operators), J. Vicenz, R. Skorup, James Murphy, Rich Blane, Joseph Sokota, John Lincoln, Walter Soucy, Frank McSpedon, Stanley Gould, Dennis

McBride, Barry Drago, G. Erickson, D. Finca, David C. Graham, Robert Jamieson, Neil McCaffrey, G. Naeder, George Rothweiler, James McCarthy, Alfred Loreto, Herman Lang, George Klimcsak, Hans Singer, Nicholas Lauria, Gordon Sweeney and William Murphy (electronic camerpersons), *1982 Masters* (CBS)

☐ Sanford Bell, Robert Brown and Anthony Hlavaty (technical directors), Anthony Filippi, Robert Pieringer and Robert Squittieri (senior video operators), James Murphy, Neil McCaffrey, Steve Gorsuch, Herman Lang, Barry Drago, Joseph Sokota, Frank McSpedon, George Rothweiler, Jeffrey Pollack, George Naeder, George Graffeo, Thomas McCarthy, Sigmund Meyers, Sol Bress, James McCarthy, Hans Singer and Walter Soucy (electronic camerapersons), *1982 Daytona 500* (CBS)

James Anngerame, Stanford Bell, Charles D'Onofrio, George Naeder, Robert Brown and Gilbert Miller (technical directors), Anthony Filippi, Robert Hanford, Robert Squittieri, Thomas DeLilla, William Berridge, David Fruitman, Frank Florio, Nancy Stevenson, Ronald Resch and Robert Pieringer (senior video operators), Rick Blane, Steve Gorsuch, Michael Denny, George Klimcsak, Gordon Sweeney, Joseph Vicenz, David Finch, James Murphy, George Rothweiler, Robert Jamieson, Robert Welch, Walter Soucy, Gorm Erickson, Frank McSpedon, Herman Lang, Stanley Gould, Hal Hoffman, John Lincoln, John Brennan, David Dorsett, Michael English, Jeffrey Pollack, Al Loreto, Dennis McBride, Gene Savitt, Neil McCaffrey, Joseph Sokota, Sig Meyer and Anthony Cucurullo (electronic camerapersons), *Super Bowl XVI*, January 24, 1982 (CBS)

Bob Brown and Steve Cunningham (technical directors), Lou Leger and Frank Florio (senior video operators), John Aguirre, Sol Bress, Barry Drago, Steve Gorsuch, Bob Jameison, Herman Lang, Tom McCarthy, Jeff Pollack, Joe Sakota, Paul Sherwood, Joe Vicens and Bob Welsh (electronic camerpersons), *NCAA Basketball Championship Final*, March 29, 1982 (CBS)

Sal Nigita (technical director), Scotty McCarthy (senior video operator), Lenny Basile, Mario Ciarlo, Steve Gonzales, Barry Frischer, Dave Hagen, Roger Harbaugh, Tom

Hogan, James Johnson, George Loomis, John Pinto, Olonzo Roberts and Brian Russo (electronic camerapersons), *C.A.R.T. Michigan 500 Indy,* "Race Live," July 25, 1981 (NBC)

☐ John Allen (technical director), Mike Michales (senior video operator), John Morreale, Frank Melchiore, Diane Cates, John Dukewich, Evan Baker, Mike Freedman, Sal Folino, Warren Cress, Dan Langford and Dale Welsh (electronic camerapersons), *Sugar Bowl,* January 1, 1982 (ABC)

☐ Gene Affrunti, John Figer, Rich Gelber and Wink Gunther (technical directors), John Monteleone (senior video operator), Mort Levin, F. Merklein, J. Sapienza, A. Best, John Cordone, D. Spanos, George Montanez, D. Lamothe, Jack Cronin, J. Woodle, A. Demamos, R. Westline, J. Schafer, Tony Gambino, Kenneth Sanborn, R. Wolff, Phil Fontana, A. Peffer, R. Hammond, T. Mortellaro, Serf Menduina, W. Sullivan, R. Bernstein, S. Madjanski and J. Stefanoni (electronic camerapersons), *New York Marathon,* October 25, 1981 (ABC)

Joe Schiavo (technical director), Robert Greenseth (senior video operator), Frank Celecia, Joe Cotugno, A. DeRosa, Tom O'Connell, Gary Donatelli, Steve Nikifor, Jim Heneghan, Jack Savoy, Roy Hutchings, Steve Wolff, Jesse Kohn, Jack Dorfman and Andy Armentani (electronic camerapersons), *NFL Football,* December 17, 1981 (ABC)

☐ Wink Gunther and Chet Mazurek (technical directors), Cyril Tywang and Ken Amow (senior video operators), A. Peffer, W. Sullivan, Steve Nikifor, J. Morreale, R. Hammond, A. DeRosa, Joe Cotugno, Jesse Kohn, Andy Armentani, Jack Savoy, Gene Wood, Jack Dorfman, Tom O'Connell, Joe Stefanoni, Frank Melchiore, Mort Levin, Joe Sapienza, Serf Menduina, Gary Donatelli and Steve Wolff (electronic camerapersons), *Indianapolis "500",* May 29, 1981 (ABC)

Wink Gunther, Ernie Buttleman and Gary Larkins (technical directors), Mike Michaels, Robert Greenseth and Hugo Dilonardo (senior video operators), Joe Sapienza, Richie Westline, George Montanez, A. DeRosa, Andrew Armentani, Mort Levin, Joe Puleo, Serf Menduina, Tom Mortellaro, Greg Ciccone,

Steve Wolff, Jack Cronin, Gene Kelly, Jack Dorfman, Bob Bernstein, Jim Heneghan and J. Morreale (electronic camerapersons), *U.S. Open,* June 20, 1982 (ABC)

John Allen (technical director), Ken Amon (senior video operator), Warren Cress, Sal Folino, Don Langford, Evan Baker, Joseph Puleo, Mike Freedman, John V. Morreale, Frank Melchiorre and John Dukewich (electronic camerapersons), *NCAA Football,* January 1, 1982 (ABC)

Senior audio engineers

James J. Davis Jr., *NCAA Football,* January 1, 1982 (ABC)

Brian Wickham, *Spirit of Competition: A Celebration of Sports,* July 3, 1982 (NBC)

Jack Newman and Phil Spieller, *NFL Weekly Magazine/Week 14,* December 7, 1981 (Syndicated)

John Lory, *New York Marathon,* October 25, 1981 (ABC)

Jim Davis, *Sugar Bowl,* January 1, 1982 (ABC)

Jack Kestenbaum, *NFL Football,* December 17, 1981 (ABC)

Jim Davis, Jack Hughes and Jack Kelly, *Indianapolis "500",* May 29, 1981 (ABC)

☐ Jack Brandes, Jim Davis, Jack Hughes, Norm Kiernan and Morley Lang, *U.S. Open,* June 20, 1982 (ABC)

Jonathon Lory, Hesh Yarmark and Alan James, "The Ironman Endurance Triathalon," *ABC's Wide World of Sports,* February 21, 1982 (ABC)

Graphics

☐ Peggy Hughes, *NCAA College Football* (ABC)

☐ James W. Grau, *Super Bowl XVI Show Opening Title Sequences,* January 24, 1982 (CBS)

Eric Buonamassa and Joe Flynn, *The NFL Today,* November 29, 1981 (CBS)

Mark Howard, *ABC's NFL Monday Night Football,* September 7–December 21, 1981 (ABC)

Hy Bley and Roger Goodman, *1982 Indianapolis "500",* May 30, 1982 (ABC)

OUTSTANDING SPORTS PERSONALITY-ANALYST

Nelson Burton Jr. (ABC)
Dick Button (ABC)
☐ John Madden (CBS)
Dave Marr (ABC)
Billy Packer (CBS)

OUTSTANDING INDIVIDUAL ACHIEVEMENT IN SPORTS PROGRAMMING

This is an "Area" where there is a possibility of one award, more than one award or no award.
Nominations in this "Area" include:

Writing:

Mark Durand and Warner Fusselle, *This Week in Baseball,* "Episode #607," May 15, 1982 (Syndicated)

George Bell, *The American Sportsman,* April 4–July 11, 1982 (ABC)

Gary Cohen, Mark Durand and Mike Tollin, *The Baseball Bunch,* "Episode #204," March 22, 1982 (Syndicated)

John Mosedale, *The NFL Today,* October 11, 1981 (Syndicated)

☐ Steve Rotfeld, *The Legend of Jackie Robinson—Greatest Sports Legends,* April 1, 1982 (Syndicated)

Theodore Strauss, *Hillary's Challenge: Race to the Sky,* May 12, 1982 (PBS)

Steve Stern, *Super-Duper All-Star Bloopers,* July 13, 1982 (Syndicated)

Peter Benchley and Hank Whittemore, *The American Sportsman,* April 4–July 11, 1982 (ABC)

Bud Greenspan, *The Heisman Trophy Award '81,* December 5, 1981 (Syndicated)

Hal Fisher, *Once in a Lifetime,* October 13, 1981 (Syndicated)

Music:

☐ Jon Silbermann, *Super Bowl XVI Theme,* January 24, 1982 (CBS)

Bob Israel, *USA vs. the World,* January 31–April 25, 1982 (ABC)

SPECIAL CLASSIFICATION OF OUTSTANDING PROGRAM

This is an "Area" where there is a possibility of one award, more than one award or no award.

Program:

☐ *Reggie Jackson,* May 23, 1982 (CBS)

Ironman World Endurance Triathlon, Roone Arledge (executive producer), Dennis Lewin (coordinating producer), Brice Weisman (producer), Craig Janoff (director), February 21, 1982 (ABC)

Jockey Safety, Roone Arledge (executive producer), Maryann Grabavoy (producer), May 1, 1982 (ABC)

They Shoot Horses, Don't They, Robert Fishman (producer), May 22, 1982 (CBS)

Matters of Life and Death: Football in America, Carol Brandenberg (executive producer), Robert Carmichael (producer), May 14, 1982 (PBS)

☐ Indicates winner

□ *The Baseball Bunch*, Larry Parker
(executive producer), Jody Shapiro
and Gary Cohen (producers), March
22, 1982 (Syndicated)
□ *ABC Sportsbeat*, February 7, May 16,
June 27, 1982 (ABC)
Superman III, David Segal (producer),
December 19, 1982 (CBS)

SPECIAL CLASSIFICATION FOR INDIVIDUAL ACHIEVEMENT

**This is an "Area" where there is a
possibility of one award, more than
one award or no award.**

Individuals:

ABC Sports' On-Air Promotions, Amy
Sacks (producer), Joe Novello
(director), July 16, 1982–July 15,
1982 (ABC)
Clemson, Chuck Howard (senior
producer), Jeff Ruhe (producer), Jim
Lampley (reporter), November 28,
1981 (ABC)
New York City Marathon, Ken Wolfe
(producer), Craig Janoff (director),
October 25, 1981 (ABC)
□ *Racecam at the Daytona 500*, Jim
Harrington (executive producer),
Robert D. Stenner (producer),
Robert Fishman (director), Walter
Pile (field technical manager), John
Porter, Peter Larsson, David Curtis
(engineers), George Graffeo
(cameraman), February 14, 1982
(CBS)
Sports Promo—On the Road Again,
Douglas E. Towey, December, 1981
(CBS)
CBS Chalkboard, Terry O'Neil, January
2, 1982 (CBS)
The Baseball Bunch, Johnny Bench,
March 22, 1982 (Syndicated)
Legend of Jackie Robinson, Ken
Howard, April 1, 1982 (Syndicated)
NBC Sports Image Display, Paul
Hammons, May 23, 1982 (NBC)
This Week in Baseball, Mel Allen
(Syndicated)

OUTSTANDING SPORTS PERSONALITY-HOST
□ Jim McKay (ABC)
Keith Jackson (ABC)
Brent Musburger (CBS)
Al Michaels (ABC)
Pat Summerall (CBS)

OUTSTANDING LIVE SPORTS SPECIAL

**Emmy(s) to executive producer(s)
and producer(s) and director(s)**

1982 Kentucky Derby, Roone Arledge
(executive producer), Chuck Howard
(producer), Jim Jennett (director),
May 1, 1982 (ABC)
1982 U.S. Open, Roone Arledge
(executive producer), Chuck Howard

□ Indicates winner

(producer), Terry Jastrow, Jim
Jennett and Bob Goodrich
(directors), June 17–20, 1982 (ABC)
Super Bowl XVI, Charles H. Milton III
(senior producer), Terry O'Neil
(producer), Sandy Grossman
(director), January 24, 1982 (CBS)
□ *NCAA Basketball Championship Final*,
Kevin O'Malley (executive producer),
Rick Sharp (producer), Robert
Fishman (director), March 29, 1982
(CBS)
The Masters, Frank Chirkinian
(producer), Bob Dailey (director)
(CBS)

OUTSTANDING ACHIEVEMENT IN THE SCIENCE OF TELEVISION ENGINEERING
□ Bosch Fernseh
□ British Broadcasting Corporation,
Research Department
□ Arthur C. Clarke
□ Eastman Kodak Company
□ Fuji Photo Film Co., Ltd.
□ Rank Cintel Limited

1982/83

*(For programs aired between July 1,
1982 and June 30, 1983.
Entertainment and individual
achievement awards presented
September 25, 1983. Creative Arts
awards presented September 18,
1983. Daytime awards presented June
6, 1983 for programs aired between
March 6, 1982 and March 5, 1983.
News and Documentary awards
presented August 30, 1984. Sports
award presented November 30, 1983
for programs aired between July 16,
1982 and July 15 1983. Science
Engineering in Television award
presented September 12, 1983.)*

Prime Time Program Awards

OUTSTANDING DRAMA SERIES

**Emmy(s) to executive producer(s)
and producer(s):**
□ *Hill Street Blues*, Steven Bochco
(executive producer), Gregory Hoblit
(co-executive producer), Anthony
Yerkovich (supervising producer),
David Anspaugh, Scott Brazil
(producers) (NBC)
Cagney & Lacey, Barney Rosenzweig
(executive producer), Harry R.
Sherman, Richard M. Rosenbloom
(supervising producers), April Smith,
Joseph Stern, Terry Louise Fisher,
Steve Brown (producers) (CBS)

Fame, William Blinn (executive
producer), Mel Swope (producer)
(NBC)
Magnum, P.I., Donald P. Bellisario
(executive producer), Douglas
Green, Joel Rogosin (supervising
producers), Chas. Floyd Johnson
(producer), Rick Weaver, Reuben
Leder (co-producers) (CBS)
St. Elsewhere, Bruce Platrow
(executive producer), Mark Tinker,
John Masius, John Falsey, Joshua
Brand (producers) (NBC)

OUTSTANDING COMEDY SERIES

**Emmy(s) to executive producer(s)
and producer(s):**
□ *Cheers*, James Burrows, Glen Charles,
Les Charles (executive producers),
Ken Levine, David Isaacs (co-
producers) (NBC)
Buffalo Bill, Bernie Brillstein, Tom
Patchett, Jay Tarses (executive
producers), Dennis Klein, Carol Gary
(producers) (NBC)
*M*A*S*H*, Burt Metcalfe (executive
producer), John Rappaport
(supervising producer), Dan Wilcox,
Thad Mumford (producers) (CBS)
Newhart, Barry Kemp (executive
producer), Sheldon Bull (producer)
(CBS)
Taxi, James L. Brooks, Stan Daniels,
Ed. Weinberger (executive
producers), Ken Estin, Sam Simon,
Richard Sakai (producers) (NBC)

OUTSTANDING LIMITED SERIES

**Emmy(s) to executive producer(s)
and producer(s):**
□ *Nicholas Nickleby*, Colin Callender
(producer) (Syndicated)
Smiley's People, "Jonathan Powell,"
(producer) (Syndicated)
The Thorn Birds, David L. Wolper,
Edward Lewis (executive producers),
Stan Margulies (producer) (ABC)
*"To Serve Them All My Days,"
Masterpiece Theatre*, Ken
Riddington (producer) (PBS)
The Winds of War, Dan Curtis
(producer) (ABC)

OUTSTANDING VARIETY, MUSIC OR COMEDY PROGRAM

**For a special or a series. Emmy(s)
to executive producer(s),
producer(s) and star(s), if
applicable:**
□ *Motown 25: Yesterday, Today,
Forever*, Suzanne de Passe
(executive producer), Don Mischer,
Buz Kohan (producers), Suzanne
Coston (producer for Motown), May
16, 1983 (NBC)
*Kennedy Center Honors: A Celebration
of the Performing Arts*, George

Stevens Jr., Nick Vanoff (producers), December 25, 1982 (CBS)

SCTV Network, Andrew Alexander (senior executive producer), Andrew Alexander, Len Stuart, Jack E. Rhodes, Doug Holtby (executive producers), Patrick Whitley (supervising producer), Patrick Whitley, Nancy Geller, Don Novello (producers), Series (NBC)

The Tonight Show Starring Johnny Carson, Fred de Cordova (producer), Peter Lassally (co-producer), Johnny Carson (host), Series (NBC)

37th Annual Tony Awards, Alexander H. Cohen (executive producer), Hildy Parks (producer), Roy A. Somlyo (co-producer), June 5, 1983 (CBS)

OUTSTANDING CLASSICAL PROGRAM IN THE PERFORMING ARTS

For a special or a series. Emmy(s) to executive producer(s), producer(s) and star(s), if applicable:

☐ *Pavarotti in Philadelphia: La Boheme*, Margarett Anne Everitt (executive producer), Clemente D'Alessio (producer), Luciano Pavarotti (star), August 28, 1982 (PBS)

Dance in America, Jac Venza (executive producer), Judy Kinberg, Barbara Horgan (producers), Series (PBS)

In Concert at the Met: Price, Horne, Levine, Michael Bronson (executive producer), Clemente D'Alessio (producer), Leontyne Price, Marilyn Horne, James Levine (stars), December 4, 1983 (PBS)

Lincoln Center Special: Stravinsky and Balanchine—Genius Has a Birthday!, John Goberman, Barbara Horgan (producers), October 4, 1982 (PBS)

Wagner's Ring: The Bayreuth Centennial Production, Horant H. Hohlfeld (executive producer), David Griffiths (supervising producer), Dietrich von Watzdorf, Peter Windgassen (producers), Series (PBS)

OUTSTANDING DRAMA SPECIAL

Emmy(s) to executive producer(s) and producer(s):

☐ *Special Bulletin*, Don Ohlmeyer (executive producer), Marshall Herskovitz, Edward Zwick (producers), March 20, 1983 (NBC)

Little Gloria. . . Happy at Last, Edgar J. Scherick, Scott Rudin (executive producers), David Nicksay, Justine Heroux (producers), October 24–25, 1982 (NBC)

M.A.D.D.: Mothers Against Drunk Drivers, David Moessinger (executive

☐ Indicates winner

producer), Douglas Benton (supervising producer), Michael Braverman (producer), March 14, 1983 (NBC)

The Scarlet Pimpernel, Mark Shelmerdine (executive producer), David Conroy (producer), November 9, 1982 (CBS)

Who Will Love My Children?, Paula Levenback, Wendy Riche (producers), February 14, 1983 (ABC)

OUTSTANDING INFORMATIONAL SPECIAL

Emmy(s) to executive producer(s), producer(s) and host(s), if applicable:

☐ *The Body Human: The Living Code*, Thomas W. Moore (executive producer), Robert E. Fuisz, M.D., Alfred R. Kelman (producers), Charles A. Bangert, Franklin Getchell, Nancy Smith (co-producers), June 13, 1983 (CBS)

IBM Presents, I, Leonardo: A Journey of the Mind, Chandler Cowles, Helen Kristt Radin (executive producers), Lee R. Bobker (producer), April 26, 1983 (CBS)

King Penguin: Stranded Beyond the Falklands, Lord Aubrey Buxton (executive producer), Colin Willock (producer), June 22, 1983 (CBS)

The Making of "Gandhi": Mr. Attenborough and Mr. Gandhi, Jenny Barraclough (producer) (Syndicated)

Mario Lanza: The American Caruso, John Musilli, Stephan Chodorov (executive producers), Jo Ann G. Young (producer), March 18, 1983 (PBS)

OUTSTANDING INFORMATIONAL SERIES

Emmy(s) to executive producer(s), producer(s) and host(s), if applicable:

☐ *The Barbara Walters Specials*, Beth Polson (producer), Barbara Walters (host) (ABC)

Entertainment Tonight/Entertainment this Week, George Merlis, Jim Bellows (executive producers), Vin di Bona (producer), Bruce Cook (coordinating producer) (Syndicated)

Over Easy with Mary Martin & Jim Hartz, Richard Rector, Jules Power (executive producers), Ben Bayol, Janice Tunder (producers), Mary Martin, Jim Hartz (hosts) (PBS)

Real People, George Schlatter (executive producer), Bob Wynn (producer) (NBC)

Screenwriters/Word into Image, Terry Sanders, Freida Lee Mock (producers) (PBS)

OUTSTANDING ANIMATED PROGRAM

For a special or a series. Emmy(s) to executive producer(s) and producer(s):

☐ *Ziggy's Gift*, Lena Tabori (executive producer), Richard Williams, Tom Wilson, Lena Tabori (producers), December 1, 1982 (ABC)

Here Comes Garfield, Jay Poyner (executive producer), Lee Mendelson, Bill Melendez (producers), October 25, 1982 (CBS)

Is This Goodbye, Charlie Brown?, Lee Mendelson, Bill Melendez (producers), February 21, 1983 (CBS)

The Smurfs Christmas Special, Joseph Barbera, William Hanna (executive producers), Gerard Baldwin (producer), December 13, 1982 (NBC)

What Have We Learned, Charlie Brown?, Lee Mendelson (executive producer), Bill Melendez (producer), May 30, 1983 (CBS)

OUTSTANDING CHILDREN'S PROGRAM

For a special or a series. Emmy(s) to executive producer(s) and producer(s):

☐ *Big Bird in China*, Jon Stone (executive producer), David Liu, Kuo Bao-Xiang, Xu Ja-Cha (producers), May 29, 1983 (NBC)

Grandpa, Will You Run with Me?, Ken Ehrlich (producer), April 3, 1983 (NBC)

Skeezer, Bill McCutchen (executive producer), Lee Levinson (producer), December 27, 1982 (NBC)

The Snow Queen—A Skating Ballet, Gregory G. Harney (executive producer), Bernice Olenick (producer), December 6, 1982 (PBS)

Prime Time Performing Awards

OUTSTANDING LEAD ACTOR IN A COMEDY SERIES

For a continuing or single performance in a regular series:

☐ Judd Hirsch, *Taxi* (NBC)
Alan Alda, *M*A*S*H* (CBS)
Dabney Coleman, *Buffalo Bill* (NBC)
Ted Danson, *Cheers* (NBC)
Robert Guillaume, *Benson* (ABC)

OUTSTANDING LEAD ACTOR IN A DRAMA SERIES

For a continuing or single performance in a regular series:

☐ Ed Flanders, *St. Elsewhere* (NBC)
William Daniels, *St. Elsewhere* (NBC)
John Forsythe, *Dynasty* (ABC)
Tom Selleck, *Magnum, P.I.* (CBS)

Daniel J. Travanti, *Hill Street Blues* (NBC)

OUTSTANDING LEAD ACTOR IN A LIMITED SERIES OR A SPECIAL

For a continuing role in a limited series or for a single appearance in a limited series or a special:

☐ Tommy Lee Jones, *The Executioner's Song*, November 28 and 29, 1982 (NBC)
Robert Blake, *Blood Feud* (OPT)
Richard Chamberlain, *The Thorn Birds* (ABC)
Sir Alec Guinness, *Smiley's People* (Syndicated)
Roger Rees, *Nicholas Nickleby* (Syndicated)

OUTSTANDING LEAD ACTRESS IN A COMEDY SERIES

For a continuing or single performance in a regular series:

☐ Shelley Long, *Cheers* (NBC)
Nell Carter, *Gimme a Break!* (NBC)
Mariette Hartley, *Goodnight, Beantown* (CBS)
Swoosie Kurtz, *Love, Sidney* (NBC)
Rita Moreno, *9 to 5* (ABC)
Isabel Sanford, *The Jeffersons* (CBS)

OUTSTANDING LEAD ACTRESS IN A DRAMA SERIES

For a continuing or single performance in a regular series:

☐ Tyne Daly, *Cagney & Lacey* (CBS)
Debbie Allen, *Fame* (NBC)
Linda Evans, *Dynasty* (ABC)
Sharon Gless, *Cagney & Lacey* (CBS)
Veronica Hamel, *Hill Street Blues* (NBC)

OUTSTANDING LEAD ACTRESS IN A LIMITED SERIES OR A SPECIAL

For a continuing role in a limited series or for a single appearance in a limited series or a special:

☐ Barbara Stanwyck, *The Thorn Birds*—Part 1, March 27, 1983 (ABC)
Ann-Margret, *Who Will Love My Children?*, February 14, 1983 (ABC)
Rosanna Arquette, *The Executioner's Song*, November 28 and 29, 1982 (NBC)
Mariette Hartley, *M.A.D.D.: Mothers Against Drunk Drivers*, March 14, 1983 (NBC)
Angela Lansbury, *Little Gloria... Happy at Last*, October 24 and 25, 1982 (NBC)

OUTSTANDING SUPPORTING ACTOR IN A COMEDY, VARIETY OR MUSIC SERIES

For a continuing or single performance in a regular series:

☐ Christopher Lloyd, *Taxi* (NBC)
Nicholas Colasanto, *Cheers* (NBC)

☐ Indicates winner

Danny De Vito, *Taxi* (NBC)
Harry Morgan, *M*A*S*H* (CBS)
Eddie Murphy, *Saturday Night Live* (NBC)

OUTSTANDING SUPPORTING ACTOR IN A DRAMA SERIES

For a continuing or single performance in a regular series:

☐ James Coco, *St. Elsewhere*, "Cora and Arnie," November 23, 1982 (NBC)
Ed Begley Jr., *St. Elsewhere* (NBC)
Michael Conrad, *Hill Street Blues* (NBC)
Joe Spano, *Hill Street Blues* (NBC)
Bruce Weitz, *Hill Street Blues* (NBC)

OUTSTANDING SUPPORTING ACTOR IN A LIMITED SERIES OR A SPECIAL

For a continuing role in a limited series or for a single appearance in a limited series or a special:

☐ Richard Kiley, *The Thorn Birds*—Part 1, March 27, 1983 (ABC)
Ralph Bellamy, *The Winds of War* (ABC)
Bryan Brown, *The Thorn Birds* (ABC)
Christopher Plummer, *The Thorn Birds* (ABC)
David Threlfall, *Nicholas Nickleby* (Syndicated)

OUTSTANDING SUPPORTING ACTRESS IN A COMEDY, VARIETY OR MUSIC SERIES

For a continuing or single performance in a regular series:

☐ Carol Kane, *Taxi* (NBC)
Eileen Brennan, *Private Benjamin* (CBS)
Marla Gibbs, *The Jeffersons* (CBS)
Rhea Perlman, *Cheers* (NBC)
Loretta Swit, *M*A*S*H* (CBS)

OUTSTANDING SUPPORTING ACTRESS IN A DRAMA SERIES

For a continuing or single performance in a regular series:

☐ Doris Roberts, *St. Elsewhere*, "Cora and Arnie," November 23, 1982 (NBC)
Barbara Bosson, *Hill Street Blues* (NBC)
Christina Pickles, *St. Elsewhere* (NBC)
Madge Sinclair, *Trapper John, M.D.* (CBS)
Betty Thomas, *Hill Street Blues* (NBC)

OUTSTANDING SUPPORTING ACTRESS IN A LIMITED SERIES OR A SPECIAL

For a continuing role in a limited series or for a single appearance in a limited series or a special:

☐ Jean Simmons, *The Thorn Birds* (ABC)

Dame Judith Anderson, *Medea, Kennedy Center Tonight*, April 20, 1983 (PBS)
Polly Bergen, *The Winds of War* (ABC)
Bette Davis, *Little Gloria... Happy at Last*, October 24 and 25, 1982 (NBC)
Piper Laurie, *The Thorn Birds*—Part 3, March 29, 1983 (ABC)

OUTSTANDING INDIVIDUAL PERFORMANCE IN A VARIETY OR MUSIC PROGRAM

For a continuing or single performance, lead or support, in a variety or music series or special:

☐ Leontyne Price, *Live from Lincoln Center: Leontyne Price, Zubin Mehta and The New York Philharmonic*, September 15, 1982 (PBS)
Carol Burnett, *Texaco Star Theater... Opening Night*, September 11, 1982 (NBC)
Michael Jackson, *Motown 25: Yesterday, Today, Forever*, May 16, 1983 (NBC)
Luciano Pavarotti, *Live from Lincoln Center: Luciano Pavarotti and The New York Philharmonic*, April 4, 1983 (PBS)
Richard Pryor, *Motown 25: Yesterday, Today, Forever*, May 16, 1983 (NBC)

Prime Time Writing and Directing Awards

OUTSTANDING DIRECTING IN A COMEDY SERIES

For a single episode of a regular series:

☐ James Burrows, *Cheers*, "Showdown"—Part 2, March 31, 1983 (NBC)
Alan Alda, *M*A*S*H*, "Goodbye, Farewell and Amen," February 28, 1983 (CBS)
Jim Drake, *Buffalo Bill*, "Woody Quits," June 15, 1983 (NBC)
Burt Metcalfe, *M*A*S*H*, "The Joker Is Wild," November 15, 1982 (CBS)
Tom Patchett, *Buffalo Bill*, "Pilot," June 1, 1983 (NBC)
Bob Sweeney, *The Love Boat*, "The Dog Show," March 26, 1983 (ABC)

OUTSTANDING DIRECTING IN A DRAMA SERIES

For a single episode of a regular series:

☐ Jeff Bleckner, *Hill Street Blues*, "Life in the Minors," February 24, 1983 (NBC)
Marc Daniels, *Fame*, "And the Winner Is," September 30, 1982 (NBC)
Leo Penn, *The Mississippi*, "Old Hatreds Die Hard," May 6, 1983 (CBS)

Robert Scheerer, *Fame*, "Feelings," October 14, 1982 (NBC)

OUTSTANDING DIRECTING IN A VARIETY OR MUSIC PROGRAM

For a single episode of a regular or limited series or for a special:

☐ Dwight Hemion, *Sheena Easton. . . Act One*, March 24, 1983 (NBC)

Emile Ardolino, *Lincoln Center Special: Stravinsky and Balanchine—Genius Has a Brithday!*, October 4, 1982 (PBS)

John Blanchard, John Bell, *SCTV Network*, "The Energy Ball/Sweeps Week Show," February 25, 1983 (NBC)

Kirk Browning, *Live from Lincoln Center: Zubin Mehta Conducts Beethoven's Ninth with The New York Philharmonic*, February 2, 1983 (PBS)

Don Mischer, *Motown 25: Yesterday, Today, Forever*, May 16, 1983 (NBC)

Marty Pasetta, *55th Annual Academy Awards Presentation*, April 11, 1983 (ABC)

OUTSTANDING DIRECTING IN A LIMITED SERIES OR A SPECIAL

For a single episode of a limited series or for a special:

☐ John Erman, *Who Will Love My Children?*, February 14, 1983 (ABC)

Dan Curtis, *The Winds of War*, "Into the Maelstrom," February 13, 1983 (ABC)

Daryl Duke, *The Thorn Birds*—Part 2, March 28, 1983 (ABC)

Simon Langton, *Smiley's People*—Part 6 (Syndicated)

Edward Zwick, *Special Bulletin*, March 20, 1983 (NBC)

OUTSTANDING WRITING IN A COMEDY SERIES

For a single episode of a regular series:

☐ Glen Charles, Les Charles, *Cheers*, "Give Me a Ring Sometime," September 30, 1982 (NBC)

Ken Estin, *Taxi*, "Jim's Inheritance," October 7, 1982 (NBC)

Ken Levine, David Isaacs, *Cheers*, "The Boys in the Bar," January 27, 1983 (NBC)

David Lloyd, *Cheers*, "Diane's Perfect Date," February 10, 1983 (NBC)

Tom Patchett, Jay Tarses, *Buffalo Bill*, "Pilot," June 1, 1983 (NBC)

OUTSTANDING WRITING IN A LIMITED SERIES OR A SPECIAL

For a single episode of a limited series or for a special:

☐ Marshall Herskovitz, (teleplay), Edward Zwick, Marshall Herskovitz (story),

☐ Indicates winner

Special Bulletin, March 20, 1983 (NBC)

Michael Bortman, *Who Will Love My Children?*, February 14, 1983 (ABC)

David Edgar, *Nicholas Nickleby*—Part 4 (Syndicated)

William Hanley, *Little Gloria. . . Happy at Last*, October 24 and 25, 1982 (NBC)

Norman Mailer, *The Executioner's Song*, November 28 and 29, 1982 (NBC)

OUTSTANDING WRITING IN A DRAMA SERIES

For a single episode of a regular series:

☐ David Milch, *Hill Street Blues*, "Trial by Fury," September 30, 1982 (NBC)

Steven Bochco, Anthony Yerkovich, Jeffrey Lewis, *Hill Street Blues*, "A Hair of the Dog," November 25, 1982 (NBC)

Karen Hall, *Hill Street Blues*, "Officer of the Year," October 28, 1982 (NBC)

Michael Wagner, David Milch (teleplay), Steven Bochco, Anthony Yerkovich, Jeffrey Lewis (story), *Hill Street Blues*, "No Body's Perfect," December 9, 1982 (NBC)

Anthony Yerkovich, David Milch, Karen Hall (teleplay), Steven Bochco, Anthony Yerkovich, Jeffrey Lewis (story), *Hill Street Blues*, "Eugene's Comedy Empire Strikes Back," March 3, 1983 (NBC)

OUTSTANDING WRITING IN A VARIETY OR MUSIC PROGRAM

For a single episode of a regular or limited series or for a special:

☐ John Candy, Joe Flaherty, Eugene Levy, Andrea Martin, Martin Short, Dick Blasucci, Paul Flaherty, John McAndrew, Doug Steckler, Bob Dolman, Michael Short, Mary Charlotte Wilcox, *SCTV Network*, "The Energy Ball/Sweeps Week," February 25, 1983 (NBC)

John Candy, Joe Flaherty, Eugene Levy, Andrea Martin, Martin Short, Dick Blasucci, Paul Flaherty, John McAndrew, Doug Steckler, Bob Dolman, Michael Short, Jeffrey Barron, Mary Charlotte Wilcox, John Hemphill, *SCTV Network*, "Towering Inferno," December 10, 1982 (NBC)

John Candy, Joe Flaherty, Eugene Levy, Andrea Martin, Martin Short, Dick Blasucci, Paul Flaherty, John McAndrew, Doug Steckler, Bob Dolman, Michael Short, Jeffrey Barron, Mary Charlotte Wilcox, Dave Thomas, *SCTV Network*, (with Robin Williams and America), November 26, 1982 (NBC)

John Candy, Joe Flaherty, Eugene Levy, Andrea Martin, Martin Short, Dick Blasucci, Paul Flaherty, John McAndrew, Doug Steckler, Bob Dolman, Michael Short, Jeffrey Barron, Mary Charlotte Wilcox, *SCTV Network*, (with Joe Walsh), March 15, 1983 (NBC)

John Candy, Joe Flaherty, Eugene Levy, Andrea Martin, Catherine O'Hara, Martin Short, Dick Blasucci, Paul Flaherty, John McAndrew, Doug Steckler, Bob Dolman, Michael Short, Mary Charlotte Wilcox, *SCTV Network*, "The Chirstmas Show," December 17, 1982 (NBC)

Creative Arts Awards

OUTSTANDING CINEMATOGRAPHY FOR A SERIES

For a single episode of a regular series:

☐ Joseph Biroc, A.S.C., *Casablanca*, "The Masterbuilder's Woman," April 17, 1983 (NBC)

Emmett Bergholz, *Fantasy Island*, "Curse of the Moreaus/My Man Friday," October 16, 1982 (ABC)

Harry Wolf, A.S.C., *Little House: A New Beginning*, "The Wild Boy"—Part 1, November 1, 1982 (NBC)

OUTSTANDING CINEMATOGRAPHY FOR A LIMITED SERIES OR A SPECIAL

For a single episode of a limited series or for a special:

☐ Charles Correll, A.S.C., Stevan Larner, A.S.C., *The Winds of War*, "Into the Maelstrom," February 13, 1983 (ABC)

Bill Butler, *The Thorn Birds*—Part 1, March 28, 1983 (ABC)

Al Francis, A.S.C., *The Blue and the Gray*—Part 3, November 17, 1982 (CBS)

Arthur F. Ibbetson, B.S.C., "Witness for the Prosecution," *Hallmark Hall of Fame*, December 4, 1982 (CBS)

Gayne Rescher, A.S.C., *Mickey Spillane's Mike Hammer*, "Murder Me, Murder You," April 9, 1983 (CBS)

OUTSTANDING ART DIRECTION FOR A SERIES

For a single episode of a regular series:

☐ John W. Corso (production designer), Frank Grieco Jr. (art director), Robert George Freer (set decorator), *Tales of the Gold Monkey*, "Pilot," September 22, 1982 (ABC)

E. Preston Ames (production designer), Bill Harp (set decorator),

Casablanca, "Jenny," April 24, 1983 (NBC)

Hub Braden (art director), Don Remacle (set decorator), *Seven Brides for Seven Brothers*, "The Rescue," February 9, 1983 (CBS)

Ira Diamond (art director), Joseph Stone (set decorator), *Fame*, "Not in Kansas Anymore," February 24, 1983 (NBC)

James Hulsey, Jacqueline Webber (art directors), Ernie Bishop, Michele Guiol (set decorators), *St. Elsewhere*, "Pilot," October 26, 1982 (NBC)

Richard Sylbert (production designer), George Gaines (set decorator), *Cheers*, "Give Me a Ring Sometime," September 30, 1982 (NBC)

Tom Trimble, Paul Sylos (art directors), Brock Broughton (set decorator), *Dynasty*, "Fathers and Sons," March 9, 1983 (ABC)

OUTSTANDING ART DIRECTION FOR A LIMITED SERIES OR A SPECIAL

For a single episode of a limited series or for a special:

☐ Robert MacKichan (art director), Jerry Adams (set decorator), *The Thorn Birds*—Part 1, March 27, 1983 (ABC)

Tony Curtis (production designer), Carolyn Scott (set decorator), *The Scarlet Pimpernel*, November 9, 1982 (CBS)

Jackson De Govia (production designer), John Cartwright, Michael Minor, Malcolm Middleton (art directors), Tom Roysden, Francesco Chianese, Herta Pischinger (set decorators), *The Winds of War*, "The Winds Rise," February 6, 1983 (ABC)

John Napier (designer), *Nicholas Nickleby*—Part 4, January 13, 1983 (Syndicated)

Stuart Wurtzel (production designer), Guy Comtois (art director), Enrico Campana, Doug Kraner, Maurice Le Blanc (set decorators), *Little Gloria. . . Happy at Last*, October 24 and 25, 1982 (NBC)

OUTSTANDING ART DIRECTION FOR A VARIETY OR MUSIC PROGRAM

For a single episode of a regular or limited series or for a special:

☐ Ray Klausen (art director), Michael Corenblith (set decorator), *55th Annual Academy Awards Presentation*, April 11, 1983 (ABC)

Romain Johnston (art director), *Sheena Easton. . . Act One*, March 24, 1983 (NBC)

☐ Indicates winner

Bob Keene (art director), *Motown 25: Yesterday, Today, Forever*, May 16, 1983 (NBC)

René Lagler, Larry Wiemer (art directors), *Solid Gold Christmas Special, 82*, December 12, 1982 (Syndicated)

René Lagler (art director), *George Burns and Other Sex Symbols*, November 8, 1982 (NBC)

OUTSTANDING ACHIEVEMENT IN CHOREOGRAPHY

For a single episode of a regular or limited series or for a special:

☐ Debbie Allen, *Fame*, "Class Act," October 21, 1982 (NBC)

Walter Painter, *55th Annual Academy Awards Presentation*, April 11, 1983 (ABC)

Twyla Tharp, *The Catherine Wheel*, March 28, 1983 (PBS)

Lester Wilson, *Motown 25: Yesterday, Today, Forever*, May 16, 1983 (NBC)

OUTSTANDING ACHIEVEMENT IN MUSIC COMPOSITION FOR A SERIES (DRAMATIC UNDERSCORE)

For a single episode of a regular series. Emmy(s) to composer(s):

☐ Bruce Broughton, *Dallas*, "The Ewing Blues," January 7, 1983 (CBS)

William Goldstein, *Fame*, "Not in Kansas Anymore," February 24, 1983 (NBC)

Jerrold Immel, *Knots Landing*, "Loss of Innocence," February 17, 1983 (CBS)

David Rose, *Father Murphy*, "Sweet Sixteen," December 28, 1982 (NBC)

Nan Schwartz, *The Devlin Connection*, "Ring of Kings, Ring of Thieves," November 27, 1982 (NBC)

OUTSTANDING ACHIEVEMENT IN MUSIC COMPOSITION FOR A LIMITED SERIES OR A SPECIAL (DRAMATIC UNDERSCORE)

For a single episode of a limited series or for a special. Emmy(s) to composer(s):

☐ Billy Goldenberg, *Rage of Angels*, February 20 and 21, 1983 (NBC)

Bruce Broughton, *The Blue and the Gray*—Part 2, November 16, 1982 (CBS)

Joe Harnell, *V*, May 1 and 2, 1983 (NBC)

Henry Mancini, *The Thorn Birds*—Part 1, March 27, 1983 (ABC)

Peter Matz, *Drop-Out Father*, September 27, 1982 (CBS)

Laurence Rosenthal, *Who Will Love My Children?*, February 14, 1983 (ABC)

OUTSTANDING ACHIEVEMENT IN MUSIC DIRECTION

For a single episode of a limited series or for a special. Emmy(s) to music director and principal arranger(s):

☐ Dick Hyman (music director and principal arranger), *Eubie Blake: A Century of Music, Kennedy Center Tonight*, May 7, 1983 (PBS)

Mercer Ellington (music director and principal arranger), *Ellington: The Music Lives On, Great Performances*, March 7, 1983 (PBS)

Ian Fraser (music director), Billy Byers, Chris Boardman (principal arrangers), *Epcot Center: The Opening Celebration*, October 23, 1982 (CBS)

Peter Matz (music director and principal arranger), *Sheena Easton. . . Act One*, March 24, 1983 (NBC)

Nick Perito (music director), Nick Perito, Jon Charles (principal arrangers), *Perry Como's Christmas in Paris*, December 18, 1982 (ABC)

OUTSTANDING ACHIEVEMENT IN MUSIC AND LYRICS

For a song (which must have both music and lyrics), whether it be for a single episode of a regular or limited series or for a special. Emmy(s) to composer(s) and lyricist(s):

☐ James Di Pasquale (composer), Dory Previn (lyricist), "Two of a Kind," *G.E. Theater*, song: "We'll Win This World," October 9, 1982 (CBS)

Bruce Broughton (composer), Mark Mueller (lyricist), *Quincy, M.E.*, "Quincy's Wedding"—Part 2, song: "Quincy's Wedding Song," February 23, 1983 (NBC)

Earl Brown, Artie Butler (composers and lyricists), *Suzanne Somers and 10,000 G.I.'s*, song: "We're Not So Dumb," January 3, 1983 (CBS)

Billy Goldenberg, Carol Connors (composers and lyricists), *Bare Essence*, song: "In Finding You, I Found Love," October 4 and 5, 1982 (CBS)

William Goldstein (composer), Molly-Ann Leikin (lyricist), *Happy Endings*, song: "Happy Endings Theme Song," March 1, 1983 (CBS)

Larry Grossman (composer), Buz Kohan (lyricist), *55th Annual Academy Awards Presentation*, song: "And It All Comes Down to This," April 11, 1983 (ABC)

Gary Portnoy, Judy Hart Angelo (composers and lyricists), *Cheers*, "Pilot," song: "Where Everybody

Knows Your Name," September 30, 1982 (NBC)

OUTSTANDING COSTUME DESIGN FOR A SERIES

For a single episode of a regular or limited series:

□ Theadora Van Runkle, *Wizards and Warriors*, "Dungeon of Death," May 7, 1983 (CBS)

Jean-Pierre Dorleac, *Tales of the Gold Monkey*, "Naka Jima Kill," March 18, 1983 (ABC)

Bob Mackie, Ret Turner, *Mama's Family Wedding*—Part 2, February 12, 1983 (NBC)

Nolan Miller, *Dynasty*, "La Mirage," December 15, 1982 (ABC)

Warden Neil, *Filthy Rich*, "Town and Gown," August 23, 1982 (CBS)

OUTSTANDING COSTUME DESIGN FOR A LIMITED SERIES OR A SPECIAL

For a single episode of a limited series or for a special:

□ Phyllis Dalton, *The Scarlet Pimpernel*, November 9, 1982 (CBS)

Ray Aghayan, *55th Annual Academy Awards Presentation*, April 11, 1983 (ABC)

Warden Neil, *Happy Birthday, Bob!*, May 23, 1983 (NBC)

Travilla, *The Thorn Birds*—Part 1, March 27, 1983 (ABC)

Julie Weiss, *Little Gloria. . . Happy at Last*, October 24 and 25, 1982 (NBC)

OUTSTANDING ACHIEVEMENT IN MAKEUP

For a single episode of a regular or limited series or for a special:

□ Del Acevedo, *The Thorn Birds*—Part 4, March 30, 1983 (ABC)

Zoltan Elek, Monty Westmore, *Who Will Love My Children?*, February 14, 1983 (ABC)

Leo L. Lotito Jr. (makeup supervisor), Werner Keppler, *V*, May 1 and 2, 1983 (NBC)

Jack Wilson, *Fame*, "Not in Kansas Anymore," February 24, 1983 (NBC)

OUTSTANDING ACHIEVEMENT IN HAIRSTYLING

For a single episode of a regular or limited series or for a special:

□ Edie Panda, *Rosie: The Rosemary Clooney Story*, December 8, 1982 (CBS)

Janice D. Brandow, *Missing Children: A Mother's Story*, December 1, 1982 (CBS)

Mark Nelson, *Nicholas Nickleby*—Part 4, January 13, 1983 (Syndicated)

□ Indicates winner

Sharleen Rassi, *Wizards and Warriors*, "The Rescue," March 12, 1983 (CBS)

OUTSTANDING FILM EDITING FOR A SERIES

For a single episode of a regular series:

□ Ray Daniels, *Hill Street Blues*, "Phantom of the Hill," December 2, 1982 (NBC)

Jeanene Ambler, *Quincy, M.E.*, "Quincy's Wedding"—Part 2, February 23, 1983 (NBC)

Fred W. Berger, A.C.E., *Dallas*, "Ewing's Inferno," May 6, 1983 (CBS)

Bob Bring, A.C.E., *Matt Houston*, "The Showgirl Murders," March 20, 1983 (ABC)

Andrew Chulack, *Cheers*, "Endless Slumper," December 2, 1982 (NBC)

Stanford L. Tischler, A.C.E., Larry L. Mills, A.C.E., *M*A*S*H*, "Goodbye, Farewell and Amen," February 28, 1983 (CBS)

Bob Blake (film editor), *Dynasty*, "La Mirage," December 15, 1982 (ABC)

OUTSTANDING FILM EDITING FOR A LIMITED SERIES OR A SPECIAL

For a single episode of a limited series or for a special:

□ C. Timothy O'Meara, *The Thorn Birds*—Part 3, March 29, 1983 (ABC)

Fred A. Chulack, A.C.E., Bud Friedgen, A.C.E., *The Blue and the Gray*—Part 1, November 14, 1982 (CBS)

Bernard Gribble, A.C.E., Peter Zinner, A.C.E., John F. Burnett, A.C.E., Jack Tucker, Earle Herdan, Gary Smith, *The Winds of War*, "Into the Maelstrom," February 13, 1983 (ABC)

Jerrold L. Ludwig, A.C.E., *Who Will Love My Children?*, February 14, 1983 (ABC)

Robert F. Shugrue, *The Thorn Birds*—Part 1, March 27, 1983 (ABC)

Benjamin A. Weissman, A.C.E., *The Scarlet and the Black*, February 2, 1983 (CBS)

OUTSTANDING FILM SOUND EDITING FOR A SERIES

For a single episode of a regular series:

□ Sam Horta (supervising editor), Don Ernst, Avram Gold, Eileen Horta, Constance A. Kazmer, Gary Krivacek (editors), *Hill Street Blues*, "Stan the Man," November 4, 1982 (NBC)

Sam Horta (supervising editor), Don Ernst, Jerelyn Golding, Avram Gold, Constance A. Kazmer, Gary Krivacek (editors), *St. Elsewhere*, "Working," April 5, 1983 (NBC)

Walter Jenevein (supervising editor), Bernard P. Cabral, John Detra, Dennis Diltz, Sam Gemette, Robert Grovenor, Phil Haberman, Jerry M. Jacobson, Marvin I. Kosberg, Billy Mauch, Tony Palk, Edward Sandlin, Kyle Wright, Sam Shaw, William Shenberg, Bruce Stambler, Andy Torres (editors), *Knight Rider*, "Pilot," September 25, 1982 (NBC)

Ed Rossi (supervising editor), William Hartman, David Ice, Don V. Isaacs, Godfrey Marks, Richard A. Sperber (editors), *M*A*S*H*, "Goodbye, Farewell and Amen," February 28, 1983 (CBS)

Sam Shaw (supervising editor), Bernard P. Cabral, John Detra, Sam Gemette, Donlee Jorgensen, Mark Roberts, Erik Schrader, John Stacy, Bob Weatherford, Paul Wittenberg, William Shenberg, *Tales of the Gold Monkey*, "Honor Thy Brother," November 24, 1982 (ABC)

OUTSTANDING FILM SOUND EDITING FOR A LIMITED SERIES OR A SPECIAL

For a single episode of a limited series or for a special:

□ Jim Troutman (supervising editor), Dave Caldwell, Paul Clay, Paul Laune, Tony Magro, Richard Rederman, Karen Rasch, Jeff Sandler, William Shenberg, Dan Thomas, Ascher Yates (editors), *The Executioner's Song*, November 28 and 29, 1982 (NBC)

Michael Hilkene, Russ Tinsley (supervising editors), William R. Jackson, Joe Mayer, Jill Taggart, Rusty Tinsley, Benjamin Wong (editors), *Who Will Love My Children?*, February 14, 1983 (ABC)

Joseph Melody, Russ Tinsley (supervising editors), Tom Cornwell, David R. Elliott, Michael Hilkene, Fred Judkins, John Kline, Rusty Tinsley, Christopher T. Welch (editors), *The Blue and the Gray*—Part 1, November 14, 1982 (CBS)

Keith Stafford (supervising editor), Richard W. Adams, Denis Dutton, James Fritch, Robert Gutknecht, Carl K. Mahakian, Lee Osborne, Bernard F. Pincus, Edward Sandlin, Ian MacGregor-Scott (editors), *The Winds of War*, "Into the Maelstrom," February 13, 1983 (ABC)

Christopher T. Welch, Russ Tinsley (supervising editors), Cathey Burrow, Greg Dillon, John Kline, Bill Manger (editors), "Uncommon Valor," January 22, 1983 (CBS)

OUTSTANDING FILM SOUND MIXING FOR A SERIES

For a single episode of a regular series:

☐ William B. Marky, C.A.S., (production mixer), John B. Asman, William Nicholson, Ken S. Polk (rerecording mixers), *Hill Street Blues*, "Trial by Fury," September 30, 1982 (NBC)

Maury Harris (production mixer), John B. Asman, William Nicholson, Ken S. Polk (rerecording mixers), *Cagney & Lacey*, "Recreational Use," December 27, 1982 (CBS)

John Kean (production mixer), Michael Casper, Stanley H. Polinksy, B. Tennyson Sebastion II (rerecording mixers), *Tales of the Gold Monkey*, "Pilot," September 22, 1982 (ABC)

"Fast" Eddie Mahler (production mixer), James R. Cook, John Norman, Robert Harman (rerecording mixers), *The A-Team*, "Pilot," January 23, 1983 (NBC)

Jimmy Rogers (production mixer), T.A. Moore Jr., Earl M. Madery, B. Tennyson Sebastion II (rerecording mixers), *Magnum, P.I.*, "Did You See the Sunrise?," September 30, 1982 (CBS)

Dean S. Vernon (production mixer), John B. Asman, William Nicholson, Ken S. Polk (rerecording mixers), *St. Elsewhere*, "The Count," March 8, 1983 (NBC)

OUTSTANDING FILM SOUND MIXING FOR A LIMITED SERIES OR A SPECIAL

For a single episode of a limited series or for a special:

☐ John Mitchell (production mixer), Gordon L. Day, Stanley A. Wetzel, Howard Wilmarth (rerecording mixers), *The Scarlet and the Black*, February 2, 1983 (CBS)

Alan Bernard (production mixer), Robert W. Glass Jr., William L. McCaughey, C.A.S., Mel Metcalfe (rerecording mixers), *The Winds of War*, "Defiance," February 9, 1983 (ABC)

Robin Gregory (production mixer), Robert W. Glass Jr., William L. McCaughey, C.A.S., Allen L. Stone (rerecording mixers), *The Winds of War*, "Cataclysm," February 8, 1983 (ABC)

Robin Gregory (production mixer), Robert W. Glass Jr., Mel Metcalfe, William L. McCaughey, C.A.S., (rerecording mixers), *The Winds or War*, "Into the Maelstrom," February 13, 1983 (ABC)

Steve Marlowe (production mixer), Robert W. Glass Jr., David J.

☐ Indicates winner

Hudson, Ray West (rerecording mixers), *The Executioner's Song*, November 28 and 29, 1982 (NBC)

OUTSTANDING VIDEOTAPE EDITING FOR A SERIES

For a single episode of a regular series:

☐ Larry M. Harris, *The Jeffersons*, "Change of a Dollar," March 13, 1983 (CBS)

Andy Ackerman, *Newhart*, "Grandma, What a Big Mouth You Have," April 3, 1983 (CBS)

Diane Block, Tee Bosustow, Cary Gries, Michael Kelly, Doug Loviska, Bruce Motyer, Bill Paulsen, Nicholas Stein, Cynthia Vaughn, Joe Walsh, *Real People*—Show 502, November 3, 1982 (NBC)

Tucker Wiard, *Alice*, "Vera, the Torch," April 24, 1983 (CBS)

Marco Zappia, *Archie Bunker's Place*, "Three Women," January 16, 1983 (CBS)

OUTSTANDING VIDEOTAPE EDITING FOR A LIMITED SERIES OR A SPECIAL

For a single episode of a limited series or for a special:

☐ Arden Rynew, *Special Bulletin*, March 20, 1983 (NBC)

Ken Denisoff, *David Frost Presents: the Fourth International Guinness Book of World Records*, May 15, 1983 (ABC)

Ken Gutstein, *Big Bird in China*, May 29, 1983 (NBC)

Danny White, *Motown 25: Yesterday, Today, Forever*, May 16, 1983 (NBC)

OUTSTANDING TAPE SOUND MIXING FOR A SERIES

For a single episode of a regular series:

☐ Frank Kulaga (production), Ken Hahn (postproduction), *Dance in America*, "The Magic Flute," April 25, 1983 (PBS)

Paul Dobbe (preproduction), Dick Sarter (production), Jerald Clemans, C.A.S., (postproduction), Craig Porter (sound effects), *Solid Gold* (with Barry Manilow), January 22, 1983 (Syndicated)

Don Helvey (production), Jerald Clemans, C.A.S., (postproduction), *Alice*, "The Secret of Mel's Diner," October 20, 1982 (CBS)

Matt Hyde (preproduction), Rich Jacob (production), Chris Haire (postproduction), Dick Wilson (sound effects), *Star of the Family*—Show 1, September 30, 1982 (ABC)

Richard Jacob (production), Al Patapoff (postproduction), Ross Davis (sound effects), *Benson*,

"Death in a Funny Position," October 22, 1982 (ABC)

OUTSTANDING TAPE SOUND MIXING FOR LIMITED SERIES OR A SPECIAL

For a single episode of a limited series or for a special:

☐ Edward J. Greene (preproduction), Ron Estes (production), Carroll Pratt (postproduction), *Sheena Easton. . . Act One*, March 24, 1983 (NBC)

Barton Chiate (preproduction), Phillip J. Seretti (production), Jerald Clemans, C.A.S., (postproduction), *Andy Williams' Early New England Christmas*, December 7, 1982 (CBS)

Russ Terrana (preproduction), Don Worsham (production), Jerald Clemans, C.A.S., (postproduction), Bruce Burns (sound effects), *The Eddie Rabbitt Special*, March 24, 1983 (CBS)

OUTSTANDING TECHNICAL DIRECTION AND ELECTRONIC CAMERAWORK FOR A SERIES

For a single episode of a regular series:

☐ Heino Ripp (technical director), Mike Bennett, Al Camoin, Jan Kasoff, John Pinto, Maurey Verschoore (camerapersons), *Saturday Night Live* (with Sid Caesar and Joe Cocker), February 5, 1983 (NBC)

Gerry Bucci (technical director), D.J. Diomedes, Art La Combe, Carol A. Wetovich, Blair White (camerapersons), *It Takes Two*, "An Affair to Remember," December 16, 1982 (ABC)

Herm Falk (technical director), William Pope, Donna Quante, John Rago, Iris Rosenthal (camerapersons), *Benson*, "The Honeymooners," January 7, 1983 (ABC)

Cal Slater (technical director), Luis Fuerte, Larry Heider, Robert Keyes, Wayne Orr, Ken Patterson (camerapersons), *Sound Festival*, (with Flora Purim and W.O. Airto), November 9, 1982 (PBS)

OUTSTANDING TECHNICAL DIRECTION AND ELECTRONIC CAMERAWORK FOR A LIMITED SERIES OR A SPECIAL

For a single episode of a limited series or for a special:

☐ Hank Geving (cameraperson), *Special Bulletin*, March 20, 1983 (NBC)

Gene Crowe (technical director), Greg Cook, Tom Geren, Larry Heider, Robert Keys, Dave Levisohn, Wayne Orr, Ken Patterson, Ron Sheldon (camerapersons), *Motown 25:*

Yesterday, Today, Forever, May 16, 1983 (NBC)

Gene Crowe, Gene Schwartz (technical directors), Joe Epperson, Larry Heider, Roy Holm, Roy Ratliff, Ron Sheldon (camerapersons), *Sheena Easton. . . Act One*, March 24, 1983 (NBC)

John B. Field (technical director), John King, Dave Levisohn (camerapersons), *Rocky Mountain Holiday with John Denver and The Muppets*, May 12, 1983 (ABC)

Karl Messerschmidt (technical director), Les Atkinson, George Falardeau, Tom Geren, Roy Holm, Mike Stramisky, *The Member of the Wedding: An NBC Live Theater Presentation*, December 20, 1982 (NBC)

OUTSTANDING LIGHTING DIRECTION (ELECTRONIC) FOR A SERIES

For a single episode of a regular series:

☐ Robert A. Dickinson (lighting consultant), C. Frank Olivas (lighting director), *Solid Gold* (with Dolly Parton and Laura) (Syndicated)

Mikel Neiers (lighting designer), Kieran Healey (lighting director), *Rock "N" Roll Tonight* (with Molly Hatchett and Quiet Riot) (Syndicated)

Alan K. Walker (lighting director), *Benson*, "Boys' Night Out," February 4, 1983 (ABC)

John C. Zak (lighting director), Alan Walker (lighting designer), *Benson*, "Death in a Funny Position," October 22, 1982 (ABC)

OUTSTANDING LIGHTING DIRECTION (ELECTRONIC) FOR A LIMITED SERIES OR SPECIAL

For a single episode of a limited series or for a special:

☐ John Rook (lighting designer), Ken Wilcox, Bob Pohle (lighting directors), *Sheena Easton. . . Act One*, March 24, 1983 (NBC)

Robert A. Dickinson (lighting consultant), C. Frank Olivas (lighting director), *Solid Gold Christmas, Special, 82* (Syndicated)

John Freschi, *Motown 25: Yesterday, Today, Forever*, May 16, 1983 (NBC)

Carl Gibson, *Special Bulletin*, March 20, 1983 (NBC)

George Riesenberger (director of photography "E"), *Rocky Mountain Holiday with John Denver and The Muppets*, May 12, 1983 (ABC)

☐ Indicates winner

OUTSTANDING INDIVIDUAL ACHIEVEMENT—COSTUMERS

Possibility of one, more than one or no award:

☐ Tommy Welsh (costume supervisor), John Napolitano, Paul Vachon, Johannes Nikerk (wardrobe), *The Winds of War*, "The Storm Breaks," February 7, 1983 (ABC)

Albert H. Frankel (men's costumer), Rita Bennett (women's costumer), *M*A*S*H*, "Goodbye, Farewell and Amen," February 28, 1983 (CBS)

Marilyn Matthews (costume supervisor), *Fame*, "Not in Kansas Anymore," February 24, 1983 (NBC)

Mina Mittelman (women's costume supervisor), Ellis Cohen (men's costume supervisor), *Missing Children: A Mother's Story*, December 1, 1982 (CBS)

OUTSTANDING INDIVIDUAL ACHIEVEMENT—GRAPHIC DESIGN AND TITLE SEQUENCES

Possibility of one, more than one or no award:

☐ James Castle, Bruce Bryant, *Cheers*, "Showdown," March 24, 1983 (NBC)

Edie Baskin, Jeff Carpenter, *Square Pegs*, "Muffy's Bas Mitzvah," November 29, 1982 (CBS)

R.O. Blechman, Seymour Chwast, Andy Ewan, *Nicholas Nickleby*—Part 1 (Syndicated)

Phill Norman, *The Scarlet and the Black*, February 2, 1983 (CBS)

John Ridgway, Pam Bloch, Harry Marks, *Entertainment Tonight/ Entertainment This Week*—Part 373 (Syndicated)

OUTSTANDING INDIVIDUAL ACHIEVEMENT—SPECIAL VISUAL EFFECTS

Possibility of one, more than one or no award:

☐ Gene Warren Jr., Peter Kleinow, Leslie Huntley (special visual effects), Jackson De Govia (production designer), Michael Minor (art director), *The Winds of War*, "Defiance," February 9, 1983 (ABC)

Bill Goddard, Gary L. Smith (videotape editors), *SCTV Network*, "Energy Ball/Sweeps Week Show," February 25, 1983 (NBC)

OUTSTANDING INDIVIDUAL ACHIEVEMENT—INFORMATIONAL PROGRAMMING

Possibility of one, more than one or no award:

☐ Alfred R. Kelman, Charles Bangert (directors), *The Body Human: The Living Code*, June 13, 1983 (CBS)

☐ Louis H. Gorfain, Robert E. Fuisz, M.D. (writers), *The Body Human: The Living Code*, June 13, 1983 (CBS)

Chandler Cowles (writer), *IBM Presents I, Leonardo: A Journey of the Mind*, April 26, 1983 (CBS)

Steve Edwards (host), *Entertainment Tonight/Entertainment This Week* (Syndicated)

Frank Langella (performer), *IBM Presents I, Leonardo: A Journey of the Mind*, April 26, 1983 (CBS)

OUTSTANDING INDIVIDUAL ACHIEVEMENT—ANIMATED PROGRAMMING

Possibility of one, more than one or no award:

Gerard Baldwin (director), *My Smurfy Valentine*, February 13, 1983 (NBC)

Phil Roman (director), *Here Comes Garfield*, October 25, 1982 (CBS)

Len Janson, Chuck Menville (teleplay), Peyo Culliford, Yvan Delporte, Len Janson, Chuck Menville, Gerard Baldwin (story), *My Smurfy Valentine*, February 13, 1983 (NBC)

OUTSTANDING ACHIEVEMENT IN ENGINEERING DEVELOPMENT

An award to an individual, a company or an organization for developments in engineering that are either so extensive an improvement on existing methods or so innovative in nature that they materially affect the transmission, recording or reception of television:

☐ Emmy Award to Eastman Kodak Company for the development of Eastman high-speed film 5294/7294, a color negative film with improved picture quality under low light level

Citation to Ikegami Electronics and CBS Inc. for the engineering and development of the EC-35, a camera used for electronic cinematography

Citation to The AMPEX Corporation for the development of the ADO, a digital effects unit displaying unique capabilities with improved picture quality

SIXTH ANNUAL ATAS GOVERNORS AWARD

☐ Sylvester L. "Pat" Weaver Jr.

News and Documentary Awards

Nominations and Awards were determined on the basis of excellence with no limitations as to number or category.

Programs and Program segments were entered and judged in their individual content "areas". All areas had the possibility of one award, or no award judged against standards

of excellence only, non-competitively.

THE NOMINATIONS

Emmy(s) to producer(s) and reporter(s)/correspondent(s)

FOR SEGMENTS OUTSTANDING COVERAGE OF A SINGLE BREAKING NEWS STORY

□ "The Assassination of Benigno Aquino," *ABC News*, William Stewart (producer), Jim Laurie (correspondent), August 21, 22, 1983 (ABC)

□ "The Grenada Coverage," *The MacNeil/Lehrer News Hour*, Lester M. Crystal (executive producer), Dan Werner (senior producer), Robert MacNeil, Jim Lehrer and Charlayne Hunter-Gault (correspondents), October 25, 26, 27, 28, 31, 1983 (PBS)

"PLO Exodus from Tripoli," *Nightline*, Tom Yellin (producer), Al Dale (correspondent), December 22, 1983 (ABC)

"The Kal Crash," *The CBS Evening News with Dan Rather*, Mark Harrington (senior producer), Don McNeill, Marquita Pool, Jennifer Siebens, Tom Bettag, Suzanne Allen, William Willson, Sharon Houston, Andrew Heyward, Lane Venardos (producers), Don McNeill, Bill McLaughlin, David Martin, Gordon Joseloff, Sandy Gilmour and Dan Rather (reporter/correspondents), September 1, 1983 (CBS)

□ "The Beirut Bombing," *The CBS Evening News with Dan Rather*, Howard Stringer (executive producer), Lane Venardos (senior producer), Harry Radliffe, Roxanne Russell, Al Ortiz, Susan Zirinsky, Phil O'Connor, Marquita Pool (producers), Tom Fenton, Bruce Morton, David Martin, Alan Pizzey, Bruce Hall and Leslie Stahl (reporter/correspondents), October 24, 1983 (CBS)

PROGRAMS OUTSTANDING BACKGROUND ANALYSIS OF A SINGLE CURRENT STORY

Is Anyone Home on the Range, Bobbie Birleffi (producer/reporter, correspondent), October 25, 1983 (PBS)

"Who Decides Disability," *Frontline*, Sherry Jones (producer), June 20, 1983 (PBS)

□ *A Doomsday Scenario: Banking at the Brink*, Stephen D. Atlas (executive producer), Glenda Baugh Manzi (producer), Paul Solman

□ Indicates winner

(correspondent), December 1, 1983 (PBS)

"Vietnam Memorial," *Frontline*, Steve York, Foster Wiley (producers), May 30, 1983 (PBS)

□ "Abortion Clinic," *Frontline*, Mark Obenhaus (producer), Rita Stern, Michael Schwarz (co-producers), Jessica Savitch (reporter/correspondent), April 18, 1983 (PBS)

□ "Nicaragua: A House Divided," *Inside Story*, Christopher Koch (executive producer), Hodding Carter (correspondent), October 13, 1983 (PBS)

□ *Crime in America: Myth and Reality*, Paul Friedman, Bob Roy (executive producers), Charles C. Stuart (producer), Richard Threlkeld (reporter/correspondent), March 2, 1983 (ABC)

FOR SEGMENTS OUTSTANDING BACKGROUND ANALYSIS OF A SINGLE CURRENT STORY

□ "US/USSR: A Balance of Powers," *World News Tonight*, Robert E. Frye (executive producer), David Guilbault (coordinating producer), Bob Aglow, Amy Entelis, Sally Holm, Steve Jacobs, David Kaplan, John Lower, Charles Stuart, Jonathan Talmadge (producers), Peter Jennings, John McWethy, Bob Zelnick, Sam Donaldson, Pierre Salinger, Richard Threlkeld, Rick Inderfurth, Dan Cordtz (correspondents), November 14, 25, 1983 (ABC)

□ "The Countdown Against Cancer," *The CBS Evening News with Dan Rather*, Howard Stringer (executive producer), Linda Mason (senior producer), David Browning (producer), Terry Drinkwater (reporter/correspondent), May 2, 3, 4, 5, 1983 (CBS)

□ "The Computers Are Coming," *The CBS Evening News with Dan Rather*, Howard Stringer (executive producer), Linda Mason (senior producer), David Browning (producer), Dan Rather (reporter/correspondent), September 12, 13, 14, 15, 16, 1983 (CBS)

"Toxic," *Our Times with Bill Moyers*, Martin Smith (producer), Bill Moyers (reporter/correspondent), July 26, 1983 (CBS)

"Our Man Who Went Into the Cold," *First Camera*, Patricia Lynch (producer), Lloyd Dobyns (correspondent), December 4, 1983 (NBC)

"Postmortem in Detroit," *Monitor*, Peter Jeffries (producer), Steve Delaney (reporter/correspondent), October 30, 1983 (NBC)

"Tragic Assumptions," *60 Minutes*, Monika R. Jensen (producer), Ed Bradley (reporter/correspondent), October 30, 1983 (CBS)

□ "Marines in Beirut," *The MacNeil/Lehrer Newshour*, Michael Joseloff (producer), Jim Webb (correspondent), October 14, 1983 (PBS)

□ "Quest for Justice," *20/20*, Janice Tomlin (producer), Tom Jarriel (reporter/correspondent), September 22, 1983 (ABC)

□ "Crime in America," *World News Tonight*, Charles C. Stuart (producer), Richard Threlkeld (reporter/correspondent), February 14, 25, 1983 (ABC)

FOR PROGRAMS OUTSTANDING INVESTIGATIVE JOURNALISM

"Oh, Tell the World What Happened," *Closeup*, Steve Singer, Judy Crichton (producers), Bill Redeker, Bill Sherman (correspondents), John Cooley, Chris Harper (reporters), January 7, 1983 (ABC)

"88 Seconds in Greensboro," *Frontline*, William Cran, Stephanie Tepper (producers), James Reston (reporter/correspondent), January 24, 1983 (PBS)

"In Our Water," *Frontline*, Meg Switzgable (producer/correspondent), June, 1983 (PBS)

□ "Uncounted Enemy, Unproven Conspiracy," *Inside Story*, Rose Economou, Joseph Russin (producers), Hodding Carter (correspondent), April 21, 1983 (PBS)

FOR SEGMENTS

□ "Poison on Your Plate," *First Camera*, Chuck Collins, Brian McTigue (producers), Mark Nykanen (correspondent), September 25, 1983 (NBC)

□ "Growing Up in Smoke," *20/20*, Alice Irene Pifer (producer), John Stossel (correspondent), October 20, 1983 (ABC)

FOR SEGMENTS OUTSTANDING INVESTIGATIVE JOURNALISM

□ "Lenell Geters in Jail," *60 Minutes*, Suzanne St. Pierre (producer), Morley Safer (reporter/correspondent), December 4, 1983 (CBS)

"Prescription for Despair," *The CBS Evening News with Dan Rather*, Linda Mason (senior producer), William Willson (producer), Susan Spencer (reporter/correspondent), November 28, 29, 30, 1983 (CBS)

"For-Profit Hospitals," *The CBS Evening News with Dan Rather*, Linda Mason (senior producer),

David Gelber, Terry Plantinga (producers), Steve Kroft (reporter/correspondent), March 29, 30, 1983 and October 13, 1983 (CBS)

"The Meat you Eat," *First Camera*, Stephanie Meagher (producer), Steve Delaney (correspondent), September 18, 1983 (NBC)

FOR PROGRAMS OUTSTANDING INTERVIEW/INTERVIEWER(S)

"Assessing John Paul II," *ABC News Directions*, William Blakemore (producer and correspondent), December 18, 1983 (ABC)

☐ "The Day After," *Viewpoint*, William Lord (executive producer), George Watson, William Moore, Stuart Schwartz, Robert Jordan (senior producers), Carla De Landri (producer), Ted Koppel (reporter/correspondent), November 20, 1983 (ABC)

"The Pleasure of Finding Things Out," *Nova*, Bebe Nixon, Christopher Sykes (producers), January 25, 1983 (PBS)

FOR SEGMENTS

☐ "Michael Doyle's Camden," *60 Minutes*, Elliot Bernstein (producer), Harry Reasoner (correspondent), March 20, 1983 (CBS)

FOR SEGMENTS OUTSTANDING INTERVIEW/INTERVIEWER(S)

☐ "Larry," *60 Minutes*, Jeanne Solomon (producer), Ed Bradley (reporter/correspondent), January 2, 1983 (CBS)

☐ "There But for the Grace of God: The Parents of John W. Hinckley, Jr.," *20/20*, Marion Goldin (producer), Barbara Walters (correspondent), April 28, 1983 (ABC)

"Man of Honor," *60 Minutes*, Ira Rosen (producer), Mike Wallace (reporter/correspondent), March 27, 1983 and May 1, 1983 (CBS)

"The World of John Huston," *20/20*, Jeff Diamond (producer), Sylvia Chase (reporter/correspondent), March 3, 1983 (ABC)

FOR PROGRAMS OUTSTANDING COVERAGE OF A CONTINUING NEWS STORY

☐ "Dateline: Moscow/Inside the USSR," *Inside Story*, Ned Schnurman (executive producer), Philip Burton, Christopher Koch Joseph Russin (producers), Hodding Carter (correspondent), April 7 and 14, 1983 (PBS)

FOR SEGMENTS

"Beirut Marines," *Nightline*, Terry Irving, Betsy Aaron (producers), Betsy Aaron (reporter/

☐ Indicates winner

correspondent), September 14, 1983 and October 24, 1983 (ABC)

☐ "After the Parades," *Sunday Morning*, Kathy Sulkes (producer), David Culhane (reporter/correspondent), November 13, 1983 (CBS)

☐ "Nicaragua 1983," *Today Show*, Jon Alpert (producer and reporter/correspondent), March 1983 (NBC)

FOR SEGMENTS OUTSTANDING COVERAGE OF A CONTINUING NEWS STORY

"Till Death Do Us Part," *20/20*, Steve Brand (producer), Hugh Downs (reporter/correspondent), April 14, 1983 (ABC)

"Afghanistan Under the Gun," *The CBS Evening News with Dan Rather*, Tom Bettag (senior producer), Harry Radliffe, Eric Durschmeid (producers), Dan Rather (reporter/correspondent), 4/5/83; 5/6/83; 4/7/83 (CBS)

"The New Industrialization," *The CBS Evening News with Dan Rather*, Linda Mason (senior producer), Terrace Martin, Andrew Heyward, David Gelber, Arden Ostrander (producers), Ed Rabel, Bernard Goldberg, Ray Brady, Jane Bryant Quinn (reporter/correspondents), 1/10; 1/11; 11/21; 11/22; 11/23 (CBS)

FOR PROGRAMS OUTSTANDING INFORMATIONAL, CULTURAL OR HISTORICAL PROGRAMS

The Pope and His Vatican, Ellen Rossen (producer), William Blakemore (reporter/correspondent), April 3, 1983 (ABC)

☐ "Rain Forest," *A National Geographic Special*, David Hughes and Carol Hughes (producers), January 12, 1983 (PBS)

Everest North Wall, Laszlo Pal (producer), May 4, 1983 (PBS)

The Oil Kingdoms, Jo Franklin-Trout (producer, reporter/correspondent), October 10, 17, 24, 1983 (PBS)

American Journey, Malcolm Clarke (producer), Richard Reeves (reporter/correspondent), March 30, 1983 (PBS)

A Normal Face, Ted Bogosian (producer, reporter/correspondent), November 22, 1983 (PBS)

FOR PROGRAMS OUTSTANDING INFORMATIONAL, CULTURAL OR HISTORICAL PROGRAMS

☐ *Vietnam: A Television History*, Richard Ellison (executive producer), Stanley Karnow (chief correspondent), "America Takes Charge," Andrew Pearson (producer), October 25, 1983 (PBS)

☐ *Vietnam: A Television History*, "LBJ Goes to War," Austin Hoyt (producer), October 18, 1983 (PBS)

☐ *Vietnam: A Television History*, "Peace Is At Hand," Martin Smith (producer), November 29, 1983 (PBS)

☐ *Vietnam: A Television History*, "Legacies," Richard Ellison (producer), December 20, 1983 (PBS)

☐ *Vietnam: A Television History*, "Roots of a War," Judith Vecchione (producer), October 4, 1983 (PBS)

☐ *Vietnam: A Television History*, "The End of the Tunnel," Elizabeth Deane (producer), December 13, 1983 (PBS)

FOR SEGMENTS

"Holocaust Remembrance," *Nightline*, Pamela Kahn (producer), April 13, 1983 (ABC)

"Aging," *Sunday Morning*, James Houtrides (producer), Bruce Morton (reporter/correspondent), September 25, 1983 (CBS)

FOR SEGMENTS OUTSTANDING INFORMATIONAL, CULTURAL OR HISTORICAL PROGRAMS

"Music of the Jedi," *20/20*, Joe Pfifferling (producer), Bob Brown (reporter/correspondent), June 16, 1983 (ABC)

☐ "Mel Torme," *20/20*, Joe Pfifferling (producer), Bob Brown (reporter/correspondent), August 11, 1983 (ABC)

☐ "Black Family," *The CBS Evening News with Dan Rather*, Howard Stringer (executive producer), Marquita Pool, Chris Weicher (producers), Lem Tucker (reporter/correspondent), August 22, 23, 24, 1983 (CBS)

☐ "The Mien People," *The CBS Evening News with Dan Rather*, Brian Healy (senior producer), Beth Pearlman, Charles Wolfson (producers), Bruce Morton (reporter/correspondent), February 2, August 25, November 25, 1983 (CBS)

"Japaning of America," *The CBS Evening News with Dan Rather*, Tom Bettag (senior producer), Peter Schweitzer (producer), Bob Simon (reporter/correspondent), May 17, 19, 20, 1983 (CBS)

"Back to His Roots with Chicken George," *Sunday Morning*, Irina Posner (producer), Charles Osgood (reporter/correspondent), February 17, 1983 (CBS)

"Missing Dads," *20/20*, Rob Wallace (producer), Tom Jarriel (reporter/correspondent), March 17, 1983 (ABC)

FOR PROGRAMS SPECIAL CLASSIFICATION OF OUTSTANDING PROGRAM ACHIEVEMENT

☐ "The Crisis Game," *Nightline*, William Lord (executive producer), William Moore (senior producer), Ted Koppel (reporter/correspondent), November 22–25, 1983 (ABC)

The Miracle of Life, John Mansfield (executive producer), Bo G. Erikson, Carl O. Lofman (producers), Bo Erikson and Carl O. Lofman (reporter/correspondents), February 15, 1983 (PBS)

Children of Darkness, Richard Kotuk and Ara Chekmayan (producers), Richard Kotuk (reporter/correspondent), May 4, 1983 (PBS)

The Constitution: That Delicate Balance, Stuart Sucherman (executive producer), Jude Dratt (producer), January 12, 1983 (PBS)

FOR SEGMENTS

"The Black Bears of Maine," *World News Tonight*, Don Wall (producer), Roger Caras (reporter/correspondent), April 13, 1983 (ABC)

"1983 Yearender," *World News Tonight*, Jonathan Talmadge (producer), Mark Bogni (co-producer), December 30, 1983 (ABC)

☐ "A Stranger in the Home," *Monitor*, Chirstine Huneke (producer), Rebecca Sobel (reporter/correspondent), April 23, 1983 (NBC)

"What Happened to Baby Gene," *Monitor*, Ray Farkas (producer), Rebecca Sobel (reporter/correspondent), May 21, 1983 (NBC)

"Viewpoint," *ABC News*, William Lord (executive producer), George Watson, William Moore, Stuart Schwartz, Robert Jordan (senior producers), Carla De Landri (producer), Ted Koppel (reporter/correspondent), November 20, 1983 (ABC)

FOR OUTSTANDING INDIVIDUAL ACHIEVEMENT IN NEWS AND DOCUMENTARY PROGRAMMING

Writers

Barbara Jampel, "Australia's Animal Mysteries," *National Geographic Special*, February 9, 1983 (PBS)

John Fielding, Steve Singer, Judy Crichton, Kathy Slobogin, Richard Gerdau, *JFK*, November 11, 1983 (ABC)

☐ Judy Crichton, Andrew Schlesinger, Steve Singer, Bill Redeker, *Oh, Tell*

☐ Indicates winner

the World What Happened, January 7, 1983 (ABC)

Nelson E. Breen, *Grand Central*, June 29, 1983 (PBS)

Miriam Birch, "Save the Panda," *National Geographic Special*, March 9, 1983 (PBS)

Theodore Strauss, "Born of Fire," *National Geographic Special*, April 6, 1983 (PBS)

Directors

☐ Paul Fine and Holly Fine, *The Plane that Fell from the Sky*, July 14, 1983 (CBS)

Laszlo Pal, *Everest North Wall*, May 4, 1983 (PBS)

FOR OUTSTANDING INDIVIDUAL ACHIEVEMENT IN NEWS AND DOCUMENTARY PROGRAMMING

Directors

☐ Jim Brown, *The Weavers: Wasn't That a Time*, March 16, 1983 (PBS)

Patrick M. Cook, "Adapt or Die," *ABC News Closeup*, April 1, 1983, (ABC)

Karyn J. Taylor, *The Vanishing America*, June 5, 1983 (ABC)

Cinematographers

Ted Haimes, *The American Inquisition*, June 23, 1983 (ABC)

Norris Brock, "Save the Panda," *National Geographic Special*, March 9, 1983 (PBS)

David and Carol Hughes, "Rain Forest," *National Geographic Special*, January 12, 1983 (PBS)

☐ Gregory Andracke, *American Journey*, March 30, 1983 (PBS)

Joe Seamans, Jim Frazier, "Australia's Animal Mysteries," *National Geographic Special*, February 9, 1983 (PBS)

FOR OUTSTANDING INDIVIDUAL ACHIEVEMENT IN NEWS AND DOCUMENTARY PROGRAMMING

Electronic camerapersons: Videographers

☐ George J. Fridrich, "Repeat Offenders Segment," *First Camera*, November 27, 1983 (NBC)

Phil G. Giriodi, "Kilauea Erupts," *CBS Evening News*, April 8, 1983 (CBS)

David Green, "Northern Ireland," *Nightline*, March 16, 1983 (ABC)

Foster Wiley (videographer), "Niacaragua: A House Divided," *Inside Story*, October 13, 1983 (PBS)

Sound: Audio sweetening (including editors, mixers, and effects), studio audio mixers, film sound mixers (including re-recording mixers and editors), live/location videotape and sound recordist (video and film)

Jon Alpert, "Nicaragua 1983," *Today Show*, March, 1983 (NBC)

Jeffrey S. Goodman (location video sound recordist), "Repeat Offenders Segment," *First Camera*, November 27, 1983 (NBC)

☐ David Clark, "Save the Panda," *National Geographic Special*, March 9, 1983 (PBS)

FOR OUTSTANDING INDIVIDUAL ACHIEVEMENT IN NEWS AND DOCUMENTARY PROGRAMMING

Tape editors: Videotape editors and videotape post production editors

Bob Bailey (video tape editor), "In Pursuit of the American Dream," *Today Show*, February 15, November 29, 1983 (NBC)

☐ John J. Godfrey, Jon Alpert, John Custodio (tape editors), "Nicaragua 1983," *Today Show*, March, 1983 (NBC)

☐ Wayne Dennis (tape editor), "Repeat Offenders Segment," *First Camera*, November 27, 1983 (NBC)

Michael M. Siegel, Barry Gingold, Mario Schencman, Wayne Weiss (post production editors), *JFK*, November 11, 1983 (ABC)

Film editors: Film editors and film post production editors

Barry Nye (editor), "Rain Forest," *National Geographic Special*, January 12, 1983 (PBS)

☐ Kris Liem, James Flanagan, Ara Chekmayan, Patrick M. Cook, John Martin, Bernard Stone (film editors), *JFK*, November 11, 1983 (ABC)

Holly Fine (production film editor), *The Plane That Fell from the Sky*, July 14, 1983 (CBS)

Jerry J. Siegel (film editor), "Willie Loman Goes to China," *Our Times with Bill Moyers*, July 5, 1983 (CBS)

Peter Eliscu (editor), "Pentagon/Underground," *Our Times with Bill Moyers*, July 19, 1983 (CBS)

FOR OUTSTANDING INDIVIDUAL ACHIEVEMENT IN NEWS AND DOCUMENTARY PROGRAMMING

Lighting directors:

Morton Gorowitz (lighting director), *The Plane That Fell from the Sky*, July 14, 1983 (CBS)

Walter Palmer (lighting director), *Viewpoint*, November, 1983 (ABC)

Scenic designers

☐ Francis Mahard (scenic designer), "Crisis in Zimbabwe," *Frontline*, April 25, 1983 (PBS)

Daytime Awards

OUTSTANDING DAYTIME DRAMA SERIES

Emmy(s) to executive producer(s) and producer(s):
All My Children, Jacqueline Babbin (producer) (ABC)
Days of Our Lives, Mrs. Ted Corday (executive producer), Al Rabin (supervising executive producer), Patricia Wenig (supervising producer), Ken Corday (producer) (NBC)
General Hospital, Gloria Monty (producer) (ABC)
One Life to Live, Joseph Stuart (producer) (ABC)
☐ *The Young & the Restless*, William J. Bell (executive producer), H. Wesley Kenney (executive producer), Edward Scott (producer) (CBS)

OUTSTANDING GAME OR AUDIENCE PARTICIPATION SHOW

Emmy(s) to executive producer(s) and producer(s):
The Price Is Right, Frank Wayne (executive producer), Barbara Hunter (co-producer), Phillip Wayne (co-producer) (CBS)
☐ *The $25,000 Pyramid*, Bob Stewart (executive producer), Anne Marie Schmitt and Sande Stewart (producers) (CBS)
Family Feud, Howard Felsher (producer) (ABC)

OUTSTANDING TALK/SERVICE SERIES

Emmy(s) to executive producer(s) and producer(s):
Phil Donahue, Richard Mincer (executive producer), Patricia McMillen (senior producer), Darlene Hayes and Sheri Singer (producers) (Syndicated)
Hour Magazine, Martin M. Berman (executive producer), Steve Clements (producer) (Syndicated)
The Richard Simmons Show, Woody Fraser and Nora Fraser (executive producers), Noreen Friend (producer) (Syndicated)
☐ *This Old House*, Russell Morash (producer) (PBS)

OUTSTANDING VARIETY SERIES

Emmy(s) to executive producer(s) and producer(s):
Fantasy, Merrill Heatter (executive producer), E.V. DiMassa Jr. (producer) (NBC)
☐ *The Merv Griffin Show*, Peter Barsocchini (producer) (Syndicated)

☐ Indicates winner

OUTSTANDING CHILDREN'S ENTERTAINMENT SERIES

Emmy(s) to executive producer(s) and producer(s):
☐ *Captain Kangaroo*, Robert Keeshan and Jim Hirschfeld (executive producer) (CBS)
☐ *Smurfs*, William Hanna and Joseph Barbera (executive producer), Gerard Baldwin (producer) (NBC)

OUTSTANDING CHILDREN'S INFORMATIONAL/INSTRUCTIONAL SERIES

Emmy(s) to executive producer(s) and producer(s):
Mister Rogers' Neighborhood, Fred Rogers (executive producer), Sam Newbury (producer) (PBS)
ABC Weekend Specials (ABC)
☐ *Sesame Street*, Dulcy Singer (executive producer), Lisa Simon (producer) (PBS)

OUTSTANDING CHILDREN'S ENTERTAINMENT SPECIALS

Emmy(s) to executive producer(s) and producer(s):
The Shooting, June 1, 1982 (CBS)
Just Pals, Peter Walz (executive producer), Bob Johnson and Nick Anderson (producers) September 14, 1982 (CBS)
Oh, Boy! Babies!, Bruce Hart and Carole Hart (executive producers), Carole Hart (producer) (NBC)
"Help Wanted," *CBS Afternoon Playhouse*, Stephen Gyllenhaal (producer), October 12, 1982 (CBS)
☐ *The Woman who Willed a Miracle*, Dick Clark and Preston Fischer (executive producers), Joanne A. Curley and Sharron Miller (producers), February 9, 1983 (ABC)

OUTSTANDING CHILDREN'S INFORMATIONAL/INSTRUCTIONAL SPECIAL

Emmy(s) to executive producer(s) and producer(s)
☐ *Winners*, Tom Robertson (producer), May, 1982 (Syndicated)

OUTSTANDING INFORMATIONAL/ INSTRUCTIONAL PROGRAMMING— SHORT FORM

Emmy(s) to executive producer(s) and producer(s):
Willie Survives, Lynn Ahrens (producer) (ABC)
In the News, Joel Heller (executive producer), Walter Lister (producer) (CBS)

OUTSTANDING ACTOR IN A DAYTIME DRAMA SERIES

Peter Bergman, (Role: Dr. Cliff Warner), *All My Children* (ABC)

James Mitchell, (Role: Palmer Cortlandt), *All My Children* (ABC)
Stuart Damon, (Role: Dr. Alan Quartermaine), *General Hospital* (ABC)
Anthony Geary, (Role: Luke Spencer), *General Hospital* (ABC)
☐ Robert Woods, (Role: Bo Buchanan), *One Life to Live* (ABC)

OUTSTANDING ACTRESS IN A DAYTIME DRAMA SERIES

Susan Lucci, (Role: Erica), *All My Children* (ABC)
☐ Dorothy Lyman, (Role: Opal Gardner), *All My Children* (ABC)
Leslie Charleson, (Role: Monica Quartermaine), *General Hospital* (ABC)
Erica Slezak, (Role: Victoria Buchanan), *One Life to Live* (ABC)
Robin Strasser, (Role: Dorian Lord Callison), *One Life to Live* (ABC)

OUTSTANDING ACTOR IN A SUPPORTING ROLE IN A DAYTIME DRAMA SERIES

☐ Darnell Williams, (Role: Jesse Hubbard), *All My Children* (ABC)
Howard E. Rollins Jr., (Role: Ed Harding), *Another World* (NBC)
David Lewis, (Role: Edward Quartermaine), *General Hospital* (ABC)
John Stamos, (Role: Blackie Parrish), *General Hospital* (ABC)
Anthony Call, (Role: Herb Callison), *One Life to Live* (ABC)
Al Freeman Jr., (Role: Ed Hall), *One Life to Live* (ABC)

OUTSTANDING ACTRESS IN A SUPPORTING ROLE IN A DAYTIME DRAMA SERIES

Eileen Herlie, (Role: Myrtle Fargate), *All My Children* (ABC)
Kim Delaney, (Role: Jenny Gardner), *All My Children* (ABC)
Marcy Walker, (Role: Liza Colby), *All My Children* (ABC)
Robin Mattson, (Role: Heather Webber), *General Hospital* (ABC)
Brynn Thayer, (Role: Jenny Janssen), *One Life to Live* (ABC)
☐ Louise Shaffer, (Role: Rae Woodard), *Ryan's Hope* (ABC)

OUTSTANDING HOST/HOSTESS IN A GAME OR AUDIENCE PARTICIPATION SHOW

Dick Clark, *The New $25,000 Pyramid* (CBS)
Richard Dawson, *Family Feud* (ABC)
☐ Betty White, *Just Men!* (NBC)

OUTSTANDING HOST/HOSTESS IN A TALK/SERVICE SERIES

Gary Collins, *Hour Magazine* (Syndicated)
☐ Phil Donahue, *Donahue* (Syndicated)

Mary Martin, *Over Easy* (PBS)

OUTSTANDING HOST/HOSTESS IN A VARIETY SERIES

Merv Griffin, *The Merv Show* (Syndicated)
Peter Marshall, *Fantasy* (NBC)
☐ Leslie Uggams, *Fantasy* (NBC)

OUTSTANDING PERFORMER IN CHILDREN'S PROGRAMMING

Kevin Dobson, (Role: Jim Welsh), "Help Wanted," *CBS Afternoon Playhouse*, October 12, 1982 (CBS)
☐ Cloris Leachman, (Role: May Lemke), "The Woman Who Willed a Miracle," *ABC Afterschool Special* (ABC)
Molly Picon, (Role: Grandma), "Grandma Didn't Wave Back," *Young People's Special* (Syndicated)
Lynn Redgrave, (Role: Sarah Cotter), "The Shooting," *CBS Afternoon Playhouse* (CBS)
Fred Rogers, (Role: Mister Rogers), *Mister Rogers' Neighborhood* (PBS)

OUTSTANDING DIRECTION FOR A DAYTIME DRAMA SERIES

For the entire series

Lawrence Auerbach, Jack Coffey, Sherrel Hoffman, Francesca James, *All My Children* (ABC)
Marlena Laird, Alan Pultz, Phillip Sogard, *General Hospital* (ABC)
☐ Allen Fristoe, Norman Hall, Peter Miner, David Pressman, *One Life to Live* (ABC)

OUTSTANDING INDIVIDUAL DIRECTION FOR A GAME OR AUDIENCE PARTICIPATION SHOW

For a single episode

Paul Alter, *Family Feud* (ABC)
☐ Mark Breslow, *The Price Is Right*, December 30, 1982 (CBS)
Bruce Burmester, *The New $25,000 Pyramid* (CBS)

OUTSTANDING INDIVIDUAL DIRECTION FOR A TALK/SERVICE SERIES

For a single episode of a series

☐ Glen Swanson, *Hour Magazine*, November 10, 1982 (Syndicated)
Ron Weiner, *Donahue* (Syndicated)

OUTSTANDING INDIVIDUAL DIRECTION FOR A VARIETY SERIES

For a single episode

☐ Dick Carson, *The Merv Griffin Show*, September 17, 1982 (Syndicated)
Barry Glazer, *American Bandstand*, October 23, 1982 (ABC)

☐ Indicates winner

OUTSTANDING INDIVIDUAL ACHIEVEMENT IN CHILDREN'S PROGRAMMING FOR DIRECTING

For a single episode of a series or for a special program

Jim Hirschfeld, *Captain Kangaroo Show*, February 5, 1983 (CBS)
Jon Stone, *Sesame Street*, January 3, 1983 (PBS)
☐ Sharon Miller, "The Woman Who Willed a Miracle," *ABC Afterschool Special*, February 9, 1983 (ABC)

OUTSTANDING WRITING FOR A DAYTIME DRAMA SERIES

For the entire series

Agnes Nixon, Wisner Washam, Lorraine Broderick, Jack Wood, Mary K. Wells, Clarice Blackburn, Carolyn Franz, Elizabeth Wallace, John Saffron, *All My Children* (ABC)
Anne Howard Bailey, A.J. Russell, Leah Laiman, Thom Racina, Jack Turley, Jeanne Glynn, Robert Guza Jr., Charles Pratt Jr., Robert Shaw, *General Hospital* (ABC)
Sam Hall, Peggy O'Shea, S. Michael Schnessel, Victor Miller, Don Wallace, Lanie Bertram, Fred Corke, Craig Carlson, *One Life to Live* (ABC)
☐ Claire Labine, Paul Avila Mayer, Mary Ryan Munisteri, Eugene Price, Judith Pinsker, Nancy Ford, B.K. Perlman, Rory Metclaf, Trent Jones, *Ryan's Hope* (ABC)

OUTSTANDING ACHIEVEMENT IN TECHNICAL EXCELLENCE FOR A DAYTIME DRAMA SERIES

For the entire series—Emmys to Individuals

☐ *All My Children*, Howard Zweig, Henry Enrico Ferro (technical directors), Diana Wenman, Jean Dadario (associate directors), Lawrence Hammond, Robert Ambrico, Trevor Thompson, Vincent Senatore, Robert Ballairs, Thomas French, Richard Westlein (electronic camera), Len Walas (senior video engineer), Fran Gertler, Kathryn Tucker-Bachelder (audio engineers), Roger Haenelt (video tape editor), Barbara Woods (sound effects engineer) (ABC)
General Hospital, Dave Smith, John Cochran (technical directors), Jim Angel, Jack Denton, Steve Jones, Barry Kirsten, Bill Scott, Jan Lowry, Rich Kenney, Warren Cress, John Rago, Dale Walsh, Sal Folino, Carol Wetovich (electronic camera), Len Grice, Sam Potter, Guy Tyler (senior video engineers), Robert Miller, Zoli Osaze (senior audio engineers), Bob Lanham, Jose Galvez, Jack Moody (video tape editors) (ABC)

One Life to Live, Martin Gavrin, Lou Marchand (technical directors), John Morris, Gene Kelly, John Wood, Howie Zeidman, Charlie Henry, Frank Schiraldi, Nancy Kriegel, Rick Schiaffo, Carla Nation Reid, Genevieve Twohig (electronic camera), Herb Segall (senior video engineer), Frank Bailey, Ken Hoffman (senior audio engineers), Stuart Silver, John W. Sullivan (associate directors), Al Forman, Tony Greco (videotape editors) (ABC)

OUTSTANDING ACHIEVEMENT IN DESIGN EXCELLENCE FOR A DAYTIME DRAMA SERIES

For the entire series—Emmys to Individuals

☐ *All My Children*, William Mickley (scenic designer), William Itkin, Donna Larson, Donald Gavitt, Robert Griffin (lighting directors), Carol Luiken (costume designer), Sylvia Lawrence (make-up), Scott Hersh (make-up designers), Richard Greene (hair), Robert Chui (hair designers), Teri Smith (music director), Sid Ramin (music composer) (ABC)
General Hospital, Jim Ellingwood (art director), Mercer Barrows, Greg Strain (set decorators), Grant Velie, Tom Markle, John Zak, Rae Creevey (lighting directors), Jim O'Daniel, Robert Berdell, Jackie Eifert, Alice Jackson, Jim Christopherson, Emma Trenchard, Dolores Lampano (costume designers), P.K., Becky Bowen, Sundi Martino, Catherine McCann, Wendy Pennington, Diane Lewis (make-up designers), Katherine Kotarakos, Debbie Holmes, Mary Guerreo, Catherine Marcotte (Hair designers), Dominic Messinger, Jill Farren Phelps (music directors), Charles Paul (music composer) (ABC)
One Life to Live, Charles Brandon (scenic designer), Jo Mayer, Howard Sharrott (lighting directors), Don Sheffield (costume designer), Paul Gebbia, Robert O'Bradovich (make-up designers), Tony Anthony, Willis Hanchett (hair designers), John Anthony (music director), Jack Urbont (music director) (ABC)

OUTSTANDING INDIVIDUAL ACHIEVEMENT IN CHILDREN'S PROGRAMMING FOR WRITING

Bob Brush, Harry Crossfield, Martin Donoff, Howard Friedlander, Matt Robinson, *Captain Kangaroo*, February 5, 1983 (CBS)

☐ Arthur Heinemann, "The Woman Who Willed a Miracle," *ABC Afterschool Special*, February 9, 1983 (ABC)

Joe Bailey, Sara Compton, Tom Dunsmuir, Judy Freudberg, Tony Geiss, Emily Kingsley, David Korr, Jeff Moss, Luis Santeiro, Ray Sipherd, Norman Stiles, *Sesame Street*, April 12, 1982 (PBS)

Daryl Warner, Carolyn Miller, "Sometimes I Don't Love My Mother," *ABC Afternoon Special*, October 13, 1982 (ABC)

OUTSTANDING MUSIC COMPOSITION/DIRECTION IN CHILDREN'S PROGRAMMING

For a single episode of a series or for a special program
Jeff Moss, Tony Geiss, Richard J. Freitas, Chris Cerf, Gerri Brioso (composers), *Sesame Street*, January 3, 1983; February 4, 1983; November 22, 1982 (PBS)

☐ Elliot Lawrence (music director), "Sometimes I Don't Love My Mother," *ABC Afterschool Special*, October 13, 1982 (ABC)

OUTSTANDING CINEMATOGRAPHY IN CHILDREN'S PROGRAMMING

For a single episode of a series or for a special program
☐ Terry Meade, "The Shooting," *CBS Afternoon Playhouse*, June 2, 1982 (CBS)

Peter Stein, "Robbers, Rooftops and Witches," *CBS Library*, April 20, 1982 (CBS)

OUTSTANDING FILM EDITING IN CHILDREN'S PROGRAMMING

For a single episode of a series or for a special program
Jennifer Boyd, Jim Burgess, Paul Fisher, Karl Keleman, Dick Langenbach, Andre Marcel, Chuck Penn, *The Great Space Coaster: A Special Kind of Courage: The Special Olympics*, October 15, 1982 (Syndicated)

☐ Scott McKinsey, "The Shooting," *CBS Afternoon Playhouse*, June 2, 1982 (CBS)

Bob Beherens, Garry Seidel, Leslie Smith, Christopher Stock, Dan Swielik, Judy Verda, *Kidsworld*, February 26, 1982 (Syndicated)

☐ Indicates winner

THIS IS AN "AREA" WHERE THERE IS A POSSIBILITY OF MORE THAN ONE AWARD, ONE AWARD OR NO AWARD.

OUTSTANDING ACHIEVEMENT IN RELIGIOUS PROGRAMMING— SERIES

Emmy(s) to executive producer(s) and producer(s):
☐ *Insight*, Ellwood E. Kieser, Paulist (executive producer), Mike Rhodes and Terry Sweeney, S.J. (producers) (Syndicated)

Directions, Sid Darion (executive producer), Della Lowe (producer) (ABC)

OUTSTANDING ACHIEVEMENT IN RELIGIOUS PROGRAMMING— SPECIALS

Emmy(s) to executive producer(s) and producer(s):
☐ *The Juggler of Notre Dame*, Ellwood E. Kieser, Paulist (executive producer), Mike Rhodes and Terry Sweeney, S.J. (producers) (Syndicated)

☐ *Land of Fear, Land of Courage*, Helen Marmor (executive producer) (NBC)

SPECIAL CLASSIFICATION OF OUTSTANDING PROGRAM ACHIEVEMENT

Emmy(s) to executive producer(s) and producer(s)
☐ *American Bandstand*, Dick Clark (executive producer), Larry Klein (producer), Barry Glazer (co-producer) (ABC)

FYI, Yanna Kroyt Brandt (producer), Mary Ann Donahue (coordinating producer) (ABC)

OUTSTANDING ACHIEVEMENT IN THE COVERAGE OF SPECIAL EVENTS

Emmy(s) to executive producer(s) and producer(s):
☐ *Macy's Thanksgiving Day Parade*, Dick Schneider (producer) (NBC)

The Ninth Annual Daytime Emmy Awards, Bill Carruthers (executive producer), Joel Stein (producer) (CBS)

OUTSTANDING PROGRAM ACHIEVEMENT IN THE PERFORMING ARTS

Emmy(s) to executive producer(s) and producer(s):
☐ *Hansel and Gretel: Live from the Met*, Michael Bronson (executive producer), Clemente D'Alessio (producer) (PBS)

☐ *Zubin and the I.P.O.*, Samuel Elfert (producer) (NBC)

OUTSTANDING INDIVIDUAL ACHIEVEMENT IN RELIGIOUS PROGRAMMING—PERFORMERS

☐ Lois Nettleton, (Role: Mandy), *Insight: "A Gun for Mandy"*, December 26, 1982 (Syndicated)

☐ Edwin Newman, (Role: Moderator), *Kids, Drugs and Alcohol*, April 18, 1982 (NBC)

SPECIAL CLASSIFICATION OF OUTSTANDING INDIVIDUAL ACHIEVEMENT—PERFORMERS

☐ Hal Linden, (Role: Host), *FYI* (ABC)

SPECIAL CLASSIFICATION OF OUTSTANDING INDIVIDUAL ACHIEVEMENT—WRITING

Mary Ann Donahue, Joseph Gustaitis, Linda Kline, Robin Westen, Elaine Whitley, *FYI* (ABC)

SPECIAL CLASSIFICATION OF OUTSTANDING INDIVIDUAL ACHIEVEMENT—DIRECTING

Mike Gargiulo, *FYI* (ABC)

Al Rabin, *Days of Our Lives*, Remote: Helicopter sequence at Lake Arrowhead (NBC)

OUTSTANDING INDIVIDUAL ACHIEVEMENT IN THE COVERAGE OF SPECIAL EVENTS—DIRECTING

Dick Schneider, *Macy's Thanksgiving Day Parade*, November 25, 1982 (NBC)

OUTSTANDING INDIVIDUAL ACHIEVEMENT IN THE COVERAGE OF SPECIAL EVENTS—TECHNICAL DIRECTION/ELECTRONIC CAMERAWORK

☐ Terry Rohnke (technical director), Mike Bennett, Carl Eckett, Eric Eisenstein, Barry Frischer, Bill Goetz, Steve Gonzalez, Dave Hagen, John Hillyer, Gene Martin, Don Mulvaney, John Pinto (electronic camera), *Macy's Thanksgiving Day Parade*, November 25, 1982 (NBC)

OUTSTANDING INDIVIDUAL ACHIEVEMENT IN ANY AREA OF CREATIVE TECHNICAL CRAFTS— TECHNICAL DIRECTION/ ELECTRONIC CAMERAWORK

Robert Hoffman (technical director), *One Life to Live*, Remote: Silver Springs, Florida, May 13 – June 1, 1982 (ABC)

Anthony L. Gambino (electronic camera), *One Life to Live*, Remote: Silver Springs, Florida, May 13 – June 1, 1982 (ABC)

Howard Zweig (technical director), Lawrence Hammond, Trevor Thompson, Diana Cates-Cantrell (electronic camera), *All My Children*, Remote: Backstage Ramp, February 5 and 28, 1982 (ABC)

Harvey L. Clavon (electronic camera), *The Richard Simmons Show* (Syndicated)

OUTSTANDING ACHIEVEMENT IN ANY AREA OF CREATIVE TECHNICAL CRAFTS—ASSOCIATE DIRECTION/VIDEOTAPE EDITING
Nick Martino (associate director and videotape editor), Mike Beltran, Mort Smith, David Dunlap, Jeffrey C. Smith (videotape editors), *Fantasy*, November 24, 1982 (NBC)
Jean L. Dadario, Roger Haenelt (associate directors), *All My Children*, Remote: Backstage Ramp, February 25 and 28, 1983 (ABC)

OUTSTANDING INDIVIDUAL ACHIEVEMENT IN CHILDREN'S PROGRAMMING—ASSOCIATE DIRECTION/VIDEOTAPE EDITING
□ Ilie Agopian (videotape editor), *Young People's Specials* (Syndicated)

OUTSTANDING INDIVIDUAL ACHIEVEMENT IN RELIGIOUS PROGRAMMING—ASSOCIATE DIRECTION/VIDEOTAPE EDITING
Matty Powers (videotape editor), *Priceless Treasure*, April 25, 1982 (NBC)

OUTSTANDING ACHIEVEMENT IN ANY AREA OF CREATIVE TECHNICAL CRAFTS— CINEMATOGRAPHY
□ Robert Ryan, *Lorne Greene's New Wilderness* (Syndicated)

OUTSTANDING INDIVIDUAL ACHIEVEMENT IN RELIGIOUS PROGRAMMING—FILM EDITING
□ Scott McKinsey, *Insight—"Every 90 Seconds"* (Syndicated)
□ Ed Williams, *Land of Fear, Land of Courage*, December 5, 1982 (NBC)

OUTSTANDING INDIVIDUAL ACHIEVEMENT IN ANY AREA OF CREATIVE TECHNICAL CRAFTS— FILM EDITING
□ Les Brown, *Lorne Greene's New Wilderness* (Syndicated)

OUTSTANDING INDIVIDUAL ACHIEVEMENT IN ANY AREA OF CREATIVE TECHNICAL CRAFTS— AUDIO
□ John N. Castaldo (audio engineer), *Donahue*, April 20, 1982 (Syndicated)

OUTSTANDING INDIVIDUAL ACHIEVEMENT IN ANY AREA OF THE PERFORMING ARTS—AUDIO
□ Jay David Saks (audio director), *Hansel and Gretel: Live from the Met*, December 25, 1982 (PBS)
□ Indicates winner

OUTSTANDING INDIVIDUAL ACHIEVEMENT IN ANY AREA OF CREATIVE TECHNICAL CRAFTS— MUSIC COMPOSITION/DIRECTION
□ Jack Urbont (composer/director), *Lorne Greene's New Wilderness* (Syndicated)

OUTSTANDING INDIVIDUAL ACHIEVEMENT IN THE COVERAGE OF SPECIAL EVENTS—MUSIC COMPOSITION/DIRECTION
Milton Delugg (composer/director), Anne Delugg (lyricist), *Macy's Thanksgiving Day Parade*, November 25, 1982 (NBC)

OUTSTANDING INDIVIDUAL ACHIEVEMENT IN CHILDREN'S PROGRAMMING—ART DIRECTION/ SCENIC DESIGN/SET DECORATION
□ Victor Dinapoli (art director), *Sesame Street*, November 24, 1982 (PBS)

OUTSTANDING INDIVIDUAL ACHIEVEMENT IN ANY AREA OF CREATIVE TECHNICAL CRAFTS— ART DIRECTION/SCENIC DESIGN/ SET DECORATION
Matthew Stoddart, John Orberg, Christopher Lyall, Robert Lovett, Jim Kroupa (puppet design and construction), *The Great Space Coaster: A Special Kind of Courage: The Special Olympics* (Syndicated)
Bruce Ryan (art director), *American Bandstand*, September 25, 1982 (ABC)
Don Shirley (scenic designer), *Daytime Emmy Awards*, June 11, 1982 (CBS)

OUTSTANDING INDIVIDUAL ACHIEVEMENT IN CHILDREN'S PROGRAMMING—LIGHTING DIRECTION
William Knight, *Sesame Street*, November 24, 1982 (PBS)
Randy Nordstrom, *Sesame Street*, October 14, 1982 (PBS)

OUTSTANDING INDIVIDUAL ACHIEVEMENT IN RELIGIOUS PROGRAMMING—LIGHTING DIRECTION
George Riesenberger, *It Is Written: "Prophet in the House"* (Syndicated)

OUTSTANDING INDIVIDUAL ACHIEVEMENT IN THE COVERAGE OF SPECIAL EVENTS—LIGHTING DIRECTION
Carl Vitelli Jr., *Daytime Emmy Awards*, June 11, 1982 (CBS)

OUTSTANDING INDIVIDUAL ACHIEVEMENT IN THE PERFORMING ARTS—LIGHTING DIRECTION
Gil Weschler, *Hansel and Gretel: Live from the Met*, December 25, 1982 (PBS)

OUTSTANDING ACHIEVEMENT IN ANY AREA OF CREATIVE TECHNICAL CRAFTS—LIGHTING DIRECTION
□ Nicholas Hutak, *The Guiding Light*, Remote: Franconia Notch, April 26 and 30, 1982 (CBS)
Everett R. Melosh, *One Life to Live*, Remote: Silver Springs, Florida, May 13 – June 1, 1982 (ABC)

OUTSTANDING INDIVIDUAL ACHIEVEMENT IN CHILDREN'S PROGRAMMING—COSTUME DESIGN
Robert Turturice, "The Shooting," *CBS Afternoon Playhouse*, June 2, 1982 (CBS)
Bill Griffin, *Captain Kangaroo*, February 19, 1983 (CBS)

OUTSTANDING INDIVIDUAL ACHIEVEMENT IN ANY AREA OF CREATIVE TECHNICAL CRAFTS— COSTUME DESIGN
Robert O'Hearn, *Hansel and Gretel: Live from the Met*, December 25, 1982 (PBS)

OUTSTANDING INDIVIDUAL ACHIEVEMENT IN CHILDREN'S PROGRAMMING—MAKE-UP DESIGN AND HAIR DESIGN
Steve Atha (hair/make-up designer), "Robbers, Rooftops and Witches," *CBS Library*, April 20, 1982 (CBS)
Scott Hamilton (make-up designer), "The Woman Who Willed a Miracle," *ABC Afterschool Special*, February 9, 1983 (ABC)
Carla White (hair-make-up designer), "Amy and the Angel," *ABC Afterschool Special*, September 22, 1982 (ABC)

OUTSTANDING INDIVIDUAL ACHIEVEMENT IN ANY AREA OF CREATIVE TECHNICAL CRAFTS— MAKE-UP AND HAIR DESIGN
Victor Callegari (make-up designer), *Hansel and Gretel: Live from the Met*, December 25, 1982 (PBS)
Nina Lawson (hair and Wig Designer), *Hansel and Gretel: Live from the Met*, December 25, 1982 (PBS)

OUTSTANDING INDIVIDUAL ACHIEVEMENT IN CHILDREN'S PROGRAMMING—GRAPHIC DESIGN
□ Gerri Brioso, *Sesame Street* (PBS)

OUTSTANDING ACHIEVEMENT IN ANY AREA OF CREATIVE TECHNICAL CRAFTS—GRAPHIC DESIGN
Jacqueline A. Frazier, Jim Sterling, *Fantasy*, November 24, 1982 (NBC)
Larry Ferguson, *Over Easy*, October 15, 1982 (PBS)

OUTSTANDING INDIVIDUAL ACHIEVEMENT IN THE COVERAGE OF SPECIAL EVENTS—PERFORMERS

Bryant Gumbel, *Macy's Thanksgiving Day Parade*, Role: Host, November 25, 1982 (NBC)

OUTSTANDING INDIVIDUAL ACHIEVEMENT IN THE PERFORMING ARTS—PERFORMERS

☐ Zubin Mehta, *Zubin and the I.P.O.*, Role: Symphony conductor, May 30, 1982 (NBC)

Sports Awards

OUTSTANDING EDITED SPORTS SPECIAL

Emmy(s) to executive producer(s) and producer(s) and director(s):

1982 U.S. Tennis Open Highlights, Frank Chirkinian (executive producer), David Winner (producer), Larry Cavolina (director), David Segal, Bob Mansbach, Bob Matina, Cathy Barreto, John McDonough (feature producers) (CBS)

Wake Up the Echoes. . . The History of Notre Dame Football, Ed Sabol (executive producer), Steve Sabol (producer), Phil Tuckett (director) (Independent)

Indianapolis "500" '83, Roone Arledge (executive producer), Chuck Howard, Bob Goodrich (producers), Dennis Lewin (co-ordinating producer), Larry Kamm, Roger Goodman (directors), Jim Jennett (post production director) (ABC)

The Game and the Glory, Larry Parker (executive producer), Jody Shapiro, Gary Cohen, Tim Parker (producers) (Syndicated)

☐ *Wimbledon '83*, Michael Weisman (executive producer), Ted Nathanson (coordinating producer), Geoffrey Mason (producer), Ted Nathanson, Bob Levy (directors), Richard Cline (producer/director), Terry Ewert (videotape producer) (NBC)

ASSOCIATE DIRECTORS

This is an "Area" where there is a possibility of one award, more than one award or no award.
Nominations in this "Area" include:
"Closing Segment," *NCAA Basketball Championship Game*, Patti Tuite, Bob Dekas (CBS)

Indianapolis "500", Norm Samet, Ned Simon, John Bessone, Garland Peete (ABC)

☐ *The American Sportsman*, "Triumph on Mt. Everest," Angelo Bernarducci, Jean MacLean (ABC)

☐ Indicates winner

U.S. Tennis Open Highlights, Cathy Barreto, Bob Rowe, Bob Matina (CBS)

Caesars Palace Grand Prix, J.D. Hansen, John Libretto, Brian Orentreich (NBC)

ABC's Wide World of Sports, John Bessoni, Alan Brum, Dick Buffinton, Jeff Cohan, Kathy Cook, Robbie Cowen, Vince DeDario, John DeLisa, Woody Freiman, Jack Graham, Ben Harvey, Bob Hersh, Paul Hutchinson, Bob Lanning, Brian McCullough, Garlant Peete, Jimmy Roberts, Norm Samet, Ned Simon, Tony Slotkin (ABC)

GRAPHIC DESIGNERS

Sonny King, Paul Hammons, *1982 NBC Sports World Series* (NBC)

☐ Douglas E. Towey, Bill Feigenbaum, *NBA World Championship Series* (CBS)

Kristin Stromquist, James R. Sterling II, *John Denver Ski Classic* (NBC)

Matthew McCarthy, James R. Sterling II, Stacey McDonough, *Sportsworld* (NBC)

SPECIAL CLASSIFICATION OF OUTSTANDING ACHIEVEMENT: INNOVATIVE TECHNICAL ACHIEVEMENT

☐ "Microwave Transmission from the summit of Mt. Everest," *The American Sportsman—Triumph on Mt. Everest*, David Breashears, Randy Hermes, Allan Weschler, John Wilcox (ABC)

"2 Way Audio with Driver," *'83 Daytona 500*, John Porter, David Curtis, Peter Larsson, Robert Seiderman (CBS)

Air to Air Competition Coverage, ABC's Wide World of Sports, "U.S. National Skydiving Championships," Roone Arledge (executive producer), Dennis Lewin (co-ordinating producer), Carol Lehti (producer), Andy Sidaris (director), Norm Kent, Mike Sisemore, Jim Baker, Ken Crabtree, Mike Kurtgis (cameramen), Dick Horan (engineering supervisor) (ABC)

OUTSTANDING EDITED SPORTS SERIES/ANTHOLOGIES

☐ *The American Sportsman*, Roone Arledge (executive producer), John Wilcox (senior producer), Chris Carmody (co-ordinating producer), Bob Nixon, Curt Gowdy (producers) (ABC)

NFL Today, Ted *Shaker (executive producer), Bob Dekas, Sherman Eagan, Bob Mansbach, David Blatt, Mark Wolff (feature producers), George Veras (producer), Duke Struck (director) (CBS)

This Is The U.S.F.L., Michael Tollin, Alan Lubell, Gary Cohen (producers) (Syndicated)

ABC's Wide World of Sports, Roone Arledge (executive producer), Dennis Lewin (co-ordinating producer), Carol Lehti, Curt Gowdy Jr., Ken Wolfe, Eleanor Riger, Bob Goodrich, Alex Wallau, Jeff Ruhe, Joel Feld (producers), Chet Forte, Doug Wilson (producer/directors), Jim Jennett, Andy Sidaris, Ken Fouts, Larry Kamm (directors) (ABC)

Sportsworld, Michael Weisman, Linda Jonsson, Hilary Cosell, Kenneth Edmundson, Terry Ewert, John Gonzalez, Jay Hansen, Matthew McCarthy, Peter M. Rolfe, Ginny Seipt (producers), Bob Levy, Richard Cline, Ted Nathanson (directors) (NBC)

FILM EDITORS

☐ Yale Nelson, *The 79th World Series* (NBC)

Ted Winterburn, *ABC's Wide World of Sports*, "Great American Bike Race" (ABC)

Steve Sabol, *Wake Up the Echoes: The History of Notre Dame Football* (Independent)

SPECIAL CLASSIFICATION OF OUTSTANDING ACHIEVEMENT. SPORTS JOURNALISM

NFL Highs, NFL Lows, Dan Lauck (producer) (Independent)

☐ *ABC Sports Beat*, Michael Marley, Ed Silverman (producing managing editor), Howard Cosell (Sr. producer), Maury Rubin, Noubar Stone, Rob Beiner (directors), (1) Cal State, (2) Herschel Walker (ABC)

Alexis Arguello, David Michaels, Pat O'Brien (CBS)

Wimbledon '83, "Burnout," Michael Weisman, Ted Nathanson, Geoffrey Mason, Terry Ewert (producers) (NBC)

CBS Sports Saturday & Sunday, "Landon Turner, Bill Kunkel, Jimmy Piersall," Michael Arnold (CBS)

MUSIC COMPOSERS, MUSIC DIRECTORS

☐ John Tesh, *World University Games* (CBS)

Paul Hammons, Roger Tallman, *1983 NBC Sports Super Bowl XVII* (NBC)

WRITING

☐ George Bell Jr., *The American Sportsman*, "A Retrospective of William Holden's Africa" (ABC)

Bud Greenspan, *Time Capsule: The Los Angeles Olympic Games of 1932* (Syndicated)

Bud Greenspan, *The 1982 Heisman Trophy Award Special* (Syndicated)
☐ Steve Sabol, Phil Tuckett, *Wake Up the Echoes: The History of Notre Dame Football* (Independent)

OUTSTANDING SPORTS PERSONALITY—ANALYST

Commentary
Frank Broyles (ABC)
☐ John Madden (CBS)
Joe Garagiola (NBC)
Al McGuire (NBC)
Merlin Olsen (NBC)

ENGINEERING/TECHNICAL SUPERVISORS
The New York City Marathon, Frank Quitoni, Harold Robbins, Rick Okulski, Geoff Felger and John Partyka (ABC)
NFL '82 Super Bowl XVII, Ernest A. Thiel Jr. (NBC)
☐ *Daytona "500"*, Walter Pile, John Pumo (CBS)
"50th Anniversary All Star Game", H. Calvin Shadwell, John W. Haynes, Jack Signorelli (NBC)
79th World Series, Robert McKearnin, Garfield Ricketts, Keith Scammahorn, H. Clavin Shadwell, Robert Brydon (NBC)

OUTSTANDING LIVE SPORTS SERIES

Emmy(s) to executive producer(s) and producer(s) and director(s):
NCAA Football '82, Roone Arledge (executive producer), Chuck Howard (senior producer), Ken Wolfe (producer), Mike Pearl (studio producer), Andy Sidaris, Larry Kamm, Dick Buffington (directors) (ABC)
☐ *CBS Sports Presents the National Football League*, Terry O'Neil (executive producer), Charles Milton, Michael Burks, Bob Stenner, David Dinkins, John Faratzis, Ed Goren, David Michaels, Jim Silman, David Winner (producers), Sandy Grossman, Andrew Kindle, Joe Aceti, Bob Dunphy, John McDonough, Peter Bleckner, Bob Dailey, Larry Cavolina (directors) (CBS)
Major League Baseball Game of the Week, Michael Weisman (executive producer), Harry Coyle, Larry Cirillo, Terry Ewert, George Finkel, Kenneth Edmundson (producers), Richard Cline, Harry Coyle, John Gonzalez, Andy Rosenberg (directors) (NBC)
Professional Bowlers Tour '83, Roone Arledge (executive producer), Peter Lasser, Peter Engelhart (producers),

☐ Indicates winner

Bob Lanning, Norm Samet (directors) (ABC)
NCAA Football on CBS, Kevin O'Malley (executive producer), Ric La Civita, Rick Sharp, Jim Silman, Jean Harper, Mike Burks, Don McGuire, David Dinkins (producers), Robert Fishman, Larry Cavolina, John McDonough, Bob Dailey, Sandy Grossman, Patti Tuite, Joe Carole, Peter Bleckner (directors) (CBS)

LIGHTING DIRECTORS

This is an "Area" where there is a possibility of one award, more than one award or no award. Nomination in this "Area" include:
ABC's Wide World of Sports, "International Professional Figure Skating Championships," Melvin B. Handelman (ABC)
☐ *NCAA Football on CBS*, Joe Crookham (CBS)
Professional Bowlers Tour—Akron, Ohio, Tony Azzolino (ABC)

CINEMATOGRAPHERS

This is an "Area" where there is a possibility of one award, more than one award or no award.
Nominations in this "Area" include:
☐ *The American Sportsman*, "Mt. Everest East Face," Kurt Diemburger, David Breashears (ABC)
☐ *The Iditarod Sled Dog Race*, Peter Henning, Bill Philbin (CBS)
ABC's Wide World of Sports, "Great American Bike Race," Don Shoemaker, Joe Longo (ABC)
Sportworld Episode: Survival of the Fittest, Don Burgess, Steve Confer, Bill Philbin, Mark Zavad, Bob Carmichael, Steve Bridge, Wallack Axle, Mosh Levin, Jim Birdwell, Robert Bagley, Linton Diegle, Chris Woods (NBC)

SPECIAL CLASSIFICATION OF OUTSTANDING ACHIEVEMENT: PROGRAM ACHIEVEMENT
☐ *ABC's Wide World of Sports*, "Great American Bike Race," Roone Arledge (executive producer), Dennis Lewin (co-ordinating producer), Larry Kamm (producer), Peter Lasser, Larry Kamm (directors) (ABC)
CBS Sports Saturday, "The Iditarod," Terry O'Neil, Ed Goren, Peter Henning (producers) (CBS)
☐ *Football in America*, Robert Carmichael (producer) (PBS)
☐ *The American Sportsman*, "Triumph on Mt. Everest," John Wilcox (producer/director) (ABC)
CBS Sports Saturday/Sunday, "Top to Bottom Coverage of America's

Downhill," Terry O'Neil, David Dinkins Jr., Andy Kindle, Peter Bleckner (producers) (CBS)
NFL Pro Magazine, "A Man to Match the Mountains," Steve Sabol, Phil Tuckett (producers) (Syndicated)

TECHNICAL DIRECTORS, ELECTRONIC CAMERAPERSONS, SENIOR VIDEO OPERATORS, SENIOR AUDIO ENGINEERS (TECHNICAL TEAM)

This is an "Area" where there is a possibility of one award, more than one award or no award.
Nominations in this "Area" include:
The NCAA Basketball Final Four, Bob Brown, Steve Cunningham (technical directors), Bob Seiderman, Mark Radulovick (audio), Frank Florio, Ed Ambrosini, Lou Lecer, Dave Orlich (video), Jeff Pollack, Gordon Sweeney, Joe Vicens, Bob Jamieson, Sol Baess, Tom McCarthy, Joel Solofsky, David Finch, Terry Clark, Bob Welsh (camera) (CBS)
The New York City Marathon, John Fider, W. Gunther, Rich Gelber, Gene Affrunti (technical directors), Mike Michaels, Bob Shultis, Paul Hurney, Ed Garofalo, M. Janklow, Danny Cahn, R. Ahrens, D. Brown, Harold Gordon, Gary Paparello, Marv Bronstein, Lloyd Lynch, T. McMurray (senior video operators), John Lory, Jerry Cudmore, Fran Gertler (audio), W. Maisch, A. Demammos, Steve Wolff, Richie Westline, J. Sapienza, Mort Levin, Nick Karas, Jerry Dowd, Jack Cronin, M. Hoffman, J. Cordone, D. Dragonetti, A. Peffer, George Montanez, Serf Menduina, J. Shafer, Tony Gambino, R. Hammond, W. Sullivan, K. Sanborn, J. Stefanoni, Phil Fontana, R. Bernstein, V. Senatore, R. Theodore, E. Wood (camera) (ABC)
Kentucky Derby, Joe Schiavo, John Fider (technical directors), Mike Michaels, Ken Amow (senior video operators), Jim Davis, Jack Kestenbaum, Norm Kiernan, Bill Sandreuter (audio), L. Stenman, A. Armentani, J. Morreale, Jim Heneghan, Tom O'Connell, Jesse Kohn, Gary Donatelli, A. DeRosa, Steve Nikifor, Frank Melchiorre, Jack Dorfman, Bill Sullivan, Jack Cronin, Roy Hutchings, E. Wood, Mort Levin, J. Stefanoni, T. Thompson, Bob Bernstein (camera) (ABC)
Super Bowl XVII, Lenny Stucker, Steven Cimino, William Tobey, Rick Lombardo (technical directors), Billy Kidd, Bill Parinello, Jim Blaney Sr. (senior audio engineers), Jim

Marshall, Scott McCartney (senior video operators), Dayne Adams, Leonard Basile, Rodney Batten, Jim Bragg, Phil Cantrell, Mario Ciarlo, Jim Culley, Eric Eisenstein, Barry Frischer, Lou Gerard, Steve Gonzalez, David A. Hagen, Roger Harbaugh, Ken Harvey, James Herring, Jim Johnson, Buddy Joseph, Joe Klimovitz, Cory Leible, George Loomis, Gene Martin, Roy Ratliff, Al Rice, George Simpson, Bailey Stortz, Mike Stramisky, Vickie Walker (camera) (NBC)

☐ *Daytona 500*, Sandy Bell, Bob Brown, Anthony Filippi (technical directors), Bob Siderman, Tom Jimenez (audio), Robert Pieringer, Tom Delilla, Bill Berridge, Ron Rasch (video), Jim Murphy, Neil McCaffrey, Tom McCarthy, Herman Lang, Barry Drago, Joe Sokota, Jim McCarthy, Jeff Pollack, Frank McSpedon, George Rothweiler, George Neader, George Graffeo, Ray Chiste, Hans Sincer, Sig Meyer, Walt Soucy (camera) (CBS)

The 79th World Series, Lenny Stucker, Steven Cimino, William Tobey (technical directors), Jerry Caruso, Bill Parinello (senior audio engineers), Jim Sunder, Sal Benza (senior video operators), Leonard Basile, Al Camoin, Phil Cantrell, Mario Ciarlo, Jim Culley, Russ Diven, Eric Eisenstein, Barry Frischer, Lou Gerard, Bill Boetz, Steve Gonzalez, David A. Hagen, Tom Hogan, Jim Johnson, Buddy Joseph, Cory Leible, George Loomis, Albert Rice, Bryan Russo, George Simpson, Mike Straminsky, Vickie Walker (camera) (NBC)

VIDEOTAPE EDITORS

**This is an "Area" where there is a possibility of one award, more than one award or no award.
Nominations in this "Area" include:**
Caesars Palace Grand Prix, Richard Leible, Jim McQueen, Scott Rader, Jeff U'ren (NBC)
Daytona 500 Opening, Steven Babb, Mario R. Marino (CBS)
Sportsworld, Richard Leible, Jim McQueen, Sam Patterson, Scott Rader, Brian Wickham (NBC)
NBC Baseball Pre-Game/Major League Baseball: An Inside Look, Mike Kostel, Rick Reed, Rich Domich, John Servideo (NBC)
This is the USFL "What A Feeling," Bob Klug, Mark King, James Walton (syndicated)
☐ *1982 World Series Pre-Game Show*, Mike Kostel, Rick Reed, Rich Domich, John Servideo (NBC)

☐ Indicates winner

ABC's Wide World of Sports – Ironman Triathlon World Championship, Harvey Beal, Marvin Gench, Joe Longo, Gary Moscato, Alex Moskovic, Pam Peterson, Mario Schencman, Mike Siegel (ABC)
☐ *"Closing Segment" NCAA Basketball Championship Game*, Bob Hickson, George Joanitis, Lito Magpayo (CBS)

OUTSTANDING SPORTS PERSONALITY – HOST

☐ Dick Enberg (NBC)
Al Michaels (ABC)
Brent Musburger (CBS)
Jim McKay (ABC)
Vin Scully (NBC)

OUTSTANDING LIVE SPORTS SPECIAL

Emmy(s) to executive producer(s) and producer(s) and director(s):
Daytona 500, Robert D. Stenner, Ted Shaker, Dan Forer (producers), Robert Fishman (director) (CBS)
☐ *The 79th World Series*, Michael Weisman, George Finkel (producers), Harry Coyle, Andy Rosenberg (directors) (NBC)
The Belmont Stakes, Robert D. Stenner, Robert Fishman (producers), Robert Fishman (director) (CBS)
1983 NCAA Basketball Championship Game, Kevin O'Malley, (executive producer), Rick Sharp, Ted Shaker, Dan Forer, Patti Tuite (producers), Robert Fishman, Duke Struck (directors) (CBS)
50th Anniversary All Star Game, David Neal, Harry Coyle, George Finkel (producers), Andy Rosenberg, Harry Coyle (directors), Michael Weisman (executive producer) (NBC)

FOR OUTSTANDING ACHIEVEMENT IN THE SCIENCE OF TELEVISION ENGINEERING

The Ampex Corporation
The International Radio Consultative Committee of the International Telecommunication Union (CCSR)
The European Broadcasting Union
RCA CCSD Video Systems
SMPTE
3M Corporation
Xerox Corporation
Mel Sater
Richard Shoup

1983/84

(For programs aired between July 1, 1983 and June 30, 1984. Entertainment and individual achievement awards presented September 23, 1984. Creative Arts awards presented September 16, 1984. Daytime awards presented June 27, 1984 for programs aired between March 6, 1983 and March 5, 1984.)

Prime Time Program Awards

OUTSTANDING COMEDY SERIES

Emmy(s) to executive producer(s) and producer(s):
Buffalo Bill, Bernie Brillstein, Tom Patchett, Jay Tarses (executive producers), Dennis Klein, Carol Gary (producers) (NBC)
☐ *Cheers*, James Burrows, Glen Charles, Les Charles (producers) (NBC)
Family Ties, Gary David Goldberg, Lloyd Garver (executive producers), Lloyd Garver, Michael J. Weithorn (producers), Carol Himes (co-producer) (NBC)
Kate & Allie, Mort Lachman, Merrill Grant (executive producers), Bill Persky, Robert Randall (producers), George Barimo (coordinating producer) (CBS)
Newhart, Barry Kemp (executive producer), Sheldon Bull (producer) (CBS)

OUTSTANDING DRAMA SERIES

Emmy(s) to executive producer(s) and producer(s):
Cagney & Lacey, Barney Rosenzweig (executive producer), Peter Lefcourt (producer) (CBS)
Fame, William Blinn (executive producer), Ken Ehrlich (producer) (SYN)
☐ *Hill Street Blues*, Steven Bochco (executive producer), Gregory Hoblit (co-executive producer), Scott Brazil (supervising producer), Jeffrey Lewis, Sascha Schneider (producers), David Latt (co-producer) (NBC)
Magnum P.I., Donald P. Bellisario (executive producer), Douglas Benton (supervising producer in Hollywood), Charles Floyd Johnson (supervising producer in Hawaii), Reuben Leder (producer), Rick Weaver, Nick Thiel (co-producers) (CBS)
St. Elsewhere, Bruce Paltrow (executive producer), Mark Tinker (supervising producers), John Masius, Tom Fontana (producers),

Abby Singer (coordinating producer) (NBC)

OUTSTANDING LIMITED SERIES

Emmy(s) to executive producer(s) and producer(s):
Chiefs, Martin Manulis (executive producer), Jerry London (supervising producer), John E. Quill (producer) (CBS)
□ "Concealed Enemies" *American Playhouse*, Lindsay Law, David Elstein (executive producers) Peter Cook (producer) (PBS)
George Washington, David Gerber (executive producer), Buzz Kulik (supervising producer), Richard Fielder (producer) (CBS)
"Nancy Astor" *Masterpiece Theatre*, Philip Hinchcliffe (producer) (PBS)
"Reilly: Ace of Spies" *Mystery!*, Verity Lambert (executive producer) C.J. Burt (producer) (PBS)

OUTSTANDING VARIETY, MUSIC OR COMEDY PROGRAM

Emmy(s) to executive producer(s) and producer(s), and host, if name appears in the title of the program
The American Film Institute Salute to Lillian Gish, Georges Stevens Jr. (producer), April 17, 1984 (CBS)
□ *The 6th Annual Kennedy Center Honors: a Celebration of the Performing Arts*, Nick Vanoff, George Stevens Jr. (producers), December 27, 1983 (CBS)
Late Night with David Letterman, Jack Rollins (executive producer), Barry Sand (producer), David Letterman (host), Series (NBC)
The Tonight Show Starring Johnny Carson, Fred de Cordova (executive producer), Peter Lassaly (producer), Johnny Carson (co-producer), Johnny Carson (host), Series (NBC)
The 1984 Tony Awards, Alexander H. Cohen (executive producer), Hildy Parks (producer), Martha Mason (co-producer), June 3, 1984 (CBS)

OUTSTANDING DRAMA/COMEDY SPECIAL

Emmy(s) to executive producer(s) and producer(s): (Includes all scripted specials that have a story with a beginning, middle and end, and performers portraying characters other than themselves.)
Adam, Alan Landsburg, Joan Barnett (executive producers), Linda Otto (producer) October 10, 1983 (NBC)
The Day After, Robert A. Papazian (producer), November 20, 1983 (ABC)

□ Indicates winner

The Dollmaker, Bruce Gilbert (executive producer), Bill Finnegan (producer), May 13, 1984 (ABC)
□ *Something About Amelia*, Leonard Goldberg (executive producer), Michele Rappaport (producer), January 9, 1984 (ABC)
A Streetcar Named Desire, Keith Barish, Craig Baumgarten (executive producers), Marc Trabulus (producer), March 4, 1984 (ABC)

OUTSTANDING CLASSICAL PROGRAM IN THE PERFORMING ARTS

Emmy(s) to executive producer(s) and producer(s), and star(s) if name appears in the title of the program
"Bernstein: Conductor, Soloist and Teacher" *Great Performances*, Horant H. Hohfeld, Harry J. Kraut (executive producers), Thomas Burger (producer), Leonard Bernstein (host), April 2, 1984 (PBS)
The Compleat Gilbert & Sullivan, George Walker (executive producer), Judith De Paul (producer), Series (PBS)
A Lincoln Center Special: New York City Ballet's Tribute to George Balanchine, John Goberman, Barbara Horgan (producers), October 10, 1983 (PBS)
Live from Lincoln Center: James Galway and Zubin Mehta with the New York Philharmonic, John Goberman (producer), James Galaway, Zubin Mehta (hosts), February 29, 1984 (PBS)
□ "Placido Domingo Celebrates Seville" *Great Performances*, Horant H. Hohlfeld (executive producer), David Griffiths (producer), Placido Domingo (host), December 5, 1983 (PBS)

OUTSTANDING INFORMATIONAL SPECIAL

Emmy(s) to executive producer(s) and producer(s), and host, if name appears in the title of the program
□ *America Remembers John F. Kennedy*, Thomas F. Horton (producer) (SYN) May 28, 1984
Balanchine, June 4, 1984 (PBS)
Great Performances Dance in America, Jac Venza (executive producer), Judy Kinberg (producer)
The Body Human: The Journey within, John D. Backe, Thomas W. Moore (executive producers), Alfred R. Kelman, Fuisz, Robert E. M.D. (producers), Robert Eisenhardt, Nancy Smith (co-producers), February 29, 1984 (CBS)
Lifestyles of the Rich and Famous, Robin Leach (executive producer), Jim Cross (supervising Producer) (SYN)

The Lions of Etosha: King of the Beasts, Aubrey Buxton (executive producer), Colin Willock (producer), June 6, 1984 (CBS)

OUTSTANDING INFORMATIONAL SERIES

Emmy(s) to executive producer(s) and producer(s), and host, if name appears in the title of the program
At the Movies, Joseph Antelo (executive producer), Nancy De Los Santos (producer) (SYN)
The Barbara Walters Specials, Beth Polson (producer), Barbara Walters (host) (ABC)
Cousteau/Amazon, Jacques-Yves Cousteau, Jean-Michel Cousteau (executive producers), Mose Richards, John Soh (producers), (SYN)
Entertainment Tonight/Entertainment this Week, George Merlis (executive producer), Jack Reilly (producer) Stu Crowner, Bruce Cook (coordinating producers) (SYN)
□ *A Walk Through the 20th Century with Bill Moyers*, Merton Y. Koplin (senior executive producer), Charles Grinker, Sanford H. Fisher (executive producers), Betsy McCarthy (coordinating producer), David Grubin, Ronald Blumer (producers) (PBS)

OUTSTANDING ANIMATED PROGRAM

Emmy(s) to executive producer(s) and producer(s):
A Disney Christmas Gift, December 20, 1983 (CBS)
□ *Garfield on the Town*, Jay Poynor (executive producer), Lee Mendelson, Bill Melendez (producers), October 28, 1983 (CBS)
It's Flashbeagle, Charlie Brown, Lee Mendelson, Bill Melendez (producers), April 16, 1984 (CBS)
The Smurfic Games, William Hanna, Joseph Barbera (executive producers), Gerard Baldwin (producer), May 20, 1984 (NBC)

OUTSTANDING CHILDREN'S PROGRAM

Emmy(s) to executive producer(s) and producer(s):
The Best Christmas Pageant Ever Merrill H. Karpf, (executive producer), George Schaefer (producer), December 5, 1983 (ABC)
Don't Eat the Pictures: Sesame Street At the Metropolitan Museum of Art, Dulcy Singer (executive producer), Lisa Simon, Arlene Sherman, Tony Geiss (producers), November 16, 1983 (PBS)

☐ *He Makes Me Feel Like Dancin'*, Edgar J. Scherick, Scott Rudin (executive producers), Emile Ardolino (producer), Judy Kinberg (co-producer), June 24, 1984 (NBC)

Prime Time Performing Awards

OUTSTANDING LEAD ACTOR IN A COMEDY SERIES

For a continuing or single performance in a regular series

NOTE: SINGLE PERFORMANCES ARE INDICATED BY EPISODE TITLE AND AIR DATE

Dabney Coleman, as: Bill Bittinger, *Buffalo Bill*, Series (NBC)

Ted Danson, as: Sam Malone, *Cheers*, Series (NBC)

Robert Guillaume, as: Benson Dubois, *Benson*, Series (ABC)

Sherman Hemsley, as: George Jefferson, *The Jeffersons*, Series (CBS)

☐ John Ritter, as: Jack Tripper, *Three's Company*, Series (ABC)

OUTSTANDING LEAD ACTOR IN A DRAMA SERIES

For a continuing or single performance in a regular series

NOTE: SINGLE PERFORMANCES ARE INDICATED BY EPISODE TITLE AND AIR DATE

William Daniels, as: Craig, Mark Dr., *St. Elsewhere*, Series (NBC)

Ed Flanders, as: Westphall, Donald Dr., *St Elsewhere* Series (NBC)

John Forsythe, as: Blake Carrington, *Dynasty* Series (ABC)

☐ Tom Selleck, as: Thomas Magnum, *Magnum, P.I.* Series (CBS)

Daniel J. Travanti, as: Frank Furillo, *Hill Street Blues* Series (NBC)

OUTSTANDING LEAD ACTOR IN A LIMITED SERIES OR A SPECIAL

For a continuing or single performance in a limited series or for a special

NOTE: SINGLE PERFORMANCES ARE INDICATED BY EPISODE TITLE AND AIR DATE

Ted Danson, as: Steven Bennett, *Something About Amelia*, January 9, 1984 (ABC)

Louis Gossett Jr., as: Anwar El Sadat, *Sadat* (OPT)

☐ Laurence Olivier, as: King Lear, *Laurence Olivier's King Lear* (SYN)

Mickey Rooney, as: Bill Sackter, *Bill: On His Own*, November 9, 1983 (CBS)

Daniel J. Travanti, as: John Walsh, *Adam*, October 10, 1983 (NBC)

☐ Indicates winner

OUTSTANDING LEAD ACTRESS IN A COMEDY SERIES

For a continuing or single performance in a regular series

NOTE: SINGLE PERFORMANCES ARE INDICATED BY EPISODE TITLE AND AIR DATE

Joanna Cassidy, as: Jo-Jo, *Buffalo Bill*, Series (NBC)

☐ Jane Curtin, as: Allie Lowell, *Kate & Allie*, Series (CBS)

Shelley Long, as: Diane Chambers, *Cheers*, Series (NBC)

Susan Saint James, as: Kate McArdle, *Kate & Allie*, Series (CBS)

Isabel Sanford, as: Louise Jefferson, *The Jeffersons*, Series (CBS)

OUTSTANDING LEAD ACTRESS IN A DRAMA SERIES

For a continuing or single performance in a regular series

NOTE: SINGLE PERFORMANCES ARE INDICATED BY EPISODE TITLE AND AIR DATE

Debbie Allen, as: Lydia Grant, *Fame*, Series (SYN)

Joan Collins, as: Alexis Carrington Colby, *Dynasty*, Series (ABC)

☐ Tyne Daly, as: Mary Beth Lacey, *Cagney & Lacey*, Series (CBS)

Sharon Gless, as: Chris Cagney, *Cagney & Lacey*, Series (CBS)

Veronica Hamel, as: Joyce Davenport, *Hill Street Blues*, Series (NBC)

OUTSTANDING LEAD ACTRESS IN A LIMITED SERIES OR A SPECIAL

For a continuing or single performance in a limited series or for a special

NOTE: SINGLE PERFORMANCES ARE INDICATED BY EPISODE TITLE AND AIR DATE

Jane Alexander, as: Calamity Jane, *Calamity Jane*, March 6, 1984 (CBS)

Ann Margret, as: Blanche Dubois, *A Streetcar named Desire*, March 4, 1984 (ABC)

Glenn Close, as: Gail Bennett, *Something About Amelia*, January 9, 1984 (ABC)

☐ Jane Fonda, as: Gertie Nevels, *The Dollmaker*, May 13, 1984 (ABC)

Jobeth Williams, as: Reve Walsh, *Adam*, October 10, 1983 (NBC)

OUTSTANDING SUPPORTING ACTOR IN A COMEDY SERIES

For a continuing or single performance in a regular series

NOTE: SINGLE PERFORMANCES ARE INDICATED BY EPISODE TITLE AND AIR DATE

Rene Auberjonois, as: Clayton Endicott III, *Benson*, Series (ABC)

Nicholas Colasanto, as: Coach Ernie Pantusso, *Cheers*, Series (NBC)

☐ Pat Harrington Jr., as: Dwayne Schneider, *One Day at a Time*, Series (CBS)

Tom Poston, as: George Utley, *Newhart*, Series (CBS)

George Wendt, as: Norm Peterson, *Cheers*, Series (NBC)

OUTSTANDING SUPPORTING ACTOR IN A DRAMA SERIES

For a continuing or single performance in a regular series

NOTE: SINGLE PERFORMANCES ARE INDICATED BY EPISODE TITLE AND AIR DATE

Ed Begley Jr., as: Ehrlich, Victor Dr., *St. Elsewhere*, Series (NBC)

Michael Esterhaus, as: Phil Esterhaus, *Hill Street Blues*, Series (NBC)

John Hillerman, as: Jonathan Higgins, *Magnum, P.I.*, Series (CBS)

James B. Sikking, as: Lt. Howard Hunter, *Hill Street Blues*, Series (NBC)

☐ Bruce Weitz, as: Mick Belker, *Hill Street Blues*, Series (NBC)

OUTSTANDING SUPPORTING ACTOR IN A LIMITED SERIES OR A SPECIAL

For a continuing or single performance in a limited series or for a special

NOTE: SINGLE PERFORMANCES ARE INDICATED BY EPISODE TITLE AND AIR DATE

☐ Art Carney, as: Troy, *Terrible Joe Moran*, March 27, 1984 (CBS)

Keith Carradine, as: Foxy Funderburke, *Chiefs*, Series (CBS)

John Gielgud, as: Lord Durrisdeer, *The Master of Ballantrae*, January 31, 1984 (CBS)

John Lithgow, as: Jo Huxley, *The Day After*, November 20, 1983 (ABC)

Randy Quaid, as: Mitch, *A Streetcar Named Desire*, March 4, 1984 (ABC)

David Ogden Stiers, as: Sloan, William Milligan Dr., *The First Olympics – Athen 1896*, May 20, 1984, May 21, 1984 (NBC)

OUTSTANDING SUPPORTING ACTRESS IN A COMEDY SERIES

For a continuing or single performance in a regular series

NOTE: SINGLE PERFORMANCES ARE INDICATED BY EPISODE TITLE AND AIR DATE

Julia Duffy, as: Stephanie Vanderkellen, *Newhart*, Series (CBS)

Marla Gibbs, as: Florence, *The Jeffersons*, Series (CBS)

Paula Kelly, as: Liz Williams, *Night Court* , Series (NBC)

☐ Rhea Perlman, as: Carla, *Cheers*, Series (NBC)

Marion Ross, as: Marion Cunningham, *Happy Days*, Series (ABC)

OUTSTANDING SUPPORTING ACTRESS IN A DRAMA SERIES

For a continuing or single performance in a regular series

NOTE: SINGLE PERFORMANCES ARE INDICATED BY EPISODE TITLE AND AIR DATE

Barbara Bosson, as: Fay Furillo, *Hill Street Blues*, Series (NBC)

Piper Laurie, as: Fran Singleton, *St. Elsewhere*, November 2, 1983 (NBC)

Madge Sinclair, as: Ernestine Shoop, *Trapper John, M.D.*, Series (CBS)

Betty Thomas, as: Officer Lucy Bates, *Hill Street Blues*, Series (NBC)

☐ Alfred Woodard, as: Doris Robson, *Hill Street Blues*, November 10, 1983 (NBC)

OUTSTANDING SUPPORTING ACTRESS IN A LIMITED SERIES OR A SPECIAL

For a continuing or single performance in a limited series or for a special

NOTE: SINGLE PERFORMANCES ARE INDICATED BY EPISODE TITLE AND AIR DATE

Patty Duke Astin, as: Martha Washington, *George Washington*, Series (CBS)

Beverly D'Angelo, as: Stella Kowalski, *A Streetcar Named Desire*, March 4, 1984 (ABC)

Cloris Leachman, as: Mary Kovacs, *Ernie Kovacs: Between the Laughter*, May 14, 1984 (ABC)

Tuesday Weld, as: Margie Young-Hunt, *"John Steinbeck's the Winter of our Discontent"*, December 6, 1983 (CBS)

☐ Roxana Zal, as: Amelia Bennett, *Something About Amelia*, January 9, 1984 (ABC)

OUTSTANDING INDIVIDUAL PERFORMANCE IN A VARIETY OR MUSIC PROGRAM

For a continuing or single performance, lead or support, in a variety or music series or special

NOTE: SINGLE PERFORMANCES ARE INDICATED BY EPISODE TITLE AND AIR DATE

Debbie Allen, *Live. . . and in Person*— Part 1, September 27, 1983 (NBC)

George Burns, *George Burns Celebrates 80 Years in Show Business*, September 19, 1983 (NBC)

☐ Indicates winner

Cloris Leachman, *Screen Actors Guild 50th Anniversary Celebration*, May 29, 1984 (CBS)

Eddie Murphy, *Saturday Night Live*, Series (NBC)

Joe Piscopo, *Saturday Night Live*, Series (NBC)

Lily Tomlin, as: Ernestine, *Live. . . and in Person*— Part 3, September 29, 1983 (NBC)

OUTSTANDING DIRECTING IN A COMEDY SERIES

For a single episode of a regular series

James Burrows, *Cheers* "Old Flames", November 17,1983 (NBC)

Ellen Chaset Falcon, *Buffalo Bill*, "Abortion Part 2", February 2, 1984 (NBC)

Larry Gelbart, *After MASH*, "Fall Out", December 5, 1983 (CBS)

☐ Bill Persky, *Kate & Allie*, "Very Loud Family", March 26, 1984 (CBS)

OUTSTANDING DIRECTING IN A DRAMA SERIES

For a single episode of a regular series

☐ Corey Allen, *Hill Street Blues*, "Goodbye, Mr. Scripps", November 24, 1983 (NBC)

Thomas Carter, *Hill Street Blues*, "Midway to What?", December 1, 1983 (NBC)

Robert Scheerer, *Fame*, "Sheer Will" (SYN)

Arthur Allan Seidelman, *Hill Street Blues*, "Doris in Wonderland", November 10, 1983 (NBC)

OUTSTANDING DIRECTING IN A VARIETY OR MUSIC PROGRAM

For a single episode of a regular series or for a special

☐ Dwight Hemion, *Here's Television Entertainment*, December 4, 1983 (NBC)

Clark Jones, *1984 Tony Awards*, June 3, 1984 (CBS)

Don Mischer, *The 6th Annual Kennedy Center Honors: A Celebration of the Performing Arts*, December 27, 1983 (CBS)

Marty Pasetta, *Burnett "Discovers" Domingo*, January 27, 1984 (CBS)

OUTSTANDING DIRECTING IN A LIMITED SERIES OR A SPECIAL

For a single episode of a limited series or for a special

☐ Jeff Bleckner, "Concealed Enemies" *American Playhouse*, "Part 3: Investigation", May 8, 1984 (PBS)

John Erman, *A Streetcar Named Desire*, March 4, 1984 (ABC)

Randa Haines, *Something About Amelia*, January 9, 1984 (ABC)

Lamont Johnson, *Ernie Kovacs: Between the Laughter*, May 14, 1984 (ABC)

Nicholas Meyer, *The Day After*, November 20, 1983 (ABC)

OUTSTANDING WRITING IN A COMEDY SERIES

For a single episode of a regular series

☐ David Angell, *Cheers*, "Old Flames", November 17, 1983 (NBC)

Glen Charles, Les Charles, *Cheers*, "Power Play", September 29, 1983 (NBC)

David Lloyd, *Cheers*, "Homicidal Ham", October 27, 1983 (NBC)

Tom Patchett, *Buffalo Bill*, "Wilkinson's Sword", December 15, 1983 (NBC)

Jay Tarses, *Buffalo Bill*, "Jo-Jo's Problem— Part 2", February 2, 1984 (NBC)

OUTSTANDING WRITING IN A DRAMA SERIES

For a single episode of a regular series

Tom Fontana, John Masius, *St. Elsewhere*, "All About Eve", December 14, 1983 (NBC)

Jeffery Lewis, Michael Wagner, Karen Hall, Mark Frost (teleplay), Steven Bochco, Jeffery Lewis, David Milch (story), *Hill Street Blues*, "Grace Under Pressure", February 2, 1984 (NBC)

John Masius, Tom Fontana, Garn Stephens, Emilie R. Small, *St. Elsewhere*, "Newhart", November 9, 1983 (NBC)

☐ John Ford Noonan (teleplay), John Masius, Tom Fontana (story), *St. Elsewhere*, "The Women", March 28, 1984 (NBC)

OUTSTANDING WRITING IN A DRAMA SERIES

For a single episode of a regular series

Peter Silverman (teleplay), Steven Bochco, Jeffery Lewis, David Milch (story), *Hill Street Blues*, "Doris in Wonder Land", November 10, 1983 (NBC)

Mark Tinker, John Tinker (teleplay), John Masius, Tom Fontana (story), *St. Elsewhere*, "Qui Transtulit Sustinet", November 16, 1983 (NBC)

OUTSTANDING WRITING IN A VARIETY OR MUSIC PROGRAM

For a single episode of a regular series or for a special

James Downey, Gerard Mulligan, George Meyer, Steve O'Donnell, Sandy Frank, Joe Toplyn, Chris Elliott, Matt Wickline, Merrill Markoe,

David Letterman, *Late Night With David Letterman*, "Show #291", October 3, 1983 (NBC)

James Downey, Gerard Mulligan, Andy Breckman, George Meyer, Steve O'Donnell, Sandy Frank, Merrill Markoe, David Letterman, *Late Night With David Letterman*, "Show #285," September 21, 1983 (NBC)

☐ Steve O'Donnell, Gerard Mulligan, Sandy Frank, Joe Toplyn, Chris Elliott, Matt Wickline, Jeff Martin, Ted Greenberg, David Yazbek, Merrill Markoe, David Letterman, *Late Night With David Letterman*, "Show #312", November 15, 1983 (NBC)

Hildy Parks, *The 1984 Tony Awards*, June 3, 1984 (CBS)

Andrew Smith, Jim Belushi, Andy Breckerman, Robin Duke, Adam Green, Mary Gross, Nate Herman, Tim Kazurinsky, Kevin Kelton, Andrew Kurtzman, Michael McCarthy, Eddie Murphy, Pamela Norris, Margaret Oberman, Joe Piscopo, Herb Sargeant, Bob Tischler, Eliot Wald, *Saturday Night Live*, "Show #378," May 12, 1984 (NBC)

OUTSTANDING WRITING IN A VARIETY OR MUSIC PROGRAM

For a single episode of a regular series or for a special

George Stevens Jr., Joseph McBride, *The American Film Institute Salute to Lillian Gish*, April 17, 1984 (CBS)

George Stevens Jr., L.T. Ilehart Jr., Sara Lukinson, Marc London, *The 6th Annual Kennedy Center Honors: A Celebration of the Performing Arts*, December 27, 1983 (CBS)

OUTSTANDING WRITING IN A LIMITED SERIES OR A SPECIAL

For a single episode of a limited series or for a special

Susan Cooper, Hume Cronyn, *The Dollmaker*, May 13, 1984 (ABC)

☐ William Hanley, *Something About Amelia*, January 9, 1984 (ABC)

Edward Hume, *The Day After*, November 20, 1983 (ABC)

Allan Leicht, *Adam*, October 10, 1983 (NBC)

April Smith, *Ernie Kovacs: Between the Laughter*, May 14, 1984 (ABC)

Daytime Awards

OUTSTANDING DAYTIME DRAMA SERIES

Emmy(s) to executive producer(s) and producer(s):

All My Children, Jacqueline Babbin (producer) (ABC)

☐ Indicates winner

Days of Our Lives, Mrs. Ted Corday (executive producer), Al Rabin (supervising executive producer), Ken Corday (producer), Shelley Curtis (producer) (NBC)

☐ *General Hospital*, Gloria Monty (producer) (ABC)

OUTSTANDING GAME OR AUDIENCE PARTICIPATION SHOW

Emmy(s) to executive producer(s) and producer(s):

Family Feud, Howard Felsher (executive producer), Cathy Hugart Dawson (producer) (ABC)

The Price is Right, Frank Wayne (executive producer) (CBS)

☐ *The $25,000 Pyramid*, Bob Stewart (executive producer) (CBS)

The Wheel of Fortune, Nancy Jones (producer) (NBC)

OUTSTANDING TALK/SERVICE SERIES

Emmy(s) to executive producer(s) and producer(s):

All New this Old House, Russell Morash (producer) (PBS)

Donahue, Richard Mincer (producer) (SYN)

Hour Magazine, Steve Clements (producer), Martin M. Berman (executive producer) (SYN)

☐ *Woman to Woman*, Mary Muldoon (producer) (SYN)

OUTSTANDING VARIETY SERIES

Emmy(s) to executive producer(s) and producer(s):

Fantasy, Merrill Heatter (executive producer), F. V. DiMassa Jr. (producer) (NBC)

☐ *The Merv Griffin Show*, Bob Murphy (executive producer), Peter Barsocchini (producer) (SYN)

OUTSTANDING CHILDREN'S ENTERTAINMENT SERIES

Emmy(s) to executive producer(s) and producer(s):

Captain Kangaroo, Bob Keeshan, Jim Hirschfeld (executive producer), Bettte Chichon, Ruth Manecke (producers) (CBS)

Smurfs, William Hanna, Joseph Barbera (executive producers), Gerard Baldwin (producer) (NBC)

Revenge of the Nerd, CBS Afternoon Playhouse, Frank Doelger, Bob Keeshan (executive producers), Jim Hirschfeld, Patrick McCormick (producers) (CBS)

☐ *The Great Love Experiment, ABC Afterschool Special*, Jane Startz (executive producer), Doro Bachrach (producer) (ABC)

He Makes Me Feel Like Dancin', Edgar J. Scherick, Scott Rudin,

(executive producers), Emile Ardolino (producer) (NBC)

Andrea's Story: A Hitchhiking Tragedy, (ABC) Afterschool Special, Martin Tahse (producer) (ABC)

OUTSTANDING CHILDREN'S INFORMATIONAL/INSTRUCTIONAL SPECIAL

Emmy(s) to executive producer(s) and producer(s):

☐ *Dead Wrong: The John Evans Story*, S. Bryan Hickox, Jay Daniel (executive producers) (CBS)

OUTSTANDING CHILDREN'S INFORMATIONAL/INSTRUCTIONAL PROGRAMMING – SHORT FORM

Emmy(s) to executive producer(s) and producer(s):

☐ *Just Another Stupid Kid*, Tom Robertson (producer) (SYN)

OUTSTANDING CHILDREN'S INFORMATIONAL/INSTRUCTIONAL SERIES

Emmy(s) to executive producer(s) and producer(s):

Mister Rogers' Neighborhood, Fred M. Rogers (producer) (PBS)

Sesame Street, Dulcy Singer (executive producer), Lisa Simon (producer) (PBS)

☐ *ABC Weekend Specials* (ABC)

OUTSTANDING ACTOR IN A DAYTIME DRAMA SERIES

James Mitchell, (Role: Palmer Cortlandt), *All My Children* (ABC)

☐ Larry Bryggman, (Role: Dr. John Dixon), *As the World Turns* (CBS)

Joel Crothers, (Role: Dr. Miles Cavanaugh), *Edge of Night* (ABC)

Larkin Malloy, (Role: Sky Whitney), *Edge of Night* (ABC)

Stuart Damon, (Role: Dr. Alan Quartermaine), *General Hospital* (ABC)

Terry Lester, (Role: Jack Abbott), *The Young and the Restless* (CBS)

OUTSTANDING ACTOR IN A SUPPORTING ROLE IN A DAYTIME DRAMA SERIES

Louis Edmonds, (Role: Langley Wallingford), *All My Children* (ABC)

Paul Stevens, (Role: Brian Bancroft), *Another World* (NBC)

☐ Justin Deas, (Role: Tom Hughes), *As The World Turns* (CBS)

David Lewis, (Role: Edward Quartermaine), *General Hospital* (ABC)

Anthony Call, (Role: Herb Callison). *One Life to Live* (ABC)

OUTSTANDING ACTRESS IN A DAYTIME DRAMA SERIES

Susan Lucci, (Role: Erica Kane Chandler), *All My Children* (ABC)

Deidre Hall, (Role: Marlena Evans Brady), *Days of Our Lives* (NBC)

Ann Flood, (Role: Nancy Karr), *Edge of Night* (ABC)

Sharon Gabet, (Role: Raven Whitney), *Edge of Night* (ABC)

□ Erika Slezak, (Role: Victoria Lord Buchanan), *One Life to Live* (ABC)

OUTSTANDING ACTRESS IN A SUPPORTING ROLE IN A DAYTIME DRAMA SERIES

Eileen Herlie, (Role: Myrtle Fargate), *All My Children* (ABC)

Marcy Walker, (Role: Liza Colby), *All My Children* (ABC)

Lois Kibbee, (Role: Geraldine Saxon), *Edge of Night* (ABC)

Loanne Bishop, (Role: Rose Kelly), *General Hospital* (ABC)

□ Judi Evans, (Role: Beth Raines), *The Guiding Light* (CBS)

Christine Ebersole, (Role: Maxie McDermot), *One Life to Live* (ABC)

OUTSTANDING HOST/HOSTESS IN A GAME OR AUDIENCE PARTICIPATION SHOW

□ Bob Barker, *The Price is Right* (CBS)

Richard Dawson, *Family Feud* (ABC)

Betty White, *Just Men!* (NBC)

OUTSTANDING HOST/HOSTESS IN A TALK/SERVICE SERIES

□ Gary Collins, *Hour Magazine* (SYN)

Phil Donahue, *Donahue* (SYN)

OUTSTANDING HOST/HOSTESS IN A VARIETY SERIES

□ Merv Griffin, *Merv Griffin Show* (SYN)

Leslie Uggams, *Fantasy* (NBC)

OUTSTANDING PERFORMER IN CHILDREN'S PROGRAMMING

Carrie Snodgress, (Role: Mrs. Cranston), *Andrea's Story: A Hitchhiking Tragedy, ABC Afterschool Special* (ABC)

□ Dick Van Dyke, (Role: Father), *The Wrong Way Kid, CBS Library* (CBS)

Fred M. Rogers, (Role: Mister Rogers), *Mister Rogers' Neighborhood* (PBS)

Bob Keeshan, (Role: Captain Kangaroo & others), *Captain Kangaroo* (CBS)

OUTSTANDING DIRECTION FOR A DAYTIME DRAMA SERIES

For the entire series:

Jack Coffey, Sherrell Hoffman, Henry Kaplan, Francesca James, *All My Children* (ABC)

□ Larry Auerbach, George Keathley, Peter Miner, David Pressman, *One Life to Live* (ABC)

OUTSTANDING INDIVIDUAL DIRECTION FOR A GAME OR AUDIENCE PARTICIPATION SHOW

Paul Alter, *Family Feud* (ABC)

□ Indicates winner

□ Marc Breslow, *The Price is Right* (CBS)

OUTSTANDING INDIVIDUAL DIRECTION FOR A TALK/SERVICE SERIES

Mary Hardwick, *Woman to Woman* (SYN)

□ Ron Weiner, *Donahue* (SYN)

OUTSTANDING INDIVIDUAL ACHIEVEMENT IN CHILDREN'S PROGRAMMING – DIRECTING

Harry Harris, *Have You Ever Been Ashamed of Your Parents?* (ABC) *Afterschool Special* (ABC)

□ Robert Mandel, *Andrea's Story: The Hitchhiking Tragedy, ABC Afterschool Special* (ABC)

Claudia Weill, *The Great Love Experiment, ABC Afterschool Special* (ABC)

Marc Daniels, *All the Money in the World, ABC Weekend Special* (ABC)

OUTSTANDING WRITING FOR A DAYTIME DRAMA SERIES

For the entire series:

Agnes Nixon, Wisner Washam, Lorraine Broderick, Dani Morris, Jack Wood, Mary K. Wells, Clarice Blackburn, Elizabeth Wallace, Roni Dengel, Susan Kirshenbaum, Carolina Della Pietra, *All My Children* (ABC)

Margaret De Priest, Sheri Anderson, Maralyn Thoma, Michael Robert David, Susan Goldberg, Bob Hansen, Leah Markus, Dana Soloff, *Days of our Lives* (NBC)

Anne Howard Bailey, A.J. Russell, Leah Laiman, Norma Monty, Thom Racina, Doris Silverton, Robert Guza, Jr., Charles Pratt, Jr., Peggy Schibi, Robert Shaw, *General Hospital* (ABC)

□ Claire Labine, Paul Avila Mayer, Mary Ryan Munisteri, Judith Pinsker, Nancy Ford, B.K. Perlman, *Ryan's Hope* (ABC)

OUTSTANDING INDIVIDUAL ACHIEVEMENT IN CHILDREN'S PROGRAMMING – WRITING

For a single episode of a series or for a special program:

Rod Baker, Glen Olson, *All the Money in the World, ABC Weekend Special* (ABC)

Virginia Carter, Fern Field, Michael McGreevey, *The Celebrity and the Arcade Kid, ABC Afterschool Special* (ABC)

Chris Manheim, *Have You Ever Been Ashamed of Your Parents? ABC Afterschool Special* (ABC)

□ Norman Stiles, Gary Belkin, Sara Compton, Tom Dunsmuir, Judy Freudberg, Tony Geiss, Emily P.

Kingsley, David Korr, Sonia Manzano, Jeff Moss, Luis Santeiro, *Sesame Street* (PBS)

OUTSTANDING ACHIEVEMENT IN TECHNICAL EXCELLENCE FOR A DAYTIME DRAMA SERIES

For the entire series – Emmy(s) to individuals:

All My Children, Howard Zweig, Michael Pomarico, Henry Enrico Ferro (technical director), Robert Ambrico, Mary Flood, Lawrence Hammond, Paul Mertens, Greg Saccaro, Vincent Senatore, Trevor Thompson, Richard Westlein (electronic camerpersons), Len Walas (senior video), Kathryn Tucker-Bachelder, Fran Getler, David Gould (senior audio), Jean Dadario Burke, Diana Wenman, Barbara Martin-Simmons (associate directors), Roger Haenelt (video tape editor), Barbara Woods (sound effects) (ABC)

General Hospital, Dave Smith, John Cochran (technical director), Guy Tyler, Len Grice, Bud Hendricks (senior video engineer), Robert Miller, Zoli Osaze, Ralph Waldo Emerson, Lisa Holly (audio engineer), Jim Angel, Jack Denton, Ritch Kenney, Bill Pope, Randy Baer, Dale Walsh. Bruce Bonnett, Ed Payne, Sal Folino, Ron Brooks, Bud Holland, D. J. Diomedes (electronic camerapersons), Bob Lanham, Jose Galvez, Jack Moody (video tape editor) (ABC)

□ *One Life to Live*, Martin Gavrin, Louis Marchand (technical director), Charlie Henry, John Morris, Rich Schiaffro, Frank Schiraldi, Wallace Hewitt, Howie Zeidman (electronic camerapersons), Herb Segall, Frank Bailey, Marianne Malitz (senior video engineer), Susan Pomerantz, Stuart Silver (associate director), Al Forman, Leona K. Zeira (video tape editor) (ABC)

OUTSTANDING ACHIEVEMENT IN DESIGN EXCELLENCE FOR A DAYTIME DRAMA SERIES

For the entire series – emmy(s) to individuals:

All My Children, William Mickley (scenic designer), William Itkin, Donna Larson, Alan Blacher (lighting director), Carol Luiken (costume designer), Sylvia Lawrence, Scott Hersh (make-up), Robert Chiu, Jim Nelson, Richard Greene (hair stylist), Teri Smith (music director), Sid Ramin (music composer) (ABC)

General Hospital, Jim Ellingwood (art director), Mercer Barrows, Greg Strain (set decorator), Grant Velie,

Tom Markle, Rae Creevey (lighting director), Jim O'Dnaiel, Robert Berdell (costume designer), Pam "P.K." Cole (make-up designer), Debbie Holmes, Katherine Kotarakos (hair designer), Dominic Messinger, Jill Farren Phelps (music director), Charles Paul (music composer) (ABC)

□ *Guiding Light*, Richard Hankins, Harry Miller (art director), Paul Hickey, Wes Laws (set decorator), Ralph Holmes, Lincoln Stulik (lighting director), Robert Anton, David Dangle (costume designer), Joseph Cola, Susan Saccavino (make-up), Linda Williams, Alba Samperisi (hair designer), Barbara Miller (music supervisor) (CBS)

Cinematography

OUTSTANDING CINEMATOGRAPHY IN CHILDREN'S PROGRAMMING

□ Hanania Baer (cinematographer), *Andrea's Story: A Hitchhiking Tragedy, ABC Afterschool Special* (ABC)

Kees Van Oostrum (cinematographer), *The Hand Me Down Kid, (ABC) Afterschool Special* (ABC)

Richard Leitteman (cinematographer), *Cougar, ABC Weekend Special* (ABC)

Film Editing

OUTSTANDING FILM EDITING IN CHILDREN'S PROGRAMMING

Pamela S. Arnold (film editor), *The Hand Me Down Kid, ABC Weekend Special* (ABC)

Michael R. Miller (film editor), *It's no Crush, I'm in Love, ABC Afterschool Special* (ABC)

□ Thomas Haneke, Charlotte Grossman (film editors), *He Makes Me Feel Like Dancing* (NBC)

Sally Coryn (film editor), *Have You Ever Been Ashamed of Your Parents? ABC Afterschool Special* (ABC)

OUTSTANDING MUSIC COMPOSITION IN CHILDREN'S PROGRAMMING

Howard Goodall (composer), *It's no Crush, I'm in love, ABC Afterschool Special* (ABC)

Doug Katsaros (composer), *The Great Love Experiment, ABC Afterschool Special* (ABC)

Misha Segal (composer), *Andrea's Story: a Hitchhiking Tragedy, ABC Afterschool Special* (ABC)

Elliot Lawrence (director), *Zack of all Trades* "Jack and Jill" (ABC)

□ Indicates winner

NOTE: ALL THE FOLLOWING ARE "AREAS" WHICH MEANS THAT THERE IS A POSSIBILITY OF ONE AWARD, MORE THAN ONE AWARD OR NO AWARD. THESE ACHIEVEMENTS ARE VOTED ON NON-COMPETITIVELY, AGAINST STANDARDS OF EXCELLENCE ONLY. THIS APPLIES TO EACH OF THE "AREAS" LISTED BELOW.

OUTSTANDING ACHIEVEMENT IN RELIGIOUS PROGRAMMING SPECIALS

Emmy(s) to executive producer(s) and producer(s):

The Last Journey, Philip Gittleman (producer) (CBS)

OUTSTANDING ACHIEVEMENT IN RELIGIOUS PROGRAMMING-SERIES

Emmy(s) to executive producer(s) and producer(s)

□ *Directions*, Sid Darion (executive producer) (ABC)

□ *Insight*, Ellwood Kieser, Paulist (executive producer), Mike Rhodes, Terry Sweeney (producers) (SYN)

SPECIAL CLASSIFICATION OF OUTSTANDING PROGRAM ACHIEVEMENT

Emmy(s) to executive producer(s) and producer(s):

□ *FYI*, Yanna Kroyt Brandt (producer), Mary Ann Donahur (coordinating producer) (ABC)

I Remember It Well: ABC Daytime's 25th Anniversary Minutes, Merle Goldberg, Mike Nichols, Donna Swajeski (producers) (ABC)

American Bandstand, Dick Clark (executive producer), Larry Klein (producer), Barry Glazer (co-producer) (ABC)

OUTSTANDING ACHIEVEMENT IN COVERAGE OF SPECIAL EVENTS

Emmy(s) to executive producer(s) and producer(s):

Macy's Thanksgiving Day Parade, Dick Schneider (producer) (NBC)

95th Tournament of Roses Parade, Dick Schneider (producer) (NBC)

OUTSTANDING PROGRAM ACHIEVEMENT IN THE PERFORMING ARTS

Emmy(s) to executive producer(s) and producer(s):

□ *Live from the Met: Metropolitan Opera Centennial Gala— Part 1*, Michael Bronson (executive producer), Clemente D'Allessio (producer) (PBS)

OUTSTANDING INDIVIDUAL ACHIEVEMENT IN RELIGIOUS PROGRAMMING – PERFORMERS

Patty Duke Astin, (Role: Peters), *Insight* "The Hit Man" (SYN)

Edwin Newman, (Role: Moderator), *The Bishop and the Bomb* (NBC)

SPECIAL CLASSIFICATION OF OUTSTANDING INDIVIDUAL ACHIEVEMENT – PERFORMERS

□ Carol Spinney, (Role: Big Bird Oscar Puppetter), *Sesame Street* (PBS)

SPECIAL CLASSIFICATION OF OUTSTANDING INDIVIDUAL ACHIEVEMENT – HOST/HOSTESS

□ Hal Linden, (Role: Host), *FYI* (ABC)

OUTSTANDING ACHIEVEMENT IN THE COVERAGE OF SPECIAL EVENTS – HOST/HOSTESS

□ Bryant Gumbel, (Role: Host), *Macy's Thanksgiving Day Parade* (NBC)

OUTSTANDING INDIVIDUAL ACHIEVEMENT IN THE PERFORMING ARTS – HOST/HOSTESS

□ Dorothy Hamill, (Role: Juliet), *Romeo & Juliet on Ice* (CBS)

SPECIAL CLASSIFICATION OF OUTSTANDING INDIVIDUAL ACHIEVEMENT – WRITING

□ Mary Ann Donahue, Joseph Gustaitis, Linda Kline, Robin Westen, Elaine Whitley, *FYI* (ABC)

OUTSTANDING INDIVIDUAL ACHIEVEMENT IN RELIGIOUS PROGRAMMING DIRECTING

□ Jay Sandrich, *Insight* "The Day Everything Went Wrong" (SYN)

OUTSTANDING CLASSIFICATION OF OUTSTANDING INDIVIDUAL ACHIEVEMENT – DIRECTING

□ Mike Gargiulo, *FYI* (ABC)

OUTSTANDING ACHIEVEMENT IN ANY AREA OF CREATIVE TECHNICAL CRAFTS – DIRECTING

(Outside Daytime Drama Teams)

□ Raymond J. Hoesten, *One Life to Live*, "The Delila Fantasy" (ABC)

□ Ira Cirker, *Another World*, "Glen Cove Remote: Double Wedding" (NBC)

OUTSTANDING INDIVIDUAL ACHIEVEMENT IN THE COVERAGE OF SPECIAL EVENTS – DIRECTORS

□ Dick Schneider, *Macy's Thanksgiving Day Parade* (NBC)

OUTSTANDING INDIVIDUAL ACHIEVEMENT IN THE PERFORMING ARTS DIRECTING

Kirk Browning, *Live from the Met: The Metropolitan Opera Centennial—Part 1*

□ Rob Iscove, *Romeo & Juliet on Ice* (CBS)

Technical Direction/ Electronic Camerawork

OUTSTANDING INDIVIDUAL ACHIEVEMENT IN TECHNICAL CRAFTS IN CHILDREN'S PROGRAMMING
Erik Daarstad, (electronic camera) *Have You Ever Been Ashamed of Your Parents? ABC Afterschool Special* (ABC)
□ Ralph Mensch (technical director), *Sesame Street* (PBS)

OUTSTANDING INDIVIDUAL ACHIEVEMENT IN RELIGIOUS PROGRAMMING
Jim Vrieling, Bob Gabrielson (technical directors), *Kalikimaka: Christmas in Hawaii* (ABC)

SPECIAL CLASSIFICATION OF OUTSTANDING INDIVIDUAL ACHIEVEMENT
Frank Gaeta (electronic camera), Noreen Falk, (technical director) *Another World* Remote: Glen Cove (NBC)

OUTSTANDING INDIVIDUAL ACHIEVEMENT IN THE COVERAGE OF SPECIAL EVENTS
Louis Fusari, Richard Lombardo (technical directors), Reed Howard, John O'Neill, Roy Holm, Kurt Tonnessen, Raymond Liu, George Falardau, Leslie Atkinson, Mike A. Higuera, George Simpson, Wayne Nostaja (cameras), *95th Tournament of Roses Parade* (NBC)
□ Terry Rohnke (technical director), Bill Goetz, John Hillyer, Steve Gonzales, Barry Fisher, John Pinto, Don Mulvaney, Michael Bennett, Gene Martin, Karl Eckett (electronic camera), *Macy's Thanksgiving Day Parade* (NBC)

OUTSTANDING ACHIEVEMENT IN ANY AREA OF CREATIVE TECHNICAL CRAFTS

(Other than Daytime Drama Technical and Design Team Members)
□ William J. Millard III (electronic camera), *Edge of Night*, Remote: Gateway National Park (ABC)
John Cordone (electronic camera), *One Life to Live*, Remote: Red Hook (ABC)

□ Indicates winner

Audio: Live, tape, film sound editors and mixers

OUTSTANDING INDIVIDUAL ACHIEVEMENT IN TECHNICAL CRAFTS IN CHILDREN'S PROGRAMMING
Lee Dichter (re-recording mixer), Mark Dichter (sound mixer), Michael Miller (audio editor), *It's no Crush, I'm in Love, ABC Afterschool Special* (ABC)
□ Blake Norton (audio), *Sesame Street* (PBS)

OUTSTANDING INDIVIDUAL ACHIEVEMENT IN RELIGIOUS PROGRAMMING
Art Dupont (audio coordinator), *Kalikimaka: Christmas in Hawaii* (ABC)

SPECIAL CLASSIFICATION OF OUTSTANDING INDIVIDUAL ACHIEVEMENT
Paul Colten, Jack Hughes (audio mixers), *All My Children*, Remote: Air Plane Crash (ABC)

OUTSTANDING INDIVIDUAL ACHIEVEMENT IN THE COVERAGE OF SPECIAL EVENTS
Joe Ralston (audio), *95th Tournament of Roses Parade* (NBC)

OUTSTANDING ACHIEVEMENT IN ANY AREA OF CREATIVE TECHNICAL CRAFTS
Dick Roes (audio), *All My Children*, "Yacht Remote" (ABC)

OUTSTANDING INDIVIDUAL ACHIEVEMENT IN THE PERFORMING ARTS
□ Jay David Saks (audio mixer), *Live from the Met*, "Metropolitan Opera Centennial Gala Part I"— (PBS)

Associate Direction/ Videotape Editing

OUTSTANDING INDIVIDUAL ACHIEVEMENT IN TECHNICAL CRAFTS IN CHILDREN'S PROGRAMMING
Ted May (post production supervisor/ associate director), *Sesame Street* (PBS)
□ Arthur Schneider (videotape editor), *Andrea's Story: A Hitchhiking Tragedy, ABC Afterschool Special* (ABC)

OUTSTANDING INDIVIDUAL ACHIEVEMENT IN RELIGIOUS PROGRAMMING
Mike Wenig (videotape editor), *Kalikimaka: Christmas in Hawaii* (ABC)

OUTSTANDING ACHIEVEMENT IN ANY AREA OF CREATIVE TECHNICAL CRAFTS
Nick V. Giordano, Louis Torino (videotape editors), *General Hospital*, Remote: Luke/Laura Reunion (ABC)

SPECIAL CLASSIFICATION OF OUTSTANDING INDIVIDUAL ACHIEVEMENT– MUSIC
Lee Holdridge (composer), *Woman to Woman* (SYN)

OUTSTANDING INDIVIDUAL ACHIEVEMENT IN THE PERFORMING ARTS
□ James Levine (music director/ conductor), *Live from the Met*, "Centennial Gala—Part I" (PBS)

OUTSTANDING INDIVIDUAL ACHIEVEMENT IN THE COVERAGE OF SPECIAL EVENTS
Milton DeLugg (music director), *Macy's Thanksgiving Day Parade* (NBC)

Art Direction/Scenic Design/Set Decoration

OUTSTANDING INDIVIDUAL ACHIEVEMENT IN CHILDREN'S PROGRAMMING
Virginia Field (art director), *It's no Crush, I'm in Love, ABC Afterschool Special* (ABC)
Bill Bohnert (art director), *Willie Tyler & Lester, ABC Weekend Special* (ABC)
□ Cary White (art director), *Andrea's Story: A Hitchhiking Tragedy, ABC Afterschool Special* (ABC)

OUTSTANDING ACHIEVEMENT IN ANY AREA OF CREATIVE TECHNICAL CRAFTS
Val Strazovec (scenic designer), *Romeo & Juliet on Ice* (CBS)

Lighting Direction

OUTSTANDING INDIVIDUAL ACHIEVEMENT IN CHILDREN'S PROGRAMMING
□ Randy Nodstrom (lighting director), *Sesame Street* (PBS)

OUTSTANDING INDIVIDUAL ACHIEVEMENT IN RELIGIOUS PROGRAMMING
Dennis Calligan, *Kalikimaka: Christmas in Hawaii* (ABC)

OUTSTANDING INDIVIDUAL ACHIEVEMENT IN ANY AREA OF CREATIVE TECHNICAL CRAFTS
Everett Melosh (lighting director), *All My Children*, "Yacht Remote" (ABC)

Costume Design

OUTSTANDING INDIVIDUAL ACHIEVEMENT IN DESIGN CRAFTS IN CHILDREN'S PROGRAMMING

Jean Blackburn, *Andrea's Story: A Hitchhiking Tragedy, ABC Afterschool Special* (ABC)

Barbara Murphy, *All the Money in the World, ABC Weekend Special* (ABC)

OUTSTANDING ACHIEVEMENT IN ANY AREA OF CREATIVE TECHNICAL CRAFTS

(Other than Daytime Drama Technical and Design Team Members)

Bob Carlton, *Sale of the Century* (NBC)

Make-up and Hair Design

OUTSTANDING INDIVIDUAL ACHIEVEMENT IN DESIGN CRAFTS IN CHILDREN'S PROGRAMMING

☐ Marie-Ange Ripka, *The Great Love Experiment, ABC Afterschool Special* (ABC)

Make-up Artist

OUTSTANDING ACHIEVEMENT IN ANY AREA OF CREATIVE TECHNICAL CRAFTS

(Other than Daytime Drama Technical and Design Team Members)

Deanna Fry, *Woman to Woman* (SYN)

Costume Design

OUTSTANDING INDIVIDUAL ACHIEVEMENT IN THE PERFORMING ARTS

☐ Zandra Rhodes, *Romeo & Juliet on Ice* (CBS)

Graphic Design

OUTSTANDING INDIVIDUAL ACHIEVEMENT IN CHILDREN'S PROGRAMMING

Philomena Morano (graphic artist), *Uncle Sam* (NBC)

OUTSTANDING INDIVIDUAL ACHIEVEMENT IN RELIGIOUS PROGRAMMING

Rick Fitch (graphic artist), *Kalikimaka: Christmas in Hawaii* (ABC)

OUTSTANDING ACHIEVEMENT IN ANY AREA OF CREATIVE CRAFTS

Sandy Dvore (graphic designer), *The Young and the Restless, Open and Close* (CBS)

☐ Indicates winner

Creative Arts Awards

OUTSTANDING ART DIRECTION FOR A SERIES

For a single episode of a regular series

James Hulsey (art director), Bruce Kay (set decorator), *The Duck Factory*, "Pilot", April 12, 1984 (NBC)

OUTSTANDING ART DIRECTION FOR A LIMITED SERIES OR SPECIAL

For a single episode of a limited series or for a special

James Hulsey (production designer), George R. Nelson (set decorator), *A Streetcar named Desire*, March 4, 1984 (ABC)

OUTSTANDING ART DIRECTION FOR A VARIETY OR MUSIC PROGRAM

For a single episode of a regular series or for a special

Roy Christopher (art director), *The 56th Annual Academy Awards*, April 9, 1984 (ABC)

OUTSTANDING INDIVIDUAL ACHIEVEMENT – GRAPHIC DESIGN AND TITLE SEQUENCES

For a single episode of a regular or limited series or for a special (possibility of one, more than one or no award)

Ted Woolery, Gerry Woolery, *The Duck Factory*, "Filling Buddy's Shoes", April 12, 1984 (NBC)

OUTSTANDING COSTUME DESIGN FOR A SERIES

For a single episode of a regular series

Bod Mackie (original costume concept), Ret Turner (costumes), *Mama's Family*, "Mama's Birthday", March 17, 1984 (NBC)

Nolan Miller, *Dynasty*, "The Wedding", December 28, 1983 (ABC)

OUTSTANDING COSTUME DESIGN FOR A LIMITED SERIES OR A SPECIAL

For a single episode of a limited series or for a special

Julie Weiss, *The Dollmaker*, May 13, 1984 (ABC)

OUTSTANDING ACHIEVEMENT IN MAKEUP

For a single episode of a regular or limited series or for a special

Michael G. Westmore, (special makeup), *Why Me?*, March 12, 1984 (ABC)

OUTSTANDING ACHIEVEMENT IN HAIRSTYLING

For a single episode of a regular or limited series or for a special

Dino Ganziano, *The Mystic Warrior*, May 20, 1984, May 21, 1984 (ABC)

OUTSTANDING CINEMATOGRAPHY FOR A LIMITED SERIES OR A SPECIAL

For a single episode of a limited series or for a special

Bill Butler, (A.S.C.), *A Streetcar Named Desire*, March 4, 1984 (ABC)

OUTSTANDING TECHNICAL DIRECTION/CAMERAWORK/VIDEO FOR A SERIES

For a single episode of a regular series

Gene Crowe (technical director), Sam Drummy, Larry Heider, Dave Levisohn, Wayne Orr, Ron Sheldon (camerapersons), Mark Sanford (senior video control), *On Stage America* "#5" (SYN)

OUTSTANDING TECHNICAL DIRECTION/CAMERAWORK/VIDEO FOR A LIMITED SERIES OR A SPECIAL

For a single episode of a limited series or for a special

Lou Fusari (technical director), Les Atkinson, Bruce Bottone, George Falardeau, Dean Hall, Dave Hilmer, Roy Holm, David Nowell (camerapersons), Jerry Smith (senior video control), *The Magic of David Copperfield VI*, April 6, 1984 (CBS)

OUTSTANDING INDIVIDUAL ACHIEVEMENT – SPECIAL VISUAL EFFECTS – ANIMATION OR GRAPHIC DESIGN AND TITLE SEQUENCES, OR LIGHTING DIRECTION (ELECTRONIC)

Robert Blalack, Nancy Rushlow, Dan Pinkham, Chris Regan, Larry Stevens, Dan Nosenchuck, *The Day After*, November 20, 1983 (ABC)

William M. Klages, *The 26th Annual Grammy Awards*, February 28, 1984 (CBS)

OUTSTANDING LIGHTING DIRECTION (ELECTRONIC) FOR A LIMITED SERIES OR A SPECIAL

For a single episode of a limited series or for a special

William M. Klages. *The 6th Annual Kennedy Center Honors: A Celebration of the Performing Arts*, December 27, 1983 (CBS)

OUTSTANDING LIGHTING DIRECTION (ELECTRONIC) FOR A SERIES

For a single episode of a regular series

Robert A. Dickinson (lighting consultant), Frank C. Olivas (lighting director), *Solid Gold*, "#198 with Cyndi Lauper, Alabama and Christine McVie" (SYN)

OUTSTANDING ANIMATED PROGRAM

Jay Poynor (executive producer), Lee Mendelson, Bill Melendez (producers), *Garfield on the Town*, October 28, 1983 (CBS)

OUTSTANDING INDIVIDUAL ACHIEVEMENT – ANIMATED PROGRAMMING – DIRECTING

R. O. Blechman, *The Soldier's Tale*, March 19, 1984 (PBS)

OUTSTANDING INFORMATIONAL SPECIAL

Thomas F. Horton (producer), *America Remembers John F. Kennedy* (SYN)

OUTSTANDING INFORMATIONAL SERIES

Merton Y. Koplin (senior executive producer), Charles Grinker, Sanford H. Fisher (executive producers), Betsy Mc Carthy (coordinating producer), David Grubin, Ronald Blumer (producers), *A Walk Through the 20th Century with Bill Moyers* (PBS)

OUTSTANDING INDIVIDUAL ACHIEVEMENT – INFORMATIONAL PROGRAMMING – DIRECTING OR WRITING

For a single episode of a regular or limited series or for a special (possibility of one, more than one or no award)

Emile Ardolino, *He Makes Me Feel Like Dancin'*, June 14, 1984 (NBC)

Bill Moyers, *A Walk Through the 20th Century with Bill Moyers*, "Marshall, Texas, Marshall, Texas", January 11, 1984 (PBS)

OUTSTANDING FILM EDITING FOR A SERIES

For a single episode of a regular series

Andrew Chulack, *Cheers*, "Old Flames", November 17, 1983 (NBC)

OUTSTANDING FILM EDITING FOR A LIMITED SERIES OR A SPECIAL

For a single episode of a regular or limited series or for a special

Jerrold L. Ludwig, A.C.E., *A Streetcar Named Desire*, March 4, 1984 (ABC)

□ Indicates winner

OUTSTANDING FILM SOUND EDITING FOR A SERIES

For a single episode of a regular series

Airwolf, "Pilot", January 22, 1984 (CBS)

OUTSTANDING FILM SOUND EDITING FOR A LIMITED SERIES OR A SPECIAL

For a single episode of a regular or limited series or for a special

The Day After, November 20, 1984 (ABC)

OUTSTANDING FILM SOUND MIXING FOR A SERIES

For a single episode of a regular series

Hill Street Blues, "Parting is such Sweep Sorrow", February 16, 1984 (NBC)

OUTSTANDING FILM SOUND MIXING FOR A LIMITED SERIES OR A SPECIAL

For a single episode of a limited series or for a special

A Streetcar Named Desire, March 4, 1984 (ABC)

OUTSTANDING VIDEO TAPE EDITING FOR A SERIES

For a single episode of a regular series

Howard Brock, *Fame*, "Gonna Learn How to Fly— Part 2" (SYN)

OUTSTANDING VIDEO TAPE EDITING FOR A LIMITED SERIES OR A SPECIAL

For a single episode of a limited series or for a special

Jim McQueen (video tape editor), Catherine Shields (film editor), *American Film Institute Salute to Lillian Gish*, April 17, 1984 (CBS)

OUTSTANDING LIVE AND TAPE SOUND MIXING AND SOUND EFFECTS FOR A SERIES

For a single episode of a regular series

Mark Hanes (prod), Stu Fox (pre), Dean Okrand (post), Ed Suski (sfx), *Real People*, "Hawaii Show – Sarah's Wedding", November 2, 1983 (NBC)

OUTSTANDING ACHIEVEMENT IN CHOREOGRAPHY

For a single episode of a regular or limited series or for a special

Debbie Allen, *Fame Takes a Look at Music '83*, (SYN)

Peter Martins, "Choreographer's Songbook: Stravinsky Piano Ballets by Peter Martins", *Dance in America*, February 13, 1984 (PBS)

□ Michael Smuin, "A Song for Dead Warriors San Francisco Battet", *Dance in America*, January 16, 1984 (PBS)

Albert Stephenson, *1984 Tony Awards*, June 3, 1984 (CBS)

OUTSTANDING ACHIEVEMENT IN MUSIC DIRECTION

For a single episode of a regular or limited series or for a special

Ian Fraser (music director), Billy Byers, Chris Boardman, J. Hill, Lenny Stack (principal arrangers), *The Screen Actors Guild 50th Anniversary Celebration*, May 29, 1984 (CBS)

OUTSTANDING ACHIEVEMENT IN MUSIC COMPOSITION FOR A SERIES (DRAMATIC UNDERSCORE)

For a single episode of a regular series

Bruce Broughton, *Dallas*, "The Letter", October 14, 1983 (CBS)

OUTSTANDING ACHIEVEMENT IN MUSIC COMPOSITION FOR A LIMITED SERIES OR A SPECIAL (DRAMATIC UNDERSCORE)

For a single episode of a limited series or for a special

Bruce Broughton, *The First Olympics – Athens 1896— Part 1*, May 20, 1984 (NBC)

OUTSTANDING ACHIEVEMENT IN MUSIC AND LYRICS

Larry Grossman (composer), Buz Kohan (lyricist), *Here's Television Entertainment*, "Gone Too Soon", December 4, 1983 (NBC)

OUTSTANDING INDIVIDUAL ACHIEVEMENT – CLASSICAL MUSIC/DANCE PROGRAMMING – FOR PERFORMING OR DIRECTING

For a single episode of a classical music/dance series or special (possibility of one, more than one or no award)

James Levine, *Live from the Met*, Series (PBS)

Leontine Price, *In Performance at the White House: an Evening of Spirituals and Gospel Music*, December 14, 1983 (PBS)

Merrill Brockway, *Dance in America*, "A Song for Dead Warriors: San Francisco Ballet", January 16, 1984 (PBS)

**OUTSTANDING CLASSICAL
PROGRAM IN THE PERFORMING
ARTS**
Horant H. Hohfeld (executive
    producer), David Griffiths (producer),
    Placido Domingo (host), *Great
    Performances*, "Placido Domingo
    Celebrates Seville", December 5,
    1983 (PBS)*

2/LOOK MAGAZINE'S ANNUAL TELEVISION AWARDS

TELEVISION HAS GROWN up, *Look* Magazine declared in 1950. Well, cameramen were still cutting off heads "now and then" and yes, women on TV still looked too "stocky," and yes, television was still being viewed with "alarm in rarefied intellectual circles," but generally there were growing signs that TV had ceased to become "a mania" and had begun to take "its proper place in American life." Television—leaving behind its "bungling amateurism"—had come of age.

In recognition of the constantly increasing importance and vast influence of TV in the entertainment and communications fields, *Look* Magazine initiated the presentation of TV Awards in 1950. It presented these prizes annually through 1959.

Initially, people within the television industry cast the votes. Approximately 1,000 network executives, producers, directors, agency directors and TV columnists were polled to select the year's outstanding programs and performers. In 1955, however, a new approach was used in selecting the jury. Only TV critics and editors (some 1,500 of them) were asked to choose the awards starting with the 1955 poll. Persons directly involved in making television shows were excluded to insure impartiality.

The voting procedures throughout the Awards' 10 years remained simple and direct: in the first ballot the participants were asked to name their three favorites in each of the various categories. The three persons or programs receiving the most votes in each category were then listed in alphabetical order on the final ballot sent to voters. In both ballots, the accounting firm of Ernst & Ernst tabulated the votes. Programs telecast between Nov. 1 of one year and Oct. 31 of the next were eligible for recognition; programs sold locally by syndicators were ruled ineligible.

When *Look* made its first appearance on newstands in 1937, there were only 17 experimental TV stations in the country and less than 8,000 receiving sets. By the time the magazine announced its Seventh Annual Awards (1957), 482 commercial stations crossed the nation and there were said to be more TV sets than bathtubs in the U.S. The average set was watched 5½ hours per day and stars were made—and unmade—overnight.

As early as 1952 *Look* realized TV's "full stature" as an on-the-scene reporter. And in 1959 the magazine was already complaining that TV was burdened "with murder and mayhem" and that its performance as a whole, in the words of Edward R. Murrow, was "trivial, timid and esca-

pist." Thus, *Look's* awards reflect many of the important changes in TV's early years—its growth, its scandals, its controversies and increasing importance to the nation:

1950

Best Program of the Year:
Jimmy Durante, *Four Star Revue* (NBC)
Best Dramatic Program:
Studio One (CBS)
Best Sports Program:
Cavalcade of Sports (NBC)
Best Public Affairs Program:
News Caravan (NBC)
Best Children's Program:
Mr. I. Magination (CBS)
Best Variety Show:
Star Theater with Milton Berle (NBC)
Most Appealing Personalities:
Faye Emerson (ABC)
Arthur Godfrey (CBS)
Most Original TV Personality:
Dave Garroway (NBC)
Best Comedian:
Sid Caesar (NBC)
Best M.C.:
Ed Sullivan, *Toast of the Town* (CBS)
Best Producer:
Max Liebman, *Your Show of Shows* (NBC)
Best Director:
Robert Montgomery, "Ride the Pink Horse," *Robert Montgomery Presents* (NBC)
Best Writer:
Charles Andrews, *Garroway at Large: Stud's Place* (ABC)
Best Stage Sets:
ABC's by James McNaughton
Special Award:
TV's coverage of the United Nations

1951

Best Variety Program:
Your Show of Shows (NBC)
Best News Program:
News Caravan (NBC)
Best Public Affairs Program:
Kefauver Committee Hearings
Special Achievement Award:
Kefauver Committee Hearings
Best Educational Program:
Zoo Parade (NBC)
Best Sports Program:
Cavalcade of Sports (NBC)
Best Dramatic Program:
Studio One (CBS)
Best Children's Program:
Kukla, Fran and Ollie (CBS)
Best Comedy Team:
Sid Caesar, Imogene Coca, *Your Show of Shows (NBC)*
Best Producer:
Max Liebman, *Your Show of Shows* (NBC)

Best M.C.:
Milton Berle (NBC)
Best Director:
Alex Segal, *Pultizer Prize Playhouse* (ABC)

1952

Best Variety Program:
Your Show of Shows (NBC)
Best Public Affairs Program:
Convention Coverage of ABC, CBS, NBC, and DuMont
Best Dramatic Program:
Robert Montgomery Presents (NBC)
Best Sports Program:
Blue Ribbon Bouts (CBS)
Best Educational Program:
Zoo Prade (NBC)
Best News Program:
See It Now (CBS)
Best Children's program:
Kukla, Fran and Ollie (NBC)
Best Producer:
Max Liebman, *Your Show of Shows* (NBC)
Best Director:
Max Liebman, *Your Show of Shows* (NBC)
Best Comedian or Comedy Team:
Lucille Ball, Desi Armaz (CBS)
Best M.C.:
John Daly (CBS)

1953

Best Dramatic Program:
Studio One (CBS)
Best Variety Program:
Toast of the Town (CBS)
Best Quiz or Panel Program:
What's My Line? (CBS)
Best News Program:
See It Now with Edward R. Murrow (CBS)
Best Public Affairs Program:
See It Now (CBS)
Best Educational Program:
Omnibus (CBS)
Best Sports Program:
Blue Ribbon Boxing Bouts (CBS)
Best Children's Program:
Ding Dong School (NBC)
Best Religious Program:
Life is Worth Living with Rev. Fulton J. Sheen (DuMont)
Best Comedian or Comedy Team:
Sid Caesar, Imogene Coca, *Your Show of Shows* (NBC)
Best M.C.:
John Daly (CBS)

Best Producer:
Fred Coe, *Mr. Peepers, Bonino, Television Playhouse* (NBC)
Best Director:
Jack Webb, *Dragnet* (NBC)

1954

Best Dramatic Program:
U.S. Steel Hour (ABC)
Best Educational Program:
Omnibus (CBS)
Best News Program:
John Cameron Swayze (NBC)
Best Variety Program
Toast of the Town (CBS)
Best Sports Program:
Cavalcade of Sports (NBC)
Best Quiz or Panel Program:
You Bet Your Life (NBC)
Best Children's Program:
Ding Dong School (NBC)
Best Religious Program:
Life Is Worth Living (Dumont)
Best Public Affairs Program:
See it Now (CBS)
Best Comedy Team or Comedian:
George Gobel (NBC)
Best Producer:
Fred Coe, *Television Playhouse, Mr. Peepers* (NBC)
Best Director:
Jack Webb, *Dragnet* (NBC)
Best Master of Ceremonies:
Garry Moore (CBS)

1955

Best Special Program:
Peter Pan (NBC)
Best Quiz or Panel Program:
The $64,000 Questions (CBS)
Best Educational Program:
Omnibus (CBS)
Best Variety Program:
The Ed Sullivan Show (CBS)
Best Children's Program:
Disneyland (ABC)
Best Public Affairs Program:
Meet the Press (NBC)
Best News Program:
John Cameron Swayze (NBC)
Best Sports Program:
Cavalcade of Sports (NBC)
Best Religious Program:
Life Is Worth Living (ABC)
Best Comedian or Comedy Team:
George Gobel (NBC)
Best Producer:
Robert Montgomery, *Robert Montgomery Presents* (NBC)

Best Director:
Alfred Hitchcock, *Alfred Hitchcock Presents* (CBS)
Best Master of Ceremonies:
Garry Moore (CBS)

1956

Best Dramatic Series (Hour or More):
Playhouse 90 (CBS)
Best Dramatic Series (1/2 Hour):
Alfred Hitchcock Presents (CBS)
Best Comedy Series (Straight):
Caesar's Hour (NBC)
Best Comedy Series (Situation):
The Phil Silvers Show (CBS)
Best Public Affairs Series:
See It Now (CBS)
Best Religious Series:
Life Is Worth Living (ABC)
Best Quiz or Panel Series:
I've Got a Secret (CBS)
Best Educational Series:
Omnibus (ABC)
Best Sports Series:
N.C.A.A. Football (NBC)
Best Novelty Series:
Person to Person (CBS)
Best Musical Series:
The Perry Como Show (NBC)
Best Variety Series:
The Ed Sullivan Show (CBS)
Best Dramatic Show:
The Cain Mutiny Court-Martial (CBS)
Best Musical Show:
Peter Pan (NBC)
Best Children's Series:
Disneyland (ABC)
Best Special Program:
Project 20 (NBC)

1957

Best Children's Series:
Disneyland (ABC)
Best Musical Show:
The Edsel Show (CBS)
Best Musical Series:
The Perry Como Show (NBC)
Best Dramatic Show:
"Green Pastures," *Hallmark Playhouse* (NBC)
Best Dramatic Series (One Houre or More):
Playhouse 90 (CBS)
Best Dramatic Series (1/2 Hour):
Alfred Hitchcock Presents (CBS)
Best Public Affairs Series:
See It Now (CBS)
Best Educational Series:
Omnibus (ABC, NBC)

Best Comedy Series (Straight):
The Jack Benny Program (CBS)
Best Comedy Series (Situation):
The Phil Silvers Show (CBS)
Best Variety Series:
The Steve Allen Show (NBC)
Best Novelty Series:
Tonight (NBC)
Best Quiz or Panel Series:
I've Got a Secret (CBS)
Best Religious Series:
Life Is Worth Living (ABC)
Best Sports Series:
The World Series (NBC)
Best Special Program:
The World Series (NBC)

1958

Best Dramatic Series:
Playhouse 90 (CBS)
Best Dramatic Show:
"The Plot to Kill Stalin," *Playhouse 90* (CBS)
Best Musical Series:
The Perry Como Show (NBC)
Best Musical Show:
An Evening With Fred Astaire (NBC)
Best Special Program:
An Evening With Fred Astaire (NBC)
Best Comedy Series (Straight):
The Jack Benny Program (CBS)
Best Comedy Series (Situation):
Father Knows Best (CBS)
Best Novelty Series:
The Steve Allen Show (NBC)
Best Variety Series:
The Steve Allen Show (NBC)
Best Quiz or Panel Series:
What's My Line? (CBS)
Best Action Series:
Gunsmoke (CBS)
Best Sports Series:
The World Series (NBC)
Best Public Affairs Series:
See It Now (CBS)
Best Educational Series:
Omnibus (NBC)

1959

Best Special Program:
Khrushchev Visit Coverage (CBS)
Best Musical Show:
An Evening With Fred Astaire (repeat broadcast) (NBC)
Best Musical Series:
The Bell Telephone Hour (NBC)
Best Dramatic Series:
Playhouse 90 (CBS)
Best Dramatic Show:
"The Untouchables," *Desilu Playhouse* (CBS)

Best Action Series:
77 Sunset Strip (ABC)
Best Comedy Series (Situation):
Father Knows Best (CBS)
Best Quiz or Panel Series:
I've Got a Secret (CBS)
Best Public Affairs Show:
Huntley-Brinkley Report (NBC)
Best Sports Show or Series:
The World Series (NBC)
Best Educational Show:
Twentieth Century (CBS)
Best Variety Series:
The Garry Moore Show (CBS)
Best Comedian:
Red Skelton, *The Red Skelton Show* (CBS)
Best Playwright:
Rod Serling, "The Velvet Alley," *Playhouse 90* (CBS)

3/Time Magazine's "TV's Most" Awards

Time Magazine did not present its first annual "TV's Most" awards until 1970, although by that time the magazine had been reviewing television for years and had long since been presenting similar awards for achievements in motion pictures.

Whereas most TV awards are given in a serious vein to honor television's best, *Time*'s prizes also cite the tube's worst. Like the *Harvard Lampoon's* "Movie Worsts" awards, *Time*'s prizes—wry, cynical, and often outrageous—provide a welcomed antidote to many of the entertainment industry's more pious and predictable awards. Ready to attack big targets such as the President of the United States or the seemingly relentless popularity of pro football on TV, *Time*'s "TV's Most" awards actually reflect some of TV's mad-as-a-hatter habits, whereby the worst often rises to the top and the best barely makes it through the season.

A special note: From 1969 through 1976, the "Most" awards were given strictly in the field of television. From 1977 through 1980, however, the prizes were extended to cover other areas of show business. These other non-TV awards are not included here, and hence there are not 10 annual prizes listed below for certain years. In 1981 the "Most" awards were replaced by a more conventional annual "Ten Best" format.

1969

TOP OF THE DECADE

First Kennedy-Nixon debate, 1960.

FCC Chairman Newton Minow's "Vast waste land" speech, 1961.

Lee Harvey Oswald murdered by Jack Ruby on-camera, 1963.

First instant replay adds new dimension to sports coverage, 1963.

Vietnam War becomes the first in history to be brought directly into the living room, 1964.

A black, Bill Cosby, costars in NBC series, *I Spy*, 1965.

All network shows are now broadcast in color, 1967.

Peter Goldmark of CBS Labs announces invention of Electronic Video Recording (EVR), 1968.

Television shows Men on the Moon, 1969.

Vice President Spiro Agnew attacks the networks, 1969.

1970

Most Embarrassing Special:
John Wayne, *Swing Out, Sweet Land* (NBC); Raquel Welch, *Raquel!* (CBS)

Most Cynically Derivative and Generally Despicable New Series:
Nancy (NBC); dishonorable mention, *Nanny and the Professor* (ABC)

Most Enterprising Reportage:
Mike Wallace, *60 Minutes* (CBS); Tom Pettit, *First Tuesday* (NBC)

Most Distinguished (not to mention only new) Cultural Series:
Kenneth Clark, *Civilisation* (PBS)

Most Impressive Vietnam Coverage:
John Laurence, *The World of Charlie Company* (CBS)

Most Worthwhile Exposes on Environment
Special:
Pollution Is a Matter of Choice (NBC)
Series:
Our Vanishing Wilderness (PBS)

Most Evocative Cinema-Verite Documentary:
Frederick Wiseman, *Hospital* (PBS)

Most Edifying Public-Service Programming:
Trial—The City and County of Denver v. Loren R. Watson (PBS)

Most Appealing Performances:
Tony Randall, Jack Klugman in *The Odd Couple* (ABC)

Most Interesting Innovation in Old Format:
David Frost's 90-minute, in-depth probing of only one guest at a time on his talk show (syndicated).

1971

Most Enlivening New Series:
All in the Family (CBS)

Most Venturesome TV Documentary:
The Selling of the Pentagon (CBS)

Most Crushing Blow ($10.6 million) to TV Revenues:
Banning of cigarette ads.

Most (and only) Creative New Program Resulting from the Extra Half-Hour of Prime Time Given to Local Stations:
Story Theater (Syndicated).

Most Endangered Species Worth Preserving:
The Great American Dream Machine (PBS)

Most Vital Dramatic Programming:
Hollywood Television Theater (PBS)

Most Ambitious, Albeit Only Partly Successful, Attempt to Upgrade Children's TV:
Make a Wish (ABC).

Most Disastrous Debut of a Movie Star in a Series:
Shirley MacLaine in *Shirley's World* (ABC).
Most Encouraging Sign of Improved Network Taste:
Cancellation of The Beverly Hillbillies (CBS).
Most Popular Game Show:
Pro football, which ran on—and on—for a total of 177 network hours (42 weekend games, 17 night games).

1972

Most Promising New U.S. Network:
The BBC, ever more visible as the producer of such literate entertainments as *Elizabeth R., Vanity Fair, and America.*
Most Unwelcome Conversation Stoppers:
The cancellation of The David Frost Show (Group W) and three-fourths cancellation of The Dick Cavett Show (ABC).
Most Slickly Scripted and Produced Special:
The Republican National Convention in Miami, whose predictable plot line made it even more boring than its Democratic competition.
Most Dramatic Live Moments:
The tragic terrorist raid at the Munich Olympics, which erupted during ABC's impressive running coverage of the sports event.
Most Lonely Program:
NBC Reports, the only regularly scheduled network public affairs show in prime time.
Most Venturesome Single Show:
VD Blues (PBS).
Most Tiresome Repetition of a Single Gag:
Bridget Loves Bernie (CBS).
Most Effective Force in Children's TV:
Action for Children's Television (ACT), whose campaigning reduced the number and subdued the tone of exploitative commercials (vitamins disguised as candy, product pitches by hosts of shows), during kiddie hours.
Most Entertaining New Series:
Sanford and Son (NBC)
Most Potent Ratings Organization:
Nixon, Inc., whose disapproval of broadcasting trends showed up in speeches, law-suits, proposed legislation and, above all, in the drastic revamping of public broadcasting to tone down, among other things, its national news and documentaries.

1973

Most Rewarding Viewing:
The Senate Watergate hearings, which combined public service, comedy, drama and some boredom in what, for this year, was the medium's finest hour—or rather 200 hours.
Most Gripping Soap Opera:
An American Family (PBS), about the Louds, which showed how the world turns in the upper-middle-class, California division.
Most Irritating Development:
The spread of comedy "roasts"—rarely well done.
Most Impressive Debut:
Katharine Hepburn, who poignantly played her first TV role in *The Glass Menagerie*, and gave an even more varied

and captivating performance as herself on The Dick Cavett Show (both ABC).
Runner-up: Sen. Sam Ervin as that perennial favorite, the shrewd, aw-shucks folk hero.
Most Ballyhooed Fizzle:
Ex-Washington *Post* Reporter Sally Quinn in CBS's pallid Morning News.
Most Lively Cultural Fare:
Alistair Cook's *America* (NBC).
Most Welcome Survivors:
The PBS public affairs shows whose funding was threatened by Administration-inspired pressure, notably *Bill Moyers' Journal, Firing Line* and *Washington Week in Review.*
Most Engaging Characterization:
Peter Falk's rumpled, resourceful Columbo (NBC), which freshened the overworked cop-and-crime formula.
Most Unprofessional Sports Coverage:
The sexist sniping by Rosemary Casals, Gene Scott and Howard Cosell at the Bobby Riggs-Billie Jean King tennis match (ABC).
Most Nourishing Drama:
Laurence Olivier and Britain's National Theater in *Long Day's Journey into Night* (ABC) and Joseph Papp's New York Shakespeare Festival production of *Much Ado About Nothing* (CBS)—a tie.

1974

Most Consistently Rewarding Show:
60 Minutes, the CBS magazine program, which features TV's best interviewer, Mike Wallace. Week-in, week-out (except during the N.F.L. season), the show blends investigative reporting, responsible social commentary and oddball features to provide the most instructive, entertaining hour in broadcast journalism.
Most Gratifying Statistic:
The drop in the audience for pro football. If the trend continues, maybe *60 Minutes* could stay on all year long.
Most Satisfying Coverage of a Special Event:
Rhoda's Wedding.
Best Single Performance:
Anthony Hopkins' merciless yet endlessly engaging portrayal of an ambitious man in *The Edwardians: Lloyd George.* Alone it made PBS's apparently irreducible trade deficit with the BBC worthwhile.
Most Dismaying New Program:
Feeling Good, the Children's Television Workshop's ghastly attempt to talk up good health practices, mostly by talking down to its audience. It is 19th century do-gooderism dressed up in 20th century electronic finery.
Most Solid Old Salt of the Earth:
Edward Asner as News Editor Lou Grant on *The Mary Tyler Moore Show.* Not even Walter Cronkite has more deftly represented the reality principle in a medium that mostly has nothing to do with it. Asner is not only the rock on which this great sitcom rests but sometimes seems to be the only reliable source of common sense in all of prime time.
Most Expert Made-for-TV Movie:
The Law, with a street smart performance by Judd Hirsch as a deputy public defender, some of the snappiest dialogue this side of *The Maltese Falcon* and a well-observed view of our clanking machinery for meting out

criminal justice. The film was a model of what can be accomplished in a throwaway form.

Most Welcome Return to the Medium:

Button-bright, flip lipped James Garner—back from a dismal movie carreer—in *The Rockford Files*, a modestly witty private-eye series.

Most Rewarding Long-run Dramas:

Tie between *Upstairs, Downstairs* and *The Richard Nixon Show (cancelled)*.

Most Devoutly Wished-for Episode:

An Hour on *The Waltons* in which Pop and Grandpa sell green lumber to the builders of an orphanage, Mom entertains a traveling salesman and John Boy's siblings discover him committing an unnatural act back of the sawmill.

1975

Most Satisfying Acting out a National Fantasy:

When, as Cher's closing credits rolled guest star Jerry Lewis simultaneously pulled the star's hair and tickled her tummy button.

Most Scroogelike Corporate Behavior:

The network's insistence on spoiling Christmas before it gets started by scheduling annual reruns (some for the eighth and tenth times) of animated fairy tales that were lousy to begin with. Like the broken-down crooners propped up in front of too many holiday "specials" this time of year, the cartoons cannot be said to improve with age.

Most Salutary Contribution to the Creation of the Proper Bicentennial Spirit:

Frederick Wiseman's *Welfare* (PBS). With his customary cool compassion, TV's only great documentarian showed us not a bland and idealized portrait of what we have been but the inhumane and bureaucratized future that has already arrived for the poor and could dominate everyone's life by our 300th birthday.

Most Dismally Earnest Tooth Fairy:

Mr. Doowdin, the busybody druggist who is letting his musty store run photogenically down while he campaigns against cavities. Maybe a discount chain will drive him off the block in the new year.

Most Underrated Show:

Lily Tomlin's comedy special (ABC). Audiences and critics generally ignored the year's brightest hour of humor by the medium's most solidly gifted talent.

Most Absorbing Programs No Grownup Should Have Been Absorbed By:

Tie between Guilty or Innocent: The Sheppard Murder Case (NBC) and *Valentino* (ABC). Trashy subject matter redeemed by the total sobriety—and professionalism—of its presentation.

Most Prominent Third Wheel:

Dan Rather on *60 Minutes* (CBS). The program remains the best commercial TV has to offer and its rescheduling in prime time is the only known benefit of a disastrous season. But Mike Wallace and Morley Safer really don't need any help from underemployed White House correspondents.

Most Impressive Evidence that Age has its Blessings:

Laurence Olivier (68) and Katharine Hepburn (66) under the direction of George Cukor (76) in the delicious *Love Among the Ruins (ABC)*.

Most Effective Counterprogramming to the Commercial Networks:

Great Performances and *In Performance at Wolf Trap* (PBS). The Fifth Freedom—freedom from yammer—is eloquently defended in programs that do not educate us about music or sell it to us, but offer it well performed without self-congratulation or apology.

1976

Most Blatant—and Longest—Commercial Interruption:

A 90-minute plug masquerading as live coverage of a celebrity jolly up, which launched NBC's *Big Event* series. Besides hyping the series, the stars tediously promoted their upcoming films—all, by an odd coincidence, Paramount releases.

Most Honest Fella:

Dustin Hoffman, at the aforementioned blast. Asked why his *Marathon Man* co-star, Laurence Olivier, was absent, Dusty gave the short answer, "He has too much class."

Most Appealing Argument for Feminism:

Lindsay Wagner as the Bionic Woman.

Most Appalling Argument for Feminism:

Barbara Walters. ABC's celebrated anchorperson, who in her first prime time special led a tour of her own apartment, and then reduced Jimmy and Rosalynn Carter to the level of her other guests, Barbra Streisand and Jon Peters.

Most Newsworthy News Show:

The *MacNeil-Lehrer Report* (PBS), which every night does what commercial broadcasting cannot, or perhaps will not, do—dives intelligently behind the headlines for reflective reporting on the day's major story.

Most Attractive Example of a Trendy Trend:

The Moneychangers (NBC). It dealt with a subject—commercial banking—that is not exactly fraught with romance. Craftsman-like writing, directing and acting (notably by Christopher Plummer as a thoroughgoing heel, and by Susan Flannery, (playing that television rarity, a genuinely mature woman) have turned it into the most amusingly melodramatic of the currently fashionable miniseries.

Most Gratefully Received Programming Euthanasia:

Tie between *Homes* and *Yo-Yo*, *Ball Four* and *Mr. T. and Tina*.

Most Logical Candidate for Similar Treatment:

The Captain and Tennille.

Most Deplorable Success:

Laverne & Shirley (ABC), a deliberate insult to some of our nation's most estimable citizens.

Most Distinguished Documentary:

Michael Roemer's *Dying* (PBS). A sentive exploration of the emotions of three people confronting the ultimate crisis, it is that least common of television phenomena—a program that continues to reverberate in the mind.

1977

Sourest Grapes:

From executives at CBS and NBC who accused top-ranking ABC of running junk—then launched a desperate search for the same kind of junk.

Best Look at an Old Face:

Jason Robards' portrayal of a vile President, Richard Monckton, a dead ringer for Richard Nixon, in ABC's *Washington: Behind Closed Doors*.

Best Argument for Divorce:

PBS's pretentious series about three New York clans, *The Best of Families*.

Television's Biggest Sleeper:

ABC's *Roots*, the eight-part saga of the black in America and the most successful show in history.

Greatest Cause of Woe and Wailing:

The demise of *The Mary Tyler Moore Show* after seven enchanting years.

Best Remembered:

Bing Crosby, Groucho Marx, Elvis Presley.

Most Provocative New Pinup:

Suzanne Somers of ABC's *Three's Company*, who proves that gentlemen still prefer blondes, preferably dumb.

1978

The Year's Biggest Rip-off:

ABC's *Battlestar Galactica*, which tries to imitate *Star Wars* without characters or talent.

Greatest Source of Fear and Trembling Along Network Row:

Reports that TV viewing is off for the first time in history.

Second Greatest Source of F & T Along Network Row:

Appointment of ABC's Fred Silverman as new chief of NBC.

Cleanest Sweep:

Fred Silverman cancels within three months of their debuts all the new fall NBC series that he inherited.

Most Promising Newcomer:

Robin Williams in ABC's *Mork & Mindy*.

Most Predictable TV Trend:

In the wake of the *National Lampoon's Animal House*, all three networks have announced frat-house sitcoms to premiere in early 1979.

1979

THE BEST OF THE SEVENTIES

Best Sitcom:

The Mary Tyler Moore Show, which beginning in 1970, provided seven seasons of sophisticated humor and showed a woman succeeding in what was once a man's job.

The Game Is On:

ABC took long odds by introducing sport to primetime in 1970 with *Monday Night Football*. Since then just about everything except golf has been played at night, doubling in a decade, to nearly 1,400 hours in 1979, the amount of sport on network TV and giving the fans World Series games played in arctic conditions and, of course, *Thursday Night Football*.

The Last Puff:

By act of Congress, cigarette ads were banned from TV and radio in 1971. The long-range effect on profits—none at all.

Most Influential Series:

All in the Family, which was launched in 1971 and proved that controversial subjects and adult language could bring high ratings.

Most Compelling Soap Opera:

The Watergate hearings 319 hours of hightension coverage centered on that age-old theme—Did he or didn't he? He did.

Most Convincing Evidence that the U.S. Is Still a British Colony:

Upstairs, Downstairs; Elizabeth R; The Six Wives of Henry VIII; Civilisation; I, Claudius; The Pallisers; The Duchess of Duke Street; Monty Python's Flying Circus.

The Horatio Alger Award:

To ABC, the little engine that could, for puffing its way into the Nielsen station and becoming the top-rated network in 1976, after a lifetime in last place.

Most Watched Show:

Roots, which not only broke all records of the 1970s, but was also the most popular TV entertainment in history.

Most Promising Development:

The new technology—cable TV, video-cassette recorders and video discs—that is finally giving viewers the choice of what they want to watch.

1980

Loudest Shot:

The shooting of *Dallas'* J.R. Ewing, which prompted three-quarters of the globe to ask: Who dunit?

Fastest Comeback:

CBS, which defied all predictions and took the No. 1 spot in the ratings back from ABC, which had grabbed the title in 1976.

Biggest Sushi:

NBC's *Shogun*, which ranked just behind *Roots* (1977) as the highest-rated mini-series of all time.

Words Least Likely to Be Remembered:

NBC President Fred Silverman's statement July a year ago, that if he could not raise ratings significantly by Christmas 1980, someone else should be given "a shot at this job." As of last week, NBC was distant third in the ratings, further behind, in fact, than it was last Christmas and the Christmas before.

Most Sadistic Show:

ABC's *That's Incredible*, which, in the search for thrills and ratings, has caused one man nearly to lose a foot, another to burn his fingers to stumps, and a third to suffer several fractures and a ruptured aorta.

Biggest Omission:

NBC's coverage of the Moscow Summer Olympics, all 152 hours of which were canceled after the U.S. withdrew from the Games to protest the Soviet invasion of Afghanistan.

Oddest Couple:

Tom Snyder and Rona Barrett, who got along so famously as co-hosts of NBC's *Tomorrow* that Miss Rona finally walked out in a huff.

1981

***Dallas* (CBS):**

Will Brave Bobby and Barren Pamela adopt the love child of J.R. and his dead mistress Kristin? Enter the Ewing labyrinth and be hooked or be damned.

Early Days (CBS Cable):
David Storey's memorable song at twilight, adapted by Director Anthony Page from Lindsay Anderson's National Theater production in London. Storey wrote this meditation on age and regret especially for Ralph Richardson, who gives one of his greatest performances.

The Golden Age of Television (PBS):
A selection of golden oldies from the '50s, including *Marty* and *The Days of Wine and Roses*, demonstrated that, yes, they really did do things better back then.

Hill Street Blues (NBC):
Probing the soul of the inner-city cop with compassion and flipped-out wit, *Hill Street* won critical raves, eight Emmys and—finally!—enough viewers to make it a hit.

The Patricia Neal Story (CBS):
Prime time offered enough triumph-over-a-bizarre-disease TV movies to choke a hospital, but Dirk Bogarde and the redoubtable Glenda Jackson made this particular version wrenching and true.

The Phil Donahue Show: "Missing Kids" (Syndicated):
A heartfelt and harrowing episode from what is consistently the best national talk show.

SCTV (NBC):
The funniest nights on television, with TV itself the target of repeated maulings by a company of six comic assassins. Their "Sammy Maudlin Show," an excursion into late-night chat and sleaze, has a kind of purgatorial hilarity, like a Friars' roast written by Sartre.

The Shock of the New (PBS):
A spirited tour, in an eight-part series, by Time Art Critic Robert Hughes through the art and architecture of that most difficult of all centuries, the 20th.

Steve Martin's Best Show Ever (NBC):
A well-turned hour of live, zoned-out comedy, which featured everything from Belushi to Bartok and raised the question, "Did dinosaurs build Stonehenge?"

Taxi (ABC):
A fourth season of high-quality laughs from the Sunshine Cab Co. *Taxi, WKRP in Cincinnati* (CBS) and *Bosom Buddies* (ABC) are the win, place and show-off of current sitcoms.

1982

Brideshead Revisited (PBS):
Faithful, sometimes to a fault, to Evelyn Waugh's most popular novel, this visually ravishing series offered a lovely elegy to a time that never was. Eleven episodes that warmed an Anglophile's winter.

CBS Cable:
An arts showcase that, in its 14 months on the air, presented some of the medium's finest theater *Sizwe Banzi Is Dead*, dance (Twyla Tharp's *Confessions of a Cornermaker*), film (*The Tree of Wooden Clogs*), music (a series on Broadway composers) and conversation (Gregory Jackson's *Signature*). After losing an estimated $30 million, it expired on Dec. 16—one of 1982's saddest death notices.

Donkey Kong (Coleco Industries Inc.):
Video games continue to crowd TV programs off the family tube. This one, probably the best translation of an arcade game to home use, boasts bemusing graphics and the most congenial cast (savage ape, imperiled heroine, undaunted hero) this side of *Dallas*.

Late Night with David Letterman (NBC):
Laid-back and amiably hip, Letterman presides over a menagerie of stupid pet tricks, oddball celebrities and the man with the worm farm. A lullaby for the eccentric insomniac.

Life on Earth (PBS):
A tale of wonders, the saga of evolution and the ascent of life, from bacteria to man, lovingly told by British host David Attenborough.

MTV (Warner Amex Satellite Entertainment Co.):
Basically FM with pictures, MTV (Music Television) is a 24-hour cable service whose imaginative videotapes illustrating rock recordings expand TV's generally unadventurous visual vocabulary.

NBC News Overnight:
TV's wittiest, toughest, least snazzy news strip. The late hour (1:30 a.m. E.S.T.) allows for lengthy and caustic reports, sutured by two droll, articulate anchors: Lloyd Dobyns (now succeeded by Bill Schechner) and Linda Ellerbee.

Police Squad! (ABC):
The folks responsible for the hit movie *Airplane!* found TV a congenial medium to spoof cop shows with a bizarre deadpan wit. This superior sitcom came and went in six spring episodes; it should have stayed.

Roses in December (PBS):
A taut documentary by Ana Carrigan and Bernard Stone about the killing of Jean Donovan, a lay missionary who worked with the Maryknoll nuns in El Salvador. An exemplary piece of humane film making that avoided political sentimentality and glib answers.

Sweeney Todd (The Entertainment Channel):
Terry Hughes directed Stephen Sodheim's operatic musical for cable with seamless theater and TV technique. George Hearn was magnificent as Sweeney, the misanthropic cutthroat; Angela Lansbury was delectably deranged as his helpmeet.

1983

Cheers (NBC):
Now in its second season, this barroom sitcom has found its saucy stride and, in stars Ted Danson and Shelley Long, has created a mismatched pair that could give Tracy and Hepburn a run for their moxie.

Faerie Tale Theater (Showtime):
These slightly fractured but never completely Grimm tales, produced by Actress Shelley Duvall, give a hip, witty twist and dreamy visual style to storybook classics.

The Life and Adventures of Nicholas Nickleby (Mobil Showcase Network):
Even squeezed to fit the small screen, the Royal Shakespeare Company's epic entertainment still ranked as a unique theatrical treat. The nine-hour drama preserved 150 great performances in a format Dickens would have loved: the mini-series.

Motown 25: Yesterday, Today, Forever (NBC):
A stirring video jukebox of the most memorable sounds of a quarter-century of soul, from the still irresistible Temptations through the stylized showmanship of Michael Jackson.

Nicklodeon (Warner Amex Satellite Entertainment Co.):
A channel devoted to children without being childish. Among its most notable enticements: the *Pinwheel* puppets for pre-schoolers, and *Livewire*, an exuberant variety talk show for early teens.

NBC News Overnight:
"Being best is not enough," rued NBC News Chief Reuven Frank in canceling this late-night paragon after 17 months. Insomniacs will miss *Ovenight*'s tough reporting, its springtly sense of the absurd and especially its Queen of Tart, Co-Anchor Linda Ellerbee. The first nightly news show good enough to warrant reruns.

Special Bulletin (NBC):
Gripping in a way that *The Day After* was not, this docudrama presented a fictional nuclear crisis as a news event actually in progress. The result was a dark parody of the pontifical way in which the networks package disaster.

Sunday Morning with Charles Kuralt (CBS):
Light but never lightweight, this 90-minute eye opener demonstrates that long-form magazine shows can work, and that Kuralt is as nimble off the road as on.

Swan Lake, Minnesota (ARTS):
Swan maidens in tutus riding bales of hay up a conveyor belt? This poetic, disarmingly simple adaptation of the classic ballet inventively mixed a country-and-western twang with Tchaikovskian lyricism.

Viet Nam: A Television History (PBS):
With its painstaking marshaling of detail, this 13-hour documentary was television as the first draft of history. It was, by turns, poignant and chilling and never blinked.

1984

THE BURNING BED (NBC):
Farrah Fawcett proved she could act, and television proved it could do an "issue drama" without preaching, simplifying or sentimentalizing, in this gripping TV movie about a woman who takes incendiary revenge on her brutal husband.

CAT ON A HOT TIN ROOF (Showtime):
Jessica Lange was a sizzling Maggie and Rip Torn an offbeat Big Daddy in this lively and well-directed (by Jack Hofsiss) classic. TV's finest posthumous tribute to Tennessee Williams.

CONCEALED ENEMIES (PBS):
Alger Hiss, the alleged spy: Whittaker Chambers, his accuser, and Congressman Richard Nixon, the investigator. These were the true-life protagonists of the year's most intriguing mystery story, deftly dramatized in a *American Playhouse* miniseries.

DOMESTIC LIFE (CBS):
Before Bill Cosby revived the sitcom genre in the fall, Martin Mull poked juicy fun at it last January, playing the father of a slightly loony family in a very funny, undeservedly short-lived series.

THE GLITTER DOME (HBO):
James Garner and John Lithgow were two burned-out detectives in this taut, cynical adaptation of Joseph Wambaugh's novel about murder in movieland. Possibly the best movie yet made for pay TV.

JEWEL IN THE CROWN (PBS):
With understated urgency, this 14-week series (which runs until March) sketched a sovereign vision of the long, sad twilight of the British raj in India.

KING LEAR (syndicated):
In what may prove to be his last great role, Laurence Olivier acts up a storm—and, in the heath scene, outacts one—scaling the majesty of Shakespeare's mad monarch. Will this *Lear* be surpassed on TV? Never, never, never, never, never.

MIAMI VICE (NBC):
Unlike most of the season's new shows, this hard-nosed police series has actually improved since its pilot. The first network series since *Hill Street Blues* to establish a unique look and tone: an alluring mix of *cinéma vérité* grit and rock-video glitz.

PRESIDENTIAL DEBATE NO. 1.
Walter Mondale's unexpected humor; President Reagan's awkward pauses; Moderator Barbara Walters' lecturing of the audience between two dull conventions and a runaway election, this face-off to chart the course of the Free World was the political year's most interesting TV news event.

LOS ANGELES SUMMER OLYMPICS (ABC):
With half the globe watching, the extensive and authoritative coverage of the XXIII Olympiad was breathtaking to behold.

4/THE PEABODYS (HENRY W. GRADY SCHOOL OF JOURNALISM

THE GEORGE FOSTER Peabody Awards—presented in memory of the eminent Georgian banker and philanthropist (1852–1938)—were established in 1940 to honor outstanding achievements in broadcasting. The Henry W. Grady School of Journalism at the University of Georgia administers the awards with the aid of a National Advisory Board. The School screens the applicants; the Board makes the final decisions.

Initially the awards only honored achievements in the field of radio, but as television became increasingly important in American life, it took more of the awards. (The radio prizes are not included here.) Through 1973 the awards were given in various categories, e.g. Entertainment, News, Education, Children's Programming, etc. But in 1974 the Board eliminated the category designations and adopted the policy of merely announcing the complete list of Peabody winners for that calendar year. Under this new system, the Board can select one or more programs from any particular field, or it may choose not to honor any achievements in that field.

The awards—now considered among the most prestigious in broadcasting—can be given to networks, programs or individuals. As of Jan. 1, 1980 the Board has presented 568 awards and 56 citations.

1948

Outstanding Contribution to the Art of Television:
   Actor's Studio

1949

Outstanding Entertainment Program:
   The Ed Wynn Show (CBS)
Outstanding Education Program:
   Crusade in Europe (ABC)
Outstanding Reporting and Interpretation of the News:
   United Nations in Action (CBS)
Outstanding Children's Program:
   Kukla, Fran, and Ollie (NBC)

1950

Outstanding Entertainment Award:
   Jimmy Durante (NBC)
Outstanding Children's Program:
   Zoo Parade (NBC)
   Saturday at the Zoo (ABC)
Outstanding Education Program (citation):
   The Johns Hopkins Science Riview (WAAM—TV, Baltimore)
Other Awards:
   To ABC, its president Robert E. Kintner, and his associates, Robert Saudek and Joseph McDonald, for their courageous stand in resisting organized pressures and their reaffirmation of basic American principles.

1951

Best Educational Program:
   What in the World (WCAU, Philadelphia)
Outstanding News and Interpretation:
   Ed Murrow, *See It Now* (CBS)
Outstanding Entertainment Program (music):
   Gian Carlo Menotti, *Amahl and the Night Visitors* (NBC)
Outstanding Entertainment Program (non-musical):
   Celanese Theater (ABC)
Meritorious Regional Public Service by Radio and Television:
   WSB, Atlanta for *The Pastor's Study and Our World Today*

1952

Outstanding Educational Program:
   The Johns Hopkins Science Review (WAAM-TV, Baltimore)
Outstanding News Program:
   Meet the Press (NBC)
Outstanding Entertainment Program:
   Mister Peepers (NBC)
   Your Hit Parade (NBC)
Outstanding Youth and Children's Program:
   Ding Dong School (NBC)
Local Public Service:
   WEWS, Cleveland
Television Award:
   Victory at Sea (NBC)

1953

Outstanding Achievement in News:
Gerald W. Johnson WAAM-TV, Baltimore for his scholarly commentary on the news.
Outstanding Achievement in Music:
NBC Opera Theater
Outstanding Achievement in Entertainment:
Television Playhouse (NBC)
Imogene Coca (NBC)
Outstanding Achievement in Education:
Cavalcade of Books (KNXT, Los Angeles)
Camera Three (WCBS-TV, New York)
Outstanding Youth and Children's Program:
Mr. Wizard (NBC)
Promotion of International Understanding Through Television:
British Broadcasting Corp. for their coverage of the coronation.
Individual Award:
Edward R. Murrow (CBS)

1954

Outstanding Achievement in Entertainment:
George Gobel (NBC)
Outstanding Achievement in Education:
Adventure (CBS)
Outstanding Youth and Children's Program:
Disneyland (ABC)
National Public Service:
Industry on Parade, National Association of Manufacturers
Regional Public Service:
WJAR-TV, Providence, Rhode Island *Hurricane Carol*
Special Television Awards:
Omnibus (CBS)
The Search (CBS)
Outstanding Radio-Television News:
John Daly (ABC)

1955

Outstanding Achievement in News:
Douglas Edwards (CBS)
Outstanding Achievement in Entertainment:
Perry Como (NBC)
Jackie Gleason (CBS)
Outstanding Achievement in Dramatic Entertainment:
Producer's Showcase (NBC)
Outstanding Youth and Children's Program:
Lassie (CBS)
Outstanding Achievement in Education:
Dr. Frank Baxter, KXNT, Los Angeles
Television Citation Recipients:
Education:
Omnibus
Adams Family Series
Local Public Service:
WMT-TV, Cedar Rapids
KOED, San Francisco

Promotion of International:
Understanding:
Assignment: India (NBC)
Radio-Television Music:
Voice of Firestone (ABC)
Radio-Television Public Service:
Sylvester L. Weaver Jr. (NBC) for pioneering program concepts, especially.
Monitor, Weekday, Wide Wide World and *Spectaculars*
Radio-Television Promotion of International Understanding:
Quincy Howe (CBS)

1956

Outstanding Achievement in News:
ABC, John Daly, and their associates for converage of the national political conventions.
Outstanding Achievement in Entertainment:
The Ed Sullivan Show (CBS)
Outstanding Achievement in Education:
You Are There (CBS)
Outstanding Youth and/or Children's Program:
Youth Wants to Know (NBC)
Outstanding Achievement in Public Service:
World in Crisis (CBS)
Outstanding Achievement in Promotion of International Understanding:
The Secret Life of Danny Kaye (UNICEF)
Outstanding Television Writing:
Rod Serling, *Requiem for a Heavyweight* (CBS)
Other Awards:
Radio-Television Local-Regional Public Service:
Regimented Raindrops (WOW, Omaha)
Radio-Television Promotion of International Understanding:
United Nations Radio and Television
Special Award:
Jack Gould, for his outstanding contribution to radio and television through his *New York Times* writings.

1957

Outstanding Achievement in News:
ABC, for *Prologue '58* and other significant news coverage by John Charles Daly and associates.
Outstanding Achievement in Entertainment (musical):
The Dinah Shore Chevy Show (NBC)
Outstanding Achievement in Entertainment (non-musical):
Hallmark Hall of Fame (NBC) with special mention of "The Green Pastures," "There Shall Be No Night," "On Borrowed Time," "Twelfth Night," "The Lark," and "Yeoman of the Guard."
Outstanding Achievement in Education:
The Heritage Series (WQED, Pittsburgh)
Outstanding Youth and Children's Program:
Captain Kangaroo (CBS)
Outstanding Local Youth and Children's Program:
Wunda Wunda (KING-TV, Seattle)
Outstanding Public Service:
The Last Word (CBS)

Outstanding Local Public Service:
Panorama (KLZ-TV, Denver)
Outstanding Contribution to International
Understanding:
Bob Hope (NBC)
Radio and Television News:
CBS, for depth and range, including Face the Nation, See it Now,
The Twentieth Century and This Is New York.
Local Radio-Television News:
Louis M. Lyons (WGBH, Boston)
Special Radio-Television Awards:
NBC, for its outstanding contribution to education through (a) the series of educational programs fed to educational stations, across the nation; and (b) the Know Your Schools project by NBC-owned and operated stations.
Westinghouse Broadcasting Company, Inc. for its Boston Conference on Programming and the high quality of its public service broadcasting.

1958

Outstanding Achievement in News:
NBC News, The Huntley-Brinkley Report
Outstanding Achievement in Dramatic Entertainment:
Playhouse 90 (CBS)
Outstanding Achievement in Musical Entertainment:
Lincoln Presents Leonard Bernstein and the New York Philharmonic (CBS)
Outstanding Achievement in Entertainment with
Humor:
The Steve Allen Show (NBC)
Outstanding Achievement in Education:
Continental Classroom (NBC)
Outstanding Achievement in Programs for Youth:
College News Conference (ABC)
Outstanding Achievement in Programs for Children:
The Blue Fairy (WGN-TV, Chicago)
Outstanding Contribution to International
Understanding:
M.D. International (NBC)
Outstanding Public Service:
CBS, with special recognition given to Dr. Frank Stanton.
Outstanding Television Writing:
James Costigan, "Little Moon of Alban," Hallmark Hall of Fame (NBC)
Special Television Awards:
An Evening With Fred Astaire (NBC)
Orson Welles, "Fountain of Youth," Colgate Theater (NBC)

1959

Outstanding Achievement in News:
Khrushchev Abroad (ABC)
Outstanding Achievement in Entertainment (non-musical):
The Play of the Week (WNTA-TV, Newark)
David Susskind for The Moon and Sixpence (NBC)
Outstanding Achievement in Entertainment (musical):
The Bell Telephone Hour (NBC)
Great Music From Chicago (WGN-TV, Chicago)

Outstanding Achievement in Education:
The Population Explosion (CBS)
Decisions (WGBH-TV, Boston and World Affairs Council)
Outstanding Contribution to International
Understanding:
The Ed Sullivan Show (CBS)
Small World (CBS)
Outstanding Local Public Service:
WDSU-TV, New Orleans
Special Television Awards:
Dr. Frank Stanton (CBS)
Ed Murrow, Fred Friendly, The Lost Class of '59 (CBS)

1960

Outstanding Achievement in News:
The Texaco Huntley-Brinkley Report (NBC)
Outstanding Achievement in Entertainment:
The Fabulous Fifties (CBS)
Outstanding Achievement in Education:
White Paper series (NBC)
Outstanding Youth Program:
G.E. College Bowl (CBS)
Outstanding Children's Program:
The Shari Lewis Show (NBC)
Outstanding Contribution to International
Understanding:
CBS, 1960 Olympic Games
Outstanding Public Service:
CBS Report
Individual Award:
Dr. Frank Stanton (CBS)
Radio-Television Education:
Broadcasting and Film Commission, National Council of Churches of Christ in the U.S.A., for such programs as Look Up and Live (CBS-TV), Frontiers of Faith (NBC-TV), Pilgrimage (ABC), and Talk-Back (local stations).
Locally Produced Radio-Television Programs:
WOOD and WOOD-TV, Grand Rapids
KPFK, Los Angeles
WCKT, Miami
WCCO-TV, Minneapolis

1961

Outstanding Achievement in News:
David Brinkley's Journal (NBC)
Outstanding Achievement in Entertainment:
The Bob Newhart Show (NBC)
Outstanding Achievement in Education:
An Age of Kings (BBC)
Vincent Van Gogh: A Self-Portrait (NBC)
Outstanding Youth and Children's Program:
Expedition! (ABC)
Outstanding Contribution to International
Understanding:
Walter Lippman, (CBS)
Outstanding Public Service:
Let Freedom Ring (KSL-TV, Salt Lake City)
Special Television Award:
Capital Cities Broadcasting Corp, Verdict for Tomorrow: The Eichmann Trial on Television.

Individual Awards:
Fred Friendly (CBS)
Newton M. Minow (FCC)

1962

Outstanding Achievement in News:
Walter Cronkite (CBS)
Outstanding Achievement in Entertainment:
DuPont Show of the Week (NBC)
Carol Burnett (CBS)
Outstanding Achievement in Education:
Biography (Official Films, Inc)
Outstanding Youth and Children's Program:
Exploring (NBC)
Walt Disney's Wonderful World of Color (NBC)
Outstanding Contribution to International Understanding:
Adlai Stevenson Reports (ABC)
Outstanding Public Service:
A Tour of the White House with Mrs. John F. Kennedy (CBS)
Outstanding Locally-Produced Television:
Elliot Norton Reviews (WGBH-TV, Boston)
Books for Our Time (WNDT, New York City)
San Francisco Pageant (KPIX-TV, San Francisco)
Individual Award:
William R. McAndrew, Executive Vice President of NBC News
Special Award:
Television Information Office (NAB) for study resulting in the book, For the Young Viewer: Television Programming for Children. . . At the Local Level

1963

Outstanding Achievement in News:
Eric Sevareid (CBS)
Outstanding Achievement in Entertainment:
The Danny Kaye Show (CBS)
Mr. Novak (NBC)
Outstanding Achivement in Education:
American Revolution of '63 (NBC)
Saga of Western Man (ABC)
Outstanding Children's Programs:
Treetop House (WGN, Chicago)
Outstanding Youth Program:
The Dorothy Gordon Forum (WNBC-TV, New York City)
Outstanding Contribution to International Understanding:
Town Meeting of the World (CBS); Frank Stanton
Outstanding Public Service:
CBS Reports: Storm Over the Supreme Court (CBS)
Special Award:
To the broadcasting industry of the U.S.A. for its coverage of the assassination of President Kennedy and related events.

1964

Outstanding Achievement:
CBS Reports, for judicious selection of material, first-rate editing, and superb production
Profiles in Courage (NBC). To Robert Saudek and his associates, and to NBC, for their faithful, artistic, and sensitive portrayal of some of the most moving episodes in American History.
Joyce Hall Hallmark Hall of Fame, (NBC) for being an enlightened patron of the television arts.
Julia Child, for her appetizing program, The French Chef (WGBH, Boston).
The Louvre (NBC), an exciting hour-long excursion into the world of art and history.
Burr Tillstrom, puppeteer, for appearances on That Was the Week That Was (NBC)
Outstanding Contribution to International Understanding:
INTERTEL (International Television Federation: Australian Broadcasting Corporation, Canadian Broadcasting Corporation, Rediffusion Television, Ltd. (London), Westinghouse Broadcasting Company, and National Educational Television).
Outstanding Public Service:
Off the Cuff (WBWB, Chicago)
Individual Award:
William H. Lawrence, White House Correspondent and American News Editor for ABC.
Special Award:
The networks and the broadcasting industry for inescapably confronting the American public with the realities of racial discontent.

1965

Outstanding Achievement in News:
Frank McGee (NBC)
Morley Safer (CBS)
KTLA (Los Angeles)
Outstanding Achievement in Entertainment:
The Julie Andrews Show (NBC)
My Name is Barbra (CBS)
Frank Sinatra—A Man and His Music (NBC)
Outstanding Achievement in Education:
National Educational Television (NET)
Outstanding Youth and Children's Program:
A Charlie Brown Christmas (CBS)
Outstanding Achievement in Public Service:
CBS Report: KKK—The Invisible Empire
Outstanding Achievement in Television Innovation
The National Driver's Test (CBS)
Television's Most Inventive Art Documentary:
The Mystery of Stonehenge (CBS)
Outstanding Contribution to International Understanding:
Xerox Corporation, with reference to The Making of the President—1964, Let My People Go, The Louvre, and the series on the United Nations.
Special Television Award:
A Visit to Washington with Mrs. Lyndon B. Johnson—On Behalf of a More Beautiful America (ABC)

1966

Outstanding Achievement in News:
Harry Reasoner (CBS)
Outstanding Achievement in Entertainment:
"A Christmas Memory," *ABC Stage '67* (ABC)
Outstanding Achievement in Education:
National Geographic Specials (CBS)
American White Paper: Organized Crime in the United States (NBC)
Outstanding Youth and Children's Program:
The World of Stuart Little (NBC)
Outstanding Achievement in Promotion of International Understanding:
The Wide World of Sports (ABC)
Siberia: A Day in Irkutsk (NBC)
Outstanding Achievement in Local News-Entertainment:
Kup's Show (WBKB-TV, Chicago)
Outstanding Achievement in Local Public Service:
Assignment Four (KRON-TV, San Francisco)
Outstanding Achievement in Local Music:
Artists' Showcase (WGN-TV, Chicaco)
A Polish Millennium Concert (WTJM-TV, Milwaukee)
Special Television Awards
Bell Telephone Hour (NBC)
Tom John (CBS) *Death of a Salesman, The Strollin' Twenties, Color Me Barbra*
CBS Reports: The Poisoned Air
National Educational Television
Outstanding Achievement in Television-Radio Public Service:
The Dorothy Gordon Youth Forum: Youth and Narcotics—Who Has the Answer? (WNBC-TV and NBC Radio)

1967

Outstanding Achievement in Entertainment:
CBS Playhouse (CBS)
An Evening At Tanglewood (NBC)
Outstanding Achievement in Youth or Children's Programs:
The Children's Film Festival (CBS)
Mr. Knozit (WIS-TV, Columbia, South Carolina)
Outstanding Contribution in Promotion of International Understanding:
Africa (ABC)
Outstanding Achievement in Public Service:
The Opportunity Line (WBBM-TV, Chicago)
Special Television Award:
The Ed Sullivan Show (CBS)
Radio-Television News Analysis and Commentary:
Eric Sevareid (CBS)
Radio-Television Special Awards:
Meet the Press (NBC)
Bob Hope (NBC)
Broadcasting Education Award:
Dr. James R. Killian Jr.

1968

Outstanding Achievement in News:
Charles Kuralt, *On the Road* (CBS)
Outstanding Achievement in Education:
Robert Cromie, *Book Beat* (WTTW, Chicago)
Outstanding Achievement in Entertainment:
Playhouse (NET)
Outstanding Achievement in Promotion of International Understanding:
ABC
Outstanding Youth or Children's Programs:
Misterogers' Neighborhood (NET)
Outstanding Achievement in Public Service:
Westinghouse Broadcasting Co., *One Nation Indivisible*
Special Television Award:
CBS Reports: Hunger in America

1969

Outstanding Achievement in News:
KQED-TV (San Francisco) *Newsroom*
Frank Reynolds (ABC-TV, New York)
Outstanding Achievement in Education:
WGBH-TV (Boston), KCET (Los Angeles) for *The Advocates*
NBC-TV (New York) for *Who Killed Lake Erie?*
Outstanding Achievement in Entertainment:
NBC-TV (New York) *Experiment in Television*
Curt Gowdy
Outstanding Youth or Children's Program:
Children's Television Workshop (New York), *Sesame Street*
Outstanding Achievement in Promotion of International Understanding:
CBS-TV (New York), *The Japanese*
Outstanding Achievement in Network Television Public Service:
Tom Pettit (NBC-TV, New York)
Outstanding Local Television Public Service:
WFBM-TV, Indianapolis, *The Negro in Indianapolis*
Television Award for Writing:
CBS-TV, *J.T.*
Individual Awards:
Chet Huntley, for his contributions to television news.
Bing Crosby, for his outstanding service to broadcasting

1970

Outstanding Achievement in News:
CBS-TV (New York), *60 Minutes*
WPBT (Miami), *Politithon '70*
Outstanding Achievement in Entertainment:
Flip Wilson Show (NBC)
Evening at Pops (PBS, Washington, D.C.)
The Andersonville Trial (PBS and KCET, Los Angeles)
Outstanding Achievement in Education:
Eye of the Storm (ABC)
Outstanding Youth or Children's Programs:
Hot Dog (NBC)
Dr. Seuss Programs (CBS)

Outstanding Achievement in Promotion of International Understanding:
Civilisation (BBC)
This New Frontier (WWL-TV, New Orleans)
Outstanding Achievement in Public Service:
KMEX-TV (Los Angeles), *Peace. . . On Our Time*: KMEX and the Death of Ruben Salazar
NBC-TV (New York), *Migrant: An NBC White Paper.*
Special Television Award:
CBS-TV (New York), *The Selling of the Pentagon*

1971

Outstanding Achievement in Entertainment:
NBC-TV (New York), Dramatic programming
CBS-TV (New York), The American Revolution: 1770–1783, A Conversation with Lord North
ABC-TV (New York), William Blinn, *Brian's Song*
Outstanding Achievement in Education:
WQED (Pitsburgh), *The Turned On Crisis*
Outstanding Youth or Children's Program
Make A Wish (ABC-TV News)
Outstanding Achievement in Television Education:
Mississippi Authority For Educational Television and executive director William Smith (Jackson, Miss.)
Outstanding Achievement in Promotion of International Understanding:
United Nations Television (New York), *United Nations Day Concert with Paplo Casals*
Outstanding Public Service:
NBC-TV (New York), *This Child is Rated X)*
Individual Awards:
George Heinemann (NBC-TV, New York)
Dr. Frank Stanton (CBS, New York)
Outstanding Achievement in Broadcast News:
John Rich (NBC Radio and Television, New York)

1972

BILL MONROE, Washington editor of the *Today* show, NBC, for his excellence in news reporting.
CBS-TV, for *The Waltons*, a sensitive dramatic representation of life during the depression.
NBC-TV, for three special programs devoted to 20th Century American music: *Jack Lemmon in 'S Wonderful, 'S Marvelous, 'S Gershwin, Singer presents Liza with a Z,* and *The Timex All-Star Swing Festival.*
WHRO-TV, Norfold, Va. for its overall classroom programming as evidenced by *Animals and Such, Writing Time, People Puzzle,* and *Dollar Data—A Matter of Choice.*
BBC and NBC-TV, for *The Search for the Nile*, an outstanding series of documentaries depicting the 35 year search for the source of the Nile River.
ABC-TV, for *ABC Afterschool Specials* an innovative series for young people.
CBS-TV, for *Captain Kangaroo*, a long-running show for young children.
WNET, New York, and BBC, for *The Restless Earth*, an outstanding use of television as a medium for the promotion of international understanding.
WWL-TV, New Orleans, for *China '72: A Hole in the Bamboo Curtain*, one of the first non-network documentaries about life in China.

NBC-TV, for *Pensions: The Broken Promise*, an investigative documentary about the private pension system.
WABC-TV, New York, for *Willowbrook: The Last Great Disgrace*, a documentary about living conditions of the mentally retarded.
ABC-TV, for *XX Olympiad*, an outstanding example of a network's coverage of a worldwide sports event.
ALISTAIR COOKE, British social historian, for a meaningful perceptive look at America in a series presented by BBC and NBC: *America—A Personal View By Alistair Cooke.*

1973

Outstanding Achievement in News:
ABC News, *Close-Up*
Peter Lisagor of Chicago *Daily News* for his contribution to broadcast news.
Outstanding Achievement in Entertainment:
WTIU (Bloomington), *Myshkin*
NBC, ABC, and CBS for their outstanding contributions to television drama as evidenced by *Red Pony* (NBC), *ABC-TV Theater* "Pueblo" and "The Glass Menagerie" (ABC), *CBS Playhouse 90* "The Catholics" (CBS).
Outstanding Achievement in Education:
ABC for its contribution to education as evidenced by *The First and Essential Freedom*
KNXT (Los Angeles), *Learning Can Be Fun* and *Dusty's Treehouse*
Outstanding Youth and Children's Program:
NBC for "The Borrowers," *Hallmark Hall of Fame* and "Street of the Flower Boxes," *NBC Children's Theater.*
Outstanding Achievement in Promotion of International Understanding:
WCAU-TV (Philadelphia) *Overture to Friendship: The Philadelphia Orchestra in China.*
Pamela Llott of CBS News for *Lamp Unto My Feet* and *Look Up and Live.*
Outstanding Achievement in Sports:
Joe Garagiola (NBC) for *The Baseball World of Joe Garagiola*
Special Television Award:
NBC, for *The Energy Crisis. . . An American White Paper.*

1974

WCKT-TV, Miami, for a suberb series of investigative reports which brought considerable response and change.
NBC, New York, for the distinguished variety and quality of its dramatic programs as evidenced by *The Execution of Private Slovik, The Law,* and *IBM Presents Clarence Darrow.*
CBS, New York, for exceptionally well-done four-part series of dramatic specials based on the life of Benjamin Franklin.
WNET-TV, New York, and PBS, Washington, D.C., for bringing *The Theater In America* to national television, giving the viewer the finest in regional American theater.
WGBH-TV, Boston, for the exceptional *Nova* series, recognizing particularly those programs which were produced in the United States.
ABC, New York, for *Free To Be. . . You and Me*, a program or young people which the Board said meets the highest

standards for excellence both in its production quality and in its concept.

NBC, New York, for *Go!*, an action oriented program for children which the Board found to be consistently of the best to be found in today's television world for children.

KING-TV, Seattle, for *How Come?*, a well-paced, fully literate program which neither talks down to nor over the level of the young audience for which it is intended.

WCCO-TV, Minneapolis, for *From Belfast with Love*, a superb effort to promote understanding of the situation in Northern Ireland.

ABC, New York, for *Sadat: Action Biography*, the story of the personal and public life of this pivotal mid-East leader, which the Board found to be exceptionally well done, particularly by interviewer Peter Jennings.

NBC, New York, for *Tornado! 4:40 P.M., Xenia, Ohio*, not only for its dramatic impact but for its searching analysis of how the community reacted in the months following.

NPACT (The National Public Affairs Center for Television), Washington, D.C., for its outstanding overall effort to bring meaningful public affairs programming to the nation.

KPRC-TV, Houston, for *The Right Man*, the story of the dedication of one man, Dr. Robert Hayes (President of Wiley College) both to a school and to his fellow man, which the Board found to be a rewarding, innovative and exceptionally well done television documentary.

CARL STERN of NBC News, New York, for his exceptional journalistic enterprise during a time of national crisis.

FRED GRAHAM of CBS News, New York, for his thoroughly professional and consistently penetrating reporting during a time of national crisis.

MARILYN BAKER, San Francisco, for her work as an investigative reporter of the highest order during the time she was a staff member of KQED-TV.

JULIAN GOODMAN, Chairman of the Board of NBC for his outstanding work in the area of first amendment rights and privileges for broadcasting.

1975

WTOP-TV, Washington, D.C., for their overrall public service effort with particular reference to *Harambee: For My People* and *Everywoman: The Hidden World*.

WCKT-TV, Miami, for compiling an envious record of outstanding investigative reporting during 1975.

Charles Kuralt, CBS News, New York, for *On The Road to '76*, a first rate effort to acquaint Americans with what each state is really like in a pre-bicentennial year.

KABC-TV, Los Angeles, for *The Dale Car: A Dream or a Nightmare* as a fine example of how an enterprising television news operation can successfully serve the community interests and needs by exposing a notorious con game.

CBS-TV, New York, for *M*A*S*H*, a creative entertainment effort that has delighted millions of Americans with first-rate humor.

ABC-TV, New York, for *ABC Theater: Love Among The Ruins* as television entertainment programming of the highest order.

NBC-TV, New York, for *Weekend*, a new and refreshing approach to television programming, providing the viewer with a quality experience.

WCVB-TV, Boston, for a viewer-oriented programming package which exhibits a quality of service too rarely seen in today's television.

Group W, New York, for *Call It Macaroni*, a first-rate series of children's programs which permits children to expand their minds through the discovery of new life styles and adventures.

ABC-TV, New York, for *The ABC Afterschool Specials* which, as a series, has opened new frontiers of children's television programming.

Kaiser Broadcasting, San Francisco, for *Snipets*, as an excellent way in which children can learn from television with brief and to-the-point educational and instructional vignettes.

Alphaventure, New York, for *Big Blue Marble*, a program which makes children very much aware of the world which lies beyond the borders of the United States.

CBS News, New York, for *Mr. Rooney Goes to Washington*, a program which rendered an outstanding and meritorious service to the citizens of this nation.

WWL-TV, New Orleans, for *A Sunday Journal*, a locally-produced magazine-concept program which reflects the finest in local television.

CBS News, New York, for *The American Assassins*, as a shining example of what quality broadcasting service to the American public can be.

WAPA-TV, San Juan, Puerto Rico, for *Las Rosas Blancas*, reflecting local television drama at its finest.

Dr. James Killian, Boston, for his outstanding contributions to educational television in the United States.

Posthumous Award

Paul Porter, Member Peabody Awards National Advisory Board.

1976

WLBT-TV, Jackson, Mississippi, for *Power Politics in Mississippi*, an example of greatly needed documentary reporting in an area seemingly untouched in the recent past.

FRANKIN MCMAHON, WBBM-TV, Chicago, for *Primary Colors, An Artist on the Campaign Trail*, showing how an artist can serve as a reporter on the Presidential Campaign trail, lending a new dimension to political reporting.

CHARLES BARTHOLD, WHO-TV, Des Moines, Iowa for his filming of a powerful and destructive tornado in action as it struck and demolished the small town of Jordan, Iowa.

HUGHES RUDD and BRUCE MORTON of *The CBS Morning News*, for their inventive and creative writing coupled with their reporting of significant and insignificant events through pointed humorous features.

SY PEARLMAN, NBC-TV, New York, as producer of *Weekend*'s *Sawyer Brothers'* segment, an outstanding example of the power of television to investigate and uncover new facts resulting in a reexamination of criminal justice in this case.

KCET/28, Los Angeles, for *Visions*, for giving extensive new opportunities to writers and independent filmmakers to display their talents before sizeable audiences.

NBC-TV, New York, for *Sybil*, one of the truly outstanding dramatic programs of the year.

ABC-TV, New York, for *Eleanor and Franklin*, a well written, superbly acted, capably directed, moving treatment of a segment of the lives of two of America's best known historical personalities.

ABC NEWS, New York, for *Animals Animals Animals*, a quality mixture of graphics, animation and live actions focusing on a particular animal in each segment as seen through the eyes of man.

ABC SPORTS, New York, for *The 1976 Winter Olympic Games, Innsbruch, Austria* and *The 1976 Summer Olympic Games, Montreal, Canada*, for reaching new heights in television sports journalism.

TOMORROW ENTERTAINMENT, INC., New York, for *Judge Horton and the Scottsboro Boys*, a program representative of the excellence one has come to expect from Thomas W. Moore and his associates.

WETA-TV, Washington, D.C., for *In Performance at Wolf Trap*, a superb example of the use of television to expand exponentially the audience for great cultural events to all America.

PERRY COMO, with especial reference to the NBC-TV presentation of *Perry Como's Christmas in Austria*, which provided viewers with a sparkling and moving musical experience.

CBS NEWS, for *In The News*, which enables children to better understand events, people, and concepts they encounter during the course of their daily lives.

KERA-TV, Dallas, for *A Thirst in the Garden*, an incisive look at the problems produced by the handling of water in one of the most productive farming areas in the world.

JIM KARAYN AND THE LEAGUE OF WOMEN VOTERS, Washington, D.C., for *'76 Presidential Debates*, for persistence against formidable obstacles which resulted in a series of joint appearances of the Presidential and Vice Presidential candidates during the 1976 political campaign.

WNET-13, New York, for *The Adams Chronicles*, an impressive endeavor which enabled Americans to more realistically comprehend the great contributions to the American heritage by one of the great patriots of the founding days of this Nation.

CBS-NEWS, New York, for *In Celebration of US* which significantly highlighted the nation's 200th birthday with their most extensive coverage on any single day since man landed on the moon.

ABC NEWS, New York, for *Suddenly An Eagle*, documenting how key events, ideas, and problems led ultimately to the Revolutionary War and the founding of the United States of America.

WETA-TV, Washington, D.C. and WNET/13, New York for *A Conversation with Jimmy Carter* in which principal reporter, Bill Moyers, demonstrated the tremendous impact through which television brought Candidate Jimmy Carter to the attention of the American people.

CBS NEWS, New York, for *60 Minutes*, as a program which clearly indicates there is a large and important audience for serious broadcast journalism.

1977

KABC-TV, Los Angeles, for *Police Accountability*, a part of *Eyewitness News*, an example of local TV station serving the public interest in the vital issue of access to information.

KCMO-TV, Kansas City, Missouri, for *Where Have all the Flood Cars Gone*, a part of *Eyewitness News*, an investigative effort in which KCMO traced flood-damaged

automobiles to the buyers, resulting in a major insurance company reclaiming the damaged cars and making proper settlement with purchasers.

WNBC-TV, New York, for *F.I.N.D., Investigative Reports*, for an impressive use of resources of a great metropolitan television, station to effet something for the common good.

WNET-TV, New York, and WETA, Arlington for *The MacNeil/Lehrer Report*, consistently thorough and well-balanced views of timely and important issues.

WBTV, Charlotte, for *The Rowe String Quartet Plays on Your Imagination*, in which the Rowe String Quartet and the North Carolina Dance Theater combined to "act out" the fantasies of people attending a concert.

LORIMAR PRODUCTIONS, for the *ABC Theater* presentation of "Green Eyes," a touching, moving treatment of the story of a young, black veteran of the Vietnam War who goes back to the scene of that conflict searching for the child he fathered but left behind.

DAVID WOLPER and ABC-TV, for the *ABC Novel for Television* presentation of *Roots*, dramatically exposing us to an aspect of our history that many of us never knew but all of us will never forget.

NORMAN LEAR for *All In the Family*, for giving us comedy with a social conscience.

LONDON WEEKEND TELEVISION, London, for *Upstairs, Downstairs*, that superb British series which captured the hearts of Americans and added luster to the PBS stations that carried it.

MTM ENTERPRISES FOR *The Mary Tyler Moore Show*, for a consistant standard of excellence—and for a sympathetic portrayal of a carrer woman in today's changing society.

STEVE ALLEN of KCET, Los Angeles, *Meeting of Minds*, for his ingenious recreation of the essence of historical personages who come alive in a theatrical form rich in philosophical fireworks and engaging wit.

NBC-TV, New York, *Tut: The Boy King*, for this exceptional accomplishment in bringing outstanding cultural treasures to a widespread public with dramatic force.

METROPOLITAN OPERA ASSOCIATION, New York, for *Live from the Met*, as exemplified by performances of La Boheme and Rigoletto which brought millions of music lovers into the Metropolitan Opera House without disturbing the patrons who are in the audience.

WNET-TV, New York, for *A Good Dissonance Like a Man*, an affectionate look at the life of the American composer Charles Ives.

MULTIMEDIA PROGRAM PRODUCTIONS, Cincinnati, for *Joshua's Confusion*, the touching story of a young Amish boy as he deals with his eighteenth century lifestyle in a twentieth century world.

NBC-TV, ARTHUR RANKIN and JULES BASS for *The Hobbitt*, a vividly original and enchanting version of J.R.R. Tolkien's classic.

WCBS-TV, New York, for *Camera Three*, for the consistent high quality of this long-running series which explores the art world.

WPIX, New York, for *The Lifer's Group—I Am My Brother's Keeper*, a slice of prison life from the inside. . . a stark, startling and effective documentary.

WNBC-TV, New York, for *Buyline: Betty Furness* for her in-depth reporting and her distinction as a public conscience.

WNET-TV, New York for *Police Tapes*, a documentary depicting the South Bronx from a squad car.

1978

BOB KEESHAN, who as Captain Kangaroo has provided superior entertainment for children and as Bob Kesshan has promoted quality television in all forms.

RICHARD S. SALANT, for his staunch defense of the First Amendment guarantee of a free press, especially in the field of electronic journalism.

THE MUPPETS, brain-children of Jim Henson, for gentle satire, clever characters, genuine good humor and for high standards for family viewing.

TITUS PRODUCTIONS, INC., and NBC for *Holocaust*, a truly distinguished series that has won international acclaim despite the controversial nature of its subject in some countries of the world.

THE BAPTIST RADIO AND TV COMMISSION, Fort Worth, for *A River to the Sea*, broadcast by CBS, a fascinating look at English history from the Roman occupation of Britain to modern times.

WDVM-TV, Washington, D.C., for *Your Health and Your Wallet*, an exceptional mini-series focusing on rising medical costs.

WENH-TV, Durham, for *Arts in New Hampshire*, which proves that news of the arts can indeed be news, particularly when enhanced by good photography and excellent editing.

CBS NEWS, New York, for *The Battle for South Africa*, as a first rate, in-depth look by anchorman Bill Moyers at the terrorist war waged against the South African government.

TOMORROW ENTERTAINMENT/MEDCOM COMPANY and CBS for *The Body Human: The Vital Connection* as a marvelous and absorbing excursion into the working of the human brain, with particular focus on medical miracles used to correct brain-related illnesses.

SURVIVAL ANGLIA LTD./WORLD WILDLIFE FUND and NBC for *Mysterious Castels of Clay* which explored the functioning of termite societies within the huge earthen mounds—some more than 20 feet tall—they build to live in.

KGO-TV, San Francisco, for *Old Age: Do Not Go Gentle*, which was two years in preparation and which reveals with candor the worlds of poverty, neglect and fear in which many of our elderly citizens find themselves enmeshed.

WDVM-TV, Washington, D.C., for *Race War in Rhodesia*. This one hour special report by columnist/commentator Carl T. Rowan captured the essence of the conflict which has prevailed in that nation and did so in a manner which enabled viewers to clearly perceive the issues and the situation.

KQED, San Francisco, for *Over Easy*. Host Hugh Downs and an able staff have come to grips with the rights, options and issues of concern to older Americans and they have done so in such a manner as to be meaningful both to the old and the not-so-old.

FOUR D PRODUCTIONS/TRISENE CORPORATION OF HOLLYWOOD and ABC for *Barney Miller* cited by the Peabody Board as an example of excellence in scripting, the use of humor with a message and providing Americans with entertainment of value.

NEWSWEEK BROADCASTING, New York City, for *Cartoon-A-Torial*, which has successfully translated the editorial cartoon from the newspaper page to the television screen and has done it with humor, style and meaning.

KHET, Honolulu, for *Damien*, the moving story of the life of the leper priest of Molokai, Joseph deVeuster, who battled bureaucracy, both lay and clerical, to become a legend in his own time.

CBS NEWS, New York, for *30 Minutes*, the excellent television magazine for teenagers which has effectively grappled with many of the major issues facing the young people of this nation.

M.T.M. PRODUCTIONS, Hollywood, and CBS for *Lou Grant*, the entertaining yet realistic look at the problems and issues which face those who are involved in the "Fourth Estate."

WAVE-TV, Louisville, for *Whose Child Is This?*, a highly realistic documentary which looks at child abuse from the perspective of the teacher, who is ofter instrumental in recognizing the problem.

WQED, Pittsburgh, for *A Connecticut Yankee in King Arthur's Court*, the first all American production presented as part of the highly acclaimed *Once Upon a Classic* family series.

Gertrude G. Broderick, Washington, D.C., and Dr. I Keith Tyler, Columbus, Ohio, for their distinguished service on the Peabody Board.

1979

KTVI, Saint Louis, Missouri, for *The Adventures of Whistling Sam*, locally produced cartoon comments on issues of importance produced with great humor, sharp satire and sound common sense.

WMAQ-TV, Chicago, for *Strip and Search*, a "Unit 5 Investigative Report" which exposed the practice by Chicago police of routinely strip-searching women brought in on minor charges, including traffic violations.

CBS News, New York, for *CBS News Sunday Morning*, hosted by Charles Kuralt.

Sylvia Fine Kaye, Beverly Hills, California, for "Musical Comedy Tonight," an entertaining look at American comedy through four significant eras.

ABC-TV, New York, *Valentine*, a sensitive and sentimental love story of two people in their declining years.

ABC-TV, New York, for *Friendly Fire*, a powerful dramatization of the human tragedy of an American family's involvement in the Vietnam War.

NBC-TV, New York, for *Dummy*, the story of an illiterate black deaf youth, who suffered injustice after his arrest as a murder suspect because of his handicap.

NBC-TV, New York, for *When Hell Was In Session*, an *NBC Theater* presentation detailing the true story of Navy Commander Jeremiah Denton, a Vietnam prisoner of war for 7 1/2 years.

KOOL Television, Phoenix, Arizona, for *The Long Eyes of Kitt Peak*, which gave viewers a look at what has been called "the largest and most complex astronomical research facility on earth."

NBC and the BBC for *Treasures of the British Crown*, an intriguing look at the priceless paintings and crown jewels of the Royal Collection in Britain, as described by members of the Royal Family.

ABC-TV, New York, for *A Special Gift*, an "ABC Afterschool Special," the fascinating story of a young boy with two talents: ballet and basketball, and how he comes to reconcile the problems brought on by his unique abilities.

KRON-TV, San Francisco, for *Politics of Poison*, which exposed public health problems caused by herbicide sprayings in northern California.

WTTW-TV, Chicago, for *Miles to Go Before We Sleep*, a documentary about age discrimination growing out of mandatory retirement.

WTTW-TV, Chicago, for *Little Rock Central High School*, a moving story looking at the years since the desegregation crisis which shook the campus.

KNXT, Hollywood, California, for *Down at the Dunbar*, which recalls the jazz greats who made the Dunbar Hotel famous.

WGBH-TV, Boston, for *World*, a series of international documentaries on diverse topics.

Roger Mudd, CBS News, for his searching questions of Senator Edward Kennedy on the CBS Reports *Teddy*, an incisive search for new information which added special depth and interest to the Kennedy profile.

CBS News, New York for *The Boston Goes to China*, coverage of the Boston Symphony Orchestra's trip and the combined concert presented by the Symphony and the Peking Philharmonic.

Robert Trout of ABC News for his nearly fifty years of service as a thoroughly knowledgeable and articulate commentator on national and international affairs.

1980

CBS NEWS, New York, for *Universe*

Mary Nissenson, WTVJ, Miami, Florida, for *Poland: Changing Nation*

CBS ENTERTAINMENT, New York, for *Gideon's Trumpet*

NBC and Paramount Television, for *Shogun*

Sol Taishoff, Editor, *Broadcasting* magazine

Public Broadcasting Service and Robert Geller, Executive Producer, for *The American Short Story* series

ABC, New York, for *IBM Presents Baryshnikov on Broadway*

Elaine Green, WCPO/TV, Cincinnati, Ohio, for the *Hoskins Interview*

ABC, New York, for *Amber Waves*

CBS ENTERTAINMENT, New York, for *Playing For Time*

BRITISH BROADCASTING CORPORATION, London, for *All Creatures Great and Small*

Carroll O'Connor, CBS, for "Edith's Death," an episode of *Archie Bunker's Place*

KCET, Adrian Malone and Carl Sagan, for *Cosmos*

Maryland Instructional Television, Owings Mills, for *Terra: Our World*

WQED and National Geographic Society, for National Geographic Specials as exemplified by *Mysteries of the Mind*, *The Superliners: Twilight of an Era*, and *The Invisible World*

KTEH, Carol Mon Pere and Sandra Nichols, for *The Battle of Westland*

Phil Donahue, host, *The Phil Donahue Show*

KQED-TV, San Francisco, for *Broken Arrow: Can A Nuclear Weapons Accident Happen Here?*

KUED-TV, Salt Lake City, Utah, and WNET/13, New York, for "The MX Debate," a special edition of *Bill Moyers' Journal*

Walter Cronkite, CBS News

1981

WLS-TV, Chicago, for *Eyewitness News*, a quality investigative reporting effort as exemplified by "Traffic Court: Justice or a Joke?" and "So You Need a Driver's License."

Bill Leonard, CBS News, New York, in recognition of his outstanding role in developing the CBS News organization, a group which has developed such outstanding programs as *Sunday Morning*, *CBS Reports: Defense of the United States*, and *CBS News Special: The Cowboy, the Craftsman, and the Ballerina*.

John Goldsmith of WDVM-TV, Washington, for *Now That We've Got Your Interest*, a year-end report which provided the viewer with a humorous, yet perceptive, look at the events which made news during 1981.

NBC and MTM Enterprises, a joint award for *Hill Street Blues* as an outstanding example of excellent writing, excellent production and first-rate entertainment.

The Nebraska Educational Television Network and the Great Amwell Company for *The Private History of a Campaign That Failed*, based on Mark Twain's brief stint in the Confederate militia, a superb example of television's ability to make history informative as well as entertaining.

CBS-TV and Alan Landsburg Productions for *Bill*, a *General Electric Theatre* special, in which Mickey Danny Kaye for his superb and stimulating entertainment efforts in *An Evening with Danny Kaye and the New York Philharmonic; Zubin Mehta, Music Director*, produced by the Lincoln Center for the Performing Arts for PBS, and *Skokie*, produced by Titus Productions for CBS.

WNET/THIRTEEN, New York and the Public Broadcasting System for *Dance In America: Nureyev and the Joffrey Ballet/In Tribute to Nijinsky* as an outstanding contribution to the understanding of the arts in America.

KJRH-TV, Tulsa, Oklahoma, for *Project: China* a beautifully photographed and produced program special detailing an eight-week long adventure in China for a group of Tulsa high school students.

HOME BOX OFFICE and Ms. Magazine for *She's Nobody's Baby: The History of American Women In the 20th Century*, a retrospective look at the emergence of American women and their changing roles in society. This is the first Peabody Award in history to a television production intended to be distributed by non-broadcast means.

SOCIÉTÉ RADIO-CANADA, Montréal, for *Klimbo: Le lion et la souris (The Lion and the Mouse)*, as an outstanding example of televised programming for children.

ABC and T.A.T. Communications for *The Wave*, a presentation of the "ABC Theatre for Young Americans which vividly demonstrated how passions for an ideal outside the self can bind the masses.

WSMV, Nashville, Tennessee, for a series of significant television documentaries which included *Crime's Children, Hot Cars, Cold Cash, Split Second Justice*, and *Crime's Carousel*.

KATU-TV, Portland, Oregon, for an outstanding series of documentary programs, as exemplified by *Ready on the Firing Line, Out of the Ashes*, and *To Begin Again. . .*

WGBH, Boston, and Granada TV, London, for *The Red Army*, a program in the *World* series which sought to analyze the strengths—and weaknesses—of the military forces of the Soviet Union, a task which it did exceptionally well.

The Eighth Decade Consortium, Seattle, Washington, for *Fed Up With Fear*, a program looking at how people in five cities are acting against crime. This well done program involved five television stations: KOMO-TV, Seattle; KSTP-TV, Minneapolis-St. Paul; WCVB-TV, Boston; WJLA-TV, Washington; and WRAL-TV, Raleigh, N.C.

ABC NEWS for three excellent program efforts: *Viewpoint*, *Nightline* and *America Held Hostage: The Secret Negotiations*, as representative of the outstanding talents of the ABC News organization, with special mention of the superb work of Ted Koppel.

KTEH, San Jose, California, for *The Day After Trinity: J. Robert Oppenheimer and the Atomic Bomb*, a candid recollection of Dr. Oppenheimer's contributions, a production of outstanding quality by Jon Else.

1982

KOCO-TV, Oklahoma City for *OKLAHOMA SHAME*

WCVB-TV, Needham, Massachusetts for *GROUND ZERO: VICTORY ROAD*

KYW-TV, Philadelphia, Pennsylvania for *SWEET NOTHING*

BRITISH BROADCASTING CORPORATION, London, England, PARAMOUNT TELEVISION, Los Angeles, California, and OPERATION PRIME TIME, New York for *SMILEY'S PEOPLE*

WWL-TV, New Orleans, Louisiana for *THE SEARCH FOR ALEXANDER*

WARNER AMEX SATELLITE ENTERTAINMENT COMPANY, New York for *NICKELODEON*

NBC-TV, MARGIE-LEE ENTERPRISES, INC., and ITC PRODUCTIONS, INC. for *SKEEZER*

CBS ENTERTAINMENT and CINETEX INTERNATIONAL for *THE WALL*

WQED, Pittsburgh, Pennsylvania for 'STRAVINSKY'S FIREBIRD' by the DANCE THEATER OF HARLEM

NBC and HIGHGATE PICTURES for *PROJECT PEACOCK/THE ELECTRIC GRANDMOTHER*

KQED-TV, San Francisco, California for *CURRENT AFFAIRS/THE CASE OF DASHIELL HAMMETT*

NBC NEWS for *THE MAN WHO SHOT THE POPE: A STUDY IN TERRORISM*

ABC NEWS for *ABC NEWS CLOSEUP/VIETNAM REQUIEM*

CBS NEWS for *JUILLIARD AND BEYOND: A LIFE IN MUSIC*

KGMB-TV and LEE PRODUCTIONS, Honolulu, Hawaii for *BEYOND THE GREAT WALL: JOURNEY TO THE END OF CHINA*

WAGA-TV, Atlanta, Georgia for *PARADISE SAVED*

WBBM-TV, Chicago, Illinois for *KILLING CRIME: A POLICE COP-OUT*

WTSP-TV, St. Petersburg, Florida for *PRISONERS OF THE HARVEST*

DANIEL WILSON PRODUCTIONS, New York and TAURUS FILM for *BLOOD AND HONOR: YOUTH UNDER HITLER*

TELEVISION CORPORATION OF AMERICA, Washington, D.C. for *784 DAYS THAT CHANGED AMERICA— FROM WATERGATE TO RESIGNATION*

ALISTAIR COOKE

1983

WNBC-TV, New York, NY for *ASYLUM IN THE STREETS*

CBS NEWS, New York, NY for *THE PLANE THAT FELL FROM THE SKY* — an exhaustively researched, flawlessly executed recreation of the events surrounding the mysterious, nearly-fatal plunge of a jet airliner.

WCCO-TV, Minneapolis, MN for *I-TEAM: AMBULANCES*, — a series of reports on ambulance service which documented the life-threatening practices of an ambulance company, ultimately leading to the revocation of its license.

CBS NEWS, New York, NY for *60 MINUTES: LENELL GETER'S IN JAIL* — an investigation into the armed-robbery conviction and life sentence imposed upon a black engineer — despite contradictory evidence and his lack of a prior criminal record. The program was instrumental in gaining Mr. Geter's release from prison early in 1984.

NBC and MOTOWN PRODUCTIONS for *MOTOWN 25: YESTERDAY, TODAY, FOREVER* — a dazzling entertainment special celebrating twenty-five years of a unique style of American music, featuring many of our premier artists and performers.

WTTW, Chicago, IL for *THE MERRY WIDOW* — featuring America's leading ballet artists and a score performed by the Chicago Symphony, this program is a delightful celebration of the life and career of choreographer Ruth Page.

CHRYSALIS-YELLEN PRODUCTIONS and NBC for *PRISONER WITHOUT A NAME, CELL WITHOUT A NUMBER* — a dramatic recreation of the imprisonment and ultimate release of journalist Jacobo Timerman in Argentina featuring outstanding writing, superb performances, and distinguished cinematography.

WTTW, Chicago, IL and the BBC for *THE MAKING OF A CONTINENT* — an educational and informative documentary describing the forces that shaped the American West. Distinguished by its location photography, geological research and its focus on the effects of ecology on human history.

WTBS, Atlanta, GA for *PORTRAIT OF AMERICA* — an ambitious series which reveals the character and diversity of the United States state by state and region by region.

WGBH, CENTRAL INDEPENDENT TELEVISION, and ANTENNE-2 for *VIETNAM: A TELEVISION HISTORY* — a definitive visual record of the Vietnam war in thirteen 60 minute episodes which the Peabody Board found to be an objective, authoritative, and thorough treatment of the conflict.

SUNBOW PRODUCTIONS, New York, NY for *THE GREAT SPACE COASTER* — a creative series for children which combines animation, live-action, puppets, and musical performances resulting in an exciting and educational achievement.

CBS ENTERTAINMENT and SMITH-HEMION PRODUCTIONS for *ROMEO AND JULIET ON ICE* — an unusual restaging of Shakespeare as an ice ballet. Acrobatic performances by leading figure skaters, including Dorothy Hamill as Juliet, give this performance a lustre rarely seen in television.

ABC and DICK CLARK PRODUCTIONS for *THE WOMAN WHO WILLED A MIRACLE* — dramatic recreation of the true story of a woman whose faith and commitment helped a severely handicapped child mature into a musical prodigy.

CBS ENTERTAINMENT and MENDELSON-MELENDEZ PRODUCTIONS for *WHAT HAVE WE LEARNED, CHARLIE BROWN?* — *while tourists in France, the "Peanuts" gang is touched by the memory of men who lost their lives struggling for freedom in World War 11. An excellent program which is instructive for both children and adults.*

WBBM-TV, Chicago, IL for *STUDEBAKER: LESS THAN THEY PROMISED* — an examination of the rise and fall of the Studebaker Car Company and its effects on the people of South Bend, Indiana. The program serves as a metaphor for the problems of post-industrial America.

WBRZ-TV, Baton Rouge, LA for *GIVE ME THAT BIGTIME RELIGION* — an intensive examination of the phenomenon of television evangelism which investigates the theology and business practices of Jimmy Swaggart.

KRON-TV, San Francisco, CA for *CLIMATE OF DEATH* — an unusual look into the role of the United States in El Salvador told in human terms by tracing the paths of nine Americans who have died there since 1980.

WGBH-TV, Boston, MA for *NOVA: THE MIRACLE OF LIFE* — revolutionary microphotographic techniques present a fascinating and informative picture of the human reproductive process.

NBC and EDGAR J. SCHERICK ASSOCIATES for *HE MAKES ME FEEL LIKE DANCIN* — which traces the aspirations and tribulations of young dancers in New York City, culminating in the "Event of the Year" at Madison Square Garden in which 1000 children participate.

KCTS, Seattle, WA for *DIAGNOSIS: AIDS* — a comprehensive inquiry into the diagnosis and treatment of AIDS which presents valuable information and debunks a variety of persistent myths associated with the epidemic.

CABLE NEWS NETWORK, Atlanta, GA for *SIGNIFICANT NEWS AND INFORMATION PROGRAMMING* — in the view of the Peabody Board, CNN has become an integral part of the lives of millions of Americans by providing significant, reliable, up-to-the-minute news coverage on a 24-hour basis.

DON McGANNON, Westinghouse Broadcasting Corporation — presented by the Peabody Board in recognition of a lifetime of achievement and distinguished service to the broadcasting industry with Westinghouse Broadcasting.

THE GRAND OLE OPRY — in recognition of the rich heritage which "The Opry" has achieved while making an important mark on music and entertainment on radio and television for almost 60 years, a Peabody Award.

1984

KDFW-TV, Dallas, Texas for a series of investigative reports into the operations of the Emergency Medical Service Division of the Dallas Fire Department, resulting in significant changes of great benefit to Dallas citizens.

WMAQ-TV, Chicago, Illinois for *Political Parasites*, an incisive inquiry into abuses in the Illinois state legislature, resulting in sweeping reform and substantial taxpayer savings.

WDVM-TV, Washington, DC for *Eyewitness News* reports examining a medical clinic operating without a license, and which, following these reports, was closed.

WCAX-TV, Burlington, Vermont for *Patterns Of Practice*, a penetrating look into wide variations in the length of hospital stays for surgical patients undergoing routine operations in Vermont hospitals.

ABC Theater for *Heartsounds*, a sensitive and highly emotional teleplay dramatizing the triumph of love over illness and despair.

WNET, New York, NY for *Heritage: Civilization and the Jews*, which examined 3000 years of history in 9 hours of intelligent and thought-provoking television.

KGW-TV, Portland, Oregon for *Rajneesh Update*, a series of special inquiries into the role which a religious/political group played in county elections and local community life.

WCCO TELEVISION, Minneapolis, Minnesota for *The Hollow Victory: Vietnam Under Communism*, a documentary based upon one of the most extensive tours into that country by American journalists since the end of the war.

ABC NEWS CLOSEUP for *To Save Our Schools, To Save Our Children*, a substantial inquiry, in prime viewing time, into problems of education in the United States.

FRONTLINE, Boston, for the overall excellence with which it continues to serve the people of the United States, presenting documentary television programming of significance and importance.

WNET THIRTEEN, New York, for *The Brain*, a fascinating, instructive, and entertaining trip to the landscape of the mind.

CBS ENTERTAINMENT and the David Gerber Company for *George Washington*, a miniseries of unusual scope, historical insight and intelligence.

WCVB, Boston, for *Somerville High*, an exceptionally well-done television examination of the realities of daily life in a typical urban high school.

NBC and MTM Enterprises for *St. Elsewhere*, which examines the medical profession in human terms, avoiding television's usual trends toward high technology and hero worship.

CENTRAL INDEPENDENT TELEVISION of ENGLAND for *Seeds of Despair*, an early and exhaustive report on the widespread famine in Ethiopia.

SHOWTIME for *Faerie Tale Theatre*, a thoroughly entertaining retelling of classic fairy tales, making for highly enjoyable family viewing.

TURNER BROADCASTING SYSTEM, Atlanta for *Costeau/Amazon*, a series of three documentary programs which enabled viewers to travel the length of this 4,000 mile river with one of the world's most authoritative researchers.

Ted Koppel *Nightline*, New York, as an invaluable source for timely and insightful news commentary.

The Roger Rosenblatt Essays as presented on the *MacNeil/Lehrer NewsHour*, for a combination of still and moving images blended with Mr. Rosenblatt's skillful narrative to produce some of television's finest commentary.

A Walk Through The 20th Century with Bill Moyers, produced by The Corporation for Entertainment and Learning/Bill Moyers, New York, a television series which has brought viewers information coated with excitement and which has made learning fun.

Granada Television of England for *The Jewel in the Crown*, a masterwork of extraordinary scope vividly depicting the last years of the British empire in India.

Roone Arledge of ABC, New York, for significant contributions to television news and sports programming.

5/THE GOLDEN GLOBE AWARDS (HOLLYWOOD FOREIGN PRESS ASSOCIATION)

THE HOLLYWOOD FOREIGN Press Association, established in 1940, is an association of foreign journalists who cover the entertainment industries in Los Angeles. In 1944 the association presented its first Golden Globe Awards (honoring film achievements of 1943) and in 1956 the group announced its first television prizes (for 1955 achievements). The Categories of TV awards have been increasing ever since.

There are now more than 80 active members in the association, representing some 100 million readers in over 50 countries. All members vote for both the nominees and winners in the various categories.

The Golden Globes are usually announced in late January-early February. The presentation ceremonies have occasionally been televised.

1955

BEST TELEVISION PROGRAMS
Dinah Shore
Lucy and Desi
The American Comedy
Davy Crockett

1956

BEST TELEVISION PROGRAMS
Cheyenne
Mickey Mouse Club
Playhouse 90
Theater Matinee
This Is Your life

1957

BEST TELEVISION PROGRAMS
Eddie Fisher
Alfred Hitchcock
Jack Benny
Mike Wallace

1958

BEST TELEVISION PROGRAMS OR PERFORMERS
Paul Oates
Ann Sothern
Loretta Young
Red Skelton
Ed Sullivan
William Orr (Producer)

1959

BEST TELEVISION PROGRAMS OR PERFORMERS
David Susskind
Chuck Conners
Pat Boone
77 Sunset Strip
Dinah Shore
Ed Sullivan
Edward R. Morrow

1960

BEST TELEVISION PROGRAMS OR PERFORMERS
Hanna-Barbera Presents
Perry Mason

Bell Telephone Hour
Hong Kong
Walter Cronkite

1961

BEST TELEVISION SHOWS
What's My Line
My Three Sons
BEST TELEVISION STAR, FEMALE
Pauline Fredericks
BEST TELEVISION STAR, MALE
Bob Newhart
John Daly

1962

BEST TELEVISION SHOWS
The Dick Powell Show
The Defenders
Mr. Ed
Telstar
BEST TELEVISION STAR, FEMALE
Donna Reed
BEST TELEVISION STAR, MALE
Richard Chamberlain
Rod Serling

1963

BEST TELEVISION SHOWS
The Richard Boone Show
The Danny Kaye Show
The Dick Van Dyke Show
BEST TELEVISION STAR, FEMALE
Inger Stevens
BEST TELEVISION STAR, MALE
Mickey Rooney

1964

BEST TELEVISION SHOWS
The Rouges
Burke's Law
BEST TELEVISION STAR, FEMALE
Mary Tyler Moore
BEST TELEVISION STAR, MALE
Gene Barry

1965

BEST TELEVISION SHOW
The Man From U.N.C.L.E.
BEST TELEVISION STAR, FEMALE
Anne Francis

BEST TELEVISION STAR, MALE
David Janssen

1966

BEST TELEVISION SHOW
I SPY
BEST TELEVISION STAR, FEMALE
Marlo Thomas
BEST TELEVISION STAR, MALE
Dean Martin

1967

BEST TELEVISION SHOW
Mission Impossible
BEST TELEVISION STAR, FEMALE
Carol Burnett
BEST TELEVISION STAR, MALE
Martin Landau

1968

BEST TELEVISION SHOW
Laugh-In
BEST TELEVISION STAR, FEMALE
Diahann Carroll, *Julia*
BEST TELEVISION STAR, MALE
Carl Betz, *Judd for the Defense*

1969

BEST TELEVISION SHOW, DRAMA
Marcus Welby, M.D.
BEST TELEVISION SHOW, MUSICAL OR COMEDY
The Governor and J.J.
BEST TELEVISION ACTRESS, DRAMA
Linda Cristal, *High Chapparrel*
BEST TELEVISION ACTOR, DRAMA
Mike Connors, *Mannix*
BEST TELEVISION ACTRESS, MUSICAL OR COMEDY
Carol Burnett
Julie Somers
BEST TELEVISION ACTOR, MUSICAL OR COMEDY
Dan Dailey, *The Governor and J.J.*

1970

BEST TELEVISION SHOW, DRAMA
Medical Center

BEST TELEVISION SHOW, MUSICAL OR COMEDY
The Carol Burnett Show
BEST TELEVISION ACTRESS, DRAMA
Peggy Lipton, *Mod Squad*
BEST TELEVISION ACTOR, DRAMA
Peter Graves, *Mission Impossible*
BEST TELEVISION ACTRESS, MUSICAL OR COMEDY
Mary Tyler Moore
BEST TELEVISION ACTOR, MUSICAL OR COMEDY
Flip Wilson
BEST SUPPORTING ACTRESS
Gail Fisher, *Mannix*
BEST SUPPORTING ACTOR
James Brolin, *Marcus Welby, M.D.*

1971

BEST TELEVISION SHOW, DRAMA
Mannix
BEST TELEVISION SHOW, MUSICAL OR COMEDY
All in the Family
BEST TELEVISION ACTRESS, DRAMA
Patricia Neal, *The Homecoming*
BEST TELEVISION ACTOR, DRAMA
Robert Young, *Marcus Welby, M.D.*
BEST TELEVISION ACTRESS, MUSICAL OR COMEDY
Carol Burnett, *The Carol Burnett Show*
BEST TELEVISION ACTOR, MUSICAL OR COMEDY
Carroll O'Connor, *All in the Family*
BEST SUPPORTING ACTRESS
Sue Ann Langdon, *Arnie*
BEST SUPPORTING ACTOR
Edward Asner, *The Mary Tyler Moore Show*
BEST MADE-FOR-TELEVISION MOVIE
The Snow Goose

1972

BEST TELEVISION SHOW, DRAMA
Columbo
BEST TELEVISION SHOW, MUSICAL OR COMEDY
All in the Family
BEST TELEVISION ACTRESS, DRAMA
Gail Fisher, *Mannix*
BEST TELEVISION ACTOR, DRAMA
Peter Falk, *Columbo*
BEST TELEVISION ACTRESS, MUSICAL OR COMEDY
Jean Stapleton, *All in the Family*

BEST TELEVISION ACTOR, MUSICAL OR COMEDY
Redd Foxx, *Sanford and Son*
BEST SUPPORTING ACTRESS
Ruth Buzzi, *Laugh-In*
BEST SUPPORTING ACTOR
James Brolin, *Marcus Welby, M.D.*
BEST MADE-FOR-TELEVISION MOVIE
That Certain Summer
BEST TELEVISION SPECIAL
Life of Leonardo Da Vinci

1973

BEST TELEVISION SHOW, DRAMA
The Waltons
BEST TELEVISION SHOW, MUSICAL OR COMEDY
All in the Family
BEST TELEVISION ACTRESS, DRAMA
Lee Remick, *The Blue Knight*
BEST TELEVISION ACTOR, DRAMA
James Stewart, *Hawkins*
BEST TELEVISION ACTRESS, MUSICAL OR COMEDY
Jean Stapleton, *All in the Family*
Cher Bono, *Sonny and Cher*
BEST TELEVISION ACTOR, MUSICAL OR COMEDY
Jack Klugman, *The Odd Couple*
BEST SUPPORTING ACTRESS
Ellen Corby, *The Waltons*
BEST SUPPORTING ACTOR
McLean Stevenson, *M*A*S*H*

1974

BEST TELEVISION SHOW, DRAMA
Upstairs, Downstairs
BEST TELEVISION SHOW, MUSICAL OR COMEDY
Rhoda
BEST TELEVISION ACTRESS, DRAMA
Angie Dickinson, *Police Woman*
BEST TELEVISION ACTOR, DRAMA
Telly Savalas, *Kojak*
BEST TELEVISION ACTRESS, COMEDY OR MUSICAL
Valerie Harper, *Rhoda*
BEST TELEVISION ACTOR, MUSICAL OR COMEDY
Alan Alda, *M*A*S*H*
BEST SUPPORTING ACTRESS
Betty Garrett, *All in the Family*
BEST SUPPORTING ACTOR
Harvey Korman, *The Carol Burnett Show*

1975

BEST TELEVISION SHOW, DRAMA
Kojak
BEST TELEVISION SHOW, MUSICAL OR COMEDY
Barney Miller
BEST TELEVISION ACTRESS, DRAMA
Lee Remick, *Jennie*
BEST TELEVISION ACTOR, DRAMA
Robert Blake, *Baretta*
Telly Savalas, *Kojak*
BEST TELEVISION ACTRESS, MUSICAL OR COMEDY
Cloris Leachman, *Phyllis*
BEST TELEVISION ACTOR, MUSICAL OR COMEDY
Alan Alda, *M*A*S*H*
BEST SUPPORTING ACTRESS
Hermione Baddeley, *Maude*
BEST SUPPORTING ACTOR
Edward Asner, *The Mary Tyler Moore Show*
Tim Conway, *The Carol Burnett Show*
BEST MADE-FOR-TELEVISION MOVIE
Babe

1976

BEST TELEVISION SHOW, DRAMA
Rich Man, Poor Man (Book I)
BEST TELEVISION SHOW, MUSICAL OR COMEDY
Barney Miller
BEST TELEVISION ACTRESS, DRAMA
Susan Blakely, *Rich Man, Poor Man* (Book I)
BEST TELEVISION ACTOR, DRAMA
Richard Jordan, *Captains and the Kings*
BEST TELEVISION ACTRESS, MUSICAL OR COMEDY
Carol Burnett, *The Carol Burnett Show*
BEST TELEVISION ACTOR, MUSICAL OR COMEDY
Henry Winkler, *Happy Days*
BEST SUPPORTING ACTRESS
Josette Banzet, *Rich Man, Poor Man* (Book I)
BEST SUPPORTING ACTOR
Ed Asner, *Rich Man, Poor Man* (Book I)
BEST MADE-FOR-TELEVISION
Eleanor and Franklin

1977

BEST TELEVISION SHOW, DRAMA
Roots
BEST TELEVISION SHOW, MUSICAL OR COMEDY
All in the Family

1978

BEST TELEVISION SHOW, DRAMA
Sixty Minutes
BEST TELEVISION SHOW, MUSICAL OR COMEDY
Taxi
BEST TELEVISION ACTRESS, DRAMA
Rosemary Harris, *Holocaust*
BEST TELEVISION ACTOR, DRAMA
Michael Moriarty, *Holocaust*
BEST TELEVISION ACTRESS, MUSICAL OR COMEDY
Linda Lavin, *Alice*
BEST TELEVISION ACTOR, MUSICAL OR COMEDY
Robin Williams, *Mork and Mindy*
BEST SUPPORTING ACTRESS
Polly Holliday, *Alice*
BEST SUPPORTING ACTOR
Norman Fell, *Three's Company*
BEST MADE-FOR-TELEVISION MOVIE
A Family Upside Down

1979

BEST TELEVISION SHOW, DRAMA
Lou Grant
BEST TELEVISION SHOW, MUSICAL OR COMEDY
Taxi
Alice
BEST TELEVISION ACTRESS, DRAMA
Nathalie Wood, *From Here to Eternity*
BEST TELEVISION ACTOR, DRAMA
Ed Asner, *Lou Grant*
BEST TELEVISION ACTRESS, MUSICAL OR COMEDY
Linda Lavin, *Alice*
BEST TELEVISION ACTOR, MUSICAL OR COMEDY
Alan Alda, *M*A*S*H*
BEST SUPPORTING ACTRESS
Polly Holliday, *Alice*
BEST SUPPORTING ACTOR
Danny De Vito, *Taxi*
Vic Tayback, *Alice*
BEST MADE-FOR-TELEVISION
All Quiet on the Western Front

1980

BEST TELEVISION SHOW, DRAMA
Shogun
BEST TELEVISION SHOW, MUSICAL OR COMEDY
Taxi
BEST MADE-FOR-TELEVISION MOVIE
The Shadow Box
BEST TELEVISION ACTRESS, DRAMA
Yoko Shimada, *Shogun*
BEST TELEVISION ACTOR, DRAMA
Richard Chamberlain, *Shogun*
BEST TELEVISION ACTRESS, MUSICAL OR COMEDY
Katherine Helmond, *Soap*
BEST TELEVISION ACTOR, MUSICAL OR COMEDY
Alan Alda, *M*A*S*H*
BEST TELEVISION SUPPORTING ACTRESS
Valerie Bertinelli, *One Day at a Time*
Diane Ladd, *Alice*
BEST TELEVISION SUPPORTING ACTOR
Pat Harrington, *One Day at a Time*
Vic Tayback, *Alice*

1981

BEST TELEVISION SHOW, DRAMA
Hill Street Blues
BEST TELEVISION SHOW, MUSICAL OR COMEDY
*M*A*S*H*
BEST MINISERIES OR MADE-FOR-TELEVISION MOVIE
East of Eden
Bill
BEST SPECIAL, VARIETY OR MUSICAL
The Kennedy Center Honors: A Celebration of the Performing Arts
BEST TELEVISION ACTRESS, DRAMA
Barbara Bel Geddes, *Dallas*
Linda Evans, *Dynasty*
BEST TELEVISION ACTOR, DRAMA
Daniel J. Travanti, *Hill Street Blues*
BEST TELEVISION ACTRESS, MUSICAL OR COMEDY
Eileen Brennan, *Private Benjamin*
BEST TELEVISION ACTOR, MUSICAL OR COMEDY
Alan Alda, *M*A*S*H*
BEST TELEVISION ACTRESS, MINISERIES OR MADE-FOR-TV MOVIE
Jane Seymour, *East of Eden*

BEST TELEVISION ACTOR, MINISERIES OR MADE-FOR-TV MOVIE
Mickey Rooney, *Bill*
BEST TELEVISION SUPPORTING ACTRESS
Valerie Bertinelli, *One Day at a Time*
BEST TELEVISION ACTOR
John Hllerman, *Magnum, P.I.*

1982

BEST TELEVISION SHOW, DRAMA
Hill Street Blues
BEST TELEVISION SHOW, MUSICAL OR COMEDY
Fame
BEST TELEVISION MINISERIES OR MADE-FOR-TV MOVIE
Brideshead Revisited
BEST TELEVISION ACTRESS, DRAMA
Joan Collins, *Dynasty*
BEST TELEVISION ACTOR, DRAMA
John Forsythe, *Dynasty*
BEST TELEVISION ACTRESS, MINISERIES OR MADE-FOR-TV MOVIE
Ingrid Bergman, *A Woman Called Golda*
BEST TELEVISION ACTOR, MINISERIES OR MADE-FOR-TV MOVIE
Anthony Andrews, *Brideshead Revisited*
BEST TELEVISION SUPPORTING ACTRESS
Shelley Long
BEST TELEVISION SUPPORTING ACTOR
Lionel Stander

1983

BEST TELEVISION SHOW, DRAMA
Dynasty
BEST TELEVISION SHOW, MUSICAL OR COMEDY
Fame
BEST MINISERIES OR MADE-FOR-TELEVISION MOVIE
The Thorn Birds
BEST TELEVISION ACTRESS, DRAMA
Jane Wyman, *Falcon Crest*
BEST TELEVISION ACTOR, DRAMA
John Forsythe, *Dynasty*
BEST TELEVISION ACTRESS, MUSICAL OR COMEDY
Joanna Cassidy, *Buffalo Bill*
BEST TELEVISION ACTOR, MUSICAL OR COMEDY
John Ritter, *Three's Company*

BEST TELEVISION ACTRESS, MINISERIES OR MADE-FOR-TV MOVIE
Ann-Margret, *Who Will Love My Children*
BEST TELEVISION ACTOR, MINISERIES OR MADE-FOR-TV MOVIE
Richard Chamberlain, *The Thorn Birds*
BEST TELEVISION SUPPORTING ACTRESS
Barbara Stanwyck, *The Thorn Birds*
BEST TELEVISION SUPPORTING ACTOR
Richard Kiley, *The Thorn Birds*

1984

BEST TELEVISION SHOW, DRAMA
Murder, She Wrote
BEST TELEVISION SHOW, MUSICAL OR COMEDY
The Bill Cosby Show
BEST MINISERIES OR MADE-FOR-TELEVISION MOVIE
Something About Amelia
BEST TELEVISION ACTRESS, DRAMA
Angela Lansbury, *Murder, She Wrote*
BEST TELEVISION ACTOR, DRAMA
Tom Selleck, *Magnum P.I.*
BEST TELEVISION ACTRESS, MUSICAL OR COMEDY
Shelly Long, *Cheers*
BEST TELEVISION ACTOR, MUSICAL OR COMEDY
Bill Cosby, *The Bill Cosby Show*
BEST TELEVISION ACTRESS, MINISERIES OR MADE-FOR-TV MOVIE
Ann-Margret, *Streetcar Named Desire*
BEST TELEVISION ACTOR, MINISERIES OR MADE-FOR-TV MOVIE
Ted Danson, *Something About Amelia*
BEST TELEVISION SUPPORTING ACTRESS
Faye Dunaway, *Ellis Island*
BEST TELEVISION SUPPORTING ACTOR
Paul LeMat, *The Burning Bed*

6/TELEVISION CHAMPION AWARDS (QUIGLEY PUBLICATIONS)

From 1949 through 1972, Quigley Publications—publisher of the indispensable trade journals *Motion Picture Almanac* and *Television Almanac*—polls television critics in the United States to determine its "Television Champion" awards. This survey—like Quigley's annual "Top Ten" Box Office Film Stars—is more fascinating than exact.

1949

Best Network Program:
Texaco Star Theater
Best Television Performer:
Milton Berle
Most Promising Female Star:
Felicia Montealegre
Most Promising Male Star:
Dave Garroway
Best Comedy Show:
Texaco Star Theater
Best Variety Show:
Texaco Star Theater
Best Dramatic Program:
Studio One
Best Quiz Show:
Who Said That?
Best Children's Program:
Kukla, Fran and Ollie
Best Commercial (Audience Viewpoint):
Texaco

1950

Best Network Program:
Your Show of Shows
Best Television Performer:
Sid Caesar
Most Promising Female Star:
Imogene Coca
Most Promising Male Star:
Jerry Lewis
Best Comedian:
Sid Caesar
Best Comedienne
Imogene Coca
Best Comedy Show:
Colgate Comedy Hour
Best Variety Program:
Your Show of Shows
Best Dramatic Program:
Studio One
Best Mystery Program:
Suspense
Best Musical Show (Classical):
Voice of Firestone
Best Musical Show (Popular):
Fred Waring Show
Best Quiz Show:
You Bet Your Life
Best Master of Ceremonies:
Bert Parks
Best Announcer:
Bud Collyer
Best News Commentator:
John Cameron Swayze
Best Sportscaster:
Dennis James
Best Daytime Program:
Ransom Sherman

Best Children's Program:
Kukla, Fran & Ollie
Best Commercial and (Audience Viewpoint):
Lucky Strike

1951

Best Network Program:
Your Show of Shows
Best Television Performer:
Jimmy Durante
Most Promising Female Star:
Lucille Ball
Most Promising Male Star:
Herb Shriner
Best Comedian:
Sid Caesar
Best Comedienne:
Imogene Coca
Best Comedy Show:
Your Show of Shows
Best Variety Program:
Your Show of Shows
Best Dramatic Program:
Studio One
Best Mystery Program:
Man Against Crime
Best Musical Show (Classical):
Voice of Firestone
Best Musical Show (Popular):
Fred Waring Show
Best Quiz Show:
You Bet Your Life
Best Master of Ceremonies:
John Daly
Best Announcer:
George Fenneman
Best News Commentator:
John Cameron Swayze
Best Sportscaster:
Jimmy Powers
Best Daytime Program:
Kate Smith Show
Best Children's Program:
Kukla, Fran and Ollie
Best Commercial:
Lucky Strike

1952

Best Network Program:
Playhouse 90
Best Television Performer:
Lucille Ball
Most Promising Female Star:
Maria Riva
Most Promising Male Star:
Wally Cox
Best Comedian:
Sid Caesar
Best Comedienne:
Lucille Ball

Best Comedy Show:
I Love Lucy
Best Variety Program:
Your Show of Shows
Best Panel Discussion Program:
Meet the Press
Best Dramatic Program:
Studio One
Best Mystery Program:
Dragnet
Best Male Vocalist:
Perry Como
Best Female Vocalist:
Dinah Shore
Best Musical Show (Classical):
Voice of Firestone
Best Musical Show (Popular):
Your Hit Parade
Best Audience Participation Quiz Show:
Groucho Marx Show
Best Panel Quiz Show:
What's My Line
Best Master of Ceremonies:
John Daly
Best Announcer:
Dennis James
Best News Commentator:
John Cameron Swayze
Best Sportscaster:
Mel Allen
Best Daytime Program:
Kate Smith Hour
Best Children's Program:
Kukla, Fran and Ollie
Best Commercial (Audience Viewpoint):
Ford

1953

Best Network Program:
Playhouse 90
Best Television Performer:
Donald O'Connor
Most Promising Female Star:
Audrey Meadows
Most Promising Male Star:
Julius LaRosa
Best Comedian:
Jackie Gleason
Best Comedienne:
Lucille Ball
Best Comedy Team:
Sid Caesar and Imogene Coca
Best Comedy Show:
Colgate Comedy Hour
Best Variety Program:
Toast of the Town
Best Panel Discussion Program:
Meet the Press
Best New Dramatic Program:
United States Steel Hour
Best Dramatic Program:
Studio One

Best Mystery Program:
Dragnet
Best Male Vocalist:
Perry Como
Best Female Vocalist:
Dinah Shore
Best Musical Show (classical):
Voice of Firestone
Best Musical Show (Popular):
Your Hit Parade
Best Audience Participation Quiz Show:
Groucho Marx Show
Best Panel Quiz Show:
What's My Line
Best Master of Ceremonies:
Ed Sullivan
Best Announcer:
George Fenneman
Best News Commentator:
John Cameron Swayze
Best Sportscaster:
Mel Allen
Best Daytime Program:
Gary Moore Show
Best Children's Program:
Ding Dong School
Best Commercial (Audience Viewpoint):
Ford

1954

Best Network Program:
Toast of the Town
Best Television Performer:
George Gobel
Most Promising Female Star:
Eva Marie Saint
Most Promising Male Star:
Dick Shawn
Most Effective Use of Color:
Max Liebman Presents
Best Comedian:
George Gobel
Best Comedienne:
Lucille Ball
Best Comedy Team:
Lucille Ball, Desi Arnez
Best Comedy Show:
The Jackie Gleason Show
Best Variety Program:
Toast of the Town
Best Panel Discussion Program:
Meet the Press
Best New Dramatic Program:
Medic
Best Dramatic Program:
Studio One
Most Unique New Program:
Disneyland
Best Mystery Program:
Dragnet

Best Male Vocalist:
Perry Como
Best Female Vocalist:
Dinah Shore
Best Musical Show (Classical):
Voice of Frestone
Best Musical Show (Popular):
Your Hit parade
Best Audience Participation Quiz Show:
Groucho Marx Show
Best Panel Quiz Show:
What's My Line
Best Master of Ceremonies:
Ed Sullivan
Best Announcer:
George Fenneman
Best News Commentator:
John Cameron Swayze
Best Sportscaster:
Mel Allen
Best Daytime Program:
Today
Best Children's Program:
Ding Dong School
Best Commercial (Audience Viewpoint):
Lucky Strike

1955

Best Network Program:
The Ed Sullivan Show
Best Television Performer:
Phil Silvers
Most Promising Female Star:
Jeannie Carson
Most Promising Male Star:
Johnny Carson
Best Effective Use Of Color:
Max Liebman Presents
Best Comedian:
George Gobel
Best Comedienne:
Lucille Ball
Best Comedy Team:
George Burns, Gracie Allen
Best Comedy Show:
You'll Never Get Rich
Best Variety Program:
The Ed Sullivan Show
Best Panel Discussion Program:
Meet the Press
Best New Dramatic Program:
Playwrights '56
Most Unique New Program:
Wide, Wide World
Best Dramatic Program:
Studio One
Best Mystery Program:
Alfred Hitchcock Presents
Best Male Vocalist:
Perry Como
Best Female Vocalist:
Dinah Shore

Best Musical Show (Classical):
Voice of Firestone
Best Musical Show (Popular):
Your Hit Parade
Best Country Music Show:
Grand Ole Opry
Best Audience Participation Quiz Show:
The $64,000 Question
Best Panel Quiz Show:
What's My Line
Best Master Of Ceremonies:
Garry Moore
Best Announcer:
George Fenneman
Best News Commentator:
John Cameron Swayze
Best Sportscaster:
Mel Allen
Best Daytime Program:
Matinee Theatre
Best Children's Program:
Disneyland
Best Commercial (Audience Viewpoint):
Ford

1956

Best Network Program:
Playhouse 90
Best Television Performer:
Steve Allen
Most Promising Female Star:
Erin O'Brien
Most Promising Male Star:
Buddy Hackett
Most Effective Use Of Color:
Producers Showcase
Best Comedian:
Phil Silvers
Best Comedienne:
Lucille Ball
Best Comedy Team:
Lucille Ball, Desi Arnez
Best Comedy Show:
You'll Never Get Rich
Best Variety Program:
The Ed Sullivan Show
Best Panel Discussion Program:
Meet the Press
Best Unique New Program:
Playhouse 90
Best Dramatic Program:
Playhouse 90
Best Mystery Program:
Alfred Hitchcock Presents
Best Male Vocalist:
Perry Como
Best Female Vocalist:
Dinah Shore
Best Musical Show (Classical):
Voice of Firestone
Best Musical Show (Popular):
The Ford Show

Best Country Music Show:
Ozark Jubilee
Best Audience Participation Quiz Show:
The $64,000 Question
Best Panel Quiz Show:
What's My Line
Best Master of Ceremonies:
Garry Moore
Best Announcer:
George Fenneman
Best News Commentator:
Douglas Edwards
Best Sportscaster:
Mel Allen
Best Daytime Program:
Matinee Theatre
Best Children's Program:
Disneyland
Best Commercial (Audience Viewpoint):
Piel's Beer

1957

Best Network Program:
Playhouse 90
Best Television Performer:
Perry Como
Most Promising Female Star:
Polly Bergen
Most Promising Male Star:
Pat Boone
Most Effective Use Of Color:
The Dinah Shore Chevy Show
Best Comedian:
Jack Benny
Best Comedienne:
Lucille Ball
Best Comedy Team:
George Burns, Gracie Allen
Best Comedy Show:
You'll Never Get Rich
Best Variety Program:
Steve Allen Show
Best Panel Discussion Program:
Meet the Press
Best Dramatic Program:
Playhouse 90
Most Unique New Program:
Seven Lively Arts
Best Mystery Program:
Suspicion
Best Male Vocalist:
Perry Como
Best Female Vocalist:
Dinah Shore
Best Musical Show (Classical):
Voice of Firestone
Best Musical Show (Popular):
Perry Como Show
Best Country Music Show:
Jimmy Dean

Best Audience Participation Quiz Show:
Twenty-One
Best Panel Quiz Show:
What's My Line
Best Master Of Ceremonies:
Steve Allen
Best Announcer:
George Fenneman
Best News Commentator:
Douglas Edwards
Best Sportscaster:
Mel Allen
Best Daytime Program:
Matinee Theatre
Best Children's Program:
Disneyland
Best Commercial (Audience Viewpoint):
Piel's Beer

1958

Best Network Program:
Playhouse 90
Best Television Performer:
Dinah Shore
Most Promising Female Star:
Barrie Chase
Most Promising Male Star:
Chuck Conners
Most Effective Use Of Color:
The Dinah Shore Chevy Show
Best Comedian:
Red Skelton
Best Comedienne:
Lucille Ball
Best Comedy Team:
Mike Nichols, Elaine May
Best Comedy Show:
Jack Benny Show
Best Variety Program:
Steve Allen Show
Best Panel Discussion Program:
Meet the Press
Most Unique New Program:
Small World
Best Dramatic Program:
Playhouse 90
Best Mystery Program:
Perry Mason
Best Male Vocalist:
Perry Como
Best Female Vocalist:
Dinah Shore
Best Musical Show (Classical):
Voice of Firestone
Best Musical Show (Popular):
Perry Como Show
Best Country Music Show:
Jubilee U.S.A.
Best Audience Participation Quiz Show:
Groucho Marx

Best Panel Quiz Show:
What's My Line
Best Master Of Ceremonies:
Garry Moore
Best Announcer:
Hugh Downs
Best News Commentator:
Chet Huntley
Best Sportscaster:
Mel Allen
Best Daytime Program:
Today
Best Children's Program:
Captain Kangaroo
Best Commercial (Audience Viewpoint):
Piel's Beer

1959

Best Network Program:
Playhouse 90
Best Television Performer:
Fred Astaire
Most Promising Female Star:
Tuesday Weld
Most Promising Male Star:
Ed Byrnes
Most Effective Use Of Color:
The Dinah Shore Chevy Show
Best Comedian:
Jack Benny
Best Comedienne:
Lucille Ball
Best Comedy Team:
Mike Nichols, Elaine May
Best Comedy Show:
Jack Benny Show
Best Variety Program:
The Ed Sullivan Show
Best Dramatic Program (One Hour Or More):
Playhouse 90
Best Dramatic Program (1/2 Hour):
General Electric Theatre
Most Unique New Program:
Twilight Zone
Best Mystery Program:
Perry Mason
Best Male Vocalist:
Perry Como
Best Female Vocalist:
Dinah Shore
Best Musical Show (Popular):
The Perry Como Show
Best Country Music Show:
Jubilee, U.S.A.
Best Audience Participation Quiz Show:
The Price Is Right
Best Panel Quiz Show:
I've Got a Secret
Best Master Of Ceremonies:
Garry Moore

Best Announcer:
Hugh Downs
Best News Commentator:
Chet Huntley
Best Western:
Gunsmoke
Best Sportscaster:
Mel Allen
Best Daytime Program:
Today
Best Children's Program:
Captain Kangaroo
Best Commercial (Audience Viewpoint):
Piel's Beer
Best Network Publicity Service:
NBC
Best Advertising Agency Publicity Service:
Young & Rubicam
Best Independent Publicity Service:
Rogers & Cowan

1960

Best Network Program:
The Untouchables
Best Television Performer:
Perry Como
Most Promising Female Star:
Annie Farge
Most Promising Male Star:
Bob Newhart
Most Effective Use of Color:
The Dinah Shore Chevy Show
Best Comedian:
Red Skelton
Best Comedienne:
Carol Burnett
Best Comedy Team:
Mike Nichols, Elaine May
Best Comedy Show:
Red Skelton Show
Best Variety Program:
The Ed Sullivan Show
Most Unique New Program:
The Untouchables
Best Dramatic Program (One Hour Or More):
The Untouchables
Best Dramatic Program (1/2 Hour):
Twilight Zone
Best Mystery Program:
Alfred Hitchcock Presents
Best Male Vocalist:
Perry Como
Best Female Vocalist:
Dinah Shore
Best Musical Show (Popular):
Perry Como's Kraft Music Hall
Best Western:
Wagon Train
Best Country Music Show:
Jubilee U.S.A.

Best Audience Participation Quiz Show:
The Price Is Right
Best Panel Quiz Show:
What's My Line
Best Master Of Ceremonies:
Garry Moore
Best Announcer:
Hugh Downs
Best News Commentator:
David Brinkley
Best Sportscaster:
Mel Allen
Best Daytime Program:
Today
Best Children's Program:
Captain Kangaroo
Best Commercial (Audience Viewpoint):
Piel's Beer, Bert & Harry
Best Network Publicity Service:
NBC
Best Advertising Agency Publicity Service:
J. Walter Thompson Co.
Best Independent Publicity Service:
Rogers & Cowan

1961

Best Network Program:
The Power and the Glory
Best Television Performer:
Laurence Olivier
Most Promising Female Star:
Cynthia Pepper
Most Promising Male Star:
Vincent Edwards
Most Effective Use Of Color:
Walt Disney's Wonderful World of Color
Best Comedian:
Red Skelton
Best Comedienne:
Carol Burnett
Best Comedy Team:
Johnny Wayne, Frank Schuster
Best Comedy Show:
Bob Newhart
Best Variety Program:
The Garry Moore Show
Best Dramatic Program (One Hour Or More):
The Power and the Glory
Best Dramatic Program (1/2 Hour):
Thriller
Best Male Vocalist:
Perry Como
Best Female Vocalist:
Dinah Shore
Best Musical Show (Popular):
Sing Along With Mitch
Best Audience Participation Quiz Show:
The Price Is Right

Best Panel Quiz Show:
What's My Line
Best Master Of Ceremonies:
Garry Moore
Best Announcer:
Hugh Downs
Best News Commentator:
David Brinkley
Best Sportscaster:
Mel Allen
Best Daytime Program:
Today
Best Children's Program:
Captain Kangaroo
Best Commercial (Audience Viewpoint):
Jax Beer
Best Network Publicity Service:
NBC
Best Independent Publicity Service:
Rogers & Cowan

1962

Best Network Program:
The Defenders
Best Television Performer:
Danny Kaye
Most Promising Female Star:
Donna Douglas
Most Promising Male Star:
Vincent Edwards
Most Effective Use of Color:
Walt Disney's Wonderful World of Color
Best Comedian:
Red Skelton
Best Comedienne:
Lucille Ball
Best Comedy Team:
Johnny Wayne, Frank Schuster
Best Comedy Show:
The Beverly Hillbillies
Best Variety Program:
The Garry Moore Show
Most Unique New Program:
It's a Man's World
Best Dramatic Program (One Hour Or More):
G.E. True
Best Dramatic Program (1/2 Hour):
No Award This Year
Best Mystery Program:
The Alfred Hitchcock Hour
Best Male Vocalist:
Perry Como
Best Female Vocalist:
Dinah Shore
Best Musical Show (Popular):
The Andy Williams Show
Best Audience Participation Quiz Show:
The Price Is Right
Best Panel Quiz Show:
To Tell the Truth

Best Master Of Ceremonies:
Garry Moore
Best Announcer:
Hugh Downs
Best News Commentator:
David Brinkley
Best Sportscaster:
Mel Allen
Best Daytime Program:
The Merv Griffin Show
Best Children's Program:
Captain Kangaroo
Best Commercial (Audience Viewpoint):
Ford Motor Co.
Best Network Publicity Service:
NBC
Best Independent Publicity Service:
Rogers & Cowan
Best Western:
Bonanza

1963

Best Network Program:
The Danny Kaye Show
Best Television Performer:
Danny Kaye
Most Promising Female Star:
Patty Duke
Most Promising Male Star:
James Franciscus
Most Effective Use of Color:
Walt Disney's Wonderful World of Color
Best Comedian:
Danny Kaye
Best Comedienne:
Lucille Ball
Best Comedy Team:
Dick Van Dyke, Mary Tyler Moore
Best Comedy Show:
The Dick Van Dyke Show
Best Variety Program:
The Danny Kaye Show
Most Unique New Program:
The Richard Boone Show
Best Dramatic Program (One Hour Or More):
The Richard Boone Show
Best Dramatic Program (1/2 Hour):
Twilight Zone
Best Mystery Program:
The Alfred Hitchcock Hour
Best Male Vocalist:
Andy Williams
Best Female Vocalist:
Judy Garland
Best Musical Show (Popular):
The Andy Williams Show
Best Audience Participation Quiz Show:
Password

Best Panel Quiz Show:
What's My Line
Best Master Of Ceremonies:
Garry Moore
Best Announcer:
Hugh Downs
Best News Commentator:
Walter Cronkite
Best Sportscaster:
Mel Allen
Best Daytime Program:
Today
Best Children's Program:
Captain Kangaroo
Best Commercial (Audience Viewpoint):
Gravy Train
Best Network Publicity Service:
NBC
Best Independent Publicity Service:
Rogers & Cowan
Best Western:
Bonanza

1964

Best Network Program:
Profiles in Courage
Best Television Performer:
Danny Kaye
Most Promising Female Star:
Elizabeth Montgomery
Most Promising Male Star:
Jim Nabors
Most Effective Use of Color:
Walt Disney's Wonderful World of Color
Best Comedian:
Dick Van Dyke
Best Comedienne:
Lucille Ball
Best Comedy Team:
Dick Van Dyke, Mary Tyler Moore
Best Comedy Show:
The Dick Van Dyke Show
Best Variety Program:
The Danny Kaye Show
Best Dramatic Program (One Hour Or More):
The Defenders
Best Dramatic Program (1/2 Hour):
Peyton Place
Best Mystery Program:
The Alfred Hitchcock Hour
Best Male Vocalist:
Andy Williams
Best Female Vocalist:
Caterina Valente
Best Musical Show (Popular):
The Andy Williams Show
Best Audience Participation Quiz Show:
Password
Best Panel Quiz Show:
To Tell the Truth

Best Master Of Ceremonies:
Johnny Carson
Best Announcer:
Ed McMahon
Best News Commentator:
Walter Cronkite
Best Sportscaster:
Chris Schenkel
Best Daytime Program:
Today
Best Children's Program:
Walt Disney's Wonderful World of Color
Best Commercial (Audience Viewpoint):
Jax Beer
Best Network Publicity Service:
NBC
Best Western:
Bonanza

1965

Best Network Program:
The Hallmark Hall of Fame
Best Television Performer:
Danny Kaye
Most Promising Female Star:
Sally Field
Most Promising Male Star:
Bill Cosby
Most Effective Use Of Color:
Walt Disney's Wonderful World of Color
Best Comedian:
Dick Van Dyke
Best Comedienne:
Lucille Ball
Best Comedy Team:
Smothers Brothers
Best Comedy Show:
The Dick Van Dyke Show
Best Variety Program:
The Hollywood Palace
Most Unique New Program:
Get Smart
Best Dramatic Program (One Hour Or More):
Chrysler Theater
Best Dramatic Program (1/2 Hour):
Peyton Place
Best Western:
Bonanza
Best Mystery Program:
Perry Mason
Best Male Vocalist:
Andy Williams
Best Female Vocalist:
Barbra Streisand
Best Musical Show (Popular):
The Andy Williams Show
Best Audience Participation Quiz Show:
Password

Best Panel Quiz Show:
To Tell the Truth
Best Master Of Ceremonies:
Johnny Carson
Best Announcer:
Ed McMahon
Best News Commentator:
Walter Cronkite
Best Sportscaster:
Chris Schenkel
Best Daytime Program:
Today
Best Children's Program:
Captain Kangaroo
Best Commercial (Audience Viewpoint):
Alka Seltzer
Best Network Publicity Service:
NBC

1966

Best Network Program:
Stage 67
Best Television Performer:
Jackie Gleason
Most Promising Female Star:
Marlo Thomas
Most Promising Male Star:
Peter Deuell
Best Comedian:
Red Skelton
Best Comedienne:
Lucille Ball
Best Comedy Team:
Jackie Gleason, Art Carney
Best Comedy Show:
The Jackie Gleason Show
Best Variety Program:
The Andy Williams Show
Most Unique New Program:
Stage 67
Best Dramatic Program (One Hour Or More):
Stage 67
Best Dramatic Program (1/2 Hour):
Rat Patrol
Best Mystery Program:
I Spy
Best Male Vocalist:
Andy Williams
Best Female Vocalist:
Barbra Streisand
Best Musical Show (Popular):
The Andy Williams Show
Best Audience Participation Quiz Show:
Password
Best Panel Quiz Show:
What's My Line
Best Master Of Ceremonies:
Johnny Carson
Best Announcer:
Ed McMahon

Best News Commentator:
Walter Cronkite
Best Sportscaster:
Chris Schenkel
Best Daytime Program:
Today
Best Children's Program:
Captain Kangaroo
Best Commercial (Audience Viewpoint):
Alka Seltzer
Best Network Publicity Service:
NBC
Best Western:
Bonanza

1967

Best Network Program:
The Jackie Gleason Show
Best Television Performer:
Dean Martin
Most Promising Female Star:
Paula Prentiss
Most Promising Male Star:
Monte Markham
Best Comedian:
Red Skelton
Best Comedienne:
Carol Burnett
Best Comedy Team:
Smothers Brothers
Best Comedy Show:
The Smothers Brothers Comedy Hour
Most Unique New Program:
Flying Nun
Best Dramatic Program (One Hour Or More):
No Award This Year
Best Dramatic Program (1/2 Hour):
Peyton Place
Best Mystery Program:
Ironside
Best Male Vocalist:
Andy Williams
Best Female Vocalist:
Barbra Streisand
Best Musical Show (Popular):
The Dean Martin Show
Best Audience Participation Quiz Show:
Newlywed Game
Best Panel Quiz Show:
To Tell the Truth
Best Master Of Ceremonies:
Johnny Carson
Best Announcer:
Ed McMahon
Best News Commentator:
Walter Cronkite
Best Sportscaster:
Curt Gowdy
Best Daytime Program:
Today

Best Children's Program:
Captain Kangaroo
Best Commercial (Audience Viewpoint):
Benson and Hedges
Best Network Publicity Service:
NBC
Best Western:
Bonanza

1968

Best Network Program:
Rowan & Martin's Laugh-In
Best Television Performer:
Dean Martin
Most Promising Female Star:
Diahann Carroll
Most Promising Male Star:
Robert Morse
Best Comedian:
Bob Hope
Best Comedienne:
Carol Burnett
Best Comedy Team:
Dan Rowan, Dick Martin
Best Comedy Show:
Rowan and Martin's Laugh-In
Best Variety Program:
The Dean Martin Show
Most Unique New Program:
That's Life
Best Dramatic Program (One Hour Or More):
Mission: Impossible
Best Dramatic Program (1/2 Hour):
N.Y.P.D.
Best Mystery Program:
Ironside
Best Male Vocalist:
Dean Martin
Best Female Vocalist:
Barbra Streisand
Best Musical Show (Popular):
Kraft Music Hall
Best Audience Participation Quiz Show:
Let's Make a Deal
Best Panel Quiz Show:
Hollywood Squares
Best Master of Ceremonies:
Johnny Carson
Best Announcer:
Ed McMahon
Best News Commentator:
Walter Cronkite
Best Sportscaster:
Curt Gowdy
Best Daytime Program:
Today
Best Children's Program:
Captain Kangaroo
Best Commercial (Audience Viewpoint):
Alka Seltzer

Best Network Publicity Service:
NBC
Best Western:
Gunsmoke

1969

Best Network Program:
Rowan & Martin's Laugh-In
Best Television Performer:
Bill Cosby
Most Promising Female Star:
Julie Sommars
Most Promising Male Star:
Lloyd Haines
Best Comedian:
Bob Hope
Best Comedienne:
Carol Burnett
Best Comedy Team:
Dan Rowan, Dick Martin
Best Comedy Show:
Rowan & Martin's Laugh-In
Best Variety Program:
The Dean Martin Show
Most Unique New Program:
Love American Style
Best Dramatic Program (One Hour Or More):
Marcus Welby, M.D.
Best Dramatic Program (1/2 Hour):
Room 222
Best Mystery Program:
Ironside
Best Male Vocalist:
Andy Williams
Best Female Vocalist:
Leslie Uggams
Best Musical Show (Popular):
The Andy Williams Show
Best Audience Participation Quiz Show:
Let's Make a Deal
Best Panel Quiz Show:
Hollywood Squares
Best Master of Ceremonies:
Johnny Carson
Best Announcer:
Ed McMahon
Best News Commentator:
Walter Cronkite
Best Sportscaster:
Curt Gowdy
Best Daytime Program:
Today
Best Children's Program:
Sesame Street
Best Commercial (Audience Viewpoint):
Alka Seltzer
Best Network Publicity Service:
1969
Best Western:
Gunsmoke

1970

Best Network Program:
Marcus Welby, M.D.
Best Television Performer:
Robert Young
Most Promising Female Star:
Renee Jarett
Most Promising Male Star:
Flip Wilson
Best Comedian:
Flip Wilson
Best Comedienne:
Carol Burnett
Best Comedy Team:
Dan Rowan, Dick Martin
Best Comedy Show:
The Flip Wilson Show
Best Variety Program:
The Carol Burnett Show
Most Unique New Program:
4 in 1
Best Dramatic Program (One Hour or More):
Marcus Welby, M.D.
Best Dramatic Program (1/2 Hour):
Room 222
Best Mystery Program:
Ironside
Best Male Vocalist:
Andy Williams
Best Female Vocalist:
Petula Clark
Best Musical Show (Popular):
Kraft Music Hall
Best Audience Participation Quiz Show:
Let's Make a Deal
Best Panel Quiz Show:
Hollywood Squares
Best Master of Ceremonies:
Johnny Carson
Best Announcer:
Ed McMahon
Best News Commentator:
Walter Cronkite
Best Sportscaster:
Curt Gowdy
Best Daytime Program:
Today
Best Children's Program:
Sesame Street
Best Commercial (Audience Viewpoint):
Alka Seltzer
Best Network Publicity Service:
NBC

1971

Best Network Program:
All in the Family

Best Television Performer:
Carroll O'Connor
Most Promising Female Star:
Sandy Duncan
Most Promising Male Star:
William Conrad
Best Comedian:
Flip Wilson
Best Comedienne:
Carol Burnett
Best Comedy Team:
Rowan and Martin
Best Comedy Show:
All in the Family
Best Variety Program:
The Carol Burnett Show
Best Dramatic Program (One Hour Or More):
Six Wives of Henry VIII
Best Dramatic Program (1/2 Hour):
Adam-12
Best Mystery Program:
NBC Mystery Movie
Best Male Vocalist:
Glen Campbell
Best Female Vocalist:
Edie Gorme
Best Musical Show (Popular):
Glen Campbell Show
Best Audience Participation Quiz Show:
Let's Make a Deal
Best Panel Quiz Show:
Hollywood Squares
Best Master of Ceremonies:
Johnny Carson
Best Announcer:
Ed McMahon
Best News Commentator:
Walter Cronkite
Best Sportscaster:
Howard Cosell
Best Daytime Program:
Today
Best Children's Program:
Sesame Street
Best Commercial (Audience Viewpoint):
Alka Seltzer
Best Network Publicity Service:
ABC
Best Western:
Gunsmoke

1972

Best Network Program:
The Waltons
Best Television Performer:
Carroll O'Connor
Most Promising Female Star:
Beatrice Arthur
Most Promising Male Star:
Richard Thomas

Best Comedian:
Flip Wilson
Best Comedienne:
Carol Burnett
Best Comedy Team:
Dan Rowan, Dick Martin
Best Comedy Show:
All in the Family
Best Dramatic Program (One Hour Or More):
The Waltons
Best Dramatic Program (1/2 Hour):
Adam-12
Best Variety Program:
The Julie Andrews Hour
Most Unique New Program:
The Waltons
Best Western Program:
Gunsmoke
Best Mystery Program:
Colombo
Best Male Vocalist:
Dean Martin
Best Female Vocalist:
Julie Andrews
Best Musical Show (Popular):
The Julie Andrews Hour
Best Audience Participation Quiz Show:
Let's Make a Deal
Best Panel Quiz Show:
Hollywood Squares
Best Master of Ceremonies:
Johnny Carson
Best Announcer:
Ed McMahon
Best News Commentator:
Walter Cronkite
Best Sportscaster:
Howard Cosell
Best Daytime Schow:
Today
Best Children's Program:
Sesame Street
Best Commercial (Audience Viewpoint):
Alka Seltzer
Best Network Publicity Service:
ABC

7/WRITERS GUILD OF AMERICA AWARDS

In 1954 THE Screen Writers Guild merged with the Radio Writers Guild and the Television Writers Guild to form the Writers Guild of America (WGA), East and West, determined geographically by the Mississippi River. The Guild is a two-headed creature: at once a labor union occupied with economics (the Guild is the collective-bargaining agent for writers) and an art guild concerned with the freedom of creativity (the Guild, for example, presides over credit jurisdiction).

In 1949 the Guild presented its first motion picture writing awards (for 1948 achievements), and in 1957 its first TV writings prizes were announced (for 1956 achievements). These awards have filled an important gap, for although the National Academy of Television Arts and Sciences has honored teleplay writing since 1954, screenwriting—for TV or for the movies— has been neglected by many other organizations. There are, for example, no Pulitzer Prizes for screenwriters, no Nobels.

The Guild, with a membership of more than 4,000, traditionally announces its awards in late March-early April. Ceremonies are held both in New York and Los Angeles. The Guild's special awards are:

THE LAUREL AWARD FOR ACHIEVEMENT, given annually to that member of the Guild who has advanced the literature of television through the years, and who has made outstanding contributions to the profession of the TV writer. Renamed the Paddy Chayefsky Award in 1981.

THE MORGAN COX AWARD, Presented to that member or group of members whose vital ideas, continuing efforts and personal sacrifices best exemplify the ideal service to the Guild which the life of Morgan Cox so fully represented.

THE JOHN MERIMAN MEMORIAL AWARD, given annually to a journalism student, commemorates the achievements of John Merriman, past president of WGA(e), editor of The CBS Evening News with Walter Cronkite.

THE VALENTIVE DAVIES AWARD, presented in memory of Valentine Davies, whose contribution to the motion picture community brought dignity and honor to writers everywhere.

THE EVELYN BURKEY AWARD, given annually for service to the television community.

1956

Best One-Half Hour TV Anthology Drama:
Donald S. Sandforc, John Nesbitt, "The Golden Junkman," *Telephone Time*.
Best One-Half Hour TV Episodic Drama:
Kenneth Kolb, "She Walks in Beauty," *Medic*
Best One-Hour TV Situation Comedy:
Leonard Stern, Sydney Zelinka, "The $99,000 Answer," *The Jackie Gleason Show*.
Best One Hour or more TV Drama:
Rod Serling, "Requiem for a Heavyweight," *Playhouse 90*.
Best One Hour TV Comedy:
J. Harvey Howells, "Goodbye, Grey Flannel," *Robert Montgomery Presents*.
Best TV Documentary:
John Whedon, George Roy Hill, "A Night to Remember," *Kraft TV Theatre*.
Best Children's Program:
Thelma Robinson (teleplay), Warren Wilson, Claire Kennedy (story), "The Visitor," *Lassie*.
Comedy-Variety Certificate of Excellence:
Hal Kanter, Howard Leeds, Harry Winkler, Everett Greenbaum, *The George Gobel Show*.

1957

Best One-Half Hour TV Anthology Drama:
Joseph Mindel, *Degree of Freedom*
Best One-Half Hour TV Episodic Drama:
Everett De Baun, "Pearls of Talimeco," *Jim Bowie*.
Best One Hour Anthology Drama:
Jerry McNeely, "The Staring Match," *Studio One*.
Best Television Western:
Gene Roddenberry, "Helen of Abajinian," *Have Gun, Will Travel*.
Best Children's Program:
Kenneth Enochs, "Elmer the Rainmaker," *Circus Boy*.
Best Program more than One Hour in Length:
Erick Moll, "The Fabulous Irishman," *Playhouse 90*
Best One-Half Hour or Less TV Comedy and Sketches:
Sydney Zelinka, A. J. Russell, "Papa Bilko," *The Phil Silvers Show*.
Best TV Documentary:
Irwin Rosten, *The Human Explosion*
Best One Hour TV Comedy:
Devery Freeman, *The Great American Hoax*

1958

Best Script, Thirty Minutes or Less:
Valentine Davies, Kurt Vonnegut Jr, "Auf Wiedersehen," *GE Theatre.*

Best Script, Sixty Minutes or Less, but more than Thirty Minutes:
Shimon Wincelberg, "The Sea is Boiling Hot," *Kraft Television Theatre.*

Best Script, more than Sixty Minutes:
Rod Serling, "A Town Has Turned to Dust," *Playhouse 90.*

Best TV Documentary-News Analysis or News in Depth:
Steven Fleishman, "Face of Crime," *20th Century.*

Best Comedy/Variety or Variety:
Sherwood Schwarz, Jesse Goldstein, Dave O'Brien, "Freddie's Thanksgiving," *The Red Skelton Show.*

1959

Best One-Half Hour TV Anthology Drama:
Christopher Knopf, "Interrogation," *Zane Grey Theatre.*

Best One-Half Hour TV Episodic Drama:
Richard Matheson, "Yawkey," *Lawman.*

Best TV Anthology, more than One-Half Hour:
Tony Webster, "Call Me Back," *The Art Carney Show.*

Best TV Episode, more than One-Half Hour:
William Spier, "The Assassination of Cermak," *The Untouchables.*

Best Television Adaptation, any Length:
Irving G. Nieman, "Child of Our Times," *Playhouse 90.*

Best TV Episodic Comedy, any Length:
Dorothy Cooper, "Margaret's Old Flame," *Father Knows Best.*

Best TV Variety, any Length:
Max Wilk, A. J. Russell, *The Fabulous Fifties.*

Best TV Documentary, any Length:
Richard Hanser, "Mark Twain's America," *Project XX.*
Earle Luby, "Down Range," *20th Century.*

1961

Best Anthology Drama:
Christopher Knopt, "Death of the Temple Bay," *The June Allyson Show.*

Best Episodic Drama:
Barry Trivers, "The Fault in Our Stars," *Naked City.*

Best Adaptation:
Bernard C. Schoenfeld, "The Little Mermaid," *The Shirley Temple Show.*

Best TV Documentary:
Philip H. Reisman, Jr., "The Real West," *NBC Project 20.*

1962

Best Anthology Drama:
Richard Alan Simmons, "The Price of Tomatoes," *Dick Powell Show.*

Best Episodic Drama:
Kenneth Rosen, Howard Rodman, "Today the Man Who Kills the Ants Is Coming," *Naked City.*

Best TV Comedy-Variety:
Gary Belkin, Nat Hiken, "I Won't Go!" *Car 54, Where Are You?*

Best Adaptation:
Gordon Russell, "The Forgery," *DuPont Show of the Month.*

Best TV Documentary:
Arthur Holch, "Walk in My Shoes," *Close-Up.*

Valentine Davies Award:
Allen Rivkin

1963

Best Anthology Drama:
Richard Alan Simmons, "The Last of the Big Spenders," *The Dick Powell Show.*

Best Episodic Drama:
Lawrence B. Marcus, "Man Out of Time," *Route 66.*

Best TV Comedy-Variety:
Everett Greenbaum, Jim Fritzell, "Barney's First Car," *The Andy Griffith Show.*

Best Adaptation:
Richard DeRoy, Iris Dornfeld, "Jeeney Ray," *Alcoa Premiere.*

Best TV Documentary:
Frank DeFelitta, Robert Northshield, *Chosen Child.*

Valentine Davies Award:
Morgan Cox

1964

Best Anthology Drama:
Howard Rodman, "The Game with Glass Pieces," *Chrysler Theatre.*

Best Episodic Drama:
Arnold Perl, "Who Do You Kill?" *East Side, West Side.*

Best Comedy, Episodic:
Bill Idelson, Sam Bobrick, "The Shoplifters," *The Andy Griffith Show.*

Best Comedy Variety:
Herbert Baker, Sheldon Keller, Saul Ilson, Ernest Chambers, Gary Belkin, Paul Mazursky, Larry Tucker, Mel Tolkin, *The Danny Kaye Show.*

Best Adaptation:
Mark Rodgers, Russel Crouse, Clarence Green, "One Day in the Life of Ivan Denisovitch," *Chrysler Theatre.*

Best TV Documentary:
Albert Waller, "In the American Grain: William Carlos Williams," *Eye on New York.*
Martin Ragaway, "My Husband is the Best One," *The Dick Van Dyke Show.*

Valentine Davies Award:
James R. Webb

1965

Best Anthology Drama:
Harlan Ellison, "Demon With a Glass Hand," *Outer Limits.*

Best Episodic Drama:
John D.F. Black, "With a Hammer in His Hand, Lord, Lord!," *Mr. Novak.*

Best Comedy, Episodic:
Dale McRaven, Carl Kleinschmitt, "Br-room Br-room," *The Dick Van Dyke Show.*

Best Comedy Variety:
Sheldon Keller, Gary Belkin, Ernest Chambers, Larry Tucker, Paul Mazursky, Billy Barnes, Ron Freidman, Mel Tolkin, *The Dany Kaye Show.*

Best Adaptation:
Robert Hartung, "The Magnificent Yankee," *Hallmark Hall of Fame.*

Best TV Documentary:
Robert Rogers, *Vietnam: It's a Mad War.*

Valentine Davies Award:
Leonard Spigelglass

1966

Best Anthology Drama:
S. Lee Pogostin, "The Game," *Chrysler Theatre.*

Best Episodic Drama:
David Ellis, "No Justice for the Judge," *Trials of O'Brien.*

Best Comedy, Episodic:
Jack Winter, "You Ought to Be in Pictures," *The Dick Van Dyke Show.*

Best Comedy, Variety:
Garry Marshall, Jerry Belson, "The Road to Lebanon," *Danny Thomas Special.*

Best Adaptation:
Robert Hartung, "Lamp at Midnight," *Hallmark Hall of Fame.*

Best TV Documentary:
Andrew A. Rooney, Richard Ellison, *The Great Love Affair.*

Special Award:
Shimon Wincelberg, *The Long, Long Curfew.*

Valentine Davies Award:
Edmund L. North

1967

Best Anthology Drama:
S. Lee Pogostin, "Crazier Than Cotton," *Chrysler Theatre.*

Best Episodic Drama:
Harlan Ellison, "The City on the Edge of Forever," *Star Trek.*

Best Comedy, Episodic:
Marvin Marx, Walter Stone, Gordon Rod Parker, "Movies Are Better Than Ever," *The Jackie Gleason Show.*

Best Comedy, Non-Episodic:
Mel Brooks, Sam Denoff, Bill Persky, Carl Reiner, Mel Tolkin, *The Sid Caesar, Imogene Coca, Carl Reiner, Howard Morris Special.*

Best Documentary: Currents Events:
Robert Rogers, "The Battle for Asie, Part 1: Thailand, The New Front," *NBC News.*

Best Documentary: Features:
Theodore Strauss, Terry Sanders, *The Legend of Marilyn Monroe.*

Valentine Devies Award:
George Seaton

1968

Best Anthology Drama:
Earl Hamner, *Heidi.*

Best Episodic Drama:
Robert Lewin, "To Kill a Madman," *Judd for the Defense.*

Best Comedy, Episodic:
Bill Idelson, Sam Bobrick, "Vive Smart," *Get Smart.*

Best Comedy, Non-Episodic:
Sam Bobrick, Ron Clark, Danny Simon, Marthy Farrell, Martin Ragaway, *Alan King's Wonderful World of Aggravation.*

Best Documentary: Features:
James Fleming, Blain Littell, Richard F. Siemanowski, *Africa.*
Perry Wolff, Andrew Rooney, "Black History—Lost, Stolen or Strayed," *Of Black America.*

Best Documentary: Current Events:
Peter Davis, Martin Carr, "Hunger in America," *CBS Reports.*

Valentine Davies Award:
Dore Schary

1969

Best Anthology Drama:
George Bellak, "Sadbird," *CBS Playhouse.*

Best Episodic Drama:
Robert Lewin, "An Elephant in a Cigar Box," *Judd for the Defense.*

Best Comedy Episodic:
Allan Burns, "Funny Boy," *Room 222.*

Best Variety:
Herbert Baker, Treva Silverman, *Norman Rockwell's America.*

Best Documentary: Features:
David Davidson, *The Ship That Wouldn't Die: U.S.S. Franklin.*
Shimon Wincelberg, *Max Brod: Portrait of the Artist in His Own Right.*

Best Documentary: Current Events:
Harry E. Morgan, *Fathers and Sons.*

Morgan Cox Award:
Barry Trivers

Valentine Davies Award:
Richard Murphy

1970

Best Anthology Drama:
Tracy Keenan Wynn, Marvin Schwartz, "Tribes," *ABC Movie of the Week.*

Best Episodic Drama:
David Rintels, "A Continual Roar of Musketry," *The Bold Ones.*

Best Comedy, Episodic:
Richard DeRoy, "The Valediction," *Room 222.*

Best Variety:
Gary Belkin, Peter Bellwood, Thomas Meehan, Herb Sargent, Judith Viorst, *Annie, the Women in the Life of a Man.*

Best Documentary: Features:
Marianna Norris, *Gertrude Stein: A Biography.*

Best Documentary: Current Events:
Craig B. Fisher, *Survival on the Prairie.*

Morgan Cox Award:
Leonard Spigelgass

Valentine Davies Award:
Daniel Taradesh

1971

Best Anthology Drama:
Carol Sobieski, Howard Rodman, "The Neon Ceiling," *NBC World Premiere.*

Best Episodic Drama:
Thomas Y. Drake, Herb Bermann, Jerold Freedman, Bo May, "Par for the Course," *The Psychiatrist.*

Best Comedy, Episodic:
Martin Cohan, "Thoroughly Unmilitant Milly," *The Mary Tyler Moore Show.*

Best Variety:
Don Hinkley, Jack Mendelsohn, Stan Hart, Larry Siegel, Woody Kling, Roger Beatty, Arnie Rosen, Kenny Solms, Gail Parent (writing supervised by Arthur Julian), *The Carol Burnett Show.*

Best Adaptation:
William Blinn, "Brian's Song," *ABC Movie of the Week.*

Best Documentary: Features:
Andrew A. Rooney, *An Essay on War.*

Best Documentary: Current Events:
Peter Davis, *Vietnam Hindsight, Part I and II.*

Morgan Cox Award:
Allen Rivkin

Valentine Davies Award:
Michal Blankfort, Norman Corin

1972

Best Anthology Drama:
Richard Levinson, William Link, "That Certain Summer," *ABC Movie of the Week.*

Best Episodic Drama:
Herman Miller, "King of the Mountain," *Kung Fu.*

Best Comedy, Episodic:
Larry Gelbart, "Chief Surgeon Who," *M*A*S*H.*

Best Variety:
Neil Simon, *The Trouble with People.*

Best Adaptation:
Richard Matheson, "The Night Stalker," *ABC Movie of the Week.*

Best Documentary: Features:
Robert Northshield, *Guilty by Reason of Race.*

Best Documentary: Current Events:
Robert Northshield, *Suffer the Little Children.*

Best TV Newswriting:
Charles West, Rabun Matthews, Gary Gates, John Merriman, *CBS Evening News with Walter Cronkite.*

Best Daytime Serial:
Loring Mandel, Nancy Ford, Kim Louis Ringwald, Max McClellan, *Love of Life.*

Valentine Davies Award:
William Ludwing

Morgan Cox Award:
David Harmon

1973

Best Anthology Drama:
Abby Mann, "The Marcus-Nelson Murders," *CBS Movie of the Week.*

Best Episodic Drama:
Harlan Ellison, "Phoenix Without Ashes," *The Starlost.*

Best Comedy, Episodic:
Bob Weiskopf, Bob Schiller, "Walter's Problem, Part II," *Maude.*

Best Variety:
Norman Barasch, Jack Burns, Avery Schreiber, Bob Ellison, Bob Garland, Caroll Moore, George Yanok, *The Burns & Schreiber Comedy Hour.*

Best Adaptation:
Carol Sobieski, "Sunshine," *CBS Movie of the Week.*

Best Documentary: Features:
Marc Siegel, *Rendezvous With Freedom.*

Best Documentary: Current Events:
James Fleming, *The First and Essential Freedom.*

Best TV Newswriting:
Charles West, Rabun Matthews, Carol Ross, *CBS Evening News with Walter Cronkite.*

Best Daytime Serial:
Ralph Ellis, Eugene Hunt, Bibi Wein, Jane Chambers, *Search for Tomorrow.*

Valentine Davies Award:
Ray Bradbury, Philip Dune

Morgan Cox Award:
James R. Webb

1974

Best Original Anthology Drama:
Joel Oliansky (teleplay), William Sackheim, Joel Oliansky (story), "The Law," *NBC World Premiere.*

Best Episodic Drama:
Jim Byrnes, "Thirty a Month and Found," *Gunsmoke.*

Best Comedy, Episodic:
Larry Gelbart, Lawrence Marks, "O.R.," *M*A*S*H.*

Best Variety:
Ed Simons, Gary Belkin, Roger Beatty, Arnie Kogen, Bill Richmond, Gene Perret, Rudy DeLuca, Barry Levinson, Dick Clair, Jenna McMahon, *The Carol Burnett Show.*

Best Variety Special:
Norman Steinberg, Alan Uger, Howard Albrecht, Sol Weinstein, John Boni, Thad Mumford, Chevy Chase, Herb Sargent, Alan King, *Alan King's Energy Crisis, Rising Prices* and *Assorted Vices Comedy Hour.*

Best Anthology Adaptation:
Tracy Keenan Wynn, "The Autobiography of Miss Jane Pittman," *CBS Movie of the Week.*

Best Documentary: Features:
Marlene Sanders, *The Right to Die.*
Best Documentary: Current Events:
Howard Stringer, *The Palestinians.*
Best TV Newswriting:
Charles West, *Two Presidents: Transitions in the White House.*
Best Daytime Serial:
Ann Marcus, Joyce Perry, Pamela Wylie, Ray Goldstone, *Search for Tomorrow.*
Valentine Davies Award:
Fay Kanin
Morgan Cox Award:
Edmund North
John Meriman Memorial Award:
John C. Blattner

1975

Best Original Anthology Drama:
Jerome Kass, *Queen of the Stardust Ballroom.*
Best Adapted Anthology:
Fay Kanin, "Hustling," *ABC Movie of the Week.*
David W. Rintels, "Fear on Trial," *CBS Movie of the Week.*
Best Dramatic Episode:
Arthur Ross (teleplay), Stephen Kandel (story), "Prior Consent," *The Law.*
Best Comic Episode:
Everett Greenbaum, Jim Fritzell, Larry Gelbart, "Welcome to Korea," *M*A*S*H.*
Best Variety:
Sybil Adelman, Barbara Gallagher, Gloria Banta, Pat Nardo, Stuart Birnbaum, Matt Neuman, Leorne Michaels, Marilyn Miller, Earl Pomerantz, Rosie Rithchild, Lily Tomlin, Jane Wagner, *Lily.*
Best Documentary: Feature:
Irv Drasnin, *The Guns of Autumn.*
Best Documentary: Current Events:
Andrew Rooney, *Mr. Rooney Goes to Washington.*
Best TV Newswriting:
Sandor Polster, William H. Moran, Carol Ross, *CBS Evening News with Walter Cronkite.*
Best Daytime Serial:
Claire Labine, Paul Mayer, Mary Munisteri, Allan Leicht, *Ryan's Hope.*
Best Children's Show:
Yanna Brandt, *The Superlative Horse.*
Laurel Award:
Rod Serling
Valentine Davies Award:
Winston Miller
Morgan Cox Award:
William Ludwig

1976

Best Original Anthology:
Robert Collins, "The Quality of Mercy," *NBC Thursday Night Movie.*
Best Adapted Anthology:
Stewart Stern, "Sybil," *NBC Movie.*
Best Dramatic Episode:
Loring Mandel, "Crossing the River," *Sandburg's Lincoln.*

Best Comic Episode:
Alan Alda, "Dear Sigmund," *M*A*S*H.*
Best Variety:
Anne Beatts, Chevy Chase, Al Franken, Tom Davis, Lorne Michaels, Marilyn Suzanne Miller, Michael O'Donoghue, Herb Sargent, Tom Schiller, Rosie Schuster, Alan Zweibel, *NBC Saturday Night Live.*
Best Documentary: Features:
Paul W. Greenberg, *Friends, Romans, Communists.*
Best Documentary: Current Events:
Andrew Rooney, *Mr. Rooney Goes to Dinner.*
Best TV Newswriting:
William Moran, Ran Gandolf, Charles L. West, *In Celebration of U.S., July 4, 1976.*
Best Daytime Serial:
Claire Labine, Paul Avila Mayer, Mary Munisteri, *Ryan's Hope.*
Best Children's Show:
Arthur Barron, *Blind Sunday.*
Laurel Award:
Everett Greenbaum, James Fritzell.
Morgan Cox Award:
Herbert Baker
Valentine Davies Award:
Carol Foreman
John Merriman Memorial Award:
Ralph Buglass

1977

Best Original Anthology:
Carol Sobieski, "Christmas Sunshine," *NBC World Premiere.*
Best Adapted Anthology:
Steven Gethers, "A Circle of Children," *CBS Movie.*
Best Comic Episode:
Larry Rhine, Mel Tolin, "Archie Gets the Business," *All in the Family.*
Best Dramatic Episode:
Mark Rodgers, "Pressure Point," *Police Story.*
Best Variety:
Elon Packard, Fred S. Fox, Seaman Jacob, *The George Burns One-Man Show.*
Best Documentary: Features:
George Crile III., *The CIA's Secret Army.*
Best Documentary: Current Events:
Marc Siegel, *The Panama Canal—A Test of Conscience.*
Best TV Newswriting:
Lee Townsend, Sandor M. Polster, Charles West, Allison Owings, Mary Earle, *CBS Evening News with Walter Cronkite.*
Best Daytime Serial:
Claire Labine, Paul Avila Mayer, Judith Pinsker, Mary Munisteri, *Ryan's Hope.*
Best Children's Show:
Art Wallace, *Little Vic..*
Laurel Award:
Ernest Kinoy
Valentine Davies Award:
Norman Lear
Morgan Cox Award:
John Furia, Jr.

1978

Best Original Anthology:
Christopher Knopf, "Scott Joplin: King of Ragtime," *NBC Movie.*

Best Adapted Anthology:
Stewart Stern, *A Christmas to Remember.*
Lonne Elder III., *A Woman Called Moses.*

Best Dramatic Episode:
Seth Freeman, "Prisoner," *Lou Grant.*

Best Comic Episode:
Gary David Holdberg, "Baby, It's Cold Outside," *M*A*S*H.*

Best Variety:
Jerry Juhl, Chris Langham, Jim Henson, Don Hinkley, *The Muppet Show.*

Best Documentary: Features:
Robert E. Fuisz, M.D., *The Body Human: The Vital Connection.*

Best Documentary: Current Events:
Perry Wolff, *CBS News Special*, 1968.

Best TV Newswriting:
Hugh Heckman, John Mosedale, Sandor M. Polster, Lee Townsend, *CBS Evening News.*

Best Daytime Serial:
Claire Labine, Jeffrey Lane, Paul Avila Mayer, Mary Munisteri, Judith Pinsker, *Ryan's Hope.*

Best Mini-Series:
John Wilder, "Only the Rocks Live Forever," *Centennial.*

Laurel Award:
James Costigan

Valentine Davies Award:
Melville Shavelson

Morgan Cox Award:
George Seaton

1979

Best Original Anthology:
Millard Lampell, *Orphan Train* (story by Dorothea Petrie).

Best Adapted Anthology:
Fay Kanin, *Friendly Fire.*

Best Dramatic Episode:
Leon Tokatyan, "Vet," *Lou Grant.*

Best Comic Episode:
Thad Mumford, Dan Wilcox, "Are You Now, Margaret?," *M*A*S*H.*
Ken Estin, "The Reluctant Fighter," *Taxi.*

Best Variety:
Jerry Juhl, David Odell, Jim Henson, Don Hinkely, *The Muppet Show* (with Liza Minnelli).
Dan Aykroyd, Anne Beatts, James Downey, Brian Doyle-Murray, Al Franken, Tom Davis, Brian McConnachie, Lorne Michaels, Don Novello, Herb Sargent, Tom Schiller, Rosie Shuster, Walter Williams, Alan Zweibel, *Saturday Night Live* (host: Richard Benjamin).

Best Miniseries:
Gwen Bagni, Paul Dubov, *Backstairs at the White House*—Part I.

Best Documentary: Features:
Robert E. Fuisz, Hank Whittemore, *The Body Human: The Magic Sense.*

Best Documentary: Current Events:
William Peters, *Death of a Family.*

Best TV Newswriting:
John M. Mosedale, Gordon Joseloff, Charles West, *CBS Evening News* (March 20, 1979).

Best Daytime Serial:
Jerome Dobson, Bridget Bobson, Charles Dizenso, Patti Dizenso, Phyllis White, Robert White, Robert Solderberg, Jean Rouverol, *Guiding Light.*

Best Children's Show:
Edward Pomerantz, *New York City Too Far from Tampa Blues.*

Laurel Award:
Howard Rodman

Valentine Davies Award:
David W. Rintels

Morgan Cox Award:
Fay Kanin

1980

Best Original Drama Anthology:
David Chase, *Off the Minnesota Strip.*

Best Adapted Drama Anthology:
David W. Rintels, *Gideon's Trumpet* (from the book by Anthony Lewis).

Best Original or Adapted Comedy Anthology:
Carmen Culver, *To Race the Wind* (from the book by Harold Krents).

Best Dramatic Episode:
Stephen J. Cannell, *Tenspeed and Brown Show* (pilot episode).

Best Comic Episode:
Stan Daniels, Ed Weinberger, "Ten Censors," *The Associates.*

Best Variety:
Michaels Elias, Jack Handey, Carmen Finestra, Robert Garland, Connie Turner, Steve Martin, *Comedy Is Not Pretty.*

Best Miniseries:
Ernest Tidyman, *Guyana Tragedy: The Story of Jim Jones*—Part I.

Best Documentary: Current Events:
Michael Connor, Kathy Slobogin, Steve Singer, Peggy Brim, *The Killing—An Update.*

Best Documentary: Features:
Irwin Rosen, *Mysteries of the Mind.*

Best TV Newswriting:
Mervin Block, *A Selection of Anchor Lead-ins at the 1980 National Political Conventions.*
Raphael Rothstein, *Obituary of the Shah of Iran.*

Best Children's Show:
Paul A. Bolding, "The Secret of the Lost Valley," *Wonderful World of Disney* (story by David Irving and Paul A. Golding).

Best Daytime Serial:
Claire Labine, Paul Avila Mayer, Mary Ryan Munisteri, Jeffrey Lane, *Ryan's Hope.*

Laurel Award:
Larry Gerbart

Valentine Davies Award:
Arthur Orloff

Morgan Cox Award:
Ron Austin

Evelyn Burkey Award:
Elmer Lower
John Merriman Memorial Award:
Rae K. Nelson

1981

Best Original Drama Anthology:
Suzanne Clauser, *Pride of Jesse Hallam.*
Arnold Peyser, Lois Peyser, The Violation of Sarah McDavid.
Best Adapted Drama Anthology:
Richard Friedenberg, *Bitter Harvest* (from the book by Frederic and Sandre Halbert).
Best Dramatic Episode:
Michael Kozoll, Steve Bochco, *Hill Street Blues* (pilot episode).
Best Comic Episode:
Nat Mauldin, "Stormy Weather," *Barney Miller.*
Best Variety:
Steve Martin, Neil Israel, Jeffrey Barron, Earl Brown, Carmen Finestra, Denny Johnston, Sean Kelly, Pat McCormick, Michael McManus, Pat Proft, Mason Williams, *All Commercials.*
Best Miniseries:
John Sacret Young, *A Rumor of War*—Part II.
Joel Iliansky, *Masada*—Part IV.
Best Documentary: Features:
Stephen Fleischman, Andrew Schlesinger, *The Gene Merchants.*
Best Documentary: Current Events:
Judy Crichton, Leslie Cockburn, *The Nuclear Battlefield.*
Best TV Newswriting:
John Mosedale, Charles West, Sander Polster, Paul Enger, *CBS Evening News* (Dec. 9, 1980).
Best Children's Show:
W.W. Lewis, *Sunshine's on the Way.*
Best Daytime Serial:
Claire Labine, Paul Avila Mayer, Mary Ryan Munisteri, Jeffrey Lane, *Ryan's Hope.*
Laurel Award (renamed the Paddy Chayefsky Laurel Award):
John McGreevey
Valentine Davies Award:
Mort R. Lewis
Morgan Cox Award:
Brad Radnitz
Evelyn Burkey Award:
Herbert Brodkin
John Merriman Memorial Award:
Regina Laurel Anderson

1982

Best Orinigal Drama Anthology:
Ernest Kinoy, *Skokie.*
Best Adapted Drama Anthology:
E. Nick Alexander, *Of Mice and Men,* (from the screenplay by Eugene Solow, based on the novel by John Steinbeck).
Best Original Comedy Anthology:
Oliver Hailey, *Sidney Shorr.*

Best Dramatic Episode:
Machael Wagner, "The World According to Freedom," *Hill Street Blues.*
Best Comic Episode:
Tony Sheehan, "Hunger Strike," *Barney Miller* (story by Sheehan and Stephen Neigher).
Best Miniseries:
E. Jack Neuman, *Inside the Third Reich*—Part 1 (based on the book by Albert Speer).
Best Variety:
Richard Alfieri, Rita Mae Brown, Rick Mitz, Arthur Allan Seidelman, Norman Lear, *I Love Liberty.*
Best Documentary: Current Events:
Judy Reemtsma, *People Like Us.*
Best Documentary: Feature:
Perry Wolff, *The Museum of Modern Art Presents Pablo Picasso: A Retrospective, Once in a Lifetime.*
Best TV Newswriting:
Indsay Miller, *News in Reviews, CBS Sunday Morning* (July 25, 1982).
Best Children's Show:
Josef Anderson, "First Kill," *CBS Afternoon Playhouse.*
Best Daytime Serial:
Claire Labine, Mary Ryan Ministeri, Eugene Price, Barbara Perlman, Rory Metcalf, *Ryan's Hope.*
Paddy Chayefsky Laurel Award:
Herbert Baker
Valentine Davies Award:
Hal Knater
Morgan Cox Award:
Oliver Crawford
Evelyn Burkey Award:
Alan Wagner
John Merriman Memorial Award:
Heidi Hughes

1983

Best Original Drama Anthology:
Marshall Herskovitz, *Special Bulletin.*
Best Adapted Drama Anthology:
Ossie Davis, J. Kenneth Rotcop, *For Us, the Living: The Story of Medgar Evers,* (based on the book by Mrs. Medgar Evers with William Peters).
Best Original Comedy Anthology:
Lila Garrett, Anne Meara, *The Other Woman.*
Best Dramatic Episode:
David Milch, "Trial by Fury," *Hill Street Blues.*
Best Comic Episode:
Glen Charles, Les Charles, "Give Me a Ring Sometime," (*Cheers,* pilot) and Ken Levine, David Isaacs, The Boys in the Bar (*Cheers*).
Best Miniseries:
Robert Boris, *Blood Feud*—Part 1.
Best Variety:
George Stevens, Jr., Joseph McBride, *The American Film Institute Salute to John Houston.*
Best Documentary: Current Events:
Theodore Bogosian, *The Cobalt Blues.*
Best Documentary: Feature:
Jonathan Ward, Dale Minor, *1984 Revisited in a Lifetime.*
Best TV Newswriting:
Mervin Block, *A Selection of Television Spot News Scripts.*

Best Children's Show:
   Arthur Heinemann, *The Woman Who Willed a Miracle*, and
      John Stone, Joseph Bailey, *Big Bird in China*
Best Daytime Serial:
   Claire Labine, Paul Avila Mayer, Mary Ryan Munisteri,
      Nancy Ford, B.K. Perlman, Judith Pinsker, *Ryan's Hope*.
Paddy Chayefsky Laurel Award:
   John Gay
Valentine Davies Award:
   Jerome Lawrence, Robert E. Lee.
Morgan Cox Award:
   Nat Monaster
Evelyn Burkey Award:
   Leonard Wasser

8/THE DIRECTORS GUILD OF AMERICA AWARDS

IN 1960 THE Screen Directors Guild merged with the Radio and Television Directors Guild to form the Directors Guild of America (DGA). Like the Writers Guild, the DGA is the official bargaining agent for its membership, which includes directors, assistant directors and unit production managers alike. The Guild thus has the power to provide for its members' creative rights, working conditions, residual payments and minimum wage scales.

The Guild presented its first film directing awards in 1948 (these are not included here) and its first TV awards in 1954, for 1953 achievements. Through 1970 the Guild presented only one annual prize for excellence in television directing, but beginning with the 1971 awards a new system was established to honor directorial achievements in 5 different categories: Comedy Series, Dramatic Series, Documentary, Musical and Variety, and Specials. Awards for direction in commercials and live broadcasts were subsequently added.

There are two ballots in each year's prizes: one to establish three nominees in each category and a second to select the winner in each category. In addition to choosing one winner in each of the six categories, each Guild member votes for one of the six winners to receive the DGA award for TV Director of the Year.

1953

☐ Robert Florey, "The Last Voyage," *Four Star Playhouse*

1954

☐ Roy Kellino, "The Answer," *Four Star Playhouse*

1955

☐ Don Weis, "The Little Guy," *Fireside Theatre*

1956

☐ Herschel Daugherty, "The Road That Led Afar," *G.E. Theatre*

1957

☐ Don Weis, "The Lonely Wizard," *Schlitz Playhouse of Stars*

1958

☐ Richard Bare, "All Our Yesterdays," *77 Sunset Strip*

1959

☐ Phil Karlson, "The Untouchables," *Westinghouse-Desilu Playhouse*

1960

☐ George Schaefer, "Macbeth," *Hallmark Hall of Fame*

1961

☐ Ernie Kovacs, Joseph Behar, *A Study in Silence*

1962

☐ David Friedkin, "The Price of Tomatoes," *Dick Powell Show*

1963

☐ Goerge Schaefer "Pygmalion," *Hallmark Hall of Fame*

1964

☐ Lamont Johnson, "Oscar Underwood Story," *Profile in Courage*

1965

☐ Dwight Hemion, *My Name is Barbra*

1966

☐ Alex Segal, *Death of a Salesman*
Ted Yates, *Congo: Victim of Independence*
Dwight Hemion, *Sinatra: A Man and His Music*, Part II
Fielder Cook, *Brigadoon*
George Schaefer, *Barefoot in Athens*

1967

☐ George Schaefer, *Do Not Go Gentle Into That Good Night*
Earl Bellamy, *I Spy*
Dwight Hemion, *Herb Albert and the Tijuana Brass*
Paul Stanley, *The Council*

1968

☐ George Schaefer, "My Mother and My Father," *CBS Playhouse*
Paul Bogart, *CBS Playhouse*
Lee Katzin, *The Mod Squad*
Delbart Mann, *Heidi*
Gordon Wiles, *Laugh-In*

1969

☐ Fielder Cook, *Teacher, Teacher*
Joel Banow, *First Manned Landing on the Moon*
Paul Bogart, "Shadow Game," *CBS Playhouse*
William A Graham, "Sadbird," *CBS Playhouse*
Daniel Petrie, *Silent Night, Lonely Night*

1970

☐ Lamont Johnson, *My Sweet Charlie*
Dwight Hemion, *Kraft Music Hall Presents Mr. Anthony Quinn and Miss Peggy Lee*
Buzz Kulik, "A Storm in Summer," *Hallmark Hall of Fame*
Delbart Mann, *David Copperfield*
Joseph Sargent, *Tribes*

1971

BEST DIRECTION IN A COMEDY SERIES (ONE HOUR OR LESS)
☐ John Rich, *All in the Family*
Bruce Bilson, "Being Divorced Is Never Having to Say I Do," *The Odd Couple*
Jay Sandrich, "Baby Sit-Com," *Mary Tyler Moore Show*

BEST DIRECTION IN A DRAMATIC SERIES (ONE HOUR OR LESS)
☐ Daniel Petrie, "Hands of Love," *The Man and the City*
Lewis Freedman, *Beginning to End*
Lamont Johnson, *Birdbath*

BEST DIRECTION IN DOCUMENTARIES (INCLUDING NEWS SPECIALS)
☐ Phillip Beigel, "Anatomy of a Decision—The F.B.I. and the Great American Dream Machine," *Behind the Lines*
Joel Banow, *Louis Armstrong 1900-1971*
Anthony Messuri, *Apollo: A Trip to the Moon*

BEST DIRECTION IN MUSICAL AND VARIETY SHOWS (ONE HOUR OR LESS)
☐ Tim Kiley, *The Flip Wilson Show*
Arthur N. Fisher, *The Sonny and Cher Show*
Greg Garrison, *The Dean Martin Show*

BEST DIRECTION IN SPECIALS (INCLUDING FEATURE-LENGTH TV FILMS)
☐ Buzz Kulik, *Brian's Song*
Fielder Cook, *The Price*
Delbert Mann, *Jane Eyre*

TV DIRECTOR OF THE YEAR
☐ John Rich

1972

BEST DIRECTION IN A COMEDY SERIES
☐ Gene Reynolds, *M*A*S*H*

Bill Hobin, *Maud's Dilemma*
John Rich, Bob La Hendro, "The Bunkers and the Swingers," *All in the Family*

BEST DIRECTION IN A DRAMATIC SERIES

☐ Robert Butler, "Dust Bowl Cousins," *The Waltons*
Marc Daniels, "Love Is When They Say They Need You," *Marcus Welby, M.D.*
Charles S. Dubin, "V for Vashon," *Hawaii Five-O*

BEST DIRECTION IN MUSICAL-VARIETY SHOWS

☐ Bob Fosse, *Liza with a Z*
Bill Davis, *The Julie Andrews Hour*
Art Fisher, *The Sonny and Cher Show*

BEST DIRECTION IN DOCUMENTARY-NEWS PROGRAMS

☐ Aram Boyajian, *The American Indian: This Land was His Land*
Julian Krainin, *Oceans: The Silent Crisis*

BEST DIRECTION IN SPECIALS

☐ Lamont Johnson, *That Certain Summer*
Paul Bogart, *The House Without a Christmas Tree*
Tom Gries, *The Glass House*

TV DIRECTOR OF THE YEAR

☐ Lamont Johnson

1973

BEST DIRECTION IN A COMEDY SERIES

☐ Gene Reynolds, "Deal Me Out," *M*A*S*H*
Hal Cooper, *Maude*
Jay Sandrich, "Lou's First Date Is 80 Years Old," *The Mary Tyler Moore Show*

BEST DIRECTION IN A DRAMATIC SERIES

☐ Charles S. Dubin, "Knockover," *Kojak*
Harry Harris, "The Journey," *The Waltons*
Jerry Thrope, "Eye For An Eye," *Kung Fu*

BEST DIRECTION IN MUSICAL-VARIETY SHOWS

☐ Dwight Hemion, *Barbra Streisand & Other Musical Instruments*
Art Fisher, *The Sonny and Cher Comedy Hour*
Dave Powers, *The Carol Burnett Show*

BEST DIRECTION IN DOCUMENTARY-NEWS SPECIALS

☐ Arthur Bloom, *60 Minutes*

Dennis Azzarella, "The Killer Instinct," *Primal Man*
Alvin R. Mifelow, "JFK—A Time to Remember," *ABC Wide World of Entertainment*

BEST DIRECTION IN SPECIALS

☐ Joseph Sargent, *The Marcus/Nelson Murders*
Robert Butler, *The Blue Knight*
Anthony Harvey, *The Glass Menagerie*

1974

BEST DIRECTION IN A COMEDY SERIES

☐ Hy Averback, "Alcoholics Unanimous," *M*A*S*H*
Robert Moore, "Rhoda's Wedding," *Rhoda* .
Jay Sandrich, "Mary Richards Goes To Jail," *Mary Tyler Moore Show*

BEST DIRECTION IN A DRAMATIC SERIES

☐ David Friedkin, "Cross Your Heart, Hope To Die," *Kojak*
Corey Allen, "Cry Help," *Streets of San Francisco*
Harry Falk, "Mask of Death," *Streets of San Francisco*

BEST DIRECTION IN MUSICAL-VARIETY SHOWS

☐ Roger Englander, "What Makes A Gershwin Tune a Gershwin Tune?," *New York Philharmonic Young People's Concerts*
Art Fisher, *The Sonny and Cher Comedy Hour*
Nick Vanoff, *The Perry Como Christmas Show*

BEST DIRECTION IN DOCUMENTARY-NEWS SPECIALS

☐ Bill Foster, *American Film Institute Salutes James Cagney*
Arthur Bloom, *60 Minutes*
Charles D. Braverman, *David Hartman. . . Birth and Babies*

BEST DIRECTION IN SPECIALS

☐ John Korty, *The Autobiography of Miss Jane Pittman*
Tom Gries, *QB VII*
Lamont Johnson, *The Execution of Private Solvik*

TV DIRECTOR OF THE YEAR

☐ John Korty

1975

BEST DIRECTION IN A COMEDY SERIES

☐ Hy Averback, "Bombed," *M*A*S*H*

Hal Cooper, *Maude*
Joan Darling, "Chuckles Bites the Dust," *Mary Tyler Moore Show, The*

BEST DIRECTION IN A DRAMATIC SERIES

☐ James Cellan-Jones, *Jennie, Lady Randolph Churchill*
David Friedkin, "How Cruel The Frost, How Bright The Stars," *Kojak*
George Schaefer, *Sandburg's Lincoln*

BEST DIRECTION IN MUSICAL-VARIETY SHOWS

☐ Jay Sandrich, *The Lily Tomlin Show*
Bill Davis, *John Denver Rocky Mountain Christmas*
Dwight Hemion, *Our Love Is Here To Stay*

BEST DIRECTION IN DOCUMENTARY-NEWS SPECIALS

☐ Irv Drasnin, *CBS Reports: The Guns of Autumn*
Martin Morris, "Kennedy Assassination," *Good Night America*
Howard Stringer, *CBS Reports: A Tale of Two Irelands*

BEST DIRECTION IN SPECIALS

☐ Sam O'Steen, *Queen of the Stardust Ballroom*
Lamont Johnson, *Fear on Trial*
Buzz Kulik, *Babe*

TV DIRECTOR OF THE YEAR

☐ Sam O'Steen

1976

BEST DIRECTION IN A COMEDY SERIES

☐ Alan Alda, "Dear Sigmund," *M*A*S*H*

BEST DIRECTION IN A DRAMATIC SERIES

☐ Glenn Jordan, *Rites of Friendship*

BEST DIRECTION IN A MUSICAL-VARIETY SHOW

☐ Tony Charmoli, *Shirley MacLaine—Gypsy in My Soul*

BEST DIRECTION IN A SPECIAL

☐ Daniel Petrie, *Eleanor and Franklin*

BEST DIRECTION IN A DOCUMENTARY-NEWS SPECIAL

☐ Arthur Bloom, coverage of Democratic and Republican Conventions. *CBS News*

1977

BEST DIRECTION IN A COMEDY SERIES
☐ Paul Bogart, "Edith's 50th Birthday," *All in the Family*

BEST DIRECTION A DRAMATIC SHOW
☐ John Erman, *Roots*, Part 2 (Second Hour)

BEST DIRECTION IN A MUSICAL-VARIETY SHOW
☐ Art Fisher, *Neil Diamond: Glad You're Here with Me Tonight*

BEST DIRECTION IN A SPECIAL
☐ Daniel Petrie, *Eleanor and Franklin: The White House Years*

BEST DIRECTION IN NEWS SPECIALS/SPORTS
☐ Ray Lockhart, "A Day with President Carter," *NBC Reports*

BEST DIRECTION IN DOCUMENTARY
☐ Perry Miller Adato, *Georgia O'Keef*

1978

BEST DIRECTION IN A COMEDY SERIES
☐ Paul Bogart, "California, Here We Are," *All in the Family*

BEST DIRECTION IN A DRAMATIC SERIES
☐ Gene Reynolds, "Prisoner," *Lou Grant*

BEST DIRECTION IN A MUSICAL-VARIETY SHOW
☐ Merrill Brockway, "Choreography by Balanchine, Part 3," *Dance in America*

BEST DIRECTION IN A SPECIAL
☐ Marvin Chomsky, *Holocaust*

BEST DIRECTION IN DOCUMENTARY
☐ John Korty, *Who Are the Debolts?*

BEST DIRECTION IN ACTUALITY
☐ Don Mischer, *The Kennedy Center Honors*

1979

BEST DIRECTION IN A COMEDY SERIES
☐ Charles S. Dubin, "Period of Adjustment," *M*A*S*H*

BEST DIRECTION IN A DRAMATIC SERIES
☐ Roger Young, "The Cop," *Lou Grant*

BEST DIRECTION IN A MUSICAL-VARIETY SHOW
☐ Tony Charmoli, *John Denver and the Muppets*

BEST DIRECTION IN A SPECIAL
☐ Michael Mann, *The Jericho Mile*

BEST DIRECTION IN ACTUALITY
☐ Don Mischer, *The Kennedy Center Honors*

BEST DIRECTION IN DOCUMENTARY
☐ Alfred R. Kelman, "The Magic Sense," *The Body Human*

1980

BEST DIRECTION IN A COMEDY SERIES
☐ Noam Pitlik, "Fog," *Barney Miller*

BEST DIRECTION IN A DRAMATIC SERIES
☐ Roger Young, "Lou," *Lou Grant*

BEST DIRECTION IN A MUSICAL-VARIETY SHOW
☐ Dwight Hemion, *IBM Presents Baryshnikov on Broadway*

BEST DIRECTION IN DOCUMENTARY
☐ Alfred R. Kelman, "Body Beautiful," *The Body Human*
☐ Perry Miller Adato, *Picasso: A Painter's Diary*

BEST DIRECTION IN ACTUALITY
☐ Don Mischer, *The Kennedy Center Honors*

BEST DIRECTION IN A SPECIAL
☐ Jerry London, *Shogun*

BEST DIRECTION IN COMMERCIALS
☐ George Gomes, for advertisements for Sara Lee, The Bell System and A&W Root Beer

1981

BEST DIRECTION IN A COMEDY SERIES
☐ Alan Alda, "The Life You Save," *M*A*S*H*

BEST DIRECTION IN A DRAMATIC SERIES
☐ Robert Butler, "Hill Street Station," *Hill Street Blues*

BEST DIRECTION IN A MUSICAL-VARIETY SHOW
☐ Emile Ardolino, "The Spellbound Child," *Dance in America*

BEST DIRECTION IN ACTUALITY
☐ Stan Harris, *Command Performance at Ford's Theatre—The Stars Meet the President*

BEST DIRECTION IN DOCUMENTARY
☐ Robert Guenette, *Great Movie Stunts: Raiders of the Lost Ark*

BEST DIRECTION IN A SPECIAL
☐ Herbert Wise, *Skokie*

BEST DIRECTION IN COMMERCIALS
☐ Rick Levine, for advertisements for Pepsi Cola and Kodak

1982

BEST DIRECTION IN A COMEDY SERIES
☐ Alan Alda, "Where There's a Will, There's a War," *M*A*S*H*

BEST DIRECTION IN A DRAMATIC SERIES
☐ David Anspaugh, "Personal Foul," *Hill Street Blues*

BEST DIRECTION IN A MUSICAL-VARIETY SHOW
☐ Don Mischer, *Shirley MacLaine—Illusions*

BEST DIRECTION IN DOCUMENTARY/ACTUALITY
☐ Perry Miller Adato, *Carl Sandburg—Echoes and Silences*

BEST DIRECTION IN A SPECIAL
☐ Marvin J. Chomskey, *Inside the Third Reich*

BEST DIRECTION IN COMMERCIALS
☐ Joe Pytka, for advertisements for Budweiser Light ("Baseball" and "Basketball" spots) and for Henry Weinhard Beer ("Future/Gallup" spot)

1983

BEST DIRECTION IN A COMEDY SERIES
☐ James Borrows, "Showdown—Part II," *Cheers*

BEST DIRECTION IN A DRAMATIC SERIES
☐ Jeff Bleckner, "Life In The Minors," *Hill Street Blues*

**BEST DIRECTION IN A MUSICAL-
VARIETY SHOW**
☐ Don Misher, *Motown 25: Yesterday,
Today, Forever*

**BEST DIRECTION IN
DOCUMENTARY/ACTUALITY**
☐ Harry Mosses, *Willie Loman Comes To
China*

BEST DIRECTION IN A SPECIAL
☐ Edward Zwick, *Special Bulletin*

BEST DIRECTION IN COMMERCIALS
☐ Bob Brooks, Hallmark Cards ("Music
Professor") and Stu Hagman, IBM
Home Computers and LDS ("Hats"
and "Hold On")

9/ACHIEVEMENT IN CHILDREN'S TELEVISION AWARDS (ACTION FOR CHILDREN'S TELEVISION. . .)

ACTION FOR CHILDREN'S Television (ACT) was formed in 1968 by four women in Newton, Mass. who wanted to improve the quality of children's programming and advertising. Like many other consumer groups in the late 1960s and early 1970s, ACT deplored the sophisticated and often deceptive advertising techniques used to seduce children to buy products advertised on TV. (According to a report by the Council on Children, Media and Merchandising, 10% of the commercials on children's programs from 1965 to 1975 were for vitamins, 30% for toys and nearly 50% for food, especially for sugared cereals, soft drinks, cookies and candy. In 1974 alone, the three major networks grossed approximately $80 million from their Saturday morning children's shows.)

In 1970 ACT petitioned the Federal Communications Commission to eliminate commercials from children's programming and to require TV stations to provide a minimum of 14 hours per week of children's shows. Although ACT's demands were never completely met, the FCC hearings elicited more than 100,000 letters from parents across the nation who were outraged by the low standards of children's programs. Because of the effective pressures of ACT and other watchdog groups, (1)drug companies stopped advertising vitamins in the guise of candy, (2)the hosts of children's shows were no longer permitted to sell products on TV, (3)the violent content of kid-vid, especially of cartoons, was considerably reduced, and, (4)the networks agreed to reduce the commercials on children's show from 16 minutes to 9½ minutes, the standard for adult prime time programs.

ACT—which has grown to include members across the nation and which is now housed in Boston—has continued its pionnering work. One of its tasks since 1972 has been to confer annual awards for significant achievements toward improving children's television. Individuals, stations, networks, and companies or organizations that provide funding for outstanding programs or set exemplary advertising policies are eligible for ACT's awards.

1972

POST-NEWSWEEK TELEVISION STATION in Washington, D.C. and Florida, for seeking quality programs and clustering commercials on such programs.
HALLMARK CARDS, for sponsoring The Snow Goose.

HEALTH-TEX, for institutional advertising on Babar Comes to America.
CHILDREN'S TELEVISION WORKSHOP, for conceiving a creative unit devoted to producing children's shows and experimenting in television education for young children.
FRED ROGERS, for pionnering efforts to meet the emotional needs of young children through television.
ROBERT KEESHAN, for 16 years of creative children's television on Captain Kangaroo.
THE KID'S THING, WHDH-TV, Boston, for noncommercial school vacation week programs.
PUBLIC BROADCASTING STATIONS, for Misterogers' Neighborhood, Sesame Street, Electric Company, Masquerade, ZOOM, Hodge Podge Lodge and What's New.
COMMENDATIONS (for programs which were cited but did not meet ACT's criteria for limited commercialism):
Earth Lab
Children's Film Festival
In the News
You Are There
Jackson Five
Curiosity Shop
Make a Wish
Take A Giant Step
Mr. Wizard

1973

SEARS ROEBUCK FOUNDATION, for Misterogers' Neighborhood.
XEROX CORP., for Spanish and Portuguese versions of Sesame Street.
MOBIL OIL CORP., for Electric Company.
INTERNATIONAL BUSINESS MACHINES, for Sleeping Beauty ballet, aired when many children were watching.
MILES LABORATORIES, SAUTER LABS/HOFFMAN-LA ROCHE and BRISTOL-MYERS, for withdrawing vitamin pill advertising from children's programs.
AVCO AND MEREDITH BROADCASTING CORP., for combining resources to produce meaningful children's programs.
ABC-TV., for Afterschool Specials, one hour monthly.
CBC NEWS, for What's An Election all About and What's A Convention All About, news specials for children.
NBC-TV for Watch Your Child, an attempt at a daily half-hour program with limited commercialism.
WESTINGHOUSE BROADCASTING, for continued commitment to science for children, especially Earth Lab.
WCVB-TV, Boston, for commitment to needs of community's children, specifically Jabberwocky and Young Reporters.
WMAL-TV, Washington, for daily children's program with clustered commercials, The Magic Door.

WPIX-TV, New York, for two local children's programs with clutered commercials, *Magic Garden* and *Joya's Fun School*.

THE 350,000 CHILDREN who contributed creative material and ideas to *Zoom*.

FORTY-EIGHT COMMERCIAL STATIONS who aired *Vision On*, the first children's programs designed for both deaf and hearing children.

FORTY-FOUR COMMERCIAL STATIONS, for airing *Sesame Street* without commercials.

SPECIAL MENTION
The Waltons
National Geographic Society Specials
Jacques Cousteau's Specials

1974

ABC-TV STATIONS, for *Over 7* a magazine format for family viewing.

ALPHAVENTURE, for creating *Big Blue Marble* with ITT noncommercial backing and teacher materials to supplement the program.

CBS-TV NEWS, for *In the News*, brief Saturday morning reports.

CHINESE COMMITTEE FOR AFFIRMATIVE ACTION, San Francisco, for *Yut, Yee, Sahm* (Here We Come).

EXXON USA FOUNDATION, for supporting *Villa Alegre* on PBS.

PRIME TIME SCHOOL TELEVISION, Chicago for developing and distributing educational materials for classroom use about televised prime-time specials and documentaries.

WBZ TV, Boston, for *Something Else*, featuring local children in a constructive alternative to Saturday morning viewing.

WNET, New York, for two-week festival of quality daytime programming.

1975

CBS-TV, for *The CBS Children's Film Festival*.

CBS-TV NEWS, for *Marshall Efron's Illustrated, Simplified and Painless Sunday School*.

CHILDREN'S TELEVISION WORKSHOP, for *The Electric Company*.

ROBERT KEESHAN ASSOCIATES, producers of *Captain Kangaroo*.

KLRN-TV, Austin, for *Carrascolendas*, bilingual program.

NBC-TV, for *GO-USA*, a series of historical dramas.

POST NEWSWEEK STATIONS, for *The Reading Show*, combining broadcast and published materials.

TAFT BROADCASTING CO., for *Max B. Nimble*.

MARTIN TAHSE PRODUCTIONS, for bringing back *Kukla, Fran and Ollie*.

WESTINGHOUSE BROADCASTING CO., for *Call it Macaroni*, adventure series.

WGBH, Boston, for *The Spider's Web*, daily radio storybook.

WXYZ, Detroit, for *Hot Fudge*, contributing to preventive medicine in mental health.

SPECIAL AWARD Agency For Instructional Television, for informational and informative classroom programs.

1976

ABC-TV, for *ABC Afterschool Special*, dramatic series.

ABC-TV NEWS, for *Animals Animals Animals*.

BEHRENS CO., Miami, for *Kidsworld*, national news magazine for children with contributions for participating stations.

EDUCATIONAL DEVELOPMENT CENTER, Newton, Mass., for *Infinity Factory*.

KETC-TV, St. Louis, for *Common Cents*.

KOMO-TV, Seattle, for *Boomerang*.

KRON-TV, San Francisco, for *Kidswatch*.

NBC-TV, for *Muggy*.

NBC-TV, for *Special Treat*.

WGBH-TV, Boston, for *Rebop*.

WMAQ-TV, Chicago, for *Bubblegum Digest*.

WQED-TV, for *Once Upon a Classic*.

WSB-TV, Atlanta, for *Operation Education*.

SEARS ROEBUCK FOUNDATION for *Misterogers' Neighborhood*.

SPECIAL AWARD Public Broadcasting Service

1977

ABC *Weekend Specials*.

CBS, *Fat Albert*.

CORPORATIONS FOR ENTERTAINMENT AND LEARNING INC.

FIELD COMMUNICATIONS for *Snipets*.

SOUTH CAROLINA ETV, for *Studio See*.

WALT DISNEY PRODUCTIONS, for *The New Mickey Mouse Club*.

WGBH, Boston, for *Captioned Zoom*.

WIIC-TV, Pittsburgh, for *Catercousins*.

WRC-TV, Washington, D.C., for *Beth and Bower Half Hour*.

WSB-TV, Atlanta, for *Super 2*.

WTTW-TV, Chicago, for *As *We *See *It*.

SPECIAL AWARD Westinghouse Broadcasting Co.

10/THE MOST MEMORABLE MOMENTS IN TV HISTORY

Film Comment, THE widely-respected magazine published by the Film Society of Lincoln Center, usually covers (as its name suggest) the world of film. But the journal's editors decided to devote their July-August 1979 issue entirely to American commercial TV. Why? Three reasons, the editors wryly confessed. One, *Mork and Mindy* is watched by more Americans than have seen any movie in a theater. Two, television produces more film per year than Hollywood does. And three, they wanted to see what a dozen or so good writers, whose first professed love is film, had to say about a medium that "everyone looks at but few think about out loud—or in print."

One of the issue's articles was Paul Slansky's list of The Most Memorable Moments in TV History, a wacky compilation of bloopers, foibles, gaffes and faux pas that records some television's most dubious achievements. When asked his definition of art, Jean Cocteau demanded only that it "astonish" him. By this criterion, Slansky noted, the vast wasteland clearly measures up.

You can starve if it's Westinghouse
During a live commercial for a Westinghouse frost-free refrigerator, Betty Furness is unable to get the appliance's door open. "Yick! Someone's playing games," she says, as she struggles in vain. "Well. . . ordinarily it's completely automatic." After 30 seconds, the director has the cameraman dolly in for an unplanned—and unattractive—close-up of Betty, while stagehands yank the goddamn door open. (1954)

And they still have to call Toilet Paper 'Bathroom Tissue.'
The two-hour shoot-out between the Symbionese Liberation Army and the Los Angeles Police Department (and the resulting inferno) is broadcast live by KNX-TV in Los Angeles. (May 17, 1974)

A Wedding
48,000,000 viewers (the largest audience in the history of *The Tonight Show*) witness the wedding of Tiny Tim and his briefly beloved Miss Vicki. The couple exchange promises to be sweet, gentle, kind, patient and "not puffed up," then move to the couch to chat with Johnny and Ed. (Dec. 17, 1969)

Like it is
Early in his TV carrer, Howard Cosell is preparing to interview a baseball star on the WABC-TV news. Not realizing they're on the air, Cosell says to the ballplayer, "Now are you gonna bullshit me or am I gonna bullshit you?" (1961)

Didn't anything happen between RFK'S Assasination and the Chicago Convention?
Co-host Regis Philbin stuns the nation by walking off *The Joey Bishop Show*. "It's one thing to lose your own show, but it's another to lose someone else's," says Regis, in response to critics. "I'm leaving," He returns a few days later. (July 11, 1968)

Of course, I realize I'll probably die eventually
"I'm so healthy that I expect to live on and on," says nutrition expert J. I. Rodale, immediately before dropping dead of a heart attack on *The Dick Cavett Show*. The program is not aired. (June 8, 1971)

You know, these Podiums are very interesting, if you really study them
The sound is lost for 27 minutes on the first Ford-Carter debate. Neither man moves from his podium or acknowledges his opponent during the delay. (Sept. 23, 1976)

The public has a right to know
While broadcasting a Cubs-Pirates game on *Monday Night Baseball*, ABC's Keith Jackson tells the nation that Chicago's Bobby Murcer spent the afternoon visiting a 12-year-old child who is dying of cancer. The boy, who has not been told the nature of his illness, watches the game from his hospital bed. (Aug. 8, 1977)

The day the clown died
The 31st Academy Awards show ends 22 minutes ahead of schedule, forcing host Jerry Lewis to fill time with such attempts at humor as asking the audience to applaud "again" for Best Actress Susan Hayward. *New York Times* critic calls Lewis's performance "a tour de force of uncompromising ineptitude." (April 6, 1959)

Do I see a waltz?
Susan Davidoff, Miss Deaf America, uses sign language and dance movement to communicate songs on "Sing a Sign," the first nationally televised original musical review in sign language. (May 20, 1978)

"Nixon has a face like a foot," says David Steinberg. "Every time I see it on TV I want to put a sock on it."
From the 1952 Checkers speech to the 1964 East Room farewell ("My mother was a saint"), Richard Nixon provides the nation with the greatest political theater in its history. The highlight of his television career occurs just before he goes on the air to announce his resignation: with the cameras rolling during the last-minute sound check, Nixon tells his photographer to stop snapping pictures. Explains the President of the United States: "I'm afraid he'll catch me pickin' muh nose." (Aug. 8, 1974)

Super-Blow 1
With the Jets leading the Raiders 32-29 with 50 seconds to play, NBC shifts away from the game so that *Heidi* can start on time; Oakland goes on to win, 43-32, scoring two touchdowns in nine seconds. Irate New York fans, unable to get through the jammed network switchboard, tie up the Police Department's emergency number for several hours. (NBC later runs a streamer reporting the outcome of the game—

just as Heidi's paralytic cousin Klara is summoning up the courage to try to walk.) (Nov. 17, 1968)

The Pope is dead but the Yankees are still alive. Details at eleven.

Following a bulletin reporting the death of Pope Paul VI, Yankee sportscaster Phil Rizzuto says, "Well, that puts the damper on even a Yankee win." (Aug. 6, 1978)

Et Tu, Fultie?

Bishop Fulton J. Sheen delivers an impassioned reading of the burial scene from *Julius Caesar*, substituting the names of several Russian leaders for those of the original characters. "Stalin," declares Sheen, "must one day meet his judgement." (The Soviet dictator dies within two weeks.) (Feb. 24, 1953)

Happy News

Following a report on the attempted rape of an eight year old, Tex Antoine begins his WABC-TV weather report by saying, "Confucius say If rape is inevitable, relax and enjoy it." Five days later, anchorman Roger Grimsby introduces the suspended Antoine's replacement thus: "Lie back, relax, and enjoy the weather with Storm Field." (Nov. 24, 1976)

A Star Is Born

Lee Harvey Oswald is shot on national television. (Nov. 24, 1963)

The Politics of Joy

While the two are covering the 1968 Democratic convention for ABC, Gore Vidal calls William Buckley a "crypto-Nazi." Buckley replies, "Now listen, you queer. Stop calling me a crypto-Nazi or I'll sock you in your goddam face and you'll stay plastered." Meanwhile, on NBC, John Chancellor is manhandled on the convention floor by several members of Chicago's finest. He says, "This is John Chancellor reporting from somewhere in custody." (Aug. 28, 1968)

Mad as Hell and not Going to Take it Anymore

Chris Chubbuck, 30-year-old hostess of Sarasota, Florida's morning talk show, *Suncoast Digest*, interrupts her reading of the news and says, "In keeping with channel 40's policy of bringing you the latest in blood and guts and in living color, you are going to see another first— attempted suicide." She takes a .38 revolver out of a shopping bag and shoots herself in the head. The attempt succeeds. (July 15, 1974)

Well Done, Bert!

Manfred Weber, a contestant on the game show, *County Fair*, is seated center stage with an enormous "firecracker" in his lap, while his blindfolded wife futilely attempts to stamp out the fuse and host Bert Parks does a grotesque burlesque of her efforts. The "cracker" goes off, buckets of flour fall on the hapless Manny, and then the unexpected piece de resistance: he suddenly *goes up in flames!* He leaps out of his chair and runs offstage while the audience screams; stagehands smother the flames. "Whoa, we goofed," says Bert Parks, bringing the nervously smiling wife back on camera. "That was a close thing, but he's all right. We're gonna have him out here for you to *see!* Let's give him a nice hand, and she's gonna receive a thousand dollars." The wife is hustled off stage, the show cuts to a commercial, and no further mention is made of Mr. Weber, who is taken to a hospital with burns on his face, neck and hands. "Lots more fun and excitement coming up in this half," says Bert when the show returns. (April 7, 1959)

1/A Brief History of the Networks and Stations

IN THE BEGINNING there were stations, not networks. During the early years of broadcasting, radio stations were largely independent and autonomous with regard to their programming: what was aired in one city was not necessarily aired in another. Because there was no national chain of stations, radio was initially a local medium.

Yes, for special occasions several stations would get together for simultaneous broadcast: President Coolidge's first message to Congress on Dec. 4, 1923, for example, was carried by several stations, some as far west as Texas. And by the time Coolidge was inaugurated in March 1925, there was a small network of more than 20 stations centered on WEAF New York and owned by A.T.&T.

But national network broadcasting did not really begin until 8:00 P.M. on Nov. 15, 1926 when the National Broadcasting Co. (NBC) kicked off its operations with an extravagant four-hour show from the Grand Ballroom of the Waldorf-Astoria Hotel. Lavish entertainment was provided by five orchestras, a brass band, stars from the Metropolitan Opera, and Will Rogers among others. A thousand guests attended the historic event which was carried live by 25 stations in 21 cities.

The potential of network broadcasting was so great that just a few weeks later, on Jan. 1, 1927, NBC established a two-network organization: the Red Network with 25 stations originated from WEAF New York; and the Blue Network with six stations originated from WJZ Newark.

General Electric initially owned 50% of NBC, RCA 30%, and Westinghouse 20%. But on Jan. 1, 1930 RCA bought out the other two and ever since NBC has been a wholly-owned subsidiary of RCA.

When talent agent Arthur Judson was unable to do business with NBC, he created his own network, the United Independent Broadcasters, in January 1927. Unfortunately, the enterprise was underfinanced and had to be rescued by Louis Sterling of the Columbia Phonograph. Sterling changed the network's name to Columbia Phonograph Broadcasting System and the new web began broadcasting on Sept. 19, 1927 with the presentation of an American opera, *The King's Henchman.*

But the company was still plagued by financial difficulties, loosing $100,000 in its first month on the air: not surprisingly, Columbia Phonograph wanted out. Philadelphia millionaire Jerome H. Louchheim was persuaded to buy the ailing network, with WCAU-owners Ike and Leon Levy as smaller investors. Once again the web was renamed: it would now be known as the Columbia Broadcasting System (CBS). But the new name did not bring new revenues, and with continued losses Louchheim, like his predecessor, soon wanted out.

Young William S. Paley, heir to the Congress Cigar fortune, bought controlling interest on Jan. 8, 1929 for a sum between $250,000 and $400,000. As president of the company, Paley re-organized the network from top to bottom—moving the web back to New York, hiring the best and the brightest of staffs, making smart financial deals. CBS was finally off and running.

The networks grew stronger throughout the 1930s: by 1937, in fact, the webs and their owned and operated radio stations had cornered an impressive 50% of industry revenues. The F.C.C. became wary of network power and began investigating the phenomenon in 1938. In its 1941 Report of Chain Broadcasting, the F.C.C. delivered its historic ruling: "no license shall be issued to a station affiliated with a network organization maintaining more than one network." NBC, in short, would have to divest itself of one of its two chains.

In October 1943, RCA sold its Blue Network for $8 million (the largest sum paid for a broadcasting organization at that time) to Edward J. Noble of the Life Savers candy corporation. Noble renamed the network the American Broadcasting Co. (ABC) and thus the third of our major three webs was born.

* * *

Both NBC and CBS had shown interest in television from their very beginnings. On April 4, 1928 the F.C.C. had granted NBC permission to run an experimental TV station, W2XBS, which began operations on Oct. 30, 1931. Regular broadcasts started April 30, 1939 as President Roosevelt opened the New York World's Fair. And on Jan. 12, 1940 NBC became a real "network" with two stations—WNBC-TV, New York and WRGB-TV, Schenectady. The F.C.C. granted NBC the first commercial-TV license in June 1941. CBS was similarly busy with its TV developments: by August 1940 the company was able to demonstrate a successful color broadcast.

But World War II brought these advances to a halt; the networks could not continue their TV work until after the war. The post-war years gave birth to a fourth network: the DuMont Television Network (DTN), owned by the Allen B. Dumont Laboratories which was in turn partially owned by Paramount Pictures.

Television business was booming after the war: *Howdy Doody* and *Kraft Television Theatre* started in 1947, *The Texaco Star Theatre* with Milton Berle in 1948, followed by the transfer of many other radio stars and shows to TV. Coast-to-coast service was inaugurated on Sept, 4, 1951, when the networks aired the signing of the Japanese peace treaty in San Francisco. Television had so much potential, in fact, that there was considerable confusion as to which station should broadcast on which frequency, which companies should be granted licences, etc. To have time to develop "a fair, efficient and equitable system" of TV operation, the F.C.C. ordered a "freeze" on TV licences in October 1948. The freeze lasted until the Commission's historic Sixth Order and Report issued on April 1, 1952. According to the report, there would be 2,053 stations in 1,291 markets: 617 stations on VHF and 1,436 on UHF. Of these, 242 were to be reserved for non-commercial stations, 80 on VHF. (These figures were later revised.)

The move to TV was difficult and costly. Expensive equipment had to be purchased, stations built, crews assembled, marketing and distribution techniques discovered, etc. And as TV executive Bob Shanks amusingly put it, "if CBS and NBC were climbing the Matterhorn in their adaptation to television, ABC was climbing Mount Everest—with one leg missing and an arm tied behind its back."

In 1952 ABC, in desperate need of money, entered into a $25 million merger with United Paramount Theaters. The web had its first major success in 1954 thanks to Walt Disney: ABC had lent Disney $500,000 to build Disneyland in return for which Disney gave ABC the rights to two TV shows—*The Mickey Mouse Club* and *Disneyland*.

ABC's second coup came in 1955 when the network signed an exclusive agreement with Warner Brothers. The collaboration gave ABC a slew of popular shows — *Cheyenne, Colt 45, Wyatt Earp, Maverick, The Rifleman, Sugarfoot*. Despite such success, ABC was perennial third-place network to CBS and NBC. (DuMont network, which had specialized in quiz and sports programs, folded in 1955, raising ABC's billing by 68% that year.)

During the early 1960s ABC lost money every year, and the switch to color TV was going to require money the network simply did not have. In 1965 ABC and the international conglomerate I.T.T. announced a proposed merger that would bring ABC some $400 million. Although the merger was approved by the F.C.C., the Justice Department wanted the case reopened. I.T.T. withdrew its offer in January 1968.

Although both Howard Hughes and Norton Simon tried to buy control of ABC thereafter, the network decided to raise money not by another merger but by selling $50 million worth of convertible debentures. ABC got another break in 1971 when the F.C.C. ruled that the networks could only provide their affiliates with three hours of prime time programming—not three and a half as had been the previous custom.

With fewer hours available for national advertisers, ABC's billings rose accordingly. When former CBS executive Fred Silverman moved to ABC and took charge of programming, ABC's fortunes increased beyond anyone's expectations: by the end of the 1975/76 season, ABC—the perennial loser—was the top-rated network. The following year, thanks in no small part to the overwhelming success of the miniseries *Roots*, ABC again won the season, earning the largest rating advantage ever amassed by a network over its competitors. (Industry experts claimed that ABC's rise was worth approximately $60 million in profits.) But by the early 1980s, CBS, which had dominated television prime-time ratings for 20 years prior to ABC's surge, regained the No. 1 title, as the following chart shows:

	1st Place	2nd Place	3rd Place
1977/78	ABC (20.6)	CBS (18.7)	NBC (18.0)
1978/79	ABC (20.9)	CBS (18.7)	NBC (17.0)
1979/80	CBS (19.6)	ABC (19.5)	NBC (17.4)
1980/81*	CBS (19.1)	ABC (18.0)	NBC (16.6)
1981/82	CBS (19.0)	ABC (18.1)	NBC (15.2)
1982/83	CBS (18.2)	ABC (17.7)	NBC (15.1)

Each of the networks has had its specialities. CBS has been known for its quality, for getting the best of the best, especially with regard to situation comedies like *I Love Lucy, The Honeymooners, The Dick Van Dyke Show, The Mary Tyler Moore Show*, and *All in the Family*. CBS was also the pioneer in that afternoon staple of TV: the soap opera. (CBS aired the first episode of *Search for Tomorrow* on September 3, 1951). CBS, moreover, nurtured what many critics claim are the two best news reporters in TV history—Edward R. Murrow and Walter Cronkite.

NBC's forte has been specials and movies—it was the first network to have a weekly film series of big, recent-vintage Hollywood movies. And for years the early morning and late night hours belonged to NBC, thanks to *The Today Show, The Tonight Show* and *Saturday Night Live*. Color TV, moreover, was primarily NBC's baby: NBC was the first "all-color" web. Comfortable as the #2 network throughout the 1950s and 1960s, NBC was pushed into third place by ABC in 1976, and the web has been having problems ever since producing successful series, so much so that industry wags have renamed the network *Nothing But Clinkers*. By 1979, in fact, the profit differential between NBC and ABC was an alarming $100 million a year.

As mentioned, ABC's strength in the late 1950s was Westerns. By the late 1960s sports and movies-made-for-TV became the web's crowning glory: ABC was the first network to put football in a regular primetime series (*Monday Night Football*) and the first web to have an en-

---

* The season was delayed due to an actors' strike. Figures listed for this year nevertheless are for the regular season, September 15 through April 19. For the poststrike measurement of 25 weeks, running from October 27 through April 19, CBS had a 19.8 average, compared to 18.2 for ABC and 16.6 for NBC.

tire series devoted to made-for-TV flics (*ABC Movie of the Week*). For the past several years, the network has been most successful with youth-oriented series like *Three's Company, Laverne & Shirley, Happy Days, Soap, Eight Is Enough, Charlie's Angels* and *Love Boat*.

As part of large corporations, the networks' holdings extend way beyond the field of television. NBC, as mentioned, is part of RCA which owns a record company, real estate, Hertz Rental Co., and (at one time) Random House. ABC owns a motion picture theater chain, a recording company, a publishing division, a film production company, and a chain of retail stores. CBS can claim a wholly owned record company, a publishing house, a film company, and at one time, the New York Yankees.

Each of the three networks owns and operates five television stations:

ABC Owned & Operated Stations	CBS Owned & Operated Stations	NBC Owned & Operated Stations
WABC-TV New York	WCBS-TV New York	WNBC-TV New York
WLS-TV Chicago	KNXT-TV Los Angeles	KNBC-TV Los Angeles
WXYZ-TV Detroit	WBBM-TV Chicago	WMAQ-TV Chicago
KABC-TV Los Angeles	KMOX-TV St. Louis	WRC-TV Washington, D.C.
KGO-TV San Francisco	WCAU-TV Philadelphia	WKYC-TV Cleveland

According to F.C.C. rules, broadcast stations in this country are privately owned but are licensed by the F.C.C. and subject to government regulation. The stations are licensed for three-year periods. The F.C.C. reviews their performance when they apply for renewal to ensure they have operated in the public interest and in accord with the Communications Act. Licenses may also be reviewed if there are serious complaints against the station. The Commission may grant short-term renewals, impose forfeitures up to $10,000 or, in severe cases, revoke licenses. The public may challenge renewals.

The Commission assigns frequencies and call letters, sets power limits and operating hours, and licenses technicians who operate broadcast equipment. The broadcaster must ascertain the needs and interest of the community by surveying civic leaders and others, and must keep logs of programs, commercials, and technical data.

The Fairness Doctrine requires licensees to broadcast contrasting views if they present programs on controversial public issues. In political broadcasting, if a station presents one candidate for an office, it must grant equal time to all other legally qualified candidates for that office, under section 315 of the Communications Act. The station must keep records of all requests for political time.

The F.C.C. acts as arbiter in disputes concerning political or Fairness Doctrine complaints. The Commission may not censor programming, although obscenity, for example, is prohibited.

To avoid concentration of control, the Commission limits any individual or company to no more than seven AM, seven FM, and seven TV station (no more than five of which can be VHF). No one can operate two commercial stations in the same service covering the same geographical area.

Networks are licensed (except for stations they own), but the Commission issues rules to further competition in network broadcasting. For example, a network may not operate dual networks sumultaneously or in overlapping territory, and certain terms of network affiliation contracts are regulated.

The television broadcast band consists of 68 channels—VHF 2 through 13 (54-72, 76-88, and 174-216 MHz) and UHF 14 through 69 (470-806 MHz). TV stations are allocated on the basis of the Table of Assignments in the Commission's rules, providing specific channels for some 850 communities in the United States. More than one-third of approximately 1,850 channels are reserved for noncommercial educational stations. The others are available for commercial or noncommercial stations.

UHF has long been a thorn in the F.C.C.'s side. In 1952 when the Commission provided for 1,462 UHF and 617 VHF stations, few TV sets were even equipped to receive UHF waves. What good were UHF stations, F.C.C. critics asked, if viewers could not receive their programs? Shouldn't the F.C.C. have made sure that UHF and VHF broadcasts were equally accessible?

Given the distinct disadvantage of UHF, it's not surprising that its early history was a rocky one: UHF stations seldom stayed on the air very long. The first commercially licensed UHF station—KPTV in Portland—began broadcasting Sept. 20, 1952 but went off the air April 17, 1957. Even major networks like CBS and NBC couldn't make a go of UHF and gave up their UHF stations in 1959. And by 1960 there were only 85 UHF stations on the air, compared to 474 VHF.

But in 1962 Congress passed the All-Channel Law: any TV sets sold in interstate commerce after April 30, 1964 would have to have UHF capacity. Later the F.C.C. ruled that UHF and VHF must have "comparable tuning," that is, that all UHF channels must be turned on with a "click" like VHF channels, rather than with a continuous dial as was the case with many UHF sets. This ruling further strengthened the UHF band and today 92% of all TV homes in this country can receive UHF programs, as the following chart shows:

YEAR	PERCENT OF TV HOMES WITH UHF
1957	9.2%
1958	8.1
1959	8.0
1960	7.0
1961	7.1
1962	7.3
1963	9.6

1964	15.8
1965	27.5
1966	38.0
1967	47.5
1968	57.0
1969	66.0
1970	73.0
1971	80.0
1972	81.0
1973	86.0
1974	89.0
1975	91.0
1976	92.0
1977	92.0

Like UHF, noncommercial stations suffered a slow and tortuous start in this country. In 1952 when the F.C.C. reserved 242 stations for noncommercial use (80 on VHF, 162 on UHF),* educators around the country rejoiced, and in May 1953 KUHT Houston became the nation's first educational TV Licensee. But officials did not realize the obstacles educational TV would have to face: TV stations were expensive to build and operate; funding was not readily available; and the predominance of educational stations of UHF certainly did not help matters.

The Ford Foundation did provide some funds to help fledgling educational stations get started, and in 1952 the Foundation gave $1.5 million to create the Educational Television and Radio Center (ETRC) in Ann Arbor, Mich. The Center, which stored and produced material for educational stations, moved to New York in 1962 when it became NET, supported by an annual $6 million grant from Ford.

In 1962 Congress passed the Educational Broadcasting Facilities Act, enabling HEW to provide $32 million in matching grants over the next five years to help build ETV facilities. The grants certainly helped: by 1967, 127 ETV stations were on the air, compared to only 59 in 1962.

The Carnegie Corp. began investigating the status of noncommercial American TV in 1965, and two years later the 15-member panel headed by James R. Killian, Jr. issued its historic report, *Public Television: A Program for Action.* The report proposed a non-profit corporation be formed to act as a central agent for public television stations. Such stations, the panel advised, should not limit themselves to classroom programs, but should expand their fare to include everything of cultural interest. And perhaps most importantly, the panel urged a considerable increase in government appropriations for noncommercial TV.

Most of the panel's recommendations were heeded in the Public Broadcasting Act of 1967 and thus educational TV became public TV. The Corporation for Public Broadcasting (CPB) was created in 1967 to adminster funds and keep public television free from political influence. In November 1969 CPB created the Public Broadcasting System to act as a central programmer.

During the 1970s, public television enjoyed much success, thanks to several British imports (*Upstairs, Downstairs, Civilisation, Monty Python*) and to its own popular series (*The Adams Chronicles, Nova, Sesame Street, The Electric Company, Great Performances, Live from Lincoln Center*). Although audiences are still small by network standards (the average prime-time commercial TV show in March 1978 had an 18.8 rating, the average public TV show a 1.5 rating), they are growing. In recent years, PBS has enjoyed particular success with its miniseries and serialized novels such as *Brideshead Revisted.* Today there are more than 260 public TV stations. Funding comes from federal and state appropriations, contributions from individual viewers and corporate grants. (In Europe funds for public stations usually come from an annual tax on television receivers.)

A second Carnegie study was issued in early 1979. The report urged that the budget for public broadcasting be increased so that by 1985 federal appropriations would amount to $630 million. Public TV, the report urged, should be a viable alternative to commercial broadcasting. Under the Reagan administration, however, federal funding was cut from $172 million to $130 million in 1983, and PBS, which in the late 1970s appeared on the brink of major success, is currently plagued with internal strife and insufficient funding.

*Later increased to 116 VHF and 516 UHF stations.

2/STATIONS ON THE AIR, 1949-1983

THE TABLE LISTS the number of stations on the air (regardless of license status) as of June 30 each year.

Figures are compiled from F.C.C. annual reports.

STATIONS ON THE AIR

Year	Total	Commercial	Educational	UHF	VHF	UHF Commercial	VHF Commercial	UHF Educational	VHF Educational
1949	69	69	0						
1950	104	104	0						
1951	107	107	0						
1952	108	108	0						
1953	199	198	1						
1954	408	402	6						
1955	469	458	11						
1956	516	496	20						
1957	545	519	26						
1958	588	556	32						
1959	609	566	43						
1960	626	579	47						
1961	607	553	54						
1962	630	571	59						
1963	651	581	70						
1964	661	582	79						
1965	681	589	92						
1966	721	613	108						
1967	753	626	127	180	573	122	504	58	69
1968	811	655	156	232	579	150	505	82	74
1969	857	680	177	274	583	174	605	100	77
1970	881	691	190	289	592	181	510	108	82
1971	894	695	199	297	597	183	512	114	85
1972	915	701	214	315	600	190	511	125	89
1973	933	705	228	329	604	193	512	136	92
1974	940	706	234	335	605	192	514	143	91
1975	949	706	243	342	607	195	511	147	96
1976	961	708	253	350	611	195	513	155	98
1977	984	725	259	369	615	211	514	158	101
1978	988	728	260	370	618	212	516	158	102
1979	1,002	738	264	380	622	221	517	159	105
1980	1,013	746	267	392	621	230	516	162	105
1981	1,035	766	269	406	629	244	522	162	107
1982	946	679	267	319	627	156	523	163	104
1983	1,149	870	279	506	643	334	536	172	107

3/AUTHORIZED AND LICENSED STATIONS, 1949-1983

THE FOLLOWING TABLE lists the number of authorized, licensed, and operating broadcast stations, and stations deleted since 1949. Due to reorganization of F.C.C. record-keeping practices, figures on pending applications in the various categories have been discontinued since 1970.

As you can see, not all licensed stations are on the air and operating. And conversely, not all stations on the air and operating are licensed.

AUTHORIZED AND LICENSED STATIONS, 1949-83

Year	Grants	Deletions	Pending applications	Licensed	CPs on air	Total on air	Not on air	Total authorized
Commercial TV								
1949	15	7	338	13	56	69	48	117
1950	0	8	351	47	57	104	5	109
1951	0	0	415	81	26	107	2	109
1952	0	1	716	96	12	108	0	108
1953	381	6	572	101	97	198	285	483
1954	174	81	200	104	298	402	171	573
1955	67	58	127	137	321	458	124	582
1956	60	25	128	186	310	496	113	609
1957	55	13	129	344	175	519	132	651
1958	35	21	125	427	129	556	109	665
1959	24	22	114	475	91	566	101	667
1960	22	36	105	481	98	579	74	653
1961	83	36	80	497	56	553	97	650
1962	24	20	114	494	77	571	83	654
1963	30	18	120	525	56	581	85	666
1964	15	10	136	526	56	582	86	668
1965	34	13	132	559	30	589	100	689
1966	58	12	173	558	55	613	122	735
1967	61	9	186	595	31	626	161	787
1968	63	15	118	610	45	655	180	835
1969	38	17	81	615	65	680	176	856
1970	18	51	—	630	61	691	129	820
1971	15	42	—	668	27	695	101	796
1972	12	34	—	688	13	701	73	774
1973	9	18	—	695	10	705	60	765
1974	3	9	—	695	11	706	53	759
1975	9	11	—	699	7	706	53	754
1976	9	3	—	700	8	708	56	764
1977	14	4	—	722	3	725	49	774
1978	16	5	—	725	3	728	57	785
1979	23	0	—	734	4	738	69	807
1980	36	1	—	744	3	746	97	844
1981	42	0	—	766	0	766	118	884
1982	65	0	—	827	*	*	148	975
1983	86	1	—	870	*	*	219	1,089

*On-air figures for these years are not available because separate applications for program test authority are no longer required in most cases.

AUTHORIZED AND LICENSED STATIONS, 1949-83

Year	Grants	Deletions	Pending applications	Licensed	CPs on air	Total on air	Not on air	Total authorized
Educational TV								
1952	0	0	1	0	0	0	0	0
1953	17	0	29	0	1	1	16	17
1954	13	0	17	0	6	6	24	30
1955	5	1	14	1	10	11	23	34
1956	7	0	11	1	19	20	21	41
1957	8	0	8	14	12	26	23	49
1958	4	0	9	29	3	32	21	53
1959	6	0	7	37	6	43	16	50
1960	6	1	7	40	7	47	17	64
1961	4	1	9	43	11	54	13	67
1962	13	1	8	43	16	59	20	79
1963	12	1	16	57	13	70	21	91
1964	13	0	30	72	7	79	28	107
1965	19	1	37	83	9	92	33	125
1966	21	2	37	94	14	108	36	144
1967	4	0	12	100	27	127	56	183
1968	6	1	23	123	33	156	32	188
1969	7	2	29	160	17	177	18	195
1970	19	2	—	173	17	190	22	212
1971	14	9	—	181	18	199	18	217
1972	12	2	—	205	9	214	13	227
1973	12	1	—	210	18	228	9	237
1974	8	0	—	219	15	234	12	246
1975	13	12	—	224	19	243	13	256
1976	14	2	—	231	22	253	14	267
1977	5	1	—	245	14	259	6	265
1978	3	0	—	248	12	260	8	268
1979	7	0	—	253	11	264	11	275
1980	12	0	—	258	9	267	21	288
1981	4	0	—	262	7	269	23	292
1982	9	0	—	285	*	*	18	303
1983	11	2	—	279	*	*	27	306

*On-air figures for these years are not available because separate applications for program test authority are no longer required in most cases.

4/NETWORK-AFFILIATED STATIONS, 1949-1977

THE NETWORKS, AS this chart clearly demonstrates, *are* powerful: 84% of all stations were affiliated with a network in 1977. And the webs have been dominant from the very beginning of TV: in 1950, for example, 98% of all stations had network affiliations.

NBC, with its early start, has traditionally been the largest web, with CBS right on its tail in second place. ABC, the youngest of the three webs, has for most of its history had the fewest affiliates. But since ABC's dramatic rise to first place in 1976, several stations have switched to ABC: in 1977, for example, ABC boasted 190 affiliates, up from 182 the previous year.

The chart below does not include statistics for the DuMont Television Network which left the air in October 1955. DuMont figures are as follows:

1949	45
1950	52
1951	62
1952	62
1953	133
1954	195
1955	158

Through the 1950s, the separate network affiliation listings may not add to the number of network stations shown: multiple affiliations were more common in those years.

All data is as of January 1 each year.

Percentages are based on total number of stations.

NETWORK-AFFILIATED STATIONS, 1949-

Year	NBC Number	NBC Percentage	CBS Number	CBS Percentage	ABC Number	ABC Percentage	Total Stations	Network Stations Number	Network Stations Percentage
1949	25	49.0	15	29.4	11	21.6	51	50	98
1950	56	57.1	27	27.6	13	13.3	98	96	98
1951	63	58.9	30	28.0	14	13.1	107	107	100
1952	64	59.3	31	28.7	15	13.9	108	108	100
1953	71	56.3	33	26.2	24	19.0	126	125	99
1954	164	46.3	113	31.9	40	11.3	354	317	90
1955	189	46.0	139	33.8	46	11.2	411	374	91
1956	200	45.4	168	38.1	53	12.0	441	421	95
1957	205	43.5	180	38.2	60	12.7	471	445	94
1958	209	42.2	191	38.8	69	13.9	495	469	95
1959	213	41.8	193	37.8	79	15.5	510	485	95
1960	214	41.6	195	37.9	87	16.9	515	496	96
1961	201	38.1	198	37.6	104	19.7	527	503	95
1962	201	37.2	194	35.9	113	20.9	541	508	94
1963	203	36.4	194	34.8	117	21.0	557	514	92
1964	212	37.6	191	33.9	123	21.8	564	526	93
1965	198	34.8	190	33.4	128	22.5	569	516	91
1966	202	34.5	193	33.0	137	23.4	585	532	91
1967	205	33.6	191	31.3	141	23.1	610	537	88
1968	207	32.6	192	30.2	148	23.3	635	547	86
1969	211	31.9	190	28.7	156	23.6	662	557	84
1970	215	31.8	193	28.5	160	23.6	677	568	84
1971	218	32.0	207	30.4	168	24.6	682	593	87
1972	218	31.5	209	30.2	172	24.8	693	599	86
1973	218	31.3	210	30.1	176	25.3	697	604	87
1974	218	31.3	212	30.4	181	26.0	697	611	88
1975	219	30.8	213	30.0	185	26.0	711	617	87
1976	218	30.7	213	30.0	182	25.6	710	613	86
1977	212	29.1	210	28.8	190	26.1	728	612	84

5/PERCENT OF TV STATIONS REPORTING PROFIT, 1955-1980

EVERETT C. PARKER of the Office of Communication of the United Church of Christ has argued that television is such a profitable enterprise that not even "incredibly incompetent management" can prevent TV stations from making large yearly profits.

Parker's claim is almost but not quite validated by the following chart, which lists the percentage of TV stations reporting profit from 1955 to 1980. As you can see, most but not *all* stations enjoy profits each year: in 1980, for example, 79% of all stations were in the black, 21% in the red.

Not surprisingly, network-affiliated stations are more likely to make money than independent stations, and VHF stations tend to be more profitable than UHF stations. But the most impressive gain listed in this chart is exactly that made by independent UHF stations. In 1969 a measly 4% of such stations showed a profit, but just seven years later, in 1976, an impressive 64% were in the black. With those kinds of leaps and bounds, it was thought that Parker's rule would soon be in effect and that TV would become a failureproof business. But the fortunes of independent UHF stations have declined dramatically: in 1980, for example, only 46% of such stations showed a profit, down 22% from the peak year 1976.

PERCENT OF TV STATIONS REPORTING PROFIT, 1955-1980

Year	Total		Network Affiliated		Independent	
	VHF	UHF	VHF	UHF	VHF	UHF
1955	63	27				
1956	73	39				
1957	81	32				
1958	71	37				
1959	78	51				
1960	81	50				
1961	79	39				
1962	81	57				
1963	83	58				
1964	85	68				
1965	87	66				
1966	87	59				
1967	83	42	84	53	72	8
1968	86	45	87	63	67	5
1969	83	35	85	51	62	4
1970	82	32	84	43	62	10
1971	81	32	83	41	45	13
1972	86	44	87	55	67	21
1973	86	47	88	55	66	30
1974	86	48	87	57	55	29
1975	86	52	87	52	73	52
1976	91	67	91	68	83	64
1977	92	73	93	76	86	68
1978	92	73	93	83	83	57
1979	—	—	—	—	—	—
1980	89	58	90	67	79	46

Excludes part-time stations and satellites.
Profits are before federal income tax.
Figures compiled from F.C.C. Annual Reports.

OUTSTANDING CHILDREN'S ENTERTAINMENT SPECIALS

Emmy(s) to executive producer(s) and producer(s):

The Shooting, June 1, 1982 (CBS)

Just Pals, Peter Walz (executive producer), Bob Johnson and Nick Anderson (producers) September 14, 1982 (CBS)

Oh, Boy! Babies!, Bruce Hart and Carole Hart (executive producers), Carole Hart (producer) (NBC)

"Help Wanted," *CBS Afternoon Playhouse*, Stephen Gyllenhaal (producer), October 12, 1982 (CBS)

☐ *The Woman who Willed a Miracle*, Dick Clark and Preston Fischer (executive producers), Joanne A. Curley and Sharron Miller (producers), February 9, 1983 (ABC)

OUTSTANDING CHILDREN'S INFORMATIONAL/INSTRUCTIONAL SPECIAL

Emmy(s) to executive producer(s) and producer(s)

☐ *Winners*, Tom Robertson (producer), May, 1982 (Syndicated)

OUTSTANDING INFORMATIONAL/ INSTRUCTIONAL PROGRAMMING— SHORT FORM

Emmy(s) to executive producer(s) and producer(s):

Willie Survives, Lynn Ahrens (producer) (ABC)

In the News, Joel Heller (executive producer), Walter Lister (producer) (CBS)

OUTSTANDING ACTOR IN A DAYTIME DRAMA SERIES

Peter Bergman, (Role: Dr. Cliff Warner), *All My Children* (ABC)

James Mitchell, (Role: Palmer Cortlandt), *All My Children* (ABC)

Stuart Damon, (Role: Dr. Alan Quartermaine), *General Hospital* (ABC)

Anthony Geary, (Role: Luke Spencer), *General Hospital* (ABC)

☐ Robert Woods, (Role: Bo Buchanan), *One Life to Live* (ABC)

OUTSTANDING ACTRESS IN A DAYTIME DRAMA SERIES

Susan Lucci, (Role: Erica), *All My Children* (ABC)

☐ Dorothy Lyman, (Role: Opal Gardner), *All My Children* (ABC)

Leslie Charleson, (Role: Monica Quartermaine), *General Hospital* (ABC)

Erica Slezak, (Role: Victoria Buchanan), *One Life to Live* (ABC)

Robin Strasser, (Role: Dorian Lord Callison), *One Life to Live* (ABC)

☐ Indicates winner

OUTSTANDING ACTOR IN A SUPPORTING ROLE IN A DAYTIME DRAMA SERIES

☐ Darnell Williams, (Role: Jesse Hubbard), *All My Children* (ABC)

Howard E. Rollins Jr., (Role: Ed Harding), *Another World* (NBC)

David Lewis, (Role: Edward Quartermaine), *General Hospital* (ABC)

John Stamos, (Role: Blackie Parrish), *General Hospital* (ABC)

Anthony Call, (Role: Herb Callison), *One Life to Live* (ABC)

Al Freeman Jr., (Role: Ed Hall), *One Life to Live* (ABC)

OUTSTANDING ACTRESS IN A SUPPORTING ROLE IN A DAYTIME DRAMA SERIES

Eileen Herlie, (Role: Myrtle Fargate), *All My Children* (ABC)

Kim Delaney, (Role: Jenny Gardner), *All My Children* (ABC)

Marcy Walker, (Role: Liza Colby), *All My Children* (ABC)

Robin Mattson, (Role: Heather Webber), *General Hospital* (ABC)

Brynn Thayer, (Role: Jenny Janssen), *One Life to Live* (ABC)

☐ Louise Shaffer, (Role: Rae Woodard), *Ryan's Hope* (ABC)

OUTSTANDING HOST/HOSTESS IN A GAME OR AUDIENCE PARTICIPATION SHOW

Dick Clark, *The New $25,000 Pyramid* (CBS)

Richard Dawson, *Family Feud* (ABC)

☐ Betty White, *Just Men!* (NBC)

OUTSTANDING HOST/HOSTESS IN A TALK/SERVICE SERIES

Gary Collins, *Hour Magazine* (Syndicated)

☐ Phil Donahue, *Donahue* (Syndicated)

Mary Martin, *Over Easy* (PBS)

OUTSTANDING HOST/HOSTESS IN A VARIETY SERIES

Merv Griffin, *The Merv Show* (Syndicated)

Peter Marshall, *Fantasy* (NBC)

☐ Leslie Uggams, *Fantasy* (NBC)

OUTSTANDING PERFORMER IN CHILDREN'S PROGRAMMING

Kevin Dobson, (Role: Jim Welsh), "Help Wanted," *CBS Afternoon Playhouse*, October 12, 1982 (CBS)

☐ Cloris Leachman, (Role: May Lemke), "The Woman Who Willed a Miracle," *ABC Afterschool Special* (ABC)

Molly Picon, (Role: Grandma), "Grandma Didn't Wave Back," *Young People's Special* (Syndicated)

Lynn Redgrave, (Role: Sarah Cotter), "The Shooting," *CBS Afternoon Playhouse* (CBS)

6/TV STATIONS REPORTING PROFIT OR LOSS BY AMOUNT OF PROFIT OR LOSS, 1967-1980

THE FOLLOWING TABLES provide more detailed data than the overview in the previous section.

Once again, the advantages of VHF and network affiliation are obvious. In 1976, for example, whereas 53 VHF stations enjoyed profits of $5 million or more, only one independent UHF station could boast similar earnings—and 1976 was the first time in TV history that a independent UHF station earned more than $5 million in profits.

All tables are from F.C.C. Annual Reports.

1967

Item	Total VHF	Total UHF	Network Affilated VHF	Network Affilated UHF	Independent VHF	Independent UHF
Total number of stations reporting	449	105	424	79	25	26
Number of stations reporting profits	374	44	356	42	18	2
Profitable stations as percent of total	83.3	41.9	84.0	53.2	72.0	7.7
Number of stations reporting profits of:						
$5,000,000 or over	17	—	16	—	1	—
$3,000,000 to $5,000,000	16	—	16	—	—	—
$1,500,000 to $3,000,000	41	—	37	—	4	—
$1,000,000 to $1,500,000	28	—	28	—	—	—
$600,000 to $1,000,000	33	—	28	—	5	—
$400,000 to $600,000	21	—	20	—	1	—
$200,000 to $400,000	91	12	87	11	4	1
$100,000 to $200,000	47	11	45	10	2	1
$50,000 to $100,000	29	7	29	7	—	—
$25,000 to $50,000	22	5	22	5	—	—
Less than $25,000	29	9	28	9	1	—
Number of stations reporting losses	75	61	68	37	7	24
Unprofitable stations as percent of total	16.7	58.1	16.0	46.8	28.0	92.3
Number of stations reporting losses of:						
Less than $10,000	9	3	8	2	1	1
$10,000 to $25,000	11	6	11	5	—	1
$25,000 to $50,000	7	10	6	7	1	3
$50,000 to $100,000	14	13	14	9	—	4
$100,000 to $200,000	13	8	12	6	1	2
$200,000 to $400,000	11	7	10	5	1	2
$400,000 and over	10	14	7	3	3	11

Excludes part-time stations and satellite stations. Profits are before federal income tax.

1968

Item	Total VHF	Total UHF	Network Affiliated VHF	Network Affiliated UHF	Independent VHF	Independent UHF
Total number of stations reporting	452	118	422	81	30	37
Number of stations reporting profits	387	53	367	51	20	2
Profitable stations as percent of total	85.6	44.9	87.0	63.0	66.7	5.4
Number of stations reporting profits of:						
$5,000,000 or over	22	—	20	—	2	—
$3,000,000 to $5,000,000	16	—	15	—	1	—
$1,500,000 to $3,000,000	53	—	48	—	5	—
$1,000,000 to $1,500,000	31	—	30	—	1	—
$600,000 to $1,000,000	33	—	29	—	4	—
$400,000 to $600,000	34	2	33	2	1	—
$200,000 to $400,000	85	11	83	10	2	1
$100,000 to $200,000	45	8	44	8	1	—
$50,000 to $100,000	34	18	32	17	2	1
$25,000 to $50,000	19	6	18	6	1	—
Less than $25,000	15	8	15	8	—	—
Number of stations reporting losses	65	65	55	30	10	35
Unprofitable stations as percent of total	14.4	55.1	13.0	37.0	33.3	94.6
Number of stations reporting losses of:						
Less than $10,000	7	3	7	3	—	—
$10,000 to $25,000	4	2	4	2	—	—
$25,000 to $50,000	9	6	9	5	—	1
$50,000 to $100,000	12	11	11	8	1	3
$100,000 to $200,000	16	14	14	8	2	6
$200,000 to $400,000	10	12	6	2	4	10
$400,000 and over	7	17	4	2	3	15

Excludes part-time stations and satellite stations. Profits are before Federal income tax.

1969

Item	Total VHF	Total UHF	Network Affiliated VHF	Network Affiliated UHF	Independent VHF	Independent UHF
Number of stations reporting	456	142	422	94	34	48
Stations reporting profits	378	50	357	48	21	2
Profitable stations as percent of total	82.9	35.2	84.6	51.1	61.8	4.2
Number of stations reporting profits of:						
$5,000,000 or over	24		23		1	
$3,000,000 to $5,000,000	20		17		3	
$1,500,000 to $3,000,000	56		52		4	
$1,000,000 to $1,500,000	32		30		2	
$600,000 to $1,000,000	35	1	33	1	2	
$400,000 to $600,000	39	1	36	1	3	
$200,000 to $400,000	73	12	71	12	2	
$100,000 to $200,000	39	10	36	9	3	1
$50,000 to $100,000	28	13	28	12		1
$25,000 to $50,000	20	8	20	8		
Less than $25,000	12	5	11	5	1	
Stations reporting losses	78	92	65	46	13	46
Unprofitable stations as percent of total	17.1	64.8	15.4	48.9	38.2	95.8
Stations reporting losses of:						
Less than $10,000	4	2	4	2		
$10,000 to $25,000	9	3	9	3		
$25,000 to $50,000	12	7	11	7	1	
$50,000 to $100,000	18	10	18	7		3
$100,000 to $200,000	13	18	10	10	3	8
$200,000 to $400,000	13	19	9	9	4	10
$400,000 and over	9	33	4	8	5	25

Excludes part-time stations and satellite stations. Profits are before Federal income tax.

1970

Item	Total VHF	Total UHF	Network Affilated VHF	Network Affilated UHF	Independent VHF	Independent UHF
Number of stations reporting	453	146	424	98	29	48
Stations reporting profits	373	47	355	42	18	5
Profitable stations as percent of total	82.3	32.2	83.7	42.9	62.1	10.4
Number of stations reporting profits of:						
$5,000,000 or over	19		18		1	
$3,000,000 to $5,000,000	24		22		2	
$1,500,000 to $3,000,000	46		42		4	
$1,000,000 to $1,500,000	34		33		1	
$600,000 to $1,000,000	30		27		3	
$400,000 to $600,000	33	4	32	4	1	
$200,000 to $400,000	68	5	65	5	3	
$100,000 to $200,000	54	11	51	10	3	1
$50,000 to $100,000	25	13	25	12		1
$25,000 to $50,000	22	4	22	2		2
Less than $25,000	18	10	18	9		1
Stations reporting losses	80	99	69	56	11	43
Unprofitable stations as percent of total	17.7	67.8	16.3	57.1	37.9	89.6
Stations reporting losses of:						
Less than $10,000	5	2	5	2		
$10,000 to $25,000	10	9	10	9		
$25,000 to $50,000	8	8	8	7		1
$50,000 to $100,000	24	13	22	9	2	4
$100,000 to $200,000	10	14	7	9	3	5
$200,000 to $400,000	15	19	13	14	2	5
$400,000 and over	8	34	4	6	4	28

Excludes part-time stations and satellite stations. Profits are before Federal income tax.

1971

Item	Total VHF	Total UHF	Network Affilated VHF	Network Affilated UHF	Independent VHF	Independent UHF
Number of stations reporting	453	149	422	101	31	48
Stations reporting profits	366	47	352	41	14	6
Profitable stations as percent of total	80.8	31.5	83.4	40.6	45.2	12.5
Stations reporting profits of:						
$5,000,000 or over	14	—	14	—	—	—
$3,000,000 to $5,000,000	22	—	22	—	—	—
$1,500,000 to $3,000,000	36	—	32	—	4	—
$1,000,000 to $1,500,000	41	—	38	—	3	—
$600,000 to $1,000,000	33	1	31	—	2	1
$400,000 to $600,000	40	3	57	3	3	—
$200,000 to $400,000	64	8	63	7	1	1
$100,000 to $200,000	46	11	45	9	1	2
$50,000 to $100,000	36	9	36	8	—	1
$25,000 to $50,000	15	5	15	5	—	—
Less than $25,000	19	10	19	9	—	1
Stations reporting losses	87	102	70	60	17	42
Unprofitable stations as percent of total	19.2	68.5	16.6	60.0	53.1	85.7
Stations reporting losses of:						
Less than $10,000	5	4	4	3	1	1
$10,000 to $25,000	9	8	9	8	—	—
$25,000 to $50,000	15	8	14	7	1	1
$50,000 to $100,000	16	16	15	11	1	5
$100,000 to $200,000	19	19	16	15	3	4
$200,000 to $400,000	14	20	10	13	4	7
$400,000 and over	9	27	2	3	7	24

Excludes part-time stations and satellite stations. Profits are before Federal income tax.

1972

Item	Total VHF	Total UHF	Network Affilated VHF	Network Affilated UHF	Independent VHF	Independent UHF
Number of stations reporting	461	164	428	111	3	53
Stations reporting profits	395	72	373	61	22	11
Profitable stations as percent of total	85.7	43.9	87.1	55.0	66.7	20.8
Stations reporting profits of:						
$5,000,000 or over	15		15			
$3,000,000 to $5,000,000	24		22		2	
$1,500,000 to $3,000,000	53		49		4	
$1,000,000 to $1,500,000	40	1	36		4	1
$600,000 to $1,000,000	37	2	35		2	2
$400,000 to $600,000	46	4	44	4	2	
$200,000 to $400,000	69	15	64	12	5	3
$100,000 to $200,000	50	15	48	13	2	2
$50,000 to $100,000	33	8	33	7		1
$25,000 to $50,000	13	10	13	10		
Less than $25,000	15	17	14	15	1	2
Stations reporting losses	66	92	55	50	11	42
Unprofitable stations as percent of total	14.3	56.1	12.9	45.0	33.3	79.2
Stations reporting losses of:						
Less than $10,000	7	3	6	3	1	
$10,000 to $25,000	6	3	6	3		
$25,000 to $50,000	8	11	8	8		3
$50,000 to $100,000	11	15	9	10	2	5
$100,000 to $200,000	14	20	13	13	1	7
$200,000 to $400,000	13	18	8	10	5	8
$400,000 and over	7	22	5	3	2	19

Excludes part-time stations and satellite stations. Profits are before Federal income tax.

1973

Item	Total VHF	Total UHF	Network Affilated VHF	Network Affilated UHF	Independent VHF	Independent UHF
Number of stations reporting	457	165	425	112	32	53
Stations reporting profits	395	77	374	61	21	16
Profitable stations as percent of total	86.4	46.6	88.0	54.5	65.6	30.2
Stations reporting profits of:						
$5,000,000 or over	18	—	18	—	—	—
$3,000,000 to $5,000,000	26	—	25	—	1	—
$1,500,000 to $3,000,000	56	1	51	—	5	1
$1,000,000 to $1,500,000	37	—	33	—	4	—
$600,000 to $1,000,000	44	6	41	4	3	2
$400,000 to $600,000	40	6	39	5	1	1
$200,000 to $400,000	66	16	60	13	6	3
$100,000 to $200,000	45	12	45	9	—	3
$50,000 to $100,000	27	16	26	15	1	1
$25,000 to $50,000	16	7	16	4	—	3
Less than $25,000	20	13	20	11	1	2
Stations reporting losses	62	88	51	51	11	37
Unprofitable stations as percent of total	13.6	53.3	12.0	45.5	34.4	69.8
Stations reporting losses of:						
Less than $10,000	4	2	4	1	1	1
$10,000 to $25,000	4	9	4	5	—	4
$25,000 to $50,000	6	9	6	7	—	2
$50,000 to $100,000	18	18	17	13	1	5
$100,000 to $200,000	12	15	7	9	5	6
$200,000 to $400,000	12	18	10	14	2	4
$400,000 and over	6	17	3	2	3	15

Excludes part-time stations and satellite stations. Profits are before Federal income tax.

1974

Item	Total VHF	Total UHF	Network Affiliated VHF	Network Affiliated UHF	Independent VHF	Independent UHF
Total Number of stations reporting	464	167	433	122	31	55
Number stations reporting profits	395	80	378	64	17	16
Profitable stations as percent of total	85.1	47.9	87.3	57.1	54.8	29.1
Number of stations reporting profits of:						
$5,000,000 or over	23	—	23	—	—	—
$3,000,000 to $5,000,000	24	—	24	—	—	—
$1,500,000 to $3,000,000	62	1	56	—	6	1
$1,000,000 to $1,500,000	36	1	34	1	2	—
$600,000 to $1,000,000	50	7	46	4	4	3
$400,000 to $600,000	39	5	38	3	1	2
$200,000 to $400,000	68	20	66	18	2	2
$100,000 to $200,000	48	13	47	12	1	1
$50,000 to $100,000	22	13	21	10	1	3
$25,000 to $50,000	7	8	7	6	—	2
Less than $25,000	16	12	16	10	—	2
Number of stations reporting losses	69	87	55	48	14	39
Unprofitable stations as percent of total	14.9	52.1	12.7	42.9	45.2	70.9
Number of stations reporting losses of:						
Less than $10,000	4	3	4	3	—	—
$10,000 to $25,000	4	5	4	2	—	3
$25,000 to $50,000	13	11	13	10	—	1
$50,000 to $100,000	9	14	7	7	2	7
$100,000 to $200,000	13	22	8	11	5	11
$200,000 to $400,000	15	17	15	12	—	5
$400,000 and over	11	15	4	3	7	12

Stations operating full year only, excluding satellite stations. Profits are before Federal income tax.

1975

Item	Total VHF	Total UHF	Network Affiliated VHF	Network Affiliated UHF	Independent VHF	Independent UHF
Total number of stations reporting	462	166	432	114	30	52
Number of stations reporting profits	398	86	376	59	22	27
Profitable stations as percent of total	86.1	51.8	87.0	51.8	73.3	51.9
Number of stations reporting profits of:						
$5,000,000 or over	24	—	24	—	—	—
$3,000,000 to $5,000,000	32	—	29	—	3	—
$1,500,000 to $3,000,000	60	1	54	—	6	1
$1,000,000 to $1,500,000	40	4	38	1	2	3
$600,000 to $1,000,000	52	5	49	3	3	2
$400,000 to $600,000	51	9	48	7	3	2
$200,000 to $400,000	53	21	51	15	2	6
$100,000 to $200,000	46	17	44	12	2	5
$50,000 to $100,000	23	15	22	11	1	4
$25,000 to $50,000	5	5	5	4	—	1
Less than $25,000	12	9	12	6	—	3
Number of stations reporting losses	64	80	56	58	8	25
Unprofitable stations as percent of total	13.9	48.2	13.0	48.2	26.7	48.1
Number of stations reporting losses of:						
Less than $10,000	7	5	7	4	—	1
$10,000 to $25,000	7	8	7	6	—	2
$25,000 to $50,000	6	5	5	4	1	1
$50,000 to $100,000	14	23	14	19	—	4
$100,000 to $200,000	7	16	5	8	2	8
$200,000 to $400,000	10	13	9	9	1	4
$400,000 and over	13	10	9	5	4	5

Stations operating full year only, excluding satellite stations. Profits are before Federal income tax.

1976

Item	Total VHF	Total UHF	Network Affilated VHF	Network Affilated UHF	Independent VHF	Independent UHF
Total number of stations reporting	460	178	430	117	30	61
Number of stations reporting profits	418	119	393	80	25	39
Profitable stations as percent of total	90.9	66.9	91.4	68.4	83.3	63.9
Number of stations reporting profits of:						
$5,000,000 or over	53	1	46	0	7	1
$3,000,000 to $5,000,000	33	4	29	0	4	4
$1,500,000 to $3,000,000	78	6	72	1	6	5
$1,000,000 to $1,500,000	49	6	48	2	1	4
$600,000 to $1,000,000	55	22	54	14	1	8
$400,000 to $600,000	32	14	32	13	0	1
$200,000 to $400,000	68	21	62	17	6	4
$100,000 to $200,000	21	17	21	11	0	6
$50,000 to $100,000	15	14	15	12	0	2
$25,000 to $50,000	4	8	4	6	0	2
Less than $25,000	10	6	10	4	0	2
Number of stations reporting losses	42	59	37	37	5	22
Unprofitable stations as percent of total	9.1	33.1	8.6	31.6	16.7	36.1
Number of stations reporting losses of:						
Less than $10,000	2	6	2	5	0	1
$10,000 to $25,000	4	4	3	2	1	2
$25,000 to $50,000	6	12	5	8	1	4
$50,000 to $100,000	15	11	14	7	1	4
$100,000 to $200,000	7	12	6	9	1	3
$200,000 to $400,000	4	10	4	5	0	5
$400,000 and over	4	4	3	1	1	3

Stations operating full year only, excluding satellite stations. Profits are before federal income tax.

1977

Item	Total VHF	Total UHF	Network Affilated VHF	Network Affilated UHF	Independent VHF	Independent UHF
Total number of stations reporting	458	173	429	117	29	56
Number of stations reporting profits	422	127	397	89	25	38
Profitable stations as percent of total	92.1	73.4	92.5	76.1	86.2	67.9
Number of stations reporting profits of:						
$5,000,000 or over	49	1	42		7	1
$3,000,000 to $5,000,000	48	4	43		5	4
$1,500,000 to $3,000,000	79	9	72	1	7	8
$1,000,000 to $1,500,000	51	6	51	2		4
$600,000 to $1,000,000	50	18	49	14	1	4
$400,000 to $600,000	43	20	41	15	2	5
$200,000 to $400,000	38	20	36	17	2	3
$100,000 to $200,000	31	17	30	13	1	4
$50,000 to $100,000	12	14	12	13		1
$25,000 to $50,000	12	10	12	8		2
Less than $25,000	9	8	9	6		2
Number of stations reporting losses	36	46	32	28	4	18
Unprofitable stations as percent of total	7.9	26.6	7.5	23.9	13.8	32.1
Number of stations reporting losses of:						
Less than $10,000	5	2	5	1		1
$10,000 to $25,000	1	5	1	4		1
$25,000 to $50,000	4	3	3	3	1	
$50,000 to $100,000	3	13	3	8		5
$100,000 to $200,000	9	11	8	6	1	5
$200,000 to $400,000	7	6	7	4		2
$400,000 and over	7	6	5	2	2	4

Stations operating full year only, excluding satellite stations. Profits are before federal income tax.

1978

Item	Total VHF	Total UHF	Network Affilated VHF	Network Affilated UHF	Independent VHF	Independent UHF
Total number of stations reporting	461	186	432	116	29	70
Number of stations reporting profits	426	136	402	96	24	40
Profitable stations as percent of total	92.4	73.1	93.1	82.8	82.8	57.1
Number of stations reporting profits of:						
$15,000,000 and over	7		7			
$10,000,000 to $15,000,000	15		13		3	
$5,000,000 to $10,000,000	42	1	37		5	1
$3,000,000 to $5,000,000	62	9	54		8	9
$1,500,000 to $3,000,000	79	10	76	4	3	6
$1,000,000 to $1,500,000	48	10	47	9	1	1
$600,000 to $1,000,000	56	24	55	16	1	8
$400,000 to $600,000	38	20	38	18		2
$200,000 to $400,000	33	22	30	16	3	6
$100,000 to $200,000	15	11	15	10		1
$50,000 to $100,000	20	9	20	8		1
$25,000 to $50,000	3	8	3	7		1
Less than $25,000	7	12	7	8		4
Number of stations reporting losses	35	50	30	20	5	30
Unprofitable stations as percent of total	7.6	26.9	6.9	17.2	17.2	42.9
Number of stations reporting losses of:						
Less than $10,000	3	3	3	2		1
$10,000 to $25,000	4	3	4	2		1
$25,000 to $50,000	3	5	2	1	1	4
$50,000 to $100,000	4	6	3	3	1	3
$100,000 to $200,000	9	12	8	3	1	9
$200,000 to $400,000	5	10	5	5		5
$400,000 and over	7	11	5	4	2	7

Stations operating full year only, excluding satellites. Profits are before federal income tax.

1979

Item	Total VHF	Total UHF	Network Affilated VHF	Network Affilated UHF	Independent VHF	Independent UHF
Total number of stations reporting	455	184	428	117	27	67
Number of stations reporting profits	408	122	387	89	21	33
Profitable stations as percent of total	89.7	66.3	90.4	76.1	77.8	49.3
Number of stations reporting profits of:						
$15,000,000 and over	10		9		1	
$10,000,000 to $15,000,000	18		14		4	
$5,000,000 to $10,000,000	47	2	42		5	2
$3,000,000 to $5,000,000	57	9	51	1	6	8
$1,500,000 to $3,000,000	71	7	70	1	1	6
$1,000,000 to $1,500,000	46	8	46	6		2
$600,000 to $1,000,000	47	24	47	17		7
$400,000 to $600,000	30	15	29	14	1	1
$200,000 to $400,000	33	25	33	20		5
$100,000 to $200,000	25	8	23	8	2	
$50,000 to $100,000	10	11	10	10		1
$25,000 to $50,000	8	6	7	5	1	1
Less than $25,000	6	7	6	7		
Number of stations reporting losses	47	62	41	28	6	34
Unprofitable stations as percent of total	10.3	33.7	9.6	23.9	22.2	50.7
Number of stations reporting losses of:						
Less than $10,000	2	1	2			1
$10,000 to $25,000	2	5	2	5		
$25,000 to $50,000	4	5	4	2		3
$50,000 to $100,000	6	6	5	2	1	4
$100,000 to $200,000	12	10	12	5		5
$200,000 to $400,000	8	11	8	7		4
$400,000 and over	13	24	8	7	5	17

Stations operating full year only, excluding satellites. Profits are before federal income tax.

1980

Item	Total VHF	Total UHF	Network Affilated VHF	Network Affilated UHF	Independent VHF	Independent UHF
Total number of stations reporting	453	197	424	116	29	81
Number of stations reporting profits	401	115	378	78	23	37
Profitable stations as percent of total	88.5	58.4	89.2	67.2	79.3	45.7
Number of stations reporting profits of:						
$15,000,000 and over	14		14			
$10,000,000 to $15,000,000	17		13		4	
$5,000,000 to $10,000,000	46	4	38		8	4
$3,000,000 to $5,000,000	55	5	50		5	5
$1,500,000 to $3,000,000	70	12	68	5	2	7
$1,000,000 to $1,500,000	41	6	40	3	1	3
$600,000 to $1,000,000	55	18	54	15	1	3
$400,000 to $600,000	32	17	31	13	1	4
$200,000 to $400,000	34	14	33	12	1	2
$100,000 to $200,000	17	18	17	15		3
$50,000 to $100,000	14	3	14	2		1
$25,000 to $50,000	4	11	4	10		1
Less than $25,000	2	7	2	3		4
Number of stations reporting losses	52	82	46	38	6	44
Unprofitable stations as percent of total	11.5	41.6	10.8	32.8	20.7	54.3
Number of stations reporting losses of:						
Less than $10,000	4	3	4	1		2
$10,000 to $25,000	2		2			
$25,000 to $50,000	3	6	3	2		4
$50,000 to $100,000	2	9	2	8		1
$100,000 to $200,000	7	7	6	4	1	3
$200,000 to $400,000	13	11	13	5		6
$400,000 and over	21	46	16	18	5	28

Stations operating full year only, excluding satellite and religious stations. Profits are before federal income tax.

7/Network Profits vs. Station Profits

MEDIA WATCHDOG GROUPS have often complained that the networks are simply too big—too powerful, too profitable.

The following table would do little to invalidate that complaint. In 1977 the networks and their fifteen owned and operated stations captured 40% of all TV profits. The other 682 stations had 60% of the market. This 40/60 split was typical of the industry almost from its beginnings through 1977. In the late 1970s, however, the networks' share of profits began to drop, falling to 32% by 1980, a loss repeatedly bemoaned by the networks. Despite this drastic reduction, the networks still, it should be remembered, capture a hefty one-third of all industry profits.

Media activists have frequently advocated that the networks should be divested of their owned and operated stations to diminish their power. The networks have replied that without their owned and operated stations, they wouldn't make enough money to survive.

It is true that in the 1950s the webs' O & O stations accounted for more profits than the webs themselves: in 1959, for example, the webs earned $32 million in profits (14% of all industry profits), while their 15 owned and operated stations could boast of $55.9 million in profits (25% of industry profits). But by the mid-1970s, that ratio was reversed, as the webs made much *more* money than their O & Os. In 1977, for example, network profits amounted to a staggering $406.1 million (29% of the industry), while the 15 owned and operated stations made $149.3 million in profits (11%).

NETWORK PROFITS vs. STATION PROFITS

Year	Network Profits (In Million $)	(%)	Network's O&O Profits (In Millions $)	(%)	Total NetWork Profits (In Millions $)	(%)	All Other Station's Profits (In Millions $)	(%)
1951					$11.0	(26.4%)	30.6	(73.6%)
1952					10.0	(18.0%)	45.7	(82.0%)
1953					18.0	(25.2%)	53.3	(74.8%)
1954					36.5	(40.4%)	53.8	(59.6%)
1955					68.1	(45.3%)	82.1	(54.7%)
1956					85.4	(45.0%)	104.2	(55.0%)
1957					70.7	(44.1%)	89.3	(55.9%)
1958					77.0	(44.8%)	94.9	(55.2%)
1959	32.0	(14.4%)	55.9	(25.1%)	87.9	(39.5%)	134.4	(60.5%)
1960	33.6	(13.8%)	61.6	(25.2%)	95.2	(39.0%)	148.9	(61.0%)
1961	24.7	(10.4%)	62.3	(26.3%)	87.0	(36.7%)	150.0	(63.3%)
1962	36.7	(11.8%)	74.7	(24.0%)	111.4	(35.8%)	200.2	(64.2%)
1963	56.4	(16.4%)	79.8	(23.3%)	136.2	(39.7%)	207.0	(60.3%)
1964	60.2	(14.5%)	96.3	(23.2%)	156.5	(37.7%)	259.1	(62.3%)
1965	59.4	(13.3%)	102.2	(22.8%)	161.6	(36.1%)	286.3	(63.9%)
1966	78.7	(16.0%)	108.1	(21.9%)	186.8	(37.9%)	306.1	(62.1%)
1967	55.8	(13.5%)	104.3	(25.1%)	160.1	(38.6%)	254.5	(61.4%)
1968	56.4	(11.4%)	122.4	(24.8%)	178.8	(36.2%)	316.0	(63.8%)
1969	92.7	(16.8%)	133.4	(24.0%)	226.1	(40.8%)	327.5	(59.2%)
1970	50.1	(11.0%)	117.3	(25.9%)	167.4	(36.9%)	286.4	(63.1%)
1971	53.7	(13.8%)	91.2	(23.4%)	144.9	(37.2%)	244.3	(62.8%)
1972	110.9	(20.1%)	102.5	(18.6%)	213.4	(38.7%)	338.8	(61.3%)
1973	184.8	(28.2%)	102.8	(15.8%)	287.6	(44.0%)	365.4	(56.0%)
1974	225.1	(30.6%)	105.7	(14.3%)	330.8	(44.9%)	406.3	(55.1%)
1975	208.5	(26.7%)	105.7	(13.5%)	314.2	(40.2%)	466.1	(59.8%)
1976	295.6	(23.7%)	159.0	(12.7%)	454.6	(36.4%)	795.6	(63.6%)
1977	406.1	(29.0%)	149.3	(10.6%)	555.4	(39.6%)	845.7	(60.4%)
1978	373.5	(22.5%)	186.3	(11.2%)	559.8	(33.8%)	1,093.5	(66.1%)
1979	370.2	(21.9%)	205.1	(12.1%)	575.3	(34.0%)	1,114.9	(65.9%)
1980	325.6	(19.6%)	208.1	(12.5%)	533.7	(32.2%)	1,119.8	(67.6%)

All profits are before federal income tax. Figures compiled from F.C.C. Annual Reports.

8/GROUP OWNERSHIP OF TV STATIONS

TV STATIONS ARE potentially so profitable that it's not surprising that an individual or company should want to own more than one: group stations ownership has been an industry phenomenon since TV's first days, as the following chart shows.

The F.C.C., for obvious reasons, has been wary of multiple station ownership. In 1940 the Commission limited broadcast ownership to three television stations and six FM radio stations. Revisions were made in 1944 to allow five TV stations to be owned by any one individual or group.

Regulations were once again revised in November 1953 and September 1954 which stipulated that a company or person could own seven AM and seven FM radio stations as well as seven TV stations, no more than five of which could be VHF.

In 1975 only four groups owned the maximum complement of seven stations; nine companies had six stations; 14 owned five stations; 27 groups had four stations; and 25 owned three TV stations.

GROUP OWNERSHIP OF TV STATIONS

Year	Number of Groups	Number of Group-Owned Stations	Total Commercial Stations	% of Group Control
1948	3	6	16	37.5%
1949	10	24	51	47.1
1950	17	52	98	53.1
1951	19	53	107	49.5
1952	19	53	108	49.1
1953	38	104	126	82.5
1954	48	126	354	35.6
1955	62	165	411	40.1
1956	60	173	441	39.2
1957	65	192	471	40.8
1958	82	241	495	48.7
1959	85	249	510	48.8
1960	84	252	515	48.9
1961	87	260	527	49.3
1962	89	268	541	49.5
1963	97	280	557	50.3
1964	106	299	564	53.0
1965	109	310	569	54.5
1966	111	324	585	55.4
(Data for 1967-1974 not available.)				
1975	115	405	711	57.0
1976	119	415	710	58.0

9/Top 15 Group Owners, 1959, 1967, 1975

1959

Ownership Unit	Number of Stations Owned	Net Weekly Circulation (millions)	Percent of Households
1. CBS	5	11.3	22%
2. RCA (NBC)	5	10.8	21
3. ABC	5	9.6	19
4. RKO General	4	5.4	11
5. Westinghouse	5	4.7	9
6. WGN-Continental	2	4.5	9
7. Metropolitan	4	3.9	8
8. Storer	5	3.3	6
9. Triangle	6	2.8	5
10. Avco	5	1.9	4
11. Scripps-Howard	3	1.9	4
12. Newhouse	6	1.8	4
13. Hearst	3	1.7	3
14. Times-Mirror	1	1.7	3
15. Time Inc.	4	1.6	3

1967

Ownership Unit	Number of Stations Owned	Net Weekly Circulation (millions)	Percent of Households
1. CBS	5	13.9	23%
2. ABC	5	13.3	22
3. RCA (NBC)	5	13.3	22
4. Metromedia	4	9.1	15
5. RKO	5	7.9	13
6. Group W	5	7.0	12
7. WGN-Continental	4	6.7	11
8. Storer	6	4.5	8
9. Cox	5	3.7	6
10. Triangle	6	3.5	6
11. Chris-Craft	3	3.1	5
12. Taft	6	3.0	5
13. Autry-Golden West	3	2.7	5
14. Scripps-Howard	4	2.6	4
15. Avco	5	2.6	4

1975

Ownership Unit	Number of Stations Owned	Net Weekly Circulation (millions)	Percent of Households
1. CBS	5	15.1	22%
2. RCA (NBC)	5	14.5	21
3. ABC	5	14.5	21
4. Metromedia	6	11.7	17
5. RKO	4	8.7	13
6. Westinghouse	5	8.6	12
7. WGN-Continental	4	7.3	11
8. Kaiser	7	6.2	9
9. Capital Cities	6	5.1	7
10. Storer	7	5.0	7
11. Cox	5	4.5	6
12. Taft	6	4.3	6
13. WKY-System	6	3.4	5
14. Scripps-Howard	5	3.3	5
15. Post-Newsweek	4	3.3	5

Note: "Net Weekly Circulation" figures indicate how many millions of households are served by each of the group owners. "Percent of Households" represent the proportion of households included in the market in which each group owner operates.

10/NEWSPAPER/TV CROSS-OWNERSHIP

THE FOLLOWING TABLE provides information on newspaper/TV station cross-ownership. Such cross-ownership has been the target of heated debate for decades—ever since newspaper began buying up radio stations in the 1930s.

Cross-ownership has decreased since television's early years, when in 1953 an alarming 69% of all TV stations were owned by newspapers. Today approximately one quarter of all TV stations are owned by newspaper publishers. And today's cross-ownership is less likely to be within the same market than it was in previous years: in 1955, for example, 82% of newspaper-owned TV stations operated in the same community as the owning newspaper. By 1974, the percentage had decreased to 46%.

Under current F.C.C. regulations, same-market newspaper/TV station cross-ownerships are no longer legal, and existing combinations should be broken up if sold.

NEWSPAPER/TV CROSS-OWNERSHIP

Year	Total TV Stations	Newspaper-Owned	
		Number	Percent of Total
1949	51	13	25.5%
1950	98	41	41.8%
1951	107	45	42.1%
1952	108	49	45.4%
1953	126	87	69.0%
1954	354	130	36.7%
1955	411	149	36.3%
1956	441	160	36.3%
1957	471	156	33.1%
1958	495	168	33.9%
1959	510	181	35.5%
1960	515	175	33.9%
1961	527	n.a.	n.a.
1962	541	161	29.8%
1963	557	n.a.	n.a.
1964	564	174	30.9%
1965	569	181	31.8%
1966	585	174	29.7%
1967	610	172	28.2%
1968	635	177	27.9%
1969	662	183	27.6%
1970	677	189	27.9%
1971	682	191	28.0%
1972	693	176	25.4%
1973	697	178	25.5%
1974	697	179	25.7%
1975	711	193	27.1%
1976	710	n.a.	n.a.
1977	728	209	28.7%

Source: *The Mass Media: Aspen Institute Guide to Communication Industry Trends.* All data is as of January 1 of each year and figured on stations actually on-air, with these exceptions: 1965 is actually as of October 31, 1964; 1970 is actually December 1, 1969; 1975 is actually December 1, 1974; and 1977 is actually December 1, 1976.
"Total" column includes only commercial stations.
Because the courses of these statistics are numerous, caution should be taken in making strict year-to-year comparisons.

11/NETWORK/STATION EMPLOYMENT

THE TELEVISION INDUSTRY was not a large one in the late 1940s: the F.C.C. had "frozen" TV licenses and the industry's growth was inhibited. But once the freeze was lifted in 1952, the industry was off and running: the 1954 TV employment was twice that of 1952. Employment increases were gradual after that first great advance: it would take another 20 years for TV employment to double once again.

How does TV employment compare with radio's? Although TV is now the bigger moneymaker and the more influential of the two media, radio employs more people. For example:

	Total Radio Employment	Total TV Employment
1952	51,000	14,000
1957	48,900	37,800
1962	56,100	41,900
1967	67,200	51,700
1972	76,200	59,300
1976	86,300	64,800

Remember, the statistics listed below are for station/network employment. They do not include people in Hollywood film production.

Figures are compiled from F.C.C. reports.

NETWORK/STATION EMPLOYMENT

Year	Total TV Employees	Networks	All Other Stations	(15 Network O&O Stations)
1949	3,800			
1950	9,000			
1951	n.a.			
1952	14,000			
1953	18,200			
1954	29,400			
1955	32,300			
1956	35,700			
1957	37,800			
1958	39,400			
1959	40,300			
1960	40,600	9,600	31,000	
1961	40,100	8,800	31,300	
1962	41,900	9,100	32,800	
1963	43,700	9,700	34,000	
1964	45,700	10,700	35,000	(3,500)
1965	47,700	11,000	36,700	(3,700)
1966	50,300	11,200	39,100	(4,000)
1967	51,700	11,500	40,200	(3,900)
1968	53,300	12,200	43,100	(4,100)
1969	57,800	12,900	44,900	(4,600)
1970	58,400	13,200	45,200	(4,700)
1971	58,100	12,000	46,100	(4,700)
1972	59,300	12,400	46,900	(4,800)
1973	60,200	12,400	47,800	(5,000)
1974	61,900	13,200	48,800	(5,100)
1975	62,300	13,300	49,000	(5,100)
1976	64,800	13,800	51,000	(5,200)
1977	67,200	14,200	53,000	(5,400)
1978	70,800	14,600	56,200	(5,400)
1979	75,500	16,000	59,500	(5,600)
1980	78,300	16,600	61,700	(5,800)

Figures are compiled from F.C.C. Annual Reports. Statistics are rounded off to the nearest hundred.

INDEX

BRESSE, Gerry—228
BRET Maverick—299, 300
BREWER, Jameson—219
BREWER, Solomon—244
BREWSTER, Allen—246
BRIAN Keith Show—53
BRIAN'S Song—114, 357, 387
BRIDESHEAD Revisited—299, 300, 301, 303, 350, 367
BRIDGE on the River Kwai—114
BRIDGE, Steve—331
BRIDGES, James—185
BRIDGES, Lloyd—171
BRIDGET Loves Bernie—51, 108, 347
BRIGADOON—190, 191, 192, 387
BRIGGS, Fred—200
BRILL, Fran—227
BRILL, Frank—304
BRILLSTEIN, Bernie—315, 332
BRIM, Peggy—278, 383
BRINCKERHOFF, Burt—260, 269, 284
BRING, Bob—320
BRING 'Em Back Alive—70
BRINGING Up Buddy—26
BRINKERHOFF, Burt—226
BRINKLEY, David—173, 188, 191, 200, 205, 215, 220, 310, 373, 374
BRIOSO, Gerri—240, 262, 291, 328, 329
BRITISH Broadcasting Corp.—178, 195, 353
BRITISH Broadcasting Corporation, Research Department—315
BROADCASTING—361
BROADSIDE—34
BROADWAY '68—The Tony Awards—198
BROADWAY to Hollywood—6, 9, 11, 13
BROAN, Lewis—226
BROCK, Howard—341
BROCK, Keith—248
BROCK, Norris—310, 325
BROCKWAY, Merrill—341, 389
BROCKWAY, Richard—194
BRODERICK, James—249
BRODERICK, John—233, 248
BRODERICK, Lorraine—304, 327, 337
BRODINE, Norbert—168, 170, 172, 174
BRODKIN, Herbert—170, 298, 384
BROEKMAN, David—170
BROKAW, Tom—278
BROKEN Arrow—18, 20
BROKEN Arrow: Can A Nuclear Weapons Accident Happen Here?—361
BROKEN Promise, Pensions: The—357
BROLIN, James—202, 207, 212, 217, 366
BRONCO—24
BRONFMAN, Edgar, Jr.—247
BRONK—56, 237, 245
BRONSON, Charles—179
BRONSON, Michael—298, 316, 328, 338
BRONSTEIN, Marv—331
BRONWELL, William F.—254
BROOKING, Dorothea—263
BROOKS, Bob—390
BROOKS, Chip—254
BROOKS, Donald—301
BROOKS, Foster—222
BROOKS, Geraldine—180
BROOKS, Holly Holmberg—300
BROOKS, James L.—208, 218, 231, 243, 267, 282, 297, 315
BROOKS, Mel—170, 172, 174, 188, 191, 380
BROOKS, Ron—224, 232, 272, 303, 337
BROSTEN, Harve—250
BROTHERS—18
BROUGHTON, Brock—226, 285, 319
BROUGHTON, Bruce—223, 270, 285, 301, 319, 341
BROUN, Heywood Hale—205, 235
BROWN, Andrew—267
BROWN, Barry A.—262
BROWN, Bill—280, 308, 312
BROWN, Bob—233, 266, 278, 279, 295, 296, 313, 324, 331, 332
BROWN, Bryan—317
BROWN, Carl—233

BROWN, D.—331
BROWN, Earl—213, 218, 232, 253, 319, 384
BROWN, Edward R., Sr.—238
BROWN, Elaine Meryl—306
BROWN, Fred—219
BROWN, Gary—248, 258
BROWN, Georg Stanford—284
BROWN, Henry—296
BROWN, James—208
BROWN, Jim—325
BROWN, Joan—297
BROWN, Johnny—223
BROWN, Jon Lomberg—288
BROWN, Les—329
BROWN, Lewis—275
BROWN, Pamela—180, 197
BROWN, Rita Mae—300, 385
BROWN, Robert—259, 261, 293, 294, 313
BROWN, Robert O.—228
BROWN, Roger—293
BROWN, Skip—308
BROWN, Steve—315
BROWN, Susan—263
BROWN, Thomas—253
BROWN, Toby—257
BROWN, W. Earl—286
BROWN, Zack—277
BROWNE, Daniel Gregory—237
BROWNE, Ken—293
BROWNE, Reg—201
BROWNE, Roscoe Lee—236
BROWNING, David—308, 323
BROWNING, Kirk—172, 196, 274, 277, 318, 338
BROWNING, Susan—240
BROYLES, Frank—331
BRUCE Verran—199
BRUCK, Paul—177
BRUM, Alan—330
BRUMETT, Dan—264
BRUNNER, Bob—297
BRUNNER, Robert F.—256
BRUNTON, Greg—253
BRUNTON, Gregory—288, 303
BRUSH, Bob—291, 327
BRYAN, Ron—253
BRYAN, William—213
BRYANT, Bruce—303, 322
BRYANT, Lee—265
BRYANT Quinn, Jane—324
BRYDON, Robert—331
BRYGGMAN, Larry—289, 304, 336
BRYSAC, Shareen Blair—278, 310
BUBBLE Gum Digest—259, 392
BUCCANEERS—19
BUCCI, Gerry—224, 281, 303, 321
BUCHIGNANI, Louis—209
BUCHMAN, Harry—264
BUCICH, Mario—293, 312
BUCK Rogers—6, 121, 285, 286
BUCK Rogers in 25th Century—81, 65, 270, 271
BUCKAGE, Charles—248
BUCKLEY, Bruce—240
BUCKNER, Art—312
BUCKNER, Bob—288
BUCKSKIN—23
BUDA, Edward—279, 297, 311
BUDDY, Can You Spare a Dime?—235
BUFFALO Bill—315, 316, 317, 318, 332, 334, 335, 367
BUFFINTON, Dick—248, 280, 293, 312, 330 331
BUGENHAGEN, Tom—270
BUGLASS, Ralph—382
BUGS Bunny: All American Hero—283
BUGS Bunny's Bustin' Out All Over—273
BUGS Bunny Show—26, 28
BUICK Berle Show—12, 14, 77, 105
BUICK Circus Hour—105
BUJOLD, Genevieve—193
BUKSBAUM, David—295
BULL, Sheldon—315, 332
BULLWINKLE Show—28

BUNIN, Elinor—211, 234, 292
BUNKER—283, 284, 287
BUNNY—225
BUONAMASSA, Eric—314
BURDEN of Shame—183
BURDETT, Winston—196
BURDITT, George—213, 223, 237, 243
BURGENSEN, William—244
BURGER, Thomas—333
BURGESS, Don—331
BURGESS, Jim—328
BURGHOFF, Gary—217, 222, 230, 236, 242, 250, 259
BURKE, Jean Dadario—337
BURKE, Jonnie—204
BURKE, Paul—180, 182
BURKE'S Law—33, 34, 365
BURKE, Tom—253
BURKHART, John—233
BURKS, Mike—293, 312, 331
BURLING, Jerry—246
BURMAN, Ellis—218
BURMAN, Tom—228
BURMESTER, Bruce—327
BURNES, Karen—310
BURNETT, Carol—180, 182, 222, 226, 260, 285, 317, 355, 365, 366, 373, 375, 376, 377
BURNETT "Discovers" Domingo—335
BURNETT, John F.—320
BURNEY, Alfonso—297
BURNHAM, Charlie—239
BURNIER, Jeanine—237
BURNING BED—351, 368
BURNS, Allan—193, 208, 218, 231, 243, 269, 380
BURNS & Allen—166, 167, 169, 171, 175
BURNS & Allen Show—168, 173
BURNS, Bruce—271, 321
BURNS, David—187, 207
BURNS, George—335, 371, 372
BURNS, Jack—243, 381
BURNS, Ralph—271
BURNS & Schreiber Comedy Hour—381
BURNS, Stan—176, 194, 198, 213, 218
BURR, Raymond—175, 177, 179, 193, 197, 202, 207, 212
BURRELL, Jack—166
BURROW, Cathey—168, 320
BURROW, Milton C.—224, 232, 245
BURROW, Richard—224, 232
BURROWS, James—269, 284, 299, 315, 317, 332, 335
BURSTYN, Ellen—283
BURT Bacharach in Shangri-La—219
BURT, C.J.—333
BURTON, Claudio Zeitlin—292
BURTON, Jay—172, 176, 218
BURTON, Levar—242
BURTON, Nelson, Jr.—314
BURTON, Philip, Jr.—308, 324
BURTON, Thomas—292
BURTON, Warren—274
BURTON, Willie D.—245
BURUM, Steve—288
BUS Stop—28, 180, 181
BUSH, Raymond M.—287, 302
BUSH, Warren V.—201, 206, 215
BUSHELMAN, Jeff—253, 302, 303
BUSHELMAN, John—253
BUSHELMAN, Johnny—168
BUSHELMAN, Steve—302, 303
BUSSAN, Mark R.—233, 257, 261
BUSTER and Billie—115
BUSTING Loose—60
BUTCH Cassidy & the Sundance Kid—114
BUTLER, Artie—271, 319
BUTLER, Bill—318, 340
BUTLER, Elliot—296
BUTLER, Helen—256
BUTLER, Lyn—289
BUTLER, Robert—222, 223, 284, 299, 388, 389
BUTLER, Wilmer C.—244
BUTON, Philip, Jr.—296

D

H

J

K

O

S

T

W